The Essential
Gaelic–English,
English–Gaelic
Dictionary

The *Essential*
Gaelic–English,
English–Gaelic
Dictionary

Compiled by
Angus Watson

BIRLINN

First published in 2012 by
Birlinn Limited
West Newington House
10 Newington Road
Edinburgh
EH9 1QS

www.birlinn.co.uk

ISBN: 978 1 84158 367 9

British Library Cataloguing-in-Publication Data
A catalogue record for this book is available from the British Library

Chuidich Comhairle nan Leabhraichean am foillsichear
le cosgaisean an leabhair seo.

Designed and typeset by Sharon McTier
Printed and bound by MPG Books Ltd, Bodmin

CONTENTS

Foreword

This volume brings together the 'Essential' Gaelic–English and English–Gaelic dictionaries, published by Birlinn since 2001 and 2005 respectively. The approach, which has been generally well received by reviewers and users, remains the same, but the opportunity has been taken to add some vocabulary and to make some emendations to the texts. For example, the treatment of gender-specific and non gender-specific terms relating to occupations etc has been improved, in response to comments from some readers. This new edition takes account of the spelling changes proposed by the Gaelic Panel of the Scottish Examination Board.

I am happy to reiterate my thanks to the Gaelic Books Council for a grant towards the costs of compiling the original English–Gaelic volume, and to Ailean Boyd for his meticulous reading of, and suggestions anent, the original texts of both volumes. Any errors remaining are, of course, mine entirely.

In particular I wish once more to thank my wife for her patience, encouragement and good humour, when the preparation of this combined edition yet again rendered her man so often incommunicado in front of the word processor!

General Introduction

Dictionary makers often point out that their work is a compromise – between completeness on the one hand and space and expense on the other. Even the monumental Dwelly dictionary of Gaelic is not fully comprehensive, and there are stories of copies of Dwelly in Highland homes, their pages speckled with words added by the family from their own Gaelic. Another common defence mechanism among dictionary makers is for them to acknowledge that their choice of words and expressions will not please everyone. They are usually right!

In the present volume the aim has been to present as rich a cross-section of the Gaelic language as possible in the space available, giving due weight both to the new contexts of our times and to the riches of the past, as well as to both colloquial and more formal language. The registers, styles and contexts represented in the dictionary include: vulgar, familiar, colloquial, formal and traditional words and expressions; examples drawn from modern poetry, modern and traditional song (an area that attracts many learners to the language); proverbs and sayings; and, occasionally, placenames. The more common vocabulary of administration, politics and government, journalism and information technology also figures here.

As a learner of Gaelic myself, I have had the learner in mind throughout – though I naturally hope the fluent learner, and perhaps even the native speaker, will find value and interest here also. The aim is to help the user of these dictionaries to access a wide range of core or 'essential' Gaelic taken from a wide variety of contexts, and a priority has been to include in the entries as many examples as space would allow, showing words and expressions *in actual use*. There are many cases where merely giving a translation equivalent of the headword would not be adequate. A further aim has been to include the kind of explanatory information that I would have found useful myself (and still do!), as a learner of the language.

Novel features include the cross-references given in many entries in the Gaelic–English dictionary. These refer the reader to related words and expressions (NB not necessarily exact synonyms), with the aim of increasing the learner's vocabulary or reminding the more advanced user of alternative words that might be appropriate in a particular context. This gives to the

Gaelic–English dictionary a little of the nature of a thesaurus, by leading the reader to more than one possible Gaelic equivalent for a given word or concept in English. It is hoped that the cross-references might also encourage the learner to learn by browsing – and of course once the reader has located a word in the English–Gaelic section, he or she can look it up in the Gaelic–English section and benefit from the examples and cross-references that are given there.

Many regret the decline of the pithy, idiomatic Gaelic of the past, and find the Gaelic used today in administration, journalism and broadcasting, for example, pale and fushionless in comparison. But a dictionary has to embrace a language as it is. I make no apology for giving samples of these barer registers of Gaelic, and for going so far as to include examples of calques (expressions closely based on an English model) such as **àrdaich ìomhaigh na Gàidhlig** (raise/promote the image of Gaelic), and some other expressions or constructions that may well be questionable from the point of view of approved grammar and usage, but which form a part of the language as it is used today. Language inevitably evolves in step with a society, its technologies, attitudes and preoccupations, and Gaelic has been no exception. And in an age where even a world language such as French has been seriously penetrated by Anglicisms – in spite of a centuries-old official policy of keeping the language 'pure' – it is not surprising if Gaelic too has been radically affected in many of its registers.

At the same time, a good deal of traditional Gaelic survives in the modern language, especially in the form of set expressions, idioms, proverbs and sayings. Users of the language who so wish, therefore, can cultivate a style and vocabulary that include a goodly leavening of traditional language, enriching their Gaelic without running the risk of sounding too old-fashioned, or perhaps pretentious. A good selection of such material is included in this dictionary, though it should be noted that the kind of items that are *specifically* marked '*trad*' would not always fit comfortably into ordinary conversation. They are given as the kinds of words and expressions that might be useful in a fairly specialised context, or as information that the more advanced learner might find of interest. For example **is math seachad e** – it's good that it's over – has the traditional feel to it, but would be appropriate and expressive in an everyday context, on completion of some task or other. On the other hand, the traditional dative **ann an Albainn** – in Scotland – or the phrase **fhuair e bàs le nàimhdean** – he died at the hand of enemies – would seem archaic. It goes without saying, though, that many of the items marked '*trad*' will be met with in reading Gaelic from earlier decades or centuries, which is another excellent reason for their inclusion here. It is my view that the learner of a language should, especially in the earlier stages, err on the side of conservatism and not immediately take up the latest changes in colloquial usage. There is the obvious risk of sounding foolish by trying to be trendy when your grasp of the language may not yet be secure! Or at times native speakers may feel you are trying to be *too* clever.

In the entries, for the sake of consistency, I have made one or two conservative choices in presentation. In particular, I have regularly used the genitive case of the noun after a present participle, as in **a' cosnadh airgid** – earning money. I have done this because the genitive is 'grammatically' correct. In fact, though, many speakers have ceased to observe this 'rule', and the construction with the radical form of the noun – **a' cosnadh airgead** – would be acceptable in most contexts except, say, an examination, or a formal talk or speech.

At the end of the volume will be found a table of the forms of the Gaelic article, tables giving the forms of irregular verbs that are most likely to be encountered in mainstream Gaelic, and a list of the forms of the prepositional pronouns. The reader is referred to this latter list, when appropriate, within the English–Gaelic dictionary entries under the relevant English preposition. The prepositional pronouns are also listed in full within the Gaelic–English section of the dictionary, under the Gaelic preposition concerned, and listed individually, in their alphabetical place.

List of Abbreviations

abbrev	abbreviation		fut	future
abstr	abstract		gen	genitive case
acc	accusative		geog	geography, geographical
adj	adjective, adjectival		gram	grammar, grammatical
admin	administration		hist	history, historical
adv	adverb, adverbial		hort	horticulture, gardening
agric	agriculture, agricultural		imper	imperative (case)
alt	alternative		incl	including
anat	anatomy		infin	infinitive
approx	approximate,		inter	interrogative
	approximately		invar	invariable
arch	archaeology		irreg	irregular
art	article		IT	information technology,
Bibl	Bible, Biblical			computing
biol	biology		lang	language
bot	botany, botanical		lit	literally
chem	chemistry, chemical		Lit	literature, literary
cf	compare		m	masculine
coll	collective		med	medical
comp	comparative		mil	military
con	concrete		misc	miscellaneous
conj	conjunction		mus	music, musical
cons	consonant		n	noun
corres	correspondence,		nec	necessarily
	corresponding		neg	negative
dat	dative case		nf	noun, feminine
def	defective		nm	noun, masculine
derog	derogatory		nmf	noun, masculine & feminine
dimin	diminutive		nom	nominative case
ed	education, educational		num(s)	numeral(s), numerical
elec	electric, electrical		obs	obsolete
emph	emphasis, emphatic		occas	occasionally
Eng	English		orthog	orthography
engin	engineering		past	part
esp	especially		PC	politically correct
excl(s)	exclamation(s)		pej	pejorative
expr(s)	expression(s), expressing		pers pron	personal pronoun
f	feminine		philo	philosophy, philosophical
fam	familiar		phys	physical, physically
fig	figurative, figuratively		pl	plural
fin	financial, financially		poet	poetry, poetic(al)
freq	frequent, frequently		pol	politics, political

poss	possessive	sp	spelling
prep	prepositional	sup	superlative
pron	pronoun	topog	topography
pres	present	trad	traditional, traditionally
pres part	present participle	typog	typography
pron	pronoun	usu	usual, usually
prov	proverb	v	verb, verbal
psych	psychology, psychological	veg	vegetable
pt	part	vi	verb intransitive
rel	relative	vt	verb transitive
relig	religion, religious	vti	verb transitive & intransitive
Sc	Scots (language), Scottish		
sing	singular	voc	vocative, vocative case
sing coll	singular collective	vulg	vulgar

GAELIC–ENGLISH

Layout of the Entries, Gaelic–English Section

Within this section all Gaelic material is in bold type. Italics are used for all text in English that is not translation of the Gaelic material, ie abbreviations, instructions such as *see* and *cf*, and all notes, comments, explanatory material and grammatical information. A generous number of translation equivalents are given for the headwords, without straying too far into the more rarefied areas of English. Where appropriate the different senses or usages a headword may have are subdivided into numbered sections, separated by semi-colons.

The Gaelic spelling used corresponds to up-to-date norms. Exceptions to this occur when an older spelling still occasionally used by some is given for completeness, e.g. '**no** (*older sp* **neo**) *conj*'. In a good number of instances, two acceptable spellings are given. Usually this happens where both spellings correspond to modern spelling conventions and both versions are established in present usage. In other instances a recent loan word, for example, may not yet have settled down into one accepted spelling, so variants are given. Sometimes alternative spellings are indicated by means of brackets as in '**san (fh)radharc** in sight/view'. This of course means that this form of the word can be found as either **fhradharc** or **radharc.** The same example shows how oblique strokes (/) are used in the English translations to save space when giving alternatives. Clearly, in this case 'in sight' and 'in view' would be equally appropriate.

NOUNS

When the headword is a noun the forms normally given are the nominative singular (also called the radical), the genitive singular and the nominative plural, unmarked for case, and in that order. To avoid confusion, in entries where the noun departs from this basic pattern in some way, the forms other than the radical are marked for case, as in '**lasgan,** *gen & pl* **lasgain,** *nm* an outburst', where the genitive singular and the nominative plural are the same, or '**làthair,** *gen* **làthaire,** *nf* presence', where no plural exists, or '**là & latha,** *gen* **là & latha,** *pl* **làithean, lathachan & lathaichean** *nm* a day', where there are variant or alternative forms, or '**leannanachd** *nf invar* courtship', where the noun has only the one form. Nouns are marked for masculine or feminine gender. Some nouns are marked as having both genders, a situation that typically came about when neuter nouns in the older language took on different genders in different dialects as the neuter went out of use.

It is easy to use a noun in a wrong aspect and so I have tried to indicate, for instance, whether a noun is best used in a concrete or abstract sense, collectively, and so on. An entry such as '**amharas,** *gen & pl* **amharais** *nm* suspicion, a suspicion, doubt, a doubt' shows that **amharas** can mean 'suspicion' and 'doubt' the abstract concepts, as well as a particular doubt or suspicion one might have at a particular time. This may be thought to take up a lot of space, but is felt to be worthwhile for the sake of clarity.

VERBS

In the case of verbs, it should be explained that in Gaelic the basic form that is given in grammar books etc corresponds to the second person singular imperative, rather than to the infinitive, which is the form usually given for English verbs. Thus in this dictionary the verbs **gabh**, **can**, **siubhal**, for example, are given the equivalents 'take', 'say', 'travel' rather than 'to take', 'to say', 'to travel'.

The verbal forms given in the entries are the imperative form, followed by the present participle, as in '**faighnich** *vi, pres part* **a' faighneachd**, ask', or '**fàillig** *vti, pres part* **a' fàilligeadh**, fail'. It is important to know whether a verb can be used transitively or intransitively, that is, whether it can be used with or without a direct object, and this is conveyed by the abbreviations *vi, vt* and *vti* given immediately after the imperative of the verb. Taking **faighnich** as an example (see previous paragraph), '*vi*' shows that it cannot be followed by a direct object. To say 'ask a question' we would have to use a different Gaelic verb (**cuir,** with the noun **ceist**), and to say 'ask Morag' we would have to use an *indirect* object in Gaelic (**faighnich de Mhòrag**). The verb **fàillig**, though (see previous paragraph), can be used without a direct object (intransitively) as in **dh'fhàillig mi** 'I failed', or with a direct object (transitively) as in **dh'fhàillig e deuchainn** 'he failed an exam', and this is shown by the label '*vti*'. The label '*vt*' means that the verb concerned is used with a direct object (transitively) and is not normally likely to be used intransitively.

CROSS-REFERENCES

In many entries the reader is referred by the instruction '*cf*' to other headwords given in the Gaelic–English section of the dictionary, as in '**tastan, tastain, tastanan** *nm* (*former currency*) a shilling, *cf* **sgillinn 2**'. Here, obviously, it is section 2 of the entry under **sgillinn** that is being compared to this sense of **tastan.** The respective entries show that both Gaelic words relate to the idea 'shilling' but in different ways, and that in fact **sgillinn** no longer means 'shilling' but 'penny'. The overall aim, then, is to draw the reader's attention to other items covered in the dictionary that relate to the headword being consulted. As the above example shows, it should not be assumed that the items being compared are exact, or necessarily even close, synonyms. They may in fact even be opposites, in which case this is made clear in the entry, as in section 2 of **smior** 'the best part of something, the best example of something', which ends '*cf* **brod** *n* **2**, & *opposite* **diù**'.

In most cases the cross-references relate to the basic senses of the headword given at the beginning of the entry, or section of the entry, concerned. Taking the entry '**a-cheana** *adv* already, **mar a thuirt mi a cheana** as I've already said, *cf* **tràth** *adj* **3**', this means that under the adjective **tràth**, in section 3 of that entry, will be found a word or expression (in this case **mu thràth**, a close synonym), which relates to the basic sense given for **a-cheana** (in this case 'already').

In a number of entries the cross-reference is in brackets, indicating that it relates only to the part of the entry immediately preceding it. Thus in the entry '**allaidh** *adj* wild (*ie not domesticated*), *usu in set compounds, eg* **madadh-allaidh** *m* a wolf (*cf* **faol**), **damhan-allaidh** *m* a spider, *cf* **fiadhaich 1**', the cross-reference '(*cf* **faol**)' relates only to the immediately preceding item '**madadh-allaidh** a wolf' (**faol** is in fact a synonym), whereas '*cf* **fiadhaich 1**' relates to the basic sense 'wild'. Occasionally a cross-reference is applicable to all the sections of an entry. Take the example '**acainn** & **acfhainn**, *gen* **ac(fh)ainne**, *pl* **ac(fh)ainnean** *nf coll* **1** apparatus, equipment, tools, **ball-acainn** *m* a (*single*) tool; **2** a set of tools; **3** (*horse*) harness; **4** (*boat*) rigging; *cf* **uidheam**'. In this case the word **uidheam** has a sense corresponding to each of the four sections of **acainn** and so the reader is referred for comparison to the entire entry for **uidheam**. This is indicated by the fact that '*cf* **uidheam**' comes at the very end of the entry for **acainn**, and is separated from it by a semi-colon.

Finally, a rough and ready guide to the relative frequency of words is sometimes given in the cross-references, as in '**iarmad, iarmaid, iarmadan** *nm* a remnant, a residue, *cf more usu* **fuidheall 1**', or '**ifrinn, ifrinn, ifrinnean** *nf* hell, a hell, *cf less usu* **iutharn(a)**'. Not all Gaelic speakers will necessarily agree with all such indications of relative frequency, but they are based on my own experience of spoken and written Gaelic.

Note: The cross-references are mainly intended to help the intermediate and more advanced learner, and beginners in Gaelic should perhaps ignore them until they have acquired a certain degree of confidence in the language. The cross-references are not, of course, exhaustive. Through them I have tried to give a good amount of useful and stimulating information, but was anxious not to clutter the text unduly.

A

a *a particle introducing the numerals 1 to 10 in counting, or when not followed by a noun,* **a h-aon, a dhà, a trì** one, two, three, **cia mheud a th' agad? a seachd** how many have you got? seven, *in combination with higher numerals* **a h-aon deug** eleven, **a dhà-dheug** twelve, **fichead 's a deich** thirty, **ceithir fichead 's a naoi-deug** ninety-nine

a *sign of the voc, lenites following cons where possible,* **a Chatrìona!** Catherine!, *in corres* **A Charaid** Dear Sir, **A Phàdraig, a charaid** Dear Patrick

a *poss adj* his, her, its, **chunnaic e a mhac 's a mhàthair** he saw his son and his mother, **chunnaic i a mac 's a màthair** she saw her son and her mother, (*ie* **a** *for* his *lenites a following cons whereas* **a** *for* hers *does not*), **chunnaic i a h-athair,** she saw her father (*ie possessive* **a** *for* her *becomes a* h- *before a vowel*), **chunnaic e athair** he saw his father (*ie possessive* **a** *for* his *is omitted before a vowel*). *Note: before a verbal noun the poss adj can express the object of the verb or the subject of a passive construction,* **chan urrainn dhomh a dhèanamh** I can't do it (*lit* I am not capable of its doing), **gus am faicinn** in order to see them (*lit* to their seeing), **bha an leabhar ga fhoillseachadh** the book was being published (*lit* was at its publishing)

a (*in neg* **nach**) *rel pron* who, whom, that, which, **am balach a rinn sin** the boy who did that, **an deoch a dh'òl mi** the drink that I drank, **am film nach fhaca mi** the film I didn't see; *Note: cf rel pron* **a** & *conj* **gu,** *eg* **nach math a rinn thu e!** didn't you do it well! (*lit*) isn't it well that you did it! & **nach math gun do rinn thu e?** isn't it a good thing that you did it?

a *combines with a following verbal noun (lenited where possible) to form an infinitive,* **tha mi a' dol a shnàmh** I am going to swim, **cha bu chòir dhut do bhràthair a bhualadh** you ought not to hit your brother

a¹ *prep* (*for* **de** *prep*) of, (*causes lenition where possible*) **a dhà no a thrì a bhliadhnaichean** two or three years, **uair a thìde** an hour (*lit* an hour of time), *cf* **de** & **dhe 1**

a² *prep* (*for* **do**) to, (*causes lenition where possible*) **thèid i a Ghlaschu** she'll go to Glasgow, (*poem*) **is duilich leam do dhol air ais a dh'Eirinn** (Meg Bateman) hard/sad for me is your going back to Ireland, *cf* **do** *prep* **2**

a' *art, see* **an** *art*

a' *sign of the pres part, see* **ag**

à (*before the art,* **às**) *prep. The prep prons formed with* à/às, *in the order first, second, third person singular, first, second, third person plural, and with the reflexive/emphatic particles in brackets, are as follows:* **asam(sa), asad(sa), às(-san), aiste(se), asainn(e), asaibh(se), asta(san),** from me, from you (*fam*), *etc.* **1** from, out of, **còmhlan-ciùil à Alba/às an Fhraing** a band from Scotland/from France, **cò às a tha thu?** where are you from? **cò às a thàinig sin?** where did that come from? **biadh à Tesco's/às a' bhùth** food from Tesco's/from the shop, **bha/chaidh am bus à sealladh** the bus was/went out of sight, **bha mi às mo rian/às mo chiall** I was out of my mind, **cuir às an solas** put out/switch off the light, **a-mach à seo!** (get) out of here! **leig mi sgreuch asam** I let out a shriek; **2** *other uses & idioms* **a' bruidhinn à(s) beul a chèile** speaking with one voice/as one, **tha an fhuil a' tighinn às mo chorraig** my finger's bleeding, **bheir mi an ceann às an amhaich aige!** I'll wring his neck! **chaidh e às mo chuimhne** I forgot it/him, **bha i a' tarraing às** she was teasing him, **tha sinn uabhasach pròiseil asad** we're terribly proud of you, **thug iad na buinn asta** they took to their heels/got the hell out of it, **às aonais sgillinn ruaidh** without a brass farthing, without a penny (to his *etc* name), **dè a nì sinn às d' aonais?** what will we do without you? **chuir na saighdearan às dha** the soldiers finished him off/did away with him, **cha robh dol às aca a-nis** there was no way out/escape for them now, **dinnear** (*etc*) **ann no às** dinner (*etc*) or no dinner, **saor-làithean ann no às, tha mi a'dol don oifis!**

holidays or no holidays, I'm going to the office!,
fhuair e às leis he got away with it

ab & **aba**, *gen* **aba**, *pl* **abachan** *nm* an abbot

abachadh, *gen* **abachaidh** *nm* (*fruits etc*)
ripening, **àm abachadh nan ubhal** apple
ripening time

abaich *adj* 1 (*of person*) mature; 2 (*of fruit etc*)
ripe

abaich *vti*, *pres part* **ag abachadh**, ripen,
mature

abaichead, *gen* **abaicheid** *nm* maturity,
ripeness, **bha an t-ubhal a' dol an abaichead**
the apple was getting riper and riper

abaid, **abaide**, **abaidean** *nf* an abbey

abair *vt irreg* (*see tables p 493*), *pres part* **ag**
ràdh, 1 say, **thuirt iad riumsa e** they said
it to me, **chan eil mi ag ràdh gu bheil thu**
ceàrr I'm not saying you're wrong, *cf* **can** 1; 2
in exclamations, **abair duine gòrach!** what
a stupid man! **abair gun robh i sgìth!** how
tired she was! **abair bùrach!** what a mess!, talk
about a mess!, **abair e!** it sure is!, you bet!

abairt, **abairte**, **abairtean** *nf* 1 a phrase, an
expression; 2 (*gram*) a phrase

àbhacas & **àbhachdas**, *gen* **àbhac(hd)ais** *nm* 1
mirth; 2 ridicule, **bha e na bhall-àbhachdais**
he was a laughing-stock, *cf* **fanaid** 1, **magadh** 2

àbhachd *nf invar* humour, amusement

àbhachdach *adj* amusing, humorous, *cf more*
usu **èibhinn**

abhag, **abhaig**, **abhagan** *nf* a terrier

abhainn, **aibhne**, **aibhnichean** *nf* a river, a
large burn

àbhaist, **àbhaiste**, **àbhaistean** *nf* 1 a habit, a
custom, *cf* **cleachdadh** 2, **gnàth** 1; 2 *usu in*
exprs **mar as àbhaist** (*in past* **mar a**
b' àbhaist) as usual, & **b' àbhaist dhomh**
(**a bhith a' seinn etc**) I used (to sing etc), *cf*
cleachd 3

àbhaisteach *adj* usual, normal, habitual, **anns**
an àite àbhaisteach aig an àm àbhaisteach
in the usual place at the usual time, *cf less usu*
gnàthach

a-bhàn *adv* down, (*song*) **shruth mo dheòir**
a-bhàn my tears ran down, *also in expr* **suidh** *v*
a-bhàn sit down, (*song*) **suidhidh sinn**
a-bhàn gu socair we will sit down at our ease,
cf usu **sìos**

a bharrachd air *prep see* **barrachd** 4

a' bhòn-dè *adv* the day before yesterday

abhlan, **abhlain**, **abhlanan** *nm*, a wafer, *esp*
abhlan coisrigte a consecrated *or* communion
wafer

a bhòn-raoir *adv* the night before last

a bhòn-uiridh *adv* the year before last

a-bhos *adv* here, over here (*with or without*
implied movement), hither, **tha e a-bhos**
airson banais he is over for a wedding, **thall**
's a-bhos here and there, hither and thither, **bi**
air an taobh a-bhos be on this side

ablach, **ablaich**, **ablaichean** *nm* 1 a mangled
carcase, carrion; 2 *usu as term of abuse or*
contempt, a wretch, a wreck, **ablach bochd**
poor creature, poor wretch, *cf more sympathetic*
truaghan; 3 (*fam*) a brat

abradh, **abraibh**, **abrainn**, **abram**, **abramaid**,
pts of irreg v **abair** (*see tables p 493*)

abstol, **abstoil**, **abstolan** *nm* an apostle, (*Bible*)
Gnìomharan nan Abstol The Acts of the
Apostles

aca *prep pron, see* **aig**

acadaimigeach *adj* academic

acadamh, **acadaimh**, **acadamhan** *nmf* an
academy, **Acadamh Rìoghail na h-Alba** the
Royal Scottish Academy

acaid, **acaide**, **acaidean** *nf* a stabbing pain, a
stitch

acainn & **acfhainn**, *gen* **ac(fh)ainne**, *pl*
ac(fh)ainnean *nf coll* 1 apparatus, equipment,
tools, accoutrements, **ball-acainn** *m* a (*single*)
tool; 2 a set of tools; 3 (*for horse*) harness; 4 (*for*
boat) rigging; *cf* **uidheam**

acainneach & **acfhainneach** *adj* 1 equipped,
tooled up, *cf* **uidheamaichte** 1; 2 energetic

acair(e)[1], *gen* **acaire** & **acrach**, *pl* **acraichean**
nmf an anchor, **air an acaire**, *also* **aig**
acarsaid, at anchor

acair(e)[2], *gen* **acaire** & **acrach**, *pl* **acraichean**
nmf an acre

acarsaid, **acarsaide**, **acarsaidean** *nf* an
anchorage, a harbour, a mooring, *cf* **cala**, **port**[2]

acasan *prep pron* (*emph*), *see* **aig**

ach *conj* 1 but, **bha dùil againn ris, ach cha**
tàinig e we were expecting him, but he didn't
come; 2 except, but, apart from, **chan eil**
duine comasach air ach Dàibhidh no-one is
capable of it except David, *cf* **a-mhàin**; 3 (*with*
a verb in the neg) only, **chan eil agam ach a**
trì I only have three; 4 (*occas*) in case, **sheall**
e oirre ach am b' e fealla-dhà a bha i ris he
looked at her in case/to see if she was joking

achadh, **achaidh**, **achaidhean** *nm* (*agric*) a
field

a-chaoidh *adv* 1 always, for ever, **bidh gaol**
agam ort a-chaoidh I will love you for ever;
2 (*with a verb in the neg*) never, **cha till mi**
a-chaoidh do thìr nam beann àrda I will
never return to the land of the high bens; *Note:*
a-chaoidh *is only used with reference to the*

future – when referring to the past use
a-riamh; *cf* **bràth 2 & 3, a-riamh, sìorraidh
2**

achd, achd, achdannan *nf* (*pol, law*) an act,
Achd Pàrlamaid an Act of Parliament, **Achd
an Aonaidh** the Act of Union (*of the Scots and
English parliaments in 1707*)

a-cheana, *also* **cheana,** *adv* already, **mar a
thuirt mi (a-)cheana** as I've already said, *cf*
tràth *adj* 3

a chionn *prep* because of, **a chionn sin** because
of that, accordingly, *cf* **brìgh 5, sgàth 3**

a chionn is gu *conj* because, **chaill mi an
trèana a chionn 's gun robh m' uaireadair
briste** I missed the train because my watch was
broken

achlais, achlaise, achlaisean *nf* 1 an armpit,
(*Sc*) an oxter, **bha neasgaid oirre na
h-achlais** she had a boil in her armpit; **2** arm,
bha màileid aice fo a h-achlais she had a bag
under her arm/oxter, **bha iad a' coiseachd
romhpa, air achlaisean a chèile** they were
walking along with their arms around each
other, **thig nam achlais!** come to my arms! (*cf*
com 1)

achlasan, *gen & pl* **achlasain** *nm* an armful, *cf*
ultach 1

achmhasan, *gen & pl* **achmhasain** *nm* reproof,
reproach, adverse criticism, a reprimand, a
rebuke

a chum *prep* (*trad*) for, for the purpose of, **a
chum sin** for that purpose, **a chum stad a
chur air an trioblaid** (in order) to stop the
trouble, *cf more usu* **airson 5, gus** *conj*

a chum is gu *conj* so that, in order that, *cf more
usu* **gus** *conj*

acrach *adj* hungry, *cf* **acrasach**

acrachadh, *gen* **acrachaidh** *nm* (*the act of*)
anchoring, mooring

acraich *vt, pres part* **ag acrachadh,** (*boat*)
anchor, moor

acranaim, acranaim, acranaimean *nm* an
acronym

acras, *gen* **acrais** *nm* hunger, *usu with the art,*
tha/thàinig an t-acras orm I am/I grew
hungry

acrasach *adj* hungry, *cf* **acrach**

actair, actair, actairean *nm* an actor, *cf*
cleasaiche 1

ad, aide, adan *nf* a hat

adag, adaig, adagan *nf* a haddock

àdha, àdha, àinean *nm* (*anat*) a liver, *cf*
grùthan

a dh'aindeoin *prep see* **aindeoin 2**

a dh'aithghearr *adv see* **aithghearr 3**

adhaltraiche, adhaltraiche, adhaltraichean
nm an adulterer, **ban-adhaltraiche** *nf* an
adulteress

adhaltranach *adj* adulterous

adhaltranas, *gen* **adhaltranais** *nm* adultery

adhar, *gen* **adhair** *nm* sky, air, **shuas san
adhar** up in the sky/air, *cf* **speur 1**

adhar-fhànas, *gen* **adhar-fhanais** *m* aerospace

adharc, adhairc, adharcan *nf* horn, a horn (*of
animal*), **bò air leth-adhairc** a one-horned
cow, **spàin adhairc** a horn spoon

adharcach *adj* horned, horny, like horn

adharcan-luachrach, *gen & pl* **adharcain-
luachrach** *nm* a lapwing, a peewit, a green
plover, (*Sc*) a peesie, *cf* **curracag**

adhart, *gen* **adhairt** *nm* 1 progress, *cf more usu*
adhartas, piseach; **2** *usu in expr* **air adhart**
adv forwards, on, onwards, **tha iad a' tighinn
air adhart gu math** they're coming on/along
well, **tha i a' faighinn air adhart** she's getting
on/along, she's making progress, **ceum air
adhart** a step forward (*lit & fig*), *cf less usu*
aghaidh 4

adhartach *adj* progressive, forward-looking

adhartaich *vt, pres part* **ag adhartachadh**
advance, further (*a cause, process etc*)

adhartas, *gen* **adhartais** *nm* progress, **chan eil
sinn a' dèanamh adhartais** we're not making
(any) progress, *cf* **piseach 1**

adhbhar, *gen* **adhbhair,** *pl* **adhbharan** *nm*
1 a reason, a cause, **cha robh adhbhar aca
greasad dhachaigh** they had no reason to
hurry home, **adhbhar mo bhròin** the cause of
my sadness, **adhbhar gàire** a laughing-stock
(*cf* **cùis 4, culaidh 4**); **2** a cause (*ie a principle,
belief system etc*), **shaothraich i ann an
adhbhar còraichean nam ban** she laboured
in the cause of women's rights; **3** materials,
adhbhar bhròg shoe-making materials, *cf*
stuth 2

adhbharaich *vt, pres part* **ag adhbharachadh,**
cause, occasion, give rise to, **is i a' ghort a
dh'adhbharaich bàs am measg an
t-sluaigh** it is/was famine that caused death
among the population

adhbrann, adhbrainn, adhbrainnean *nf* an
ankle, *cf* **caol na coise** (*see* **caol** *n* 3)

a dh'ionnsaigh *prep see* **ionnsaigh 3**

a dhìth *adv see* **dìth 2**

adhlacadh, *gen* **adhlacaidh** *nm* 1 (*the act
of*) burying, interring; **2** burial, a burial, an
interment, a funeral, *cf* **tiodhlacadh 2,
tòrradh**

adhlaic *vt, pres part* **ag adhlacadh,** bury, inter,
cf **tiodhlaic 1**

adhradh, adhraidh, adhraidhean *nm*, worship, **dèan** *v* **adhradh** worship, **dèan/ thoir** *v* **adhradh do Dhia** worship God

Afganach *gen & pl* **Afganaich** *nm*, an Afghan, *also adj* **Afganach** Afghan

Afraga *nf invar* Africa

Afraganach, *gen & pl* **Afraganaich** *nm* an African, **ban-Afraganach** *nf* an African woman, *also as adj* **Afraganach** African

ag *with following verbal noun forms the pres part, eg* **ag èisteachd** listening, *Note: before cons usu* **a**, *eg* **a' briseadh** breaking, **a' tionndadh** turning, *though note exception* **ag ràdh** saying; **ag** *combines with the poss adjs* **mo, do, a** *etc to form the particles* **gam, gad, ga, gar, gur, gan/gam** *which express the object of the verb or the subject of a passive construction*, **tha iad gam bhrìodal** they're flattering/courting me, **bidh sinn gur faicinn!** we'll be seeing you! **bha a' bhò ga bleoghann** the cow was being milked

agad (*emph form* **agadsa**), **againn** (*emph form* **againne**), **agaibh** (*emph form* **agaibhse**), *prep prons, see* **aig**

agair *vt, pres part* **ag agairt**, *similar uses to* **tagair**

agalladh, *gen* **agallaidh** *nm* (*media etc*) interviewing

agallaich *vt, pres part* **ag agalladh**, (*media etc*) interview

agallamh, agallaimh, agallamhan *nm* **1** (*media etc*) an interview; **2** conversation, *cf* **còmhradh 1, conaltradh 1**

agam (*emph form* **agamsa**) *prep pron, see* **aig**

àgh & **àigh**, *gen* **àigh** *nm* **1** joy, *cf* **gàirdeachas**; **2** good fortune, *cf more usu* **fortan, sealbh 1**; **3** *in excl* **an ainm an àigh!** in heaven's name!

agh, aighe, aighean *nf* a heifer

aghaidh, aghaidhe, aghaidhean *nf* **1** a face, **aghaidh ri aghaidh** face to face, **air aghaidh na beinne** on the face of the mountain, *cf* **aodann 1 & 2**; **2** cheek, nerve, **nach (ann) airsan a tha an aghaidh!** hasn't he got a cheek! **abair aghaidh!** what a cheek! *cf* **bathais 2**; **3** *in expr* **an aghaidh** *prep* against, in the face of (*with gen*), **an aghaidh na gaoithe** against the wind, **chaidh e nam aghaidh** he went against me; **4** *in expr* **air aghaidh** *adv* forward(s), *cf more usu* **air adhart** (*see* **adhart 2**); **5** (*weather*) a front, **aghaidh bhlàth** a warm front

aghaidh-choimheach, aghaidh-coimhich, aghaidhean-coimheach *nf* (*fancy dress etc*) a mask, *cf* **aodannan, masg**

aghann, aigh(ain)ne, aghannan *nf*, a pan, *esp* a frying pan

aghastar, aghastair, aghastaran *nm* a halter

àghmhor *adj* **1** pleasant, *cf more usu* **taitneach, tlachdmhor 1**; **2** joyful, happy, *cf* **aighearach, aoibhneach 3**

agus, *also* **is** *or* **'s**, *conj* **1** and, **rugadh agus thogadh mi an sin** I was born and brought up there, *Note:* **agus** *often occurs as* **is** *or* **'s**, *esp in set phrases, eg* **m' athair 's mo mhàthair** my father and mother, **aran is ìm** bread and butter; **tha mi sgìth; tha agus mise!** I'm tired! and me!/me too!/so am I!, **2** *in comp constructions as*, **chan eil mi cho òg agus/is a bha mi** I'm not as young as I was, **cho luath 's a b' urrainn dhomh** as quickly as I could, **dè cho fliuch 's a tha e?** how wet is it?; **3** *in concessive clauses* **air cho anmoch 's gu bheil e** however late it is/may be, **gabh e, beag 's gu bheil e** take it, small as/though it is; **4** *usu* **is** *or* **'s** (*trad*) *expressing simultaneity, & corres to Eng* with, while, though *etc, as implied by the context*, **boireannach is triùir mhac aice** a woman with three sons, **cha chaidil iad 's an solas air** they won't sleep with the light on, **chaidil mi gu math is an solas air fad na h-oidhche** I slept well even though the light was on all night, **ghoid e is ise ri thaobh** he stole it while (*also* even though) she was beside him, (*song*) **tè eile chan iarrainn 's tu beò** I wouldn't want any other woman as long as you live, **bha iad 's an gàirdeanan mun cuairt air a chèile** they had their arms around each other

a h-uile *adj see* **uile 2**

àibheis *nf invar* an abyss, *cf* **dubh-aigeann 2**

àibheiseach *adj* huge, enormous

aibidil, aibidile, aibidilean *nf* an alphabet

aibidealach *adj* alphabetical, **òrdugh aibidealach** alphabetical order

aice (*emph form* **aicese**) *prep pron, see* **aig**

àicheadh, *gen* **àicheidh** *nm* **1** (*the act of*) denying, renouncing; **2** denial, a denial, **dèan** *v* **àicheadh** deny, *NB note the double neg in exprs such as* **cha dèan mi àicheadh nach do smaoinich mi . . .** I won't deny that I thought . . . ; **3** renunciation, a renunciation (*of belief etc*)

àicheidh *vt, pres part* **ag àicheadh**, **1** deny, **ag àicheadh a chionta** denying his guilt; **2** deny, renounce, **ag àicheadh a chreideimh** denying/renouncing his faith

àicheil *adj* (*gram*) negative

aideachadh, aideachaidh, aideachaidhean
nm **1** (*the act of*) confessing, admitting; **2**
confession, a confession (*not in RC sense, see*
faoisid), an admission (*of guilt etc*)

aidich *vti, pres part* **ag aideachadh**, confess,
admit, **dh'aidich e a chionta** he confessed/
admitted his guilt, **tha iad air aideachadh**
they have confessed

aifreann, *gen* **aifrinn** *nm* (*relig*) a Mass

aig *prep. The prep prons formed with* **aig**, *in
the order first, second, third person singular,
first, second, third person plural, and with the
reflexive/emphatic particles in brackets, are
as follows:* **agam(sa), agad(sa), aige(san),
aice(se), againn(e), agaibh(se), aca(san)**,
at me, at you *etc*. **1** at, **aig an doras** at the
door, **aig a' Mhòd** at the Mod, **aig baile** at
home; **2** belonging to, in the possession of,
an cù aig Dòmhnall Donald's dog, **a bheil
teaghlach aig Iain?** does John have a family?
tha cù agam I have a dog, **an cù aca** their dog,
Uilleam againn(e) our William, **a bheil an
iuchair agad?** have you got the key?, **seo agad
ugh** here's an egg (for you), *cf* **le 4**; **3** *for mental
and emotional states* **tha cuimhn' agam**
(**ort** etc) I remember (you etc), **tha dùil agam**
(**rithe** etc) I expect (her etc), **tha gaol agam**
(**oirre** etc) I love (her etc); **4** *in expr* **tha agam**
(etc) **ri . . .** I (etc) have to . . . , **bha bileag aice
ri phàigheadh** she had a bill to pay, **tha aca
ri goc a chàradh** they have to repair a tap, *cf*
feudar 2, **feum** *v* **1**; **5** *in expr* **dè a' Ghàidhlig
a th' agad air 'continental drift'** (etc)? what
do you say in Gaelic for 'continental drift' (etc)?;
6 *misc idioms* **tha iad mòr aig a chèile** they're
great friends, **chaidh agam air** I managed it,
also I got the better of him/it, **tha not agam
air** he owes me a pound, **tha e ag obair aig
an uachdaran** he's working for the landlord,
a' fuireach aig Ailig staying (*ie* lodging) with
Alec, **pòsta aig Peigi** married to Peggy, **bha
i air a dearg-mhilleadh aig a màthair** her
mother had got her completely spoiled, she'd
been completely spoiled by her mother

àigeach, *gen & pl* **àigich** *nm* a stallion

aige (*emph form* **aigesan**) *prep pron, see* **aig**

àigh *nm see* **àgh**

aighear, *gen* **aigheir** *nm* merriment, joy,
cheerfulness

aighearach *adj* cheerful, merry, joyful, (*song*)
b' aighearach an-uiridh mi merry was I last
year, *cf* **aoibhneach 3**

aighearachd *nf invar* cheerfulness, joyfulness

aigne *nf invar* **1** mind, *esp in expr* **air m' aigne/
air d' aigne** etc on my/your (etc) mind, *cf* **aire**

1, cùram 2, fa-near 1; **2** character, disposition,
cf **mèinn 1, nàdar 2**

ailbhinn, *gen* **ailbhinne** *nf* flint, a flint

àile, *also* **àileadh, fàile & fàileadh**, *gen*
(f)àileidh, *pl* **(f)àileachan, fàilean &
fàilidhean** *nm* **1** air, atmosphere, *cf* **èadhar**;
2 smell **bha droch àile a' tighinn às** *or*
bha droch àile dheth it had a bad smell, *cf*
boladh, *& usu pleasant* **boltrach**

àileach *adj* **1** airy, **2** pertaining to the air or
atmosphere

aileag, aileig, aileagan *nf* hiccups (*with the
art*), **tha an aileag orm** I've got (the) hiccups

àill *nf invar* **1** (*trad*) desire, will, *now usu in expr*
's àill leam (etc) I (etc) desire, **'s àill leatha
beartas** she desires wealth, *cf* **iarr 1, miann
1**; **2** *in expr* **B' àill leibh?** (*also*) **Bàillibh?**
Pardon?, *cf less polite* **dè an rud?** (*see* **rud 1**)

àilleag, àilleig, àilleagan *nf* **1** a jewel, (*song*)
àilleagan (*dimin*) **nan gillean** a jewel among
youths, *cf* **leug, seud**; **2** a pretty girl

àillidh *adj* **1** shining, bright, resplendent, *cf more
usu* **boillsgeach, deàlrach 1**; **2** beautiful,
lovely, *cf more usu* **àlainn, bòidheach,
sgèimheach**

ailm *see* **failm**

ailse *& aillse* *nf invar* cancer, **aillse sgamhain**
lung cancer

ailseag, ailseig, ailseagan *nf* a caterpillar

ailtire, ailtire, ailtirean *nm* an architect

ailtireachd *nf invar* architecture

aimhleas, *gen* **aimhleis** *nm* **1** (*trad*) misfortune,
ruination, *cf more usu* **creach n 2, sgrios n**; **2**
mischief, *cf* **donas 1, olc n**

aimhreit, aimhreite, aimhreitean *nf* **1**
disorder, a disorder, disturbance, a disturbance,
trouble, *cf* **trioblaid, ùpraid 2**; **2** (*hist*)
Aimhreit an Fhearainn the 19th-century
Land League agitation

aimhreiteach *adj* quarrelsome, argumentative,
turbulent, trouble-making, *cf* **buaireasach**

aimsir, aimsire, aimsirean *nf* **1** (*occas*) time,
cf more usu **tìde 1, ùine 1**; **2** (*occas*) a season,
cf **ràith 1, tràth n 1**; **3** (*more often*) weather,
droch aimsir bad weather, *cf* **sìde**

aimsireil *adj* **1** temporal; **2** climatic

ain- *a prefix corres to Eng* un-, *see examples
below, cf* **do-, mì-, neo-**

aindeoin *nf* **1** reluctance, unwillingness, *cf
opposite* **deòin**; **2** *usu in expr* **a dh'aindeoin**
(*with gen*) in spite of, against the will of, **a
dh'aindeoin na thubhairt i** in spite of what
she said, **a dh'aindeoin cùise** nonetheless, all
the same, in spite of everything, **a dheòin no a
dh'aindeoin** whether he was/is willing or not,

(*prov*) **fear a chuirear a dh'aindeoin don allt, bristidh e na soithichean** a man sent unwilling to the burn will break the water jugs; **3** *also as conj, eg* **a dh'aindeoin 's gun robh i sgìth** despite the fact that she was tired

aindeònach *adj* reluctant, unwilling, *cf* **leisg** *adj* **2**

àineach & **àithneach** *adj* imperative (*gram*), **am modh àithneach** the imperative mood

aineolach *adj* **1** ignorant; **2** not knowledgeable, unfamiliar, (**air** about, with), **aineolach air coimpiutairean** unfamiliar with computers, *cf less usu* **ainfhiosrach**

aineolas, *gen* **aineolais** *nm* **1** ignorance; **2** unfamiliarity (**air** with)

ainfhios, *gen* **ainfhiosa** *nm* ignorance, *cf more usu* **aineolas 1**

ainfhiosrach *adj* ignorant, *cf more usu* **aineolach**

aingeal, aingil, ainglean *nm* an angel

aingidh *adj* wicked, *cf more usu* **olc** *adj*

ainm, *gen* **ainme**, *pl* **ainmean** & **ainmeannan** *nm* a name, **dè an t-ainm a th' ort?** what's your name? **'s e Stiùbhart an t-ainm a th' orm** my name is Stewart, **ainm àite** a placename (*pl* **ainmean àite/àiteachan**), (*excl*) **an ainm an duine mhaith!** in the name of the wee man!, *also in expr* **cuir** *v* **m'** (etc) **ainm ri pàipear** sign a document

ainmeachadh, *gen* **ainmeachaidh** *nm* (*the act of*) naming, mentioning

ainmear, ainmeir, ainmearan *nm* (*gram*) a noun, **ainmear gnìomhaireach** a verbal noun

ainmeil *adj* famous, celebrated, renowned, *cf* **cliùiteach, iomraiteach**

ainmh- *prefix corres to Eng* zoo-, *eg* **ainmh-eòlas**, *gen* **ainmh-eòlais** *nm* zoology

ainmhidh, ainmhidhe, ainmhidhean *nm* an animal, *cf* **beathach, biast 1**

ainmich *vt*, *pres part* **ag ainmeachadh**, **1** name; **2** mention, **an tè a dh' ainmich mi roimhe** the woman I mentioned before, *cf* **thoir iomradh air** (*see* **iomradh 1**)

ainmneach *adj* (*gram*) nominative, **an tuiseal ainmneach** the nominative case

ainneamh *adj* **1** (*trad*) unusual, scarce, *cf* **tearc** & *more usu* **gann 1**; **2** (*trad*) *usu in expr* **is ainneamh a . . .** it's not often that . . . , **is ainneamh a chì thu a leithid** you won't often/you'll rarely see the likes of him/her/it

ainneart, *gen* **ainneirt** *nm* violence, *cf* **fòirneart**

ainneartach *adj* violent

ainnir, ainnire, ainnirean *nf* a virgin, *cf* **maighdeann 2, òigh 1**

ainnis, *gen* **ainnise** *nf* poverty, *cf more usu* **bochdainn 1**

ainniseach *adj* poor, indigent, needy, *cf* **bochd 1, easbhaidheach 1, uireasbhach 1**

aintighearn(a), aintighearna, aintighearnan *nm* a tyrant

aintighearnail *adj* tyrannical

aintighearnas, *gen* **aintighearnais** *nm* tyranny

air *prep* (*with dat*). *The prep prons formed with* **air**, *in the order first, second, third person singular, first, second, third person plural, and with the reflexive/emphatic particles in brackets, are as follows:* **orm(sa), ort(sa), air(san), oirre(se), oirnn(e), oirbh(se), orra(san)** on me, on you (*fam*), etc. **1** on, **air a' mhullach** on the roof, **cuir air an coire** put the kettle on, **air m' aire** on my mind; **2** *for phys, mental and emotional states*, **thàinig am pathadh orm** I grew thirsty, **tha smùid orra** they're drunk, **tha an cnatan oirre** she's got the cold, **tha mulad oirre** she's sad, **tha eagal orm** I'm afraid (*ie* I'm sorry to say *etc*), **tha an t-eagal orm** I'm afraid (*ie* I'm frightened); **3** *expr disadvantage*, **ghoid e mo sgian orm** he stole my knife 'on me', **dè tha a' cur ort?** what's the matter with you? **gabh brath air cuideigin** take advantage of somebody, **faigh spòrs air cuideigin** have fun at someone's expense; **4** on, about, **film air murtair** a film about a murderer, **òraid air feallsanachd** a lecture on philosophy, **cò air a tha thu a-mach?** what are you (going) on about?, *cf* **mu 2 & 3**; **5** at, **air banais/tòrradh** at a wedding/a funeral, **tha iad math air iomain** they're good at shinty, **thug iad greis mu seach air an spaid** they each took a turn for a while at the spade; **6** during, in the course of, **bidh cèilidhean ann air a' mhìos seo** there'll be ceilidhs this month, **thig gam fhaicinn air an fheasgar** come to see me in the evening; **7** in exchange for, **reic air deagh phrìs** sell at a good price, **thug mi nota air** I paid/gave a pound for it; **8** however, **air cho bochd 's gu bheil e** however poor he might be; **9** by, judging by, **bha fhios aice air a ghuth gun robh e sgìth** she knew by his voice that he was tired; **10** *expr a completed action in the past*, **tha iad air falbh** they have gone, **bha mi air an doras a dhùnadh** I had closed the door, **tha iad air fhaicinn** they have seen him, **bha iad air am moladh** they had praised them, *also* they had been praised; **11** *misc idioms & exprs* **chaidh sinn air seachran** we got lost *or* went astray, **càite air an t-saoghal a bheil i?** where in the world is she? **cò tha**

sgìth? **tha mise air aon** who's tired? I am
for one, **bha iad air an dòigh** they were
contented *or* delighted, **air an dòigh seo** in
this way, **chan eil air sin ach sin fhèin** that's
all there is to it, **chan eil cothrom air** there's
nothing to be done about it/it can't be helped,
chan eil air ach (falbh etc) there's nothing
for it but (to leave etc), **tha nota agam ort** you
owe me a pound, **mo mhallachd ort!** curse
you!, **air dheireadh** lagging behind, **thàinig
i air deireadh** she came last, **air mo sgàth**
for my sake, **air chor/air dhòigh 's gun
do chaochail iad** so that they died, **thug e
Ameireaga air** he went off to America, **thoir
an t-siteag ort** get out/outside! **air neo** or
else, otherwise, **thig sinn air chèilidh oirbh**
we'll come to 'ceilidh' on you/to visit you, **cùm
ort** keep it up, keep going, **greas ort!** (*pl*
greasaibh oirbh) hurry up!, **a' coimhead
a-mach air an uinneig** looking out (of) the
window, **'s beag orm do cheòl** I dislike your
music, **beag air bheag** little by little, **rug e
air làimh oirre** he shook her hand; *Note:* air
*sometimes causes lenition in a following noun
eg* **ceum air cheum** step by step
air *prep pron, see* **air** *prep*
air adhart *adv see* **adhart 2**
air aghaidh *adv see* **aghaidh 4**
air ais *adv* back, backwards, **cuir air ais e!** put
it back! **chùm e air ais mi** he kept/held me
back, he delayed me, **mìos air ais** a month
back/ago, **ghabh e ceum air ais** he stepped
back, *also* he took a retrograde step, **sùil air ais**
a backward glance/look, *also* (*ed etc*) revision,
air ais 's air adhart backwards and forwards,
to and fro
air ball *adv* at once, immediately, *cf* **bad 5**
air beulaibh *prep* in front of (*with gen*), **chì mi
thu air beulaibh na h-eaglaise** I'll see you in
front of the church, **air am beulaibh** in front of
them, *cf* **beulaibh, air cùlaibh, cùl 3**
air b(h)onn *adv see* **bonn 3**
air chall *adv see* **call 3**
airchealladh, *gen* **aircheallaidh** *nm* sacrilege
air chois *adv see* **cas** *n* 1 & 6
air choreigin *adj* some, some or other, **air
dòigh air choreigin** somehow or other, **neach
air choreigin** some person or other, **ann an
àite air choreigin** somewhere or other, (in)
some place or other
air cùl *prep see* **cùl 3**
air cùlaibh *prep* behind (*with gen*), **air cùlaibh
na h-eaglaise** behind the church, **bha e air
an cùlaibh** he was behind them, **dh'fhag mi/
chuir mi air mo chùlaibh e** I left/I put it

behind me, **thoir an aire air do chùlaibh**
look/watch out behind you, *cf* **air beulaibh, cùl
3, cùlaibh**
àird(e), àirde, àirdean *nf* 1 (*usu topog*) a
height, a high place, *also in expr* **bha mi a'
seinn (aig) àird mo chlaiginn** I was singing
at the top of my voice; 2 a point, a promontory,
cf **maol** *n* 1, **rinn** *n* 2, **rubha, sròn** 2; 3 a
compass point, a direction, *(Sc)* an airt, **an àird
an iar** the East, **an àird an ear** the West; 4 *in
expr* **an-àird** *adv* up, **cuiridh mi sgeilp an-
àird** I'll put a shelf up, **bha sanas an-àird air
a' chlàr** there was a notice up on the board, *cf*
shuas, suas
àirde *nf invar* 1 height, **dè an àirde a tha ann?
tha sia troighean a dh'àirde ann** what
height/how tall is he? he's six feet tall/in height,
tha troigh a dh'àirde ann it's a foot tall/high;
2 (*hill, plane etc*) altitude; 3 (*musical note*) pitch
air do *conj* after, **air dhuinn am bealach a
ruigsinn** after we had reached the top of the
pass, *cf* **an dèidh 2**
aire *nf invar* 1 mind, **tha rudeigin air a h-aire**
there's something on her mind/preoccupying
her, *cf* **aigne 1, cùram 2, fa-near 1**; 2
attention, heed, *usu in phrase* **thoir** *v* **an aire**
pay attention, pay heed, notice, **cha tug e an
aire don chàr** he paid no attention/heed to/
he ignored the car, *also* he didn't notice the car,
cf **fa-near 3, feart** *nf*, **for, sùim 2**; 3 care, *esp
in expr* **thoir an aire (ort fhèin)!** take care (of
yourself)!, **thoir an aire nach tuit thu** mind/
watch/take care you don't fall
aireachail *adj* attentive, *cf* **faiceallach**
àireamh, àireimh, àireamhan *nf* a number,
àireamh a trì number three, **àireamh
fòn** a phone number, **àireamh mhòr
bhoireannach** a large number of women
àireamhach *adj* numerical
àireamhaich *vti, pres part* **ag
àireamhachadh**, (*sums etc*) calculate, work
out, *cf* **obraich 3**
àireamhair, àireamhair, àireamhairean *nm*
a (*pocket etc*) calculator
air èiginn *see* **èiginn 4**
air fad *adv see* **fad** *nm* 3
air falbh *adv see* **falbh 1**
air feadh, *also* **feadh**, *prep* through,
throughout, all over (*with gen*), **air feadh an
taighe** through/throughout the house, **bha
glainneachan falamh air feadh an àite**
there were empty glasses all over the place, **bha
fàileadh air feadh an rùim** a scent filled the
room, **air feadh an là** all through the day, all

day, **chuir sin an ceòl air feadh na fìdhle!** that put the cat among the pigeons!

airgead, gen **airgid** nm 1 money, **airgead-pòcaid** pocket money, **airgead ullamh** ready money, cash, **tha e a' cosnadh mòran airgid** he's earning a lot of money, **'s e airgead mòr a tha sin!** that's a lot of money!; 2 silver, (song) **An Fhìdeag Airgid** The Silver Whistle, **bonn airgid** a coin, also a silver medal

airgeadach adj 1 well-off, comfortably off, cf **seasgair**; 2 lucrative

airidh adj worthy, deserving, **duine airidh** a worthy man, **airidh air moladh** worthy of praise, **bha sibh airidh air** you deserved it, also you were entitled to it, (without prep) **duais a b' airidh an t-ainm** a prize worthy of the name, (trad) **'s math an airidh** it's richly deserved, he (etc) richly deserves it, cf less usu **toillteanach**

airidheachd nf invar (usu of persons) merit, worth, worthiness

àirigh, àirighe, àirighean nf (trad) summer pasture(s), a sheiling, **bha na boireannaich air àirigh** the women were at the summer pastures, **bothan àirigh** a sheiling bothy, cf less usu **ruighe 3**

air leth adv see **leth 2**

air muin adv see **muin 1 & 3**

àirneis nf invar (coll) 1 furniture, **àirneis taighe** household furniture, **ball-àirneis** a piece/an item of furniture; 2 (trad) gear, accoutrements, trappings, (theatre etc) props, cf **uidheam 2**

air neo conj or, or else, otherwise, **gabh do dhìnnear air neo chan fhaigh thu suiteis** eat your dinner or (else) you won't get any sweeties, **dùin an doras air neo gabhaidh sinn an cnatan** shut the door or we'll catch cold, cf **no**

airsan prep pron (emph), see **air** prep

air sgàth prep, see **sgàth** n 3

airson prep (with gen) 1 for, **sgrìobh i aiste airson a bràthar** she wrote an essay for (ie to oblige) her brother, **na bi duilich air a son** don't be sorry for her (cf **do** prep 3), **chaidh sinn don bhùth airson uighean** we went to the shop for eggs; 2 of time for, **ghabh i e air iasad airson dà sheachdain** she borrowed it for two weeks; 3 for, for the sake of, **chaill e a bheatha airson a' Phrionnsa** he lost his life for the Prince, cf **sgàth** n 3; 4 for, in support of, in favour of, ready or willing (to do something), **bha mi airson falbh** I was for leaving/felt like leaving/was about to leave, **bhòt iad airson an riaghaltais** they voted for the government,

chan eil mi airson sin idir I don't approve of/I'm not in favour of that at all, (fam) **a bheil thu airson pinnt?** are you for/do you fancy a pint?; 5 to, in order to (less formal & trad than **gus**), **chaidh mi don bhaile airson caraid fhaicinn** I went to town to see a friend, cf **a chum, gus**[1] conj; 6 in expr **air a shon sin** in spite of that, for all that, cf **aindeoin 2**

air thoiseach adv see **toiseach 3**

airtnealach adj (trad, in songs etc) weary, woeful, sorrowful, cf **brònach, muladach, tùrsach**

aiseag, aiseig, aiseagan nm a ferry, (trad) a ferry crossing, **a' gabhail an aiseig** taking/crossing the ferry, **bàt'-aiseig** m a ferry boat, **aiseag-charbad** a car ferry

aiseal, aiseil, aisealan nf an axle

aiseal nm see **asal**

aisean, gen **aisne**, pl **aisnean, aisnichean** & **asnaichean** nf a rib

aiseirigh nf invar 1 (relig) resurrection, a resurrection; 2 resurgence, revival, a revival, **aiseirigh na Gàidhlig** the resurgence of Gaelic, cf **ath-bheothachadh 2**

Àisia nf invar Asia (used with the art), **thachair e san Àisia** it happened in Asia

Àisianach, gen & pl **Àisianaich** nm an Asian, also as adj **Àisianach** Asian

aisling, aislinge, aislingean nf a dream, a vision, **bha thu ag aisling** you were dreaming or seeing things, cf **bruadar 2**

aiste prep pron, see **às**

aiste, aiste, aistidhean nf 1 (school etc) an essay; 2 (journalism etc) an article

aistese prep pron (emph), see **às**

àite, gen **àite**, pl **àiteachan, àitichean** & **àiteannan** nm 1 a place, **'s e àite brèagha a th' ann** it's a bonny/beautiful place, **bha a h-uile rud na àite fhèin** everything was in its (proper) place, **àite-coise** pedestrian crossing, **àite-fuirich** & **àite-còmhnaidh**, a dwelling, a dwelling-place, accommodation, **àite-falaich** a hiding-place, cf **bad 1, ionad**; 2 **an àite** prep instead of, in place of (with gen), **sìth an àite cogaidh** peace instead of war, **thàinig Iain na h-àite** Iain came in her place/instead of her

àiteach, gen **àitich** nm cultivation (of land or crops), **talamh àitich** arable/cultivable land, cf **àiteachadh 1 & 2**

àiteachadh, gen **àiteachaidh** nm 1 (the act of) cultivating (land); 2 (also abstr) cultivation (of land), cf **àiteach**; 3 occupation of, dwelling on, (land etc), **luchd-àiteachaidh** m coll inhabitants, dwellers, cf **còmhnaidh 1, tuineachadh 1 & 2**

àiteachail *adj* agricultural

àiteachas, *gen* **àiteachais** *nm* & **àiteachd** *nf invar* agriculture, (*knowledge of*) farming

aiteal, *gen* & *pl* **aiteil** *nm* a glimpse, **fhuair iad aiteal den tìr** they got a glimpse of the land, **aiteal grèine** a glimpse/blink of sunshine, *cf* **plathadh** 1

aiteamh, *gen* **aiteimh** *nm* a thaw, thawing, **an uair a thig an t-aiteamh** when the thaw comes

àiteigin *nm invar* somewhere, (*lit*) some place, **chaill mi ann an àiteigin e** I lost it somewhere (or other)

àite-pàighidh, **àite-pàighidh**, **àiteachan-pàighidh** *nm* (*in supermarket etc*) a checkout, a paypoint, a till, *cf* **cobhan**

aithghearr *adj* 1 short, brisk, quick, **sùil aithghearr air a' ghleoc** a quick look at the clock; 2 (*manner etc*) abrupt, *cf* **cas** *adj* 3; 3 *esp in expr* **a dh'aithghearr** *adv* soon, shortly, **bidh sinn ann a dh'aithghearr** we'll be there soon

aithghearrachd *nf invar* 1 abbreviation, an abbreviation, *cf* **giorrachadh** 2; 2 a short cut, **ghabh sinn aithghearrachd** we took a short cut, *cf* **bealach** 4; 3 *in expr* **an aithghearrachd** *adv* swiftly, promptly, 'sharpish', **sgrìobh e an litir an aithghearrachd** he wrote the letter in no time (at all), *cf* **grad** 3

aithisg, **aithisge**, **aithisgean** *nf* a report (*esp formal & written*), an account, *cf* **aithris** 1

aithne *nf invar* 1 knowledge, acquaintance (*usu of people*); 2 *esp in expr* **cuir aithne air** get to know, get acquainted with; 3 *esp in expr* **an aithne dhuibh e** (etc)? **chan aithne** do you know him (etc)? no; *cf* **eòlach** 2, **eòlas** 3

aithneachadh & **faithneachadh**, *gen* **(f)aithneachaidh** *nm* (*the act of*) knowing etc (*see senses of* **aithnich** *v*)

àithneach *adj* imperative (*gram*)

aithnich & **faithnich**, *vt, pres part* **ag aithneachadh** & **a' faithneachadh**, 1 know, recognise (*of people*), **aithnichidh sinn a-rithist sibh** we'll know/recognise you another time, **chan aithnichinn e ged a thachradh e nam bhrochan orm** I wouldn't know him if I came upon him in my porridge/gruel; 2 know, experience, **cha do dh'aithnich ar clann na duilgheadasan a bh' againn** our children didn't know/experience the problems we had; 3 acknowledge, **dh'aithnich e a mhearachd** he acknowledged his mistake

aithreachail *adj* repentant, remorseful

aithreachas, *gen* **aithreachais** *nm* (*relig*) repentance, remorse, **rinn iad/ghabh iad aithreachas** they repented

aithris *vt, pres part* **ag aithris**, 1 report or recount something; 2 recite, **dh'aithris i pìos bàrdachd** she recited a piece of poetry; 3 (*play etc*) rehearse

aithris, **aithrise**, **aithrisean** *nf* 1 a report, an account (*verbal or written*), **tha *Aithris na Maidne* air an rèidio gach là** 'Morning Report'/'Morning Bulletin' is on the radio every day, **beul-aithris** oral tradition, *cf* **cunntas** 4, **iomradh** 2; 2 recitation, a recitation; 3 (*play etc*) rehearsal, a rehearsal

àitich *vt, pres part* **ag àiteachadh**, 1 cultivate (*land or crops*), *cf* **obraich** 2; 2 inhabit, dwell on, occupy (*land etc*), *cf* (*vi*) **còmhnaich**

aitreabh, **aitreibh**, **aitreabhan** *nm* a building, a dwelling, *cf more usu* **fàrdach** 1, **togalach**

àl, *gen* **àil** *nm* (*trad*) a litter, a brood, progeny, the young of a bird or mammal, *cf* **cuain**

àlainn *adj* 1 lovely, fine, splendid, **abair bad àlainn!** what a lovely spot! **taigh àlainn** a lovely/fine house, *cf* **àillidh** 2, **brèagha**, **grinn** 1; 2 (*more fam*) fine, grand, **bha sin dìreach àlainn!** that was just grand!, *cf* **sgoinneil**

Alba, *gen* **Alba**, *trad gen* **Albann**, *trad dat* **Albainn** *nf* Scotland, **ann an Alba** or (*trad*) **ann an Albainn** in Scotland, **Gàidhlig na h-Alba** or (*trad*) **na h-Albann** the Gaelic of Scotland, Scottish/Scots Gaelic, **à Alba** or (*trad*) **à/às Albainn** from Scotland

Albàinia *nf invar* Albania

Albàinianach *gan* & *pl* **Albàinianaich** *nm* an Albanian, *also as adj* Albanian

Albais, *gen* **Albaise** *nf* the Scots language, Scots, *cf* **A' Bheurla Ghallta** (*see* **Beurla** 2)

Albannach, *gen* & *pl* **Albannaich** *nm* a Scotsman, a Scot, **ban-Albannach** *f* a Scotswoman, *also as adj* **Albannach** Scottish, Scots

alcol, *gen* **alcoil** *nm* alcohol

allaban, *gen* **allabain** *nm* (*trad*) wandering(s), (*trad*) **rach air allaban** take to wandering, become a wanderer, *cf* **fuadan** 1

allaidh *adj* wild (*ie not domesticated*), *usu in* set compounds, *eg* **madadh-allaidh** *m* a wolf (*cf* **faol**), **damhan-allaidh** *m* a spider, *cf* **fiadhaich** 1

allt, *gen* & *pl* **uillt** *nm* a mountain stream, a stream, a burn, *cf* **abhainn**, **sruth** *n* 1

alltan, *gen* & *pl* **alltain** *nm* (*dimin of* **allt**) a (*usu small*) stream, a water, (*stream name*) **an t-Alltan Dubh** Black Water

alt, uilt, altan *nm* **1** (*anat*) a joint, **alt na h-uilne** the elbow joint; **2** a method, a way (*of doing something*), a knack, **cha robh an t-alt againn air eòin a ghlacadh** we didn't know the way to catch/the method/art of catching birds, **air alt 's gun . . .** in such a way that . . . , so that . . . , *cf* **dòigh 1, liut, seòl**[2] **1; 3** (*gram*) **an t-alt** the article; **4** *in expr* **an altan a chèile** *or* (*trad*) **an altaibh a chèile** together (*ie consecutive, one after the other*), **chan urrainn dha dà fhacal a chur an altaibh/an altan a chèile** he can't string two words together, *cf* **an ceann a chèile** (*see* **ceann 3**)

altachadh, *gen* **altachaidh** *nm* grace (*before meals etc*), **dèan** *v* **altachadh** say grace, (*prov*) **dh'ith e am biadh mun do rinn e an t-altachadh** he ate the food before he said the grace

altair, altarach, altairean *nf* an altar

altraim *vt, pres part* **ag altram** & **ag altramas,** **1** foster; **2** nurse (*esp a sick person*), *cf* **eiridnich**

altram, *gen* **altraim, 1** fosterage, fostering; **2** nursing, *cf exprs* **banaltram** *f* a nurse, **fear-altraim** *m* a male nurse, **taigh-altraim** *m* a nursing home, *cf* **eiridinn**

am *poss adj see* **an** *poss adj*

am *art see* **an** *art*

àm, ama, amannan *nm* time, *Note: not used for clock time (see* **uair 1**); **bho àm gu àm** from time to time, **bha i bochd aig an àm** she was poorly at the time, **aig an àm seo den bhliadhna** at this time of the year, **thàinig i ron àm** she came early, **tha an t-àm againn falbh** it's time for us to go/leave, **bha an t-àm ann** it was high time/not before time, **san àm a dh'fhalbh** in the past, in olden times, **anns na h-amannan ùra/nodha seo** in these modern times, **aig amannan tha** (*or* **bidh**) **e crosta, aig amannan eile tha** (*or* **bidh**) **e solta** at times he's naughty, at other times he's good (*cf* **uaireannan**)

a-mach *adv* **1** out (*expressing motion*), **leum iad a-mach às an trèan** they jumped out of the train, **sheall iad a-mach air an uinneig** they looked out of the window, **biadh a-mach à Tesco's** food from/out of Tesco's, **a-mach à seo (leat)!** out of here (with you), get out of here!, *cf* **a-muigh; 2** *other idioms* **chaidh iad a-mach air a chèile** they fell out (with each other), **bha e (a' dol) a-mach air staid na dùthcha,** he was going on about the state of the country, **cha toigh leam an dol-a-mach a th' aige** I don't like his manner/his behaviour/his 'carry on'/way of carrying on, **b' fheudar**

dhomh cur a-mach I had to be sick/vomit, **a-mach air doras** out of doors

amadan, *gen & pl* **amadain** *nm* a fool, **'s e amadan a th' ann dheth** he's a fool, **abair amadan!** what a fool! **na dèan sin, amadain!** don't do that, you fool!, (*also with milder sense*) **tha fios gu bheil gaol agam ort, amadain!** of course I love you, silly!, *cf* **òinseach**

amaideach *adj* foolish, silly, stupid, **duine/film amaideach** a stupid man/film, *cf* **baoth, faoin 1, gòrach 1 & 2**

amaideas, *gen* **amaideis** *nm* **1** (*esp in behaviour*) foolishness, silliness; **2** (*esp spoken*) nonsense, rubbish; *cf* **gòraiche 2**

a-màireach *adv* tomorrow, **nì mi a-màireach e** I'll do it tomorrow, **madainn a-màireach** tomorrow morning

amais *vti, pres part* **ag amas,** (at **air**) **1** aim (*weapon etc*), **dh'amais mi air an damh** I aimed at the stag, *cf* **cuimsich; 2** *in expr* **amais air** hit upon, find, come across, **dh'amais mi air deagh thàillear** I've found (etc) a good tailor, *cf* **faigh 2, lorg 2, tachair 3**

amaiseach *adj* (*of weapon, marksman, aim*) accurate, *cf* **cuimseach**

amalach *adj* complicated, *cf* **iomadh-fhillte** (*see* **fillte 2**)

amar, amair, amaran *nm* **1** a basin (*cf* **mias 1**), a pool (*cf* **linne 1**); **2** *now usu in compounds, eg* **amar-ionnlaid** a wash basin, **amar-snàimh** a swimming pool

amas, amais, amasan *nm* **1** (*weapons; the act of*) aiming etc (*see senses of* **amais** *v*); **2** (*fig*) an aim, an objective, a goal

am bitheantas *adv* usually, commonly, normally, generally, **am bitheantas bidh ìm buidhe** usually butter is yellow, *cf* **an cumantas, tric 2**

am broinn *prep, see* **broinn 2**

Ameireaga(idh) *nf invar* America

Ameireaganach, *gen & pl* **Ameireaganaich** *nm* an American, *also as adj* **Ameireaganach** American

am-feasd & **am-feast** *adv* ever, for ever, (*with verb in neg*) never, *cf much more usu* **a-chaoidh, bràth 2 & 3, sìorraidh 2**

amh *adj* **1** raw, uncooked, **muilt-fheòil amh** raw mutton, **stuth amh** raw materials; **2** unripe, **ubhal amh** an unripe apple, *cf* **an-abaich 1**

amha(i)ch, amhaiche, amhaichean *nf* **1** a neck, **ròpa mu amhaich** a rope around his neck, **bheir mi an ceann às an amhaich aige!** I'll wring his neck!, **amhaich botail** neck of a bottle, *cf* **muineal; 2** throat, **bha cnàimh**

aice na h-amhaich she had a bone in her throat, *cf* **sgòrnan**

a-mhàin *adv* **1** only (*more emph than* **ach 3 & 4**), **aon laogh a-mhàin** only one calf, **chan e a-mhàin gu bheil e gun airgead ach . . .** it's not only that he's got no money but . . . ; **2 ach a-mhàin** *prep* except, apart from, **cha robh duine beò ann ach mi fhìn a-mhàin** there wasn't a living soul except myself; *cf* **ach 3 & 4**

àmhainn, àmhainne, àmhainnean *nf* an oven

amhairc *vi, pres part* **ag amharc**, look (at **air**)

amharas, *gen pl* **amharais** *nm* suspicion, a suspicion, doubt, a doubt, *usu in expr* **tha amharas agam** (**agad** *etc*) I (you *etc*) suspect, **tha amharas agam gun deachaidh e a-null thairis** I suspect/(*Sc*) doubt he went abroad, **tha amharas agam air** I suspect him, **fo amharas** under suspicion, *cf* **teagamh 1**

amharasach *adj* suspicious, distrustful, doubting, *cf* **teagmhach**

amharc, *gen* **amhairc** *nm* **1** sight, view, *usu in exprs* **san amharc** in sight, **às an amharc** out of sight, *cf more usu* **fradharc 2, sealladh 3**; **2** sight (*of firearm*)

amhran *see* **òran**

am measg *prep* among (*with gen*), **am measg an fhraoich** among the heather, **am measg an luchd-èisteachd** among the listeners/the audience, **tha tòrr dhaoine, is mise nam measg, den bheachd gu . . .** many people, myself among them, believe that . . . , *cf less usu in this sense* **eadar 2**

a-muigh *adv* outside (*ie position*), **cà'il am bodach? tha e a-muigh** where's the old fellow? he's outside, (**air**) **an taobh a-muigh** (on) the outside, **a-muigh 's a-staigh** inside and out(side), (*more fig*) **oileanach an taobh a-muigh** an external student, *cf* **a-mach 1, a-staigh**

an *art* (*for forms see table p 491*) the

an (**am** *before b, f, m, p*) *poss adj* their, **chaill iad an airgead** they lost their money, **chaill iad am pàrantan** they lost their parents, *Note: before a verbal noun the poss adj can express the object of the verb or the subject of a passive construction,* **chan urrainn dhomh am faicinn** I can't see them, **bha e gan leantainn** he was following them (*lit* he was at their following), **an dèidh am fuadach** after they were/had been exiled

an (**am** *before b, f, m, p*) *prep, & its duplicated form* **ann an** (**ann am** *before b, f, m, p*). *The prep prons formed with* **an** *&* **ann an***, in the order first, second, third person singular, first, second, third person plural, and with*

the reflexive/emphatic particles in brackets, are as follows: **annam(sa), annad(sa), ann(san), innte(se), annainn(e), annaibh(se), annta(san)**, in me, in you *etc. For some examples of their use see* **2 *a*)** *&* ***b*)** *below.* **1** in (*mostly found in poetry & set phrases, & much less common than* **ann an**), **an treun a neirt** in his prime, at the height of his powers, **am beul na h-oidhche** at dusk, **an aithghearrachd** in a jiffy, **thèid mi an urras gu bheil e onarach** I guarantee/vouch that he is honest, **cuiridh mi an geall gur e slaightire a th' ann (dheth)!** I'll bet/wager he's a scoundrel!, *cf* **ann an 1**; **2 *a*)** *expressing identity* **is e sgrìobhadair a th' annam** I am a writer, **is e òinseach a th' annad** you are an idiot, **'s e poileasmain a th' annta** they are policemen, **is e là brèagha a th' ann!** it's a fine day! ***b*)** *expressing location, attributes, existence* **seo a' phoit, cuir an tì innte** here's the pot, put the tea in it, **is e inntinn mhath a th' innte** she's got a good mind, **a bheil Iain ann?** is Iain here/there/in? **creididh mi/tha mi a' creidsinn gu bheil taibhsean ann** I believe that there are ghosts (*ie* here), *or* I believe that ghosts exist; **3** *Note: the poss adjs* **mo, do, a, ar, ur, an** *combine with* **an** *to give* **nam, nad, na, na, nar, nur, nan** (*before b, f, m, p* **nam**) in my/your etc, *also found as* **na mo, na do** *etc, examples of use:* **tha e nam phòcaid** it's in my pocket, **cur nad mhàileid e** put it in your bag, **chaidh e na shaighdear** he became a soldier, (*Sc*) he went for a sodger, **tha i na banaltram** she's a nurse, **bha sinn nar cadal** we were asleep/sleeping, (*bodily positions*) **a bheil sibh nur laighe?** are you lying down/in bed? **tha iad nan seasamh** they are standing/standing up, **bha mi nam shuidhe** I was sitting/sitting down/seated; *Note:* **nam** *etc can often express more temporary situations than* **annam** *etc, eg cf* **tha e na chìobair pàirt-ùine an-dràsta** he's a part-time shepherd just now, **'s e dotair a th' innte** she's a doctor (*ie permanently*); **4** *emphasising or 'highlighting' use of* **ann** *prep pron,* **is ann an-dè a thachair e** it's yesterday that it happened, **an ann le foill a cheannaich e e? is ann** is it/was it fraudulently that he bought it? yes, **an robh iad sgìth? cha robh, is ann leisg a bha iad!** were they tired? no, they were lazy (*emph*), *Note: this construction is used with adjs, advs & phrases, not with prons, nouns & proper nouns, contrast* **is e an trèana a chunnaic mi** it's/it was the train (*emph*) that I saw

an (**am** *before b, f, m, p, but note also second pers sing form* **a bheil**), *with neg v*, **nach**, *inter particle*, **an robh e ann?** was he there? **a bheil e ann?** is he there? **nach bi e ann?** won't he be there? **an do rinn iad e?** did they do it? **am faigh sinn e?** will we get it?

ana- (**an-** *before a vowel*) *a negativising prefix, but note that an apparently identical prefix can also intensify the sense of the following word, eg* **ana-blasta** *adj* tasteless, insipid, **ana-cothrom** *f* disadvantage, unfairness, *but* **ana-chùram** *m* extreme anxiety, **anabarrach** *adj* exceeding, extreme

an-abaich *adj* **1** (*fruit etc*) unripe, *cf* **amh 2**; **2** premature, **bha asaid an-abaich aice** she had a miscarriage, **bha breith an-abaich aice** she had a premature baby/gave birth prematurely, *cf* **ron mhithich** *under* **mithich** *nf invar*

anabarrach *adj* **1** extreme; **2** *often used as adv* **bha am biadh anabarrach math** the food was extremely good/excellent, *cf* **eagalach 3**, **uabhasach 2**

ana-cainnt, *gen* **ana-cainnte** *nf* abusive language, **dèan ana-cainnt** (*with prep* **air**) abuse (verbally)

an aghaidh *prep see* **aghaidh 3**

anail, **analach**, **anailean** *nf* breath, a breath, **on a tharraing mi mo chiad anail** since I first drew breath, **bha i a' gearan fo a h-anail** she was grumbling under her breath, **leig d' anail!** get your breath back!, take a breather!, *cf less usu* **deò 1**

anainn, **anainne**, **anainnean** *nf* eaves (*of building*)

an àite *prep see* **àite 2**

a-nall *adv* here (*ie movement*), hither, *Note: expressing point of view of person(s) towards whom the movement is made*, (*song*) **teann a-nall 's thoir dhomh do làmh** come hither/ over here and give me your hand, (*song*) **thoir a-nall Ailean thugam** bring Alan over (here) to me (*cf* **a-bhos**, **a-null**, **thall 1**), **a-null 's a-nall** hither and thither (*cf* **thall 's a-bhos** – *see* **thall 1**), **bha sinn a' bruidhinn/a' còmhradh a-null 's a-nall** we were talking about this and that

anam, **anma**, **anman** *nm* a soul, (*trad*) **air m' anam!** upon my soul!

ana-miann *nmf invar* lust, *cf* **drùis**

anart, **anairt**, **anartan** *nm* **1** (*the material*) linen, **lèine anairt** (*gen*) a linen shirt; **2** (*coll*) linen, **cuir** *v* **an t-anart sa phreas** put the linen in the cupboard, **anart bùird** table linen, **anart leapa** bed linen, (*trad*) **anart bàis** a shroud

an-asgaidh *adv see* **asgaidh 2**

an ath-bhliadhna *adv* next year

an ath-oidhch(e) *adv* tomorrow night

an ceann *prep see* **ceann 3**

an-ceart(u)air *adv* just now (*used for immediate past, present & immediate future*), **bha e ann an ceartair** he was here just now, **tha mi trang an ceartair** I'm busy just now, **bidh mi agad an ceartair** I'll be with you in a moment, *cf more usu* **an-dràsta**

an cèin *adv* abroad, *cf more usu* **thall thairis** (*see* **thairis 1**)

an cois *prep see* **cas** *n* **4**

an comhair *prep* in the direction of (*with gen*), *usu in phrases, eg* (**thuit e etc**) **an comhair a chinn/an comhair a chùil** (he fell etc) head first/backwards, *see* **comhair 1**

an-còmhnaidh *adv* always, **tha i còmhla ris an-còmhnaidh** she's always with him, *cf* **daonnan**, **sgur 2**

an-dè *adv* yesterday, **chunna mi an-dè i** I saw her yesterday

an dèidh & **às dèidh**, **1** *prep* after (*with gen*), **an dèidh na stoirme** after the storm, **bhruidhinn e nam/nad** (*etc*) **dhèidh** he spoke after me/you (*etc*), **tha am poileas nan dèidh** the police are after them, **an dèidh sin 's na dhèidh** after all (is said and done), **tha thu ceàrr! 's an dèidh sin?** you're wrong! so?; **2 an dèidh do** *conj* after, **an dèidh dhomh an sgoil fhàgail chaidh mi nam shaighdear** after leaving/after I left school I became a soldier, *cf* **air 11**; **3 an dèidh sin** *adv* nevertheless, however

an-diugh *adv* today, **madainn/feasgar an-diugh** this morning/afternoon, **bidh sin a' tachairt gu tric san là an-diugh** that often happens today/these days

an-dràsta (& **an-dràsda**) *adv* just now (*used for immediate past & present*) **bha e ann an-dràsta** he was here just now, **tha mi trang an-dràsta** I'm busy just now, **tha sinn ga dhèanamh an-dràsta fhèin** we're doing it this very instant/moment, **bha e agam an-dràsta fhèin** I had it just a moment ago, **an-dràsta 's a-rithist** now and again, from time to time, (*fam*) **tìoraidh an-dràsta** cheerio just now, (*less fam*) **mar sin leibh an-dràsta!** goodbye just now!, *cf* **an ceart(u)air, a-nis(e)**

an ear *adv see* **ear**

an-earar *adv* the day after tomorrow

anfhann *adj* infirm, *cf* **euslainteach** *adj*

anfhannachd *nf invar* infirmity, *cf* **euslaint(e)**, **tinneas**

an-fhoiseil *adj* restless, uneasy, *cf* **anshocrach**

an iar *adv see* **iar** *nf invar*

an impis *prep* about to, on the point of, **an impis falbh** about to leave/go, **an impis an dùthaich fhàgail** on the point of leaving the country, *cf* **beul 3, bi 11**

an-iochdmhor *adj* merciless, pitiless

a-nìos *adv* up, *Note: lit* 'from below', *expressing point of view of person(s) towards whom the ascent is made*, **thig a-nìos thugainn!** come up to us!, *cf* **a-nuas, sìos, suas**

a-nis(e) *adv* now (*usu more permanent or lasting than* **an-dràsta**), **tha iad a' fuireachd ann an Canada a-nis** they're living in Canada now, **tha thu gun obair, dè a nì thu a-nis?** you've no job, what will you do now? **A-nis, a Dhonnchaidh . . .** Now, Duncan . . . , *cf more transient* **an-ceart(u)air, an-dràsta**

an làthair *see* **làthair 2**

anmoch *adv* late, at a late hour, **anmoch san oidhche/san fheasgar** late in the night/in the evening, *cf* **fadalach 1** & *opposite* **moch**

annad (*emph form* **annadsa**), **annaibh** (*emph form* **annaibhse**), **annainn** (*emph form* **annainne**), **annam** (*emph form* **annamsa**), *prep prons, see* **an** *prep* 2

ann an (**ann am** *before b, f, m, p*) *prep, Note: this is a duplicated form of* **an** *prep, q.v*; **1** in, **dhùisg e ann an uaimh** he woke up in a cave, **bha an rùm ann am bùrach** the room was in a mess, **bidh mi an sin ann an tiotag** I'll be there in an instant, *cf* **an** & **anns an** *preps*; **2** *expressing identity* **is e caraid dhomh a tha ann an Dòmhnall** Donald is a friend of mine, *cf* **an** *prep* 2 *a*)

annas, annais, annasan *nm* a rarity, a novelty, **o chionn ghoirid bha coimpiutairean nan annas fhathast** not long ago computers were still a novelty, **chan eil sinn air an t-annas a thoirt às fhathast** we haven't got used to it, the novelty of it hasn't worn off for us yet, *cf* **suaicheantas 2**

annasach *adj* novel, unusual, odd, *cf* **neònach, nuadh**

anns an, anns a', anns na, *the forms taken by the preps* **an** & **ann an** *when combined with the art (often shortened to* **san, sa, sna**), in the, **anns an taigh** *or* **san taigh** in the house, **anns a' bhaile** *or* **sa bhaile** in the town, **anns na** *or* **sna Stàitean Aonaichte** in the United States, **anns an dol-seachad** in passing, incidentally, **san t-sabhal** in the barn, *Note:* **anns** *can also occur as* **as**, *eg,* (*fam*) **bha mi as a' bhùth** I was in the shop; *note also exprs with seasons as* **t-earrach, as t-samhradh, as t-fhoghar** in (the) spring, in (the) summer, in (the) autumn

(*but* **sa gheamhradh** in (the) winter), *cf* **an** *prep*, **ann an**

ann (*emph form* **annsan**), **annta** (*emph form* **anntasan**), *prep prons, see* **an** *prep* 2 & 4

a-nochd *adv* tonight

an sàs *see* **sàs 1**

an seo, ann an s(h)eo *advs see* **seo** *pron*

anshocair, anshocair, anshocran *nf* **1** unease, uneasiness; **2** discomfort; **3** sickness

anshocrach *adj* **1** uneasy, *cf* **an-fhoiseil**; **2** uncomfortable

an sin, ann an s(h)in *advs see* **sin** *pron*

an siud, ann an s(h)iud *advs see* **siud** *pron*

an tòir air *see* **tòir 2**

an toiseach *adv see* **toiseach 1**

an uair a & **nuair a**, *conj* when (*not used in questions, cf* **cuine**), (*song*) **nuair (a) bha mi òg** (Màiri Mhòr) when I was young, **an uair a thig Ùisdean bidh a h-uile duine ann** when Hugh comes everybody will be here

an uair sin *adv* then (*ie next, after that*), **ghabh e pinnt is an uair sin drama** he had a pint and then a dram/a whisky, **gabhaidh mi mo dhìnnear 's an uair sin bidh mi a' coimhead an telebhisean** I'll have my dinner and then I'll be watching the television

a-nuas *adv* down, *Note: lit* 'from above', *expressing point of view of person(s) towards whom the descent is made*, **thig a-nuas thugainn!** come down to us! *cf* **a-nìos, sìos, suas**

an-uiridh *adv* last year

a-null *adv* there (*ie movement*), thither, over, across, *Note: envisaged from the point from which the movement is made*, **thèid mi a-null do Ghlaschu** I'll go over/across to Glasgow (*cf* **a-bhos, a-nall, thall 1**), **thèid sinn a-null thairis** we'll go abroad/overseas, **a-null 's a-nall** hither and thither (*cf* **thall 's a-bhos** – *see* **thall 1**), (*idiom*) **bha sinn a' còmhradh a-null 's a-nall** we were chatting about this and that

an urra *see* **urra**

ao- *prefix see* **eu-**

aobhar *nm see* **adhbhar**

aobrann *nmf see* **adhbrann**

aodach, aodaich, aodaichean *nm* **1** cloth, material, *cf* **clò[1] 1, stuth 1**; **2** *more usu* clothes, clothing, **m' aodach** *or* **mo chuid aodaich** my clothes, **chuir i oirre a h-aodach/a cuid aodaich** she put on her clothes, she got dressed, **ball-aodaich** *m* a garment, a piece *or* item of clothing, **aodach-leapa** bedclothes,

aodach-oidhche night clothes, **fo-aodach** underclothes, *cf less usu* **trusgan 1**

aodann, aodainn, aodainnean *nm* **1** a face, **mhaisich i a h-aodann** she made up her face, **clàr an aodainn** the brow/forehead, **bhuail e e an clàr a aodainn** he struck him full in the face, *cf* **aghaidh 1**; **2** (*topog*) a hillface, a hillslope, (*placename*) **An t-Aodann Bàn** Edinbane (the white/pale hillface), *cf* **leathad, leitir, ruighe 2**

aodannan, *gen & pl* **aodannain** *nm* (*fancy dress etc*) a mask, *cf* **aghaidh-choimheach, masg**

aoibhneach *adj* **1** pleasant, *cf* **taitneach, tlachdmhor 1**; **2** glad, happy, *cf* **sona, toilichte**; **3** joyful, *cf* **àghmhor 2, aighearach**

aoidion, aoidiona, aoidionan *nm* (*tap etc*) a leak

aoidionach & **aoidion** *adj*, not waterproof or watertight, leaky

aoigh, aoigh, aoighean *nm* **1** a guest; **2** (*hotel etc*) a resident

aoigheachd, *nf* hospitality, **air aoigheachd aig teaghlach Sgitheanach** enjoying the hospitality of/as guests of a Skye family

aoigheil *adj* **1** generous; **2** hospitable; *cf* **fial 1**

aoir, aoire, aoirean *nf* (*Lit etc*) satire, a satire

aois, aoise, aoisean *nf* **1** age, **dè an aois a tha Iain? tha e trì bliadhna a dh'aois** how old is Iain? he's three years old; **2** old age, (*idiom*) **tha iad a' tarraing gu h-aois a-nis** they're getting on in years/getting quite old now

aol, *gen* **aoil** *nm* (*mineral*) lime

aom *vi, pres part* **ag aomadh, 1** bend, incline (*phys*), *cf* **crom** *v* **1, fiar** *v* **1, lùb** *v* **1**; **2** tend, be inclined (*to do something*)

aomadh, *gen* **aomaidh** *nm* **1** bending, tending etc (*see senses of* **aom** *v*); **2** a tendency, an inclination, a trend, **aomadh eaconomach** an economic trend

aon *num adj* **1** one (*lenites following cons where possible*), **aon fhireannach is aon bhoireannach** one male and one female, one man and one woman, **thachair e aon là** it happened one day, **bidh smùid air gach aon là** he's drunk every single day; **2** *with art* the only, **is esan an t-aon mhac a th' aca** he's the only son they have; **3** *with art* the same, **bha sinn a' fuireachd san aon taigh** we were living in the same house, *in expr* (*trad*) **ag iomairt an aon ràimh** (*lit* rowing the same oar) pulling together, working together, co-operating, *cf* **ceudna 1**

aon *nmf* **1** one, **cia mheud a th' agad? a h-aon** how many have you got? one, **ceithir fichead**

's a h-aon eighty-one, **cò a tha airson falbh? tha mise air aon!** who's for leaving? I am, for one!; **2** (*cards*) **an t-aon** the ace

aonach, aonaich, aonaichean *nm* (*topog*) an extensive upland moor, *cf* **mòinteach, monadh 1, sliabh 1**

aonachadh, *gen* **aonachaidh** *nm* **1** (*the act of*) uniting, combining; **2** (*pol*) coalition, a coalition

aonad, aonaid, aonadan *nm* **1** (*maths etc*) a unit, **aonad tomhais** a unit of measurement; **2** (*building, department etc*) a unit, **aonad mhàthraichean** a maternity unit, **aonad-leasachaidh** a development unit

aona deug *num adj* eleventh, **an t-aona là deug den Ògmhios** the eleventh of June

aonadh, aonaidh, aonaidhean *nm* union, a union, a merger, **aonadh-ceàird/ciùird** a trade(s) union, **na h-Aonaidhean** the (Trades) Unions, **Aonadh Nàiseanta nam Maraichean** the National Union of Seamen, (*pol, law*) **An t-Aonadh** the Union (*between Scotland & England*), **Achd an Aonaidh** the Act of Union, **Aonadh na h-Eòrpa** the European Union

aonaich *vti, pres part* **ag aonachadh**, unite, combine, merge

aonaichte *adj & past part*, united, **na Stàitean Aonaichte** the United States

aonan *adj & pron* one, *similar uses to* **aon** *num adj* **1**, *but can be more emphatic*, **aonan dhiubh co-dhiù** one of them at least, *cf more usu* **aon** *num adj* **1**

aonar, *gen* **aonair** *nmf*, (*usu in phrase* **nam/ nad** (*etc*) **aonar**) **1** one person, **dhìrich i Everest na h-aonar** she climbed Everest alone/solo (*lit* as one person); **2** aloneness, solitude, the state of being by oneself, **tha i a' fuireachd na h-aonar** she is living alone/by herself, in solitude

aonaran, aonarain, aonaranan *nm* a hermit, a recluse, a loner

aon(a)ranach *adj* **1** (*of place*) lonely, desolate, deserted, isolated, *cf* **fàs** *adj* **1, uaigneach 2**; **2** (*of person*) lonely, **bha iad a' faireachdainn aonaranach** they were feeling lonely, *cf* **uaigneach 1**

aon(a)ranachd *nf invar* loneliness, desolation etc (*see senses of* **aonaranach** *adj*)

aon-deug 1 *n* eleven, **cia mheud taigh a bh' ann? bha a h-aon-deug** how many houses were there? eleven; **2** *as num adj* eleven, **aon chù deug** eleven dogs, **aon uair deug** eleven o'clock

aon-fhillte *adj* simple, uncomplicated, **buidheachas aon-fhillte** simple gratitude, *cf* **sìmplidh 1 & 2**

aon-inntinneach *adj* unanimous, of one/the same mind

aon-sheasmhach *adj* (*of equipment etc*) stand-alone

aonta & **aontadh**, *gen* **aontaidh**, *pl* **aontaidhean** *nm* agreement, assent, consent, an agreement, a settlement, **thàinig an dà riaghaltas gu aonta** the two governments came to an agreement/reached a settlement, **feumaidh sinn aonta a' bhaile fhaighinn** we must get the township's agreement/consent, *cf* **còrdadh 2**

aontachadh, *gen* **aontachaidh** *nm* (*the act of*) agreeing etc (*see* **aontaich** *v*)

aontaich *vi*, *pres part* **ag aontachadh**, agree, **dh'aontaich iad le chèile** they agreed with each other, **chan eil mi ag aontachadh ris na molaidhean agaibh** I don't accept/agree to your proposals

aosmhor *adj* ancient, *cf* **àrsaidh**, **sean 2**

aosta & **aosda** *adj* (*of people*) old, aged, elderly, **tha am pàrantan air fàs gu math aosta** their parents have grown quite old, *cf* **sean 1**

aotrom *adj* 1 light, **bha na clachan aotrom a dh'aindeoin am meud** the stones were light in spite of their size; 2 light (*ie not serious*), **na h-òrain mhòra 's na h-òrain aotrom** the big/great/classic songs and the light songs, **a' bruidhinn mu rudan aotrom** talking about unimportant/trivial/flippant things

aotromachadh, *gen* **aotromachaidh** *nm* (*the act of*) lightening etc (*see senses of* **aotromaich** *v*)

aotromaich *vt*, *pres part* **ag aotromachadh**, 1 lighten, (*burden etc*) make light or lighter, alleviate; 2 (*ship etc*) unload, *cf* **falmhaich 2**

aotroman, *gen* & *pl* **aotromain** *nm* (*anat*) a bladder

aparan, **aparain**, **aparanan** *nm* an apron

ar (leam/leat etc) *defective verb* (*trad & formal*) (I/you etc) think, it seems (to me/you etc), **ar leam gu bheil e ro anmoch** I think/I consider that it is too late, *cf more usu* **creid 2, saoil**

ar (ar n- before a vowel) poss adj our, **ar dachaigh** our home, **ar n-athair** our father, *Note: before a verbal noun the poss adj can express the object of the verb or the subject of a passive construction*, (*trad*) **rinn iad ar sgriosadh** they destroyed us/wrought our destruction, **chaidh ar moladh** we were praised, **an dèidh dhaibh ar fògradh** after they had driven us out

àr, àir, àir *nm* slaughter, *cf less strong* **marbhadh**

àra, àrann, àirnean *nf* (*anat*) a kidney, *cf* **dubhag**

Arabach, *gen* & *pl* **Arabaich** an Arab, *also as adj* **Arabach** Arab, Arabic, **figearan** *m* **arabach** arabic numerals

Arabais *nf invar* (*lang*) Arabic

àrach, *gen* **àraich** *nm* raising, upbringing, rearing, (*song*) **soraidh leis an àit' an d' fhuair mi m' àrach òg** (Màiri Mhòr) farewell to the place in which I was raised (*lit* got my raising) when young, *cf* **togail**

àrachas, *gen* **àrachais** *nm* insurance, **àrachas beatha/nàiseanta** life/national insurance, **dìon/poileasaidh àrachais** insurance cover/policy, **tagairt àrachais** an insurance claim, *cf* **urras 3**

àradh & **fàradh**, *gen* **(f)àraidh**, *pl* **(f)àraidhean** *nm* a ladder, **a' dìreadh àraidh** climbing a ladder

Aràbia, *nf invar* Arabia

àraich *vt*, *pres part* **ag àrach**, raise, rear, bring up, **ag àrach cloinne/uan** raising/rearing children/lambs, *cf* **tog 3**

àraid *adj* 1 particular, *see* **àraidh 1**; 2 peculiar, strange, unusual, **bha dìthis bhan aige, nach robh sin àraid?** he had two wives, wasn't that strange?, *cf* **neònach**, & *stronger* **iongantach**

àraidh, *also* **àraid**, *adj* 1 particular, in particular, **'s e taigh àraidh a tha mi airson a cheannach** it's a particular house/one house in particular that I want to buy, *cf* **sònraichte 1**; 2 exceptional, unusual, special, **'s e duine àraidh a bh' ann** he was an exceptional/unusual man, *cf* **leth 2**; 3 *in expr* **gu h-àraid(h)** *adv* especially, particularly, **is toigh leam am foghar, is gu h-àraid(h) an t-Sultain** I like the autumn, and especially September, *cf* **sònraichte 3** & *see* **seac**

àrainneachd *nf invar, with art*, (*ecology*) **an àrainneachd** the environment

ar-a-mach *nm invar* rebellion, a rebellion, an uprising, **rinn an sluagh ar-a-mach an aghaidh an luchd-riaghlaidh** the people rebelled/rose up against their rulers, *cf* **èirigh 2**

aran, *gen* **arain** *nm* bread, *Note: formerly restricted to home baked bread*, **lof** *being used for shop bread*

a-raoir *adv* last night, **feasgar a-raoir** last/yesterday evening, (*song*) **chan eil fios aig duin' air thalamh far an robh mi (a-)raoir** no-one on earth knows where I was last night

araon *adv* (*rather trad*) both, **araon air Ghàidhealtachd agus air Ghalltachd** both in Highlands and Lowlands, *cf* **le chèile** (*see* **le 1**), **cuid 4, eadar 3**

arbhar, *gen* **arbhair** *nm* corn

àrc, àirce, àrcan *nf* cork, a cork, *cf* **corcais**

Arcach, *gen & pl* **Arcaich** *nm* an Orcadian, *also as adj*, **Arcach** Orcadian, of, from or pertaining to Orkney

Arcaibh *nm invar* Orkney

arc-eòlaiche, arc-eòlaiche, arc-eòlaichean *nm* an archaeologist

àrd *adj* **1** (*person, building, hill etc*) high, tall; **2** (*sounds*) loud, **tha an ceòl sin uabhasach àrd!** that music is terribly loud! *cf trad* **labhar**; **3** *often as prefix* **àrd-** high, principal, supreme, **àrd-shagart** *m* a high priest, **àrd-chuidiche** *m* a principal assistant, **àrd-chumhachd** *mf* supreme power (*& see examples below*), *cf* **prìomh**

àrdachadh, *gen* **àrdachaidh** *nm* **1** (*the act of*) increasing etc (*see senses of* **àrdaich** *v*); **2** promotion, a promotion, a rise, **fhuair e àrdachadh** he got promotion, **fhuair sinn àrdachadh pàighidh** we got a pay rise

àrdaich *vt*, *pres part* **ag àrdachadh**, **1** increase, raise, **dh'àrdaich an luchd-stiùiridh tuarastal an luchd-obrach** the management increased/raised the salary of the workforce; **2** promote, further, (*calque*) **àrdaich ìomhaigh na Gàidhlig** promote the image/raise the profile of Gaelic

àrdaichear, àrdaicheir, àrdaichearan *nm* a lift, an elevator

àrdan, *gen* **àrdain** *nm* arrogance, pride (*usu excessive*), (*song*) **leis an àrdan nach d' rinn feum dhomh** through the pride that did me no good at all, *cf* **pròis, uaibhreas 2**

àrdanach *adj* arrogant, (*usu excessively*) proud, *cf* **dàna 4, uaibhreach 2**

àrd-doras, àrd-dorais, àrd-dorsan *nm* a lintel

àrd-easbaig, àrd-easbaig, àrd-easbaigean *nm* an archbishop

àrd-ìre *nf invar & adj* higher, high-grade, high-level, **rinn e Gàidhlig aig Àrd-ìre** he did Higher Gaelic/Gaelic at Higher Grade/Highers, (*adjectivally*) **tha na sgoilearan a' feuchainn nan deuchainnean Àrd-ìre aca** the pupils are taking/sitting their Higher Exams/their Highers, **foghlam àrd-ìre** Higher/Further (*ie Tertiary*) Education

àrd-sgoil, àrd-sgoile, àrd-sgoiltean *nf* a high school, a secondary school, (*Sc*) an academy, **Àrd-sgoil Phort Rìgh** Portree High School, **dh'ionnsaich iad Spàinnis anns an àrd-sgoil** they learnt/studied Spanish at secondary school

àrd-ùrlar, àrd-ùrlair, àrd-ùrlaran *nm* (*theatre, hall etc*) a stage, a platform

àrd-urram, *gen* **àrd-urraim** *nm* distinction, high honour, **ghabh i ceum le àrd-urram** she graduated with First Class Honours/with Distinction

a rèir *prep* **1** according to (*with gen*), **a rèir na mòr-chuid** in most people's opinion, according to the majority, **do gach fear a rèir a chomais** to each one according to his ability; **2** *as adv* accordingly, pro rata, proportionately, **thug iad còig notaichean do Mhàiri agus don fheadhainn eile a rèir** they gave Mary five pounds and the others pro rata/accordingly/proportionately; **3** *in expr* **a rèir choltais** apparently, seemingly, *see* **coltas 2**

a-rèist(e) & **a-rèisd(e)** *adv* then, in that case, **cha do ghoid mise e! cò a ghoid e a-rèist?** I didn't steal it! who stole it then?, *cf* **ma 2**

argamaid, argamaide, argamaidean *nf* **1** an argument, a line of reasoning, **cha do lean mi an argamaid aice** I didn't follow/understand her argument; **2** (*philo etc*) discussion, disputation; **3** (*more hostile*) arguing, an argument, *cf* **trod 2**

argamaidich *vi*, *pres part* **ag argamaid**, argue

a-riamh *adv* **1** ever, always, (*poem*) **'s tha mo ghaol aig Allt Hallaig . . . 's bha i riamh** (Somhairle MacGill-Eain) and my love is at the Burn of Hallaig . . . and she has always been, *cf* **daonnan**; **2** *more usu with a neg verb*, never, **an robh thu san Èipheit? cha robh a-riamh** have you been to Egypt? never, *Note: used only to refer to past time, for* ever *&* never *in the future cf* **a-chaoidh 2, bràth 2 & 3, sìorraidh 2**

a-rithist *adv* again, **na dèan a-rithist e!** don't do it again! (*on parting*) **chì sinn a-rithist sibh!** we'll see you again! (*cf* **fhathast 3**), (*calque*) **an-dràsta 's a-rithist** now and again, from time to time, occasionally

arm, *gen & pl* **airm** *nm* an army, **bha sinn san arm aig an àm sin** we were in the army at that time, (*song*) **nuair a thèid mi fhìn dhan arm, gheibh mi fèileadh 's sporan garbh** when I go to the army, I will get a kilt and a rough sporran, *cf less usu* **armailt**

armachadh, *gen* **armachaidh** *nm* (*the act of*) arming

armachd *nf invar* **1** armour; **2** arms, weapons

armaich *vt*, *pres part* **ag armachadh**, arm, **dh'armaich iad an sluagh airson a'**

chogaidh a bha a' tighinn they armed the people for the coming war

armailt, armailte, armailtean *nm* an army, *cf more usu* arm

armlann, armlainn, armlannan *nf* an armoury (*ie store for weapons*), an arsenal

arsa, *before a vowel usu* ars, *def verb used after direct speech*, said (*ie past tense only*), 'Gu sealladh orm!' ars Eòghann. 'Dè tha ceàrr ort?' arsa Tormod 'Good heavens/Good grief!' said Ewan. 'What's the matter with you?' said Norman, *Note: used in speech and in writing to report conversations; more trad than* can & abair

àrsaidh *adj* 1 ancient, togalaichean/beul-oideas àrsaidh ancient buildings/lore, *cf* aosmhor, sean 2; 2 archaic

àrsaidheachd *nf invar* 1 antiquarianism; 2 archaeology

àrsair, àrsair, àrsairean *nm* 1 an antiquarian; 2 an archaeologist

arspag *see* farspag

Artach *adj* Arctic

Artaig, *gen* Artaige *nf, used with art*, an Artaig the Arctic

as (*for* a is that is, who is) *see* is *v* 6

as *prep, see* anns an *Note*

às *prep, see* à *prep*

às *prep pron, see* à *prep*

asad (*emph form* asadsa), asaibh (*emph form* asaibhse), asainn (*emph form* asainne), *see* à *prep*

asaid, asaide, asaidean *nf* 1 (*gynaecology*) delivery, a delivery, childbirth, asaid an-abaich a premature birth/delivery

às-aimsireil *adj* anachronistic

asal, asail, asalan *nf, also* aiseal, aiseil, aisealan *nm*, an ass; a donkey

asam (*emph form* asamsa) *prep pron, see* à *prep*

às aonais *prep* without, in the absence of, (*with gen*), às aonais chàirdean without friends/relations, tha mi brònach às d' aonais I'm sad without you/in your absence, *cf* às eugmhais & gun *preps*

às dèidh *prep see* an dèidh

às eugmhais *prep* without, in the absence of, *cf more usu* às aonais, *which is used in a similar way* (*see above*) & gun *prep*

asgaidh, asgaidhe, asgaidhean *nf* 1 a present, a gift, *cf more usu* tabhartas, tiodhlac; 2 *usu in exprs* an asgaidh free, as a gift, & saor 's an-asgaidh *adv* free, free of charge, fhuair mi mo làithean-saora saor 's an asgaidh I got my holidays completely free, *cf* saor *adj* 3

asgair, asgair, asgairean *nm* (*orthog*) an apostrophe

às leth *prep see* leth 6 & 7

às-san *emph prep pron, see* à *prep*

asta (*emph form* astasan), *prep pron, see* à *prep*

a-staigh *adv* in, *Note: traditionally* a-staigh *expresses 'position within' and* a-steach *'movement into', but this distinction is not always observed, cf both* thig a-steach! *and* thig a-staigh! *for* come in/inside!; (*prov*) cha robh thu a-staigh an uair a chaidh a' chiall a roinn you weren't in/at home when sense was shared out, bha an coitheanal a-staigh san eaglais the congregation was inside the church, taobh a-staigh is taobh a-muigh an togalaich inside and outside the building, the inside/interior and the outside/exterior of the building, *cf* broinn 2, a-mach, a-muigh, a-steach

asta *prep pron, see* à *prep*

astar, *gen & pl* astair *nm* 1 distance, a distance, 's e astar math a tha sin that's a good distance/a fair step; 2 speed, a speed, ag itealaich aig astar gun tomhas flying at an incalculable speed, bha astar math aca they were going at a good speed, astar gun chiall an insane speed, *cf* luas 1

astarach *adj* fast, speedy, *cf more usu* luath *adj* 1

astasan *emph prep pron, see* à *prep*

a-steach *adv* 1 in, into, inside, *Note: traditionally* a-staigh *expresses 'position within' and* a-steach *'movement into', but this distinction is not always observed, cf both* thig a-steach! *and* thig a-staigh! *for* come in/inside!; chaidh sinn a-steach don eaglais we went into the church, cuir a' bhò a-steach don bhàthaich put the cow in/into the byre, *cf* a-staigh; 2 *also in expr* thàinig e a-steach oirre (etc) gu . . . it occurred to her (etc) that . . ., she (etc) realised that . . .

Astràilia *nf invar* Australia

Astràilianach, *gen & pl* Astràilianaich *nm* an Australian, *also as adj* Astràilianach Australian

at, at, atan *nm* swelling, a swelling, tha at na mo ghlùin I've a swelling in my knee, *cf* bòcadh 2

at *vi, pres part* ag at & ag atadh, swell, puff up, tha mo shròn ag at/air at my nose is swelling/is swollen, *cf* bòc 1, sèid 2

atachas, *gen & pl* atachais *nm* (*fin*) inflation

atadh, *gen* ataidh *nm* (*the act of*) swelling etc (*see senses of* at *v*)

ataireachd *nf invar* swelling, a swell (*esp of sea*), (*song*) **an ataireachd àrd** the lofty swell, *cf* **sumainn**

atamach *adj* atomic

ath *adj* next, *precedes the noun (which is lenited where possible) & is usu used with the art,* **an ath là/sheachdain/mhìos** (the) next day/ week/month, **chaidh an obair a chur air ath là** the work was left till another day/put off, **bidh iad a' fuireachd an ath-dhoras** they'll be staying/living next door

àth, àtha, àthan *nf* a kiln

àth, àth, àthan *nm* a ford

ath- *prefix usu corres to Eng* re-, *see examples below*

ath- *prefix corres to Eng* after-, *eg* **ath-bhreith** *f* afterbirth, **ath-fhrithealadh** *m* aftercare, **ath-bhlas** *m* aftertaste

athach, *gen & pl* **athaich** *nm* a giant, *cf more usu* **famhair** 1

athair, athar, athraichean *nm* 1 a father, **m' athair 's mo mhàthair** my father and (my) mother, **athair-cèile** a father-in-law, **bràthair d' athar** your uncle, **piuthar d' athar** your aunt (*ie on the father's side*); 2 a progenitor, a forefather, **ar n-athraichean** our forefathers

athaireil *adj* fatherly, paternal

athaiseach *adj* dilatory, tardy

ath-aithris *vt, pres part* **ag ath-aithris**, repeat, reiterate, **dh'ath-aithris e na naidheachdan air fad** he repeated/told again all the news

a thaobh *prep see* **taobh** 5

ath-aonachadh, ath-aonachaidh, ath-aonachaidhean *nm* 1 (*the act of*) reuniting, reunifying; 2 reunification, a reunification

ath-aonaich *vt, pres part* **ag ath-aonachadh**, reunite, reunify

atharrachadh, atharrachaidh, atharrachaidhean *nm* (*the act of*) changing, altering, varying; 2 change, a change, alteration, an alteration, a variation, **thàinig atharrachadh air** a change came over him, he changed, *cf* **caochladh** 2, **mùthadh** 2

atharraich *vti, pres part* **ag atharrachadh**, change, alter, vary, **dh'atharraich mi mo chuid aodaich** I changed my clothes, **tha am baile air atharrachadh gu mòr** the township/town has changed considerably, *cf* **caochail** 1, **mùth** 1

atharrais *nf invar* 1 (*the act of*) copying etc (*see senses of* **atharrais** *v*); 2 imitation, an imitation, mimicry, **dèan atharrais air a' Phrìomhair** imitate/mimic the Prime Minister, *cf* **atharrais** *v*

atharrais *vt, pres part* **ag atharrais**, *with prep* **air**, copy, mimic, imitate, **atharrais air a' Phrìomhair** imitate/mimic the Prime Minister, *cf* **atharrais** *n*

ath-bheachd, ath-bheachda, ath-bheachdan *nm* an afterthought, a revised opinion, *cf* **ath-smuain**

ath-bheothachadh, *gen* **ath-bheothachaidh** *nm* 1 (*the act of*) reviving etc (*see senses of* **ath-bheothaich** *v*); 2 revival, a revival, **ath-bheothachadh cultair** a revival of culture, (*trad*) **rinn thu m' ath-bheothachadh** you revived me/brought me back to life; 3 (*hist*) **an t-Ath-bheothachadh** the Renaissance, **Linn an Ath-bheothachaidh** the Renaissance Period

ath-bheothaich *vt, pres part* **ag ath-bheothachadh**, revive, bring back to life, **molaidhean airson na mion-chànain ath-bheothachadh** proposals to revive the lesser-used languages

ath-chruthaich *vt, pres part* **ag ath-chruthachadh**, recreate

ath-chuairtich, *pres part* **ath-chuairteachadh**, recycle

athchuinge, athchuinge, athchuingean *nf* (*pol etc*) an entreaty, a petition, **chuir trì mìle neach an ainm ris an athchuinge** three thousand individuals signed the petition

ath-chuir *vt, pres part* **ag ath-chur**, (*hort*) replant, transplant

ath-dhìol *vt, pres part* **ag ath-dhìoladh**, repay, pay back, **ath-dhìolaidh mi a-màireach na tha agad orm** I'll pay back what I owe you tomorrow, *cf* **dìoghail** 1, **pàigh** *v* 1

ath-leasachadh, ath-leasachaidh, ath-leasachaidhean *nm* 1 (*the act of*) redeveloping, reforming; 2 redevelopment, a redevelopment, **ath-leasachadh nam bailtean mòra** (the) redevelopment of the big cities; 3 reform, a reform, **ath-leasachadh nan seann phoileasaidhean** (the) reform of the old policies; 4 (*hist, relig*) **an t-Ath-leasachadh** the Reformation

ath-leasaich *vt, pres part* **ag ath-leasachadh**, redevelop, reform, **feumaidh sinn am pàrtaidh ath-leasachadh** we need to reform the party

ath-nuadhachadh, *gen* **ath-nuadhachaidh** *nm* 1 (*the act of*) renewing etc (*see senses of* **ath-nuadhaich** *v*); 2 renewal, a renewal, renovation, a renovation

ath-nuadhaich *vt, pres part* **ag ath-nuadhachadh**, 1 renew (*ie replace*), **b' fheudar dhuinn pìoban an uisge ath-**

nuadhachadh we had to renew the water pipes; **2** renew, renovate; **3** renew, re-affirm, **dh'ath-nuadhaich iad an creideamh/an geallaidhean** they renewed their faith/their vows, **ath-nuadhaich fo-sgrìobhadh** renew a subscription

ath-sgrìobh *vt, pres part* **ag ath-sgrìobhadh,** re-write; copy (*a text etc*)

ath-sgrùdadh, ath-sgrùdaidh, ath-sgrùdaidhean *nm* **1** re-appraisal, reassessment, a review, **sgrìobh i/rinn i ath-sgrùdadh mòr air sgrìobhaidhean nam bàrd** she wrote/carried out a major reassessment/re-appraisal of the writings of the poets, **ath-sgrùdadh phoileasaidhean** a review of/a new look at policies; **2** (*education etc*) revision, **ath-sgrùdadh airson deuchainn(e)** revision for an exam

ath-smuain, ath-smuaine, ath-smuaintean *nf* an afterthought

a thuilleadh air *prep, see* **tuilleadh 3**

B

babag, babaig, babagan *nf* **1** a tassel; **2** a tuft, *cf* **bad 2**

bàbhan, bàbhain, bàbhanan *nm* **1** a rampart, a bulwark, *cf* **mùr**

babhstair, babhstair, babhstairean *nm* **1** a bolster, a large pillow, *cf* **cluasag**; **2** a mattress

bac, *gen* **baca** & **baic**, *pl* **bacan** *nm* **1** a hindrance, a delay, an obstacle, *cf more usu* **bacadh 2**; **2** a hollow or bend *esp on the body*, **bac na ruighe** the hollow/bend of the arm, **bac na h-iosgaid** the back of the knee; **3** a peat bank, *cf* **poll 3**; **4** a sand bank

bac *vt, pres part* **a' bacadh**, prevent, obstruct, hinder, restrain, *cf* **bacadh 3**

bacach *adj* **1** lame, crippled, **tha e bacach air aon chois** he's lame in one leg, **Eachann Bacach** Lame Hector (*a 17ᵗʰ century MacLean poet*); **2** *in expr* **tha e (*etc*) bacach** he (*etc*) is lame, he (*etc*) limps/has a limp; *cf* **crùbach** *adj*, **cuagach**

bacach, *gen* & *pl* **bacaich** *nm* a cripple, someone who is lame *or* who limps, *cf* **crioplach**, **crùbach** *n*

bacadh, bacaidh, bacaidhean *nm* **1** (*the act of*) preventing etc (*see senses of* **bac** *v*); **2** an obstacle, hindrance, a hindrance, restraint, prevention, delay, a delay, **is bacadh mòr an aois** old age is a great hindrance, *cf less usu* **bac** *n* **1**, **cnap-starra** (*see* **cnap 1**); **3** *often in expr* **cuir** *v* **bacadh air** obstruct, prevent etc, **chuir a pàrantan bacadh air ar pòsadh** her parents obstructed/put obstacles in the way of our getting married, **chuir dìth airgid bacadh air a' ghnothach** lack of money held the business back

bacan, *gen* & *pl* **bacain** *nm* (*agric*) a hobble, a tether post *or* stake, *cf* **teadhair, feiste**

bachall, bachaill, bachallan *nm* a crozier, a (*cleric's*) staff

bachlach & **bachallach** *adj* (*of hair*) curled, curly, ringleted, (*song*) **b' e siud an cùl, seo an cùl bachallach** yonder, here, is the ringleted hair, *cf* **camagach**

bachlag, bachlaig, bachlagan *nf* **1** a curl, a ringlet, *cf* **camag 1, dual² 1**; **2** (*of plant etc*) a shoot, a sprout, *cf* **gas, ògan**

bachlaich *vt, pres part* **a' bachlachadh**, curl, **bhachlaich an gruagaire m' fhalt** the hairdresser curled my hair, *cf* **dualaich**

bad, baid, badan *nm* **1** a place, a spot, **bad grianach** a sunny spot, *cf* **àite 1, ionad 1**; **2** a tuft, a bunch, **bad fraoich/fuilt/feòir** a tuft of heather/hair/grass, *cf* **bagaid 2**; **3** a flock, a group, **bad ghobhar/chaorach** a flock of goats/sheep (*ie in the concrete sense of a group together at one time*), *cf* **buar, treud**; **4** a clump of trees, a thicket; **5** *in exprs* **anns a' bhad** immediately, this instant, **thig an seo anns a' bhad!** come here this instant! **bheir mi dhuibh an cofaidh anns a' bhad** I'll bring you your coffee right away, & (*calque*) **air a' bhad** on the spot, straight away, *cf* **air ball**

badan, *gen* & *pl* **badain** *nm* **1** (*dimin of* **bad** *nm*) little spot etc (*see senses of* **bad**); **2** a nappy

baga, *gen* **baga**, *pl* **bagannan** & **bagaichean** *nm* a hand-bag, (*paper, polythene, luggage etc*) a bag, *cf more trad* **màileid, poca**

bagaid, bagaide, bagaidean *nf* a bunch, a cluster, **bagaid fhìon-dhearcan** a bunch of grapes, **bagaid chnò** a cluster of nuts

bagair *vti, pres part* **a' bagairt** & **a' bagradh**, **1** threaten, **bhagair e orm** he threatened me, **bhagair iad mo mharbhadh** they threatened to kill me, **bha an abhainn a' bagairt cur thairis** the river was threatening to overflow, *cf* **maoidh**; **2** (*vi*) bluster

bagairt, bagairt, bagairtean *nf* & **bagradh, bagraidh, bagraidhean** *nm* **1** (*the act of*) threatening, blustering (*see senses of* **bagair** *v*); **2** a threat, **bagairt cogaidh** a threat of war, (*prov*) **cha tèid plàst air bagairt** you don't put a poultice on a threat (*roughly equivalent to* sticks and stones will hurt my bones but words will never harm me); **3** bluster

bàgh, *gen* **bàigh**, *pl* **bàghan** & **bàghannan** *nm* a bay, a cove, *cf* **camas 1, òb**

bagradh *see* **bagairt**

bàidh, *gen* **bàidhe** *nf* 1 affection, fondness, (*song*) **cur mo chùil ri càirdean nochd am bàidh cho treun** as I turned away from (my) dear ones their great affection became evident, *cf* **dèidh 2**, **spèis 2**; 2 a favour, an act of kindness, a good turn, **an dèan thu bàidh dhomh?** will you do me a favour?, *cf* **fàbhar**, **seirbheis 2**

bàidheil & **bàigheil** *adj* kind, kindly (*of person, act*), *cf* **coibhneil**

baidhsagal, **baidhsagail**, **baidhsagalan** *nm* a bicycle, *cf more trad* **rothar**

baile, **baile**, **bailtean** *nm* 1 a (crofting) township, **bha fang ùr aig a' bhaile** the township had a new fank/sheepfold, **clàrc a' bhaile** the township clerk; 2 *esp with* **beag**, a village, **baile beag Ùige** the village of Uig, *cf* **clachan 1 & 2**; 3 *esp with* **beag**, a small town, **baile beag Chuimrigh** the small town of Comrie; 4 **baile mòr** a town, a city, **chaidh iad a dh'fhuireach sa bhaile mhòr** they went to live in the town/city, **'s e baile mòr a th' ann an Glaschu** Glasgow is a big city (*cf* **cathair 2**), **talla a' bhaile** the village/town/city hall; 5 *in expr* **aig baile** at home, **cà' il am bodach? chan eil e aig baile** where's the old fellow? he's not at home, *cf* **taigh 2**

bailead, **baileid**, **baileadan** *nm* a ballad

baileat, **baileit**, **baileatan** *nm* a ballot, *cf* **taghadh 3**

baile-puirt, **baile-puirt**, **bailtean-puirt** *nm* a seaport, **'s e baile-puirt a th' ann an Obar-Dheathain** Aberdeen is a seaport

bàillidh, **bàillidh**, **bàillidhean** *nm* 1 (*law*) a bailiff; 2 (*civic admin etc*) a baillie; 3 a magistrate; 4 (*on estate etc*) a factor, *cf* **maor 1**

bàine *comp of* **bàn** *adj* whiter, whitest, **an t-aodann as bàine** the whitest face

bàinead, *gen* **bàineid** *nf* whiteness, fairness (*ie of colouring*)

bàinidh *nf invar* 1 madness, fury, rage; 2 *esp in expr* **air bhàinidh** (*of person*) extremely angry, mad with rage, absolutely furious; *cf* **boile**, **cuthach**

bainne, *gen* **bainne** *nm* milk

baintighearna, **baintighearna**, **baintighearnan** *nf* a lady (*ie female equivalent of a lord*)

bàirlinn *nf invar* (*law*) 1 a summons; 2 an eviction order or notice

bàirneach, **bàirnich**, **bàirnich** *nf* 1 a barnacle; 2 a limpet

baist *vt*, *pres part* **a' baisteadh**, baptise, christen

Baisteach, **Baistich**, **Baistich** *nm* a Baptist

baisteadh, **baistidh**, **baistidhean** *nm* 1 (*the act of*) baptising or christening; 2 baptism, a baptism, a christening

bàl, *gen & pl* **bàil** *nm* a ball (*ie a dance*), *cf less formal* **danns(a)**

bàla, **bàla**, **bàlaichean** *nm* (*for games etc*) a ball

balach, *gen & pl* **balaich** *nm* 1 a boy, a lad, **cha robh aon bhalach anns an sgoil an-diugh** there wasn't a single boy at school today, **balach beag** a little/small/wee/young boy; 2 *affectionate or fam for a male of any age*, (*song*) **Balaich an Iasgaich** The Fishing Lads/Boys, *expr admiration or irony* **nach esan am balach!** isn't he the boy/the boyo/the clever one/the rogue! *common as form of address* **thig a-steach is gabh drama, a bhalaich!** come inside and take a dram, boy!; *cf* **gille 2 & 3**

balachan, *gen & pl* **balachain** *nm*, *dimin of* **balach**, a small boy, a wee boy

balaiste *nf invar* ballast

balbh *adj* 1 dumb, mute, **creutairean balbha** dumb animals/creatures; 2 silent, speechless, **bha e balbh ro fheirg na mnà aige** he was silent/speechless in the face of his wife's anger, **bog balbh** speechless, struck dumb, *cf* **tosdach**; 3 (*place, scene etc*) quiet, silent, peaceful, *cf more usu* **sàmhach**, **sìtheil 1**

balbhan, *gen & pl* **balbhain** *nm* a dumb person

balg & **bolg**, *gen & pl* **builg** *nm* 1 (*anat*) an abdomen, a belly, *cf* **brù 2**, **stamag**; 2 a blister, **bha balg air mo làimh an dèidh dhomh fiodh a shàbhadh** I had a blister on my hand after sawing wood, *cf* **leus 3**; 3 (*trad*) a bag

balgair, **balgaire**, **balgairean** *nm* 1 a fox, *cf* **madadh 2**, **sionnach**; 2 a cunning person, a sly person, a rogue, *cf* **slaightear**

balgam, **balgaim**, **balgaman** *nm* 1 a sip (*of liquid*), **balgam bùirn/uisge** a sip of water, *cf* **drùdhag 2**; 2 a mouthful, a swig, **thug e balgam math às a' bhotal** he took a good swig from the bottle, *cf* **sgailc** *n* **3**, **steallag**

balgan, *gen & pl* **balgain** *nm* a mushroom; a toadstool

balgan-buachair, *gen & pl* **balgain-buachair** *nm*, *also* **balg-bhuachair**, **balg-buachrach**, **balgan-buachrach** *nm*, the edible field mushroom

ball[1], *gen & pl* **buill** *nm* 1 (*anat*) a limb, an organ, **is e buill a th' ann an casan is gàirdeanan** legs and arms are limbs, **buill a' chuirp** the parts of the body, **ball-bodhaig** a (bodily) organ, **na buill-ghineamhainn** the reproductive/sexual organs, the genitals; 2 a member (*of organisation etc*) **a bheil thu nad bhall den Chomunn Ghaidhealach/de**

Chomann an Luchd-Ionnsachaidh? are you a member of An Comunn Gaidhealach/of the Gaelic Learners' Association?, **Ball Pàrlamaid** a Member of Parliament; **3** *used with coll nouns*, a piece of, an item of *etc*, **ball-acfhainn** a tool, a piece of equipment, **ball-airm** a weapon, **ball-àirneis** a piece/an item of furniture, **ball-aodaich** an item of clothing, a garment; **4** a rope (*esp part of ship's tackle*), *cf* **ròp(a)**; **5** *in exprs* **ball-àbhachdais** a laughing-stock, a butt of ridicule, **air ball** immediately, straight away, right away, *cf similarly used* **bad 5**

ball², *gen & pl* **buill** *nm* a ball (*ie for games etc*), *cf* **bàl(l)a**

balla, *gen* **balla**, *pl* **ballachan** & **ballaichean** *nm* a wall (*usu inner or outer wall of building, but occas free-standing*), **ballachan cloiche** stone walls, *cf* **gàrradh 1**

bàl(l)a, bàl(l)a, bàl(l)aichean *nm* a ball (*ie for games etc*), *cf* **ball²**

ballach *adj* (*cloth etc*) spotted, speckled, *cf* **breac** *adj*, & *trad* **riabhach 1**

ballan, ballain, ballanan *nm* a tub

ball-basgaid, *gen & pl* **buill-basgaid** *nm* basketball, a basketball

ball-coise, *gen & pl* **buill-coise** *nm* football, a football, **ball-coise chòignear** five-a-side football

ball-dòbhrain, *gen & pl* **buill-dòbhrain** *nm* a mole (*on skin*)

ball-lìn, *gen & pl* **buill-lìn** *nm* netball, a netball

ball-maise, *gen & pl* **buill-maise** *nm* an ornament, **bha tòrr bhall-maise aice air oir na h-uinneige** she had a lot of ornaments on the windowsill, **is seud-muineil mu h-amhaich na bhall-maise** with a necklace round her neck as an ornament

ballrachd, *gen* **ballrachd** *nf* (*abstr*) membership, (*coll*) a membership, **bhòtaidh a' bhallrachd airson atharrachaidhean** the membership/members will vote for changes, **bha ballrachd beatha aca** they had life membership

bàn¹ *adj* **1** fallow, **talamh bàn** fallow land; **2** (*paper etc*) blank

bàn² *adj* **1** white, fair (*in colouring*), **Dàibhidh Bàn** fair-haired David, **an cù bàn** the white dog, *cf* **fionn, geal** *adj*; **2** *prefixed to other colours* light, pale, **bàn-dhearg** pale red, pink, **bàn-ghorm** pale/light blue

bana- & **ban-** *prefix, corres to Eng* female, woman, -ess, *see examples below*

ban-aba, ban-aba, ban-abaichean *nf* an abbess

bana-bhuidseach, bana-bhuidsich, bana-bhuidsichean *nf* a sorceress, a witch

banacharaid, banacharaide, banachàirdean *nf* **1** a (female *or* woman) friend or relative, **bha i na deagh bhanacharaid don mhnaoi agam** she was a good friend to my wife/of my wife's; **2** (*in corres*) **A Bhanacharaid**, Dear Madam, **A Mhàiri, a bhanacharaid** Dear Mary

banachdach, *gen* **banachdaich** *f* vaccination

bana-chliamhainn, bana-chleamhna, bana-chleamhnan *nf* a daughter-in-law

bànag, bànaig, bànagan *nf* a sea-trout, (*also coll*) **tha e mì-laghail lìontan a chur airson bànaig** it's illegal to set nets for sea-trout

bana-ghaisgeach, bana-ghaisgich, bana-ghaisgich *nf* a heroine

banail *adj* womanly, feminine, **dòighean banail** womanly/feminine ways, *cf opposites* **duineil, fearail**

banais, bainnse, bainnsean *nf* a wedding, **bean** *f* **na bainnse** the bride, **fear** *m* **na bainnse** the groom, **cuirm** *f* **bainnse** a wedding reception, (*trad song*) **òlar am fìon air do bhanais** wine will be drunk at your wedding, *cf* **pòsadh 2**

banaltram, banaltraim, banaltraman *nf* a nurse, **banaltram sgìreachd** a district nurse, *cf* **bean-eiridinn** & *less trad* **nurs**

bana-mhaighstir-sgoile, bana-mhaighstir-sgoile, bana-mhaighstirean-sgoile a schoolmistress (*usu primary*)

bana-phrionnsa, bana-phrionnsa, bana-phrionnsan *nf* a princess

banarach, banaraich, banaraichean *nf* a milk-maid, a dairy-maid

banas-taighe *nm invar* housekeeping, the running of a house(hold), housewifery, home economics

banc & **banca**, *gen* **banca**, *pl* **bancaichean** & **bancan** *nm* a (*clearing, savings etc*) bank, **Banca Dhail Chluaidh** the Clydesdale Bank, **banca-siubhail** a mobile/travelling bank

bancair, bancair, bancairean *nm* a banker

bancaireachd *nf invar* banking

ban-dia, ban-dè, ban-diathan *nf* a goddess

ban-diùc, ban-diùc, ban-diùcan *nf* a duchess

bàn-ghlas *adj* (*of complexion etc*) ashen

ban-ìompaire, ban-ìompaire, ban-ìompairean *nf* an empress, **b' e Bhictòria Ban-Ìompaire nan Innseachan** Victoria was Empress of India

ban-leòmhann, *gen & pl* **ban-leòmhainn** *nf* a lioness

bann, bainne, bannan *nm* **1** a strip (*of material etc*), **chàirich e cas na spaide le bann teip** he mended the spade handle with a strip of tape, *cf* **stiall** *n* **2**; **2** a bandage; **3** a hinge, *cf* **banntach**; **4** (*fin*) a bond, **bann tasgaidh** an investment bond

banntach, banntaich, banntaichean *nm* a hinge, *cf* **bann 3**, **lùdag 2**

ban(n)trach, ban(n)traich, ban(n)traichean *nf* **1** a widow, (*trad tale*) **Mac na Bantraich** the Widow's Son; **2** (*as nm*) a widower

ban-ogha, ban-ogha, ban-oghaichean *nf* a grand-daughter

banrigh, banrighe, banrighean *nf, also* **banrighinn, banrighinn, banrighinnean** *nf,* a queen

ban-rùnaire, ban-rùnaire, ban-rùnairean *nf* a (female) secretary

baoghalta *adj* stupid, *cf* **gòrach**

baoghaltachd *nf invar* stupidity, *cf* **gòraiche**

baoit *nf invar, also* **baoiteag,** *gen* **baoiteige** *nf,* a fly, worm or other bait for fishing, *cf* **maghar**

baoth *adj* foolish, silly, simple, **dh'ath-cheannaich am ministear baoth an t-each aige fhèin air an fhèill** the foolish minister bought back his own horse at the fair, *cf* **amaideach, faoin 1, sìmplidh 3**

bàr, bàir, bàraichean *nm* (*hotel, pub etc*) a bar, **cuir na glainneachan falamh air a' bhàr** put the empty glasses on the bar, **Bàr na Camanachd** The Camanachd Bar (*in Portree*)

barail, baraile, barailean *nf* an opinion, **dè do bharail?** what's your opinion?, what do you think? **nam bharail-sa tha e sgriosail!** in my (*emph*) opinion it's dreadful!, *cf* **beachd 2**

baraille, baraille, baraillean *nm* a barrel, a cask, (*cf* **tocasaid**), **baraille ola** a barrel of oil, **baraille gunna** a gun barrel

baralach *adj* conceited, *cf* **mòrchuiseach**

bàrd, *gen & pl* **bàird** *nm* a bard, a poet, (*title of anthology*) **Sàr Obair nam Bàrd Gàidhealach** The Master Work of the Gaelic Poets, *cf* **filidh 1**

bàrdachd *nf invar* poetry, **sgrìobh e bàrdachd mun chogadh** he wrote poetry about the war, **rinn mi bàrdachd** I have written/I wrote poetry/a poem, **dh'ath-aithris e pìos bàrdachd leis fhèin** he recited a piece of his own poetry, *cf* **dànachd, rann 1**

bàrdail *adj* poetic, bardic

bargan, *gen* **bargain,** *pl* **bargain & barganan** *nm* a bargain (*ie a good buy or deal*)

bàrr, barra, barran *nm* **1** the top or uppermost surface of anything, **bàrr a' bhainne** the cream, the top of the milk, **air bàrr na**

talmhainn on the surface of the earth, **cop air bàrr an leanna** foam on the top/surface of the beer, **a' seòladh air bhàrr nan tonn** sailing on the crest of the waves, **thig** *v* **am bàrr** surface, come to the surface, (*abstr*) manifest itself/oneself, *cf* **ceann as àirde** (*see* **ceann 2**), **mullach 1, uachdar 1, 2 & 3**; **2** (*agric etc*) a crop, **bàrr feòir/buntàta** a crop of hay/potatoes, **prìomh bhàrr** a main crop; **3** *in expr* **thoir** *v* **bàrr air** top, cap or beat something, **tha do bhathais a' toirt bàrr air na chunnaic mi a-riamh** your cheek caps/beats anything I ever saw; **4** *in expr* **a bhàrr air,** *same as* **a bharrachd air** (*see* **barrachd 4**); **5** *in expr* **bhàrr & far** *prep* (*for de bhàrr*) from, from off, down from, (*with gen*), **thug e leabhar bhàrr na sgeilp/a' bhùird** he took a book from the shelf/the table, **seiche bhàrr laoigh** hide from a calf, **chaidh e à sealladh mar sneachd bhàrr gàrraidh** he disappeared like snow off a dyke

Barrach, *gen & pl* **Barraich** *nm* someone from the Isle of Barra, *also as adj* **Barrach** of, from or pertaining to Barra

barrachd *nf invar* **1** (*trad*) superiority; a surplus; **2** (*now usu*) more, **tha mi ag iarraidh barrachd!** I want (some) more!, **barrachd ime/feòla** more butter/meat, *cf* **tuilleadh 1**; **3** *in expr* **barrachd air** *prep* more than, **barrachd air dà fhichead** more than forty, **barrachd air na bha mi an dùil fhaicinn** more than I was hoping/expecting to see, (*prov*) **chì dithis barrachd air aon fhear** two will see more than one, *cf* **còrr** *nm* **1**; **4** *in expr* **a bharrachd (air)** in addition (to), as well (as), besides, **chan eil mi ag iarraidh càil a bharrachd** I don't want anything else/another thing, **dithis neach-obrach a bharrachd** two more/additional/extra workers, **A bharrachd air sin . . .** Moreover . . . , Also . . . , In addition . . . , **cò na seinneadairean as toigh leat a bharrachd oirrese?** what/which singers do you like apart from/besides her?

barragach *adj* creamy, *cf* **uachdarach 4**

barraichte *adj* truly excellent, top-class, supreme

Barraigh *f* (the Isle/Island of) Barra

barrail *adj* excellent, first-rate

barrall, barraill, barraillean *nm* a shoe-lace, *cf* **iall**

barrantaich *vt, pres part* **a' barrantachadh, 1** guarantee, *cf* **rach an urras** (*see* **urras 1**); **2** commission, authorise, appoint *cf* **ùghdarraich**

barrantaichte *adj* accredited, guaranteed

bar(r)antas, bar(r)antais, bar(r)antasan *nm* **1** a pledge, a guarantee; **2** security (*for loan etc*); *cf* **urras 1**

bas & **bois**, *gen* **boise**, *pl* **basan** & **boisean**, *nf* palm of the hand, **bas-bhualadh** *m* applause, clapping, **bhuail iad am basan** they applauded/clapped, (*prov*) **bonnach air bois, cha bhruich e is cha loisg** a bannock in the hand will neither cook nor burn (*roughly equivalent to* 'nothing ventured, nothing gained'), *cf* **glac** *n* 2

bàs, *gen* **bàis** *nm* 1 death, **urras bàis** a death certificate, **ri uchd bàis** at the point of death, at death's door, **grèim-bàis** *m* death throe(s), (*poem*) **Glac a' Bhàis** (Somhairle MacGill-Eain) Death Valley, (*song title*) **Bàs an Eich** The Death of the Horse; 2 *in expr* **a' dol bàs** dying out, fading away, **tha na seann dòighean a' dol bàs** the old ways are dying out, (*as infinitive*) (*prov*) **faodaidh a' chaora dol bàs a' feitheamh ris an fheur ùr** the sheep may die waiting for the new grass; 3 *in expr* **faigh bàs** die, be killed, **am faigh a' Ghàidhlig bàs?** will Gaelic die? (*trad*) **fhuair e bàs le nàimhdean** he died at the hand of enemies

bàsachadh, *gen* **bàsachaidh** *nm* (*the act of*) dying

bàsaich *vi*, *pres part* **a' bàsachadh**, die, *Note: not used by some speakers when referring to humans*, *cf* **bàs** 3, **caochail** 2, **siubhail** 3

basdalach *adj* (*of dress etc*) showy, flashy, garish

Basgach, *gen* & *pl* **Basgaich** *nm* a Basque, *also as adj* Basque, pertaining to the Basque Country

basgaid, **basgaide**, **basgaidean** *nf* a basket, **basgaid-sgudail** & **basgaid-truileis** waste-paper/rubbish basket, **cuir sa bhasgaid e!** put it in the (rubbish) basket!

Basgais *nf* Basque (*ie the language*)

bàsmhor *adj* 1 mortal, **do chorp bàsmhor is d' anam neo-bhàsmhor** your mortal body and your immortal soul; 2 deadly, fatal, *cf* **marbhtach**

bàsmhorachd *nf invar* mortality, the state of being mortal

bata, **bata**, **bataichean** *nm* 1 a stick, *cf* **maide** 2; 2 a walking stick (*also* **bata-coiseachd**)

bàta, **bàta**, **bàtaichean** *nm* a boat, a ship, *Note: though* **bàta** *is masculine the pron* **i**, she, *is used*, (*song*) **chì mi am bàta 's i tighinn** I see the boat as she comes, **bàt'-aiseig** a ferry boat, **bàt'-iasgaich** a fishing boat, **bàta-marsantachd** a merchant ship/vessel, **bàta-ràmh** a rowing boat (*cf* **eathar**), **bàta-sàbhalaidh** & **bàta-teasairginn**, a lifeboat, a rescue boat, **bàta-siùil** a sailing boat, **bàta-smùide** a steam-boat, (*song*) **Fear a' Bhàta** The Boatman, *cf* **long**, **soitheach** 2

bataraidh, **bataraidh**, **bataraidhean** *nmf* (*elec*) a battery

bàth *vt*, *pres part* **a' bàthadh**, 1 drown, **bhàth e na piseagan** he drowned the kittens, **chaidh Ùisdean a bhàthadh ann am boglaich** Hugh was drowned in a quagmire/a bog; 2 drown out, muffle (*sounds*)

bàthach, **bàthcha**, **bàthchannan** *nf* & **bàthaich**, **bàthaich**, **bàthaichean** *nm* a byre, a cow-shed

bàthadh, *gen* **bàthaidh** *nm* 1 (*the act of*) drowning etc (*see senses of* **bàth** *v*); 2 a drowning

bathais, **bathais**, **bathaisean** *nf* 1 a forehead, a brow, *cf* **clàr** 2, **mala** 2, **maoil** 2; 2 cheek, nerve, impudence, effrontery, **nach ann airsan a tha a' bhathais!** what a cheek/nerve he's got!, *cf* **aghaidh** 2

bathar, *gen* **bathair** *nm coll* 1 goods, merchandise, wares, **bathar ri reic** goods/merchandise for sale, **bathar a-steach** imports, an import, **trèana bathair** a goods train; 2 (*IT*) **bathar cruaidh** hardware, **bathar bog** software

bàthte *adj* drowned (*see also* **dìle**)

beach, **beacha**, **beachan** *nm* 1 a bee (*cf more usu* **seillean**), **beachlann** *m* a beehive; 2 a wasp, *cf more usu* **speach**

beachd, **beachda**, **beachdan** *nm* 1 an idea, a thought, a surmise, (*also* **beachd- smuain**), **thàinig beachd(-smuain) thugam air sin** a thought/an idea occurred to me about that, *cf* **smaoin**; 2 *more usu* an opinion, **dè do bheachd air a' bhiadh?** what's your opinion/what do you think of the food? **thug mi seachad mo bheachd air na molaidhean aca** I gave my opinion of their proposals, **nam bheachd-sa, tha iad uabhasach math** in my opinion, they're extremely good, **tha sinn den bheachd gu . . .** we are of the opinion that . . . , **chan eil sinn den aon bheachd** we are not of the same opinion, **gabh** *v* **beachd air rudeigin** form an opinion on/observe something, *cf* **barail**; 3 *in expr* **bi am beachd a . . .** be thinking of . . . , be intending/aiming to . . . , **dè a tha thu am beachd a dhèanamh a-nise?** what are you intending to do/thinking of doing now?; 4 *in expr* **rach** *v* **às mo (etc) b(h)eachd** go out of/lose my (etc) mind, *cf* **ciall** 2, **rian** 3

beachdaich *vi*, *pres part* **a' beachdachadh**, consider, meditate, speculate (**air** about)

beachdail *adj* 1 observant, *cf* **mothachail** 1; 2 abstract, theoretical, *cf opposites* **nitheil**, **rudail**; 3 self-satisfied, opinionated

beachd-smaoin(t)eachadh, *gen* **beachd-smaoin(t)eachaidh** *nm* **1** (*the act of*) meditating or contemplating; **2** meditation, a meditation, contemplation

beachd-smaoin(t)ich *vi, pres part* **a' beachd-smaoin(t)eachadh,** meditate, contemplate, **feallsanach a' beachd-smaointeachadh air ceist an uilc** a philosopher meditating on the problem of evil, *cf less rigorous* **cnuasaich, meòraich 1**

beadaidh *adj* cheeky, impudent, impertinent, pert, saucy, forward, *cf* **dàna 3**

beag *adj, comp* **(n)as (etc) lugha, 1** small, little, wee, **balach beag** a little/wee boy, **caileag bheag** a little/wee girl, **tuarastal beag** a small/low salary, **ann an ùine bheag** in a short time/a little while, (*whisky*) **tè bheag** a wee one, a nip, **'s beag an ùidh a th' agam ann am poilitigs** I'm not very interested/have little interest in politics; **2** slight, light, **ceò beag air a' mhonadh** a slight/light mist on the hill, **bha uisge beag ann** it was raining slightly, **thàinig eagal beag orm** I grew a little bit afraid; **3** *in some usages* **beag** *is treated as a noun with the senses* little, the least bit, few, **beag is beag** *or* **beag air bheag** little by little, **an d' fhuair thu a bheag?** did you get some/any?, (*with a neg sense*) **cha robh a bheag de shiùcar sa phreas** there wasn't any/the least bit of sugar in the cupboard, **cha robh ach a bheag de rùm sa bhàta** there was only the smallest amount of room in the boat, **tha glè bheag de chàirdean aige** he has very few friends, *cf* **beagan** *n*; **4** *in expr* **rud beag** *adv* a bit, a wee bit, somewhat, **bha i rud beag sgìth** she was a bit/rather tired, *cf* **beagan** *adv*, **rudeigin 2**; **5** *in expr* **is beag orm (do chàr ùr etc)** I don't like (your new car etc)

beagaich *vti, pres part* **a' beagachadh** reduce, lessen, **beagaich air** cut down on, make cuts in (*budget, activity*)

beagan *adv* a little, a bit, slightly, **tha i beagan nas sine na Màiri** she's a bit/slightly older than Mary, *cf* **rudeigin 2, car** *n* **7, caran, rud beag** (*see* **beag 4**)

beagan, *gen* **beagain** *nm* a little, a bit of, a few, *can be used more positively than* **a bheag** (*see* **beag 3**), **bha beagan siùcair sa phreas/beagan rùim sa bhàta** there was a bit of sugar in the cupboard/a little room in the boat, **chan eil ach beagan chàirdean aige** he only has a few friends, **a bheil airgead agad? tha beagan** have you any money? a little, **a' gluasad anns a' bheagan gaoithe** moving in the little wind (that there was)

beag-nàrach, also **beag-nàire,** *adj* shameless

beairt *see* **beart**

beairteach, beairteas *see* **beartach, beartas**

bealach, *gen & pl* **bealaich** *nm* **1** a mountain or hill pass, (*placename*) **Bealach na Bròige** the Pass of the Shoe (Ross-shire); **2** the top of a pass, **ràinig e am bealach** he reached the top of the pass/the col; **3** a detour, a roundabout way, **gabhaidh sinn bealach tron choille** we'll make/take a detour through the wood; **4 bealach goirid** a short cut, *cf* **aithghearrachd 2**

bealaidh *nm invar* (*bot*) broom

Bealltainn, *gen* **Bealltainne** *nf* May Day, the first of May, Beltane

bean, *gen* **mnà,** *dat* **mnaoi,** *pl* **mnathan,** *gen pl* **ban** *nf* **1** a wife, **seo a' bhean agam** this is/here is my wife, (*song*) **a' bhean agam fhìn** my very own wife/that wife of mine, **bean-phòsta** a married woman, *also as form of address*, Mrs, **a Bhean-phòsta NicAoidh** (*voc*) Mrs MacKay; **2** (*trad*) a woman, (*song*) **a bhean** (*voc*) **ud thall a rinn an gàire** woman over there who laughed, *cf* **boireannach, tè 2**; **3** *in compounds & set exprs* woman, female, lady, **bean an taighe** lady of the house, housewife, landlady, *see further examples below*

bean *vi, pres part* **a' beantainn 1** (*with preps* **ri & do**) touch, handle, meddle with, **na bean ris na buill-maise** don't touch/meddle with the ornaments, *cf* **buin 3, làimhsich 1**; **2** (*with prep* **ri**) brush against, *cf* **suath 2**; **3** (*with prep* **ri**) deal with, touch upon, **bhean an òraid ris an t-suidheachadh ann an Afraga** the talk touched upon the situation in Africa

bean-bainnse, mnà-bainnse, mnathan-bainnse *nf* a bride, **bean na bainnse** the bride

bean-eiridinn, mnà-eiridinn, mnathan-eiridinn *nf* a nurse, *cf more usu* **banaltram** & *less trad* **nurs**

bean-ghlùine, mnà-glùine, mnathan-glùine *nf* a midwife

beannachadh, beannachaidh, *pl* **beannachaidhean** *nm* **1** (*the act of*) blessing etc (*see senses of* **beannaich** *v*); **2** beatification; **3** a blessing, (*song*) **oir tha beannachadh Dhè agus sìth ann** for peace and God's blessing are there; **4** a greeting, a farewell, *cf* **beannachd 4, soraidh**

beannachd, beannachd, beannachdan *nf* **1** a blessing, **mo bheannachd oirbh** my blessing on you, *cf* **beannachadh 3**; **2** (*without religious overtones*) a blessing, a boon, (*trad*) **is i beannachd deagh shlàinte** good health is a blessing; **3** compliments, regards,

mo bheannachd don mhnaoi agad! my compliments/regards to your wife!; **4** *on parting,* **beannachd leat/leibh** goodbye!, *cf* **mar 2, slàn 3, soraidh 1, tìoraidh**

beannaich *vti, pres part* **a' beannachadh, 1** beatify; **2** bless; **3** *as vi in expr* **beannaich do chuideigin** greet someone

beannaichte *adj* blessed

bean-shìthe, mnà-sìthe, mnathan-sìthe *nf* a fairy woman, a female fairy

bean-taighe, mnà-taighe, mnathan-taighe *nf* **1** a housewife; **2** *with art* **bean an taighe** the woman/lady/mistress of the house, the lady householder, (*of lodgings, pub etc*) the landlady, (*song*) **a bhean an taighe** (*voc*), **dùin an seòmar, cha bhi aon dhen t-seòrsa leinn!** close up the room, landlady, we won't have one of that sort among us!

bean-teagaisg, mnà-teagaisg, mnathan-teagaisg *nf* a (*female*) teacher (*usu secondary*)

bean-uasal, mnà-uaisle, mnathan-uaisle *nf* **1** a noblewoman; **2** *as polite form of address* (*trad*) **A Bhean-Uasal** Madam

beàrn, *gen* **bèirn** & **beàirn,** *pl* **beàrnan** *nmf* a notch, a gap, a breach, a space or opening in anything, **tro bheàrnan sna neòil** through gaps in the clouds, *cf* **fosgladh 2**

beàrnan-brìde, *gen* & *pl* **beàrnain-bhrìde** *nm* a dandelion

Beàrnarach, *gen* & *pl* **Beàrnaraich** *nm* someone from Bernera/Berneray, *also as adj* **Beàrnarach** of, from or pertaining to Berneray/Bernera

Beàrnaraigh *nf* Berneray/Bernera

beàrr *vt, pres part* **a' bearradh, 1** (*sheep etc*) shear, *cf* **rùisg 2**; **2** (*more usu*) shave, **bheàrr am bearradair m' fheusag** the barber shaved my beard

bearradair, bearradair, bearradairean a barber, *cf less trad* **borbair**

bearradh[1], *gen* **bearraidh** *nm* (*the act of*) shaving, shearing (*see* **beàrr** *vt*)

bearradh[2], *gen* **bearraidh, bearraidhean** *nm* a (steep) cliff, a precipice

beart & **beairt,** *gen* **beairt,** *pl* **beartan** & **beairtean** *nf* **1** (*trad*) a deed, a feat, **droch-bheart** a vice, an evil deed, *cf* **cleas 1, euchd 1, gnìomh**; **2** a machine, *cf* **inneal**; **3** *esp* a (weaving) loom (*also* **beart-fhighe**), **bha a' bheart aige ann an seada air cùlaibh an taighe** his loom was in a shed behind the house

beartach & **beairteach** *adj* rich, wealthy, *cf* **saidhbhir**

beartas & **beairteas,** *gen* **beartais** & **beairteis** *nm* riches, wealth, *cf* **ionmhas 2, saidhbhreas, stòras**

beatha, beatha, beathannan *nf* **1** life, a life, **beatha chruaidh** a hard life, **bha e sona fad a bheatha** he was happy all his life, **chaith iad/chuir iad seachad am beatha san arm** they spent their lives in the army; **2** *in expr* **'s e do bheatha** you're welcome, **mòran taing! 's e ur beatha/do bheatha!** thank you very much! you're welcome!; **3** *in expr* **mar mo** (etc) **b(h)eatha** for dear life, **bha i a' ruith mar a beatha** she was running as fast as she could/for dear life/for all she was worth

beathach, beathaich, beathaichean *nm* a beast, an animal, *usu domestic, often cattle,* **a' togail/a' biathadh nam beathaichean** raising/feeding the beasts/animals, (*also of wild creatures, eg*) **beathach-mara** a sea-creature, a marine animal, *cf* **ainmhidh**

beathachadh, *gen* **beathachaidh** *nm* **1** (*the act of*) feeding, maintaining (*see* **beathaich** *v*); **2** (*of livestock etc*) maintenance, keep

beathaich *vt, pres part* **a' beathachadh,** feed, maintain, (*prov*) **beathaich thusa mis' an-diugh is beathaichidh mise thus' a-màireach** you feed me today and I'll feed you tomorrow, *cf* **biath**

beath-eachdraidh, beath-eachdraidhe, beath-eachdraidhean *nf* biography, a biography

beic, beice, beiceannan *nf* a curtsey, **dèan** *v* **beic** curtsey

bèicear, bèiceir, bèicearan *nm* a baker, *cf more trad* **fuineadair**

bèile, bèile, bèilichean *nm* a bale

Beilg *nf, used with art,* **a' Bheilg** Belgium

Beilgeach, *gen* & *pl* **Beilgich** *nm* a Belgian, *also as adj* **Beilgeach** Belgian

being, beinge, beingean *nf* a bench (*ie seat*), *cf* **furm 1**

beinn, *gen* **beinne,** *pl* **beanntan,** *gen pl* **beann** *nf* **1** *in mountain and hill names* Ben, **Beinn Nibheis** Ben Nevis, **Beinn Laoigh** Ben Lui; **2** a mountain, a ben, **a' streap beinne** climbing a mountain, **tìr nam beann àrda** the land of the high bens, (*song collection*) **Ceòl nam Beann** The Music of the Mountains, *cf other terms for hills* **cnoc, mòinteach, monadh, sgùrr, tom, tulach**

beinn-theine, beinn-teine, beanntan-teine *nf* a volcano

beir *vti irreg* (*see tables p 494*), *pres part* **a' breith, 1** (*vt*) bear, give birth to, **rug i nighean** she bore/had/gave birth to a daughter, (*song*) **'s**

ann an Ìle (a) rugadh mi it was in Islay that I was born, **rugadh is thogadh mi an sin** I was born and brought up there, **a' breith uighean** laying eggs, **a' breith cloinne/laoigh/uain** giving birth to children/a calf/a lamb; **2** (*vi*) *with prep* **air**, overtake, catch up with, catch, **cha robh e luath gu leòr airson breith air a' chù** he wasn't fast enough to catch up with/catch the dog, **beiridh am poileas air ann an Lunnainn** the police will catch up with him in London; **3** (*vi*) *with prep* **air**, seize, take hold of, **rug mi air a' bhaga** I seized the bag, **beir air!** take hold of it!, *cf* **gabh grèim air** (*see* **grèim 1**)

beireadh, beiream, beireamaid, beiribh, beiridh, beirinn *pts of irreg v* **beir** (*see tables* p 494)

beirm, *gen* **beirme** *nf* yeast

beithe *nf invar* a birch(-tree)

beò *adj* **1** alive, living, animate, **chan fhaca sinn duine beò** we didn't see a living soul, (*fam*) **dè do chor? tha mi beò fhathast** how are you doing? I'm still in the land of the living, (*trad*) **ma mhaireas mi beò** if I survive/remain alive, if I'm spared, (*trad*) **cho fad 's as beò mi** as long as I live; **2** *used as m noun* (*trad*) **rim** (etc) **b(h)eò** throughout my (etc) life, all my (etc) life, **cha do dh'fhàg e an t-eilean ri bheò** he never left the island as long as he lived, *cf* **beatha, maireann 2, saoghal 2**

beò-ghlacadh, beò-ghlacaidh, beò-ghlacaidhean *nm* obsession, an obsession

beòshlaint, beòshlainte, beòshlaintean *nf* a living, a livelihood, *cf* **teachd-an-tìr**

beothachadh, *gen* **beothachaidh** *nm* (*the act of*) reviving etc (*see senses of* **beothaich** *v*)

beothaich *vti, pres part* **a' beothachadh,** revive, liven up, bring to life, animate, **tha na malairtean ùra a' beothachadh a' bhaile** the new businesses are livening up/reviving the town (*cf* **ath-bheothaich**), **bheothaich mi an dèidh norraig** I revived after a snooze/nap

beothail *adj* lively, active, vivacious, animated, vital, **beothail a dh'aindeoin a h-aoise** lively/active/spry in spite of her age

beothalachd *nf invar* liveliness, vivacity, animation, vitality

beuc, beuc, beucan *nm* (*of humans & animals*) a roar, a bellow, **leig e beuc às** he let out a roar/bellow, (*fig*) **beuc na mara** the roar of the sea, *cf* **geum** *n*

beuc *vi, pres part* **a' beucadh,** (*of humans & animals*) roar, bellow, *cf* **geum** *v*, **nuallaich**

beucadh, *gen* **beucaidh** *nm* roaring, bellowing

beud, beud, beudan *nm* (*trad*) harm, loss, a blow, *usu in expr* **is mòr am beud (e)** it's a great shame/pity (*cf* **bochd 2, truagh 3**)

beul, *gen & pl* **beòil** *nm* **1** a mouth, **fosgail/dùin do bheul** open/shut your mouth, **làn-beòil bìdh** a mouthful of food, (*trad*) **chaochail iad/chaidh an tiodhlacadh air am beul fòdhpa** they died/they were buried face downwards (*considered to be the most unfortunate form of death or burial*), **beul na h-aibhne** the river mouth (*cf* **bun 4**), **beul na h-uamha** the cave mouth, *cf* (*fam*) **bus² 1, cab, gob 3**; **2** (*trad*) *referring to the beginning or proximity of anything, esp* **(am) beul an latha/na h-oidhche** (at) the onset of the day/the night; **3** (*as adv*) nearly, about, **beul a bhith deiseil** nearly ready (*cf more usu* **bi 11**), **beul ri dà mhìle leabhar** almost/about two thousand books (*cf more usu* **timcheall air** – *see* **timcheall 3**)

beulach *adj* **1** talkative, *cf* **cabach**; **2** plausible (*ie misleadingly, falsely*), smooth-talking, *cf* **beulchair**

beulaibh *nm invar* the front part of anything, *cf* **cùlaibh** *& see also* **air beulaibh**

beul-aithris *nf invar* oral tradition, **chruinnich e òrain is sgeulachdan o bheul-aithris** he collected songs and stories from oral tradition, *cf* **beul-oideachas, seanchas 1**

beulchair *adj* plausible, *cf* **beulach 2**

beul-oideachas, *gen* **beul-oideachais** *nm*, *&* **beul-oideas,** *gen* **beul-oideis** *nm*, oral tradition, *Note: comparable to* **beul-aithris** *but with more emphasis on trad lore and learning as opposed to song, story etc*

beum, *gen* **beuma,** *pl* **beuman** *&* **beumannan** *nm* **1** a stroke, a blow, *cf more usu* **buille 1**; **2** a taunt, a cutting or sarcastic remark

Beurla *nf invar*, **1** (*earlier, now obs in this sense*) a language; **2** (*now*) the English language, English, *often used with the art,* **bhruidhinn e rinn anns a' Bheurla/ann am Beurla** he spoke to us in English, **chan eil facal Beurla agam** I don't have/speak a word of English, (*trad*) **luchd na Beurla** English speakers, English people, *also* non-Gaelic Scots, **Beurla Shasannach** the English of England, **Beurla Ghallta** Scots, Lowland Scots, **Beurla leathann** broad Scots (*cf* **Albais**)

beus, beusa, beusan *nf* **1** moral character, virtue, *in pl* morals, **deagh-bheusan** virtuous morals; **2** behaviour, conduct, manners, **droch-**

bheus bad behaviour/manners, *cf* giùlan 3, modh 3

beus *adj* (*music*) bass

beusach *adj* 1 (*morally, sexually etc*) modest, *cf* nàrach 2; 2 moral, well-behaved, decent, *cf* modhail

beus-eòlas, *gen* beus-eòlais *nm* ethics

bha, bhathar, bheil, *pts of irreg v* bi (*see tables p 505*)

bhan(a), bhan(a), bhanaichean *nf* a van

bhàrr *prep see* bàrr 5

Bhatarsach, *gen & pl* Bhatarsaich *nm* someone from Vatersay (*see next*), *as adj* of from or pertaining to Vatersay

Bhatarsaigh *nf* Vatersay

Bheunas *nf* the planet Venus

bheir, bheireadh, bheirinn *pts of irreg verbs* beir & thoir (*see tables p 494 & 505*)

bheireas *pt of irreg v* beir (*see tables p 494*)

bhi, bhiodh, bhios, bhitheas, bhitheadh, bhitheamaid, bhithinn, *pts of irreg v* bi (*see tables p 505*)

bhidio, bhidio, bhidiothan *nmf* video, a video, cèiseag bhidio *nf* a video cassette

bho (*also* o) *prep* from. *For senses & examples of use, see* o *prep. The prep prons formed with* bho, *in the order first, second, third person singular, first, second, third person plural, and with the reflexive/emphatic particles in brackets, are as follows:* bhuam(sa), bhuat(sa), bhuaithe(san), bhuaipe(se), bhuainn(e), bhuaibh(se), bhuapa(san); *from me, from you* (*fam*), *etc, used exactly as* uam(sa), uat(sa) *etc, see under* o *prep*

bhòt(a), bhòt(a), bhòtaichean *nf* a vote

bhòt *vi, pres part* a' bhòtadh, vote, cha do bhòt sinn san taghadh we didn't vote in the election, bhòt mise airson a' Phàrtaidh Uaine I (*emph*) voted for the Green Party, *cf* tagh 2

bhuaibh (*emph form* bhuaibhse), bhuainn (*emph form* bhuainne), bhuaipe (*emph form* bhuaipese), bhuat (*emph form* bhuatsa), bhuaithe (*emph form* bhuaithesan), bhuam *emph form* bhuamsa), bhuapa (*emph form* bhuapasan) *prep prons, see* bho & o *preps*

bhur *see* ur

bi *vi irreg* be, *for forms see tables p 505, Note: Unlike* is, bi *cannot be used with a noun complement – cf* is boireannach i she is a woman (*see irreg vb* is) *with* tha i na ban-rùnaire & is e ban-rùnaire a tha innte she is a secretary; 1 *with adj complement* tha mi

àrd/fadalach/tinn I'm tall/late/ill; 2 *with adv* tha i an seo/gu bochd/gu dòigheil she's here/poorly/fine; 3 *with pres part* cha robh e a' coiseachd/ag òl/a' sealltainn he wasn't walking/drinking/looking; 4 *with* ann, *expressing existence, presence,* bidh Iain ann Iain will be here/there/present, chan eil sìthichean ann! there are no fairies, fairies don't exist!; 5 *in constr* is e . . . a tha (*etc*) ann *expressing identity, occupation, attributes etc,* cò esan? is e Niall a th' ann who's he? It's Neil, is e duine comasach a bh' ann an Dòmhnall, 's e lannsair a bh' ann Donald was an able man, he was a surgeon; 6 *with prep pron* nam, nad *etc* (*see p 509*), *expr a* (*usu*) *more temporary state, position, occupation etc than* 5, an uair a bha i na caileig òig when she was a young girl, tha iad nan laighe they're lying down, cha bhi thu nad aonar you won't be on your own; 7 *with* ri, ris, *engaged in, up to, at,* dè tha thu ris? what are you up to? a bheil thu ri bàrdachd fhathast? are you still at the poetry/writing poetry? tha iad ri iasgach they're fishing/at the fishing, *Note:* ri *is used after* bi *by some speakers as an alternative to* ag/a', *before the pres part, eg* bha i ri seinn she was singing; 8 *with* air & *the verbal noun or the infin, expr a passive sense or a perfect/pluperfect tense,* tha sinn air seinn we have sung, bha sinn air seinn we had sung, bha sinn air òrain a sheinn we had sung songs, bha an doras air a dhùnadh the door had been closed; 9 *with* aig, *indicates possession,* cha bhi sgillinn ruadh agam/ aig Màiri I/Mary won't have a brass farthing; 10 *with* aig . . . ri, *expresses obligation, tasks ahead,* tha tòrr agam ri dhèanamh I've got lots to do, bha aig Peigi ri aran fhuineadh Peggy had to bake bread; 11 *in expr* gu(s) bhith . . . , nearly . . . , ready to . . . , bha i gu bhith deiseil she was nearly/almost ready, tha iad gus falbh they are ready to/about to leave; *Note: when* bi & is *can both be used* is *usu implies more permanence &/or emphasis, eg* is math bùrn fuarain spring water is good, tha bùrn an fhuarain seo math the water from this spring is good, tha mi fèineil I'm selfish, I'm being selfish, (*more emph*) is fèineil mi I'm (*inherently*) selfish

biadh, *gen* bìdh & bidhe, *pl* biadhan *nm* 1 food, deasaich *v* biadh prepare/cook food, gabh do bhiadh! eat your food/meal! blasad *m* bìdh *or* grèim *m* bìdh a bite to eat, taigh-bìdh *m* a restaurant, thoir *v* biadh do na

beathaichean feed/fodder the animals; **2** a meal, *cf* **diathad 1**, **lòn 2**

biadh *v*, *same as* **biath** *v*

biadhlann, biadhlainn, biadhlannan *nf* a refectory, a canteen, a dining hall

bian, *gen & pl* **bèin** *nm* **1** fur, a fur; **2** skin, a skin, hide, a hide, a pelt, *cf* **seiche**

biast *& **bèist**, *gen* **bèiste**, *pl* **biastan** & **bèistean** *nf* **1** a beast, an animal (*wild or domestic*), *cf* **ainmhidh, beathach**; **2** *as term of abuse* **'s e biastan a th' annta!** they're beasts/animals!, *cf* **brùid 2**

biath *vt*, *pres part* **a' biathadh**, feed (*persons, stock* etc), *cf* **beathaich**

biathadh, *gen* **biathaidh** *nm* (*the act of*) feeding (*see* **biath** *v*)

bìd, bìde, bìdean *nm* **1** (*of bird*) a cheep, a chirp; **2** *of humans* (*fam*) a sound, a word, **cha tuirt e bìd** he didn't say a word, **cha chluinn i bìd** she can't hear a sound/a thing, *cf* **bìog, smid**

bìd *vt*, *pres part* **a' bìdeadh**, bite

bìdeadh, bìdidh, bìdidhean *nm* **1** (*the act of*) biting (*see* **bìd** *v*); **2** a bite

bìdeag, bìdeig, bìdeagan *nf* **1** a fragment, a crumb, a morsel, a small piece of anything, *cf* **criomag, mìr**; **2** (*IT*) a bit

bidh *pt of irreg v* **bi** (*see tables p 505*)

bidse *nf invar* **1** a bitch; **2** *as oath/swear* (*fam/vulg*) **taigh na bidse!** sod it/bugger it!

bile, bile, bilean *nf* **1** a lip (*of mouth*), **a' bhile uachdarach/ìochdarach** the upper/lower lip, **thàinig faite-gàire bheag gu a bilean** a wee smile came to her lips, *cf* **lip**; **2** a rim, a lip (*of container* etc), *cf* **iomall 2, oir** *n* **2**

bile, bile, bilean *nm* (*parliament*) a bill, *cf* **achd**

bileag, bileig, bileagan *nf* **1** a petal; **2** a blade (*of grass*); **3** (*also* **bileag cunntais**), (*household* etc) an account, a bill, **bha bileag bheag agam ri phàigheadh** I had a wee bill to pay, *cf* **cunntas 3**; **4** a ticket, *cf* **tigead**; **5** a label; **6** a leaflet; a pamphlet

billean, billein, billeanan *nm* a billion

binid, *gen* **binide** *nf* rennet

binn *adj* **1** (*of sound*) sweet, **a guth binn** her sweet voice, (*song*) **bha na h-eòin air na crannaibh 's iad ri caithream gu binn** the birds were on the trees, singing away sweetly, *Note: not usu for sweet smell or taste – see* **cùbhraidh, milis**; **2** melodious, *cf* **ceòlmhor**

binn, *gen* **binne** *nf* a judgement, a sentence, **thoir** *v* **a-mach binn** pronounce/give judgement, *cf* **breith²**

binnean, *gen & pl* **binnein** *nm* a hilltop, a peak, a pinnacle

binneas, *gen* **binneis** *nm* (*of sounds*) sweetness

bìoball, *gen* **bìobaill**, *pl* **bìobaill** & **bìoblaichean** *nm* a Bible, **Am Bìoball** The Bible

bìoballach *adj* biblical

bìobhar, bìobhair, bìobharan *m* a beaver

bìodach *adj* **1** tiny; **2** trifling; *cf* **crìon** *adj* **1** & **2**, **meanbh, suarach 1**

biodag, biodaig, biodagan *nf* a dirk, a dagger, (*trad*) **ag iomairt biodaig** wielding/using a dirk

biodh, *pt of irreg v* **bi** (*see tables p 505*)

bìog, bìoga, bìogan *nf* a cheep, a sound, *same uses as* **bìd** *n*

bìog *vi*, *pres part* **a' bìogail**, (*of bird*) chirp, cheep

biolair, *gen* **biolair** *nf* cress, water-cress

biona, biona, bionaichean *nmf* a bin, **cuir sa bhiona e!** bin it! **biona-sgudail** a dustbin

bior, biora, bioran *nm* **1** a point (*of stick* etc); **2** a pointed object, *esp* a pointed stick, a goad, *cf* **bioran, brod** *n* **1**; **3** a prickle, a thorn, *cf* **dealg 1**; **4** (*cookery*) **bior-ròstaidh** a spit; **5** *in expr* **air bhioran** *adv* on tenterhooks

biorach *adj* **1** pointed, sharp, (*trad*) **claidheamh caol biorach** a pointed rapier, **maide biorach** a pointed/sharp stick, **sùil bhiorach** a sharp eye; **2** prickly, thorny

bioran, *gen & pl* **biorain** *nm* a stick, *esp* a pointed stick, **a' brosnachadh na sprèidhe le bioran** urging on the cattle/the stock with a stick, *cf* **bior 2, brod** *n* **1**

biorra-crùidein, biorra-crùidein, biorrachan-crùidein *nm* a kingfisher

biotais *nm sing & coll* beet, beetroot; **biotais (siùcair)** sugarbeet

birlinn, birlinn, birlinnean *nf* (*trad*) a galley, a birlinn, (*poem*) **Birlinn Chlann Raghnaill** The Galley of Clan Ranald

bith *nf invar* **1** life, existence, being, **thoir** *v* **rudeigin am bith** bring something into existence/into being, **a' dol à bith** passing out of existence, ceasing to be, **bith-eòlas** *m* biology (*lit* knowledge of life *or* being); **2** the world, the earth, *esp in exprs* **air bith** & **sam bith**, any, any at all (*lit* on earth, in the world), **cò air bith a bha sin?** whoever/who on earth was that? (*cf* **fon ghrèin** – *see* **grian**), **bhiodh duine air bith/sam bith comasach air** anyone at all would be capable of it, **chan fhaca sinn duine sam bith** we didn't see anyone at all, **thoir dhomh leabhar – leabhar sam bith** give me a book – any book at all, (*emph*) **chan eil airgead agam, airgead sam bith** I've no money, no money at all (*cf* **idir**); **3** *esp in expr* **às bith** *also* **ge bith** (who-, what- etc) ever, **às**

bith cò a rinn e, às bith càite an d' fhuair thu e, tha e sgoinneil! whoever made it, wherever you got it from, it's smashing/great!

bìth, *gen* bìthe *nf* 1 tar, tarmacadam, pitch, *cf* teàrr; 2 gum

bith- *a prefix corres to Eng* ever-, bith-bheò *adj* ever-living, bith-bhuan *adj* eternal, everlasting, *cf* sìor-

bitheadh, bitheam, bitheamaid, bithear *pts of irreg v* bi (*see tables p 505*)

bitheag, bitheige, bitheagan *nf* a microbe, a germ

bitheanta *adj* frequent, common, *cf* cumanta

bitheantas *see am* bitheantas

bithibh, bithidh, bithinn *pts of irreg v* bi (*see tables p 505*)

bithis, bithis, bithisean *nf* (*joinery*) a screw, *cf* sgriubha

bithiseach *adj* spiral

blais *vt, pres part* a' blasad(h), taste, bhlais e an càise ach cha do chòrd e ris he tasted the cheese but he didn't like it

blàr, blàir, blàran *nm* 1 a plain, (*placename*) Blàr Dhruiminn Blair Drummond, *lit* 'the plain/level place of Drummond'; 2 (*trad*) a battle, a battlefield, blàr Chùil Lodair the battle of Culloden, air blàr Chùil Lodair on the field/battlefield of Culloden

blas, *gen* blais *nm* 1 taste, flavour, pògan air bhlas na meala kisses tasting of honey, tha droch bhlas air it has a bad taste; 2 (*language*) accent, tha blas na Beurla air a chuid Gàidhlig fhathast there's an English accent/flavour to his Gaelic still

blasachadh, *gen* blasachaidh *nm* (*the act of*) flavouring

blasad, *gen* blasaid *nm* 1 (*the act of*) tasting; 2 *usu in phrase* blasad bìdh a taste/a small amount of food, gabhaidh mi/gheibh mi blasad bìdh I'll take/get a bite to eat/a snack, *cf* grèim bìdh (*see* grèim 2)

blasaich *vt, pres part* a' blasachadh, flavour, add flavour to something

blasmhor, *adj* full of flavour, delicious, delectable, *cf* blasta

blasta & blasda *adj* tasty, full of flavour, biadh/ubhal blasta tasty food/a tasty apple, *cf* blasmhor

blàth *adj* 1 warm, tha i blàth an-diugh it's warm/a warm day today, bainne blàth warm milk; 2 (*of people, feelings etc*) warm, affectionate, tender, *cf* bàidheil, coibhneil

blàth, blàith, blàthan *nm* 1 a bloom, a blossom, blàth an ubhail apple blossom, preas fo bhlàth a shrub in bloom/blossom/flower; 2

flower (*of smaller plants*), *cf* dìthean & *more usu* flùr²

blàthachadh, *gen* blàthachaidh *nm* (*the act & process of*) warming, warming up, blàthachadh na cruinne global warming

blàthaich *vt, pres part* a' blàthachadh, 1 warm, warm up, *cf* teasaich, teòthaich; 2 (*fig*) blàthaich ri warm to (*develop sympathy or liking for*), bhlàthaich iad ris they warmed to him

blàth-chridheach *adj* tender-hearted, warm-hearted, affectionate

blàths, *gen* blàiths *nm* warmth (*phys, & of affections etc*)

bleadraig *vi, pres part* a' bleadraigeadh (*fam*) blether, chatter

bleideag, bleideig, bleideagan *nf* a flake, bleideagan sneachda/siabainn snowflakes/soapflakes, bleideagan-coirce cornflakes

bleith, *gen* bleithe *nf* 1 (*the act of*) grinding etc (*see senses of* bleith *v*); 2 attrition

bleith *vt, pres part* a' bleith, 1 (*of grain*) grind, mill, chaidh an t-arbhar a bhleith sa mhuileann the corn was ground in the mill, *cf* meil; 2 (*more generally*) grind, pulverise, *cf more usu* pronn *v* 1

bleoghain(n) *vt, pres part* a' bleoghan(n), milk, bhleoghainn a' bhanarach a' bhò the dairymaid milked the cow

bleoghann *nf invar* (*the act of*) milking

bliadhna, *gen* bliadhna, *pl* bliadhnachan & bliadhnaichean *nf* a year, *Note: usu in singular after numerals*; ceithir bliadhna a dh'aois four years of age, bliadhnachan air ais years ago, bha e san arm fad bhliadhnachan he was in the army for years, bidh sin a' tachairt gach bliadhna/a h-uile bliadhna that happens each/every year, Bliadhna Theàrlaich the period of the Jacobite Rising of 1745–6 (*lit* Charlie's Year), ceann-bliadhna *m* a birthday, am-bliadhna *adv* this year, chan eil biadh daor am-bliadhna food isn't dear this year, an ath-bhliadhna *adv* next year, bliadhna-lèim a leap year, Bliadhna Mhath Ur (dhut/dhuibh)! a Good/Happy New Year (to you)!

bliadhnach, *gen & pl* bliadhnaich *nm* a yearling

bliadhnail *adj* annual, yearly, coinneamh bhliadhnail a' Chomuinn Ghàidhealaich the annual meeting of An Comunn Gaidhealach

blian *vi, pres part* a' blianadh, sunbathe, sun oneself, bask in the sun

blianadh, *gen* blianaidh *nm* (*the act of*) sunbathing etc (*see senses of* blian *v*)

blianna *see* **bliadhna**

blobhsa, blobhsa, blobhsaichean *nm* a blouse

bloigh & **bloidh**, *gen* **bloighe**, *pl* **bloighean** *nf* **1** (*trad*) half of something, *cf more usu* **leth** 3; **2** a bit or piece of something, a fragment, *cf* **criomag, mìr, pìos** 1; **3** (*maths*) a fraction

bloighd, bloighd, bloighdean *nf* a fragment, a splinter, **bha am bata-coiseachd na bhloighdean** the walking stick was in splinters, *cf* **sgealb** *n*, **spealg** *n*

bloinigean-gàrraidh, *gen* **bloinigein-gàrraidh** *nm* spinach

blonag, *gen* **blonaig** *nf* lard, fat

bò, *gen* **bà**, *dat* **boin** & **bò**, *pl* **bà**, *gen pl* **bò** *nf* a cow, **a' tional/a' bleoghann bhò** herding/milking cows, **bò laoigh** a cow in calf, **bò bhainne** a milk cow, a milker, (*song*) **on a dh'fhàg mi i 'n Raineach nam bò** since I left her in Rannoch of the cattle, (*saying*) **bò mhaol odhar agus bò odhar mhaol** six and half a dozen, *cf* **crodh, sprèidh**

bobhla, bobhla, bobhlaichean *nm* a bowl, *cf more trad* **cuach**

bòc *vi*, *pres part* **a' bòcadh**, swell, bloat, blister, *cf more usu* **at** *v*, **sèid** 2

bòcadh, bòcaidh, bòcaidhean *nm* **1** (*the act of*) swelling etc (*see senses of* **bòc** *v*); **2** a swelling, *cf* **at** *n*

boc, *gen* & *pl* **buic** *nm* **1** a male goat, a billygoat, *cf* **gobhar**; **2** (*also* **boc-earba**) a buck, a roebuck, *cf* **damh** 1

bòcan, *gen* & *pl* **bòcain** *nm* **1** a spectre, an apparition, *cf* **taibhse, tannasg**; **2** a bog(e)y-man, (*Sc*) a bogle

bochd *adj* **1** poor, badly off, **fad làithean m' òige bha sinn bochd, bochd** all through my young days we were very, very poor, *cf* **ainniseach**; **2** unfortunate, poor, **an duine bochd!** the poor man!, **tha sin bochd** that's unfortunate/sad/a pity, *cf* **duilich** 4, **truagh** 3; **3** not well, poorly, in a bad way, ailing, **ciamar a tha thu? chan eil ach bochd** how are you? I'm not too good at all, *also as adv* **gu bochd** poorly, **tha mi gu bochd** I'm poorly/in a bad way, *cf* **tinn**

bochdainn, *gen* **bochdainne** *nf* **1** poverty, *cf* **ainnis**; **2** misfortune, bad luck, *cf* **dosgainn**

bocsa & **bogsa**, *gen* **bogsa**, *pl* **bogsaichean** *nm* **1** a box, **bogsa-fòn** a (tele)phone box *or* kiosk, **bogsa-litrichean** a letter box, a post box, **bogsa mhaidsichean** a match box, a box of matches, *cf* **bucas**; **2** **bogsa** (*fam*) *for* **bogsa-ciùil**, *gen* **bogsa(-ciùil)**, *pl* **bogsaichean (-ciùil)** *nm* an accordeon, (*fam*) a box, **bha Phil Cunningham air a' bhogsa (-ciùil)** Phil Cunningham was on/was playing the box

bocsair, bocsair, bocsairean, *also* **bogsair, bogsair, bogsairean** *nm*, (*sport*) a boxer

bod, *gen* & *pl* **buid** & **boid** *nm* a penis, *cf* **slat** 4

Bòd *n* Bute

bodach, *gen* & *pl* **bodaich** *nm* (*fam*) **1** an old man, an old guy, an old fellow, **cà'il am bodach?** where's the old fellow? **Bodach na Nollaig(e)** Father Christmas, Santa Claus; **2** *sometimes more derog*, (*song*) **bodachan** (*dimin*) **le pinnt air, bidh e leis an daoraich** a little old man with a pint in him, he'll be drunk; **3** *not necessarily with implication of age*, **is esan bodach an airgid** he's the money man/the guy who looks after the money, **bodach nam bucaidean** the bucket man, the bin man, **bodach-sneachda** a snowman, **bodach-ròcais** a scarecrow, (*of one's husband*) **am bodach** the old man, my old man, *cf* **cailleach**

bodhaig, bodhaige, bodhaigean *nf* a (*human*) body (*usu living*), *cf* **colann, corp** 1

bodhair *vt*, *pres part* **a' bòdhradh**, deafen, make deaf

bodhar *adj* deaf

bodhar, bodhair, bodharan *nm* a deaf person, (*prov*) **cluinnidh am bodhar fuaim an airgid** (even) the deaf man will hear the sound of money

bòdhradh, *gen* **bòdhraidh** *nm* (*the act of*) deafening

bòdhran, bòdhrain, bòdhranan *nm* (*music*) a bodhran

bodraig *vti*, *pres part* **a' bodraigeadh**, **1** (*vt*) (*fam*) bother, **na bodraig mi!** don't bother me!, *cf more trad* **sàraich**; **2** (*vi*) bother oneself, take the trouble, **an do dheasaich thu biadh dhomh? cha do bhodraig mi** did you prepare me some food? I didn't bother

bodraigeadh, *gen* **bodraigidh** *nm* (*the act of*) bothering (*see senses of* **bodraig** *v*)

bog *adj* **1** soft, **stuth bog** soft material/fabric, **talamh bog** soft (*often boggy*) ground; **2** (*of character etc*) soft, **tha e bog on a mhill a mhàthair e** he's soft since his mother spoiled him, *cf* **maoth** 1; **3** tender, **cridhe bog** a tender heart; **4** *in expr* **bog fliuch**, soaking wet, **bha sinn bog fliuch mus do sguir an t-uisge** we were soaking wet before the rain stopped; **5** moist, humid, *cf* **tais**; **6** limp, flabby

bog, buig, bogachan *nm* **1** a bog *cf* **boglach, fèith(e)**; **2** *in expr* **air bhog** floating, afloat, **cuir** *v* **air bhog** launch, *cf* **fleòdradh, flod**

bog *vti*, *pres part* **a' bogadh**, **1** *vt* dip, soak, steep (*in liquid*); **2** *vi* (*movement*) bob, dip, (*of tail*) wag, **bha earball a' choin a' bogadh** the dog's tail was wagging

bogachadh, *gen* **bogachaidh** *nm* (*the act of*) wetting etc (*see senses of* **bogaich** *v*)

bogadaich *nf invar* **1** a bouncing or bobbing movement; **2** *also as pres part* **a' bogadaich** bouncing, bobbing (**ri** against), jumping up and down

bogadh, *gen* **bogaidh** *nm* **1** (*the act of*) soaking etc (*see sense of* **bog** *v*); **2** *in expr* **cuir** *v* **aodach** (etc) **am bogadh** put clothes (etc) to soak/steep; **3** immersion, (*also fig*) **bogadh cànain** language immersion, (*lang*) **cùrsa** *m* **bogaidh** an immersion course

bogaich *vti*, *pres part* **a' bogachadh 1** (*vt*) wet, make wet, *cf* **fliuch** *v*; **2** (*vti*) soften, make or become soft

bogha, bogha, boghachan *nm* **1** a bow or curve in anything, a bulge, **tha bogha air a' bhalla** the wall has a bulge in it, *cf* **lùb** *n* **1**; **2** an arch, a vault; **3** a bow (*ie weapon*); **4** (*mus*) a bow (*for violin etc*)

boghadair, boghadair, boghadairean *nm* an archer, a bowman

bogha-frois, bogha-fhrois/ bogha-froise, boghachan-frois *nm* a rainbow

boglach, boglaich, boglaichean *nf* a bog, soft or marshy ground, a swamp, **bha e an sàs ann am boglaich** he was stuck in a bog, *cf* **bog** *n* **1**, **fèith(e)**

bogsa *see* **bocsa**

bòid, bòide, bòidean *nf* **1** an oath, a vow, a solemn promise, *cf less strong* **geall** *n* **2**; **2** an oath, swearing, (*Sc*) a swear, *cf* **droch cainnt** (*see* **cainnt 2**), **mionn 1 & 2**

Bòideach, *gen & pl*, **Bòidich** *nm* a Bute man, someone from Bute (**Bòd**), *also as adj*, **Bòideach** of from or pertaining to Bute

bòideachadh, *gen* **bòideachaidh** *nm* (*the act of*) vowing etc (*see senses of* **bòidich** *v*), *cf* **mionnachadh**

bòidhchead, *gen* **bòichdheid** *nf* beauty, loveliness, prettiness, *cf* **maise**

bòidheach, *comp* **(n)as** (etc) **bòidhche** *adj* beautiful, pretty, bonny, *esp of places, human females & other living things*, **àite bòidheach** a beautiful/bonny place, **caileag bhòidheach** a beautiful/bonny girl, (*song*) **isein bhòidhich tha ri siubhal null gud nead an Tìr an Fhraoich** O bonny wee bird travelling yonder to your nest in the Land of the Heather, (*song*) **'s e Siabost as bòidhche . . .** Siabost is the bonniest (place) . . . , *cf* **àlainn, brèagha, maiseach**

bòidich *vi*, *pres part* **a' bòideachadh 1** (*in legal context*) vow, swear; **2** curse, swear, (*ie use bad or foul language*); *cf* **mionnaich** *vi* **1 & 2**

boile *nf invar* **1** madness; **2** frenzy, rage, passion, (*trad*) **boile chatha** battle frenzy, battle madness (*cf* **misg chatha**, *see* **misg**); **3** *in expr* **air bhoile** in a frenzy, in a rage, **bha e air bhoile an dèidh dha obair a chall** he was mad/in a rage/furious after losing his job; *cf* **bàinidh, cuthach**

boillsg, boillsge, boillsgean *nm* **1** a flash of light; **2** a gleam

boillsg *vi*, *pres part* **a' boillsgeadh**, gleam, flash, glitter, shine, dazzle (*esp intermittently*), **bha an uaimh a' boillsgeadh le òr** the cave was shining/glittering with gold, *cf* **deàlraich 2**

boillsgeach *adj* gleaming, flashing, glittering, shining, dazzling *cf* **deàlrach 1**

boillsgeadh, *gen* **boillsgidh** *nm* (*the act of*) gleaming, flashing etc (*see senses of* **boillsg** *v*)

boin *nf see* **bò**

boinne, *gen* **boinne**, *pl* **boinnean & boinneachan** *nmf* **1** a drop (*of liquid*), **boinne bainne** a drop of milk; **2** a very small quantity (*of liquid*), **chan eil boinne bùirn** (*or* **uisge**) **againn** we don't have a drop of water; *cf* **boinneag, braon** *n* **1**

boinneag, boinneige, boinneagan *nf* **1** a small drop, *cf* **drùdhag 1**; **2** *in expr* **boinneag ri shròin** a drop on his nose

boireann *adj* female, feminine, **cù/each boireann** a female dog/horse, (*biol etc*) **an cineal boireann** the female sex/gender, (*gram*) **a' ghnè bhoireann** the feminine gender, **'s e facal boireann a th' ann an 'uiseag'** 'uiseag' is a feminine word, *cf* **fireann**

boireannach, *gen & pl* **boireannaich** *nm* a woman, a (*human*) female, *Note: though* **boireannach** *is grammatically masculine the pronoun* **i** *is used*, **chuala mi boireannach is i a' seinn** I heard a woman singing, *cf* **bean** *n* **2**, **fireannach, tè 2**

boireannta *adj* effeminate

boiseag, boiseig, boiseagan *nf* **1** a slap or blow with the palm of the hand; **2** a palmful of anything

boiteag, boiteig, boiteagan *nf* a worm, *cf* **cnuimh**

boladh, bolaidh, bolaidhean *nm* a smell (*pleasant or unpleasant*), an odour, a scent, a stink, *cf* **àile 2, boltrach, tòchd**

bolgan, *gen* **bolgain**, *pl* **bolgain & bolganan** *nm* **1** (*hort*) a bulb; **2** a light bulb

boltrach, *gen & pl* **boltraich** *nm* a smell (*usu pleasant*), a scent, a perfume, *cf* **àile 2, boladh, tòchd**

boma, boma, bomaichean *nm* a bomb, **leag** *v* **boma** drop a bomb

bonaid, bonaide, bonaidean *nmf* **1** a bonnet, **bonaid b(h)iorach** a Glengarry bonnet, **bonaid càir** a car bonnet; **2** (*headgear*) a cap
bonn, *gen & pl* **buinn** *nm* **1** the lowest part, base, foot or foundation of anything, **bonn taighe** foundations of a house, **bonn na coise/na bròige** the sole of the foot/of the shoe, **bonn na beinne** the foot/bottom of the mountain (*cf* **bun 1**), **bonn-dubh** heel of the foot (*cf more usu* **sàil**); **2** *esp* **bonn airgid** a coin, a piece of money, (*trad*) **bonn-a-sia** & **bonn-a-sè** (*orig*) sixpence Scots, (*subsequently*) a halfpenny; **3** a medal, **choisinn i am Bonn Airgid/Òir aig a' Mhòd** she won the Silver/Gold Medal at the Mod, **bonn-cuimhne** a military medal, a medal for bravery, a commemorative medal; **4** *in expr* **thug iad na buinn asta** they took to their heels; **5** *in expr* **cuir** *v* **air b(h)onn** found, establish, set up, **chaidh an gnothach a chur air bonn le mo sheanair** the business was founded/set up by my grandfather, **tha a' chomhairle a' cur air bonn cròileagan tro mheadhan na Gàidhlig** the Council is setting up a Gaelic-medium playgroup, *cf* **cas** *n* **5**, **stèidhich**
bonnach, *gen & pl* **bonnaich** *nm* **1** a bannock; **2** a cake; **3** a scone (*cf less trad* **sgona**); *cf* **breacag**; **4** **bonnach-uighe** an omelette
borb *adj* wild, savage, barbarous, uncouth, **sluagh borb** a wild/savage people, **duine borb** a barbarous *or* uncouth man, **dòighean/dol-a-mach borb** uncouth behaviour, *cf* **garbh 3**, **garg**
borbair, borbair, borbairean *nm* a barber, *cf more trad* **bearradair**
bòrd, *gen & pl* **bùird** *nm* **1** (*furniture*) a table, **bha sinn nar suidhe mun bhòrd** we were sitting/seated round the table, **bòrd-iarnaigidh** an ironing-board, **bòrd-sgrìobhaidh** a writing table/desk; **2** (*joinery etc*) a board or plank of wood, *cf* **clàr 1**, **dèile**; **3** (*in school etc*) a board, **bòrd-dubh** a blackboard, **bòrd-geal** a whiteboard, **bha liosta an-àird air a' bhòrd** there was a list up on the (notice) board; **4** (*business, admin etc*) Board (*of Directors etc*), **Bòrd na Slàinte** the Health Board, **Bòrd nan Deuchainnean** the Examinations Board; **5** *in exprs* (*of boats, planes*) **air bòrd** on board, aboard, & (**thuit e etc**) **far bòrd** (he fell etc) overboard, **bha sinn/chaidh sinn air bòrd na luinge** we were/we went on board the ship
bòst, bòsta, bòstan *nm* a boast, boasting, **dèan** *v* **bòst** boast
bòstail *adj* boastful, *cf* **bragail**

botal & **buideal**, *gen & pl* **botail** *nm* a bottle, **botal fìon(a)** a bottle of wine *or* a wine bottle, **amhaich** *f* **botail** neck of a bottle, **botal-teth** a hot-water bottle
bòtann, bòtainn, bòtannan *nmf* a boot, *usu* a Wellington boot, a wellie, *cf* **bròg throm, bròg-mhòr** (*see* **bròg**)
bothan, *gen & pl* **bothain** *nm* **1** a cottage; **2** a hut, a shed, *cf less trad* **seada**; **3** a bothy, *esp* (*trad*) **bothan àirigh(e)** a sheiling bothy; **4** a shebeen (*a place where illicitly distilled whisky is/was drunk*), *cf* **taigh-dubh** (*see* **taigh 1**)
bracaist, bracaiste, bracaistean *nf* breakfast, **dè a ghabhas tu air/gu do bhracaist?** what will you have for your breakfast?
brach *vti, pres part* **a' brachadh**, **1** (*esp of beer, wine etc*) ferment; **2** (*vi*) (*of boil, spot*) gather, fill with pus
brachadh, brachaidh, brachaidhean *nm* **1** (*the act of*) fermenting (*see senses of* **brach** *v*); **2** fermentation; **3** pus, matter
bradan, *gen & pl* **bradain** *nm* a salmon, (*coll*) salmon
brag, *gen* **braig** *nm* a bang (*esp sharp, not dull*), **rinn an dèile brag an uair a thuit i chun an ùrlair** the plank made a bang when it fell to the floor
bragail *adj* **1** boastful, *cf* **bòstail**; **2** cheeky, *cf* **beadaidh**
braich, *gen* **bracha** *nf* malt, malted barley, (*trad*) **Mac na Bracha** Son of the Malt, *a nickname for malt whisky*
braid(e), *gen* **braide** *nf* theft, thieving, pilfering, stealing, *cf* **goid** *n*, **mèirle**
bràigh¹, *gen* **bràighe** & **bràghad**, *pl* **bràigheachan** *nm* **1** the upper part of anything, **bràigh a' bhaile** the upper part of the township, the top of the town, **bràigh a' ghlinne** the head/the upper part of the glen, **bràigh a' chuirp** the upper part of the body, the chest area (*cf more usu* **broilleach 2**), **losgadh-bràghad** heartburn; **2** *in placenames*, upland, *often rendered as* Brae(s), **Bràigh Dhùin** the Braes of Doune, **Bràigh Loch Abair** Brae Lochaber
bràigh², **bràighe, bràighdean** *nmf* a prisoner, a captive, *esp* a hostage, *cf* **ciomach, prìosanach**
braighdeanas, *gen* **braighdeanais** *nm* captivity, imprisonment, **am braighdeanas** in captivity, held hostage, *cf* **ciomachas, daorsa, làmh 2, sàs 1**
braim, brama, bramannan *nm* breaking of wind, a fart, **leig e braim** he broke wind/farted

braisead, *gen* **braiseid** *nf* **1** (*of persons, behaviour*) hastiness, impetuosity; **2** (*of soldier etc*) intrepidity, boldness, *cf* **dànadas 1**

bràiste, bràiste, bràistean *nf* a brooch, a badge

bràithreil *adj* brotherly, fraternal

bràmair, bràmair, bràmairean *nm* (*fam*) a girlfriend *or* boyfriend, *cf* **car(a)bhaidh, leannan**

branndaidh *nf invar* brandy

braoisg, braoisge, braoisgean *nf* a grin *or* a grimace, **chuir i braoisg oirre** she grinned *or* she grimaced, *cf* **bus² 2**

braoisgeil *adj* (*not usu complimentary*) grinning

braon, *gen & pl* **braoin** *nm* **1** a drop (*of liquid*), *cf* **boinne 1**; **2** drizzle, *cf* **ciùbhran 1**

braon *vi, pres part* **a' braonadh**, drizzle

bras *adj* **1** (*of persons, behaviour*) hasty, impetuous, impulsive, *cf* **cas** *adj* **3**; **2** (*of soldier etc*) intrepid, bold, *also* rashly bold, *cf* **dàna 2**; **3** (*of stream etc*) rushing, precipitous, *cf* **cas** *adj* **2**

brat, brata, bratan *nm* **1** a cover, a covering (*cf* **còmhdach**), **brat-leapa(ch)** a bed cover, a coverlet, a quilt; **2** (*trad*) a cloak; **3** a mat, *also* **brat-ùrlair** & **brat-làir** a (*larger*) floor-covering, a carpet

bratach, brataich, brataichean *nf* a banner, a flag, colours (*of a regiment etc*), **a' Bhratach Shìth** the Fairy Flag (*of Dunvegan*), (*song*) **Mhic Iarla** (*voc*) **nam bratach bàna** O Son of the Earl of the white banners

bràth, *gen* **bràtha** *nm* **1** (*trad*) judgement, doom, **là a' bhràtha** judgement day, doomsday; **2** *esp in expr* **gu bràth** for ever, always, **bidh na beanntan ann gu bràth** the mountains will be there for ever/will always be there, (*more emph*) **gu sìorraidh bràth** for ever and ever; **3 gu bràth** *with neg v* never, **cha bhruidhinn mi ris gu bràth (tuilleadh)** I'll never speak to him (again); *cf* **a-chaoidh, sìorraidh 2**; *Note:* **gu bràth** *is used only to refer to future time, for ever* & *never in the past see* **a-riamh**

brath, *gen* **bratha** *nm* **1** knowledge, information, *esp in exprs* **'s ann aig Dia tha brath!** God alone knows! & **aig Sealbh tha brath carson!** Heaven knows why!, *cf more usu* **fios 1** & **2**; **2** (*usu* unfair) advantage, **ghabh am fear-reic brath air** the salesman took advantage of him, *cf* **fàth 3**; **3** betrayal, a betrayal

brath *vt, pres part* **a' brathadh**, **1** betray, give away, inform on (*someone*); **2** give away (*a secret*)

brathadair, brathadair, brathadairean *nm* **1** a betrayer, an informer; **2** a traitor

brathadh, *gen* **brathaidh** *nm* **1** (*the act of*) betraying etc (*see senses of* **brath** *v*); **2** treason, betrayal

bràthair, bràthar, bràithrean *nm* a brother, **bràthair-athar** an uncle (*on father's side*), **bràthair-màthar** an uncle (*on mother's side*), **bràthair m' athar/mo mhàthar** my uncle, **bràthair-cèile** a brother-in-law

breab, breaba, breaban *nmf* a kick

breab *vti, pres part* **a' breabadh**, **1** kick; **2** stamp the foot, *cf* **stamp** *v*

breabadair, breabadair, breabadairean *nm* **1** one who kicks; **2** (*usu*) a weaver, one who works a loom, *cf* **figheadair 1**; **3** a daddy-longlegs

breabadh, *gen* **breabaidh** *nm* (*the act of*) kicking etc (*see senses of* **breab** *v*)

breac *adj* speckled, spotted, variegated (*pattern, appearance, material etc*), (*more fig*) **tha an t-eilean breac le bailtean beaga** the island is dotted with villages, *cf* **ballach** & *trad* **riabhach 1**

breac¹, *gen & pl* **bric** *nm* a trout

breac², *gen* **brice** *nf* (*used with the art*) **a' bhreac** smallpox, **a' bhreac-òtraich** chicken-pox, **a' bhreac-sheunain** & **(am) breacadh-seunain** freckles

breacach, *gen* **breacaich** *nm* fishing (*esp for trout*), *cf* **iasgach**

breacag, breacaig, breacagan *nf* **1** a cake; **2** a bannock; *cf* **bonnach**

breacan, *gen* **breacain**, *pl* **breacain** & **breacanan** *nm* **1** (*trad*) a plaid, *cf* **fèile 1**; **2** tartan cloth, **pìos breacain** a piece of tartan, (*song*) **soraidh leis a' bhreacan ùr** farewell to the fair tartan plaid; **3** a variegated pattern, **bha am fearann na bhreacan de fhraoch 's de raineach** the land was a patchwork of heather and bracken

breacanach *adj* tartan, of tartan, **aodach breacanach** tartan cloth, tartan clothing

breac-bhallach *adj* freckled

brèagha *adj* fine, lovely, beautiful, **là brèagha** a lovely/beautiful day, (*Sc*) a braw day, **sìde bhrèagha** fine/grand weather, **àite brèagha** a fine/bonny/lovely place, **nighean bhrèagha** a pretty/bonny/beautiful girl, *cf* **àlainn, bòidheach, grinn 1** & **2**

brèaghachadh, brèaghachaidh, brèaghachaidhean *nm* **1** (*the act of*) embellishing, beautifying; **2** (*more con*) an embellishment, *cf* **sgeadachadh 2**

brèaghaich *vt, pres part* **a' brèaghachadh**, beautify, embellish, *cf* **maisich 1, sgeadaich 1, sgèimhich**

Breatainn *nf* Britain; **A' Bhreatainn Bheag**
Britanny

Breatannach, *gen & pl* **Breatannaich** *nm* a
British person, (*modern & hist*) a Briton, *also as*
adj **Breatannach** British

Breatnais *nf invar* (*lang*) Breton

brèid, brèide, brèidean *nm* 1 (*trad*) a kerchief
worn formerly by married women; 2 a patch,
cuir brèid air seann bhriogais put a patch
on an old pair of trousers, *cf* **tuthag**; 3 a cloth,
(*Sc*) a clout, **brèid-shoithichean** a dish-cloth,
cf **clobhd, clùd** 2

brèig, brèige, brèigichean *nf* a brake (*ie*
stopping device), *cf* **casgan**

breige, breige, breigichean *nmf* a brick

brèige *adj* 1 false, deceitful, **leannan brèige** a
deceitful lover, *cf* **fallsa, meallta(ch)**; 2 false
(*ie artificial*), **fear-brèige** *m* a puppet, **gruag-**
bhrèige *f* a wig, *cf* **fuadain**

breigire, breigire, breigirean *nm* a bricklayer

breisleach, *gen* **breislich** *nm* 1 confusion,
chuir am fuaim mòr am breisleach mi
the great noise confused me, *cf* **buaireas** 1,
bruaillean; 2 delirium

breisleachadh, *gen* **breisleachaidh** *nm* (*the*
act of) confusing, raving *etc* (*see* **breislich** *v*)

breisleachail *adj* delirious, raving

breislich *vti*, *pres part* **a' breisleachadh**, 1 (*vt*)
confuse, cause to be confused; 2 (*vi*) rave, talk
irrationally, **bha i a' breisleachadh na cadal**
she was raving/delirious in her sleep

breith[1], *nf invar* birth, a birth, **o là mo bhreith**
since the day of my birth, **co-là-breith** a
birthday (*cf* **ceann-bliadhna**), **breith**
an-abaich a premature birth

breith[2] *nf invar* a judgement, a decision, (*law*)
a sentence, *usu in expr* **thoir** *v* **breith** pass
judgement/sentence, give a decision, *cf* **binn** *n*

breitheamh *see* **britheamh**

breithneachadh, *gen* **breithneachaidh**
nm (*the act of*) judging etc (*see senses of*
breithnich *v*)

breithnich *vti*, *pres part* **a' breithneachadh**,
judge, assess, appraise

breug, brèige, breugan *nf* 1 a lie, **innis** *v*
breug & **dèan** *v* **breug** lie, tell a lie; 2 *as excl*
breugan! (*not necessarily in serious context*),
nach eil thu a' streap ris an dà fhichead?
Breugan! aren't you're getting on for forty?
that's not true!/Rubbish!/Nonsense!

breugach *adj* lying, false, **faclan/briathran**
breugach lying words, **duine breugach** a
lying/mendacious man

breugnaich *vt*, *pres part* **a' breugnachadh**, 1
refute, disprove, give the lie to; 2 falsify

breugaire, breugaire, breugairean *nm* a liar

breug-riochd, breug-riochda, breug-
riochdan *nm* 1 disguise, a disguise; 2
camouflage

breun *adj* 1 putrid, corrupt, *cf* **coirbte**; 2 filthy,
disgusting, vile, *cf* **grànda, sgreamhail,**
sgreataidh

briathar, briathair, briathran *nm* 1
(*language*) a term, **is e 'sgaoileadh-**
cumhachd' am briathar a th' againn air
'devolution' 'sgaoileadh-cumhachd' is the
term we have/use for 'devolution', **briathran**
teicneolach technical terms; 2 *esp in pl*,
words, statements, pronouncements, **briathran**
amaideach foolish words/statements,
briathran ciallach sensible words/statements,
cha chreid mi briathran luchd-poilitigs
I don't believe politicians' words/statements, I
don't believe what politicians say

briathrach *adj* wordy, verbose, *cf* **faclach**

briathrachas, *gen* **briathrachais** *nm* 1
verbosity; 2 terminology

brìb, *gen* **brìbe**, *pl* **brìbean** & **brìbeachan** *nf*
a bribe

brìb *vt*, *pres part* **a' brìbeadh**, bribe

brìbeadh, *gen* **brìbidh** *nm* (*the act of*) bribing

brìgh & **brìogh** *nf invar* 1 meaning, sense,
(*dictionary title*) **Brìgh nam Facal** the
Meaning/Sense of Words, *cf* **ciall** 3, **seagh**; 2
virtue, quality, substance, essence of anything,
leabhar gun bhrìgh a book without substance,
brìgh na feallsanachd aige the essence of his
philosophy, *cf* **susbaint**; 3 (*plants, fruit etc*)
pith, sap, juice, *cf* **sùgh**; 4 strength, energy, **bha**
mi gun bhrìgh an dèidh na tubaiste I had
no strength/energy after the accident, *cf* **lùth** 3,
neart, spionnadh; 5 *prep* **do bhrìgh** because
of, on account of, **do bhrìgh sin** because of
that, for that reason, *cf* **a chionn, sgàth** 3

brìghmhor & **brìoghmhor** *adj* 1 sappy, juicy,
pithy, full of sap or juice or pith, *cf* **smiorach,**
sùghmhor; 2 energetic, zestful, full of zest or
energy, *cf* **lùthmhor** 3

brìodail *vt*, *pres part* **a' brìodal**, 1 caress, *cf*
cnèadaich; 2 flatter; 3 court, woo, *cf* **dèan**
suirghe (*see* **suirghe**)

brìodal, *gen* **brìodail** *nm* 1 (*the act of*) caressing
etc (*see senses of* **brìodail** *v*); 2 endearments;
3 flattery, *cf* **miodal, sodal**; 4 courtship,
courting, wooing, *cf* **leannanachd, suirghe**

briogais, briogais, briogaisean *nf* trousers,
a pair of trousers, (*Sc*) breeks, (*song*) **chuir e**
bhriogais ghlas an gèill he made the grey
trousers compulsory (*ie he banned Highland*
dress), *cf* **triubhas**

brìogh, brìoghmhor *see* brìgh, brìghmhor

briosgaid, briosgaide, briosgaidean *nf* a
  biscuit

brisg *adj* 1 crisp; 2 brittle

brisgean, brisgein, brisgean *nm* 1 silverweed;
  2 a (potato) crisp

bris(t) *vti*, *pres part* a' bris(t)eadh, 1 break,
  smash, (*as vi*) bhris an uinneag the window
  broke, brisidh an aimsir a-màireach the
  weather will break tomorrow, bhris iad
  a-mach às a' phrìosan they broke out of
  prison, (*as vt*) bhris i an lagh/an gealladh/
  an t-uaireadair she broke the law/the
  promise/the watch, brisidh e mo chridhe it
  will break my heart, *cf* smuais, smùid *v* 2; 2
  (*contract etc*) breach; 3 *in expr* bhris an latha
  day broke, day dawned

briste *adj* broken, smashed, tha an uinneag/
  mo chridhe briste the window/my heart is
  broken

bris(t)eadh, *gen* bris(t)idh *nm* 1 (*the act of*)
  breaking, smashing, breaching *etc*, *see senses*
  of bris(t) *vti*; 2 bankruptcy; 3 (*of contract,*
  conditions etc) a breach; 4 *in expr* (*church hist*)
  Briseadh na h-Eaglaise the Disruption

bris(t)eadh-cridhe, bris(t)idh-cridhe,
  bris(t)idhean-cridhe *nm* heartbreak, a cause
  of heartbreak, (*poem*) nist tha mi a' faicinn
  nad shùilean briseadh-cridhe na cùise
  (Meg Bateman) now I see in your eyes the heartbreak of the matter

bris(t)eadh-dùil, bris(t)idh-dùil,
  bris(t)idhean-dùil *nm* disappointment,
  a (cause of) disappointment, a blow, is e
  bristeadh-dùil a bh' ann an toradh an
  taghaidh dha the result/outcome of the
  election was a disappointment/a blow to/for him

bris(t)eadh-là, bris(t)idh-là, bris(t)idhean-
  là (*also* bris(t)eadh an là) *nm* daybreak,
  dawn, *cf* camhanach

britheamh, *gen* britheimh, *pl* britheamhan
  nm a judge, tha e na bhritheamh ann an
  Cùirt an t-Seisein/aig a' Mhòd Nàiseanta
  he is a Judge in the Court of Session/at the
  National Mod

broc, *gen & pl* bruic *nm* a badger

brochan, *gen & pl* brochain *nm* porridge, gruel,
  (*song*) brochan lom, tana lom, brochan
  lom sùghain plain porridge, thin and plain,
  plain sowans porridge, *cf* lite

brod, bruid, brodan *nm* 1 (*a stick used as*)
  a goad, a prod, *cf* bioran; 2 the best part of
  anything, the best example of anything, brod a'
  bharra the best part/the pick of the crop, brod

na croite the best of crofts, an excellent croft, *cf*
  smior 2 & *opposite* diù

brod *vt*, *pres part* a' brodadh, 1 goad, drive on
  (*stock etc*), *cf* greas 2, iomain *v* 1; 2 stimulate,
  encourage, stir up, animate, *cf* brosnaich,
  spreig, stuig

brodadh, *gen* brodaidh *nm* 1 (*the act of*)
  goading, driving etc (*see senses of* brod *v*); 2
  (*also* fèin-bhrodadh) masturbation

bròg, bròige, brògan *nf* a shoe, a boot (*not a*
  Wellington, *cf* bòtann), bròg aotrom a light
  shoe, bròg-mhòr *or* bròg throm a (*stout*)
  boot, brògan ball-coise football boots,
  brògan tacaideach nailed boots, (*Sc*) tackety
  boots, bròg-eich a horse-shoe (*cf more trad*
  crudha), *cf* bòtann

broilleach, *gen* broillich, *pl* broilleachan &
  broillichean *nm* 1 (*of male or female*) a breast,
  a bosom, (*song*) cìochan corrach 's iad glè-
  gheal ann am broilleach na lèine pointed
  breasts, and they so white, in the bosom of the
  shirt, *cf* com 1, uchd 1; 2 a chest, the chest area,
  cf cliabh 4

broinn, *dat of* brù (*see below*) used as a nom, *nf*
  1 a belly, a womb, *cf* balg 1, machlag, maodal;
  2 the interior (*esp of a building*), *esp in exprs*
  am broinn in, inside, within, *and* na (etc)
  b(h)roinn inwards, in, bha amar-snàimh
  am broinn an taighe there was a swimming
  pool inside/within the house, thuit am
  mullach na bhroinn the roof fell in, *cf* taobh
  a-staigh (*see* taobh 1)

bròn, *gen* bròin *nm* 1 sadness, sorrow, adhbhar
  mo bhròin the cause of/reason for my sadness,
  tha mi fo bhròn I am sorrowful/sad, *cf*
  mulad; 2 mourning, tha an teaghlach ri
  bròn the family is in mourning, *cf* caoidh

brònach *adj* sad, sorrowful, miserable, òrain
  bhrònach sad songs, tha mi muladach
  brònach I'm sad and miserable, *cf* dubhach 1,
  muladach, truagh 2, tùrsach

brosnachadh, *gen* brosnachaidh *nm* 1 (*the act*
  of) encouraging etc (*see senses of* brosnaich
  v); 2 encouragement, stimulus, feumaidh e
  brosnachadh mus dèan e a dhìcheall he
  needs encouragement before he'll do his best,
  cf misneachadh 2; 3 incitement, exhortation,
  (*trad*) brosnachadh catha incitement to
  battle, *cf* earalachadh 2; 4 (*trad*) the name of a
  class of martial bagpipe music

brosnachail *adj* encouraging, fear-teagaisg
  brosnachail an encouraging teacher, *cf*
  misneachail 3

brosnaich *vt, pres part* **a' brosnachadh,**
encourage, urge on, arouse, animate, inspire, *cf*
brod *v*, **misnich 2, spreig, stuig**

brot, brota, brotan *nm* broth, soup, *cf trad*
eanraich

broth, brotha, brothan *nm* a rash

brù, *gen* **bronn** & **broinne,** *dat* **broinn,** *pl*
bruthan *nf* 1 a womb, **leanabh na broinn** a
baby/child in her womb, *cf* **broinn 1, machlag;**
2 a belly, **fhuair mi làn mo bhronn de**
bhiadh I got a bellyful of food, *cf* **balg 1,**
maodal, stamag; 3 a bulge, **tha brù air a'**
bhalla there's a bulge in the wall, the wall is
bulging; 4 *see* **broinn**

bruach, bruaich, bruaichean *nf* a bank (*of a*
river, loch etc), **bruach an lòin** the bank of
the pond

bruadair *vi, pres part* **a' bruadar** & **a'**
bruadarachd, dream, **bha mi a' bruadar ort**
a-raoir I dreamt about you last night

bruadar, bruadair, bruadaran *nm* 1 (*the*
act of) dreaming, **tha thu ri bruadar!** you're
dreaming!; 2 a dream, *cf* **aisling**

bruaillean, *gen* **bruaillein** *nm* trouble,
confusion, upset (*esp moral &/or emotional*), *cf*
breisleach 1, buaireas 1

brùchd, brùchda, brùchdan *nm* a belch, *cf*
rùchd *n* 2

brùchd *vi, pres part* **a' brùchdadh,** 1 belch, *cf*
rùchd *v* 2; 2 burst out, **bhrùchd iad a-mach**
às an taigh-dhealbh they burst out/came
pouring out of the cinema, **bhrùchd na**
h-òganan ùra a-mach às an talamh the new
shoots burst out of the ground

brùchdadh, *gen* **brùchdaidh** *nm* (*the act of*)
belching etc (*see senses of* **brùchd** *v*)

brù-dhearg, brù-dheirge, brù-dheargan *nm*
a robin

bruich *adj* cooked, boiled

bruich *nf invar* (*the act of*) boiling, cooking

bruich *vt, pres part* **a' bruich,** cook, boil (*esp*
food), *cf* **deasaich biadh** (*see* **biadh 1**)

bruicheil *adj* (*of weather*) sultry, *cf*
bruthainneach

brùid, brùide, brùidean *nmf* 1 (*trad*) a brute
beast; 2 (*esp as term of abuse or condemnation*)
a brute, a brutal person; *cf* **biast 1** & **2**

brùidealachd *nf invar* brutality

brùideil *adj* (*person, act etc*) brutal, brutish

bruidhinn, *gen* **bruidhne** *nf* 1 (*the act of*)
speaking, talking, conversing; 2 talk, **aig**
deireadh na bruidhne when all is said and
done

bruidhinn *vti, pres part* **a' bruidhinn,** speak,
talk, converse, **bruidhinn ri cuideigin** talk

to/converse with someone, **bruidhinn ri**
chèile talk together/to each other, **bha sinn**
a' bruidhinn Frangais/Gàidhlig we were
speaking French/Gaelic, **a' bruidhinn às beul**
a chèile speaking with one voice/unanimously,
cf less usu **labhair**

bruidhneach *adj* talkative, fond of talking,
chatty, *cf* **còmhraideach**

bruis, bruise, bruisean *nf* a brush (*cf more*
trad **sguab** *n* 1), **bruis-aodaich** a clothes
brush, **bruis-chinn** & **bruis-fhuilt,** a hair
brush, **bruis-fhiaclan** a toothbrush, **bruis-**
pheant a paint brush

bruisig *vt, pres part* **a' bruisigeadh,** brush,
bhruisig i a falt she brushed her hair, *cf more*
trad **sguab** *v*

bruisigeadh, *gen* **bruisigidh** *nm* (*the act of*)
brushing

brùite *adj* 1 bruised, crushed, broken, **tha mo**
chridhe briste brùite my heart is broken
and bruised; 2 oppressed, **sluagh brùite** an
oppressed/downtrodden people

brùth *vt, pres part* **a' bruthadh,** 1 bruise; 2
push (*roughly*), shove, thrust, press (*forcefully*),
cf **put** *v* 1, **sàth 2, spàrr** *v*

bruthach, bruthaich, bruthaichean *nmf*
1 a slope, a hillside, (*Sc*) a brae, **a' ruith ris**
a' bhruthaich running uphill/against the
slope/up the brae, **a' ruith leis a' bhruthaich**
running downhill/with the slope/down the brae,
cf **aodann 2, leathad, leitir, ruighe 2;** 2 a
bank (*of a river, loch etc*), *cf* **bruach**

bruthadh, *gen* **bruthaidh** *nm* 1 (*the act of*)
bruising, pushing etc (*see senses of* **brùth** *v*);
2 (*esp science*) pressure, **bruthadh fala** blood
pressure, **bruthadh an àile** atmospheric
pressure

bruthainneach *adj* (*of weather*) sultry, *cf*
bruicheil

bu *see* **is** *v*

buachaille, buachaille, buachaillean *nm* a
cowherd, a herdsman, (*occas*) a shepherd, (*Sc*)
a herd, (*placename*) **Buachaille Èite Mòr** the
Big Herdsman of Etive

buachailleachd *nf invar* (*the act of*) herding or
tending cattle

buachaillich *vt, pres part* **a' buachailleachd,**
herd *or* tend cattle, (*song*) **na glinn san robh**
mi buachailleachd the glens where I herded
cattle

buachar, *gen* **buachair** *nm* cow-dung, *cf*
innear

buadh, buaidh, buadhan *nf* 1 a
quality, a property, an attribute; a
talent, an accomplishment, **buadhan**

nàdarra(ch) natural qualities, **buadhan inntinn** intellectual/mental qualities *or* accomplishments, *cf* **comas, tàlann; 2** virtue, goodness, excellence (*ie having ability to raise spirits or to nourish*) **tha buadh air an uisge-bheatha/air a' bhainne** whisky/milk has virtue/goodness in it, *cf* **brìgh 2**

buadhair, buadhair, buadhairean *nm* (*gram*) an adjective

buadhmhor *adj* **1** effective, successful, *cf* **èifeachdach; 2** victorious

buaic, buaice, buaicean *nf* a wick (*of lamp etc*), *cf* **siobhag**

buaidh, buaidhe, buaidhean *nf* **1** victory, a victory, **bheir sinn buaidh orra** we will gain victory over them/defeat them; **2** success, **fhuair na h-iomairtean aige buaidh aig deireadh an latha** his efforts gained success/were successful at the end of the day, *cf* **soirbhich; 3** influence, **fo bhuaidh duine nimheil** under the influence of a venomous/pernicious man, *cf* **cumhachd 1; 4** an effect, a consequence of something, **thoir** *v* **buaidh air** affect, have an effect on, **buaidh an taigh-ghlainne** the greenhouse effect, *cf* **buil 1, èifeachd, toradh 2**

buail *vt, pres part* **a' bualadh, 1** hit, strike, **bha am balach bochd ga bhualadh leis na gillean mòra** the poor laddie was being hit by the big boys, **bhuail an t-itealan mullach an togalaich** the plane struck the top/roof of the building; **2** (*expr almost random appearance of something or someone*) **bhuail e a-steach do thaigh Sheumais** he dropped by at/dropped in to Seumas's house, **bhuail e na cheann pòg a thoirt dhi** it came into his head/occurred to him to give her a kiss

buaile, buaile, buailtean *nf* a sheep-fold, a cattle-fold, *cf* **crò 1**

buailteach *adj* liable, apt, inclined, prone (**do** to), **buailteach do ghàire/do dh'fheirg** prone to laughter/to anger, **buailteach do chaochladh** prone/liable to change, **tha e buailteach airgead a chosg** he is liable to spend/waste money; **2** *also with prep* **air, tha sinn buailteach air fàs sgìth** we're apt to/we tend to get tired; **3** *with conj* **gun, bha an t-sìde cheudna buailteach gun leanadh i** the same weather was liable/likely to continue; *cf* **dual(t)ach**

buailteachd *nf* a tendency, a propensity, *cf* **aomadh**

buain, *gen* **buana** *nf* reaping, cutting, harvesting of crops, **buain an eòrna/an arbhair** the barley/the corn harvest, *cf* **foghar 1**

buain *vt, pres part* **a' buain**, reap, cut, harvest (*crops*), (*prov*) **ge b' e nach cuir san là fhuar, cha bhuain san là theth** the man who (*lit* whoever) doesn't sow on the cold day will not reap/harvest on the hot day

buair *vt, pres part* **a' buaireadh, 1** disturb, upset, trouble, perturb (*person, atmosphere etc*), **bhuair thu sìth nam beann** you have disturbed the peace of the mountains, **bhuair an droch naidheachd mi gu mòr** the bad news troubled/upset me greatly, **bhuair am fion a smaointean** the wine troubled her thoughts; **2** tempt, **bhuair an Donas mi** the Evil One tempted me, *cf* **meall** *v* **3, tàlaidh 2**

buaireadair, buaireadair, buaireadaran *nm* a troublemaker, a disruptive person

buaireadh, buairidh, buairidhean *nm* **1** (*the act of*) disturbing, tempting etc (*see senses of* **buair** *v*); **2** temptation, a temptation

buaireas, buaireis, buaireasan *nm* **1** (*esp emotional*) trouble, confusion, anxiety, **chuir e buaireas ann an cridhe òg** he introduced (*emotional or moral*) confusion into a young heart, *cf* **breisleach 1, bruaillean; 2** (*eg social, civil*) turbulence, disorder, *cf* **aimhreit 1**

buaireasach *adj* troublesome, annoying, disturbing, rurbulent, **leanabh buaireasach** a troublesome child, **neach buaireasach** a disruptive person/individual (*cf* **buaireadair** *n*), **naidheachd bhuaireasach** disturbing news, *cf* **aimhreiteach, draghail**

buaireasachd *nf invar* (*eg in society*; *of weather*) turbulence

bualadh, *gen* **bualaidh** *nm* **1** (*the act of*) striking, hitting (*see senses of* **buail** *v*), **aig àm bualadh nan dòrn** at the time of fist blows/of the striking of fists; **2** a blow, *cf* **beum, buille 1**

buan *adj* lasting, long-lasting, durable, **stuth buan** durable stuff/material, **bodach buan** a long-lived/tough old man, (*song*) **an ataireachd bhuan** the everlasting swell of the sea, *cf* **maireannach**

buannachadh, *gen* **buannachaidh** *nm* (*the act of*) winning etc (*see senses of* **buannaich** *v*)

buannachd, buannachd, buannachdan *nf* **1** profit, gain, advantage, **là/obair gun bhuannachd** a fruitless day/task, *cf* **tairbhe; 2** (*fin*) profit, **chan eil an gnothach a' cosnadh buannachd sam bith** the business isn't making/earning any profit, (*prov*) **cha dèanar buannachd gun chall** profit is never made without some loss, *cf less trad* **prothaid**

buannachdail *adj* advantageous, of advantage, profitable (**do** to)

buannaich *vti, pres part* **a' buannachadh, 1** (*vi*) win, succeed, (*in race, battle, competition etc*), *cf* **buinnig; 2** (*vt*) win, gain, acquire, **bhuannaich i bonn òir** she won a gold medal, **bhuannaich iad cliù** they won fame; **3** (*vt*) reach, (*Sc*) win to, **bhuannaich sinn am baile am beul na h-oidhche** we made it to/reached the village at dusk; *cf* **buidhinn, coisinn 2**

buar, *gen & pl* **buair** *nm* a herd (*esp of cattle*), *cf* **treud 1**

bucaid, bucaide, bucaidean *nf* **1** a bucket, *cf* **peile** & *more trad* **cuinneag, cuman; 2** a dustbin, **cuir sa bhucaid e!** bin it!

bucas, *gen & pl* **bucais** *nm* a box, *cf* **bocsa 1**

bugair, bugaire, bugairean *nm* (*fam, vulg*) a bugger, *usu in excls, eg* **na bugairean!** the buggers!, **na bugair rudan!** the bloody things!

buideal *see* **botal**

buidhe *adj* **1** yellow, **buidhe-ruadh** auburn; **2** (*trad*) lucky, fortunate, *cf more usu* **fortanach, sealbhach 1**

buidhe *nm* (*the colour*) yellow

buidheach *adj* **1** grateful, thankful, **tha mi buidheach airson ur cuideachaidh** I am grateful for your help, **bi buidheach do do phàrantan!** be grateful to your parents!, *cf* **taingeil**

buidheachas, *gen* **buidheachais** *nm* gratitude, *cf* **taing 1**

buidheagan, *gen & pl* **buidheagain** *nf* an egg-yolk, the yolk of an egg

buidheann, buidhne, buidhnean *nmf* **1** a group, a band, a party (*of people*), a company (*of soldiers*), **buidheann (de) luchd-turais** a group/party of tourists, **buidheann-cluich(e)** a playgroup (*cf* **cròileagan**), **buidheann-obrach** a working party, **buidheann- rannsachaidh** a research group/team, **buidheann-strì** a pressure group, *cf* **còmhlan, cuideachd** *n* **3; 2** (*business*) a firm, a company, *cf* **companaidh**

buidhinn *vti, pres part* **a' buidhinn**, win, *cf similarly used* **buannaich**

buidhre *nf invar* (*abstr noun corres to* **bodhar**) deafness

buidseach, buidsich, buidsichean *nmf* a wizard, a sorcerer, a witch, a sorceress, **bana-bhuidseach** *f* a witch, a sorceress, *cf* **draoidh 2**

bùidsear, bùidseir, bùidsearan *nm* **1** a butcher, *cf more trad* **feòladair; 2** a butcher, *ie* someone thought of as murderous or brutal, (*hist*) **Am Bùidsear** 'Butcher' Cumberland, the Duke of Cumberland (*Commander of the Government forces in 1745–6*)

buidseat, buidseit, buidseatan *nm* a budget

buige *nf invar* (*abstr noun corres to* **bog** *adj*) **1** softness (*phys, & of character etc*); **2** moistness; **3** humidity; **4** limpness

buil, *gen* **buile** *nf* **1** a consequence, a result, an effect, (*saying*) **an rud a nithear gu ceart, chithear a bhuil** when a thing is done properly the effect/result of it will be visible/evident, *cf* **buaidh 4, èifeachd, toradh 2; 2** completion, a conclusion, *esp in expr* **thoir** *v* **gu buil** complete, bring to a conclusion, achieve, implement, realise, **thoir pròiseact gu buil** complete a project, **cha tug thu càil gu buil a-riamh!** you never achieved anything! *or* you never saw anything through!, *cf* **crìoch 1**

buileach *adj used as adv*, *also* **gu buileach** *adv*, completely, quite, entirely, **tha mi buileach cinnteach** I am quite sure (*cf* **làn** *adj* **2**), **chan eil i buileach deiseil** she's not quite ready, **gu buileach eadar-dhealaichte** completely/totally different, **nì mi an gnothach air gu buileach** I'll beat him completely, I'll get the better of him entirely, *cf* **tur 2, uile-gu-lèir** (*see* **uile 4**)

buileann, builinn, buileannan *nf* a loaf (*of bread, sugar etc*), *cf* **lof**

builgean, builgein, builgeanan *nm* a bubble

builgeanach *adj* bubbly, **'s toigh leam siaimpèan a chionn 's gu bheil e builgeanach** I like champagne because it's bubbly

builich *vt, pres part* **a' buileachadh**, bestow, grant (**air** on)

buille, buille, *pl* **buillean** & **builleannan** *nf* **1** a blow, a stroke, **buille cuip** a whip stroke, a stroke with a whip, *cf* **beum, bualadh 2, stràc 1; 2** emphasis, stress, importance, **bidh a' chompanaidh a' cur buille shònraichte air pongalachd** the company will place particular stress/importance on punctuality, *cf* **cudthrom 2; 3** (*speech , music, rhythm*) stress, a stress, a beat, **buille-cridhe** a heartbeat, **ceithir buillean sa char** four beats to the bar, **anns an fhacal 'caraid' thig a' bhuille air a' chiad lide** in the word 'caraid' the stress comes on the first syllable; **4** (*sport*) a stroke

buin *vi, pres part* **a' buntainn, 1** belong (**do** & **ri** to), **am buin e dhutsa?** does it belong to you (*emph*)? **às bith cò dha a bhuineas e** whoever it belongs to, *cf* **bi aig** (*see* **aig 2**), **is le** (*see* **le 4**); **2** be related to, **buinidh iad do Chlann Dòmhnaill** they belong to Clan Donald, they are MacDonalds, *cf* **càirdeach; 3** interfere with, meddle with, have to do with, (*prov*) **an rud nach buin dhut, na buin dha** do not interfere with something that doesn't concern you, *also* *with prep* **ri**, *cf* **bean** *v* **1**, **gnothach 4; 4** be relevant, affect, apply to, **buinidh seo dhutsa** this applies to you (*emph*), **fianais a bhuineas don chùis** evidence relevant to the case, *cf* **buntainneach**

buinneach, *gen* **buinnich** *nf*, *with the art*, **a' bhuinneach** diarrhoea, *cf* **sgàird, spùt 3**

buinneag Bhruisealach, buinneig Bruisealaich, buinneagan Bruisealach *nf* a Brussels sprout

buinnig & **buintig**, *vi, pres part* **a' buintig**, win, (*fam, calque*) **a bheil thu a' buintig?** are you winning/getting there?

buinteanas, buntainneas & **buntanas**, *gen* **buinteanais** *nm* **1** link(s), connection(s) *esp with a particular place*, **bha buinteanas aige ris an Eilean Sgitheanach** he had Skye connections, he had (family) links with Skye; **2** relevance, pertinence

buirbe *nf invar* (*abstr noun corres to* **borb**), barbarity, wildness, savageness, uncouthness

bùirdeasach *adj* bourgeois

bùirdeasach, *gen* & *pl* **bùirdeasaich** *nm* a bourgeois

bùirdeasachd *nf invar, usu with art,* **a' bhùirdeasachd** the bourgeoisie

Bulgàrianach, *gen* & *pl* **Bulgàrianaich** a Bulgarian, *also as adj,* **Bulgàrianach** Bulgarian **Bulgàrais** *nf invar* (*lang*) Bulgarian

bumailear, bumaileir, bumailearan *nm* (*fam*) a fool, a blockhead, an oaf, a buffoon, a no-user, (*Sc*) an eejit, *cf* **stalcaire, ùmaidh**

bun, *gen* **buna** & **buin**, *pl* **buin** & **bunan** *nm* **1** the base, bottom or foot of anything, **bun na beinne** the foot of the mountain, *cf* **bonn 1**; **2** *esp in expr* **bun-os-cionn** upside down, topsy-turvy, (*Sc*) tapsalteerie, **cuir** *v* **bun-os-cionn** turn upside down, upend, **bha seòmar mo mhic bun-os-cionn** my son's room was topsy-turvy/in a shambles (*cf* **bùrach**), *cf* **tro 2**; **3** a root, a source or an origin of something, **bun na craoibhe** the root (*or* the foot *or* the trunk) of the tree, **bun an uilc** the root/source of evil (*cf* **freumh**), **bun-dealain** an electric socket, a power point, **bun-stuth** *m* basic/raw material(s); **4** (*topog*) mouth of a river or stream, (*placename*) **Bun Abha** Bonawe, the mouth of the River Awe, *cf* **beul 1**

bunai(l)teach *adj* **1** stable, steady, well founded, *cf* **seasmhach 1**; **2** (*beliefs etc*) fundamental, radical, *cf less usu* **bunasach 1**; **3** basic (*ie*

essential), **còraichean bunaiteach** basic rights

bunait, bunaite, bunaitean *nmf* the basis or foundation of anything (*esp abstr things*), **bunait a' chreideimh/na feallsanachd** the foundation/the fundamentals of religion/of philosophy, *cf* **stèidh 2**, & *more con* **bonn 1**

bunasach *adj* **1** radical, fundamental, basic, *cf more usu* **bunaiteach 2**; **2** *esp in gram,* **an tuiseal bunasach** (*the case in Gaelic corres to the nom and the acc in Eng, Latin etc*) the radical case

bun-os-cionn *see* **bun 2**

bun-sgoil, bun-sgoile, bun-sgoiltean *nf* a primary school

buntainn, *gen* **buntainne** *nm* (*the act of*) belonging, interfering with etc (*see senses of* **buin** *v*)

buntainneach *adj* relevant, *cf* **buin** *vi* **4**

buntanas *see* **buinteanas**

buntàta *nm invar, sing* & *coll,* a potato, potatoes, **buntàta pronn** mashed potato(es)

bùrach, *gen* **bùraich** *nm* a mess, a shambles, (*Sc*) a guddle, (*Highland Eng*) a b(o)urach, **an dèidh na h-imriche bha a h-uile càil ann am bùrach** after the flitting everything was in a mess/a guddle/a b(o)urach, *cf* **bun 2, tro 2**

bùrn, *gen* **bùirn** *nm* water, *used by some speakers as alternative to* **uisge** *to refer to fresh running water, tap water etc, but not to salt water or rain,* (*prov*) **is tighe fuil na bùrn** blood is thicker than water, *cf* **uisge 1**

burraidh, burraidh, burraidhean *nm* **1** a fool, a blockhead, *cf* **amadan, bumailear, ùmaidh**; **2** a bully, *cf* **maoidhear**

bus[1], bus, busaichean *nm* a bus, **àite-stad bus** a bus-stop, **bha am bus làn** the bus was full, **tha am bus gun tighinn fhathast** the bus hasn't come/arrived yet

bus[2], buis, busan *nm* **1** (*derog*) a mouth, *cf* **beul 1, cab, gob 3**; **2** a grimace, a pout (*of anger, pique etc*), **chuireadh i bus oirre an uair a chàineadh a màthair i** she would grimace/pout when her mother gave her a row, *cf* **braoisg**; **3** *in expr* (*fam*) **a-mach air a bhus le . . .** overflowing with . . . , *cf* **cuir thairis** (*see* **thairis 1**)

bùth, *gen* **bùtha**, *pl* **bùthan, bùithean** & **bùithtean** *nmf* a shop, a store, **bùth-èisg** a fish shop, **bùth-chungaidhean** a chemist's shop, a pharmacy, **bùth-chiùird** a craft shop

C

cab, *gen & pl* **caib** *nm* (*fam*) a mouth, a gob, **duin do chab!** shut your mouth/your gob! *cf* **beul 1** & (*fam*) **bus² 1, gob 3**

cabach *adj* (*fam*) talkative, garrulous, apt to talk too much, *cf* **beulach 1, gobach**

cabadaich, *gen* **cabadaiche** *nf* **1** chatter, chattering, (*Sc*) blether, *cf* **cabaireachd, goileam**; **2** *used as a pres part*, **a' cabadaich** chattering, blethering

cabaireachd *nf invar, same senses as* **cabadaich**

càball, càbaill, càballan *nm* cable, a cable

cabar, *gen & pl* **cabair** *nm* **1** an antler, *esp in phrase* **cabair fèidh** a deer's antlers, *also* (*trad*) a war cry of the Mackenzies and the name of a pipe tune, *cf* **crò(i)c**; **2** a pole, *esp* a rafter, **cabar-droma** (*also* **maide-droma**) a ridge pole (*of a house*); **3** (*Highland Games*) a caber

cabhag, *gen* **cabhaig** *nf* **1** haste, hurry, **na cùm air ais sinn, tha cabhag oirnn!** don't keep us back, we're in a hurry!, **dèan** *v* **cabhag** hurry up, get a move on, **ann an cabhaig** in a hurry, *cf less usu* **deann 2**; **2** *in expr* **cuir** *v* **cabhag air cuideigin** press, hurry someone, *cf* **greas 2**

cabhagach *adj* **1** (*of person*) hurried, in a hurry; **2** (*of actions etc*) hurried, cursory, hasty; **3** urgent, pressing

cabhlach, cabhlaich, cabhlaichean *nm* a fleet (*trad of boats or ships, now also of vehicles, planes etc*), a navy, *cf less usu* **loingeas 2**

cabhsair, cabhsair, cabhsairean *nm* a pavement, a causeway, (*Sc*) a causey

cabstair, cabstair, cabstairean *nm* a (*horse's*) bit

cac, *gen* **caca** *nm* **1** excrement; **2** (*fam, vulg*) crap, shit, cack, (*derog of person, action, statement etc*) **tòrr caca** a load of crap

cac *vi, pres part* **a' cac** & **a' cacadh**, defecate

caca *adj* (*fam*) nasty, unpleasant, 'yukky'

cacadh, *gen* **cacaidh** *nm* **1** (*the act of*) defecating; **2** defecation

càch, *gen* **càich** & **chàich** *pron* (*used of persons*) **1** the rest, others, other people, the others, **rinn i na b' fheàrr na càch** she did better than the rest/the others, **coltach ri càch** like the rest, like everybody else; **2** *in expr* **càch-a-chèile** each other, **a' faicinn càch-a-chèile** seeing each other, *cf* **cèile 2**

cachaileith, cachaileithe, cachaileithean *nf* a gate, a gateway, an entrance

cadal, *gen* **cadail** *nm* **1** (*the act of*) sleeping; **2** sleep, **dèan** *v* **cadal** sleep, go to sleep, **rach** *v* **a chadal** go to bed, **bha mi nam chadal/ bha sinn nar cadal** I was/we were asleep/ sleeping, **norrag chadail** *f* a wink of sleep, a nap, a snooze, **cha d' fhuair mi norrag chadail a-raoir** I didn't get a wink of sleep last night, **oidhche gun chadal** a sleepless night, **cadal sàmhach** peaceful sleep, **tha an cadal orm** I'm sleepy, **cadal math dhut!** sleep well!, **cadal-geamhraidh** hibernation, *cf* **dùsal, norrag, suain** *n*; **3** *also in expr* **an cadal-deilgneach** pins and needles

cadalach *adj* sleepy, drowsy

cafaidh, cafaidh, cafaidhean *nmf* a café

cagailt, cagailte, cagailtean *nf* a hearth, **na shuidhe ris a' chagailt** sitting beside the hearth/at the fireside, *cf* **teallach, teinntean**

cagainn *vt, pres part* **a' cagnadh**, chew, gnaw, *cf* **cnàmh** *v* **1, creim 2**

cagair *vti, pres part* **a' cagar, a' cagarsaich** & **a' cagartaich**, whisper

cagar, cagair, cagairean *nm* **1** (*the act of*) whispering; **2** a whisper; **3** a secret, *cf* **rùn 5**

cagnadh, *gen* **cagnaidh** *nm* (*the act of*) chewing, gnawing

caibe, caibe, caibeachan *nm* **1** a spade, *cf more usu* **spaid**; **2** a mattock

caibeal, caibeil, caibealan *nm* a chapel

caibideil, caibideil, caibideilean *nmf* a chapter (*of book*), **caibideil a h-aon** chapter one

caidil *vi, pres part* **a' cadal**, sleep, **caidil gu math!** sleep well! *cf* **dèan cadal** (*see* **cadal 2**)

caidreabhach, *gen & pl* **caidreabhaich** *nm* an ally

caidreabhas, *gen* **caidreabhais** *m* **1** alliance, an alliance; **2** friendship, *cf* **càirdeas 2**

càil, càile, càiltean *nf* (*trad*) desire, (*now esp for food*) appetite, an appetite, *also* **càil bìdh** (*lit* desire for food)

càil *nm invar* **1** a thing, **bha a h-uile càil troimh-a-chèile** everything was in a mess, *cf* **dad** 1, **nì** *n* 1, **rud** 1, **sìon** 3; **2** *with verb in neg* nothing, (not) anything, **chan eil càil againn ri dhèanamh** we've nothing/ we haven't anything to do, **cha robh càil ann** there was nothing there; **3** *in expr* **càil sam bith** anything, anything at all, anything whatsoever, **a bheil càil sa phreas? chan eil càil sam bith!** is there anything in the cupboard? there's nothing at all/not a thing!; **4** *in expr* **càil a** (*for* **càil de**), any, *esp* **càil a dh'fhios** any information, knowledge, **a bheil càil a dh'fhios agad càit a bheil e?** have you any idea where he is? **chan eil càil a dh'fhios agam** I haven't the faintest idea/don't know anything about it

cailc, cailce, cailcean *nf* 1 (*the substance*) chalk; **2** (blackboard) chalk, a piece of (blackboard) chalk

caileag, caileige, caileagan *nf* 1 a (small) girl, a female child, (*Sc*) a lassie, *esp* **caileag bheag** a little girl, **an uair a bha mi nam chaileig (bhig) bha mi am Bun-sgoil Phort Rìgh** when I was a (little) girl I was at Portree Primary School; **2** (*a female up to the end of her teens approx*) a girl, (*Sc*) a lass, a lassie, **tha e daonnan an dèidh nan caileagan** he's always after/chasing the girls; *cf* **clann-nighean, nighean, nìghneag**

cailin, cailin, cailinean *nf* (*trad*) a girl, a maid, (*song*) **mo chailin donn òg** my brown-haired young girl

caill *vti, pres part* **a' call**, **1** lose, **chaill mi an t-uaireadair agam** I lost my watch, **chaill i a pàrantan ann an tubaist** she lost her parents in an accident, (*vi*) **chaill an sgioba ball-coise an-dè** the football team lost yesterday, (*fam*) **bha mi gus mo mhùn a chall leis cho èibhinn 's a bha e!** I was nearly wetting myself, he was so funny!; **2** miss, **chaill mi an trèana** I missed the train, **nach robh thu aig a' chèilidh? cha do chaill thu mòran!** weren't you at the ceilidh? you didn't miss much!

cailleach, cailliche, cailleachan *nf* 1 an old woman, (*Sc*) an old wifie; **2** (*not nec implying age*) a woman, a wifie, **bodach is cailleach nam faochagan** the guy/fellow and wifie who gather whelks, **cailleach nan cearc** the hen wife/wifie; **3** (*fam, of spouse*) **a' chailleach**

the/my old woman; **4** (*esp* **cailleach-dhubh**) a nun; **5** (*pej*) an old witch, an old hag; *cf* **bodach**

cailleach-oidhche, caillich-oidhche, cailleachan-oidhche *nf* an owl, *cf* **comhachag**

cailleachag, cailleachaige, cailleachagan *nf* a little old lady/woman

caime, caime, caimean *nf* curvature, a bend, a curve, *cf* **lùb** *n* 1

càin, gen cànach & càine, pl càintean *nf* 1 taxation, tax, a tax, *cf* **cìs**; **2** a fine, **cuir** *v* **càin air** fine, **chuir am britheamh càin air** the judge fined him

càin *vt, pres part* **a' càineadh**, **1** scold, criticise, (*Sc*) give a row to, (*song*) **bhiodh m' athair 's mo mhàthair gam chàineadh gu bràth, nam pòsainn do leithid** my father and mother would be at me for evermore if I married the likes of you, *cf* **cronaich, sàs** 3; **2** slander

cainb, gen cainbe *nf* 1 hemp, **lus-cainb** the cannabis plant; **2** canvas, *cf less trad* **canabhas**

càineadh, gen càinidh *nm* 1 (*the act of*) scolding, criticising etc (*see senses of* **càin** *v*); **2** (verbal) abuse

caineal, gen caineil *nm* cinnamon

cainnt, cainnte, cainntean *nf* 1 speech, language (*in general & abstr sense*), **gun chainnt** not possessed of speech, unable to speak, **comas cainnte** the faculty of speech/ language, the ability to speak, *cf* **labhairt** 1; **2** speech, language, tongue (*as used by a particular individual or group*), (*song*) **cainnt mo mhàthar, Gàidhlig Bharraigh** my mother tongue, the Gaelic of Barra (*cf* **teanga** 2, **cànain, cànan**), (*song*) **bha mi eòlach air a cainnt** I was familiar with her speech/ way of speaking, **droch cainnt** bad language, swearing, **dual-chainnt** (*also* **dualchainnt**) a dialect

caiptean, caiptein, caipteanan *nm* 1 (*of boat, plane, team etc*) a captain, a skipper, a master, *cf* **sgiobair**; **2** (*military rank*) a captain

càir *n see* **càrr**

càir *vt see* **càirich**

càirdeach *adj* related, kin (**do** to), **chan eil mi càirdeach dhut** I'm not related to you, *cf* **buin** *v* 2

càirdeas, gen càirdeis *nm* 1 family relationship, kinship, **càirdeas fala** blood relationship, **càirdeas pòsaidh** kinship by marriage (*cf* **cleamhnas** 1); **2** friendship, ties of friendship, **an càirdeas eadar Alba is Canada** the ties between Scotland & Canada (*cf* **caidreabhas** 2); *cf* **dàimh** 1

càirdeil *adj* friendly (**ri** to, with)

càirdineal, càirdineil, càirdinealan *nm* a Cardinal

càirean, càirein, càireinean *nm* gum(s) (*of mouth*), palate

cairidh, cairidh, cairidhean, *also* **caraidh, caraidh, caraidhean,** *nf* a weir

cairgein, *gen* **cairgein** *nm, also* **carraigean,** *gen* **carraigein** *nm,* edible seaweed, carrageen

càirich (*also* **càir**), *vt, pres part.* **a' càradh,** repair, mend, fix, (*Sc*) sort, *in expr* **càirich do leabaidh** make your bed

cairt¹, cartach, cairtean *nf* 1 card, **cairt-bhòrd** cardboard; 2 a card, **cairt Nollaig** a Christmas card, **cairt-chluiche** a playing card, **cairt-phuist** a postcard, **cairt-iasaid** & **cairt-creideis** a credit card; 3 a chart, **cairt-iùil** a sea-chart, a navigation chart; 4 (*hist etc*) a charter; 5 tree bark, *cf* **rùsg**

cairt², cartach, cairtean *nf* a cart

cairt *also* **cart** *vt, pres part* **a' cartadh,** 1 tan (*leather*); 2 muck out, clean out (*byre etc*)

cairteal, cairteil, cairtealan *nm* 1 a quarter (*usu for clock time*), **cairteal/trì chairteil na h-uarach** a quarter/three-quarters of an hour, **cairteal gu ceithir** a quarter to four, **cairteal an dèidh a deich** a quarter past ten, *cf* **ceathramh**; 2 (*measure*) a quart

caisbheart, *gen* **caisbheirt** *nf* footwear

caise *nf invar* (*abstr n corres to* **cas** *adj*) 1 irritability, shortness of temper; 2 (*of gradient*) steepness, abruptness *cf* **caisead**

càise, càise, càisean *nmf* cheese, a cheese

caisead, *gen* **caiseid** *nm* steepness (*of gradient*)

Càisg, *gen* **Càisge** *nf, used with the art,* **a' Chàisg** Easter, **Diluain na Càisge** Easter Monday

caisg *vti, pres part* **a' casgadh,** 1 (*vt*) prevent, stop, restrain, interrupt, staunch, *cf* **bac** *v,* **bacadh** 3, **casg, stad** *n* 3; 2 (*vi*) subside, abate, **chaisg an stoirm** the storm abated

caismeachd, caismeachd, caismeachdan *nf* 1 (*trad*) a call to arms, an alarm; 2 a march (*ie tune*), a martial song or piece of music; 3 (*the act of*) beating time, *also in expr* **cùm** *v* **caismeachd ri** keep time with

caisteal, caisteil, caistealan *nm* a castle

càite (*before a vowel* **càit**) *inter adv* where, **càit a bheil Iain? a bheil fios agad càit a bheil e?** where's Iain? do you know where he is?, *Note difference between* **càite** *and* **far a,** *eg* **an uair a gheibh mi a-mach càit a bheil e, thèid mi far a bheil e** when I find out where he is (*interrogative*), I'll go where he is (*non-interrogative*)

caith *vt, pres part* **a' caitheamh,** 1 *usu of clothing,* wear, wear out, (*trad wish or greeting – of new clothing*) **gum meal 's gun caith thu e** may you enjoy it and wear it, *cf* **giùlain** 2; 2 (*of time*) spend, pass, (*song*) **chaith mi 'n oidhche cridheil coibhneil mar ri maighdeannan na h-àirigh** I spent the night in warm-hearted kindliness in the company of the sheiling maidens, *cf* **seachad** 2; 3 (*esp of wealth, money*) waste, squander, consume, *cf* **cosg** *v* 3, **struidh**; 4 cast, throw, **fiodh air a chaitheamh don chladach** wood cast up onto the shore, *cf* **tilg** 1

caitheadair, caitheadair, caitheadairean *nm* a consumer

caitheamh, *gen* **caitheimh** *nf* 1 (*the act of*) wearing, spending etc (*see senses of* **caith** *v*); 2 (*with the art*) **a' chaitheamh** tuberculosis, consumption; 3 (*business, fin etc*) consumption, **luchd-caitheimh** *m* consumers, **caitheamh ola** oil consumption

caitheamh-beatha *nm invar* way of life, lifestyle

caithte *adj* 1 worn out, used up; 2 (*gram*) past, **an tràth caithte** the past tense

caith(t)each *adj* wasteful, extravagant, spendthrift, prodigal, *cf* **struidheil**

Caitligeach, *gen* & *pl* **Caitligich** *nm* a Catholic, *also as adj* **Caitligeach** Catholic

càl, *gen* & *pl* **càil** *nm* cabbage, a cabbage, (*trad*) kail

cala(dh), cala(idh), calaidhean *nm* a harbour, *cf* **acarsaid, port²**

calaraidh, calaraidh, calaraidhean *nm* a calorie

càl-colaig, *gen* & *pl* **càil-cholaig** *nm* cauliflower, a cauliflower

calg, *gen* **cuilg** *nm* 1 a prickle, *cf* **bior** 3, **dealg** 1; 2 a bristle, *cf* **frioghan**

calg-d(h)ìreach *adv* directly, completely, *esp in expr* **calg-dhìreach an aghaidh** completely against, diametrically opposed to, dead against, **tha na pàrtaidhean calg-dhìreach an aghaidh a chèile** the parties are diametrically opposed to each other/in total disagreement, **tha mi calg-dhìreach na aghaidh** I am completely against him/it

call, *gen* **calla** *nm* 1 (*the act of*) losing, missing etc (*see senses of* **caill** *v*); 2 loss, a loss, (*book title*) **Call na h-Iolaire** The Loss of the Iolaire; 3 *in expr* **air chall** lost, **bha/chaidh sinn air chall** we were/got lost, *cf* **seachran** 2; 4 a waste, **is e call a bh' ann** it was a waste, **call ùine/airgid** a waste of time/money, *cf* **cosg** *n* 3

calla & **callda** *adj* 1 tame; 2 domesticated

callachadh, *gen* **callachaidh** *nm* (*the act of*) taming, domesticating

callaich, *vt, pres part* **a' callachadh**, **1** tame, *cf* **ceannsaich 3**; **2** domesticate

callaid, **callaide**, **callaidean** *nf* **1** a hedge *cf* **fàl 1**; **2** a fence, *cf less trad* **feansa**

Callainn, *gen* **Callainne** *nf* (*trad*), *used with art*, **a' Challainn** New Year's Day, *see* **oidhche 2**

callda *see* **calla**

calltainn, *gen* **calltainne** *nm* (*bot*) hazel, **cnò-challtainn** a hazelnut, *often in placenames as* cowden, colden

calma *adj* (*morally or phys*) stout, sturdy, robust, *cf* **tapaidh 2**

calman, *gen* **calmain**, *pl* **calmain** & **calmanan** *nm* a dove, a pigeon

calpa[1], **calpa**, **calpannan** *nm* a calf (*of leg*)

calpa[2], **calpa**, **calpannan** *nm* (*fin*) capital

calpachas, *gen* **calpachais** *nm* capitalism

cam *adj* bent, curved, *cf* **crom** *adj*, **fiar** *adj* **1**, **lùbte**

cama-chasach *adj* bow-legged

camag, **camaig**, **camagan** *nf* **1** a curl, a ringlet, *cf* **bachlag 1**, **dual**[2] **1**; **2** (*typog*) a bracket

camagach *adj* (*of hair*) curled, in ringlets, *cf* **bachlach**

caman, *gen* **camain**, *pl* **camain** & **camanan** *nm* **1** a shinty stick; **2** a golf club; **3** (*mus*) a quaver

camanachd *nf invar* shinty, *cf* **iomain** *n*

camara, **camara**, **camarathan** *nm* a camera

camas, *gen* & *pl* **camais** *nm* **1** a bay, *cf* **bàgh**, **òb**; **2** a curve or bend in a river

càmhal, *gen* & *pl* **càmhail** *nm* a camel

camhana(i)ch, *gen* **camhanaich** *nf* **1** dawn, *cf* **bris(t)eadh-là**; **2** twilight, **camhana(i)ch an là** morning twilight, **camhana(i)ch na h-oidhche** evening twilight, *cf* **duibhre**, **eadar-sholas**

campa, **campa**, **campaichean** *nm* a camp

campachadh, *gen* **campachaidh** (*the act of*) camping

campaich *vi, pres part* **a' campachadh**, camp

can *vti def pres part* **a' cantainn** & **a' cantail** (*for forms see table p 495*) **1** say, *used by some speakers instead of* **abair**, *mainly in imperative, fut, pres continuous, past continuous and conditional tenses*, **canaidh mi seo ribh** . . . I'll say this to you . . . , **can a-rithist e** say it again, (*name of Gaelic course*) **Can Seo** Say This, *also in expr* **mar a chanas iad** as they say, *esp after using Eng words or phrases*, **tit for tat**, **mar a chanas iad sa Bheurla** tit for tat, as they say in English, *cf* **abair 1**; **2** *in expr* **can air** say for, **dè a chanas**

sibh air 'spade' sa Ghàidhlig? what do you say in Gaelic for 'spade'?, *cf* **aig 5**; **3** *in expr* **can ri** (*of people, places*) call, **Dàibhidh Bàn**, **mar a chanadh iad ris** Fair-haired Davie, as they called him/used to call him

cana, **cana**, **canaichean** *nm* a can, a tin (*ie for drinks, food etc*), *cf* **canastair**

canabhas, *gen* **canabhais** *nm* **1** canvas, *cf* **cainb 2**; **2** (*painting*) a canvas

canach, *gen* **canaich** *nm* **1** (*bot*) bog-cotton; **2** cotton, *cf* **cotan**

Canada *nf invar* Canada

cànain, **cànaine**, **cànainean** *nf* & **cànan**, *gen* & *pl* **cànain** *nm* a language, (*song*) **Cànan nan Gàidheal** (Murchadh MacPhàrlain) The Language of the Gaels, **cànainean cèin** foreign languages, **mion- chàna(i)n** & **càna(i)n b(h)eag** a minority language, a lesser-used language, (*IT*) **cànan (prògramaidh)** a (programming) language, *cf* **cainnt 2**

cànanach *adj* **1** linguistic, pertaining to language(s); **2** *in adj exprs* **dà-chànanach** bilingual, **trì-chànanach** trilingual, **ioma-chànanach** multilingual, polyglot

cànanaiche, **cànanaiche**, **cànanaichean** *nm* a linguist

canastair, **canastair**, **canastairean** *nm* a can, a tin (*for drinks, food etc*), *cf* **cana**

Canèidianach, *gen* & *pl* **Canèidianaich** *nm* a Canadian, *also as adj* **Canèidianach** Canadian

cantainn, *gen* **cantainne** *nm* (*the act of*) saying etc (*see senses of* **can** *v*)

caochail *vi, pres part* **a' caochladh**, **1** change, alter, **bha i air caochladh gu mòr** she had changed/altered greatly, *cf* **atharraich**, **mùth 1**; **2** (*of persons*) die, pass away, *cf* **bàsaich**, **siubhail 3**

caochladh, **caochlaidh**, **caochlaidhean** *nm* **1** (*the act of*) changing, dying etc (*see senses of* **caochail** *v*); **2** change, alteration, a change, an alteration, *cf* **atharrachadh 2**; **3** a variety, *esp with gen pl* a variety of, various, **ann an caochladh àiteachan** in various places

caochlaideach *adj* **1** variable, changeable, **sìde chaochlaideach** changeable/unsettled weather; **2** (*of people, fate etc*) fickle, volatile, capricious, moody, apt to change, (*song*) **tha an saoghal caochlaideach na dhòigh** the world is fickle in its conduct/ways, *cf* **carach 2**, **cugallach 2**, **luaineach**

caog *vi, pres part* **a' caogadh**, blink, wink, *cf more usu* **priob**

caogad, **caogaid**, **caogadan** *nm* **1** the number fifty (*now used in the alternative Gaelic*

numbering system); **2** (*trad*) a group of fifty
men; *cf* **leth-cheud**

caogadh, *gen* **caogaidh** *nm* (*the act of*) blinking,
winking, *cf more usu* **priobadh 1**

caoidh, *gen* **caoidhe** *nf* **1** (*the act of*) lamenting,
mourning etc (*see senses of* **caoidh** *v*); **2**
lamentation

caoidh *vi*, *pres part* **a' caoidh**, **1** lament, mourn,
grieve, *cf* **bròn 2, caoin** *v* **1**; **2** moan, *cf* **caoin**
v **2**

caoimhneas, caoimhneil *see* **coibhneas,
coibhneil**

caoin *adj* (*esp of character*) gentle, mild

caoin *vi*, *pres part* **a' caoineadh**, **1** lament,
mourn, *cf* **bròn 2, caoidh** *v* **1**; **2** weep, cry, wail,
moan, *cf* **guil**

caoineadh, *gen* **caoinidh** *nm* lamenting,
weeping etc (*see senses of* **caoin** *v*)

caol *adj* **1** narrow, thin, slender, **sràidean caola**
narrow streets, (*trad*) **claidheamh caol** a
rapier, (*trad*) **an taigh caol** the narrow house,
the grave, (*Gaelic spelling rule*) **leathann ri
leathann is caol ri caol** broad (vowel) next to
broad and slender next to slender, *cf* **cumhang
1**; **2** (*of angle*) acute; **3** (*of people*) thin, skinny,
lanky, **bodach fada caol** a tall lanky old guy, *cf*
seang, tana 1

caol, *gen* **caoil**, *pl* **caoil** & **caoiltean** *nm* **1** a
strait, narrows, a narrow place in a river or arm
of the sea, (*Sc*) a kyle, **chaidh iad tarsainn air
a' chaol** they crossed the narrows, (*placenames*)
An Caol Kyle of Lochalsh, **Na Caoil Bhòdach**
Kyles of Bute, *cf* **caolas**; **2** the narrow part of
anything, *esp in exprs* **caol an dùirn** the wrist,
caol na coise the ankle (*cf* **adhbrann**), **caol
an droma** the small of the back

caolan, *gen* **caolain**, *pl* **caolain** & **caolanan**
nm an intestine, a gut, (*vulg*) **chuir mi a-mach
rùchd mo chaolanan** I spewed my guts up,
beul a' chaolain the duodenum, *cf* **greallach,
innidh, mionach 1**

caolas, *gen* & *pl* **caolais** *nm* a strait, narrows,
(*Sc*) a kyle, kyles, *cf* **caol** *n* **1**

caol-shràid, caol-shràide, caol-shràidean *nf*
a vennel, a wynd, an alley, a lane, *cf* **lònaid**

caomh *adj* **1** (*esp of character*) gentle, kind, mild,
humane; **2** dear, beloved, *cf* **ionmhainn**; **3** *esp
in expr* **is caomh leam** (*etc*) I (etc) like (*used
by some, esp Lewis speakers, as equivalent to*
is toigh le), **is caomh leis ceòl traidiseanta**
he likes traditional music, **cha chaomh leatha
creamh** she doesn't like garlic, *cf* **toigh 2**

caomhain *vt*, *pres part* **a' caomhnadh**, save,
economise on, be thrifty with, **caomhain
gus a-màireach e** save it till tomorrow,

a' caitheamh airgid gun chaomhnadh
spending money unsparingly, *cf* **glèidh 2,
sàbhail 3**

caomhnadh, *gen* **caomhnaidh** *nm* (*the act
of*) saving, economising etc (*see senses of*
caomhain *v*)

caon *adj* wily, cunning, *cf more usu* **carach 1,
fiar** *adj* **4, seòlta 1**

caora, *gen* **caorach**, *dat* **caora**, *pl* **caoraich**,
gen pl **chaorach** *nf* a sheep, a ewe, **rùisg** *v* **na
caoraich** shear the sheep, **caora uain** a ewe
in lamb

caorann, *gen* **caorainn** *nmf* (*bot*) a rowan, a
mountain ash

car, cuir, caran *nm* **1** a twist, a turn, (*prov*) **an
car a bhios san t-seann mhaide, is deacair
a thoirt às** the twist that is in the old stick
is hard to get out (*roughly equivalent to* you
can't teach an old dog new tricks); **2** a (circular)
movement, a turn, a spin, **bheir mi car
a-muigh** I'll take a stroll/a 'turn' outside, **cuir
car den chuibhle!** give the wheel a turn/a spin!
cuir car den bhrot! give the soup a stir! **car a'
mhuiltein** a somersault, **a' dol car mu char
leis a' bhruthaich** rolling over and over down
the brae; **3** a movement, *esp in expr* **cuir** *v* **car
de** move, **na cuir car dheth!** don't move/upset
it! **cuir car dhìot!** move yourself, get a move
on!, *cf* **caraich, gluais 1**; **4** a trick, *esp in expr*
thoir *v* **an car às** trick, cheat, **thug iad an car
aiste** they tricked her, (*prov*) **cha tugadh an
donas an car às** the devil couldn't cheat him, *cf*
cleas 2, meall *v* **1**; **5** *in expr with a superlative*
aig a' char as miosa/lugha (etc) at worst/least
(etc), **aig a' char as mò cha chaill sinn ach
fichead nota** at most we will only lose twenty
pounds; **6** *in expr* **a' chiad char sa mhadainn**
first thing in the morning; **7** *as adv* a bit, rather,
car anmoch rather late, (*song*) **ged tha mi car
sgìth** though I'm a bit tired, *cf* **beag 4, beagan**
adv, **caran, rudeigin 2**

car *prep* (*with dat*) during, for, **car mìosa** for a
month, **bha sinn ann an Glaschu car uair**
we were in Glasgow for a while/a time, *cf* **fad** *n* **2**

càr, càir, càraichean *nm* a car, *cf trad* **carbad**

**car(a)bhaidh, car(a)bhaidh, car(a)
abhaidhean** *nm* (*fam*) a boyfriend, *cf*
bràmair, leannan

carach *adj* **1** wily, sly, crafty, cunning, up
to tricks, *cf* **caon, fiar** *adj* **4, seòlta 1**; **2**
changeable, unreliable, *cf* **caochlaideach 2,
cugallach 2, luaineach**

carachadh, *gen* **carachaidh** *nm* (*the act of*)
moving, *cf* **gluasad 1**

carachd *nf invar* wrestling

caractar, caractair, caractairean *nm* (*in play etc*) a character, *cf less usu* **pearsa 2**

càradh, *gen* **càraidh** *nm* **1** (*the act of*) repairing, mending etc (*see senses of* **càirich** *v*); **2** a repair, **luchd-càraidh** repairers; **3** (*trad*) state, condition, **is truagh mo chàradh** sad is my condition, *cf now more usu* **cor 1, staid**

caraich *vti, pres part* **a' carachadh,** move, **na caraich am bòrd!** don't move the table! **na caraich bhon bhòrd!** don't move from the table!, *cf* **car** *n* **3, gluais 1**

caraiche, caraiche, caraichean *nm* a wrestler

caraid, caraid, càirdean *nm* **1** a friend, (*Note: in this sense, the pl can be* **caraidean**), **tha thu nad dheagh charaid dhomh** you're a good friend to me/of mine, (*prov*) **cha chall na gheibh caraid** what a friend gets is no loss, **banacharaid** a female/woman friend, **Caraid nan Gàidheal** The Friend of the Gael (*the Rev Norman MacLeod 1783–1862*); **2** a relative, *esp in pl,* **tha mo chàirdean air fad ann an Steòrnabhagh** all my relatives/folks/family are in Stornoway; **3** (*corres*) **A Charaid** Dear Sir, **A Chàirdean** Dear Sirs, **A Sheumais, a charaid** Dear James/Hamish, **A Bhanacharaid** Dear Madam, **A Mhòrag, a bhanacharaid** Dear Morag, *cf* **còir** *adj* **2**

càraid, càraide, càraidean *nf* **1** a pair, a brace, a couple, **càraid (phòsta)** a married couple, *cf* **dithis 2**; **2** a pair of twins, **caora-càraid** a sheep with twin lambs

caraidh *nf see* **cairidh**

caran *dimin of* **car** *n*, used adverbially, a little, a bit, (*Sc*) a wee bit, **tha thu caran fadalach!** you're a wee bit late! **bha sinn caran sgìth** we were a bit tired, *cf* **beag 4, beagan** *adv,* **car** *n* **7, rudeigin 2**

carbad, carbaid, carbadan *nm* a vehicle, a conveyance, a carriage, (*trad*) a motorcar (*cf* **càr**), (*trad*) **carbad-iarainn** a railway train (*cf* **trèana**), **carbad-eiridinn** an ambulance, **carbad-smàlaidh** a fire engine, **carbad-adhair** an aircraft, **carbad-speura** a spacecraft

Carghas, *gen* **Carghais** *nm* (*used with def art*), **An Carghas** Lent

cargu & carago, *gen* **carago,** *pl* **caragothan** *nm* a cargo, *cf more trad* **luchd**[1]

càrn, *gen* **càirn & cùirn,** *pl* **càirn & cùirn** *nm* **1** a cairn, a heap of stones, (*trad*) **cuiridh sinn clach air a chàrn** we will put a stone on his cairn, we will remember him/honour his memory, **càrn-cuimhne** a monument; **2** (*topog*) a hill (*often stony*)

càrn *vt, pres part* **a' càrnadh,** heap, pile up, accumulate, **càrn maoin is airgead** accumulate possessions and money, **càrn am buntàta air an làr** heap the potatoes on the ground, *cf* **cruach** *v*

càrnadh, *gen* **càrnaidh** *nm* (*the act of*) heaping, accumulating etc (*see senses of* **càrn** *v*)

càrnaid, càrnaide, càrnaidean *nf* a carnation

càrnan[1], *gen* **càrnain,** *pl* **càrnain & càrnanan** *nm* (*dimin of* **càrn** *n*) a small cairn, a small heap of stones

càrnan[2], **càrnain, càrnanan** *nm* a cockroach

càrr, *gen* **càrra** *nf, also* **càir,** *gen* **càire** *nf,* **1** a scab; **2** dandruff

carragh, carraigh, carraighean *nf* **1** a rock, a pillar (*of rock*); **2** a standing stone, *cf* **gallan, tursa**

carraig, carraige, carraigean *nf* a rock (*often by the sea*)

carraigean *see* **cairgein**

carson *inter adv* why, **carson a dh'fhalbh e?** why did he leave? **chan eil Màiri ag obair, carson a tha sin?** Mary's not working, why's that? **na faighnich carson** don't ask why

cartadh, *gen* **cartaidh** *nm* (*the act of*) tanning, mucking out etc (*see senses of* **cairt** *v*)

carthannachd *nf invar & ***carthannas,** *gen* **carthannais** *nm* **1** (*trad*) kindness, (Christian) charity, (*poem*) **Spiorad a' Charthannais** The Spirit of Charity, *cf* **seirc 2**; **2** charity (*ie charitable giving and the work of charities*), **buidheann-carthannachd** a charity, a charitable organisation, *cf* **dèirc**

cas *adj* **1** steep, abrupt, **leathad cas** a steep slope, **bruthach c(h)as** a steep brae; **2** precipitous, fast-flowing (*burn, current etc*), *cf* **bras 3**; **3** (*of person*) irritable, hasty, abrupt, impetuous, *cf* **aithghearr 2, bras 1**

cas, *gen* **coise,** *dat* **cois,** *pl* **casan** *nf* **1** a foot, **ball-coise** football, a football, (*command to dog*) **cùl mo chois!** *also* **rim chois!** heel! **de chois** on foot, **thèid mi ann dhem chois** I'll go there on foot, I'll walk there, **air mo** (*etc*) **chois** up, up and about, **nach tràth a bha thu air do chois an-diugh!** weren't you up and about early today!; **2** a leg, **thoir do chasan leat!** (*lit* take your legs/feet with you) get out, take yourself off! **caol mo choise** my ankle (*cf* **adhbrann**), **cas-lom & casruisgte,** barefoot, *also* barelegged; **3** a handle, **cas na spaide** the spade handle, **cas sgeine** a knife handle; **4** *also in expr* **an cois** near, accompanying, associated with, **caora is uan na cois** a ewe with a lamb at foot, **cha tàinig iad nam chois** they didn't come with me, **bochdainn agus na duilgheadasan a thig na cois** poverty and its associated difficulties, (*also in corres*) **an**

cois na litreach enclosed with the letter, **cuir** *v* **rudeigin an cois** enclose something, *cf* **lùb** *n* 3; **5** *in expr* **cuir** *v* **air chois** found, set up, organise, *cf* **bonn 5, stèidhich**

càs, càis, càsan *nm* a difficulty, a predicament, *esp* **(ann an) cruaidh-chàs** (in) serious difficulty, (in) an extreme predicament

casad, casaid, casadan *nm* a cough (*the action and the ailment*), **rinn i casad** she coughed, *cf* **casadaich** *n*

casadaich *nf invar* **1** (*the act of*) coughing, **dè a' chasadaich a th' ort!** what a lot of coughing you're doing!; **2** *also as verbal noun,* **tha i a' casadaich** she's coughing; **2** a cough; *cf* **casad**

casa-gòbhlach *adj & adv* astride, **casa-gòbhlach air a' chathair/air an stairsnich** astride the chair/the threshold, **a' marcachd casa-gòbhlach** riding astride

casaid, casaide, casaidean *nf* a complaint (*esp official, legal*), an accusation, **dèan** *v* **casaid** make/bring a complaint, make an accusation, **rinn e casaid orm/nam aghaidh** he accused me, **fear-casaid & neach-casaid** an accuser, a prosecutor, **Fear-casaid/Neach-casaid a' Chrùin** the Procurator Fiscal, the Crown Prosecutor, **tha e fo chasaid muirt** he is accused of murder

cas-chrom, cois(e)-cruim(e), casan-croma *nf* (*trad*) a foot plough

casg, *gen* **caisg** *nm* prevention, restraint, **cuir** *v* **casg air** stop, prevent, restrain, *cf* **casgadh 2**

casgadh, *gen* **casgaidh** *nm* **1** (*the act of*) subsiding, preventing etc (*see senses of* **caisg** *v*); **2** prevention, restraint, interruption, *cf* **casg**

casgair *vt, pres part* **a' casgairt & a' casgradh,** slay, slaughter, massacre, butcher, *cf* **marbh** *v*, **murt** *v*

casgairt *nf invar, also* **casgradh,** *gen* **casgraidh** *nm,* **1** (*the act of*) slaying etc (*see senses of* **casgair** *v*); **2** slaughter, butchery, massacre, a massacre, *cf* **murt** *n*

casgan, *gen* **casgain,** *pl* **casgain & casganan** *nm* **1** (*on wheel etc*) a brake, *cf* **brèig; 2** a condom

casg-breith *nm invar* abortion, an abortion, **bha casg-breith aice** she had an abortion

casg-gineamhainn *nm invar* **1** contraception; **2** a contraceptive

cat, *gen & pl* **cait** *nm* a cat, **cat-fiadhaich** a wild cat

Catalanach, *gen & pl* **Catalanaich** *nm* a Catalan, *as adj* **Catalanach** Catalan

Catalanais *nf invar* (*lang*) Catalan

cath, *gen* **catha,** *pl* **cathan & cathannan** *nm* a battle, warfare, (*trad dance*) **cath nan coileach** the battle of the cocks, the cockfight, (*trad*)

misg-catha (*also* **mire-catha**) battle frenzy (*lit* battle drunkenness), *cf* **blàr 2, cogadh**

càth, *gen* **càtha** *nf* chaff, *cf* **moll**

cathadh, cathaidh, cathaidhean *nm* **1** a snowstorm, (*poem*) **An Cathadh Mór** (Aonghas MacNeacail) (*translated as*) The Great Snow Battle; **2** *in expr* **cathadh-mara** sea-spray

cathag, cathaig, cathagan *nf* a jackdaw

cathair, cathrach, cathraichean *nf* **1** a chair, **cùl cathrach** a chair back, **cathair-ghàirdeanach** an armchair, **cathair-chuibhle** a wheelchair, *cf less trad* **sèithear; 2** a big city, a cathedral city, **cathair-eaglais** *nf* a cathedral

cath-bhuidheann, cath-bhuidhinn, cath-bhuidhnichean *nf* a batallion

cathraiche, cathraiche, cathraichean *nm* a chairman *or* chairperson (*of meeting*)

cèaban, cèabain, cèabainean *nm* (*on ship etc*) a cabin

cead *nm invar* **1** permission, leave, (*trad*) **le ur cead** by your leave, with your permission, **thug mi cead dhaibh falbh** I gave them permission to leave/go; **2** a permit, a licence, **cead-dràibhidh** a driving licence, **cead-dol-thairis** a passport; **3** farewell, leave, a leave-taking, **ghabh sinn ar cead dhiubh** we took our leave of them/bade them farewell, (*poem*) **Cead Deireannach nam Beann** The Last Farewell to the Mountains, taking leave of the mountains for the last time

ceadach *adj* tolerant

ceadachadh, *gen* **ceadachaidh** *nm* (*the act of*) permitting, licensing etc (*see senses of* **ceadaich** *v*), **bòrd** *m* **ceadachaidh** a licensing board

ceadachail *adj* permissive

ceadachas, *gen* **ceadachais,** *nm* permissiveness, tolerance

ceadaich *vti, pres part* **a' ceadachadh,** **1** permit, allow, tolerate, (*song*) **Nan Ceadaicheadh an Tìde Dhomh** If Time Would Allow Me, *cf* **leig 1; 2** license, grant or issue licences

ceadaichte *adj* allowed, permitted, permissible, admissible, licit

ceàird, ceàirde, ceàirdean *nf* a trade, a craft, **fear-ceàirde** a skilled tradesman, a craftsman, an artisan

cealg, *gen* **ceilge** *nf* deceit; hypocrisy, *cf* **foill 1**

cealgach *adj* deceitful, hypocritical

cealgair(e), cealgair(e), cealgairean *nm* a deceiver, a cheat, a hypocrite, *cf* **mealltair**

cealla, cealla, ceallan *nf* (*biol*) a cell

ceanalta *adj* **1** pretty, comely, (*song*) **chunnaic mi caileag a bha ceanalta grinn** I saw a girl who was comely and neat, *cf more usu*

bòidheach, grinn 2; **2** kind, gentle, *cf more usu* **coibhneil, sèimh**

ceangail *vt, pres part* **a' ceangal**, tie, link, join, unite, connect (**ri** to), **cheangail e iallan a bhrògan** he tied his shoe-laces, **ceangail ri chèile** join together

ceangal, ceangail, ceanglaichean *nm* **1** (*the act of*) tying, linking etc (*see senses of* **ceangail** *v*); **2** (*abstr & con*) a connection, a link, a bond, **bha dlùth-cheangal aca ris a' Ghàidhealtachd** they had a close link with the Highlands, **chan fhaic mi an ceangal eadar an dealbh 's na faclan** I don't see the connection between the picture and the words, *cf* **dàimh** 2

ceangaltach *adj* (*of a promise etc*) binding

ceann, *gen & pl* **cinn** *nm* **1** a head, **bha a ceann goirt** her head ached/was sore, (*song*) **ged tha mo cheann air liathadh** though my head has turned grey, **ceannruisgte** bare-headed; **2** the end of anything, **ceann an rathaid** the end of the road, **bho cheann gu ceann** from end to end, **phòs iad aig a' cheann thall** they married in the end/eventually, **ceann as àirde/ as ìsle (a' mhullaich etc)** the top/bottom (of the roof etc); **3** *in expr* **an ceann** *prep* after, in (*of time*), **an ceann greiseig** in/after a little while, (*of time & space*) **an ceann a chèile** together, one after the other, in succession, **chan urrainn dha dà fhacal a chur an ceann a chèile** he can't string/put two words together, **trì tubaistean an ceann a chèile** three accidents one after the other/in succession/in a row (*cf* **sreath** 3); **4** *in expr* **ag obair** (*etc*) **air a cheann fhèin** working (*etc*) on his own account/for himself

ceannach, *gen* **ceannaich** *nm* (*the act of*) buying, purchasing, trading

ceannachd *nf invar* trade, commerce, *cf* **malairt** 1

ceannaich *vt, pres part* **a' ceannach(d),** buy, purchase, **ceannaich air deagh phrìs** buy at a good price

ceannaiche, ceannaiche, ceannaichean *nm* **1** a purchaser; **2** (*more usu*) a merchant, a dealer, a buyer

ceannard, ceannaird, ceannardan *nm* **1** a head, a boss (*of firm etc*), a principal (*of ed institution etc*), a leader *or* commander (*of military unit etc*)

ceannbheart, *gen* **ceannbheairt** *nf* headgear

ceann-bliadhna, *gen & pl* **cinn-bliadhna** *nm* a birthday, **bha ceann-bliadhna agam an-dè** it was my birthday yesterday, *cf* **co-là-breith**

ceann-cinnidh, *gen & pl* **cinn-chinnidh** *nm* *also* **ceann-feadhna,** *gen & pl* **cinn-fheadhna** *nm* a clan chief, **ceann-cinnidh nan Dòmhnallach** chief of the MacDonalds

ceann-là, *gen & pl* **cinn-là** *nm* a (*calendar*) date

ceann-làidir *adj* headstrong

ceann-naidheachd, *gen & pl* **cinn-naidheachd** *nm* (*news*) a headline

ceann-obrach, *gen & pl* **cinn-obrach** (*IT*) a (*computer*) terminal

ceann-pholan, ceann-pholain, ceann-pholanan *nm* *also* **ceann-simid, ceann-simide, ceann-simidean** *nm* a tadpole

ceannsachadh, *gen* **ceannsachaidh** *nm* **1** (*the act of*) conquering, quelling etc (*see senses of* **ceannsaich** *v*); **2** conquest, repression

ceannsaich *vt, pres part* **a' ceannsachadh,** **1** conquer, overcome (*army, enemy etc*); **2** (*people, emotions etc*) quell, master, control, repress, **cheannsaich am poileas an aimhreit** the police quelled/controlled the disturbance, **cheannsaich mi m' fhearg** I controlled/mastered my anger, *cf* **mùch** 3; **3** (*animal etc*) tame, *cf* **callaich** 1

ceannsaiche, ceannsaiche, ceannsaichean *nm* a conqueror, a vanquisher

ceannsaichte *adj* (*of animal etc*) tamed

ceannsal, *gen* **ceannsail** *nm* rule, authority, subjugation, **fo cheannsal a nàmhaid** under his enemy's rule, *cf* **smachd**

ceannsalach *adj* **1** authoritative, commanding, *cf* **smachdail**; **2** dictatorial, domineering

ceann-simid *see* **ceann-pholan**

ceann-suidhe, *gen & pl* **cinn-suidhe** *nm* a president (*of firm, company, also of country*)

ceann-uidhe, *gen & pl* **cinn-uidhe** *nm* a destination, **'s e Glaschu mo cheann-uidhe** Glasgow's my destination

ceap, *gen* **cip,** *pl* **ceapan** & **ceapannan** *nm* **1** a block *or* lump of anything, **ceap mòna/fiodha** a block *or* a lump of peat/wood, *cf* **cnap** 1; **2** (*also* **ceap-bròige**) a cobbler's last

ceap, ceapa, ceapan *nm* a cap (*ie headgear*), *cf* **bonaid** 2

ceapach, *gen & pl* **ceapaich** *nmf* (*hort*) a plot, a bed

ceapaire, ceapaire, ceapairean *nm* a sandwich

cearb, cirbe, cearban *nf* **1** a rag, *cf* **luideag**; **2** a defect, a fault, *cf* **easbhaidh**

cearbach *adj* **1** (*person, action*) clumsy, awkward, ungainly; **2** ragged, untidy, tatty, *cf* **luideach**

cearbair(e), cearbair(e), cearbairean *nm* an awkward or clumsy person, a bungler, *cf* **uaipear**

cearc, circe, cearcan nf **1** a (*domestic*) hen; **2** a female game bird, **cearc-ruadh** a red grouse

cearcall, gen **cearcaill,** pl **cearcaill &** **cearcallan** nm a circle, a ring, **a' dannsadh ann an cearcall** dancing in a circle/a ring, (*song*) **Cearcall a' Chuain** The Circle of the Ocean

cearclach adj circular

ceàrd, gen **ceàird,** pl **ceàrdan** nm **1** a tinker; **2** (*usu in compounds*) a smith, **ceàrd-airgid** a silversmith, **òr-cheàrd** a goldsmith, **ceàrd-copair** a coppersmith, cf **gobha**

ceàrdach, ceàrdaich, ceàrdaichean nf a smithy, a blacksmith's shop; a forge

ceàrn, gen **ceàrnaidh,** pl **ceàrnaidhean &** **ceàrnan** nm an area, a district, a corner, a zone, **sa cheàrn seo den dùthaich** in this part/corner of the country, **ceàrnaidhean iomallach** remote areas/districts, cf **sgìre 1, tìr 3**

ceàrnach adj square

ceàrnag, ceàrnaig, ceàrnagan nf **1** (*geometry*) a square; **2** a square (*in a town etc*), **Ceàrnag Shomhairle** Somerled Square (*in Portree, Skye*)

ceàrnagach adj square, **meatair ceàrnagach** a square metre

ceàrr adj wrong, amiss, **bha mi cinnteach gun robh mi ceart, ach bha mi ceàrr** I was sure I was right, but I was wrong, **fada ceàrr** far wrong, **tha rudeigin ceàrr air mo dhruim** there's something wrong with my back; **2** left, **mo làmh cheàrr** my left hand, cf **clì**

ceàrrachas, gen **ceàrrachais,** also **ceàrrachadh,** gen **ceàrrachaidh** nm, gambling

ceàrraiche & cèarraiche, gen **ceàrraiche,** pl **ceàrraichean** nm a gambler

ceart adj **1** right, correct, exact, accurate, **tha thu pòsta a-nis, a bheil sin ceart?** you're married now, is that right? **tha na cunntasan/ na freagairtean ceart** the accounts/the answers are correct, **ann an ceart-mheadhan a' bhaile** right in the centre/in the exact centre of the town, *as excl* **ceart, ma-thà!** right, then!; **2** just, right, **binn cheart** a just sentence, **duine ceart** a just/upright man, **cuir** v **ceart na tha ceàrr** put right what is wrong; **3** same, very, **Iain bràthair Mòraig, a bheil thu a' minigeadh? an ceart duine!** Iain, Morag's brother, do you mean? the very man!/ the very same!, **ach feumaidh mi ràdh aig a' cheart àm . . .** but I have to say at the same time . . ., cf **aon 3, ceudna 1, dearbh** adj **1, fèin 5; 4** right, right-hand, cf more usu **deas**

nf **2; 5** as adv **a cheart cho** just as, every bit as, **tha margarain a cheart cho math ri ìm** margarine is just as good as butter; **6** used as noun, right, **cho ceart ri ceart** as right as can be, perfectly correct, (*prov*) **thèid neart thar ceart** might before right, cf **ceartas, còir** n **4; 7** in expr **ceart gu leòr!** OK!, right!, fine!

ceartachadh, ceartachaidh, ceartachaidhean nm **1** (*the act of*) correcting, marking etc (*see senses of* **ceartaich** v); **2** correction, a correction; cf **comharrachadh**

ceartaich vt, pres part **a' ceartachadh,** correct, rectify, put right, (*teacher etc*) mark, **bha i a' ceartachadh obair a sgoilearan** she was correcting/marking her pupils' work, cf **comharraich 2**

ceartas, gen **ceartais** nm justice, right, cf **còir** n **4, ionracas 2**

ceartuair see **an-ceartuair**

ceart-uilinn, ceart-uilinn, ceart-uilnean nf a right angle

ceas, ceasa, ceasaichean nm a (suit)case, cf **baga, màileid**

ceasnachadh, ceasnachaidh, ceasnachaidhean nm **1** (*the act of*) questioning etc (*see senses of* **ceasnaich** v); **2** a questionnaire, cf **ceisteachan; 3** interrogation, an interrogation; **4** a quiz

ceasnachail adj inquisitive, questioning, cf **faighneach**

ceasnaich vti, pres part **a' ceasnachadh, 1** question; **2** interrogate; **3** (*relig*) catechise

ceathach, gen & pl **ceathaich** nm mist, (*poem*) **Òran Coire a' Cheathaich** Song to (the) Misty Corrie, cf more usu **ceò 1**

ceathrad, ceathraid, ceathradan nm the number forty (*in alt numbering system*), cf **dà fhichead** (*see* **fichead**)

ceathramh num adj fourth, **an ceathramh fear** the fourth man/one, **ceathramh deug** fourteenth

ceathramh, ceathraimh, ceathramhan nm **1** a quarter, a fourth part of anything, (*placename*) **An Ceathramh Cruaidh** Kerrycroy, the hard quarter (*ie division of land*); **2** (*of time*) a quarter (of an hour), **ceathramh gu sia** a quarter to six, cf **cairteal 1**

ceathrar nm invar (people numbering) four, a foursome, *takes the gen,* **bha ceathrar mhac aice** she had four sons, **tha ceathrar mun bhòrd** there are four people round/at the table

cèic, cèice, cèicean nf cake, a cake

cèidse, cèidse, cèidsichean nf a cage

ceil vt, pres part **a' ceileadh, a' cleith & a' ceiltinn,** hide, conceal (**air** from), **ceil an**

fhìrinn air do mhàthair! hide the truth from your mother!, *cf* **falaich**

cèile *nmf invar* 1 a spouse, a wife, a husband, **a chèile** his spouse/wife, **a cèile** her spouse/husband, *cf* **bean 1, duine 4**; 2 a counterpart, a fellow, *esp in exprs based on* **a chèile**, each other, **phòg iad a chèile** they kissed each other, **a' bruidhinn ri chèile** talking to each other, **tha na bràithrean thar a chèile** the brothers are at loggerheads/have fallen out with each other, **tha sinn mòr aig a chèile** we are good friends (with each other); 3 *for* **le chèile** *see* **le 1**

ceileadh, *gen* **ceilidh** *nm, also* **ceiltinn** *nf invar & * **cleith**, *gen* **cleithe** *nmf* 1 (*the act of*) hiding, concealing; 2 concealment, a hiding place; *cf* **falach**

ceileir *vi, pres part* **a' ceileireadh**, 1 sing (*esp of birds*), warble; 2 sing sweetly

cèilidh, cèilidh, cèilidhean *nmf* 1 a visit (*to someone's house*), **thàinig i a chèilidh oirnn a-raoir** she came to visit us/to ceilidh on us last night, *cf* **tadhal 2**; 2 a ceilidh, **bidh cèilidh ann an talla a' bhaile an ath-oidhch** there'll be a ceilidh in the village hall tomorrow night

cèilidheach *adj* companionable, sociable, fond of company

ceilp, *gen* **ceilpe** *nf* (*trad*) kelp, (*hist*) **losgadh** *m* **na ceilpe** kelp burning

Ceilteach, *gen & pl* **Ceiltich** *nm* a Celt, *also as adj* **Ceilteach** Celtic, **na cànainean Ceilteach** the Celtic languages

ceiltinn *nf & pres part, see* **ceil** *v*, **ceileadh** *n*

ceimig, ceimig(e), ceimigean *nf* a chemical substance, a chemical

ceimigeachd *nf invar* chemistry

ceimigear, ceimigeir, ceimigearan *nm* a chemist (*not a pharmacist – see* **cungaidh 3**)

cèin *adj* 1 foreign, **dùthaich/cànain chèin** a foreign country/language, **an cèin** *adv* abroad; 2 distant, faraway, *cf* **cian** *adj* 1

cèir, *gen* **cèire** *nf* wax, **cèir-chluaise** ear-wax

cèis, cèise, cèisean *nf* 1 a frame, **cèis dealbha/baidhsagail** a picture/bicycle frame, **cèis streap** a climbing frame, *cf* **frèam**; 2 (*also* **cèis litreach**) an envelope

cèiseag, cèiseig, cèiseagan *nf* a cassette, *cf* **teip 2**

ceist, ceiste, ceistean *nf* 1 a question, a query, **chuir e ceist dhoirbh orm** he asked me a difficult question; 2 a problem, a question, a point at issue, **a bheil e ro chosgail? 's e sin a' cheist!** is it too costly? that's the question/the point/the problem!

ceisteachan, *gen & pl* **ceisteachain** *nm* a questionnaire, *cf* **ceasnachadh 2**

ceistear, ceisteir, ceistearan *nm* 1 a questioner, an interrogator; 2 a question-master; 3 (*relig*) a catechist

Cèitean, *gen* **Cèitein** *nm* the month of May, *usu with art* **an Cèitean** May, *also adjectivally* **air madainn Chèitein** on a May morning, *cf less trad* **Màigh**

ceithir *n & num adj* four, **ceithir coin** four dogs, **cia mheud a th' ann? a ceithir** how many are there? four, **ceithir-chuibhleach** *adj* four-wheeled, **ceithir-chasach** *adj & nm* (a) quadruped

ceithir-deug *n & adj* fourteen

ceò, ceò, ceothannan *nm* 1 mist, a mist, a haze, **Eilean a' Cheò** The Misty Isle (Skye), **bha na beanntan fo cheò** the mountains were in/covered in mist, *cf* **ceathach 1**; 2 fog, a fog; 3 smoke, *cf* **toit 2**

ceòl, *gen* **ciùil** *nm* music, **luchd-ciùil** musicians, **còmhlan-ciùil** a band, a group, **bogsa-ciùil** an accordeon, **inneal-ciùil** a musical instrument, **ceòl na mara** the music/song of the sea, **ceòl-mòr** the 'great music' or classical music of the Highland bagpipe, **ceòl-beag** light music, dance music (for the pipes), (*idiom*) **cuir** *v* **an ceòl air feadh na fìdhle** put the cat among the pigeons

ceòlmhor *adj* musical, harmonious, melodious, tuneful, *cf* **binn** *adj* 2, **fonnmhor**

ceòthach *also* **ceòthar** *adj* 1 misty, covered in mist, hazy; 2 foggy

ceud, ceud, ceudan *nm* a hundred, **ceud duine** a/one hundred people, **thàinig iad nan ceudan** they came in their hundreds, hundreds of them came, **iomadh ceud bliadhna** many hundreds of years, **a ceithir** (*etc*) **às a' cheud** four (*etc*) percent, **ceud taing!** thanks a lot! (*trad greeting*) **ceud mìle fàilte!** a hundred thousand welcomes!

ceudameatair, ceudameatair, ceudameatairean *nm* a centimetre

ceudamh *num adj* hundredth

ceudna *adj* 1 same, very, **chunnaic mi srainnsear an-dè is chunnaic mi an srainnsear ceudna an-diugh** I saw a stranger yesterday and I saw the same stranger today, **an e Seòras a th' ann? an duine ceudna!** is it George? the very man!, *cf more usu* **aon 3, ceart 3, dearbh** *adj* 1; 2 *also in expr* **mar an ceudna** similarly, likewise, also, too, **bha mi math air dannsadh, mo phiuthar mar an ceudna** I was good at dancing, my sister likewise/too, *cf* **cuideachd** *adv*

ceum, *gen* **ceuma** & **cèim**, *pl* **ceuman** &
ceumannan *nm* **1** (*in walking etc*) a step, a
pace, a stride, **ghabh i ceum air adhart** she
took a step/pace forwards, she stepped forward,
ceum air cheum step by step; **2** a footstep
chuala mi ceumannan fad' air falbh I heard
footsteps far away; **3** a step (*of staircase etc*) **a'**
dol suas na ceumannan going up the steps;
4 a track, a (foot)path, *cf* **frith-rathad**; **5** a
(university) degree, **thug i a-mach ceum** she
graduated (*cf* **ceumnaich 2**)

ceumnachadh, ceumnachaidh,
ceumnachaidhean *nm* **1** (*the act of*) pacing,
graduating (*see* **ceumnaich** *v*); **2** (*ed*) (*also*
ceumnachd *nf invar*) graduation, a graduation

ceumnaich *vi, pres part* **a' ceumnachadh**, **1**
pace; **2** (*ed*) graduate, *cf* **ceum 4**

ceus *vt, pres part* **a' ceusadh**, crucify

ceusadh, ceusaidh, ceusaidhean *nm*
crucifixion, a crucifixion

cha (*before a vowel, or fh followed by a vowel,*
chan), *neg particle expressing concepts* 'not',
'No', **cha robh sinn ann** we weren't there,
cha toigh leatha ìm she doesn't like butter, **a**
bheil thu sgìth? chan eil are you tired? No
or I'm not, **an sibhse Ailean? cha mhi** are
you Alan? No *or* I am not, **an d' fhuair thu an**
duais? cha d' fhuair did you get the prize? No
or I didn't

chaidh *pt of irreg v* **rach** (*see tables p 501*)

cheana *adv, see* **a-cheana**

chì, chitheadh, chithinn *pts of irreg vb* **faic**
(*see tables p 498*)

chluinn, chluinneadh, chluinneas,
chluinninn, chluinntinn *pts of irreg v*
cluinn (*see tables p 496*)

cho *adv* **1** so, **bha e cho trang!** he was so busy!
chan eil mi cho math an-diugh I'm not so
good today; **2** *in comparisons* **cho . . . sin** as . . .
as that, **cha robh e cho math sin** he wasn't
that good/as good as (all) that, **chan eil mi cho**
aosta sin! I'm not that old!; **3** *in comparisons*
cho . . . ri as . . . as, **cho mòr ri taigh** as big
as a house, **cho beag ri a trì** as few as three;
4 *in comparisons involving a verb* **tha mi (a**
cheart) cho luath 's a bha mi a-riamh I'm
(just) as fast as I ever was, **chan eil an aimsir**
cho math agus a chleachd i (a bhith) the
weather isn't as good/so good as it used to be; **5**
in questions **dè cho . . . 's/agus . . . ?**
how . . . ?, *eg* **dè cho fada 's a bhios sibh a'**
fuireach againn? how long will you be staying
with us? **dè cho trom agus a tha e?** how
heavy is it?

choreigin, *see* **air choreigin** *adv*

chuala *pt of irreg v* **cluinn** (*see tables p 496*)

chuca (*emph form* **chucasan**), **chugad**
(*emph form* **chugadsa**), **chugam** (*emph*
form **chugamsa**), **chugainn** (*emph form*
chugainne), **chugaibh** (*emph form*
chugaibhse, chuice (*emph form* **chuicese**),
chuige (*emph form* **chuigesan**) *prep prons,*
see **chun**

chun, *prep, see also* **gu**[1] & **gus** *prep* **1** & **2**. *The*
prep prons formed with **chun**, *in the order first,*
second, third person singular, first, second,
third person plural, and with the reflexive/
emphatic particles in brackets, are as follows:
chugam(sa), chugad(sa), chuige(san),
chuice(se), chugainn(e), chugaibh(se),
chuca(san), *to me, to you* (*fam*) *etc, used*
exactly as **thugam(sa), thugad(sa)** *etc, for*
which see **gu 2** & **gus** *prep*

chum *see* **a chum**

chunna, chunnaic *pts of irreg v* **faic** (*see tables*
p 498)

ciad *adj* first, *used with art*, **a' chiad leasan** the
first lesson, **a' chiad turas** the first time, **anns**
a' chiad àite in the first place

ciad-fhuasgladh, *gen* **ciad-fhuasglaidh** *nm*
(*medical*) first aid

ciall, *gen* **cèille**, *dat* **cèill** & **ciall**, *pl* **ciallan** *nf*
1 sense, good sense, reasonableness, **briathran**
làn cèille words full of good sense, *cf* **toinisg,**
tuigse 1; **2** reason, mind (*ie sanity*), **chaill mi**
mo chiall I've lost my mind/my reason, **tha i**
gu bhith às a ciall le iomagain she's nearly
out of her mind with worry, *cf* **reusan, rian**
3; **3** meaning, sense, (*trad & emph*) **gu dè as**
ciall dhut? what on earth/whatever do you
mean?, **faclan gun chiall** meaningless words,
also senseless words, *cf* **brìgh 1, seagh**; **4** *in*
expr **cuir an cèill** (*ideas, feelings etc*) express,
put into words; **5** *excl* **a chiall!** goodness! good
heavens!

ciallach *adj* **1** sensible, reasonable, *cf* **toinisgeil**
1, tuigseach 1, tùrail; **2** sane, in possession of
one's faculties, of sound mind

ciallaich *vt, pres part* **a' ciallachadh**, mean, **dè**
a tha thu a' ciallachadh? what do you mean?,
dè a tha am facal seo a' ciallachadh? What
does this word mean? *cf* **minig** *v*

ciamar *inter adv* how, **ciamar a tha thu an-**
diugh? how are you today? **ciamar a chaidh**
dhut? how did you get on? **chan eil fhios**
agam ciamar a rinn e e I don't know how he
did it

cia mheud & **co mheud**, *inter adv* how many,
how much, *Note: takes a sing noun,* **cia mheud**
duine a bha ann? how many people were there?

cian *adj* **1** distant, remote (*in time or space*), *cf* **cèin, iomallach**; **2** long, weary, (*poetry collection*) **An Rathad Cian** (Ruaraidh MacThòmais) The Far Road

cian, *gen* **cèin** *nm* distance, remoteness (*in time or space*), (*song*) **'s cian nan cian bho dh'fhàg mi Leòdhas** it is a very long time (*lit* the age of the ages) since I left Lewis, *cf more usu* **is fhada** (*see* **fad(a) 2**)

cianail *adj* **1** sad, *cf* **brònach, muladach**; **2** plaintive, melancholy; **3** terrible, *as intensifying element* (*also* **cianail fhèin**), **tha e cianail (fhèin) mòr** it's very big indeed/terribly big, *cf* **eagalach 3, uabhasach 2**

cianalach *adj* sad (*esp through homesickness*)

cianalas, *gen* **cianalais** *nm* **1** sadness, *cf* **bròn, mulad**; **2** homesickness; **3** nostalgia

ciar *adj* **1** (*of persons, complexion*) dark, swarthy, *cf* **lachdann 2**; **2** (*of atmosphere, setting*) dark, gloomy, *cf* **doilleir**; **3** (*of colour*) dun, *cf* **odhar 1**; **4** *in expr* **is** *v* **ciar leam . . .** I take a dim view of . . . , *cf* **beag 5**

ciar *vi, pres part* **a' ciaradh**, darken, grow dark, **mus do chiar am feasgar** before the evening grew dark, before dusk fell, *cf* **doilleirich**

ciaradh, *gen* **ciaraidh** *nm* (evening) twilight, dusk, *cf* **duibhre, camhana(i)ch 2, eadar-sholas**

ciatach *adj* **1** pleasant, attractive, agreeable, *cf* **taitneach, tarraingeach**; **2** *in expr* **bu chiatach air . . .** he ought to/should . . . , it would be fitting for him to . . . , *cf more usu* **còir** *n* **1**

cidhe, cidhe, cidhean *nm* a quay, a pier, *cf* **laimrig**

cidsin, cidsin, cidsinean *nm* a kitchen

cileagram, cileagraim, cileagraman *nm* a kilogram, a kilo

cilemeatair, cilemeatair, cilemeatairean *nm* a kilometre

cill, *gen* **cille**, *pl* **cillean** & **cilltean** *nf* **1** (*trad*) a cell of a saint, monk or hermit, a holy site associated with such a saint etc, (*placenames*) **Cill Aonghais** Killanish, the cell or church of (St) Angus, **Cille Mhoire** Kilmore, Kilmuir, Mary's church; **2** (*trad*) a kirkyard, a burial ground, *cf* **clachan 3, cladh**

cineal, cineil, cinealan *nm* **1** race, a race, **dàimh-chinealan** *f* race relations; **2** a species, *cf* **gnè 2, seòrsa 2**

cinealtach *adj* racist, racialist

cinealtas, *gen* **cinealtais** *nm* racism, racialism

cinn *vi, pres part* **a' cinntinn**, grow, increase, multiply, prosper, (*trad*) **chinn a shliochd** his progeny increased, *cf* **fàs** *v* **2, meudaich**

cinneach, *gen* & *pl* **cinnich** *nm* a heathen

cinneadail *adj* **1** clannish; **2** racial, **leth-bhreith chinneadail** racial discrimination

cinne-daonna *see* **daonna**

cinneadh, cinnidh, cinnidhean *nm* **1** (*in Scotland & Ireland*) a clan, **ceann-cinnidh** a clan chief, the head of a clan, **fear-cinnidh** a (fellow) clansman, *also* a (male) namesake, **bean-chinnidh** a (fellow) clanswoman, *also* a (female) namesake, *cf* **clann 2, fine 2**; **2** (*in general*) a race, a tribe, a people, *esp of real or supposed common ancestry*; **3** a surname, one's second *or* family name, **dè an cinneadh a th' agad?** what's your surname/second name?, *cf more usu* **sloinneadh 2**

cinneas, *gen* **cinneis** *nm* growth (*abstr & con*), **cinneas eaconomach** economic growth, *cf* **fàs** *n*

cinnt, *gen* **cinnte** *nf* certainty, a certainty

cinnteach *adj* certain, sure, confident, **a bheil thu cinnteach gun tig i? tha mi làn-chinnteach às!** are you certain/sure she'll come? I'm quite certain/sure of it! *cf more trad* **deimhinn(e)**

cinntinn *nm invar* (*the act of*) growing etc (*see senses of* **cinn** *v*)

cìobair, cìobair, cìobairean *nm* a shepherd, (*song*) **Duanag a' Chìobair** The Shepherd's Song

cìoch, cìche, cìochan *nf* **1** a (*woman's*) breast; **2** a nipple; **3** *in expr* **cìoch an t-slugain** the uvula

cìochag, cìochaig, cìochagan *nf* a valve

ciod *inter pron, corres to much more common* **dè** & **cò** *inter prons*, **ciod e a tha thu a' ciallachadh?** what(ever) do you mean?, **ciod air bith a dh'fhosgail an doras sin?** whoever opened that door?

ciomach, *gen* & *pl* **ciomaich** *nm* a prisoner, a captive, a detainee, *cf* **prìosanach**

ciomachas, *gen* **ciomachais** *nm* imprisonment, captivity, detention, *cf* **bràighdeanas, daorsa, làmh 2, sàs 1**

cion *nm invar* **1** a lack, a want, a shortage, **cion-ùidhe** apathy, (*song*) **Cion a' Bhuntàta** Lack/Want of Potatoes, the potato shortage, *cf* **dìth 1, easbhaidh, gainne**; **2** desire, a desire (*for something or someone*), **mo chion ort fhèin** my desire for you, *cf more usu* **miann 1 & 2**

cion-fala *nm invar* anaemia

cionn, chionn *preps, see* **a chionn, o chionn**, & **os cionn** (*see under* **os**) *preps*

cionnas *conj* how, *cf more usu* **ciamar** *conj*

ciont(a), cìont(a), ciontan *nm* **1** guilt; **2** a guilty action, a sin, a transgression, a fault, *cf* **peacadh**

ciontach *adj* guilty, *cf* **coireach** *adj* 1

ciontach, *gen & pl* **ciontaich** *nm* a guilty person, an offender, *cf* **coireach** *n*, **eucorach**

ciontachadh, *gen* **ciontachaidh** *nm* (*the act of*) offending etc (*see senses of* **ciontaich** *v*)

ciontaich *vi, pres part* **a' ciontachadh,** offend, commit an offence, commit a guilty action, transgress, *cf* **peacaich**

cion-ùidhe *nm invar* apathy

ciora, cìora, *pl* **cioran & ciorachan** *nf, an affectionate word for a lamb or sheep,* **trobhad, a chiora bheag!** come to me, little sheep!

ciorram, ciorraim, ciorraman *nm* disability, a disability, a (*phys*) handicap, **cuibhreann-ciorraim** *m* a disability allowance

ciorramach *adj* disabled, (*phys*) handicapped

ciorramach, *gen & pl* **ciorramaich** *nm* a disabled person, a handicapped person, **na ciorramaich** the disabled

ciotach *adj* left-handed, (*hist*) **Colla Ciotach** Colkitto (left-handed Colla)

cipean, cipein, cipeanan *nm* **1** a stake, *cf less trad* **post**; **2** a tether post, *cf* **bacan**

cìr, cìre, cìrean *nf* **1** a (*hair*) comb; **2** (*also* **cìr-mheala**) a honeycomb; **3** cud, **a' cnàmh na cìre** (*of animals*) chewing the cud, (*fam, of humans*) talking things over, chewing the fat, talking of this and that

cìr *vt, pres part* **a' cìreadh,** comb, **cìr d' fhalt anns a' bhad!** comb your hair this instant! (*trad*) **cìr do cheann** comb your hair

cìreadh, *gen* **cìridh** *nm* (*the act of*) combing

cìrean, *gen* **cìrein,** *pl* **cìrein & cìreanan** *nm* **1** a comb or crest of a cock or game bird; **2** a crest of a clan or other group or body, *cf* **suaicheantas** 1

cìs, cìse, cìsean *nf* **1** taxation, a tax, customs (*etc*) duty, **saor o chìsean** tax free, duty free, (*formerly*) **a' chìs-chinn** the poll tax, *cf* **càin**

cìs-bhuailteach *adj* liable to tax(ation), taxable

ciste, ciste, cisteachan *nf* **1** (*household*) a chest, **ciste anairt** a linen chest; **2** (*used for box-like spaces of various kinds, eg*) **ciste-càir** a car boot, **ciste-laighe** a coffin

ciùb, ciùb, ciùban *nm* a cube

ciùbach *adj* cubic

ciùbhran & ciùthran, *gen & pl* **ciùbhrain,** *also* **ciuthrach,** *gen & pl* **ciuthraich,** *nm* **1** drizzle, *cf* **braon** 2; **2** a shower of rain, *cf* **fras** *n* 1

ciudha, ciudha, ciudhaichean *nf* a queue

ciùin *adj* mild, gentle, quiet, calm, **madainn chiùin** a calm/still morning, **oiteag chiùin** a gentle/mild breeze, (*trad*) **maighdeann chiùin** a gentle maiden, *cf* **sàmhach** 2, **sèimh** 1

ciùineachadh, *gen* **ciùineachaidh** *nm* (*the act of*) quietening etc (*see senses of* **ciùinich** *v*)

ciùineas, *gen* **ciùineis** *nm* calm, calmness, quiet, quietness, tranquillity, *cf* **sàmhchair** 2

ciùinich *vti, pres part* **a' ciùineachadh,** quieten, calm, calm down, pacify, still, soothe, *cf* **sìthich** 1 & 2, **socraich** 1, **tàlaidh** 3

ciùraig *vt, pres part* **a' ciùraigeadh,** cure (*bacon, fish etc*)

ciùrr *vt, pres part* **a' ciùrradh, 1** (*phys*) hurt intensely, pain, torture, *cf* **cràidh, goirtich, pian** *v* 2; **2** harm, injure (*someone's feelings, situation etc*)

ciùrradh, ciùrraidh, ciùrraidhean *nm* **1** (*the act of*) hurting, harming etc (*see senses of* **ciùrr** *v*); **2** a hurt, *cf* **creuchd**

ciùrrte *adj* hurt, injured (*phys or emotionally*)

ciuthrach & ciùthran, *see* **ciùbhran**

clabar-snàimh, clabair-snàimh, clabaran-snàimh *nm* a flipper (*as worn by divers etc*)

clabhstair, clabhstair, clabhstairean *nm* a cloister

clach, cloiche, clachan *nf* **1** stone, a stone, **thilg e clach orm** he threw a stone at me, **ballachan cloiche** stone walls, **Clach Sgàin** *also* **Clach na Cineamhainn** the Stone of Destiny/of Scone, **clach-chuimhne** *or* **clach-chuimhneachain** a memorial, a memorial stone, a monument, **clach phlumaise/shirist** a plum/cherry stone, **clach-mheallain** a hailstone, **clach-mhuilinn** a millstone, **clach-iùil** a magnet, **clach uasal** a precious stone, **clach na sùla** the eyeball, the apple of the eye; **2** a stone (*ie measure of weight*), **clach bhuntàta** a stone of potatoes; **3** a testicle, *cf* **magairle**

clach *vt, pres part* **a' clachadh,** stone, pelt with stones

clachach *adj* stony

clachadh, *gen* **clachaidh** *nm* (*the act of*) stoning, pelting with stones

clachair, clachair, clachairean *nm* a mason, a stonemason

clachan, *gen & pl* **clachain** *nm* **1** (*trad*) a village with a parish church, (*Sc*) a kirktoun; **2** a hamlet; **3** (*trad*) a kirkyard, a cemetery, *cf* **cill** 2, **cladh**

clach-bhalg, clach-bhuilg, clach-bhalgan *nf* **1** a rattle (*ie toy etc*); **2** a scrotum

clach-ghràin, *gen* **cloich-gràin** *nf* granite

cladach, cladaich, cladaichean *nm* a shore,
a beach, a stony beach, *usu of sea, but can also
be of loch,* (*prov*) **is lom an cladach air an
cunntar na faochagan** it's a bare beach on
which the whelks can be counted, *cf* **tràigh** *n* 1

cladh, *gen* **cladha** & **claidh,** *pl* **cladhan** *nm* a
churchyard, a kirkyard, a cemetery, a graveyard,
cf **cill** 2, **clachan** 3

cladhach, *gen* **cladhaich** *nm* (*the act of*) digging

cladhaich *vi, pres part* **a' cladhach,** 1 dig,
cf **ruamhair** 1; 2 (*fig*) **fiosrachadh a
chladhaich i à leabhraichean** information
she dug out of books

cladhaire, cladhaire, cladhairean *nm* a
coward, *cf* **gealtaire**

cladhaireach *adj* cowardly, *cf* **gealtach**

cladhaireachd *nf invar* cowardice, *cf* **gealtachd**

clag, *gen* & *pl* **cluig** *nm* a bell, **clag-rabhaidh** an
alarm bell

clagarsaich *nf invar* 1 a clinking, a rattling (*as
of glasses etc*); 2 *as pres part,* **a' clagarsaich**
clinking, rattling

claidheamh, claidheimh, claidhnean *nm* a
sword, **claidheamh leathann** a broadsword,
claidheamh caol a rapier, **claidheamh
dà-làimh** a two-handed sword, *Note: the
latter of these is properly referred to in Gaelic
as* **claidheamh-mòr** *but both it and the
broadsword can be found as* 'claymore' *in Sc/
Eng*

**claidheamhair, claidheamhair,
claidheamhairean** *nm* a swordsman

claigeann, claiginn, claignean *nm* a skull, *also
in expr* (**aig**) **àird mo** (*etc*) **c(h)laiginn** at the
top of my (etc) voice, **bha i a' seinn àird a
claiginn** she was singing at the top of her voice

clàimhean, clàimhein, clàimheanan *nm* (*on
door etc*) a latch

clais, claise, claisean *nf* 1 a ditch, a trench, a
channel, *cf* **dìg**; 2 a drain, *cf* **drèana**; 3 (*agric*) a
furrow, *cf* **sgrìob** 2; 4 a rut; 5 a groove

claisneachd & **claisteachd,** *nf invar* the faculty
of hearing, **tha mi a' call mo chlaisneachd**
I'm losing my hearing

clamhan, *gen* & *pl* **clamhain** *nm* a buzzard

clann, *gen* **cloinne** *nf coll* 1 children, **càraid
gun chlann** a childless couple, **clann bheaga**
little children, **dithis chloinne** two children,
Note: **clann** *is sing but has coll or pl sense,*
duine cloinne, *a child, can be more strictly
and logically used to refer to individual
children,* **cia mheud duine cloinne a
th' agaibh? aon duine cloinne** how many
children do you have? one child; 2 a clan, the
descendants of the real or supposed progenitor
of a clan, **Clann Dòmhnaill** Clan Donald, the
MacDonalds, **Clann 'IcLeòid** Clan MacLeod,
(*trad*) **Clann a' Cheò** the Children/Clan of
the Mist *a nickname for the MacGregors, cf*
cinneadh 1, **fine** 2

clann-nighean, *gen* **cloinn-nighean** *nf coll*
1 girl children; 2 girls *up to and incl late teens
approx*; 3 young women of a variety of ages, *eg
in expr* (*trad*) **clann-nighean an sgadain** the
herring girls/lasses

claoidh *nf invar,* & **claoidheadh** *gen*
claoidhidh *nm,* (*the act of*) exhausting, vexing
etc (*see senses of* **claoidh** *v*)

claoidh *vt, pres part* **a' claoidh** & **a'
claoidheadh,** (*of people*) 1 exhaust, wear out, *cf*
sgìthich; 2 vex, weary, harass, *cf* **sàraich** 2

claoidhte *adj* tired out, worn out, exhausted

claoin *vi, pres part* **a' claoineadh,** (*of verbs*)
decline

claon *adj* 1 awry, oblique, askew, (*Sc*) squint, *cf*
fiar *adj* 2; 2 sloping; 3 perverse

claon, *vti, pres part* **a' claonadh,** 1 slope,
incline; 2 go astray, lead astray; 3 (*vt*) pervert, *cf*
coirb *v,* **truaill** 3; 4 veer, move obliquely

claonadh, *gen* **claonaidh** *nm* 1 (*the act of*)
inclining etc (*see senses of* **claon** *v*); 2 a slant,
a slope, an incline; 3 obliqueness; 4 a squint,
cf **fiaradh** 2, **spleuchd** *n* 2; 5 perversion, a
perversion; 6 prejudice, bias, discrimination

claon-bhàidh, *gen* **claon-bhàidhe** *nf* bias,
prejudice

clàr, clàir, clàran *nm* 1 *used for many types
of smooth, level surface, esp wooden,* a board,
a plank, a table, *cf more usu* **bòrd** 2, **dèile**; 2
clàr aodainn a brow, a forehead, *esp in exprs*
bhuail i e an clàr aodainn she struck him
full in the face, (*fig*) **dh'innis mi an fhìrinn
dhi an clàr a h-aodainn** I told her the truth to
her face; 3 (*in book etc*) a table, a list, a register,
clàr-innse a table/list of contents, **clàr-amais**
an index, **clàr ainmean/dhaoine** a list of
names/people, **clàr an luchd-taghaidh** the
register of electors, **clàr-gnothaich** an agenda,
clàr-ama a timetable, **clàr-oideachais** a
curriculum, (*IT*) **clàr-ruith** a flow chart, *cf less
trad* **liosta**; 4 a map (*also* **clàr-dùthcha**),
clàr den Eilean Sgitheanach a map of
Skye, *cf* **mapa**; 5 a (gramophone) record, a
recording, **inneal-chlàr** a record-player; 6
misc uses, (*med*) **clàr sgiorrte** a slipped disc,
(*IT*) a disc, **meanbh-chlàr** a compact disc,
(*IT*) **clàr cruaidh/sùbailte** a hard/floppy
disc, (*IT*) **clàr-inneal** *m* a disc drive, (*IT*)
clàr-iùil a menu, (*oil industry*) **clàr tollaidh/
ola** a drilling/an oil platform, **clàr seòlaidh**

a signpost, a direction board, **clàr-iarrtais** an application form

clàrachadh, *gen* **clàrachaidh** *nm* (*the act of*) recording, registering (*see* **clàraich** *v*)

clàraich *vti, pres part* **a' clàrachadh**, **1** (*on paper, electronically etc*) register, record; **2** (*at college etc*) register, enrol

clàrc, *gen & pl* **clàirc** *nm* a clerk, *esp* (*crofting*) **clàrc a' bhaile** the township/grazings clerk, *cf* more *trad* **clèireach 2**

clàr-fhiacail, clàr-fhiacail, clàr-fhiaclan *nf* (*tooth*) an incisor

clàrsach, clàrsaich, clàrsaichean *nf* a harp, *esp* a Celtic harp, a clarsach, (*poetry collection*) **Creachadh na Clàrsaich** (Ruaraidh MacThòmais) Plundering the Harp, *cf less usu* **cruit 1**

clàrsair, clàrsair, clàrsairean *nm* a harper, *cf less usu* **cruitear¹**

clas, clas, clasaichean *nm* (*school etc*) a class, **cò an clas sa bheil thu?** which class are you in? **tha clas agam an-dràsta** I have a class just now

clasaigeach *adj* classical, **ceòl clasaigeach** classical music, **eachdraidh chlasaigeach** classical history

cleachd *vti, pres part* **a' cleachdadh**, **1** (*vt*) use, **cha chleachd mi salann sa chidsin** I don't use salt in the kitchen, *cf less usu* **gnàthaich 1**; **2** (*vt*) accustom, get used to, **cleachd thu fhèin ris an fhuachd!** accustom yourself/get used to the cold!, *cf less usu* **gnàthaich 2**; **3** (*vi*) *in the past tense* used to, was/were accustomed to, **chleachd mi a bhith droch-nàdarach** I used to be bad-tempered, *in comp expr* **is/agus a chleachd** as it (*etc*) used to, **chan eil iad cho fàilteach 's a chleachd iad a bhith** they're not so/as welcoming as they used to be, **cha tèid sinn ann cho tric agus a chleachd sinn** we won't go as often as we used to, *cf* **àbhaist 2**

cleachdadh, cleachdaidh, cleachdaidhean *nm* **1** (*the act of*) using etc (*see senses of* **cleachd** *v*); **2** a custom, a habit, a practice, **bha na chleachdadh agam a bhith a' coiseachd a h-uile là** it was a habit of mine to walk every day; **3** (*musical instrument etc*) practice, (*prov*) **is e an cleachdadh a nì teòma** practice makes perfect; **4** (*IT*) *esp in pl*, **cleachdaidhean** applications

cleachdte *adj* used, accustomed (**ri** to), **dh'fhàs i cleachdte ris aig a' cheann thall** she got/grew used to it/him in the end, **chan eil mi cleachdte ris a' bhiadh a tha seo** I'm not used to this food

cleamhnas, *gen* **cleamhnais** *nm* **1** relationship by marriage, *cf* **càirdeas pòsaidh** (*see* **càirdeas 1**); **2** sex, sexual relations, intercourse, *cf* **feis(e)**

cleas, cleasa, cleasan *nm* **1** (*trad*) a feat, an exploit, **Cù Chulainn nan cleas** Cuchulainn of the exploits, *cf* **euchd 1**; **2** (*now usu*) a trick, a joke, a stunt, **rinn iad cleas orm** they played a trick/a joke on me, *cf* **car** *n* **4**; **3** a conjurer's trick; **4** (*children etc*) play, playing, *cf more usu* **cluich** *n* **1**

cleasachd *nf invar*, **1** (*usu of children*) play, (*the action of*) playing, *cf more usu* **cluich** *n*; **2** conjuring; **3** juggling

cleasaich *vi, pres part* **a' cleasachd**, (*of children*) play, *cf more usu* **cluich** *v*

cleasaiche, cleasaiche, cleasaichean *nm* **1** (*film, theatre*) an actor, a player, *cf less trad* **actair**; **2** a comedian, a comic, a clown; **3** a conjurer; **4** a juggler

cleas-chluich, cleas-chluiche, cleas-chluichean *nf* a comic film or play, a comedy

clèir, *gen* **clèire** *nf* **1** (*coll*) clergy; **2** (*Presbyterian churches*) a Presbytery

clèireach *adj* presbyterian, **an Eaglais Chlèireach** the Presbyterian Church, **an Eaglais Shaor Chlèireach** the Free Presbyterian Church

clèireach, *gen & pl* **clèirich** *nm* **1** (*trad*) a clergyman, *cf* **ministear 1, pears-eaglais, sagart**; **2** a clerk, *cf less trad* **clàrc**; **3** a Presbyterian

clèireachail *adj* clerical, **luchd-obrach clèireachail** clerical staff

cleith *n & pres part, see* **ceil** *v*, **ceileadh** *n*

cleoc *see* **gleoc**

cleòc, cleòca, cleòcan *nm* a cloak

clì *adj* left, **mo chas chlì** my left foot, **air a làimh chlì** on his/her left, *cf* **ceàrr 2**

CLI *nm, the acronym of* **Comann an Luchd-Ionnsachaidh**, the Gaelic Learners' Association

cliabh, *gen & pl* **clèibh** *nm* **1** (*trad*) a pannier (*for a horse or pony*); **2** (*trad*) a creel (*for carrying peats etc*); **3** a creel (*to set for crabs etc*), **cliabh ghiomach** a lobster creel, a lobsterpot; **4** (*human*) chest, a thorax, *cf* **broilleach 2**; **5** (*mus notation*) a stave

cliamhainn, cleamhna, cleamhnan *nm* a son-in-law, **bana-chliamhainn** *f* a daughter-in law

cliath, clèithe, cliathan *nf* **1** a grating, a grid, **cliath-uinneig** a lattice, window bars, **cliath-theine** a fire grate, **cliath cruidh** a cattle grid, (*maps*) **ceàrnag clèithe** a grid square; **2** (*agric*) a harrow

cliath *vti, pres part* **a' cliathadh**, (*agric*) harrow

cliatha(i)ch, cliathaich, cliathaichean *nf* a side, **tha pian agam nam chliathaich** I've a pain in my side, **dhìrich sinn cliathach na beinne** we climbed the side of the mountain, *cf more usu* **taobh 1**

cliathan, cliathain, cliathanan *nm* (*anat*) a sternum, a breastbone

clìomaid, clìomaide, clìomaidean *nf* climate, a climate

clis *adj* nimble, agile, swift; *also* sudden, **Na Fir Chlis** Aurora Borealis, the Northern Lights, *also the name of a sadly defunct Gaelic theatre company*, *cf* **lùthmhor 1, deas, ealamh**

cliseachd *nf invar* nimbleness, quickness, agility, *cf* **lùth 2**

clisg, *pres part* **a' clisgeadh**, start, jump (*through fear or surprise*), **chlisg e** he jumped/started

clisgeach *adj* **1** jumpy, nervy, nervous, on edge; **2** timid; *cf* **sgeunach**

clisgeadh, clisgidh, clisgidhean *nm* **1** (*the act of*) starting, jumping etc (*see senses of* **clisg** *v*); **2** a start, a jump, a fright, a shock, **chuir thu clisgeadh orm!** you gave me a start/a fright, you startled me/made me jump

clisgear, clisgeir, clisgearan *nm* (*gram*) an exclamation, an interjection

clisg-phuing, clisg-phuinge, clisg-phuingean *nf* (*typog*) an exclamation mark

cliù *nm invar* **1** fame, reputation, a reputation, renown, glory, (*prov*) **is buaine cliù na saoghal** reputation (*ie* honour) lasts longer than life, **choisinn e cliù ann an saoghal na poilitigs** he won fame/ made a reputation in the world of politics, **choisinn an rèiseamaid cliù sa bhlàr** the regiment won glory in the battle (*cf* **glòir 2**); **2** praise, (*song*) **fàilte, fàilte, mùirn is cliù dhut!** welcome, welcome, love and praise to you!, *cf* **luaidh** *n* **2**, **moladh**

cliùiteach *adj* famous, celebrated, renowned, *cf* **ainmeil, iomraiteach**

clò¹, *gen* **clò(tha)**, *pl* **clòitean** & **clòithean** *nm* **1** cloth, woven material, *cf* **aodach 1**; **2** woollen cloth, tweed, **An Clò Mòr** *also* **Clò na Hearadh** & **An Clò Hearach** Harris Tweed

clò² & **clòdh**, *gen* **clòdha**, *pl* **clòdhan** *nm* **1** print, **cuir** *v* **leabhar** (*etc*) **an clò** to print/ bring out/publish a book (*etc*), **nochd a' bhàrdachd aige an clò an-uiridh** his poetry appeared in print last year (*cf* **clò-bhuail, foillsich 1**), **ùr on chlò** newly published, hot off the presses, **mearachd clò** a printing error, a misprint; **2** a printing press; **3** a publishing house, an imprint, **Clò Ostaig** the Ostaig Press

clòbha, clòbha, clòbhan *nf* a clove

clobha, clobha, clobhan *nm* tongs

clòbhar, *gen* **clòbhair** *nm* clover, *cf more trad* **seamrag 2**

clobhd, clobhda, clobhdan *nm* a cloth (*for cleaning etc*), (*Sc*) a clout, *cf* **brèid 3, clùd 2**

clobhsa, clobhsa, clobhsaichean *nm* (*in tenement etc*) a close

clò-bhuail *vt, pres part* **a' clò-bhualadh**, print, **air a chlò-bhualadh le** . . . printed by . . .

clò-bhuailte *adj* printed, **clò-bhuailte le A Learmonth 's a Mhac, Sruighlea** printed by A Learmonth & Son, Stirling

clò-bhualadair, clò-bhualadair, clò-bhualadairean *nm* **1** a printer; **2** a printing firm

clò-bhualadh, clò-bhualaidh, clò-bhualaidhean *nm* **1** (*the act of*) printing; **2** publication, an imprint, **Clò-bhualaidhean Gairm** Gairm Publications

cloc *see* **gleoc**

clò-chadal, *gen* **clò-chadail** *nm* dozing, a doze, **chaidh mi nam chlò-chadal** *or* **thàinig clò-chadal orm** I dozed off/dropped off

clochar, clochair, clocharan *nm* a convent

clòdh *see* **clò²**

cloga(i)d, clogaide, clogaidean *nmf* a helmet, **clogad-dìona** a crash helmet, a hard hat

clòimh, *gen* **clòimhe** *nf* wool, **aodach clòimhe** woollen clothing, *cf* **olann**

clòimhteachan, *gen* & *pl* **clòimhteachain** *nm* an eiderdown

closach, closaich, closaichean *nf* **1** a dead body (*usu not human*), *cf* **corp 2**; **2** a carcase (*ie to be processed by butcher*)

clòsaid, clòsaide, clòsaidean *nf* a closet

clò-sgrìobh *vti, pres part* **a' clò-sgrìobhadh**, type, use a typewriter

clò-sgrìobhadair, clò-sgrìobhadair, clò-sgrìobhadairean *nm* a typewriter

clò-sgrìobhadh, clò-sgrìobhaidh, clò-sgrìobhaidhean *nm* **1** (*the act of*) typing; **2** typescript, a typescript

clò-sgrìobhaiche, clò-sgrìobhaiche, clò-sgrìobhaichean *nm* a typist

clua(i)n, *gen* **cluaine**, *pl* **cluainean** & **cluaintean** *nf* a meadow, a pasture, *cf* **dail 1, faiche, ionaltradh 2**

cluaineas, *gen* **cluaineis** *nm* retirement, **thàinig e air ais bho chluaineas** he came out of retirement, **peinnsean cluaineis** *m* a retirement pension

cluaran, cluarain, cluaranan *nm* a thistle, *cf* **fòghnan**

cluas, cluaise, cluasan *nf* **1** an ear, (*song*) **toirm mum chluais** a din about my ear,

cluas-fhail f an ear-ring, **cèir-cluaise** f ear-wax, **grèim-cluaise** m earache, **tolladh-chluasan** m ear-piercing; **2** a handle of a vessel or container, (Sc) a lug

cluasag, cluasaig, cluasagan nf a pillow, cf **babhstair**

club, club, clubaichean nm a club (ie association), cf **comann 1**

clùd, clùid, clùdan nm **1** a rag, cf **luideag**; **2** a cloth, (Sc) a clout, cf **brèid 3, clobhd**

cluich & cluiche, gen **cluiche**, pl **cluichean & cluicheannan** nm **1** play, (the activity of) playing, cf less usu **cleas 4**; **2** a game, **cluich-bùird** a board game, cf less trad **geama 1**

cluich vti, pres part **a' cluich(e)**, **1** (games, music) play, **cha bhi mi a' cluich sa mhaidse an-diugh** I won't be playing in the match today, **cluich ball-coise/rugbaidh** play football/rugby, **bidh sinn a' cluich (an aghaidh) Rangers** we'll be playing (against) Rangers, **tha a' chlann a' cluich sa ghàrradh** the children are playing in the garden (cf less usu **cleasaich**), **cò tha a' cluich a' bhogsa/air a' bhogsa?** who's playing/playing on the accordeon?; **2** (in theatre, films) act, play, **cluich Hamlet air an àrd-ùrlar** play Hamlet on the stage

cluicheadair, cluicheadair, cluicheadairean nm **1** a player (of a game, instrument); **2** (on stage, screen) a player, an actor, cf more usu **actair**

cluinn, vt irreg (see tables p 496), pres part **a' cluinntinn**, hear, **chuala mi gun robh thu tinn** I heard you were ill, **cha chluinn e bìd/guth** he can't hear a thing/a sound, he's as deaf as a post, **'s math a bhith a' cluinntinn bhuat!** it's good to be hearing from you!

cluinneadh, cluinneam, cluinneamaid, cluinnibh pts of irreg v **cluinn** (see tables p 496)

cluinntinn nf invar (the act of) hearing

cnag, cnaig, cnagan nf **1** a bang, a knock; **2** a peg, **cnag-aodaich** a clothes peg; **3** a knob, cf **cnap 2**; **4** a plug (for sink, container etc); **5** in expr **cnag na cùise**, the nub/crux of the matter, the fundamental issue, the crucial question, **am bi clann bheaga a' togail na Gàidhlig aig an taigh? 's e sin cnag na cùise** are small children picking up Gaelic at home? that's the crucial question

cnag vti, pres part **a' cnagadh**, **1** (vi) crunch (ie make a crunching noise), **bha am mol a' cnagadh fo chasan** the shingle was crunching beneath his feet; **2** (vti) bang, knock

CNAG n, the acronym of **Comunn na Gàidhlig**, the Gaelic Association, a body set up to promote Gaelic language and culture

cnag-dealain, cnaig-dealain, cnagan-dealain nf an electric plug, a power plug, cf **bun-dealain** (see **bun 3**)

cnàimh, gen **cnàmha**, pl **cnàmhan & cnàimhean** nm, also **cnàmh, cnàimh, cnàmhan** nm, bone, a bone, **cnà(i)mh an droma** the backbone, the spine, **cnà(i)mh an uga** the collarbone

cnàimhneach, gen & pl **cnàimhnich** nm a skeleton

cnàimhseag, cnàimhseig, cnàimhseagan nf **1** a pimple, cf **guirean, plucan**; **2 cnàimhseagan** pl acne

cnàmh[1] nm see **cnàimh**

cnàmh[2], gen **cnàimh** nm potato blight, cf **gaiseadh**

cnàmh vt, pres part **a' cnàmhadh & a' cnàmh**, **1** chew, masticate; **2** digest; **3** in expr **a' cnàmh na cìre**, (of animals) chewing the cud, (fam, of humans) talking things over, chewing the fat, talking of this and that; cf **cnuas**

cnàmhach adj bony

cnàmhadh, gen **cnàmhaidh** nm (the act of) chewing etc (see senses of **cnàmh** v)

cnàmh-loisg see **loisg 1**

cnap, cnaip, cnapan nm **1** a block or a lump or a chunk of anything, cf **ceap 1, geinn 1**; **2** a knob, a boss, cf **cnag 3**; **3** a small (lumpy) hill, cf **meall n 2**

cnapach adj lumpy, knobby, nobbly

cnap-starra(dh) nm (lit) an obstruction, a barrier, an obstacle (cf **bacadh 2**), (fig) a stumbling block

cnatan, gen & pl **cnatain** nm a cold, (Sc) the cold, used with the art, **tha an cnatan a' tighinn orm** I'm getting a/the cold, cf **fuachd 2**

cnead, cneada, cneadan nm a groan (of pain or grief), **rinn i cnead** or **leig i cnead (aiste)** she groaned/let out a groan

cnèadachadh, gen **cnèadachaidh** nm (the act of) caressing etc (see senses of **cnèadaich** v)

cnèadaich & cniadaich vt, pres part **a' cnèadachadh**, caress, fondle, stroke affectionately or amorously, **bha e a' cnèadachadh a fuilt** he was stroking her hair

cneutag, cneutaig, cneutagan, nf a small ball (for ball games, esp shinty)

cniadaich see **cnèadaich**

cnò, gen **cnò & cnotha**, pl **cnothan** nf **1** (bot) a nut, **cnò Fhrangach & gall-chnò** a walnut, **cnò-challtainn** a hazelnut, **cnò-thalmhainn**

a peanut, **cnò-bhainne** & **cnò-còco** a coconut;
2 (*engin etc*) a nut, **cnò is crann** a nut and (a)
bolt

cnoc, *gen & pl* **cnuic** *nm* a hill, *usu small to
medium-sized*, **mullach nan cnoc** the top of
the hills, *in placenames usu rendered as* Knock,
An Cnoc Liath Knocklea, the grey hill, *cf*
**beinn 2, mòinteach, monadh, sgùrr, tom,
tulach**

cnocach *adj* hilly, **sgìre chnocach** a hilly area/
district, *cf* **monadail**

cnocan, *gen & pl* **cnocain** (*dimin of* **cnoc**) *nm* a
small hill, a hillock, *cf* **tulach**

cnòthach *adj* (*of taste*) nutty

cnuasaich (*also found as* **cnuas**) *vti, pres part*
a' cnuasa(cha)dh, 1 chew (*food*); **2** (*vi*) (*ideas,
topics etc*) chew over, reflect, ruminate, think,
contemplate, ponder, (**air** on, about, upon)
**bha e a' cnuasachadh air na thubhairt i
ris** he was turning over in his mind/thinking
over what she (had) said to him; *cf* **cnàmh** *v*,
meòraich 1

cnuas *vti see* **cnuasaich**

cnuimh, cnuimhe, cnuimhean *nf* **1** a maggot,
a grub; **2** a worm, **cnuimh-thalmhainn** an
earthworm, *cf* **boiteag**

cò *inter pron, Note: in some constrs the v* **is** *can
be understood as implicitly following* **cò**, *eg* **cò
esan?** who's he?; *Note: in senses* **4, 5** & **6** *below
the accent is usu omitted;* **1** (*of persons only*)
who, *in direct questions* **cò a rinn e?** who did
it? *in indirect questions* **chan eil fhios a'm
cò a th' ann** I don't know who it is, **is coma
leam cò ris a bha i a' bruidhinn** I don't care
who she was talking to; **2** (*of persons & things*)
which, what, **cò na seinneadairean as fheàrr
leat?** which are the singers you like best? **cò na
leabhraichean a tha thu airson fhaighinn
air iasad?** which/what books would you like/do
you want to borrow? **cha robh mi cinnteach
cò aca** (*also* **cò dhiubh**) **a phòsainn** I wasn't
sure which of them I would marry, (*prov*) **chan
eil fios cò as glice – fear a chaomhnas no
fear a chaitheas** there's no knowing which is
wiser – a man who saves or a man who spends;
3 *in expr* **cò às . . . ?** where . . . from?, **cò
às a tha thu?**, where are you from? **cò às a
nochd esan?** where did he (*emph*) appear/
spring from?; **4** *in exprs* **co aca** & **co-dhiù** *conj*
whether, **tha thu ciontach co-dhiù a ghoid
thu e no nach do ghoid** you're guilty whether
you stole it or not; **5** *in expr* **co-dhiù** anyway,
in any case, at least, **fuirich ma thogras tu,
tha mise a' falbh co-dhiù!** stay if you like/
want, I'm leaving anyway/in any case!, **bha dà**

mhìle ann co-dhiù there were two thousand
there at least/anyway, **tha mi coma co-dhiù** I
don't mind/care either way, I'm indifferent; **6 co
mheud** *see* **cia mheud**

co- *a prefix often corres to Eng* co-, con-, fellow-,
also found in older spellings as **comh-** &
coimh(-); **co-** *does not usu change the basic
sense of the word it precedes, but it stresses
mutuality, reciprocity, co-operation etc; see
examples below*

co-aimsireil *adj* **1** contemporary, living at the
same time; **2** belonging to the present time

co-alta (*also* **co-dhalta**), *gen* **co-alta**, *pl* **co-
altan** *nmf* a foster brother or sister

co-aois & **comhaois**, *gen* **co-aois**, *pl* **co-
aoisean** *nm* a person of roughly the same age
as another, a contemporary, **bha Iain Mac a'
Ghobhainn is Domhnall MacAmhlaigh
nan co-aoisean** Iain Crichton Smith and
Donald MacAulay were contemporaries

co-aoiseach *adj* having roughly the same age as
another

co-aonaich *vi, pres part* **co-aonachadh**
(*companies etc*) amalgate

co-aonar, co-aonair, co-aonaran *nm* (*maths*)
an equation

co-aontachadh, *gen* **co-aontachaidh** *nm* **1**
(*the act of*) consenting etc (*see senses of* **co-
aontaich** *v*); **2** agreement, an agreement,
accord, an accord

co-aontaich *vti, pres part* **co-aontachadh, 1**
vi be in agreement, consent, come together in
agreement; **2** *vt* consent to, agree to

cobhair, *gen* **cobhrach** & **coibhre** *nf* **1**
help, aid, relief, **bàta-coibhre** a life boat (*cf*
bàta-teasairginn), **an dèan thu cobhair
orm?** will you help me? *cf more general*
cuideachadh 2; **2** *as excl* **cobhair orm!** help!

cobhan, cobhain, cobhanan (*also* **cobhan-
airgid**) *nm* a till, a cash register, *cf* **àite-
paighidh**

cobhar, *gen* **cobhair** *nm* foam, froth, *cf* **cop**

cobhartach, *gen* **cobhartaich** *nmf* **1** booty,
plunder *cf* **creach** *nf* **1**; **2** prey

**co-bhualadh, co-bhualaidh, co-
bhualaidhean** *nm* **1** (*the act of*) colliding; **2**
collision, a collision, an impact

co-bhuail *vi, pres part* **a' co-bhualadh**, collide

còc *nm invar* (*fuel, also the drink*) coke

còcaire, còcaire, còcairean *nm* a cook, a chef,
ban-chòcaire *f* a (female) cook *or* chef

còcaireachd *nf invar* cooking, cookery

cochall, *gen & pl* **cochaill** *nm* **1** (*of a seed
etc*) a husk, (*peas, beans*) a pod, *cf* **plaosg**; **2**
(*headgear*) a hood

co-cheangail *vt, pres part* **a' co-cheangal**, link, connect, tie together

co-cheangailte *adj* linked together, connected, **tha blàthachadh na cruinne is a' chlìomaid co-cheangailte ri chèile** global warming and the climate are linked to one another

co-cheangal, co-cheangail, co-cheanglaichean *nm* **1** (*the act of*) linking etc; **2** linkage, a link, connection, a connection, **co-cheangal smaointean** association of ideas

co-chomann, *gen & pl* **co-chomainn** *nm* **1** a community, a commune; **2** (*business*) a co-operative, **co-chomann chroitearan** a crofters' co-operative, **Co-chomann Stafainn** Staffin Co-operative, *cf* **co- obrachadh 3**

co-chòmhragaiche, co-chòmhragaiche, co-chòmhragaichean *nm* an adversary, an opponent (*in argument, debate etc*)

co-chòrd, *vi, pres part* **a' co-chòrdadh**, agree mutually, come to a mutual agreement

co-chòrdadh, co-chòrdaidh, co-chòrdaidhean *nm* **1** (*the act of*) agreeing etc (*see senses of* **cò-chòrd** *v*); **2** concord, agreement, an agreement, an accord, a treaty, an alliance

co-chothrom, *gen* **co-chothruim** *nm* balance, equilibrium

co-chruinnich *vti, pres part* **a' co-chruinneachadh**, gather together, assemble, collect (*people & things*)

co-chruinneachadh, co-chruinneachaidh, co-chruinneachaidhean *nm* **1** (*the act of*) gathering etc (*see senses of* **co-chruinnich** *v*); **2** assembly, an assembly, a gathering, a convention, **Co-chruinneachadh Ùghdarrasan Ionadail na h-Alba** the Convention of Scottish Local Authorities; **3** (*Lit etc*) a collection, a compilation, an anthology, **co-chruinneachadh de sgeulachdan goirid** a collection of short stories

còco *nm invar* cocoa

còd, còd, còdaichean *nm invar* (*cypher etc*) code, a code, (*IT*) **còd dà-fhillte** binary code, (*IT*) **còd inneil** machine code

co-dhèanta *adj* composed, made up, assembled, put together

co-dhiù *adv & conj see* **cò 4** & **5**

co-dhlùthaich *vti, pres part* **a' co-dhlùthachadh**, condense

co-dhùin *vti, pres part* **a' co-dhùnadh**, **1** (*process, meeting etc*) conclude, bring to a conclusion, end; **2** come to a decision, come to a conclusion, decide

co-dhùnadh, co-dhùnaidh, co-dhùnaidhean *nm* **1** (*the act of*) concluding, ending etc (*see senses of* **co-dhùin** *v*); **2** a conclusion, an end, an ending, (*song*) **nì mi nis co-dhùnadh is bheir mi an dàn gu crìch** now I will conclude and bring the song to an end; **3** a decision, a conclusion, **cha tàinig na comhairlichean gu co-dhùnadh** the councillors didn't reach a decision/come to a conclusion

co-èigneachadh, *gen* **co-èigneachaidh** *nm* **1** (*the act of*) forcing, compelling; **2** compulsion

co-èignich *vt, pres part* **a' co-èigneachadh**, force, compel, **cho-èignich a chàirdean e gus sin a dhèanamh** his friends forced/compelled him to do that, *cf* **thoir 4**

cofaidh, cofaidh, cofaidhean *nmf* coffee, a coffee, **a bheil thu ag iarraidh cofaidh?** do you want/would you like a coffee?

co-fharpais (*also* **farpais**), *gen* **co-fharpaise**, *pl* **co-fharpaisean** *nf* a competition, **co-fharpaisean a' Mhòid** the Mod competitions

co-fhlaitheachd *nf invar* **1** a republic; **2** republicanism; **3** *in expr* **a' Cho-Fhlaitheachd Bhreatannach** the British Commonwealth (*cf next*)

co-fhlaitheas, co-fhlaitheis, co-fhlaitheasan *nm* a confederation (*of countries*), **An Co-fhlaitheas** the (British) Commonwealth

co-fhoghar, co-fhoghair, co-fhoghairean *nm* a consonant, *cf* **connrag, consan**

co-fhoghlam, *gen* **co-fhoghlaim** *nm* co-education

co-fhreagair *vti, pres part* **a' co-fhreagairt**, match, correspond, cause to match or correspond (**do** to)

co-fhreagairt, co-fhreagairte, co-fhreagairtean *nf* **1** (*the act of*) matching etc (*see senses of* **co-fhreagair** *v*); **2** (*general, incl letter-writing*) correspondence

co-fhulangach *adj* sympathetic, compassionate

co-fhulangas, *gen* **co-fhulangais** *nm* sympathy, fellow-feeling

cofhurtachadh, *gen* **cofhurtachaidh** *nm* (*the act of*) comforting, consoling

cofhurtachd *nf invar* **1** consolation, comfort (*spiritual, emotional*); **2** (*phys*) comfort

cofhurtaich *vt, pres part* **a' cofhurtachadh**, comfort, console, *cf* **faothaich, furtaich**

cofhurtail *adj* comfortable, **a bheil thu cofhurtail? a bheil a' chathair sin cofhurtail gu leòr?** are you comfortable? is that chair comfortable enough?, *cf* **seasgair 1**

cogadh, cogaidh, cogaidhean *nm* war, warfare, a war, **An Cogadh Mòr** The Great War, **A' Chiad Chogadh, An Dàrna Cogadh** the

First (World) War, the Second (World) War,
cuimhneachan-cogaidh *m* a war-memorial,
rinn iad cogadh they made/waged war
cogais, cogaise, cogaisean *nf* conscience,
a conscience, **bha mo chogais gam
shàrachadh fad na h-oidhche** my conscience
was tormenting me all night
cogaiseach *adj* conscientious, trustworthy, *cf*
dìcheallach
co-ghin *vi, pres part* **a' co-ghineadh**, mate,
have sexual intercourse, copulate, *cf* **cuplaich,
muin 4**
co-ghineadh, *gen* **co-ghinidh** *nm* 1 (*the act
of*) mating etc (*see senses of* **co-ghin** *v*); 2
copulation, intercourse, *cf* **cuplachadh 2**
**co-ghnìomhair, co-ghnìomhair, co-
ghnìomhairean** *nm* (*gram*) an adverb
coibhneas, *gen* **coibhneis** *nm* kindness,
kindliness
coibhneil *adj* kind, kindly, (*song*) **chaith mi
'n oidhche cridheil coibhneil mar ri
maighdeannan na h-àirigh** I spent the night
in warm-hearted kindliness in the company of
the sheiling maidens, *cf* **bàidheil**
coidse, *gen* **coidse**, *pl* **coidseachan** *nf*
(*transport*) a coach
còig *n & num adj* the number five, five, **còig
mionaidean** five minutes **còig-deug** *n & adj*
fifteen, **còig mionaidean deug** fifteen minutes
còigeamh *adj* fifth, **air a' chòigeamh latha** on
the fifth day
còigeamh-deug *adj* fifteenth, **an còigeamh là
deug den Ògmhios** the fifteenth of June
còignear *nm invar* (people numbering)
five, a fivesome, *takes gen pl*, **còignear
mhinistearan** five ministers
coigreach, *gen & pl* **coigrich** *nm* 1 a foreigner,
an alien, *cf* **eilthireach 1, Gall 1**; 2 a stranger,
cf **coimheach** *n* 2**, srainnsear 1**; 3 an
incomer, *cf* **seatlair, srainnsear 2**
coileach, *gen & pl* **coilich** *nm* a cock (*game
bird or male domestic fowl*), **coileach-dubh** a
blackcock, a male black grouse, **coileach-coille**
a woodcock, **coileach-gaoithe** a weathercock
coilean *pres part* **a' coileanadh** (*also found as*
coilion & *earlier* **coimhlion**) *vt,* accomplish,
achieve, complete, *cf* **thoir gu buil** (*see* **buil 2**),
crìochnaich
coileanadh, *gen* **coileanaidh** *nm* (*the act of*)
accomplishing etc (*see senses of* **coilean** *v*)
coileanta *adj* 1 accomplished, achieved, finished,
completed; 2 perfect (*not usu in moral sense, cf*
foirfe), (*gram*) **an tràth coileanta** the perfect
tense
coileapach *nmf, see* **coimhleapach**

coilear, coileir, coilearan *nm* a collar
coilion *vt, see* **coilean**
coill *nf invar* 1 guilt, sin; 2 *in expr* **bha e fon
choill** he was outlawed/an outlaw
coille, coille, coilltean *nf* a wood, a forest,
(*poem*) **Coilltean Ratharsair** (Somhairle
MacGill-Eain) The Woods of Raasay, **coille-
uisge** a rainforest
coilleag, coilleig, coilleagan *nf* a cockle, *cf*
srùban
coillear, coilleir, coillearan *nm* a woodcutter
coillteach *adj* (*of landscape etc*) wooded
coillteachadh, *gen* **coillteachaidh** *nm*
afforestation
coilltear, coillteir, coilltearan *nm* a forester,
cf **forsair**
coilltearachd *nf invar* forestry
coimeas, *gen* **coimeis** *nm* 1 (*the act
of*) comparing, likening; 2 comparison,
resemblance, **dèan** *v* **coimeas eadar dà rud**
compare two things; 3 *esp in expr* **an coimeas
ri** compared to, in comparison to, **is tana
bainne an coimeas ri uachdar** milk is thin in
comparison to/compared to cream, *cf* **seach 2,
taca 2**; 4 a match, the like(s) of, an equal, (*trad*)
chan fhaca mi a choimeas a-riamh I never
saw the like of him/it, I never saw his/its equal,
cf **leithid, samhail**
coimeas *vt, pres part* **a' coimeas**, compare,
liken, *cf* **dèan coimeas eadar** (*see* **coimeas**
n 2)
coimeasach *adj* 1 comparable; 2 (*gram*)
comparative, **buadhair coimeasach** an
adjective of comparison, a comparative adjective
coimeasgaich *see* **co-mheasgaich**
coimheach *adj* 1 strange, foreign, unfamiliar,
(*prov*) **a h-uile cù air a' chù choimheach** all
dogs against/down on the strange dog, *in expr*
aghaidh-choimheach a mask
coimheach, *gen & pl* **coimhich** *nm* 1 a
foreigner; 2 a stranger; *cf more usu* **coigreach**
n, **eilthireach, Gall, srainnsear**
coimhead, *gen* **coimhid** *nm*, (*the act of*)
watching, looking etc (*see senses of* **coimhead**
v), **luchd-coimhid** *m* watchers, onlookers,
spectators, (*TV etc*) viewers
coimhead *vti, pres part* **a' coimhead**, 1 (*vt*)
watch, **coimhead film/TV** watch a film/TV,
coimheadaidh mi dol fodha na grèine
I will watch the sunset; 2 (*vi*) look (**air** at),
coimhead oirre look at her, **a' coimhead
air dealbhan** looking at pictures/photos, *cf*
seall 1; 3 (*vi*) *in exprs* **coimhead ri** expect,
tha sinn a' coimhead ri stoirmean we're
expecting storms (*cf* **dùil** 2, **sùil** 3), & (*calque*)

coimhead air adhart gu/ri look forward to, **bha iad a' coimhead air adhart chun/ris an fhogha(i)r** they were looking forward to the autumn; **4** (*vi*) (*calque*) look (*ie appear*), **tha sin a' coimhead math!** that looks/is looking good!

coimhearsnach, *gen & pl* **coimhearsnaich** *nm* a neighbour, *cf more usu* **nàbaidh**

coimhearsnachd *nf invar* a neighbourhood, a locality, a community, *cf* **nàbaidheachd**

coimheatailt, coimheatailte, coimheatailtean *nf* (*metals*) an alloy

coimhleapach *also* **coileapach**, *gen & pl* **coi(mh)leapaich** *nmf* a mistress, a live-in lover, a (sexual) partner, (*Sc*) a bidie-in; a bedfellow

coimhlion *vt*, *see* **coilean**

coimisean, coimisein, coimiseanan *nm* a commission, **Coimisean na Croitearachd** the Crofting Commission, **Coimisean na Roinn Eòrpa** the European Commission

coimpiutair, çoimpiutair, coimpiutairean *nm* a computer, *cf older, less usu* **rianadair 2**

coineanach, *gen & pl* **coineanaich** *nm* a rabbit, *cf less trad* **rabaid**

còinneach, *gen* **còinnich** *nf* (*bot*) moss

coinneachadh, *gen* **coinneachaidh** *nm* (*the act of*) meeting etc (*see senses of* **coinnich** *v*)

coinneal, coinnle, coinnlean *nf* a candle

coinneamh, coinneimh, coinneamhan *nf* **1** (*business, societies etc*) a meeting, **coinneamh bhliadhnail** an annual meeting; **2** *in expr* **mu choinneimh** opposite, facing, **bha mi nam shuidhe mu coinneimh** I was sitting opposite/facing her, *cf* **comhair 2**; **3** *in expr* **an coinneimh** towards, to meet, **rachamaid nan coinneimh** let's go to meet them, *cf* **ionnsaigh 3**

coinnich *vi*, *pres part* **a' coinneachadh**, **1** meet, congregate, come together, **bidh sinn a' coinneachadh ann an talla a' bhaile** we'll be meeting in the town/village hall, *cf more usu* **cruinnich 1**; **2** *in expr* **coinnich ri** meet (*by chance or by arrangement*), **'s ann sa phàirc a choinnich mi riutha** it was in the park that I met them, *cf* **tachair 3, 4 & 5**

coinnlear, coinnleir, coinnlearan *nm* a candlestick, a candle holder

co-ionann & co-ionnan, *adj* identical, equal, the same, equivalent **tha bùrn agus uisge co-ionann (ri chèile)** 'bùrn' and 'uisge' are the same (as each other), (*maths*) **tha x uiread x** (or **x air iomadachadh le x) co-ionann ri x²** x times x equals x², *cf* **ionann**

còir *adj* **1** (*trad*) *of people* decent, worthy, kindly, (*prov*) **duine còir an rathaid mhòir is bèist mhòr a-staigh** a fine fellow when he's out and about and a monster at home; **2** (*esp in corres*) dear, **A Dhòmhnaill chòir** Dear Donald, *more personal &/or affectionate than* **A Dhòmhnaill, a charaid** (*see* **caraid 3**)

còir, *gen* **còire & còrach**, *pl* **còraichean** *nf* **1** an obligation, a (*usu moral*) duty, *esp in expr* **bu chòir dhomh** (etc) I (etc) should, I (etc) ought, **bu chòir dhut sgrìobhadh thuice an-diugh** you should/ought to write to her today, **bu chòir dhomh a bhith a' falbh** I ought to be going/leaving, *in neg,* **cha bu chòir dhomh** (etc) I (etc) shouldn't, I (etc) ought not to, **cha bu chòir dhut goid/smocadh** you shouldn't steal/smoke, **chan eil e cho math agus bu chòir** it's not as good as it should be; **2** a right, **Còraichean (a' Chinne-) Daonna** Human Rights, **còir-slighe** a right of way, **chan eil còir aig a' Chomhairle an taigh-òsta agam a dhùnadh** the Council has no right to close my hotel; **3** *esp in expr* **tuilleadh 's a' chòir** more than enough, too much, far too much, **an robh biadh gu leòr agaibh aig a' phàrtaidh? bha tuilleadh 's a' chòir againn!** did you have plenty food at the party? we had more than enough!; **4** justice, right, (*trad*) **a' seasamh na còrach** maintaining/standing up for justice, *cf* **ceartas, ionracas 2**

coirb *vt*, *pres part* **a' coirbeadh**, corrupt, *cf* **claon v 3, truaill 3**

coirbte *adj* corrupt, corrupted

coirce *nm invar* oats, **aran-coirce** oatmeal bread, **min-choirce** *f* oatmeal

coire¹, coire, coireannan *nf* **1** a wrong, an offence, *cf* **eucoir 2**; **2** blame, **cuir v coire air duine eile** blame/lay blame on someone else (*cf* **coirich**), *cf* **cron 2 & less usu** **lochd 1**

coire², coire, coireachan *nm* **1** a kettle, **cuir air an coire!** put the kettle on!; **2** (*trad, esp as* **coire mòr**) a cauldron; **3** (*topog*) a corrie

coireach *adj* **1** guilty, at fault, (*trad*) **is e Seumas as** (*for a is*) **coireach** James is guilty/to blame/at fault, *cf* **ciontach** *adj*; **2** responsible, the reason or explanation for something (*often without implication of guilt or blame*), **tha an gàrradh a' coimhead uabhasach math am-bliadhna, cò as coireach ri sin?** the garden's looking great this year, who's responsible for that?, to whom do we owe that? **dè as coireach nach eil duine beò air an t-sràid an-diugh?** what's the explanation/reason for there being nobody on the street today?

coireach, *gen & pl* **coirich** *nm* a guilty person, an offender, *cf* **ciontach** *n*, **eucorach**

coireachadh, *gen* **coireachaidh** *nm* (*the act of*) blaming

coireachail *adj* apt to blame or rebuke, censorious, *cf* **cronachail**

coirich *vti, pres part* **a' coireachadh**, blame, *cf* **coire** *nf* 2

coiseachd *nf invar*, walking, the act of walking, **an dèidh pìos math coiseachd ràinig sinn am bàgh** after a good bit of walking we reached the bay

coisich *vi, pres part* **a' coiseachd**, walk, **choisich mi romham fad an latha** I walked on/onwards all day

coisiche, coisiche, coisichean *nm* 1 a walker; 2 a pedestrian

coisinn *vt, pres part* **a' cosnadh**, 1 earn, **tha mi a' cosnadh airgid mhòir a-nis** I'm earning big money now; 2 win, gain, **choisinn i cliù air an àrd-ùrlar** she won fame on the stage, **cha do choisinn mi duais aig a' Mhòd** I didn't win a prize at the Mod, *cf* **buannaich** 2

còisir & **còisir-chiùil**, *gen* **còisre(-ciùil)** & **còisire(-ciùil)**, *pl* **còisirean(-ciùil)** *nf* a choir, **Còisir Ghàidhlig Shruighlea** Stirling Gaelic Choir

coisrig *vt, pres part* **a' coisrigeadh**, 1 consecrate (*a church etc*) (**do** to); 2 devote (**do** to), **choisrig e a bheatha do dh'adhbhar na saorsa** he devoted his life to the cause of freedom; 3 (*book, music etc*) dedicate (**do** to)

coisrigeadh, coisrigidh, coisrigidhean *nm* 1 (*the act of*) consecrating etc (*see senses of* **coisrig** v); 2 consecration, a consecration, dedication, a dedication

coisrigte *adj* sacred, consecrated, **abhlan coisrigte** a consecrated (communion) wafer

coitcheann *adj* 1 communal, shared, public, common, **amar-snàimh coitcheann** public baths/swimming pool, (*formerly*) **Am Margadh Coitcheann** The Common Market, *cf* **poblach**; 2 general, **eòlas/foghlam coitcheann** general knowledge/education, **taghadh-pàrlamaid coitcheann** a general election, **stailc choitcheann** a general strike

coiteachadh, *gen* **coiteachaidh** *nm* (*the act of*) pressing etc (*see senses of* **coitich** v)

coitheanal & **coithional**, *gen* **coitheanail**, *pl* **coitheanalan** *nm* a (church) congregation

coitich *vt, pres part* **a' coiteachadh**, press, urge, encourage (*someone to do something*), *cf* **spreig, stuig**, & *more usu* **brosnaich**

col, *gen* **cola** *nm* incest

colach *adj* incestuous

co-labhairt *nf invar* a conference, a symposium, (*business etc*) a seminar, *cf* **còmhdhail**

co-là-breith, co-là-breith, co-làithean-breith *nm* a birthday **tha co-là-breith agam an-diugh** it's my birthday today, *cf* **ceann-bliadhna**

cola-deug *nm invar* a fortnight, **bidh sinn air ais an ceann cola-deug** we'll be back in/after a fortnight, **tha mi a' falbh airson cola-deug** I'm going away for a fortnight, **bidh mi air falbh fad cola-deug** I'll be away for a (whole) fortnight

colaiste (*also found as* **colaisde**), *gen* **colaiste**, *pl* **colaistean** *nmf* a college, **colaiste phrìobhaideach** a private college

colann, *gen* **colainn** & **colna**, *pl* **colainnean** *nf* a body, *cf more usu* **bodhaig, corp** 1

colbh, *gen & pl* **cuilbh** *nm* 1 (*architecture*) a column, a pillar; 2 (*in newspaper etc*) a column

co-leagh *vti, pres part* **co-leaghadh**, (*of substances*) fuse, amalgamate

Col(l)ach, *gen & pl* **Col(l)aich** *nm* someone from Coll (**Col(l)a**), *also as adj* **Col(l)ach** of, from or pertaining to Coll

collaidh *adj* 1 sensual, carnal, *cf* **feòlmhor** 2; 2 lewd, *cf more usu* **drabasta, draosta**

coltach *adj* 1 likely, probable, **tha e coltach gun tig i** it's likely that she'll come, it seems she'll come; 2 *in expr* **coltach ri** *prep* like, similar to, resembling, **chan eil i coltach ri a bràthair** she's not like her brother, **bha a ghuth coltach ri guth ròcais** his voice was like a rook's voice, **bha na togalaichean air fad coltach ri chèile** all the buildings were alike/resembled each other

coltachadh, *gen* **coltachaidh** *nm* (*the act of*) comparing, likening (**ri** to)

coltachd *nf invar* likelihood, possibility, probability

coltaich *vt, pres part* **a' coltachadh**, compare, liken (**ri** to)

coltas, *gen* **coltais** *nm* 1 appearance, look, **tha coltas saighdeir ort** you look like a soldier, **cha do chaidil mi idir a-raoir, tha a choltas (sin) ort!** I didn't sleep at all last night, you look like it!, *cf* **dreach** 1; 2 *esp in expr* **a rèir c(h)oltais** by the look of it, judging by appearances, seemingly, apparently, **chaill e obair, a rèir coltais** he lost his job, it seems, **a rèir choltais bidh stoirm ann a dh'aithghearr** it looks as if/by the look of it there'll be a storm soon

com, *gen & pl* **cuim** *nm* **1** a bosom (*male or female*), the chest area (*cf* **broilleach 1**, **uchd 1**), **thig nam chom!** come to my arms!, come and let me hug you! (*cf* **achlais 2**); **2** a trunk (*of a human body*), the chest cavity, **a chridhe a' bualadh na chom** his heart beating in his chest/bosom

coma *adj* indifferent, unconcerned, of no concern, **is coma sin** that doesn't matter, that's of no concern (*cf* **diofar 2**), **coma leat!** don't worry!, never mind!, **thig an saoghal gu crìch a-màireach! tha mise coma, is coma leam an tig no nach tig** the world ends tomorrow! I (*emph*) don't care/mind, I don't care if it ends or not, *also more emph* **coma co-dhiù** indifferent either way, **ge b' e cò a bhuannaich, tha mi coma co-dhiù** whoever won, I don't care either way

comain, comain, comainean *nf* **1** an obligation, a debt (*moral, not fin*), **fo chomain aig cuideigin** under an obligation to someone; **2** *esp in expr* **(fada) nad** (etc) **c(h)omain** (very much) obliged to you (etc), **chuidich sibh gu mòr sinn, tha sinn fada nur comain** you helped us greatly, we are very much obliged to you

comanachadh, comanachaidh, comanachaidhean *nm* **1** (*the act of*) taking (Holy) Communion, going to the Lord's Table; **2** (Holy) Communion, *cf* **òrdugh 4**; **3** the Communion season, *cf* **òrdugh 4**

comanaich *vi, pres part* **a' comanachadh**, take (Holy) Communion, go to the Lord's Table

comanaiche, comanaiche, comanaichean *nm* a communicant, someone taking (Holy) Communion/going to the Lord's Table

comann (*also found as* **comunn**), *gen & pl* **comainn** *nm* **1** an association, a society, a club, **Comann Gàidhlig Ghlaschu** The Gaelic Society of Glasgow, **comann togalaich** a building society, **chuir sinn air bonn comann do dheugairean** we set up/started a club for teenagers; **2** a commune, a community; **3** company, fellowship, society, **is toigh leam comann na h-òigridh** I like the company of young people, *cf* **conaltradh 2** & *more usu* **cuideachd** *n* **1**

comar, comair, comaran *nf* a confluence of rivers, burns, *esp in placenames, eg* **Comar nan Allt** Cumbernauld, the confluence of the burns

comas, comais, comasan *nm* ability, capacity, faculty, power, **comas bruidhne** power/faculty/capacity of speech, ability to speak, **comas inntinn** intellectual ability/powers,

rinn i na bha na comas she did what she could/what she was capable of, *also in expr* **thar mo chomais** beyond my ability/capacity/power, **na (h-)iarr sin orra, tha e thar an comasan** don't ask that of them, it's beyond their capabilities,

comasach *adj* able, capable (**air** of), **duine comasach** an able/a capable man, **chan eil mi comasach air mìorbhailean a dhèanamh** I'm not capable of performing miracles

comataidh, comataidh, comataidhean *nf* a committee

combaist, combaiste, combaistean *nf* a compass

co-measgaich *see* **co-mheasgaich**

comhachag, comhachaig, comhachagan *nf* an owl, *esp* a barn owl, *cf* **cailleach-oidhche**

comhair *nf invar* **1** a direction (*in which something, & esp someone, faces or moves*), *esp in exprs* **thuit** (etc) **e an comhair a chinn, an comhair a chùil, an comhair a thaoibh** he fell (etc) headlong/head first, backwards, sideways, (*of vehicle etc*) **an comhair a thoisich** front end first, forwards; **2** *in expr* **fa chomhair** *prep* opposite, in front of, before (*with the gen*), **stad e fa mo chomhair** he stopped opposite/in front of me, *cf* **mu choinneimh** (*see* **coinneamh 2**)

comhairle, comhairle, comhairlean *nf* **1** advice, a piece of advice, **thoir** *v* **comhairle air/do** advise, give advice to, **rinn ur comhairle feum mòr dhomh** your advice did me a great deal of good/was very useful to me, **fear-comhairle** *m* & **neach-comhairle** *m* an adviser (*cf* **comhairleach**), *also in expr* **ann an iomadh-chomhairle dè a dhèanainn** (etc) in a quandary/undecided (as to) what I would do (*etc*); **2** (*elected or appointed body*) a Council, **Comhairle nan Eilean Siar** The Western Isles Council, *esp a local authority* council **comhairle sgìre** a district council, **comhairle roinne** a regional council, **taigh-comhairle** a council house, *cf* **ùghdarras 2**

comhairleach, *gen & pl* **comhairlich** *nm* an adviser *cf* **fear-comhairle** & **neach-comhairle** (*see* **comhairle 1**)

comhairleachadh, *gen* **comhairleachaidh** *nm* (*the act of*) advising

comhairlich *vt, pres part* **a' comhairleachadh**, advise, *cf* **thoir comhairle air/do** (*see* **comhairle 1**)

comhairliche, comhairliche, comhairlichean *nm* a (local authority) councillor

comhaois, comhaoiseach see **co-aois, co-aoiseach**

comharrachadh, gen **comharrachaidh** nm 1 (the act of) marking etc (see senses of **comharraich** v); 2 (teacher etc) correction (of work), marking, cf **ceartachadh** 2

comharra(dh), comharraidh, comharraidhean nm 1 a mark, **fhuair Eilidh deagh chomharran san sgoil an-dè** Eilidh got good marks at school yesterday, **comharradh cluaise** an ear-mark (on livestock), **comharradh-stiùiridh** a landmark (for navigation, cf **iùl** 3); 2 a sign, a mark, a symbol, **is e deagh/droch chomharradh a tha sin!** that's a good/bad sign!, **comharradh urraim** a mark/sign of respect, **comharradh inbhe** a status symbol, **comharradh-ceiste** a question mark; 3 a mark (left by someone or something), cf **lorg** n 2, **làrach** 1; 4 (med) a symptom; 5 in expr (maps) **comharradh-clèithe** a grid reference

comharraich vt, pres part **a' comharrachadh**, 1 mark, put a mark on; 2 (teacher) mark, correct (work), cf **ceartaich**; 3 mark, observe (anniversaries etc) cf **cùm** vt 3, first example

comhart, comhairt, comhartan nm a bark (of dog)

comhartaich nf invar, barking (of dog), **dèan** vt **comhartaich** bark, cf **tabhannaich** v

còmhdach, còmhdaich, còmhdaichean nm a cover, a covering, **còmhdach leapa/leapach** a bed cover, **còmhdach ùrlair** a floor covering (cf **brat** 1)

còmhdaich vt, pres part **a' còmhdachadh**, cover

còmhdaichte adj covered

còmhdhail, còmhdhalach, còmhdhailean nf 1 transport (general & abstr), **Comataidh na Còmhdhalach** The Transport Committee, cf **giùlan** 2; 2 a congress, a conference, cf **co-labhairt**

co-mheadhanach adj concentric

co-m(h)easgachadh, gen **co-m(h)easgachaidh** nm (the act of) mixing etc (see senses of **co-mheasgaich** v); 2 a blend, a mixture

co-mheasgaich, also **co-measgaich** & **coimeasgaich**, vti, pres part **a' co-m(h)easgachadh**, mix, blend, intermix, mingle, intermingle, amalgamate, merge

co mheud see **cia mheud**

còmhla(dh) adv 1 together, **thig** v **còmhla** come together, congregate, unite, assemble, **thàinig an dà thaobh còmhla airson co-labhairt** the two sides came together for a conference, cf **co-chruinnich, tionail** 1; 2 **còmhla ri** prep with, along with, together with, **is toigh leam a bhith còmhla riut** I like being with you, **tha iad uile a' fuireach còmhla ri chèile** they're all living together, cf **cuide ri, le** 1, **mar** 5

còmhla(dh), gen **còmhla** & **còmhlaidh**, pl **còmhlan, còmhlaidhean** & **còmhlaichean** nmf 1 (trad) a door, ie the leaf of a door (**doras**, now used for door and doorway, earlier designated the door opening/doorway), (song) **biodh e muigh air cùl na còmhla** let him be outside, behind the door, cf **doras** 1 & 2; 2 a shutter

còmhlan, gen & pl **còmhlain** nm a band, a group (of people), **còmhlan actairean** a troupe of actors, **còmhlan-ciùil** (mus) a band, a group, **còmhlan shaighdearan** a company of soldiers, cf **buidheann** 1, **cuideachd** n 3

còmhnaich vi, pres part **a' còmhnaidh**, live, dwell, inhabit, reside, (Sc) stay, **a' còmhnaidh anns an sgìre** dwelling/living/staying in the district, cf **fuirich** 2

còmhnaidh, còmhnaidhe, còmhnaidhean nf 1 (the act of) dwelling etc (see senses of **còmhnaich** v), **cead còmhnaidh** a residence permit; 2 esp in compounds **àite-còmhnaidh** a dwelling place, an abode, **gun àite-còmhnaidh seasmhach** of no fixed abode, **taigh-còmhnaidh** a dwelling house; 3 in expr **an-còmhnaidh** adv always, **tha i an sàs annam an-còmhnaidh airson an gàrradh a sgioblachadh** she's always on at me to tidy the garden, cf **daonnan**

còmhnard adj (of ground, surface etc) 1 flat, level, even, smooth, cf **rèidh** 1; 2 horizontal

còmhnard, còmhnaird, còmhnardan nm 1 a plain, a piece of level ground, cf **blàr** 1; 2 (railway etc) a platform; 3 (abstr) a level, esp in expr **còmhnard na mara** sea level

còmhradh, còmhraidh, còmhraidhean nm 1 conversation, talk, chat, a conversation, a talk, a chat, **dèan** v **còmhradh** talk, converse, chat, **rinn sinn còmhradh beag an-dè** we had a wee chat yesterday, **bonn còmhraidh** a bit of conversation, a chat, **cuspair a' chòmhraidh againn** the subject of our conversation, cf less usu **agallamh** 1, **conaltradh** 1; 2 occas used as pres part, eg **a' còmhradh a-null 's a-nall** talking/chatting of this and that

còmhrag, còmhraig, còmhragan nf combat, conflict, fighting, a combat, a conflict, a fight, **còmhrag-dithis** a duel, cf more usu **sabaid** n

còmhraideach adj talkative, fond of talking, chatty, cf **bruidhneach**

còmhstri, còmhstri, còmhstrithean *nf* **1** strife, conflict; **2** competition, rivalry

com-pàirt, com-pàirte, com-pàirtean *nf* (*mus*) accompaniment, an accompaniment

com-pàirteachadh, *gen* **com-pàirteachaidh** *nm* (*the act of*) communicating, accompanying etc (*see senses of* **com-pàirtich** *v*)

com-pàirtich *vti, pres part* **a' com-pàirteachadh, 1** communicate (*information etc*); **2** participate, take part; **3** (*mus*) accompany, *cf* **taic 3**

companach, *gen & pl* **companaich** *nm* **1** a companion, a comrade, a pal, *cf* **caraid 1**; **2** a colleague, an associate, *cf* **co-obraiche; 3** (*trad, affectionate*) a husband, **bha i ag ionndrain a companaich** she was missing her husband, *cf* **cèile 1, duine 4**

companaidh, companaidh, companaidhean *nmf* (*commerce etc*) a firm, a company, **na companaidhean mòra eadar-nàiseanta** the big international companies

companas, *gen* **companais** *nm* companionship

comraich, comraiche, comraichean *nf* sanctuary, a place of sanctuary, *cf* **tèarmann**

còn, còn, cònaichean *nm* (*geometry etc*) a cone

cònail *adj* coniferous

conair(e), conair(e), conairean *nf* (*relig*) a rosary (*the prayers & the string of beads*), *cf* **paidirean 1 & 2**

conaltrach *adj* (*of person*) social, sociable, *cf* more usu **cuideachdail**

conaltradh, *gen* **conaltraidh** *nm* **1** conversation, *cf* **agallamh 2** & more usu **còmhradh 1**; **2** company, *cf* **comann 3, cuideachd** *n* **1**; **3** sociability; **4** communication

conasg, *gen* **conaisg** *nm* (*bot*) gorse, (*Sc*) whins

con(a)stabal, con(a)stabail, conastabalan *nm* (*crofting*) a land/township constable

connadh, *gen* **connaidh** *nm coll* fuel

connadh-làmhaich, *gen* **connaidh-làmhaich** *nm coll* munitions, ammunition

connlach, *gen* **connlaich** *nf coll* straw, fodder

connrag, connraig, connragan *nf* a consonant, *cf* **consan, fuaimreag**

connsachadh, *gen* **connsachaidh** *nm* **1** (*the act of*) arguing etc (*see senses of* **connsaich** *v*); **2** an argument, a dispute, a squabble, *cf* **tuasaid 1**

connsachail *adj* quarrelsome, argumentative, disputatious

connsaich *vi, pres part* **a' connsachadh, 1** argue, row, squabble, quarrel, **bidh iad ri connsachadh gun sgur** they're continually squabbling/rowing, *cf* **argamaid 3, troid; 2** (*less confrontational, philo etc*) argue, dispute, debate

connspeach, connspeach, connspeachan *nf* a hornet; a wasp

connspaid, connspaide, connspaidean *nf* dispute, a dispute, controversy, a controversy, wrangling, contention

connspaideach *adj* **1** disputatious, litigious; **2** contentious, controversial

con(n)traigh, con(n)traighe, con(n)traighean *nf* a neap tide (*ie the lowest tide*), (*poetry collection*) **Reothairt is Contraigh** (Somhairle MacGill-Eain) Spring tide and Neap tide

consal, consail, consalan *nm* a consul

consan, *gen & pl* **consain** *nm* a consonant, *cf* **connrag, fuaimreag**

co-obrachadh, co-obrachaidh, co-obrachaidhean *nm* **1** (*the act of*) cooperating, working together; **2** co-operation; **3** a co-operative, *cf* **co-chomann 2**

co-obraich *vi, pres part* **a' co-obrachadh,** co-operate, work together

co-obraiche, *gen* **co-obraiche,** *pl* **co-obraichean** *nm* **1** one who co-operates or collaborates with others; **2** a fellow worker, a colleague, a workmate, *cf* **companach 2**

co-ogha, *gen* **co-ogha,** *pl* **co-oghachan &** **co-oghaichean** *nm* (*trad*) a cousin, *Note:* '**cousin**' is used in Gaelic by many speakers

cop, *gen* **coip & cuip** *nm* foam, froth, *cf* **cobhar**

copach *adj* frothy, foaming

copag, copaig, copagan *nf* (*bot*) a dock, (*Sc*) a docken

copan, copain, copanan *nm* a (drinking) cup, *cf* **cupa, cùp**

copar, *gen* **copair** *nm* copper, **ceàrd-copair** *m* a coppersmith

cor, coir, cuir *nm* **1** a condition, a state, **chunnaic mi cor truagh nam fògarrach** I saw the pitiful state of the refugees, *esp in expr* (*fam*) **dè do chor?** how are you doing?, how are you? (*lit* what is your condition?), *cf* less trad **staid; 2** a condition, an eventuality, a circumstance, **air chor** on condition, **gheibh thu e air chor 's gum pòs thu mi** you'll get it on condition that you marry me (*cf* **cumha** *nf*, **cùmhnant 2**), **na buin dha air chor sam bith!** don't touch it under any circumstances!; **3** a method, a manner, *esp in expr* **air chor is gu/nach . . .** so that . . . (*lit* in such a manner that), **ghlas e an doras air chor is nach b' urrainn dhomh faighinn a-steach** he locked the door so that I couldn't get in, *cf* similarly used **dòigh 5**

còrcair & corcair *adj* purple, *cf* **purpaidh**

corcais, **corcais**, **corcaisean** *nf* cork, (*esp*) a bottle cork, **tarraing** *v* **corcais** draw/pull a cork, *cf* **àrc**

còrd, *gen & pl* **cùird** *nm* cord, a cord, line, a line (*of a thickness between string and rope*)

còrd *vi*, *pres part* **a' còrdadh**, **1** agree with, be agreeable to, please, get on with, **a' còrdadh ri chèile** getting on (well) with each other; **2** *followed by the prep* **ri**, **còrd** *is commonly used to express the idea* enjoy, **ciamar a tha sin a' còrdadh ribh?** how are you enjoying that? **cha do chòrd an ceòl rium idir** I didn't enjoy the music at all

còrdadh, **còrdaidh**, **còrdaidhean** *nm* **1** (*the act of*) agreeing etc (*see senses of* **còrd** *v*); **2** agreement, an agreement, an understanding, **thàinig iad gu còrdadh** they reached an agreement/an understanding, **bha droch chòrdadh eatarra** they were on bad terms; **3** a contract, *cf* **cùmhnant 1**

coreigin, *see* **air choreigin**

co-rèir *nf* accordance, *in expr* **ann an co-rèir ri ...** in accordance with ...

còrn, *gen & pl* **cùirn** *nm* **1** (*trad*) a drinking horn; **2** (*mus*) a horn; **3** a corn (*on foot*)

Còrnach, *gen & pl* **Còrnaich** *nm* a Cornishman, someone from Cornwall (**a' Chòrn**), *also as adj* **Còrnach** Cornish

còrnair, **còrnair**, **còrnairean** *nm* a corner, (*short story*) **Granny anns a' Chòrnair** Granny in the Corner, *cf more trad* **cùil 1**, **oisean**, **uileann 2**

corp, *gen & pl* **cuirp** *nm* **1** a body (*of any living creature*), **buill a' chuirp** the parts of the body, **corp is anam** body and soul, *cf* **bodhaig**; **2** a dead (*human*) body, a corpse, **fhuair iad a chorp dà là an dèidh a bhàis** they found his body/corpse two days after his death, *cf* **marbhan**

corpailear, **corpaileir**, **corpailearan** *nm* (*army*) a corporal, **bha e na chorpailear sna Seaforths** he was a corporal in the Seaforths

corp-eòlaiche, **corp-eòlaiche**, **corp-eòlaichean** *nm* an anatomist

corp-eòlas, *gen* **corp-eòlais** *nm* anatomy

corp-làidir *adj* able-bodied, (*bodily*) strong

corporra *adj* bodily, corporal, corporeal

còrr *adj* odd (*ie not even*), **àireamh chòrr** an odd number, *cf* **cothrom** *adj*

còrr *nm invar* **1** *in expr* **còrr is**, more than, **tha iad còrr is fichead mìle air falbh** they're more than twenty miles away; **2** *with art* **an còrr** the rest, **dh'ith mise mo leòr, an gabh thusa an còrr?** I've eaten my fill/had enough, will you take the rest?; **3** *with art* **an còrr**, anything else, **thubhairt i, 'Obh! Obh!', ach an uair sin cha tubhairt i an còrr** she said, 'Dear, oh dear', but then she didn't say anything else, **cha robh an còrr ann ach sin** that's all there was to it, there was no more to it than that

corra *adj* odd, occasional, **gabhaidh mi corra phinnt còmhla ris na co-obraichean agam** I have the odd/occasional pint with my workmates/the people from work, **chaidh corra dhuine seachad oirnn** the odd person went past us

corra-biod *nm invar*, *in expr* **air mo** (etc) **c(h)orra-biod** on tiptoe, on the tip of my (etc) toes

corrach *adj* **1** unsteady, unstable, *cf more usu* **critheanach 2**, **cugallach 1**; **2** (*terrain etc*) steep, rough

corrag, **corraig**, **corragan** *nf* a finger, *cf* **meur 1**

corra-ghritheach, **corra-grithich**, **corrachan-gritheach** *nf* a heron, (*poem*), **thàinig corra-ghritheach ghiùigeach, sheas i air uachdar tiùrra** (Somhairle MacGill-Eain) a demure heron came and stood on top of sea-wrack

corran, *gen & pl* **corrain** *nm* **1** a sickle; **2** a crescent

còs, **còis**, **còsan** *nm* (*topog*) a hollow, *cf more usu* **lag** *n*, **sloc 1**

còsach *adj* hollow

cosamhlachd, **cosamhlachd**, **cosamhlachdan** *nf* a parable

cosg *nm invar* **1** (*also* **cosgadh**, *gen* **cosgaidh**) (*the act of*) costing etc (*see senses of* **cosg** *v*); **2** cost, *cf* **cosgais 1**, **prìs**; **3** a waste, **cosg airgid/tìde** a waste of money/time, *cf* **call** *n* **4**

cosg *vt*, *pres part* **a' cosg** & **a' cosgadh**, **1** cost, **dè a chosgas briogais ùr? cosgaidh i dà fhichead not** what will some new trousers cost? they'll cost forty pounds; **2** spend, **bidh ise a' cosnadh airgid 's bidh esan ga chosg** she earns money and he spends it; **3** waste, **cosg airgead** waste money, *cf* **caith 3**

cosgail *adj* expensive, dear, costly, **'s e stuth cosgail a tha sin!** that's expensive stuff!, *cf* **daor**

cosgais, **cosgaise**, **cosgaisean** *nf* **1** cost, the monetary cost of anything, **cosgais bith-beò** the cost of living, *cf* **cosg** *n* **2**; **2** *in pl* costs, expenses, **dh'fhàillig an gnothach air sgàth chosgaisean àrda** the business failed because of/on account of high costs, **cosgaisean siubhail** travelling costs/expenses

co-sheirm, *gen* **co-sheirme** *nf* (*music*) harmony

co-shìnte *adj* parallel, **loidhnichean co-shìnte** parallel lines

cosnadh, cosnaidh, cosnaidhean *nm* **1** (*the act of*) earning, winning etc (*see senses of* **coisinn** *v*); **2** (*abstr*) employment, a job, **ionad cosnaidh** (*also* **ionad obrach**) a job centre, **gun chosnadh** unemployed, without work/a job, *cf* **dreuchd, obair 4**; **3** (*con*) work, **am beagan cosnaidh a rinn iad** the little work that they did, *cf* **obair 1**; **4** earnings, *cf more usu* **pàigh, tuarastal**

costa, costa, costaichean *nm* a coast, *cf* **oirthir**

còta, còta, còtaichean *nm* a coat, **còta-mòr** an overcoat, a greatcoat, **còta-leapa** a dressing gown, a housecoat, **còta-bàn** a petticoat, **còta-froise** a raincoat

cotan, *gen* **cotain** *nm* cotton

cothrom *adj* even (*ie not odd*), **àireamh chothrom** an even number, *cf* **còrr** *adj*

cothrom, cothruim, cothroman *nm* **1** a chance, an opportunity, **an do ghlan thu na h-uinneagan? cha d' fhuair mi an cothrom fhathast** did you clean the windows? I didn't get the chance yet, **cothrom air foghlam àrd-ìre** opportunity for access to higher education, (*prov*) **far am bi càil bidh cothrom** (*roughly equivalent to*) where there's a will there's a way, **gabh** *v* **cothrom air** take advantage of (*not nec unfairly – cf* **brath** *n* **2, fàth 3**), (*trad expr*) **cothrom na Fèinne** a sporting chance, fair odds; **2** *in expr* **chan eil cothrom air** there's nothing to be done, it can't be helped, **ma tha sin an aghaidh nan riaghailtean, chan eil cothrom air** if that's against the regulations, it can't be helped; **3** *in expr* **air chothrom a (dhol a-mach** etc) able/fit to (go out etc), *cf* **comasach**; **4** equilibrium, balance, *cf* **meidh 2**; **5** a pair of scales, a balance, *cf* **meidh 1**

cothromach *adj* fair, just, decent, reasonable, **tuarastal cothromach** a decent/reasonable salary, **duine cothromach** a fair/decent man, **breith chothromach** a just/fair decision, *cf* **dìreach 2, reusanta 2**

cothromachadh, *gen* **cothromachaidh** *nm* (*the act of*) weighing, balancing

cothromaich *vt, pres part* **a' cothromachadh**, weigh, balance, assess

co-thuit *vi, pres part* **a' co-thuiteam**, coincide

co-thuiteamas, co-thuiteamais, co-thuiteamasan *nm* coincidence, a coincidence, **abair co-thuiteamas!** what a coincidence!

cràbhach *adj* devout, pious, very religious, *cf* **diadhaidh**

cràbhadh, *gen* **cràbhaidh** *nm* piety, devoutness, *cf* **cùram 3, diadhachd 3**

crac, *also* **craic**, *gen* **craice** *nf* (*fam*) chat, conversation, 'crack'

cràdh, *gen* **cràidh** *nm* **1** (*the act of*) paining, torturing etc (*see senses of* **cràidh** *v*); **2** (*mental or phys*) pain, anguish, suffering, torture, torment, **cuir** *v* **an cràdh** torture, put to torture (*cf* **cràidh** *v*); *cf* **ciùrradh**

craiceann, *gen* **craicinn** & **craicne**, *pl* **craicnean** *nm* skin, a skin

cràidh *vt, pres part* **a' cràdh**, pain, torture, torment (*mentally or phys*), **bha pian is dòrainn ga chràdh** pain and grief were tormenting him, *cf* **ciùrr, goirtich, pian** *v* **2**

crài(dh)teach *adj* grievous, painful, causing grief or pain (*mentally or phys*), **cuimhneachan cràiteach** a painful reminder, *cf* **dòrainneach**

cràin, cràine, cràintean *nf* a sow, *cf* **cullach, muc, torc**

crann, *gen* & *pl* **crainn** & **croinn** *nm* **1** a tree, now usu restricted to tree names, eg **crann-fìogais** *m* a fig tree, **crann-fìona** *m* a vine, *cf more usu* **craobh**; **2** a (ship's) mast; **3** a bar (*of wood, metal*), **crann-tarsainn** a crossbar, (*trad*) **cuir** *v* **an crann air an doras** bar the door; **4** a plough, **crann-sneachda** a snow plough, (*astronomy*) **An Crann-arain** The Plough; **5** (*engin*) a bolt, **cnò is crann** a nut and bolt; **6** (*also* **crann-togail**) a crane (*for lifting*), a derrick; **7** *in expr* **crann-ola** an oil rig (*also* an olive tree!); **8** (*heraldry etc*) a saltire, a St Andrew's cross, **An Crann** the Saltire; **9** *also in expr* **cuir** *v* **crainn** (*pl*) draw lots, toss a coin (*to decide something*), **chuir iad crainn feuch cò a phàigheadh** they drew lots/tossed a coin to see who would pay

crannag, crannaig, crannagan *nf* **1** a pulpit, *cf more usu* **cùbaid**; **2** a milk churn, *cf* **muidhe**; **3** (*hist*) a crannog, an artificial island

crann-ceusaidh, *gen* & *pl* **crainn-cheusaidh** & **croinn-cheusaidh** *nm* a cross (*for crucifixion*), **An Crann-Ceusaidh** Our Lord's Cross, *cf* **crois 2**

crannchur, crannchuir, crannchuran *nm* **1** the casting or drawing of lots, **an Crannchur Nàiseanta** the National Lottery, **crannchur-gill** a raffle; **2** (*trad*) one's fate, one's lot, **mas e sin mo chrannchur** if that is my fate/lot, *cf* **dàn¹ 1**

crann-sgaoilidh, *gen* & *pl* **crainn-sgaoilidh** *nm* (*radio, TV*) a transmitter, a radio or television mast

craobh, craoibhe, craobhan *nf* a tree, **craobh mheas** a fruit tree, (*song*) **Craobh nan Ubhal** The Apple Tree, *Note:* **craobh-** *can be prefixed to the name of a species to give the tree name* *eg* **craobh-challtainn** a hazel tree, **craobh-dharaich** an oak tree; *cf less usu* **crann 1**

craobh-sgaoil *vti, pres part* **a' craobh-sgaoileadh, 1** (*trad*) diffuse, propagate; **2** (*more recently*) broadcast, transmit (*by radio or TV*), **'s e seo Rèidio Alba, a' craobh-sgaoileadh air feadh na dùthcha** this is Radio Scotland, broadcasting/transmitting throughout the country

craobh-sgaoileadh, *gen* **craobh-sgaoilidh** *nm* **1** (*the act of*) diffusing, broadcasting etc (*see senses of* **craobh-sgaoil** *v*); **2** (*radio, TV*) a broadcast, a transmission, *cf* **prògram**

craos, craois, craosan *nm* **1** (*pej when used of humans*) a mouth, a wide or gaping mouth, (*of animal*) a maw; **2** gluttony, *cf* **geòcaireachd**

craosach *adj* **1** gluttonous, *cf* **geòcach**; **2** having a wide or gaping mouth

craosaire, craosaire, craosairean *nm* a glutton, *cf* **geòcaire**

crasg, craisg, crasgan *nf* a crutch (*ie walking aid*), *cf* **croitse**

crasgag & **crosgag**, *gen* **crasgaig**, *pl* **crasgagan** *nf* a starfish

crath *vti, pres part* **a' crathadh, 1** (*deliberately*) shake, wave, brandish, **chrath e a cheann** he shook his head, **crath dhìot an cadal!** wake up!, look lively! (*lit* shake the sleep from you!), **bha a' chlann a' crathadh rithe** the children were waving to her (*cf* **smèid 2**), **chrath e a dhòrn** he shook/brandished his fist, **cù a' crathadh earbaill** a dog wagging its tail; **2** (*vt*) sprinkle, shake (*on or over something*), **crath salann air an iasg** sprinkle salt on the fish

crè *nf, see* **crèadh**

creach, creiche, creachan *nf* **1** (*trad, hist*) booty, plunder (*often stolen cattle in particular*), *cf* **cobhartach**; **2** a disaster, destruction, ruin or ruination befalling someone, *esp in excl expr surprise or dismay*, **O, mo chreach!** Good heavens!, Dear me!, *also* (*stronger*) **O, mo chreach-sa (a) thàinig!** Good gracious me!, Mercy me!, Good grief! etc (*lit* O my very destruction has come!), *cf* **sgrios** *n*

creach *vti, pres part* **a' creachadh, 1** rob, plunder, *cf* **spùill**; **2** ruin, bring ruin upon (*someone*), *cf* **sgrios** *v*

creachadh, *gen* **creachaidh** *nm* (*the act of*) robbing, ruining etc (*see senses of* **creach** *v*)

creachan(n), creachain(n), creachan(n)an *nm* a scallop, **slige *f* chreachain** a scallop shell

crèadh, *also* **criadh** & **crè**, *gen* **creadha** & **creadhadh** *nf* clay

crèadhadair, crèadhadair, crèadhadairean *nm* a potter

crèadhadaireachd *nf invar* pottery

creag, creige, creagan *nf* **1** a rock, a crag, an outcrop of rock, a cliff, (*placename*) **Creag an Iubhair** Craignure, the rock or crag of the yew tree; **2** a hill (*usu rocky*)

creagach *adj* rocky, craggy

creamh, *gen* **creamha** *nm* garlic

creamh-gàrraidh *nm invar* a leek, (*coll*) leeks

creapan, *gen* & *pl* **creapain** *nm* (*trad*) a stool, *cf* **furm 2, stòl**

creathail (*also* **creathall**), *gen* **creathaile** & **creathlach**, *pl* **creathailean** *nf* a cradle

creid *vti, pres part* **a' creidsinn** & **a' creids, 1** believe, **cha bu mhise a ghoid e! chan eil mi gad chreidsinn** it wasn't me who stole it! I don't believe you, **chan eil mi a' creidsinn anns na sìthichean** I don't believe in fairies; **2** *with double neg constr and understated positive sense* **cha chreid mi nach eil** (etc) I wouldn't be surprised if it is (etc), **am faigh i duais? cha chreid mi nach fhaigh** will she get a prize? I wouldn't be surprised if she does, *more emph* **bidh mi air an daoraich a-nochd! cha chreid mi nach bi!** I'll be drunk tonight! I'm sure you will!/I know fine you will!; **3** think, believe, **a bheil e ann? cha chreid mi gu bheil** is he there? I don't think so, I don't think/believe he is

creideamh, creideimh, creideamhan *nm* **1** belief, a belief; **2** faith, religious belief, a faith, a creed, a religion, **daoine gun chreideamh** people without faith, unbelievers, **an creideamh Ioslamach** the Islamic faith/religion

creideas, *gen* **creideis** *nm* **1** trust; **2** belief; **3** *in expr* **thoir** *v* **creideas do** believe, trust, **thubhairt e gun tigeadh e agus tha mi a' toirt creideas dha** he said he would come and I believe/trust him, **an toir thu creideas dhomh? cha toir!** will you/do you trust me? no!; *cf* **earbsa**

creidsinn *nm invar* (*the act of*) believing etc (*see senses of* **creid** *v*)

creim (*also* **criom**) *vti, pres part* **a' creimeadh, 1** nibble, pick (*at food*), *cf* **pioc 2**; **2** gnaw, *cf* **cagainn**

creimeach, creimich, creimich *nm* a rodent

creimeadh (*also* **criomadh**), *gen* **creimidh** *nm* (*the act of*) nibbling etc (*see senses of* **creim** *v*)

crèis, *gen* **crèise** *nf* grease, fat, (*Sc*) creesh, *cf* **geir 2, saill** *n*

crèiseach *adv* greasy, fatty

creithleag, creithleig, creithleagan *nf* a cleg, a horsefly

creuchd, creuchda, creuchdan *nf* a wound, a hurt, *cf* **ciùrradh 2, leòn** *n*, **lot** *n*

creud, creuda, creudan *nf* (*relig etc*) a creed

creutair, creutair, creutairean *nm* a creature, a being, **is creutairean daoine agus beathaichean** people and animals are creatures, (*with affective meaning*) **tha e gun sgillinn ruadh, an creutair bochd** he hasn't a penny to his name, the poor creature/soul, (*cf* **truaghan**)

criadh *nf, see* **crèadh**

criathar, criathair, criatharan *nm* a sieve, a riddle

criathraich *vt, pres part* **a' criathradh** & **a' criathrachadh**, sieve, sift, riddle

cridhe, cridhe, cridheachan *nm* **1** a heart, **buille cridhe** *f* a heartbeat, **tinneas cridhe** *m* heart disease, a heart ailment, **clisgeadh-cridhe** *m* a heart attack, **bris(t)eadh-cridhe** *m* heartbreak, (*trad*) **a charaid** (etc) **mo chridhe** my dear friend (etc); **2** courage, heart, **cha robh iad air a shon agus cha robh a** (*for* de) **chridhe agam na rachadh nan aghaidh** they didn't approve and I hadn't the heart/courage to go against them, *cf* **misneach**

cridhealas, *gen* **cridhealais** *nm* heartiness, jollity, merriment, hilarity, conviviality (*sometimes with implication of intoxication*), (*song*) **siud far an robh 'n cridhealas!** that was where conviviality was to be found!

cridheil *adj* (*person, atmosphere etc*) hearty, cheery, jovial, **fàilte chridheil** a hearty welcome

crìoch, crìche, crìochan *nf* **1** the end or completion of something, **aig a` chrìch** (*dat*) at the end, **thàinig a' choinneamh gu crìch** (*dat*) the meeting came to an an end, (*song*) **aig crìch mo là** at the end of my days/life, **cuir** *v* **crìoch air** finish, complete, **chuir i crìoch air an nobhail aice a-raoir** she finished her novel last night; **2** a boundary, a border, a frontier, a limit, (*Sc*) a march, **is e seo crìoch an fhearainn agam** this is the boundary/march of my land, **crìoch na sgìre** the parish boundary, **Na Crìochan** or **Crìochan Shasainn** The (Scottish-English) Borders, **Na Crìochan-Grèine** The Tropics, **crìoch astair** a speed limit

crìoch(n)ach *adj* finite, **neo-chrìoch(n)ach** infinite

crìochnachadh, *gen* **crìochnachaidh** *nm* (*the act of*) finishing etc (*see senses of* **crìochnaich** *v*)

crìochnaich *vt, pres part* **a' crìochnachadh**, finish, end, complete, *cf* **cuir crìoch air** (*see* **crìoch 1**)

crìochnaichte *adj* finished, completed, *cf* **coileanta 1**

criom *vti* & **criomadh** *nm, see* **cream** & **creamadh**

criomag, criomaige, criomagan *nf* a bit, a piece, a crumb of anything, **bha na dèideagan aice a' dol nan criomagan** her toys were falling to pieces/dropping to bits, (*title of newspaper column*) **Criomagan** Bits and Pieces, Odds and Ends

crìon *adj* **1** tiny, *cf* **meanbh, mion 1**; **2** petty, mean, trifling, insignificant, *cf* **suarach 1**; **3** withered, dried up, wizened

crìon *vti, pres part* **a' crìonadh**, wither, dry up, fade, fade away, *cf* **searg**

crìonadh, *gen* **crìonaidh** *nm* (*the act of*) withering etc (*see senses of* **crìon** *v*)

crioplach & **cripleach,** *gen* & *pl* **crioplaich** *nm* a cripple, *cf* more *usu* **bacach** *n*, **crùbach** *n*

crios, criosa, criosan *nm* a belt, a band, **tha mo chrios ro theann** my belt's too tight, **crios-sàbhalaidh,** *also* **crios-teasairginn,** a lifebelt, **crios-muineil** a neckband, a necklace, **crios-rubair** a rubber band

Crìosdachd *nf invar,* with *art* **A' Chrìosdachd** Christendom

Crìosdaidh, Crìosdaidh, Crìosdaidhean *nm* a Christian

Crìosdaidheachd *nf invar* Christianity

Crìosdail (*also* **Crìosdaidh**), *adj* Christian, **An Eaglais Chrìosdail** the Christian Church

Crìosdalachd *nf invar* Christian behaviour and beliefs, way of life characteristic of a Christian

criostal, criostail, criostalan *nm* crystal, a crystal

cripleach *see* **crioplach**

crith, crithe, crithean *nf* **1** (*the act of*) trembling, shaking etc (*see senses of* **crith** *v*), *esp in expr* **air chrith** *adv* trembling, shaking, shivering, **bha e air chrith leis an fhiabhras** he was shaking/trembling with the fever, **rach** *v* **air chrith** start to tremble, shake etc; **2** a tremble, a tremor, a quake, a shake, a shiver (*through fear, cold, illness etc*), **crith-thalmhainn** an earthquake

crith *vi, pres part* **a' crith**, tremble, shiver, shake, quake, *cf more usu* **bi air chrith** (*see* **crith** *n* **1**)

critheanach *adj* **1** liable to shake or tremble; **2** shaky, unsteady, (*Sc*) shooglie, *cf* **cugallach 1**; **3** liable to give one the shivers, scary

crò, *gen* **cròtha**, *pl* **cròithean** & **cròthan** *nm* **1** a pen, a fold (*for livestock, esp sheep*), *cf* **buaile**; **2** *in expr* **crò snàthaid**, the eye of a needle

croch *vt, pres part* **a' crochadh**, **1** hang, **croch am murtair gu h-àrd!** hang the murderer high!, **chrochadh na dealbhan aige san taisbeanlann** his pictures were hung in the art gallery

crochadair, crochadair, crochadairean *nm* **1** a hangman; **2** a hanger, (*also* **crochadair-còta**) a coat hanger

crochadh, *gen* **crochaidh** *nm* **1** (*the act of*) hanging (*see* **croch** *v*), (*trad, hist*) **am maide-crochaidh** *lit* the hanging stick, *a piece of wood hung as a punishment around the neck of a child caught speaking Gaelic at school*; **2** *in expr* **an crochadh** *adv* (*of objects*) hanging, hung, **seann chòta an crochadh air cùl dorais** an old coat hanging/hung behind a door; **3** *in expr* **an crochadh air** *prep* depending on, **am bi thu a' ceannachd an taighe? bidh sin an crochadh air a' phrìs** will you be buying the house? that will depend on the price, **tha sinn an crochadh ort** we're depending on you

crochte *adj* hung, hanged, hanging

crodh, *gen* **cruidh** *nm coll* cattle, stock, livestock (*esp cattle*), (*song*) **ged nach eil mo chrodh air bhuailidh** though I have no cattle in the fold, **crodh-bainne** milking cows, dairy cows, *cf* **bò, sprèidh**

crò-dhearg *adj* crimson

cròg, cròige, crògan *nf* **1** (*of animal*) a paw, *cf* **màg, spòg 1**; **2** (*of humans*) a large hand, (*derog*) a clumsy hand, a paw, a (great) fist, **bha am botal a' coimhead beag sa chròig mhòir aige** the bottle looked small in his great fist

cròic, cròice, cròicean *nf* a deer's antler, *cf* **cabar 1**

croich, croiche, croichean *nf* **1** gallows, a gibbet; **2** *in excl* (**òrd** etc) **na croiche!** the damned/bloody (hammer etc)!, *cf* **bugair, galla 2**

cròileagan, *gen* & *pl* **cròileagain** *nm* a playgroup

crois, croise, croisean *nf* **1** a cross, **chuir e crois air a' phàipear o nach robh sgrìobhadh aige** he put a cross on the paper, as he couldn't write, **crois rathaid** a cross-roads; **2** (*relig*) a cross, a crucifix, **rinn e comharradh na croise** he made the sign of the cross, he crossed himself, *cf* **crann-ceusaidh**

croit & **cruit**, *gen* **croite**, *pl* **croitean** *nf* **1** a croft, **bhiodh e a' togail bheathaichean 's a'**

cur eòrna air a' chroit aige he used to rear animals and sow barley on his croft, *cf* **lot** *nf*; **2** a hump (*on the back*)

croitear & **cruitear**, *gen* **croiteir**, *pl* **croitearan** *nm* a crofter, **Aonadh nan Croitearan** The Crofters' Union

croitearachd *nf invar* crofting

croitse, croitse, croitseachan *nf* a crutch (*ie walking aid*), *cf* **crasg**

crom *adj* bent, crooked, curved, **bata crom** a bent/crooked stick, (*poem*) **dìreach an druim, crom an ceann** (Somhairle MacGill-Eain) straight their backs, bent their heads, **crom-chasach** bandy-legged, *cf* **cam, fiar** *adj* **1**, **lùbte**

crom *vti, pres part* **a' cromadh**, **1** (*vt*) bend, incline, bow, stoop, **chrom i a ceann** she bent/bowed her head, *cf* **crùb 2, lùb** *v* **1**; **2** (*vi*) *in expr* **crom air an obair** set to work, 'get stuck in'; **3** (*vti*) bend, curve, *cf* **lùb** *v* **1**; **4** (*vi*) descend, climb down, **chrom e bhon asail** he climbed/got down from the donkey's back, **chrom e leis a' chreig** he climbed down the rock, *cf* **teirinn 1** & **2**

cromadh, *gen* **cromaidh** *nm* (*the act of*) bending etc (*see senses of* **crom** *v*)

cromag, cromaig, cromagan *nf* **1** a hook, a clasp, a clip, *cf* **dubhan**; **2** a (shepherd's) crook, a cromag; **3** (*typog*) a comma, **cromagan turrach** inverted commas

cron, *gen* & *pl* **croin** *nm* **1** harm, injury (*not usu phys*), **dèan** *v* **cron air cuideigin** harm/injure someone, *cf* **dochann**; **2** fault, blame, **'s ann ortsa a tha a chron** it's with you that the blame for it lies, it's you who are to blame for it, **faigh** *v* **cron do chuideigin** blame someone; *cf* **coire** *nf* & *less usu* **lochd**

cronachadh, *gen* **cronachaidh** *nm* (*the act of*) chiding, scolding, rebuking (*see* **cronaich** *v*)

cronachail *adj* apt to blame or rebuke, censorious, *cf* **coireachail**

cronaich *vt, pres part* **a' cronachadh**, chide, scold, rebuke, *cf* **càin** *v* **1**

cronail *adj* harmful, hurtful, injurious

crònan, *gen* **crònain** *nm* **1** (*a low, continuous, usu musical sound*) humming, buzzing (*eg of insects*), murmuring (*eg of voices, water*), purling, purring, *cf* **torman 1, monmhar**; **2** belling, bellowing (*of red deer stags*), *cf* **dàmhair 1**

crost(a) & **crosda**, *adj* **1** cross, irritable, grumpy, grouchy, *cf* **diombach 1, gruamach 4**; **2** (*usu of child*) naughty, badly behaved, peevish

crotach *adj* hump-backed

crotal, *gen* **crotail** *nm* (*bot*) lichen

cruach, cruaiche, cruachan *nf* **1** a heap, a pile, *esp* a stack, a rick (*esp of peats, hay, corn etc*), *cf less usu* **dùn 1, tudan 1**; **2** (*topog*) a hill (*usu conical*)

cruach *vt, pres part* **a' cruachadh**, heap, pile, stack, *cf* **càrn** *v*

cruachan, cruachain, cruachanan *nm*, little heap etc (*dimin of* **cruach** *n, see senses above*)

cruachann, cruachainn, cruaichnean *nf* (*anat*) a hip

cruadal, *gen* **cruadail** *nm* **1** adversity, hardship, a tight corner, *cf* **cruaidh-chàs 2**; **2** hardihood, intrepidity, courage

cruadalach *adj* **1** difficult, dangerous (*situation etc*); **2** (*of person*) bold, hardy, intrepid, *cf* **cruaidh** *adj* **3, fulangach 1**

cruadhaich *vti, pres part* **a' cruadhachadh**, harden, solidify

cruadhachadh, *gen* **cruadhachaidh** *nm* (*the act of*) hardening, solidifying

cruaidh *adj* **1** hard, (*song*) **bheir mi às a' ghreabhal chruaidh do mo luaidh teachd-an-tìr** I will win from the hard gravel a living for my love, **obair chruaidh** hard work; **2** (*of person, situation*) cruel, harsh, hard, **tìr chruaidh** a hard/harsh land, **cruaidh-chridheach** hard-hearted; **3** (*usu of person*) hardy, tough, *cf* **cruadalach 2, fulangach 1**

cruaidh, *gen* **cruaidhe** *nf* steel, *cf* **stàilinn**

cruaidh-chàs, cruaidh-chàis, cruaidh-chàsan *nm* **1** an emergency, a sudden crisis; **2** a difficult, dangerous, dicy situation, a tight corner, *cf* **cruadal 1, staing**

cruan, *gen* **cruain** *nm* enamel

cruas, *gen* **cruais** *nm* **1** hardness; **2** harshness, cruelty; **3** hardiness, hardihood, toughness, endurance, *cf* **fulang 3**

crùb *vi, pres part* **a' crùbadh**, **1** crouch, squat, (*Sc*) coorie, *cf* **dèan crùban** (*see* **crùban**); **2** stoop, bend, *cf* **crom** *v* **3**; **3** cringe, *cf* **strìochd 2**; **4** crawl, *cf* **snàig 1**

crùbach *adj* **1** lame, limping; **2** *in expr* **tha e** (*etc*) **crùbach,** he (*etc*) is lame, he (*etc*) limps/has a limp; *cf* **bacach, cuagach** *adjs*

crùbach, *gen & pl* **crùbaich** *nm* a lame person, *cf* **bacach** *n*, **crioplach**

crùbadh, *gen* **crùbaidh** *nm* (*the act of*) crouching etc (*see senses of* **crùb** *v*)

crùbag, crùbaig, crùbagan *nf* a crab, *cf smaller* **partan**

crùbagan *nm in exprs* **bha e na chrùbagan** he was crouched down, **chaidh iad nan crùbagan** they crouched down, *cf* **crùban**

crùban, *gen* **crùbain** *nm* a crouch, a squat, a crouching or squatting position, *esp in exprs*

dèan *v* **crùban** crouch, squat, **rinn e crùban san oisean** he crouched down in the corner, **& na c(h)rùban** crouching, in a crouch, squatting, **bha iad nan crùban air bruaich na h-aibhne** they were crouched on the river bank, *cf* **crùbagan**

crùdh *vt, pres part* **a' crùidheadh**, shoe (*a horse*), *cf* **cuir crudha air** (*see* **crudha**)

crudha, cruidhe, cruidhean *nm* a horseshoe, **cuir crudha air** shoe (*horse*), *cf less trad* **bròg-eich** (*see* **bròg**)

cruineachd *see* **cruithneachd**

cruinn *adj* **1** round, circular, spherical, **tha bàla, ubhal agus planaid cruinn** a ball, an apple and a planet are round/spherical; **2** (*of sums etc*) accurate, *cf* **grinn 4**; **3** assembled, gathered, **bha an coitheanal cruinn san eaglais** the congregation was assembled in the church

cruinne (*m*), *gen* **cruinne** (*f*), *pl* **cruinnean** (*m*) *nmf* **1** roundness; **2** a sphere, a globe, **leth-chruinne** a hemisphere; **3** (*with art*) **an cruinne** the world, the earth, the globe, **crìoch na cruinne** the end of the world, **uachdar na cruinne** the surface of the globe, (*football etc*) **Cuach na Cruinne** the World Cup, *cf* **cruinne-cè 1, saoghal 1, talamh 1**; **4** (*of sums etc*) accuracy

cruinneachadh, cruinneachaidh, cruinneachaidhean *nm* **1** (*the act of*) gathering etc (*see senses of* **cruinnich** *v*); **2** a gathering, an assembly (*of people*); **3** a collection (*of objects*), an anthology (*of writing*); *cf* **co-chruinneachadh**

cruinnead *nf invar* roundness

cruinne-cè (*m*), *gen* **cruinne-cè** (*f*), *nmf, used with art*, **an cruinne-cè**, **1** the world, the earth, *cf* **cruinne 3, saoghal 1, talamh 1**; **2** the universe, *cf* **cruitheachd, domhan**

cruinneil *adj* global, **blàthachadh cruinneil** global warming

cruinn-eòlas, *gen* **cruinn-eòlais** *nm* geography, *cf* **tìr-eòlas** (*see* **tìr 2**)

cruinnich *vti, pres part* **a' cruinneachadh**, **1** (*of people*) gather, assemble, collect, come or bring together, **bha an sluagh a' cruinneachadh** the people were gathering, **chruinnich e a' chlann san leabharlann** he assembled the children in the library, *cf* (*vi*) **coinnich, thig còmhla** (*see* **còmhla** *adv* **1**); **2** gather, collect, accumulate (*objects*), pick (*flowers etc*); **3** gather, round up (*livestock*), **a' cruinneachadh nam bò** gathering the cattle, *cf* **tionail 2, tru(i)s 3**

cruinn-leum, cruinn-lèim, cruinn-leuman *nm* a standing jump

cruìsgean, cruìsgein, cruìsgeanan *nm* (*trad*)
an oil lamp, a cruisie
cruit[1], **cruite, cruitean** *nf* **1** a harp (*cf more usu*
clàrsach), **cruit-chòrda** a harpsichord
cruit[2] *see* **croit**
cruitear[1], **cruiteir, cruitearan** *nm* a harper, *cf*
more usu **clàrsair**
cruitear[2] *see* **croitear**
cruitheachd, cruitheachd, cruitheachdan *nf*
creation, a creation, **a' Chruitheachd** Creation,
the World, the Universe (*cf* **cruinne-cè**)
cruithear, cruitheir, cruithearan *nm* a
creator, **an Cruithear** the Creator, God
Cruithneach, *gen & pl* **Cruithnich** *nm* (*hist*) a
Pict, *also as adj* **Cruithneach** Pictish
cruithneachd & **cruineachd** *nf invar* wheat
crùn, crùin, crùintean *nm* a crown
crùn *vt, pres part* **a' crùnadh,** crown (*a*
monarch etc)
crùnadh, crùnaidh, crùnaidhean *nm* **1** (*the*
act of) crowning, **chaidh a chrùnadh** he was
crowned; **2** a coronation
cruth, *gen* **crutha,** *pl* **cruthan** & **cruthannan**
nm **1** a shape, a form, a figure, an appearance
or aspect (*of a person etc*), **rinn iad a-mach**
a cruth san dorchadas they made out her
form/appearance in the darkness, **cruth-tìre**
landscape, *cf* **cumadh 2, dealbh** *n* **5**; **2** (*Lit etc*)
form, **cuspair is cruth** matter and form
cruthachadh, *gen* **cruthachaidh** *nm* **1** (*the act*
of) creating; creation
cruthachail *adj* creative
cruthaich *vt, pres part* **a' cruthachadh,** create
cù, *gen & pl* **coin,** *gen pl* **chon** *nm* a dog, **cù-**
chaorach a sheepdog, *cf obs* **madadh 1**
cuachag, cuachaige, cuachagan *nf* (*esp in*
songs) a girl, a maiden, *cf* **gruagach, nìghneag**
2, rìbhinn
cuach, cuaich, cuachan *nf* **1** a bowl; **2** (*as*
trophy etc) a cup, a quaich
cuagach *adj* **1** bent, twisted; **2** lame, limping, *in*
expr **tha e** (*etc*) **cuagach** he (*etc*) is lame, he
(*etc*) limps/has a limp, *cf* **bacach, crùbach** *adjs*
cuaille, cuaille, cuaillean *nm* a cudgel, a club,
a bludgeon
cuain, cuaine, cuainean *nf* (*of animals*) a litter,
cf **àl**
cuairt, cuairte, cuairtean *nf* **1** a circuit, a cycle,
a round, an orbit, **cuairt na grèine** the sun's
orbit, **cuairt a' phosta** the postman's round,
cuairt goilf a round of golf, **cuairt-rathad** *m* a
ring road; **2** a stroll, a walk, **tha iad a' gabhail**
cuairt a-muigh they're taking a stroll/walk/
turn outside, *cf* **car** *n* **2**; **3** a trip, an excursion, a
tour, **thèid sinn air chuairt do na**

h-eileanan we'll go on a trip/tour to the
islands, *cf* **sgrìob 3, turas 1 & 2**; **4** *in adv expr*
mun cuairt, *also* **mu chuairt,** about, around,
tha an cnatan a' dol mun cuairt the cold's
going around, *cf* **timcheall 1**; **5** *in expr* **mun**
cuairt air *prep* around, **bha seallaidhean**
brèagha fada mun cuairt oirre there were
fine views all around her, *cf* **timcheall 2 & 3**
cuairtich *vti, see* **cuartaich**
cuan, cuain, cuantan *nm* a sea, an ocean, **an**
Cuan Sgìth(e) the Little Minch, **an Cuan Siar**
the Atlantic, (*song*) **slighe cuain eadar mi 's**
m' eudail a sea journey between me and my
darling, (*prov*) **a' dèanamh cuain mhòir de**
chaolas cumhang making a great ocean of a
narrow strait
cuaraidh, cuaraidh, cuaraidhean *nmf* a
(stone-)quarry
cuaran, *gen* **cuarain,** *pl* **cuarain** & **cuaranan**
nm a light shoe, a sandal
cuartachadh & **cuairteachadh,** *gen*
cuartachaidh *nm* **1** (*the act of*) surrounding
etc (*see senses of* **cuartaich** *v*); **2** circulation (*of*
blood, air etc)
cuartaich & **cuairtich** *vti, pres part* **a'**
cuartachadh, 1 surround, enclose, encircle, *cf*
iadh; 2 (*movement*) circle (around); circulate
cùbaid, cùbaide, cùbaidean *nf* a pulpit
cubhaidh *adj* fitting, befitting, (*trad*) **rinn thu**
do dhleastanas, mar bu chubhaidh dhut
you did your duty, as was fitting for you
cùbhraidh *adj* (*of smells*) sweet, fragrant, (*song*)
fàile cùbhraidh an fhraoich tighinn thar
mullach nam beann the fragrant scent of the
heather coming over the mountain tops
cucair, cucair, cucairean *nm* a cooker, **cucair**
gas a gas cooker, **cucair dealain** an electric
cooker
cùdainn, cùdainn, cùdainnean *nf* a large tub,
(*trad, hist*) **Clach na Cùdainn** the washtub
stone (*a stone in Inverness where women used*
to rest their washtubs)
cudrom *see* **cudthrom**
cudthrom & **cudrom,** *also* **cuideam,** *gen*
cud(th)ruim & **cuideim** *nm* **1** weight, a
weight, **b' fheudar dhomh cudthrom a**
chur orm I had to put on weight, **bha i a'**
giùlan cudthruim mhòir she was carrying
a great weight, **cileagram de chudthrom** a
kilogram in weight, **cuir cudthrom eile air**
a' chothrom put another weight on the scales;
2 importance, stress, emphasis, **leigidh a'**
chompanaidh cudthrom mòr air trèanadh
a luchd-obrach the company lays great

importance/stress on training its workforce, *cf* **buille 2**

cudthromach *also* **cudromach** *adj* 1 (*phys*) heavy, *cf more usu* **trom** 1; 2 (*in abstr sense*) weighty, important, serious, **gnothaichean cudthromach** serious/weighty matters, **duine mòr cudthromach** a big important man, (*ironic*) a bigwig, a big shot

cugallach *adj* 1 unsteady, shaky, wobbly, (*Sc*) shooglie, **bòrd cugallach** a wobbly table, **cugallach air a chasan** unsteady on his feet, *cf* **critheanach 2**; 2 (*in abstr sense*) shaky, dodgy, precarious, unreliable, dubious, **na buin ris a' ghnothach ud, tha e gu math cugallach** don't get involved in yon affair/business, it's pretty dodgy/shaky, (*trad*) **is cugallach an saoghal** the world is precarious/unreliable

cuibheall *nf see* **cuibhle**

cuibheas, cuibheis, cuibheasan *nm* (*maths*) an average

cuibheasach *adj* 1 (*maths*) average; 2 (*in quality etc*) middling, average, so-so

cuibhle, cuibhle, *pl* **cuibhlean** & **cuibhlichean,** *also* **cuibheall, cuibhle, cuibhleachan,** *nf* a wheel, (*cf more trad* **roth**), **cuibhle-stiùiridh** a steering wheel

cuibhreach, cuibhrich, cuibhrichean *nm* a chain, *cf* **slabhraidh**

cuibhreachadh, *gen* **cuibhreachaidh** *nm* (*the act of*) chaining (*see* **cuibhrich** *v*)

cuibhreann, *gen* **cuibhrinn,** *pl* **cuibhrinnean** & **cuibhreannan** *nm* 1 a portion, a share, *cf* **cuid 1, roinn** *n* 1; 2 (*fin*) an allowance, an allocation; 3 an instalment

cuibhrich *vt, pres part* **a' cuibhreachadh,** chain, chain up, put in chains

cuibhrig, cuibhrige, cuibhrigean *nmf* a quilt, a coverlet, a bed-cover

cuid, codach, codaichean *nf* 1 a share, a portion, a part, **tha fichead nota againn, sin agad do chuid-sa dheth** we've twenty pounds, there's your (*emph*) share of it, (*prov*) **feumaidh an talamh a chuid fhèin** the earth (*ie* grave) must have its due share, (*trad*) **mo chuid den t-saoghal** my share of worldly goods, my possessions, **bha cuid den chirc nach deachaidh ithe** there was part of the chicken that wasn't eaten, **mòr-chuid** a greater part, **a' mhòr-chuid de a bheatha** most/the greater part of his life, (*of people*) a majority, **tha a' mhòr-chuid air a shon** the majority/most people are in favour of it, **leth-chuid** a half, a half share, **cia mheud a tha thu ag iarraidh? a leth-chuid** how many do you want? half, **a' chuid as lugha/as motha** the smallest/biggest

part, *cf* **cuibhreann 1, roinn** *n* 1; 2 *with following gen noun,* what one possesses or has acquired of anything, **ar cuid mhac** our sons, **mo chuid aodaich** my clothes/clothing, **càit an do thog thu do chuid Gàidhlig?** where did you learn/pick up your Gaelic?, (*can be derog, dismissive*) **còmhlan-ciùil 's an cuid fuaim** a band with their noise/din; 3 (*of people*) some, **tha cuid dhiubh a' cumail a-mach gu bheil e às a rian, tha a' chuid eile coma co-dhiù!** some of them are making out that he's out of his mind, the rest/the others don't care! *cf* **feadhainn 1; 4** *in expr* **an dà chuid** both, **leann no uisge-beatha? an dà chuid!** beer or whisky? both!, **chan fhaodar an dà chuid dràibheadh agus òl** you/one can't/it's not permitted to both drink and drive, *cf* **dara 3, gach 3; 5** *in expr* **aon chuid . . . no** neither . . . nor, **cha phòs e aon chuid Mòrag no Màiri** he'll marry neither Morag nor Mary; **6** *in expr* **an dara cuid . . . no** either . . . or, **gabhaidh sinn an dara cuid trèana no bus** we'll take either a train or a bus

cuideachadh, *gen* **cuideachaidh** *nm* 1 (*the act of*) helping etc (*see senses of* **cuidich** *v*); 2 help, assistance, aid, **mòran taing airson do chuideachaidh** many thanks for your help, **làmh-chuideachaidh** a helping hand, *cf* **cobhair 1**

cuideachail *adj* helpful

cuideachd *adv* also, too, as well, **an do dh'fhalbh Eòghann? dh'fhalbh, agus Iain cuideachd** has Ewan left? yes, and Iain too, *cf* **ceudna 2**

cuideachd, cuideachd, cuideachdan *nf* 1 company, society, **nam chuideachd** in my company, **is toigh leis cuideachd na h-òigridh** he likes the company/society of young people, *cf* **comann 3, conaltradh 2**; 2 one's companions, (*trad*) one's people, one's followers, (*song*) **mo chuideachd air m' fhàgail** my people/followers having left me, *cf* **muinntir 1**; 3 a group, a company, **cuideachd shaighdearan** a company of soldiers, *cf* **buidheann 1, còmhlan**

cuideachdail *adj* sociable, fond of company, *cf less usu* **conaltrach**

cuideam *nm see* **cudthrom**

cuideigin *nmf invar* someone, somebody, **tha cuideigin air tighinn a-steach** someone's come in, *cf* **duine 2**

cuide ri *prep* with, along with, together with, (*song*) **an uair a bha mi ann an Ìle, bha Catrìona cuide rium** when I was in Islay,

Catriona was with me, *cf more usu* **còmhla 2, le 1**

cuidhteag & **cùiteag**, *gen* **cuidhteig**, *pl* **cuidhteagan** *nf* a whiting

cuidhteas, cuidhteis, cuidhteasan *nm* 1 a receipt (*for money etc*); 2 *in expr* **faigh** *v* **cuidhteas** get rid/shut of, **fhuair sinn cuidhteas na loidsearan mu dheireadh thall** we got rid of the lodgers at last, *cf* **saor** *adj* 2; 3 *in expr* **cùm cuidhteas** keep/stay clear (of), give a wide berth (to), **cùm cuidhteas boireannaich gun nàire!** keep away from shameless women!

cuidhtich, *pres part* **a' cuidhteachadh** *vt* (*fin*) compensate

cuidich *vti*, *pres part* **a' cuideachadh**, help, assist, **cuidich iad**, (*more trad*) **cuidich leotha**, help them

cuidiche, cuidiche, cuidichean *nm* a helper, a help, **cuidiche-taighe** *nm* a home help

cuid oidhche *nf* a night's lodging/ accommodation, **fhuair sinn ar cuid oidhche** (*or* **fhuair sinn cuid na h-oidhche**) **aig an taigh-òsta** we were put up for the night at the hotel,

cùil, cùile, cùiltean *nf* 1 a corner (*esp internal*), **na shuidhe sa chùil** sitting in the corner (*cf* **oisean** & *less trad* **còrnair**), (*calque*) **ann an cùil-chumhang** in a tight corner/a fix; 2 a nook, (*Sc*) a neuk, a tucked away part of a place or building, (*placename*) **Cùil na Muice** Cuilmuick, pig neuk

cuilbheart, cuilbheirt, cuilbheartan *nf* a trick, a wile, a plot, a stratagem, *cf* **innleachd 4**

cuilc, cuilce, cuilcean *nf* 1 a reed; 2 cane, a cane, **cuilc Innseanach** bamboo

cuileag, cuileig, cuileagan *nf* a fly, a house-fly

cuilean, cuilein, cuileanan *nm* 1 (*of dog*) a pup, a puppy; 2 (*of fox, bear, lion, seal etc*) a cub, a whelp, a pup

cuileann, *gen* **cuilinn** *nm* holly

cuimhne *nf invar* memory (*incl IT*), remembrance, recollection, *esp in exprs* **chan eil cuimhne agam**, *also* (*trad*) **cha chuimhne leam**, I don't remember, I've no recollection (of it), **mas math mo chuimhne** if I remember rightly, if my memory doesn't deceive me, **chaidh e às mo chuimhne** I forgot/have forgotten it, **chuir sin nam chuimhne nuair bha mi òg** that reminded me of when I was young, (*IT*) **cuimhne bhuan** ROM, *cf less usu* **meomhair**; *Note that to express Eng* **I** (*etc*) **remember** *followed by a direct object, Gaelic has* **tha cuimhne agam**

(*etc*) *followed by prep* **air**, *eg* **tha cuimhne aice air sin** she remembers that

cuimhneachadh, *gen* **cuimhneachaidh** *nm* (the act of) remembering, commemorating, *cf less usu* **meòrachadh**

cuimhneachan, *gen* & *pl* **cuimhneachain** *nm* 1 a memorial, a commemoration; 2 a remembrance, a souvenir, a keepsake; 3 a memorandum

cuimhnich *vi*, *pres part* **a' cuimhneachadh** (*with prep* air), remember, recall, *cf less usu* **meòraich 1**

cuimir *adj* 1 (*report, document etc*) succinct; 2 (*person, figure etc*) neat, trim, shapely, tidy, **calpa cuimir** a shapely/well-turned calf, *cf* **grinn 3, sgiobalta 2, snasail**

Cuimreach, *gen* & *pl* **Cuimrich** *nm* a Welshman, someone from Wales, *also as adj* **Cuimreach** Welsh

Cuimrigh *nf*, used with def art, **a' Chuimrigh** Wales

Cuimris *nf invar* (*lang*), *usu with def art*, **a' Chuimris** Welsh

cuimseach *adj*, (*of aim*) accurate, *cf* **amaiseach**

cuimseachadh, *gen* **cuimseachaidh** *nm* (the act of) aiming

cuimsich *vti*, *pres part* **a' cuimseachadh**, aim (*gun etc*), (*more fig*) **cuimsich air**, target, have in one's sights, *cf* **amais 1**

cuine & **cuin** *inter adv* when, **cuin a bha sin?** when was that? **cuine bhios a' bhracaist deiseil?** when will the breakfast be ready?

cuing[1], **cuinge, cuingean** *nf* a yoke, (*fig*) **fo chuing an aintighearna** beneath the tyrant's yoke

cuing[2], *gen* **cuinge** *nf* (*with art*) **a' chuing** asthma, *cf* **sac 2**

cuingealaich & **cuingich** *vt*, *pres part* **a' cuingealachadh** & **a' cuingeachadh**, restrict, limit, narrow down, **air a chuingealachadh gu còig mionaidean** restricted/limited to five minutes

cuinneag, cuinneige, cuinneagan *nf* a bucket, a pail, *esp* a milking pail, *cf* **cuman** & *less trad* **bucaid 1, peile**

cuinnean, cuinnein, cuinneanan *nm* a nostril

cuip, *gen* **cuipe**, *pl* **cuipean** & **cuipeachan** *nf* a whip, *cf* **sgiùrsair**

cuip *vt*, *pres part* **a' cuipeadh**, whip, *cf* **sgiùrs**

cuipeadh, *gen* **cuipidh** *nm* (the act of) whipping

cuir *vti*, *pres part* **a' cur**, there are very many idioms & exprs using this verb and only a selection can be given here, 1 *involving the notions* put, place, set, **cuir gual air an teine** put coal on the fire, **cuiridh mi sa phreas e**

I'll put it in the cupboard, **cuir rudeigin air an spàrr** stow/store something away, **cuir ort** (*more trad* **cuir umad**) **do chuid aodaich** put your clothes on, **cuir dhìot do chòta** (etc) take your coat (etc) off, **cuir x ri y** add x to y, **cuir air an solas** put the light on, **cuir air an teine** light the fire, **cuir às an solas/an teine** put the light/the fire out, **cuir an cèill** put into words, express, **cuir Beurla air Gàidhlig** translate Gaelic into English, **cuir às do rudeigin no chuideigin** put an end to/destroy/abolish something or someone, **cuir rudeigin air ath là** put something off (till another day), **cuir an dàil** adjourn (*meeting etc*), **cuir mu seach** put by, save, keep, **cuir an suarachas** belittle, **cuir gnothach** (etc) **air chois** set up/start up/found a business (etc), **chuir iad orm/chuir iad às mo leth nach robh mi onarach** they accused me of not being honest, **cuir aithne/ eòlas air cuideigin** get to know/get acquainted with someone, **cuir dragh air** worry/trouble (someone), **cuir aghaidh ri** face up to, address (*problem etc*), **cuir an gnìomh** put into effect, adopt (*measure etc*), **cuir an dreuchd** appoint (*job applicant etc*), **cuiridh mi (an) geall nach bi (an t-)uisge ann** I bet it won't rain, **cuir seachad ùine** spend/pass time, **tha e a' cur (an t-sneachda)** it's snowing, **cuir sìol** sow seed, **cuir buntàta** plant potatoes, **dè a tha a' cur ort?** what's wrong/the matter with you?, **chuir mi romham a' bhùth a dhùnadh** I decided to close the shop, **cuir an ceòl air feadh na fidhle** set/put the cat among the pigeons, **chuir seo gu smaoineachadh mi** this set me thinking; **2** *involving the notions* send, bring, turn, **cuir air falbh** send away, **cuir a dh'iarraidh** send for, **chuir mi litir thugad** I sent you a letter, **chuir i a-mach a dinnear** she brought up her dinner, **bha am ministear a' cur dheth** the minister was talking away/was in full flow, **cuir fios thuige** (etc) let him (etc) know/send him (etc) word, **chuir Gairm a-mach leabhar ùr** Gairm brought out/published a new book, **cha do chuir e suas no sìos mi** it didn't worry/affect/bother me in the least, **bha e gus mo chur dhìom fhìn** it was nearly driving me demented/out of my mind, **cuir fodha bàta** sink a boat, **cuir thairis** overflow, **chuir e nam aghaidh** he opposed me, **cò ris nach cuireadh e a làmh?** what couldn't he turn his hand to? **cuir mo** (etc) **c(h)ùl ri** turn my (etc) back on, leave, forsake, abandon, **cuir prìosanach** (etc) **mu sgaoil** set free/release a prisoner (etc)

cuireadh, cuiridh, cuiridhean *nm* an invitation, **cuireadh gu banais** an invitation to a wedding, **thoir** *v* **cuireadh do chuideigin** invite someone, *cf* **fiathaich, iarr 3, iarraidh 3**

cuirm, cuirme, cuirmean *nf* **1** a feast, a banquet (*cf* **fèis 2, fleadh**), **cuirm-chnuic** a picnic, **cuirm-chiùil** a concert; **2** a treat

cuirmeach *adj* festive

cùirt, cùirte, cùirtean *nf* **1** a (royal etc) court; **2** a law court (*also* **cùirt-lagha**)

cùirtean, cùirtein, cùirteanan, *also* **cùirtear, cùirteir, cùirtearan,** *nm* a curtain

cùirteil *adj* **1** courteous, *cf* **modhail**; **2** courtly

cùis, cùise, cùisean *nf* **1** a matter, an affair, a business, **ciamar a chaidh a' chùis?** how did the matter/affair go/turn out? **cnag na cùise** the nub/crux of the matter, the fundamental issue, the crucial question, **aig crìch na cùise** in the end, finally, *in expr (in argument, discussion etc)* **chan e sin a' chùis!** that's not the point!, *cf* **gnothach 2**; **2** (*in pl*) matters, things, **tha cùisean gu math dripeil an-dràsta** things are pretty busy just now; **3** (*legal*) a case (*also* **cùis-lagha**), a lawsuit, an action, **chaidh a' chùis na h-aghaidh** the case went against her; **4** a cause, a reason, a butt, an object, **cùis mo bhròin** the cause of/reason for my sadness, **bha iad nan cùis-mhagaidh an dèidh sin** they were a laughing-stock/a butt of ridicule after that, **cùis-ghearain** a cause for complaint, a grievance, *cf* **adhbhar 1, culaidh 4**; **5** *in expr* **dèan** *v* **a' chuis air** manage (*a task etc*), get the better of *or* defeat (*someone*), *cf* **gnothach 6, uachdar 5**; **6** *in expr* **nì sin a' chùis!** that'll do!, that'll do the job/trick!, *cf* **gnothach 7**

cùis-bheachd, cùis-bheachd, cùis-bheachdan *nf* an abstraction, an abstract idea

cùisear, cùiseir, cùisearan *nm* (*gram*) a subject, *cf* **cuspair 4**

cuisle, cuisle, cuislean *nf* **1** a vein, *cf less usu* **fèith 3**; **2** (*also* **cuisle mhòr**) an artery, **a' chuisle-chinn** the aorta; **3** a pipe, **cuisle-chiùil** a flute, *cf next*

cuislean, cuislein, cuisleanan *nm* a flute

cùiteag *see* **cuidhteag**

cùl, cùil, cùiltean *nm* **1** (*trad*) the back or nape of the neck, the hair on the nape, the hair of the head in general, **Gàidheal gu chùl** a Gael/Highlander through and through, every bit a Gael/Highlander; **2** *more generally* a back (*of human, animal, object etc*), **chuir mi mo chùl ris** I turned my back to/on him, **cùl na làimhe** the back of the hand, **cùl na h-amhaich** the back of the neck, **shad e an cùl na làraidh e** he shoved it in the back of the lorry, *Note:* **druim** *is used for the phys human back* ; **3** *in expr* **air cùl** *prep* behind (*with gen*), **air cùl na h-eaglaise** behind the church, *cf* **air cùlaibh**

cùlaibh *nm invar* the back part of anything, **cùlaibh air beulaibh** back to front, vice versa, *cf* **beulaibh** *& see* **air cùlaibh**

culaidh, culaidhe, culaidhean *nf* **1** (*trad*) a garment, *cf* **ball-aodaich** (*see* **aodach 2**); **2** (*also* **culaidh-aodaich**) a suit of clothes, *cf* **deise, trusgan 2**; **3** (*theatre, party etc*) a costume, **culaidh-choimheach** a fancy dress costume; **4** an object, a butt (*of emotions, reactions etc*), **culaidh-fharmaid** an object of envy, **culaidh-mhagaidh** an object of mockery, a butt of ridicule, *cf* **adhbhar 1, cùis 4**

cùlaist, cùlaiste, cùlaistean *nf* a scullery, a back kitchen, a utility room

cularan, cularain, cularanan *nm* a cucumber

cùl-chàin *vt, pres part* **a' cùl-chàineadh**, slander, back-bite

cùl-chàineadh, *gen* **cùl-chàinidh** *nm* **1** (*the act of*) slandering; **2** slander, back-biting, calumny

cullach, *gen & pl* **cullaich** *nm* **1** a boar, a male (domestic) pig; **2** a wild boar; *cf* **cràin, muc, torc**; **3** a male cat, a tom-cat

cùl-mhùtaire, cùl-mhùtaire, cùl-mhùtairean *nm* a smuggler

cùl-mhùtaireachd *nf invar* smuggling

cultar, cultair, cultaran *nm*, (*mental, artistic*) culture, a (*national etc*) culture, **cultar na Gàidhlige** Gaelic culture

cultarach *adj* cultural

cum *vt, pres part* **a' cumadh**, shape, form, fashion, **chum e ìomhaigh às a' chloich** he formed/fashioned an image/a figure out of the stone, *cf* **dealbh** *v* **2**

cùm *vt, pres part* **a' cumail, 1** keep, hold, hold on to, **cùm seo dhomh gu Dihaoine** keep this for me until Friday, **an cùm a' mhàileid sin mo chuid aodaich air fad?** will that bag hold all my clothes? **cùm grèim air rudeigin** keep a grip on/keep hold of something, **cumaibh air ais!** keep back! **cha chùm mi air ais sibh** I won't keep/hold you back, I won't delay you, *cf* **glèidh 1**; **2** continue, keep (on), (*calque*) **ciamar a tha thu a' cumail?** how are you keeping? **tha mi a' cumail beò** I'm surviving/still in the land of the living, **cùm ort!** keep going!, keep at it!, (*work, a task etc*) **cùm ris!** stick at it!, persevere!, don't give up!; **3** (*misc senses*) **cha do chùm sinn a' Bhliadhna Ur an-uiridh** we didn't keep/observe New Year last Year (*cf* **comharraich 3**), **cùm suas** keep, maintain, support, **tha teaghlach agam ri chumail suas** I have a family to support, **cùm cuidhteas iad** keep clear of them/give them a wide berth, **cùm a-mach** assert, maintain, claim, make out, **tha iad a' cumail a-mach gun tig an saoghal gu crìch a-màireach** they are making out that the world will end tomorrow,

cumadh, cumaidh, cumaidhean *nm* **1** (*the act of*) shaping etc (*see senses of* **cum** *v*); **2** a shape, a form, **rinn iad a-mach a chumadh san dorchadas** they made out his/its shape in the darkness, **chunnaic mi clach air chumadh eich** I saw a stone in the shape of a horse, *cf* **cruth 1, dealbh 5**

cumail, *gen* **cumalach** *nf* (*the act of*) keeping etc (*see senses of* **cùm** *v*)

cuman, *gen & pl* **cumain** *nm* (*trad*) a pail, a bucket (*esp for milking*), *cf* **cuinneag** *& less trad* **bucaid 1, peile**

cumanta *adj* common, frequently met with, **facal cumanta** a common word, *cf* **àbhaisteach, gnàthach**

cumantas, *gen* **cumantais** *nm* the quality of being common or usual, normality, *esp in exprs* **an cumantas** *adv* usually, commonly, normally (*cf* **am bitheantas**), *&* **às a' chumantas** *adv* out of the ordinary, out of the common run of things, unusual, (*calque*) **chan eil mòran aca an cumantas** they haven't much in common

cumha[1], cumha, cumhachan *nf* **1** (*trad, esp in contracts etc*) a stipulation, a condition; **2** *also in expr* **air chumha is gu . . .** on condition that . . . , as long as . . . , provided that . . . ; *cf* **cor 2, cùmhnant 2**

cumha[2], cumha, cumhachan *nm* (*trad*) *esp as genre of poetry or music*, a lament, an elegy, *cf* **marbhrann**

cumhach *adj* (*gram*) conditional, **an tràth cumhach** the conditional tense

cumhachd *nmf invar* **1** (*mainly abstr, pol, military etc*) power, might, force, influence, **cumhachd na h-Ìompaireachd Ròmanaich** the might of the Roman Empire; **2** (*industrial, domestic etc*) energy, power, **cumhachd niùclasach** nuclear energy/power

cumhachdach *adj* **1** powerful, mighty; **2** influential

cumhang *adj* **1** narrow, *cf more usu* **caol 1**; **2** (*of people, attitudes*) limited, narrow, narrow-minded

cùmhnant, cùmhnaint, cùmhnantan *nm* **1** (*legal, official, fin etc*) a covenant, a contract, a bargain, an agreement, *cf* **cunnradh**; **2** *also in*

cur-seachad

expr **air a' chùmhnant seo** on this condition, *cf* **cor 2, cumha** *nf* 1 & 2

cunbhalach *adj* 1 even, regular, constant, firm, steady; 2 tidy

cungaidh, cungaidh, cungaidhean *nf* 1 (*trad*) stuff, materials, ingredients; 2 (*trad*) a tool, an implement; 3 (*also* **cungaidh-leighis**) a medicine, a (medical) drug, **bùth-chungaidh** a chemist's shop, a pharmacy, **fear/neach-chungaidhean** a pharmacist, a (pharmaceutical) chemist

cunnart, cunnairt, cunnartan *nm* danger, risk, a danger, a risk, (**ann**) **an cunnart** in danger, at risk, endangered, **cuir** *v* **cuideigin/ rudeigin an cunnart** endanger/put at risk someone/something, **cunnart bàis** danger/risk of death, mortal/deadly danger, *cf* **gàbhadh** 1

cunnartach *adj* dangerous, risky, hazardous, *cf usu stronger* **gàbhaidh**

cunnradh, cunnraidh, cunnraidhean *nm* 1 a covenant, a contract, an agreement, *cf more usu* **cùmhnant** 1; 2 (*business, fin*) a bargain, a deal

cunnt *vti, pres part* **a' cunntadh**, count, **a' cunntadh chaorach** counting sheep, **chan urrainn do mo bhràthair beag cunntadh fhathast** my wee brother can't count yet, **chan eil Teàrlach ann ach chan eil esan a' cunntadh** Charles/Charlie isn't here but he doesn't count

cunntachail *adj* accountable

cunntadh, gen cunntaidh, also cunntais, gen cunntais, nm (*the act of*) counting

cunntair *see* **cuntair**

cunntas, cunntais, cunntasan *nm* 1 arithmetic; 2 a (bank etc) account, **tha cunntas agam aig a' Bhanca Rìoghail** I have an account at the Royal Bank, **cunntas tasgaidh/ sàbhalaidh** an investment/savings account; 3 an account, an invoice, a bill **chuir an grosair cunntas thugainn** the grocer sent us an account/bill, *cf more fam* **bileag** 3; 4 a written or verbal account, a narration, a narrative, a description, **sgrìobh e cunntas (air) a bheatha fhèin** he wrote an account of his own life, **cunntas-beatha** a CV; 5 (*sports, games*) a score, *cf* **sgòr**

cunntasachd *nf invar* accountancy, accounting

cunntasair, cunntasair, cunntasairean *nm* an accountant

cuntair (*also* **cunntair**), **cuntair, cuntairean** *nm* (*shop etc*) a counter, (*song*) **chosg mi de dh'airgead aig cuntair a' bhàir na cheannaicheadh trì taighean-òsta** I spent/ squandered as much money at the bar counter as would buy three hotels/pubs

cùp, cùpa, cùpannan *nm* cup

cupa, cupannan *nm* a cup, **nach gabh sibh cupa teatha?** won't you have a cup of tea? *cf* **copan**

cuplachadh, gen cuplachaidh *nm* 1 (*the act of*) copulating etc (*see senses of* **cuplaich** *v*); 2 copulation

cuplaich *vi, pres part* **a' cuplachadh**, copulate, couple, mate, have sexual intercourse, *cf* **co-ghin, muin** 4

cùpon, cùpoin, cùponan *nm* a coupon, a voucher

cur, gen cuir *nm* (*the act of*) placing, putting, sending etc, (*see senses of* **cuir** *v*)

curach, curaich, curaichean *nf* 1 (*trad, hist*) a curach *or* curragh, a coracle, *a light, usu round, boat of timber or wattle, covered with hide*; 2 **curach Innseanach** a canoe

curaidh, curaidh, curaidhean *nm* a hero, *cf* **gaisgeach, laoch, seòd**

cùram, cùraim, cùraman *nm* 1 care, responsibility, **air cùram Dhòmhnaill** in Donald's care/charge, under Donald's responsibility, entrusted to Donald, *cf* **uallach** 2, **urra** 2; 2 anxiety, preoccupation, **fo chùram** anxious, worried, (*song*) **tha i daonnan air mo chùram anns gach nì** she is always on my mind in every situation, *cf* **iomagain** 1; 3 (*Presbyterianism*) conversion, becoming very devout or religious, *esp in expr* **ghabh e (etc) an cùram** he (*etc*) became converted/became very devout, (*Highland Eng*) he's (*etc*) got the cùram

cùramach *adj* 1 careful, cautious, acting responsibly, *cf* **faiceallach**; 2 anxious, prone to anxiety or worry, *cf* **iomagaineach** 1

cur na mara *nm invar* sea-sickness, *cf* **tinneas-mara** (*see* **tinneas**)

curracag, curracaig, curracagan *nf* a lapwing, a peewit, a green plover, (*Sc*) a peesie, *cf* **adharcan-luachrach**

curran, gen currain, pl currain & curranan *nm* a carrot

cùrsa, cùrsa, cùrsaichean *nm* 1 (*academic etc*) a course, **rinn mi cùrsaichean sa Ghàidhlig agus sa Bheurla anns an Oilthigh** I did/took courses in Gaelic and English at University, (*lang teaching*) **cùrsa-bogaidh** an immersion course; 2 a course, a direction of travel, *cf* **iùl** 1, **seòl** 2

cùrsair, cùrsair, cùrsairean *nm* (*IT etc*) a cursor

cur-seachad, cuir-seachad, cur-seachadan *nm* a hobby, a pastime, a (leisure) pursuit *or* activity, **is e ball-coise an cur-seachad as**

fheàrr leam/as fheàrr a th' agam football is my favourite hobby/pastime

cur-sìos *adj* derogatory, belittling, **briathran cur-sìos** derogatory statements

cùrtair *see* **cùirtean**

cus, *gen* **cuis** *nm* an excess, too much, **dh'òl mi cus a-raoir!** I drank too much last night! **cus bruidhne** too much talking

cusbainn *nf invar* customs (*ie levying of import duty*), **cìs-chusbainn** *f* customs duty

cusp, cusp, cuspan *nf* a chilblain

cuspair, cuspair, cuspairean *nm* **1** a subject, a topic, a theme, **cuspair a h-òraid** the subject of her talk; **2** (*school etc*) a subject, **b' e ceimigeachd an cuspair a b' fheàrr leis** chemistry was his favourite subject; **3** (*trad*) an object (*of emotion etc*), **cuspair a ghràidh** the object of his love; **4** (*gram*) an object (*ie of a verb*), *cf* **cùisear**; **5** (*Lit, art etc*) a subject, subject matter, **cuspair is cruth** matter and form

cuspaireach *adj* (*gram*) accusative, **an tuiseal cuspaireach** the accusative case

cut *vti, pres part* **a' cutadh**, gut (*esp fish*)

cutair, cutair, cutairean *nm* a gutter (*esp of fish*)

cuthach, *gen* **cuthaich** *nm* **1** madness, insanity; **2** rage, fury, extreme anger, **chaidh e air chuthach** he went mad/insane, *also* he went mad (*with rage*), he became furious, **ghabh e an cuthach (dearg)** he went mad with rage; *cf* **bàinidh, boile**

cuthag, cuthaig, cuthagan *nf* a cuckoo

D

dà *n & adj* **1** two (*takes the dat, lenites following noun*), **dà chù** two dogs, **dà chloich** two stones, **uair no dhà** a time or two, once or twice, *also* an hour or two; **2** *in compound adjs & nouns* two-, bi-, **dà-bharaileach** *adj* in two minds, undecided, ambivalent, *see other examples below*

dà-bhitheach *adj* amphibious, *cf* **muir-thìreach**

dachaigh, dachaigh(e), dachaighean *nf* a home, one's home, **1** (*one's dwelling*) **am faic thu an taigh ud thall? 's e sin mo dhachaigh** do you see the house over yonder? that's my home, (*house name*) **Ar Dachaigh** Our Home, *cf* **baile 5, taigh 2**; **2** (*district, country etc one belongs to*) (*song*) **eilean beag Leòdhais, dachaigh nan seòid** the little isle of Lewis, home of heroes, *cf* **dùthaich 3**; **3** (*as adv expressing movement, lenited*) **dhachaigh** home, homewards, **tha mi a' falbh/a' dol dhachaigh** I'm away/going home

dà-chànanach *adj* bilingual

dad *nf invar* **1** a thing, anything, **chan eil dad agam** I haven't a thing/anything, *cf* **càil 1 & 2, nì n 1, rud 1, sìon**; **2** *also in expr* **dad ort!** never mind, don't worry!

dadaidh, dadaidh, dadaidhean *nm* (*fam*) Daddy, a Daddy, *cf* **athair, mamaidh**

dadam, *gen & pl* **dadaim** *nm* **1** an atom; **2** a tiny piece of anything

dà-dheug *n & adj* twelve, **dà uair dheug** twelve o'clock

dà-fhillte *adj* **1** two-fold; **2** (*IT*) binary

daga & dag, *gen* **daige,** *pl* **dagan & dagaichean** *nm* a handgun, a pistol, a revolver

dail, dalach, dailean *nf* **1** a meadow (*cf* **clua(i)n**), a haugh (*cf* **innis** *n* **2**); **2** a dale, a small valley

dàil, dàlach, dàlaichean *nf* **1** delay, a delay, **thig dhachaigh gun dàil** come home without delay, *cf* **maille 2**; **2** *in exprs* **cuir** *v* **dàil ann/air** delay, **chuir an aimsir dàil anns a' chùis** the weather delayed the business/matter, *cf* **cùm**

air ais (see **cùm 1**); **3** (*fin*) credit, **ceannaich** *v* **air dàil** buy on credit/hire purchase

dalma *adj* blatant, *cf* **ladarna**

dàimh, *gen* **dàimhe** *nmf* **1** a relationship, ties (*of kinship, friendship*), **an dàimh eadar an dà theaghlach** the relationship/ties between the two families, *cf* **càirdeas**; **2** (*in general*) a connection, a tie, a link (**ri** with), **cha robh dàimh agam ris a' chompanaidh sin** I had no connection with that firm, *cf* **buinteanas, ceangal 2**

dàimheach *adj* relative, (*gram*) **mion-fhacal/mìrean dàimheach** a relative particle

dàimheil *adj* friendly; affectionate

daingeann *adj* (*structure, building etc*) firm, solid, *cf* **teann** *adj* **2**

daingneach, daingnich, daingnichean *nf* a fort, a fortress, a stronghold, a (*fortified*) castle, *cf* **dùn 2**

daingneachadh, *gen* **daingneachaidh** *nm* (*the act of*) fortifying, confirming etc (*see senses of* **daingnich** *v*)

daingnich *vt, pres part* **a' daingneachadh, 1** (*structure, building etc*) fortify, strengthen, consolidate, make firm or solid; **2** (*truths, principles etc*) confirm, prove, **dhaingnich i a creideamh le a bhith a' dol na caillich-dhuibh** she confirmed her faith by becoming a nun, *cf* **dearbh** *v* **1**

dàir, *gen* **dàra** *nf* (*of cattle*) breeding, coupling, **crodh-dàra** breeding *or* calving cattle, **bò fo dhàir** a cow in season, a bulling cow

dall *adj* blind, **an Clàrsair Dall** the Blind Harper (*a 17th–18th century Gaelic poet*)

dall, *gen & pl* **doill** *nm* a blind person, (*prov*) **chì sinn, mar a thuirt an dall** we'll see, as the blind man said

dall *vt, pres part* **a' dalladh, 1** blind; **2** delude

dalladh, *gen* **dallaidh** *nm* **1** (*the act of*) blinding, (*the state of*) blindness; **2** (*fig*) infatuation, delusion

dàmais *nf invar* draughts (*ie the game*), **bòrd-dàmais** *m* a draught board

damh

damh, *gen & pl* **daimh 1** *nm* a stag (*usu red deer*), *cf* **boc 2, eilid**; **2** an ox; **3** a bullock

dàmhair, dàmhair, dàmhairean *nf* **1** rutting of red deer, rutting time or season; **2** (*with art*) **An Dàmhair** October

damaiste, damaiste, damaistean *nf* **1** damage; **2** *in pl* **damaistean** (*fin, legal etc*) damages

damhan-allaidh, *gen & pl* **damhain-allaidh** *nm* a spider

dàn¹, *gen* **dàin** *nm* **1** fate, destiny, **na cuir an aghaidh dàin!** don't oppose/go against fate!; **2** *in expr* **an dàn do** fated, destined, ordained (*for someone*), **ghabh e ris na bha an dàn dha** he accepted his fate/what fate had ordained for him

dàn², *gen* **dàin**, *pl* **dàna** & **dàin** *nm* **1** a poem, (*title of poem sequence*) **Dàin do Eimhir** (Somhairle MacGill-Eain) Poems to/for Eimhir, *cf* **bàrdachd, rann 1**; **2** (*trad*) a song, (*song*) **nì mi nis co-dhùnadh is bheir mi an dàn gu crìch** I'll conclude now and bring the song to an end, **dàn spioradail** a spiritual song, a hymn (*cf* **laoidh 2**); *Note: before the 20th century the distinction between poem and song hardly existed in Gaelic culture*

dàna *adj* **1** bold, daring, intrepid, adventurous, *cf* **gaisgeil**; **2** rashly brave, *cf* **bras 2**; **3** impudent, *cf* **ladarna**; **4** arrogant, *cf* **àrdanach, uaibhreach 2**

dànachd *nf invar* poetry, verse, *cf more usu* **bàrdachd, rann 1**

dànadas, *gen* **dànadais** *nm* **1** boldness, daring, intrepidity; **2** impudence; **3** arrogance

Danmhairg *nf invar*, used with the art, **an Danmhairg** Denmark

Danmhairgeach, Danmhairgich, Danmhairgich *nm* a Dane, *also as adj*, **Danmhairgeach** Danish

danns *vti, pres part* **a' dannsa(dh)**, dance

dannsa, dannsa, dannsaichean *nm* a dance (*individual dance and social event*), **bidh cèilidh agus dannsa ann a-nochd** there'll be a ceilidh-dance tonight

dannsadh, *gen* **dannsaidh** *nm* (*the act of*) dancing, **an toigh leat dannsadh? cha toil!** do you like dancing? no!

dannsair, dannsair, dannsairean *nm* a dancer

daoimean, daoimein, daoimeanan *nm* a diamond

daoine *see* **duine**

daolag, daolaig, daolagan *nf* a beetle, **daolag-bhreac-dhearg** a ladybird

daonna (*also* **daonda**) *adj* **1** human, *freq in expr* **an cinne-daonna** *m* humanity, humankind, mankind, the human race, *cf* **mac-an-duine** (*see* **duine 3**); **2** humane, *cf more usu* **caomh, truacanta**

daonnachd (*also* **daondachd**) *nf invar* humanity (*ie both humaneness and the quality or state of being human*)

daonnan *adv* always, constantly, *cf similarly* used **an-còmhnaidh, fad na h-ùine** (*see* **ùine 1**)

daor *adj* dear, expensive, costly (*opposite of* **saor**), (*song*) **'s daor a cheannaich mi 'n t-iasgach** I paid dearly for the fishing, *cf* **cosgail**

daorach, *gen* **daoraich** *nf* **1** drunkenness, intoxication, *esp in exprs* **tha an daorach air, tha e air an daoraich, tha e leis an daoraich** he's drunk, **ceann daoraich** *m* a hangover, *cf* **misg, smùid** *n* **4**; **2** (*trad*) a (drinking) spree, (*song, pibroch*) **An Daorach Mhòr** The Big Spree

daorachail *adj* intoxicating

daorsa *nf invar* captivity (*opposite of* **saorsa**), *cf more usu* **braighdeanas, ciomachas, làmh 2, sàs 1**

dara & **dàrna** *adj* **1** second, **an dara là den mhìos** the second day of the month; **2** (*when in contrast to* **eile**) one, **tha an dara mac dèanadach ach tha am fear eile leisg** one son is industrious but the other one is lazy, *in expr* **cuir** *v* **an dara taobh** put to one side, set aside; **3** *in expr* **an dara cuid**, either, **thoir dhomh an dara cuid feòil no iasg** give me either meat or fish

darach, *gen & pl* **daraich** *nm* oak

dara-deug *adj* twelfth, **an dara là deug** the twelfth day

da-rìribh & **da-rìreadh** *adv* **1** *in expr* (**cha robh iad** etc) **ann an da-rìribh** (they weren't etc) serious/in earnest, they didn't mean it, *see* **fealla-dhà** & *cf less usu* **stòlda 2**; **2** *often in expr* **math dha-rìribh** very good indeed, excellent, extremely good, *cf* **eagalach 3, uabhasach 2**

dàrna *see* **dara**

dà-sheaghach *adj* ambiguous, ambivalent, equivocal

dà-sheaghachd *nf invar* ambiguity, ambivalence

dà-shùileach *adj* two-eyed

dàta *nm invar* data, information, (*IT*) **stòr-dàta** *m* a database

dath *vt, pres part* **a' dathadh**, **1** colour; **2** dye; *cf* **cuir dath air** (*see* **dath** *n*)

dath, datha, dathan *nm* **1** colour, a colour, **dè an dath a th' air a' chòta?** what colour's the coat? **cuir** *v* **dath air** colour, dye, **dath-lipean** lipstick, **dath-dhall** *adj* colour blind, **dath-bhacadh** *m* a colour bar; **2** dye, a dye

dathail *adj* colourful, highly coloured

dà-thaobhach *adj* bilateral

dathte *adj* coloured; dyed

dè *pron* **1** what, **dè an t-ainm a th' oirbh?** what's your name?, **dè a tha a' tachairt?** what's happening? **dè am math a bhith bruidhinn!** what's the good/use of talking! **dè do bheachd?** what do you think?, **Dè an rud?** What?, Pardon? (*cf more polite* **B' àill leibh?** *– see* **àill 2**), **dè na tha e?** how much is it?, (*in indirect questions*) **chan eil fhios a'm dè a nì mi** I don't know what I'll do; **2** *in constr* **dè cho . . . agus/'s a . . . ?** how . . . ?, **dè cho feumail 's a tha e?** how useful is it?; **3** (*trad, now more emph*) **gu dè** what, whatever, **gu dè as ciall dhut?** whatever do you mean?

de & **dhe** *prep, with the dat, lenites following cons where possible. The prep prons formed with* **de** & **dhe**, *in the order first, second, third person singular, first, second, third person plural, and with the reflexive/emphatic particles in brackets, are as follows:* **dhìom(sa), dhìot(sa), dheth(san), dhith(se), dhinn(e), dhibh(se), dhiubh(san)**, of/from me, of/from you (*fam*), *etc* **1** of, **a' chuid as mò dheth** most of it, **aig an àm seo den bhliadhna** at this time of the year, **am ficheadamh là den mhìos** the twentieth of the month, **làn de bhainne** full of milk, **fear de na bh' ann** one of those who were there, **amadan de dhuine** a fool of a man, **fear dhiubh sin** one of those; **de** *sometimes occurs as* **a**, *eg* **chan eil càil a dh'fhios agam** I haven't the faintest idea (*lit* I have nothing of knowledge); **2** of (*ie made of*), **bràiste de dh'airgead** a brooch of silver; **3** of, out of, (*song*) **dèan am foghar den gheamhradh** make autumn (out) of winter; **4** from, off, **cuir dhìot do chòta** take your coat off, (*fam*) **tha e dheth an-diugh** he's off (*work etc*) today, **tog** *v* **clachan den làr** lift stones from the ground; **5** *in expr* **ullamh de** finished with, **bha am poileas ullamh de a cheasnachadh** the police had finished questioning him

deacair *adj* hard, difficult, abstruse, **leabhar deacair** a difficult book (*ie to understand*), *cf* **doirbh, duilich 1**

deach, deachaidh *pts of irreg v* **rach** (*see tables p 501*)

deachd *vti, pres part* **a' deachdadh**, dictate (*letter etc*)

deachdadh, deachdaidh, deachdaidhean *nm* **1** (*the act of*) dictating; **2** dictation, a dictation

deachdaire, deachdaire, deachdairean *nm* (*pol etc*) a dictator

deachdaireachd *nf invar* dictatorship

deadhan, gen & pl deadhain *nm* (*relig, ed*) a dean

deagh *adj* (*precedes & lenites the noun*) **1** good, **is e deagh sheinneadair a th' ann** he's a good singer, (*corres etc*) **leis gach deagh dhùrachd!** with best wishes! (*lit* with every good wish), **tha e air a dheagh dhòigh** he's pleased/delighted, **tha mi ann an deagh thriom** I'm in good trim; **2** *also in compounds, eg* **deagh-thoil** *f* goodwill, **deagh-chridheach** *adj* good-hearted, **deagh bheusan** *f* (good) morals; **3** *as adv* well, **tha e air a dheagh chumadh/dhèanamh** (etc) it's well shaped/made (etc); *cf* **math** & *opposite* **droch**

dealachadh, dealachaidh, dealachaidhean *nm* **1** (*the act of*) parting etc (*see senses of* **dealaich** *v*), **thug i nota dha anns an dealachadh** she gave him a pound on parting/as they parted; **2** separation, a separation, **dealachadh-pòsaidh** (a) separation, (a) divorce, *cf* **sgaradh 3**; **3** segregation; **4** (*elec etc*) insulation

dealaich *vti, pres part* **a' dealachadh**, **1** part, separate, segregate, detach (**ri** from), **dhealaich na càirdean ri chèile** the friends parted/separated, **cha dealaich thu bho chuid airgid e!** you won't part him from his money!, **dhealaich am bàs iad** death parted them; **2** (*elec etc*) insulate

dealan, gen dealain *nm* electricity, **Bòrd an Dealain** the Electricity Board, (*song*) **solas an dealain** the electric light, **dealan-uisge** hydro-electricity, *cf* **cumhachd 2**; **2 dealain** (*gen of* **dealan** *used as adj*) electric, electronic, **teine** *m* **dealain** an electric fire, (*IT*) **post-dealain** *m* electronic mail, e-mail

dealanach, gen & pl dealanaich *nm* lightning

dealanaich *vt, pres part* **a' dealanachadh**, electrify (*not in fig sense*)

dealanair, dealanaire, dealanairean *nm* an electrician

dealan-dè, dealain-dè, dealanan-dè *nm* a butterfly

dealantach *adj* electronic

dealas, gen dealais *nm* eagerness, zeal, commitment

dealasach *adj* eager, zealous, *cf* **deònach, èasgaidh**

dealbh, gen dealbha & deilbh, pl dealbhan, deilbh & dealbhannan *nmf* **1** a picture, **taigh-dhealbh** a picture house, a cinema; **2** a painting; **3** a photograph, **tog** *v* **dealbh** take a photograph; **4** a drawing, **dealbh-èibhinn**

a cartoon (*single sketch, strip cartoon or animated film*); **5** a form, a shape, a figure, **rinn mi a-mach dealbh duine/dealbh taighe san dorchadas** I made out the shape/figure of a man/the shape/form of a house in the darkness, *cf* **cruth 1, cumadh 2**; **6** *also in compounds, eg* **dealbh-chluich** a (stage) play, **dealbh-chumadh** a (*usu technical*) plan or diagram

dealbh *vt, pres part* **a' dealbhadh**, **1** picture (*mentally*), imagine, **tachartas nach b' urrainn dhut a dhealbhadh** an event you couldn't imagine; **2** make, shape, construct, *cf* **cum**; **3** design, plan (*technical & artistic objects*), **dealbh innealan** design machines

dealbhadh, *gen* **dealbhaidh** *nm* (*the act of*) picturing, shaping, planning etc (*see senses of* **dealbh** *vt*), **cead dealbhaidh** *m* planning permission

dealbh-èibhinn *nmf, see* **dealbh** *nmf* 4

dealg, deilg, dealgan *nf* **1** a prickle, a thorn, *cf* **bior 3**; **2** a thorn (*ie the plant*); **3** a skewer; **4** a pin, *cf more usu* **prìne**

deàlrach *adj* **1** shining, radiant, *cf* **boillsgeach**; **2** shiny

deàlradh, *gen* **deàlraidh** *nm* **1** (*the act of*) shining etc (*see senses of* **deàlraich** *v*); **2** radiance

deàlraich *vi, pres part* **a' deàlradh**, (*of lights*) **1** shine, *cf* **soillsich 2**; **2** flash, glitter, *cf* **boillsg**

dealt, *gen* **dealta**, *nmf* dew, (*song*) **dealt na h-oidhche a' sileadh coibhneis** the dew of the night shedding kindliness, *cf* **driùchd**

deamhais, deamhais, deamhaisean *nmf* (a pair of) shears

deamhan, *gen & pl* **deamhain** *nm* a demon, a fiend, *cf* **diabhal**

deamocrasaidh, deamocrasaidh, deamocrasaidhean *nm* democracy, a democracy

deamocratach *adj* democratic

deamocratach, *gen & pl* **deamocrataich** *nm* a democrat

dèan *vt irreg* (*see tables p 497*), *pres part* **a' dèanamh**, **1** do, **dèan do dhleastanas** do your duty, **na dèan sin!** don't do that! **rinn mi mo dhìcheall** I did my best, **nach math a rinn thu!** well done!, didn't you do well! **nì sin an gnothach** that will do!, that's just the job; **2** make, **nì mi silidh a-màireach** I'll make jam tomorrow, (*poem*) **ma bha siud an dàn dhaibh, dhèanadh iad daoine** (Ruaraidh MacThòmais) if that were their lot, they would make men, **rinn iad adhartas** they made progress, **rinn e air a' bhàta** he made for the

boat; **3** (*art etc*) compose, **rinn mi bàrdachd/òran** I've made/composed some poetry/a song; **4** (*trad*) *as auxiliary verb with poss adj & verbal noun* **rinn iad ar sgriosadh/ar sàbhaladh** (etc) they ruined/saved (etc) us (*lit* they did our ruining/our saving etc); **5** *other common exprs* **dèan cabhag!** hurry up! **dèan cadal!** go to sleep!, **dèan suidhe** be seated, **nì e feum dhut** it will do you good

dèanadach *adj* industrious, hardworking, active, *cf* **dìcheallach, gnìomhach**

dèanadas, *gen* **dèanadais** *nm* industry, industriousness, *cf* **gnìomhachas 1**

dèanadh, dèanaibh, dèanainn, dèanam, dèanamaid *pts of irreg v* **dèan** (*see tables p 497*)

dèanamh, *gen* **dèanaimh** *nm* **1** (*the act of*) doing, making etc (*see senses of* **dèan** *v*); **2** one's form, figure, build, physique, constitution, **'s e iasg is min-choirce a thug an deagh dhèanamh dhaibh** it's fish and oat-meal that gave them their fine build/constitution

deann, deanna, deannan *nf* **1** (*trad*) force, impetus; **2** haste, speed, *usu in expr* **na (etc) dheann** rushing, in a rush, in (great) haste, **chaidh iad dhachaigh nan deann** they rushed home, *cf* **cabhag 1, deann-ruith**

deannan *nm* (*followed by gen*) a good *or* fair number (of), quite a few, **deannan dhaoine** a good number of people

deann-ruith *nf* a headlong rush, (*usu in exprs such as*) **dh'fhalbh e** (*etc*) **na** (*etc*) **dheann-ruith** he (*etc*) left in a headlong rush/at full speed

deanntag *see* **feanntag**

dèanta & dèante *adj* made, done, completed, **duine dèanta** a grown man (*cf* **foirfe**), **dèanta ri cogadh** raised/trained to war

dearbh *adj* **1** very, same, exact, **an e Tormod a tha a' tighinn? an dearbh dhuine!** is it Norman who's coming? the very man! **'s e òrd an dearbh rud a bha dhìth orm** a hammer was the very/exact thing I needed, *cf* **ceart 3, ceudna 1, fèin 5**; **2** *as adv* **gu dearbh** indeed, certainly, definitely, really, **a bheil thu sgìth? tha gu dearbh!** are you tired? I certainly am! **tha e beartach! a bheil gu dearbh?** he's rich! is he really?/is he indeed?

dearbh *vt, pres part* **a' dearbhadh**, **1** prove, demonstrate, **dearbh a chionta/gu bheil Dia ann** prove his guilt/that there is a God; **2** test, put to the test, try, *cf* **deuchainn 2, feuch 2**

dearbhadh, dearbhaidh, dearbhaidhean *nm* **1** (*the act of*) proving etc (*see senses of* **dearbh** *v*); **2** proof, a proof, evidence, a piece of evidence (air of), **dearbhadh air a chionta** proof/ evidence of his guilt, *cf* **fianais 2, teisteanas 1; 3** a test, a trial, **dearbhaidhean air càr ùr** tests on/trials of a new car

dearbhte, *also* **dearbhta**, certain, definite, proven, proved

dearc, dearc, dearcan *nf, also dimin* **dearcag, dearcaig, dearcagan** *nf*, a berry, *cf* **sùbh**

dearg *adj* **1** red (*usu for a brighter red than* **ruadh**), **fride dhearg** red corpuscle, **brù-dhearg** a robin, **dearc-dhearg** a redcurrant; **2** *with other colours*, reddish-, reddy-, **dearg-dhonn** reddish-brown; **3** *as pej intensifying element*, complete, utter, **dearg amadan** *m* an utter fool; **4** *as adv* completely, utterly, **tha i air a dearg mhilleadh** she's utterly spoilt, **dearg rùisgte** stark naked

deargad, deargaid, deargadan *nf &* **deargann, deargainn, deargannan** *nf*, a flea, (*poem*) **Deargadan na Pòlainn** the Fleas of Poland

deargnaich *vt, pres part* **a' deargnachadh**, make *or* colour red, redden

dearmad, dearmaid, dearmadan *nm* **1** (*the act of*) neglecting, omitting (*see senses of* **dearmaid** *v*); **2** neglect, negligence, omission, **peacaidhean dearmaid** sins of omission; **3** *also in exprs* **cuir** *v* **rudeigin air dhearmad** neglect to do something, **leig** *v* **rudeigin/ cuideigin air dhearmad** neglect something/ someone, *cf* **dearmaid** *v* **1** & **2**

dearmadach *adj* neglectful, negligent

dearmaid *vt, pres part* **a' dearmad**, **1** omit *or* neglect (*to do something*); **2** neglect (*something or someone*)

deàrrs *vi, pres part* **a' deàrrsadh**, *also* **deàrrsaich** *vi, pres part* **a' deàrrsachadh**, shine, (*often of sun*) **chan eil a' ghrian a' deàrrs(ach)adh** the sun's not shining

deas *nf invar & adj* **1** south, **an àird(e) deas** south (*ie the compass direction*), **Uibhist a Deas** South Uist, **a' fuireach/a' dol mu dheas** living in/going to the south, **oiteag on deas** a breeze from the south, **an taobh deas den dùthaich** *also* **taobh a deas na dùthcha** the southern part/the south of the country, **tha Ceann Rois deas air Peairt** Kinross is south of Perth; **2** *in expr* **an làmh dheas**, right, **tha a' bhùth air an làimh dheis** (*dat*) the shop is on the right(-hand side), *cf less usu* **ceart 4**

deas *adj* **1** ready, **a bheil thu deas?** are you ready? *Also* have you finished?, *cf more usu* **deiseil 1 & 2, ullamh 1 & 2**; **2** (*of person, action*) active, quick, adroit, prompt, **rinn e gu deas e** he did it promptly, *cf* **clis, ealamh**

deasachadh, *gen* **deasachaidh** *nm* **1** (*the act of*) preparing etc (*see senses of* **deasaich** *v*); **2** preparation; **3** editing, **fear-deasachaidh** *m* an editor

deasaich *vt, pres part* **a' deasachadh**, **1** prepare, get ready, **deasaich am bòrd** set the table, **deasaich biadh** prepare/cook food, *cf* **ullaich 1**; **2** (*publishing etc*) edit

deasbad, deasbaid, deasbadan *nmf* **1** discussion, a discussion, debate, a debate

deasg, deasga, deasgan *nm* a desk

deas-ghnàth, deas-ghnàith, deas-ghnàthan *nm* ceremony, a ceremony

deatach, deataiche, deataichean *nf* fumes, gas, smoke, vapour, **cuir** *v* **deatach** emit/give out fumes, *cf* **smùid** *n* **3**

deataich *vi, pres part* **a' deatachadh** evaporate

deatamach *adj* crucial, essential, *cf* **riatanach**

deich *n invar & adj* ten

deicheach *adj* decimal

deichead, deicheid, deicheadan *nm* ten years, a decade

deicheamh, *gen* **deicheimh** *nm* **1** a decimal; **2** a tenth

deicheamh *adj* tenth

deichnear *nmf invar* (*people numbering*) ten, (*takes gen pl*) **deichnear mhac** ten sons

dèideadh, *gen* **dèididh** *nm* toothache, (*used with art*) **tha an dèideadh orm** I've got (the) toothache

dèideag, dèideig, dèideagan *nf* **1** a toy; **2** a pebble

dèidh, dèidhe, dèidhean *nf* **1** a wish, a desire, *cf more usu* **miann 1, rùn 3, togradh 2**; **2** fondness, *cf* **rùn 1, spèis 1**

dèidheil *adj* fond (*air* of), keen (*air* on), **ro dhèidheil air deoch-làidir** over-keen on drink, **bha i dèidheil orm** she was fond of me, *cf* **measail 2**

deidhinn *see* **mu 3**

deifrichte *adj see* **diof(a)rach**

deigh *see* **eigh**

deilbh *v & n same as* **dealbh** *v & n*

dèile, *gen* **dèilidh**, *pl* **dèilean** & **dèileachan** *nf* a (wooden) board, a plank, *cf* **bòrd 2, clàr 1**

dèilig *vi, pres part* **a' dèiligeadh**, deal (*ri* with), **dèiligidh mi ris a-màireach** I'll deal with it tomorrow

deimhinn(e), *also* **deimhinnte** *adj* sure, certain, **bidh (an t-)uisge ann, tha mi deimhinne** it'll rain, I'm certain, *cf more usu* **cinnteach**

dèine, *nf invar* (*abstr n corres to* **dian** *adj*) eagerness, keenness, fervour, ardour

dèirc

dèirc, dèirce, dèircean *nf* charity, alms, charitable gifts, *cf* **carthannachd 2**

dèirceach *adj* charitable, apt to give charitably

dèirceach, *gen & pl* **dèircich** *nm* **1** a beggar; **2** someone dependent on charity

deireadh, deiridh, deiridhean *nm* **1** end (*usu of period of time*), **deireadh a' mhìosa** the end of the month, **aig deireadh an là** at the end of the day, in the end, finally, *cf* **ceann 2**; **2** *in expr* **air dheireadh** *adv* behind, lagging behind; **3** *in expr* **(thàinig i etc) air deireadh** *adv* (she came etc) last, *also* late, **còig mionaidean air deireadh** five minutes late; **4** *in expr* **mu dheireadh** *adj* last, *adv* at last, **'s e seo an cothrom mu dheireadh a gheibh thu** this is the last opportunity you'll get, **sguir an t-uisge mu dheireadh (thall)** the rain stopped at (long) last

deireannach *adj* last, final, **air an latha dheireannach** on the last day, (*song*) **Cead Deireannach nam Beann** The Last/Final Farewell to the Mountains, *cf less emph* **mu dheireadh** (*see* **deireadh 4**)

deisciobal, *gen & pl* **deisciobail** *nm* a disciple

deise, deise, deiseachan *nf* a suit (*of clothes*), *cf* **culaidh 2, trusgan 2**

dèiseag, dèiseige, dèiseagan *nf* a smack, a slap, a skelp, *cf* **sgailc 1**

deiseil *adj* **1** ready, **tha am biadh deiseil** the food's ready, **tha mi deiseil** I'm ready, *cf* **ullamh 1** & *less usu* **deas** *adj* **1**; **2** having finished (*a task etc*), **a bheil thu deiseil fhathast?** have you finished yet? **deiseil dhe a bhracaist** having finished his breakfast, **chan eil iad deiseil den fòn** they haven't finished with the phone, *cf* **ullamh 2**; **3** handy (*ie convenient*) **bidh sin deiseil dhut** that'll be handy for you, *cf* **ullamh 3**; **4** *as adv* clockwise, *cf opposite* **tuathal 1**; **5** *as adv* (*trad*) sunwise (*opposite of Sc* widdershins), *cf opposite* **tuathal 2**

deit, deite, deitichean *nf* (*fruit*) a date

deò *nf invar* **1** breath, a breath, **deò gaoithe** a breath of wind (*cf* **ospag 2**), *cf more usu* **anail**; **2** life, the breath of life, **fhad 's a bhios an deò annam** as long as there's life in me/breath in my body, *cf* **rong** *nf*

deoc *vti, pres part* **a' deocadh**, *same senses as* **deothail** *vti* (*see below*)

deoch, dighe, deochannan *nf* **1** a drink (*of any liquid*), **deoch bhainne/uisge** a drink of milk/ of water; **2** an alcoholic drink, drink, *also more specifically* **deoch-làidir** strong drink, alcoholic drink, **thoir** *v* **dhomh deoch** give me a drink, (*prov*) **an uair a bhios an deoch a-staigh**

bidh a' chiall a-mach when drink's in sense is out, **tha e measail air an deoch** he's fond of the drink/booze, (*trad*) **deoch-an-dorais** a 'Jock and Doris', a parting drink, 'one for the road', **tinneas na dighe** *m* alcoholism

deothail, *also* **deoghail**, *vti, pres part* **a' deothal**, suck, suck up, absorb (*esp liquids*), *cf* **sugh** *vti*

deothail, *gen* **deothail** *nm* (*the act of*) sucking, absorbing; suction

deòin, *gen* **deòine** *nf* consent, willingness, *usu in expr* **a dheòin no a dh'aindeoin** willing(ly) or not, willy-nilly, *cf opposite* **aindeoin 1**

deònach *adj* willing, prepared (*to do something*), **chan eil iad deònach** (*more trad* **deònach air**) **a dhèanamh** they're not willing/prepared to do it, *cf* **airson 4, toileach 1** & *opposite* **aindeònach**

deuchainn, deuchainne, deuchainnean *nf* **1** (*ed etc*) an examination, a test, **feuch/suidh** *v* **deuchainnean** sit *or* take exams; **2** a test, a trial, **chuir iad na h-innealan ùra gu deuchainn** they tried out/tested the new machines, *cf* **dearbh** *v* **2, feuch 2**; **3** (*science etc*) an experiment, **deuchainn-lann** *m* a laboratory; **4** a trying time or experience, a trial, **'s e deuchainn a bh' ann an tinneas mo mhàthair dhomh** my mother's illness was a trial for me

deudach *adj* dental, *cf* **fiaclach 3**

deug *num suffix in numbers* 11 *to* 19, **a h-aon-deug** eleven, **sia cait dheug** sixteen cats

deugaire, deugaire, deugairean *nm* a teenager, *cf* **òigear**

deur, *gen & pl* **deòir** *nm* a tear, a teardrop, (*song*) **'s na deòir a' sileadh** with the tears flowing

deurach *adj* tearful, weeping, *cf* **silteach**

dha, *with sing art* **dhan**, *prep used by some speakers for* **do**, to, **a' dol dhan bhùth** going to the shop, *see* **do** *prep*

dha (*emph form* **dhàsan**) *prep pron, see* **do** *prep*

dhachaigh *adv see* **dachaigh 3**

dhaibh (*emph form* **dhaibhsan**) *prep pron, see* **do** *prep*

dhèanadh, dhèanainn *pts of irreg v* **dèan** (*see tables p 497*)

dheth *adv* off, (*calques*) **tha an dealan dheth** the electricity's off, **cuir dheth an rèidio** turn the radio off, **tha an t-uachdar a' dol dheth** the cream's going off

dheth (*emph form* **dhethsan**) *prep pron, see* **de** *prep*

dhi (*emph form* **dhìse**) *prep pron, see* **do** *prep*

dhibh (*emph form* dhibhse), dhinn (*emph form* dhinne), dhìom (*emph form* dhìomsa), dhìot (*emph form* dhìotsa), dhith (*emph form* dhithse), dhiubh (*emph form* dhiubhsan) *prep prons, see* de *prep*

dhomh (*emph form* dhòmhsa), dhuibh (*emph form* dhuibhse), dhuinn (*emph form* dhuinne), dhu(i)t (*emph form* dhu(i)tsa) *prep prons, see* do *prep*

dia, dè, diathan *nm* 1 Dia, God; 2 a god, diathan nan Ròmanach the gods of the Romans, ban-dia *f* a goddess; 3 (*excl after a sneeze*) Dia leat! Bless you!

diabhal, diabhail, diabhail & diabhlan *nm* 1 a devil, *cf* deamhan; 2 an Diabhal the Devil

diabhlaidh *adj* diabolical, devilish, fiendish

diadhachd *nf invar* 1 godhead, deity, the quality of being a god; 2 theology; 3 godliness, devoutness, piety, *cf* cùram 3, cràbhadh

diadhaidh *adj* 1 devout, pious, godly, religious, *cf* cràbhach; 2 divine

diadhaire, diadhaire, diadhairean *nm* a theologian

diallaid *see* dìollaid

dia-mhaslachadh, *gen* dia-mhaslachaidh *nm* blasphemy, *cf* toibheum

dian *adj* (*trad*) 1 eager, fierce, keen (*pursuit, fighting, endeavour etc*); 2 intense, intensive, fervent, ardent (*persons, emotions, deeds*)

Diardaoin *nm invar* Thursday

dias, dèise, diasan *nf* an ear of corn

diathad, diathaid, diathadan *nf* 1 a meal, *cf* biadh 2, lòn¹ 2; 2 *with art* an diathad dinner, *cf more usu* dinnear

dibhearsan, *gen* dibhearsain *nm* fun, entertainment, amusement, *cf* spòrs 2

dìblidh *adj* vile, abject

dìcheall, *gen* dìchill *nm* 1 (*trad*) diligence, effort, application, *cf* dèanadas, gnìomhachas 1; 2 *now usu in expr* rinn mi (*etc*) mo (*etc*) dhicheall (air . . .) I (*etc*) did my (*etc*) best (to . . .)

dìcheallach *adj* diligent, hardworking, conscientious, *cf* dèanadach, gnìomhach

dì-cheannachadh, *gen* dì-cheannachaidh *nm* 1 (*the act of*) beheading, decapitating; 2 decapitation

dì-cheannaich *vt, pres part* a' dì-cheann(ach)adh, behead, decapitate

dì-chuimhnich *see* dìochuimhnich

Diciadain *nm invar* Wednesday

Didòmhnaich *nm invar* Sunday, *trad used by Catholic communities, cf* Sàbaid

didseatach *adj* (*IT etc*) digital, *cf* figearail

difir *see* diofar

dìg, dìge, dìgean *nf* a ditch, *cf* clais 1

Dihaoine *nm invar* Friday, feasgar Dihaoine Friday afternoon/evening

dìle, *gen* dìleann & dìlinn *nf* 1 heavy rain, a deluge, a downpour, bha dìle bhàthte ann it was bucketing down/raining cats and dogs; 2 a flood, *cf* tuil

dìleab, dìleib, dìleaban *nf* a legacy (*lit or fig*), heritage, a heritage, a bequest, dìleab na h-eachdraidh the legacy of history

dìleas *adj* faithful, trusty, loyal (*also popular as a dog's name*)

dìlseachd *nf invar* loyalty, faithfulness

Diluain *nm invar* Monday

Dimàirt *nm invar* Tuesday

dìmeas *nm invar* contempt, disrespect, (*poem*) Alba fo dhìmeas (Meg Bateman) Scotland despised

dìnichean *npl invar* jeans

dinn *vti, pres part* a' dinneadh, stuff, cram, *cf* sàth 2

dinnear, *gen* dinneir & dinnearach, *pl* dinnearan *nf* dinner, dè a th' againn gu/ air ar dinnear? what have we got/what are we getting/having for our dinner? àm dinnearach dinner time, *cf more trad* diathad 2

dìobair *vt, pres part* a' dìobradh, desert, abandon, dhìobair e a' bhean aige he deserted his wife, *cf* fàg, trèig

dìobhair *vti, pres part* a' dìobhairt, vomit, throw up, be sick, sick up, *cf* sgeith, tilg 3

dìobhairt *nm invar* 1 (*the act of*) vomiting etc (*see senses of* dìobhair *v*); 2 vomit, sick (*ie the substance*)

dìobradh, *gen* dìobraidh *nm* (*the act of*) deserting, abandoning; desertion, abandonment

dìochuimhne *nf invar* 1 forgetfulness, absent-mindedness; 2 the state of being forgotten, oblivion, *esp in expr* rach *v* air dìochuimhne be forgotten, pass into oblivion

dìochuimhneach *adj* forgetful, absent-minded

dìochuimhneachadh, *gen* dìochuimhneachaidh *nm* (*the act of*) forgetting

dìochuimhnich, *vt, pres part* a' dìochuimhneachadh, forget

diofar, *gen* diofair *nm, also* difir *nm invar* & deifir, *gen* deifire *nf*, 1 difference, a difference dè an diofar a tha eadar A agus B? what's the difference between A and B?, *cf* eadar-dhealachadh 2; 2 importance, *esp in exprs* chan eil diofar ann! & chan eil e gu diofar! it's not important!, it doesn't matter!, it makes no difference!

diof(a)rach, *also* **deifrichte** & **diofaraichte**, *adj* different, *cf* **eadar-dhealaichte**

diog, **diog**, **diogan** *nm* (*clock time*) a second, *cf* **tiota 1**

diogail *vti, pres part* **a' diogladh**, tickle, *cf vi* **tachais 2**

diogalach *adj* ticklish, tickly

dìoghail & **dìol** *vt, pres part* **a' dìo(gh)ladh**, 1 repay (*esp loan, debts*); 2 take revenge, get one's own back, pay someone back

dìoghaltas, *gen* **dìoghaltais** *nm* revenge, vengeance

dìo(gh)ladh, *gen* **dìo(gh)laidh** *nm* 1 (*the act of*) repaying etc (*see senses of* **dìoghail** *v*); 2 payment, a payment

dìoghras, *gen* **dìoghrais** *nm* zeal, enthusiasm, fervour, passion (*for a cause, idea etc*)

dìoghrasach *adj* zealous etc (*see senses of* **dìoghras**)

dìol *see* **dìoghail**

dìolain *adj* bastard, illegitimate, **duine/neach dìolain** a bastard

dìollaid & **diallaid**, *gen* **dìollaide**, *pl* **dìollaidean** *nf* a saddle

diomb *nm invar* indignation, displeasure (*esp towards another person*)

diombach *adj* 1 out of sorts, in a dark mood or temper, *cf* **crost(a) 1**, **dubhach 1**, **gruamach 4**; 2 annoyed, indignant, disgruntled, put out (*with prep* **de**), **diombach dhìom fhìn** annoyed with myself, *cf* **feargach**

diombuan *adj* transient, fleeting, ephemeral, *cf* **siùbhlach 3**

dìomhain *adj* 1 vain, empty, without substance, **cur-seachadan dìomhain** vain/pointless pastimes, *cf* **faoin 2**; 2 idle (*ie lazy*), *cf* **leisg 1**; 3 idle (*ie unoccupied, unemployed*), *cf* **tàmh** *n* 3

dìomhair *adj* 1 secret, private (*ie confidential*); 2 mysterious, deep

dìomhaireachd *nf invar* 1 secrecy, confidentiality; 2 mystery

dìomhanas, **dìomhanais**, **dìomhanasan** *nm* vanity, **dìomhanas nan dìomhanas** vanity of vanities, *cf* **faoineas 2**

dìon, *gen* **dìona** *nm* protection, shelter, defence, **fo dhìon an rìgh/a' chaisteil** protected by the king/the castle, *cf* **fasgadh**, **tèarmann**

dìon *vt, pres part* **a' dìon** & **a' dìonadh**, shelter, protect, guard, defend

dìonach *adj* 1 sheltering, safe, secure; 2 leakproof, waterproof, rainproof, (*house, ship etc*) wind and watertight

dìonadh, *gen* **dìonaidh** *nm* (*the act of*) sheltering, protecting, defending

dìorrasach *adj* keen, tenacious, stubborn

dìosail *nm invar* & *adj* diesel

dìosgan, *gen* **dìosgain** *nm, also* **dìosgail** *nf invar*, 1 a creaking, crunching, grating or squeaking noise; 2 *also as pres part* **a' dìosgail** creaking etc

diosgo *nm invar* a disco

dìreach *adj* & *adv* 1 straight, **seas** *v* **dìreach** stand (up) straight, **loidhne dhìreach** a straight line, (*song*) **'s fheudar dhomh fhìn a bhith gabhail dhachaigh dìreach** I must be going straight home; 2 upright (*fig* & *lit*), just, **duine dìreach** an upright man, *cf* **ionraic 2**; 3 (*as adv*) just, (*calques*) **bhiodh sin dìreach sgoinneil!** that would be just great! **tha e dìreach an dèidh falbh** he's just left, (*Sc*) he's just after leaving; 4 *as excl expr agreement* **dìreach!** exactly!, quite!, just so!

dìreachadh, *gen* **dìreachaidh** *nm* (*the act of*) straightening etc (*see senses of* **dìrich¹** *v*)

dìreadh, *gen* **dìridh** *nm* (*the act of*) climbing, *cf* **streap(adh)**

dìrich¹ *vti, pres part* **a' dìreachadh**, straighten, make or become straight

dìrich² *vt, pres part* **a' dìreadh**, climb (*hill etc*), *cf* **streap**

Disathairne *nm invar* Saturday

dìsinn *nm* & **dìsne** *nmf, gen* **dìsne**, *pl* **dìsnean**, a die, *pl* dice (*ie for gaming etc*)

dìt *vt, pres part* **a' dìteadh** 1 condemn (*ie disapprove of*), **dhìt iad ar dol-a-mach** they condemned our conduct; 2 (*legal*) condemn, convict, sentence, **dìt gu bàs** condemn/sentence to death

dìteadh, **dìtidh**, **dìtidhean** *nm*, condemning, sentencing *etc*, *see senses of* **dìt** *vt*

dìth, *gen* **dìthe** *nm* 1 a lack, a want, a deficit, **dìth cleachdaidh** lack of practice/experience, **dìth cèille** a lack of common sense; 2 *often in expr* **a** (*for* **de**) **dhìth** lacking, wanting, needed, **tha biadh a dhìth** food is lacking/in short supply, **dè tha a dhìth oirbh?** what do you want/need?, (*in shop etc*) what would you like?, what are you wanting?, **tha còta a dhìth orm** I need/want a coat, **cha tèid sinn a dhìth** we won't go short, *cf* **easbhaidh**

dìthean, **dìthein**, **dìtheanan** *nm* a flower, *cf* **blàth** *n* 2, **flùr²**

dithis, **dithis**, **dithisean** *nf* (*usu used of people only*) 1 two, a twosome (*with gen pl*) **bha dithis aig a' bhòrd** there were two people at the table, **dithis shaighdearan** two soldiers, **an dithis agaibh** both/the two/the pair of you; 2 a couple, a pair, **bha iad nan suidhe nan dithisean** they were sitting in pairs/couples, *cf* **càraid 1**

dìthreabh, dìthreibh, dìthreabhan *nf* a desert, a wilderness, *cf more usu* **fàsach**

diù *nm invar* the worst, the worst thing, (*proverb*) **diù an domhain droch bhean** the worst thing in the world (is) a bad wife, **diù nan dreuchdan** the worst of jobs/professions, *cf opposites* **brod** *n* 2, **smior** 2

diùc, diùc, diùcan *nm* a duke (*cf* **ban-diùc** *nf* a duchess)

diùid *adj* shy, bashful, timid, *cf* **nàrach** 2

diùide *nf invar* bashfulness, shyness, timidity, *cf* **nàire** 2

diùlt *vti, pres part* **a' diùltadh**, 1 refuse, **dhiùlt sinn biadh** we refused food, **dhiùlt an athair an leigeil air falbh** their father refused to let them go, **a' diùltadh èirigh** refusing to get up; 2 deny, disown, **cha diùlt i a nighean fhèin** she won't deny/reject/disown her own daughter

diùltadh, gen diùltaidh *nm* 1 (*the act of*) refusing, denying etc (*see senses of* **diùlt** *v*); 2 refusal, a refusal; 3 denial, a denial

diùmb, diùmbach *see* **diomb, diombach**

Diùrach, gen & pl Diùraich *nm* someone from Jura, *also as adj* **Diùrach** of, from or pertaining to Jura

Diùra(igh) *nf* Jura

diùraidh, diùraidh, diùraidhean *nm* a jury

dleas, dleasa, dleasan *nm* 1 *same as more usu* **dleastanas**; 2 a due, a right, an entitlement, **dleas ùghdair** royalties (*for book etc*)

dleastanas, *also* **dleasdanas & dleasnas,** *gen* **dleas(ta)nais,** *pl* **dleas(ta)nasan** *nm* duty, a duty, **rinn iad an dleastanas** they did their duty

dlighe *nf invar* 1 a right, one's due

dligheach *adj* lawful, rightful, legitimate, valid

dlùth, gen dlùtha *nm* warp (*of cloth*)

dlùth *adj* 1 close, near, adjacent, (**ri/air** to), **dlùth ri chèile** close to each other, **dlùth air a' bhaile** close to the village/township, *cf more usu* **faisg**; 2 (*hair, woodland, crowd etc*) thick, dense, closely packed, *cf* **dòmhail** 2, **tiugh** 1

dlùthachadh, gen dlùthachaidh *nm* (*the act of*) approaching etc (*see senses of* **dlùthaich** *v*)

dlùthaich *vi, pres part* **a' dlùthachadh,** approach, come near, draw close (**ri** to), **bha sinn a' dlùthachadh ris a' mhuir** we were nearing/drawing near to the sea

dlùth-cheangal, dlùth-cheangail, dlùth-cheanglaichean *nm* a close link *or* tie (**ri** with, **eadar** between)

dlùths *nm invar* density

do *poss adj* (*sometimes found as* **t'** *before a vowel, or before* **fh** *followed by a vowel*), your (*corres to the sing/fam pron* **thu**), **gabh do**

dhìnnear take/eat your dinner, **'s math d' fhaicinn!** it's good to see you!, *cf* **ur**

do *verbal particle used in some neg & inter contexts,* **cha do rinn mi e** I didn't do it, **an do dh'fhalbh i?** did she leave? **nach d' fhuair sibh iad?** didn't you find/get them? **càit an do rugadh e?** where was he born?

do *prep, takes the dat, lenites following cons where possible. The prep prons formed with* **do,** *in the order first, second, third person singular, first, second, third person plural, and with the reflexive/emphatic particles in brackets, are as follows:* **dhòmh(sa), dhu(i)t(sa), dhà(san), dhì(se), dhuinn(e), dhuibh(se), dhaibh(san)** to/for me, to/for you (*fam*), etc 1 to, **thoir do dh'Iain e** give it to Iain, **innis do Mhàiri e** tell it to Mary, **dè a thachair dhut?** what happened to you?; 2 to (*phys movement*) *Note: in this usage* **do** *can appear as* **a,** *and* **don** & **do na** *can appear as* **dhan** & **dha na;** **a' dol do** (*or* **a**) **Ghlaschu** going to Glasgow, **thèid mi don** (*or* **dhan**) **eaglais** I'll go to (the) church, **sgrìob do na** (*or* **dha na**) **h-eileanan** a trip to the islands, **cuir màileid dhan chàr** put a bag in the car, **tilg clach dhan loch** throw a stone in(to) the loch; 3 for, **nì mi sin dhut** I'll do that for you, **ciamar a chaidh dhuibh?** *or more trad* **ciamar a dh'èirich dhuibh?** how did you get on? (*lit* how did it go/turn out for you?*); 4 misc usages* **tha e na dheagh charaid dhomh** he's a good friend of mine/to me, **co-ogha dhomh** a cousin of mine, **cha b' aithne dha i** he didn't know her, **an urrainn dhaibh a dhèanamh?** can they do it? **b' fheudar do Sheumas falbh** James had to leave, **air dha am bealach a ruigsinn . . .** on (his) reaching/when he reached the pass . . . , **an dèidh dhomh mo shùilean a dhùnadh** after I closed/had closed my eyes

do- *a prefix corres to Eng* un-, in-, im-, *eg* **do-àireamh** *adj* innumerable, uncountable, **do-dhèanta** *adj* impossible, **do-labhairt** *adj* unspeakable, *cf* **ain-, mì-, neo-**

dòbhran, gen & pl dòbhrain *nm* an otter

do bhrìgh *see* **brìgh** 5

doca, doca, docannan *nm* a dock (*ie in seaport etc*)

docair, docair, docairean *nm* a docker

dòcha *comp adj* 1 (*trad*) more likely, probable; 2 *now in expr* **'s dòcha!** *adv* perhaps!, maybe!, *also* probably!; 3 *also as conj* **'s dòcha gun tig e a-màireach** maybe he'll come tomorrow, *cf* **faod** 2, **teagamh** 2

dochainn *vt, pres part* **a' dochann,** 1 hurt, injure (*phys*) *cf* **goirtich**; 2 thrash, beat up, *cf* **buail, slac**; **3** prejudice, harm (*someone's situation etc*), *cf* **dèan cron air** (*see* **cron 1**)

dochann, dochainn, dochannan *nm* **1** a (*physical*) hurt, an injury *cf* **leòn** *nm*; **2** a thrashing, a beating *cf* **pronnadh, slacadh**; **3** prejudice, harm, injury, damage (*esp done to someone's situation etc*), *esp in expr* **dèan dochann** (*wth prep* **air**) damage, *cf* **cron 1**

dòchas, dòchais, dòchasan *nm* **1** hope, a hope, **'s e sin mo dhòchas** that is my hope (*cf* **dùil1** **1**, *less usu in this sense*), **gun dòchas** hopeless, without hope, *also in expr* **cuir** *v* **dòchas ann an . . .** put one's hope in . . . (*something, someone*); **2** *often in expr* **an dòchas** (*lit* in hope), **tha mi an dòchas nach tig i** I hope she won't come, **bidh là math ann, tha mi an dòchas** it'll be a good day, I hope

dòchasach *adj* hopeful, optimistic

do(c)tair, do(c)tair, do(c)tairean *nm* a (*medical*) doctor, *cf trad* **lighiche**

dòigh, dòighe, dòighean *nf* **1** a way, a manner (*of doing something*), **dèan e air an dòigh seo** do it (in) this way, **dòigh-beatha** a way of life, a lifestyle, *cf less usu* **modh 1, nòs 2**; **2** *in pl* ways, manners, customs, **chan eil iad cleachdte ri ar dòighean** they aren't used to our ways; **3** a (*good, proper*) state, condition or situation, **bha a h-uile rud air dòigh** everything was in good order/as it should be, **cuir** *v* **air dòigh** put in order, organise, sort (out); **4** form, a mood, a state of mind, **bha Murchadh air a (dheagh) dhòigh** Murdo was on good form/in fine fettle, *also* very pleased (with himself), (*fam*) **dè an dòigh (a th' ort)?** how are you doing?, *cf* **cor 1, fonn 2, gean, gleus** *n* **2**; **5** *in expr* **air dhòigh is gu/nach . . .** *conj* so that, in such a way that, **bhruidhinn e air dhòigh 's nach cuala mi e** he spoke so that/in such a way that I didn't hear him, *cf similarly used* **air chor is gu** (*see* **cor 3**)

dòigheil *adj* **1** well-ordered, proper, in good order, as it (*etc*) should be; **2** *esp as adv*, **rinn e gu dòigheil e** he did it properly/well, **ciamar a tha thu? tha gu dòigheil** how are you? I'm fine

dòil *nm invar* dole, unemployment benefit, (*Sc*) broo

doille *nf invar* blindness

doilleir *adj* dark, gloomy, obscure, dim (*opposite of* **soilleir**), *cf* **ciar** *adj* **2, dorch(a)**

doilleirich *vti, pres part* **a' doilleireachadh**, become or make dark, darken, dim, obscure (*opposite of* **soilleirich**), *cf* **ciar** *v*

doimhne *nf invar, usu with art* **an doimhne** the Deep

doimhneachd *nf invar* depth

doimhnich *vti, pres part* **a' doimhneachadh**, deepen

doineann, doininn, doineannan *nf* a storm, a tempest, a hurricane, *cf* **gailleann, sian 1, stoirm 1**

doineannach *adj* stormy, tempestuous

doirbh *adj* difficult, hard (*opposite of* **soirbh**), **ceist dhoirbh** a difficult question/problem, **tha sin uabhasach doirbh a ràdh** that's terribly hard to say, *cf* **deacair, duilich 1**

doire, *gen* **doire**, *pl* **doirean** & **doireachan** *nmf* a grove, a thicket, a small wood, (*poetry collection*) **Clàrsach an Doire** (Niall MacLeòid) The Harp of the Grove, *can occur in placenames as* Derry, *cf* **bad 4**

dòirt *vti, pres part* **a' dòrtadh** (*of liquids*) **1** (*vt*) pour; **2** (*vi*) flow, pour down, **uisge a' dòrtadh tron mhullach** water pouring through the roof; **3** (*vt*) spill, shed, (*song*) **dhòirt iad fhuil mu làr** they spilled/shed his blood upon the ground

dol *nm invar* (*the act of*) going, happening, becoming, etc, etc (*see senses of* **rach** *v*)

dolaidh *nf invar* harm, detriment, deterioration, *esp in exprs* **chan eil dolaidh ann!** there's no great harm done! *or* it's no great loss!, **rach** *vi* **a dholaidh** go off, go to waste, go to ruin

dolair, dolair, dolairean *nm* a dollar

dol-air-adhart *nm invar* **1** behaviour, conduct, way of carrying on, **cha toigh leam an dol-air-adhart (a th')** aice I don't like the way she behaves/carries on, *cf* **dol-a-mach 1, giùlan 3**

dol-a-mach *nm invar* **1** *same as* **dol-air-adhart** *above*; **2** *in expr* **sa chiad dol-a-mach** at first, initially, in the first instance

dòlas, *gen* **dòlais** *nm* **1** grief, *cf sometimes less strong* **bròn, mulad**; **2** *as excl* **an dòlas!** 'woe is me'!, how terrible!, good grief!

dol-às *nm invar* (*means of*) escape, a way out, **cha robh dol-às againn a-nis ach . . .** there was no way out/escape for us now except . . .

dòmhail & **dùmhail**, *adj* **1** (*of places, buildings, gatherings etc*) crowded, congested, packed; **2** (*trees, hair, vegetation etc*) thick, dense, *cf* **dlùth 2, tiugh 1**

domhainn *adj* **1** deep, **uisge domhainn** deep water, (*opposite*) **eu-domhainn** shallow; **2** (*fig*) deep, profound, **leabhar domhainn** a profound book

domhan, *gen* **domhain** *nm, with art, esp in exprs* **an domhan** the universe, **An Treas Domhan** the Third World, *cf* **cruinne-cè 2**

dona *adj, comp* **(n)as** (*etc*) **miosa**, bad, **tha siùcar dona dhut** sugar's bad for you, **gille dona** a bad/naughty boy (*cf* **crost(a)**), **ciamar**

a tha thu? chan eil gu dona, chan eil mi cho dona 's a bha mi how are you? not bad, I'm not as bad as I was, ciamar a chaidh dhut? cha deach ach gu dubh dona! how did it go? just terrible!; 2 *occas* (*trad*) unlucky, unfortunate

donas, *gen* donais *nm* 1 badness, evil, mischief, *cf stronger* olc *n*; 2 *with art* an Donas the Devil, the evil one, *excl* mac an donais! the devil!, damn it!, (*prov*) cha d' fhuaradh an Donas a-riamh marbh air cùl gàrraidh the Devil was never found dead behind a dyke

donn *adj* 1 brown, brat-ùrlair donn a brown carpet, dubh-dhonn dark brown, (*song*) eilean beag donn a' chuain the little brown island of the ocean (Lewis); 2 brown-haired, (*song*) an tèid thu leam, mo nighean donn? will you go with me, my brown-haired lass?

donnal, donnail, donnalan *nm* a howl (*esp of dog*), rinn e donnal he howled

donnalaich, *gen* donnalaiche *nf* howling

dòrainn, dòrainne, dòrainnean *nf* (emotional) anguish, torment, (deep) sorrow

dòrainneach *adj* anguished, (*emotionally*) tortured, pained, sgeulachd dhòrainneach a painful/harrowing/tragic story, *cf* cràidhteach

doras, dorais, dorsan *nm* 1 (*trad*) a doorway, *see* còmhla(dh); 2 a door, an doras mòr the main/front door, làmh an dorais the door handle, a' fuireach an ath-dhoras living next door

dorch(a) *adj* dark, neul dorcha a dark cloud, (*story anthology*) Dorcha tro Ghlainne Through a Glass Darkly, (*hist*) na Linntean Dorcha the Dark Ages, *cf* doilleir

dorchadas, *gen* dorchadais *nm* darkness

dòrlach, *gen & pl* dòrlaich *nm* 1 a fistful, a handful; 2 a batch

dòrn, *gen & pl* dùirn *nm* a fist, (*poem*) san taigh-òsta 'n àm nan dòrn a bhith gan dùnadh (Somhairle MacGill-Eain) in the pub in the time of (the) fists being clenched

dòrn *vt*, *pres part* a' dòrnadh, thump

dorsair, dorsair, dorsairean *nm* a doorman, a porter, a janitor, a concierge, *cf* portair 2

dòrtadh, *gen* dòrtaidh *nm* shedding, spilling, dòrtadh fala bloodshed, spilling of blood

dos, *gen* dois, *pl* dois & dosan *nm* 1 a bush, *cf* preas¹; 2 a drone of a bagpipe

dosgainn, dosgainn, dosgainnean *nf* calamity, a calamity, misfortune, a misfortune

dotair *see* do(c)tair

dòth *vt*, *pres part* a' dòthadh, scorch, singe, burn

dòthadh, *gen* dòthaidh *nm* (the act of) scorching etc (*see senses of* dòth *v*)

drabasta & drabasda *adj* obscene, lewd, bawdy, smutty, coarse, *cf* draosta

drabastachd & drabasdachd *nf invar* smut, obscenity, lewdness, bawdiness, *cf* draostachd, rabhd 2

dràbhail *adj* grotty, *cf* grodach, mosach 1

drabhair *see* drathair

dràc, dràic, dràcan *nm* a drake, *cf* ràc *n*

dragh, dragha, draghannan *nm* 1 trouble, bother, chan eil mi airson dragh a chur oirbh I don't want to bother you/put you to any trouble (*cf* bodraig *vti*); 2 annoyance, tha fuaim a' chiùil sin a' cur dragh orm the noise of that music is annoying me; 3 worry, anxiety, gabh/dèan *v* dragh worry, get worried, tha dìth airgid a' dèanamh dragh dhomh lack of money is causing me worry, *cf* iomagain 1

draghail *adj* (*of person, situation*) worrying, troublesome, annoying

dràibh *vti*, *pres part* a' dràibheadh, *also* dràibhig *vti*, *pres part* a' dràibhigeadh, drive (a vehicle)

dràibhear, dràibheir, dràibhearan *nm* a driver (*of a vehicle*)

dràibhig *see* dràibh

dram, drama, dramannan *nmf*, *also* drama, drama, dramaichean *nm*, (*fam*) a dram, a drink of whisky, an gabh thu drama? will you take a dram?

dràma, dràma, dràmathan *nmf* drama, a drama (*play or crisis*), bidh i a' teagasg dràma she teaches drama

dranndan, *gen & pl* dranndain *nfm*, (*of dog etc*) snarling, a snarl, growling, a growl, rinn an cù dranndan the dog snarled/growled, *cf* grànsgal

dranndanach *adj* 1 (*esp of dog*) apt to snarl or growl; 2 (*of people*) snappy, irritable, (*Sc*) crabbit

draoidh, draoidh, draoidhean *nm* 1 (*trad, hist*) a druid; 2 a wizard, a sorcerer, a magician, *cf* buidseach

draoidheachd *nf invar* wizardry, sorcery, magic

draoidheil *adj* magic, magical

draosta *adj* smutty, lewd, obscene, *cf* drabasta

draostachd & draosdachd *nf invar* smut, obscenity, lewdness, *cf* drabastachd, rabhd 2

drathair (*also found as* drabhair), drathair, dràthraichean *nm* (*furniture*) a drawer

drathais & drathars *nf invar* 1 pants, knickers; 2 underpants; *cf* fo-aodach *nm* (*see under* fo *prep* 2)

dreach, dreacha, dreachan *nm* **1** (*phys*) appearance, aspect, **air dhreach taibhse** with the appearance of/looking like a ghost, *cf* **coltas 1**; **2** complexion, *cf* **fiamh 1, snuadh 2, tuar**

dreachd, dreachd, dreachdan *nf* a draft (*of document etc*)

dreachd *vt, pres part* **a' dreachdadh**, draft (*a document etc*)

dreachmhor *adj* handsome, good-looking

dreag, dreige, dreagan *nf* a meteor

dreallag, dreallaige, dreallagan *nf* a (*child's*) swing

drèana, drèana, drèanaichean *nf* **1** a drain; **2** a drainage ditch, *cf* **clais 1 & 2, dìg**

dreasa, dreasa, dreasaichean *nf* a dress

dreasair, dreasair, dreasairean *nm* (*furniture*) a dresser

dreathan-donn, dreathain-duinn, dreathain-donna *nm* a wren

drèin, drèine, drèinean *nf* a scowl, a 'face', **chuir e drèin air** he scowled, pulled a face, *cf* **gruaim 2, mùig, sgraing**

dreuchd, dreuchd, dreuchdan *nf* a job, an occupation, a profession, a career, *usu non-manual work*, **leigidh mi dhìom mo dhreuchd an ath-bhliadhna** I'll give up my job/I'll retire next year, *cf* **cosnadh 2, obair 4**

dreuchdail *adj* professional **1** (*relating to a job or profession*) **briathrachas dreuchdail** professional terminology; **2** (*working for payment*) **seinneadair dreuchdail** a professional singer; *cf* **proifeiseanta**

driamlach, driamlaich, driamlaich(ean) *nmf* a fishing line

drile, drile, drilichean *nf* a drill, an auger, *cf more trad* **snìomhair(e)**

drioftair, drioftair, drioftairean *nm* (*fishing*) a drifter

drip, *gen* **dripe** *nf* bustle, animation, the state of being busy, *cf* **sàs 2 & dripeil** *adj*

dripeil *adj* busy, **tha cùisean garbh dripeil an-dràsta** things are hell of a busy just now, *cf* **trang**

dris, drise, drisean *nf* the bramble, the brier, the blackberry (*ie the plant, cf* **smeur** *n*)

drithleann, *gen & pl* **drithlinn** *nm* a sparkle, a flash

dr(i)ùchd, dr(i)ùchd, dr(i)ùchdan *nmf* dew, (*song*) **is an sliabh fo dhriùchd** and the hill with dew upon it, *cf* **dealt**

dròbh, dròibh, dròbhan *nmf* (*hist*) a drove (of cattle)

dròbhair, dròbhair, dròbhairean *nm* (*hist*) a cattle drover

droch *adj* **1** bad (*precedes the noun, which it lenites where possible*), **droch aimsir** *or* **droch shìde** bad weather, **droch anail** bad breath, halitosis, **tha an togalach ann an droch staid** the building's in a bad state/condition; **2** (*also in compounds*) bad-, ill-, *eg* **droch-c(h)ainnt** *f* bad language, swearing, (*trad*) **an droch-shùil** *f* the evil eye, **droch-nàdarrach** *adj* ill-/evil-natured, ill-/evil-tempered; *cf* **dona 1 &** *opposite* **deagh**

drochaid, drochaide, drochaidean *nf* a bridge, **Drochaid an Eilein Sgitheanaich** the Skye Bridge

droga, droga, drogaichean *nf* a drug (*medical, illegal etc*)

droigheann, *gen* **droighinn** *nm* a thorntree

droighneach *adj* thorny

droman, *gen & pl* **dromain** *nm* an elder tree

drùchd *see* **dr(i)ùchd**

drùdhag, drùdhaig, drùdhagan *nf* **1** a drop (*of liquid*), *cf* **boinneag 1**; **2** a small sip, **nach gabh thu drùdhag tì?** won't you take a drop of tea?, *cf* **balgam 1**

druid, druid, druidean *nf* a starling, (*song*) **thig an smeòrach, thig an druid, thig gach eun a dh'ionnsaigh nid** the thrush will come, the starling will come, each bird will make for its nest

drùidh *vti, pres part* **a' drùidheadh**, **1** penetrate/soak to the skin, drench, *esp in expr* **dhrùidh an t-uisge orm/oirnn** (*etc*) the rain soaked me/us (*etc*) to the skin; **2** affect, make an impression on, move, 'get to', **cha do dhrùidh an naidheachd oirre** the news didn't affect/'get to' her/made no impression on her

drùidheadh, *gen* **drùidhidh** *nm* **1** (*the act of*) penetrating etc (*see senses of* **drùidh** *v*); **2** an effect, an impression (*made on someone*)

drùidhteach *adj* impressive, moving, affecting

druim, droma, dromannan *nm* **1** a back (*ie considered as part of a human or animal body, cf* **cùl 2, muin 1**), **air do dhruim-dìreach** flat on your back, **tha mo dhruim goirt** my back aches/is sore, (*trad*) **bha ultach a droma aice** she had as much as she could carry (*lit* her back's load), **caol an droma** *m* the small of the back, **cnà(i)mh an droma** *m* the backbone/spine; **2** (*topog*) a ridge, *usu in placenames as* Drum

drùis, *gen* **drùise** *nf* lust, lechery, *cf* **ana-miann**

drùiseach *adj* & **drùiseil** *adj* lustful, lecherous, randy

druma, druma, drumaichean *nmf* (*mus*) a drum

drumair, drumair, drumairean *nm* a drummer, a percussionist

duais, duaise, duaisean *nf* **1** (*trad*) wages, reward (*for services etc performed*), *cf usu* **pàigh** *n*, **tuarastal**; **2** (*now usu*) a prize, an award, **choisinn i duais aig a' Mhòd** she won a prize at the Mod

dual¹, duaile, dualan *nm* (*trad*) **1** what might be expected of one because of one's descendance, one's character considered as inherited, (*prov*) **bu dual dha sin** that was to be expected of him (*ie he being the man he is*), **bu dual dha bàrdachd bho thaobh athar** he inherited a talent for poetry from his father's side of the family (*lit* poetry was hereditary for him from his father's side); **2** a hereditary right, a birthright, (*song*) **MacGriogair à Ruadhshruth dam bu dual bhith 'n Gleann Lìobhann** MacGregor of Roro whose birthright it was to be in Glen Lyon; *cf* **dualchas 2, dùthchas**

dual², duail, dualan *nm* **1** a curl, lock or ringlet of hair, *cf* **bachlag 1, camag 1**; **2** (*in hair, rope etc*) a plait

dualach *see* **dual(t)ach**

dualachadh, *gen* **dualachaidh** *nm* (*the act of*) curling etc (*see senses of* **dualaich** *v*)

dualaich *vt, pres part* **a' dualachadh**, **1** curl (*hair*), *cf* **bachlaich**; **2** twist, plait, braid (*hair, rope etc*)

dualchainnt, dualchainnte, dualchainntean *nf* a dialect, speech of an area

dualchas, *gen* **dualchais** *nm* **1** heritage (*esp cultural*), tradition; **2** (*trad*) one's character or characteristics (*with a suggestion of hereditary influence*), one's inheritance, what one is, what might be expected of one, or what one might be entitled to, by reason of one's descent, **is e a dhualchas a bhith àrdanach** it's in his character/nature to be proud, *cf* **dual¹, dùthchas 2**

dualchasach *adj* **1** traditional, **ceòl dualchasach** traditional music

dual(t)ach *adj* natural, inherent, innate, typical, in one's nature or temperament (*with a suggestion of hereditary influence*), **tha e dualtach dhut a bhith ag innse bhreugan!** it's in your nature/just like you/typical of you to tell lies! **tha iad dualach a bhith spìocach** they are inclined/apt to be stingy/mean, *cf* **buailteach**

duan, *gen & pl* **duain** *nm* **1** a poem, *cf more usu* **dàn² 1**; **2** *esp as dimin* **duanag, duanaig, duanagan** *nf*, a song, **Duanag a' Chìobair** The Shepherd's (little) Song

duanaire, duanaire, duanairean *nm* an anthology (*of poetry*)

dùbailte *adj* double, dual, **gunna dùbailte** a double-barrelled shotgun, **rathad dùbailte** a two-lane road, a dual carriageway

dubh *adj* **1** black, **bha an oidhche cho dubh ri gual** the night was as black as coal, **boireannach dubh** a black woman, (*mus*) **dubh-nota** *m* a crotchet; **2** *with other colours,* dark, **dubh-ghorm** dark blue; **3** *of colour of human hair, colour of coat, feathers etc of other creatures,* black, dark, **boireannach dubh** a black-haired/dark-haired woman, **coileach-dubh** a blackcock; **4** *as intensifying element,* very, extremely, **tha e leisg agus dubh leisg!** he's utterly lazy!, (*also* **gu dubh**) **ciamar a chaidh dhuibh? cha deachaidh ach gu dubh dona!** how did it go? it went absolutely terribly!

dubh, *gen* **duibh** *nm* **1** the colour black, (*story anthology*) **An Dubh is an Gorm** The Black and the Blue; **2** ink, *cf less trad* **inc**; **3** pupil (*of the eye*)

dubh *vti, pres part* **a' dubhadh**, **1** blacken, make black, become black; **2 dubh às** *vt*, erase; black out, blot out

dubhach *adj* **1** sad, gloomy, (*song*) **chan eil adhbhar (a) bhith dubhach no sgìth ann** there's no reason to be gloomy or weary there, *cf* **smalanach** (*see* **smalan**); **2** moody, in a bad mood, **nach tusa tha dubhach an-diugh!** aren't you the moody one today!, *cf* **diombach 1**

dubhadh, dubhaidh, dubhaidhean *nm* **1** (*the act of*) blackening etc (*see senses of* **dubh** *v*); **2** (*astronomy*) an eclipse, **dubhadh na grèine/ na gealaich** an eclipse of the sun/of the moon (*though note also* **dubhadh grèine** suntan, a tan)

dubhag, dubhaig, dubhagan *nf* (*anat*) a kidney, *cf* **àra**

dubh-aigeann *nm invar* **1** the deep, the ocean; **2** an abyss, *cf* **àibheis**

dubhan, *gen & pl* **dubhain** *nm* a hook (*for fastenings, hanging objects, fishing, etc*), *cf* **cromag 1**

dubhar, *gen* **dubhair** *nm* shade, shadow, **thàinig iad gu stad fo dhubhar nam ballachan** they came to a halt in the shade/ shadow of the walls, *cf* **sgàil(e) 1**

Dùbhlachd & **Dùdlachd** *nf invar, used with the art*, **an Dùbhlachd** December

dùbhlan *nm* a challenge, *also in expr* **thoir** *v* **dùbhlan do** challenge, defy, **thug e dùbhlan dhomh an fhìrinn innse** he challenged/defied me to tell the truth

dùbhlanach *adj* challenging, demanding (*tasks, situations etc*)

dùblaich *vti, pres part* **a' dùblachadh**, (*numbers, quantities etc*) double

dùdach, dùdaiche, dùdaichean *nmf &* **dùdag, dùdaig, dùdagan** *nf* **1** a bugle; **2** a hooter, a siren

Dùdlachd *see* **Dùbhlachd**

duibhre *nf invar* dusk, evening twilight, *cf* **camhanaich, eadar-sholas**

duibhreachadh, *gen* **duibhreachaidh** *nm* (*the act of*) shading etc (*see senses of* **duibhrich** *v*)

duibhrich *vti, pres part* **a' duibhreachadh**, shade, darken, eclipse, *cf* **sgàil** *v*

Duidseach *see* **Duitseach**

dùil[1], **dùile, dùilean** *nf* **1** hope, a hope, (*trad song*) **gun dùil ri tilleadh** without hope of returning, *cf more usu* **dòchas** 1 & 2; **2** expectation, an expectation, **dùil-aoise** life expectancy, **tha dùil agam gun tig e** I expect he'll come, **tha dùil agam rithe** I expect her, **chan eil mi an dùil gun tèid aige air** I don't expect he'll manage it, *cf* **sùil 3, sùilich**

dùil[2], *gen* **dùile**, *pl* **dùil(t)ean**, *gen pl* **dùl** *nf* **1** (*trad*) a creature, a created being, **Rìgh nan Dùl** the King/Lord of the Universe/of Creation, God; **2** (*chemistry etc*) an element

duileasg, *gen* **duilisg** *nm* (*bot*) dulse

duilgheadas, duilgheadais, duilgheadasan *nm* a difficulty, a problem, **tha duilgheadasan againn a thaobh airgid** we've got difficulties/ troubles where money is concerned, **cha bhi sin na dhuilgheadas dhàsan** that won't be a problem for him (*emph*), **duilgheadasan sòisealta** social problems

duilich *adj* **1** difficult, hard (*to solve*), **ceist dhuilich** a difficult question/problem, *cf* **deacair, doirbh**; **2** difficult, hard (*to bear*), (*poem*) **is duilich leam do dhol air ais a dh'Eirinn** (Meg Bateman) hard for me is your going back to Ireland, *cf* **cruaidh** *adj* 2; **3** sorry, **tha mi duilich!** I'm sorry!, (*calque*) **bha i a' faireachdainn duilich air a son fhèin** she was feeling sorry for herself; **4** *in expr* **tha sin duilich!** that's a pity/shame!, *cf more usu* **bochd 2, truagh 3**

duilleach, *gen* **duillich** *nm* foliage

duille, duille, duillean *nf* a sheath

duilleachan, *gen & pl* **duilleachain** *nm* (*publicity etc*) a leaflet

duilleag, duilleige, duilleagan *nf* **1** a leaf (*of tree, plant*); **2** a sheet (*of paper*); **3** (*also* **taobh-duilleige** *m*) a page (*of a book etc, abbrev* **d** *or* **td**, *in pl* **dd** *or* **tdd**), **Na Duilleagan Buidhe** The Yellow Pages

dùin *vti, pres part* **a' dùnadh**, **1** close, shut, **dùin an doras!** shut the door! **bha a' bhùth a' dùnadh** the shop was closing, (*vulg*) **dùin do chab!** shut your gob! **dhùin an uinneag le brag** the window shut with a bang; **2** bring or come to a close, **dùinidh am fear-cathrach a' choinneamh aig sia uairean** the chairman will close the meeting at six o'clock

duine, duine, daoine *nm* **1** a man (*as opposed to a child or youth*), **an uair a bhios mi nam dhuine gabhaidh mi san arm** when I'm a man I'll join the army, **is duine Iain** Iain is a man, *Note also* **duine dèanta** a (grown *or* adult) man, *cf* **inbheach** *n*; **2** a man (*as opposed to a woman*), **is duine Iain** Ian is a man, *cf* **fear** 1 *which stresses male gender more*; **3** a person (*irrespective of gender or age*), one, someone, somebody, anybody, anyone, (*in neg contexts*) no-one, nobody, **a bheil duine ann?** is someone/anybody (*etc*) there?, **chan fhaca duine duine sam bith** no-one/nobody saw anyone/anybody at all, **chuireadh e iongnadh air duine** it would amaze one/you/(*Sc*) a body, *cf* **neach** 1; **4** (*fam*) husband, *usu in expr* **an duine agam, mo dhuine** my husband, (*Sc*) my man, *cf* **bodach** 3, **cèile** 1, **companach** 3; **5** *in pl* people, folk, **mòran dhaoine** many people, **na daoine-sìth** the fairies, fairy folk; **6** *in pl* one's people, relatives, folks, **tha buinteanas aig mo dhaoine ris an Eilean Dubh** my people/folks have links with the Black Isle, (*song*) **gun duine de mo dhaoine ris am faod mi mo ghearan** without anyone of my people/kin to whom I might make my complaint, *cf less usu* **muinntir** 1; **7** *in excl* **dhuine! dhuine!** oh dear! oh dear!

duinealas, *gen* **duinealais** *nm* **1** manliness; **2** decisiveness, firmness of character

duineil *adj* **1** manly, virile, having manly qualities, *cf* **fearail, smiorail 2, tapaidh 2**; **2** (*of woman*) mannish; **3** (*of both sexes*) decisive, enterprising, resourceful, firm (*in actions, character*)

dùinte *adj* **1** (*buildings, objects etc*) closed, shut; **2** (*of persons*) reserved, withdrawn, introvert, *cf* **fad(a) 4**

dùisg *vti, pres part* **a' dùsgadh**, **1** wake up, waken, awaken, **dhùisg mi aig a sia** I woke up at six, **dùisg mi an ceann dà uair a thìde** wake me in/after two hours, (*poem*) **dùisg suas, a Ghàidhlig!** Gaelic, awake!; **2** *as noun in expr* **nam (etc) d(h)ùisg** awake, **chan eil iad nan dùisg** they're not awake, *cf* **dùsgadh 2**

Duitseach (*also found as* **Duidseach**), *gen & pl* **Duitsich** *nm* a Dutchman, someone from the Netherlands, *also as adj* **Duitseach** Dutch

dùlan *see* **dùbhlan**

dùmhail *see* **dòmhail**

dùn, *gen* **dùin**, *pl* **dùin** & **dùintean** *nm* **1** a heap, a pile, *cf* **cruach** *n* **1**, **tòrr** **1**; **2** (*trad*) a (*usu fortified*) castle, a fortress, (*song*) **chaidh Mac-alla às an dùn** Echo left the castle (*ie* it fell silent), *cf* **daingneach**; **3** a (*Pictish or Iron Age*) hill fort; **4** (*topog*) a hill (*usu rounded & suitable for fortification*), occurs in placenames as Dun

dùnadh, **dùnaidh**, **dùnaidhean** *nm* **1** (*the act of*) closing, shutting; closure, a closure; **2** (*Lit, music*) a cadence, a fall

dùnan, *gen & pl* **dùnain** *nm*, *dimin of* **dùn**, **1** a small hill; **2** a dung-heap, a manure heap, a midden, *cf* **òtrach**, **siteag**

dup *vti*, *pres part* **a' dupadh**, dip (sheep)

dùr *adj* **1** stubborn, obstinate, (*Sc*) thrawn, *cf* **rag 2**, **rag-mhuinealach**; **2** stolid, (*Sc*) dour

dùrachd, **dùrachd**, **dùrachdan** *nm* **1** (*trad*) earnestness, seriousness, sincerity; **2** (*now usu*) an expression of good will, a good wish, (*radio programme*) **dùrachdan** greetings, good wishes, *cf more trad* **soraidh 2**; **3** *formulae closing letter etc* **le dùrachd** yours sincerely, **le deagh dhùrachd** with compliments, **leis gach deagh dhùrachd** with best wishes/kindest regards

dùrachdach *adj* **1** serious, earnest; **2** eager, fervent, keen, *cf* **dealasach**, **dian 1 & 2**

dùraig *vi*, *pres part* **a' dùraigeadh**, dare (*to do something*), **bha an stoirm cho garbh 's nach do dhùraig sinn an taigh fhàgail** the storm was so wild we didn't dare leave the house

durcan, *gen & pl* **durcain** *nm* a pine cone, a fir cone

dùrdail, *gen* **dùrdaile** *nf* (*of doves, pigeons*) cooing, **dèan** *v* **dùrdail** coo

dùsal, *gen & pl* **dùsail** *nm* slumber, light sleep, a snooze, a nap, **dèan** *v* **dùsal** snooze, take a snooze/nap, *cf* **cadal 2**, **norrag**, **suain** *n*

dusan, *gen & pl* **dusain** *nm* **1** a dozen; **2** (*fam*) twelve, **dusan bliadhna a dh'aois** twelve years old

dùsgadh, *gen* **dùsgaidh** **1** (*the act of*) awakening, waking up etc (*see senses of* **dùisg** *v*); an awakening; **2** an awakened state, *esp in expr* **tha mi nam dhùsgadh** I am awake, **bha i na leth-dhùsgadh** she was half-awake, *cf* **dùisg 2**; **3** religious revival

duslach, *gen* **duslaich** *nm* **1** dust, *cf* **dust**, **stùr**; **2** mortal remains

dust *nm invar* dust, *cf* **duslach**, **stùr**

dustach *adj* dusty

dustaig *vti*, *pres part* **a' duataigeadh**, dust, do the dusting

dustair, **dustair**, **dustairean** *nm* a duster

dùthaich, **dùthcha**, **dùthchannan** *nf* **1** a country, a land, **dùthaich chèin** a foreign country, *cf* **tìr 2**; **2** a land, a territory, a country (*associated with a particular clan, group, individual etc*), eg (*trad*) **dùthaich MhicAoidh** the Mackay country/lands (*in Sutherland*); **3** one's homeland *or* home district, (*song*) **O mo dhùthaich, 's tu th' air m' aire** O my homeland, it is you who are on my mind; **4** country (*as opposed to town*), countryside, **bha sinn a' fuireach air an dùthaich** we lived/were living in the country, (*formerly*) **Ùghdarras Dùthcha na h-Alba** the Countryside Commission for Scotland

dùthchail *adj* rural, pertaining to or characteristic of the couhtryside

dùthchas, *gen* **dùthchais** *nm* **1** (*trad*) the ancestral land(s) of a clan or an individual, (*prov*) **cha bhi dùthchas aig mnaoi no aig sagart** a woman and a priest have no homeland, *cf* **dùthaich 2**; **2** (*trad*) one's cultural inheritance or heritage, what one is by reason of the place one belongs to, *cf* **dualchas 2**

dùthchasach *adj* **1** native, indigenous, aboriginal; **2** hereditary (*esp in sense of* **dùthchas 2**)

dùthchasach, *gen & pl* **dùthchasaich** *nmf* a native, an aborigine, *cf* **tùsanach**

E

e *pron m sing, emph form* **esan**, he, him, (**e** *only, ie not* **esan**) it (*nm*), **chunnaic e e** he saw him/it, **is esan a rinn e** he (*emph*) did it; *also impersonal* it, **is e mo bràthair a dh'fhalbh** it's my brother who left

eabar, *gen* **eabair** *nm* mire, mud, sludge, silt, **bha a chasan a' dol fodha san eabar** his feet were sinking into the mire, *cf* **poll 1**

eabarach *adj* muddy *etc* (*see senses of* **eabar**)

Eabhra *nf invar* (*lang*) Hebrew

Eabhrach *adj* Hebrew

eacarsaich, eacarsaiche, eacarsaichean *nf* (*phys, ed, etc*) exercise, an exercise

each, *gen & pl* **eich** *nm* a horse, **each dìollaid** a saddle horse, a riding horse, **each-obrach** a workhorse, (*trad*) **each-uisge** a kelpie, a water-horse

each-aibhne, *gen & pl* **eich-aibhne** *nm* a hippopotamus

eachdraiche, eachdraiche, eachdraichean *nm* a historian

eachdraidh, eachdraidhe, eachdraidhean *nf* history, **eòlach air eachdraidh na dùthcha** familiar with the country's history, **rinn i eachdraidh aig an/anns an oilthigh** she did history at university

eachdraidheil *adj* historical, pertaining to history or its study

eachraidh *nm coll* cavalry, horse soldiers

eaconamachd *nf invar* economics

eaconomaidh, eaconomaidh, eaconomaidhean *nmf* an economy, **eaconomaidh na dùthcha** the country's/the national economy

eaconomair, eaconomair, eaconomairean *nm* an economist

Eadailteach, *gen & pl* **Eadailtich** *nm* an Italian, *also as adj* **Eadailteach** Italian

Eadailt *nf, used with art,* **an Eadailt** Italy

Eadailtis *nf invar, used with art,* (*lang*) **an Eadailtis** Italian

eadar *prep*: **eadar** combines with the pl pers prons **sinn, sibh, iad** to give the prep prons **eadarainn, eadaraibh, eatarra** (*also* **eatorra**), between/among us, between/among you (*pl*), between/among them. **1** between, **thàinig i eadarainn** she came between us, **tha iad a' fuireach eadar Port Rìgh agus Dùn Bheagain** they stay between Portree and Dunvegan, *also in expr* **eadar-dhà-lionn** undecided, hesitating, *also* neither one thing nor another; **2** among, **a bheil dotair eadaraibh?** is there a doctor among you?, *cf more usu* **am measg**; **3** both, *Note: in this usage* **eadar** *lenites both words qualified, cf* **thàinig iad, eadar bheag agus mhòr** they came, both small and great, *and* **tha e eadar beag agus mòr** he is between small and big, *ie* neither small nor big, *cf* **cuid 4, gach 3**; **4** *in compounds* inter-, **eadar-ùine** *f* an interval, an interlude, **eadar-phòsadh** *m* intermarriage, *see further examples below*

eadarach *adj* interim, temporary, stop-gap, **beart eadarach** an interim measure

eadar-aghaidh, eadar-aghaidhe, eadar-aghaidhean *nf* (*IT etc*) an interface

eadaraibh, eadarainn *prep prons, see* **eadar**

eadar-dhealachadh, eadar-dhealachaidh, eadar-dhealachaidhean *nm* **1** (*the act of*) differentiating, distinguishing; **2** a difference, **dè an t-eadar-dhealachadh eadar A agus B?** what's the difference between A and B?, *cf* **diofar 1**; **3** differentiation, a distinction, **cha dèan mi eadar-dhealachadh eadar saorsa is neo-eisimeileachd** I make no distinction/don't differentiate between freedom and independence

eadar-dhealaich *vt, pres part* **ag eadar-dhealachadh**, differentiate, distinguish, *cf* **eadar-dhealachadh 3**

eadar-dhealaichte *adj* distinct, separate, **tha an dà cheist gu tur eadar-dhealaichte** the two questions/matters are totally distinct/separate, *cf less strong* **diof(a)rach**

eadar-lìon, eadar-lìn, eadar-lìontan *nm, usu with art,* (*IT*) **an t-eadar-lìon** the internet

eadar-nàiseanta *adj* international

eadar-sholas, *gen & pl* **eadar-sholais** *nm* morning or evening twilight, *cf* **camhana(i)ch 2**, **duibhre**

eadar-theangachadh, **eadar-theangachaidh**, **eadar-theangachaidhean** *nm* **1** (*the act of*) translating; translation; **2** a translation

eadar-theangaich *vt, pres part* **ag eadar-theangachadh**, translate (**do** into), *cf* **cuir Beurla air Gàidhlig** (*see* **cuir 1**)

eadar-theangair, **eadar-theangair**, **eadar-theangairean** *nm* a translator

eadh *obs neut pron see* **seadh** *adv*

èadhar, *gen* **èadhair** *nf* air, *cf* **àile 1**

eadhon *adv* even, **cha robh eadhon dà nota agam** I didn't even have two pounds, *cf* **fiù** *n* **2**, **uiread 3**

eadradh, **eadraidh**, **eadraidhean** *nm* (*formerly*) milking time *or* place of milking, *now esp in expr* **crodh-eadraidh** milk/milch cows

eag, **eige**, **eagan** *nf* a nick, a notch, an indentation

eagach *adj* notched, indented, serrated

eagal & *occas* **feagal**, *gen* **(f)eagail** *nm* **1** fear, fright, **bha an t-eagal oirre ron mhèirleach** she was afraid of the robber, **bha eagal mo bheatha orm** I was scared stiff/to death, **gabh** *v* **eagal** become afraid, take fright, **cuir** *v* **eagal air cuideigin** frighten someone, (*expr polite regret*) **chan eil fhios a'm, tha eagal orm** I don't know, I'm afraid, *cf less usu* **fiamh 2**; **2** *in conj* **air eagal 's gu** lest, for fear, in case, **gabh greum air an fhàradh air eagal 's gun tuit mi** get hold of the ladder in case/for fear I fall, *cf* **fios 5**, **mus 2**

eagalach *adj* **1** fearful, prone to fear; **2** terrible, awful, dreadful (*now usu with attenuated sense*), **ciamar a chaidh an dealbh-chluich? bha e dìreach eagalach!** how did the play go? it was just dreadful!, *cf* **uabhasach 1**; **3** *also as adv* **bha na h-actairean eagalach math!** the actors were awfully/terribly good!, *cf* **uabhasach 2**

eaglais, **eaglaise**, **eaglaisean** *nf* a church (*ie building & institution*), (*Sc*) a kirk, **Eaglais na h-Alba** the Church of Scotland, **cathair-eaglais** *f* a cathedral

eala, **eala(idh)**, **ealachan** *nf* a swan, (*song*) **An Eala Bhàn** The White Swan

èalaidh *vi, pres part* **ag èala(i)dh**, **1** creep, *cf* **snàig 2**; **2** creep or sneak away (*from gathering etc*), **bha iad ag èalaidh dhachaigh** they were sneaking/creeping off home, *cf* **siolp**

ealain, *gen* **ealaine**, *pl* **ealain(ean)**, *gen pl* **ealain** *nf* **1** art, a branch of the arts, **is e tè de na h-ealain(ean) a th' ann am bàrdachd**

poetry is one of the arts, **Ministear na h-Ealain**, the Minister for the Arts, **neach-ealain** *m* an artist; **2** a specific art or skill, **ealain snaighidh** the art of sculpture

ealamh *adj* quick, nimble, swift (*in performing tasks etc*), *cf* **clis**, **deas** *adj* **2**

ealanta *adj* **1** artistic; **2** expert, accomplished, skilled, sgilful, adept, *cf* **sgileil**, **teòma 1**

ealantach, *gen & pl* **ealantaich** *nm* an expert, *cf* **eòlaiche 1**

eallach, *gen & pl* **eallaich** *nm* (*lit & fig*) a burden, a load, (*song*) **is trom an t-eallach an gaol** love is a heavy burden, *cf* **uallach 1**, **ultach 1**

ealt(a), **ealta**, **ealtan** *nf* a flock, a flight (*of birds*)

ealtainn, **ealtainne**, **ealtainnean** *nf* a razor

eanchainn, **eanchainne**, **eanchainnean** *nmf* **1** (*anat*) brain, a brain, (*fam*) **chuir e an eanchainn às** he brained him; **2** a brain, brains, mental or intellectual ability, **tha eanchainn mhath innte** she's got a good brain, *cf* **inntinn 1**

eangarra *adj* bad-tempered, irritable

eanraich, *gen* **eanraiche** *nf* (*trad*) soup, broth, *cf* **brot**

ear *nf invar* east, **on ear** from the east, **an ear air Èden** east of Eden, **gaoth às an ear** a wind from/out of the east, **gaoth an ear** an easterly wind, *Note that* **an** *of* **an ear** *does not behave as an article in the following exprs* **an àird(e) an ear** the east (*ie compass direction*), **an taobh an ear** the east coast/east side of the country, **a' dol an ear** going east, *see* **sear** & *cf* **deas 1**, **iar**, **siar**, **tuath**[1]

earalachadh, **earalachaidh**, **earalachaidhean** *nm* **1** (*the act of*) exhorting etc (*see senses of* **earalaich** *v*); **2** an exhortation, *cf* **brosnachadh 3**; **3** a caution, a warning, *cf* **rabhadh**

earalaich *vt, pres part* **ag earalachadh**, **1** exhort, *cf* **brosnaich**; **2** caution, warn (**air** about)

earalas, *gen* **earalais** *nm* caution, foresight (*in case of trouble*), *esp in expr* **cuir** *v* **air earalas** forewarn, put on (his etc) guard, *cf* **faiceall**

earb *vti, pres part* **ag earbsa(dh)**, **1** (*vi*) trust (*with prep* **à**, **às**) **cha robh iad ag earbsadh às na nàbaidhean aca** they didn't trust their neighbours, *cf* **creideas 3**; **2** (*vt*) entrust (*with prep* **ri**), **na h-earb thu fhèin riutha** don't entrust yourself to/rely on them, *also* don't confide in them

earb(a), **earba**, **earbaichean** *nf* a roe-deer

earball, *gen & pl* **earbaill** *nm* a tail, **cù (is e) a' crathadh earbaill** a dog wagging its tail, **earball daimh** ox-tail

earbsa *nf invar* trust, confidence, reliance, **cuir** *v* **earbsa ann an rudeigin** trust/put one's trust in something, rely on something, **chan eil earbsa aca annaibh** *or* **asaibh** they don't trust you, *cf* **creideas 1 & 3**

earbsach *adj* 1 trusting; 2 trustworthy, *cf* **urrasach**

eàrlas, *gen & pl* **eàrlais** *nm* (*fin*) an advance, **thug am foillsichear eàrlas dha** the publisher gave him an advance

earrach, *gen & pl* **earraich** *nm* (*the season*) spring, **as t-earrach** in (the) spring

Earra-Ghàidheal, *gen* **Earra-Ghàidheal** *n* Argyll

Earra-Ghàidhealach, *gen & pl* **Earra-Ghàidhealaich** *nm* someone from Argyll, *also as adj* **Earra-Ghàidhealach** of, from, or pertaining to Argyll

earrann, **earrainn**, **earrannan** *nf* 1 a part, a piece, a section (*of something*), (*of play*) an act, **a' chiad earrann den nobhail aice** the first part of her novel, *cf* **pàirt 1**, **roinn** *n* 2; 2 (*fin*) a share, a stock, **margadh nan earrannan** the stock market, *cf* **sèar**

earranta *adj* (*business*) limited, **companaidh earranta** a limited company, **Birlinn Earranta** Birlinn Limited

eas, **easa**, **easan** *nm* a waterfall, falls, a cascade, (*prov*) **cha tèid stad ort nas mò na air eas na h-aibhne** you don't stop any more than the waterfall in the river, *cf* **leum-uisge**, **linne 3**, **spùt** *n* 2

eas(-) *a prefix implying negation; can corres to Eng* in-, un-, dis- *etc*; *cf* **eu-**, **mì-**, **neo-** *& see examples below*

easag, **easaig**, **easagan** *nf* a pheasant

eas-aonta, **eas-aonta**, **eas-aontan** *nf* disagreement, discord, dissent, **dh'èirich eas-aonta mhòr eadar na ministearan** there arose considerable disagreement/dissent among/between the ministers

easbaig, **easbaig**, **easbaigean** *nm* a bishop

Easbaigeach, *gen & pl* **Easbaigich** *nm* an Episcopalian, *also as adj* **Easbaigeach 1** Episcopalian; 2 episcopal

easbhaidh, **easbhaidhe**, **easbhaidhean** *nf* 1 lack, want, need, a deficiency or deficit, *esp in expr* **a** (*for* de) **dh'easbhaidh** lacking, wanting, missing, **dè (a) tha a dh'easbhaidh orra?** what do they lack/want/need?, **bha còmhdach an leabhair a dh'easbhaidh** the cover of the book was missing, *cf more usu* **dìth**; 2 a fault, a defect, *cf* **cearb 2**

easbhaidheach *adj* 1 needy, in need, *cf* **feumach**; 2 lacking, wanting, in short supply, *cf* **dìth 2**; 3 faulty, defective

eascaraid *m* a foe, an enemy (*lit* a non-friend)

eas-chruthach *adj* abstract

èasgaidh *adj* (*of persons*) active, willing, keen, prompt, obliging (*with implication of ability, handiness*), **èasgaidh gus a dhèanamh** willing/keen to do it, **èasgaidh gu èirigh sa mhadainn** keen to get up in the morning, *cf* **dealasach**, **deas 4**, **deònach**

easgann, **easgainn**, **easgannan** *nf* an eel

eas-umhail *adj* insubordinate, disobedient, irreverent

eas-urramach *adj* dishonourable

eatarra (*also* **eatorra**) *prep pron*, *see* **eadar**

eathar, **eathair**, **eathraichean** *nmf*, *also* **eithear**, **eitheir**, **eithrichean** *nmf*, a small boat, *also specifically* a rowing boat, (*saying*) **eathar ùr is seana chreagan** a new boat and old rocks, *cf* **geòla**

èibh *v see* **èigh** *v*

èibhinn *adj* funny, amusing, humorous, comic(al), *cf less usu* **àbhachdach**

èibhleag, **èibhleige**, **èibhleagan** *nf* an ember, a cinder, **bheothaich i èibhleagan an teine** she revived/stirred up the embers of the fire

èideadh, **èididh**, **èididhean** *nm* dress (*esp a particular mode of dress*), a garb, a uniform, (*song*) **chuir e bhrìogais ghlas an gèill gus an t-èideadh seo (a) thoirt bhuainn** he made the grey breeks compulsory in order to take this garb/dress away from us, **an t-èideadh Gàidhealach** the garb of the Gael, Highland dress

eidheann, *gen* **eidhne** *nf* ivy

èifeachd *nf invar* an effect, a consequence, **gun èifeachd** without effect, of no avail, *cf* **buaidh 4**, **buil 1**, **toradh 2**

èifeachdach *adj* 1 effective, *cf* **buadhmhor**; 2 efficient

èifeachdas, *gen* **èifeachdais** *nf* efficiency, effectiveness

Eigeach, *gen & pl* **Eigich** *nm* someone from Eigg (**Eilean Eige**), *also as adj* **Eigeach** of, from or pertaining to Eigg

èigeantach *adj* compulsory

èigh, **èighe**, **èighe(ach)an** *nf* a shout, a cry, *cf* **gairm** *n* 3, **glaodh** *n*

eigh, *gen* **eighe** *nf*, *also* **eighre**, *gen* **eighre** *nf*, *also* **deigh**, *gen* **deighe** *nf*, ice

eighe, **eighe**, **eigheachan** *nf* (*for metalwork etc*) a file

èigh & **èibh** *vi, pres part* **ag èigheach(d)**, shout, cry, call, *cf* **gairm** *v* **1**, **glaodh** *vi*

èigheachd *nf invar* shouting, crying, calling

eighre *see* **eigh**

eigin *a suffix corres to Eng* some-, *appended to nouns, eg* **rudeigin** something, **latheigin** one day, some day (or other), **tha cuideigin air a thighinn a-steach** someone's come in, **chaill mi an àiteigin e** I lost it somewhere, **chì mi uair no uaireigin thu** I'll see you sometime or other

èiginn *nf invar* **1** difficulty, trouble, a difficult situation, an emergency, a crisis, **tha mi ann an èiginn** (*also* **nam èiginn**) I'm in trouble/in a fix (*cf more con* **staing**), **itealan ann an èiginn os cionn a' phuirt-adhair** an aeroplane in difficulty/difficulties above the airport, **doras-èiginn** an emergency exit; **2** necessity; **3** violence, *esp in expr* **thoir** *v* **air èiginn** rape, *also* take (*something*) by force; **4** *in expr* **air èiginn** hardly, scarcely, barely, with difficulty, **'s ann air èiginn a dh'fhosgail e a shùil** it was with difficulty that he opened his eye, *also* he barely opened his eye, *cf* **gann 2**

èiginneach *adj* (*of situation etc*) critical, difficult, desperate

èigneachair, èigneachair, èigneachairean *nm* a rapist, a ravisher

èignich *vt, pres part* **ag èigneachadh**, **1** force, compel (*someone to do something*); **2** rape, ravish

eil *pt of irreg vb* **bi** (*see tables p 505*)

Eilbheiseach, *gen & pl* **Eilbheisich** *nm* someone from Switzerland (**an Eilbheis** *f*), *also as adj* **Eilbheiseach** Swiss

èildear, èildeir, èildearan *nm* a (church) elder, *cf more trad* **foirfeach**

eile *adj* other, another, else, **b' fheàrr leam leabhar eile** I'd prefer another (*ie different*) book, **cha ghabh mi pinnt eile** I won't take another (*ie additional*) pint, **air an dara làimh . . . ach air an làimh eile . . .** on the one hand . . . but on the other hand . . . , (*set expr*) **mar a thuirt am fear eile** as someone once said, **rud eile** another thing, something else, (*set expr*) **agus rud eile dheth . . .** and another thing . . . , **cò eile a bh' ann?** who else was there? **chan eil mi ag iarraidh càil eile** I don't want another thing/anything else (*cf* **barrachd 4**)

èile, èileadh, *see* **fèileadh**

eileamaid, eileamaide, eileamaidean *nf* **1** (*science*) an element; **2** (*general*) an element, a factor (*in a situation etc*)

eilean, eilein, eileanan *nm* an island, **air an eilean**, *or more usu* **anns an eilean**, on the island, **Na h-Eileanan Siar** The Western Isles, **Comhairle nan Eilean Siar** the Western Isles Council, **Eilean Fraoich** Isle of Heather (*ie Lewis*), *often prefixed to island name in gen or adj form* **Eilean Mhuile/An t-Eilean Muileach** Mull, **Eilean Leòdhais** Lewis, *cf less usu* **innis** *n* **1**

eileanach, *gen & pl* **eileanaich** *nm* an islander

eilid, èilde, èil(i)dean *nf* a hind (*of red deer*), *cf* **boc 2, damh 1, earb(a)**

eilthireach, *gen & pl* **eilthirich** *nm* **1** someone from another country, a foreigner, *cf* **coigreach 1**; **2** an exile, *esp* (*trad, hist*) a Highlander who emigrated as a result of the Clearances, an emigrant, an émigré, *cf* **fògarrach 2, fear-fuadan**; **3** a pilgrim

eilthireachd *nf invar* **1** (*abstr*) exile; **2** emigration

einnsean, einnsein, einnseanan *nm* an engine, **einnsean càir** a car engine, **einnsean-smàlaidh** a fire engine

einnseanair, einnseanair, einnseanairean *nm* an engineer

Èipheit *nf invar, used with art*, **an Èipheit** Egypt

Èipheiteach, *gen & pl* **Èipheitich**, an Egyptian, *also as adj*, **Èipheiteach** Egyptian

eireachdail *adj* handsome, graceful, elegant, *cf* **gasta 1, grinn 1**

eireag, eireig(e), eireagan *nf* a pullet, (*port-à-beul*) **b' fheàrr leam fhìn gum beireadh an tèile 'màireach dhe na h-eireagan** I would dearly like the other one of the pullets to lay tomorrow

Èireannach, *gen & pl* **Èireannaich** *nm* an Irishman, *also as adj*, **Èireannach** Irish

èirich *vi, pres part* **ag èirigh**, **1** rise, arise, get up (*from bed, sitting position etc*), stand up, **dh'èirich mi anmoch an-dè** I got up late yesterday, **dh'èirich e na sheasamh** he stood up/rose to his feet, **dh'èirich i air a leth-uilinn** she raised herself up onto one elbow; **2** rise up, rebel, revolt, **èirichibh suas an aghaidh nan aintighearnan!** rise up against the tyrants!, *cf* **ar-a-mach**; **3** happen, befall, **dè a dh'èirich dha?** what happened to him? *or* what became of him? (*cf* **tachair 1**), **ciamar a dh'èirich dhaibh?** how did they get on? **'s math a dh'èireas dha mura tèid a mharbhadh** it will go well with him (*ie he'll be lucky*) if he isn't killed (*cf* **rach 2**)

eiridinn *nm invar* (*trad*) nursing, care of the sick, **taigh-eiridinn** *m* a hospital (*cf less trad* **ospadal**), an infirmary, **carbad-eiridinn** *m* an ambulance, *cf* **altram 2**

eiridnich *vt, pres part* **ag eiridneachadh**, nurse, tend (*the sick*), **eiridnich na h-euslaintich** tend/care for the sick/ill, *cf* **altraim 2**

èirig, èirige, èirigean *nf* a payment (*in reparation for something*), *esp* a ransom

èirigh *nf invar* **1** (*the act of*) rising etc (*see senses of* **èirich** *v*); **2** a rising, a rebellion, *cf* **ar-a-mach**

Èirinn, *gen* **Èireann** *nf* Ireland, **Gàidhlig na h-Èireann** Irish (Gaelic)

Èirisgeach, *gen & pl* **Èirisgich** *nm* someone from Eriskay (**Èirisgeigh**), *also as adj* **Èirisgeach** of, from or pertaining to Eriskay

eirmseach *adj* **1** witty; **2** sharp, smart, intelligent

èisd *vi see* **èist**

eisimeil, *gen* **eisimeile** *nf*, dependence, *esp in expr* **an eisimeil** (*with gen*) dependent on, **bha a' chompanaidh an eisimeil an luchd-earrann aice** the company was dependent on its shareholders, *also with prep* **air, an eisimeil air a bhràthair** dependent on his brother

eisimeileach *adj* dependent (**air** on), (*opposite*) **neo-eisimeileach** *adj* independent

eisimeileachd *nf invar*, dependence, (*opposite*) **neo-eisimeileachd** independence, *cf* **eisimeil**

eisimpleir, eisimpleir, eisimpleirean *nm* an example, *esp in expr* **mar eisimpleir** for example (*abbrev* **m.e.**)

eist *excl see* **ist**

èist *vi* (*also found as* **èisd**), *pres part* **ag èisteachd**, listen (**ri** to), **ag èisteachd ris na h-òrain** listening to the songs

èisteachd *nf invar* (*also found as* **èisdeachd**), **1** (*the act of*) listening, hearing; **2** (*more con*) a hearing, an audience; **3** *in expr* **nam** (*etc*) **èisteachd** in my (*etc*) hearing

eitean, *gen* **eitein & eitne**, *pl* **eitnean** *nm* **1** a kernel, **eitean cnotha** a nut kernel; **2** a core, **eitean ubhail** an apple core

eòlach *adj* **1** knowledgeable, familiar, conversant, (**air** with, about) **duine eòlach** a knowledgeable man, **eòlach air coimpiutairean** familiar/conversant with, knowledgeable about computers, **bha an t-each eòlach air an rathad dhachaigh** the horse knew the way home, *cf* **fiosrach**; **2** (*of people*) acquainted, **tha iad eòlach air a chèile** they're acquainted (with one another), **'s e sin Ùisdean, a bheil thu eòlach air?** that's Hugh, do you know him?; *cf* **aithne 1, 2 & 3**

eòlaiche, eòlaiche, eòlaichean *nm* **1** an expert, *cf* **ealantach**; **2** a scientist; **3** a savant, a scholar

eòlas, eòlais, eòlasan *nm* **1** knowledge, **tha e làn eòlais air filmichean** he's full of knowledge about films; **2** (*in compounds*) a branch of knowledge, **bith-eòlas** biology, **eòlas-leighis** medicine, **eòlas-inntinn** psychology, **luibh-eòlas** botany; **3** acquaintance, familiarity, **cuir** *v* **eòlas air cuideigin** get to know/get acquainted with someone, **luchd-eòlais** acquaintances, (*trad*) **tìr m' eòlais** the land I am familiar with/know best (*ie* my homeland *or* home district), *cf* **aithne 1**

eòrna *nm invar* barley, **eilean an eòrna** the barley island, Tiree, (*song*) **gealach abachaidh an eòrna, bheir i sinne 'Leòdhas dhachaigh** the barley-harvest moon will get us home to Lewis, (*prov*) **cha dèan làmh ghlan eòrna** clean hand(s) won't make barley

Eòrpa *nf invar* Europe, *more usu* **an Roinn Eòrpa** Europe, the continent of Europe

Eòrpach, *gen & pl* **Eòrpaich** *nm* a European, *also as adj* **Eòrpach** European

esan *see* **e**

eu(-), *occas* **ao(-)**, *a negating prefix, can corres to Eng* in-, un-, dis-, -less, *see examples below*, *cf* **eas-, mì-, neo-**

euchd, euchd, euchdan *nm* **1** (*trad*) a feat, a deed, an exploit (*of heroes etc*), *cf* **cleas 1**; **2** (*now more usu*) an achievement

eucoir, eucorach, eucoirean *nf* **1** crime, a crime; **2** wrong, a wrong, **rinn iad eucoir orm** they wronged me, *cf* **coire 1**

eu-coltach *adj* unlikely, improbable; dissimilar

eucorach, *gen & pl* **eucoraich** *nm* a criminal

eud (*also* **iad**) *nm invar* **1** jealousy (*often sexual*), *cf* **farmad**; **2** zeal

eudach (*also* **iadach**) *adj* jealous, (*song*) **A' Bhean Eudach** The Jealous Woman

eudach (*also* **iadach**), *gen* **eudaich** *nm* jealousy (*often sexual*), *also used as pres part*, **bha i ag eudach ris mu bhoireannaich eile** she was jealous about him and other woman, (*lit* she was showing/feeling jealousy towards him concerning other women)

eudail *occas* **feudail**, *gen* **eudail & eudalach**, *pl* **eudailean** *nf* **1** (*trad*) treasure, cattle, valuable possessions; **2** *now usu in affectionate address or excl* **m' eudail!** my darling! (*less intimate*) (my) dear! (*to children*) pet!, love!, precious!; *cf* **ulaidh**

eudmhor *adj* **1** jealous (*often sexually*); **2** zealous

eu-dòchas, *gen* **eu-dòchais** *nm* hopelessness

eu-domhainn *adj* shallow, superficial

eug, *gen* **èig** *nm* (*trad*) death, *cf more usu* **bàs**

eug *vi, pres part* **ag eugadh,** (*trad*) die, *cf much more usu* **bàsaich, caochail, siubhail**

eugmhais *see* **às eugmhais**

eun, *gen & pl* **eòin** *nm* a bird, **eòin-mhara** sea birds, **eòin-àir** birds of prey, **eòin-uisge** waterfowl, (*prov*) **ge beag an t-ugh, thig eun às** though the egg be small, a bird will come out of it

eun-eòlas, *gen* **eun-eòlais** *nm* ornithology

eunlaith *nf pl coll* birds, **ealt eunlaith** a flock of birds

euslaint(e), euslainte, euslaintean *nf* illness, ill-health, *cf* **anfhannachd, tinneas**

euslainteach *adj* ill, unhealthy, in bad health, sick, *cf* **anfhann, tinn**

euslainteach, *gen & pl* **euslaintich** *nm* an invalid, a patient, a sick or ill person

F

fàbhar, fàbhair, fàbharan *nm* a favour, **rinn e fàbhar dhut** he did you a favour, *cf* **bàidh 2, seirbheis 2**

fàbharach *adj* favourable, propitious

faca *pt of irreg v* **faic** (*see tables p 498*)

fabhra, fabhra, fabhran *nm* **1** an eyelash, *cf* **rosg²**; **2** an eyelid

facal, *gen* **facail**, *pl* **facail** & **faclan** *nm* **1** a word (*written or spoken*), **is e facal boireann a tha ann an 'eaglais'** 'eaglais' is a feminine word, **thubhairt i facal no dhà anns a' Ghàidhlig** she said a word or two/a few words in Gaelic, **cha do bhruidhinn sinn facal Gàidhlig air a' bhàt'-aiseig** we didn't speak a word of Gaelic on the ferry, **an toir thu dhomh d' fhacal (air)?** will you give me your word (on it)/swear (to it)? **2** a saying, **is e facal a th' ann an 'is tighe fuil na bùrn'** 'blood is thicker than water' is a saying, *cf* **ràdh 1, seanfhacal**

fa chomhair *see* **comhair 2**

faclach *adj* wordy, verbose, *cf* **briathrach**

facladair, facladair, facladairean *nm* (*IT*) a word processor

facladaireachd *nf invar* (*IT*) word processing

faclair, faclair, faclairean *nm* a dictionary, **am faclair as ainmeile sa Ghàidhlig, 's e am fear aig Dwelly** the most famous dictionary in Gaelic is Dwelly's one

faclaireachd *nf invar* lexicography

facs, facsa, facsaichean *nm* (*IT*) a fax, **inneal facsa** *m* a fax machine

factaraidh, factaraidh, factaraidhean *nf* a factory

fad, *gen* **faid** *nm* **1** (*spatial*) length, **mìle a** (*for* **de**) **dh'fhad** a mile long/in length, **tha dà throigh de dh'fhad ann** it's two feet long, **dh'itealaich e air fad an taighe** it flew the length of the house, **cuir** *v* **rudeigin am fad** lengthen something, **a' dol am fad** getting longer, *cf less usu* **faide**; **2** length (*of time*), *prepositional use corres to Eng* for, whole, all, **bha sinn sa bhaile mhòr fad cola-deug** we were in the town for a fortnight (*lit* the length of a fortnight), **fad na h-ùine** the whole/all

the time, **bha mi bochd fad mo bheatha** I was poor my whole/all my life, **bidh mi nam dhùisg fad na h-oidhche** I'll be awake the whole night; **3** *in expr* **air fad** *adv* all, the whole, completely, **chaidh na taighean air fad a losgadh** all the houses were burned, **sgrios iad an dùthaich air fad** they ravaged the whole country, **mhill e air fad e** he spoiled it completely; **4** **fhad is a** *conj* while, **fhad 's a bha i anns an Fhraing dh'ionnsaich i an Fhraingis** while she was in France she learnt French

fàd, fàid, fàdan *nm* a (single) peat (*also* **fàd mònach**), *cf* **fòid 3**

fad(a) *adj* **1** (*spatially*) long, a long way, far, (*of people*) tall, **druim fada** a long ridge, **dè cho fada 's a tha e?** how long is it? *or* how far is it? (*song*) **'s fhada bhuam Grìminis** a long way/far from me is Griminish, (*prov*) **fada bhon t-sùil, fada bhon chridhe** (*approx equivalent to*) what the eye doesn't see the heart doesn't grieve over, **tìr fad' air falbh** a faraway/distant land, **boireannach fada caol** a tall lanky woman, **còta/film làn-fhada** a full-length coat/film; **2** long (*in time*), **bha na làithean fada dhuinn** the days were/seemed long for us, **na bi fada!** don't be long! **'s ann o chionn fhada a thachair sin** it's long ago/a long time ago that that happened, **is fhada o nach fhaca mi thu** it's a long time since I saw you, long time no see, **chan fhada thuige a-nis** it won't be long now; **3** *in comparative exprs* **fada nas fheàrr, fada nas sine** far/much better, far/much older, *cf* **mòran 3**; **4** *in expr* **fad' às** (*of persons*) distant, remote, withdrawn (*cf* **dùinte 2**), *also* preoccupied, absent-minded; **5** *in compounds* long-, *eg* **fad- fhulangas** *m* long-suffering, **fad-shaoghalach** *adj* long-lived

fadachd *nf invar, also* **fadal**, *gen* **fadail** *nm*, **1** longing, yearning, nostalgia for *or* feeling of missing a place, person or thing, **thàinig fadachd orm ris** a longing/nostalgia came over me for it/him; **2** weariness, tedium, boredom, impatience (*for something to be finished*), **bha**

fadachd orm fhad 's a bha e a' bruidhinn I was bored/impatient all the time he was talking, **gabh** *v* **fadachd** grow weary

fadal *nm, see* **fadachd**

fadalach *adj* **1** late (*ie after the appropriate moment*), tardy, **bha mi fadalach, bha a h-uile duine air falbh** I was late, everyone had left, *cf* **deireadh 3**; **2** tedious, boring, long drawn out, **òraid fhadalach** a boring/ long drawn out talk, *cf* **liosta, màirnealach 2, ràsanach, slaodach 2**

fadhail, *gen* **fadhail** & **fadhlach,** *pl* **fadhlaichean** *nf* a tidal ford between two islands

fàg *vt, pres part* **a' fàgail, 1** leave, quit, abandon, (*songs*) **a' fàgail Steòrnabhaigh** leaving Stornoway, **on dh'fhàg thu mi 's mulad orm** since you left me with sadness upon me, **càit na dh'fhàg thu an fhichead gini?** where did you leave the twenty guineas?; **2** leave in a particular state, make, cause to be, (*song*) **dh'fhàg thu tana-ghlas mo shnuadh** you made my complexion pale and wan, **dh'fhàg an turas sgìth iad** the journey made/left them tired

fàgail, fàgaile *nf* (*the act of*) leaving, quitting *etc* (*see senses of* **fàg** *v*)

faic *vt irreg* (*see tables p 498*), *pres part* **a' faicinn,** see, **chan fhaic mi càil** I can't see anything/a thing, (*song*) **chì mi 'm bàta 's i tighinn** I see the boat approaching, **bidh sinn ga fhaicinn gu math tric** we see him pretty often, **chì sinn** we'll see

faiceall, *gen* **faicill** *nf* care, caution, circumspection, *cf* **earalas**

faiceallach *adj* careful, cautious, prudent, circumspect, **bi faiceallach!** be careful! *cf* **cùramach 1**

faiceadh, faiceam, faiceamaid *pts of irreg v* **faic** (*see tables p 498*)

faiche, faiche, faichean *nf* a meadow, a grass park, a lawn, *cf* **clua(i)n, dail 1, lòn² 3**

faicinn *nf invar* (*the act of*) seeing, **'s math d' fhaicinn** it's good to see you

faicsinneach *adj* **1** visible, *cf less usu* **lèirsinneach 1**; **2** conspicuous

faide *nf invar* length, *cf more usu* **fad 1**

fàidh, fàidhe, fàidhean *nm* (*Bibl, trad*) a prophet, a seer, (*poem*) **A' Cluich air Football le Fàidh** (Ruaraidh MacThòmais) Playing Football with a Prophet, *cf* **fiosaiche 1**

fàidheadaireachd, fàidheadaireachd, fàideadaireachdan *nf* prophecy, a prophecy, *cf* **fàisneachd**

faidhir, faidhreach, faidhrichean *nf* a fair, *cf* **fèill 1**

faidhle, *gen* **faidhle,** *pl* **faidhlean** & **faidhlichean** *nm* (*IT & documents*) a file

faigh *vt irreg* (*see tables p 500*), *pres part* **a' faighinn** & **a' faotainn, 1** get, obtain, acquire, **faigh iasg on bhan** get/fetch some fish from the van, (*song*) **gu dè nì mi mur faigh mi thu?** what will I do if I don't get you?, (*prov*) **cha d' fhuair droch bhuanaiche a-riamh deagh chorran** bad reaper never got good sickle (a bad workman always blames his tools), **cha d' fhuair mi an obair ud** I didn't get yon job, **fhuair i duais** she got/won a prize (*cf* **coisinn 2**); **2** find, **fhuair i sgillinn air a' chabhsair** she found a penny on the pavement, **gheibh sibh san taigh-òsta e** you'll find him in the pub, *cf* **lorg** *v* **2; 3 faigh a-mach** find out, discover, **fhuair iad a-mach gun robh e briste** they found out that he was broke/bankrupt; **4** *in expr* **faigh seachad air (opairèisean** *etc***)** get over, recover from (an operation *etc*); **5** *in expr* **faigh air** manage to, **gheibh mi air tilleadh ann uair no uaireigin** I'll manage to go back there some time or other, *cf* **rach 5**

faigheadh, faigheam, faigheamaid *pts of irreg v* **faigh** (*see tables p 500*)

faighean, faighein, faigheanan *nm* a vagina, *cf* **pit 1, ròmag**

faighinn *nf invar* & **faotainn** *nf invar* (*the act of*) getting, finding *etc* (*see senses of* **faigh** *v*)

faighneach & **faighneachail** *adj* inquisitive, enquiring, *cf* **ceasnachail**

faighneachd *nf invar* (*the act of*) asking, enquiring

faighnich *vi, pres part* **a' faighneachd,** ask, enquire, **faighnich de Mhòrag** ask Morag, **dh'fhaighnich i an robh beatha air Mars** she asked whether there was life on Mars, *cf less usu* **feòraich**

fail, faile, failean *nf* (*agric*) a sty

failc *vti, pres part* **a' failceadh,** bathe, *cf* **ionnlaid, nigh**

fàile & **fàileadh** *see* **àile**

faileas, faileis, faileasan *nm* **1** a shadow, **laigh a faileas orm** her shadow fell on me; **2** a reflection, **chì mi faileas na gealaich air uachdar an locha** I can see the reflection of the moon on the surface of the loch

faileasach *adj* shadowy

faillean, faillein, failleanan *nm* an eardrum

faillich *see* **fairtlich**

fàillig *vti, pres part* **a' fàilligeadh,** fail, **fàillig deuchainn** fail an exam, **dh'fhàillig an t-àrdaichear orm** the lift failed on me

fàilligeadh, fàilligidh, fàilligidhean *nm* 1 (*the act of*) failing; 2 a failing, a deficiency; 3 failure, a failure

fàillinn, fàillinne, fàillinnean *nf* 1 a failing, a fault, a blemish (*in personality etc*), *cf* **meang** 1; 2 weakening, falling off, deterioration, (*song*) **chan eil fàillinn san teangaidh aig a' bhean agam fhìn!** there's no weakening in the tongue of my very own wife!; 3 failure; *cf* **fàilligeadh**

failm & **ailm**, *gen* **(f)ailme**, *pl* **(f)ailmean** *nf* (a boat's) tiller

failmean & **falman**, *gen* **failmein**, *pl* **failmeanan** *nm* a kneecap

fail-mhuc, fail-mhuc, failean-mhuc *nf* a pigsty

fàilte, fàilte, fàiltean *nf* 1 a welcome, **cuir** *v* **fàilte air cuideigin** welcome someone (*cf* **fàiltich**), **fàilte oirbh don bhaile!** welcome to the village! **fhuair sinn fàilte chridheil** we got a hearty welcome (*cf* **gabhail** 4), (*trad*) **ceud mìle fàilte!** a hundred thousand welcomes!, (*hotel etc*) **an t-ionad fàilte** reception, the reception desk, *cf less usu* **furan**; 2 a greeting, a salute; 3 (*pibroch*) a salute, **Fàilte an t-Siosalaich** Chisholm's Salute

fàilteach & **fàilteachail** *adj* welcoming, hospitable

fàilteachadh, *gen* **fàilteachaidh** *nm* (*the act of*) welcoming, greeting, saluting

fàiltich *vt, pres part* **a' fàilteachadh**, welcome, salute, greet, *cf more usu* **cuir fàilte air** (*see* **fàilte** 1)

fàiltiche, fàiltiche, fàiltichean *nm* (*hotel etc*) a receptionist

faing, fainge, faingean *nf, also* **fang, faing, fangan** *nm*, 1 a sheepfold, (*Sc*) a (sheep-) fank; 2 a fank (*ie the activity and occasion of gathering, dipping, shearing etc carried out at the sheep-fank*), **bidh faing ann a-màireach** there'll be a fank tomorrow

fàinne, fàinne, fàinneachan *nmf* a ring (*esp for finger*), **fàinne-pòsaidh/fàinne-pòsta** a wedding ring, **fàinne gealladh-pòsaidh** an engagement ring

fàinne-solais, fàinne-solais, fàinneachan-solais *nf* a halo

fairche, fairche, fairchean *nm* a mallet

faire, faire, fairean *nf* 1 (*the action of*) guarding, watching, **dèan/cùm** *v* **faire** be on guard, keep watch, keep a look-out, **faire na h-oidhche** the night watch (*abstr*); 2 (*coll, con*) a guard, **cuir** *v* **faire air** put a guard on it, **fear-faire** *m* a (*single*) guard, a member of the guard, *cf* **freiceadan**

fàire, fàire, fàirean *nf* 1 a horizon, a skyline, **air fàire** on the horizon; 2 *in expr* **faigh** *v* **fàire air** spot, catch sight of (*usu at a distance or on horizon*)

faireachdainn, faireachdainne, faireachdainnean *nf* 1 (*the act of*) feeling, smelling (*see* **fairich** *v*); 2 (*phys*) feeling, a feeling, sensation, a sensation, *cf* **mothachadh** 2; 3 (*emotional, mental*) a feeling, *in pl* feelings

fàireag, fàireig, fàireagan *nf* (*anat*) a gland, **fàireag-fhallais** a sweat gland

fairge, *gen* **fairge**, *pl* **fairgeachan** & **fairgeannan** *nf* (*trad, in poetry etc*) an ocean, a sea, (*song*) **air luing mhòir air bhàrr na fairge** on a great ship on the crest of the ocean, *cf* **sàl** 2 & *more usu* **cuan, muir**

fairich *vti, pres part* **a' faireachdainn** & **a' faireachadh**, 1 (*vti*) feel (*phys*), **fairich fuachd is teas** feel cold and heat, **ciamar a tha thu a' faireachdainn an-diugh?** how are you feeling/how do you feel today?; 2 (*vi*) feel (*emotionally, mentally*), **a' faireachdainn diombach** feeling disgruntled; 3 (*vt*) smell, **am fairich thu ceò na mòna/boladh an èisg?** can you smell the peat reek/the smell of the fish?

fairtlich *vi, pres part* **a' fairtleachadh**, *also* **faillich** *vi, pres part* **a' faillicheadh**, overcome, *esp in expr* **fairtlich air** get the better of, defeat, baffle (*something, someone*), **bha mi airson a' bheinn a dhìreadh ach dh'fhairtlich i orm** I wanted to climb the mountain but it defeated/got the better of me, *or*, I failed, **fairtlichidh sinn air an nàmhaid** we will overcome/defeat the enemy

faisg *adj* near, close (**air** to), **faisg air a chèile** close together, **tha àm na Nollaige faisg a-nis** Christmas time is near now, *cf less usu* **dlùth** 1

fàisg *vt, pres part* **a' fàsgadh**, compress, press, squeeze, wring, *cf* **teannaich** 2

faisge *nf invar* nearness, closeness

fàisneachd *nf invar* prophecy, a prophecy, *cf* **fàidheadaireachd**

fàisnich *vti, pres part* **a' fàisneachadh**, prophesy, foretell, predict

faite, faite, faitichean *nf* a smile, *now esp as* **faite-gàire** *nf* a smile, **dèan** *v* **faite-gàire** smile (*cf less usu* **faitich**), *cf* **fiamh-gàire** (*see* **fiamh** 3), **snodha-gàire**

fàitheam, fàitheim, fàitheaman *nm* a hem (*on material or garment*)

faitich *vi, pres part* **a' faiteachadh**, smile

fàl, *gen* & *pl* **fàil** *nm* 1 a hedge, *cf* **callaid**; 2 a turf, a sod, a divot, *cf* **fòid** 1; 3 (*at roadside*) a verge

falach, *gen* falaich *nm* hiding, the act of hiding, concealment, **am falach** in hiding, **rach** *v* **am falach** go into hiding, **cuiridh mi am falach thu** I will hide/conceal you

falach-fead *nm invar* hide-and-seek

falachd *nf invar* a feud

falaich *vti, pres part* **a' falach** & **a' falachadh**, hide, conceal, secrete (**air** from), *cf more usu* **rach/cuir am falach** (*see* falach)

falaichte *adj* hidden, concealed, secret, (*song*) **chuir iad a ghleann falaicht' mi** they sent me to a hidden glen

falaid, *gen* falaide *nm* varnish

falamh *adj* 1 empty, **tha na glinn/mo stamag falamh** the glens are/my stomach is empty, *cf* **fàs** *adj* 1, *less usu in this sense*; 2 hollow

fal(a)mhachd *nf invar* 1 emptiness; 2 a void, a vacuum, *cf* fànas 2

falbh *vi, pres part* **a' falbh**, 1 leave, go (away), depart, **dh'fhalbh iad an-dè** they left/went away yesterday, **tha i air falbh** she's left/gone, she's away, **ceart! tha mi (a') falbh** right! I'm going, I'm off, I'm away, *imper also occurs as* **thalla, f(h)albh/thalla don bhùth dhomh** away you go to the shop for me, (*eg to dog*) **falbh/thalla dhachaigh!** away/get off home!; 2 *in expr* **falbh a dh'iarraidh rudeigin** go to fetch/get something

fallain *adj* 1 (*persons*) sound, healthy, well, able-bodied, (*song*) **fallain gum bi thu!** may you be safe and sound/in perfect health! **ràinig sinn an cala slàn is fallain** *or* (*trad*) **gu slàn fallain** we reached the harbour safe and sound/in one piece; 2 wholesome, health-giving, **biadh fallain** wholesome/healthy food; *cf* **slàn** 1 & 2

fallas, *gen* fallais *nm* sweat, perspiration, **tha mi a' cur fallas dhìom** *or* **tha fallas orm** *or* **tha mi nam fhallas** I'm sweating

fallasach *adj* sweaty

fallsa *adj* false, deceitful, *cf* **brèige** *adj* 1, **meallta(ch)**

falmadair, falmadair, falmadairean *nm* a helm (*of boat*)

falman *see* failmean

falmhachadh, *gen* falmhachaidh *nm* (*the act of*) emptying, unloading

falmhaich *vti, pres part* **a' falmhachadh**, 1 empty, make empty, become empty; 2 unload, *cf* **aotromaich** 2

falt, *gen* fuilt *nm* hair (*of human head*), *cf* **gruag** 1

famh, faimh, famhan *nmf* a mole (*ie the animal*)

famhair, famhair, famhairean *nm*, *also* fuamhaire, fuamhaire, fuamhairean *nm*, 1 a giant, *cf less usu* **athach**; 2 (*trad*) a champion, a hero, *cf usu* **curaidh, gaisgeach**

fan *vi, pres part* **a' fantainn, a' fantail** & **a' fanachd**, 1 wait (**air** for), stay, **fan thusa an seo!** you wait/stay here! **bha mi a' fantainn ort** I was waiting for you/(*Sc*) on you, *cf* **feith** 1, **fuirich** 1; 2 live, stay, **fan aig cuideigin** stay/lodge with someone, *cf* **fuirich** 2

fanaid, *gen* fanaide *nf* 1 mockery, ridicule (*of person, his/her possessions etc*), *esp in expr* **dèan** *v* **fanaid air** mock, ridicule, scoff at, make fun of, *cf* **magadh** 2 & *less usu* **àbhacas** 2; 2 *also found as pres part* **bha iad a'/ri fanaid air a chuid aodaich** they were making fun of his clothes; *cf* **mag** *v*

fànas, fànais, fànasan *nm* 1 space (*ie extra-terrestrial*), **fànas-long** *f* a spaceship, *cf* **speur** 3; 2 a void, *cf* **fal(a)mhachd** 2

fa-near *adv* 1 *in expr* **fa-near dhomh** (etc) on my (etc) mind, (*song*) **nuair (a) bhios mi leam fhìn bidh tu tighinn fa-near dhomh** when I'm alone you come into my thoughts, *cf* **aigne** 1, **aire** 1, **cùram** 2; 2 *expr intention, inclination,* **bha e fa-near dhi an taigh a sgioblachadh rud beag** it was on her mind/she was minded/had a mind to tidy the house a wee bit, *cf* **beachd** 3; 3 *as noun, in expr* **thoir** *v* **fa-near (do)** notice, *cf* **aire** 2, **mothaich** 1

fang *see* faing

fann *adj* (*phys*) weak, feeble, faint, **guth fann** a weak/feeble voice, *cf* **lag** *adj*

fannachadh, *gen* fannachaidh *nm* (*the act of*) weakening etc (*see senses of* **fannaich** *v*)

fannaich *vti, pres part* **a' fannachadh**, 1 weaken, make or become weak, feeble or faint, *cf more usu* **lagaich**; 2 (*vi*) faint, *cf* **fanntaig laigse** 2, **neul** 3

fanntaig *vi, pres part* **a' fanntaigeadh**, faint, *cf* **fannaich** 2, **laigse** 2, **neul** 3

faobhar, faobhair, faobharan *nm* an edge (*of blade, tool etc*), **faobhar gearraidh** a cutting edge

faobharachadh, *gen* faobharachaidh *nm* (*the act of*) sharpening etc (*see* **faobharaich** *v*)

faobharaich *vt, pres part* **a' faobharachadh**, sharpen, put an edge on (*blade, tool etc*), *cf* **geuraich**

faochadh *see* faothachadh

faochag, faochaig, faochagan *nf* (*Sc*) a whelk, (*Eng*) a winkle, (*prov*) **is lom an cladach far an cunntar na faochagan** it's a bare beach on which the whelks can be counted

faod *vti def, no pres part,* 1 may, can, might (*ie be permitted, allowed to – for can physically see* **urrainn** 2), **am faod sinn falbh?**

faodaidh may/can we go? yes, **chan fhaodar smocadh** smoking not allowed, no smoking, **dh'fhaodadh e a bhith gu bheil beatha air Mars** it could/might be that there is life on Mars, **faodaidh gu bheil e tinn** he may/might be ill, perhaps he's ill; **2** *past part* **faodte** *in adv & conj* **(is) ma(th) dh'fhaodte**, *also* **is mathaid**, maybe, perhaps, possibly, **bidh là brèagha ann, math dh'fhaodte** it'll be a fine day, perhaps, **math dh'fhaodte nach cuir i** maybe it won't snow, *cf* **dòcha 2** & **3**, & *less usu* **teagamh 2**

faoighe *nf invar* (*trad*) cadging, thigging, begging for gifts of food etc, *now in expr* **dèan faoighe** *v* beg

faoileag, faoileig, faoileagan *nf* a seagull

faoilidh *adj* **1** hospitable, generous, *cf* **fial 1**; **2** frank (*in nature, speech etc*), *cf* **fosgailte 3, fosgarra 1**

Faoilleach, *gen* **Faoillich** *nm, also* **Faoilteach,** *gen* **Faoiltich** *nm, used with art* **am Faoilleach, am Faoilteach, 1** (*trad*) the last two weeks of January and the first two weeks of February, approximately; **2** (*now*) January, **am ficheadamh là den Fhaoilteach** the 20th of January

Faoilteach *see* **Faoilleach**

faoin *adj* **1** silly, empty-headed, foolish, brainless, *cf* **amaideach, baoth; 2** vain, futile, **ionnsaighean faoin mhic-an-duine** the vain/futile endeavours of mankind, *cf* **dìomhain 1**

faoineas, *gen* **faoineis** *nm* **1** silliness, foolishness, vacuity; **2** vanity, futility, *cf* **dìomhanas**

faoinsgeul, *gen & pl* **faoinsgeòil** *nm* **1** a myth, a legend, *cf* **fionnsgeul; 2** idle talk

faoisid, faoiside, faoisidean *nf* confession, a confession, (*rel*) **dèan** *v* **faoisid** make confession, *cf* **aideachadh 2**

faoisidich *vti, pres part* **a' faoisidich**, confess, *cf* **dèan faoisid** (*see* **faoisid**)

faol, *gen & pl* **faoil** *nm* a wolf, *cf* **madadh 3**

faotainn *see* **faigh** & **faighinn**

faothachadh & **faochadh,** *gen* **fao(tha)chaidh** *nm* **1** (*the act of*) alleviating etc (*see senses of* **faothaich** *v*); **2** relief, respite, alleviation (*of pain, suffering*), **thàinig faothachadh air** he experienced some respite, his suffering/pain lessened, *cf* **furtachd**

faothaich *vti, pres part* **a' fao(tha)chadh**, alleviate, relieve, ease, bring or experience relief or respite (*of pain, suffering*), *cf* (*vi*) **furtaich**, (*vt*) **lasaich 2**

far *prep see* **bàrr 5**

far a *conj* where, *Note: used in non-interrogative contexts* (*cf interrogative* **càite**); **gheibh thu e far na dh'fhàg thu e** you'll find it where you left it

faradh, faraidh, faraidhean *nm* (*transport etc*) **1** a fare; **2** a freight charge, carriage, haulage (*ie the charges*)

fàradh *see* **àradh**

far-ainm, *gen* **far-ainme,** *pl* **far-ainmean** & **far-ainmeannan** *nm* a nickname, *cf* **frith-ainm**

faram, *gen* **faraim** *nm* loud noise, a loud noise, (*of various kinds*) *cf* **fuaim, gleadhraich, toirm**

faramach *adj* noisy, loud, *cf* **fuaimneach**

farchluais, *gen* **farchluaise** *nf* eavesdropping, **dèan** *v* **farchluais** eavesdrop, listen in (*on conversations etc*)

fàrdach, fàrdaich, fàrdaichean *nf* **1** a dwelling, a house, *cf more usu* **taigh 1; 2** a lodging, *cf more usu* **lòistinn**

farmad, *gen* **farmaid** *nm* envy, **dèan/gabh** *v* **farmad ri cuideigin** feel envious of someone, envy someone, (*song*) **cha bhi agad eud no farmad ri luchd-cruit ged tha iad ainmeil** you will have no (need to feel) jealousy or envy towards crofter folk, though they are famous (*for being well-off!*)

farmadach *adj* envious

farpais *see* **co-fharpais**

farpaiseach *adj* (*sport, business etc*) competitive

farpaiseach, *gen & pl* **farpaisich** *nm* a competitor, an entrant, a participant (*in a competition*)

farranaich *vt, pres part* **a' farranachadh, 1** tease, *cf* **tarraing** *v* **6; 2** vex

farsaing *adj* **1** wide, broad, extensive, *cf* **leathann; 2** *also in expr* **fad' is farsaing** *adv* far and wide, **sgaoil a cliù fad' is farsaing** her fame spread far and wide

farsaingeachd *nf invar* **1** breadth, width, *cf* **leud; 2** extent, area; **3** *in expr* **san fharsaingeachd** generally, in general, broadly speaking, by and large, on the whole, **san fharsaingeachd tha a' mhòr-chuid na aghaidh** generally speaking the majority are against it/him

farspag & **arspag,** *gen* **(f)arspaig,** *pl* **(f)arspagan** *nf* a great black-backed gull, **farspag bheag** a lesser black-backed gull

fàs *adj* **1** empty, *cf* **falamh 1; 2** waste, uncultivated, barren, **talamh fàs** waste ground *or* uncultivated ground

fàs, *gen* **fàis** *nm* **1** (*the act of*) growing, becoming (*see* **fàs** *v*); **2** (*of crops etc, con & abstr*) growth, *cf* **cinneas**

fàs *vi, pres part* **a' fàs**, **1** grow (*of crops etc*), **'s e eòrna a tha a' fàs ann an sheo** it's barley that's growing here; **2** grow (*ie increase in size*) **tha am balach a' fàs gu math luath** the boy's growing pretty quickly, *cf* **cinn, meudaich**; **3** grow, become, **dh'fhàs iad sgìth dheth** they grew/became tired of it/him

fàsach, fàsaich, fàsaichean *nmf* **1** a desert, **fàsaichean Afraga** the deserts of Africa; **2** a wilderness, a deserted place or area, (*song*) **Coille an Fhàsaich** The Wood in (*lit of*) the Wilderness/in the Deserted Place; *cf less usu* **dìthreabh**

fàsachadh, *gen* **fàsachaidh** *nm* **1** (*the act of*) emptying, depopulating etc (*see senses of* **fàsaich** *v*); **2** clearance, depopulation

fàsaich *vt, pres part* **a' fàsachadh**, **1** empty; **2** (*hist, esp with ref to the Highland Clearances*) depopulate, clear (*a district etc of people*)

fàsail *adj* desolate (*not used of people*), **tìr fhàsail** a desolate land

fasan, fasain, fasanan *nm* **1** fashion, a fashion, **san fhasan, às an fhasan** in fashion, out of fashion, **fasan ùr** a new fashion; **2** a habit, a custom

fasanta *adj* fashionable, modish, trendy

fasdachadh, fasdaich, fasdaidhear *see* **fastachadh, fastaich, fastaidhear**

fasgach *adj* **1** sheltering, **coille fhasgach** a sheltering wood; **2** sheltered, **bad fasgach** a sheltered spot

fasgadh, fasgaidh, fasgaidhean *nm* shelter, a shelter, protection, **gabh** *v* **fasgadh on dìle** take shelter from the downpour, *cf* **dìon** *n*

fàsgadh, *gen* **fàsgaidh** *nm* (*the act of*) compressing, pressing, etc (*see senses of* **fàisg** *v*)

fasgain *vt, pres part* **a' fasgnadh**, winnow (*grain*)

fastachadh, fasdachadh & fastadh, *gen* **fastachaidh & fastaidh** *nm* (*the act of*) hiring etc (*see senses of* **fastaich** *v*)

fastaich, *also* **fasdaich & fastaidh**, *vt, pres part* **a' fastachadh & a' fastadh**, hire, employ, take on (*workers*)

fastaidhear (*also found as* **fasdaidhear**), **fastaidheir, fastaidhearan** *nm* an employer

fàth *nm invar* **1** a cause, a reason, **fàth mo mhulaid** the cause of my sadness, **fàth magaidh** a cause/object of mockery, *cf more usu* **adhbhar 1, cùis 4**; **2** an opportunity, **fàth airson spòrsa** an opportunity for some fun, *cf* *more usu* **cothrom 1**; **3** *in expr* **gabh** *v* **fàth air** take (unfair) advantage of, *cf* **brath** *n* **2**

fathann, *gen & pl* **fathainn** *nm* a rumour, **bha fathann mun deidhinn a' dol timcheall** a rumour about them was going round/circulating, **sgeul no fathann cha robh air Murchadh** (*lit*) there was neither news nor rumour concerning Murdo, there was no trace of Murdo

feabhas, *gen* **feabhais** *nm* improvement, excellence, superiority, *esp in expr* **rach** *v* **am feabhas** improve, get better, **chaidh an t-euslainteach am feabhas** the invalid got better/recovered, **tha na seirbheisean ionadail a' dol am feabhas** the local services are improving

feachd, feachd, feachdan *nf* (*trad*) an army, a host, a force, **Feachd an Adhair** the Air Force, **feachd obrach/oibre** a work force, *cf* **armailt** *& more usu* **arm**

fead, fead, feadan *nf* **1** a whistle (*the noise not the instrument*), **rinn mi fead** *or* **leig mi fead (asam)** I whistled (*ie a single whistle*); **2** *also for more continuous whistling, eg* **fead na gaoithe** the whistling of the wind

fead *vi, pres part* **a' feadail**, whistle, **bha am balach beag a' feadail** the wee boy was whistling

feadag, feadaige, feadagan *nf* **1** a whistle (*ie penny whistle, Irish flute etc*), **ghabh e port air an fheadaig** he played a tune on the whistle, *cf* **fìdeag**; **2** a plover

feadaireachd *nf invar, also* **feadalaich** *nf invar, &* **feadarsaich** *nf invar*, **1** whistling (*ie with mouth, usu continuous, cf* **fead** *n*), **chuala sinn feadaireachd** we heard whistling; **2** (*the act or art of*) playing a whistle

feadalaich *see* **feadaireachd**

feadan, feadain, feadanan *nm* **1** a bagpipe chanter; **2** *objects of tubular shape such as a* tube, a pipe (*cf* **pìob 1**), a spout

feadarail *adj* federal

feadarsaich *see* **feadaireachd**

feadh *see* **air feadh**

feadhainn, *gen* **feadhna** *nf* **1** some, some people, **tha feadhainn air a shon, tha feadhainn eile na aghaidh** some (people) are in favour, others are against, *cf* **cuid 3**; **2** *with art*, **tha an fheadhainn seo a' dol dhachaigh** these/these ones/this group are going home, **an fheadhainn eile** the others, the other ones, the rest, (*also of objects*) **tha an fheadhainn a th' air an sgeilp briste** the ones that are on the shelf are broken

feagal *see* **eagal**

feàirrde *adj* (*trad*) better, made better, *now esp in expr* **is fheàirrde e** (*etc*) he (*etc*) is the better for, **b' fheàirrde sinn cuairt bheag** we'd be/we were the better for a wee stroll, a wee stroll would do us good/did us good, **'s fheàirrd' thu Guinness** you're better for a Guinness, Guinness is good for you, *cf* **feum** *n* 4 & *opposite* **miste**

feairt *see* **feart¹**

fealladh, feallaidh, feallaidhean *nm* (*sports & games*) a foul, foul play

fealla-dhà *nf invar* joking, a joke, a jest, **chan ann ri fealla-dhà a tha mi!** I'm not joking! **eadar fealla-dhà is da-rìribh** half in jest, half joking(ly), half in jest and half in earnest, *cf* **da-rìribh** 1, **fìor** 4

feall-fhalach, feall-fhalaich, feall-fhalaichean *nm* an ambush

feallsanach, *gen & pl* **feallsanaich** *nm* a philosopher

feallsanachd, feallsanachd, feallsanachdan *nf* 1 philosophy, a philosophy, **feallsanachd Aristotle** the philosophy of Aristotle; 2 the rationale or thinking behind something, (*ed*) **feallsanachd a' chùrsa** the course rationale

feallsanachd-maise *nf invar* aesthetics

fealltach *adj* fraudulent *cf* **foilleil** 3

feamainn, *gen* **feamann, feamnach & feamad**, *nf* (*the generic name for*) seaweed

feamainn *vt, pres part* **a' feamnadh**, manure (*with seaweed*), **a' feamnadh an fhearainn** manuring the land

feannag¹, feannaige, feannagan *nf* a crow, **feannag dhubh** a carrion crow, **feannag ghlas** a hooded crow, (*Sc*) a hoodie

feannag², feannaige, feannagan *nf* a rig or ridge of land (*for cultivation*), (*trad, hist*) a lazybed

feanntag, feanntaige, feanntagan *nf*, & **deanntag, deanntaige, deanntagan** *nf*, a nettle

feansa, feansa, feansaichean *nmf* (*agric etc*) a fence, *cf* **callaid** 2

feansaig *vti, pres part* **a' feansaigeadh**, fence (*a field, garden etc*)

fear, *gen & pl* **fir** *nm* 1 a man, **tha fear agus boireannach/tè a' tighinn** there's a man and a woman coming, **fear an taighe** the man of the house *or* the landlord (*of pub etc*) *or* the MC/compère (*at a ceilidh etc*), **thug fear Caimbeulach dhomh e** a Campbell/a man of the name of Campbell/some Campbell guy gave me it, *cf* **duine** *which stresses male gender less*, *cf also* **fireannach**; 2 *in numerous compounds denoting a function, role or profession of*

some kind, corres to Eng -man, -er, -ian *etc, eg* **fear-labhairt** *m* a spokesman, **fear-siubhail** *m* a traveller, **fear-ciùil** *m* a musician, **fear-stiùiridh** *m* a director, **fear-ealain** *m* an artist, *see remarks under* **neach**; *Note: the pl of such nouns is usu* **luchd** (*eg* **luchd-ciùil** musicians) *see* **luchd²**; 3 *representing a m sing n*, one, **seo leabhraichean, gabh fear no dhà dhiubh** here are some books, take one or two of them, **cò am fear as fheàrr leat?** which one do you prefer? *Note: in this usage the pl can be supplied by* **an fheadhainn**, ones (*see* **feadhainn** 2); *cf* **tè** 1

fearachas, *gen* **fearachais** *nm* virility

fearail *adj* manly, of manly character, **feartan fearail** manly characteristics, **giùlan fearail** manly conduct, *cf* **duineil** 1, **tapaidh** 2

fearalachd *nf invar* manliness, *cf* **duinealas** 1

fearann, *gen* **fearainn** *nm* ground, land, **àitich** *v* **am fearann** cultivate/till the land, **pìos fearainn** a piece of ground/land, *cf* **talamh** 3, **tìr** 4

fearas-chuideachd, *gen* **fearais-chuideachd** *nf* 1 sport, fun, *cf more usu & fam* **spòrs**; 2 a pastime, *cf more usu* **cur-seachad**

fearas-feise *nf invar* homosexuality

fear-brèige, *gen & pl* **fir-bhrèige** *nm* a puppet

fear-fuadain, *gen & pl* **fir-fuadain** *nm* an exile, (*song*) **is cianail dùsgadh an fhir-fhuadain, 's e sìor-ionndrainn tìr a bhruadair** sad is the waking of the exile, forever longing for the land he sees in his dream, *cf* **fògarrach** 1

fearg, *gen* **feirge** *nf* anger, ire, wrath, **thàinig fearg oirre** she grew angry, **chuir i fearg air** she made him angry

feargach *adj* angry, indignant, *cf* **diombach** 2

feàrna *nf invar* alder

feàrr *adj* 1 (*trad*) better, best (*comp of* **math** *adj*); 2 *now usu with v* **is**, *eg* **an tè as** (*for a is*) **fheàrr** the best one (*f*), **tha A nas fheàrr na B** A is better than B, **'s e Ailean as fheàrr a bhitheas** Alan will be best, **mar a b' fheàrr a chaidh aige** as best he could, **b' fheàrr leam càise** I would prefer/rather have cheese; 3 *in expr* **b' fheàrr dhomh** (etc) ... I (etc) had better ... , **b' fheàrr dhut fuireach** you'd better stay, you'd be better staying, **b' fheàrr dhuibh a bhith a' falbh** you'd better be going

feart¹ & **feairt**, *gen* **feirt**, *pl* **feartan** *nf* attention, heed, *esp in expr* **thoir** *v* **fea(i)rt air** pay attention to, heed, *cf* **aire** 2, **for**

feart², fearta, feartan *nm* an inherent quality, an attribute, a characteristic, **gheibh sinn mòran fheartan bhor sinnsirean** we get many characteristics from our forebears/ ancestors

feasgar, gen **feasgair**, pl **feasgair** & **feasgaran** (also found as **feasgraichean**) nm **1** afternoon, an afternoon, evening, an evening, **feasgar samhraidh** a summer afternoon or evening, **feasgar an-dè** yesterday afternoon/evening, **feasgar math!** good afternoon! or good evening! **air an fheasgar** in/during the afternoon/evening, **bidh sinn ann feasgar** we'll be there in the afternoon/evening; **2** (with times) pm, **seachd uairean feasgar** seven in the evening, 7 pm

fèath, **fèatha**, **fèathan** nmf (of weather) calm, a calm, **thàinig fèath air a' bhàta** the boat was becalmed

fèichear, **fèicheir**, **fèichearan** nm a debtor

fèileadh & **èileadh** (also found as **(f)èile**), gen **(f)èilidh**, pl **(f)èilidhean** (also found as **(f)èilichean** & **(f)èileachan**) nm, **1** (trad) **(f)èileadh** or **(f)èileadh-mòr**, a kilted plaid, ie the earlier form of this dress, stretching from the shoulder to the knee or calf; **2 (f)èileadh** or **(f)èileadh-beag** or **(f)èile-beag** the kilt, the later forms of kilted plaid, either (trad) passing between the legs, or as the modern kilt, (song) **èileadh beag os cionn mo ghlùin ann am pleataibh** (dat pl) **dlùth mun cuairt** a kilt above my knee in close enfolding pleats; cf **breacan 1**

fèill, **fèille**, **fèill(t)ean** nf **1** (trad) a (religious) feast or festival, **latha-fèille** a feast day, **An Fhèill Brìde** the Feast of St Bride/Bridget, Candlemas; **2** a fair (trad often linked to a saint's day), (song) **nam faicinn air an fhèill thu, an Glaschu no 'n Dùn Èideann** if I should see you at the fair, in Glasgow or in Edinburgh, cf **faidhir**; **3** a market, a sale (esp of livestock), **fèill uan** a lamb sale, cf **margadh 1**; **4** (economics, business) demand, a market, **am bi fèill air?** will there be a market/demand for it? cf **margadh 2**; **5** a fair (ie rides, amusements etc)

fèin reflexive pron (usu lenited as **fhèin**, after **mi** & **sinn** often becomes **fhìn**) **1** corres to Eng -self, **am fear a thug buaidh air fhèin, thug e buaidh air nàmhaid** the man who has conquered himself has conquered an enemy, **chunnaic e e fhèin san sgàthan** he saw himself in the mirror, **bha i ga tiormachadh fhèin** she was drying herself, **thoir an aire ort fhèin** take care of yourself, **rinn Ealasaid fhèin a' chèic** Ealasaid herself made the cake, **air mo shon fhìn . . .** for my part . . . , as for myself . . . , **'s math thu fhèin!** well done!, good

for you! **leam fhìn** by myself, Note: in direct address **thu fhèin** & **sibh fhèin** are more polite than **thusa** & **sibhse**; **2** emphasising identity, **rinn mi fhìn e** I (emph) did it, **tha mi gu math, ciamar a tha thu fhèin?** I'm well, how are you (emph)/how's yourself? **nach aithnich thu mi?** 's mi fhìn a th' ann!** don't you know me? It's me (emph)!, cf emph prons **mise, thusa** etc; **3** own, **an taigh aige fhèin** his own house, **bhris e a chas fhèin** he broke his own leg; **4** even, **thàinig an t-eagal air Calum fhèin** even Calum grew afraid, **chaill mi am barrall fhèin às mo bhròig** I lost even the lace/I lost the very lace out of my shoe, cf **eadhon**, **fiù** n **2**; **5** same, very (same), **sin an duine fhèin a chunna mi an-dè** there's the very (same) man I saw yesterday, cf **aon 3, ceart 3, ceudna 1, dearbh** adj **1**; **6** as emphasising element, **bha an ceòl uabhasach fhèin math** the music was very good indeed/ really excellent, **cianail fhèin fada** exceedingly long; **7** as noun **am fèin** the self, the ego, (poem) **Eadh is Fèin is Sàr-Fhèin** (Somhairle MacGill-Eain) Id and Ego and Super-Ego; **8** in compound nouns & adjs, eg **fèin-riaghladh** m self-government, **fèin-fhrithealadh** m self-service, **fèin-spèis** f self-love, self-importance, **fèin-mheas** m self-respect, **fèin-mholadh** m conceit (lit self-praise), **fèin-mhurt** m suicide, **fèin-ìsleachadh** m self-abasement, **fèin-fhoghainteach** adj self-sufficient, **fèin-chùiseach** adj selfish

fèin-eachdraidh, **fèin-eachdraidhe**, **fèin-eachdraidhean** nf autobiography, an autobiography

fèinealachd nf invar selfishness

fèineil adj selfish, cf **fèin-chùiseach** (see **fèin 8**)

fèin-ghluaiseach adj (machine etc) automatic

fèis, fèise, fèisean nf a festival, **fèis litreachais/ciùil** a literature/a music festival

feis(e), gen **feise** nf sex, sexual intercourse, cf **cleamhnas 2**

fèist (also found as **fèisd**), **fèiste**, **fèistean** nf a feast, a banquet, cf **cuirm, fleadh**

feiste, feiste, feistean nf a tether

fèistear, fèisteir, fèistearan nm an entertainer

fèisteas, gen **fèisteis**, nm entertainment

feith vi, pres part **a' feitheamh**, **1** wait (**air** & **ri** for), **a' fèitheamh ris a' bhus** waiting for the bus, cf **fan 1**; **2** stay, remain, cf more usu **fuirich 1**

fèith, fèithe, fèithean nf **1** a muscle; **2** a sinew; **3** a vein, cf more usu **cuisle 1**

fèith(e), **fèithe**, **fèitheachan** *nf* a bog, a marsh, *cf* **bog** *n* 1, **boglach**

fèitheach *adj* 1 muscular; 2 sinewy

feitheamh, *gen* **feithimh** *nm* (*the act of*) waiting etc (*see senses of* **feith** *v*)

feòil, *gen* **feòla(dh)** *nf* 1 meat, **feòil-caorach** & **muilt-fheòil** mutton, **feòil-muice** & **muic-fheòil** pork, **mairt-fheòil** beef; 2 flesh

feòladair, **feòladair**, **feòladairean** *nm* a butcher, *cf less trad* **bùidsear** 1

feòlmhor *adj* 1 fleshy; 2 sensual, carnal, fleshly, *cf* **collaidh** 1

feòlmhorachd *nf invar* sensuality

feòrag, **feòraig**, **feòragan** *nf* a squirrel

feòrachadh, *gen* **feòrachaidh** *nm* (*the act of*) asking

feòraich *vi, pres part* **a' feòrachadh**, ask, *cf more usu* **faighnich**

feuch & **fiach**, *vti, pres part* **a' feuch(d)ainn**, 1 try, attempt, **feuchaidh mi ri/ris an doras fhosgladh** I'll try to open the door, **dh'fheuch iad ri ar togail** they attempted to lift us, **bi math! feuchaidh mi** be good! I'll try, **feuch deuchainn** attempt/take/sit an exam; 2 try, try out, test, **feuch an leann a tha seo** try/taste this beer, **feuch air** give it a try, try it out, *cf* **dearbh** *v* 2, **deuchainn** 2; 3 *as imperative*, try, see, **feuch gum bi thu ann ron àm** see that you're/try to be there early, **feuchaibh a bheil am buntàta deiseil** see if the potatoes are done/ready, **fosgail an doras feuch a bheil an t-uisge ann fhathast** open the door to/and see if it's still raining (*cf* **ach** 5); 4 (*trad*) **feuch!** behold!, lo!

feudail *see* **eudail**

feudar *n* 1 (*trad*) ability, possibility, *cf* **urrainn** 1; 2 *now in expr* **'s fheudar dhomh** (*etc*) I (*etc*) must, **'s fheudar/b' fheudar dhi sgur** she has to/had to stop, (*song*) **'s fheudar dhomh fhìn a bhith gabhail dhachaigh dìreach** I must be getting straight home, *cf* **feum** *v* 1, **aig** 4

feum, *gen* **feuma** & **fèim** *nm* 1 need, **is e feum bìdh a thug air a bhith a' goid** it's need of food that made him steal, *cf* **dìth** 1; 2 *esp in expr* **tha feum agam** (*etc*) **air . . .** I (*etc*) need . . . , **tha feum aca air comhairle** they need advice *cf* **feum** *v* 2; 3 use, good, **dè am feum a bhith a' bruidhinn?** what's the good/use of talking? (*cf* **math** *n*), **chan eil feum anns an inneal seo** this machine's no good/useless, **duine/obair gun fheum** a useless man/job, **cuir** *v* **gu feum** use, **dèan** *v* **feum de** use, utilise, make use of; 4 *in expr* **dèan** *v* **feum (do)** do good (to), *also* be useful (to), **nì na saor-làithean**

feum dhuibh the holidays will do you good (*cf* **feàirrde**), **dhèanadh siosar feum an-dràsta** scissors would be useful/come in handy just now (*cf* **feumail** 1)

feum *vti def, no pres part*, 1 must, have to, **feumaidh mi aideachadh gu . . .** I have to/must admit that . . . , **am feum sibh falbh?** Must you/do you have to go? **feumaidh (e bhith) gu bheil stailc ann** there must be a strike, it must be that there's a strike, *Note: the past tense of this verb can be supplied by* **b' fheudar dhomh** (*etc*) I (*etc*) had to (*see* **feudar** 2), *cf* **aig** 4; 2 (*vt*) need, **feumaidh e beagan sgioblachaidh fhathast** it needs a bit of tidying up yet, **feumaidh mi airgead!** need money!, *cf* **feum** *n* 2

feumach *adj* 1 needy, in need, *cf* **easbhaidheach** 1; 2 *in expr* **feumach air** in need of, **tha mi feumach air fois** I need some peace, **feumach air leasachadh** in need of improvement

feumail *adj* 1 useful, handy, **bhiodh airgead feumail an-dràsta** money would be useful/handy just now, **bha do chomhairle feumail dhomh** your advice was useful to me, *cf* **feum** *n* 4; 2 needful, necessary, *cf stronger* **deatamach**, **riatanach**

feumalachd *nf invar* usefulness

feur, *gen* **feòir** *nm* 1 grass; 2 hay

feurach *adj* grassy, covered with grass

feurach, *gen* **feuraich** *nm* grazing, pasture

feuraich *vt, pres part* **a' feurachadh**, graze, pasture, put (*cattle etc*) out to graze, (*song*) **sprèidh a-mach gam feurach(adh) madainn ghrianach chiùin** (Màiri Mhòr) cattle out grazing/put out to graze on a mild sunny morning

feusag, **feusaig**, **feusagan** *nf* a beard

feusgan, *gen* & *pl* **feusgain** *nm* a mussel

fhad is a *conj see* **fad** *n* 4

f(h)asa *see* **furasta**

fhathast *adv* 1 yet, **cha do sguir an t-uisge fhathast** the rain hasn't stopped yet, **a bheil a' bhracaist deiseil? chan eil fhathast** is breakfast ready? not yet, **nì sinn a' chùis air fhathast** we'll get the better of it/crack it yet; 2 still, **tha an t-uisge ann fhathast** it's still raining; 3 again, **chì mi fhathast sibh** I'll see you again, I'll be seeing you (*similar to au revoir*), I'll see you later, **dèan fhathast e!** do it again!, *cf* **a-rithist**

fheàrr *see* **feàrr**

fhèin, **fhìn** *see* **fèin**

fhuair *pt of irreg v* **faigh** (*see tables p 500*)

fiabhras, fiabhrais, fiabhrasan *nm* fever, a fever, **am fiabhras dearg/buidhe** scarlet/ yellow fever

fiacail(l), fiacla, fiaclan *nf* a tooth, **clàr-fhiacail** an incisor, **fiacail-chùil** a molar, **fiacail-forais** & **fiacail a' ghliocais** a wisdom tooth, **sgrùdadh fhiacail** *m* a dental check-up/ examination, **fiacail sàibh** a tooth of a saw

fiach *adj* worth, worthwhile, of value, *usu in expr* **is/b' fhiach (do)** is/was worth (to), **aon uair eile? chan fhiach e!** one more time? it's not worth it! **rud as fhiach fhaicinn** a thing worth seeing, **an fhiach seo dhut? chan fhiach** is this of value/worth anything to you? no, **airson na 's fhiach e** for what it's worth, **duine nach fhiach tromb gun teanga** a worthless/good for nothing man (*lit* not worth a jew's harp without a tongue)

fiach, fèich, fiachan *nm* **1** value, worth, **thoir dhomh fiach dà nota dheth** give me two pounds'-worth of it, *cf* **luach 1**; **2** debt, a debt, **dìoghail** *v* **fiach** repay a debt, (*Bibl*) **maith dhuinn ar fiachan** forgive us our debts, (*prov*) **cha tèid fiach air beul dùinte** a closed mouth doesn't run into debt; **3** *exprs with* **fiachaibh** (*obs dat pl*), (*formal*) **tha e mar fhiachaibh orm facal no dhà a ràdh** it is incumbent upon me to say a few words, **chuir iad mar fhiachaibh orm an dreuchd a ghabhail** they obliged me/made me feel obliged to accept the post, **tha mi fo fhiachaibh dhaibh** I'm indebted to them (*not nec financially, cf* **comain 2**)

fiach *vti see* **feuch**

fiachaibh *see* **fiach** *n* **3**

fiaclach *adj* **1** toothed; **2** toothy; **3** dental, *cf* **deudach**

fiaclair(e), fiaclaire, fiaclairean *nm* a dentist, **ionad fiaclaire** *m* a dental surgery

fiadh, *gen* & *pl* **fèidh** *nm* a deer

fiadhaich *adj* **1** wild (*ie not domesticated*), **cat-fiadhaich** *m* a wildcat, *cf* **allaidh**; **2** (*fam*) angry, furious, **bha mi fiadhaich an dèidh na thuirt e rium** I was wild/furious after what he said to me; **3** (*fam*) wild (*ie given to uninhibited behaviour, heavy drinking etc*), **'s e duine fiadhaich a th' ann dheth, ceart gu leòr!** he's a wild man, right enough!

fial & **fialaidh** *adj* **1** generous, open-handed, hospitable, *cf* **faoilidh 1**; **2** tolerant, easy-going, liberal

fialaidh *see* **fial**

fiamh, *gen* **fiamha** *nm* **1** hue, tinge, tint, complexion, *cf* **dreach 2, snuadh 2, tuar**; **2** fear, *cf more usu* **eagal 1**; **3** a (*transient*) look,

an expression (*on face, in eye*), **fiamh-ghàire**, *also* **fiamh a' ghàire**, a smile (*lit* a look of laughter, *cf* **faite, snodha-gàire**), *cf more permanent* **gnùis**

fianais, fianais, fianaisean *nf* **1** the act or fact of witnessing something; **2** evidence, witness, testimony, **neach-fianais** *m* (*also* **fianais**) a witness (*at scene of crime, at trial*), **thoir** *v* **fianais** give evidence, testify, bear witness, *cf* **dearbhadh 2, teisteanas 1**; **3** sight, bha/ **thàinig e am fianais** he was/he came in sight, **à fianais** out of sight (*cf* **fradharc 2** & *more usu* **sealladh 3**), **bha sinn am fianais an eilein** we were in sight of the island; **4** (*trad*) presence, **nam fianais** in their presence, **a-mach às m' fhianais!** out of my presence/ sight!, *cf* **làthair 1**

fiar *adj* **1** bent, crooked, *cf* **cam, crom, lùbte**; **2** slanting, aslant, oblique, distorted, (*Sc*) squint, *cf* **claon** *adj* **1**; **3** (*of eyes*) squinting, having a squint, **seall** *v* **fiar** squint, **fiar-shùileach** *adj* squint-eyed; **4** wily, cunning, devious, *cf* **caon, carach 1, seòlta 1**

fiar & **fiaraich** *vti, pres part* **a' fiaradh**, **1** bend, become or make curved, *cf* **crom** *v* **3, lùb** *v* **1**; **2** (*lit* & *fig*) slant, distort

fiaradh, *gen* **fiaraidh** *nm* **1** (*the act of*) bending etc (*see senses of* **fiar** *v*); **2** a squint (*in eye*), *cf* **claonadh 4, spleuchd** *n* **2**; **3** a slant, **air fhiaradh** slanting, at a slant, at an angle, (*Sc*) squint

fiaraich *vti, see* **fiar** *vti*

fiathaich *vt, pres part* **a' fiathachadh**, invite, *cf* **iarr 3, thoir cuireadh** (*see* **cuireadh** *n*)

fichead, fichid, ficheadan *nm* twenty, a score, *takes the nom sing (radical) of the noun,* **fichead sgillinn/bliadhna** twenty pence/ years, **dà fhichead** forty

ficheadamh *adj* twentieth

ficsean, *gen* **ficsein** *nm* fiction

fìdeag, fìdeig, fìdeagan *nf* a whistle, (*song*) **cò (a) sheinneas an fhìdeag airgid?** who will sound the silver whistle?, *cf* **feadag 1**

fidheall, *gen* **fidhle,** *dat* **fidhill,** *pl* **fidhlean** *nf* a fiddle, a violin, **port** *m* **air an fhidhill** a tune on the fiddle, (*idiom*) **cuir** *v* **an ceòl air feadh na fidhle** put the cat among the pigeons

fìdhlear, fìdhleir, fìdhlearan *nm* a fiddler, a violinist

fidir *vti, pres part* **a' fidreadh**, sympathise with, appreciate, comprehend, take into account, (*prov*) **chan fhidir an sàthach an seang** the well-fed don't sympathise with the hungry, (*song*) **chan fhidir thu idir mar tha mise**

led ghràdh you don't appreciate at all the state I'm in through loving you

fìge *see* **fìogais**

figear, figeir, figearan *nm* (*arith etc*) a figure, a digit, a numeral, *cf* **àireamh**

figearail *adj* (*IT etc*) digital, **gleoc/sealladh figearail** a digital clock/display, *cf* **didseatach**

figh *vti, pres part* **a' fighe(adh)**, **1** weave; **2** knit

fighe *nf invar* **1** weaving, **beart-fhighe** *f* a weaving loom; **2** knitting, **bior-fighe** *m* a knitting needle

figheachan, *gen & pl* **figheachain** *nm* a pigtail, a plait; a pony-tail (*on head*)

figheadair, figheadair, figheadairean *nm* **1** a weaver, *cf* **breabadair 2**; **2** a knitter

fighte *adj* **1** woven; **2** knitted

fileanta *adj* **1** eloquent, articulate, good at expressing oneself; **2** (*now esp*) good at speaking a language, fluent, **tha i fileanta sa Ghàidhlig** she's fluent in Gaelic/speaks Gaelic fluently

fileantach, *gen & pl* **fileantaich** *nm* **1** someone fluent in a language; **clas nam fileantach** the fluent speakers' class; **2** (*esp*) a fluent speaker

filidh, filidh, filidhean *nm* **1** (*trad*) a poet, *cf* **bàrd**; **2 filidh (aig Sabhal Mòr Ostaig** (*etc*)) writer-in-residence (at Sabhal Mòr Ostaig (*etc*))

fill *vt, pres part* **a' filleadh**, **1** (*paper*) fold; **2** (*cloth*) fold, pleat; **3** (*hair etc*) braid, plait; **4** (*material, parcel etc*) wrap (up), roll (up), *cf* more *usu* **paisg**

filleadh, *gen* **fillidh**, *pl* **filltean** & **filleachan** *nm* **1** (*the act of*) folding, pleating, braiding, plaiting; **2** a fold, a pleat, a braid, a plait

fillte *adj* **1** folded, pleated, plaited; **2** implied, implicit; **3** *in compounds, eg* **trì-fillte** *adj* folded three times, threefold, triple, three-ply, **iomadh-fhillte** *adj* complex, complicated, manifold

film, film, filmichean *nm* (*cinema, TV etc*) film, a film

fine, fine, fineachan *nf* **1** a tribe; **2** *esp* a (Highland) clan, (*song*) **òran nam fineachan a fhuair am fearann air ais** the song of the clans who got their land back, *cf* **cinneadh 1, clann 2**

finealta *adj* elegant, refined

fiodh, *gen* **fiodha** *nm* wood, timber, **pìos fiodha** a piece of wood, **taigh fiodha** a wooden house, *cf* **maide 1** *which is usu wood when shaped, fashioned etc*

fiodhrach, *gen* **fiodhraich**, *nm* timber, wood (*not shaped, finished etc*)

fìogais, fìogais, fìogaisean *nf, also* **fìge, fìge, fìgean** *nf*, a fig, **crann-fìogais** *m* a fig-tree,

(*song*) **gur mìlse na fìogais a pòg** sweeter than a fig is her kiss

fiolan, fiolain, fiolanan *nm, also* **fiolan-gòbhlach, fiolain-ghòbhlaich, fiolanan-gòbhlach** *nm*, an earwig, *cf* **gòbhlag 2**

fìon, *gen* **fiona** *nm* wine, **crann-fìona** *m* a vine

fìonan, *gen & pl* **fionain** *nm* a vine, *cf* **crann-fìona** (*see* **fìon**)

fìon-dhearc, fìon-dhearc, fìon-dhearcan *nf* a grape

fìon-geur, *gen* **fìon-ghèir** *nm* vinegar

fionn *adj* (*trad*) white, *often in placenames as* Fin-, *cf* **bàn² 1, geal** *adj*

fionnach *adj* hairy, rough, shaggy, *cf* **molach, ròmach 1**

fionnadh, *gen* **fionnaidh** *nm coll* hair (*of animal*)

fionnairidh *nf invar* evening, **air an fhionnairidh** in the (cool air of) evening

fionnan-feòir, *gen & pl* **fionnain-fheòir** *nm* a grasshopper

fionnar *adj* **1** (*of weather*) cool, fresh, **2** (*of welcome, attitude etc*) cool, cold, off-hand, **fhreagair i gu fionnar** she answered coolly/coldly, *cf* **leth-fhuar, fuaraidh**

fionnarachadh, *gen* **fionnarachaidh** *nm* **1** (*the act of*) cooling etc (*see senses of* **fionnaraich** *v*); **2** refrigeration

fionnaraich *vti, pres part* **a' fionnarachadh**, cool, refrigerate, make or become cool

Fionnlainn *nf, used with art* **an Fhionnlainn** Finland

fionnsgeul, *gen & pl* **fionnsgeòil** *nm* a legend, a myth, *cf* **faoinsgeul 2**

fìor *adj* **1** true, **tha am fathann/an sgeul fìor** the rumour/story is true; **2** true, real, genuine, actual, (*precedes the noun, which it lenites where possible*), **'s e fìor Albannach a th' ann** he's a real/true Scot, **fìor òr** real gold, **fìor chosgaichean** true/actual costs; **3** *as emphasising element*, **bha am biadh fìor mhath** the food was very/truly/really good, **am Fìor Urramach Uilleam Caimbeul** the Very/Right Reverend William Campbell, *cf* **garbh 4, glè, uabhasach 2**; **4** *in expr* **mas fhìor** kidding, pretending, **thuirt mi gun robh mi gu bhith ann am film ach cha robh mi ach mas fhìor** I said I was to be in a film but I was only kidding

fìoreun, *gen & pl* **fìoreòin** *nm* (*trad*) an eagle, *cf usu* **iolaire**

fios, *gen* **fiosa** *nm* **1** knowledge, **chan eil fios càit a bheil e** no-one knows/it's not known where he is, **gun fhios do Mhàiri** without Mary's knowledge, unknown to Mary; **2** *esp in* *expr* **tha fios agam (etc)** I *(etc)* know *(of facts, information)*, *often lenited eg* **chan eil fhios agam** I don't know (it *understood*), *lit* I do not have its knowledge, **air na bha a dh'fhios aca** as far as they knew, **cha robh mi air fhaicinn bho nach b' fhios cuin** I hadn't seen him since Heaven knows when; **3** information, word, a message, news, *(song)* **thoir am fios seo thun a' bhàird** give this information/message to the poet, tell the poet this, **cuir fios orra** send (word) for them, **chuir sinn fios thuige** we sent him word/let him know; **4** *in expr* **tha fios** obviously, of course, naturally, **bidh sin saor 's an-asgaidh, tha fios** that will be free of charge, of course/naturally, **a bheil thu toilichte? tha fios gu bheil!** are you pleased? of course I am!; **5** *in expr* **gun fhios nach** *conj* lest, in case, **chuir e pìos na phòca gun fhios nach tigeadh an t-acras air** he put a piece in his pocket in case he should grow hungry, *cf* **eagal 2, mus 2**

fiosaiche, fiosaiche, fiosaichean *nm* **1** *(trad)* a prophet, a soothsayer, a seer, *cf* **fàidh; 2** a fortune teller

fiosrach *adj* (well-)informed, knowledgeable (**air** about), *cf* **eòlach 1**

fiosrachadh, fiosrachaidh, fiosrachaidhean *nm* information *(coll)*, a piece of information, **bu toigh leam fiosrachadh fhaighinn air a' chompanaidh** I'd like to receive information about the company/firm, *(IT)* **teicneolas fiosrachaidh** *m* information technology

Fir-Chlis *see* **clis**

fireann *adj* masculine, male, **cat fireann** a male cat, a tomcat, *(gram)* **facal/ainmear fireann** a masculine word/noun, *cf* **fireannta**

fireann-boireann *adj* androgynous, hermaphrodite

fireannach, gen & pl fireannaich *nm* a man, a male, **fireannaich air an làimh dheis is boireannaich air an làimh chlì, mas e ur toil e!** men on the right and women on the left, please!, *cf* **fear 1**

fireannta *adj (of living things)* masculine, of the male gender, *cf* **fireann**

fìrinn, fìrinne, fìrinnean *nf* **1** truth, **'s e an fhìrinn a th' aige** he's telling the truth, **leis an fhìrinn innse, chan eil fhios a'm** to tell the truth, I don't know, *(of devout person)* **tha e/i làn den Fhìrinn** he/she is full of the *(scriptural)* Truth; **2** fact, a fact, **'s e an fhìrinn a th' ann!** it's a fact!, *cf* **rud 2**

fìrinneach *adj* **1** *(of person)* truthful, reliable; **2** *(of statements etc)* true, accurate

fitheach, gen & pl fithich *nm* a raven

fiù *adj corres to Eng* worth, *takes v* **is, chan fhiù e deich sgillinn** it's not worth 10p, **chan fhiù i a màthair** she's not worth/the equal of her mother, she's not the woman her mother was

fiù *nm invar* **1** worth, value, **sgrìobhaidhean gun fhiù** worthless writings, *cf* **luach 1; 2** *in expr* **fiù agus/is** even, as much as, **cha robh fiù is pìos arain air fhàgail** there wasn't even/as much as a piece of bread left (*cf* **uiread 3**), **cha do rinn iad fiù agus sùil a thoirt oirnn** they didn't even/didn't so much as look at us, *cf* **eadhon**

fiùdalach *adj* feudal

flaitheas, gen flaitheis *nm* heaven, paradise, *cf* **nèamh 1, Pàrras**

flanainn, flanainne, flanainnean *nf* **1** flannel; **2** *(for washing face etc)* a flannel

flat, flat, flataichean *nm* **1** a flat (*ie* dwelling), *cf* **lobht(a); 2** a saucer, *(Sc)* a flat, *cf* **sàsar**

flath, gen flaith, pl flathan & flaithean, nm **1** *(trad)* a king, prince or ruler; **2** a noble, *cf* **uasal n 1**

flathail *adj* **1** princely; **2** noble, *cf* **uasal** *adj* **1**

fleadh, fleadha, fleadhan *nm* a feast, a banquet, *cf* **cuirm, fèist**

fleadhach *adj* festive, celebratory

fleasgach, gen & pl fleasgaich *nm* **1** *(trad)* a young man, a youth, a stripling, *cf* **òganach; 2** *(now usu)* a bachelor, **seann fhleasgaich** old bachelors

fleisg, fleisge, fleisgean *nf (elec)* flex

fleòdradh, gen fleòdraidh *nm* the act of floating, buoyancy, *esp in expr* **(tha am ball etc) air fleòdradh** (the ball etc is) floating, *cf* **bog** *n* **2, flod**

flin, flinne *nm invar* sleet

fliuch *adj* wet, **tha mi bog fliuch** I'm wet through/soaking wet, *(of weather)* **tha i fliuch, fliuch!** it's gey wet!

fliuch *vt, pres part* **a' fliuchadh**, wet, make wet, **chuir an t-uisge thairis, a' fliuchadh a h-uile càil** the water overflowed, wetting everything, **chaidh a fhliuchadh chun na seiche** he got soaked to the skin, *(fam)* **fliuch do ribheid!** wet your whistle!

fliuchadh, gen fliuchaidh *nm (the act of)* wetting *(see* **fliuch** *v)*

flod, gen floda *nm* the state of being afloat, **air flod** afloat, floating, **cuir** *v* **air flod** float, launch, *cf* **bog** *n* **2, fleòdradh**

flùr[1], flùir, flùraichean *nm* a flower, *cf less usu* **blàth** *n* **2, dìthean**

flùr[2], gen flùir *nm* flour, *cf* **min** *n* **2**

flùranach *adj* flowery, covered in flowers, floral

fo *prep, lenites following noun where possible & takes the dat. The prep prons formed with* **fo**, *in the order first, second, third person singular, first, second, third person plural, and with the reflexive/emphatic particles in brackets, are as follows:* **fodham(sa), fodhad(sa), fodha(san), fòidhpe(se)** (*also* **fodhainn(e), fodhaibh(se), fòdhpa(san)**, under/beneath me, under/beneath you (*fam*), *etc.* **1** under, beneath, below, **fon uachdar** below the surface, **fo chraoibh** under a tree, **chaidh am bàta fodha** the boat went under/ sank, (*fig*) **chaidh a' chompanaidh fodha** the company failed/folded, **fo smachd** under control; **2** influenced *or* affected by, suffering from (*emotions, situations etc*), **fo eagal** afraid, **fo mhulad** sad, **fo chomain** under/having an obligation, **fo amharas** under suspicion, suspected; **3** *in compounds, as* **fo-**, *corres to Eng* sub-, under-, infra-, *eg* **fo-aodach** *m* underwear, underclothes, **fo-chomataidh** *f* a sub-committee, **fo-thiotalan** *mpl* subtitles, **fo-mhothachail** *adj* subconscious, **fo-dhearg** *adj* infra-red

fòd *see* **fòid**

fodar, *gen* **fodair** *nm* fodder

fodha (*emph form* **fodhasan**), **fodhad** (*emph form* **fodhadsa**), **fodhaibh** (*emph form* **fodhaibhse**), **fodhainn** (*emph form* **fodhainne**), **fodham** (*emph form* **fodhamsa**), **fòdhpa** *or* **fòpa** (*emph forms* **fòdhpasan** *or* **fòpasan**), *prep prons, see* **fo**

fògair *vt, pres part* **a' fògradh** & **a' fògairt**, **1** (*mainly trad & hist, referring to the Highland Clearances*) banish, exile, expel, drive out, **dh'fhògradh an sluagh às a' ghleann** the people were driven/banished from the glen, **chaidh am fògradh** they were exiled/expelled, *cf* **fuadaich 2**; **2** (*more generally*) exile, deport; *cf* **fuadaich 3**

fògairt *see* **fògradh**

fògarrach, *gen & pl* **fòg(ar)raich**, also found as **fògrach**, *nm* **1** an exile, a fugitive, a refugee; **2** *esp with reference to Highland Clearances*, someone cleared from his/her home district, *cf* **eilthireach 2, fuadan 2**

foghain *vi, pres part* **a' fòghnadh**, suffice, be enough, do, **am foghain sin?** will that be enough? will that do? (*saying*) **fòghnaidh na dh'fhòghnas** enough is enough, enough is as good as a feast, (*to children etc*) **fòghnaidh siud!** that's enough!, that will do! **chan fhòghnadh leis gun mise dhol còmhla ris**

he wouldn't be satisfied unless/until I went with him

foghar, foghair, fogharan *nm* **1** (*trad*) harvest, harvest time, **foghar an eòrna** the barley harvest, *cf* **buain** *n*; **2** autumn, fall, (*novel title*) **Deireadh an Fhoghair** (Tormod Caimbeul) The End of Autumn, **as t-fhoghar** in autumn

foghlaim *vt, pres part* **a' foghlam**, educate, *cf* **teagaisg 2**

foghlaimte, *also* **foghlaimichte**, *adj* educated, learned, *cf* **ionnsaichte**

foghlam, *gen* **foghlaim** *nm* **1** (*the act of*) educating; **2** education, learning, scholarship, **foghlam fo-sgoile** pre-school/nursery education, **foghlam inbhidh** adult education, **foghlam tro meadhan na Gàidhlig** Gaelic-medium education, **Roinn an Fhoghlaim** the Education Department, *cf* **ionnsachadh 2, oideachas 1**

fòghnadh, *gen* **fòghnaidh** *nm* sufficiency, a sufficiency, enough, *cf more usu* **leòr 1**

fòghnan, fòghnain, fòghnanan *nm* a thistle, (*song*) **Fòghnan na h-Alba** the Thistle of Scotland, *cf* **cluaran**

fògrach *see* **fògarrach**

fògradh, *gen* **fògraidh** *nm, also* **fògairt** *nf invar*, **1** (*the act of*) banishing etc (*see senses of* **fògair** *v*); **2** exile, banishment, *cf* **fuadan 2**

fòid & **fòd**, *gen* **fòide**, *pl* **fòidean** *nf* **1** turf, a turf, a sod, (*trad*) **an uair a bhios mi fon fhòid** when I'm beneath the sod/in my grave, *cf* **fàl 2, ploc 1**; **2** a clod *or* clump of earth, *cf* **ploc**; **3** a (single) peat (*occas m in this sense*), (*song*) **gun solas lainnteir (= lanntair) ach ceann an fhòid** (Màiri Mhòr) with the (burning) end of the peat as my only lamp light, *cf* **fàd**

fòidhpe (*emph form* **fòidhpese**) *prep prons, see* **fo** *prep*

foighidinn, *gen* **foighidinne** *nf* patience, *opposite* **mì-fhoighidinn** impatience

foighidneach *adj* patient, *opposite* **mì-fhoighidneach** impatient

foileag, foileig, foileagan *nf* a pancake

foill, *gen* **foille** *nf* **1** deceit, *cf* **cealg, mealladh 2**; **2** cheating, **tha iad ri foill!** they're cheating! **neach-foille** *m* a cheat, **rinn thu foill orm** you cheated me; **3** fraud, deception, **a' faighinn bathair le foill** obtaining goods fraudulently

foilleil *adj* **1** deceitful; **2** treacherous; **3** fraudulent, *cf* **fealltach**

foillseachadh, *gen* **foillseachaidh** *nm* **1** (*the act of*) publishing, revealing etc (*see senses of* **foillsich** *v*); **2** publication; **3** revelation, disclosure

foillsear, foillseir, foillsearan *nm* (*IT etc*) a monitor

foillsich *vt, pres part* **a' foillseachadh 1** publish, bring out (*books etc*), *cf* **cuir an clò** (*see* **clò²** 1); **2** reveal, disclose, make public (*facts etc*)

foillsichear, foillsicheir, foillsichearan *nm* a publisher

foinne, foinne, foinnean *nm* a wart

foireann, foirinn, foireannan *nm* **1** (*unruly etc*) gang, *cf* **gràisg, prabar**; **2** (*office etc*) staff, personnel, *cf* **luchd-obrach** (*see* **luchd²**)

foirfe *adj* perfect (*usu morally, cf* **coileanta** 2), **duine foirfe** a man without fault, *also* a full-grown man (*cf* **dèanta**)

foirfeach, *gen & pl* **foirfich** *nm* an elder (*of church*), *cf less trad* **èildear**

foirfeachd *nf invar* perfection (*esp moral*)

foirm, foirm, foirmean *nm* a form (*ie document*)

foirmeil *adj* formal, **tha mi a' cur fios thugaibh gu foirmeil gu . . .** I am informing you formally that . . . , **cainnt fhoirmeil** formal language/speech

fòirneart, *gen* **fòirneirt** *nm* violence, oppression, force, **neach-fòirneirt** an oppressor, *cf* **ainneart**

fois, *gen* **foise** *nf* **1** rest, peace (*ie tranquility*), (*story collection*) **Gun Fhois** (Eilidh Watt) Without Peace/Rest, (*esp of dead*) **tha iad aig fois a-nise** they are at peace/rest now, *cf* **sìth** *n* 2; **2** rest, leisure, relaxation, ease, **gabh** *v* **fois** have a rest, take a break, take one's ease, *cf* **tàmh** 3

foiseil *adj* restful, peaceful

fo-lèine, fo-lèine, fo-lèintean *nf* a vest, *cf* **peitean** 1

follais *nf invar* evidentness, obviousness, clarity, openness, *esp in exprs* **am follais** *adv* obvious, clear, evident, **thoir** *v* **am follais** bring into the open, bring to light, expose, **thig** *v* **am follais** come to light, become apparent

follaiseach *adj* **1** evident, obvious, clear, apparent, **tha e follaiseach nach eil e ciontach** it's obvious he's not guilty, *cf* **soilleir** 2; **2** public (*esp of knowledge, information etc*), **rannsachadh follaiseach** a public enquiry, **coinneamh fhollaiseach** a public meeting, *cf* **fosgailte** 2

fòn, fòn, fònaichean *nmf* **1** a phone, a telephone, **bha mi a' bruidhinn ris air a' fòn** I was talking to him on the phone, **dè an àireamh-fòn agad?** what's your phone number?; **2** a phone call, *in expr* **chuir e fòn thuice** he phoned her, he gave her a call

fòn *vi, pres part* **a' fònadh**, *also* **fònaig** *vi, pres part* **a' fònaigeadh** (*with prep* **gu**), phone, telephone, **dh'fhòn e thuice** he phoned her

fonn, *gen & pl* **fuinn** *nm* **1** a tune, an air, a melody, **air fonn 'Fill-ò-ro'** (*words to be sung*) to the tune of 'Fill-ò-ro', (*song*) **togaidh sinn fonn air eilean beag donn a' chuain** we will raise a tune to the little brown island of the ocean (*Lewis*), *cf* **port¹**; **2** a mood, frame of mind, *esp in expr* (*fam*) **dè am fonn a th' ort?** how are you?, how are you doing?, *cf* **dòigh** 4, **gean, gleus**

fonnmhor *adj* tuneful, melodious, *cf* **ceòlmhor**

for *nm invar* attention, notice, heed, concern, **gun for a thoirt air** without paying attention/heed to it, **gun for aige ach air a ghnothaichean fhèin** with concern for nothing but his own affairs, *cf* **aire** 2, **feart** *nf*

fo-rathad, fo-rathaid, fo-rathaidean *nm* an underpass, a subway

forc(a), *gen* **forca**, *pl* **forcan & forcaichean** *nf* a (*table*) fork, **forc agus sgian** a fork and a knife, *cf* **greimire** 1

fòrladh, *gen* **fòrlaidh** *nm* (*army etc*) furlough, leave

forsair, forsair, forsairean *nm* a forester, a forestry worker, *cf* **coilltear**

fortan, *gen* **fortain** *nm* fortune, luck, **fortan leat!** good luck (to you)!, **deagh/droch fhortan** good/bad luck, (*song*) **Cuibhle an Fhortain** The Wheel of Fortune, *cf* **àgh** 2, **dàn¹** 1, **sealbh** 1

fortanach *adj* lucky, fortunate, *cf* **sealbhach** 1 & *less usu* **buidhe** 2

for-thalla, for-thalla, for-thallachan *nm* a foyer (*of public building*)

fosgail *vti, pres part* **a' fosgladh**, open, **fosgail an doras!** open the door! **dh'fhosgail an doras** the door opened, **tha a' bhùth a' fosgladh** the shop's opening

fosgailte *adj* **1** open, opened, **uinneag fhosgailte** an open window, **tha a' bhùth/a' choinneamh fosgailte** the shop/meeting is open; **2** public, **coinneamh fhosgailte** a public/an open meeting, *cf* **follaiseach** 2; **3** (*of character etc*) open, frank, approachable, amenable, *cf* **faoilidh** 2, **fosgarra** 1

fosgailteachd *ni invar* frankness, openness, candour

fosgarra *adj* (*of person*) **1** frank, candid; **2** approachable, accessible; *cf* **fosgailte** 3, **faoilidh** 2

fosgladh *gen* **fosglaidh** *nm* **1** (*the act of*) opening; **2** an opening, a gap, an aperture, *cf* **beàrn; 3** an opening, a chance, an opportunity, *cf* **cothrom 1**

fosglair, fosglair, fosglairean *nm* (*for tins, bottles etc*) an opener

fo-sgrìobhadh, fo-sgrìobhaidh, fo-sgrìobhaidhean *nm* **1** a postscript, a PS; **2** (*magazine etc*) a subscription

fo-shlighe, fo-shlighe, fo-shlighean *nf same as* **fo-rathad**

fradharc (*also found as* **radharc**), *gen* **(f)radhairc** *nm* **1** eyesight, vision, *cf* **lèirsinn 1; 2** sight, view, **san fhradharc** in sight/view, **às an fhradharc** out of sight/view, *cf* **fianais 3, sealladh 3**

Fraing *nf, used with art* **an Fhraing** France

Fraingis *nf, usu with the art,* (*lang*) **an Fhraingis** French

Frangach, *gen & pl* **Frangaich** *nm* a Frenchman, a French person, *also as adj,* **Frangach** French

fraoch, *gen* **fraoich** *nm* heather, heath, ling (*ie the plants*), **coileach-fraoich** *m* a heather-cock, a (male) grouse

fraoidhneas, fraoidhneis, fraoidhneasan *nm* a fringe (*on material, hair etc*)

fras, froise, frasan *nf* **1** a shower (*of rain, sleet, snow*), *cf* **meall** *n* **3; 2** (*coll*) seed, *cf more usu* **sìol 1**

fras *vi, pres part* **a' frasadh,** rain lightly, shower

frasair, frasair, frasairean *nm* a (*bathroom*) shower

freagair *vti, pres part* **a' freagairt, 1** answer, reply, **nach freagair thu mi?** won't you answer me? **cha do fhreagair e fhathast** he hasn't replied yet; **2** suit, **chan eil an ad sin a' freagairt ort!** that hat doesn't suit you!, **cha fhreagair dhomh a bhith nam thàmh** it doesn't suit me to be unoccupied/idle, **a bheil an obair a' freagairt dhut?** is the job suiting you?, *cf* **thig 4; 3** match, correspond to, (*prov*) **freagraidh a' bhriogais don mhàs** the breeks will match the backside

freagairt, freagairt, freagairtean *nf* **1** (*the act of*) answering etc (*see senses of* **freagair** *v*); **2** an answer, a reply, **cha d' fhuair mi freagairt** I didn't get/haven't got a reply, **bheir sinn freagairt dhaibh a dh'aithghearr** we'll reply to you/give you an answer soon

freagarrach *adj* suitable, appropriate, fitting, **cha robh an taigh freagarrach dha** the house wasn't suitable for him, **àite freagarrach airson snàimh** a place suitable for swimming/a swim

frèam, frèama, frèamaichean *nm* a frame, a framework, *cf* **cèis 1**

freastail, *vti, pres part* **a' freastal** (*also found as* **freasdail**), attend, serve, wait on (*someone*), **freastail don bhòrd** wait/serve at table, *cf* **fritheil**

freastal, *gen* **freastail** *nm* (*also found as* **freasdal**) **1** (*the act of*) attending, serving, waiting (*on someone*); **2** service, attendance, *cf* **frithealadh 1; 3** providence, *cf* **sealbh 2**

freiceadan, freiceadain, freiceadanan *nm* a watch, a guard (*sing & coll*), **freiceadan-oirthire** a coast guard (*cf more usu* **maor-cladaich** – *see* **maor**), **Am Freiceadan Dubh** The Black Watch, **freiceadan cloinne** a babysitter, a child minder, *cf* **faire 2**

freumh, freumha, freumh(aiche)an *nm* **1** a root (*lit & fig*), **freumh craoibh** a tree root, **thug e na h-eileanan air, an tòir air a fhreumhaichean** he went off to the islands, in search of his roots; **2** a source, an origin, (*of words, placenames*) a derivation, a root

frìde, frìde, frìdean *nf, also* **meanbh-fhrìde** *nf,* an insect

frids, frids, fridsichean *nm* a fridge, a refrigerator, *cf less usu* **fuaradair**

frighig *vt, pres part* **a' frighigeadh,** fry, *cf* **ròist 2**

frioghan, *gen & pl* **frioghain** *nm* a bristle (*esp on body of animals*), *cf* **calg 2**

frionas, *gen* **frionais** *nm* **1** upset, annoyance, vexation; **2** touchiness, irritability, over-sensitivity

frionasach *adj* **1** (*of people*) upset, fretful; **2** (*of people*) irritable, touchy, *cf* **frithearra; 3** (*situations etc*) vexing, annoying, niggling, irritating, upsetting, **bidh iad a' cur cheistean frionasach orm gun sgur** they're constantly asking me niggling questions, *cf* **leamh**

frìth, frìthe, frìthean *nf* **1** (*trad*) a deer forest, (*placename*) **Achadh na Frìthe** Achnafrie, the field of the deer forest; **2** moor, moorland, *cf more usu* **mòinteach, sliabh 1**

frith-ainm, *gen* **frith-ainme,** *pl* **frith-ainmean & frith-ainneannan** *nm* a nickname, *cf* **far-ainm**

frithealadh, *gen* **frithealaidh** *nm* **1** (*the act of*) serving, attending; waiting (*at table etc*), service, attendance (*on someone*), **luchd-frithealaidh** *m coll* attendants, **gille-frithealaidh** *m* a waiter, **caileag-fhrithealaidh** *f* a waitress, *cf* **freastal 1; 2** attendance (*at an event etc*)

frithearra *adj* touchy, peevish, *cf* **frionasach 2**

fritheil *vti, pres part* **a' frithealadh,** serve, wait on, attend, *cf* **freastail**

frith-rathad, frith-rathaid, frith-rathaidean
nm a path, a footpath, a track, *cf* **ceum 4**

froga (*also found as* **froca**), *gen* **froga**, *pl*
frogaichean *nm* a frock

fuachd, fuachd, fuachdan *nmf* **1** cold, coldness,
chan fhuiling mi fuachd a' gheamhraidh
I can't stand/bear the cold of winter; **2** *with art*,
am fuachd a cold, (*Sc*) the cold, **tha am fuachd**
aice she's got a/the cold, *cf* **cnatan**

fuadach *see* **fuadachadh**

fuadachadh, *gen* **fuadachaidh** *nm*, *also*
fuadach, fuadaich, fuadaichean *nm*,
banishing, banishment, clearance, driving
or being driven away (*esp in relation to
the Highland Clearances*), (*song*) **òigridh**
ghuanach tha nis air fuadach (Màiri
Mhòr) happy-go-lucky young folk who are now
banished/driven away, (*hist*) **na Fuadaichean**
the (Highland) Clearances, *cf* **fògradh 2**,
fuadan 2

fuadaich *vt, pres part* **a' fuadachadh** & **a'**
fuadach, **1** chase, chase away, **dh'fhuadaich**
an cù an sionnach the dog chased away the
fox; **2** *esp in relation to the Highland Clearances*,
clear, banish, drive away, *cf* **fògair 1**; **3** (*more
generally*) exile, deport, *cf* **fògair 2**

fuadain *adj* false, artificial, synthetic, **fiaclan**
fuadain false teeth, dentures, *cf* **brèige** *adj* **2**

fuadan, *gen* **fuadain** *nm* **1** wandering, **air**
fhuadan *adv* wandering, astray, *in expr* **cù**
fuadain a stray dog, *cf* **allaban, seachran 1**; **2**
(*the state of*) exile (*see, eg*, **fear-fuadain** *above*),
cf **fògarradh 2**

fuaigh & **fuaigheil** *vti, pres part* **a' fuaigheal**,
sew, stitch, seam

fuaigheal, *gen* **fuaigheil** *nm* **1** (*the act of*) sewing,
stitching, seaming; **2** a piece of sewing; **3** a seam

fuaighte *adj* **1** sewn, stitched; **2** connected

fuaim, fuaime, fuaimean *nmf* (*the general word
for*) noise, sound

fuaimeadair, fuaimeadair, fuaimeadairean
nm a megaphone

fuaimneach *adj* noisy, *cf* **faramach**

fuaimnich *vt, pres part* **a' fuaimneachadh**,
(*lang*) pronounce

fuaimneachadh, *gen* **fuaimneachaidh** *nm*
(*lang*) pronunciation, a pronunciation

fuaimreag, fuaimreig, fuaimreagan *nf* a
vowel, *cf* **connrag, consan**

fual, *gen* **fuail** *nm* urine, *cf* **mùn**

fuamhaire *see* **famhair**

fuar *adj* **1** (*phys*) cold, **là fuar** a cold day, **tha am**
brochan a' fàs fuar! the porridge is getting
cold!; **2** (*emotionally etc*) cold, impersonal,
unfeeling, **bodach fuar** a cold chiel, **is i fàilte**

fhuar a gheibh thu an sin! it's a cold welcome
you'll get there!; *cf* **fionnar 2, fuaraidh, leth-**
fhuar

fuarachadh, *gen* **fuarachaidh** *nm* (*the act of*)
cooling etc (*see senses of* **fuaraich** *v*)

fuaradair, fuaradair, fuaradairean *nm* a
refrigerator, a fridge, *cf more usu* **frids**

fuaraich *vti, pres part* **a' fuarachadh**, cool, chill,
make or become cold or colder, *cf* **meilich**

fuaraidh *adj* (*lit & fig*) cool, chill, chilly, damp *cf*
fionnar 1 & 2, leth-fhuar

fuaran, *gen* **fuarain**, *pl* **fuarain** & **fuaranan**
nm a spring, a well (*usu in its natural state*), *cf*
tobar 1 & 2

fuasgail *vt, pres part* **a' fuasgladh**, **1** release, set
free, liberate, (*legal*) acquit, *cf* **saor** *v* **1, sgaoil**
v **2, sgaoil** *n*; **2** untie, loosen, undo, disentangle,
fuasgail snaidhm/barrall untie a knot/a
shoelace, *cf* **lasaich 1**; **3** solve, resolve, **fuasgail**
tòimhseachan-tarsainn solve a crossword

fuasgladh, *gen* **fuasglaidh** *nm* **1** (*the act of*)
releasing, loosening, solving etc (*see senses
of* **fuasgail** *v*); **2** a solution, a resolution (*to
problem etc*), **ceist gun fhuasgladh** an
unsolved/unresolved problem

fuath, fuatha, fuathan *nm* hate, hatred, loathing,
cf **gràin 1**

fuathach *adj* hateful, loathsome, detestable, *cf*
gràineil 1

fuathachadh, *gen* **fuathachaidh** *nm* (*the act of*)
hating, loathing, detesting

fuathaich *vt, pres part* **a' fuathachadh**, hate,
loathe, detest, *cf* **tha gràin agam orra** (*see*
gràin 1)

fùdar, fùdaraich *see* **pùdar, pùdaraich**

fuidheall (*also found as* **fuigheall**), *gen* **fuidhill**
nm **1** a relic, a remnant, a remainder, a residue,
leavings, what is left (*after some activity,
operation etc*), **fhuair esan a roghainn dheth,**
fhuair mise am fuidheall he got his pick of
it, I got what was left/the leavings, *cf less usu*
iarmad; **2** (*arith, fin*) a balance, a remainder

fuidhleach, *gen* **fuidhlich** *nm* rubbish, refuse, *cf*
more usu **sgudal 1**

fuil, *gen* **fola** & **fala**, *nf* blood, gore, **tha an fhuil**
a' tighinn às it's bleeding, **caill** *v* **fuil** bleed,
dòrtadh-fala *m* bloodshed, **càirdeas-fala** *m*
kinship, blood relationship, (*saying*) **is tighe fuil**
na bùrn blood is thicker than water

fuilear *adv* **1** (*trad*) too much; **2** *now in expr*
chan fhuilear dhut you need . . . (at least), *lit*
it is not too much for you, **chan fhuilear dha**
cola-deug dheth he needs (at least) a fortnight

fuiling & **fulaing** *vti, pres part* **a' fulang**, 1 (*vi*) suffer, **cha do dh'fhuiling e an uair a bha e tinn** he didn't suffer when he was ill; 2 (*vt*) bear, stand, put up with, tolerate, endure, abide, (*Sc*) thole, **chan fhuilinginn a dhèanamh** I couldn't bear to do it, **b' fheudar dhaibh fuachd is acras fhulang** they had to put up with/endure cold and hunger, **chan urrainn dhomh a fulang!** I can't stand/abide her!

fuil-mìos(a), *gen* **fala-mìos(a)**, *nf* menstruation, a period

fuil(t)each *adj* bloody, gory, **cath fuilteach** a bloody battle

fuiltean, fuiltein, fuilteana(n) *nm* a (single) hair (*of the head*), **fuilteana do chinn** the hairs of your head, *cf* **ròineag**

fuin *vt, pres part* **a' fuine(adh)**, 1 bake; 2 knead (*dough*)

fuine *see* **fuineadh**

fuineadair, fuineadair, fuineadairean *nm* a baker, *cf less trad* **bèicear**

fuineadh, *gen* **fuinidh** *nm*, *also* **fuine** *nf invar*, 1 (*the act of*) baking, kneading; 2 (*a batch of*) baking

fuireach(d), *gen* **fuirich** *nm* 1 (*the act of*) staying, waiting etc (*see senses of* **fuirich** *v*); 2 (*in compounds*) **àite-fuirich** *m* a dwelling place, accommodation, **taigh-fuirich** *m* a dwelling house; *cf* **còmhnaidh** 1 & 2

fuirich *vi, pres part* **a' fuireach(d)**, 1 stay, remain, **fuirich thusa far a bheil thu!** you stay where you are! *cf* **fan** 1; 2 live, dwell, (*Sc*) stay, bide, **bha sinn a' fuireach ann an Ìle aig an àm** we were living in Islay at the time, **a' fuireach aig Calum** staying/lodging with Calum, *cf* **còmhnaich, fan** 2; 3 wait, **fuirich (ort)!** wait! **chan fhuirich sinn rithe** we won't wait for her, **thachair sin . . . , fuirich ort . . . ,** **ann an Steòrnabhagh** that happened . . . , wait a minute/let me see now . . . , in Stornoway

fùirneis, fùirneis, fùrneisean *nf* a furnace

fulaing *see* **fuiling** & **fulang**

fulang, *gen* **fulaing** *nm* 1 (*the act of*) suffering, bearing etc (*see senses of* **fuiling** *v*); 2 suffering (*through pain etc*); 3 endurance, hardiness, toughness, capacity for bearing suffering and hardship, *cf* **cruas** 3

fulangach *adj* 1 capable of bearing suffering and hardship, hardy, tough, long-suffering, *cf* **cruadalach** 2, **cruaidh** *adj* 3; 2 passive, (*gram*) **an guth fulangach** the passive voice

fulangas, *gen* **fulangais** *nm* 1 tolerance; 2 endurance, resistance to suffering; 3 Christ's suffering on the Cross, the Passion

fulmair, fulmaire, fulmairean *nm* a fulmar

furachail *adj* 1 watchful, observant, alert, attentive, vigilant; 2 attentive (*to task, someone's needs etc*)

furan, *gen* & *pl* **furain** *nm* hospitality, a welcome, (*trad*) **fàilte is furan** welcome and hospitality

furasta (*also found as* **furasda**), *comp* **(n)as** (etc) **fhasa**, *adj* easy, **obair/ceist fhurasta** an easy job/question, **bidh sin nas fhasa** that will be easier, **b' e an rud a b' fhasa tilleadh** the easiest thing was to come back, *cf* **soirbh**

furm, fuirm, fuirm(ean) *nm* 1 a form, a bench (*ie seat*), *cf* **being**; 2 a stool

furtachadh, *gen* **furtachaidh** *nm* (*the act of*) consoling etc (*see senses of* **furtaich** *v*)

furtachd *nf invar* consolation, relief (*from pain, worry etc*), comfort, solace, **furtachd air a dhòrainn** comfort/relief for his anguish, *cf* **faothachadh** 2, **sòlas** 1

furtaich *vi, pres part* **a' furtachadh**, (*with prep air*) console, relieve (*from pain, worry etc*), comfort, bring solace, **furtaichidh sinn oirbh** we will comfort/console you, *cf* **faothaich**

G

gabaireachd *see* **gobaireachd**

gabh *vt, pres part* **a' gabhail,** *Note: there are many idioms & expressions with this verb and only a selection can be given here;* **1** *corres to the notion* take, **gabh àite** take place, **gabh a-steach** take in, include, **gabh cupan tì** take/have a cup of tea, **gabh mi mo dhìnnear mu thràth** I've already taken/had my dinner, **gabh mo leisgeul** excuse me (*lit* take/accept my excuse), **gabh comhairle** take counsel, get advice, **gabh truas de chuideigin/ri cuideigin** take pity on someone, **gabh eagal** take fright, become afraid, **ghabh na saighdearan e** the soldiers took/captured him, **ghabh sinn an cnatan** we took/caught the cold, **gabh d' anail** take a breather/a rest (*cf* **leig d' anail** – *see* **leig 3**), **gabhaidh an talla trì cheud duine** the hall will take/hold 300 people, **gabh cead de** take leave of, (*prov*) **bidh teine math an sin an uair a ghabhas e** that will be a good fire when it takes hold/kindles, **gabh gnothach os làimh** take a matter in hand; **2** *corres to the notion* go, **ghabh i an rathad** *also* **ghabh i roimhpe** she went her way/set off, **ghabh iad chun a' mhonaidh** they went to/made for the hill, **ghabh i ris an leabaidh** she took/went to her bed, **ghabh e san Nèibhidh** he went into/joined the Navy; **3** *corres to the notions* give, perform, deliver, **gabh òran!** give us/sing a song! **gabh port air an fhidhill!** give us/play a tune on the fiddle!; **4** *corres to the notion* can, **cha ghabh sin a dhèanamh** that can't be done, **tha an àmhainn cho teth 's a ghabhas** the oven's as hot as can be/as hot as possible; **5** *misc exprs* **gabh gnothach ri rudeigin** interfere in/meddle in something, **na gabh gnothach ris!** don't have anything to do with him/it!, **na gabh ort!** don't let on!, **na gabh ort fàgail** (*etc*)! don't you dare leave (*etc*)!, don't take it upon yourself to leave (*etc*)!, **ghabh iad ris an t-suidheachadh ùr** they accepted/agreed to/went along with the new situation, **dè tha a' gabhail riut?** what's troubling you/wrong with

you?, **ghabh iad dha chèile** they set about each other

gàbhadh, gàbhaidh, gàbhaidhean *nm* **1** danger, a danger, peril, a peril, **ann an gàbhadh** in danger/peril, *usu stronger than* **cunnart; 2** a crisis, *cf* **cruaidh-chàs**

gàbhaidh *adj* dangerous, perilous, *cf usu less strong* **cunnartach**

gabhail, gabhalach, gabhalaichean *nmf* **1** (*the act of*) taking *etc* (*see senses of* **gabh** *v*); **2** a lease, **thug an t-uachdaran seachad tuathanas air gabhail** the landlord leased (out) a farm; **3** a course, a bearing, a tack (*of boat, plane*), *also fig in expr* **chuir thu às mo ghabhail mi** you made me lose my drift/wander from the point (*also* you disappointed me); **4** a welcome, a reception, **dè an seòrsa gabhail a fhuair sibh?** what sort of a reception/welcome did you get?, *cf* **fàilte 1**

gabhal *see* **gobhal**

gabhaltach *adj* infectious, catching, contagious, **tinneasan gabhaltach** infectious diseases, **a bheil e gabhaltach?** is it catching?

gabhaltas, *gen* **gabhaltais** *nm* **1** a piece of rented land; **2** a tenancy, tenure

gach *adj* **1** each, every, **fhuair gach gille dà nota** each boy got two pounds, **leis gach deagh dhùrachd** with every good wish, *cf* **uile 1; 2** (*more emph*) **gach aon** every single, **gach uile** each and every, **bha an t-uisge ann gach aon là** it rained every single day, **bidh i an sàs annam mu gach uile nì** she's on at me about each and every thing; **3** *in expr* **gach cuid** both, **thoir dhomh gach cuid siùcar is salann** give me both sugar and salt, *cf* **cuid 4, dara 3**

gad, goid, gadan *nm* a supple stick, a withy, a switch

gad *conj see* **ged**

gadaiche, gadaiche, gadaichean *nm* a thief, a robber, *cf* **mèirleach**

gagach *adj* stammering, stuttering, **bruidhinn** *v* **gagach** stutter, stammer

gagachd *nf invar* stammering, stuttering, a stammer, a stutter

gagaire, gagaire, gagairean *nm* a stammerer, a stutterer

Gaidheal & **Gàidheal**, *gen* & *pl* **Gaidheil** & **Gàidheil** *nm* **1** someone of Goidelic race, a Gael, (*song*) **Cànan nan Gàidheal** the tongue/language of the Gaels; **2** a Highlander; **3** *restricted by some to those who speak Gaelic, sometimes including fluent non-native speakers*

Gaidhealach & **Gàidhealach**, *adj* **1** (*trad*) belonging or pertaining to the Gaels; **2** *now usu* Highland, **An Comunn Gàidhealach** The Highland Association, **Geamannan Gàidhealach** Highland Games

Gaidhealtachd & **Gàidhealtachd**, *nf invar*, *with art* **a' Ghàidhealtachd** the Highlands, **Roinn na Gàidhealtachd** Highland Region, **air (a') Ghàidhealtachd** in the Highlands

Gàidhlig, *gen* **Gàidhlig(e)** *nf* (*lang*) Gaelic, **tha Gàidhlig agam** I speak Gaelic, **cuir Gàidhlig air Beurla** put/translate English into Gaelic, *often with art*, **bruidhinn Gàidhlig/sa Ghàidhlig** speaking (in) Gaelic, **Comunn na Gàidhlig** the Gaelic Association, **luchd na Gàidhlig** Gaelic people, Gaelic speakers, *also as adj* **is e facal Gàidhlig a th' ann** it's a Gaelic word

gail *see* **guil**

gailbheach *adj* (*of sea, weather*) stormy

gailearaidh, *gen* **gailearaidh**, *pl* **gailearaidhean** *nm* an art gallery, *cf more trad* **taisbean-lann**

gailleann, gaillinn, gailleannan *nf* a storm, a tempest, *cf* **doineann, sian 1, stoirm 1**

gainmheach, *gen* **gainmhich** *nf* sand, **gainmheach an fhàsaich** the desert sand(s), **pàipear-gainmhich** *m* sandpaper

gainmheil *adj* sandy

gainne *nf invar*, *also* **gainnead** *nm invar*, scarcity, shortage, want, *cf* **cion 1**

gàir, gàir, gàirean *nm* a cry, a call, an outcry

gàir *vi*, *pres part* **a' gàireachdainn**, laugh, *cf* **dèan gàire** (*see* **gàire**)

gairbhe *nf invar*, *also* **gairbhead**, *gen* **gairbheid** *nm* (*abstr nouns corres to* **garbh**), roughness, coarseness, wildness

gairbhead *see* **gairbhe**

gàirdeachas, *gen* **gàirdeachais** *nm* joy, gladness, rejoicing, **dèan** *v* **gàirdeachas** rejoice (**ri** at), *cf* **àgh 1**

gàirdean, gàirdein, gàirdeanan *nm* an arm (*of person, chair*)

gàire *nmf invar* a laugh, laughter, **cò a tha a' dèanamh gàire?** who's laughing?

gàireachdaich *nf invar* **1** (*the act of*) laughing; **2** laughter, *cf* **gàire**

gàireachdainn *nf invar*, *same as* **gàireachdaich**

gairge *nf invar* (*abstr noun corres to* **garg**) **1** fierceness, ferocity; **2** wildness, unruliness

gairm, gairme, gairmean(nan) *nf* **1** (*the act of*) calling, crying, crowing; **2** a crow (*ie the sound*), **gairm coilich** a cock-crow; **3** a cry, a call, **gairm-chogaidh** a warcry (*cf* **sluagh-ghairm 1**), *cf* **èigh** *n*, **glaodh**[1] *n*; **4** a vocation, a calling; **5** a proclamation; **6 Gairm** *the Gaelic quarterly magazine* (*now sadly defunct*)

gairm *vi*, *pres part* **a' gairm**, **1** call, cry, **a' gairm ri chèile** calling to each other, (*fig*) **ghairm iad oirre sin a dhèanamh** they called on her to do that, *cf* **èigh** *v*, **glaodh** *vi*; **2** (*cock etc*) crow; **3** *in expr* **gairm cogadh** declare war

gairmeach *adj* (*gram*) vocative, **an tuiseal gairmeach** the vocative case

gàirnealair, gàirnealair, gàirnealairean *nm* a gardener

gàirnealaireachd *nf invar* gardening

gaiseadh, *gen* **gaisidh** *nm*, *used with art*, **an gaiseadh** potato blight, *cf* **cnàmh**[2]

gaisge *nf invar*, *also* **gaisgeachd** *nf invar*, (*esp phys*) bravery, valour, heroism, *cf* **dànadas 1**

gaisgeach, *gen* & *pl* **gaisgich** *nm* a hero, a champion, *cf* **curaidh, laoch, seòd**

gaisgeachd *see* **gaisge**

gaisgeil *adj* (*esp phys*) heroic, brave, *cf* **dàna 1**

gal *see* **gul**

galan, galain, galanan *nm* a gallon

galar, galair, galaran *nm* a disease, an illness, a malady, (*song*) **is trom an galar an gaol** love is a heavy malady/affliction, *cf* **gearan, tinneas**

Gall, *gen* & *pl* **Goill** *nm* **1** (*trad*) a non-Gael, a foreigner, *cf* **coigreach 1**; **2** *now usu* a Lowlander, a Lowland Scot, **tìr nan Gall** the Lowlands (*cf* **Galltachd**)

galla, galla, gallachan *nf* **1** a bitch; **2** *as a swear*, damned, bloody, **càr** (*etc*) **na galla!** bloody car (*etc*)!, **taigh na galla dhaibh!** damn them!, sod them!

gallan, *gen* **gallain**, *pl* **gallain** & **gallanan** *nm* a branch; **2** (*fig*) a youth; **3** a standing stone, *cf* **carragh 2, tursa**

gall-chnò, gall-chnotha, gall-chnothan *nf* a walnut

Gallta (*also found as* **Gallda**, *esp formerly*) *adj* Lowland, **A' Bheurla Ghallta** (*lang*) Lowland Scots, **air a' Mhachair Ghallta** in the Lowlands

Galltachd (*also found as* **Galldachd,** *esp formerly*) *nf* invar, used with art, **a' Ghalltachd** the Lowlands, **air a' Ghalltachd** in the Lowlands, *cf* **machair 2**

gàmag, gàmaig, gàmagan *nf* (*music*) an octave

gamhainn, *gen & pl* **gamhna** & **gaimhne** *nm* a stirk, a six-month or year-old calf

gamhlas, *gen* **gamhlais** *nm* malice, ill-will, spite

gamhlasach *adj* malevolent, spiteful

gann *adj* **1** scarce, scant(y), sparse, in short supply, **bha airgead gann air a' mhìos sin** money was in short supply/scarce/tight that month, **bàrr gann** a sparse/scanty crop; **2** *in expr* **is gann** scarcely, hardly, barely, **is gann a rinn sinn a-mach dè a bha e ag ràdh** we barely/scarcely made out what he was saying (*cf* **èiginn 4**), **is gann a chì thu a leithid** it's rare that you'll see/you'll hardly ever see the likes of him (*cf* **ainneamh 2**)

gànraich *vt, pres part* **a' gànrachadh,** soil, make dirty *or* filthy, *cf* **salaich 1**

gaoid, gaoide, gaoidean *nf* a blemish, a defect, a flaw, *cf more usu* **fàillinn 1, meang 1**

gaoir, gaoire, gaoirean *nf* **1** a cry (*usu of pain, anguish etc*), (*poem*) **Gaoir na h-Eòrpa** (Somhairle MacGill-Eain) Europe's Anguished Cry; **2** a thrill, **cuir** *v* **gaoir air/an** thrill, give a thrill to

gaoisid & **gaosaid,** *gen* **gaoiside** *nf* **1** hair (*of animals*), *esp* horsehair; **2** pubic hair, *cf* **ròm**

gaol, *gen* **gaoil** *nm* **1** love, (*song*) **thig trì nìthean gun iarraidh, an t-eagal, an t-iadach 's an gaol** three things come unsought, fear, jealousy and love, **tha i ann an gaol** she's in love, **gaol na h-òige** young love, **mo chiad ghaol** my first love, **thug mi mo ghaol dhut 's mi òg** I gave my love to you when I was young, **tha gaol agam ort** I love you, *cf* **gràdh 1** *which can be less intimate*; **2** *in voc expr* **a ghaoil** (my) love, (my) dear, (my) darling, *cf* **a ghràidh** (*see* **gràdh 2**), *which can be less intimate*

gaolach *adj* **1** loving, affectionate, *cf* **gràdhach;** **2** beloved, dear

gaoth, *gen* **gaoithe,** *pl* **gaothan** & **gaoithean** *nf* **1** wind, a wind, (*prov*) **an nì a thig leis a' ghaoith, falbhaidh e leis an uisge** what comes with the wind will go with the rain (easy come, easy go), **a' ghaoth an iar** the west wind, **tha gaoth ann** it's windy; **2** *with art,* **a' ghaoth** (intestinal) wind, flatulence

gaothach, *also* **gaothar,** *adj* **1** windy; **2** flatulent

gaotharan, gaotharain, gaotharanan *nm* a fan, **gaotharan teasachaidh** a fan heater

gàradh *see* **gàrradh**

garaids, garaids, garaidsean *nf* a garage (*household garage, service station etc*)

garbh *adj* **1** (*phys*) rough, wild, rugged, harsh, **oidhche gharbh** a wild/rough night, **allt garbh** a wild/impetuous stream, **tìr gharbh** a wild/rugged/harsh/land, wild etc country, *can occur in placenames as* garve-, *cf* **cruaidh** *adj* **2**; **2** coarse, rough (*to the senses*) **stuth garbh** coarse/rough material, **guth garbh** a harsh/hoarse voice; **3** vulgar, uncouth, coarse, **duine garbh** a coarse/vulgar man, (*also* a wild man, *or* a harsh man), *cf* **borb**; **4** *as intensifying adv* very, terribly, dreadfully, **tha cùisean garbh dripeil an-dràsta** things are terribly/hell of a busy just now, *cf* **glè, uabhasach 2**

garbhlach, *gen* **garbhlaich,** *pl* **garbhlaichean** *nm,* wild, rough *or* rugged terrain

garg *adj* **1** fierce, ferocious, brutal; **2** wild, turbulent, unruly, **sluagh garg** a wild/turbulent people, *cf* **borb**

gàrradh & **gàradh,** *gen* **gàrraidh,** *pl* **gàrraidhean** *nm* **1** a wall (*free-standing*), a stone dyke, *cf* **balla;** **2** a garden, *cf* **lios 1**

gartan, *gen* **gartain,** *pl* **gartain** & **gartanan** *nm* **1** a tick (*ie the insect*); **2** a garter

gas, *gen* **gaise,** *pl* **gasan** & **gaisean** *nf* (*of plants*) a stalk, a stem, a shoot, *cf* **bachlag 2, ògan**

gas, *gen* **gais** *nm* gas, a gas

gasta (*also found as* **gasda**), *adj* **1** handsome, fine, splendid, **bha na saighdearan a' coimhead gasta** the soldiers looked fine/splendid (*cf* **eireachdail**), **duine calma gasta** a sturdy handsome man; **2** (*fam*) great, fine, **bha sin dìreach gasta!** that was just great!, *cf* **glan** *adj* **2, sgoinneil, taghta 2**

gath, gatha, gathan(nan) *nm* **1** *a small sharp point such as* a dart, a sting, a barb, **gath speacha** a wasp's sting, **cuir** *v* **gath ann** sting (*cf* **guin** *v*); **2** a spear, a javelin, *cf* **sleagh;** **3** a ray, a beam, **gath solais** a light ray, a ray/beam of light, **gath-grèine** a sunbeam, **gathan na gealaich** the rays of the moon, *cf* **leus 1**

ge *conj* **1** (*trad*) though, *cf usu* **ged;** **2** *now usu in expr* **ge b 'e** whatever, however *etc*, **ge b' e cò a dh'innis e dhut, chan eil e fìor!** whoever told you it, it isn't true! **ge b' e cuin a ràinig iad** . . . whenever they arrived . . ., (*prov*) **ge b' e mar a bhios an t-sian, cuir do shìol anns a' Mhàrt** whatever the weather may be, sow your seed in March

gèadh, *gen & pl* **geòidh** *nmf* a goose

geal *adj* white, **dubh is geal** black and white, **duine geal** a white man (*cf* **duine bàn** a fair-haired/blonde man), *cf* **bàn²** **1** & *trad* **fionn**

geal, *gen* **gil** *nm* the white part of anything, *eg*
geal na sùla the white of the eye

gealach, gealaich, gealaichean *nf, used
with art,* **a' ghealach** the moon, **gealach an
abachaidh** the harvest moon, **ghealach
(sh)làn** a full moon

gealachadh, *gen* **gealachaidh** *nm* (*the act of*)
whitening, bleaching

gealagan, *gen & pl* **gealagain** *nm* an egg white,
the white of an egg

gealaich *vti, pres part* **a' gealachadh**, **1** whiten,
blanch, make or become white; **2** bleach, *cf*
todhair 2

gealbhonn, gealbhuinn, gealbhonnan *nm* a
sparrow

geall, *gen & pl* **gill** *nm* **1** a bet, a wager, **bùth
gheall** *f* a betting shop, **cuir** *v* **geall (air
each** etc) bet, put/lay/place a bet (on a horse
etc), **cuiridh mi an geall nach tig e** I bet he
won't come; **2** a promise, a pledge, *cf more usu*
gealladh

geall *vti, pres part* **a' gealltainn**, promise,
pledge, vow, (*with prep* **do**), **gheall e dhomh
nach dèanadh e a-rithist e** he promised me
he wouldn't do it again

gealladh, geallaidh, geallaidhean *nm* a
promise, a pledge, a vow, **thoir** *v* **gealladh**
promise, vow, make a promise, **thoir gealladh
dhomh gun sgrìobh thu thugam** promise
me you'll write to me (*cf* **geall** *v*), (*song*) **gur
òg thug mi mo ghealladh dhut** I gave you
my promise when I was young, **gealladh-
pòsaidh** an engagement, a betrothal, **thug iad
gealladh-pòsaidh dha chèile an-dè** they
got engaged yesterday, **Tìr a' Gheallaidh** the
Promised Land

gealltainn *nm invar* (*the act of*) promising etc
(*see senses of* **geall** *v*)

gealltanach *adj* **1** promising, **cluicheadair/
oileanach gealltanach** a promising player/
student; **2** (*of events etc*) auspicious

gealtach *adj* cowardly, fearful, timid, *cf*
cladhaireach

gealtachd *nf invar* cowardice, timidity, *cf*
cladhaireachd

gealtaire, gealtaire, gealtairean *nm* a coward,
cf **cladhaire**

gèam(a), geam(a), *gen* **gèama & geama**, *pl*
geamannan, geamachan & geamaichean
nm **1** a game (*of any kind*), *cf* **cluich** *n* **2**; **2** *esp*
football, a game, a match, **am bi thu a' dol
dhan gheama?** will you be going to the game/
match?, *cf* **maidse 2**

geamair, geamair, geamairean *nm* a
gamekeeper

geamhrachail *adj* wintry

geamhradh, geamhraidh, geamhraidhean
nm winter, a winter, **sneachd a' gheamhraidh**
(the) winter snow

gean, *gen* **geana** *nm* a mood, a humour, a frame
of mind, **deagh/droch ghean** a good/bad
mood, **dè an gean a th' air a' bhodach an-
diugh?** what sort of mood/frame of mind's the
old fellow in today?, *cf* **dòigh 4, fonn 2, gleus**
n **2, sunnd 2**

geanmnachd *nf invar* chastity

geanmnaidh *adj* chaste

geansaidh, geansaidh, geansaidhean *nm* a
jersey, a jumper, a pullover, (*Sc*) a gansey

gèar *see* **gìodhar**

gearain *vi, pres part* **a' gearan**, **1** complain,
grumble, moan, (**ri** to, **air** about), **gearain ris
a' mhanaidsear** complain to the manager, **cha
leig thu a leas a bhith a' gearan fad na
h-ùine!** you needn't bother grumbling/moaning
all the time! **dè a tha thu a' gearan?** what ails
you?, what's wrong with you?

gearaineach & gearanach *adj* complaining,
grumbling, querulous, apt to grumble or
complain, apt to moan and groan

gearan, gearain, gearanan *nm* **1** (*the act of*)
complaining etc (*see senses of* **gearain** *v*); **2** a
complaint, a grumble; **3** (*med*) a complaint, *cf*
galar, tinneas

gearanach *adj, see* **gearaineach**

gearastan (*also found as* **gearasdan**), *gen*
gearastain, *pl* **gearastanan** *nm* a garrison,
(*placename*) **An Gearasdan** Fort William

Gearmailt *nf invar, used with art* **a'
Ghearmailt** Germany

Gearmailteach, *gen & pl* **Gearmailtich** *nm* a
German, *also as adj* **Gearmailteach** German

Gearmailtis *nf invar, used with art* **a'
Ghearmailtis** (*lang*) German

geàrr *adj* **1** short, **an ùine gheàrr** in a short
time, shortly, *cf more usu* **goirid 1**; **2** *in
compounds* short-, *eg* **geàrr-chasach** *adj*
short-legged, **geàrr-sgrìobhadh** *m* shorthand,
geàrr-shealladh *m* short-sightedness

geàrr, gearra, gearran *nf* a hare, *cf*
maigheach

geàrr *vt, pres part* **a' gearradh**, **1** cut, **geàrr
sìos craobhan** cut down trees, **gheàrr e a
ghlùn** he cut his knee; **2** castrate, **tha iad a'
gearradh nan uan** they are castrating the
lambs, *cf more usu* **spoth**

gearradh, gearraidh, gearraidhean *nm* **1** (*the
act of*) cutting, **gearradh an fheòir** mowing/
cutting the hay/grass; **2** a cut, **bha gearradh
aige na ghlùin** he had a cut in his knee; **3**

gilb

sarcasm; **4** *in pl* (financial) cuts, **chaill e obair air sgàth nan gearraidhean** he lost his job on account of the cuts

Gearran, *gen* **Gearrain** *nm, with art,* **an Gearran** February

gearran, *gen & pl* **gearrain** *nm* **1** a gelding; **2** a garron *(a type of horse trad used in the Highlands & Islands for work and riding)*

geàrr-chunntas, geàrr-chunntais, geàrr-chunntasan *nm* **1** *(of documents etc)* an abstract, a summary, a précis; **2** *(of meeting)* minute(s)

geas, *gen* **geasa** *&* **geis,** *pl* **geasan** *nf,* **1** enchantment, a charm, a spell, *cf* **ortha, seun 1, 2** *in expr* **fo gheasaibh** *(obs dat pl; with gen)* spellbound, under a spell, enchanted, bewitched, **fo gheasaibh a bòidhcheid** spellbound *(etc)* by/under the spell of her beauty

geata, geata, geataichean *nm* a gate

ged, *also* **gad,** *conj* though, although, *(song)* **ged nach eil sinn fhathast pòst', tha mi 'n dòchas gum bi** though we are not yet married, I am hopeful that we will be, **cha do sguir i den obair ged a bha i claoidhte** she didn't stop work although she was exhausted, **chì mi e cho math 's ged a b' ann an-dè a bh' ann** I can see it/him as well as though it were yesterday, *cf trad* **ge 1**

ged-thà *see* **ge-tà**

gèile, *gen* **gèile,** *pl* **gèilean** *&* **gèileachan** *nm* a gale

gèill *vi, pres part* **a' gèilleadh,** yield, surrender, submit, give in, **(do** to), **ghèill an t-arm gu lèir (dha)** the entire army surrendered (to him), **ghèill e do/ro na h-argamaidean aca** he gave in to/in the face of their arguments, *cf* **strìochd 1**

gèilleadh, *gen* **gèillidh** *nm* **1** *(the act of)* yielding etc; **2** submission *etc; (see senses of* **gèill** *v); cf* **strìochdadh**

geimheal, geimheil, geimhlean *nm* a shackle, a fetter

geimhlich *vt, pres part* **a' geimhleachadh,** shackle, fetter

geinn, geinne, geinnean *nm* **1** a chunk of anything, *cf* **cnap 1; 2** a wedge, *(prov)* **'s e geinn dheth fhèin a sgoltas an darach** it's (only) a wedge of itself that will split the oak

geir, *gen* **geire** *nf* **1** suet; **2** fat, *cf* **crèis, saill** *n*

gèire *nf invar (abstr noun corres to* **geur** *adj)* sharpness, bitterness, harshness etc *(see senses of* **geur***)*

geòcach *adj* gluttonous, greedy *(for food), cf* **craosach**

geòcaire, geòcaire, geòcairean *nm* a glutton, *cf* **craosaire**

geòcaireachd *nf invar* gluttony, greed *(for food), cf* **craos 2**

geodha, geodha, geodhaichean *nmf* a cove, a narrow bay, *cf less specialised* **camas**

geòla, geòla(dh), geòlachan *nf* a yawl, a small boat, *cf* **eathar**

geòlas, *gen* **geòlais** *nm* geology

ge-tà *&* **ged-thà** *adv* though, however, **thug iad gealladh-pòsaidh dha chèile; cha do phòs iad, ge-tà** they got engaged; they didn't get married, though/however/(Sc) but

geug, gèige, geugan *nf* a branch *(of tree)*, a bough, *cf* **meang(l)an, meur 3**

geum, *gen* **geuma** *&* **gèime,** *pl* **geuman** *nm* *(cattle)* bellowing, a bellow, lowing, mooing, *(humans etc)* bellowing, a bellow, **leig e geum às** he let out a bellow, *cf* **beuc** *n*

geum *vi, pres part* **a' geumnaich,** *(cattle)* bellow, low, moo, *(humans)* bellow, **bha sprèidh a' geumnaich** cattle were lowing, *cf* **beuc** *v*

geur *adj* **1** sharp, having a sharp blade or point, **sgian gheur** a sharp knife; **2** *(of faculties)* sharp, acute, **sùil/cluas gheur** a sharp eye/ear, **tha e geur na inntinn** he's mentally sharp/quick/alert; **3** *(phys sensation)* bitter, sharp, biting, harsh, **gaoth gheur** a bitter/biting/(Sc) snell wind, **blas geur** a bitter/sharp/tart taste, *cf* **searbh 1; 4** *(temperament, words etc)* acerbic, sarcastic, sharp, bitter, sardonic, **teanga gheur** a sharp/cutting tongue, **briathran geura** bitter/sarcastic/cutting remarks, *cf* **guineach 1 & 2, searbh 3; 5** *(lang, orthog)* **stràc geur** an acute accent

geurachadh, *gen* **geurachaidh** *nm (the act of)* sharpening

geuraich *vt, pres part* **a' geurachadh,** sharpen, *cf* **faobharaich**

geurchuiseach *adj (mentally)* smart, shrewd, quick, subtle, *cf* **geur 2, toinisgeil 2**

gheibh, gheibheadh, gheibhinn *pts of irreg v* **faigh** *(see tables p 500)*

giall, *gen* **gialla** *&* **gèille,** *pl* **giallan** *nf* a jaw, *cf* **peirceall 1**

gibht, gibht, gibhtean *nf* a gift, a present, *cf more trad* **tabhartas, tiodhlac**

Giblean, *gen* **Giblein** *nm, also* **Giblinn,** *gen* **Giblinne** *nf, used with art,* **an Giblean/a' Ghiblinn** April

gidheadh *adv (trad)* nevertheless, yet, nonetheless, however, *cf less formal* **ge-tà**

gilb, gilbe, gilbean *nf* a chisel, *cf* **sgeilb**

gile *nf invar, also* **gilead**, *gen* **gilid** *nm*, (*abstr nouns corres to* **geal** *adj*) whiteness

gille, gille, gillean *nm* **1** (*trad*) a servant (*cf Sc* gillie), *in surnames as* Gil-, *eg* Gilchrist *from* **gille Chrìosd** servant/follower of Christ; **2** (*a young male from, say, 4 or 5 to, say, early twenties approx*) a boy, a lad, a youth, a young man, (*Sc*) a loon, **tha na gillean a' cluich ball-coise** the lads are playing football, **a bheil teaghlach agaibh? tha triùir ghillean is dithis nighean againn** do you have a family? we have three boys and two girls, **seana-ghille** a (*usu middle-aged or elderly*) bachelor (*cf* **fleasgach 2**); **3** (*fam*) *address to male of any age*, **a ghille** (*voc*) boy, lad, **tha thu ceart, a ghille!** (*or shortened to* **'ille**) you're right, boy!; *cf* **balach**

gille-brì(gh)de, gille-bhrì(gh)de, gillean-brì(gh)de *nm* an oystercatcher

gin *pron* any, *with neg v* none, **bha e ag iarraidh thàirngean ach cha robh gin agam** he was wanting nails but I hadn't any/I had none, **a bheil gin chèisean-litreach againn?** have we any envelopes?

gin *vti, pres part* **a' gineadh** *also* **a' gineamhainn 1** (*vt*) (*Bibl*) beget, conceive, **agus ghin Noah triùir mhac** and Noah begat three sons, **an nì a tha air a ghineamhainn innte** that which has been conceived in her; **2** (*vi*) breed, conceive, bear offspring, **tha an crodh a' gineadh** the cattle are breeding

gine, gine, gineachan *nf* (*biol*) a gene

gineadair, gineadair, gineadairean *nm* **1** a progenitor; **2** (*elec*) a generator

gineal, gineil, ginealan *nmf* offspring, race, progeny, *cf* **clann 2, sìol 3, sliochd**

ginealach, *gen & pl* **ginealaich** *nm* **1** a generation (*of a family*), **bha dà ghinealach den teaghlach agam ann an Canada** two generations of my family were in Canada; **2** *a whole group living in a society at the same time, or of approx the same age*, **ginealach nan Trì-ficheadan** the Sixties generation, **ginealach an donais** the wicked generation

gineamhainn *nm invar* **1** (*the act of*) begetting, breeding etc (*see senses of* **gin** *v*), **na buill-ghineamhainn** *mpl* the reproductive organs, the genitals; **2** conception, **casg-gineamhainn** *m* contraception, a contraceptive

ginean, ginein, gineanan *nm* a foetus

ginideach *adj* **1** (*gram*) genitive, **an tuiseal ginideach** the genitive case; **2** *also as noun, with art*, **an ginideach**, *gen* **a' ghinidich** *nm* the genitive

ginidich *vi, pres part* **a' ginideachadh**, germinate

giodar, *gen* **giodair** *nm* sewage

gìodhar, gìodhair, gìodhraichean *nm*, *also* **gèar** *nf invar*, a gear (*ie in machinery*)

giomach, *gen & pl* **giomaich** *nm* a lobster

gioma-goc, gioma-goc, gioma-gocan *nm* a piggy-back (*Sc* cuddy-back) ride

gionach *adj* **1** greedy (*for wealth, food*), *cf* **sanntach**; **2** keen, ambitious, 'hungry' (*for success*)

gionaiche *nm invar* **1** greed (*for wealth, food*), *cf* **sannt**; **2** ambition

giorrachadh, giorrachaidh, giorrachaidhean *nm* **1** (*the act of*) shortening etc (*see senses of* **giorraich** *v*); **2** curtailment, abbreviation, an abbreviation, abridgement, an abridgement

giorrad, *gen* **giorraid** *nm* shortness

giorraich *vt, pres part* **a' giorrachadh**, shorten, abbreviate, abridge, curtail

gìosg *vt, pres part* **a' gìosgail**, gnash, **bha e a' gìosgail fhiaclan** he was gnashing his teeth

giotàr, giotàir, giotàran *nm* a guitar

giùlain *vt, pres part* **a' giùlan**, **1** carry, transport, **bha e a' giùlan bùird** he was carrying a table, **bha an làraidh a' giùlan guail** the lorry was carrying/transporting coal; **2** (*occas*) wear (*clothing*); **3** behave, **cha robh e ga ghiùlan fhèin uabhasach math** he wasn't behaving (himself) terribly well

giùlan, giùlain, giùlanan *nm* **1** (*the act of*) carrying etc (*see senses of* **giùlain** *v*), **neach-giùlain** *m* a carrier, a bearer; **2** transport, **dòighean giùlain** means/modes of transport, *cf* **còmhdhail 1**; **3** behaviour, conduct, **is beag orm do ghiùlan** I don't think much of your conduct/behaviour, *cf* **dol-a-mach 1**; **4** carriage, deportment, bearing, posture, *cf* **gluasad 3**

giùran, giùrain, giùranan *nm* **1** a gill (*of fish*); **2** a barnacle

giuthas, *gen* **giuthais** *nmf* pine, a pine or fir tree, a Scots pine, a spruce tree, **giuthas Lochlannach** Norway spruce

giùthsach, *gen & pl* **giùthsaich** *nm* a pine wood or forest

glac *vt, pres part* **a' glacadh**, catch, capture, apprehend, trap, seize, grasp, snatch, **glac iasg** catch/trap fish, **ghlac am poileas e** the police caught/apprehended him, **cha do ghlac sinn am plèana** we didn't catch the plane, *cf* **beir 2** & **3**, **gabh grèim air** (*see* **grèim 1**), **greimich**

glac, glaice, glacan *nf* **1** a (*usu small or narrow*) valley, a hollow, (*poem*) **Glac a' Bhàis**

(Somhairle MacGill-Eain) Death Valley, *cf*
gleann, lag *n*; **2** a palm, the hollow of a hand, *cf*
more usu **bas**
glacadh, *gen* **glacaidh** *nm* **1** (*the act of*)
catching, capturing etc (*see senses of* **glac**
v); capture, seizure (*not med*), **an dèidh a**
ghlacadh after capturing him *or* after he had
been captured *or* after his capture; **2** a grasp, *cf*
grèim 1
glacte *adj* caught, captured, trapped, seized, *cf*
sàs 1
glagadaich, *gen* **glagadaiche** *nf* a clattering,
clanging, clashing or rattling noise
glaine *nf invar* (*abstr noun corres to* **glan** *adj*)
cleanliness
glainne & (*less usu*) **gloinne**, *gen* **glainne**,
pl **glainneachan** & **glainnichean** *nf* **1**
glass, a glass, **taigh-glainne** a greenhouse,
a glasshouse, (*story collection*) **Dorcha tro**
Ghlainne Through a Glass Darkly, **glainne-**
sìde a barometer; **2** *in pl* **glainneachan** &
glainnichean glasses, spectacles, *cf more trad*
speuclairean
glais *vt, pres part* **a' glasadh**, lock, **glais an**
doras lock the door
glaiste *adj* locked, (*song*) **an seòmraichean**
glaiste le claspaichean iarainn in rooms
locked with iron clasps
glam & **glamh** *vt, pres part* **a' glam(h)adh**,
gobble, devour, 'wolf', **na glam do bhiadh!**
don't gobble/wolf down your food!
glan *adj* **1** clean, **tubhailte ghlan** a clean towel,
a bheil do làmhan glan? are your hands
clean?; **2** fine, grand, **a bheil mi gad chumail**
air ais? fuirich an sin, a bhalaich, tha thu
glan! am I keeping you back? stay there boy,
you're fine!, *cf* **gasta, sgoinneil, taghta 2**
glan *vt, pres part* **a' glanadh**, clean, cleanse,
purge
glanadh, *gen* **glanaidh** *nm* (*the act of*) cleaning
etc (*see senses of* **glan** *v*)
glaodh[1], **glaoidh, glaodhan** *nm* a call, a cry, a
shout, a yell, *cf* **èigh** *n*, **gairm** *n* **3**, **sgairt**[2] **1**
glaodh[2], **glaoidh, glaodhan** *nm* glue
glaodh[1] *vi, pres part* **a' glaodha(i)ch**, call, cry,
shout, yell, bawl, *cf* **èigh** *v*, **gairm** *v* **1**
glaodh[2] *vt, pres part* **a' glaodhadh**, glue
glaodhadh, *gen* **glaodhaidh** *nm* (*the act of*)
glueing
glaodha(i)ch *nm invar* (*the act of*) calling,
crying etc (*see senses of* **glaodh** *vi*)
glaodhaire, glaodhaire, glaodhairean *nm* a
loudspeaker, a public address system, a tannoy

glaodhan, *gen* **glaodhain** *nm* **1** pulp, pith,
glaodhan-fiodha wood pulp; **2** (*flour & water*)
paste
glas *adj* **1** grey, (*song*) **chuir mi bhriogais**
ghlas fom cheann I put the grey breeks about
me, *cf* **liath** *adj*; **2** green, **tulaichean glasa**
green hillocks, *cf* **gorm 2**, **uaine**
glas, glaise, glasan *nf* (*on door etc*) a lock
glas-neulach *adj* pale-faced, wan, pasty, pallid
glas-làmh, glais-làmh, glasan-làmh *nf* a
handcuff
glasraich *nf invar, sing & coll,* a vegetable,
vegetables, greens
glè *adv* very, (*lenites following cons where*
possible), **bha sin glè mhath** that was very
good, **rinn i glè luath e** she did it very quickly,
cf **fìor 3, garbh 4, uabhasach 2**
gleac, *gen* **gleaca** *nm* **1** a struggle, a fight, *cf* **strì**
n **2**; **2** wrestling
gleac *vi, pres part* **a' gleac(adh)**, **1** fight,
struggle, (**ri** with, against), *cf* **strì** *v*; **2** wrestle
gleacadair, gleacadair, gleacadairean *nm* a
wrestler
gleacadh, *gen* **gleacaidh** *nm* (*the act of*)
struggling, fighting, wrestling
gleadhar, gleadhair, gleadharan *nm* uproar,
an uproar, *cf* **othail, ùpraid 1**
gleadhraich, gleadhraich, gleadhraichean *nf*
1 a loud rattling or clattering noise, a clamour, a
din; **2** the noise of loud talking or chattering
gleann, *gen* **glinn(e)**, *pl* **glinn** & **gleanntan** *nm*
a glen, a valley
gleans, *gen* **gleansa** *m* a shine, a lustre (*on a*
surface etc)
glèidh *vt, pres part* **a' gleidheadh**, **1** keep, hold,
retain, have custody of, *cf* **cùm 1**; **2** save (*money*
etc), *cf* **caomhain(n), sàbhail 3**; **3** keep,
preserve, save, conserve, (*phys*) **tha iad gan**
gleidheadh ann an taigh-tasgaidh they're
being kept/conserved in a museum, (*spiritually*)
gleidhidh Dia sinn God will preserve/save us
(*cf* **sàbhail 2**)
gleidheadh, *gen* **gleidhidh** *nm* (*the act of*)
keeping, saving etc (*see senses of* **glèidh** *v*)
glèidhte *adj* kept, held, saved etc (*see senses*
of **glèidh** *v*), (*copyright statement*) **na**
còraichean uile glèidhte all rights reserved
glèidhteach *adj* conservative
glèidhteachas, *gen* **glèidhteachais** *nm*
conservation, **neach-glèidhteachais** *m* a
conservationist, **glèidhteachas nàdair** nature
conservancy, conservation
gleoc, *also* **cloc** & **cleoc**, *gen* **gleoca**, *pl*
gleocaichean *nm* a clock, *cf* **uaireadair 2**

gleus *vt, pres part* **a' gleusadh**, 1 get ready, prepare, put in good order *or* trim; 2 (*machines etc*) adjust, service; 3 (*music*) tune, *cf* **gleus** *n* 3

gleus, *gen* **gleusa** & **gleois**, *pl* **gleusan** & **gleois** *nmf* 1 (*of objects*) order, condition, trim, **air (deagh) ghleus** in good order/trim/nick, **cuir** *v* **air ghleus** get ready, put in trim *or* good order; 2 (*of people*) mood, humour, trim, **air (deagh) ghleus** in good trim, in a good mood, **gleus inntinn** a frame of mind, *cf* **dòigh** 4, **fonn, gean**; 3 (*music*) a key, a tonality, (*of musical instrument*) tuning, tune, **air (deagh) ghleus** in tune, well tuned, **cuir** *v* **air ghleus** tune (*cf* **gleus** *v* 3)

gleus *vt, pres part* **a' gleusadh**, 1 get ready, prepare, put in good order *or* trim; 2 (*machines etc*) adjust, service; 3 (*musical instruments*) tune, *cf* **gleus** *n* 3

gleusadh, *gen* **gleusaidh** *nm* (*the act of*) preparing, adjusting etc (*see senses of* **gleus** *v*)

gleusta & **gleusda**, *adj* 1 ready, prepared, in good trim *or* order, (*music*) tuned, in tune; 2 (*of people*) in good trim, in a good mood *or* humour, *cf* **dòigh** 4; 3 (*of people*) handy, clever, resourceful, skilled, **gleusta ann an làimhseachadh nan arm** skilled in the handling of weapons

glic *adj* 1 wise, full of wisdom; 2 clever, mentally able; 3 sensible, *cf* **ciallach**

gliocas, *gen* **gliocais** *nm* 1 wisdom; 2 cleverness

gliog, glioga, gliogan *nm* a drip, dripping (*ie the sound*), **gliog an uisge is e a' tuiteam on mhullach** the drip of water as it falls from the roof

gliong, glionga, gliongan *nm, also* **gliongartaich** *nm invar*, a clinking, tinkling *or* jingling noise

gloc, *gen* **gloic** *nm, also* **glocail** *nf invar*, a cackle, cackling, *cf* **gogail**

gloc *vi, pres part* **a' glocail**, cackle

gloinne *nf see* **glainne**

glòir, *gen* **glòir(e)** & **glòrach** *nf* 1 (*spiritual*) glory, (*hymn*) **tha do rìoghachd làn de ghlòir** Thy kingdom is filled with glory; 2 fame, honour, *cf* **cliù** 1

glòirich *vt, pres part* **a' glòireachadh**, glorify

glòir-mhiann, *gen* **glòir-mhianna** *nmf* ambition, an ambition, **is e a' ghlòir-mhiann (a tha) agam a bhith nam phrìomhaire** it's my ambition to be prime minister

glòir-mhiannach *adj* ambitious

glòrmhor *adj* glorious, magnificent, *cf* **greadhnach, òirdheirc**

gluais *vti, pres part* **a' gluasad**, 1 (*phys*) move, **ghluais i an càr** she moved the car, **ghluais an**

talamh the earth moved (*cf* **caraich**), **ghluais an t-arm chun a' bhaile** the army moved towards the town; 2 (*emotionally*) move, touch, affect, stir, (*prov*) **an nì nach cluinn cluas, cha ghluais e cridhe** what (the) ear doesn't hear will not affect (the) heart, (*song*) **ghluais ar buadhan nàdair ann an gràdh dha chèil'** our natural feelings moved/stirred in mutual affection, **chaidh mo ghluasad** I was moved

gluasad, gluasaid, gluasadan *nm* 1 (*the act of*) moving, affecting etc (*see senses of* **gluais** *v*); 2 (*phys*) motion, mobility, movement, a movement, a gesture, **bha sinn gun ghluasad** we were motionless, **chuala mi gluasad san dorchadas** I heard a movement in the darkness, **taigh-gluasaid** a mobile home; 3 a gait, **tha gluasad cearbach aige** he has an awkward gait, *cf* **giùlan** 4; 4 agitation, excitement, emotional arousal, a 'stir'

gluasadach *adj* (*phys & emotionally*) capable of moving

glug, gluig, glugan *nm* gurgling, a gurgle, a gulp, a gulping noise, **glug caoinidh** a sob

glugan, glugain, gluganan *nm* gurgling, a gurgle

glumag, glumaig, glumagan *nf* 1 a pool *esp in a river or stream*, *cf* **linne** 1, **lòn**² 1; 2 a puddle, *cf* **lòn**² 2

glùn, glùin(e), glùin(t)ean *nf* a knee, **fèileadh-beag os cionn mo ghlùin** the kilt abune ma knee, **lùbadh na glùine** bending the knee (*esp in prayer*), **bean-ghlùine** *f* a midwife

gnàth, gnàtha, gnàthan(nan) *nm, also* **gnàth(a)s**, *gen* **gnàthais** *nm*, 1 a custom, a practice, a habit, a usage, (*trad*) **mar bu ghnàth leis** as was his custom/habit, **a rèir gnàthan na dùthcha** in accordance with the customs of the country, *cf* **àbhaist** 1, **cleachdadh** 2, **dòigh** 2, **nòs** 1; 2 a convention, **gnàth litreachail** a literary convention

gnàthach *adj* customary, normal, usual, habitual, routine, conventional, *cf* **àbhaisteach, cumanta**

gnàthaich *vt, pres part* **a' gnàthachadh**, 1 use, *cf more usu* **cleachd** 1; 2 accustom, *cf* **cleachd** 2; 3 behave towards, use, treat, **is dona a ghnàthaich e a' bhean aige** he behaved badly towards his wife, *cf* **làimhsich** 2

gnè *nf invar* 1 a kind, a sort, **nithean de gach gnè** things of all kinds, *cf more usu* **seòrsa** 1; 2 (*biol*) a species, **gnè nan gobhar** the goat species, *cf* **cineal** 2, **seòrsa** 2; 3 a sex, a gender, **daoine den dà ghnè** people of both sexes, (*gram*) **a' ghnè bhoireann/fhireann** the feminine/masculine gender

gnè(i)theach & **gnè(i)theasach** *adj* sexual, pertaining to sexuality or gender

gnìomh, gnìomha, gnìomhan *nm* 1 action, an action, a deed, an act, **cuir** *v* **an gnìomh** put into action, practise (*theory, precept etc*), **fear gnìomha** *m* a man of action, **droch ghnìomh** a bad deed/action; 2 (*esp IT*) a function, a process, **iuchair-gnìomha** *f* a function key, **gnìomh-inneal** *m* a processor, **gnìomh bodhaig** a bodily function; 3 (*of official etc*) **an gnìomh** acting (*ie standing in for*), **Prìomhaire an gnìomh** acting Prime Minister

gnìomhach *adj* active, enterprising, hardworking, industrious, *cf* **dèanadach, dìcheallach**

gnìomhachadh, *gen* **gnìomhachaidh** *nm* 1 (*the act of*) acting, carrying out *etc* (*see senses of* **gnìomhaich** *v*); 2 (*IT*) **gnìomhachadh-dàta** data processing

gnìomhachail *adj* industrial, *cf* **tionnsgalach 2**

gnìomhachas, *gen* **gnìomhachais** *nm* 1 industry, industriousness, *cf* **dèanadas**; 2 business, a business, **chuir e gnìomhachas ùr air chois** he set up a new business, **cairt-ghnìomhachais** *f* a business card, **raon gnìomhachais** *m* a business park, an industrial estate, *cf* **gnothach 1, malairt 1**; 3 an industry, **gnìomhachas an dealain/a' bhìdh** the electricity/food industry

gnìomhaich *vti, pres part* **a' gnìomhachadh,** 1 (*vi*) act; 2 (*vt*) effect, carry out, execute (*a task, process etc*)

gnìomhaiche, gnìomhaiche, gnìomhaichean *nm* 1 an executive; 2 (*pol etc*) an activist

gnìomhair, gnìomhair, gnìomhairean *nm* (*gram*) a verb, **gnìomhairean (neo-)riaghailteach** (ir)regular verbs

gnog *vt, pres part* **a' gnogadh,** 1 knock, (*Sc*) chap, **gnog an doras/an uinneag** chap/knock at the door/window; 2 **gnog an ceann** nod the head

gnogadh, *gen* **gnogaidh** *nm* 1 (*the act or noise of*) knocking; 2 a knock (*on door etc*); 3 **gnogadh cinn** a nod of the head

gnothach, gnothaich, gnothaichean *nm* 1 (*commerce*) business, a business, **fear-gnothaich** a businessman, **dèan** *v* **gnothach ri** do/transact business with, **dh'fhàillig an gnothach aige** his business failed, **chaidh e don Fhraing air ceann gnothaich** he went to France on business, *cf* **gnìomhachas 2, malairt 1**; 2 a matter, a business, an affair, **'s e droch ghnothach a bh' ann!** it was a bad business!, **chan e sin do ghnothach-sa** that's no business/affair of yours, *cf* **cùis 1**; 3 an errand, **dh'fhalbh am balach air gnothach** the boy went on an errand; 4 *in expr* **gabh gnothach ri** interfere/meddle in or with, or get involved in, have anything to do with, **na gabh gnothach ri sin!** don't meddle in that! or don't have anything to do with that! *cf* **buin** *v* **3; 5** *in expr* **a dh'aon ghnothach** *adv* expressly, deliberately, specially, on purpose, specifically, **sgrìobh mi an litir a dh'aon ghnothach gus a' chùis a thoirt gu ceann** I wrote the letter expressly to bring the matter to an end, *cf* **rùn 4; 6** *in expr* **dèan** *v* **an gnothach air** get the better of, defeat, *cf* **cùis 5, uachdar 5; 7** *in expr* **nì sin an gnothach!** that'll do!, that'll do the trick/job!, *cf* **cùis 6**

gnù *adj* surly, sullen, *cf* **mùgach 2** & *more usu* **gruamach 1**

gnùis, gnùise, gnùisean *nf* one's face, one's facial appearance or habitual expression, one's complexion, *cf more temporary* **fiamh 3, tuar**

gob, *gen & pl* **guib** *nm* 1 a beak, a bill (*of bird*); 2 the point or (sharp) end of anything, **gob rubha/snàthaid/prìne** the point of a headland/needle/pin; 3 (*vulg*) a gob, a mouth, **dùin do ghob!** shut your mouth/gob!, *cf* **beul 1, bus² 1, cab**

gobach *adj* prattling, chattering, *cf* **cabach**

gobaireachd *also* **gabaireachd** *nf invar* prattle, chatter, prattling, chattering, **chuala sinn gobaireachd na cloinne** we heard the children's prattling, *cf* **cabadaich, goileam**

gobha, gobhainn, goibhnean *nm* a (black)smith, *cf* **ceàrd 2**

gobhal & **gabhal,** *gen* **gobhail** & **goibhle,** *pl* **goibhlean** *nm* 1 a fork (*ie angle where two lines join*), an object so shaped (*NB not a table fork, see* **forc, greimire,** *nor a farm or garden fork, see* **gobhlag, gràpa**), **gobhal san rathad** a fork in the road, **gobhal-gleusaidh** a tuning fork, **gobhal baidhsagail** the fork of a bicycle; 2 the crutch (*ie at the groin*), **gobhal briogais** the crutch of a pair of trousers

gòbhar, *gen* **goibhre** & **gobhair,** *pl* **goibhrean, gobhraichean** & **gobhair** *nmf* a goat, *cf* **boc 1**

gòbhlach *adj* forked, **earball gòbhlach** a forked tail, **dealanach gòbhlach** forked lightning

gòbhlag, gòbhlaig, gòbhlagan *nf* 1 a (two-pronged) fork, a pitchfork, a hay-fork, *cf* **gràpa**; 2 an earwig, *cf* **fiolan**

gòbhlan-gaoithe, gòbhlain-ghaoithe, gòbhlanan-gaoithe *nm* a swallow (*ie the bird*)

goc, *gen* **goca,** *pl* **gocan** & **gocaichean** *nm* a tap, a stopcock, a faucet, (*Sc*) a toby, *cf* **tap**

gogail *nf invar* cackling, clucking (*of hen*), (*prov*) **gogail mhòr is ugh beag** a great deal of cackling and a little egg, *cf* **gloc** *n*

goid, *gen* **goide** *nf* **1** (*the act of*) thieving, stealing, pinching, **a bheil thu ri goid a-rithist?** are you at your thieving again?; **2** theft; *cf* **braid**, **mèirle**

goid *vt*, *pres part* **a' goid**, steal, pinch, thieve, **ghoid iad càr** they stole a car

goil *vti*, *pres part* **a' goil**, **1** (*of liquids*) boil; **2** (*fig*) **bha an loch a' goil le iasg** the loch was seething/(*Sc*) hotchin with fish

goile, **goile**, **goilea(cha)n** *nf* a stomach, *cf more usu* **stamag**

goileach *adj* boiling

goileam, *gen* **goileim** *nm* prattle, tittle-tattle, chatter, *cf* **cabadaich**, **gobaireachd**

goireas, **goireis**, **goireasan** *nm* **1** a resource, an amenity, a facility, **ionad-ghoireasan** *m* a resource centre, **tha goireasan gu leòr aig a' chlub shòisealta** the social club has lots of facilities/resources; **2** a convenience, *in pl* **na goireasan** the conveniences, the toilets, *cf* **taigh-beag** (*see* **taigh 3**)

goireasach *adj* convenient, handy, *cf* **deiseil 3**, **ullamh 3**

goirid (*comp* **(n)as (etc) giorra**) *adj* **1** short, brief, **sgeulachd ghoirid** a short story, **tha na làithean a' fàs goirid** the days are getting short, **cuairt ghoirid** a brief tour, *cf* **aithghearr 1**; **2** (*as n*) **o chionn ghoirid** a short time ago, recently, **an ceann ghoirid** in/after a short time; *cf less usu* **geàrr** *adj* **1**

goirt *adj* **1** painful, hurting, (*Sc*) sore, **ceann goirt** (*Sc*) a sore head, a headache, **tha mo dhruim goirt** my back hurts/is sore, *cf* **pianail**; **2** sour, **bainne/uachdar goirt** sour milk/cream; **3** bitter, severe, sore, **deuchainn ghoirt** a sore/severe trial, **àmhghar goirt** bitter distress, *cf* **crài(dh)teach**

goirt *n see* **gort**

goirteachadh, *gen* **goirteachaidh** *nm* (*the act of*) hurting, causing pain

goirtich *vt*, *pres part* **a' goirteachadh**, hurt, cause pain to (*usu phys*), *cf* **ciùrr**

goistidh, **goistidh**, **goistidhean** *nm* **1** a godfather; **2** a sponsor (*of sporting or cultural event etc*); **3** a gossip

gòrach *adj* **1** stupid, *cf* **baoghalta**; **2** foolish, silly, daft, *cf* **amaideach**, **baoth**

gòraiche, *nf invar* **1** stupidity; **2** foolishness, folly, silliness, absurdity, *cf* **amaideas**

gorm *adj* **1** blue, **adhar gorm** a blue sky, (*song*) **Teàrlach òg nan gorm-shùl meallach** young Charles (*ie Edward Stewart*) of the bewitching blue eyes; **2** green, **feur gorm** green grass (*a more intense green than* **glas**), *cf* **glas** *adj* **2**, **uaine**

gort, *gen* **gorta** *nf* famine, a famine, starvation, **a' Ghort Mhòr** the Great Famine, the Great Hunger (*the potato famine of 1846*)

gràbhail *vt*, *pres part* **a' gràbhal(adh)**, engrave

grad *adj* **1** sudden, abrupt, **lasair/fuaim ghrad** a sudden flash/noise, *cf* **obann**; **2** quick, sharp, agile, alert, **gluasadan grada** quick movements, **bha i grad na h-inntinn** she was mentally quick/alert, *cf* **deas 4**, **luath** *adj* **2**; **3** *as adv* **gu grad** suddenly, quickly, shortly, **dh'èirich e gu grad** he rose suddenly, **bidh e deiseil gu grad** it will be ready/finished shortly (*cf* **a dh'aithghearr**)

gràdh, *gen* **gràidh** *nm* **1** love, affection, **tha gràdh agam ort!** I love you! **thug i a gràdh dha** she gave her love to him, *cf* **gaol 1**; **2** *in voc expr* **a ghràidh**, (my) love, (my) dear, *Note: can be used more widely than* **a ghaoil** (*see* **gaol 2**), *which tends to be a mode of address for lovers & close family*

gràdhach *adj* loving, affectionate, *cf* **gaolach 1**

graf, **grafa**, **grafaichean** *nm* a graph

gràg, **gràig**, **gràgan** *nm* a croak, a caw, *cf* **ròcail**

gràgail *nf invar* (*the act & sound of*) croaking, cawing, **dèan** *v* **gràgail** croak, caw

graide *nf invar* (*abstr noun corres to* **grad**) suddenness, quickness etc (*see senses of* **grad**)

gràin, *gen* **gràine** *nf* **1** hate, hatred, abhorrence, loathing, **tha gràin agam orra** I hate/loathe/detest/abhor them, *cf* **fuath**; **2** disgust, *cf* **sgreamh**

gràineag, **gràineig**, **gràineagan** *nf* a hedgehog

gràineil *adj* **1** hateful, loathsome, abhorrent, detestable, *cf* **fuathach**; **2** disgusting, vile, *cf* **grànda 2**, **sgreamhail**

gràinne, **gràinne**, **gràinnean** *nf* a (*single*) grain (*of a cereal*)

gràinneach *adj* granular

gràinnean, **gràinnein**, **gràinneanan** *nm* a grain, **gràinnean salainn/siùcair** a grain of salt/sugar

gràisg, **gràisge**, **gràisgean** *nf* a crowd (*derog*), a mob, a rabble, *cf* **foireann 1**, **prabar**

gràisgealachd *nf invar* vulgarity, uncouthness, yobbishness, loutishness

gràisgeil *adj* vulgar, uncouth, yobbish, loutish

gram, **grama**, **graman** *nm* a gram(me) **ceud gram de shiùcar** a hundred grams of sugar

gramail & **greimeil** *adj* persistent, resolute

gràmar, *gen* **gràmair** *nm* grammar, **leabhar gràmair** *m* a grammar book

gràmarach *adj* grammatical, pertaining to grammar

gràn, *gen & pl* **gràin** *nm* **1** a cereal, a cereal crop, a grain crop; **2** (*coll*) grain (*from cereal crops*)

granaidh, granaidh, granaidhean *nf* (*fam*) a granny, a grandmother, (*story*) **Granaidh anns a' Chòrnair** (Iain Mac a' Ghobhainn) Granny in the Corner

grànda *adj* **1** ugly; **2** vile, *cf* **gràineil 2, sgreamhail**

gràpa, gràpa, gràpan *nm* a fork (*usu 4 or more prongs, for farm or garden*), (*Sc*) a graip, *cf* **gobhlag 1**

gràs, gràis, gràsan, *nm* **1** grace, graciousness, **gun ghràs** graceless; **2** (*spiritual*) grace, **gràs Dhè** God's grace, divine grace

gràsmhor *adj* gracious

greadhnach *adj* gorgeous, magnificent, splendid, *cf* **glòrmhor, òirdheirc**

greallach, *gen* **greallaiche** *nf* entrails, intestines, innards (*esp of animals*), *cf* **caolan, innidh, mionach 1**

greannach *adj* **1** ill-tempered, (*Sc*) crabbit, *cf* **crost(a) 1, diombach 1, gruamach 4**; **2** (*of weather*) gloomy, threatening

greannmhor *adj* cheerful, joyful, (*song*) **is os mo chionn sheinn an uiseag ghreannmhor** (Màiri Mhòr) and above my head sang the joyful skylark, *cf* **àghmhor**

greas *vti, pres part* **a' greasad, 1** (*trad*) (*vi*) hurry, make haste, **ghreas mi orm** I hurried/made haste, *now usu in imperative* **greas ort!**, *pl* **greasaibh oirbh!** hurry up!, **bu chòir dhaibh greasad orra** they ought to hurry, *cf* **dèan cabhag** (*see* **cabhag 1**); **2** (*vt*) hurry, drive *or* urge on (*people, animals*), *cf* **cabhag 2, iomain** *v* **1**

grèata, grèata, grèataichean *nm* a grate, grating

greideal, *gen* **greideil** & **greidealach**, *pl* **greidealan** *nf* (*baking*) a griddle, a gridiron, (*Sc*) a girdle

Grèig *nf, used with art* **a' Ghrèig** Greece

greigh, greighe, greighean *nf* a herd, a flock (*of animals*), *esp* a stud of horses

greigheach *adj* gregarious

grèim, greime, greimean(nan) *nm* **1** a grip, a grasp, a hold, **gabh** *v* **grèim air rudeigin** take hold of/grip/grasp/grab/seize something (*cf* **greimich**), **bha grèim aice air làimh air** she was holding/gripping his hand, **bha e an grèim** he was held (*ie in captivity, custody*); **2** a bite, a bit, *esp in expr* **grèim bìdh** a bite, a morsel, **tha mi airson grèim bìdh a ghabhail** I fancy getting/having a bite to eat, **cha d' fhuair sinn**

grèim bìdh fad an latha we didn't get a bite to eat all day, *cf* **blasad 2**; **3** (*needlework*) a stitch

greimeil *see* **gramail**

greimich *vi, pres part* **a' greimeachadh**, (*with prep* **ri** *or* **air**) seize, grasp, *cf more usu* **gabh grèim air** (*see* **grèim 1**), **glac** *v*

greimire, greimire, greimirean *nm* a (table) fork, **sgian is greimire** a knife and (a) fork, *cf* **forc(a)**; **2** pliers

greis, greise, greisean *nf* a while, a time, **fad/car/airson greis** for a while/a time, **o chionn greis** a while ago, (*trad*) **greis air seinn/air pìobaireachd** a while (spent) singing/piping, *cf* **greiseag, treis**

grèis, *gen* **grèise** *nf* needlework, embroidery (*ie the activity*), **obair-ghrèise** *nf is the product*

greiseag, greiseig, greiseagan *nf* (*dimin of* **greis**) a short *or* little while, (*Sc*) a whilie, *cf* **greis, treis, ùine ghoirid** (*see* **ùine 2**)

Greugach, *gen & pl* **Greugaich** *nm* a Greek, *also as adj* **Greugach** Greek

Greugais *nf invar, used with art* **a' Ghreugais** Greek (*the language*)

greusaiche, greusaiche, greusaichean *nm* a shoemaker, a shoe-repairer, a cobbler

grian, grèine, grianan *nf, used with art* **a' ghrian** the sun, **solas na grèine** *m* sunlight, **gathan na grèine** *mpl* the sun's rays, **gath-grèine** *m* a sunbeam, **èirigh na grèine** *f* sunrise, **dol fodha/laighe na grèine** *f* sunset, **gabh** *v* **a' ghrian** sunbathe, **beum-grèine** *m* sunstroke, **càite fon ghrèin a bheil e?** where on earth (*lit* beneath the sun) is he?

grinn *adj* **1** elegant, fine (*in appearance*), **aodach grinn** fine/elegant clothing, *cf* **eireachdail, brèagha**; **2** pretty, *cf* **bòidheach**; **3** neat, *cf* **cuimir 2, sgiobalta 2, snasail**; **4** accurate, correct, **tomhas grinn** an accurate/correct measurement/calculation, *cf* **cruinn 2**

grinneal, *gen* **grinneil** *nm* **1** gravel, *cf* **morghan**; **2** bottom of sea, river or well, *cf* **grunnd 1**

grinneas, *gen* **grinneis** *nm* elegance, neatness, fineness

grìogag, grìogaig, grìogagan *nf* a bead (*on necklace etc*)

Grioglachan, *gen* **Grioglachain** *nm, used with art*, **an Grioglachan** the Pleiades

Griomasach, *gen & pl* **Griomasaich** *nm* someone from Grimsay (**Griomasaigh**), *also as adj* **Griomasach** of, from or pertaining to Grimsay

grìos, grìosa, grìosachan *nm* a grill (*ie for cooking*)

grìosaich *vt, pres part* **a' grìosachadh,** (*cookery*) grill

griù(th)lach & **griù(th)rach,** *gen* **griùlaich** *nf, used with art,* **a' ghriùlach** (the) measles, **tha e sa ghriùlaich** he has (the) measles

grod *adj* rotten, rotted, putrid, *cf* **lobhte**

grod *vi, pres part* **a' grodadh,** rot, putrefy, *cf* **lobh**

grodach *adj* (*fam*) grotty, (*fam, calque*) **grodach-coimhead** *adj* grotty-looking, *cf* **dràbhail**

grodadh, *gen* **grodaidh** *nm* **1** (*the act of*) rotting, putrefying; **2** rot, putrefaction; *cf* **lobhadh**

gròiseid, gròiseide, gròiseidean *nf* a gooseberry, (*Sc*) a groset

grosair, grosair, grosairean *nm* a grocer

gruag, gruaig, gruagan *nf* **1** hair, a head of hair (*human*), (*song*) **thug thu ghruag far mo chinn** you caused my hair to fall (*lit* took the hair from my head), *cf more usu* **falt**; **2** a wig (*also* **gruag-bhrèige**)

gruagach, gruagaich(e), gruagaichean *nf* (*now mostly in love songs*) a maid, a virgin, a girl *or* young woman, (*song*) **Gruagach Òg an Fhuilt Bhàin** The Fair-haired Young Maid/ Girl, *cf* **cuachag, maighdeann 1, nighean, nìghneag**

gruagaire, gruagaire, gruagairean *nm* a hairdresser

gruaidh, gruaidhe, gruaidhean *nf* a cheek, **bha dath nan ròsan air a gruaidh** her cheek was the colour of roses, *cf* **pluic,** & *trad* **lethcheann 1**

gruaim, *gen* **gruaime** *nf* **1** gloom, gloominess, melancholy, **is tu a dh'fhàg mi fo ghruaim** it's you who plunged me into gloom/left me melancholy, *cf* **bròn 1, mulad; 2** scowling, a scowl, frowning, a frown, **chuir e gruaim air** he scowled/frowned, *cf* **drèin, mùig, sgraing; 3** sulkiness, a sulk, *cf* **mùig; 4** grumpiness, ill-humour, **fo ghruaim** gloomy, in an ill humour

gruamach *adj* **1** gloomy, melancholy, morose, sullen, surly, **stuadhan gruamach** surly/sullen waves, **aghaidh ghruamach** a gloomy/morose face, *cf* **brònach, dubhach, gnù, muladach; 2** scowling, frowning; **3** sulky, sulking; **4** grumpy, grouchy, ill-humoured, *cf* **crost(a) 1, diombach 1, greannach 1**

grùdair(e), grùdaire, grùdairean *nm* a brewer; a distiller

grùdaireachd *nf invar* brewing; distilling

grùid, *gen* **grùide,** *nf* **1** lees, dregs, grounds, sediment (*in liquids*); **2** *in expr* **taigh-grùide** *m* a brewery

grunn, *gen* **gruinn** *nm* **1** a crowd, a group, **grunn dhaoine** a crowd of people; **2** (*fam*) many, a lot of, lots of, **chuir mi seachad grunn bhliadhnachan an sin** I spent a fair number of years there, *cf* **iomadach, iomadh 1, mòran 1, tòrr 2**

grunnan, grunnain, grunnanan *nm* (*dimin of* **grunn**) a group, a small number, a few (*persons or things*)

grunnd, *gen* **gruinnd** & **grunnda,** *pl* **grunndan** *nm* **1** the base, bed, bottom *or* ground of anything, **grunnd na mara** the bottom of the sea, the sea-bed, **grunnd glinne** a valley bottom, *cf* **bonn 2, grinneal 1, ìochdar; 2** (*occas*) ground (*ie land*), (*song*) **Flòdaigearraidh sgiamhach, càit 'eil d' fhiach de ghrunnd?** lovely Flodigarry, where is your equal as a piece of ground?, *cf* **fearann, talamh 3**

grùnsgal, *gen* **grùnsgail** *nm* growling, a growl, *cf* **dranndail**

gruth, *gen* **grutha** *nm* (*dairying*) curd(s), crowdie, *cf* **slaman**

grùthan, grùthain, grùthanan *nm* (*anat*) a liver (*often of animal*), *cf* **adha**

gu[1] **1** *a particle placed before an adj to form an adv, eg* **gu mòr** greatly, **gu tric** frequently, often, **gu mì-fhortanach** unfortunately, **tha mi gu math** I'm well, **tha i gu bochd** she's poorly; **2** (*trad*) *found before first of a pair of adjectives, eg* **bha iad gu muladach brònach** they were sad and melancholy

gu[2] *prep* (*The prep prons formed with* **gu,** *in the order first, second, third person singular, first, second, third person plural, and with the reflexive/emphatic particles in brackets, are as follows:* **thugam(sa), thugad(sa), thuige(san), thuice(se), thugainn(e), thugaibh(se), thuca(san)** *to me, to you* (*fam*), *etc*) **1** to, up to, towards, **cuiridh mi leabhar thuice** I'll send a book to her, **chaidh e gu Glaschu** he went to (*ie to the outskirts of*) Glasgow (*cf* **chaidh e do Ghlaschu** he went to (*ie into*) Glasgow); *Note:* **gu** *plus the art becomes* **chun** *or* **thun** *prep* (*with gen*), **chaidh e chun a' bhaile** he went to the town, *or* he went towards the town, *cf* **ionnsaigh 3; 2** (*occas for time*) **chan fhad' thuige a-nis** it won't be long now (*lit* not long to/until it), **cha do thachair e chun a seo** it hasn't happened up to now/so far/until now, *cf* **gu ruige 2; 3** to, for (*with implication of intention*), **thig gam** (*for* **gu mo**) **fhaicinn** come to see me (*lit or* for my seeing), **thàinig e dhachaigh gu 'bhiadh** he came home to eat (*lit* to his food), *cf* **airson 5**; **4** on the point of, about to, almost, nearly, **tha mi gu bhith deiseil** I'm almost/ just about ready (*ie up to the point of being ready*), **tha sinn gu falbh** we're (just) about to go, **bha e gus a mhùn a chall ag èisteachd riutha** he was nearly wetting himself listening to them

gu³ & **gus** *prep* until, till, (*with dat*), **fanaidh sinn gu sia uairean** we'll wait/stay till six o'clock, **chan urrainn dhomh a ghleidheadh gus a-màireach** I can't keep/ save it until tomorrow

gual, *gen* **guail** *nm* coal

gualan, gualain, gualanan *nm* carbon

gualann & **gualainn**, *gen* **gualainn** & **guailne**, *pl* **guailnean** & **guaillean** *nf* a shoulder, **poca air a ghualainn** a sack on his shoulder, **gualainn ri gualainn** shoulder to shoulder, *cf* *less usu* **slinnean**; **2** a shoulder of a hill, **leig/ ghabh iad an anail an uair a ràinig iad gualann na beinne** they took a rest/a breather when they reached the shoulder of the mountain

gual-fiodha, *gen* **guail-fhiodha** *nm* charcoal

guanach *adj* **1** giddy, scatter-brained, skittish, **na h-èildean guanach** the giddy/skittish hinds, **caileag ghuanach** a giddy/scatter-brained girl, **òigridh ghuanach** happy-go-lucky young folk; **2** coquettish

guanag, guanaig, guanagan *nf* **1** a giddy or scatter-brained girl; **2** a coquettish girl

gu buileach *see* **buileach**

gucag, gucaig, gucagan *nf* **1** (*botany*) a bud; **2** a bubble

gucag-uighe, gucaig-uighe, gucagan-uighe *nf* an egg-cup

gu dè *see* **dè 3**

gu dearbh *adv* **1** certainly, definitely, indeed, **a bheil thu gu math? tha gu dearbh!** are you well? I certainly am!, I am indeed! **am bi thu ann? bithidh gu dearbh!** will you be there? definitely! *cf* **fios 4**; **2** *as intensifying element* **gu dearbh fhèin** extremely, **bha sin gu dearbh fhèin math** that was extremely good/ very good indeed, *cf* **uabhasach 2**

guga, guga, gugaichean *nm* a young gannet or solan goose (*trad gathered from cliffs & stacks for food*), *cf* **sùlaire**

guidh *vi, pres part* **a' guidhe**, **1** beg, beseech, entreat, plead, pray, **tha mi a' guidhe ort fuireach!** I'm begging/pleading with you to stay!, **ghuidh e oirnn a leigeil ma/mu sgaoil** he begged us to let him go/set him free; **2** wish (*a situation, benefit etc upon someone*), **guidhidh mi mallachd air** I wish a curse on him, **a' guidhe Nollaig Chridheil dha**

wishing him a Happy Christmas, **guidheam slàint' is sonas dhut** I wish you health and happiness; **3** (*relig*) pray, *cf more usu* **dèan ùrnaigh** (*see* **ùrnaigh**)

guidhe, guidhe, guidheachan *nmf* **1** (*the act of*) beseeching, praying etc (*see senses of* **guidh** *v*); **2** an entreaty, a plea, an appeal; **3** a wish, **droch ghuidhe** an ill wish; **4** (*relig*) a prayer, *cf more usu* **ùrnaigh**

guidheam *obs & trad present, see* **guidh** *v*

guil *vi, pres part* **a' gul**, *also* **gail** *vi, pres part* **a' gal**, weep, cry, (*poem*) **Èirinn a' Gul** Ireland Weeping, *cf* **caoin 2**

guilbneach, *gen & pl* **guilbnich** *nmf* a curlew

guin, guin, guinean *nm* **1** a sting (*part of bee etc*), *cf* **gath 1**; **2** a sting (*ie the wound inflicted*); **3** a pang

guin *vt, pres part* **a' guineadh**, sting, **ghuin speach mi** a wasp stung me, *cf* **cuir gath ann** (*see* **gath 1**)

guineach *adj* **1** sharp, bitter, acerbic, acrimonious (*remarks, character etc*); **2** stinging, cutting, wounding, hurtful (*remarks etc*); *cf* **geur 4**, **searbh 3**

guineadh, *gen* **guinidh** *nm* (*the act of*) stinging

guir *vti, pres part* **a' gur** (*vi, of hen etc*) brood, (*vti*), hatch (*eggs*)

guirean, guirein, guireanan *nm* **1** a pimple, a pustule, a spot, (*Sc*) a plook, *cf* **cnàimhseag 1**, **plucan 1**; **2 guirean dubh** a blackhead

gul, *gen* **guil** *nm*, *also* **gal**, *gen* **gail** *nm*, (*the act of*) weeping, crying (*see* **guil** *v*)

gu lèir *adv with adjectival force*, entire, complete, whole, **chaidh an t-arm gu lèir a chur an sàs** the entire/complete/whole army was captured, *cf* **fad 3**

gu leòr *see* **leòr 2**

gu leth *see* **leth 3**

gum *see* **gun** *conj*

gun *conj*, **gum** *before b, f, m, p, also in forms* **gu, nach** (*neg*) & (*with v* **is**) **gur** & **guma** (*see examples*), that, **tha mi toilichte gun tàinig sibh** I'm glad (that) you came, **'s cinnteach gu bheil i air chall** it's certain/definite that she's lost, **chan eil mi airson gum bi thu nad aonar** I don't want you to be on your own, **thuirt iad nach robh iad deiseil** they said (that) they weren't ready, **an e òr a th' ann? cha chreid mi gur e** is it gold? I don't think (that) it is, I don't think so, (*trad*) *expr wishes etc* (*prov*) **guma fada bhios tu beò agus ceò bhàrr do thaighe!** (*also* **guma fada bèo thu is ceò às do thaigh**) lang may ye live an yer lum(b) reek!, (*song*) **fallain gum bi thu** may you be in good health

gun *prep* (*takes nom, lenites following cons except for d, n & t*) **1** without, **gun fhois** without peace/rest, **càraid gun chlann** a childless couple, **thig gun dàil** come without delay, (*prov*) **fainne mun mheur 's gun snàthainn mun mhàs** a ring around the finger and not a stitch about the bum (*corres to Sc* 'fur coat an nae knickers'), *cf* **às aonais**; **2** *in neg verbal exprs* **dh'iarr e orm gun a bhith mì-mhodhail** he asked me not to be rude, **cha b' urrainn dhi gun a bhith a' gàireachdainn** she couldn't help laughing, **tha am bus gun tighinn** the bus hasn't come, (*calque*) **gun ach beagan dhiubh ainmeachadh** to name but a few of them; **3** *in conj* **gun fhios nach** in case *see* **fios 5**

gùn, gùin, gùintean *nm* a gown, **gùn-oidhche** a nightgown

gunna, gunna, gunnaichean *nm* a gun

gunnair, gunnair, gunnairean *nm* a gunner

gurraban, *gen* **gurrabain** *nm* crouching, a crouch, a crouching position, *cf* **crùbagan, crùban**

gu ruige *prep* (*with nom*) **1** (*of distance, space*) up to, as far as, **chaidh iad romhpa gu ruige an druim** they went on as far as the ridge, **thàinig na tuiltean gu ruige an taigh** the floods came (right) up to the house; **2** (*of time*) up to, until, **cha do rinn sinn mearachdan gu ruige seo** we haven't made any mistakes so far/up to now, **bidh sinn trang gu ruige a' Bhliadhna Ùr** we'll be busy until/(right) up to New Year, *cf* **gu²** **2**

gus¹, gus am, gus an, gus nach, *conj* to, in order to, so that, **cheannaich i sguab gus an taigh a ghlanadh** she bought a broom (in order) to clean the house (*cf* **a-chum** 1), **fhuair e obair bheag gus am biodh airgead-pòcaid aige** he found a little job so that he would have some pocket money, **seo an seòladh againn gus an urrainn dhut an taigh a lorg** here's our address so that you can find the house, **thug a màthair pìos dhi gus nach biodh an t-acras oirre** her mother gave her a piece so that she wouldn't be hungry, *cf* **dòigh 5, los 2** & *less trad* **airson 5**

gus², gus am, gus an, gus nach, *conj* until, **cha deasaich mi am biadh gus an tig thu dhachaigh** I won't get the meal ready until you come home, **cosnaidh mi airgead gus am bi gu leòr againn dheth** I'll earn money until we've got enough of it, **cùm e gus nach bi feum agad air** keep it until you don't need it

guth, gutha, guthan *nm* **1** a voice, **guth binn** a sweet voice, **ann an guth ìosal** in a low voice; **2** news, a word, **ciamar a chaidh do Chalum? cha chuala mi guth mu dheidhinn** how did Calum get on? I haven't heard a thing/a word/any news about him, *cf* **fios 3**; **3** a mention, an allusion, **thoir** *v* **guth air rudeigin** mention/allude to something, **tha na peuran pailt am-bliadhna, gun ghuth air na h-ùbhlan** pears are plentiful this year, not to mention/never mind apples, *cf* **iomradh 1, tarraing 5**

gu tur *see* **tur 2**

H

hàidraidean, *gen* **hàidraidein** *nm* hydrogen
halò *excl* hello, hullo
heactair, heactair, heactairean *nm* a hectare
Hearach (*also* **Tearach**), *gen & pl* **Hearaich**
   nm someone from Harris, *also as adj*
   Hearach of, from or pertaining to Harris
Hearadh *nf invar, used with art,* **Na Hearadh**
   Harris, the Island of Harris
heileacopta(i)r, heileacoptair,
   heileacoptaran *nm* a helicopter

Hiort (*also* **Hirt** & **Tirt**) *nf invar* St Kilda
Hiortach (*also* **Hirteach** & **Tirteach**), *gen & pl*
   Hiortaich *nm* a St Kildan, someone from
   St Kilda, *also as adj* **Hiortach** of, from or
   pertaining to St Kilda
hòro-gheallaidh *nm invar* **1** (*fam*) a boisterous
   party, ceilidh, get-together etc, a 'knees-up',
   a hoolie; a celebration; **2** *in expr* (*fam*) **cha**
   toir mi hòro-gheallaidh air I don't give a
   damn/a fig/a bugger for it/him

i *pron f sing, emph form* **ise**, she, her, (*representing nf*) it, **chunnaic i i** she saw her/ it, **bha ad agam uaireigin ach chaill mi i** I had a hat once but I lost it

iad *nm, see* **eud**

iad *pron m & f pl, emph form* **iadsan**, they, them

iadach *adj & noun see* **eudach**

iadh & **iath** *vt, pres part* **ag iadhadh**, surround, circle, enclose, **dh'iadh na saighdearan e** the soldiers surrounded him

iadh-shlat & **iath-shlat**, *gen* **iadh-shlait** *nf* honeysuckle

iall, **èille**, **iallan** *nf* a thong, a (dog's) lead *or* leash, a strap, a strop, **iall bròige** a shoe-lace (*cf* **barrall**)

ialtag, ialtaig, ialtagan *nf* a bat (*ie the animal*)

iar *nf invar* west, **tha sinn a' dol an iar** we're going west(wards), (*story collection*) **Oiteagan on Iar** Breezes from the West, *Note that* **an** *of* **an iar** *does not behave as an article in the following exprs* **an àird(e) an iar** the west(*ie compass direction*), **an taobh an iar** the west coast/west side of the country, **Na h-Eileanan an Iar** The Western Isles, *see* **sear** & *cf* **deas 1**, **ear, siar, tuath¹**

iar- 1 *a prefix corres to Eng* under-, vice-, deputy, (*Sc*) depute, *eg* **iar-chlèireach** *m* an under-secretary, **iar-stiùiriche** *m* a deputy director, **iar-cheann-suidhe** *m* a vice-president (*of company*); 2 *a prefix corres to Eng* post-, *eg* **iar-cheumnaiche** *m* a postgraduate; 3 (*in family relationships*) great-, **iar-ogha** *m* a great-grandchild

iarann, iarainn, iarannan *nm* 1 iron, (*song*) **seòmraichean glaiste le claspaichean iarainn** rooms locked with clasps of iron; 2 (*household*) an iron

iargalt(a) *adj* churlish, surly, *cf* **gnù, mùgach**

iarla, iarla, iarlan *nm* an earl, (*song*) **mhic iarla nam bratach bàna** son (*voc*) of the earl of the white banners

iarmad, iarmaid, iarmadan *nm* a remnant, a residue, *cf more usu* **fuidheall 1**

iarmailt, iarmailt, iarmailtean *nf, used with art*, **an iarmailt** the firmament, the sky, the skies, the heavens, *cf* **nèamh 2, speur 2**

iarnaich *vti, pres part* **ag iarnachadh**, *also* **iarnaig** *vti, pres part* **ag iarnaigeadh**, iron (*clothes etc*)

iarnachadh *gen* **iarnachaidh** *nm, also* **iarnaigeadh** *gen* **iarnaigidh** *nm*, 1 (*the act of*) ironing; 2 (*a batch of*) ironing

iar-ogha *see* **iar- 3**

iarr *vt, pres part* **ag iarraidh**, 1 want, require, **a bheil thu ag iarraidh cofaidh?** do you want/ would you like a/some coffee? **bha a' chlann ag iarraidh orm piseag a cheannach** the children wanted me to buy a kitten, *cf* **dìth 2**, **miannaich 1, togair 1**; 2 ask, ask for, request, demand, **dh'iarr iad àrdachadh pàighidh** they asked for/demanded a pay rise, **dh'iarr i orm an doras a dhùnadh** she asked me to shut the door; 3 ask, invite, **chan iarr sinn oirbh a thighinn a-steach** we won't ask/invite you to come in, **dh'iarr iad mi gu pàrtaidh** they asked/invited me to a party (*cf* **fiathaich**, **thoir cuireadh do** (*see* **cuireadh**)); 4 *in expr* **rach** *v* **a dh'iarraidh rudeigin** go to/and get something, go to/and fetch something

iarraidh, iarraidh, iarraidhean *nm* 1 (*the act of*) wanting, asking etc (*see senses of* **iarr** *v*); 2 a request, *cf more usu* **iarr(a)tas 1**; 3 an invitation, (*song*) **thig trì nithean gun iarraidh . . .** three things come unasked/ uninvited . . . , *cf more usu* **cuireadh**

iarr(a)tas, iarr(a)tais, iarr(a)tasan *nm* 1 a request, a demand, *cf less usu* **iarraidh 2**; 2 an application(*for job etc*), **foirm iarr(a)tais** *m* an application form

iasad, iasaid, iasadan *nm* borrowing, a loan, **iasad banca** a bank loan, **gabh/faigh** *v* **rudeigin air iasad** borrow something, get something on loan, **faigh/thoir** *v* **iasad de rudeigin** get/give a loan/a lend of something, borrow/lend something, (*prov*) **cha bhi each-iasaid sgìth a-chaoidh** a borrowed horse never gets tired

iasg (*sing & coll*), *gen & pl* **èisg** *nm* fish, a fish, **is toigh leam iasg** I like fish, (*prov*) **glac thusa foighidinn is glacaidh tu iasg** catch yourself some patience and you'll catch fish

iasgach, *gen* **iasgaich** *nm* **1** (*the act & activity of*) fishing (*deep sea & inshore*), **tha a h-athair ris an iasgach** her father's a fisherman/at the fishing, **bàt'-iasgaich** *m* a fishing-boat; **2** (*as hobby etc*; *also* **iasgach-slàite**) fishing, angling, **slat-iasgaich** *f* a fishing rod, *cf* **breacach**

iasgaich *vt, pres part* **ag iasgach(d)**, fish, **nam bhalach bhithinn ri/ag iasgach fad na h-ùine** as a boy I'd be fishing all the time

iasgair, iasgair, iasgairean *nm*, an angler, a fisherman, (*Sc*) a fisher

iath *see* **iadh**

idir *adv* **1** at all, (*usu with neg verb*) **a bheil thu sgìth? chan eil idir!** Are you tired? not at all!, not in the least!, *often duplicated for emphasis* **cha dèan sin a' chùis idir idir!** there's no way that will do/suffice!; **2** *in emph question* **càit idir an deach e?** where on earth did he go? *cf* **fon ghrèin** (*see* **grian**), **air an t-saoghal** (*see* **saoghal 1**)

ifrinn, ifrinn, ifrinnean *nf* hell, a hell, *cf less usu* **iutharn(a)**

ifrinneach *adj* hellish, infernal

ìghne, ìghnean *see* **nighean**

Ìle *nf invar* Islay, (*song*) **'s ann an Ìle ghorm an fheòir a rugadh mi 's a thogadh mi** it was in green grassy Islay that I was born and raised

Ìleach, *gen & pl* **Ìlich** *nm* someone from Islay, *also as adj* **Ìleach** of, from or pertaining to Islay

ìm, *gen* **ime** *nm* butter, (*prov*) **bu dual don bhlàthaich tòchd an ime** it's only to be expected that buttermilk should smell of butter

imcheist, imcheist, imcheistean *nf* **1** anxiety, **fo imcheist** *adv* anxious, *cf* **cùram 2**, **iomagain 1**; **2** perplexity, doubt, a dilemma, **an/fo imcheist** *adv* perplexed, in doubt, in a dilemma, **cuir** *v* **an imcheist** perplex

imcheisteach *adj* **1** anxious, worrying, perplexed, perplexing, *cf* **an/fo imcheist** (*see* **imcheist 1 & 2**), **iomagaineach**

imich *vi, pres part* **ag imeachd**, **1** depart, leave, go, *cf more usu* **falbh 1**; **2** go, journey, move (*from one place to another*), (*song*) **'s mi ri imeachd nam aonar anns an òg-mhadainn Mhàirt** as I walked out alone in the morning freshness of March, *cf more usu* **rach 1, triall**

imleag, imleige, imleagan *nf* a navel, a belly-button

imlich, *gen* **imliche** *nf* **1** (*the act of*) licking, lapping; **2** a lick

imlich *vt, pres part* **ag imlich**, lick, lap

imnidh, *gen* **imnidhe**, *also* **iomnaidh** *gen* **iomnaidhe**, *nf* solicitude, anxiety, *cf* **iomagain 2**

impidh, impidhe, impidhean *nm* persuasion, entreaty, an entreaty, urging, *esp in expr* **cuir** *v* **impidh air** persuade, urge, entreat, **chuir iad impidh orm mo dhreuchd a leigeil dhìom** they urged me to give up my job/to retire

impidheach *adj* persuasive, urging

impis *see* **an impis**

imrich, imriche, imrichean *nf* **1** (*the act of*) moving (*house etc*), (*Sc*) flitting; **2** a removal, a flitting, **dèan** *v* **imrich** move house, (*Sc*) flit (*cf* **imrich** *vi* **2**); **2** migration

imrich *vi, pres part* **ag imrich(d) & ag imreacheadh**, **1** move house, (*Sc*) flit, *cf* **imrich** *n* **2**; **2** migrate

inbhe, inbhe, inbhean *nf* **1** (*in hierarchy, progression etc*) rank, dignity, status, a rank, a level (*of rank, attainment, ability*), **mòr-inbhe** eminence, high rank or attainment, **comharradh inbhe** a status symbol, *cf* **ìre 1, seasamh 4**; **2** adulthood, maturity, the state of being grown up/fully grown, **thig** *v* **gu inbhe** grow up, reach adulthood, *cf* **ìre 2**

inbheach *adj* adult, grown-up, fully grown, mature, **oileanach inbheach** *m* a mature student

inbheach, *gen & pl* **inbhich** *nm* an adult, a grown-up, a fully grown individual

inbheil *adj* eminent, high-ranking

inbhidh *adj* adult, **foghlam inbhidh** adult education

inbhidheachd *nf invar* puberty

inbhir, inbhir, inbhirean *nm* a confluence, the place where watercourses meet or a watercourse joins a loch etc, the mouth of a watercourse, *now in placenames, occurring as* Inver-, Inner-, **Inbhir Nis** Inverness, the mouth of the River Ness; *also* an estuary

inc *nmf invar* ink, *cf* **dubh** *n* **2**

ìne, ìne, ìnean, *also* (*more trad*) **iong(n)a, ingne, ingnean**, *nf* **1** a nail (*of finger, toe*), (*prov*) **is ann air ìnean a dh'aithnichear duine-uasal** it's by his nails that a gentleman/nobleman can be recognised; **2** a claw, a talon (*of birds*), *cf* **spuir**; **3** a hoof (*of horse, cattle etc*), *cf* **ladhar**

inneal, inneil, innealan *nm* **1** a machine, **inneal-nighe & inneal-nigheadaireachd** a washing machine, *cf* **beart 2**; **2** *for devices of various kinds eg* **inneal-smàlaidh** a fire extinguisher, **inneal-chlàr** a record-player, inneal-ciùil a musical instrument; 3 a tool, an implement, *cf* ball-acainn (*see* acainn 1)

innealach *adj* mechanical

innean, innein, inneanan *nm* an anvil

inneir & innear, *gen* innearach *nf* (*agric*) dung, manure, (*prov*) dùnan math innearach, màthair na ciste-mine a good heap of dung (is) the mother of the meal-kist, *cf* buachar, todhar

innidh *nf invar* a bowel, bowels, innards, intestines, *cf* caolan, greallach, mionach 1

innis, innse, innsean *nf* 1 an island, *cf more usu* eilean; 2 low-lying ground or meadowland, *esp* near water, (*Sc*) a haugh, (*song*) innis nam bò the haugh of the cattle

innis *vti, pres part* ag innseadh & ag innse, (*with prep* do) tell, inform, relate, recount, mar a dh'innis mi dhuibh as I told you, innis dhomh mu dheidhinn! tell me about it/him!, innsidh mi na tha a dh'fhios agam I'll tell/ relate what I know, leis an fhìrinn innse, cha robh e cho math sin to tell the truth, it wasn't that good, innis sgeulachd tell a story

Innis Tìle *nf* Iceland

innleachadh, *gen* innleachaidh *nm* (*the act of*) inventing, conceiving, contriving etc (*see senses of* innlich *v*)

innleachd, innleachd, innleachdan *nf* 1 ingenuity, invention, an invention, (*prov*) nì airc innleachd necessity is the mother of (*lit* makes/creates) invention, *cf* tionnsgal 2; 2 artfulness, resourcefulness, cunning; 3 intelligence, *cf* inntinn 1, tuigse 1; 4 a stratagem, a plot, a plan, a ploy, ro-innleachd a strategy, *cf* cuilbheart; 5 a (*mechanical*) device, a machine, *cf more usu* inneal 1 & 2

innleachdach *adj* 1 ingenious, inventive, *cf* tionnsgalach 1; 2 artful, resourceful, adroit, cunning, *cf* carach 1; 3 intelligent, *cf* tuigseach 1

innleadair, innleadair, innleadairean *nm* an engineer, a mechanic, innleadair-dealain an electrical engineer, innleadair-thogalach a civil engineer

innleadaireachd *nf invar* engineering

innlich *vt, pres part* ag innleachadh, invent, devise, plan, plot, hatch (*a plot etc*), contrive, conceive, create, engineer (*a plan, a stratagem, a mental or mechanical device of some kind*), dh'innlich e inneal ùr airson arbhar a bhuain he invented/devised/conceived a new machine for harvesting corn, innlich cuilbheart conceive/devise a trick/a stratagem, *cf* cruthaich, dealbh *v* 3, tionnsgail

Innseachan *nmpl, used with art* Na h-Innseachan India, *also* the Indies

innse(adh), *gen* innsidh *nm* (*the act of*) telling, informing etc (*see senses of* innis *v*)

Innseanach, *gen & pl* Innseanaich *nm* someone from India, an Indian, *also as adj* Innseanach Indian

Innse Gall *fpl* the Hebrides

innte (*emph form* inntese) *prep pron*, see an *prep*

inntinn, inntinn, inntinnean *nf* 1 mind (*as seat of knowledge & intelligence*), intellect, tha inntinn mhath aice she's got a good mind, comas inntinn *m* mental/intellectual ability, mental powers, intellectual capacity, *cf* eanchainn 2; 2 mind (*as seat of memory, feeling etc*), bha i rud beag sìos na h-inntinn she was a bit down/a bit depressed

inntinneach *adj* 1 interesting, leabhar/ cuspair/duine inntinneach an interesting book/subject/man; 2 (*also* inntinneil) intellectual, mental, to do with the mind

inntrig *vi, pres part* ag inntrigeadh, enter, go in

inntrigeadh, inntrigidh, inntrigidhean *nm* 1 (*the act of*) entering, doras inntrigidh an entrance/access door; 2 (*mainly abstr*) entrance, entry, access, deuchainn inntrigidh *f* an entrance exam/test, còir inntrigidh *f* right of entry/access

ìobair *vt, pres part* ag ìobradh, (*relig*) sacrifice, offer (up) as a sacrifice

ìobairt, ìobairte, ìobairtean *nf* (*relig*) a sacrifice, a sacrificial offering

ìoc, *gen & pl* ìce *nm* payment, a payment, *cf more usu* dìo(gh)ladh 2, pàigheadh

ìoc *vti, pres part* ag ìocadh, pay, *cf more usu* pàigh *v* 1

ìochd *nf invar* compassion, mercy, clemency, pity, humaneness, *cf* daonnachd, tròcair, truacantas, truas

ìochdar, ìochdair, ìochdaran *nm* (*opposite of* uachdar), bottom, base, foundation, lowest part of anything, am beul-ìochdair the lower lip, *cf* bonn 1

ìochd(a)rach *adj* (*opposite of* uachd(a)rach), 1 lower, nether, bottom; 2 inferior, subordinate; *cf* (n)as (etc) ìsle (*comp of* ìosal)

ìochdaran, *gen & pl* ìochdarain *nm* (*opposite of* uachdaran), 1 an inferior, a subordinate, an underling; 2 (*of monarchy etc*) a subject

ìochdaranachd *nf invar* inferiority

ìochdmhor *adj* merciful, compassionate, *cf* tròcaireach, truacanta

ìocshlaint, ìocshlainte, ìocshlaintean *nf* a medicine, a remedy, *cf* **leigheas 2**

iodhal, iodhail, iodhalan *nm* an idol, *cf* **ìomhaigh 3**

iodhlann, iodhlainn, iodhlannan *nf* (*agric*) a corn-yard, a stackyard

iolach, *gen & pl* **iolaich** *nf* a shout, a cheer, **dèan/tog** *v* **iolach** shout, cheer, *cf more usu* **èigh** *n*, **glaodh¹** *n*

iolair(e), iolaire, iolairean *nf* an eagle, **iolair(e) bhuidhe** a golden eagle

iolra, iolra, iolran *nm, also as adj* **iolra,** (*gram*) plural, a plural, **ainmear iolra** a plural noun

ioma- *a prefix corres to Eng* multi-, poly-, *eg* **ioma-chànanach** *adj* multilingual, polyglot, (*IT etc*) **ioma-mheadhan** *adj* multimedia, **ioma-thìreach** *adj* multinational, **ioma-phòsadh** *m* polygamy, **ioma-sheòrsach** *adj* heterogenous, *cf* **iomadh 2**

iomadach *adj* many, many a, *Note: precedes the noun, which is in the nom sing* (*radical*); **rinn mi iomadach uair e** I did it often/many a time, **rudan de dh'iomadach seòrsa** things of many kinds, all sorts of things, *cf less usu* **iomadh 1**

iomadaich, *pres part* **ag iomadachadh,** *vt* (*maths*) multiply (**le** by)

iomadh *adj* **1** many, many a, *Note: precedes the noun, which is in the nom sing* (*radical*); **dh'fheuch iomadh duine e** many a man/ many men tried it, **iomadh là** many a day, many days, *cf more usu* **iomadach; 2** *occas in compound adjs eg* **iomadh-fhillte** complex, complicated, abstruse, manifold, *cf* **ioma-**

iomagain, iomagaine, iomagainean *nf* **1** anxiety, worry, **fo iomagain** anxious, worried, troubled, *cf* **cùram 2, dragh 3, imcheist 1; 2** solicitude, *cf* **imnidh**

iomagaineach *adj* **1** worried, anxious, prone to worry or anxiety, *cf* **cùramach 2; 2** worrying, causing worry or anxiety, *cf* **draghail;** *cf* **imcheisteach**

iomain, *gen* **iomaine** *nf* shinty, *cf* **camanachd**

iomain *vt, pres part* **ag iomain, 1** drive, drive on, urge on (*esp livestock*), *cf* **greas 2; 2** drive, propel (*machinery etc*), **stuth-iomain** propellant, **dh'iomaineadh an t-inneal le smùid** the machine was driven by steam; **3** propel (*a ball in a game, esp shinty*); **4** (*as vi*) play a ball game (*esp shinty*), **bha na gillean ag iomain** the lads were playing shinty

iomair *vti, pres part* **ag iomramh,** row (*a boat*), **ag iomramh an aon ràimh** pulling/working together, co-operating, (*lit* rowing/pulling the same oar)

iomair *vt, pres part* **ag iomairt,** use, employ, wield (*weapon, tool etc*), **ag iomairt ùird/ bhiodagan** wielding a hammer/dirks, *cf more usu* **cleachd 1, làimhsich 3**

iomairt, iomairte, iomairtean *nf* **1** (*the act of*) using, employing, wielding (*see* **iomair** *vt*); **2** an effort, an endeavour, a struggle (*in aid of something, to achieve something*), a campaign; **3 Iomairt na Gàidhealtachd** Highlands and Islands Enterprise

iomall, iomaill, iomallan *nm* **1** an edge, a border, a margin, an extremity, a limit, a verge, a fringe, a periphery, **iomall na coille** the edge of the wood, **iomall na dùthcha** the limits/ fringes of the country, **iomall a' bhaile** the suburbs/outskirts of the town, **fearann iomaill** marginal land, *cf* **crìoch 2, oir** *n* **1; 2** a rim, a lip (*of jug etc*), **iomall na poite** the rim of the pot, *cf* **oir** *n* **2**

iomallach *adj*, remote, isolated, distant, on the margins, peripheral, **ceàrnaidhean iomallach** remote areas/districts

iomchaidh & iomchuidh *adj* **1** suitable, *cf more usu* **freagarrach; 2** fitting, decent, proper, acceptable, *cf* **cothromach; 3** advisable

iomchair *vt, pres part* **ag iomchar,** bear, carry, transport, *cf more usu* **giùlain 1**

iomchar, *gen* **iomchair** *nm* **1** (*the act of*) bearing etc (*see senses of* **iomchair** *v*), **neach-iomchair** *m* a bearer, *cf more usu* **giùlan; 2** comportment, behaviour, conduct, *cf more usu* **dol-a-mach, giùlan**

ìomhaigh, ìomhaigh, ìomhaighean *nf* **1** an image or physical representation of something or someone (*in art, sculpture etc*), a likeness; **2** a visual image (*in mirror, lens etc*); **3** (*relig*) an image, an idol, *cf* **iodhal; 4** (*publicity etc*) an image, a profile, **leasaich** *v* **ìomhaigh na companaidh** improve the company's image, **tog** *v* **ìomhaigh a' phàrtaidh** raise the party's profile; **5** (*Lit*) an image

iomlaid, iomlaid, iomlaidean *nf* **1** (*trad*) exchange, barter, *cf more usu* **malairt 2; 2** *now usu* change (*ie money*), **iomlaid nota** change for a pound, **iomlaid à nota** change from a pound, **thug mi dà nota dha ach cha d' fhuair mi iomlaid** I gave him two pounds but I didn't get any change

iomlan *adj* **1** (*abstr & con*) complete, entire, whole, absolute, **mòr-chùid iomlan** an absolute majority, **chan eil a' charragh iomlan** the stone isn't complete, *cf* **slàn 4; 2** *as adv* **gu h-iomlan** absolutely, entirely, fully, completely, totally, quite, *cf* **buileach, tur 2**

iomlan, *gen* **iomlain** *nm* all *or* the whole of anything, **a bheil thu ag iarraidh an iomlain (dheth)?** do you want all/the whole of it?

iomnaidh *see* **imnidh**

iompachadh, iompachaidh, iompachaidhean *nm* **1** (*the act of*) converting, persuading etc (*see senses of* **iompaich** *v*); **2** (*esp relig*) conversion, a conversion

iompachan, *gen & pl* **iompachain** *nm* (*relig etc*) a convert, a neophyte

iompaich *vt, pres part* **ag iompachadh, 1** (*relig*) convert, **chaidh a h-iompachadh** she was converted, *cf* **cùram 3**; **2** persuade, cause someone to change his/her opinion or mind, *cf* **cuir impidh air** (*see* **impidh**)

ìompaire, ìompaire, ìompairean *nm* an emperor, **ban-ìompaire** *f* an empress

ìompaireachd, ìompaireachd, ìompaireachdan *nf* empire, an empire

ìompaireil *adj* imperial

iomradh, iomraidh, iomraidhean *nm* **1** mentioning, a mention, a remark, an allusion, a reference (**air** to), **cha tug e iomradh air an teaghlach aige** he didn't mention his family, *cf* **guth 3, tarraing 5**; **2** a report, an account, a commentary, **tha iomradh air an stailc sa phàipear-naidheachd** there's an account of the strike in the paper, *cf* **aithris** *n* **1**

iomraiteach *adj* (*esp persons*) well-known, celebrated, famous, renowned, notorious, *cf* **ainmeil, cliùiteach**

iomrall, iomraill, iomrallan *nm* **1** error, a mistake, an error, *cf more usu* **mearachd**; **2** wandering, straying, **air iomrall** *adv* astray, wandering, *cf* **seachran 1**; **3** *in expr* **rach** *v* **air iomrall** go astray (*phys, morally*), *also* make a mistake, err, go wrong

iomrallach *adj* mistaken, wrong, erroneous, *cf* **mearachdach**

iomramh, *gen* **iomraimh** *nm* (*the act of*) rowing (*a boat*) (*see* **iomair** *vti*)

ion- 1 *a prefix corres to Eng* -able, -ible, *eg* **ion-ithe** *adj* eatable, edible, **ion-dhèanta** *adj* feasible, possible, practicable, *cf* **so-**; **2** *occas corres to Eng* worthy of, fit for, *eg* **ionmholta** *adj* praiseworthy

ionad, ionaid, ionadan *nm* **1** (*trad*) a place, a spot, *cf* **àite 1, bad 1**; **2** (*now often*) a building where a particular activity is based or administered, a centre, an agency; **ionad-latha** (*for pensioners etc*) a day centre, **ionad-obrach** a job centre, *also* (*IT*) a work station, **ionad-slàinte** a health centre, **ionad-spòrsa** a sports centre/complex, **ionad-stiùiridh** a management centre, **Ionad airson Eòlas-**

dìona Centre for Defence Studies, *cf* **taigh 3; 3** (*IT*) a site, **ionad eadar-lìn** an internet site

ionadail *adj* local, **ùghdarras ionadail** *m* a local authority, **eachdraidh ionadail** *f* local history

ionaltair *vi, pres part* **ag ionaltradh,** (*livestock*) graze

ionaltradh, ionaltraidh, ionaltraidhean *nm* **1** (*the act of*) grazing; **2** grazing (*ie land*), pasture, a pasture, *cf* **clua(i)n**

ionann & ionnan *adj* same, alike, similar, identical, *takes the v* **is, chan ionann thusa is mise** you and I are not the same/are different, **cha b' ionann an uair a bha sinn òg** it wasn't the same when we were young, *in expr* **ionann agus** just/exactly like, the same as, identical with, *cf* **co-ionann, coltach 2; 2** (*maths*) equal, **is ionann X is Y** X equals/is equal to Y

ionga *see* **ìne**

iongantach *adj* strange, surprising, amazing, wonderful, marvellous, phenomenal, *cf* **mìorbhaileach,** & *less strong* **neònach**

iongantas, iongantais, iongantasan *nm* **1** amazement, wonder, **gabh** *v* **iongantas** be amazed; **2** a wonder, an amazing thing or event, a phenomenon, *cf* **mìorbhail 1**; *cf less strong* **iongnadh 1**

iongna *see* **ìne**

iongnadh, iongnaidh, iongnaidhean *nm* **1** a surprise, a surprising *or* amazing thing, a wonder, a marvel, *esp in expr* **chan iongnadh . . .** no wonder . . . , **chan iongnadh sin** that's no wonder/not surprising, **chan iongnadh gu bheil e toilichte!** no wonder he's pleased!; **2** surprise, amazement, wonder, **gabh** *v* **iongnadh** be surprised/amazed, **chuir e iongnadh orm** it surprised/amazed me, **mòr-iongnadh** astonishment; *cf stronger, less usu* **iongantas**

ionmhainn *adj* (*trad*) (*term of endearment*) dear, precious, darling, beloved, **a leannan ionmhainn** her darling (*etc*) sweetheart, *cf* **còir** *adj* **2, gaolach 2**

ionmhas, ionmhais, ionmhasan *nm* **1** treasure, *cf* **ulaidh 1**; **2** wealth, riches, *cf* **beartas, saidhbhreas, stòras; 3** (*business, public admin etc*) finance, **Roinn an Ionmhais** the Finance Department

ionmhasair, ionmhasair, ionmhasairean *nm* a treasurer

ionnan *see* **ionann**

ionnanach *adj* **1** equal, identical (*cf more usu* **ionann**); **2** (*sport*) **geama ionnanach** *m* a draw, a drawn game

ionndrainn *vt, pres part* **ag ionndrainn**, miss, long for, feel the absence or lack of, (*song*) **a' sìor-ionndrainn tìr a bhruadair** forever longing for/missing the land he dreams of, **tha mi gad ionndrainn** I miss/am missing you

ionnlad, *gen* **ionnlaid** *nm* (*the act of*) washing or bathing, ablution(s), **mias ionnlaid** *f* a wash basin, **seòmar-/rùm-ionnlaid** *m* a bathroom

ionnlaid *vti, pres part* **ag ionnlad**, wash, bathe, *cf* **failc, nigh**

ionnsachadh, *gen* **ionnsachaidh** *nm* **1** (*the act of*) learning, studying etc (*see senses of* **ionnsaich** *v*); **2** learning (*ie knowledge, scholarship*), *cf* **foghlam 2, oideachas 1**

ionnsaich *vti, pres part* **ag ionnsachadh**, **1** learn, **cha do dh'ionnsaich mi mòran anns an sgoil** I didn't learn much at school, **ionnsaich mu dheidhinn** learn/find out about it; **2** learn, study (*a particular subject etc*), **bidh sinn ag ionnsachadh na Gàidhlig aig a' cholaiste** we'll be studying Gaelic at college; **3** (*occas*) teach, train, instruct, *cf usu* **teagaisg**

ionnsaichte *adj* educated, trained, *cf* **foghlaimte**

ionnsaigh, ionnsaigh, ionnsaighean *nmf* **1** an attack, an assault, **fear-ionnsaigh** *m* an attacker/assailant, **thoir** *v* **ionnsaigh air cuideigin** attack/assault someone, (*legal*) **droch ionnsaigh** assault, an assault, **ionnsaigh dhrabasta** indecent assault; **2** an attempt, an effort, a try, (*Sc*) a shot, **thoir** *v* **ionnsaigh eile** have another try/attempt/shot (**air** at), *cf* **oidhirp 1**; **3** *in prep* **a dh'ionnsaigh** to, towards, *with gen*, **a dh'ionnsaigh a' bhaile** to/towards the town(ship), **bha am balach a' ruith dha h-ionnsaigh** the boy was running towards her, *cf* **gu¹ 1**

ionnsramaid, ionnsramaide, ionnsramaidean *nf* an instrument (*esp music*, *cf* **inneal-ciùil** – *see* **inneal 2**)

ionracas, *gen* **ionracais** *nm* **1** honesty, *cf* **onair 3**; **2** justice, justness, righteousness, *cf* **ceartas, còir** *n* **4**

ionraic *adj* **1** honest, *cf* **onarach 3**; **2** just, righteous, *cf* **ceart 2, dìreach 2**

ìoran(t)as, *gen* **ìoran(t)ais** *nm* irony

ìoranta *adj* ironic(al)

iorghail, iorghail, iorghailean *nf* tumult, a tumult, *cf* **gleadhar, othail, ùpraid 1**

iorghaileach *adj* tumultuous

Ìosa *nm invar* Jesus

ìosal & ìseal *adj* (*opposite of* **uasal**), *comp* (**n**) **as** (*etc*) **ìsle**, **1** (*phys*) low, **cnoc ìosal** a low hill, **taigh ìosal air a thogail** a low-built house; **2**

(*status etc*) low, lowly, humble, *cf* **iriosal 1; 3** (*sound*) low, quiet, **ann an guth ìosal** in a low/quiet voice, **os ìosal** *adv* quietly, *also* secretly, privately, covertly

Iosrail & Israel, *nf invar* Israel

Iosraileach, *gen & pl* **Iosrailich**, *also* **Israeleach**, *gen & pl* **Israelich**, *nm*, an Israeli, (*Bibl, hist*) an Israelite, *also as adj* **Iosraileach & Israeleach** Israeli, of, from or pertaining to Israel

Ioslamach *adj* Islamic, *cf* **Mohamadanach**

ìota(dh), *gen* **ìotaidh** *nm* thirst, *cf* **tart** & *more usu, less strong,* **pathadh**

ìotmhor *adj* parched, dry, very thirsty, *cf* **tartmhor**

ìre *nf invar* **1** a degree, a level, a stage (*of progress, development, ability etc*), **foghlam (aig) àrd-ìre** higher/tertiary/further education, **duine aig ìre na h-obrach** a man up to the job; **2** maturity, **thig** *v* **gu ìre** come to/reach maturity, become full-grown, *cf* **inbhe 2**; **3** *in expr* **an ìre mhath** *adv* quite, pretty, fairly, **bha sinn an ìre mhath sgìth** we were quite/pretty/fairly tired (*cf* **gu math** – *see* **math 4**), *also* just about, pretty well, more or less, **tha an geamhradh an ìre mhath seachad** the winter's pretty well/just about over (*cf* **bi 11**); **4** *in expr* **gu ìre bhig** almost, nearly, all but, **chaill sinn am bus gu ìre bhig** we almost/all but missed the bus, *cf* **mòr 5**

iriosal *adj* **1** (*status etc*) humble, lowly, *cf* **ìosal 2**; **2** humble (*ie self-effacing*), *cf* **umha(i)¹ 1**

irioslachadh, irioslachaidh, irioslachaidhean *nm* **1** (*the act of*) humbling, humiliating; **2** humiliation, a humiliation; *cf* **isleachadh, ùmhlachadh**

irioslachd *nf invar* **1** lowliness, humble status; **2** humility, *cf* **ùmhlachd 1**

irioslaich *vt, pres part* **ag irioslachadh**, humble, humiliate, *cf* **ùmhlaich 2**

iris, iris, irisean *nf* a periodical, a magazine, a (*literary etc*) quarterly, *cf* **ràitheachan**

is *conj see* **agus**

is (*inter* **an**, *neg* **cha(n)**, *neg inter* **nach**, *past & conditional* **bu**) *v irreg & def*, is, are, was, were, would be, **1** *as a copula linking nouns, prons,* **is duine mi** I am a man, **an ise Iseabail?** is she Isabel?, **b' iadsan an fheadhainn a rinn e** they were the ones who did it, (*trad*) **is meatailt copar** copper is a metal; **2** *when linking a noun etc and an adj* **is** *often implies a more permanent quality or greater emphasis than* **bi**, (*trad*) **is searbh fìon-geur** vinegar is bitter, **is fèineil mi!** I'm (so) selfish!, *Note:* **is** + *an adj is common in set phrases & exprs, eg* **is**

toigh leam I like, **b' fheàrr leam** I preferred/
I'd prefer, **is truagh sin!** that's a shame! **is
coma leis** he doesn't mind, **'s math seachad
e** it's good that it's finished/over; **3** *introducing
a rel clause*, **an tusa a sgrìobh e? cha mhi!**
was it you who wrote it? no! **nach iadsan a
thèid ann?** isn't it they who'll go?, **a bheil thu
deiseil? is mi a tha!** are you ready? I certainly/
sure am! **nach math a rinn thu!** didn't you do
well!, well done!; *Note: before nouns* **is e, b' e,
chan e** (*etc*) *is used*, **is e am bodach a chaill
e** it's the old man who lost it, **nach e a cèile
a chaochail?** isn't/wasn't it her husband who
died?; **4** *when introducing an adj or adv constr*
is (etc) **ann** (*often emph*) *is used*, **'s ann aosta
a tha i** she's old (*lit* it's old that she is), **an ann
a-màireach a chì sinn i? chan ann** is it
tomorrow we'll see her? no; **5 is** *with* **gun** *conj*
becomes **gur**, *conj*, that it (etc) is, **an e saor a
th' ann? cha chreid mi gur e** is he a joiner,
I don't think (that) he is, *see also* **gun** *conj*; **6**
introducing a comp or superlative, **as** (*for* **a is**),
in past tense **a bu, an tè as sine** the oldest one
(*f*), **am peann a b' fheàrr a bh' agam** the best
pen I had; *cf* **bi**
ìsbean, ìsbein, ìsbeanan *nm* a sausage
ìseal *see* **ìosal**
isean, isein, iseanan *nm* **1** a chick, a chicken,
a young bird; **2** a baby mammal, **isean cait**
a kitten (*cf usu* **piseag**); **3** *a term for a child
(sometimes affectionate)*, **droch isean** a brat, a
naughty, unruly or badly brought-up child (*also
of adult*), a bad lot
ìsleachadh, *gen* **ìsleachaidh** *nm* **1** (*the act of*)
lowering, degrading etc (*see senses of* **ìslich**
v); **2** abasement, humiliation, a humiliation, *cf*
ùmhlachadh 2
ìslich *vti*, *pres part* **ag ìsleachadh**, become or
make low or lower(*phys & fig*), degrade, debase,
demote, humble, humiliate, demean
is mathaid (gu) *adv & conj see* **faod 2**

isneach, isnich(e), isnichean *nf* a rifle, *cf usu*,
less trad, **raidhfil**
ist *pl* **istibh**, *also* **èist** *pl* **èistibh**, *excl* hush! be
quiet! (*Sc*) wheesht!, *cf* **sàmhach 1**
ite, ite, itean *nf* **1** a feather, *cf* **iteag 1**; **2** a fin (*of
fish*)
iteach *adj* feathered, having feathers, *cf* **iteagach**
iteach, *gen* **itich** *nm* plumage
iteachan, *gen* **iteachain**, *pl* **iteachain &
iteachanan** *nm* a bobbin, a spool
iteag, iteig, iteagan *nf* (*dimin of* **ite**) **1** a (small)
feather; **2** flight, flying, *esp in expr* **air iteig**
flying, on the wing, **rach** *v* **air iteig** fly (*cf*
itealaich, sgiathaich)
iteagach *adj* feathered, having feathers, *cf* **iteach**
itealaich *vi*, *pres part* **ag itealaich &** ag
itealachadh, fly, *cf* **rach air iteig** (*see* **iteag
2**), **sgiathaich**
itealan, *gen & pl* **itealain** *nm* an aeroplane, a
plane, an aircraft, *cf less trad* **plèana**
iteileag, iteileig, iteileagan *nf* a kite (*ie the
flying structure*)
ith *vti*, *pres part* **ag ithe(adh)**, eat
iubhar, iubhair, iubharan *nm* yew (*wood &
tree*), *also* **craobh-iubhair** *f* a yew tree
iuchair, iuchrach, iuchraichean *nf* a key (*for
locking, winding up, typing etc*)
Iuchar, *gen* **Iuchair** *nm*, *used with art*, **an
t-Iuchar** July
Iùdhach, *gen & pl* **Iùdhaich** *nm* a Jew, *also as
adj* **Iùdhach** Jewish
iùil-tharraing, *gen* **iùil-tharrainge** *nf*
magnetism
iùil-tharraingeach *adj* magnetic
iùl, iùil, iùilean *nm* (*trad*) **1** (*of boat etc*)
a course, *cf more usu* **cùrsa 2, seòl**[2] **2**; **2**
guidance, **neach-iùil** *m* a guide (*ie a person*), *cf
more usu* **treòrachadh 2**; **3** a landmark (*ie for
nagivation*), *cf* **comharradh-stiùiridh** (*see*
comharradh 1)
iutharn(a), *gen* **iutharna** *nf* hell, *cf more usu*
ifrinn

L

là & **latha**, *gen* **là** & **latha**, *pl* **làithean,
lathachan** & **lathaichean** *nm* a day, **làithean
na seachdain** the days of the week, **dè an là
a th' ann?** what day is it?, **là-breith** a date
of birth, **latha-fèille** a (public) holiday, a
feast-day, **làithean-saora** & **saor-làithean**
holidays, **chunna sinn an là roimhe e** we saw
him the other day, **chì mi latha no latheigin
thu** I'll see you some day or other/one of these
days, (*trad*) **nach oirnn a thàinig an dà
latha!** what a change has come upon us!, (*trad*)
Là-Luain doomsday, Nevermas (*a day that
will never come*), (*trad song*) **gu Là-Luain
cha ghluaisear mis'** I will not be moved until
doomsday

labhair *vi, pres part* **a' labhairt**, speak, talk, *cf
more usu* **bruidhinn** *v*

labhairt *nf invar* **1** (*the act of*) speaking,
talking, **neach-labhairt** a speaker, *more usu* a
spokesman, *cf* **bruidhinn** *n* 1; **2** speech, **comas
labhairt** *m* faculty/power of speech, *cf* **cainnt** 1

labhar *adj* loud, *cf more usu* **àrd** *adj* 2

Làbarach *adj* (*pol*) Labour, *for pol parties, see*
pàrtaidh

lach, lacha, lachan *nf* a (*usu* wild) duck, *cf*
tunnag

lachdann *adj* **1** dun, tawny, khaki, *cf* **odhar** 1; **2**
swarthy, *cf* **ciar** *adj* 1

ladar, ladair, ladaran *nm* **1** a ladle, a large
spoon, (*song*) **gabh an ladar no an taoman**
take the ladle or the baling dish (*ie any
expedient that comes to hand*), *cf* **liagh** 1,
spàin; **2** a scoop, *cf* **liagh** 2

ladarna *adj* bold, shameless, audacious, bare-
faced, impudent, blatant, *cf* **dàna** 3

ladhar, *gen* **ladhair** & **ladhra**, *pl* **ladhran** *nm* a
hoof, *cf* **ìne** 3

lag *adj* weak, feeble, **bha i lag leis an acras**
she was weak with/from hunger, **bha e lag na
inntinn** he was feeble-minded, *cf* **fann**

lag, *gen* **laig** & **luig**, *pl* **lagan** *nmf* **1** (*topog etc*)
a hollow, a pit, (*Sc*) a howe, a den, (*placename*)
Lag a' Mhuilinn Lagavulin, Mill Hollow, *cf*

còs, glac 1, **sloc** 1; **2** (*part of body*) **lag na
h-achlaise** the armpit

lagaich *vti, pres part* **a' lagachadh**, weaken,
grow or make weak or weaker, enfeeble,
debilitate, *cf less usu* **fannaich** 1

lagachadh, *gen* **lagachaidh** *nm* (*the act of*)
weakening etc (*see senses of* **lagaich** *v*)

lagchuiseach *adj* unenterprising,
unadventurous, **duine lag-chùiseach** a stick-
in-the-mud

lagh, lagha, laghannan *nm* (*jurisprudence,
science etc*) law, a law, **an aghaidh an lagha**
against the law, **fear-lagha** *m* a lawyer, a
solicitor

laghach *adj* (*esp of people*) nice, kind, *cf* **lurach,
snog** 2

laghail *adj* lawful, legal, **mì-laghail** unlawful,
illegal

laghairt, laghairt, laghairtean *nmf* a lizard

Laideann, *gen* **Laidinne** *nf* Latin

Laidinneach *adj* Latin

làidir *adj, Note: as well as the regular comp* **(n)
as** (etc) **làidire**, stronger, **(n)as** (etc) **treise** *or*
treasa (*see* **treun** *adj*) *is also used;* **1** strong,
physically powerful, **gàirdean làidir** a strong
arm, **corp-làidir** *adj* able-bodied, strong in
body, *cf* **neartmhor**; **2** potent, strong, **deoch-
làidir** *f* strong/potent drink, alcoholic drink,
intoxicating liquor

laigh *vi, pres part* **a' laighe**, **1** (*of people etc*) lie
(down), **laigh sìos** lie down (*esp for sleep*), **tha
sinn a' dol a laighe** we're going to bed; **2** land,
settle, lie, come to rest, perch, **laigh am plèana**
the plane landed, **gach rud air an laigheadh
a shùil** each thing his eye would rest/light/
settle upon; **3** decline, subside, go down, set, **tha
a' ghaoth a' laighe a-nis** the wind's subsiding
now, **laigh a' ghrian** the sun set/went down

laighe *nmf invar* **1** (*the act of*) lying (down),
landing etc (*see senses of* **laigh** *v*); **2** a reclining
or recumbent position, **tha i na laighe** she's
lying down, **figear na laighe** a reclining/
recumbent figure

laigse, **laigse**, **laigsean** *nf* **1** weakness, infirmity, debility; **2** a faint, a fainting fit, **chaidh mi an laigse** I fainted, *cf* **fannaich 2, fanntaig, neul 3**

làimhseachadh, *gen* **làimhseachaidh** *nm* **1** (*the act of*) feeling, handling, treating etc (*see senses of* **làimhsich** *v*); **2** treatment, behaviour, conduct (*towards another person, animal etc*), **droch-làimhseachadh** ill-treatment, *also* (physical) abuse

làimhsich *vt, pres part* **a' làimhseachadh**, **1** feel, finger, touch, handle (*person. objects etc*), *cf* **bean** *v* **1**; **2** treat, behave towards (*esp persons*), *cf* **gnàthaich 3**; **3** handle, wield (*tool, weapon etc*), *cf* **iomair** *vt*; **4** handle, manage (*situation etc*), *cf* **dèilig (ri)**

laimrig, **laimrige**, **laimrigean** *nf* a quay, a landing-place, *cf* **cidhe**

lainnir, *gen* **lainnire** *nf* (*of light*) a glint, a glitter, a sparkle; brilliance, radiance

lainnireach *adj* sparkling, brilliant, radiant, *cf* **boillsgeach**

làir, *gen* **làiridh** & **làireadh**, *pl* **làiridhean** *nf* a mare

làirne-mhàireach & **làrna-mhàireach** *adv* (on) the morrow, the next *or* following day, **bha i tinn air an oidhche ach bha i gu dòigheil làirne-mhàireach** she was ill in/during the night but she was fine the next/following day

làitheil *adj* daily, everyday

làmh, *gen* **làimh(e)**, *dat* **làimh**, *pl* **làmhan** *nf* **1** a hand, (*song*) **thoir dhomh do làmh** give me your hand, **air an làimh chlì** on the left(-hand side), **cha do rug e air làimh orm** he didn't shake hands with me, he didn't shake my hand, **crathadh-làimhe** *m* a handshake, **ghabh sinn làmh-an-uachdair orra** we got the upper hand of them, **gabh obair** (etc) **os làimh** undertake/take on work (etc); **2** captivity, arrest, **cuir** *v* **an làimh** capture, arrest, (*trad song*) **tha mis' an làimh** I am a prisoner/captive, *cf* **braighdeanas, ciomachas, daorsa, sàs 1**; **3** a handle, *cf* **cas** *n* **3**; **4** *in expr* **tha làmh aige** (*etc*) **ann an X** he (*etc*) dabbles in X

làmhach *adj* (*of person*) handy, adroit

làmhainn, **làmhainn**, **làmhainnean** *nf* a glove, *cf* **miotag 1**

làmh-lèigh, **làmh-lèigh**, **làmh-lèighean** *nm* a surgeon

làmh-sgrìobhaidh, **làmh-sgrìobhaidh**, **làmh-sgrìobhaidhean** *nmf* handwriting

làmh-sgrìobhainn, **làmh-sgrìobhainn**, **làmh-sgrìobhainnean** *nmf* a manuscript

làmhthuagh, **làmhthuaigh**, **làmhthuaghan** *nf* a hatchet, a chopper

lampa, **lampa**, **lampaichean** *nmf* a lamp, *cf* **lanntair, leus**

làn *adj* **1** full, **botal làn bainne/làn de bhainne** a bottle full of milk, **leth-làn** half full, **film làn-fhada** a full length film, **làn-chumhachd** *nmf* full *or* absolute power/ authority, **làn-thìde** *adj* full-time, **bha làn-fhios agam nach robh e fìor** I was fully aware that it wasn't true (*lit* I had full knowledge); **2** *as adv* fully, completely, **tha sinn làn-chinnteach** we're quite/completely certain, *cf* **buileach**

làn, *gen* & *pl* **làin** *nm* **1** fullness, a fill, as much as will fill something, **làn beòil** a mouthful, **làn dùirn** a handful, a fistful (*cf* **dòrlach**), **làn-spàine** a spoonful, **fhuair mi mo làn de bhrot** *or* **fhuair mi làn mo bhroinn de bhrot** I got my fill of/a bellyful of soup (*cf* **leòr 1, sàth** *n*); **2** (*also* **làn-mara**, *gen* & *pl* **làin-mhara** *nm*) a (high) tide, *cf* **muir- làn, seòl-mara** (*see* **muir**), **tràigh** *n* **2**

langa, **langa**, **langan** *nf* (*fish*) ling, a ling

lànachd *nf invar* fulness

langanaich *vi, pres part* **a' langanaich**, (*cattle* & *esp deer*) bellow, low, (*song*) **bhiodh na fèidh a' langanaich** the deer would be bellowing, *cf* **beuc** *v*, **geum** *v*, **nuallaich**

langasaid, **langasaide**, **langasaidean** *nf* a sofa, a couch, *cf* **sòfa**

lann¹, *gen* **lanna** & **lainne**, *pl* **lannan** *nf* **1** a blade, **lann sgeine** a knife blade, **tharraing e a lann** he drew his blade/sword; **2** (*of fish, reptile*) a scale

lann², **lainn**, **lannan** *nf* **1** an enclosure, an enclosed piece of ground; **2** a fence, *cf more usu* **feansa**; **3** (*in compounds*) a repository, a place where objects are kept, a place where a particular activity is carried out, **leabharlann** a library, **obair-lann** & **deuchainn-lann** a laboratory, **cainnt-lann** a language laboratory, **biadh-lann** a refectory, **taisbean-lann** an art gallery, an exhibition hall, *cf* **ionad 2**

lanntair, **lanntair**, **lanntairean** *nmf* a lantern, *cf* **lampa, leus**

laoch, *gen* & *pl* **laoich** *nm* a hero, a warrior, *cf* **curaidh, gaisgeach**

laochan, *gen* & *pl* **laochain** *nm* (*dimin of* **laoch**), a little/wee hero, *esp a term of endearment applied to a young boy*, **ciamar a tha thu an-diugh, a laochain?** how are you today, (my) wee hero?

laogh, **laoigh**, **laoghan** *nm* **1** a calf, **laoigh-fheòil** *f* veal; **2** (*as voc term of endearment*) **a laoigh!** (my) love!, (my) dear!, *cf* **eudail 2, gaol 2, gràdh 2, luaidh** *nmf*

laoidh, laoidhe, laoidhean *nmf* **1** a song, a poem, a lay, *cf* **dàn²** 1 & 2, **duan** 1; **2** a hymn; **3** an anthem

lapach *adj* **1** numb; **2** weak, feeble, *cf more usu* **fann, lag** *adj*

làr, làir, làran *nm* **1** (the) ground, (*song*) **dhòirt iad fhuil mu làr** they spilled his blood upon the ground, **sìnte air an làr** stretched out on the ground; **2** a floor, *cf* **ùrlar 1**

làrach, làraich, làraichean *nmf* **1** a trace or vestige of something, a mark, a scar, (*of building*) a ruin (*cf* **tobhta**), **cha do dh'fhàg e làrach** it didn't leave a trace, *also in expr* **an làrach nam bonn** immediately, on the spot (*lit* in the sole prints), *cf* **comharra(dh) 3, lorg** *n* 2; **2** a site (*of something past or to come*), **làrach taighe** a site for a house

làraidh, làraidh, làraidhean *nf* a lorry

las *vti, pres part* **a' lasadh**, **1** (*vt*) light, set fire to, kindle, ignite (*candle, fire etc*), **las toitean** light a cigarette, *cf* **leig 8, loisg 1**; **2** (*vi*) blaze, flame, burn brightly, flare up; **3** (*vi*) (*fig*) light up, **bhiodh aodann a' lasadh** his face would light up

lasachadh, gen lasachaidh *nm* (*the act of*) loosening etc (*see senses of* **lasaich** *v*)

lasadair, lasadair, lasadairean *nm* a match (*for lighting*), *cf less trad* **maids(e) 1**

lasadh, gen lasaidh *nm* (*the act of*) lighting, blazing etc (*see senses of* **las** *v*)

lasaich *vt, pres part* **a' lasachadh**, **1** (*fastenings etc*) loosen, slacken, *cf* **fuasgail 2**; **2** ease (*suffering etc*), *cf* **faothaich**

lasair, gen lasrach & lasair, pl lasraichean *nf* **1** a flame, flames, (*song*) **Glaschu a' dol na lasair** Glasgow going up in flames, (*fig; situation etc*) **cuir** *v* **lasair ri** inflame; **2** a flash

lasanta *adj* **1** inflammable; **2** (*person*) passionate, hot-blooded, easily inflamed

lasgan, gen & pl lasgain *nm* (*of noise, emotion etc*) a burst, an outburst, **lasgan gàire** a burst/peal of laughter, **lasgan feirge** a fit/outburst of anger

lasrach *adj* flaming, flashing, blazing, **teine lasrach** *m* a blazing fire, **sùilean lasrach** flashing eyes

lastaig *nf invar* elastic

latha *see* **là**

làthair, gen làthaire *nf* **1** presence, **a-mach às mo làthair (leat)!** out of my presence/sight (with you)!, *cf* **sealladh 3, fradharc 2**; **2** the fact of being present, **an làthair** present, there, **bha mi eòlach air na bha an làthair** I knew those who were present/there, **cùm** *v* **às an**

làthair keep out of sight, keep away, *cf less usu* **làthaireachd**

làthaireachd *nf invar* presence, **neo-làthaireachd** absence, *cf much more usu* **làthair**

le *prep* (*takes the dat*), *before the art* **leis** (*The prep prons formed with* **le**, *in the order first, second, third person singular, first, second, third person plural, and with the reflexive/emphatic particles in brackets, are as follows*: **leam(sa), leat(sa), leis(-san), leatha(se), leinn(e), leibh(se), leotha(san)**, with me, with you (*fam*) *etc* - *also* 'mine', 'yours' *etc, eg* **is ann leamsa a tha e** it's mine, it belongs to me); **1** with, along with (*Note: when referring to people* **còmhla ri** *is more usu/polite than* **le**, *except in some set exprs etc*), (*song*) **an tèid thu leam, mo nighean donn?** will you go with me, my brown-haired lass? (*song*) **nuair (a) bhios mi leam fhìn** when I am alone/by myself, **le chèile** together, *also* both, **dh'fhalbh iad le chèile** they left together *or* they both left, **air falbh leis a' ghaoith** gone with the wind, **beannachd/slàn leat!** goodbye (*lit* a blessing/health be with you), (*corres etc*) **le deagh dhùrachd** with compliments, *cf* **còmhla 2** & *less usu* **cuide ri, maille ri, mar 5**; **2** with (*expr means, instrument*), **bhuail e le òrd e** he struck it with a hammer; **3** (*expr agent*) by, **chaidh a mharbhadh le peilear** he was killed by a bullet, **sgeulachd air a sgrìobhadh le ban-sgrìobhadair** a story written by a woman writer, **faigh** *v* **le foill** obtain fraudulently/by fraud; **4** belonging to, **cò leis a tha seo?** 's ann leathase a tha e** who does this belong to? it's hers/it belongs to her, (*pibroch title*) **Is Leamsa An Gleann** The Glen Is Mine, *cf* **aig 2**; **5** *in numerous verbal exprs conveying emotion, attitude etc, eg* **is toigh leam e** (*or esp in Lewis*) **is caomh leam e** I like it, **is duilich leam e** I find it difficult *or* it is hard/painful for me, **is math leam e** I find/think it good, **b' fhada leam e** it seemed/was long/tedious for me; **6** *expr motion*, (**choisich i** *etc*) **leis a' bhruthaich** (she walked *etc*) down/with the slope (*cf* **ris a' bhruthaich** up/against the slope), **leis an t-sruth** downstream, with the current; **7** *in adv expr* **leis (a) sin** whereupon, thereupon, at that, **dhùin am bàr, is leis a sin chaidh e dhachaigh** the bar closed, and at that he went home, *cf* **an uair sin, sin** *pron* 4; **8** *in expr* **leis cho ... is ...** with it being so ..., **chan fhaic mi thu leis cho dorch 's a tha e** I can't see you with it being so dark

leabaidh, *gen* **leapa(ch)**, *pl* **leapannan** &
leapaichean *nf* a bed, **bha iad san leabaidh**
they were in bed, **aodach-leapa** *m* bedclothes
leabhar, **leabhair**, **leabhraichean** *nm* a book,
leabhar-latha a diary, a journal, **leabhar-**
mìneachaidh a manual, an instruction book,
leabhar-chlàr a bibliography
leabharlann, **leabharlainn**, **leabharlannan**
nmf a library
leabhrachan, **leabhrachain**, **leabhrachanan**
nm & **leabhran**, **leabhrain**, **leabhranan** *nm*
a booklet, a pamphlet, a brochure, a manual
leabhran *see* **leabhrachan**
leac, **lic(e)**, **leacan** *nf* 1 (*topog*) a slab or ledge
of natural stone or rock, an expanse of flat stone
or rock; 2 (*masonry etc*) a slab or flat piece of
(*usu dressed*) stone, **leac uaighe** a tombstone, a
gravestone, **leac-ùrlair** a paving/flooring stone
leacach *adj* flat, slab-like
leacag, **leacaig**, **leacagan** *nf* a tile
leag *vt, pres part* **a' leagail**, 1 (*building, tree,*
opponent etc) knock down, throw down,
demolish, fell, **leag gu làr** raze to the ground; 2
lower, bring *or* let down, **leag e an uinneag** he
lowered/let down the window; 3 lay down, put
down, **leag leacagan air ùrlar** lay tiles on a
floor; 4 drop, **leag boma** drop a bomb
leagail, *gen* **leagalach** *nf* (*the act of*) knocking
down, lowering etc (*see senses of* **leag** *v*)
leagh *vti, pres part* **a' leaghadh**, 1 melt, thaw; 2
dissolve (*in liquid*)
leaghadh, *gen* **leaghaidh** *nm* (*the act or process*
of) melting, thawing, dissolving, *see* **leagh** *v*
leam *prep pron see* **le**
leamh *adj* exasperating, vexing, galling, *cf*
frionasach 3
leamhachadh, *gen* **leamhachaidh** *nm* (*the act*
of) exasperating etc (*see senses of* **leamhaich** *v*)
leamhaich *vt, pres part* **a' leamhachadh**,
exasperate, plague, get on someone's nerves, *cf*
sàraich 2
leamhan, *gen* **leamhain** & **leamhna** *nm* elm
leamsa *emph prep pron, see* **le**
lean *vti, pres part* **a' leantainn** & **a' leantail**,
1 follow, **thog e air is ise ga leantainn** off
he went with her following him, **ionnsaich na**
faclan a leanas learn the following words;
2 follow, understand, **a bheil sibh gam**
leantainn? are you following/understanding
me?, *cf* **tuig**; 3 continue, persevere, keep *or* go
on, **an lean an droch aimsir?** will the bad
weather continue/go on?, **bha e sgìth den**
dreuchd aige ach lean e air he was tired of
his job but he kept on/persevered, **lean ort!**
keep going!, *cf* **cùm** 2; 4 (*lit & fig*) stick, adhere

(**ri** to), **lean a' chuileag ris a' bhalla** the fly
stuck to the wall
leanabail *adj* childish, juvenile, infantile
leanaban, **leanabain**, **leanabanan** *nm* (*dimin*
of **leanabh**), a baby, a small child, an infant, *cf*
leanabh, **naoidhean**, **pàiste**
leanabas, *gen* **leanabais** *nm* childhood
leanabh, **leanaibh**, **leanabhan**, **leanaban**
nm a baby, a child, an infant, *cf* **leanaban**,
naoidhean, **pàiste**
leanailteach *adj* 1 continuous, incessant; 2
sticky, adhesive
leann, **leanna**, **leannan**, **leanntan** *nm* beer, ale
leannan, **leannain**, **leannain**, **leannanan** *nm*
a lover, a sweetheart, a boyfriend, a girlfriend, *cf*
(*fam*) **bràmair**, (*fam*) **car(a)bhaidh**
leannanach *adj* amorous; fond of the opposite sex
leannanachd *nf invar* courtship, courting, *cf*
suirghe
leannra, **leannra**, **leannran** *nm* sauce (*ie for*
food), *cf* **sabhs**
leantainneach *adj* 1 continuing, continuous,
measadh leantainneach continuous
assessment, **pàipear leantainneach**
continuous paper/stationery; 2 persevering,
enduring, lasting, **stòras leanntainneach** a
renewable resource
leas, *nm invar* 1 (*trad*) benefit, profit, advantage,
improvement; 2 *now esp in expr* **cha leig/ruig**
mi (etc) **a leas . . .** I (*etc*) don't need to . . . ,
cha leig thu (a) leas tighinn còmhla rinn
you don't need to come with us, there's no point
in your coming with us, **am faigh mi fàinne**
dhut? cha leig thu a leas! will I get you a
ring? you don't need to/you needn't bother!, *cf*
feum *v* 2, **feum** *n* 2
leas- *prefix* (*in family relationships*) step-, **leas-**
bhràthair a step-brother
leasachadh, **leasachaidh**, **leasachaidhean**
nm 1 (*the act of*) improving, developing etc
(*see senses of* **leasaich** *v*); 2 improvement, an
improvement, development, a development,
bòrd leasachaidh *m* a development board,
tìr fo leasachadh a developing country,
tabhartas leasachaidh an improvement
grant; 3 a remedy, a means of putting something
right, **cha robh leasachadh air a' chùis ach**
. . . there was no remedy for the matter except
. . . , foghlam/obair leasachaidh remedial
education/work, *cf* **cothrom** *n* 2 ; 4 (*agric*)
manure, fertiliser, *cf* **mathachadh**
leasaich *vt, pres part* **a' leasachadh**, 1 improve,
develop, **tha mi airson mo chuid Gàidhlig a**
leasachadh I want to improve my Gaelic, **bidh**
a' chomhairle a' leasachadh meadhan a'

bhaile the council will be improving/developing the town centre; **2** remedy, rectify, reform, put right; **3** (*agric*) manure, fertilise (*ground*), *cf* **mathaich, todhair 1**

leasaiche, leasaiche, leasaichean *nm* a therapist, **leasaiche cainnt** a speech therapist

leasan, leasain, leasanan *nm* a lesson

leasbach, *gen & pl* **leasbaich** *nf* a lesbian, *also as adj* **leasbach** lesbian

leat & leatha *prep prons*, see **le**

leathad, leathaid, leathaidean *nm* a slope, a hillslope, a hillside, **leathaidean casa** steep hillsides, *common in placenames as* Le(a)d-, *eg* **An Leathad Beag** Ledbeg, little hillslope, *cf* **aodann 2, bruthach 1, leitir**

leathann *adj* broad, wide, (*placename*) **An t-Ath Leathann** Broadford, *cf* **farsaing 1** & *opposite* **caol** *adj* **1**

leathar, *gen* **leathair** & **leathrach** *nm* leather, **seacaid leathair** *f* a leather jacket

leathase *emph prep pron*, see **le**

leatrom, *gen* **leatruim** *nm* pregnancy

leatsa *emph prep pron*, see **le**

leibh (*emph form* **leibhse**) *prep pron*, see **le**

leig *vt, pres part* **a' leigeil** & **a' leigeadh, 1** let, permit, allow, **cha do leig e dhomh/ leam a cheannachd** he didn't let me buy it, *cf* **ceadaich 1; 2** leave, entrust, **leig leathase am pàiste a thogail** leave it to her to bring up the child; **3 leig** & **leig às** let go, drop, release, let off, let slip, (*trad*) **leig às na coin** let slip the dogs, **leig saighead** loose/fire an arrow, **leig e às braim** he farted, let off a fart, **leig iad sgreuch (asta)** they let out a yell, **leig d' anail!** take a breather!; **4 leig le** leave alone, let be, **leig leatha** let her alone, let her be, *also* let her get on with it; **5 leig de** & **leig seachad** stop, cease, discontinue, give up, relinquish, **leig mi seachad smocadh** I've given up smoking, **leig am bodach dheth an obair** the old fellow gave up his job *or* retired, **leig e dheth an crùn** he abdicated; **6 leig air** pretend, make out, **leig na saighdearan orra gun robh iad nan sìobhaltairean** the soldiers pretended/ made out they were civilians; **7 leig air** give something away, let on, **chuir iad ceistean gu leòr ach cha do leig sinn oirnn** they asked lots of questions but we didn't let on/give the game away; **8 leig na theine** set on fire, *cf* **las 1, loisg 1; 9** *for* **leig (a) leas** *see* **leas 2**

leigeadh, *gen* **leigidh** *nm*, *also* **leigeil**, *gen* **leigealach** *nf*, (*the act of*) letting, dropping etc (*see senses of* **leig** *v*)

leigheas, leigheis, leigheasan *nm* **1** (*the act & process of*) healing (*see* **leighis** *v*), **leigheas**

inntinn psychiatry; **2** a cure, a remedy, a medicine, **leigheas air a ghalar** a cure for his malady, **leigheas chasad** cough medicine, (*after drink*) **leigheas na pòit** the hair of the dog, *cf* **ìocshlaint**

leighis *vt, pres part* **a' leigheas**, cure, heal, *cf* **slànaich**

lèine, lèine, lèintean *nf* a shirt

leinn (*emph form* **leinne**) *prep pron*, see **le**

lèir *adj* **1** (*trad*) visible, clear, plain, evident, obvious; **2** *esp in expr* (*rather trad*) **is lèir dhomh** (*etc*) I (*etc*) see, **cha lèir dhomh fàire** I can't see the horizon, **bu lèir dha gun robh e air chall** it was clear/plain *etc* to him/ he could see that he was lost; *cf* **faicsinneach 1, follaiseach 1, soilleir 2**

lèir-chlais(tin)neach *adj* audio-visual

lèirmheas *nm invar* a review (*of book etc*), a critique

lèirsinn *nf invar* **1** sight, eyesight, vision, *cf* **fradharc 1; 2** insight, perceptiveness, *cf more usu* **tuigse 1**

lèirsinneach *adj* **1** visible, *cf more usu* **faicsinneach 1; 2** perceptive, *cf more usu* **mothachail 1, tuigseach 1**

leis *prep pron*, see **le**

leis, leise, leisean *nf* a thigh, *cf more usu* **sliasaid**

leisg *adj* **1** lazy, idle, indolent, slothful, **bu chòir dhomh am mullach a chàradh ach tha mi ro leisg** I ought to mend the roof but I'm too lazy, *cf less usu* **dìomhain 2; 2** reluctant, loth, unwilling, disinclined, *esp in expr* **is leisg leam** (*etc*) I (*etc*) am loth/reluctant/unwilling, I (*etc*) hesitate (to), **bu leisg leatha an teallach fhàgail** she was reluctant to leave the fireside, *cf* **aindeònach**

leisg(e), *gen* **leisge** *nf* **1** laziness, idleness, indolence, sloth, (*prov*) **cha dèan làmh na leisge beartas** the lazy hand will not earn riches; **2** reluctance, unwillingness, **bha leisg orm falbh** I was reluctant/unwilling to leave

leisgeadair, leisgeadair, leisgeadairean *nm* a lazy *or* idle person, a lazybones

leisgeul, leisgeil, leisgeulan *nm* an excuse, a pretext, *also in exprs* **gabh mo leisgeul!** excuse me! pardon me!, **dèan** *v* **leisgeul** apologise

leis-san *emph prep pron*, see **le**

leiteas, leiteis, leiteisean *nf* a lettuce

lèith, lèithe, lèithean *nf* (*anat*) a nerve

leitheach *adv* half, semi-, **leitheach làn** half-full, **leitheach-slighe eadar Port Rìgh is Dùn Bheagain** halfway between Portree and Dunvegan

leithid, leithide, leithidean *nf* the like of someone or something, *usu with poss adj*, **cha robh a leithid ann a-riamh** his/her/its like never existed, **a leithid sin** the like(s) of that, such a thing/one as that, **chan aithne dhomh a leithid de dhuine** I don't know such a man/a man the likes of him, *cf* **coltas, mac-samhail 2, samhail, seòrsa**

leitir, leitire, leitirean *nf* a slope (*often near water*), *now usu in placenames, eg* **Leitir Choill** Letterchall, wood slope, *cf* **aodann 2, leathad, ruighe 2**

Leòdhasach, *gen & pl* **Leòdhasaich** *nm* someone from (the Isle of) Lewis (**Leòdhas** *or* **Eilean Leòdhais**), *also as adj*, **Leòdhasach** of, from or pertaining to Lewis

leòghann *see* **leòmhann**

leòinteach, *gen & pl* **leòintich** *nm* a casualty, a victim (*of accident etc*), **na leòintich** the injured, the wounded, the casualties

leòm, *gen* **leòim(e)** *nf* pride, conceit, 'side', affectation, *cf more usu* **àrdan, mòrchuis, pròis**

leòman, *gen & pl* **leòmain** *nm* a moth

leòmhann, *gen & pl* **leòmhainn** *nm,* a lion

leòn, leòin, leòntan *nm* (*phys or emotional*) a wound, a hurt, an injury, (*song*) **'s e 'n gunna caol a rinn mo leòn** it's the fowler's gun that caused my hurt, *cf* **ciùrradh 2, creuchd, lot** *nm*

leòn *vt, pres part* **a' leònadh**, (*phys or emotionally*) wound, hurt, injure, *cf* **ciùrr 1 & 2, lot** *v*

leònadh, *gen* **leònaidh** *nm* (*the act of*) wounding, hurting, injuring

leònta & leònte, *adj* wounded, hurt, injured

leòr *nf invar* **1** enough, a sufficiency, **fhuair mi mo leòr de dh'òrain a-raoir** I got (more than) enough songs/all the songs I could take/ my fill of songs last night, *cf* **làn** *n* **1, sàth** *n*; **2** *esp in expr* **gu leòr** enough, sufficient, plenty (*cf* **pailteas**), **a bheil gu leòr bìdh agad?** have you enough food?, **tha gu leòr ann a tha den bheachd sin** there are plenty of/a good many people around who think that, **tha trioblaid gu leòr againn aig an taigh** we've plenty/a lot of trouble at home, **ceart gu leòr!** right enough!, quite right!, *also* OK!

leotha (*emph form* **leothasan**) *prep pron, see* **le**

leth *nm invar* **1** (*trad*) a side, **cuir** *v* **airgead air leth** put money aside/on one side, **leth ri** *prep* next to, beside, **rach** *v* **às leth cuideigin** side with someone, **chaidh i às an leth** she sided with them/took their part, *cf* **taobh 3; 2** *as adv expr* **air leth** (*lit*) apart, *also* exceptional,

excellent, outstanding, special, **duine air leth** a man apart *or* an outstanding man, **bha sin air leth math** that was extremely/especially good, *cf* **anabarrach 2, fìor 3; 3** a half, **an leth eile** the other half, **mìle/dusan gu leth** a mile and a half/a dozen and a half, **leth-uair** half an hour, **leth-bhotal** half a bottle, a half bottle, **leth mar leth** half and half, **leth an t-samhraidh/a' gheamhraidh** mid-summer/ winter (*ie the half-way point*); **4** *often used adverbially* **leth-shean** middle-aged (*lit* half old), **leth-mharbh** half dead, *cf* **leitheach; 5** one of a pair, **leth-aon & leth-chàraid** a twin, (*trad*) *often of parts of the body* **dh'èirich i air a leth-uilinn** she rose up onto one elbow, **air leth-chois** on one leg, **bò air leth-adhairc** a cow with (only) one horn; **6** *in expr* **às leth** *prep* on behalf of, **is ann às mo leth a rinn e e** it was on my behalf/for me that he did it, *cf* **airson 3, sgàth** *n* **3; 7** *in expr* **cuir** *v* **às leth** accuse, attribute, **chuir iad às mo leth gun robh mi leisg** they accused me of being/made out that I was lazy (*cf* **tilg 2**), **na cuiribh am fathann às mo leth-sa** don't attribute the rumour to me; **8** *in expr* **fa leth** *adv* separate, **nochd na h-òrain mu dheireadh aige ann an leabhar fa leth** his last songs appeared in a separate book

lethbhreac, lethbhric, lethbhreacan *nm* **1** (*trad*) a like, a fellow, an equal, a match, (*prov*) **gheibh Gàidheal fhèin a lethbhreac** even a Gael will meet his match, *cf* **coimeas 4, leithid, mac-samhail 2, samhail, seis(e); 2** a copy, a reproduction (*of book, picture etc*), a duplicate, a transcript; **3** *now esp* an individual copy (*of a book, newspaper etc*)

lethcheann, *gen & pl* **lethchinn** *nm* **1** (*trad*) a cheek, *cf more usu* **gruaidh, pluic; 2** the side of the head, the temple, **buille air a lethcheann** a blow on the side of his head

leth-cheud & lethcheud, *gen* **leth-cheud**, *pl* **leth-cheudan** *nm* fifty (*lit* half a hundred), *takes nom sing* (*radical*) **leth-cheud boireannach** fifty women, **rugadh e sna Leth-cheudan** he was born in the Fifties, *cf* (*trad*) **caogad**

leth-chuid, leth-chodach, leth-chodaichean *nf* a half, a half share, **cia mheud a tha thu ag iarraidh? a leth-chuid** how many do you want? half (of them/it etc)

leth-fhuar *adj* (*lit & fig*) tepid, lukewarm, tepid, **fhuair sinn fàilte leth-fhuar** we got a lukewarm/half-hearted welcome, **brot leth-fhuar** lukewarm broth, *cf* **fionnar 2, fuaraidh**

leth-mhisg *nf see* **misg**

leud, *gen* **leòid** *nm* breadth, width, *cf*
farsaingeachd 1

leudachadh, leudachaidh, leudachaidhean
nm **1** (*the act of*) extending etc (*see senses
of* **leudaich** *v*); **2** extension, an extension,
enlargement, an enlargement, expansion, an
expansion

leudaich *vti, pres part* **a' leudachadh**, extend,
enlarge, widen, broaden, expand, **chaidh an
rathad a leudachadh** the road was widened

leudaichte *adj* **1** extended, enlarged, widened,
broadened, expanded; **2** (*occas*) flattened, **bha
a shròn leudaichte ris an lòsan** his nose was
flattened against the window pane

leug, lèig, leugan *nf* a jewel, *cf* **seud**

leugh *vti, pres part* **a' leughadh**, read, **an do
leugh thu an leabhar ùr aige?** have you read
his new book?

leughadair, leughadair, leughadairean *nm*
a reader

leughadh, *gen* **leughaidh** *nm* (*the act of*)
reading, a reading

leum, lèim, leuman(nan) *nm* **1** (*the act of*)
jumping etc (*see senses of* **leum** *v*); **2** a jump, a
leap, a skip, a spring, *cf* **sùrdag**

leum *vti, pres part* **a' leum** *also* **a' leumadh,
a' leumnaich & a' leumadaich, 1** jump, leap,
skip, spring, **leum am balla** jump (over) the
wall; **2** (*of nose*) bleed, **tha mo shròn a' leum**
my nose is bleeding

**leum-sròine, lèim-sròine, leumannan-
sròine** *nm* a nose bleed

leum-uisge, lèim-uisge, leumannan-uisge
nm a waterfall, *cf more usu* **eas, linne 3, spùt**
n **2**

leus, *gen & pl* **leòis** *nm* **1** a light, a ray of light, *cf
more usu* **gath 3, solas; 2** a torch, *cf* **lampa,
lanntair; 3** a blister, *cf* **balg 2**

leusair, leusair, leusairean *nm* a laser,
teicneolas leusair *m* laser technology, **gath
leusair** a laser beam

liagh, lèigh, liaghan *nf* **1** a ladle, a large spoon,
cf **ladar 1, spàin; 2** a scoop, *cf* **ladar 2**

liath *adj* **1** grey, **falt liath** grey hair, **creag liath**
grey rock/crag, *cf* **glas** *adj* **1; 2** (*pale*) blue

liath *vti, pres part* **a' liathadh**, make or become
grey, (*song*) **ged tha mo cheann air liathadh**
though my head/hair has turned/gone/ become
grey

liathadh, *gen* **liathaidh** *nm* (*the act or process
of*) greying, turning grey (*see* **liath** *v*)

liath-reothadh, *gen* **liath-reothaidh** *nm* hoar
frost

libearalach *adj* **1** (*of attitudes etc*) liberal; **2** (*pol*)
for pol parties see **pàrtaidh 1**

lìbhrig *vt, pres part* **a' lìbhrigeadh**, deliver
(*goods etc*)

lìbhrigeadh, lìbhrigidh, lìbhrigidhean *nm* **1**
(*the act of*) delivering; **2** delivery, a delivery (*of
goods etc*)

lide, lide, lidean *nm* a syllable

lighiche, lighiche, lighichean *nm* a (medical)
doctor, *cf less trad* **do(c)tair**

lili(dh), lili(dh), lilidhean *nf* a lily

lìnig *vt, pres part* **a' lìnigeadh**, (*curtains etc*)
line

lìnigeadh, lìnigidh, lìnigidhean *nm* **1** (*the act
of*) lining; **2** (*material*) lining, a lining

linn, linn, linntean *nmf* **1** an age, a time, an
era, **Na Linntean Dorcha** The Dark Ages, **Na
Linntean Meadhanach** The Middle Ages,
linn an fhànais the space age, **ri linn ar
sinnsirean** in our ancestors' time, *cf* **rè** *n* **2; 2**
a generation, **bho linn gu linn** from generation
to generation, *cf more usu* **ginealach 1; 3**
a century, **san fhicheadamh linn** in the
twentieth century

linne, *gen* **linne**, *pl* **linneachan & linntean**
nf **1** a pool, (*esp in placenames*) a pool below a
waterfall, (*Sc*) a linn, *cf* **glumag 1, lòn² 1; 2** (*esp
in placenames*) a waterfall, falls, *cf* **eas, leum-
uisge, spùt** *n* **2**

liomaid, liomaide, liomaidean *nf* a lemon

lìomh, *gen* **lìomha** *nf* polish, a polish, a gloss, a
shine (*on shoes etc*)

lìomh *vt, pres part* **a' lìomhadh**, polish, shine
(*shoes etc*)

lìomharra *adj* polished, shiny, glossy

lìon *vti, pres part* **a' lìonadh**, fill (up), become
full, **lìon botal-teth dhomh** fill me a hot water
bottle, **lìon am muir/a' mhuir** the tide came
in

lìon, lìn, lìontan *nm* **1** net, netting, a net, a web,
lìon-iasgaich a fishing net, **lìon damhain-
allaidh** a spider's web, a cobweb; **2** lint, flax

lìonadh, *gen* **lìonaidh** *nm* (*the act of*) filling etc
(*see* **lìon** *v*)

lìonmhor *adj* numerous, copious, plentiful,
abundant, (*trad*) **bu lìonmhor a luchd-
leanmhainn** numerous were his followers, **na
h-èildean lìonmhor** the numerous/abundant
hinds, *cf* **pailt 1**

lìonmhorachd *nf invar* abundance, plenty, *cf*
leòr 2, pailteas

lionn, lionna, lionntan *nm* liquid, a liquid,
a fluid, **'s e lionn a th' ann am bùrn** water
is a liquid, *also in expr* **eadar-dhà-lionn**
undecided, *also* neither one thing nor the other

lionsa, lionsa, lionsaichean *nf* a lens, **lionsa-
suathaidh** a contact lens

lìonta *adj* filled, full

liopard, liopaird, liopardan *nm* a leopard

lios, *gen* **liosa** & **lise,** *pl* **liosan** *nmf* **1** a garden, *cf* **gàrradh 2; 2** (*trad*) an enclosure, *cf* **lann² 1**

Liosach, *gen* & *pl* **Liosaich** *nm* someone from Lismore (**Lios Mòr**), *also as adj,* **Liosach** from, of or pertaining to Lismore

liosda *adj* boring, tedious, *cf* **fadalach 2, màirnealach 2**

liosta, liosta, liostaichean *nf* a list (*of items*)

liotach *adj* lisping

liotachas, *gen* **liotachais** *nm* a lisp, lisping

liotair, liotair, liotairean *nm* a litre

lip, lipe, lipean *nf* a lip, *cf more usu* **bile** *nf* **1**

lite *nf invar* porridge, *cf* **brochan**

litearra *adj* literate

litearrachd *nf invar* literacy

litir, litreach, litrichean *nf* a letter, **litrichean na h-aibidile** the letters of the alphabet, **tapadh leat airson na litreach a chuir thu thugam** thank you for the letter you sent me

litireil *adj* literal

litreachadh, *gen* **litreachaidh** *nm* spelling, orthography, **tha i math air litreachadh** she's good at spelling

litreachail *adj* literary

litreachas, *gen* **litreachais** *nm* literature, **litreachas na Gàidhlig** Gaelic literature, **fèis litreachais** *f* a literature/literary festival

litrich *vti, pres part* **a' litreachadh,** spell

liùdhag, liùdhaig, liùdhagan *nf* a doll

liut, *gen* **liuit** *nf* a knack, a flair, **chan eil an liut agam air sin** I haven't got the knack of/for that

lobh *vi, pres part* **a' lobhadh,** rot, decay, decompose, go bad or rotten, putrefy, *cf* **grod** *v*

lobhadh, *gen* **lobhaidh** *nm* **1** (*the act or process of*) rotting, decaying etc (*see senses of* **lobh** *v*); **2** rottenness, putrefaction, rot, decay; *cf* **grodadh**

lobhar, *gen* & *pl* **lobhair** *nm* a leper, *cf* **luibhre**

lobht(a), lobhta, lobhtaichean *nm* **1** (*in tenement etc*) a storey, a floor, a flat (*ie both storey & individual dwelling*); **2** a loft (*ie roofspace*), *cf* **seòmar-mullaich** (*see* **seòmar**)

lobhte *adj* putrid, rotted, rotten, *cf* **grod** *adj*

locair, locair, locairean *nf also* **locar,** *gen* **locair,** *pl* **locaran** & **locraichean** *nmf* (*carpentry*) a plane

lòcast, *gen* & *pl* **lòcaist** *nm* a locust

loch, locha, lochan *nm* a loch, a lake, **loch-mara** a sea loch, a fjord, **loch-tasgaidh** a reservoir

lochan, lochain, lochanan *nm* (*dimin of* **loch**) a lochan, a small loch

lochd, lochda, lochdan *nm* **1** fault, blame; **2** harm; *cf more usu* **cron**

lochdach *adj* harmful, *cf more usu* **cronail**

Lochlann, *gen* **Lochlainn** *nf* **1** *now used for* Scandinavia; **2** (*trad*) Norway, *cf now more usu* **Nirribhidh**

Lochlannach, *gen* & *pl* **Lochlannaich** *nm* **1** *now used for* a Scandinavian; **2** (*trad*) a Norwegian; **3** (*hist*) a Norseman, a Viking

Lochlannach *adj* **1** *now used for* Scandinavian; **2** (*trad*) Norwegian; **3** (*hist*) Norse, Viking

lòchran, *gen* & *pl* **lòchrain** *nm* a lamp, a lantern, *cf more usu* **lampa, lanntair**

lof, lofa, lofaichean *nmf* a (*shop-bought*) loaf, a breadloaf, *cf* **aran** & *less usu* **buileann**

loidhne, loidhne, loidhnichean *nf* a line, **tarraing** *v* **loidhne** draw a line, **cò a th' agam air an loidhne?** who have I got on the (*phone*) line?, (*IT*) **air-loidhne** on line, online

loingeas & **luingeas,** *gen* **loingeis** *nm* **1** shipping; **2** a fleet, a navy, *cf more usu* **cabhlach, nèibhi(dh)**

lòinidh *nmf invar, with art,* **an lòinidh** rheumatism, rheumatics

loisg *vti, pres part* **a' losgadh, 1** burn, (*prov*) **fear sam bith a loisgeas a mhàs, 's e fhèin a dh'fheumas suidhe air** any man who burns his backside must sit on it himself, **cnàmh-loisg** smoulder, *cf* **las 1** & **2; 2** fire, shoot (*a firearm*), *cf* **tilg 4**

loisgte *adj* burnt

lòistear & **loidsear,** *gen* **lòisteir,** *pl* **lòistearan** *nm* a lodger

lòistinn, lòistinn, lòistinnean *nm* lodging(s), digs, accommodation, *cf less usu* **fàrdach 2**

lom *adj* **1** bare, naked, nude, *cf more usu* **lomnochd, rùisgte; 2** bare, bleak, **sliabh lom** a bare/bleak moor, (*prov*) **is lom an leac air nach buaineadh tu bàirneach** it's a bare rock from which you couldn't gather a limpet; **3** thin, threadbare, **còta lom** a worn/threadbare coat, **brochan lom** thin porridge/gruel; **4** (*weight, sum etc*) net

lom *vt, pres part* **a' lomadh, 1** bare, lay bare, strip, *cf* **rùisg 1; 2** shave (*cf* **beàrr 1**); (*esp of sheep*) shear, clip (*cf* **rùisg 2**); **3** (*lawn, grass*) mow, **feur air a lomadh** mown grass

lomadair, lomadair, lomadairean *nm* a sheep-shearer

lomadh, *gen* **lomaidh** *nm* (*the act of*) baring, shearing etc (*see senses of* **lom** *v*)

loma-làn *adj* completely full, full up, full to the brim, packed, **bha an talla loma-làn** the hall was packed

lomnochd *adj* (*of person*) naked, unclothed, undressed, bare, *cf* **lom** *adj* **1, rùisgte**

lòn[1], *gen* **lòin** *nm* **1** food, nourishment, sustenance, provisions, fare, (*song*) **cha bhi lòn oirnn a dhìth** we will not want for food, *cf more usu* **biadh 1**; **2** (*trad*) a meal, *cf* **biadh 2**, **diathad 1**

lòn[2], **lòin**, **lòintean** *nm* **1** a pool, *cf* **glumag 1**, **linne 1**; **2** a puddle, *cf* **glumag 2**; **3** a meadow, *cf* **clua(i)n**, **dail 1**, **faiche**

lònaid, **lònaide**, **lònaidean** *nf* a lane, *cf* **caol-shràid**

lon-dubh, **loin-duibh**, **loin-dubha** *nm* a blackbird

long, **luinge**, **longan** *nf* a ship, a (sailing) vessel, **long-chogaidh** a warship, a battleship, **long-bhriseadh** *m* a shipwreck

lorg, **luirge**, **lorgan** *nf* **1** (*the act of*) looking for, finding etc (*see senses of* **lorg** *v*); **2** (*left by person, animal, object*) a print, a footprint, a path, a trace, a track, a mark, a vestige, an imprint, **meur-lorg** a fingerprint, (*book title*) **Mo Lorgan Fhìn** My Own Tracks/traces, my own footsteps, **air lorg an fhèidh** on the track/path/trail of the deer, **chan eil lorg air** there's no trace/sign of him/it, *cf* **comharra(dh) 3**, **làrach 1**; **3** *in expr* **faigh** *v* **lorg air** find, locate, track down, **fhuair am poileas lorg air ann an Lunnainn** the police found/located him in London, *cf* **faigh 2**, **lorg** *v* **2**

lorg *vt, pres part* **a' lorg** & **a' lorgadh**, **1** look for, be in search of *or* on the track of, *cf* **sir** & *less usu* **siubhail 4**; **2** find, track down, trace, **lorg mi a' chaora a bha a dhìth** I found the missing sheep, *cf* **amais 2**, **faigh 2**, **lorg** *n* **3**

los *nm invar* **1** (*trad*) a purpose, an intention, **air mo los** (*trad*) for me, for my sake, on my account, because of me (*cf more usu* **airson 3**, **sgàth 3**); **2** *also in expr* **los gu(n)** *conj* so that, in order that, to, *cf more usu* **dòigh 5**, **gus** *conj*

lòsan, *gen* & *pl* **lòsain** *nm* a pane of glass

losgadh, **losgaidh**, **losgaidhean** *nm* **1** (*the act of*) burning etc (*see senses of* **loisg** *v*); **2** a burn, **losgadh-bràghad** heartburn, **losgadh-grèine** sunburn

losgann, **losgainn**, **losgannan** *nm* a frog

lot[1], **lota**, **lotaichean** *nf* a piece *or* holding of land, (*in some districts*) a croft (*cf more usu* **croit 1**)

lot[2], **lota**, **lotan** *nm* a wound, *cf more usu* **leòn** *n*

lot *vti, pres part* **a' lotadh**, wound, *cf more usu* **leòn** *v*

lotadh, *gen* **lotaidh** *nm* (*the act of*) wounding

loth, **lotha**, **lothan** *nmf* **1** a filly; **2** (*occas*) a foal, a colt, *cf more usu* **searrach**

luach *nm invar* **1** worth, value, **dè an luach a th' ann?** what's it worth? **gun luach** worthless,

cf more usu **fiù** *n* **1**; **2** (*fin*) a rate, **luach na h-iomlaide** the rate of exchange, **luach rèidh** an interest rate; **3** *in expr* **cuir** *v* **luach air** evaluate, value, *cf* **luachaich**

luachachadh, **luachachaidh**, **luachachaidhean** *nm* (*the act of*) evaluating etc (*see senses of* **luachaich** *v*); **2** (*also* **luachadh**, **luachaidh**, **luachaidhean** *nm*) valuation, a valuation, an evaluation, *cf* **meas**[1] **2**

luachaich *vt, pres part* **a' luachachadh**, evaluate, value, put a price or value on, *cf* **luach 2**, **meas** *v* **3**

luachair, *gen* **luachrach** *nf* a rush (*ie the plant*), rushes

luachmhor *adj* valuable, precious, *cf* **prìseil**

luadhadh, *gen* **luadhaidh** *nm* **1** (*trad*) (*the act of*) waulking *or* fulling cloth (*by hand or with the feet*); **2** (*also* **luadh**, *gen* **luaidh** *nm*) a waulking (*ie occasion when fulling was done*), **òrain luadhaidh** (*also* **òrain luaidh**) waulking songs (*to accompany fulling of cloth*)

luaidh[1] *nm invar* **1** (*the act of*) praising, mentioning *cf* **moladh 1**; **2** praise, **dèan luaidh (air)** praise (*cf* **mol** *v* **1**); *cf* **cliù 2**, **moladh 2**

luaidh[2], **luaidhe**, **luaidhean** *nmf* a beloved person, *often in voc*, **a luaidh!/mo luaidh!** love!/my love! darling!/my darling! *cf* **eudail 2**, **gaol 2**, **gràdh 2**, **laogh 2**

luaidh[1] *vt, pres part* **a' luaidh**, **1** praise, *cf* **mol** *v* **1**; **2** mention

luaidh[2] *vti, pres part* **a' luadhadh**, waulk *or* full cloth, hold or be engaged in a waulking

luaidhe *nmf invar* lead, **bha dath na luaidhe air a' mhuir** the sea was the colour of lead, **saighdear luaidhe** a lead soldier

luaineach *adj* restless, changeable, fickle, *cf* **caochlaideach 1 & 2**, **carach 2**

luaisg *vi, pres part* **a' luasgadh**, rock, shake, oscillate, sway, swing, toss, wave, *cf* **tulg 1**

luaithre *nf invar*, *also* **luath**, *gen* **luaith** & **luatha(inn)** *nf*, ash, ashes

luamhan, *gen* **luamhain**, *pl* **luamhain** & **luamhanan** *nm* a lever

luas & **luaths**, *gen* **luai(th)s** *nm* **1** speed, velocity, *cf* **astar 2**; **2** agility, *cf* **lùth 2**

luasgadh, *gen* **luasgaidh** *nm* (*the act of*) rocking etc (*see senses of* **luaisg** *v*)

luasgan, *gen* **luasgain** *nm* **1** a rocking, shaking etc movement (*see senses of* **luaisg** *v*), oscillation; **2** giddiness, dizziness, *cf more usu* **tuainealaich**

luath *adj* **1** (*phys*) fast, swift, speedy, rapid, quick, **each luath** a fast horse, **luath-thrèana** *f* a fast/an express train, *cf* **astarach**; **2** (*mentally*)

quick, sharp, agile, **tha e luath na inntinn**
he's quick/sharp, he's mentally agile, *cf* **grad**
2; **3** *in expr* **cho luath agus/is** as soon as, no
sooner than, **thòisich iad ri trod cho luath 's**
a thàinig iad a-steach they started squabbling
as soon as/the moment they came in; **4** *also in*
expr **luath no mall** sooner or later, eventually
luath *nf see* **luaithre**
luathachadh, *gen* **luathachaidh** *nm* **1** (*the*
act of) accelerating, hurrying etc (*see senses of*
luathaich *v*); **2** acceleration
luathaich *vti, pres part* **a' luathachadh**,
1 accelerate, speed up, **bha an càr/an**
dràibhear a' luathachadh the car/the driver
was accelerating, **luathaich sinn ar ceum** we
quickened/increased our pace; **2** *as vt* hurry
(on), **bha an tidsear gar luathachadh aig**
deireadh an leasain the teacher was hurrying
us on at the end of the lesson, *cf* **greas 2**
luaths *see* **luas**
lùb, lùib, lùban *nf* **1** a bend, a curve, a meander,
tha lùb mhòr air/anns a' bhata the stick
has a big bend in it, *cf* **caime**; **2** a loop, a noose;
3 *in expr* **an lùib** (*with gen*) involved in *or*
with, implicated in, under the influence of, *also*
associated with, connected with, attached to,
tha dealbh an lùib gach facail a picture
accompanies/is associated with each word (*cf*
cas *n* **4**)
lùb *vti, pres part* **a' lùbadh**, **1** bend, curve, bow,
lùb a' ghlùin bend/bow the knee (*esp for*
prayer), *cf* **crom** *v* **1 & 2**, **fiar** *v*; **2** (*river etc*)
meander
lùbach *adj* **1** bending, having bends; **2** pliant,
flexible, bendy, **bata lùbach** a pliant stick,
cf **sùbailte**; **3** (*road, river, argument etc*)
meandering, tortuous, winding
lùbadh, *gen* **lùbaidh** *nm* (*the act of*) bending,
curving etc (*see senses of* **lùb** *v*)
lùbte *adj* bent, curved, bowed, *cf* **cam, crom** *adj*,
fiar *adj* **1**
luch, *gen* **lucha & luchainn**, *pl* **luchan &**
luchainn *nf* a mouse
lùchairt, lùchairte, lùchairtean *nf* a palace, *cf*
less trad **pàileis**
luchd¹, luchda, luchdan *nm* a cargo, a load, *cf*
cargu, uallach
luchd² *nm invar* people, *used only in gen exprs,*
as pl of **fear** *or* **neach**, *eg* (*song*) **tha mi sgìth**
de luchd na Beurla I'm weary of people
of English speech, **luchd-casaid** accusers,
prosecutors, **luchd-eòlais** acquaintances,
luchd-frithealaidh attendants, **luchd-**
obrach workers, a workforce, staff, **luchd-**
turais tourists, *cf* **duine 5, fear 2, neach 2**

luchdachadh, *gen* **luchdachaidh** *nm* (*the act*
or process of) loading
luchdaich *vt, pres part* **a' luchdachadh**, load
(*boat, vehicle etc*)
luchdmhor *adj* capacious, able to take a large
cargo
luchraban, *gen & pl* **luchrabain** *nm* a dwarf, a
midget, *cf* **troich**
Lucsamburg *nf*, *also* **Lugsamburg,**
Luxembourg
Lucsamburgach, *gen & pl* **Lucsamburgaich**
nm someone from Luxembourg (**Lucsamburg**),
also as adj **Lucsamburgach** of, from or
pertaining to Luxembourg
lùdag, lùdaig, lùdagan *nf* **1** a little finger, (*Sc*) a
pinkie (finger); **2** a hinge, *cf* **banntach**
lugha *comp adj, in comp exprs* **(n)as** (*etc*) **lugha**
smaller *etc* (*see* **beag**), **tha am bàta seo nas**
lugha this boat is smaller, **'s e mo chùid-sa a**
bu lugha it's my share that was smaller
lùghdachadh, *gen* **lùghdachaidh** *nm* **1** (*the act*
of) lessening etc (*see senses of* **lùghdaich** *v*); **2**
shrinkage, diminution, a diminution, abatement,
an abatement, reduction, a reduction, decrease, a
decrease, **lùghdachadh màil** a rent reduction
lùghdaich *vti, pres part* **a' lùghdachadh**,
lessen, decrease, diminish, reduce, shrink, make
or become smaller, abate
luibh, luibhe, luibhean *nmf* a herb, a plant, a
weed, **luibh-eòlas** *m* botany, *cf* **lus 1 & 2**
luibheach *adj* botanical
luibhre *nf invar* leprosy, *cf* **lobhar**
luideach *adj* **1** shabby, scruffy, slovenly, untidy,
ragged, *cf* **cearbach 2**; **2** silly
luideag, luideig, luideagan *nf* a rag, *cf* **cearb 1**
luidhear, luidheir, luidhearan *nm* a ship's
funnel, a (*usu non-domestic*) chimney, *cf*
similear
luime *nf invar* (*abstr noun corres to* **lom** *adj*)
nakedness, bleakness etc
Luinneach, *gen & pl* **Luinnich** *nm* someone
from Luing (**Eilean Luinn**), *also as adj*
Luinneach of, from or pertaining to Luing
luinneag, luinneig, luinneagan *nf* a ditty, a
short song, (*song title*) **Luinneag MhicLeòid**
MacLeod's Ditty, *cf* **duan 2**
Lùnastal, *gen* **Lùnastail** *nm*, *used with art*, **an**
Lùnastal August, **Là Lùnastail** Lammas Day,
August 1st
Lunnainn *n* London
lurach *adj* (*trad*) pretty, nice; beloved, (*song*) **bò**
lurach thu, bò na h-àirigh you nice/beloved
cow you, shieling cow, *cf more usu* **àlainn,**
laghach, snog 2

lurgann, *gen* lurgainn, *pl* lurgannan &
  luirgnean *nf* a shin (*also* faobhar na
  lurgainn)
lus, *gen* luis & lusa, *pl* lusan *nm* 1 a herb, lus
  MhicCuimein cumin; 2 a plant, a weed, lus a'
  chrom-chinn the daffodil, *cf* luibh
lùth, *gen* lùtha *nm*, *also* lùths, *gen* lùiths *nm*,
  1 movement, the power or faculty of movement,
  tha e gun lùth(s) he is unable to move/

without the power of motion; 2 (*power of swift
movement*) agility, nimbleness, *cf* cliseachd,
luas 2; 3 energy, vigour, bodily strength, *cf*
brìgh 4, neart, spionnadh
lùthmhor *adj* 1 strong, (*phys*) powerful, *cf* làidir
1, neartmhor; 2 agile, nimble, athletic, *cf* clis;
3 energetic, vigorous, *cf* brìoghmhor 2
lùths *see* lùth

M

ma *conj* if, *neg* **mur(a)** if . . . not, **leig d' anail ma tha thu sgìth** have a break if you're tired, **cha tig mi ma bhios Anndra ann** I won't come if Andrew will be there, **cha tèid mise mura bheil** (*fam* **mur eil**) **thusa air a shon** I won't go if you're not keen on it, **dùin an doras, mas e** (*for* **ma is e**) **do thoil e** close the door, please (*lit* if it is your will), *cf* **nan** *conj*; **2** *in expr* **ma-thà** *or* **ma-tà** then, in that case, **tha an doras fosgailte, dùin e, ma-tà!** the door's open, close it, then!, **ceart, ma-thà!** right, then!, *cf* **a-rèist**

màb *vt, pres part* **a' màbadh**, abuse (*verbally*), revile, vilify

màbadh, *gen* **màbaidh** *nm* (*the act of*) abusing etc (*see senses of* **màb** *v*)

mac, *gen & pl* **mic** *nm* a son, **tha dithis mhac** (*gen pl*) **aca** they have two sons, **mac mo bhràthar** & **mac mo pheathar** my nephew, **am mac stròdhail/struidheil** the prodigal son; **2** *in various exprs & excls eg* **a mhic an donais!** damn it! (*lit* son (*voc*) of the evil one), **mac-na-bracha** (*a nickname for*) malt whisky (*lit* son of the malt), **mac-talla** an echo, **mac-an-aba** the ring finger (*lit* son of the abbot), **mac-an-duine** mankind (*cf usu* **an cinne-daonna**, *see* **daonna**); **3** *as* **Mac-** *in clan surnames* (*and other surnames adapted to the Gaelic system*), a (male) descendant of the real or supposed progenitor of the clan, **MacAonghais** MacInnes, a descendant of Angus, **Mac an Tàilleir** Taylor, *cf* **nic-**

macanta *adj* meek, submissive, *cf* **umha(i)l**[1] **2**

mach *see* **a-mach**

machair(e), **machrach**, **machraichean** *nmf, applied to grassy stretches of land adjoining the Atlantic seaboard, affording excellent grazing, similar to links but usu more level,* machair-land, a machair; **2** a plain, low-lying level land, *esp in* (**air**) **a' Mhachair Ghallta** (in) the (Scottish) Lowlands (*cf* **Galltachd**)

machlag, **machlaig**, **machlagan** *nf* a womb, a uterus, *cf* **broinn 1**, **brù 1**

mac-meanmna, *gen* **mic-meanmna** *nm* imagination, an imagination

mac-meanmnach *adj* **1** imaginary; **2** imaginative

mac-samhail, *gen & pl* **mic-samhail** *nm* **1** a replica, a duplicate, a facsimile of something, *cf* **lethbhreac 2**; **2** the equal, match, 'fellow' (*cf Sc* marrow), 'image', like or likeness of someone or something, *cf* **leithid**, **lethbhreac 1**, **samhail**, **seis(e)**

mac-talla *see* **mac 2**

madadh, **madaidh**, **madaidhean** *nm, an animal of the canine species,* **1** a dog, *cf more usu* **cù**; **2** (*esp* **madadh-ruadh**) a fox, (*prov*) **cho carach ris a' mhadadh-ruadh** as wily as the fox, *cf* **balgair 1**, **sionnach**; **3** (*esp* **madadh-allaidh**) a wolf, *cf* **faol**

madainn, **maidne**, *pl* **maidnean** & **madainnean** *nf* morning, (*news programme*) **Aithris na Maidne** Morning Report/Bulletin, **bha uisge ann air a' mhadainn** it rained during/in the course of the morning, **rugadh i sa mhadainn an-diugh/an-dè** she was born this/yesterday morning, **trì uairean sa mhadainn** three in the morning, 3 a.m.

ma dh'fhaodte *see* **faod 2**

màg, **màig**, **màgan** *nf* a paw, (*in expr*) **air a** (*etc*) **mhàgan** *also* **air mhàgaran**, on all fours, on (*his etc*) hands and knees, *cf* **cròg 1**, **spòg 1**

mag *vi, pres part* **a' magadh**, mock, deride, jeer, scoff, make fun, (**air** at, of), **clann (is iad) a' magadh air a' bhodach bhochd** children mocking/making fun of the poor old man, *cf* **fanaid 1**

magadh, *gen* **magaidh** *nm* **1** (*the act of*) mocking etc (*see senses of* **mag** *v*); **2** mockery; *cf* **fanaid 1**

magail *adj* mocking, jeering, scoffing, making fun; *also* apt to mock, jeer etc

magairle, **magairle**, **magairlean** *nmf* a testicle, *cf* (*more fam*) **clach** *n* **3**

maghar, **maghair**, **maghairean** *nm* **1** a fly (*for fly-fishing*); **2** bait, *cf* **baoit**

maide, maide, maidean nm 1 wood, timber, a
piece of wood or timber, *usu shaped or worked
for a specific purpose, cf* **fiodh** *which is rather
wood in general or in its natural state, eg*
maide-droma & **maide-mullaich** a ridge-
pole, a roof-tree; 2 a stick, **maide poite** a
spirtle, **am maide-crochaidh** the hanging
stick (*formerly a stick hung around the neck of
children caught speaking Gaelic at school), cf*
bata 1

maids(e), maidse, maidsichean nm 1 a match
(*ie for lighting), cf more trad* **lasadair; 2**
(*sport, esp football*) a match, *cf* **geama 2**

màidsear, màidseir, màidsearan nm (*army
etc*) a major

Màigh, *gen* **Màighe** nf, *with art* **a' Mhàigh** (the
month of) May, *cf more trad* **Cèitean**

maighdeann, *gen* **maighdinn,** *pl*
maighdeannan & **maighdinnean** nf 1
(*trad*) a maiden, a maid, a young woman,
maighdeann mo rùin my beloved maiden,
maighdeann-mhara a mermaid, *common
in songs eg* **maighdeannan na h-àirigh** the
sheiling maidens, *cf* **gruagach, nighean 2,
nìghneag 2, rìbhinn;** 2 a virgin, *cf* **ainnir;**
3 an unmarried woman, a spinster, **seana-
mhaighdeann** an elderly spinster, an old
maid; 4 *in formal address, corres,* Miss, **A
Mhaighdeann(-uasal) Chaimbeul,** *abbrev* **A
Mh(-uas) Chaimbeul,** (Dear) Miss Campbell

maighdeannas, *gen* **maighdeannais** nm (*phys
& abstr*) virginity, maidenhood, maidenhead

maigheach, maighiche, maighichean nf a
hare, *cf* **geàrr** n

maighstir, maighstir, maighstirean nm 1 a
master, **maighstir-sgoile** a schoolmaster, a
schoolteacher (*usu primary), also* a headteacher
(*usu secondary*), **ban(a)-mhaighstir-sgoile**
f a schoolmistress (*cf* **fear-teagaisg** (*see*
teagasg), **tìdsear**); 2 *in formal address, corres,*
(*abbrev* **Mgr**) Mister, Mr., **A Mhaighstir
Fhriseil** (*abbrev* **A Mhgr Fhriseil**) (Dear) Mr
Fraser

màileid, màileide, màileidean nf *various
kinds of leather etc bags*, a suitcase, a briefcase,
a (*large*) bag, a satchel, **màileid-làimhe**
a handbag, **màileid-droma** a rucksack, a
backpack (*cf* **paca 1**), *cf* **baga, ceas** n, **poca**

maille nf invar 1 (*abstr noun corres to* **mall**)
slowness; 2 delay, a delay, **cuir** v **maille air** or
ann delay, impede, hold back, retard, slow down
(*a process etc*), **ma thèid maille orra** if they're
held up/delayed, *cf* **dàil 2**

mailleachadh, *gen* **mailleachaidh** nm (*the act
of*) procrastinating etc (*see senses of* **maillich** v)

maille ri *prep* with, along with, **bidh sinn a'
falbh maille ri càch** we'll be leaving along
with the others, *cf* **cuide ri, mar 5,** & *more usu*
còmhla 2, le 1

maillich vti, *pres part* **a' mailleachadh,**
procrastinate, delay, defer, retard, *cf*
màirnealaich

mair vi, *pres part* **a' mairsinn,** *also* **a'
maireann** & **a' maireachdainn,** last, continue
(in existence), **cha mhair e dà latha** he/it
won't last two days, **mair beò** live, survive, **ma
mhaireas mi** if I live/survive, if I'm spared,
(*prov*) **cha mhair a' ghrian mhaidne rè an
latha** the morning sun won't last all day

maireann (*adj,* & *obs pres part/verbal noun of*
mair v) 1 *in expr* **rim** (*etc*) **mhaireann** during
my (etc) lifetime, as long as I (etc) live, *cf* **beò 2,
saoghal 2;** 2 *in expr* **nach maireann** the late
..., **Seonaidh Caimbeul nach maireann**
the late Johnny Campbell

maireannach adj 1 eternal, everlasting, **beatha
mhaireannach** everlasting life; 2 durable,
lasting, abiding, **sìth mhaireannach** (a) lasting
peace; 3 (*of individual*) long-lived; *cf* **buan**

mairg adj (*trad*) pitiable, to be pitied, *esp in expr*
(**is**) **mairg a** ... woe to ..., (*song*) (**'s**) **mairg
a dhèanadh mo bhualadh** woe to him who
would strike me, **is mairg a thigeadh faisg
air** woe to/pity anyone who would come near
him

màirnealach adj 1 slow, dilatory, *cf* **athaiseach**
& *more usu* **mall, slaodach 1;** 2 long drawn
out, boring, tedious, *cf* **fadalach 2, slaodach
2, ràsanach**

màirnealaich vi, *pres part* **a'
màirnealachadh,** delay, procrastinate, (*fig*)
drag one's heels, *cf* **maillich**

mairtfheoil, *gen* **mairtfheòla** nf beef

maise nf invar beauty, loveliness, gracefulness,
maise na nighinne the girl's beauty, **ball-
maise** m an ornament, *also* a beauty spot (*on
face), cf* **bòidhchead**

maiseach adj (*esp of woman*) beautiful, lovely,
graceful, handsome, *cf* **àlainn, bòidheach**

**maiseachadh, maiseachaidh,
maiseachaidhean** nm 1 (*the act of*) decorating
etc (*see senses of* **maisich** v); 2 decoration, a
decoration, embellishment, an embellishment, *cf*
sgeadachadh 2

maisich vt, *pres part* **a' maiseachadh,** 1
decorate, beautify, embellish, *cf* **brèaghaich,
sgeadaich 1;** 2 make up (*ie with cosmetics*),
mhaisich i a h-aodann she made up her face

maith *see* **math** v & n

màithreil adj motherly, maternal

màl, *gen & pl* **màil** *nm* rent, **gabh** *v* **taigh air mhàl** rent a house (*as tenant*), **thoir** *v* **seachad taigh air mhàl** rent (out) a house (*as landlord*), **taigh air mhàl** a rented house

mala, mala, malaichean *nf* 1 an eyebrow; 2 a brow, *cf* **bathais** 1, **clàr** 2, **maoil**

malairt, malairt, malairtean *nf* 1 trade, business, commerce, a business, **dèan** *v* **malairt** trade, do business (*cf* **malairtich**), *cf* **gnìomhachas** 2, **gnothach** 1; 2 barter, exchange, *cf* **iomlaid** 1

malairteach *adj* commercial, **ealain mhalairteach** commercial art

malairtich *vi, pres part* **a' malairteachadh**, 1 trade, engage in trade or commerce, *cf* **malairt** 1; 2 barter, exchange

màlda *adj* coy, bashful, modest, *cf* **nàrach** 2

mall *adj* (*of persons, events*) slow, tardy, lethargic, *cf* **athaiseach** & *more usu* **màirnealach** 1, **slaodach** 1

mallachadh, *gen* **mallachaidh** *nm* (*the act of*) cursing (*see* **mallaich** *v*)

mallachd & **mollachd**, *gen* **mallachd**, *pl* **mallachdan** *nf* a curse, malediction, a malediction, (*song*) **mallachd nan Gàidheal gu lèir air Rìgh Uilleam 's air a threud** the curse of every Gael on King William and on his gang

mallaich *vt, pres part* **a' mallachadh**, curse

mallaichte *adj* cursed, accursed, damned

mamaidh, mamaidh, mamaidhean *nf* (*child's lang*) mammy, mummy, *cf* **màthair** 1

manach, *gen & pl* **manaich** *nm* a monk

manachainn, manachainne, manachainnean *nf* a monastery

manadh, manaidh, manaidhean *nm* an omen

manaidsear, manaidseir, manaidsearan *nm* a manager, **bana-mhanaidsear** *f* a manageress, *cf* **fear-riaghlaidh** (*see* **riaghladh** 3), **fear-stiùiridh** (*see* **stiùireadh**)

Manainneach, *gen & pl* **Manainnich** *nm* a Manxman, *also as adj* **Manainneach** Manx, of, from or pertaining to the Isle of Man (**Eilean Mhanainn** & **an t-Eilean Manainneach**)

mànas, mànais, mànasan *nm* (*agric*) the mains or home farm of an estate

mang, mainge, mangan *nf* a fawn

maodal, maodail, maodalan *nf* a (large) stomach, a paunch, a belly, *cf* **balg** 1, **brù** 2, **stamag**

maoidh *vi, pres part* **a' maoidheadh**, 1 threaten, menace (*with prep* **air**), **bha e a' maoidheadh orm** he was threatening me, *cf* **bagair** 1; 2 bully

maoidheadh, maoidhidh, maoidhidhean *nm* 1 (*the act of*) threatening, menacing, bullying; 2 a threat, a menace; 3 bullying

maoidhear, maoidheir, maoidhearan *nm* a bully

maoil, maoil, maoilean *nf* a forehead, a brow (*not eyebrow, cf* **mala** 1), *cf* **bathais** 1, **clàr** 2, **mala** 2

Maoil, *gen* **Maoile** *nf, with art*, **a' Mhaoil** the Minch

maoile *nf invar, also* **maoilead**, *gen* **maoileid** *nm*, baldness (*abstr nouns corres to* **maol** *adj*)

maoin, maoine, maoinean, *nf* 1 goods (*not usu at point of sale, cf* **bathar**); 2 one's wordly goods, possessions, goods and chattels, (*Sc*) gear; 3 worldly wealth, riches, assets, *cf more usu* **beartas, saidhbhreas**

maol *adj* 1 (*knife etc*) blunt; 2 bald, *cf* **sgallach**; 3 hornless, **bò mhaol odhar agus bò odhar mhaol** six and half a dozen (*lit* a hornless dun cow and a dun hornless cow)

maol, *gen & pl* **maoil** *nm* 1 a cape, a promontory (*usu rounded*), *cf* **àird(e)** *n* 2, **rubha, sròn** 2; 2 (*topog*) a rounded bare hill

maor, *gen & pl* **maoir** *nm* 1 (*trad*) referring to a number of subordinate & middle-ranking positions in the law, land-management etc, eg a bailiff (*cf* **bàillidh** 1), a land/township constable (*cf* **con(a)stabal**), a factor (*cf* **seumarlan** 1), a (land) steward (*cf* **stiùbhard**); 2 *in compands*, **maor-eaglais** a church officer, **maor (-obrach)** a foreman, a gaffer, **maor dùthcha/ pàirce** a countryside/park ranger, **maor-cladaich** a coastguard (*cf less usu* **freiceadan-oirthire** – *see* **freiceadan**)

maorach, *gen* **maoraich** *nm* shellfish, a shellfish

maoth *adj* 1 (*phys or emotionally*) soft, tender, delicate, *cf* **bog** *adj* 1; 2 tender(-hearted), affectionate, loving, *cf* **gaolach** 1, **gràdhach**

maothachadh, *gen* **maothachaidh** *nm* (*the act of*) softening (*see senses of* **maothaich** *v*)

maothaich *vti, pres part* **a' maothachadh**, soften, make or become soft or softer

mapa, mapa, mapaichean *nm* a map, **mapa na Roinn Eòrpa** the map of Europe, *cf* **clàr** 4

mar 1 *prep*, in the manner of, like, *Note: a noun without the art after* **mar** *is in the dat, & lenited, eg* **a' cluich mar chaileig** playing like a girl, (*but cf*) **mar a' chaileag** like the girl; **thug e Canada air dìreach mar a bhràthair** he went off to Canada just like his brother, (*common saying*) **is ann mar sin a tha agus a bha agus a bhitheas** that's how/ the way it is and always was and always will be; 2 *in expr* **mar sin** so, **chaill mi mo mhàileid-**

pòca 's mar sin chan eil sgillinn ruadh
agam I lost my wallet and so I haven't a brass
farthing, *also in leave-taking* **mar sin leat/
leibh!** 'bye, then!, 'bye just now! (*cf* **tìoraidh!**
& more formal **beannachd 4**); **3** *in exprs* **mar
sin** & **mar sin air adhart** and so on, **briogais,
brògan 's mar sin** trousers, shoes and so on/
that kind of thing, **thuirt i gun robh sinn
leisg, mì-mhodhail, luideach . . . 's mar sin
air adhart** she said we were lazy, rude, scruffy
. . . and so on; **4** *in expr* **mar eisimpleir** for
example (*abbrev* **me** & **m.e.**); **5** (*trad*) **mar ri**
prep with, along with, **'s truagh nach eil thu
mar rium** it's sad that you aren't with me, *cf
more usu* **còmhla 2**; **6** *in expr* **mar an ceudna**
adv likewise, too, similarly, **bha athair an sàs
ann am poilitigs – e fhèin mar an ceudna**
his father was involved in politics – himself too/
likewise, *cf* **cuideachd** *adv*
mar a *conj* as, how, **bitheadh sin mar a
bhitheas e** be that as it may, **mar a chanas
iad** as they say, **thachair a h-uile càil mar
a thogradh sinn** everything happened as we
would wish, **tha sinn dòigheil mar a tha
sinn** we're fine/contented as we are, **dh'innis
i dha mar a chuala i** she told him what she
had heard, **is truagh mar a thachair** it's sad
the way things turned out, it's a shame what
happened, (*prov*) **mar as** (*for* **mar a is**) **sine
am boc 's ann as cruaidhe an adharc** the
older the buck the harder the horn
mar gun/nach *conj* as if, as though, **lean e air
mar nach robh e gu diofar** he carried on/
continued as if/as though it didn't matter, **bha
i, mar gum biodh, fad' às** she was, as it were,
withdrawn
mar a tha, *also* **mar-thà**, *adv* already, *see* **tràth**
adj & adv **3**
marag, maraig, maragan *nf* **1** a pudding
(*savoury, not sweet –* *cf* **mìlsean**), **marag
dhubh/gheal** black/white pudding; **2** (*occas*) a
haggis, *cf* **taigeis**
maraiche, maraiche, maraichean *nm* a sailor,
a seaman, a seafarer, a mariner, (*song*) (**'s e**) **'n
fhìrinn a th' agam nach maraiche mi** I'm
no sailor and that's the truth, *cf* **seòladair**
marbh *adj* dead, **corp marbh** a dead body, a
corpse, **a' mhìos mharbh** the dead month
(February), **ann am marbh na h-oidhche** in
the dead of night, **uisge marbh** stagnant water
marbh *vt, pres part* **a' marbhadh**, kill, slay,
(*poem*) **creachadh, losgadh agus marbhadh**
plundering, burning and killing, *cf* **murt** *v*
marbhadh, *gen* **marbhaidh** *nm* (*the act of*)
killing etc (*see senses of* **marbh** *v*)

marbhaiche, marbhaiche, marbhaichean
nm a killer, a murderer, *cf* **murtair**
marbhan, marbhain, marbhanan *nm* a
corpse, a dead body, *cf more usu* **corp 2**
**marbhphaisg, marbhphaisge,
marbhphaisgean** *nf* a shroud, a windingsheet,
trad, in curses, eg (*song*) **mìle marbhphaisg
air a' ghaol/air na fearaibh** (*obs dat pl*) a
thousand shrouds on love/on men
marbhrann, marbhrainn, marbhrannan *nm*
(*trad*) a poem in praise of a dead hero etc, an
elegy, *cf* **cumha** *nm*
marbhtach *adj* deadly, fatal, mortal, death-
dealing, **buille mharbhtach** a deadly/mortal
(etc) blow, *cf* **bàsmhor 2**
marcachadh, *gen* **marcachaidh** *nm, also*
marcachd *nf invar*, **1** (*the act of*) riding (*see
senses of* **marcaich** *v*); **2** horsemanship, **sgoil
mharcachd** a riding school
marcaich *vi, pres part* **a' marcachd** & **a'
marcachadh**, ride (*esp horses*)
marcaiche, marcaiche, marcaichean *nm* a
(*horse*) rider, a horseman
marcaid *see* **margadh**
margadh, margaidh, margaidhean *nmf,
also* **marcaid, marcaide, marcaidean** *nf*,
1 a (*weekly etc*) market, **ionad-margaidh** *m*
a market-place, **baile-margaidh** *m* a market
town, *cf* **fèill 3**; **2** (*economics*) a market, **am
Margadh Coitcheann** the Common Market,
eaconomaidh saor-mhargaidh a free market
economy, **am bi margadh air?** will there be a
market for it? (*cf* **fèill 4**)
margarain *nm invar* margarine
màrmor, *gen* **màrmoir** *nm* marble
màrsail, *gen* **màrsaile** *nf* marching, a march,
sometimes used as pres part, **a' màrsail**
marching, *cf* **caismeachd 2**, **mèarrsadh**
Màrt, *gen* **Màirt** *nm* **1** (*the planet*) Mars; **2** *with
art* **am Màrt** March
mart, *gen & pl* **mairt** *nm* (*trad*) any bovine, (*now
usu*) a beef animal, (*Sc*) a mart
màs, màis, màsan *nm* **1** a buttock; **2** (*fam*) a
bottom, a backside, *cf* **tòn 2**
mas fhìor *see* **fìor 4**
masg, masg, masgan *nm* a mask, *cf* **aghaidh-
choimheach, aodannan**
ma sgaoil (*see* **sgaoil** *n*)
maslach *adj* disgraceful, shameful, deplorable, *cf*
nàr, tàmailteach 1
maslachadh, *gen* **maslachaidh** *nm* (*the act of*)
disgracing etc (*see senses of* **maslaich** *v*)
masladh, maslaidh, maslaidhean *nm*
disgrace, shame, **'s e cùis-mhaslaidh**

maslaich

a th' ann! (*cf* **cùis 4**) it's a disgrace!, *cf* **nàire 1**, **tàmailt 1**

maslaich *vt, pres part* **a' maslachadh**, disgrace, shame, put to shame, **chaidh mo mhaslachadh** I was put to shame, *cf* **nàraich**

matamataig *nm invar* mathematics, maths

math *adj* (*comp* **(n)as** (etc) **fheàrr** better, best, *see* **feàrr**), **1** good (*in quality*) **biadh math** good food, (*in quantity*) **pìos math coiseachd** a good/fair bit of walking, (*morally*) **duine math** a good man, (*in standard, ability*) **cluicheadair math** a good player, **math air òrain** good at singing, (*in accuracy*) **mas math mo chuimhne** if I remember rightly/correctly, (*expr a wish, greeting*) **madainn/oidhche mhath!** good morning/night!, (*expr approval, pleasure*) **glè mhath!** very good/excellent! **'s math sin!** that's good/smashing!, **math dha-rìribh!** very good indeed!, splendid!, **math thu fhèin!** good for you!, well done!, **'s math d' fhaicinn!** it's good to see you, **'s math gu bheil thu a' cumail sùil air** it's good that you're keeping an eye on him; **2** *as adv* well, **nach math a rinn thu!** didn't you do well!, well done!; **3** *in expr* **cho math ri** as well as, in addition to, **dh'ith e marag cho math ri pìos math feòla** he ate a pudding as well as a good bit of meat; **4** *in expr* **gu math** *adv* well, quite, **tha mi gu math** I am well, **bha iad gu math aosta** they were quite/pretty old, (*calque*) **tha e (gu) math dheth** he's well off; **5** (is) **ma(th) dh'fhaodte** *see* **faod 2**

math, *gen* **maith** *nm* good, **am math is an t-olc** good and evil, **dè am math a bhith a' bruidhinn?** what's the good/use of talking? (*cf* **feum** *n* **3**)

math & **maith** *vi, pres part* **a' mathadh**, forgive, **math dhuinn ar peacaidhean!** forgive us our sins!, *cf* **mathanas**

mathachadh, *gen* **mathachaidh** *nm* manure, fertilizer etc (*used to enrich land*), *also* the act of adding this to land, *cf* **inneir**, **leasachadh 4**, **todhar**

mathadh, *gen* **mathaidh** *nm* (*the act of*) forgiving (*see* **math** *v*)

mathaich *vt, pres part* **a' mathachadh**, manure, enrich, fertilize land (*by adding manure etc*), *cf* **leasaich 3**

màthair, **màthar**, **màthraichean** *nf* **1** a mother, **màthair-chèile** a mother-in-law; **2** (*occas, esp in compounds*) the origin or prime example of something, *eg* **màthair-adhbhar** *m* a prime cause, **màthair-uisge** *m* a fountainhead

màthaireachd *nf invar* motherhood, maternity

mathan, **mathain**, *pl* **mathain** & **mathanan** *nm* a (brown) bear, **mathan bàn** a polar bear

mathanas, *gen* **mathanais** *nm* forgiveness, pardon, **thoir** *v* **mathanas dhomh** forgive me (*cf* **math** *v*)

mathas, *gen* **mathais** *nm* goodness

me & **m.e.** (*abbrev*) *see* **mar 4**

meadhan, **meadhain**, **meadhanan** *nm* **1** a middle, a centre, **meadhan a' bhaile** the town centre/middle of the town, **ann an teis-meadhan** (*also* **ceart-mheadhan**) **an achaidh** in the dead centre of the field; **2** an average, a mean; **3** a medium, a mechanism, a means, **foghlam tro mheadhan na Gàidhlig** Gaelic-medium education, (*press, TV etc*) **na meadhanan** the media; **4** a waist, **crios mum mheadhan** a belt around my middle/waist; **5** *adjectivally in compound exprs, eg* **meadhan-aois** *f* middle age, **meadhan-aoiseil** *adj* medieval, **am meadhan-chearcall** *m* the equator, **meadhan-latha/-oidhche** *m* noon/midnight, **meadhan-sheachnach** *adj* centrifugal

meadhanach *adj* **1** middling, tolerable, average, so-so, **chan eil mi ach meadhanach an-diugh** I'm only middling (well)/so-so today, **cha do rinn thu ach meadhanach math** you only did tolerably/middling well; **2** middle, **An Ear Mheadhanach** *f* the Middle East

Meadhan-thìreach *adj* Mediterranean

meal *vt, pres part* **a' mealadh** & **a' mealtainn**, enjoy (*cf* **còrd** *v* **2**), *esp in exprs* **meal do naidheachd!** congratulations! (*lit* enjoy your news) & **cuir** *v* **meal-a-naidheachd air cuideigin** congratulate someone

mealadh, *gen* **mealaidh** *nm, also* **mealtainn** *nm invar*, **1** (*the act of*) enjoying (*see* **meal** *v*); **2** enjoyment

meal-bhucan, **meal-bhucain**, *pl* **meal-bhucain** & **meal-bhucanan** *nm* a melon

meall, *gen* & *pl* **mill** *nm* **1** a lump of anything, *cf* **cnap 1**; **2** (*topog*) a (*usu lumpy*) hill, a lump of a hill, *cf* **cnap 3**; **3** **meall uisge** *m* a shower of rain (*heavier than* **fras** *n* **1**); **4** **meall an sgòrnain** the adam's apple

meall *vt, pres part* **a' mealladh**, **1** deceive, trick, cheat, **carson, a ghaoil, a mheall thu mi?** why, my love, did you deceive me?; **2** beguile, entice, tempt, allure, **mheall an nathair Eubha** the serpent beguiled Eve, *cf* **tàlaidh 2**

meallach *adj* alluring, enticing, beguiling, bewitching, (*song*) **Teàrlach òg nan gorm-shùil meallach** young Charles (*Edward Stewart*) of the bewitching blue eyes

mealladh, *gen* **meallaidh** *nm* 1 (*the act of*) deceiving, beguiling etc (*see senses of* **meall** *v*); 2 deceit, deception, *cf* **foill** 1; 3 enticement, allurement; 4 (*also* **mealladh-dùil**) disappointment, *cf more usu* **bris(t)eadh-dùil**

meallta(ch) *adj* deceitful, cheating, false, deceptive, *cf* **brèige** *adj* 1, **fallsa**

meallta *adj* deceived, cheated, taken in

mealltair, mealltair, mealltairean *nm* a cheat, a deceiver, *cf* **cealgair(e)**

mealtainn *see* **meal** *v* & **mealadh**

meamhair, meamhrachadh, meamhraich *see* **meomhair, meòrachadh, meòraich**

mean *adj* little, tiny, *often in expr* **mean air mhean** little by little, gradually, *cf* **beag** 1, **meanbh, mion** 1

mèanan, mèananaich *see* **mèaran, mèaranaich**

meanbh *adj* (very) little, tiny, diminutive, minute, *usu in compounds eg* **meanbh-chuileag** *f* a midge (*lit* tiny fly), **meanbh-thonn** *nf* & *adj* (a) microwave, **meanbh-reic** *m* (*commerce*) retailing, *cf* **crìon** *adj* 1, **mean, mion** 1

meang, *gen* **meanga** & **meing**, *pl* **meangan** *nf* 1 (*moral*) a fault, a defect, a flaw, a blemish, **an laoch gun mheang** the flawless hero, *cf* **fàillinn** 1, **gaoid**; 2 (*phys*) a defect, an abnormality, *cf* **fàillinn** 1

meangach *adj* (*phys*) abnormal

meang(l)an, *gen* **meang(l)ain**, *pl* **meang(l)ain** & **meang(l)anan** *nm* (*of tree*) a branch, a bough

meann, *gen* & *pl* **minn** *nm* a kid (*ie young goat*)

mear *adj* excited, animated, in high spirits

mearachd, mearachd, mearachdan *nf* a mistake, an error, a slip-up, **cha dèan mi mearachdan idir** I never make mistakes

mearachdach *adj* mistaken, wrong, incorrect, erroneous, **aithris mhearachdach** an incorrect report, **beachd mearachdach** a mistaken opinion, *cf* **iomrallach**

mèaran & **mèanan**, *gen* **mèarain**, *pl* **mèaranan** *nm* a yawn

mèaranaich & **mèananaich**, *gen* **mèaranaiche** *nf* yawning, **'s ann ort a tha a' mhèaranaich an-diugh!** you're yawning a lot today!

mèarrsadh, *gen* **mèarrsaidh** *nm* marching, a march, *cf* **caismeachd** 2, **màrsail**

meas¹ *nm invar* 1 respect, regard, esteem, **tha meas mòr agam oirre** I have a great deal of respect/regard for her, (*corres*) **is mise le meas** yours sincerely (*lit* I am, with respect …),

cf **urram** 1; 2 (*surveyor etc; abstr* & *con*) valuation, evaluation, assessment, appraisal, *cf* **luachachadh** 2

meas², **measa, measan** *nm* fruit, a fruit, **measchraobh** *f* a fruit tree, **sùgh-measa** *m* fruit juice

meas *vti, pres part* **a' meas(adh)**, 1 think, reckon, consider, *cf* **creid** 2, **saoil, smaoin(t)ich** 3; 2 esteem, respect, value; 3 (*surveyors, valuers etc*) evaluate, assess, value, appraise, estimate, *cf* **luachaich, luach** 2

measach *adj* fruity, full of *or* tasting of fruit

measadh, *gen* **measaidh** *nm* (*the act of*) considering, esteeming, valuing etc (*see senses of* **meas** *v*)

measail *adj* 1 respectable, respected, esteemed, valued, highly regarded; 2 fond (**air** of), (*poem*) **a chionn 's gu robh mi measail air** (Meg Bateman) because I was fond of him, *cf* **dèidheil**

measarra *adj* moderate, sober, temperate, modest (*ie not excessive*), *cf* **stuama** 1

measg *see* **am measg**

measgachadh, measgachaidh, measgachaidhean *nm* 1 (*the act of*) mixing etc (*see senses of* **measgaich** *v*); 2 mixture, a mixture

measgaich *vt, pres part* **a' measgachadh**, 1 mix, mingle, **air am measgachadh ri chèile** mixed/mingled together, (*calque*) **measgaich suas (rudan eadar-dhealaichte etc)** mix up/confuse (different things etc); 2 combine, *cf stronger* **co-mheasgaich**

measgaichear, measgaicheir, measgaichearan *nm* (*food, cement etc*) a mixer

meata *adj* faint-hearted, timid, feeble, lacking in spirit, *cf* **gun smior** (*see* **smior** 3)

meatailt, meatailte, meatailtean *nf* metal, (*also as adj*) **dorsan meatailt** *or* **dorsan de mheatailt** metal doors

meatair, meatair, meatairean *nm* a metre

meatrach *adj* metric

meidh, meidhe, meidhean *nf* 1 (*weighing*) a balance, a scale, scales; 2 balance, equilibrium, *esp in exprs* **air mheidh** balanced & **cuir** *v* **air mheidh** balance, **chuir i an t-eallach air mheidh air a ceann** she balanced the load/burden on her head; *cf* **cothrom** *n* 4

meil *vti, pres part* **a' meileadh**, (*corn etc*) mill, grind, *cf* **bleith** *v* 1

meileabhaid, *gen* **meileabhaide** *nf* velvet

meileachadh, *gen* **meileachaidh** *nm* (*the act of*) chilling, numbing

mèilich *nf invar* a bleat (*esp sheep*), a baa, bleating, baaing, **dèan** *v* **mèilich** bleat, baa

meilich *vti, pres part* **a' meileachadh**, chill, make or become chilled, make or become numb (*esp with cold*), *cf* **fuaraich**

mèinn, *gen* **mèinne** *nf* **1** character, disposition, temperament, nature, *cf* **aigne 2, nàdar 2**; **2** (*occas, more temporary*) look, appearance, mien, expression, *cf* **dreach 1, fiamh 3, tuar**

mèinn(e), mèinne, mèinnean *nf* **1** ore; **2** a mine, **mèinn(e)-guail** a coalmine

mèinneadair, mèinneadair, mèinneadairean *nm* a miner

mèinneach & **mèinneil** *adj* mineral

mèinnear, mèinneir, mèinnearan *nm*, *also* **mèinnearach**, *gen* & *pl* **mèinnearaich** *nm*, a mineral

mèinnearachd *nf invar* **1** mineralogy, *cf* **mèinn-eòlas**; **2** mining

mèinneil *see* **mèinneach**

mèinn-eòlas, *gen* **mèinn-eòlais** *nm* mineralogy

meirg, *gen* **meirge** *nf* rust, **meirg-dhìonach** *adj* rustproof

meirg *vti, pres part* **a' meirgeadh**, *also* **meirgich** *vti, pres part* **a' meirgeachadh**, rust, make or become rusty or rustier

meirgeach *adj* rusty, (*lit & fig*) **tha mo chuid Gàidhlig** (etc) **gu math meirgeach** my Gaelic (etc) is pretty rusty

meirgich *see* **meirg** *v*

mèirle *nf invar* theft, thieving, stealing, **dèan** *v* **mèirle** steal, thieve, (*prov*) **breac à linne, slat à coille is fiadh à fireach – mèirle nach do ghabh duine a-riamh nàire aiste** a trout from the pool, a wand from the wood and a deer from the hill – theft no man was ever ashamed of, *cf* **braid, goid** *n* & *v*

mèirleach, *gen* & *pl* **mèirlich** *nm* a thief, *cf* **gadaiche**

meomhair & **meamhair**, *gen* **meomhair(e)**, *pl* **meomhairean** *nf* (*the faculty of*) memory, **cùm** *v* **air mheomhair** memorise, *cf more usu* **cuimhne**

meòrachadh, *gen* **meòrachaidh** *nm* (*the act of*) remembering, meditating etc (*see senses of* **meòraich** *v*), *cf more usu* **cuimhneachadh**

meòraich *vi, pres part* **a' meòrachadh**, **1** meditate, ponder, muse, think, contemplate, (**air** on, about), *cf more usu* **beachd-smaoin(t)ich, cnuas 2**; **2** memorise, commit to memory; **3** remember, think over the past, *cf more usu* **cuimhnich**

meud *nm invar* **1** size, extent, **meud an taighe/ an achaidh** the size of the house/the field, **meud a h-iomagain** the extent of her anxiety, **rach** *v* **am meud** increase in size, grow bigger; **2** amount, quantity, number, (*trad*) **a mheud 's a bha an làthair** as many as were present, *cf* **uimhir 1; 3** *esp in expr* **cò** (*also* **cia**) **mheud** how many, how much, **cò mheud a th' ann?** how many are there? *or* how much is there? **cò mheud bliadhna a bha thu ann?** how many years were you there?

meudachadh, meudachaidh, meudachaidhean *nm* **1** (*the act of*) increasing etc (*see senses of* **meudaich** *v*); **2** increase, an increase, enlargement, an enlargement, addition, augmentation

meudachd *nf invar* bigness, magnitude, greatness, size, **meudachd nam fiachan aca** the greatness of their debts, **mu mheudachd muice** about the size of a pig

meudaich *vti, pres part* **a' meudachadh**, increase, enlarge, add to, augment, make or become bigger, *cf* (*vi*) **fàs** *v* **2**, (*vti*) **leudaich**

meur, *gen* & *pl* **meòir** *nf* **1** a finger, **meur-lorg** *f* a fingerprint, *cf* **corrag**; **2** (*of piano, computer etc*) a key, **meur-chlàr** *m* a keyboard; **3** (*of tree, family, river, organisation etc*) a branch

meuran, *gen* **meurain**, *pl* **meurain** & **meuranan** *nm* a thimble

mi, *emph form* **mise**, *pers pron* I, me

mì- *a common neg prefix corres to Eng* un-, in-, dis-, mis-, -less *etc* (*ie it negativises second part of compound*), *eg* **mì-bhlasta** *adj* tasteless, unsavoury, **mì-cheartas** *m* injustice, **mì-dhìleas** *adj* disloyal, **mì-earbsa** *m* mistrust, distrust, **gu mì-fhortanach** *adv* unfortunately, **mì-rùn** *m* malice, ill-will, malevolence, *cf* **eas-, eu-, neo-**

mial, miala, mialan *nf* **1** a louse; **2** a tick (*ie the parasite*), **mial-chaorach** a sheep-tick

mial-chù, *gen* & *pl* **mial-choin** *nm* a greyhound

mialaich *nf invar, also* **miamhail** *nf invar*, mewing, miauing, **rinn an cat mialaich/ miamhail** the cat mewed

miann, miann, miannan *nmf* **1** desire, a desire, longing, a longing, a wish, **tobar m(h)iann** *m* a wishing well, (*trad*) **is e mo mhiann a bhith còmhla riut** my desire/wish is to be with you, **is miann/bu mhiann leam** I wish, **bu mhiann leam gum faighinn duais sa chrannchur** I wish I could win a prize in the lottery, *cf* **rùn 3; 2** (sexual) desire, **dh'fhairich e lasair bheag miann** he felt a small flame of desire, *cf* **drùis**

miannachadh, *gen* **miannachaidh** *nm* (*the act of*) desiring etc (*see senses of* **miannaich** *v*)

miannaich *vt, pres part* **a' miannachadh**, **1** desire, long for, wish for, **na miannaich rudan**

nach faigh thu do not desire/wish for things you won't get, *cf* **togair 1**; **2** (*sexually*) desire

miann-abhartais *nmf invar* ambition (*esp in career*), *cf* **gionaiche 2**

mias, *gen* **mias** & **mèise**, *pl* **miasan** *nf* **1** a basin, **mias-ionnlaid** a wash basin; **2** a (large) dish, a platter

miastachd *nf invar* hooliganism, loutish behaviour

miastadh *gen* **miastaidh** *nm* **1** harm, damage; **2** vandalism, hooliganism

mì-ghnàthaich, *pres part* **a' mì-ghnàthachadh** (*substances, position of authority etc*) abuse, misuse

mil, meala(ch), mealan *nf* honey, **pògan air bhlas na meala** honeyed/honey-sweet kisses, **cìr-mheala** *f* a honeycomb

mìle[1], **mìle, mìltean** *nm* thousand, **dà mhìle saighdear** two thousand soldiers, **thàinig iad nam mìltean** they came in their thousands

mìle[2], **mìle, mìltean** *nmf* a mile

milis *adj*, *comp* **(n)as (etc) mìlse**, sweet, **rudan milis** sweet things (*to eat*), *also* sweet(ie)s, (*song*) **gur milis Mòrag** how sweet is Mòrag, (*song*) **'s mìlse leam do phògan gu mòr na na cìrean-meala** (Murchadh MacPhàrlain) your kisses are sweeter to me by far than (the) honeycombs

mill *vti*, *pres part* **a' milleadh**, **1** spoil, ruin, mar, damage, destroy, wreck, **mhill e an doras** he damaged the door, **mhill na gunnaichean an tùr** the guns destroyed the tower, *cf stronger* **sgrios** *v*; **2** spoil (*ie over-indulge*) **tha an cuilean ud air a mhilleadh!** yon pup's spoilt!

milleadh, *gen* **millidh** *nm* **1** (*the act of*) spoiling, ruining etc (*see senses of* **mill** *v*); **2** destruction, (*trad*) **is esan a rinn ar milleadh** it is he who brought about/wrought our destruction, *cf* **sgrios** *n*

millean, millean, milleanan *nm*, *also* **muillean, muillean, muilleanan** *nm*, a million

millte *adj* spoilt, marred, damaged

millteach *adj* destructive, ruinous, apt to spoil, damage or wreck, *cf* **sgriosail 1**

milltear, millteir, milltearan *nm* a vandal

mìlseachd *nf invar* sweetness

mìlsean, *gen* **mìlsein**, *pl* **mìlsein** & **mìlseanan** *nm* a dessert, a pudding, a sweet (course), **spàin-mhìlsein** *f* a dessert spoon

mì-mhodhail *adj* rude, ill-mannered, impolite, ill-bred, discourteous

mìn *adj* **1** smooth, soft, **aodach/falt mìn** soft/smooth material/hair; **2** dainty, fine

min, *gen* **mine** *nf* **1** meal, **min-choirce** oatmeal, **min-èisg** fish meal; **2** (*occas*) flour (*more often* **min-flùir**, *cf* **flùr 2**; **3** *other finely-ground or fragmented substances*, *eg* **min-iarainn** iron filings, **min-sàibh** sawdust

mìneachadh[1], **mìneachaidh, mìneachaidhean** *nm* **1** (*the act of*) explaining, interpreting (*see* **mìnich**[1] *vt*); **2** explanation, an explanation, interpretation, an interpretation

mìneachadh[2], *gen* **mìneachaidh** *nm* (*the act of*) smoothing, making smooth, *cf* **mìnich**[2] *vt*

mìneachail *adj* explanatory

mìnich[1] *vt*, *pres part* **a' mìneachadh**, (*vt*) explain, interpret, **bha an tidsear a' mìneachadh brìgh an fhacail** the teacher was explaining the sense/meaning of the word, *cf* **soilleirich 2**

mìnich[2] *vt*, *pres part* **a' mìneachadh**, smoothe, make smooth

minig *adj* used adverbially, frequent, (*trad*) **is minig a chì thu caora air leth-shùil** you'll often see/many's the time you'll see a one-eyed ewe, *now usu as adv* **gu minig** often, frequently, *cf more usu* **tric 1**

minig *vt*, *pres part* **a' minigeadh**, (*fam*) mean, **dè a tha thu a' minigeadh?** what do you mean?, *cf* **ciallaich**

ministear, ministeir, ministearan *nm* **1** a minister (of religion), *cf* **clèireach** *n* **1**, **pears-eaglais, sagart**; **2** a (government) minister, **Ministear na Stàite** the Minister of State, **Ministear a' Chosnaidh** the Employment Minister

ministrealachd, ministrealachd, ministrealachdan *nf* (*church, government*) ministry, a ministry

miodal, *gen* **miodail** *nm* flattery, fawning, buttering up, **dèan** *v* **miodal do chuideigin** flatter, fawn on, butter up someone, *cf* **brìodal 3, sodal**

mìog, mìoga, mìogan *nf* a smirk, a sly smile

mìogadaich *nf invar* bleating, a bleat *esp of goats*

mion *adj*, *usu used as prefix* **1** small, minute, tiny, on a small scale, **mion-bhraide** *f* petty pilfering, **mion-gheàrr** *vt* cut up finely, **mion-fhacal** *m* (*gram*) a particle, *cf* **crìon** *adj* **1, meanbh**; **2** detailed, exact, punctilious, **mion-cheasnaich** *v* question minutely/in detail, (*fam*) grill, **mion-eòlas** *m* detailed/thorough/intimate knowledge or acquaintance, **mion-phuing** *f* a detail, **mion-chùiseach** *adj* meticulous, punctilious, attentive to detail, *cf* **mionaideach, pongail 1**; **3** minor, minority, lesser, **mion-chànan** *m* a minority/lesser used language, **mion-aoiseach** *adj* minor (*ie under* *age)*, **mion-chuid** *f* a minority (*ie a lesser part*, *cf* **mòr-chuid** a majority)

mionach, mionaich, mionaichean *nm* 1 entrails, guts, innards, **mionach èisg** fish guts, *cf* **caolan, greallach, innidh**; 2 (*fam*) a stomach, a belly, a gut, *cf* **broinn** 1, **brù** 2, **stamag**

mionaid, mionaide, mionaidean *nf* a minute, **fichead mionaid** twenty minutes, **fuirich mionaid!** wait a minute!

mionaideach *adj* thorough, meticulous, detailed, in detail, **sgrùdadh mionaideach** a detailed/ thorough/meticulous enquiry *or* study, *cf* **mion** 2, **pongail** 1

mionn, mionna, mionnan *nmf*, *also* **mionnan**, *gen* **mionnain**, *pl* **mionnain** & **mionnanan** *nm*, 1 an oath, **thoir** *v* **mionnan** take/swear an oath; 2 a curse, an oath, (*Sc*) a swear, *cf* **droch cainnt** (*see* **cainnt** 2)

mionnachadh, *gen* **mionnachaidh** *nm* (*the act of*) swearing etc (*see senses of* **mionnaich** *v*)

mionnaich *vi*, *pres part* **a' mionnachadh**, 1 swear (*ie testify etc on oath*); 2 curse, swear, use bad or foul language

mionnan *see* **mionn**

mìorbhail, mìorbhaile, mìorbhailean *nf* 1 a marvel, a wonder, *cf* **iongnadh** 1; 2 a miracle

mìorbhaileach *adj* 1 marvellous, wonderful, *cf* **iongantach**; 2 miraculous

mìos, mìosa, mìosan *nmf* a month, **mìos nam pòg** a honeymoon (*lit* the month of the kisses)

miosa *see* **dona**

mìosach & **mìosail** *adj* monthly

mìosachan, *gen* & *pl* **mìosachain** *nm* a calender

miotag, miotaig, miotagan *nf* 1 a glove, *cf* **làmhainn**; 2 a mitten

mìr, mìre, mìrean *nm* a bit, a small piece, particle or scrap of anything, *cf* **bìdeag, criomag**

mire(adh) *adj* merriment, mirth, light-heartedness, (*song*) **thèid sinn le mireadh a-null air an linne** merrily we will cross the channel/sound, *cf* **aighearachd, cridhealas**

mìrean, *gen* & *pl* **mìrein** (*dimin of* **mìr**) *nm* 1 a particle of anything; 2 (*gram*) a particle

mì-reusanta *adj* 1 unreasonable; 2 (*logic, philo etc*) absurd

mì-reusantachd *nf invar* 1 unreasonableness; 2 (*logic, philo etc*) absurdity

misde *see* **miste**

miseanaraidh, miseanaraidh, miseanaraidhean *nm* a missionary, *cf trad* **teachdaire** 2

misg, *gen* **misge** *nf* drunkenness, intoxication, **air mhisg** drunk, **cuir** *v* **air mhisg** make drunk, inebriate, **air leth-mhisg** tipsy, merry, half-drunk, (*trad*) **misg-catha** battle frenzy (*lit* battle drunkenness), *cf* **daorach** 1, **pòitearachd, smùid** *n* 3

misgeach *adj* intoxicated; drunken; heady

misgear, misgeir, misgearan *nm* a drunkard, a boozer, *cf* **pòitear**

misneach, *gen* **misnich** *nf*, *also* **misneachd** *nf invar*, 1 courage, bravery, fortitude, (*esp moral*) *cf* **cridhe** 2, **smior** 3; 2 confidence, morale

misneachadh, *gen* **misneachaidh** *nm* 1 (*the act of*) inspiring with courage etc (*see senses of* **misnich** *v*); 2 encouragement, **cha d' fhuair i misneachadh bhuapa** she got no encouragement from them, *cf* **brosnachadh** 2

misneachail *adj* 1 courageous, brave (*esp morally*), *cf* **smiorail**; 2 spirited, of good cheer, in good heart; 3 encouraging, *cf* **brosnachail**

misneachd *see* **misneach**

misnich *vt*, *pres part* **a' misneachadh**, 1 inspire or fill someone with courage, awaken someone's courage or confidence; 2 encourage; *cf* **brosnaich**

miste, *also* **misde** *adj*, worse, the worse, *esp in expr* **is miste mi** (etc) . . . I am (etc) the worse for . . . , **cha mhiste sibh e** you are none the worse for it, **cha bu mhiste mi pinnt** I'd be none the worse for a pint, a pint wouldn't do me any harm, *cf opposite* **feàirrde**

mithich *adj* timeous, timely, opportune

mithich *nf invar* the proper or appointed time for something, *esp in expr* **ron mhithich** premature, prematurely, **leig mi dhìom mo dhreuchd ron mhithich** I retired prematurely

mnà, mnaoi, mnathan *see* **bean** *nf*

mo *poss adj* my, **mo dhachaigh** my home, **m' athair** my father, *cf* **aig** 2

mò *see* **mòr**

moch *adj*, *now usu as adv*, early, (*trad*) **anns a' mhoch-mhadainn** in the early morning, **moch sa mhadainn** early in the morning, *also in expr* **bho mhoch gu dubh** from morning till night/dawn to dusk (*lit* from early till darkness), *cf* **tràth** *adj* 1 & *opposite* **anmoch**

mòd, mòid, mòdan *nm* 1 (*trad*) a (*legal*) court, *cf more usu* **cùirt** 2; 2 (*now usu*) a Gaelic Mod (*a session of literary and musical events and competitions*), **Mòd ionadail** a local mod, **am Mòd Nàiseanta** the National Mod, *cf* **fèis** 1

modh, modha, modh(ann)an *nmf* 1 a way, a manner, a mode (of doing something), **feumaidh tu a dhèanamh air mhodh àraidh** you must do it in a particular way/

manner, **modh riaghlaidh** a mode/way/
system of governing, *cf* **dòigh 1** & *less usu*
nòs 2; **2** *in expr* **air mhodh eile** otherwise,
alternatively, or, on the other hand, *cf* **air neo**;
3 manners, (good) behaviour, (good) breeding,
civility, *cf* **beus 2, giùlan 3**; **4** (*gram*) a mood,
a' mhodh àithneach the imperative mood
modhail *adj* polite, well-mannered, well-bred, *cf*
cùirteil 1 & *opposite* **mì-mhodhail**
modhalachd *nf invar* politeness, courtesy
mogan, *gen* **mogain**, *pl* **moganan** *nm* **1** a
slipper, *cf* **slapag**; **2** (*fam*) a large sum of
money, a hoard of money
Mohamadanach, *gen* & *pl* **Mohamadanaich**,
a Mohammedan, a Muslim, *also as adj*
Mohamadanach Mohammedan, Muslim,
Islamic, *cf* **Ioslamach**
mòine, *gen* **mòna, mònadh** & **mònach**, *nf*
peat, **poll-mòna(ch)** *m* a peat bank/bog/hag,
fàd/fòid mònach *m* a (single) peat, **bha iad
ris a' mhòine** they were (working) at the peats,
dèan/buain mòine win/cut/gather peat
mòinteach, mòintich, mòintichean *nf* (*rough
hill land at low to medium altitude*), a moor,
moorland, *cf* **aonach, monadh 1, sliabh 1**
moit, *gen* **moite** *nf* pride, *often legitimate, cf*
àrdan, pròis
moiteil *adj* proud, *often legitimately,* **tha sinn
moiteil asad** we're proud of/pleased with you,
cf **àrdanach, pròiseil**
mol, *gen* **moil** & **mola**, *pl* **molan** *nm* **1** shingle;
2 a shingly or pebbly beach
mol *vt, pres part* **a' moladh, 1** praise, *cf* **luaidh**
vt; **2** suggest, propose, recommend, **mholainn
dha an t-airgead a thoirt seachad** I'd
advise/recommend him to give the money away,
**tha a' chomhairle a' moladh meadhan a'
bhaile a leasachadh** the council is proposing
to develop/improve the town centre
molach *adj* **1** hairy, rough, shaggy, 'wild and
woolly', (*song*) **bonaid bhiorach, mholach,
ghorm** a blue, hairy/rough, pointed bonnet, *cf*
robach 1, ròmach 1; **2** furry
moladh, molaidh, molaidhean *nm* **1** (*the act
of*) praising, proposing etc (*see senses of* **mol** *v*);
2 praise, (*song*) **Moladh Mòraig** (in) Praise of
Mòrag, *cf* **cliù 2, luaidh** *nm* **2**; **3** a proposal, a
recommendation, a suggestion, **molaidhean
Oifis na h-Alba airson drochaid ùire**
Scottish Office proposals/recommendations for
a new bridge
moll, *gen* **muill** *nm* chaff, *cf* **càth**
mollachd *see* **mallachd**
molldair, molldair, molldairean *nm* a mould
(*ie for forming, shaping*)

molt *see* **mult**
mòmaid, mòmaide, mòmaidean *nf* a moment,
an instant, (*loosely*) a second, *cf more usu*
tiota(n) 2, tiotag
monadail *adj* hilly, mountainous, *cf* **cnocach**
monadh, monaidh, monaidhean *nm* **1**
moorland, a moor, rough hill land, *cf* **aonach,
mòinteach, sliabh 1**; **2** (*crofting*) **am monadh**
the hill (*the common hill grazing land associated
with a crofting township*), **tha caoraich agam
air a' mhonadh** I've sheep on the hill
monmhar, monmhair, monmharan *m* a
murmur, murmuring (*eg of flowing water,
voices*), *cf more usu* **crònan 1**
mòr *adj, comp* **(n)as** (etc) **mò/motha, 1** big,
large, great in size, quantity or quality, **eilean
mòr** a big island, **Aonghas Mòr** Big Angus,
sluagh mòr a big/numerous/great crowd
(*cf* **lìonmhor**), **airgead mòr** 'big' money, a
lot/great deal of money, (*trad*) **bu mhòr mo
mhulad** great was my sadness; **2** important,
great, **bàrd/fear-ciùil mòr** a great poet/
musician, **tha sinn mòr aig a chèile** we
are great friends/get on famously, (*ironic*) **na
daoine mòra** the big shots/bigwigs, **mòr às**
(etc) **fhèin** self-important, 'too big for his (etc)
boots'; **3** *in compounds, eg* **a' mhòr-chuid**
the majority, **mòr-iongnadh** *m* astonishment,
mòr-roinn *f* a continent; **4** *in conj* **cha mhòr,
a)** barely, hardly, scarcely, **cha mhòr gun
do leig e às dà fhacal** he barely/scarcely
uttered two words, *cf* **gann 2, b)** *also* almost,
nearly, (*note double neg*) **cha mhòr nach
do chaill mi an sporan agam** I almost/
nearly lost my purse, *cf* **theab 2**; **5** *in adv expr*
cha mhòr, nearly, almost, just about, **bidh
sinn ga faicinn a h-uile là, cha mhòr** we
see her every day, almost, *cf* **ìre 4**; **6** *in adv
expr* **nas motha** either, neither, **cha tèid mi
dhachaigh! cha tèid mise nas motha!** I
won't go home! neither will I!/I won't either!;
7 cha mhotha (a) *conj* neither, nor, **cha
mhotha (a) chunnaic duine eile mi** nor/
neither did anyone else see me
mòrachd *nf invar* greatness, grandeur, majesty
morair, morair, morairean *nm* a lord, **Taigh
nam Morairean** the House of Lords, *cf*
tighearna 1
mòran, *gen* **mòrain** *nm* **1** many, a lot, a large
number, *with gen pl noun,* **mòran dhaoine** a
lot of/many people, **mòran dhiubh/aca** many
of them, *cf* **iomadach, iomadh 1** & *opposite*
beagan *n*; **2** much, a lot, a great deal, a large
quantity, *with gen sing n,* **mòran bìdh** much/a
lot of food, **mòran taing!** many thanks!, thanks

a lot!, **a bheil airgead agad? chan eil mòran** have you any money? not much, (*fam*) **dè tha dol? chan eil mòran** what's doing? not a lot, *cf opposite* **beagan** *n*; **3** *as adv* much, a great deal, **tha an t-sìde mòran nas fheàrr an-diugh** the weather's a great deal better today, *cf* **fada 3**

mòr-chòrdte *adj* popular, well-liked

mòr-chuid *see* **cuid 1**

mòrchuis, *gen* **mòrchuise** *nf* pride (*usu excessive*), conceit, *cf* **leòm**

mòrchuiseach *adj* **1** proud, conceited, *cf* **baralach**; **2** pompous

morgaidse, morgaidse, morgaidsean *nm* a mortgage

morghan, *gen* **morghain** *nm* **1** gravel, *cf* **grinneal 1**; **2** shingle, *cf* **mol** *n* **1**

mòr-ghràin, *gen* **mòr-ghràin** *nf* abomination, detestation, *cf* **gràin 1, fuath**

mòr-iongnadh, *gen* **mòr-iongnaidh** *nm* amazement, astonishment, **ghabh mi mòr-iongnadh** I was amazed/astonished, **chuir e mòr-iongnadh orm** he/it amazed (*etc*) me, *cf less strong* **iongnadh**, *less usu* **iongantas 1**

mòr-roinn, mòr-roinne, mor-roinnean *nf* a continent (*cf* **mòr-thìr**)

mort, mortadh, mortair *see* **murt, murtadh, murtair**

mòr-thìr, mòr-thìre, mòr-thìrean *nf* a continent, a mainland, *cf* **tìr-mòr** (*see* **tìr 1**)

mosach *adj* **1** nasty, dirty, scruffy, *cf* **dràbhail, grodach, rapach**; **2** niggardly, *cf* **spìocach**

mosg, mosga, mosgan *nm* a mosque

mosgail *vti, pres part* **a' mosgladh**, awake, wake, waken, rouse from sleep, *cf more usu* **dùisg 1**

mosgladh, *gen* **mosglaidh** *nm* (*the act of*) awakening etc (*see senses of* **mosgail** *v*), an awakening, *cf* **dùsgadh 1**

Mosgo *n* Moscow

motair, motair, motairean *nm* a motor, **motair-rothar** a motor-bike

motha *see* **mòr**

mothachadh, *gen* **mothachaidh** *nm* **1** (*the act of*) noticing, feeling etc (*see senses of* **mothaich** *v*); **2** (*the sense or faculty of*) feeling, sensibility, sensitivity, sensation; **3** consciousness, awareness

mothachail *adj* **1** aware, observant, perceptive, *cf* **beachdail 1, lèirsinneach 2**; **2** sensitive, feeling, sympathetic (*also* **co-mhothachail**), *cf* **tuigseach 2**; **3** conscious (*ie opposite of* unconscious); **4** **mothachail air** conscious/aware of, alert to

mothaich *vt, pres part* **a' mothachadh**, **1** notice, observe, perceive, **mhothaich mi e**

san dol seachad I noticed it in passing (*also* **mhothaich mi dha** I noticed it/him), *cf* **aire 2, fa-near 3**; **2** feel, experience, be conscious/aware of, **mhothaich sinn gluasad a' bhàta** we felt the movement of the boat, *cf* **fairich 1**

mu *prep, takes the dat.* (*The prep prons formed with* **mu**, *in the order first, second, third person singular, first, second, third person plural, and with the reflexive/emphatic particles in brackets, are as follows*: **umam(sa), umad(sa), uime(san), uimpe(se), umainn(e), umaibh(se), umpa(san)**, around/concerning me, around/concerning you (*fam*), *etc*) **1** around, about, **bann mu cheann** a bandage around his head (*cf* **timcheall air**), **chuir i uimpe** she got dressed, **cuir umad do chòta** put your coat on/about you, *cf* **air 1**; **2** about, concerning, **sgeulachd mu iasgair/mun chogadh** a story about a fisherman/about the war, *cf* **air 4**; **3** *in expr* **mu dheidhinn** *prep, takes gen,* about, concerning, **a' bruidhinn mum dheidhinn** talking about me, **prògram mu dheidhinn foghlaim** a programme about education, (*calque*) **dè mu dheidhinn?** what about it?; **4** about, approximately, **bidh mu dheichnear ann** there'll be about ten people there, *cf* **timcheall air** (*see* **timcheall 3**); **5** (*with* **deas** *n* & **tuath** *n*) in, to, **chaidh e mu dheas** he went to the south, **na h-eileanan mu thuath** the islands in the north, the northern/northerly islands, **anns a' chùil mu dheas de bhàgh farsaing** in the southern corner of a broad bay; *Note: for other prep exprs with* **mu** *see under second word of expr*

muc, muice, mucan *nf* a pig, a sow (*cf* **cràin**), **muicfheoil** *f* pork, *cf* **cullach, torc**

mùch *vt, pres part* **a' mùchadh, 1** (*fire*) extinguish, quench, smother, *cf* **smà(i)l, tùch 2**; **2** (*person*) choke, strangle, suffocate, smother, throttle, *cf* **tachd**; **3** (*spirit, rebellion etc*) quell, repress, put down, subdue, *cf* **ceannsaich 2**

mùchadh, *gen* **mùchaidh** *nm* **1** (*the act of*) extinguishing, choking etc (*see senses of* **mùch** *v*); **2** suffocation; **3** (*pol etc*) repression, *cf* **ceannsachadh 2**

mu choinneimh *see* **coinneamh 2**

mu chuairt *see* **cuairt 4**

muc-mhara, muice-mara, mucan-mara *nf* a whale

mu dheas *see* **mu 4**

mu dheidhinn *see* **mu 3**

mu dheireadh *see* **deireadh 4**

muga, *gen* **muga**, *pl* **mugannan** & **mugaichean** *nmf* a (*drinking*) mug

mùgach *adj* 1 morose, gloomy, *cf* **gruamach** 1; 2 surly, sullen, *cf* **gnù**, **iargalt(a)**

muicfheoil *see* **muc**

muidhe, *gen* **muidhe**, *pl* **muidhean** & **muidheachan** *nm* a churn, *cf* **crannag** 2

mùig, **mùig**, **mùigean** *nm* a frown, a scowl, a sulk, **chuir e mùig air** he frowned, he scowled he sulked, *cf* **drèin**, **gruaim** 2 & 3, **sgraing**

Muileach, *gen* & *pl* **Muilich** *nm* someone from Mull (**Muile**), *also as adj* **Muileach** of, from or pertaining to Mull, **An t-Eilean Muileach** The Isle of Mull

muileann, *gen* **muilinn**, *pl* **muilnean** & **muileannan** *nmf, also* **muilinn**, **muilne**, **muilnean** *nf*, a mill, **muileann-uisge** a water-mill, **muileann-gaoithe** a windmill, **muileann-pàipeir** a paper-mill

muile-mhàg, **muile-mhàg**, **muileacha-màg** *nf* a toad

muil(i)cheann *see* **muin(i)chill**

muilinn *see* **muileann**

muillean *see* **millean**

muillear, **muilleir**, **muillearan** *nm* a miller

muiltfheoil *see* **mult**

muime, **muime**, **muimeachan** *nf* a step-mother, *cf* **oide**

muin *nf invar* 1 a back (*esp of an animal*), **air muin eich** on horseback, on the back of a horse, **leum e air muin na h-asail** he leapt on the donkey's back, *cf* **druim** 1; 2 the top of something, **muin a' chnuic** the top of the hill (*cf more usu* **mullach** 1), **chuir i blobhs oirre agus air muin sin seacaid** she put on a blouse and on top of that a jacket; 3 *with sexual meaning* **rach** *v* **air muin** (*with gen*) have intercourse with; (*animals*) mount, serve, **chaidh e air a muin** he had intercourse with her, **chaidh an tarbh air muin na bà** the bull mounted/served the cow; 4 *also in expr* **faigh** *v* **muin** have sex, have sexual intercourse, copulate, *cf* **co-ghin**, **cuplaich**

mùin *vi, pres part* **a' mùn**, urinate, pass water, piss, *cf* **dèan** *v* **mùn** (*see* **mùn**)

muinchill & **muinichill**, *gen* **muin(i)chill**, *pl* **muin(i)chillean** *nm, also* **muil(i)cheann**, **muil(i)chinn**, **muil(i)chinnean** *nm*, a sleeve (*of garment*), **thruis e a mhuilchinnean** he rolled up his sleeves

muineal, **muineil**, **muinealan** *nm* a neck, *cf* **amha(i)ch** 1

muing, **muinge**, **muingean** *nf* (*of horse etc*) a mane, **muing an leòmhainn** the lion's mane

muinntir, *gen* **muinntire** *nf* 1 (*in the sense of one's associates, relatives, household etc*) people, folk(s) **dh'fhàg e an dùthaich ach cha**

deachaidh a mhuinntir còmhla ris he left the country but his people/folks/followers didn't go with him; 2 (*now more usu in gen exprs*) the people, folk, inhabitants *of a particular place or locality*, **muinntir a' bhaile seo** the people of this town(ship), **muinntir Uibhist** the people of Uist, Uist folk, (*prov*) **ged as e an taigh, chan e a' mhuinntir** though it's the (same) house, these are not the people; *cf* **duine** 6, **sluagh** 2

muir, **mara**, **marannan** *nmf* sea, a sea, **am muir** & **a' mhuir** the sea, **air muir 's air tìr** on land and sea, **rach gu muir** go to sea, **tha e aig muir** he's at sea, he's a sailor/seaman, **ceòl na mara** the song/sound of the sea, **seòl-mara** *m* tide, **còmhnard na mara** sea level, *cf* **cuan** & *less usu* **fairge**

muir-làn, *gen* & *pl* **muir-làin** *nm* a (high) tide, *cf* **làn** *n* 2, **seòl-mara** (*see* **muir**), **tràigh** *n* 2

Muir Mheadhan-thìreach *f, used with art* **A' Mhuir Mheadhan-thìreach** the Mediterranean

muir-thìreach *adj* amphibious, *cf* **dà-bheathach** (*see* **dà** 2)

mulad, *gen* **mulaid** *nm* grief, sadness, **tha mi fo mhulad** *or* (*less trad*) **tha mulad orm** I'm sad, *cf* **bròn** 1

muladach *adj* sad, (*song*) **gur muladach sgìth mi** I am sad and weary, *cf* **brònach**, **tùrsach**

mullach, **mullaich**, **mullaichean** *nm* 1 the top of something, **clach mhòr is eun air a mullach** a great stone with a bird on top (of it), **mullach beinne** the top/summit of a mountain, *cf less usu* **muin** 2; 2 a roof, **mullach taighe** a house roof, **bha an t-uisge a' sileadh tron mhullach** the rain was pouring through the roof

mult & **molt**, *gen* & *pl* **muilt**, a wether, a wedder (*castrated ram*)

muiltfheòil *gen* **muiltfheòla** *nf* mutton

mùn, *gen* **mùin** *nm* urine, **dèan** *v* **mùn** urinate, **theab mi mo mhùn a chall leis cho èibhinn 's a bha e** I almost wet myself, it was so funny, *cf* **fual**

mun *conj see* **mus**

mùnadh, *gen* **mùnaidh** *nm* (*the act of*) urinating; urination

muncaidh, **muncaidh**, **muncaidhean** *nm* a monkey

mun cuairt *see* **cuairt** 4 & 5

mur, **mura** *conj see* **ma**

mùr, **mùir**, **mùirean** *nm* (*trad*) a wall (*esp defensive or fortified*), a bulwark, a rampart, *cf* **bàbhan**

murt, *gen & pl* **muirt**, *nm* murder, manslaughter, assassination, (*hist*) **Murt Ghlinne Comhainn** the Massacre of Glencoe

murt *vt*, *pres part* **a' murt(adh)**, murder, assassinate, *cf* **marbh** *v*

murtadh, *gen* **murtaidh** *nm*, (*the act of*) murdering, assassinating (*see* **murt** *vt*)

murtair, murtair, murtairean *nm*, a murderer, an assassin

mus & mun *conj* 1 before, **mus/mun tig an geamhradh** before the winter comes, **cha do phàigh e mus do dh'fhalbh e** he didn't pay before he left, **an oidhche mus do chaochail i** the night before she died; 2 lest, in case, for fear, **chùm e grèim math air an fhàradh mus tuiteadh i** he kept a good grip on the ladder lest/for fear she should fall, *cf* **eagal 2**, **fios 5**

mu seach *see* **seach 3**

mu sgaoil *see* **sgaoil** *n*

mùth *vti*, *pres part* **a' mùthadh**, 1 change, alter; (*often*) change for the worse, deteriorate, *cf more usu* **atharraich**; 2 mutate

mùthadh, mùthaidh, mùthaidhean *nm* 1 (*the act of*) changing, mutating etc (*see senses of* **mùth** *v*); 2 change, a change, alteration, an alteration (*often for the worse*), *cf more usu* **atharrachadh 2**, **caochladh 2**; 3 mutation, a mutation; 4 (*phys*) corruption, decay

mu thimcheall *see* **timcheall 4**

mu thràth *see* **tràth** *adj* 3

N

na *neg imper particle* don't, do not, **na fàg air an làr e!** don't leave it on the floor! **na bi gòrach!** don't be silly/stupid!

na *inter particle equivalent to* **an do** *before v in the past*, **na chùm e air ais sibh?** did he keep you back?

na *conj* than, **tha iad nas sine na mise** they are older than I

na *rel pron* **1** that, what, (all) that which, (all) those which, **thug mi dha na bha agam de bhiadh** I gave him what food/all the food I had (*lit* that which I had of food), **chuir i iongnadh air mòran de na bha ann** she surprised many of those that were there; **2** *in comp constrs* **tha am fear seo nas** (*for* **na is**) **mò** this one's bigger, **bha an trèana na b' fhaide** the train was longer

na *form of the art* (*see table p 491*)

na *prep pron see* **an** *prep* 3

na b' (*in comp constrs*) *see* **na** *rel pron* 2

nàbaidh, nàbaidh, nàbaidhean *nm* a neighbour, *cf less usu* **coimhearsnach**

nàb(aidhe)achd *nf invar* a neighbourhood, *cf* **coimhearsnachd**

nàbaidheil *adj* neighbourly

nach *neg particle* **1** *in inter clauses*, **nach do rinn thu e?** didn't you do it?, **tha i fuar, nach eil?** it's cold, isn't it? **nach bi iad ann?** won't they be there? **nach truagh sin?** isn't that a shame/pity? **nach math a rinn thu!** didn't you do well!, well done!; **2** *in rel clauses*, **an tè nach tàinig 's nach tig** the woman who didn't come and won't come, (*prov*) **cha chaoidh duine an rud nach fhaic e** a man doesn't grieve over what he doesn't see; **3** *forming neg with conjs*, **a chionn 's nach eil stailc ann** because there isn't a strike, **ged nach robh e tinn** though he wasn't ill, **air dhòigh 's nach bithinn mì-mhodhail** so that I wouldn't be impolite

nad *prep pron see* **an** *prep* 3

nàdar, *gen* nàdair *nm*, **1** nature (*ie the natural world*), **glèidhteachas nàdair** nature conservancy, conservation; **2** nature,

temperament, character, disposition, temper, *cf* **aigne** 2, **mèinn** 1

nàdarra(ch) *adj* natural

naidheachd, naidheachd, naidheachdan *nf* **1** news, a piece of news, tidings, **meal do naidheachd!** congratulations! (*lit* enjoy your news), **bha Iain a' gabhail do naidheachd** Iain was asking after you, (*TV, Radio etc*) **na naidheachdan** the news, **fear-naidheachd** a journalist (*cf* **naidheachdair**); **2** (*at ceilidh etc*) an anecdote, a short (*& usu humorous*) story

naidheachdair, naidheachdair, naidheachdairean *nm* a journalist

nàidhlean, *gen* nàidhlein *nm* nylon

nàimhdeas, *gen* nàimhdeis *nm* (*abstr noun corres to* **nàmhaid**) enmity, hostility

nàimhdeil *adj* hostile, inimical

nàire *nf invar* **1** shame, ignominy, **a bhoireannaich** (*voc*) **gun nàire!** shameless woman!, **gabh** *v* **nàire** be/feel ashamed, **fo nàire** ashamed, **mo nàire!** for shame!, **mo nàire oirbh!** shame on you! *cf* **masladh**; **2** bashfulness, *cf* **diùide**; **3** embarassment (*through shame*)

nàireach *see* **nàrach**

nàisean, nàisein, nàiseanan *nm* a nation (*people & territory*)

nàiseanta *adj* national, **Am Mòd Nàiseanta** The National Mod

nàiseantach, *gen & pl* nàiseantaich *nm* a nationalist, *also as adj* **nàiseantach** nationalist(ic) (*for pol parties see* **pàrtaidh** 1)

nàiseantachd *nf invar* **1** nationalism; **2** nationhood

naisgear, naisgeir, naisgearan *nm* (*gram*) a conjunction

nam *prep pron, see* **an** *prep* 3

nàmhaid, nàmhad, nàimhdean *nm* an enemy, a foe, an adversary

nan *conj* (**nam** *before b, f, m, p*) if (*in hypothetical contexts in past & conditional tenses*), (*song*) **nam biodh agams' an sin cupan, dh'òlainn dith mo shàth** if I had had a cup there, I would have drunk my fill of it, **nan**

robh mi beartach, thogainn caisteal dhut if I was/were rich, I'd build you a castle, *cf* **ma 1**

nan (**nam** *before b, f, m, p*) *form of the* (*article see table p 491*)

nan *prep pron see* **an** *prep* **3**

naoi & **naodh** *num* nine, **naoi-deug** & **naodh-deug** nineteen

naoidhean, naoidhein, naoidheanan *nm* an infant, a baby, a young child, *cf* **leanaban, leanabh, pàiste**

naoinear *nmf* people numbering nine, **cha tàinig ach naoinear** only nine (people) came, **naoinear mhac/chaileag** (*gen pl*) nine sons/girls

naomh, *gen* & *pl* **naoimh** *nm* a saint

naomh *adj* holy, sacred, saintly

naomhachd *nf invar* **1** saintliness; **2** holiness, sanctity

nàr *adj* shameful, disgraceful, **is nàr sin!** that's disgraceful!, *cf* **maslach, tàmailteach 1**

nar *prep pron see* **an** *prep* **3**

nàrach & **nàireach** *adj* **1** shame-faced, sheepish, ashamed; **2** bashful, modest, diffident, *cf* **diùid, màlda**

nàrachadh, *gen* **nàrachaidh** *nm* (*the act of*) shaming etc (*see senses of* **nàraich** *v*)

nàraich *vt, pres part* **a' nàrachadh**, shame, put to shame, abash, disgrace, *cf* **maslaich**

nas (*in comp exprs*), *see* **na** *rel pron* **2**

nathair, nathrach, nathraichean *nf* **1** an adder; **2** a snake, a serpent, *also in Bibl context* **mheall an nathair Eubha** the serpent beguiled Eve

neach *nm invar* **1** a person, one, someone, an individual, (*in neg constr*) no-one, **an neach ris an do bhruidhinn mi** the person/individual I spoke to, **chan fhaca mi neach sam bith** I saw no-one/didn't see anyone at all, **gaol nach cuireadh neach an cèill** a love no-one could/one couldn't express, *cf* **duine 2, urra 1**; **2** *used in numerous compounds as a non sex-specific alternative to* **fear-** (*pl* **luchd-**), *see examples below* & *cf* **bana-, fear 2, luchd**[2], *Note: Though* **neach** *is a masculine noun it is not in itself gender-specific, thus it is available for use in compounds where the gender of the person involved is irrelevant or not known.*

neach-cathrach *nm* a chairperson

neach-ciùil *nm* a musician

neach-ionaid, *pl* **luchd-ionaid** *nm* a replacement, a proxy, an agent, a representative, (*sport etc*) a substitute, (*theatre etc*) a stand-in, (*med*) a locum

neach-labhairt *nm* a spokesperson

neach-obrach *nm* a worker, a workperson

neactar, *gen* **neactair** *nm* nectar

nead, *gen* & *pl* **nid** *nm* a nest, (*song*) **thig gach eun a dh'ionnsaigh nid** each bird will make for its nest

nèamh, nèimh, nèamhan *nm* **1** heaven, a heaven, *cf* **flaitheas, pàrras**; **2** (*occas*) the heavens, *cf* **iarmailt, speur 2**

nèamhaidh *adj* heavenly, celestial

neapaigear, neapaigeir, neapaigearan *nm* a handkerchief

neapaigin, neapaigine, neapaiginean *nf* a napkin

nèarbhach *adj* nervy, nervous

neart, *gen* **neirt** *nm* (*usu phys*) strength, force, might, vigour, (*prov*) **thèid neart thar ceart** might before right, **ann an treun a neirt** at the height of his/her strength/powers, in his/her prime, *cf* **lùth 3, spionnadh**

neartachadh, *gen* **neartachaidh** *nm* (*the act of*) strengthening etc (*see senses of* **neartaich** *v*)

neartaich *vti, pres part* **a' neartachadh**, strengthen, make or become strong or stronger, invigorate

neartmhor *adj* (*phys*) strong, mighty, powerful, *cf* **làidir 1, lùthmhor 1**

neas, neasa, neasan *nf* **1** a weasel; **2** a stoat (*also* **neas mhòr**); **3** a ferret

neasgaid (*also* **niosgaid**), **neasgaide, neasgaidean** *nf* a boil, an ulcer, a carbuncle, an abscess

nèibhi(dh), nèibhi(dh), nèibhidhean *nmf* a navy, (*song*) **saoilidh balaich . . . nach eil ceàrd as fheàrr na 'n Nèibhi gus an tèid iad innte** (Murchadh MacLeòid, Siabost) young fellows think there's no trade better than the Navy, until they join it, *cf* **cabhlach 2, loingeas 2**

neimh *see* **nimh**

Neiptiùn, *gen* **Neiptiùin** *nm* Neptune

neo *see* **no**

neo- *prefix corres to Eng* un-, in-, -less *etc* (*ie negativises second element of compound*), *cf* **eas-, eu-, mì-**, & *see examples below*

neo-àbhaisteach *adj* unusual

neo-chomasach *adj* incapable, incompetent

neo-chùramach *adj* irresponsible

neodrach *adj* (*gram etc*) neuter

neo-eisimeileachd *f* independence

neoichiontach *adj* guiltless, innocent

neòinean, *gen* **neòinein**, *pl* **neòinein** & **neòineanan** *nm* a daisy

neòinean-grèine a sunflower

neo-iomlan *adj* incomplete

neònach *adj* odd, strange, curious, (*trad expr*) **nach neònach sin?** isn't that strange?, *cf stronger* **iongantach**

neoni *nf invar* nothing, nought, zero, (*scores*) nil, (*tennis*) love, **rach** *v* **gu neoni** come to nought/nothing, **cuir** *v* **an neoni** abolish, do away with, annul

neonithich *vt, pres part* **neonitheachadh**, cancel; annihilate

neo-phàirteach *adj* unbiased, impartial, objective

neo-thruacanta *adj* pitiless

neul, *gen & pl* **neòil** *nm* **1** a cloud, (*song*) **a' fuadach neul na h-oidhche** banishing the clouds of night, *cf* **sgòth**; **2** (*of face*) a complexion, a hue, *cf* **dreach 2, tuar**; **3** a faint, a fainting fit, **rach** *v* **an neul** faint, *cf* **laigse 2**

neulach *adj* cloudy, *cf* **sgòthach**

neulaich *vti, pres part* **a' neulachadh**, cloud, cloud over, obscure

nì, nì, nithean *nm* **1** a thing, **a h-uile nì** everything, **nì sam bith** anything at all, **nitheigin** something, *cf* **càil** *nm* **1, dad 1, rud 1**; **2** a circumstance, a matter, an affair, a business, **'s e droch nì a bh' ann** it was a bad business/affair, (*song*) **bidh i daonnan air mo chùram anns gach nì** she's always on my mind in every circumstance, (*prov*) **deiseil air gach nì** sunwise in every circumstance/situation, *cf* **gnothach 2**; **3** *in expr* **(an) Nì Math** God, *cf more usu* **Dia, Tighearna 3**

nì *pt of irreg v* **dèan** (*see tables p 497*)

Nic- *a prefix found in clan surnames* (*and other surnames adapted to the Gaelic system*), female descendant of (*lit* grand-daughter of), **Mòrag NicDhòmhnaill** Morag MacDonald, **Seònaid NicBhàtair** Janet Watson, *cf* **mac 3**

nigh *vt, pres part* **a' nighe**, wash, *cf less usu* **failc, ionnlaid**

nighe *nm invar* (*the act of*) washing

nigheadair, nigheadair, nigheadairean *nm* a washer, a washing machine (*cf* **inneal-nighe** – *see* **inneal 1**), **nigheadair-shoithichean** a dishwasher

nigheadaireachd *nf invar* washing (*ie a batch of washing*)

nighean, *gen* **nighinne** *& ***ìghne**, *pl* **nigheanan** *& ***ìghnean** *nf* **1** a (*young*) girl, **clann-nighean** girls, girl children; **2** a young woman (*up to the late teens or early twenties approx*); *cf* **caileag 2, nìghneag**; **3** a daughter, **nighean bràthar/peathar** a niece

nìghneag *& ***nìonag**, *gen* **nìghneig**, *pl* **nìghneagan** *nf* (*affectionate dimin of*

nighean) **1** a (*young*) girl; **2** (*freq in songs*) a young woman (*up to the late teens or early twenties approx*), (*song*) **nìghneag a' chùil duinn, nach fhan thu?** brown-haired girl/lass, won't you wait?; *cf* **caileag 2, cuachag, gruagach, nighean 1 & 2, maighdeann 1, rìbhinn**

nimh *& ***neimh**, *gen* **n(e)imhe** *nm* **1** poison, venom, *cf* **puinnsean**; **2** (*abstr*) venom, bitterness, malice, *cf* **mì-rùn** (*see* **mì-**)

nimheil *adj* **1** poisonous, (*phys*) venomous, *cf* **puinnseanach**; **2** (*abstr*) venomous, malicious

nìonag *see* **nìghneag**

niosgaid *see* **neasgaid**

Nirribhidh *nf invar* Norway, *formerly* **Lochlann**

nis(e) *see* **a-nis(e)**

nitheil *adj* concrete, actual, real, *cf* **fìor 2, rudail**, *& opposite* **beachdail 2**

niuclasach *adj* nuclear, **sgudal niùclasach** *m* nuclear waste

no (*older sp* **neo**) *conj* or, **cogadh no sìth** war or peace

nobhail, nobhaile, nobhailean *nf* a novel

nochd *vti, pres part* **a' nochdadh**, **1** (*vt*) show, reveal, **nochd dhomh e** show me it, *cf* **seall 2**; **2** (*vi*) appear, come into view or sight, **an uair a nochd e a-staigh** when he turned up/rolled in, **cò às a nochd thusa?** where did you (*emph*) appear/spring from? (*song*) **a' nochdadh ri beanntan na Hearadh** coming in sight of the mountains of Harris, (*book etc*) **nochd an clò** appear in print, come out, be published

Nollaig, Nollaige, Nollaigean *nf* Christmas, **Nollaig Chridheil!** Merry Christmas! **Latha/Oidhche Nollaig** Christmas Day/Eve, **aig àm na Nollaige** at Christmas time

norradaich, *gen* **norradaiche** *nf* a nap (*ie short sleep*)

norrag, norraig, norragan *nf* a doze, a nap, a snooze, **cha d' fhuair mi norrag c(h)adail** I didn't get a wink of sleep, *cf* **cadal 2, dùsal, suain** *n*

nòs, nòis, nòsan *nm* **1** a custom, a habit, a usage, *cf more usu* **àbhaist 1, cleachdadh 2**; **2** a way *or* manner of doing something, *esp* (*under influence of Irish*) **an seann nòs** the traditional style/manner (*esp of singing*), *cf more usu* **dòigh 1, modh 1**

nota, nota, notaichean *nf* **1** (*money*) *earlier* a bank-note, *now usu* a pound, **tha ceithir notaichean agam oirbh** you owe me four pounds, *cf trad* **punnd 2**; **2** a (*written*) note, an aide-mémoire, **bha na h-oileanaich a'**

gabhail **notaichean** the students were taking notes; **3** a short letter or written message, a note

nuadh *adj* new, novel (*can stress difference from what has gone before rather than a pristine state*), **an Tiomnadh Nuadh** the New Testament, **nuadh-fhacal** *m* a neologism, *cf more usu* **ùr 1**, *& opposite* **sean**

nuadhachadh, *gen* **nuadhachaidh** *nm*, **1** (*the act of*) making new etc (*see senses of* **nuadhaich** *v*); **2** (*of house etc*) a renovation

nuadhaich *vt, pres part* **a' nuadhachadh**, make new, renovate, do up, *cf* **ùraich 1** *& stronger* **ath-nuadhaich 2**

nuair a *see* **an uair a**

nuallaich *vi, pres part* **a' nuallaich**, (*usu of animals*) howl, roar, bellow, *cf* **beuc** *v*, **geum** *v*, **langanaich**

nur *prep pron see* **an** *prep* **3**

nurs, nurs, nursaichean *nf* a nurse, *cf more trad* **banaltram, bean-eiridinn**

o

o (*see also* **bho**) *prep* from, *takes dat & lenites following noun where possible* (*The prep prons formed with* **o**, *in the order first, second, third person singular, first, second, third person plural, and with the reflexive/emphatic particles in brackets, are as follows:* **uam(sa), uat(sa), uaithe(san), uaipe(se), uainn(e), uaibh(se), uapa(san)**; from me, from you (*fam*), *etc*) **1** (*time*) **o mhoch gu dubh** from morn till night, **bhon àm sin air adhart** from that time forward/on, **bho Dhiluain gu Dihaoine** from Monday to Friday; **2** (*movement, direction*) **chaidh i suas bhon chladach** she went up from the beach, **litir o Mhurchadh** a letter from Murdo, (*story collection*) **Ugam agus Bhuam** To Me and from Me, *also fig in exprs* **thig** *v* **bhuaithe** recover (*from illness*), get better, & **rach** *v* **bhuaithe** go off, get worse, deteriorate; **3** *as conj*, since (*esp of time, but see also* **on a**), (*song*) **'s cian nan cian bhon dh'fhàg mi Leòdhas** it's a very long time since I left Lewis, **bho dh'fhàg mi an sgoil** since I left school, **'s fhada o nach fhaca mi thu!** I haven't seen you for a long time!, long time no see!, *cf* **on a**

òb, *gen* **òba** & **òib**, *pl* **òban** *nm* a bay, a creek *cf* **bàgh, camas 1**

obair, *gen* **obrach** & **oibre**, *pl* **obraichean** *nf* **1** work, labour, **tha obair agam ri dhèanamh** I've (got) work to do, **obair chruaidh** hard work, **obair-taighe** housework, (*prov*) **'s e obair latha tòiseachadh** it's a day's work getting started, *cf* **cosnadh 3, saothair 1**; **2** *freq as pres part* **ag obair** working, **ag obair gu trang** working busily, **bha sinn ag obair fad an latha an-dè** we were working all day yesterday; **3** work (*ie the product of labour*), **obair-ghrèis** needlework, **obair-làimhe** handiwork, (*poetry collection*) **Sàr-obair nam Bàrd Gàidhealach** The Masterworks of the Gaelic Poets; **4** a job, an occupation, employment, **a bheil obair agad?** have you got a job?, are you working?, **gun obair** unemployed, (*calque*) **a-mach à obair** out of work, **luchd-obrach** *m* workers, employees, a workforce (*cf* **obraiche**), *cf* **cosnadh 2, dreuchd**

obann *adj* sudden, *cf* **grad 1**

obh *excl, usu as* **obh! obh!** dear, oh dear!, my goodness me!, good heavens! *etc, expressing sympathy, concern, surprise etc*

obraich (*occas* **oibrich**) *vti, pres part* **ag obrachadh**, **1** (*vi*) work, (*usu in sense of*) function properly, succeed, **chan eil an t-inneal-nighe ag obrachadh** the washer isn't working, **dh'fheuch sinn ri a car a thoirt aiste ach cha do dh'obraich e** we tried to play a trick on her but it didn't work; **2** (*vt*) work, operate, work at *or* on, **obraich inneal** operate/work a machine, **obraich fearann/croit** work land/a croft (*cf* **àitich 1**); **3** *in expr* (*sums, problems etc*) **obraich** *vt* **a-mach** work out

obraiche (*occas* **oibriche**), **obraiche, obraichean** *nm* a worker, a workman, a labourer, *cf* **neach-obrach**

och *excl usu expr sadness, common in songs eg* **och nan och, tha mi fo mhulad** alas/woe is me, (for) sadness is upon me

ochd *num & adj* eight, **ochd-deug** eighteen, **ochdamh** eighth

ochdad *nm* eighty (*in alt numbering system*)

ochdnar *nmf* people numbering eight, an 'eightsome', **ruidhle-ochdnar** *m* an eightsome reel

o chionn *also* **bho chionn** *prep, with gen* (*not to be confused with* **a chionn**) **1** *corres to* ago, **bho chionn ghoirid** a short time ago, recently, **o chionn mìos(a)** a month ago/back; **2** since, for (*of time*), **tha mi ag obair aige bho chionn bliadhna** I've been working for him for a year/since a year ago

odhar *adj* **1** dun(-coloured), **bò odhar** a dun cow, *can occur in placenames as* our, **Beinn Odhar** Ben Our, dun mountain, *cf* **ciar 3, lachdann 1**; **2** sallow, **Coinneach Odhar**

Fiosaiche Sallow Kenneth the Seer (*the Brahan Seer*)

òg *adj* **1** young, **caileag òg** a young girl; **2** (*usu poet*) fresh, new, early, **san òg-mhadainn** in the early morning, **an t-Ògmhios** June, *cf* **ùr 1**

ògan, ògain, òganan *nm* (*on plants etc*) a shoot, a tendril, *cf* **bachlag 2, gas**

òganach, *gen & pl* **òganaich** *nm* **1** a young man, (*folk group*) **Na h-Òganaich** The Young Ones; **2** a youth, a stripling, an adolescent (male), (*Sc*) a halflin, *cf* **òigear**

ogha, *gen* **ogha,** *pl* **oghachan** & **oghaichean** *nm* a grandchild, a grandson, a grand-daughter, **iar-ogha** a great-grandchild

Ògmhios *see* **òg 2**

ogsaidean, *gen* **ogsaidein** *nm* oxygen

oibrich, oibriche *see* **obraich, obraiche**

oide, oide, oidean *nm* a step-father, *cf* **muime**

oideachas, *gen* **oideachais** *nm* **1** learning, education, instruction, *cf more usu* **foghlam 2, ionnsachadh 2; 2** *esp in expr* **beul-oideachas** traditional learning, knowledge and lore orally transmitted, *cf* **beul- aithris**

oidhche, oidhche, oidhcheannan *nf* **1** night, a night, **air feadh na h-oidhche** during/all through the night, **Oidhche Mhàirt** Tuesday night, **oidhche mhath (leat/leibh)!** goodnight!, **a dh'oidhche 's a là** by night and by day; **2** the eve (*of specific days*), **Oidhche Challainn** New Year's Eve, Hogmanay, **Oidhche Shamhna** Halloween

oidhirp, oidhirpe, oidhirpean *nf* **1** an attempt, a try, (*Sc*) a shot, **dèan/thoir** *v* **oidhirp** make an attempt, try (**air** at/to), **thug e oidhirp eile air** he had another try/shot at it, **oidhirp air saorsa** a bid for feedom, *cf* **ionnsaigh 2; 2** an effort (*ie the concrete result of an attempt at something*), **cha bu toigh leis an fhear-deasachaidh na h-oidhirpean agam** the editor didn't like my efforts

oifig, oifige, oifigean *nf, also* **oifis, oifise, oifisean** *nf,* **1** an office (*ie the phys place*) **tha an oifis na bùrach** the office is untidy/in a mess, **cheannaich mi stampaichean an Oifis a' Phuist** I bought some stamps at the Post Office; **2** (*abstr*) an office, a position, a function, *cf* **dreuchd, obair 4; 3** an office (*ie the institution*) **Oifis na h-Alba** the Scottish Office

oifigeach, *gen & pl* **oifigich** *nm, also* **oifigear, oifigeir, oifigearan** *nm* **1** (*forces etc*) an officer; **2** an official, **tha e na oifigeach aig a' Chomhairle** he's a Council Official/an official with the Council

oifigeil *adj* official, **cuir fios thuca gu h-oifigeil** let them know officially

òige *nf invar* youth (*abstr*), **làithean m' òige** the days of my youth, my young days, **gaol na h-òige** young love

òigeachd *nf invar* adolescence

òigear, òigeir, òigearan *nm* a youngster, an adolescent, a teenager, a youth, *cf* **deugaire, òganach 2**

òigh, òighe, òighean *nf* **1** a virgin, *cf* **ainnir; 2** a maiden, a young (*single*) woman, *cf* **caileag 2, gruagach, maighdeann 1, nighean 2, nìghneag 2, rìbhinn**

òigheil *adj* virginal, maidenly

oighre, oighre, oighreachan *nm* an heir, an inheritor

oighreachd, oighreachd, oighreachdan *nf* **1** an inheritance, an estate (*ie property left as an inheritance*), **cìs oighreachd** *f* inheritance tax, *cf* **dìleab; 2** an estate (*ie large land unit*), **tha e na gheamair air an oighreachd** he's a gamekeeper on the estate

òigridh *nf coll invar,* young people, youngsters, young folk, (*song*) **le òigridh ghuanach tha nis air fuadach** (Màiri Mhòr) with carefree young folk who are now in exile, **buidheann òigridh** *mf* a youth club/group

oilbheum, oilbheim, oilbheuman *nm* offence, **dèan/thoir** *v* **oilbheum do chuideigin** offend/give offence to someone, *cf stronger* **tàmailt 2**

oilbheumach *adj* offensive, *cf stronger* **tàmailteach 2**

oileanach, *gen & pl* **oileanaich** *nm* (*university, college etc*) a student

oileanachadh, *gen* **oileanachaidh** *nm* **1** (*the act of*) training, instructing, teaching; **2** instruction, training; *cf* **teagasg**

oileanaich *vt, pres part* **ag oileanachadh,** train, instruct, teach, *cf* **teagaisg 2**

oillt, oillte, oilltean *nf* terror, horror, dread, **cuir** *v* **oillt air** terrify, horrify, **thàinig oillt orm** dread/horror came over me, *cf* **eagal 1, uabhas 1, uamhann**

oillteil *adj* horrible, dreadful, frightful, *cf* **uabhasach 1**

oilltich *vt, pres part* **ag oillteachadh,** terrify, *cf* **cuir oillt air** (*see* **oillt**)

oilthigh, oilthigh, oilthighean *nm* a university, **Oilthigh Ghlaschu** Glasgow University, *with art,* **tha i aig an oilthigh/a' dol don oilthigh** she's at university/going to university, **an t-Oilthigh Fosgailte** the Open University

òinseach, òinsiche, òinsichean *nf* an idiot, a fool, *trad a female but also used of males, cf* **amadan**

oir, oire, oirean *nf* **1** an edge, a margin, a fringe, (*of road*) a verge, **oir na coille** the edge/margin/fringe of the wood, **oir a' chabhsair** the kerb, **air oir na creige** on the cliff-edge; **2** (*of jug etc*) a rim, a lip; *cf* **bile** *nf* **2**, **iomall 2**

oir *conj* (*rather formal*) for, **dh'fhalbh e, oir bha an oidhche a' fàs dorcha** he left, for the night was growing dark

oirbh (*emph form* **oirbhse**) *prep pron, see* **air**

òirdheirc *adj* **1** glorious, magnificent, *cf more usu* **glòrmhor**; **2** distinguished, llustrious, *cf more usu* **ainmeil, cliùiteach, iomraiteach**

òirleach, *gen & pl* **òirlich** *nmf* an inch (*ie measurement*), **is duine gach òirleach dheth** he's every inch a man

oirnn (*emph form* **oirnne**), **oirre** (*emph form* **oirrese**) *prep prons, see* **air**

oirthir, oirthire, oirthirean *nf* a coast, a littoral, a seaboard, *cf* **costa**

oisean, oisein, oiseanan *nm, also* **oisinn, oisne, oisnean** *nf*, a corner, (*external, eg*) **aig oisean an taighe** at the corner of the house, (*or internal, eg*) **anns an oisean** in the corner (*cf* **cùil 1** & *less trad* **còrnair**)

oiteag, oiteig, oiteagan *nf* a breeze, (*story collection*) **Oiteagan on Iar** Breezes from the West, *cf* **gaoth 1, osnadh 2**

òl *vti, pres part* **ag òl**, **1** (*vt*) drink, **òl cupan teatha** drink a cup of tea, *cf* **gabh 1**; **2** (*vi*) drink (*alcoholic drinks*), **cha bhi mi ag òl idir** I don't drink at all

ola, ola, olaichean *nf* oil, **ola-luis** vegetable oil, **ola-thalmhainn** mineral oil

Òlaind *nf, used with art* **an Òlaind** Holland

olann, *gen* **olainn** *nf* wool, *cf* **clòimh**

olc, *comp* **(n)as (etc) miosa**, *adj* evil, wicked, bad, **tha an t-athair olc ach tha am mac nas miosa** the father is wicked but the son is more wicked/worse, *cf less strong* **dona 1**

olc, *gen* **uilc** *nm* evil, badness, wickedness, *cf less strong* **donas 1**

ollamh, ollaimh, ollamhan *nm* **1** (*trad*) a learned man; **2** (*formerly*) a (non-medical) doctor, someone holding a doctorate; **3** a Professor, **An t-Ollamh Caimbeul** Professor Campbell

òmar, *gen* **òmair** *nm* amber

on a & **bhon a** *conj* since, as (*often causal, though cf eg* **'s fhada on a bha mi san sgoil** it's a long time since I was at school; *see also* **o 3**), **chuir iad an sprèidh dhan mhonadh on a bha an t-ionaltradh math shuas an sin** they put the stock on the hill as/since the grazing was good up there, *cf* **a chionn 2, oir** *conj*

onair, onaire, onairean *nf* **1** (personal) honour, **air m' onair!** (up)on my honour! honestly!; **2** honour, esteem, respect, *cf* **urram 1** & **2**; **3** honesty, *cf* **ionracas 1**

onarach *adj* **1** honourable; **2** honorary, **ball onarach den chomann** an honorary member of the society; **3** honest, *cf* **ionraic 1**

onarachadh, *gen* **onarachaidh** *nm* (*the act of*) honouring

onaraich *vt, pres part* **ag onarachadh**, **1** honour (*ie bestow an honour on*), *cf* **urram 2**; **2** honour (*ie respect, revere*)

opairèisean, opairèisein, opairèiseanan *nmf* an operation (*ie medical*), **tha i a' faighinn seachad air opairèisean** she's recovering from an operation

òr, *gen* **òir** *nm* **1** gold, (*song*) **bidh airgead nad phòcaidean is òr nach cuir thu feum air** you'll have silver in your pockets and more gold than you'll be able to use; **2** *gen used adjectivally,* gold, golden, of gold, **bonn òir** *m* a gold coin/medal

òraid, òraide, òraidean *nf* a speech, a talk, a lecture, an address, **thoir seachad/dèan** *v* **òraid** give a talk, **thug i seachad òraid don chomann eachdraidh ionadail** she gave a talk to/addressed the local history society

òraidiche, òraidiche, òraidichean *nm* a speaker, someone who gives talks or lectures, a lecturer

orains *adj* orange, **dè an dath a th' air? (tha) orains** what colour is it? orange

orainsear, orainseir, orainsearan *nm* an orange

òran (*in some areas* **amhran**), *gen & pl* **òrain** *nm* a song, (*19th century poetess*) **Màiri Mhòr nan Oran** Big Mary of the Songs, **òrain luadhaidh** waulking songs (*see* **luadhadh**), **na h-òrain mhòra** the big songs (*the classic songs of Gaelic tradition*), (*at ceilidh etc*) **gabh òran!** give us/sing a song!, *cf* **duan 2, luinneag**

orc, *gen* **oirc** *nm, used with art,* **an t-orc** (*muscular*) cramp, **tha an t-orc orm** I've got cramp

òrd, *gen* **ùird**, *pl* **ùird** & **òrdan** *nm* a hammer

òrdachadh, *gen* **òrdachaidh** *nm* (*the act of*) ordering, organising etc (*see senses of* **òrdaich** *v*)

òrdag, òrdaig, òrdagan *nf* **1** a thumb; **2** (*also* **òrdag-coise**) a toe, **an òrdag mhòr** the big toe

òrdaich *vti, pres part* **ag òrdachadh**, **1** (*vi*) order, command, tell, **dh'òrdaich iad dhomh na geataichean a dhùnadh** they ordered me to shut the gates; **2** (*vti*) (*in café etc*) order; **3** put in order, organise, tidy, *cf* **òrdugh 3**; **4** (*med etc*) prescribe

òrdaighean *see* **òrdugh 4**

òrdail *adj* **1** ordered, orderly, regular, methodical, *cf* **riaghailteach, rianail**; **2** (*arith*) ordinal, **cunntair òrdail** an ordinal number

òrdugh, òrduigh, òrduighean *nm* **1** an order, a command; **2** (*café etc*) an order, (*med*) **òrdugh cungaidh** a prescription; **3** orderliness, a proper order, state or sequence, **cuir** *v* **an òrdugh** put in order, organise, tidy up, *cf* **òrdaich 3**; **4** (*Presbyterianism*) *in pl, usu as* **na h-Òrdaighean**, Communion (*also the sequence of services leading up to the sacrament of Communion*), *cf* **comanachadh**

òrgan, òrgain, òrganan *nm* (*mus*) an organ

orm (*emph form* **ormsa**) *prep pron, see* **air**

òrraiseach *adj* **1** squeamish; **2** fastidious

orra (*emph form* **orrasan**), **ort** (*emph form* **ortsa**) *prep prons, see* **air**

ortha, ortha, orthannan *nf* a spell, a charm, an incantation, *cf* **geas 1, seun 1**

os (*trad*) *prep* **1** above, *now usu in compound prep* **os cionn** above, over, *with gen*, **neòil os cionn a' chuain** clouds over the ocean, (*song*) **os mo chionn sheinn an uiseag ghreannmhor** (Màiri Mhòr) above me/ overhead sang the joyful skylark; **2** *occas as prefix corres to Eng* super- *etc, eg* **os-nàdarrach** *adj* supernatural, **os-rathad** *m* a fly-over

osan, *gen* osain, *pl* osain & osanan *nm* a stocking, hose, *cf* **stocainn**

osann *see* **osna**

os cionn *see* **os 1**

os ìosal *see* **ìosal 3**

os làimh *see* **làmh 1**

osna (*nf*) & **osnadh** (*nm*), *gen* **osnaidh**, *pl* **osnaidhean** *nmf, also* **osann**, *gen & pl* **osainn** *nm*, **1** a sigh, **leig/dèan** *v* **osna** sigh, heave a sigh (*cf* **osnaich**), *cf less usu* **ospag 1**; **2** (*occas*) a breeze, a breath of wind, *cf more usu* **oiteag, ospag 2**

osnachadh *see* **osnaich** *n*

osnaich, *gen* **osnaiche** *nf, also* **osnachadh**, *gen* **osnachaidh** *nm*, (*the act of*) sighing

osnaich *vi, pres part* **ag osnaich &** ag **osnachadh**, sigh, *cf* **osna 1**

ospadal, ospadail, ospadalan *nm* a hospital, *usu with art*, **anns an ospadal** in hospital, *cf more trad* **taigh-eiridinn** (*see* **eiridinn**)

ospag, ospaig, ospagan *nf* **1** a sigh, *cf more usu* **osna 1**; **2** a breath or gentle gust of wind, *cf* **oiteag, &** (*occas*) **osna 2**

òstair & **òsdair**, *gen* **òstair**, *pl* **òstairean** *nm* a hotelier, an innkeeper, (*of pub etc*) a landlord, a licensee, *cf* **fear an taighe** (*see* **fear 1**)

Ostair, *gen* **Ostaire** *nf*, used with art **an Ostair** Austria

Ostaireach, *gen & pl* **Ostairich** *nm* an Austrian, *also as adj* **Ostaireach** Austrian, of, from or pertaining to Austria

othail, othaile, othailean *nf* a hubbub, an uproar, a tumult, a din, *cf* **gleadhar, iorghail, ùpraid 1**

othaisg, *gen* **othaisge**, *pl* **othaisgean** *occas* **òisgean** *nf* a hog(g) (*ie a ewe lamb between 1 & 2 years old*)

òtrach, òtraich, òtraichean *nm* a dunghill, a midden, a manure heap, *cf* **dùnan 2, siteag**

P

paca, paca, pacannan *nm* **1** a pack (*ie as carried on back*); **2** a pack (*ie a bundle or collection of something*), **paca clòimhe** a pack of wool, **paca chairtean** a pack of cards

pacaid, pacaide, pacaidean *nf* a packet

pàganach, *gen & pl* **pàganaich** *nm* a pagan, *also as adj* **pàganach** pagan

Pagastan (*also* **Pacastan**) *gen* **Pagastain/ Pacastain** *nf*, Pakistan

paidhir, *gen* **paidhir** (*m*) & **paidhreach** (*f*), *pl* **paidirichean** *nmf* a pair, **paidhir thrilleachan/mhiotagan** a pair of oystercatchers/of gloves

paidir, paidire, paidrichean *nf, used with art,* **a' phaidir** the Lord's Prayer, the Paternoster, *cf* **Ùrnaigh an Tighearna** (*see* **ùrnaigh**)

paidirean, paidirein, paidirean *nm* (*relig*) **1** a rosary (*ie the beads*); **2** a rosary (*ie the prayers*); *cf* **conaire**

pàigh *nm invar,* pay, remuneration, **àrdachadh pàighidh** *m* a pay rise, *cf* **cosnadh 4, pàigheadh 2, tuarasdal**

pàigh *vt, pres part* **a' pàigheadh, 1** pay, pay for, **pàigh cunntas** pay a bill, **pàigh neach-obrach** pay a worker, **cha do phàigh e am pinnt/airson a' phinnt a ghabh e** he didn't pay for the pint he had, **dh'fhalbh e gun phàigheadh** he left without paying, *cf less usu* **ìoc** *v*; **2** pay, make amends, suffer or atone for, **pàighidh tu (airson) do pheacaidhean** you'll pay (*etc*) for your sins

pàigheadh, *gen* **pàighidh** *nm* **1** (*the act of*) paying etc (*see senses of* **pàigh** *v*), payment; **2** *same as* **pàigh** *n*

pàileis, pàileis, pàileisean *nf* a palace, *cf more trad* **lùchairt**

pàillean, pàillein, pàilleanan *nm* **1** a pavilion; **2** a (*sizeable*) tent, *cf* **puball, teanta**

pailt *adj* **1** plentiful, ample, abundant, copious, **bi** *vi* **pailt** abound, be plentiful, **biadh pailt** copious food, **sitheann phailt** abundant game, *cf* **lìonmhor; 2** *expr good measure,* **trì troighean pailt de dh'fhad** a good/full three

feet in length, **punnd pailt de fhlùr** a good/ generous pound of flour

pailteas, *gen* **pailteis** *nm* plenty, abundance, an abundance, an ample sufficiency, *cf* **leòr 2, lìonmhorachd**

pàipear, pàipeir, pàipearan *nm* **1** paper, **pàipear-balla** wallpaper, **pàipear-sùghaidh** blotting paper; **2** (*for* **pàipear-naidheachd**), a newspaper, (*fam*) **Am Pàipear Beag** (*lit* the wee paper) The West Highland Free Press

pàirc(e), pàirce, pàircean *nf* **1** a field, (*Sc*) a park, *cf* **achadh; 2** a (public) park

paireafain *nm invar* paraffin

pàirt, pàirt, pàirtean *nmf* **1** a part, **bha an t-ugh math, pàirt dheth co-dhiù** the egg was good, part of it at any rate, **ghabh iad pàirt san ar-a-mach** they took part/participated in the rising (*cf* **com-pàirtich 2**), *cf* **cuid 1, earrann, roinn** *n* **2; 2** (*cars etc*) a part, **pàirtean-càraidh** spare parts, spares

pàirteacheadh, *gen* **pàirteachaidh** *nm* **1** (*the act of*) sharing, dividing etc (*see senses of* **pàirtich** *v*); **2** division, partition

pàirtich *vt, pres part* **a' pàirteachadh,** share, divide into shares or parts, *cf* **roinn** *v* **2**

pàirtiche, pàirtiche, pàirtichean *nm* **1** an associate, a partner, *cf* **companach 2, co-obraiche 2; 2** an accomplice, an abettor

pàisde *see* **pàiste**

paisg *vt, pres part* **a' pasgadh,** wrap (up), roll (up), fold (up), pack (up) (*objects, material, parcels etc*), *cf* **fill 1 & 2**

pàiste (*also* **pàisde**), *gen* **pàiste,** *pl* **pàistean** *nm* an infant, a baby, a small child, **bha pàiste aice** she had a baby/child, *cf* **leanaban, leanabh, naoidhean**

pàiteach *adj* thirsty, *cf* **ìotmhor, tartmhor**

pana, pana, panaichean *nm* (*kitchen etc*) a pan, *cf more trad* **aghann**

pannal, pannail, pannalan *nm* **1** (*building etc*) a panel, **pannal fiodha** a wooden panel; **2** (*official body etc*) a panel, **Pannal na Cloinne** the Children's Panel, *cf* **bòrd 1, comataidh**

Pàp(a), *gen* **Pàpa**, *pl* **Pàpan** & **Pàpachan** *nm*, *with art*, **am Pàp(a)** the Pope

Pàpanach, *gen* & *pl* **Pàpanaich** *nm* (*derog*) a papist, a Roman Catholic, *also as adj* **pàpanach** (*derog*) papist, popish, Catholic

pàrant, **pàrant**, **pàrantan** *nm* a parent

pàrlamaid, **pàrlamaide**, **pàrlamaidean** *nf* a parliament

pàrlamaideach *adj* parliamentary

pàrras, *gen* **pàrrais** *nm* paradise, a paradise, heaven, a heavenly or idyllic place, *cf* **flaitheas**, **nèamh** 1

parsail, **parsail**, **parsailean** *nm* a parcel, a package, *cf* **pasgan** 2

pàrtaidh, **pàrtaidh**, **pàrtaidhean** *nm* 1 (*body, group etc*) a party, **pàrtaidh poilitigeach** a political party, **Am Pàrtaidh Làborach/ Libearalach Democratach/Tòraidheach** the Labour/Liberal Democrat/Tory Party, **Pàrtaidh Nàiseanta na h-Alba** the Scottish National Party; 2 (*social gathering*) a party, *cf* **hòro-gheallaidh** 1

partan, **partain**, **partanan** *nm* a crab (*usu edible*), (*Sc*) a partan, *cf larger* **crùbag**

pasgadh, *gen* **pasgaidh** *nm* 1 (*the act of*) packing *etc* (*see senses of* **paisg**); 2 packing; a package, *cf* **parsail**, **pasgan** 1 & 2

pasgan, *gen* & *pl* **pasgain** *nm* 1 a bundle, a package, *cf* **pasgadh** 2; 2 a parcel, *cf more usu* **parsail**; 3 (*stationery etc*) a folder

pastra *nf invar* pastry

pathadh, *gen* **pathaidh** *nm* thirst, **bha/thàinig am pathadh oirre** she was/she grew thirsty, *cf stronger* **tart**

pàtran, **pàtrain**, **pàtranan** *nm* 1 a pattern (*ie a design, arrangement etc*) **pàtran brèagha air a' phàipear-balla** an attractive pattern on the wallpaper; 2 (*needlework etc, as model to be followed or copied*) a pattern, **tha am pàtran seo ro dhoirbh, chan urrainn dhomh a leantainn** this pattern's too difficult, I can't follow it

peacach *adj* sinful

peacach, *gen* & *pl* **peacaich** *nm* a sinner

peacadh, **peacaidh**, **peacaidhean** *nm* sin, a sin, **peacadh-bàis** a mortal sin, **peacadh-gin(e)** original sin, *cf* **ciont(a)** 2

peacaich *vi*, *pres part* **a' peacachadh**, (*usu in relig sense*) sin, transgress, *cf* **ciontaich**

peanas, **peanais**, **peanasan** *nm*, punishment, a punishment, a penalty, **peanas corporra** corporal punishment

peanasachadh, *gen* **peanasachaidh** *nm*, 1 (*the act of*) punishing, chastising; 2 punishment, a punishment

peanasaich *vt*, *pres part* **a' peanasachadh**, punish, chastise

peann, *gen* & *pl* **pinn** *nm* a pen

peansail, **peansail**, **peansailean** *nm* a pencil

peant *vti*, *pres part* **a' peantadh**, paint

peant(a), *gen* **peanta**, *pl* **peantan** & **peantaichean** *nm* paint

peantadh, *gen* **peantaidh** *nm* (*the act of*) painting

peantair, **peantair**, **peantairean** *nm* a painter (*artist or tradesman*)

pearraid, **pearraide**, **pearraidean** *nf* a parrot

pearsa, **pearsa**, **pearsachan** *nm* 1 a person, *cf* **duine** 3, **neach** 1; 2 (*in novel etc*) a character, *cf more usu* **caractar**

pearsanta *adj* personal, **beachd pearsanta** a personal opinion, **coimpiutair pearsanta** a personal computer

pearsantachd *nf invar* personality

pears-eaglais, *gen* **pears-eaglais**, *pl* **pearsan-eaglais** & **pearsachan-eaglais** *nm* a clergyman, *cf* **clèireach** *n* 1, **ministear** 1, **sagart**

peasair, **peasrach**, **peasraichean** *nf* a pea (*ie the vegetable*)

peasan, **peasain**, **peasanan** *nm* a brat

peata, *gen* **peata**, *pl* **peatan** & **peatachan** *nm* a pet

peathrachas, **peathrachais**, **peathrachasan** *nm* sisterhood, a sisterhood, sisterliness

peatrail, *gen* **peatrail** *nm*, *also* **peatroil**, *gen* **peatroil** *nm* petrol

peighinn, **peighinne**, **peighinnean** *nf* 1 (*trad*) a penny, *orig* a penny Scots, (*prov*) **cha dlighe do pheighinn fois** a penny has no right to be idle, *cf usu* **sgillinn** 1; 2 (*hist & in placenames*) a pennyland, **Peighinn a' Chaisteil** Pennycastle, the pennyland of the castle

peile, **peile**, **peilichean** *nm* a pail, **peile-frasaidh** a watering can, *cf* **bucaid** 1, & *more trad* **cuinneag**, **cuman**

pèileag, **pèileig**, **pèileagan** *nf* a porpoise

peilear & **peileir**, *gen* **peileir**, *pl* **peilearan** & **peileirean** *nm* a bullet, a pellet (*ie as projectile*)

peinnsean, **peinnsein**, **peinnseanan** *nm* a pension, **luchd-peinnsein** *m sing coll* pensioners

peirceall, *gen* **peircle** & **peircill**, *pl* **peirclean** & **peirceallan** *nm* 1 a jaw, *cf* **giall** 2; 2 a jawbone

pèist, **pèiste**, **pèistean** *nf* a reptile

peitean, **peitein**, **peiteanan** *nm* 1 a vest, *cf* **fo-lèine**; 2 a waistcoat

peitseag, **peitseig**, **peitseagan** *nf* a peach

peur, **peura**, **peuran** *nf* a pear

pian, **pèin**, **piantan** *nmf* pain, a pain

pian vt, pres part, **a' pianadh**, **1** pain, distress, **tha an dol-a-mach (a th') aice gam phianadh gu mòr** her behaviour pains/ distresses me greatly; **2** (stronger, fig) torment, torture, cf **ciùrr 1**, **cràidh**, **goirtich**

piàna also **piàno**, gen **piàna**, pl **piànathan** nm a piano

pianadh, gen **pianaidh** nm **1** (the act of) paining, tormenting etc (see senses of **pian** v); **2** torture

pianail adj painful (phys or mentally), cf **crài(dh)teach**, **goirt 1**

pic, **pice**, **picean** nm (tool) a pick, a pickaxe

picil, gen **picile** nf pickle, a pickle

pile, gen **pile**, pl **pilichean** & **pileachan** nf (med) a pill

pìleat, **pìleat**, **pìleatan** nm, also **poidhleat**, **poidhleit**, **poidhleatan** nm, **1** (seafaring) a pilot, **thàinig pìleat air bòrd an uair a ràinig sinn beul na h-aibhne** a pilot came on board when we reached the river mouth; **2** (aviation etc) a pilot

pill, **pilleadh** see **till**, **tilleadh**

pillean, **pillein**, **pilleanan** nm **1** a cushion; **2** a pillion seat or saddle

pinc adj pink

pinnt, **pinnt**, **pinntean** nm **1** (measure) an imperial pint; **2** a pint, esp of beer, **tha mi airson pinnt** I fancy a pint

pìob, **pìoba**, **pìoban** nf **1** a pipe, a tube, **pìoban-uisge** water pipes, cf **feadan 2**; **2** (also **pìob-thombaca**) a pipe (for smoking); **3** (music) a pipe, a bagpipe, (esp) the great Highland bagpipe (also **pìob mhòr**), a set or stand of pipes, **gabh** v **port air a' phìob** play a tune on the pipes, **ceòl na pìoba** pipe music, **pìob-uilne** uileann pipes

pìobaire, **pìobaire**, **pìobairean** nm a piper, **pìobair an aona phuirt** the piper with only one tune

pìobaireachd nf invar **1** piping, the act and art of playing on the great Highland bagpipe; **2** used at competitions etc, & often Anglicised as pibroch, a pibroch, to refer to the classical music of the pipes, which is strictly speaking **ceòl mòr**

piobar, gen **piobair** nm pepper

piobraich vt, pres part **a' piobrachadh**, **1** add pepper to; **2** (lit & fig) pep up, spice up

pioc vti, pres part **a' piocadh**, **1** (birds feeding) peck; **2** (persons etc) pick (at food), nibble, cf **creim 1**

pìos, **pìos**, **pìosan** nm **1** a bit or a piece of something, **pìos arain** a piece/bit of bread, **pìos math coiseachd** a fair bit of walking, **pìos air falbh** a bit away, some distance away;

2 a snack, a sandwich etc (esp eaten away from one's house), a (worker's, pupil's etc) packed lunch, (Sc) a piece

piseach, gen **pisich** nm **1** progress, improvement (in skill, activity etc), **tha piseach a' tighinn oirnn** we're improving/making progress/getting better, cf **adhartas**, **leasachadh 2**; **2** occas (trad) luck, good fortune

piseag, **piseig**, **piseagan** nf a kitten

pit, **pite**, **pitean** nf **1** female genitals, a vulva, cf **faighean**, **ròmag**; **2** (vulg) as **a phit!**, occas used as an oath or swear

piuthar, gen **peathar**, dat **piuthair**, pl **peathraichean** nf a sister, **piuthar-chèile** a sister-in-law, **piuthar mo mhàthar** my aunt (on mother's side)

plaide, **plaide**, **plaidean** nf a blanket, cf **plangaid**

plàigh, **plàighe**, **plàighean** nf **1** a plague, a pestilence, **plàigh de luchainn** a plague/an infestation of mice; **2** a pest, a nuisance

plàigheil adj pestiferous, pestilential

plana, **plana**, **planaichean** nm **1** a plan (ie project, intention), **planaichean na comhairle airson a' bhaile** the council's plans for the village/town, cf **moladh 3**; **2** a plan (ie map, diagram etc)

planaid, **planaide**, **planaidean** nf a planet

planaig vti, pres part **a' planaigeadh**, plan, make a plan or plans, cf **dealbh** v **3**

planaigeadh, gen **planaigidh** nm (the act of) planning, cf **dealbhadh**

plangaid, **plangaide**, **plangaidean** nf a blanket, cf **plaide**

plaoisg vt, pres part **a' plaosgadh**, (fruit, vegetables, nuts etc) shell, pod, peel, skin, husk, cf **rùisg 3**

plaosg, **plaoisg**, **plaosgan** nm (of nuts, eggs, peas & beans) shell, a shell, a pod, (of fruit, vegetables) skin, peel, husk, cf **cochall 1**, **rùsg 1**

plap nm invar fluttering (esp of heart, wings), cf more severe **plosg** n **2**

plap vi, pres part **a' plapail**, (esp wings, heart) flutter, cf more severe **plosg** v **2**

plàst & **plàsd**, gen **plàsta**, pl **plàst(aidhe)an** nm a (sticking) plaster

plastaig, **plastaige**, **plastaigean** nf plastic, a plastic, also as adj **plastaig** plastic

plathadh, **plathaidh**, **plathaidhean** nm **1** a glance, a glimpse, cf **aiteal**; **2** an instant, a flash, **chaidh e seachad orra ann am plathadh** he went past them in a flash, cf **priobadh 2**

pleadhag, **pleadhaig**, **pleadhagan** nf a paddle (of canoe etc)

pleadhagaich *vti, pres part* **a' pleadhagaich**, 1 paddle (*canoe etc*); 2 paddle (*one's feet*)

plèana, plèana, plèanaichean *nmf* a plane, an aeroplane, an aircraft, *cf more trad* **itealan**

ploc, pluic, plocan *nm* 1 (*of earth*) a clod, a turf, a divot, *cf* **fòid** 1; 2 a block of wood, (*song*) **chuir iad a cheann air ploc daraich** they placed his head on a block/stump of oak, *cf* **sgonn**; 3 a rounded piece or lump of something, **ploc-prìne** a pinhead, *cf* **ceap** 1, **cnap** 1

plosg, ploisg, plosgan *nm* 1 gasping (*for breath*), a gasp, panting, a pant; 2 (*esp of heart*) palpitation, a palpitation, throbbing, a throb, *cf less severe* **plap** *n*

plosg *vi, pres part* **a' plosgadh** *also* **a' plosgail** & **a' plosgartaich**, 1 gasp (*for breath*), pant, (*Sc*) pech; 2 (*esp heart*) palpitate, throb, **tha mo chridhe a' plosgadh** my heart is palpitating/beating very fast, *cf less severe* **plap** v

plosgadh, *gen* **plosgaidh** *nm, also* **plosgail** *nf invar* & **plosgartaich** *nf invar*, 1 (*the act of*) gasping, palpitating etc (*see senses of* **plosg** v); 2 palpitation, a palpitation

plub, pluba, pluban *nm* 1 (*sound*) a splash, a plop; 2 a sloshing or sploshing or glugging sound

plub *vi see* **plubraich**

plubraich *vi, pres part* **a' plubraich**, *also* **plub** *vi, pres part* **a' plubadaich** & **a' plubarsaich**, 1 (*sound of impact on water*) splash, plop; 2 (*sound of motion of liquids*) slosh, splosh, glug, splash

plubraich, *gen* **plubraiche** *nf* (*the act & sound of*) splashing, sloshing etc (*see senses of* **plubraich** v)

plucan, plucain, plucanan *nm* 1 a pimple, a spot, (*Sc*) a plouk, *cf* **cnàimhseag** 1, **guirean** 1; 2 a plug (*for sink, container, powerpoint etc*), *cf* **cnag** *n* 4

pluic, pluice, pluicean *nf* a cheek (*esp plump, rosy*), (*prov*) **cha dèan a' phluic a' phìobaireachd** (*loosely*) there's more to piping than puffed-out cheeks, *cf* **lethcheann** 1 & *more usu* **gruaidh**

plumair, plumair, plumairean *nm* a plumber

Pluta *nm invar* (the planet) Pluto

poball, pobaill, poballan *nm* a people, **poball na h-Èireann** the Irish people, the people of Ireland, *cf more usu* **muinntir** 2, **sluagh** 2

poblach (*less usu* **poballach**) *adj* public, **companaidh phoblach** a public company, **leabharlann poblach** a public library, **an roinn phoballach** the public sector, *cf* **coitcheann** 1, & *opposite* **prìobhaideach**

poblachd, poblachd, poblachdan *nf* a republic **Poblachd na h-Eireann** the Irish Republic **Poblachd na(n) Seic** *nf* the Czech Republic

poca, poca, pocannan *nm* 1 a bag (*usu for small purchases etc – cf Sc* poke); 2 a larger bag, a sack, **poca-cadail** a sleeping-bag, *cf* **sac**

pòcaid, pòcaide, pòcaidean *nf, also more trad* **pòca, pòca, pòcan(nan)** *nm* a pocket, **airgead pòca(id)** pocket money

pòg, pòige, pògan *nf* a kiss, (*trad dance*) **ruidhle nam pòg** the kissing reel, (*pibroch*) **thug mi pòg do làimh an Rìgh** I got a kiss of the King's hand

pòg *vti, pres part* **a' pògadh**, kiss, (*humorous car sticker*) **na pòg mo thòn** don't kiss my backside, keep your distance

poidhleat *see* **pìleat**

poidsear, poidseir, poidsearan *nm* a poacher

poileas, *gen* **poilis** *nm*, 1 police, **càr-poilis** a police car; 2 a policeman, *cf* **poileasman**

poileasaidh, poileasaidh, poileasaidhean *nm* (*government etc*) a policy, **poileasaidh-urrais** an insurance policy

poileasman, *gen & pl* **poileasmain** *nm* a policeman, **chaidh e na phoileasman ann an Glaschu** he became a policeman/joined the police in Glasgow, *cf* **poileas** 2

poilitigeach *adj* political, **pàrtaidhean poilitigeach** political parties

poilitigs *nf invar* politics, **ann an saoghal na poilitigs** in the world of politics, **luchd-poilitigs** *m* politicians

poit, poite, poitean *nf* 1 a pot (*as container, cooking utensil etc*), **poit-fhlùran** a flowerpot, **poit na lite** the porridge pot, **poit teatha** a teapot (*also* a pot of tea), *cf* **prais**; 2 **poit-dhubh** a (*whisky*) still, *cf* **stail**

poitean, *gen* **poitein** *nm* poteen, illicitly distilled whisky

pòitear, pòiteir, pòitearan *nm* a drinker, a tippler, a boozer, a drunkard, **co-phòitear** a drinking companion, a fellow boozer, *cf* **misgear**

pòitearachd *nf invar* drinking, tippling, boozing, (*Sc*) bevvying, *cf* **daorach** 1, **misg**

pòla, pòla, pòlaichean *nm* 1 a (magnetic) pole, **am Pòla a Deas** the South Pole; 2 a (*wooden etc*) pole, *cf* **cabar** 2

Pòlach, *gen & pl* **Pòlaich** *nm* a Pole, *also as adj* **Pòlach** Polish

Pòlainn *nf invar, used with art* **a' Phòlainn** Poland, (*POW poem*) **Deargadan na Pòlainn** The Fleas of Poland

poll, *gen & pl* **puill** *nm* 1 mud, mire, silt, *cf* **eabar**; 2 a bog, a mire, *cf* **boglach, fèith(e)**, sùil-chritheach; 3 *esp* **poll-mòna(ch)** a peat(y) bog, a peat hag, a peat bank

pònaidh, pònaidh, pònaidhean *nm* a pony

pònair, *gen* **pònarach** *nf* a bean, (*more often as coll*) beans, **pònair leathann/Fhrangach** broad/French beans

pong, puing, pongan *nm* (*music*) a note

pongail *adj* **1** (*person, work etc*) punctilious, meticulous, exact, painstaking, thorough, *cf* **mion 2, mionaideach; 2** (*discourse etc*) concise, pointed, to the point; **3** punctual

pòr, pòir, pòran *nm* **1** (*trad*) seed, *cf* **fras** *n* **2**, & *more usu* **sìol 1; 2** crops, *cf* **bàrr 2; 3** growth (*of plants*), *cf* **fàs** *n*

port¹, *gen & pl* **puirt** *nm* a tune, **gabh** *v* **port air an fhidhill** play a tune on the fiddle, **port-à-beul** mouth music (*ie singing to dance tunes, using vocables or nonsensical or humorous words*), *cf* **fonn 1**

port², *gen & pl* **puirt** *nm* a port, a harbour, **'s e port a th' ann an Glaschu** Glasgow is a port, **port-adhair** an airport, *cf* **acarsaid, cala**

Portagail *nf,* used with art **a' Phortagail** Portugal

Portagaileach, *gen & pl* **Portagailich** *nm* a Portuguese, *also as adj* **Portagaileach** Portuguese

portair, portair, portairean *nm* **1** a porter, a bearer, *cf more trad* **neach-giùlain** (*see* **giùlan 1**); **2** a porter, a doorman, *cf more trad* **dorsair**

pòs *vti, pres part* **a' pòsadh,** marry, get married, **phòs iad an-uiridh** they (got) married last year, **am pòs thu mi? cha phòs!** will you marry me? no!

pòsadh, pòsaidh, pòsaidhean *nm* **1** (*the act of*) marrying, getting married; **2** marriage, a marriage, **gealladh-pòsaidh** *m* an engagement (*lit* a promise of marriage - *see* **gealladh**), **sgaradh-pòsaidh** *m* divorce, a divorce, separation, *cf* **banais**

pòsda *see* **pòsta**

post¹, *gen & pl* **puist** *nm* post, mail, **am Post Rìoghail** the Royal Mail, **Oifis a' Phuist** *nf* the Post Office (*ie the institution & a branch*), *also* **Post-Oifis** *nm* a Post Office, **post-adhair** air mail, **post a-mach/a-steach** outgoing/incoming mail, **post-dealain** electronic mail, e-mail

post², *gen & pl* **puist** *nm* a (wooden) post, a stake, a stob, **post-seòlaidh** a signpost, *cf* **stob 1**

post(a), posta, postaichean *nm* a postman, (*Sc*) a postie, (*Highland Eng*) a post, **Ailig Post** Alec the Post(ie)

pòsta & **pòsda** *adj* married, wed, **pòsta aig Anndra** married to Andrew, **nuadh-phòsta** *adj* newly married, **càraid phòsta** *f* a married couple, (*song*) **ged nach eil sinn fhathast pòst', tha mi 'n dòchas gum bi** though we are not yet married, I hope we will be

prabar, prabair, prabairean *nm* a rabble, a mob, a crowd (*derog*), *cf* **foireann 1, gràisg**

prab-shùileach *adj* bleary-eyed, having rheumy or runny eyes

prais, praise, praisean *nf* a (cooking) pot, *cf* **poit**

pràis, *gen* **pràise** *nf* brass

pràiseach *adj* brass, made of brass, (*lit, not fig*) brazen

preantas, preantais, preantasan *nm* an apprentice

preas¹, *gen* **pris,** *pl* **pris** & **preasan** *nm* a bush, a shrub, *cf less usu* **dos 1**

preas², preasa, preasan *nm, also* **preasadh, preasaidh, preasaidhean** *nm,* a wrinkle

preas *vt, pres part* **a' preasadh, 1** fold, crease, *cf* **fill 1** & **2; 2** furrow, wrinkle, corrugate; **3** crush, squeeze, *cf* **fàisg**

preas(a), *gen* **pris,** *pl* **pris** & **preasan** *nm* a cupboard, (*Sc*) a press, **preas-aodaich** a wardrobe, a clothes cupboard, **preas-leabhraichean** a bookcase

preasach *adj* **1** wrinkly, wrinkled; **2** corrugated, **iarann/pàipear preasach** corrugated iron/paper

preasadh *see* **preas²**

preasag, preasaig, preasagan *nf* a crease, a wrinkle, *cf* **preas 2**

prìbheideach, prìbheiteach *see* **prìobhaideach**

prìne, prìne, prìnichean *nm* a pin (*cf Sc* preen), **prìne-banaltraim** a safety pin, *cf* **dealg 4**

priob *vti, pres part* **a' priobadh,** wink, blink, twinkle, *cf* **caog**

priobadh, priobaidh, priobaidhean *nm* **1** (*the act of*) winking, blinking, twinkling; **2** a wink, a blink, (*fig*) **ann am priobadh na sùla** in an instant, in the twinkling of an eye, *cf* **plathadh 2**

prìobhaideach, *adj* private, (*industry etc*) **an roinn phrìobhaideach** the private sector, *cf opposites* **coitcheann 1, poblach**

prìomh *adj* (*precedes the noun, which it lenites where possible*) main, foremost, principal, chief, head, prime, premier, major, **prìomh-chlèireach** *m* a chief/head clerk, **prìomh-àireamh** *f* a prime number, **a' phrìomh-oifis** the head ofice, **prìomh adhbhar a ghiùlain**

the main/principal reason for his conduct, (*ed*)
prìomh chuspair a core subject, *cf* **àrd** *adj* 3
prìomhaire, prìomhaire, prìomhairean *nm*
a prime minister, a premier
prionnsa, prionnsa, prionnsan *nm* a prince,
Bliadhna a' Phrionnsa the year of the Prince
(1745–6), **bana-phrionnsa** *f* a princess
prionnsapal (*also found as* **prionnsabal**),
prionnsapail, prionnsapalan *nm* 1 a
principle, **ann am prionnsapal** in principle; 2
a principal (*of ed or other establishment etc*), *cf*
ceannard 2
prìosan, prìosain, prìosanan *nm* a prison
prìosanach, *gen & pl* **prìosanaich** *nm* a
prisoner, *cf more trad* **bràigh**[2] *n*, **ciomach**
prìs, prìse, prìsean *nf* a price, the cost of
something, **dè a' phrìs a th' air?** how much
does it cost?, **air deagh phrìs** at a good price,
prìsean àrda high prices, *cf* **cosg** *n* 2, **cosgais**
1
prìseil *adj* precious, valuable, *cf* **luachmhor**
pròbhaist, pròbhaiste, pròbhaistean *nm*
(*civic admin*) a provost
prògram, prògraim, prògraman *nm* a
programme, (*IT*) a program(me), **a' craobh-
sgaoileadh phrògraman air an rèidio**
broadcasting programmes on the radio, (*IT*)
prògram chleachdaidhean an applications
programme
proifeasair, proifeasair, proifeasairean
nm a professor, (*children's book*) **Clann a'
Phroifeasair** (Maoilios M. Caimbeul) The
Professor's Children, *cf more trad* **ollamh**
proifeiseanta *adj* professional, *cf* **dreuchdail** 2
pròis, *gen* **pròise** *nf* pride (*often legitimate*), *cf*
moit, *& usu more excessive* **àrdan, uabhar,
uaibhreas**
pròiseact, *pl* **pròiseactan** *nmf* a project, *cf*
plana 1
pròiseil *adj* (*often legitimately*) proud, **bha sinn
pròiseil asad** we were proud of you, **pròiseil
aiste fhèin** proud of herself, *cf* **moiteil**, *& often
more excessive* **àrdanach, uaibhreach**
pronn *adj* mashed, pounded, ground, pulverised,
broken up small, **buntàta pronn** mashed
potato, **airgead pronn** small change
pronn *vt, pres part* **a' pronnadh, 1** mash,
pound, grind, pulverise, break up small, (*saying*)
chaidh a phronnadh na shùgh fhèin he
was mashed in his own juice; **2** (*fam, in f ight
etc*) bash, maul, beat up; **3** *in expr* (*fam*) **bha**

mi air mo phronnadh I was drunk/smashed/
steaming
pronnadh, *gen* **pronnaidh** *nm* (*the act of*)
mashing, bashing etc (*see senses of* **pronn** *v*)
pronnasg, *gen* **pronnaisg** *nm* sulphur,
brimstone
prosbaig, prosbaig, prosbaigean *nf* 1
binoculars, field glasses; **2** a telescope
Pròstanach, *gen & pl* **Pròstanaich** *nm* a
Protestant, *also as adj* **Pròstanach** Protestant
prothaid, prothaide, prothaidean *nf* (*usu fin*)
profit, a profit, gain, a gain, benefit, a benefit,
dèan *v* **prothaid** make a profit
puball *&* **pùball**, *gen* **pubaill**, *pl* **puballan** *nm*
a (very) large tent, a marquee, *cf* **pàillean** 1,
teanta
pùdar *&* **fùdar**, *gen* **pùdair**, *pl* **pùdaran** *nm*
powder, a powder
pùdaraich *&* **fùdaraich** *vt, pres part* **a'
pùdarachadh, 1** powder, put powder on
something; **2** reduce to powder
puing, puinge, puingean *nf* 1 a point in a scale,
series etc, (*of heat, angles*) a degree; **2** a point
(*made in an argument etc*); **3** (*typog*) a stop, a
mark, **stad-phuing** a full stop, **clisg-phuing**
an exclamation mark, **dà-phuing** a colon
puinnsean, puinnsein, puinnseanan *nm*
poison, a poison, *cf more trad* **nimh** 1
puinnseanach *also* **puinnseanta**, *adj*
poisonous, *cf more trad* **nimheil** 1
puinnseanaich *vt, pres part* **a'
puinnseanachadh**, poison
puinnseanta *see* **puinnseanach**
pumpa, pumpa, pumpaichean *nm* a pump
punnd, *gen & pl* **puinnd** *nm* 1 (*weight*) a
pound; **2** (*money*) a pound, (*formerly*) **punnd
Èireannach** an Irish pound, a punt, (*trad*)
punnd Sasannach a pound Sterling, *cf* **nota** 1
purgadair, *gen* **purgadair** *nm* purgatory
purpaidh *adj* purple, *cf* **còrcair**
purpar *&* **purpur**, *gen* **purpair** *nm* (*the colour*)
purple
put, puta, *pl* **putan** *&* **putaichean** *nm* a buoy
put *vti, pres part* **a' putadh, 1** push, shove, *cf*
brùth 2, **sàth** *v* 2; **2** jostle, *cf* **uillnich**; **3** (*IT
etc*) **put ann** key in (*data etc*)
putadh, *gen* **putaidh** *nm* (*the act of*) pushing,
shoving, jostling etc, *see* **put** *vti*
putan, putain, putanan *nm* 1 a button, **dùin/
fuasgail** *v* **putanan** fasten/undo buttons; **2** (*on
keyboards etc*) a key, a button

R

rabaid, rabaide, rabaidean *nf* a rabbit, *cf*
coineanach

rabhadh, rabhaidh, rabhaidhean *nm*
warning, a warning, an alarm, an alert, a caution,
clag-rabhaidh *m* a warning bell, an alarm
bell, **thug iad rabhadh dhomh** they warned/
alerted/cautioned me, *cf* **earalachadh 3,**
earalaich 3

rabhd, *gen* **rabhda** *nm, also* **ràbhart,** *gen*
ràbhairt *nm,* **1** idle, boastful or far-fetched
talk, tales or chatter, a 'spiel'; **2** obscene talk, *cf*
drabastachd, draostachd

ràc, ràic, ràcan *nm* a drake, *cf* **dràc**

ràc *vti, pres part* **a' ràcadh,** (*gardening etc*) rake

racaid, racaide, racaidean *nf* (*tennis etc*) a
racket

ràcan, ràcain, ràcanan *nm* (*tool*) a rake

rach *vi irreg* (*for forms see tables p 501*), *pres
part* **a' dol, 1** go, **thèid mi don bhaile** I'll go
to the town, **a bheil an trèana seo a' dol do
Ghlaschu?** is this train going to Glasgow?, **rach
air adhart** (*of troops etc*) advance, go forward,
rach a chadal go to bed, **chaidh i bhuaithe**
she went downhill/off, she deteriorated, *cf* **falbh
1, gabh 2, triall; 2** happen, go on, take place, **a
bheil/am bi na cèilidhean a' dol fhathast?**
are the ceilidhs still going (strong)?, (*fam*)
dè tha dol? what's doing/happening/going
on?, how's things?, **bha mi sa chùirt an-dè!
ciamar a chaidh dhut? cha deach ach gu
dubh dona!** I was in court yesterday! how did
you get on/how did it go? just terrible!, *cf* **èirich
2; 3** become, grow, get, *with abstract nouns* **tha
e a' dol am meud/feabhas** (*etc*) it's getting
bigger/better (*etc*), *cf* **fàs** *v* **3; 4** become, take a
job (*etc*) as, **chaidh e na phoileas** he became
a policeman; **5** *in expr* **rach agam** (*etc*) **air**
manage to, succeed in, **an tèid agad air obair
fhaighinn?** will you manage to find/get a job?
rinn i e cho math 's a rachadh aice she did
it as well as she could (manage); **6** *used to expr
passive,* **chaidh talla a' bhaile a pheantadh**
the town hall was painted, **cha tèid sin a
dhèanamh** that won't be done; **7** *misc exprs,*

rach thar a chèile fall out, quarrel (with each
other), **rach an sàs anns an obair** (*etc*) get
involved in the work (*etc*), get stuck into the
work (*etc*), **rach an urras gu . . .** guarantee
that . . . , **chaidh e às mo chuimhne** I forgot
it, **rach ri taobh cuideigin** take after (*ie*
resemble) someone

**rachadh, rachaibh, rachainn, racham,
rachamaid** *pts of irreg v* **rach** (*see tables p 501*)

radan, *gen & pl* **radain** *nm* a rat

ràdh *nm invar* **1** a saying, a proverb, an adage, *cf
more usu* **facal 2, seanfhacal; 2** *for* **ag ràdh,**
pres part, see **abair**

radharc *see* **fradharc**

rag *adj* **1** (*phys*) stiff, rigid, inflexible; **2** (*in
character etc*) stubborn, obstinate, inflexible,
(*Sc*) thrawn, *cf* **dùr 1, rag-mhuinealach**

ragaich *vti, pres part* **a' ragachadh,** stiffen,
make or become stiff or rigid

rag-bharaileach *adj* dogmatic, stubborn or
overbearing in one's opinions or beliefs

rag-mhuinealach *adj* very stubborn or
obstinate, pig-headed, *cf* **dùr 1, rag 2**

raidhfil, raidhfil, raidhfilean *nf* a rifle

raige *nf invar* (*abstr noun corres to* **rag** *adj*) **1**
stiffness, rigidity; **2** obstinacy

raineach, *gen* **rainich** *nf* bracken, fern(s)

ràinig *pt of irreg v* **ruig** (*see tables p 502*)

ràith, ràithe, ràithean *nf* **1** a season, a quarter
(*of year*); **2** a period, a while, a time, *cf* **greis,
ùine 2**

ràitheachan, *gen & pl* **ràitheachain** *nm*
(*publishing*) a quarterly (magazine), a periodical,
cf **iris**

ràmh, *gen & pl* **ràimh** *nm* an oar

ràn, *gen & pl* **ràin** *nm* a roar, a yell, a bellow, *cf*
beuc *n,* **geum** *n*

ràn *vi, pres part* **a' rànail & a' rànaich, 1** roar,
yell, bellow, *cf* **beuc** *v,* **geum** *v;* **2** cry, weep (*usu
vigorously*), *cf* **caoin 2, guil**

rànail *nm invar* **1** roaring, yelling, bellowing; **2**
(*usu vigorous*) crying, weeping

rann, *gen* **rainn,** *pl* **rannan & ranntaichean**
nf **1** verse, poetry, **rosg is rann** prose and verse,

cf **bàrdachd, dànachd; 2** a (*single*) verse, a stanza

rannaigheachd *nf invar* (*poet*) versification, metre, metrics, **saor-rannaigheachd** free verse

rannsachadh, *gen* **rannsachaidh** *nm* **1** (*the act of*) searching, rummaging etc (*see senses of* **rannsaich** *v*); **2** research

rannsaich *vti, pres part* **a' rannsachadh, 1** search; **2** rummage (*esp in search of something*), *cf* **ruamhair 2, rùraich 1; 3** research, study, investigate, **tha i a' rannsachadh eachdraidh na dùthcha** she's researching the history of the country; **4** explore; **5** (*trad*) ransack

raon, *gen* **raoin**, *pl* **raontan & raointean** *nm* **1** a field, a piece of (*usu*) level ground (*often for a specific purpose*), **raon-cluiche** a playing field, a pitch, **raon goilf** a golf course, **raon-adhair** an airfield, **raon gnìomhachais** an industrial estate, a business park, **raon-ola** an oil field; **2** (*fig*) a field, an area, an aspect (*of activity, knowledge, experience etc*), **raon eile anns an robh e fìor eòlach** another field/area he was highly knowledgeable about; **3** (*IT*) a field

rapach *adj* slovenly, scruffy, dirty, *cf* **dràbhail, grodach, luideach, mosach 1**

ràsanach *adj* boring, tedious, *cf* **fadalach 2, liosda, màirnealach 2**

rath, *gen* **ratha** *nm* (*trad*) luck, good fortune, prosperity, *now usu in proverbs, eg* **is duilich rath a chur air duine dona** it's hard to put luck on a worthless (*or* unlucky) man

rathad, *gen* **rathaid & rothaid**, *pl* **rathaidean & ròidean** *nm* **1** a road, **rathad beag** a minor road, **rathad-mòr** a main road, **rathad singilte/dùbailte** a single/double track road; **2** a way, a route, **air an rathad dhachaigh** on the way home, **chaidh iad an rathad sin** they went that way, **an rathad teaghlaich** in the family way, *cf* **slighe**

rathail *adj* auspicious

Ratharsach, *gen & pl* **Ratharsaich** *nm* someone from Raasay (**Ratharsair & Ratharsaigh**), *also as adj* **Ratharsach** of, from or pertaining to Raasay

rè *nf invar* **1** a time, a period, *cf more usu* **ùine 2; 2** one's time, day or lifetime, **an rè mo sheanar** in my grandfather's time/day, *cf more usu* **linn 2**

rè *prep, with gen,* during, through(out), in the course of, **rè nam bliadhnachan dh'fhàs i na bu shèimhe** through/over the years she became calmer, *cf* **air feadh**

reachd *nm invar* **1** rule, command, authority, **a' Ghrèig fo reachd nan Seanailearan** Greece under the Generals' rule, (*prov*) **ge cruaidh reachd a' bhàillidh, chan fheàrr reachd a' mhinisteir** though the factor's rule is harsh, the minister's is no better, *cf* **smachd; 2** a rule, a command, a statute, an ordinance, a law, *cf more usu* **lagh, riaghailt 1**

reamhar *adj* fat, *cf* **sultmhor 1**

reamhraich *vti, pres part* **a' reamhrachadh**, fatten, make or become fat

reic *nm invar* selling, a sale, **chan eil e airson a reic** it's not for sale, **fear-reic** *m* a salesman, **neach-reic** *m* a salesperson

reic *vt, pres part* **a' reic**, sell, **chan eil càil agam ri reic** I've nothing to sell, **reic air deagh phrìs** sell at a good price

reiceadair, reiceadair, reiceadairean *nm* **1** a seller, a vendor; **2** a salesman, a salesperson, *cf more usu* **fear-reic, neach-reic** (*see* **reic** *n*); **3** an auctioneer

rèidh *adj* **1** level, even, *cf* **còmhnard** *adj*; **2** smooth, *cf* **mìn; 3** (*area of ground etc*) clear, cleared, (*wool etc*) disentangled, straightened out; **4** *in expr* **bi rèidh ri cuideigin** get on well/smoothly with someone, be on good terms with someone

rèidhlean, rèidhlein, rèidhleanan *nm* a meadow, (*village etc*) a green

rèidio, rèidio, rèidiothan *nm* radio, a radio, **dè a th' air an rèidio?** what's on the radio?

rèile, rèile, rèilichean *nf* **1** a rail; **2** *pl* **rèilichean** railings

rèilig, rèilige, rèiligean *nf* a kirkyard, a churchyard, a graveyard, *cf* **cill 2, clachan 3, cladh**

rèir *see* **a rèir**

rèis, rèise, rèisean *nf* (*sports etc*) a race

rèisde, rèist *see* **a-rèist**

rèiseamaid, rèiseamaide, rèiseamaidean *nf* a regiment

rèite, rèite, rèitean *nf* **1** agreement, an agreement; **2** reconciliation, a reconciliation; **3** atonement, expiation; **4** *also used for* **rèiteach**, *see next*

rèiteach, rèitich, rèitichean *nm* (*trad*) a betrothal, *involving family discussion, agreement and associated celebrations*

rèiteachadh, *gen* **rèiteachaidh** *nm* **1** (*the act of*) conciliating, settling etc (*see senses of* **rèitich** *v*); **2** *also used for* **rèiteach**, *see above*

rèitear, rèiteir, rèitearan *nm* (*sport*) a referee

reithe, reithe, reitheachan *nm* a tup, a ram, *cf* **rùda**

rèitich *vt, pres part* **a' rèiteachadh**, **1** (*opposing parties etc*) conciliate, reconcile, appease, arbitrate; **2** (*situations, relationships etc*) settle, sort out, put right/in order, put/set on an even keel, adjust, clear up, **rèitich an gnothach** settle/sort out the matter; **3** disentangle, **rèitich a' chlòimh seo dhomh** disentangle this wool for me, *cf* **fuasgail 2**; **4** (*objects, spaces*) clear (away), clear up, **rèitich an rùm agad!** clear up/sort your room! (*cf* **sgioblaich**), **rèitich an rathad** clear the road/way

reodh *see* **reoth**

reoth *vti, pres part* **a' reothhadh & a' reodhadh**, freeze

reòdhta *see* **reòthta**

reòiteag, reòiteig, reòiteagan *nf* ice cream, an ice cream

reòthta *adj*, frozen, **biadh** *m* **reòthta** frozen food, **tha mo chasan reòthta!** my feet are frozen!

reothadair, reothadair, reothadairean *nm* a freezer, a deep freeze

reothadh, *gen* **reothaidh** *nm* frost, a frost, **bha reothadh ann sa mhadainn (an-diugh)** there was (a) frost this morning

reotha(i)rt, reothairt, reothartan *nmf* a spring-tide, (*poetry collection*) **Reothairt is Contraigh** (Somhairle MacGill-Eain) Spring tide and Neap tide, (*saying*) **reothart an-diugh is conntraigh a-màireach** too much today and too little tomorrow

reòthte *see* **reòthta**

reub *vti, pres part* **a' reubadh**, (*materials, flesh etc*) tear, rend, rip, lacerate, mangle, (*song*) **an dèidh a reubadh le claidheamh** after ripping/mangling him with a sword, *cf* **srac**

reubadh, reubaidh, reubaidhean *nm* **1** (*the act of*) tearing, rending etc (*see senses of* **reub** *v*); **2** a rip, a rent

reubalach, *gen & pl* **reubalaich** *nm* a rebel

reudan, reudain, reudanan *nm* a wood-louse, (*Sc*) a slater

reul, rèil, reultan *nf* a star, (*story*) **Iain am measg nan Reultan** (Iain Mac a' Ghobhainn) Iain among the Stars, **reul-bhad** *m* a constellation, **an reul-iùil** the pole star, **reul-eòlas** *m* astronomy, *cf* **rionnag**

reuladair, reuladair, reuladairean *nm* an astronomer

reultag, reultaig, reultagan *nf* (*typog*) an asterisk

reusan, *gen* **reusain** *nm* reason (*ie the faculty*), sanity, *cf* **ciall 2, rian 3**

reusanta *adj* **1** reasonable, sensible, *cf* **ciallach**; **2** reasonable, fair, *cf* **cothromach**

ri, *before art* **ris**, *prep, takes the dat.* (*The prep prons formed with* **ri**, *in the order first, second, third person singular, first, second, third person plural, and with the reflexive/emphatic particles in brackets, are as follows:* **rium(sa), riut(sa), ris(-san), rithe(se), rinn(e), ribh(se), riutha(san);** to me, to you (*fam*), *etc*) **1** *often expresses opposition, some degree of struggle or effort,* **chaidh i ris an t-sruth** she went upstream/against the current, **ris a' ghaoith** against the wind, **bha iad a' trod ri chèile** they were squabbling (with each other); **2** *expr proximity* **taobh ri taobh** side by side, **bha mo dhruim ris a' bhalla** my back was against/to the wall, **an tacsa ri craoibh** leaning/propped up against a tree, **còmhla rium/cuide rium/mar rium** with me, in my company, **dhealaich sinn riutha** we parted from them/took our leave of them; **3** *in exprs of comparison* **coltach ri chèile** like each other, **cho seang ri seangan** as slim as an ant; **4** *expr that something is or needs to be done* **tha mòran agam ri dhèanamh** I've lots to do, **tha an taigh sin ri reic** that house is to be sold/is for sale, **tha iad rim moladh** they are/deserve to be praised; **5** during, in (*of time*), **ri linn mo sheanar** in my grandfather's time/day, **gheibh sinn ri tìde e** we'll get it in time/in due course/eventually; **6** *expr exposure, visibility,* (*song*) **(a') nochdadh ri beanntan na Hearadh** appearing/coming in sight of the mountains of Harris, **bha a h-uileann ris** her elbow was showing/visible/bared/exposed, **ris a' ghrèin** exposed to the sun; **7** engaged in an activity, **tha iad ris an iasgach** they are at the fishing (*either just now, or as an occupation*), **dè a tha sibh ris?** what are you up to?, **a bheil thu ri bàrdachd fhathast?** are you still writing poetry?, *Note:* **ri** *in this sense is used by some speakers in the place of* **ag** *or* **a'** *to form the pres part*

riabhach *adj* (*trad*) **1** brindled, marked with spots or stripes, *freq in placenames as* -reoch, **Dail Riabhach** Dalreoch, brindled haugh or meadow, *cf* **ballach, breac** *adj*; **2** *of a range of dull colourings,* grizzled, drab, dun, yellowish-brown, *cf* **lachdann 1, odhar 1**

riadh, *gen* **rèidh** *nm* (*fin*) interest

riaghail *vti, pres part* **a' riaghladh**, *also* **riaghlaich** *vti, pres part* **a' riaghlachadh**, **1** rule, rule over, govern (a country etc); **2** regulate, administer, manage (*a body, firm etc*), *cf* **stiùir** *v* **2**

riaghailt, riaghailte, riaghailtean *nf* 1 a rule, a regulation, an ordinance, *cf* **lagh, reachd** 2; 2 system, order, *cf* **òrdugh** 3, **rian** 1

riaghailteach *adj* 1 regular, systematical, orderly, conforming to the rules or norms, *cf* **òrdail** 1

riaghailteachd *nf invar* orderliness, regularity

riaghailtich *vt, pres part* **a' riaghailteachadh**, regularise, make regular, regulate, put or keep in order

riaghaltas, riaghaltais, riaghaltasan *nm* government, a government, **riaghaltas nàiseanta/ionadail** national/local government

riaghladair, riaghladair, riaghladairean *nm* 1 a ruler (*ie head of state etc*), a governor; 2 a regulator

riaghladh, *gen* **riaghlaidh** *nm* 1 (*the act of*) ruling, regulating etc (*see senses of* **riaghail** *v*); 2 (*of country etc*) (*abstr*) government; 3 (*of business, body etc*) (*abstr*) administration, management, **neach-riaghlaidh** *m* a manager, an administrator (*cf less trad* **manaidsear**), **an luchd-riaghlaidh** the administrators, (*con*) the administration

riamh *see* **a-riamh**

rian, rian, rianan *nm* 1 method, methodicalness, orderliness, system, **cuir rian air rudeigin** impose order, system, method etc on something, *cf* **òrdugh** 3; 2 (*trad*) a mode or manner (*of doing something*), *cf more usu* **dòigh** 1; 3 reason, senses, sanity, **cha mhòr nach deach mi às mo rian** I nearly went out of my mind/lost my reason, **tha thu às do rian!** you're out of your mind! *cf* **ciall** 2, **reusan**; 4 (*music*) an arrangement

rianachd *nf invar* administration

rianadair, rianadair, rianadairean *nm* 1 (*music*) an arranger; 2 a computer, *cf now usu* **coimpiutair**

rianaich *vt, pres part* **a' rianachadh**, administer (*organisation etc*), *cf* **riaghail, seòl** *vti* 3

rianail *adj* methodical, *cf* **òrdail**

rianaire, rianaire, rianairean *nm* an administrator

riarachadh, *gen* **riarachaidh** *nm* (*the act of*) pleasing, dividing etc (*see senses of* **riaraich** *v*)

riaraich *vt, pres part* **a' riarachadh,** 1 please, content, satisfy, *cf* **còrd** *v*, **sàsaich** 1, **toilich**; 2 divide, share (out), distribute, allocate, allot, (*playing cards*) deal, *cf* **pàirtich, roinn** *v* 2

riaraichte *adj* pleased, satisfied, *cf* **sàsaichte** 1, **toilichte**

riatanach *adj* essential, necessary, indispensable, *cf* **deatamach**

rib *vt, pres part* **a' ribeadh,** trap, ensnare

ribe, ribe, ribeachan *nmf* a snare, a trap

ribh *prep pron, see* **ri**

ribheid, ribheide, ribheidean *nf* 1 (*music*) a reed; 2 *in expr* (*fam*) **fliuch do ribheid!** wet your whistle!

rìbhinn, rìbhinne, rìbhinnean *nf* (*trad, freq in songs*) a maiden, a young woman, a girl (*as object of affections*), (*song*) **a rìbhinn òg, bheil cuimhn' agad?** young lass, do you remember?, *cf* **cuachag, caileag** 2, **gruagach, nighean** 2, **nìghneag** 2, **maighdeann** 1

ribhse *emph prep pron, see* **ri**

ridhil *see* **ruidhle**

ridire, ridire, ridirean *nm* a knight

rìgh, rìgh, rìghrean *nm* 1 a king, (*prov*) 'Tiugainn,' ars an rìgh, 'Fuirich,' ars a' ghaoth 'Come,' said the king, 'Stay,' said the wind; 2 (*occas*) God, Lord (God), **a Rìgh, glèidh sinn!** Lord save us! **Rìgh nan dùl** the Lord of the elements/universe, *cf* **Dia** 1

righinn *adj* (*materials etc*) tough, (*prov*) **bidh an iall righinn gu leòr gus am brist i** the thong is tough enough until it breaks

rinn, rinne, rinnean *nm* 1 a point (*of pencil, pin etc*), *cf* **bior** 1; 2 a point of land, a promontory, *cf more usu* **àird(e)** 2, **rubha**

rinn (*emph form* **rinne**) *prep pron, see* **ri**

rinn *pt of irreg v* **dèan** (*see tables p 497*)

rioban, riobain, riobanan *nm* ribbon, a ribbon, **rioban-tomhais** a tape measure

riochd, riochda, riochdan *nm* form, likeness, appearance, **nochd an taibhse an riochd cait** the ghost appeared in the likeness of a cat, **breug-riochd** *m* a disguise (*lit* a false appearance)

riochdachadh, riochdachaidh, riochdachaidhean *nm* 1 (*the act of*) representing, portraying etc (*see senses of* **riochdaich** *v*); 2 (*by lawyer, spokesperson etc*) representation; 3 (*by actor, artist etc*) representation, a representation, portrayal, a portrayal

riochdaich *vt, pres part* **a' riochdachadh,** 1 (*lawyer, spokesman etc*) represent; 2 (*actor, artist etc*) represent, portray, impersonate

riochdair, riochdair, riochdairean *nm* (*gram*) a pronoun

riochdaire, riochdaire, riochdairean *nm* 1 a representative, **riochdaire aonaidh** a union representative, a shop steward; 2 (*film etc*) a producer

rìoghachadh, rìoghachaidh, rìoghachaidhean *nm* reigning, a reign

rìoghachd, rìoghachd, rìoghachdan *nf* a kingdom

Rìoghachd Aonaichte *nf, used with art* **an Rìoghachd Aonaichte** the United Kingdom

rìoghaich *vi, pres part* **a' rìoghachadh**, reign

rìoghail *adj* royal, kingly, regal, **is rìoghail mo dhream** royal is my race (*motto of Clan Gregor*)

rìomhach *adj* beautiful, fine, splendid, (*song*) **air luing rìomhaich nam ball airgid** on a splendid/beautiful ship with silver rigging, *cf* **àlainn, eireachdail**

rionnach, *gen & pl* **rionnaich** *nm* mackerel, a mackerel

rionnag, rionnaig, rionnagan *nf* a star, (*fam*) **chan eil fhios a'm o na rionnagan ruadha** I haven't the faintest idea, *cf* **reul**

ris (*emph form* **ris-san**) *prep pron, see* **ri**

ri taobh *see* **taobh** 1 & 4

rithe (*emph form* **rithese**), **rium** (*emph form* **riumsa**), **riut** (*emph form* **riutsa**), **riutha** (*emph form* **riuthasan**) *prep prons, see* **ri**

ro *adv, lenites following adj etc,* **1** too, excessively, **tha e ro anmoch airson cuairt a ghabhail** it's too late to go for a walk; **2** *also occurs as prefix* **ro-** over-, **ro throm** *adj* overweight, **ro-nochd** *v* over-expose; **3** (*trad*) *as intensifying element* very, extremely, (*before noun*) great, extreme, **ro-gheal** *adj* extremely white, **ro-chùram** *m* extreme anxiety/care

ro, roi- & **roimh**, *before art* **ron**, *prep* (*takes dat*), before (*in various senses*). (*The prep prons formed with* **ro**, *in the order first, second, third person singular, first, second, third person plural, and with the reflexive/emphatic particles in brackets, are as follows:* **romham(sa), romhad(sa), roimhe(san), roimhpe(se), romhainn(e), romhaibh(se), romhpa(san):** before me, before you (*fam*), *etc*) **1** before (*in time*), **dh'fhalbh sinn ron àm** we left early (*lit* before the time), **ron mhithich** *adv* before the appointed time, prematurely, **ro-làimh** *adv* beforehand, in advance, (*trad tales*) **fada, fada ron a seo** long, long ago (*lit* before this), once upon a time; **2** in front of, before (*in space*), **choisich sinn romhainn** we walked along/on (*lit* before ourselves), **bha càr ron doras** a car was in front of the door, *cf* **air beulaibh**; **3** *expr reaction to or in the presence of someone,* **bha eagal air roimhpe** he was afraid of her; **4** *prep pron* **roimhe** *used adverbially*, before (*in time*), **duine nach fhaca sinn a-riamh roimhe** a man we never saw before, (**chaidh mi ann** *etc*) **an là roimhe** (I went there *etc*) the other day; **5** *in expr* **cuir**

v **romham** (*etc*) decide, determine, resolve, propose, intend, make up my (*etc*) mind, **chuir iad romhpa taigh ùr a thogail** they resolved to build a new house

ro-, *also* **roi(mh)-**, *prefix corres to Eng* pre-, fore-, *see examples below*

ro-aithris *f* (*esp of weather*) a forecast

ro-aithris, *pres part* **a' ro-aithris** *vti*, forecast, foretell

robach *adj* **1** shaggy, hairy, *cf* **molach, ròmach 1**; **2** slovenly, untidy, *cf* **luideach**

robh *pt of irreg v* **bi** (*see tables p 505*)

roc, *gen & pl* **ruic** *nf* a wrinkle, *cf more usu* **preas²**

rocaid, rocaide, rocaidean *nf* a rocket

ròcail, *gen* **ròcaile** *nf* croaking, a croak, (*of crows etc*) cawing, a caw, *cf* **gràg, gràgail**

ròca(i)s, ròcais, ròcaisean *nf*, a rook, **bodach-ròcais** *m* a scarecrow

ro-chraiceann, *gen* **ro-chraicinn**, *pl* **ro-chraicnean** *nm* a foreskin

roghainn, roghainn, roghainnean *nmf* choice, choosing, a choice, an alternative, an option, a preference, **chan eil roghainn againn** we've no choice/no alternative, **mo roghainn fhìn de cheòl** my own choice of/preference in music, *cf* **taghadh 2**

roghnachadh, *gen* **roghnachaidh** *nm* (*the act of*) choosing etc (*see senses of* **roghnaich** *v*)

roghnaich *vti, pres part* **a' roghnachadh**, choose, select, pick, *cf* **tagh 1**

roi-, roimh, roimhe *see* **ro** *prep*

roilig *vti, pres part* **a' roiligeadh**, roll

Ròimh *nf, used with art* **An Ròimh** Rome

roimh- *prefix, see* **ro-** *also* **roi(mh)-**, *prefix*

roimhe (*emph form* **roimhesan**) *prep pron, see* **ro** *prep*

roimhe *adv* (*of time*) before, **cha do rinn mi sin a-riamh roimhe** I never did that before, *see* **ro** *prep* 4

roimhear, roimheir, roimhearan *nm* (*gram*) a preposition

roimhpe (*emph form* **roimhpese**) *prep pron, see* **ro** *prep*

ròineag, ròineig, ròineagan *nf* a (single) hair, *cf* **fuiltean**

roinn, roinne, roinnean *nf* **1** a division (*incl football*), (*arith etc*) division, a sector, (*pol*) **roinn taghaidh** a constituency, (*industry etc*) **an roinn phoblach/phrìobhaideach** the public/private sector; **2** a share, a portion, a part, a section, *cf* **cuibhreann 1, cuid 1, earrann**; **3** (*in organisation etc*) a department, **roinn na rùnaireachd** the secretarial department, (*ed*) **Roinn na Fraingis** the French Department; **4** (*local government, formerly*) a region, **Roinn na**

Gàidhealtachd Highland Region; **5** a continent *cf* **Roinn Eòrpa**

roinn *vt, pres part* **a' roinneadh**, **1** divide (up), split (up), separate (*into smaller quantities, shares etc*); **2** divide, distribute, share (out), apportion, (*cards*) deal, **roinn i an t-airgead oirnn** she divided/shared (*etc*) the money between us, *cf* **pàirtich, riaraich 2**; **3** (*arith*) divide, **72 air a roinneadh le 3** 72 divided by 3

Roinn Eòrpa *nf, used with art* **an Roinn Eòrpa** Europe, the continent of Europe

ròist & **ròsd** *vt, pres part* **a' ròstadh** & **a' ròsdadh**, **1** roast (*meat etc*); **2** fry, *cf* **frighig**

ro-làimh *adj* advance, **dìoladh ro-làimh** an advance payment

ro-làimh *adv, see* **ro** *prep* **1**

ròlaist, ròlaist, ròlaistean *nm* (*Lit*) a romance, a romantic novel

ro-leasachan, gen & pl ro-leasachain *nm* (*gram*) a prefix

ròm *nmf invar* pubes, pubic hair, *cf* **gaoisid 2**

ròmach *adj* **1** woolly, hairy, shaggy, *cf* **molach, robach 1**; **2** bearded, hirsute

ròmag, ròmaig, ròmagan *nf* female genitals, the female pubic area, *cf* **faighean, pit**

Romàinia *nf* Romania

Romàinianach, gen & pl Romàinianaich *nm* a Romanian, *also as adj* **Romàinianach** of, from or pertaining to Romania

romhad (*emph form* **romhadsa**), **romhaibh** (*emph form* **romhaibhse**), **romhainn** (*emph form* **romhainne**), **romham** (*emph form* **romhamsa**), **romhpa** (*emph form* **romhpasan**) *prep prons, see* **ro** *prep*

ròn, gen & pl ròin *nm* a seal (*ie the sea creature*)

ron *see* **ro** *prep*

rong[1]**, gen roinge** & **ronga, pl rongan** *nf, also* **rongas, gen & pl rongais** *nm*, **1** a rung; **2** a spar, a (wooden) crosspiece, a dwang; **3** a (wooden) hoop

rong[2]**, gen & pl roing** *nm* a spark, *esp* a spark of life, a vital spark, **chan eil rong innte** there's not a spark of life in her, *cf* **deò**

ronn, roinn, ronnan *nm* **1** mucus, phlegm; **2** slaver, *cf* **seile**

ro-òrdachadh, gen ro-òrdachaidh *nm* predestination

ro-phàigheadh, gen ro-phàighidh *nm* pre-payment

ròp(a), gen ròpa, pl ròpaichean & **ròpannan** *nm* a rope, **ròp-aodaich** a clothes-line, *cf* **ball**[1] **4, còrd** *n*

ro-ràdh, gen ro-ràidh, pl ro-ràidhean *nm* a foreword, a preamble, a prologue

ròs, ròis, ròsan *nm* a rose

rosg[1]**, ruisg, rosgan** *nm* prose, *cf* **rann 1**

rosg[2]**, ruisg, rosgan** *nm* an eyelash, *cf* **fabhra 1**

rosgrann *f* (*gram*) a sentence (*cf less trad* **seantans**)

ròsta & **ròsda** *adj* **1** roast, roasted; **2** fried, **buntàta ròsta** *m* fried potatoes, chips

roth, rotha, rothan *nmf* a wheel, *cf less trad* **cuibhle**

rothach *adj* wheeled, having wheels

ro-thaghadh, gen ro-thaghaidh *nm* pre-selection

rothar, rothair, rotharan *nm* a bicycle, *cf less trad* **baidhsagal**

ruadh *adj* **1** (*of hair, animal's coat etc*) red, ginger, **falt ruadh** red/ginger hair, **fear ruadh** a red-haired man, **madadh-ruadh** a fox (*lit a red dog/canine*); **2** red (*a less true red than* **dearg**), **sgillinn ruadh** a (*brass or copper*) penny, *esp in expr* **chan eil sgillinn ruadh agam** I don't have a brass farthing, I'm completely broke, *cf* **dearg 1**

ruagadh, gen ruagaidh *nm* (*the act of*) chasing, routing etc (*see senses of* **rua(i)g** *v*)

rua(i)g *vt, pres part* **a' ruagadh**, **1** chase, chase away, put to flight, pursue, drive out *or* away; **2** (*military*) rout

ruaig, ruaige, ruaigean *nf* **1** chasing, a chase, pursuing, a pursuit, *cf* **tòir 1**; **2** (*military etc*) a flight, a rout; **3** (*hunting*) a chase, a hunt

ruamhair *vi, pres part* **a' ruamhar**, **1** dig, *cf* **cladhaich 1**; **2** rummage (*esp in search of something*), *cf* **rannsaich 2, rùraich 1**

rubair, rubair, rubairean *nm* rubber, a rubber

rubha, rubha, rubhaichean *nm* (*topog, usu coastal*) a point, a promontory, *cf* **àird(e)** *n* **2, maol** *n* **1**

rùchd, rùchda, rùchdan *nm* **1** (*esp of pig*) a grunt; **2** a belch, *cf* **brùchd** *n*; **3** retching, (*vulg*) **chuir mi a-mach rùchd mo chaolanan** I spewed my guts up

rùchd *vi, pres part* **a' rùchdail**, **1** (*esp pig*) grunt; **2** belch, *cf* **brùchd** *v* **1**; **3** retch, *cf* **dìobhair, sgeith**

rud, rud, rudan *nm* **1** a thing, **rud sam bith** anything at all, (*after neg verb*) nothing at all (*cf* **rudeigin**), (*fam*) **dè an rud?** what?, what did you say? (*cf more polite* **àill 2**), *cf* **càil** *nm* **1, dad 1, nì** *n* **1, sìon 2**; **2** a fact, **mas e an rud e 's gu bheil stoirm a' tighinn oirnn** if it is true/a fact/the case that we are in for a storm, **nam b' e rud e 's gun caochladh iad** if they were to die, *cf* **fìrinn 2**; **3** a matter, an affair, a business, **'s**

e droch rud a bha ann it was a bad business/ affair; **4 rud beag** *adv, see* **beag 4**

rùda, rùda, rùdan *nm* a ram, a tup, *cf* **reithe**

rudail *adj* concrete, real, actual, *cf* **nitheil**, *& opposite* **beachdail 2**

rùdan, *gen* **rùdain,** *pl* **rùdain** *&* **rùdanan** *nm* a knuckle, a finger-joint, **tha altas nad rùdain** you've got arthritis in your knuckles

rudeigin 1 *pron* something, anything, **a bheil rudeigin ceàrr? tha rudeigin nam shùil** is anything/something wrong? there's something in my eye, *cf less usu* **nitheigin** (*see* **nì** *n* 1); **2** *as adv* a little, a bit, somewhat, rather, **bha mi rudeigin sgìth** I was a bit/rather tired, *cf* **beag 4, beagan** *adv,* **car** *n* 7, **caran**

rudhadh, *gen* **rudhaidh** *nm* **1** (*the act of*) blushing, flushing (*of face*); **2** (*also* **rudhadh-gruaidhe**) a blush, a flush (*on face*)

rug, rugadh *pts of irreg v* **beir** (*see tables p 494*)

ruidhle, ruidhle, ruidhlea(cha)n *nm, also* **ridhil, ridhle, ridhlea(cha)n** *nm,* (*dance*) a reel, **ruidhle-ochdnar** an eightsome reel, **Ruidhle Thulachain** the Reel o Tulloch, (*prov*) **tha car eile air ruidhle a' bhodaich** there's another turn left in the old man's reel

ruig *vti irreg* (*see tables p 502*), *pres part* **a' ruigsinn, 1** (*vi*) arrive, (*vt*) arrive at, reach (*a place*), **an dèidh dhuinn an cladach a ruigsinn** after we reached/arrived at the shore; **2** *in expr* **ruig air** reach, reach for, take, seize (*object etc, esp with hand*), **an ruig thu air an sgeilp as àirde?** can you reach the top shelf? **ruig air mo làimh** reach for/take my hand; **3** attain (*an aim etc*); **4** *for expr* **cha ruig mi** (*etc*) **a leas** *see* **leas 2**

ruige *see* **gu ruige**

ruighe, ruighe, ruighean *nmf* **1** a forearm; **2** (*topog*) a hillslope, *cf* **aodann 2, bruthach 1, leathad, leitir**

ruigsinneach *adj* (*of a place*) accessible

rùilear, rùileir, rùilearan *nm* a ruler, a rule (*ie for measuring*), *cf more trad* **slat-thomhais** (*see* **slat 3**)

Ruis (an) *see* **Ruisia**

ruisean, *gen* **ruisein** *nm, with art* **an ruisean** the midday meal, lunch

Ruiseanach, *gen & pl* **Ruiseanaich** *nm* a Russian, *also as adj* **Ruiseanach** Russian

Ruiseanais *nf invar* (*lang*) Russian

rùisg *vt, pres part* **a' rùsgadh, 1** (*body etc*) bare, uncover, expose, undress, strip, **rùisg e a ruighe** he bared his forearm, *cf* **lom** *v* 1; **2** (*sheep*) shear, clip, fleece; **3** (*vegetables etc*) peel, skin; **4** (*sword etc*) unsheathe, bare, draw, (*trad*) **an**

àm rùsgadh nan lann in the time of baring of blades; **5** (*peatbank*) strip, open up (*by removing turf*); **6** chafe, graze, scrape (*skin of hand etc*)

rùisgte *adj* bare, bared, naked, stripped, peeled etc (*see senses of* **rùisg** *v*), **buntàta rùisgte** peeled potatoes, **casruisgte** *adj* barefoot, **ceannruisgte** *adj* bare-headed

Ruisia *nf, also* **an Ruis** *nf,* Russia

ruiteach *adj* **1** (*of colour*) ruddy, *cf* **dearg 1; 2** (*of a face*) blushing, flushed

ruith, ruithe, ruithean *nf* **1** running, a run, **dh'fhalbh iad nan ruith** they went away at a run, **nan dian-ruith** at full tilt, hell for leather; **2** (*military etc*) a pursuit, a flight, a rout, *cf more usu* **ruaig** *n* 2; **3** a rate (*of speed, progress etc*), **air an ruith seo cha bhi e seachad ron oidhche** at this rate it won't be finished/over before night, **cùm ruith ri cuideigin** keep up/ keep pace with someone; **4** a sequence

ruith *vti, pres part* **a' ruith, 1** run, **ruith i dà mhìle an-dè** she ran two miles yesterday, **chan eil an trèana/an t-uisge a' ruith** the train's/ the water's not running, (*calque*) **ruith an gual a-mach** the coal ran out; **2** (*liquids*) run, flow, stream, *cf* **sil 2, sruth** *v;* **3** chase, run after, *cf* **rua(i)g** *v* 1

rùm, rùim, rumannan *nm* **1** room, space, **cha robh rùm sa bhàta** there was no room in the boat; **2** a room, (*Sc*) an apartment, **rùm is cidsin** a room and kitchen, **rùm-bìdh** a dining-room, **thalla don rùm agad!** go to your room!, *cf* **seòmar**

Rùmach, *gen & pl* **Rùmaich** *nm* someone from Rum (**Eilean Ruma** *&* **Eilean Rùim**), *also as adj* **Rùmach** of, from or pertaining to Rum

rùn, rùin, rùintean *nm* **1** love, affection, **tìr mo rùin(-sa)** the land I love, **mì-rùn** ill-will, malice, *cf* **dèidh 2, gaol 1, gràdh 1; 2** an object of love or affection, a thing, place or person loved, (*song*) **Mo Rùn Geal Dìleas** My Faithful Fair Loved One; **3** ambition, an ambition, a desire, an intention, a purpose, a motive; a wish, a hope, *cf* **miann 1; 4** *also in expr* **a dh'aon rùn (gu)** deliberately/on purpose (to), with the sole/express intention (of) (*cf similarly used* **gnothach 5**); **5** a secret

rùnachadh, *gen* **rùnachaidh** *nm* (*the act of*) wishing, intending etc (*see senses of* **rùnaich** *v*)

rùnaich *vi, pres part,* **a' rùnachadh,** wish, desire, propose, resolve, intend (*to do something*), *cf* **cuir** *v* **romham** (*see* **ro** *prep* 5)

rùnaire, rùnaire, rùnairean *nm* a secretary, **Rùnaire na Stàite** the Secretary of State

rùrachadh, *gen* **rùrachaidh** *nm* (*the act of*) rummaging, exploring etc (*see senses of* **rùraich** *v*)

rùraich *vi, pres part* **a' rùrachadh**, **1** rummage, grope (*esp in search of something*), *cf* **rannsaich 2, ruamhair 2**; **2** *vti* explore

rus, *gen* **ruis** *nm* rice

rùsg, rùisg, rùsgan *nm, refers to covering of many objects*, **1** (*fruit etc*) peel, skin, husk, (*sheep*) fleece, (*wood*) bark, *cf* **cochall 1, plaosg**; **2** *in expr* **rùsg na Talmhainn** the Earth's crust

rùsgadh, *gen* **rùsgaidh** *nm* (*the act of*) baring, shearing etc (*see senses of* **rùisg** *v*)

S

's *see* **agus** *conj &* **is** *v*

sa[1] (*for* **anns a'**) *see* **anns an**

sa[2] *corres to* **seo**, this, **air an t-seachdain sa** this week

-sa *a suffix used to emphasise a poss adj*, (*song*) **Cailin Mo Rùin-sa** the lass (who is) my very own love, **air do shon-sa** for you (*emph*), for your (*emph*) part

Sàbaid, (*also* **Saboìn(n)d** *etc*), **Sàbaid**, **Sàbaidean** *nf*, *v*a sabbath, (*esp in Protestant usage*) **Là na Sàbaid** the Sabbath (Day), Sunday, *cf* **Didòmhnaich**

sabaid, **sabaide**, **sabaidean** *nf* fighting, brawling, a fight, a brawl, a scrap, **dèan** *v* **sabaid** fight, have a fight, *cf* **còmhrag**, **tuasaid** 2

sabaid *vi*, *pres part* **a' sabaid**, *also* **sabaidich** *vi*, *pres part* **a' sabaidich**, fight, scrap, brawl, (**ri** with, against)

sàbh, *gen* **sàibh**, *pl* **sàbhan** & **sàibh** *nm* a saw

sàbh *vti*, *pres part* **a' sàbhadh**, saw

sàbhail *vt*, *pres part* **a' sàbhaladh**, 1 save, rescue (*from accident, danger*), **chaidh an sàbhaladh le bàta-teasairginn** they were saved by a lifeboat, *cf* **teasairg**; 2 (*spiritually*) save, **sàbhail na pàganaich** save the heathens, *cf* **saor** *v* 2; 3 (*money*) save, economise, put aside, *cf* **caomhain**, **glèidh** 2

sàbhailte *adj* safe, *cf* **tèarainte** 1

sabhal, *gen* **sabhail**, *pl* **sabhalan** & **saibhlean** *nm* a barn

sàbhaladh, *gen* **sàbhalaidh** *nm* 1 (*the act of*) saving, rescuing *etc* (*see senses of* **sàbhail**); 2 (*relig*) salvation, *cf* **saorsa** 2; 3 (*fin*) savings

sabhs, **saibhse**, **sabhsan** *nm* (*cookery*) sauce, a sauce, *cf* **leannra**

Sàboin(n)d *see* **Sàbaid**

sac, *gen* **saic**, *pl* **sacan** & **saic** *nm* 1 a sack, *cf* **poca** 2; 2 *with art*, **an sac** asthma, *cf* **cuing**[2]

sad *vt*, *pres part* **a' sadail** & **a' sadadh**, throw (*carelessly*), toss, chuck, fling, **sad an cùl na làraidh e** throw it in the back of the lorry, *cf* **tilg** 1

sagart, **sagairt**, **sagartan** *nm* a priest, *cf* **clèireach** *n* 1, **ministear** 1, **pears-eaglais**

saibhear & **sàibhear**, *gen* **saibheir**, *pl* **saibhearan** *nm* 1 a culvert, a conduit; 2 a sewer

saideal, **saideil**, **saidealan** *nm* a satellite

saidhbhir *adj* wealthy, rich, affluent, opulent, *cf* **beartach**

saidhbhreas, *gen* **saidhbhreis** *nm* wealth, riches, affluence, opulence, *cf* **beartas**, **ionmhas**, **stòras** 2

saidheans, **saidheans**, **saidheansan** *nm* science, a science, **'s e saidheans an cuspair as fheàrr leam** science is my favourite subject

saighdear, **saighdeir**, **saighdearan** *nm* a soldier, **bha e na shaighdear** he was a soldier, (*prov*) **ceannard ar fhichead air fichead saighdear** twenty-one captains leading twenty soldiers, (*hist*) **na saighdearan dearga** the redcoats (*government troops, esp in Jacobite period*)

saighead, **saighde**, **saighdean** *nf* an arrow, (*trad song*) **Saighdean Ghlinn Lìobhann** The Arrows of Glen Lyon

sail, **saile**, **sail(th)ean** *nf* (*building*) a beam, a joist, *cf* **spàrr** *n* 1

sàil, **sàile**, **sàil(t)ean** *nf* a heel (*of foot & shoe*)

sailead, **saileid**, **saileadan** *nm* salad, a salad

saill, *gen* **saille** *nf* fat (*not bodily fat, cf* **sult**), grease, *cf* **crèis**, **geir** 2

saill *vt*, *pres part* **a' sailleadh**, 1 (*fish, meat etc*) salt, preserve, pickle *etc* (*with salt*); 2 season with salt

saillear, **sailleir**, **saillearan** *nf* a salt-cellar

saillte *adj* salty, salted, salt, **sgadan saillte** salt herring

saimeant *nm invar* cement, concrete

sal, *gen* **sail** *nm* 1 filth, *cf more usu* **salchar**; 2 dross, *cf* **smùr**; 3 a stain, *cf* **smal**

sàl, *gen* **sàil(e)** *nm* 1 salt water, brine; 2 (*esp in songs*) **an sàl** the sea, the ocean, the 'briny', **thar an t-sàile** over/beyond the salt sea, *cf* **fairge**, & *more usu* **cuan**, **muir**

salach *adj* dirty, filthy, foul

salachadh, *gen* **salachaidh** *nm* (*the act of*) dirtying, defiling etc (*see senses of* **salaich** *v*)

salaich *vt, pres part* **a' salach(adh)**, **1** dirty, make dirty, soil; **2** defile, sully, *cf* **truaill** 1 & 2

salann, *gen* **salainn** *nm* salt

salchar, *gen* **salchair** *nm* dirt, filth, *cf less usu* **sal** 1

salm, *gen* & *pl* **sailm** *nmf* a psalm, (*Bibl*) **Leabhar nan Salm** the Book of Psalms

salmadair, salmadair, salmadairean *nm* **1** a psalm book, a psalter; **2 An Salmadair** The Book of Psalms; the Psalmist

saltair *vt, pres part* **a' saltairt**, tread, trample, **saltair fìon-dearcan** tread grapes

sam bith *see* **bith** *n* 2

sàmhach *adj* **1** quiet, silent, **bi sàmhach!** be quiet! (*cf* **ist!**), *cf* **tosdach**; **2** (*weather, person etc*) peaceful, still, quiet, tranquil, **feasgar sàmhach** a peaceful/quiet evening, (*prov*) **far an sàmhaiche** (*superlative*) **an t-uisge, is ann as doimhne e** where the water's at its most tranquil, that's where it's deepest, *cf* **ciùin**

samhail, samhla, samhailean *nm* an equivalent, a match, a likeness, the (spitting) image of someone, the like(s) of something or someone, **cha robh a samhail ann a-riamh** the like(s) of her never existed before, *cf* **leithid, mac-samhail** 2, **seis(e)**

Samhain, *gen* **Samhna** *nf* **1** Hallowtide, All Souls' *or* All Saints' Day (1st November), **Oidhche Shamhna** Halloween; **2** *with art,* **an t-Samhain** November

sàmhchair, *gen* **sàmhchaire** *nf* **1** quiet, quietness, silence, *cf* **tosd**; **2** peacefulness, stillness, tranquility, *cf* **ciùineas**

samhla(dh), samhlaidh, samhlaidhean *nm* **1** a resemblance, a likeness; **2** a symbol, a sign, **is e '-an' samhla an iolra** '-an' is a sign of the plural, *cf* **comharra(dh)** 2; **3** (*Lit etc*) a simile, a comparison; **4** an allegory, a parable, *cf* **cosamhlachd**

samhlaich *vti, pres part* **a' samhlachadh**, (*vt*) compare, liken (**ri** to), **samhlaich ri cuideigin** liken to someone

samhradh, samhraidh, samhraidhean *nm* summer, a summer, **as t-samhradh** in (the) summer, **sgoil shamhraidh** a summer school

san *see* **anns an**

sanas, sanais, sanasan *nm* **1** a (written) announcement, notice or message (*publicly displayed*), an advertisement, a placard, **sanas-reic** an advertisement, a commercial; **2** a hint, a sign, **thug e sanas dhomh le priobadh a shùla** he gave me a hint/sign with a wink of his eye

sanasaich *vti, pres part* **a' sanasachadh**, advertise

sannt, *gen* **sannta** *nm* avarice, greed (*esp for wealth*), avarice, covetousness

sanntach *adj* greedy (*esp for wealth*), avaricious, covetous, *cf* **gionach** 1

sanntaich *vt, pres part* **a' sanntachadh**, covet (*wealth etc of others*)

saobh *adj* foolish, misguided, wrong-headed (*applied to what is false or foolish, or goes against the established norm*), now *esp* in compounds, *eg* **saobh-smuain** *m* a whim, **saobh-shruth** *m* an eddy *or* countercurrent, **saobh-chràbhadh** *m* superstition

saobhaidh, saobhaidh, *pl* **saobhaidhean** *nf* (*of animal*) a den, a lair

saoghal, saoghail, *pl* **saoghail** & **saoghalan** *nm* **1** a world, **an saoghal** the world (*cf* **talamh** 1), **mo chuid-sa den t-saoghal** my worldly possessions (*lit* my share of the world), **càit air an t-saoghal a bheil iad?** where on earth/in the world are they? **ann an saoghal a' ghnìomhachais** in the business world/the world of business; **2** (*trad*) a life, a lifetime, **rim shaoghal** in/during my life(time) (*cf* **beò** 2, **maireann** 1), **saoghal fada dhuibh!** long life to you!, *cf* **beatha** 1

saoghalta *adj* **1** wordly, pertaining to the world, *cf* **talmhaidh**; **2** materialistic

saoil *vi, pres part* **a' saoilsinn**, think, consider, suppose, believe, **saoilidh mi gu bheil thu ceart** I think/consider that you're right, **saoil(ibh) am bi stoirm ann?** do you think there'll be a storm?, *also* I wonder if there'll be a storm, *cf* **creid** 2, **smaointich** 3

saor *adj* (*opposite of* **daor**) **1** free, at liberty, **tha na prìosanaich saor a-nis** the prisoners are free now, **saor-làithean** *mpl* & **làithean-saora** *mpl* holidays; **2** *in expr* **saor o** free from, untroubled by, without, (*song*) **gheibh thu do roghainn saor o dhearbhadh** you'll get what you want without dispute/argument, *also* **saor is** free/shut/quit of (*cf* **cuidhteas** 2); **3** free (of charge), *esp in expr* **saor 's an-asgaidh** free of charge, absolutely free, *see* **asgaidh** 2; **4** cheap, **biadh saor** cheap food

saor, *gen* & *pl* **saoir** *nm* a joiner, a carpenter, **saor-àirneis** a cabinetmaker

saor *vt, pres part* **a' saoradh**, **1** free, set free, liberate, rescue (*from captivity, oppression etc*), *cf* **sgaoil** *n*; **2** save, redeem, deliver, absolve (*esp from sin*), *cf* **sàbhail** 2

saoradh, *gen* **saoraidh** *nm* **1** (*the act of*) freeing, saving etc (*see senses of* **saor** *v*); **2** liberation, deliverance, absolution

saorsa *nf invar, also* **saorsainn**, *gen* **saorsainne** *nf*, **1** freedom, liberty; **2** salvation, redemption, deliverance (*esp from sin*), *cf* **sàbhaladh** 2

saothair, saothrach, saothraichean *nf* **1** labour, toil, hard work, **chan fhiach dhut do shaothair** it's not worth your while/effort; **2** (*childbirth*) labour; **3** (*industry etc*) labour, **cosgaisean saothrach** labour costs

saothrachadh, *gen* **saothrachaidh** *nm* **1** (*the act of*) labouring, manufacturing etc (*see senses of* **saothraich** *v*); **2** manufacture

saothraich *vti, pres part* **a' saothrachadh**, **1** labour, toil, work very hard, (*as vt*) **shaothraich iad am fearann** they laboured at the land; **2** manufacture

saothraichte *adj* manufactured

sàr *adv, adj & prefix* (*precedes noun etc, & lenites where possible*), (*trad*) very, extremely, true etc (*according to context*), **sàr-Ghàidheal** *m* a Gael through and through, a true Gael, **sàr-obair** *f* a master work, a masterpiece, **sàr-mhath** *adj* excellent

sàrachadh, *gen* **sàrachaidh** *nm* **1** (*the act of*) oppressing, vexing etc (*see senses of* **sàraich** *v*); **2** oppression

sàraich *vt, pres part* **a' sàrachadh**, **1** (*phys*) oppress, do violence to; **2** (*emotionally etc*) vex, harass, trouble, bother, weary, fatigue, distress, **air mo shàrachadh le fiachan** harassed/troubled by debts, *cf* **claoidh** *v* 2, **cuir dragh air** (*see* **dragh** 1), **leamhaich**

sàraichte *adj* boring, tedious, *cf* **fadalach** 2

sàs, *gen* **sàis** *nm* **1** the state of being caught, trapped or captured, *esp in expr* **an sàs** caught, stuck *etc*, **chaidh i an sàs sna drisean** she got caught in the brambles, **tha iad an sàs** they are in captivity, **radan an sàs ann an ribe** a rat caught in a trap, **cuir** *v* **an sàs** capture, arrest, *cf* **làmh** 2; **2** the state of being busy at, engaged or involved or active in, something, **bha mi an sàs ann am poilitigs aig an àm sin** I was involved in politics at that time; **3** *in expr* **bi** *v* **an sàs ann an cuideigin** nag, natter, pester, be on at, someone, **bha i an sàs annam fad na h-ùine airson an taigh a pheantadh** she was on at me all the time to paint the house

sàsachadh, *gen* **sàsachaidh** *nm* **1** (*the act of*) pleasing, satisfying etc (*see senses of* **sàsaich** *v*); **2** satisfaction

sàsaich *vt, pres part* **a' sàsachadh**, **1** please, content, satisfy, *cf* **riaraich** 1; **2** satisfy, fill, sate, satiate

sàsaichte *adj* **1** contented, pleased, satisfied, *cf* **riaraichte, toilichte**; **2** full, sated, satiated, glutted

Sasainn *nf invar* England

Sasannach, *gen & pl* **Sasannaich** *nm* an Englishman, *also as adj* **Sasannach** English

sàsar, sàsair, sàsaran *nm* a saucer, *cf* **flat**

sàth, *gen* **sàith** *nm* one's fill, **fhuair sinn ar sàth dheth** we got our fill/more than enough of it, (*song*) **nam biodh agams' an sin cupan, dh'òlainn dhith mo shàth** if I had had a cup there, I would have drunk my fill of it, *cf* **làn** *n* 1, **leòr** 1

sàth *vti, pres part* **a' sàthadh**, **1** stab; **2** thrust, push, shove, stuff, **sàth a-steach sa phreas e** shove/push/stuff it into the cupboard, *cf* **brùth** 2, **put** 1, **spàrr** *v*

sàthadh, sàthaidh, *pl* **sàthaidhean** *nm* **1** (*the act of*) stabbing, thrusting etc (*see senses of* **sàth** *v*); **2** a stab; **3** a thrust, a push, a shove

seabhag, seabhaig, seabhagan *nmf* a hawk, a falcon, (*prov*) **cha dèanar seabhag den chlamhan** you can't make a hawk out of a buzzard

seac & seachd, *reinforcing adverbial element, eg* **seac àraidh** (*adv*) especially, particularly (*cf* **àraidh** 3, **sònraichte** 3), **tha mi seac searbh sgìth dheth!** I'm sick and tired/heartily sick of it/him

seacaid, seacaide, seacaidean *nf* (*clothing, book etc*) a jacket

seach *prep* **1** instead of, rather than, **gabhaidh sinn iasg seach feòil** we'll take fish rather than/instead of meat; **2** compared to, in comparison to, **tha gròiseidean searbh seach mil** gooseberries are bitter compared to honey, *cf* **coimeas** *n* 3; **3** (*esp of a sequence*) after, **fear seach fear, chaidh iad tron doras** one (man) after another/one by one/each one in turn, they went through the door, *also in expr* **mu seach** *adv* in turn, alternately, turn and turn about, *also* one by one, one after the other, **thug iad greis mu seach air an spaid** they each spent a while in turn/each took a turn for a while at the spade, **thog i na piseagan tè mu seach** she picked up the kittens one after the other; **4** *Note also the usage of* **fear seach fear** (*m*) *and* **tè seach tè** (*f*) *to express* neither (one) of them, *eg* **tha dà mhac agam ach chan eil fear seach fear aca pòsta** I've two sons but neither of them is married; **5** (*trad*) *adv & prep* past, by, **chaidh i seach** she passed/went by (*cf more usu* **seachad**), **chaidh i seach an taigh**

she passed/went past the house (*cf more usu* **seachad air**)

seachad *adv* 1 (*movement*) past, by, **chaidh bus làn seachad** a full bus went past/by, **bhuail e a-steach san dol seachad** he dropped in in passing/(*Sc*) in the by-gaun; 2 (*time*) past, **cuir** *v* **seachad ùine** pass/spend time, (*Sc*) put by time, **tha an oidhche a' dol seachad gu luath** the night is passing quickly; 3 past, over, finished, **tha na làithean ud seachad** yon days are over, (*of task etc*) **is math seachad e!** it's good that it's finished!; *cf more trad* **seach** 4; 4 *in expr* **thoir** *v* **seachad** give, give away, **thoir seachad òraid** give a talk, **thoir seachad airgead** give away money

seachad air *prep* (*esp movement*) past, by, **ruith a' chlann seachad oirnn** the children ran past us, *cf more trad* **seach** 5

seachain(n) *vt, pres part* **a' seachnadh**, avoid, shun, abstain from, keep away from, **seachain meadhan a' bhaile, tha cus trafaig ann** avoid the town centre, there's too much traffic, **seachain boireannaich gun nàire** shun/ keep away from shameless women, (*at election*) **seachain bhòtadh** abstain

seachanta *adj* avoidable, **neo-sheachanta** unavoidable, inevitable

seachd *adj & num* seven

seachd *adv see* **seac**

seachdad, seachdaid, seachdadan *nm* seventy (*in alt numbering system*)

seachdain, seachdaine, seachdainean *nf* a week, **seachdain an-diugh** a week today, **air an t-seachdain sa** (during) this week

seachdamh *adj* seventh

seachdnar *nmf invar* seven (*used of people*)

seachnadh, *gen* **seachnaidh** *nm* (*the act of*) avoiding, shunning etc (*see senses of* **seachain** *v*), (*poem*) **An Seachnadh** (Aonghas MacNeacail) The Avoiding, (*on single track road*) **àite-seachnaidh** *m* passing place

seachran, *gen* **seachrain** *nm* 1 wandering, **rach** *v* **air seachran** go wandering (*see also* 2), *cf* **allaban, fuadan** 1; 2 (*the act of*) getting lost or going astray (*phys or morally*), **rach** *v* **air seachran** go astray, err, *cf* **iomrall** 2 & 3

seach-rathad, seach-rathaid, seach-rathaidean *nm* a bypass

seada, seada, seadaichean *nmf* a shed

seadag, seadaig, seadagan *nf* a grapefruit

seadh *nm see* **seagh**

seadh (*v is plus obs neuter* **eadh**) *adv, expr non-affirmative* yes, *ie not in answer to a question*, **Aonghais! seadh?** Angus! yes? **bha mi sa bhaile an-dè . . . seadh(?) . . . agus chunna**

mi Ailean, Ailean às a' bhùth . . . À, seadh! seadh! I was in town yesterday . . . yes/uh-huh/ so?/and? . . . and I saw Alan, Alan from the shop . . . Ah, yes, of course!, *in expr* **seadh dìreach!** absolutely!, definitely!

seagal, *gen* **seagail** *nm* rye, **aran seagail** rye bread

seagh *occas* **seadh**, *gen* **seagha**, *pl* **seaghan** *nm* sense, meaning, *esp of words & exprs*, **cha chleachdar am facal san t-seagh sin** the word isn't used in that sense, **tha thu ceart, ann an seagh** you're right, in a sense/way, *cf* **brìgh** 1

seàla, seàla, seàlaichean *nf* a shawl

sealbh, *gen* **seilbh** *nm* 1 luck, fortune (*usu good*), **sealbh ort!** good luck!, *cf* **fortan**; 2 providence, heaven, **gun glèidh an Sealbh mi!** Heaven help/protect me! (*see also* **seall** 3), **aig Sealbh tha brath (carson** *etc*)! Heaven knows (why *etc*)!, *cf* **freastal** 3; 3 *same senses as* **seilbh**

sealbhach *adj* 1 lucky, fortunate, **mì-shealbhach** unlucky, unfortunate, *cf* **fortanach**; 2 *same sense as* **seilbheach**

sealbhadair *see* **seilbheadair**

sealbhaich *same senses as* **seilbhich**

sealg, seilge, sealgan *nf* hunting, a hunt, a chase, (*poem*) **Òran Seachran Seilge** (Donnchadh Bàn) Song on a Hunt That Went Wrong

sealg *vti, pres part* **a' sealg**, hunt, hunt for, chase, **sealg na daimh** hunt the stags

sealgair, sealgair, sealgairean *nm* a hunter, a huntsman, **an Sealgair Mòr** (the constellation) Orion

seall *vti, pres part* **a' sealltainn**, 1 see, look (**air** at), behold, **seall orm** look at me, **seall seo!** look at/see this! *cf* **coimhead** 2; 2 (*vt*) show, **seall dhomh na dealbhan a ghabh thu** show me the photos you took, *cf* **nochd** 1; 3 watch over, preserve etc, *usu in excls, to express surprise, indignation etc,* **gu sealladh (Dia/Sealbh) orm!** My Goodness!, For Pete's/ Heaven's sake! *etc*, (*lit* God/Providence/Heaven preserve me!)

sealladh, seallaidh, seallaidhean *nm* 1 sight, eyesight, vision, (*trad*) **is lag mo shealladh** weak is my sight, **an dà shealladh** second sight (*cf* **taibhsearachd**), *cf more usu* **fradharc** 1, **lèirsinn** 1; 2 a look, **thug e sealladh neònach orm** he gave me a strange look/ looked at me strangely, **sealladh-taoibh** a sideways glance/look, *cf* **sùil** 2; 3 sight (*ie what one can see at a given time*), **a-mach às mo shealladh!** out of my sight!, **thig** *v* **an sealladh/san t-sealladh** come in(to) sight, rach *v* à **sealladh/às an t-sealladh** go out of sight, (*song*) **fad mo sheallaidh mun cuairt** as far as I could see all around me, **chaill sinn sealladh air** we lost sight of him, *cf* **fradharc** 2; **4** a sight, a view, a spectacle, a prospect, (*song*) **seallaidhean bu bhrèagha riamh chan fhaca sùil** (Màiri Mhòr) eye never saw more beautiful views/sights/prospects; **5** a point of view, **tha sin math bhon t-sealladh is gum bi i nas fhaisge a-nise** that's good from the point of view that she'll be nearer now

sealladh-aghaidh, seallaidh-aghaidh, seallaidhean-aghaidh *nm* aspect (*ie northerly, southerly etc exposure*)

Sealtainn *nm* Shetland

Sealtainneach, *gen & pl* **Sealtainnich** *nm* a Shetlander, *also as adj* **Sealtainneach** of, from or pertaining to Shetland

seamrag, seamraig, seamragan *nf* **1** shamrock; **2** clover, *cf* **clòbhar**

sean, *before d, s, t, l, n or r* **seann,** *lenites exc for d, s, & t, comp* **(n)as sine,** (*in past tense*) **(n)a bu shine,** *adj* **1** *of people,* old, aged, **tha i a' fàs sean** she's getting old, **dachaigh nan seann daoine** the old folk's/people's home, *cf* **aosta**; **2** *of objects etc,* old, **seann chaisteal** *m* an old castle, *cf* **àrsaidh**; **3** old, former, **sna seann làithean** in the old days, **is e seann phoileasman a th' ann dheth** he's a former policeman; **4** *as noun in expr* **o shean** of old, **bha mo dhaoine san sgìre o shean** my people/folks/family were in the district of old/from way back/since long ago; **5** *as prefix,* **sean(n)-** old-, **sean(n)-fhasanta** old-fashioned; **6** (*family relationships*) grand-, great-, **seann-phàrant** *m* a grandparent, *cf* **sinn-**

seana- *adj prefix* old, (*esp*) **seana-ghille** an old bachelor, **seana-mhaighdeann** an old maid, a spinster

seanailear, seanaileir, seanailearan *nm* a general

seanair, seanar, seanairean *nm* **1** a grandfather; **2** an ancestor, a forebear, **an àm ar seanairean** in our ancestors' time, *cf* **sinnsear**

seanchaidh, seanchaidh, seanchaidhean *nm* **1** a (traditional) storyteller (*cf* **sgeulaiche**), a tradition-bearer; **2** (*trad*) a shenachie, *one of the 'office-bearers' of Gaelic society, keeper of the history, tradition. genealogy etc of the clan or community*

seanchas, seanchais, seanchasan *nm* **1** (*trad*) traditional knowledge and lore, culture and tradition, the knowledge in the keeping of a **seanchaidh** (*see previous entry*), *cf* **beul-aithris, beul-oideachas**; **2** talk, chat, gossip, news, anecdote, **tha iad ri seanchas aig ceann a' bhaile** they're busy talking/gossiping at the end of the township, **seanchasan bhon taigh** news/gossip from home, **tha mi air a dhol seachad air mo sheanchas** I've strayed/wandered from the/my point

seanfhacal, seanfhacail, *pl* **seanfhacail &** **seanfhaclan** *nm* a proverb, a saying, an adage, *cf* **facal 2, ràdh 1**

seang *adj* slim, slender, skinny, lanky, thin, *cf* **caol** *adj* 3, **tana 1**

seangan, *gen* **seangain,** *pl* **seanganan &** **seangain** *nm* an ant

seanmhair, seanmhar, seanmhairean *nf* a grandmother, *cf* **seanair 1**

seann *see* **sean**

seantans, seantans, seantansan *nm* (*gram*) a sentence, *cf more trad* **rosg-rann** (*see* **rosg¹**)

Seapan, Seapanach, Seapanais, *see* **Iapan, Iapanach, Iapanais** respetively

sear *adj & adv, corres to* **an ear** (*see* **ear**), east, eastern, **an taobh sear & an taobh an ear** the east(ern side of the country), **sear air Èden** east of Eden, *cf* **deas 1, ear, iar, siar, tuath¹**

sèar, sèair, sèaraichean *nm* (*stock market*) a share

searbh *adj* **1** (*esp tastes*) bitter, sour, tart, acrid, harsh, pungent, sharp, unpleasant, *cf* **geur 3**; **2** (*situation etc*) disagreeable, hard to swallow, **searbh is gun robh sin leatha** disagreeable though that was to her, (*prov*) **ge milis am fìon, tha e searbh ri dhìol** though the wine is sweet, it is bitter to pay for; **3** sarcastic, sardonic, *cf* **geur 4**; **4** acid

searbhadair, searbhadair, searbhadairean *nm* a towel, *cf* **tubhailte**

searbhag, searbhaig, searbhagan *nf* acid, an acid

searbhagach *adj* acid, acidic

searbhanta, searbhanta, searbhantan *nmf* a servant, a maid-servant, *cf* **seirbheiseach, sgalag 2**

searg *vti, pres part* **a' seargadh,** (*vti*) dry up, fade, shrivel, wither, decay, (*vi*) fade, waste or pine away, (*vt*) blight, **shearg a' ghaoth an duilleach ùr** the wind blighted/withered the new foliage, **a' seargadh le aois** drying up/fading away/shriveling with age, *cf* **crìon** *v*

seargach *adj* **1** apt to dry up, fade etc, (*see senses of* **searg** *v*); **2** (*trees*) deciduous

seargadh, *gen* **seargaidh** *nm* (*the act of*) drying up, blighting etc (*see senses of* **searg** *v*); **2** decay; **3** blight

searmon, searmoin, searmonan nm a sermon

searmonaich vi, pres part **a' searmonachadh**, preach, give or deliver a sermon

searrach, gen & pl **searraich** nm a colt, a foal

searrag, searraig, searragan nf **1** a bottle, cf more usu **botal**; **2** a flask

seas vti, pres part **a' seasamh**, **1** (vi) stand, get on one's feet, **sheas an luchd-èisteachd** the audience stood up, **seas suas/an-àird!** Stand up!; **2** (vt) stand up for, stand by, support, **seas an còir** stand up for their rights, **cò a sheasas thu?** who will support you/take your part?; **3** (vi) endure, last, **aoibhneas a sheasas** joy that will endure, cf **mair**

seasamh, gen **seasaimh** nm **1** a standing position, esp in expr **nam** (etc) **sheasamh** standing, **bha i na seasamh** she was standing (up); **2** one's footing (also **seasamh-chas** m), **ghlèidh e a sheasamh(-chas)** he kept his footing; **3** (phys & mental) attitude, stance, position; **4** status, standing, cf **inbhe 1**; **5** in expr **an seasamh nam bonn** on the spot, on the spur of the moment

seasg adj **1** (of livestock etc) barren, sterile; **2** (of dairy or suckling animals) dry, giving no milk

seasgad, seasgaid, seasgadan nm sixty (in alt numbering system), **anns na Seasgadan** in the Sixties

seasgair adj **1** cosy, comfortable, snug, **cùil sheasgair** a cosy nook/corner, cf **cofhurtail**; **2** (fin) comfortable, comfortably off, cf **airgeadach**

seasmhach adj (phys & morally) **1** firm, stable, steady, reliable, dependable, consistent, **gun àite-còmhnaidh seasmhach** of no fixed abode; **2** constant, enduring, durable, lasting, cf **buan, maireannach**

seatlair, seatlair, seatlairean nm a settler, esp in expr (pej) **seatlair geal** a white settler, applied esp to well-to-do incomers perceived as making little attempt to integrate into or identify with the local community and way of life, cf **srainnsear 2**

seic, seice, seicichean nf a cheque, **seic-leabhar** m a chequebook

Seic, gen **Seice** nf, used with art, **an t-Seic** the Czech Republic

Seiceach, gen & pl **Seicich** nm a Czech, also as adj **Seiceach** Czech

seiche, seiche, seicheannan nf a skin, a pelt, a hide, **seiche bhàrr laoigh a bhàsaich** a hide from a calf that died, **chaidh a fhliuchadh chun na seiche** he got soaked to the skin, cf **bian 2**

sèid vti, pres part **a' sèideadh**, **1** (vi) blow, **shèid a' ghaoth an ear** the east wind blew, **a' sèideadh air mo chorragan** blowing on my fingers; **2** (vi) swell, puff up, cf **at** v, **bòc**; **3** (vt) (trad) **sèid a' phìob** blow/play the pipes, (calque) **sèid do shròn!** blow your nose!, (calque) **sèid suas (ball-coise etc)** blow up, inflate (a football etc)

seilbh (also **sealbh** nm), gen **seilbhe**, pl **seilbhean** nf property, possession, a possession, **gabh** v **seilbh air** take possession of, **cuir an seilbh** invest

seilbheach (also **sealbhach**) adj possessive, (gram) **buadhair seilbheach** a possessive adjective

seilbheadair (also **sealbhadair**), gen **seilbheadair**, pl **seilbheadairean** nm an owner, a proprietor

seilbhich vt, pres part **a' seilbheachadh**, own, possess

seilcheag, seilcheig, seilcheagan nf **1** a snail; **2** a slug

seile nm invar saliva, spittle, slaver, cf **ronn 2**

seileach, seilich, seileachan nm willow, a willow

seillean, gen **seillein**, pl **seilleanan** & **seillein** nm a bee, **seillean-mòr** a bumble-bee, cf **beach 1**

sèimh adj (of person, weather etc) calm, mild, gentle, **maighdeann shèimh** a gentle maiden, **feasgar sèimh** a calm evening, cf **ciùin**; **2** pacific, **an Cuan Sèimh** the Pacific Ocean

sèimhe nf invar (of person, weather etc) calm(ness), mildness, gentleness, cf **ciùineas**

sèimheachadh, gen **sèimheachaidh** nm (gram) lenition

seinn, gen **seinne** nf **1** singing; **2** (trad) playing (an instrument)

seinn vti, pres part **a' seinn**, **1** sing; **2** (trad) play, sound (a musical instrument), **sheinn e a' phìob** he played the pipes, cf more usu **cluich** v

seinneadair, seinneadair, seinneadairean nm a singer

seirbheis, seirbheise, seirbheisean nf **1** serving, service, ie the role or work of a servant, waiter etc; **2** a service, a favour, **an dèan thu seirbheis bheag dhomh?** will you do me a small service/favour? cf **bàidh 2, fàbhar**; **3** a (religious/church) service; **4** (misc contexts, tennis, garage etc) a service

seirbheiseach, gen & pl **seirbheisich** nm a servant, cf **searbhanta, sgalag 2**

seirc, gen **seirce** nf **1** (non-sexual) love, affection, cf more usu **gràdh 1**; **2** (in Bibl sense) charity, cf **carthannachd 1**

seirm *vti, pres part* **a' seirm**, ring, ring out, sound, **seirm na cluig** ring the bells, **sheirm a' phìob** the pipe(s) sounded/rang out

seis(e), **seise**, **seisean** *nm* **1** the like(s) of something or someone, *cf* **leithid**, **samhail**; **2** an equal, a match (*ie a worthy or superior opponent*), **fhuair i a seis an là sin!** she met her match that day!

seisean, **seisein**, **seiseanan** *nm* **1** a kirk session; **2** (*of meetings, college etc*) a session

sèist[1], **sèist**, **sèistean** *nmf* a siege, **fo shèist** under siege, **dèan/cuir** *v* **sèist air caisteal** besiege/lay siege to a castle

sèist[2], **sèist**, **sèistean** *nmf* (*song, poetry*) a refrain, a chorus

sèithear, **sèithir**, **sèithrichean** *nm* a chair, *cf* **cathair 1**, **suidhe 3**

seo & (*trad*) **so** *adj* this, **am fear seo** this man/one, **aig an àm seo** at this time, **an t-seachdain seo chaidh** last week (*lit* this week that went), **an t-seachdain seo tighinn** next week, *cf* **sa 1**, **sin** *adj* **1**, **ud**

seo & (*trad*) **so 1** *pron* this, **cò/dè a tha seo?** who's/what's this? **seo an càr agam** this is my car; **2** *pron* & *adv* here, **seo agad tiodhlac** here's a present for you, **cà'il do bhràthair? seo e** where's your brother? here he is, (*to dog etc*) **a-mach à seo (leat)!** get out of here!; **3** *in exprs* **an seo** & (*sometimes more emph*) **ann an s(h)eo**, *advs*, here, **dè a tha thu a' dèanamh an seo?** what are you doing here? (*song*) **chan eil mo leannan ann an seo** my sweetheart isn't here, **tha Seumas an seo! càite? . . . ann an sheo?** James is here! where? . . . right here?; **4** *corres to* now, *in exprs* **gu ruige seo** & **chun a seo** *advs* up until now, up to now, **cha chuala sinn sgeul air gu ruige seo** we haven't heard anything of him up to now (*lit* up to this), **bho seo a-mach** from now on; *cf* **sin** *pron*, **siud**

seòclaid *see* **teòclaid**

seòd, *gen* & *pl* **seòid** *nm* a hero, (*song*) **eilean beag Leòdhais, dachaigh nan seòid** little isle of Lewis, home of heroes, *cf* **curaidh**, **gaisgeach**, **laoch**

seòl[1], *gen* & *pl* **siùil** *nm* a sail, **seòl-toisich** a foresail

seòl[2], *gen* & *pl* **siùil** *nm* **1** a way, a method, a means, an expedient, **air an t-seòl seo** in this way, **chan eil seòl air** there's no way/ means of doing it, **faigh seòl air rudeigin a dhèanamh** find a way/contrive/manage to do something, **seòl-beatha** a way of life, *cf* **dòigh 1**; **2** a course or direction of travel, *cf more usu* **cùrsa 2**, **iùl 1**

seòl *vti, pres part* **a' seòladh**, **1** (*vi*) sail, **a' seòladh dhachaigh** sailing homewards; **2** (*vt*) sail, navigate, steer, **bha Iain ga seòladh** Iain was sailing/steering her; **3** (*vt*) guide, steer, direct, manage, administer (*persons, organisation etc*), govern (*country etc*); **4** (*vt*) direct, show (someone) the way; *cf* **stiùir** *v*

seòladair, **seòladair**, **seòladairean** *nm* a sailor, a mariner, a seaman, *cf* **maraiche**

seòladh, **seòlaidh**, **seòlaidhean** *nm* **1** (*the act of*) sailing, navigating, directing etc (*see senses of* **seòl** *v*); **2** an address (*ie postal*); **3** *usu in pl* **seòlaidhean** guidelines, instructions, directions

seòl-mara *see* **muir**

seòlta *adj* **1** cunning, artful, crafty, wily, *cf* **carach 1**, **fiar** *adj* **4**; **2** *occas in more favourable sense*, ingenious, resourceful, full of expedients, shrewd, subtle

seòmar, **seòmair**, **seòmraichean** *nm* a room, (*Sc*) an apartment (& *cf Sc* chaumer), **seòmar-cadail** & **seòmar-leapa** a bedroom, **seòmar-ionnlaid** a bathroom, **seòmar-mullaich** an attic, a garret, (*cf* **lobht(a) 2**), *cf* **rùm 2**

seòrsa, *gen* **seòrsa**, *pl* **seòrsaichean** & **seòrsachan** *nm* **1** a sort, a kind, a type, a category, **dè an seòrsa là a th' ann?** what sort of a day is it? **rudan de gach seòrsa** things of every kind, all sorts/kinds of things, **cha do leugh mi leabhar den t-seòrsa** I haven't read such a book/a book of that kind (*cf* **leithid**), *cf* **gnè 1**; **2** (*natural hist*) a genus, a species, *cf* **cineal 2**, **gnè 2**; **3** a (social) class, **chan ionann do sheòrsa 's mo sheòrsa-sa** your class and mine are not alike

seòrsachadh, *gen* **seòrsachaidh** *nm* **1** (*the act of*) classifying etc (*see senses of* **seòrsaich** *v*); **2** a classification

seòrsaich *vt, pres part* **a' seòrsachadh**, classify, sort, arrange (*according to type etc*), *cf* **òrdaich 3**

seud, *gen* **seòid**, *pl* **seudan** & **seòid** *nm* a jewel, a gem, a precious stone, *cf* **àilleag 1**, **leug**

seumarlan, *gen* & *pl* **seumarlain** *nm* **1** (*estates etc*) a factor, a land-agent, *cf* **maor 1**; **2** a chamberlain

Seumasach, *gen* & *pl* **Seumasaich** *nm* (*hist*) a Jacobite, *also as adj* **Seumasach** Jacobite

seun, **seuna**, **seun(t)an** *nm* **1** a spell, a charm, *cf* **geas 1**, **ortha**; **2** (*magic etc*) an amulet (*or other object to protect against spells etc*), a charm

seunta *adj* enchanted, bewitched, spellbound, charmed (*by magic*), *cf* **geas 2**

sgadan, *gen & pl* **sgadain** *nm* herring, a herring, (*trad, hist*) **clann-nighean an sgadain** the herring lasses/girls (*itinerant fish gutters*)

sgàil *nf see* **sgàil(e)**

sgàil *vt, pres part* **a' sgàileadh**, shade, darken, veil, mask, cloak in darkness or shade, eclipse, *cf* **duibhrich**

sgailc, sgailce, sgailcean *nf* 1 a sharp blow, a slap, a smack, (*Sc*) a skelp, **sgailc mun chluais** a crack/slap around the ear, *cf* **sgealp** 1, **sgleog**; 2 a sharp sound, a crack, *cf* **brag**; 3 a swig, a good swallow or drink of liquid, **ghabh e sgailc mhath uisge-bheatha** he took a good swig of whisky, *cf* **balgam** 2, **steallag**; 4 baldness, *cf* **sgall** 2

sgailc *vt, pres part* **a' sgailc(eadh)**, slap, smack

sgàil(e), sgàile, sgàilean *nf* 1 shade, shadow, a shade, a veil, a mask, a film, a covering, **sgàil-sùla** an eyelid, **sgàil-lampa** a lampshade, **fo sgàil na h-oidhche** under the shadow/veil/covering of night, **fo sgàil craoibhe** in/beneath the shade of a tree, *cf* **dubhar**; 2 a ghost, a spectre, a (*ghostly*) shade, *cf* **tannasg** & *more usu* **taibhse**

sgàileadh, *gen* **sgàilidh** *nm* (*the act of*) shading, masking etc (*see senses of* **sgàil** *v*)

sgàilean, sgàilein, sgàileanan *nm* 1 *dimin of* **sgàil(e)**; 2 an umbrella (*also* **sgàilean-uisge**), **sgàilean-grèine** a parasol, a sun-shade; 3 (*IT, TV etc*) a screen

sgàin *vti, pres part* **a' sgàineadh**, burst, crack, split, **bha am baraille air sgàineadh** the barrel was/had split, (*prov*) **cha sgàin màthair leanaibh** a mother with a child to raise doesn't burst (*ie with overeating*), *cf* **sgoilt**

sgàineadh, sgàinidh, sgàinidhean *nm* 1 (*the act of*) bursting, cracking, splitting; 2 a split, a crack, **sgàineadh sa chreig** a split in the rock; *cf* **sgoltadh**

sgàird, *gen* **sgàirde** *nf, with art*, **an sgàird** diarrhoea, *cf* **buinneach**

sgairt[1]**, sgairte, sgairtean** *nf* a diaphragm

sgairt[2]**, sgairte, sgairtean** *nf* 1 a yell, **dèan** *v* **sgairt** yell, *cf* **glaodh** *n*; 2 energy, activity, bustle, enthusiasm, gusto, vigour, *cf more usu* **brìgh** 4, **lùth** 3, **spionnadh**

sgairteil *adj*, 1 (*persons*) brisk, energetic, active, bustling, enthusiastic, vigorous, *cf* **brìoghmhor** 2, **lùthmhor** 3; 2 (*weather*) blowy, blustery, gusty (*ie windy but not stormy*)

sgait, sgaite, sgaitean *nf* a skate (*ie the fish*)

sgal, sgala, sgalan *nm* 1 an onset or outburst of something, *esp* a squall, a blast of wind; 2 a yell, a squeal, a cry (*esp shrill & sudden*)

sgal *vi, pres part* **a' sgaladh**, yell, squeal, cry out (*esp shrilly and suddenly*)

sgàl, *gen & pl* **sgàil** *nm* a tray

sgàla, sgàla, sgàlaichean *nf* (*music*) a scale

sgaladh, *gen* **sgalaidh** *nm* (*the act of*) yelling etc (*see senses of* **sgal** *v*)

sgalag, sgalaig, sgalagan *nf* 1 (*trad*) a farm servant; 2 a skivvy, a menial, a flunkey

sgalanta *adj* (*sound, voice*) shrill

sgall, *gen* **sgaill** *nm* 1 a bald patch (*on head*); 2 baldness, *cf* **sgailc** 4

sgallach *adj* bald(-headed), *cf* **maol** 2

Sgalpach, *gen & pl* **Sgalpaich** *nm* someone from Scalpay (**Sgalpaigh na Hearadh**), *also as adj*, **Sgalpach** of, from or pertaining to Scalpay

sgamhan, sgamhain, sgamhanan *nm* a lung

sgaoil *nm invar* liberty, freedom, *esp in exprs* **fa/ma/mu sgaoil** *adv* free, at liberty, **cuir/leig** *v* **mu sgaoil** set free, liberate, release (*cf* **fuasgail** 1, **saor** *v* 1), *cf more usu* **saorsa** 1

sgaoil *vti, pres part* **a' sgaoileadh**, 1 spread, spread out, scatter, disperse, (*vt*) strew, **sgaoil i a gàirdeanan** she stretched/spread out her arms, **sgaoil na fògarraich air feadh an t-saoghail** the cleared people scattered throughout the world, **sgaoil an sgoil** the school dispersed/(*Sc*) skailed, **seallaidhean brèagha sgaoilte/air an sgaoileadh fòdhpa** beautiful views spread out beneath them, *cf* **sgap**; 2 (*vt*) release, free, loosen, untie, disentangle, *cf more usu* **fuasgail** 1 & 2

sgaoileadh, *gen* **sgaoilidh** *nm* 1 (*the act of*) spreading, scattering, releasing etc (*see senses of* **sgaoil** *v*); 2 dispersal, (*Sc*) skailin, (*Sc*) lowsin

sgaoth, sgaotha, sgaothan *nm* 1 a great mass or multitude; 2 *esp* a swarm of insects

sgaothaich *vi, pres part* **a' sgaothachadh**, 1 flock, mass, assemble in great numbers; 2 *esp* (*of insects etc*) swarm

sgap *vti, pres part* **a' sgapadh**, scatter, *cf less brusque* **sgaoil** *v* 1

sgar *vti, pres part* **a' sgaradh**, separate, break up or apart, split up or apart, sever

sgaradh, sgaraidh, sgaraidhean *nm* 1 (*the act of*) separating etc (*see senses of* **sgar** *v*); 2 separation, a separation, severance etc, (*see senses of* **sgar** *v*); 3 (*esp of marriage*) separation, **sgaradh-pòsaidh** divorce, a divorce, *cf* **dealachadh** 2

sgarbh, *gen & pl* **sgairbh** *nm* a cormorant, **sgarbh an sgumain** a shag (*lit* tufted cormorant)

sgarfa, sgarfa, sgarfaichean *nmf* a scarf, *cf more trad* **stoc**[2]

sgàrlaid *adj* scarlet

sgath *vt, pres part* **a' sgath(adh)**, cut off, lop off, prune

sgàth, sgàtha, sgàthan *nm* **1** (*trad*) shadow, shade, protection; **2** (*trad*) fear; **3** *now usu in expr* **air sgàth** *prep, with gen,* on account of, because of, **air sgàth na h-aimsire** because of the weather, **'s ann air mo sgàth-sa a rinn e e** it was because of me/on my account/for my sake that he did it, **ealain air sgàth ealain** art for art's sake, *cf* **a chionn, airson 3, brìgh 5**

sgàthan, sgàthain, *pl* **sgàthain & sgàthanan** *nm* a mirror, a looking-glass, (*saying*) **is math an sgàthan sùil caraid** a friend's eye makes a good mirror

sgeadachadh, *gen* **sgeadachaidh** *nm* **1** (*the act of*) adorning, clothing etc (*see senses of* **sgeadaich** *v*), *cf* **sgèimheachadh; 2** embellishment, *cf* **maiseachadh 2**

sgeadaich *vt, pres part* **a' sgeadachadh, 1** adorn, decorate, ornament, embellish, beautify, prettify, *cf* **maisich, sgèimhich; 2** dress (up), clothe (*esp attractively*); **3** attend to (*various objects to tidy them or make them function better*), *eg* **sgeadaich an teine/an lampa** make up the fire, trim the lamp

sgealb, sgeilb, sgealban *nf* **1** a chip, a splinter, a fragment *esp one broken or cut from wood or stone*; **2** (*IT*) a chip

sgealb *vti,* **1** split, splinter, shatter, dash/break into pieces, (*esp wood or stone*) chip, *cf* **sgoilt, smùid** *v* **2, spealg** *v*; **2** carve, *cf* **snaigh**

sgealbag, sgealbaig, sgealbagan *nf* an index finger

sgealp, sgealpa, sgealpan *nf* **1** a sharp blow, a slap, a smack, (*Sc*) a skelp, *cf* **sgailc** *n* **1, sgleog; 2** a sharp sound, a crack, *cf* **brag, sgailc** *n* **2**

sgeama, sgeama, sgeamaichean *nm* a scheme

sgeap, sgip, sgeap(aiche)an *nf* a beehive, (*Sc*) a skep

sgeilb, sgeilbe, sgeilbean *nf* a chisel, *cf* **gilb**

sgeileid, sgeileide, sgeileidean *nf* a skillet

sgeilp, sgeilp, sgeilpichean *nf* a shelf

sgèimheach, sgiamhach *adj* beautiful, elegant, graceful, *cf* **bòidheach, eireachdail, maiseach**

sgèimheachadh, *gen* **sgèimheachaidh** *nm* **1** (*the act of*) adorning, ornamenting etc (*see senses of* **sgèimhich** *v*), *cf* **sgeadachadh 1; 2** adornment, ornamentation

sgèimhich, *also* **sgiamhaich,** *vt, pres part* **a' sgèimheachadh,** adorn, ornament, beautify, deck (**le** with), *cf* **maisich 1, sgeadaich 1**

sgeir, sgeire, sgeirean *nf* a skerry, a rock (*in the sea near the shore, usu covered & uncovered by the tide*)

sgeith *vti, pres part* **a' sgeith(eadh)**, vomit, spew, throw *or* bring up, be sick, *cf* **dìobhair, tilg 3**

sgeul, *gen & pl* **sgeòil** *nm* **1** a story, a tale (*often trad in content*), **sgeul air na daoine-sìth** a tale about the fairy folk, (*poem*) **gun bhristeadh cridhe an sgeòil** (Somhairle MacGill-Eain) without the heartbreak of the tale, *cf* **sgeulachd; 2** news, information, tidings, a piece of news, a report, (*song*) **bochd an sgeul a chuala mi** sad is the report/news I have heard, *cf* **fios 3, naidheachd 1; 3** (*fam*) a sign (*of something or someone*), **a bheil sgeul air Ruairidh?** is there any sign of Rory?

sgeulach *adj* **1** like a tale; **2** fond of tales; **3** *esp in adv expr* **gu h-aon-sgeulach** unanimously

sgeulachd, sgeulachd, sgeulachdan *nf* a story (*usu less trad in content than* **sgeul**), **sgeulachdan goirid** short stories, **innis sgeulachd dhuinn!** tell us a story! *cf* **naidheachd 2, sgeul 1, stòiridh**

sgeulaiche, sgeulaiche, sgeulaichean *nm* a storyteller

sgeunach *adj* (*esp of animals*) **1** timid, apt to take fright or bolt or shy; **2** skittish, mettlesome

sgì, sgì(the), sgìthean *nf* a ski

sgiamh, sgiamha, sgiamhan *nm* a squeal, a shriek, a yell, *cf* **sgairt² 1, sgreuch** *n*

sgiamh *vi, pres part* **a' sgiamhadh, a' sgiamhail & a' sgiamhaich,** squeal, shriek, yell, *cf* **sgreuch** *v*

sgian, *gen* **sgine & sgeine,** *dat* **sgithinn,** *pl* **sgeinean & sgineachan** *nf* a knife

sgiath, sgèithe, sgiathan *nf* **1** a wing, (*song*) **an uiseag air a sgiath** (Màiri Mhòr) the lark on the (*lit* its) wing; **2** (*armour etc*) a shield; **3** (*occas*) shelter, protection, *cf more usu* **dìon** *n;* **4** *in expr* **fo sgèith** (*with gen*) under the auspices of

sgiathaich *vi, pres part* **a' sgiathadh,** fly, *cf* **itealaich**

Sgiathanach *same as* **Sgitheanach**

sgil, sgil, sgilean *nm* skill, a skill

sgileil *adj* skilful, skilled, *cf* **ealants 2, teòma**

sgillinn, sgillinne, sgillinnean *nf* **1** a penny, **deich sgillinn** 10p, *also in expr* **gun sgillinn ruadh (no geal)** without a penny/cent/brass farthing, stony broke, penniless, skint; **2** (*trad*) a shilling Scots; **3** (*hist*) *in land valuation* a shilling-land, (*placename*) **Fichead Sgillinn** Twenty Shilling Land

sgioba, sgioba, *pl* **sgioban, sgiobachan, sgiobaidhean** *nmf* **1** a crew (*of boat etc*); **2** a team, **sgioba ball-coise** a football team

sgiobair, sgiobair, sgiobairean *nm* a skipper, a captain (*of boat, team etc*), *cf* **caiptean 1**

sgiobalta *adj* 1 (*of room, space etc*) neat, tidy, tidied up; 2 (*of person, object*) neat, tidy, trim, *cf* **cuimir 2, grinn 3, snasail**; 3 (*esp of persons*) active, quick, handy, *cf* **deas 4, èasgaidh, tapaidh 1**

sgioblachadh, *gen* **sgioblachaidh** *nm* (*the act of*) tidying etc (*see senses of* **sgioblaich** *v*)

sgioblaich *vti, pres part* **a' sgioblachadh**, tidy (up), put right or straight, arrange, **sgioblaich an rùm agad!** tidy your room!

sgiorradh, sgiorraidh, sgiorraidhean *nm* 1 an accident, *cf more usu* **tubaist**; 2 slipping, a slip, stumbling, a stumble, *cf* **tuisleadh 1 & 2**

sgiort, sgiorta, *pl* **sgiortan & sgiortaichean** *nf* a skirt

sgìos *see* **sgìths**

sgìre, sgìre, sgìrean *nf* 1 a district, an area, a locality, **muinntir na sgìre** the people of the district, the local people, (*formerly*) **comhairle na sgìre** the district council, *cf* **ceàrn**; 2 a parish, *cf* **sgìreachd**

sgìreachd, sgìreachd, sgìreachdan *nf* a parish, *cf* **sgìre 2**

sgìth *adj* tired, weary (*phys or emotionally*), *see also* **seac**

sgitheach, *gen & pl* **sgith(e)ich** *nm* whitethorn; hawthorn

sgìtheachadh, *gen* **sgìtheachaidh** *nm* (*the act of*) tiring, wearying (*see senses of* **sgìthich** *v*)

Sgitheanach, *gen & pl* **Sgitheanaich** *nm* a Skyeman, someone from Skye (**an t-Eilean Sgitheanach**), *also as adj*, **Sgitheanach** of, from or pertaining to Skye

sgìtheil *adj* tiring, wearying, wearisome

sgìthich *vti, pres part* **a' sgìtheachadh**, tire, weary, make or become tired or weary

sgìthich *vi, pres part* **a' sgitheadh**, ski

sgìths *nf invar* tiredness, weariness, fatigue, **bha coltas na sgìths oirre** she looked tired/weary

sgiùrs *vt, pres part* **a' sgiùrsadh**, scourge, whip, *cf more usu* **cuip** *v*

sgiùrsair, sgiùrsair, sgiùrsairean *nm* a scourge, a whip, *cf more usu* **cuip** *n*

sglàib *nf invar* (*building*) plaster

sglàibeadair, sglàibeadair, sglàibeadairean *nm* (*building*) a plasterer

sglèat, sglèata, sglèatan *nm* slate, a slate, **mullach sglèata** a slate roof

sglèatair, sglèatair, sglèatairean *nm* (*building*) a slater

sgleog, sgleoig, sgleogan *nf* a slap, a sharp blow, *cf* **sgailc** *n* 1, **sgealp 1**

sgob *vti, pres part* **a' sgobadh**, 1 snatch; 2 sting, bite; 3 peck

sgoch *vt, pres part* **a' sgochadh**, sprain, strain (*ankle etc*), *cf* **siach**

sgoil, sgoile, sgoiltean *nf* 1 a school, **sgoil-àraich** a nursery school, **bun-sgoil** a primary school, **àrd-sgoil** a high/secondary school, **tha i anns an sgoil** she's at school; 2 schooling, education, **fhuair sinn ar sgoil san Òban** we were educated/got our schooling in Oban, *cf* **foghlam**

sgoilear, sgoileir, sgoilearan *nm* 1 a (school) pupil; 2 a scholar

sgoilearach *adj* scholarly, learned, academic

sgoilearachd, sgoilearachd, sgoilearachdan *nf* 1 scholarship, learning, erudition; 2 a scholarship, a bursary

sgoilt & sgolt *vti, pres part* **a' sgoltadh**, split, cleave, crack, slit, *cf* **sgàin**

sgoinneil *adj* (*fam*) great, super, smashing, **duine sgoinneil** a great/super guy, **là sgoinneil** a smashing day, **bha sin dìreach sgoinneil!** that was just great/grand!, *cf* **gasta 2, glan** *adj* 2, **taghta 2**

sgol *vt, pres part* **a' sgoladh**, rinse

sgolt *see* **sgoilt**

sgoltadh, sgoltaidh, sgoltaidhean *nm* 1 (*the act of*) splitting, cleaving etc (*see senses of* **sgoilt** *v*); 2 a split, a cleft, a crack, a slit, a chink; *cf* **sgàineadh**

sgona, sgona, sgonaichean *nmf* a scone, *cf more trad* **bonnach 3**

sgonn, *gen* **sgoinn & sguinn**, *pl* **sgonnan & sguinn** *nm* a block, a lump, a hunk of anything, **sgonn cloiche** a block/lump of stone, **sgonn arain** a thick slice/a hunk of bread, *cf* **ceap 1, cnap 1, ploc 2 & 3**

sgòr, sgòir, sgòraichean *nm* (*games etc*) a score, *cf* **cunntas 5**

sgòrnan, sgòrnain, sgòrnanan *nm* a gullet, a throat, a windpipe, **meall an sgòrnain** *m* the adam's apple

sgoth, sgotha, sgothan *nf* a skiff, a sailing boat, **sgoth-long** a yacht

sgòth, sgòtha, sgòthan *nf* cloud, a cloud, *cf* **neul 1**

sgòthach *adj* cloudy, *cf* **neulach**

sgraing, sgrainge, sgraingean *nf* a frown, an angry or sullen look, a scowl, *cf* **drèin, gruaim 2, mùig**

sgreab, sgreaba, sgreaban *nf* a scab

sgread, sgreada, sgreadan *nm* a scream, a screech, a shriek, *cf* **sgreuch** *n* sgread *vi, pres part* **a' sgreadadh** & **a' sgreadail**, scream, screech, shriek, *cf* **sgreuch** *v*

sgreadhail, sgreadhaile, sgreadhailean *nf* a trowel

sgreamh, *gen* sgreamha & sgreimhe *nm* loathing, disgust, *cf* **gràin** 2

sgreamhail *adj* disgusting, loathsome, nauseating, (*Sc*) scunnersome, *cf* **gràineil** 1 & 2, **sgreataidh**

sgreataidh *adj same senses as* **sgreamhail**

sgreuch, sgreucha, sgreuchan *nm* a scream, a screech, *cf* **sgread** *n*

sgreuch *vi, pres part* **a' sgreuchail**, scream, screech, *cf* **sgread** *v*

sgrìob, sgrìoba, sgrìoban *nf* 1 a scratch, a scrape on surface of something; 2 (*farming*) a furrow, *cf* **clais** 3; 3 a trip, an excursion, a jaunt, (*song*) **bheir mi sgrìob do dh'Uibhist leat** I'll take a trip to Uist with you, *cf* **cuairt** 3, **turas** 1 & 2; 4 (*typog*) a dash

sgrìob *vti, pres part* **a' sgrìobadh**, 1 scratch or scrape the surface of something, **sgrìob e am bòrd ùr** he scratched the new table; 2 scrape or rub the surface of something (*to clean it*), **sgrìob am buntàta** scrape the potatoes; 3 scratch (*with fingernails*), *cf* **sgròb, tachais**; 4 furrow (*esp the ground*)

sgrìobadh, *gen* sgrìobaidh *nm* (*the act or sound of*) scratching, scraping etc (*see senses of* **sgrìob** *v*)

sgrìoban, sgrìobain, sgrìobanan *nm* a hoe, *cf* **todha**

sgrìobh *vti, pres part* **a' sgrìobhadh**, 1 write, **sgrìobh iad thugam** they wrote to me, **bidh e a' sgrìobhadh bàrdachd** he writes poetry

sgrìobhadair, sgrìobhadair, sgrìobhadairean *nm* a writer, *cf* **sgrìobhaiche**

sgrìobhadh, sgrìobhaidh, sgrìobhaidhean *nm* 1 (*the act of*) writing; 2 writing, a piece of writing, **tha am balach beag math air sgrìobhadh** the wee boy's good at writing, **sgrìobhaidhean Aristotle** the writings of Aristotle; 2 (*also* **làmh-sgrìobhaidh**) handwriting, script

sgrìobhaiche, sgrìobhaiche, sgrìobhaichean *nm* a writer, *cf* **sgrìobhadair**

Sgriobtar, Sgriobtair, Sgriobtairean *nm* Scripture

sgrios, sgriosa, sgriosan *nm* destruction, ruin, (*excl*) **mo sgrios!** my ruin is upon me!, woe is me!, *cf* **creach** *n* 2

sgrios *vti, pres part* **a' sgrios** & **a' sgriosadh**, destroy, ruin, wreck, *cf* **creach** *v* 2, **mill** 1

sgriosadh, *gen* sgriosaidh *nm* (*the act of*) destroying etc (*see senses of* **sgrios** *v*)

sgriosail *adj* 1 destructive, apt to ruin or wreck, *cf* **millteach**; 2 pernicious; 3 (*more fam*) terrible, dreadful, awful, **chaill mi m' obair! tha sin sgriosail!** I lost my job! that's awful!

sgriubha, sgriubha, sgriubhaichean *nmf* (*joinery*) a screw

sgriubhaire, sgriubhaire, sgriubhairean *nm* a screwdriver

sgròb *vti, pres part* **a' sgròbadh**, scratch (*with fingernails*), *cf* **sgrìob** *v* 3,**tachais** 1

sgrùd *vt, pres part* **a' sgrùdadh**, 1 scrutinize, examine, look into, investigate, study, analyse, **tha sinn a' sgrùdadh dhòighean ùra air cosgaisean a lùghdachadh** we're looking at/ into new ways of decreasing costs, *cf* **rannsaich** 3; 2 (*accounts*) audit

sgrùdadh, sgrùdaidh, sgrùdaidhean *nm* 1 (*the act of*) scrutinizing, studying etc (*see senses of* **sgrùd** *v*); 2 scrutiny, investigation, an investigation, an examination (*not school etc*), **sgrùdadh air beatha na speacha** a study of/investigation into the life of the wasp; 3 (*of accounts*) an audit

sguab, sguaibe, sguaban *nf* 1 a brush, a broom (*cf less trad, & often smaller,* **bruis**), **sguab-fhliuch** a mop; 2 a sheaf of corn

sguab *vti, pres part* **a' sguabadh**, sweep, brush

sguabadair, sguabadair, sguabadairean *nm* a hoover, a vacuum-cleaner

sgud *vti, pres part* **a' sgudadh**, chop, **a' sgudadh fiodha** chopping wood

sgudal, *gen* sgudail *nm* 1 rubbish, refuse, garbage, waste, **tha làraidh na comhairle a' togail sgudail** the council lorry's collecting/ uplifting rubbish, *cf less usu* **fuidhleach**; 2 (*fam*) rubbish, nonsense, **'s e tòrr sgudail a th' ann!** it's a load of rubbish!

sguir *vi, pres part* **a' sgur**, stop, cease, give up, leave off, desist (**de** from), **sguir sinn aig meadhan-latha** we stopped at noon, **sguir dheth!** stop it!, *cf* **stad** *v* 2

sgur, *gen* sguir *nm* 1 (*the act of*) stopping, ceasing etc (*see senses of* **sguir** *v*); 2 *esp in expr* **gun sgur** *adv* unceasingly, continually, constantly, endlessly, **ag obair/a' bruidhinn gun sgur** working/talking non-stop, **tha iad an sàs annam gun sgur** they're constantly/ always on at me

sgùrr, sgurra, sgurran *nm* a peak, a pinnacle, a steep sharp mountaintop, **Sgùrr Alasdair** Alasdair's Pinnacle

shìos *adv* down (*expr position*), **shìos bhuaithe** down below him, **am baile ud shìos** the township down yonder, *cf* **sìos**, **shuas**, **suas**

shuas *adj* up (*expr position*), **tha uiseag a' seinn shuas an sin** a lark's singing up there, *cf* **shìos**, **sìos**, **suas**

sia *adj & num* six

siab *vti, pres part* **a' siabadh**, **1** wipe, rub (*esp to clean*), **siab am bòrd** wipe the table, *cf* **suath** 1; **2** *vi* (*snow etc*) drift, blow away

siabann, *gen & pl* **siabainn** *nm* soap

siach *vt, pres part* **a' siachadh**, sprain, strain (*ankle etc*), *cf* **sgoch**

sia-deug *adj & num* sixteen

sia-deugach *adj* (*IT etc*) hexadecimal

sian, **sìne**, **siantan** *nf*, **1** a storm, a blast (*of wind, rain etc*), *cf* **doineann**, **gailleann**, **stoirm** 1; **2** *in pl*, the elements, the climate, *esp in expr* **sìde nan seachd sian** appalling weather, the worst weather imaginable, (*of face etc*) **air dath nan sian** weather-beaten

sianar *nmf invar* six (*used of people*)

siar *adj & adv*, *corres to* **an iar** (*see* **iar**), west, western, **na h-Eileanan Siar** the Western Isles, **an Cuan Siar** the Atlantic Ocean, **an taobh siar** *or* **an taobh an iar** the west(ern) side of the country), **siar air a' bhaile** west of the township/village, *cf* **deas** 1, **ear**, **iar**, **sear**, **tuath**[1]

sibh *emph* **sibhse**, *pron pl, also expr formal sing*, you, **ciamar a tha sibh? tha gu math, ciamar a tha sibh fhèin?** how are you? well, how are you yourself/yourselves? **am bi sibhse ann?** will you (*emph*) be there? *Note: There are two systems governing the use of* **sibh** *&* **thu** *in the sing, based on status and familiarity respectively. In some areas one's parent or a close friend who was, eg, a minister or an elderly neighbour, would be addressed as* **sibh** *out of respect for their status. Where the familiarity criterion prevails they might be addressed as* **thu**; **sibh** *is advisable when in any doubt!*; *cf* **thu**

sìde *nf invar* weather, **deagh/droch shìde** good/bad weather, **tuairmse sìde** a weather forecast, *see also* **sian** 2, *cf* **aimsir** 3, **tìde** 2

sil *vi, pres part* **a' sileadh**, (*of liquids*) **1** drip, drop, **uisge a' sileadh tron tughadh** rain/water dripping through the thatch, *cf* **snigh**; **2** flow, (*song*) **mo chùl rid chùl 's na deòir a' sileadh** my back to your back and the tears flowing, *cf* **ruith** *v* 2; **3** rain (*often heavily*) **tha e/i a' sileadh** it's raining/pouring, *cf* **uisge** 2

sileadh, *gen* **silidh** **1** *nm* (*the act of*) dripping, flowing etc (*see senses of* **sil** *v*); **2** rainfall, precipitation

silidh *nm invar* **1** jam, (*Sc*) jeelie; **2** jelly, a jelly

silteach *adj* fluid, dripping, dropping, flowing, apt to drip etc, (*of eye*) tearful, (*song*) **dh'fhàg thu silteach mo shùil** you caused my eye to shed tears (*cf* **deurach**)

similear, **simileir**, **similearan** *nm* a chimney, *cf* **luidhear**

sìmpleachadh, *gen* **sìmpleachaidh**, *nm* **1** (*the act of*) simplifying (*see* **sìmplich** *v*); **2** simplification

sìmplich *vt, pres part* **a' sìmpleachadh**, simplify

sìmplidh *adj* **1** simple, easy, uncomplicated, elementary, *cf* **furasta**, **soirbh**; **2** simple, plain, unpretentious, *cf* **aon-fhillte**; **3** simple, simple-minded, *cf* **baoth**

sin *adj* **1** that, those, **na coin sin** those dogs, **aig an àm sin** at that time, **thoir dhomh am fear sin** give me that one; **2** *as emphasising element* **chan eil mi cho math sin!** I'm not that (*emph*) good, **b' iad sin an fheadhainn a chunnaic mi** those ones/they (*emph*) were the ones that I saw, **chùm e grèim air an laogh ach thuit e sin air a mhuin** he kept hold of the calf but it fell on top of him; *cf* **seo** *adj*, **ud**

sin **1** *pron* that, **cò/dè a tha sin?** who's/what's that? **sin an càr agam** that is my car, **sin e** that's it, **'s e sin** . . . that is . . . , i.e . . . , namely . . . , **is e sin ri ràdh** . . . that is to say . . . , **'s e sin a' chùis!** that's the point/problem!; **2** *pron & adv* there, **sin agad leabhar** there's a book (for you), **cà'il do bhràthair? sin e** where's your brother? there he is, (*to dog etc*) **a-mach à sin (leat)!** get out of there!; **3** *in exprs* **an sin** & (*sometimes more emph*) **ann an s(h)in**, *adv*, there, **rugadh mi an sin** I was born there, **dè a tha thu a' dèanamh an sin?** what are you doing there? **tha an cat ann an sin** the cat's there; **4** *in expr* **an sin** *adv* then, thereupon, **an sin dh'fhàg e an dùthaich** then/at that he left the country; **5** *in expr* **sin thu (fhèin)!** well done!; **6** *as emphasising element* **a bheil thu sgìth? tha mi sin!** are you tired? I am that!, I sure am!; *cf* **seo**, **siud** *prons*

sìn *vti, pres part* **a' sìneadh**, **1** stretch, make or become longer by stretching, **tha an ròpa air a shìneadh** the rope has been stretched; **2** stretch, stretch out, extend (*one's body*), **shìn i a-mach a cas chlì** she stretched out her left foot/leg; **3** pass, reach, hand, **shìn i thugam am pàipear-naidheachd** she passed/handed me the newspaper

sinc *nm invar* zinc

sinc(e), **since**, **sincean** *nmf* a sink

sine, **sine**, **sinean** *nf* a nipple, a teat, **a' deothal air sine** sucking at/on a teat

sineach, *gen & pl* **sinich** *nm* a mammal; *also as adj*, **sineach** mammalian

sìneadh, *gen* **sìnidh** *nm* 1 (*the act of*) stretching, stretching out, extending etc (*see senses of* **sìn** *v*); 2 an outstretched position or posture, *esp in expr* **nam** (etc) **shìneadh** stretched out, **bha i na sìneadh air a' bheinge** she was stretched out on the bench, *cf* **laighe 2**

singilte *adj* 1 single, **leabaidh shingilte** a single bed, **rathad singilte** a single-track road; 2 single, unmarried, (*song*) **nuair a bha mi singilte, 's a bha mo phòca gliongadaich** when I was single and my pocket did jingle; 3 (*gram*) singular, **ainmear singilte** a singular noun

sinn *emph* **sinne**, *pron*, we, **is truagh nach robh sinn còmhla** it's a shame we weren't together, **sinn fhìn** ourselves

sinn- *prefix used in family relationships*, great-, **sinn-seanair** *m* a great-grandfather, **sinn-sinn-seanmhair** *f* a great-great-grandmother, *cf* **sean 6**

sinnsear, **sinnsir**, **sinnsirean** *nm* an ancestor, a forefather, a forebear, **ri linn ar sinnsirean** in the time of our ancestors, *cf* **seanair 2**

sìnteag, **sìnteig**, **sìnteagan** *nf* 1 a hop; 2 a (long) stride; 3 a stepping-stone

siobhag, **siobhaig**, **siobhagan** *nf* a wick, *cf* **buaic**

sìobhalta *adj* 1 civil, polite, courteous, (*song*) **labhair mi rithe gu sìobhalta blàth** I addressed her politely and warmly, *cf* **cùirteil 1**, **modhail**; 2 (*legal etc*) civil, pertaining to the citizens of a state, **lagh sìobhalta** civil law

sìobhaltair, **sìobhaltair**, **sìobhaltairean** *nm* a civilian

sìochail *see* **sìtheil**

sìoda, **sìoda**, **sìodachan** *nm* silk, (*song*) **sìoda reamhar ruadh na Spàinne** the full/sleek red silk of Spain

sìol, *gen* **sìl** *nm coll* 1 seed, **sìol eòrna** barley seed, **sìol-cuir** seed-corn, *cf less usu* **fras** *n* 2; 2 (*also* **sìol-ginidh**) semen; 3 a race, a clan, progeny of the same real or supposed ancestor, **sìol Diarmaid** the race/descendants/children of Dermid, the Campbells, *cf* **clann 2**, **gineal**, **sliochd**; 4 (*livestock etc*) a breed

sìolachadh, *gen* **sìolachaidh** *nm* 1 (*the act of*) engendering, seeding etc (*see senses of* **sìolaich** *v*); 2 (*med etc*) insemination, **sìolachadh fuadain** artificial insemination

sìol(t)achan, *gen & pl* **sìol(t)achain** *nm* (*for coffee etc*) a strainer, a filter

sìoladh, *gen* **sìolaidh** *nm* (*the act of*) subsiding, filtering etc (*see senses of* **sìolaidh** *v*)

sìolaich *vti*, *pres part* **a' sìolachadh**, 1 (*trad*) engender, beget, propagate; 2 (*vi*) seed; 3 (*vt*) inseminate

sìolaidh *vti*, *pres part* **a' sìoladh**, 1 subside, lower, settle, sink, cause to subside or lower, **shìolaidh na h-uisgeachan** the waters subsided/settled, *cf* **tràigh** *v* 2; 2 filter, strain (*liquids*), **tha an cofaidh a' sìoladh** the coffee's filtering

siolp *vi*, *pres part* **a' siolpadh**, (*of surreptitious movement*) slip, steal, **siolp a-steach/air falbh** slip in(side)/away, *cf* **èalaidh 2**

sìoman, **sìomain**, **sìomanan** *nm* straw rope, a straw rope

sìon a thing, something, anything, (*in neg exprs*) nothing, **a h-uile sìon** everything, **cha robh sìon againn** we had nothing, *cf* **càil** *nm* 1 & 2, **dad 1**, **nì** *n* 1, **rud 1**

Sìona *nf* China

Sìonach, *gen & pl* **Sìonaich** someone from China, *also as adj* **Sìonach** Chinese

sionnach, *gen & pl* **sionnaich** *nm* a fox, *cf* **balgair 1**, **madadh 2**

sionnsar, **sionnsair**, **sionnsaran** a bagpipe chanter, *cf* **feadan 1**

sìor- *a prefix corres to Eng* ever-, eternally, constantly, (*song*) **a' sìor-ionndrainn tìr a bhruadair** ever yearning for the land he dreams of, **sìor-mhaireannach** *adj* eternal, everlasting, immortal, **sìor-uaine** *adj* evergreen, *cf* **bith-**

siorrachd, **siorrachd**, **siorrachdan** *nf also* **siorramachd** *nf invar* 1 (*hist*) a sheriffdom; 2 (*now*) a county, a shire, **Siorrachd Rois** Ross-shire

siorraidh, **siorraidh**, **siorraidhean** *nm &* **siorram**, **siorraim**, **siorraman** *nm* a sheriff, **Cùirt an t-Siorraim** *f* the Sheriff Court

sìorraidh *adj* 1 everlasting, eternal, *cf* **bith-bhuan** (*see* **bith-**); 2 *usu as adv* ever, for ever, (*with neg verb*) never, (*song*) **cha till iad gu sìorraidh** they will never return, **gu sìorraidh bràth** for ever and ever, *cf* **a-chaoidh**, **a-riamh**, **bràth 2 & 3**; 3 *in excls*, *eg* **a shìorraidh!** Heavens!, Goodness!, for Pete's sake!, *cf* **sealbh 2**

sìorraidheachd *nf invar* eternity

siorram *see* **siorraidh**

siorramachd *see* **siorrachd**

sìos adv down (expr movement, NB from point of view of the person moving, cf **a-nìos, a-nuas**), **thuit e sìos an staidhre** he fell down the stair (cf **tha e shìos an staidhre** he's downstairs/ down the stair), **chaidh iad sìos** they went down, also (trad, of army) they charged, cf **a-bhàn, a-nìos, a-nuas, shìos, shuas, suas**

siosar, siosair, siosaran nmf scissors, a pair of scissors

siosarnaich nf invar **1** (the act or sound of) hissing, a hiss, also used as pres part **tha e a' siosarnaich** he is hissing; **2** whispering, a whisper, cf **cagar 2**; **3** a rustling noise

sìothchail see **sìtheil**

sir vt, pres part **a' sireadh**, seek, search for, look for, **tha e a' sireadh mnà/obrach** he's looking for a wife/work, **tha a' chompanaidh a' sireadh luchd-obrach** the company is looking for/requires workers, cf **lorg** v **1**

sireadh, gen **siridh** nm (the act of) seeking etc (see senses of **sir** v)

siris(t), siris(t), siris(t)ean nf a cherry

siteag, siteig, siteagan nf & **sitig, sìtig, sitigean** nf a dunghill, a manure heap, a midden, also in expr **thoir an t-siteag ort!** get out(side)!, cf **dùnan 2, òtrach**

sìth adj fairy, of or pertaining to fairies, **daoine-sìth** fairy folk, **a' Bhratach Shìth** the Fairy Flag (at Dunvegan)

sìth, gen **sìthe** nf **1** peace (ie opposite of war), **cogadh no sìth** war or peace; **2** peace, tranquillity, quiet, cf **fois 1**

sìtheachadh, gen **sìtheachaidh** nm **1** (the act of) pacifying etc (see senses of **sìthich** v); **2** pacification

sìthean, gen & pl **sìthein** nm a small rounded hill (often one thought to be a fairy hill)

sitheann, gen **sìthne** & **sithinn** nf **1** venison; **2** game in general

sìtheil & **sìo(th)chail** adj **1** peaceful, tranquil; **2** peaceable

sìthich vti, pres part **a' sìtheachadh**, **1** (vt) pacify; **2** (vti) make or become peaceful or tranquil; cf **ciùinich, socraich 1**

sìthiche, sìthiche, sìthichean nm a fairy, cf **daoine-sìth** (see **sìth** adj)

sitig see **siteag**

sitir, gen **sitire** nf braying, neighing, whinnying

siubhail vti, pres part **a' siubhal**, **1** (vi) travel, **'s toigh leam a bhith a' siubhal** I like travelling; **2** (vt) travel, cross, **a' siubhal na mòintich** travelling/crossing the moor; **3** (vi) die, pass away, cf more usu **bàsaich, caochail 2**; **4** (vt) seek, look for, cf more usu **lorg** v **1, sir**

siubhal, siubhail, siùbhlaichean nm **1** travel, travelling, **luchd-siubhail** m travellers, **cosgaisean siubhail** fpl travel(ling) costs/ expenses; **2** time, esp in expr **fad an t-siubhail** all the time, cf more usu **tìde 1, ùine 1**

siùbhlach adj **1** speedy, swift, fleet, moving easily, cf **clis, luath** adj **1**; **2** (speech) fluent, fluid; **3** transient, fleeting, cf **diombuan**

siùcar, siùcair, siùcairean nm **1** sugar; **2** in pl sweets, sweeties, cf **suiteas**

siud & **sud** pron **1** that (more distant or remote than **sin**), (Sc) yon, **dè a bha siud?** what was that/yon? (song) **siud mar chuir mi 'n geamhradh tharam** that's how I spent the winter; **2** in expr **an siud** & (sometimes more emph) **ann an s(h)iud** adv there (more distant or remote than **an sin**), (Sc) yonder, **thall an siud** over yonder, **an siud 's an seo** here and there, also hither and thither, . . . **is siud is seo** . . . and so on and so on, . . . blah, blah, blah, (can be more pej than **sin**) **tha am biadh sgriosail ann an siud!** the food's terrible in yon place!; cf **seo, sin, ud**

siuga, siuga, siugannan nmf a jug

siùrsach, siùrsaich, siùrsaichean nf a prostitute, cf **strìopach**

siùrsachd nf invar prostitution

siuthad, pl **siuthadaibh** imperatives of def verb, excl giving encouragement, on you go! go to it! get on with it! (song) **siuthadaibh, 'illean, gabhaibh am port** on you go, lads, strike up the tune

slabhraidh, slabhraidh, slabhraidhean nf a chain, cf **cuibhreach**

slaic vt, pres part **a' slaiceadh**, (esp with heavy object) thrash, drub, beat, thump, bruise, maul

slaiceadh, slaicidh, slaicidhean nm, also **slacadaich** nf invar, **1** (the act of) thrashing etc (see senses of **slac** v); **2** (**slaiceadh** only) a thrashing

slaightear, slaighteir, slaightearan nm a knave, a rascal, a rogue, a villain, cf **balgair 2**

slàinte nf invar **1** (public) health, **Seirbheis na Slàinte** the Health Service, **Ministear na Slàinte** the Health Minister, **foghlam slàinte** health education, **slàinte inntinn** mental health; **2** health (of individual), **ma cheadaicheas mo shlàinte dhomh** if my health allows/permits me; **3** freq in toasts, wishes etc, **deoch-slàinte** f a toast, **slàinte!** Good health!, cheers!, **slàinte mhath/mhòr!** the best of health!, **air do dheagh shlàinte!** (to) your very good health!

slaman, gen **slamain** nm (dairying) curds, crowdie, cf **gruth**

slàn *adj* **1** healthy, well, in good health, **pàiste slàn** a healthy child, *cf* **fallain 1**; **2** healthy (*ie healthgiving*), **biadh slàn** healthy food, *cf* **fallain 2**; **3** *in expr* **slàn leat!** goodbye!, farewell!; **4** complete, whole, entire, in one piece, intact, **facal slàn** a whole word, **àireamh shlàn** a whole number, **tursa Cruithneach slàn** a complete/intact Pictish standing stone, *cf* **iomlan** *adj* **2**

slànachadh, *gen* **slànachaidh** *nm* (*the act of*) healing, curing (*see senses of* **slànaich** *v*)

slànaich *vti, pres part* **a' slànachadh**, heal, cure, (*of ill person*) make or get better, *cf* **leighis**

slànaighear, *gen & pl* **slànaigheir** *nm* a saviour (*esp relig*), *with art*, **an Slànaighear** the Saviour

slaod, **slaoid**, **slaodan** *nm* a sledge, **slaod-uisge** a raft

slaod *vti, pres part* **a' slaodadh**, *usu of heavy objects* drag, haul, pull, **shlaod e a' chaora a-mach às a' bhoglaich** he dragged/hauled the ewe out of the bog, *cf* **tarraing** *v* **1**

slaodach *adj* **1** slow (*in a trailing, dragging way*), **chaidh an tìde seachad cho slaodach** the time dragged so, *cf* **mall 1**; **2** boring, tedious, **obair shlaodach** a tedious/long-drawn-out job, *cf* **fadalach 2**, **màirnealach 2**, **ràsanach**; **3** (*person*) slow, dilatory

slaodadh, *gen* **slaodaidh** *nm* (*the act of*) dragging etc (*see senses of* **slaod** *v*)

slaodair, **slaodair**, **slaodairean** *nm* (*transport*) a trailer

slapag, **slapaig**, **slapagan** *nf* a slipper

slat, **slait**, **slatan** *nf* **1** (*measure*) a yard; **2** a twig; **3** a rod, a switch, a wand, **slat-iasgaich** a fishing rod, **slat-thomhais** a rule, a measure, a yardstick (*also, abstr,* a criterion), **slat-rìoghail** a sceptre; **4** (*fam, vulg*) a penis, a prick, a cock, *cf* **bod**

sleagh, **sleagha**, **sleaghan** *nf* a spear, a lance, a javelin, *cf* **gath 2**

sleamhainn *adj* slippy, slippery, **cabhsair sleamhainn** a slippery pavement

sleamhnachadh, *gen* **sleamhnachaidh** *nm* (*the act of*) sliding, slipping (*see* **sleamhnaich** *v*)

sleamhnag, **sleamhnaig**, **sleamhnagan** *nf* **1** (*also* **sleamhnan**, **sleamhnain**, **sleamhnanan** *nm*) a slide (*made on ice*); **2** (*in playpark etc*) a (*children's*) slide, (*Sc*) a chute

sleamhnaich *vi, pres part* **a' sleamhnachadh**, slide, slip (*on ice etc*)

sleuchd *vi, pres part* **a' sleuchdadh**, **1** kneel, kneel down, *cf* **lùb** *v* **1**; **2** bow down, prostrate oneself

sleuchdadh, **sleuchdaidh**, **sleuchdaidhean** *nm* **1** (*the act of*) kneeling, bowing down etc (*see senses of* **sleuchd** *v*); **2** prostration; a bow

sliabh, **slèibh**, **slèibhtean** *nm* **1** a moor, an expanse of moorland, (*Sc*) a muir, (*placename*) **Sliabh an t-Siorraim** Sheriffmuir, *cf* **aonach**, **mòinteach**, **monadh 1**; **2** (*esp in upland placenames*) a hill or mountain, *cf* **beinn 2**, **cnoc**

sliasaid, **sliasaide**, **sliasaidean** *nf* a thigh, *cf less usu* **leis**

slige, **slige**, **slige(ach)an** *nf* **1** a shell (*of egg, nut, shellfish*), *cf* **cochall 1**, **plaosg**; **2** (*artillery*) a shell

slighe, **slighe**, **slighean** *nf* (*with rather abstract connotation*) a path, a road, a track, a way, a route, **gabh an t-slighe sin** take that road/route, **thachair sinn riutha air an t-slighe** we met them on the way/en route, (*at road junction etc*) **gèill** *v* **slighe** give way, **còir-slighe** *f* right of way, **fàsach** *m* **gun slighe** a trackless wilderness, **slighe na fìreantachd** the path of righteousness, *cf* **rathad 2**

slinnean, **slinnein**, **slinneanan** *nm* a shoulder, **cnàimh-slinnein** *m* a shoulder-blade, *cf more usu* **gualann 1**

slìob *vt, pres part* **a' slìobadh**, *also* **slìog** *vt, pres part* **a' slìogadh**, stroke (*dog etc*)

sliochd, **sliochda**, **sliochdan** *nm coll* descendants, offspring, progeny, lineage (*of real or supposed ancestor*), *cf* **clann 2**, **gineal**, **sìol 3**

slìog *see* **slìob**

slios, **sliosa**, **sliosan** *nm* (*of object, living thing etc*) a side, a flank, *cf more usu* **cliathaich**, **taobh 1**

slis, **slise**, **slisean** *nf*, & *dimin* **sliseag**, **sliseig**, **sliseagan** *nf*, **1** a slice cut from something, (**sliseag** *only*) a (bacon) rasher; **2** (*kitchen tool*) **sliseag-èisg** a fish-slice

slisnich *vt, pres part* **a' slisneadh**, slice

sloc, *gen* **sluic**, *pl* **slocan** *nm* **1** (*topog*) a hollow, a low-lying area surrounded by higher ground, *freq in placenames, cf* **lag** *n*; **2** a pit, **sloc-buntàta** a potato pit

sloinn *vi, pres part* **a' sloinneadh**, trace or research one's family tree

sloinneadh, **sloinnidh**, **sloinnidhean** *nm* **1** (*the act of*) tracing one's family tree (*see* **sloinn** *v*); **2** a surname, a second name, a family name, **dè an sloinneadh a th' agad/a th' ort?** what's your second name?; **3** a patronymic

sluagh, *gen* **sluaigh**, *pl* **slòigh**, *gen pl* **slògh** *nm* **1** (*trad*) an army, a host; **2** people, population, populace (*of a country, locality etc*), **aimhreit**

am measg an t-sluaigh unrest among the people/population, **an sluagh dom buineadh e** the people he belonged to, *cf* **muinntir 2, poball; 3** a crowd, **bha sluagh mòr ann** there was a big crowd (there), **mòr-shluagh** a multitude, a huge crowd

sluagh-ghairm, sluagh-ghairme, sluagh-ghairmean *nf* **1** (*trad, clan hist*) a war-cry, a gathering cry, **'s e 'Cruachan' sluagh-ghairm nan Caimbeulach** 'Cruachan' is the war-cry of the Campells; **2** (*now, pol, advertising etc*) a slogan

sluaghmhor *adj* populous, well populated

sluasaid, sluasaide, sluasaidean *nf* a shovel

slug *see* **sluig**

slugadh, slugaidh, slugaidhean *nm* **1** (*the act of*) swallowing, gulping etc (*see senses of* **sluig** *v*); **2** a swallow, a gulp

sluig & **slug** *vti, pres part* **a' slugadh**, swallow, gulp (down), devour

smachd *nm invar* authority, control, command, discipline, rule, subjection, **fo smachd nan Ròmanach** under the authority/control/rule of the Romans, **cùm** *v* **smachd air sgoilearan** keep control of/maintain discipline over pupils, **sluagh** *m* **fo smachd** a subject people, *cf* **cumhachd 1, reachd 1, ùghdarras 1**

smachdaich *vt, pres part* **a' smachdachadh, 1** discipline, punish, keep in order; **2** impose (one's) authority or power upon (*a people, country etc*)

smachdail *adj* authoritative, commanding

smà(i)l *vt, pres part* **a' smàladh**, (*esp fire*) put out, extinguish, snuff (out), quench, **smàil às an teine** put the fire out, **smàil na coinnlean** snuff the candles, *cf* **mùch 1, tùch 2**

smal, smail, smalan *nm* a stain, a spot (*on clothing etc*), *cf* **sal 3, spot 1**

smàladair, smàladair, smàladairean *nm* **1** a firefighter; **2** (*formerly*) candle-snuffers

smàladh, gen smàlaidh *nm* (*the act of*) extinguishing etc (*see senses of* **smà(i)l** *v*), **inneal-smàlaidh** *m* a fire-extinguisher, **einnsean-smàlaidh** *m* a fire engine, **luchd-smàlaidh** *m coll* firefighters, firemen

smalan, gen smalain *nm* gloom, melancholy, **fo smalan** (*also* **smalanach** *adj*) gloomy, melancholy, *cf* **bròn 1, gruaim 1**

smaoin, smaoine, smaointean *nf* & **smuain, smuaine, smuaintean** *nf* a thought, a notion, a reflection, an idea, **smaointean dubhach** melancholy thoughts, **cha do chòrd an dàn rium ach chòrd an smuain** I didn't enjoy the poem but I liked the idea/theme

smaoin(t)eachadh, gen smaoin(t)eachaidh *nm* (*the act of*) thinking, supposing, considering etc (*see senses of* **smaoin(t)ich** *v*)

smaoin(t)ich *vi, pres part* **a' smaointinn** & **a' smaoin(t)eachadh**, *also* **smuain(t)ich** *vi, pres part* **a' smuain(t)eachadh, 1** think, reflect, **is tric a bhios mi a' smaoineachadh mu dheidhinn** I often think about it/him; **2** think, imagine, suppose, **bidh an t-acras ort, tha mi a' smaoineachadh** you'll be hungry, I imagine/I'm thinking, *cf* **saoil; 3** think, consider, believe, be of the opinion, **tha mi a' smaointeachadh gun robh thu ceàrr** I think you were wrong (*some speakers would say that* **smaoin(t)ich** *should not be used in this sense*), *cf* **saoil**

smàrag, smàraig, smàragan *nf* an emerald

smèid *vi, pres part* **a' smèideadh, 1** beckon, **smèid air cuideigin** beckon to someone; **2** wave, **smèid ri cuideigin** wave to someone, *cf* **crath 1**

smèideadh, gen smèididh *nm* (*the act of*) beckoning, waving (*see* **smèid** *v*)

smeòrach, smeòraich, smeòraichean *nf* a thrush, (*prov*) **cha dèan aon smeòrach samhradh** one thrush doesn't make it summer

smeur, smeura, smeuran *nf* a bramble, a blackberry (*ie the berry, cf* **dris**), (*poetry collection*) **Smeur an Dòchais** (Ruaraidh MacThòmais) Bramble of Hope

smeur *v see* **smiùr**

smeuradh, gen smeuraidh *nm* (*the act of*) smearing etc (*see senses of* **smiùr/smeur** *v*)

smid, smide, smidean *nf* a word, a syllable, *esp in expr* (*fam*) **cha tubhairt e smid** he didn't say a word/utter a syllable, *cf* **bìd 2**

smig, smig, smigean *nm* & *more usu* **smiogaid, smiogaid, smiogaidean** *nm* a chin

smiogaid *see* **smig**

smior, gen smior & **smir** *nm* **1** marrow, (*prov*) **briseadh a' chnàimh agamsa, an smior aig càch** I get to break the bone, the others get the marrow; **2** the best part of something, the best example of something, **smior an t-sìl** the best/pick of the seed, **dhèanadh e smior a' mhaighstir-sgoile** he'd make a great schoolmaster, *cf* **brod** *n* **2**, & *opposite* **diù; 3** (*esp inner or moral*) courage, spirit, strength, pluck, 'guts', **duine gun smior** a spineless/'wet' individual, *cf* **misneach; 4** manliness, vigour, *cf* **duinealas 1**

smiorach *adj* pithy, *cf* **brìoghmhor 1**

smiorail *adj* **1** (*esp in character*) strong, spirited, plucky, *cf* **misneachail; 2** manly, vigorous, *cf* **duineil 1**

smiùr *vt, pres part* **a' smiùradh**, *&* **smeur** *vt, pres part* **a' smeuradh**, smear, daub, grease

smoc *vti, pres part* **a' smocadh**, smoke (*tobacco etc*), **a bheil thu a' smocadh?** do you smoke?

smocadh, *gen* **smocaidh** *nm* smoking, the act of smoking, (*notice*) **chan fhaodar smocadh** no smoking, smoking not allowed

smuain, smuain(t)ich *see* **smaoin, smaoin(t)ich**

smuais *vt, pres part* **a' smuaiseadh**, smash, splinter, break into pieces, *cf* **smùid** *v* 2, **spealg** *v*

smùch *vi, pres part* **a' smùchadh**, snivel

smugaid, smugaide, smugaidean *nf* spit, spittle, *esp in expr* **tilg** *v* **smugaid** spit

smùid, smùide, smùidean *nf* 1 steam, vapour, (*song*) **fàgaidh sinn Malaig air bàta na smùide** we'll leave Mallaig on the steamer/ steamboat; 2 smoke, *esp in expr* **cuir** *v* **smùid** smoke, **tha an teine a' cur smùide** the fire's smoking; 3 fumes, *cf* **deatach**; 4 (*fam*) a state of drunkenness, **ghabh e smùid mhath a-raoir** he got well and truly drunk last night, **tha smùid orra** they're drunk/steaming/ smashed, *cf* **daorach** 1, **misg**

smùid *vti, pres part* **a' smùideadh**, 1 (*of chimney etc*) smoke; 2 smash into pieces, *cf* **smuais, spealg** *v*

smùr, *gen* **smùir** *nm* dust, dross, **smùr mòna** peat dross, *cf* **sal** 2

sna *see* **anns an**

snàgadh, *gen* **snàgaidh** *nm*, *&* **snàgail**, *gen* **snàgaile** *nf*, (*the act of*) stealing, creeping etc (*see senses of* **snàig** *v*)

snagan-daraich, snagain-daraich, snaganan-daraich *nm* a woodpecker

snaidhm, snaidhm, snaidhmean(nan) *nm* a knot (*in rope etc*), *fig* (*song*) **'s mi ri cromadh leis a' ghleann, thàinig snaidhm air mo chrìdh'** as I came down the glen my heart knotted/a pang came upon my heart

snàig *vi, pres part* **a' snàgail** *&* **a' snàgadh**, 1 crawl, **shnàig mi a' dh'ionnsaigh an taighe** I crawled towards the house, *cf* **crùb** 4; 2 creep, steal (*ie walk stealthily*), **shnàig sinn sìos an staidhre** we crept/stole down the stair, *cf* **èalaidh** 1

snaigh *vt, pres part* **a' snaigheadh**, hew, chip, carve (*wood, stone etc*)

snàith *n see* **snàth**

snàmh, *gen* **snàimh** *nm* 1 (*the act or activity of*) swimming *or* floating, **math air snàmh** good at swimming, **an dèan thu snàmh?** can/ do you swim?; 2 *in expr* **air snàmh** deluged, inundated, flooded, **cuir** *v* **an seòmar air** snàmh flood the room with water, **bha an taigh air snàmh** the house was swimming in water/awash

snàmh *vi, pres part* **a' snàmh**, swim, float

snasail *&* **snasmhor** *adj* neat, trim, **eathar beag snasmhor** a trim wee boat, *cf* **cuimir** 2, **sgiobalta** 2

snàth *&* **snàith**, *gen* **snàith** *&* **snàtha**, *pl* **snàithean** *nm coll* (*needlework etc*) thread, *cf* **snàthainn**

snàthad, snàthaid, snàthadan *nf* a (*sewing*) needle, **crò snàthaid** the eye of a needle

snàthainn, *gen* **snàithne** *&* **snàithainne**, *pl* **snàithnean** *&* **snàithainnean** *nm* (*needlework etc*) a (single) thread, *cf coll* **snàth**

sneachd(a), *gen* **sneachda** *nm* snow, **tha e a' cur an t-sneachda** it's snowing, **bodach-sneachda** a snowman

snèap, snèip, snèapan *nf* a turnip, a swede, (*Sc*) a neep

snigh *vi, pres part* **a' snighe**, (*of liquids*) drip, seep, **uisge a' snighe tron tughadh** rain seeping through the thatch, *cf* **sil** 1

snighe *nm invar* (*the act of*) dripping, seeping (*see* **snigh** *v*)

snìomh *vti, pres part* **a' snìomhadh** *&* **a' snìomh**, 1 spin (*yarn etc*); 2 twist, wring, **shnìomh e an ròpa** he twisted the rope, **tha thu a' snìomhadh mo chridhe** you're wringing my heart(-strings), **na snìomh d' adhbrann!** don't twist/sprain your ankle!

snìomhadh, *gen* **snìomhaidh** *nm* (*the act of*) spinning, twisting etc (*see senses of* **snìomh** *v*)

snìomhair(e), snìomhaire, snìomhairean *nm* (*tools*) a drill, an auger, *cf less trad* **drile**

snodha-gàire, snodha-gàire, snodhan-gàire *nm* a smile, *cf* **faite**

snog *adj* (*slightly fam*) 1 (*esp of people, places*) pretty, bonny, **tha i uabhasach snog** she's ever so pretty, *cf* **brèagha**; 2 (*of people, objects, situations*) nice, **duine snog** a nice man, **chuir sinn seachad feasgar còmhla, bha e snog** we spent an evening together, it was nice, **àite snog** a nice (*also* pretty) place, *cf* **laghach**, *&* *stronger* **sgoinneil**

snuadh, *gen* **snuaidh** *nm* (*esp of people*) 1 appearance, aspect, (*song*) **dh'fhàg thu tana-ghlas mo shnuadh** you left me looking/made me look thin and wan, *cf* **coltas** 1, **dreach** 1; 2 hue, colour, complexion, *cf* **dreach** 2, **fiamh** 1, **tuar**

so *see* **seo** *adj & pron*

so- *prefix corres to Eng* -able, -ible, *eg* **so-ruighinn** *adj* attainable, reachable, accessible, **so-thuigsinn** *adj* intelligible, understandable, comprehensible, **so-dhèanta** *adj* possible, feasible, able to be done, **so-lùbadh** *adj* flexible, pliable, **so-leughte** legible *cf* ion-, neo-, mì-

sòbair, *also* **sòbarr(a)**, *adj* sober, *esp* not drunk, **cha tric a tha e sòbair** it's not often he's sober, *cf* **stuama 2**

sòbhrach, sòbhraich, sòbhraichean *nf* (also found as **seòbhrach** *etc*), and **sòbhrag, sòbhraig, sòbhragan** *nf,* a primrose

socair *adj* 1 (*weather etc*) mild, tranquil, calm, *cf more usu* **ciùin, sèimh**; 2 (*esp of people*) at ease, at peace, relaxed

socair, *gen* **socrach** & **socaire** *nf* comfort, ease, leisure, **gabh** *v* **socair** take one's ease, **gabh** *v* **air do** (etc) **shocair** take things easily/comfortably, *excl* **socair!** *or* **air do shocair!** steady on!, take it easy!, go easy!

socais, socais, socaisean *nf* a sock (*ie* footwear)

sochar, *gen* **sochair** *nf* 1 bashfulness, shyness, *cf more usu* **diùide**; 2 (*of character*) softness, weakness, (excessive) compliance or indulgence

socharach *adj* 1 bashful, shy, *cf more usu* **diùid**; 2 (*of character*) soft, weak, tame, (too) compliant or indulgent, *cf more usu* **bog** *adj* 2, **lag, maoth** 1

so-chnàmhach *adj* bio-degradable

socrach *adj* 1 at ease, sedate, comfortable, leisurely, **ceum socrach** a leisurely/comfortable pace

socrachadh, *gen* **socrachaidh** *nm* (*the act of*) settling, solving, establishing etc (*see senses of* **socraich** *v*)

socraich *vti, pres part* **a' socrachadh**, 1 settle, make or become calm or tranquil, **shocraich a' ghaoth** the wind settled/abated, **cha tèid am fearg a shocrachadh** their anger cannot/will not be calmed/assuaged, *cf* **ciùinich, sìthich** 1 & 2; 2 (*vt*) (*dispute etc*) settle, solve, arrange, sort out, **shocraich a' chomataidh na duilgheadasan air fad** the committee solved/settled all the problems, *cf* **fuasgail** 3; 3 (*vt*) set, settle, fix, establish, **socraich an ìomhaigh air a' cholbh** set the statue on the column, **shocraich i a cridhe air** she set her heart on it, **chan urrainn dhomh m' inntinn a shocrachadh air a' chùis** I can't fix/concentrate my mind on the matter, *cf* **suidhich** 1

sodal, *gen* **sodail** *nm* adulation, fawning, flattery, *also in expr* **dèan** *v* **sodal ri cuideigin** fawn on/butter up/suck up to someone

sòfa, sòfa, sòfathan *nf* a sofa, *cf more trad* **langasaid**

sògh, *gen* **sòigh** *nm* luxury

sòghail *adj* luxurious

soilire, *gen* **soilire** *nm* celery

soilleir *adj* 1 (*of light etc*) bright, clear, **là soilleir** a bright/clear day, **deàlraich** *v* **gu soilleir** shine brightly; 2 (*of facts etc*) clear, apparent, evident, obvious, manifest, **tha a chionta soilleir** his guilt is clear/obvious, *cf* **follaiseach** 1; 3 (*of argument etc*) clear, easy to follow, **mìneachadh soilleir** a clear explanation

soilleirich *vti, pres part* **a' soilleireachadh**, 1 (*vi*) (*light etc*) become bright(er), become clear(er), **shoilleirich an là** the day brightened up; 2 (*vt*) (*problems etc*) clear up, clarify, elucidate, explain, enlighten, **shoilleirich an tidsear an cuspair dhuinn** the teacher clarified/elucidated the subject for us, *cf* **mìnich**

soillse *nm invar* light (*esp natural*), *cf more usu* **solas**

soillseachadh, *gen* **soillseachaidh** *nm* 1 (*the act of*) becoming bright, clarifying, shining (*see senses of* **soilleirich** & **soillsich** *v*); 2 explanation, an explanation, clarification, enlightenment, (*hist, philo*) **an Soillseachadh** the Enlightenment

soillsich *vti, pres part* **a' soillseachadh**, 1 *same senses as* **soilleirich**; 2 (*vi*) (*of lights*) shine, gleam, *cf* **deàlraich** 1

soineannta *adj* naive

soirbh *adj, opposite of* **doirbh**, easy, **rud soirbh** an easy thing, **chan eil e soirbh a ràdh** it's not easy to say, *cf* **furasta, sìmplidh** 1

soirbheachail *adj* (*business etc*) successful, thriving, prosperous

soirbheachas, *gen* **soirbheachais,** *nm* prosperity, success (*esp material*)

soirbhich *vi, pres part* **a' soirbheachadh**, succeed, turn out well, thrive, prosper, (*with prep* **le**) **an soirbhich an gnìomhachas leotha?** Will the business succeed/turn out well for them?, (*as impersonal verb*) **shoirbhich leis** he succeeded *or* he throve/prospered

sòisealach, *gen* & *pl* **sòisealaich** *nm* & *adj* (*pol*) a socialist, *also as adj* **sòisealach** socialist, **pàrtaidh sòisealach** a socialist party

sòisealta *adj* social, **tèarainteachd shòisealta** social security, **seirbheisean sòisealta** social services

soisgeul, *gen* **soisgeil** *nm* a gospel, **an Soisgeul a rèir Mhata** the Gospel according to Matthew

soisgeulach *adj* evangelical

soisgeulaiche, soisgeulaiche, soisgeulaichean *nm* an evangelist; an evangelical preacher

soitheach, soithich, soithichean *nfm* **1** a vessel, a container, *now usu food or kitchen-related,* a dish, **nigh** *v* **na soithichean** wash the dishes, do the washing-up; **2** a ship, a (*sailing*) vessel, *cf* **bàta, long**

soitheamh *adj* gentle, tractable, good-natured, *cf more usu* **ciùin, sèimh**

sòlaimte *adj* solemn, dignified, ceremonious

solair *vt, pres part* **a' solar(adh)**, (*of trader etc*) purvey, supply, provide, procure, **buidheann a' solaradh àirneis-oifis** a firm supplying office furniture, **solair fasgadh don luchd-turais** provide shelter for the tourists

solas, *gen & pl* **solais** *nm* (*natural & artificial*) light, a light, **solas an latha** daylight, **solas dealain** electric light, **cuir** *v* **air an solas** put/switch the light on, *cf less usu* **soillse**

sòlas, *gen* **sòlais** *nm* solace, consolation, comfort (*esp spiritual or emotional*), *cf* **furtachd**; **2** joy, gladness, delight, (*song*) **seòlaidh sinn thairis le sòlas** we'll sail across joyfully, *cf more usu* **gàirdeachas**

sòlasach *adj* **1** (*esp spiritually, emotionally*) comforting, consoling; **2** joyful, glad, well contented, *cf more usu* **aoibhneach 2 & 3**

solt(a) *adj* **1** meek, harmless, gentle, quiet, *cf* **macanta** *& more usu* **ciùin, sèimh**

sòn *nm* a zone (*climatic, industrial etc*)

son (*in exprs* **air a son, air mo shon** *etc*) *see* **airson 1**

sona *adj* (*opposite of* **dona**) **1** happy, content, **phòs iad 's tha mi an dòchas gun robh iad sona** they married and I hope they were happy, *cf stronger* **toilichte**; **2** *occas* (*trad*) lucky, fortunate

sònrachadh, *gen* **sònrachaidh** *nm* (*the act of*) distinguishing, specifying, pointing out *etc* (*see senses of* **sònraich** *v*)

sònraich *vt, pres part* **a' sònrachadh**, **1** distinguish (**bho** from); **2** specify, choose, single out, **shònraich an seanailear e airson na teachdaireachd** the general singled him out/chose him to deliver the message; **3** point out; **4** (*admin*) allocate, allot (*resources etc*)

sònraichte *adj* **1** particular, **tha mi a' sireadh seòrsa sònraichte** I'm looking for a particular sort/kind/variety, *cf* **àraidh 1**; **2** special, **'s e àite sònraichte a th' ann dhomh** it's a special place to/for me, *cf* **leth 2**; **3** *in expr* **gu sònraichte** *adv* particularly, especially, **chòrd na h-òrain rium, gu sònraichte am fear mu dheireadh** I enjoyed the songs, particularly/especially the last one, *cf* **àraidh 3**, & *see* **seac**

sop, *gen* **suip**, *pl* **sopan** & **suip** *nm* a wisp (*esp of straw, hay*)

soraidh *nf invar & excl* **1** (*trad*) a farewell, **soraidh leibh!** farewell, fare ye well! *cf* **beannachd 4**; **2** (*trad*) a greeting, **thoir mo shoraidh thar a' chuain** carry my greeting beyond the ocean, *cf* **dùrachd 2**

spaid, spaide, spaidean *nf* a spade, *cf less usu* **caibe 1**

spaideil *adj* (*of dress etc*) smart (*can be in a slightly showy way*)

spai(s)dirich *vi, pres part* **a' spai(s)dearachd**, walk *or* march in a proud or showy way, strut, parade

spàin, spàine, spàin(t)ean *nf* a spoon, **spàin-mhìlsein** a dessert spoon, **làn-spàine** *m* a spoonful

Spàinn, *gen* **Spàinne** *nf*, used with art **an Spàinn** Spain

Spàinnis *nf invar*, Spanish (*ie the lang*)

Spàinn(t)each, *gen & pl* **Spàinn(t)ich** *nm* a Spaniard, *also as adj* **Spàinn(t)each** Spanish

spàirn, *gen* **spàirne** *nf* exertion, hard physical effort, an effort, struggling, a struggle, **leis gach spàirn a rinn e** with every effort he made

spanair, spanair, spanairean *nm* a spanner

spàrr, sparra, sparran *nm* **1** (*joinery etc*) a joist, a beam, *cf* **sail**; **2** *in expr* **cuir** *v* **air an spàrr** put aside, save, store/stow away, *cf* **glèidh 2 & 3, stò(i)r**; **3** a roost (*for hen etc*), *cf* **spiris**

spàrr *vt, pres part* **a' sparradh**, drive or thrust one object into another, **spàrr tarrag ann an dèile** drive a nail into a plank, **spàrr do làmh sa phoca** thrust/shove your hand into the sack, *cf* **brùth 2, put** *v* **1, sàth 2**

sparradh, *gen* **sparraidh** *nm* (*the act of*) driving, thrusting (*see senses of* **spàrr** *v*)

speach, speacha, speachan *nf* a wasp

speal, speala, spealan *nf* a scythe

spealg, speilg, spealgan *nf* a splinter, a fragment, **bhris e am bòrd na spealgan** he smashed the table into splinters/to bits, *cf* **sgealb** *n*

spealg *vti, pres part* **a' spealgadh**, splinter, smash to pieces, *cf* **smuais, smùid** *v* **2**

spealgadh, *gen* **spealgaidh** *nm* (*the act of*) splintering etc (*see* **spealg** *v*)

spèil, spèile, spèilean *nf* a skate, an ice-skate

spèil *vi, pres part* **a' spèileadh**, skate (*on ice*)

spèis, *gen* **spèise** *nf* **1** (*esp in songs*) love, affection, **gur òg thug mi mo spèis dhut** when young I gave you my love/affection, *cf* **dèidh 2**, & *more generally used* **gaol 1**; **2** (*of friends etc*) liking, fondness, affection, regard, esteem, **fèin-spèis** conceit, self-regard, (*in letter*) **le mòran spèis . . .** sincerely yours . . . , *cf* **bàidh 1**

speuclairean *nm pl* spectacles, glasses, **speuclairean-grèine** sunglasses, *cf* **glainne 2**

speur, speura, speuran *nm* **1** sky, **shuas san speur** up in the sky, *cf* **adhar**; **2** *esp in pl* **na speuran** the heavens, the firmament, **reultan nan speuran** the stars of the heavens, *cf* **iarmailt**; **3** space, **speur-sheòladh** *m* space travel, *cf* **fànas 1**

speuradair, speuradair, speuradairean *nm* **1** an astrologer; **2** a cosmonaut

speuradaireachd *nf invar* astrology

speurair, speurair, speurairean *nm* a spaceman, an astronaut

spìc, spìce, spìcean *nf* a spike

spideag, spideig, spideagan *nf* a nightingale

spìocach *adj* mean, miserly, niggardly, stingy, *cf* **mosach 2**

spìocaire, spìocaire, spìocairean *nm* a miser, a mean, stingy person

spìon *vt, pres part* **a' spìonadh**, **1** snatch, grab, tug, tear or wrench away; **2** (*less strong*) pluck (*flower, harpstring etc*)

spìonadh, *gen* **spìonaidh** *nm* (*the act of*) snatching, plucking etc (*see senses of* **spìon** *v*)

spionnadh, *gen* **spionnaidh** *nm* energy, strength, vigour, **leis na bha de spionnadh air fhàgail aige** with his remaining strength/energy, *cf* **lùth 3, neart**

spiorad, spioraid, spioradan *nm* **1** (*relig*) a spirit, **an Spiorad Naomh** the Holy Spirit/Ghost; **2** a spirit, a ghost, *cf* **taibhse, tannasg**

spioradail *adj* (*relig*) spiritual, pertaining to the spirit, **dàin spioradail** spiritual songs, hymns

spìosradh, spìosraidh, spìosraidhean *nm* (*culinary*) spice, a spice

spìosraich *vt, pres part* **a' spìosrachadh**, **1** spice, add spices to food; **2** (*body*) embalm

spiris, spirise, spirisean *nf* a perch, a roosting or perching place, *cf* **spàrr** *n* **3**

spleuchd, spleuchda, spleuchdan *nm* **1** a stare, a gaze, a 'gawping' expression; **2** a squint, *cf* **claonadh 4, fiaradh 2**

spleuchd *vi, pres part* **a' spleuchdadh**, **1** stare, gaze, gape, 'gawp' (**air** at); **2** squint

spleuchdadh, *gen* **spleuchdaidh** *nm* (*the act of*) staring, squinting etc (*see senses of* **spleuchd** *v*)

spliùchan, spliùchain, spliùchanan *nm* a pouch (*esp for tobacco*)

spòg, spòig, spògan *nf* **1** a paw, *cf* **cròg 1, màg**; **2** a hand of a clock or watch, **spòg mhòr/**

bheag a minute/an hour hand; **3** (*of wheel*) a spoke

spong, spuing, spongan *nm* sponge, a sponge

sporan, *gen & pl* **sporain** *nm* **1** a purse; **2** (*highland dress*) a sporran, (*song*) **gheibh mi fèileadh 's sporan garbh** I will get a kilt and a rough sporran

spòrs, *gen* **spòrsa** *nf* **1** sport, a sport, **'s e ball-coise an spòrs as fheàrr leam** football's my favourite sport; **2** fun, amusement, **bha spòrs againn a-raoir** we had fun/had a good time/enjoyed ourselves last night, **faigh** *v* **spòrs air cuideigin** have fun at someone's expense, *cf* **dibhearsan**

spot, spot, spotan *nm* **1** a spot, a stain, *cf* **smal**; **2** a spot, a place, (*calque*) **air an spot** on the spot, *cf* **bad 1**

spoth *vt, pres part* **a' spoth** & **a' spothadh**, castrate, geld, spay, *cf* **geàrr** *v* **2**

spothadh, *gen* **spothaidh** *nm* **1** (*the act of*) castrating (*see* **spoth** *v*); **2** castration

spreadh *vti, pres part* **a' spreadhadh**, **1** (*vi*) burst; **2** (*vti*) explode, blow up

spreadhadh, spreadhaidh, spreadhaidhean *nm* **1** (*the act of*) bursting, exploding, blowing up; **2** an explosion

sprèidh, *gen* **sprèidhe** *nf* livestock, stock, (*esp*) cattle, (*song*) **chan iarrainn sprèidh no fearann leat** I wouldn't ask for cattle or land with you (*ie as a dowry*), *cf* **bò, crodh, stoc**[1] **3**

spreig *vt, pres part* **a' spreigeadh**, incite, prompt, urge (*someone to do something*), *cf* **brod** *v* **1** & **2, brosnaich, stuig**

spreigeadh, *gen* **spreigidh** *nm* (*the act of*) inciting etc (*see senses of* **spreig** *v*)

sprùilleach, *gen* **sprùillich** *nm coll* **1** crumbs, *cf* **criomag, sprùilleag**; **2** debris

sprùilleag, sprùilleig, sprùilleagan *nf* a crumb, *cf* **criomag**, & *coll* **sprùilleach 1**

spùill *vt, pres part* **a' spùilleadh**, *also* **spùinn** *vt, pres part* **a' spùinneadh**, plunder, rob, despoil, *cf* **creach** *v* **1**

spùinn *vt see* **spùill**

spùinneadair, spùinneadair, spùinneadairean *nm* a robber, a plunderer, a despoiler, a brigand, **spùinneadair-mara** a pirate, a buccaneer

spu(i)r, spuir, spuirean *nm* a claw (*esp of bird*), a talon, *cf* **ìne 2**

spùt, spùta, spùtan *nm* **1** a spout (*ie jet of liquid*), a gush, a spurt, *cf* **steall** *n* **1**; **2** a (*large*) waterfall, *freq in placenames as* Spout, *eg* **Spùt Roilidh** Spout Rollo (*near Comrie*), *cf* **eas, leum-uisge, linne 2**; **3** *with the art*, **an spùt** diarrhoea, *cf* **buinneach, sgàird**

spùt *vti, pres part* **a' spùtadh**, *(of liquids)* spout, spurt, squirt, *cf* **steall** *v*, **srùb** *v* 1

spùtadh, *gen* **spùtaidh** *nm* *(the act of)* spouting, spurting etc *(see senses of* **spùt** *v)*

sràbh, sràibh, sràbhan *nm* a (drinking) straw

srac *vt, pres part* **a' sracadh**, tear, rip, rend, *cf* **reub**

sracadh, *gen* **sracaidh** *nm* *(the act of)* tearing, ripping, rending *(see* **srac** *v)*

sradag, sradaig, sradagan *nf* a spark

sràid, sràide, sràidean *nf* a street

sràidearaich *vi, pres part* **a' sràidearachd**, stroll, saunter, walk about, *(song)* **air madainn dhomh 's mi (a') sràidearachd** one morning as I strolled about

srainnsear, srainnseir, srainnsearan *nm* 1 a stranger, **na bi nad shrainnsear!** don't be a stranger! *(ie* keep in touch!), *cf* **coigreach** 2; 2 an incomer, **tha am baile làn shrainnsearan a-nis** the township's full of incomers now, *cf* **seatlair**

srann, srainn, srannan *nmf, also* **srannail** *nf invar*, & **srannartaich**, *gen* **srannartaiche** *nf*, snoring, a snore

srann *vi, pres part* **a' srannail**, snore

sreang, sreinge, sreangan *nf* string *(not of musical instrument, cf* **teud***)*

sreath, sreatha, sreathan *nmf* 1 *(of people, objects)* a row, a line, *(of platoon etc)* a rank, *(of hills, mountains)* a range, *(on roadway)* a lane, *also in expr* **(an treas bliadhna etc) an sreath a chèile** (the third year etc) in a row/running/in succession *(cf* **an ceann a chèile** – *see* **ceann** 3); 2 a layer, a stratum; 3 a series, **am prògram mu dheireadh san t-sreath** the last programme in the series

sreothart, sreothairt, sreothartan *nm* a sneeze, **dèan** *v* **sreothart** sneeze

sreothartaich, *gen* **sreothartaiche** *nf* sneezing, a bout or fit of sneezing, **dè an t-sreothartaich a th' ort!** what a lot of sneezing you're doing!

srian, *gen* **srèine**, *pl* **srèinean** & **sriantan** *nf* 1 a bridle, a rein, reins; 2 a streak, a stripe, *cf* **stiall** *n* 1

sròn, *gen* **sròine**, *pl* **srònan** & **sròintean** *nf* 1 a nose, **tha mo shròn a' leum** my nose is bleeding, *(idiom)* **gabh rudeigin anns an t-sròin** take offence at something, **sròn bròige** a toe of a shoe; 2 *(topog)* a ridge, point or promontory, *often in placenames as* Stron(e), **Sròn Iasgair** Stronesker, fisher's point or promontory, *cf* **àird(e)** 2, **maol** *n* 1, **rinn** 2, **rubha**

sròn-adharcach, *gen* & *pl* **sròn-adharcaich** *nm* a rhinoceros

srùb, srùib, srùban *nm* a spout *(of container, teapot etc)*

srùb *vti, pres part* **a' srùbadh**, 1 spout, spurt, *cf* **spùt** *v*, **steall** *v*; 2 suck or slurp in *(a drink etc)*

srùbadh, *gen* **srùbaidh** *nm* *(the act of)* spouting, sucking etc *(see senses of* **srùb** *v)*

srùbag, srùbaig, srùbagan *nf* 1 a sip, a small drink *(cf* **srùb** *v* 2); 2 *(esp)* a snack, a cup of tea *(plus biscuits, sandwich etc)*, *(Highland Eng)* a stroupach, **an tig thu a-steach airson srùbaig?** will you come in for a cup of tea/a stroupach?

srùban, *gen* & *pl* **srùbain** *nm* a cockle, *cf* **coilleag**

sruth, *gen* **sruith** & **srutha**, *pl* **sruthan** *nm* 1 a stream, a burn, *occurs in placenames as* Stru(ie), Strow(ie) *etc*, *cf* **allt**; 2 a flow, a rush *(of running water)*; 3 a current, **ris/leis an t-sruth** against/with the current

sruth *vi, pres part* **a' sruthadh**, *(esp of liquids)* flow, stream, run, *cf* **ruith** *v* 2, **sil** 2

sruthach *adj* 1 *(of liquids)* streaming, running, flowing; 2 liquid

sruthadh, *gen* **sruthaidh** *nm* *(the act of)* flowing etc *(see senses of* **sruth** *v)*

sruthan, *gen* & *pl* **sruthain** *nm, dimin of* **sruth** *n*, a small stream or burn, *can occur in placenames as* Struan

stàball, stàbaill, stàballan *nm* a stable

stad, stada, stadan *nm* 1 a stop, a halt, a pause *(in motion, activity etc)*, **nì sinn stad an seo** we'll stop/wait here *(usu briefly)*, **thàinig i gu stad** she came to a halt/stop, *cf* **stad** *v* 1; 2 the state or condition of being stationary, **bha am bus na stad** the bus was stationary, **tha a' chùis na stad** the affair/matter/business is at a standstill/in abeyance; 3 an end, a cessation, a stop, *esp in expr* **cuir** *v* **stad air** stop, put a stop or end to, **cuiridh mi stad air do shràidearachd!** I'll put a stop to your stravaigin! **thoir** *v* **rudeigin gu stad** bring something to an end, *cf* **crìoch** 1

stad *vti, pres part* **a' stad(adh)**, 1 stop, halt, pause, come or bring to a halt or stop, **stad iad aig bun/bonn na beinne** they halted at the foot of the mountain, **stad e an làraidh** he stopped the lorry; 2 stop, cease, desist from doing something, *cf more usu* **leig** 5, **sguir**

stad-phuing, stad-phuinge, stad-phuingean *nf* a full stop

staid, staide, staidean *nf* a state, a condition, **ann an droch staid** in a bad state/condition, *(of person)* in a bad way, *cf* **cor** 1, **dòigh** 3

staidhir, staidhreach, staidhrichean *nf*, & **staidhre, staidhre, staidhrichean** *nf*, 1 a (*single*) stair, a step (*in staircase*); **2** a staircase, a flight of stairs, (*Sc*) a stair; *cf* **ceum 3**

stail, staile, stailean *nf* a (whisky) still, *cf* **poit 2**

stailc, stailc, stailcean *nf* (*industry etc*) a strike, **air stailc** on strike

stàilinn, *gen* **stàilinne** *nf* steel, *cf* **cruaidh** *n*

staing, stainge, staingean *nf* a difficulty, a tight corner, a fix, **ann an droch staing** in a very difficult situation/a bad fix, *cf* **cruaidh-chàs 2**

stàirn, *gen* **stàirne** *nf* **1** a crashing or clattering noise; **2** a loud rumbling noise

stairs(n)each, stairs(n)ich, stairs(n)ichean *nf* a threshold

stais, staise, staisean *nf* a moustache

stàit, stàite, stàitean *nf* (*pol etc*) a state, **an stàit Bhreatannach** the British state, **Rùnaire na Stàite** the Secretary of State

Stàitean Aonaichte *fpl*, used with art **Na Stàitean Aonaichte** the United States

stàiteil *adj* stately, **ceum stàiteil** a stately pace/gait

stalc, *gen* **stailc** *nm* starch

stalcair(e), stalcaire, stalcairean *nm* a fool, a blockhead, *cf* **amadan, bumailear, ùmaidh**

stalcaireachd *nf invar* **1** stupidity; **2** a stupid action

stalla, stalla, stallachan *nm* a precipice

stamag, stamaig, stamagan *nf* a stomach, *cf* **balg 1, broinn 1, brù 2, maodal**

stamh, *gen* **staimh**, *pl* **staimh** & **stamhan** *nm* (*seaweed*) tangle

stamp *vti, pres part* **a' stampadh**, stamp (*with foot*), **bha i a' stampadh a casan ris** she was stamping her feet at him, *cf* **breab** *v* **2**

stamp(a), stampa, stampaichean *nf* a (postage) stamp

staoig, staoige, staoigean *nf* steak, a steak

staoin, *gen* **staoine** *nf* tin

steall, still, steallan *nf* **1** an outpouring of liquid, a spout, a spurt, a gush, a squirt, *cf* **spùt** *n* **1**; **2** a large drink, a swig, a slug, *cf* **balgam 2, sgailc 3, steallag**

steall *vti, pres part* **a' stealladh**, (*of liquids*) spout, squirt, spurt, gush, *cf* **spùt** *v*, **srùb** *v* **1**

stealladh, *gen* **steallaidh** *nm* (*the act of*) spouting etc (*see senses of* **steall** *v*)

steallag, steallaig, steallagan *nf*, *dimin of* **steall** *n*, a drink, a slug, a swig, **ghabh e steallag mhath às a' bhotal** he took a good swig from the bottle, *cf* **balgam 2, sgailc 3, steall** *n* **2**

steallair(e), steallaire, steallairean *nm* a syringe

stèidh, stèidhe, stèidhean *nf* **1** (*phys*) a base, a foundation, (*Bibl*) **stèidh na talmhainn** the foundation of the earth, *cf more usu* **bonn 1**; **2** (*philo, relig etc*) a basis, a foundation, a fundamental or founding principle, *cf* **bunait**

stèidheachadh, *gen* **stèidheachaidh** *nm* **1** (*the act of*) founding etc (*see senses of* **stèidhich** *v*); **2** (*abstr*) foundation, establishment

stèidhich *vt, pres part* **a' stèidheachadh**, found, establish, set up, *cf* **bonn 5, cas** *n* **6**

stèidhichte *adj* founded, established, set up, **stèidhichte ann an 1923** founded in 1923, **an Eaglais Stèidhichte** the Established Church

stèisean, stèisein, stèiseanan *nm* (*transport, radio etc*) a station

stiall, stèill, stiallan *nf* **1** a streak, a stripe (*on material, skin etc*); **2** tape, a tape, a strip (*of material etc*), *cf less trad* **teip 1**; **3** a scrap or stitch of clothing, **chuir e dheth a h-uile stiall ach a bhriogais** he took off every scrap/stitch of clothing except his trousers

stiall *vt, pres part* **a' stialladh**, stripe, streak, mark with streaks or stripes

stialladh, *gen* **stiallaidh** *nm* (*the act of*) striping etc (*see senses of* **stiall** *v*)

stìopall, *gen* & *pl* **stìopaill** *nm* a steeple, (*song*) **Glaschu mòr nan stìopall** great Glasgow of the steeples

stiùbhard, stiùbhaird, stiùbhardan *nm* a steward

stiùir, stiùire(ach), *also* **stiùrach, stiùir(ich)ean** *nf* **1** (*of boat*) a rudder; **2** a helm, *cf* **failm, falmadair**; **3** *in expr* **uisge na stiùrach** (*lit*) the wake (*of boat etc*), (*fig*) **cha tig iad** (*etc*) **an uisge na stiùrach dhut** (*etc*) they (*etc*) can't hold a candle to you/aren't in the same league as you/can't compete with you (*etc*)

stiùir *vt, pres part* **a' stiùireadh**, **1** (*boat, vehicle etc*) steer; **2** (*firm etc*) direct, run, manage, *cf* **riaghail 2**; **3** direct, lead, conduct, show the way (*to someone in street etc*); *cf* **seòl** *v*

stiùireadair, stiùireadair, stiùireadairean *nm* a steersman, a helmsman

stiùireadh, *gen* **stiùiridh** *nm* (*the act of*) steering, directing etc (*see senses of* **stiùir** *v*), **neach-stiùiridh** *m* a director, a manager (*of firm, organisation etc*), **an luchd-stiùiridh** the managers, the directors, (*coll*) the management, *cf* **manaidsear, riaghladh 3**

stiùiriche, stiùiriche, stiùirichean *nm* (*esp admin*) a director, **Stiùiriche Foghlaim/Ionmhais** Director of Education/Finance, **stiùiriche riaghlaidh** a managing director

stob, stuib, stoban *nm* **1** a fence post, a stake, a stob, *cf* **post2**; **2** a stump

stòbh(a), stòbha, stòbhaichean *nmf* a stove

stoc[1], *gen & pl* **stuic** *nm* **1** a trunk, *also* a stump (*of tree*), *cf* **stob 2**; **2** a root(-stock), *cf* **freumh**; **3** stock, livestock, *cf* **sprèidh**

stoc[2], *gen & pl* **stuic** *nm* a scarf, a cravat, *cf less trad* **sgarfa**

stocainn, stocainne, stocainnean *nf* a stocking, *cf* **osan, socais**

stoidhle, stoidhle, stoidhlichean *nf* style, a style, **tha stoidhle throm air a chuid sgrìobhaidh** there's a ponderous style about his writing

stò(i)r *vt, pres part* **a' stòradh**, store, put in store, *cf* **spàrr** *n* **2, glèidh 3**

stòiridh (& stòraidh), *gen* **stòiridh**, *pl* **stòiridhean** *nm* a story (*often a joke, a humorous story or anecdote*), *cf* **naidheachd 2, sgeul 1, sgeulachd**

stoirm, stoirme, stoirmean *nmf* **1** a storm, *cf* **doineann, gailleann, sian 1**; **2** *occas for* **toirm**

stòl, *gen* **stòil** & **stòla**, *pl* **stòil** & **stòlan** *nm* (*furniture*) a stool, *cf* **furm 2** & *trad* **creapan**

stòlda *adj* (*of temperament, behaviour*) **1** sedate, serious, slow and steady, staid, sober; **2** serious (*ie opposite of* in jest), *cf* **da-rìribh 1**

stòr, stòir, stòran *nm* **1** a store (*ie repository, shop etc, also stock, hoard etc*), (*IT*) **stòr-dàta** a database; **2** *same senses as* **stòras**

stòr *v see* **stò(i)r**

stòradh, *gen* **stòraidh** *nm* (*the act of*) storing (*see* **stò(i)r** *v*)

stòras, *gen* **stòrais** *nm* (*trad*) riches, wealth, possessions, (*song*) **ged a bhiodh mo phòcaid falamh, chì mi stòras air gach bealach** though my pocket may be empty, I see riches on every side, *cf* **beartas, ionmhas 2, saidhbhreas**

stràc, stràic, stràcan *nm* **1** a stroke (*of scythe, strap, pen etc*), a blow, *cf* **buille 1**; **2** (*lang, typog*) an accent (*ie diacritic mark*), **tha stràc air 'a' san fhacal 'stràc'** there's an accent on 'a' in the word 'stràc', *Note: in Gaelic the 'accents' are really length marks*; **3** (*lang*) stress, accentuation

stràic, stràice, stràicean *nm* (*formerly, in schools*) a belt, a strap, (*Sc*) a tawse, a lochgelly

streap *vti, pres part* **a' streap(adh)**, climb, *cf* **dìrich**[2]

streap(adh), *gen* **streapaidh** *nm* (*the act of*) climbing, **streap mhonaidhean** hill/mountain climbing, hillwalking

strì *nf invar* **1** (*the act of*) struggling, striving etc (*see senses of* **strì** *v*); **2** strife, contention, a struggle, a contest, **bhris an claidheamh anns an t-strì** the sword broke in the struggle, **buidheann strì** a pressure group, (*trad*) **strì nam bàrd** the contest of the poets, *cf* **gleac** *n* **1**

strì *vi, pres part* **a' strì**, struggle, strive, battle, contend, compete (**ri** with, against), **a' strì ri chèile** struggling (*etc*) against each other

strìoch, strìocha, strìochan *nf* (*typog*) a hyphen, *cf* **tàthan**

strìochag, strìochaig, strìochagan *nf* (*typog*) a tick

strìochd *vi, pres part* **a' strìochdadh**, **1** submit, surrender, yield, *cf* **gèill 1**; **2** cringe, *cf* **crùb 3**

strìochdadh, *gen* **strìochdaidh** *nm* **1** (*the act of*) submitting, cringing etc (*see senses of* **strìochd** *v*); **2** surrender

strìopach, strìopaiche, strìopaichean *nf* a prostitute, *cf* **siùrsach**

strìopachas, *gen* **strìopachais** *nm* prostitution

stròc, stròic, stròcan *nm* (*med*) a stroke

stròdhail *see* **struidheil**

structair, structair, structairean *nm* structure, a structure

struidh *vt, pres part* **a' struidh** waste, spend lavishly, squander, dissipate, *cf* **caith 3**

struidhear, struidheir, struidhearan *nm* a waster, a wastrel, a spendthrift

struidheil & stròdhail *adj* extravagant, prodigal, *esp in expr* (*Bibl, humorous etc*) **am mac struidheil/stròdhail** the prodigal son

struth, strutha, struthan *nmf* an ostrich

stuadh & stuagh, *gen* **stuaidh**, *pl* **stuadhan(nan)** *nf* **1** (*in sea etc*) a wave, *cf* **tonn 1**; **2** a gable (*of building*)

stuaim, *gen* **stuaime** *nf, also* **stuamachd** *nf invar*, abstemiousness, abstinence, moderation, restraint, temperance, sobriety

stuama *adj* **1** (*in general behaviour, temperament*) abstemious, moderate, temperate, restrained, demure, *cf* **measarra, stòlda 1**; **2** (*as regards drink*) sober, abstemious, abstinent, **'s e duine stuama a th' ann, cha bhi e ag òl idir** he's a sober/abstemious man, he doesn't drink at all, *cf* **sòbair**

stuamachd *see* **stuaim**

stùiceach & stùirceach *adj* surly, morose, *cf* **gnù, mùgach 2**

stuig *vt, pres part* **a' stuigeadh**, incite, prompt, urge (*someone to do something*), *cf* **brod** *v* **1** & **2, brosnaich, spreig**

stuigeadh, *gen* **stuigidh** *nm* **1** (*the act of*) inciting etc (*see senses of* **stuig** *v*); **2** incitement; *cf* **brosnachadh** 1 & 3

stùirceach *see* **stùiceach**

stùr, *gen* **stùir** *nm* dust, (*Sc*) stour, *cf* **duslach**, **dust**

stuth, **stutha**, **stuthan** *nm* **1** (*textiles etc*) material(s); **2** (*sing*) material (*for making something*), **stuth bhròg** shoe-making material(s), *cf* **adhbhar** 3; **3** stuff, matter, material, **stuth-leughaidh** reading matter, **stuth math a tha sin!** that's good stuff! **chuir an naidheachdair stuth air falbh chun an fhir-deasachaidh** the journalist sent some stuff/material off to the editor

suaicheantas, *gen* & *pl* **suaicheantais** *nm* **1** (*clan, regiment, organisation etc*) a badge, an emblem, insignia, **is e an t-aiteann suaicheantas MhicLeòid** the badge/emblem of MacLeod of MacLeod is the juniper; **2** (*occas*) a novelty, a rarity, a phenomenon, a remarkable thing, (*prov*) **cha shuaicheantas còrr air cladach** a heron on a beach is no marvel

suaimhneach *adj* calm, composed, quiet, *cf more usu* **ciùin**, **socair** 1 & 2

suain, *gen* **suaine** *nf* sleep (*usu deep*), slumber, *cf more usu* **cadal** 2

suain *vt, pres part* **a' suaineadh**, wrap, entwine (*in flexible object such as rope, foliage*), envelop

Suain *nf, used with art* **An t-Suain**, Sweden

Suaineach, *gen* & *pl* **Suainich** *nm* a Swede, *also as adj* **Suaineach** Swedish, of, from or pertaining to Sweden (**An t-Suain**)

suaineadh, *gen* **suainidh** *nm* (*the act of*) wrapping, entwining (*see* **suain** *v*)

suairc(e) *adj* **1** affable, approachable; **2** kind, gentle; **3** courteous, mannerly, *cf* **beusach** 2, **cùirteil** 1, **modhail**, **sìobhalta** 1

suarach *adj* **1** insignificant, petty, mean, trifling, paltry, *cf* **crìon** *adj* 2; **2** (*stronger*) contemptible, despicable, abject, *cf* **tàireil**

suarachas, *gen* **suarachais** *nm* **1** insignificance, pettiness, paltriness *etc* (*cf senses of* **suarach**), *esp in expr* **cuir** *v* **rudeigin/cuideigin an suarachas** belittle *or* slight something/someone; **2** contemptible or despicable nature of something

suas *adv* up (*usu expr movement, NB from point of view of the person moving, cf* **a-nìos**, **a-nuas**), **chaidh e suas an staidhre** he went up the stair (*cf* **tha e shuas an staidhre** he's upstairs), **cuiridh mi suas sanas** I'll put up a notice (*cf* **àrd** *n* 4), (*fam*) **cha do chuir e suas no sìos mi** it didn't affect me in the least/

one way or the other, *cf* **a-nìos**, **a-nuas**, **shìos**, **shuas**, **sìos**

suath *vti, pres part* **a' suathadh**, **1** rub, wipe (*esp for cleaning*), *cf* **siab** 1; **2** rub or brush (**ri** against), (*autobiography title*) **Suathadh ri Iomadh Rubha** (Aonghas Caimbeul) Rubbing/Brushing against Many a Point/Headland, (*fig*) **shuath mi ri iomadh carraig** I (have) knocked about a good deal (*lit* I (have) brushed against many a rock), *cf* **bean** *vi* 2; **3** massage

suathadh, *gen* **suathaidh** *nm* **1** (*the act of*) rubbing, brushing etc (*see senses of* **suath** *v*); **2** friction; **3** massage

sùbailte (*also* **subailte**) *adj* supple, flexible (*material, mind etc*), *cf* **lùbach** 2

sùbh, **sùibh**, **sùbhan** *nm* a berry, **sùbh-làir** strawberry, *cf more usu* **dearc**

sud *see* **siud**

sùgan, **sùgain**, **sùganan** *nm* (*trad*) rope made of twisted straw

sùgh, *gen* **sùgha** & **sùigh**, *pl* **sùghan** *nm* **1** juice, **sùgh-measa** fruit juice; **2** (*of trees, plants etc*) sap

sùgh & **sùigh** *vti, pres part* **a' sùghadh**, (*liquids*) absorb, suck (up), soak (up), **shùigh mo chòta an t-uisge** my coat absorbed/soaked up the rain, **pàipear-sùghaidh** blotting paper, *cf* **deothail** *vti*

sùghach *adj* absorbent

sùghadh, *gen* **sùghaidh** *nm* **1** (*the act of*) absorbing etc (*see senses of* **sùgh** *v*); **2** suction

sùghmhor *adj* juicy, sappy

sùgradh, *gen* **sùgraidh** *nm* **1** (*trad*) mirth, merry-making, **dèan** *v* **sùgradh** make merry, revel, (*song*) **dhèanainn sùgradh ris an nighinn duibh** I would make merry/would sport with the black-haired girl; **2** (*occas*) lovemaking

suidh *vi, pres part* **a' suidhe**, sit (down), **suidh an sin** sit there, **suidh sìos/a-bhàn!** sit down! **shuidh e sa bhus** he sat in the bus, *cf* **suidhe** *n* 1 & 2

suidhe, **suidhe**, **suidhe(ach)an** *nm* **1** the act of sitting down, **dèan** *v* **suidhe** sit down, take a seat, be seated; **2** the state of being seated, **tha mi nam shuidhe** I am seated/sitting down, **cuir** *v* **cuideigin na shuidhe** seat someone, sit someone down, **àite-suidhe** *m* a seat, a sitting place, **cha robh àite-suidhe ann** there was nowhere to sit; **3** (*occas*) a seat

suidheachadh, **suidheachaidh**, **suidheachaidhean** *nm* **1** (*the act of*) settling, arranging, placing, etc (*see senses of* **suidhich** *v*); **2** a setting, a physical situation, a site, **b' e**

sin **suidheachadh air leth math airson taigh-dhealbh** that was an exceptionally good site/situation for a cinema; **3** (*freq*) an abstract situation, a state of affairs, **tha an teaghlach ann an suidheachadh gu math cugallach** the family's in a pretty dodgy/dicy/uncertain situation

suidheachan, *gen & pl* **suidheachain** *nm* a seat (*cf* **suidhe** *n* 3), a stool (*cf* **stòl**), (*in church*) a pew

suidhich *vt, pres part* **a' suidheachadh, 1** place, seat, plant, settle or install (*an object in its location*), **suidhich stèidh** lay down a foundation, **suidhich gàrradh** plant/establish a garden, **suidhich ìomhaigh air colbh** place/install a statue on a column, *cf* **socraich** 3; **2** set, settle, arrange, agree upon (*details, plans etc*), **suidhich là na coinneimh** arrange/settle the date of the meeting; **3** appoint, set up, establish, **suidhich comataidh** appoint a committee, **modh-riaghlaidh a shuidhich na Lochlannaich** a way/mode of governing that the Vikings established/set up

suidhichte *adj* **1** settled, arranged, placed, *etc* (*see senses of* **suidhich**); **2** determined, resolute, **suidhichte nach fairtlicheadh e orm** determined it wouldn't get the better of me; **3** (*of persons, status etc*) settled, established, steady; **4** (*of persons*) sedate, grave, respectable, *cf* **stòlda** 1

suidse, suidse, suidsichean *nf* (*elec*) a switch

suigeart, *gen* **suigeirt** *nm* cheerfulness, *cf more usu* **sunnd** 1

sùigh *see* **sùgh** *v*

sùighteach *adj* absorbent

sùil, sùla, sùilean *nf* **1** an eye, **dùin** *v* **do shùilean** close your eyes, **sùil gheur** a sharp eye, **ann am priobadh na sùla** in the twinkling of an eye, in a flash, (*song*) **Teàrlach òg nan gorm-shùl meallach** young Charles (*ie Charles Edward Stewart*) of the bewitching blue eyes, **cùm** *v* **sùil air** keep an eye on him/it; **2** a look, a glance, **sùil aithghearr air a' chloc** a quick look/glance at the clock, **an toir thu sùil air a' chàr agam?** will you take/have a look at my car?; **3** *in expr* **tha sùil aig ... ri** ... expect, **tha sùil aige rithe** he's expecting her, **cha robh sùil aca ri ar faicinn** they didn't expect to see us, *cf* **dùil**[1] 2, **sùilich**

sùil-chritheach, *gen & pl* **sùil-chrithich** *nf* a quagmire

suilbhir *adj* cheerful, *cf* **aoibhneach** 2, **sunndach**

sùilich *vi, pres part* **a' sùileachadh**, expect, **chan eil mi ga shùileachadh** I don't expect it, *cf more usu* **dùil**[1] 2, **sùil** 3

sùim, suime, suimeannan *nf* **1** regard, respect; **2** attention, concern, interest, care, **chan eil sùim agam de na thubhairt iad** I'm not paying any attention to what they said, **gabh** *v* **sùim** care, **cuir** *v* **sùim ann an rudeigin** be interested/take an interest in something, *cf* **aire** 2, **ùidh** 2; **3** an amount, a sum, **sùim airgid** a sum of money; **4** a sum (*ie arithmetical problem*)

suipear & suipeir, *gen* **suipeire**, *also* **suipearach** *pl* **suipearan** *nf* a supper

suirghe & suiridhe *nf invar* courting, courtship, *also as pres part* **a'/ri suirghe** courting, **fear-suirghe** a suitor, **dèan** *v* **suirghe ri nighean** court a lass, *cf* **brìodal** 4, **leannanachd**

suiridhe *see* **suirghe**

suiteas, *gen & pl* **suiteis** *nm* a sweet, (*Sc*) a sweetie, **poca shuiteas** *m* a bag of sweet(ie)s, *cf* **siùcar** 2

sùith(e), *gen* **sùithe** *nmf* soot

sùlaire, sùlaire, sùlairean *nmf* a gannet, a solan goose, *cf* **guga**

sult, *gen* **suilt** *nm* (*bodily*) fat, fatness, plumpness, (*fig*) **cha robh a bheag de shult na talmhainn ann** there was none of the earth's fatness/abundance there

Sultain, *gen* **Sultaine** *nf &* **Sultuine** *nf invar*, *used with art*, **an t-Sultain/an t-Sultuine** September

sultmhor *adj* **1** fat, plump, corpulent, *cf* **reamhar**; **2** in rude health, lusty, sleek; **3** wealthy, prosperous, opulent

sumainn, sumainne, sumainnean *nf* billowing, a billow, surge, swell (*of sea*), *cf* **ataireachd**

sunnd *nm invar* **1** cheerfulness, alacrity, good humour, good cheer; **2** frame of mind, mood, humour, **dè do shunnd?** how are you?, (*Aberdeenshire*) fit like?, **ann an deagh/droch shunnd** in a good/bad humour/mood, in good/bad spirits, **tha deagh shunnd oirre** she's in good spirits, *cf* **cor** 1, **dòigh** 3, **fonn** 2, **gean**, **gleus** 2

sunndach *adj* lively, cheerful, merry, in good spirits, hearty, *cf* **aoibhneach** 2, **beòthail**, **cridheil**, **suilbhir**

Suòmaidh *nf* Finland, *cf* **Fionnlainn**

Suòmach, *gen & pl* **Suòmaich** *nm* a Finn, someone from Finland, *also as adj* **Suòmach** Finnish, *cf* **Fionnlannach**

sùrd, *gen* **sùird** *nm* 1 cheerfulness; **2** alacrity, eagerness, willingness, **chuir e ris le sùrd** he set to with a will

sùrdag, **sùrdaig**, **sùrdagan** *nf* a jump, a skip, a leap, a bounce, a caper, **dèan** *v* **sùrdag** jump, skip etc, *cf* **leum** *n* **2**

sùrdagaich *vi*, *pres part* **a' sùrdagaich**, jump, skip, leap, bounce, caper, *cf* **leum** *v* **1**, **dèan sùrdag** (*see* **sùrdag**)

susbaint, *gen* **susbainte** *nf*, (*of book etc*) substance, 'pith', significance, authenticity, *cf* **brìgh 2**

susbainteach *adj* substantial, 'pithy', of significance

suth, **sutha**, **suthan** *nm* (*biol, med*) an embryo

sù, **sù**, **sùthan**, **sutha**, **sutha**, **suth(ach)an** *nmf* a zoo

T

t' *see* **do** *poss adj*

tàbhachdach *adj* sound, solid, substantial, **gnìomhachas tàbhachdach** a sound/solid business, **cho tàbhachdach 's a bha a h-inntinn** how substantial her intellect was

tabhainn *see* **tabhannaich** *v*

tabhair, tabhairt *pts of irreg v* **thoir** (*see tables p 504*)

tabhairteach, *gen & pl* **tabhairtich** *nm, also* **tabhairtiche, tabhairtiche, tabhairtichean** *nm,* a giver, a donor, a benefactor

tabhann *see* **tabhannaich** *n*

tabhannaich, *gen* **tabhannaiche** *nf, also* **tabhann,** *gen* **tabhainn** *nm* (*the act & sound of*) barking, *cf* **comhart** & **comhartaich**

tabhannaich *vi, pres part* **a' tabhannaich,** *also* **tabhainn** *vi, pres part* **a' tabhann,** bark, *cf* **comhartaich**

tabhartach *adj* **1** giving, liberal, apt to give; **2** *esp* (*gram*) dative, **an tuiseal tabhartach** the dative case

tabhartas, tabhartais, tabhartasan *nm* a donation, an offering, a presentation, a grant, a gift, *cf* **tiodhlac**

taca *nf invar* **1** proximity, *cf* **taic(e) 2**; **2** *now usu in expr* **an taca ri** compared to, alongside, **tha i glic an taca ri a bràthair** she's clever compared to/alongside her brother, *cf* **coimeas** *n* **3, seach 2**

tacaid, tacaide, tacaidean *nf* **1** (*esp for footwear*) a tack, (*Sc*) a tacket, a hobnail; **2** (*also* **tacaid-balla**) a drawing-pin

tacan, tacain, tacanan *nm* a (short) time, a (little) while, (*song*) **an sin suidhidh i tacan a' tachas a cinn** then she'll sit for a while scratching her head, *cf more usu* **greis, tamall, treis**

tachair *vi, pres part* **a' tachairt, 1** happen (**do** to), occur, take place, **dè a tha a' tachairt?** **chan eil càil** what's happening? nothing, **thachair sin an-uiridh** that happened last year, **dè a thachair do Sheumas?** what happened to James? (*cf* **èirich 3**); **2** *can occur without a subject eg* **'s ann mar sin a**

thachair that's how it happened/turned out, **mar a thachair, bha trì dhiubh ann** as it happened/turned out, there were three of them; **3** *in expr* **tachair air** happen upon, chance upon, come across, **thachair mi air an-dè** I came across/happened to meet him yesterday, *cf* **amais 2**; **4** *in expr* **tachair ri,** meet (*more intentionally*), **thachair mi rithe sa bhaile** I met her in town, *cf* **coinnich 2**; **5** meet, make the acquaintance of, **an do thachair thu ris a-riamh?** did you ever meet him?, *cf* **coinnich 2**

tachais *vti, pres part* **a' tachas, 1** (*vt*) scratch, (*song*) **an sin suidhidh i tacan a' tachas a cinn** then she'll sit for a while scratching her head, *cf* **sgrìob** *v* **3, sgròb**; **2** (*vi*) itch, tickle, *cf vti* **diogail**

tachartas, tachartais, tachartasan *nm* a happening, an event, an incident, an occurrence, *cf* **tuiteamas 1**

tachas, *gen* **tachais** *nm* **1** (*the act of*) scratching (*esp an itch*); itching (*see* **tachais** *v*); **2** an itch, a tickling sensation

tachd *vt, pres part* **a' tachdadh,** smother, choke, throttle, strangle; (*aperture etc*) stop up, *cf* **mùch 2**

tachdadh, *gen* **tachdaidh** *nm* **1** (*the act of*) smothering, choking etc (*see senses of* **tachd** *v*); **2** suffocation

tadhail *vti, pres part* **a' tadhal, 1** visit, go to see, call (**air** on), **tha sinn a' dol a thadhal orra** we're going to visit/see/call on them, *cf* **cèilidh 1, tathaich**

tadhal, tadhail, tadhalaichean *nm* **1** (*the act of*) visiting etc (*see senses of* **tadhail** *v*); **2** a visit, a call, *cf* **cèilidh 1**; **3** (*sport*) a goal

tagair *vt, pres part* **a' tagairt** & **a' tagradh, 1** claim (*rights, possessions, also in insurance etc*), **a' tagairt a dhuais** claiming his prize/reward; **2** (*a cause, & esp a legal case*) plead, argue, prosecute or conduct

tagairt, tagairte, tagairtean *nf* **1** (*the act of*) claiming, pleading etc (*see senses of* **tagair** *v*); **2** a claim; a petition

tagh *vt, pres part* **a' taghadh**, **1** choose, select, appoint, **thagh e an sgioba** he chose/selected the team, *cf* **roghnaich**; **2** (*pol*) elect, vote for, vote into office, **cha deachaidh an taghadh** they weren't elected, *cf* **bhòt**

taghadh, taghaidh, taghaidhean *nm* **1** (*the act of*) choosing, electing etc (*see senses of* **tagh** *v*); **2** choice, a choice, selection, a selection, *cf* **roghainn**; **3** (*pol*) an election, a ballot, *cf* **baileat**

taghta *adj* **1** chosen, selected, elected; **2** choice, (*fam*) great!, fine!, perfect!, smashing!, *as excl* **an dèan mi na soithichean dhut? taghta!** will I do the dishes for you? great!, *cf* **gasta 2**, **glan** *adj* **2**, **sgoinneil**

tagradh, tagraidh, tagraidhean *nm* **1 & 2** *same as* **tagairt 1 & 2**; **3** (*law courts etc*) a plea, (*also*) an appeal

tagsaidh, *gen* **tagsaidh**, *pl* **tagsaidhean** *nmf* a taxi, a cab

taibhs(e), taibhse, taibhsean *nmf* a ghost, *cf* *less usu* **tannasg**

taibhsearachd *nf invar* second sight, (*the ability and activity of*) seeing visions (*freq announcing death*), *cf* **an dà shealladh** (*see* **sealladh 1**)

taic(e), *gen* **taice** *nf* **1** (*lit or fig*) support, a support, a buttress, a prop; patronage, **neach-taice** *m* a supporter, a patron, a backer, **cùm** *v* **taic ri cuideigin** support someone, **taic airgid** financial support/backing/help/aid, **taic-beatha** life support, **cuir** *v* **do thaic orm/rium** lean on me, *also* depend on me; **2** contact, proximity, *now usu in expr* **an taic ri** leaning on/against, propped up against, *cf* **taca 1**; **3** (*esp music*) accompaniment, an accompaniment, **thoir taic** (*with prep* **do**) accompany

taiceil *adj* supporting, supportive

taidhr, taidhre, taidhrichean *nf* a tyre

taifeid, taifeid, taifeidean *nm* a bowstring

taigeis, taigeise, taigeisean *nf* haggis, a haggis

taigh, taighe, taighean *nm & * **tigh, tighe, tighean** *nm* **1** a (dwelling) house, **fear an taighe** the man of the house/head of the family, *also* the landlord (*of hotel, pub etc*) & the MC (*at ceilidh etc*), **bean an taighe** the lady/woman of the house, the housewife, *also* the landlady (*of hotel, pub, boarding house etc*), **taigh-dubh** a blackhouse, *a trad type of low-walled, thatched, round-ended Highland dwelling now virtually disappeared, also* an illicit distillery, a shebeen (*cf* **bothan 3**), *cf* **fàrdach 1**; **2** home, *in exprs* **aig an taigh** at home, **on taigh** away from home, not at home, out, *cf* **baile 5, dachaigh 1**; **3** *other kinds of building, or part of a building, usu for a specific use, eg* **Taigh nan**

Cumantan/nam Morairean the House of Commons/of Lords, **taigh-beag** a toilet (*public or private*), **taigh-bìdh** a café, a restaurant, **taigh-chon** a kennel, **taigh-cluiche** a theatre, **taigh-dhealbh** a cinema, **taigh-nighe** a wash-house, a laundry, **taigh-òsta** a hotel, an inn, (*loosely*) a public house/pub, **taigh-spadaidh** an abattoir, a slaughterhouse, **taigh-siùrsachd** a brothel, **taigh-tasgaidh** a museum, **taigh-staile** a distillery, *cf* **ionad 2**

taigheadas, *gen* **taigheadais** *nm* housing, **Comataidh an Taigheadais** *f* the Housing Committee

tailceas, tailceasach *see* **tarcais, tarcaiseach**

tàileasg, *gen* **tàileisg** *nm* **1** chess; **2** backgammon

tàillear, tàilleir, tàillearan *nm* a tailor

taing, *gen* **tainge** *nf* **1** thanks, gratitude, **gus mo thaing a nochdadh** to show my thanks/gratitude, *cf* **buidheachas**; **2** *usu in exprs* **mòran taing!** many thanks! thank you very much! thanks a lot!, (*less usu*) **taing dhut/dhuibh!** thank you!, **ceud taing!** thanks very much (indeed)!, *cf* **tapadh 2**

taingeil *adj* thankful, grateful, appreciative, *cf* **buidheach**

tàinig *pt of irreg v* **thig** (*see tables p 503*)

tàir, tàire, tàirean *nf* contempt, disparagement, **dèan** *v* **tàir air cuideigin** despise, disparage someone, *cf* **tarcais 1**

tàir *v see* **tàrr**

tairbhe *nf invar* advantage, gain, profit, benefit, *cf* **leas 1** & *more usu* **buannachd 1**

tairbheach & tarbhach *adj* advantageous, beneficial, profitable (**do** to)

tairbhich *vi, pres part* **a' tairbheachadh**, *also* **tarbhaich** *vi, pres part* **a' tarbhachadh**, profit, gain, benefit

tàireil *adj* contemptible, *cf* **suarach 2**

tairg *vti, pres part* **a' tairgse**, **1** offer, propose, **thairg e a chuideachadh** he offered his help, **thairg e a dhèanamh** he offered/proposed to do it; **2** offer, bid (*at sale etc*), *cf* **tairgse 2**

tairgse, tairgse, tairgseachan *nf* **1** (*the act of*) offering etc (*see senses of* **tairg** *v*); **2** an offer, **thoir** *v* **tairgse (air)** make an offer/a bid (for); **3** *in expr* **cuir** *v* **an tairgse muinntir eile** offer/make available to other people

tàirneanach, *gen* **tàirneanaich** *nm* thunder

tairsgeir, tairsgeir, tairsgeirean *nf* a peat iron, a peat spade

tais *adj* damp, moist, humid, *cf* **bog** *adj* **5**

taisbean & taisbein *vt, pres part* **a' taisbeanadh**, display, show, present, reveal, exhibit, demonstrate, *cf* **nochd 1, seall 2**

taisbeanach *adj* **1** (*esp of sounds, sights*) clear, distinct, **chunnaic/chuala e gu taisbeanach iad** he saw/heard them clearly; **2** (*gram*) indicative, **a' mhodh thaisbeanach** the indicative mood

taisbeanadh, taisbeanaidh, taisbeanaidhean *nm* **1** (*the act of*) displaying, showing etc (*see senses of* **taisbean** *v*); **2** an exhibition, a display, a show, a demonstration, a presentation (*of art, goods, techniques etc*)

taisbeanlann, taisbeanlainn, taisbeanlannan *nf* an exhibition hall, an art gallery

taise *nf invar* & **taiseachd** *nf invar* moistness, moisture, dampness, humidity

taiseachadh, *gen* **taiseachaidh** *nm* (*the act of*) dampening etc (*see senses of* **taisich** *v*)

taisg *vt, pres part* **a' tasgadh**, **1** store, put in store, deposit (*esp in museums etc*), *cf* **stò(i)r**; **2** hoard; **3** (*fin*) invest, deposit

taisich *vt, pres part* **a' taiseachadh**, dampen, moisten, make damp, moist or humid

taitinn *vi, pres part* **a' taitinn** & **a' taitneadh**, (*with prep* **ri**), please, be pleasant, *cf* **còrd** *v* **2**

taitneach *adj* (*of persons, also things, situations*) agreeable, pleasant, pleasing, congenial (**ri** to), *cf* **ciatach 1, tlachdmhor 1**

taitneadh, *gen* **taitnidh** *nm* (*the act of*) pleasing etc (*see senses of* **taitinn** *v*)

taitneas, taitneis, taitneasan *nm* **1** pleasure, the state of being pleased, *cf* **tlachd 1**; **2** pleasantness, agreeableness

talachadh, *gen* **talachaidh** *nm* (*the act of*) complaining etc (*see senses of* **talaich** *v*)

tàladh, tàlaidh, tàlaidhean *nm* **1** (*the act of*) attracting, enticing, soothing etc (*see senses of* **tàlaidh** *v*); **2** attraction, attractiveness, appeal; **3** enticement, allurement; **4** a lullaby (*also* **òran tàlaidh** *m*)

talaich *vi, pres part* **a' talachadh**, complain, grumble, be dissatisfied, *cf more usu* **gearain**

tàlaidh *vt, pres part* **a' tàladh**, **1** attract, *cf* **tarraing 5**; **2** entice, allure, tempt, **tàlaidh an luchd-ceannachd air ais** attract/tempt the customers back, *cf* **meall** *v* **2**; **3** hush, soothe, calm, *cf* **ciùinich**; **4** sing and/or rock to sleep

tàlaidheach *adj* attractive, *cf* **tarraingeach**

talamh, talmhainn, talamhan *nm* (*f in gen sing*) **1 an Talamh** the Earth, **air aghaidh na talmhainn** on the face of the earth, *cf* **cruinne-cè, saoghal 1**; **2** earth, soil, **chuir iad san talamh e** they put him into the earth, *cf* **ùir**; **3** land, ground, **talamh-àitich** arable/cultivated land, **talamh bàn** fallow ground, *cf* **fearann, tìr 4**

tàlann, tàlainn, tàlann(t)an *nm* a talent, a (natural) gift, *cf less strong* **comas**

tàlantach *adj* talented, gifted, *cf less strong* **comasach**

talla, talla, tallachan *nm* a hall (*trad, hist*) **talla MhicLeòid** MacLeod's (*ancestral or chiefly*) hall, *now usu a public space, eg* **talla a' bhaile** the village hall, the town hall; **2** *in expr* **mac-talla** *m* an echo (*lit* son of (the) hall)

talmhaidh *adj* **1** earthly, **creutair talmhaidh** an earthly creature; **2** worldly (*opposite of spiritual*), *cf* **saoghalta**

tàmailt, tàmailte, tàmailtean *nf* **1** disgrace, shame, *cf* **masladh, nàire 1**; **2** an insult, an indignity

tàmailteach *adj* **1** scandalous, shameful, disgraceful, deplorable, *cf* **maslach, nàr**; **2** insulting

tàmailtich *vt, pres part* **a' tàmailteachadh**, insult, make ashamed

tamall, tamaill, tamallan *nm* a while, a time, **an ceann tamaill** in/after a while, (*song*) **ma dh'fhanas tu tamall** if you'll tarry a while, *cf more usu* **greis, tacan, treis**

tàmh, *gen* **tàimh** *nm* **1** (*the act of*) resting, dwelling etc (*see senses of* **tàmh** *v*); **2** rest, peace, **tha iad nan tàmh** they are at rest, (*esp of the dead*) they are at peace, *cf* **fois 1, sìth**; **3** (*not necessarily pej*) idleness, inactivity, freedom from work, **a bheil thu nad thàmh?** are you at leisure/free?, **tha an luchd-obrach nan tàmh air sgàth na stailc** the workers are idle because of the strike, (*prov*) **am fear a bhios na thàmh, cuiridh e an cat san teine** the man with nothing to do will put the cat in the fire

tàmh *vi, pres part* **a' tàmh**, **1** rest, *cf more usu* **gabh fois** (*see* **fois 2**); **2** dwell, live, stay, (*song*) **gruagach an taobh shuas dhìom a' tàmh** a girl living up the way from me, *cf* **còmhnaich** & *more usu* **fuirich 2**

tàmhadair, tàmhadair, tàmhadairean *nm* a tranquilizer

tana *adj* **1** (*of build, dimensions*) thin, *cf* **caol** *adj* **3**; **2** (*of liquids*) thin, runny, **brochan tana** thin gruel/porridge; **3** (*opposite of dense*) thin, sparse, **falt tana** thin(ning) hair, *cf* **gann 1**, & *opposite of* **dlùth 2**; **4** (*of water*) shallow; **5** (*of material etc*) flimsy

tanaich *vti, pres part* **a' tanachadh**, thin, make or become thin etc (*see senses of* **tana**)

tancair, tancair, tancairean *nm* a tanker, **tancair-ola** an oil tanker

tannasg, *gen* & *pl* **tannaisg** *nm* a ghost, *cf more usu* **taibhse**

taobh, taoibh, taobhan *nm* **1** a side, **tha pian nam thaobh** there's a pain in my side (*cf* **cliathaich**), **bhuail an làraidh taobh an taighe** the lorry struck the side of the house, **taobh-duilleige** a page (*of book etc*), (*abbrev* **td a seachd** p7), **rim thaobh** at my side, beside me, **ri taobh a' chidhe** beside/alongside the quay, **taobh ri taobh** side by side, **an taobh a-muigh/a-staigh** the outside/inside, **an taobh siar** & **an taobh an iar** the west (side of the country); **2** a way, a direction, **tha iad a' tighinn an taobh seo** they're coming this way, *cf* **rathad 2**; **3** (*in dispute etc*) a side, a part, **ghabh sinn a taobh** we took her part/side, we sided with/supported her, **cùm** *v* **taobh ri** side with, favour, *cf* **leth 1**; **4** *in expr* (*in family etc*) **rach ri taobh cuideigin** take after someone; **5** *in expr* **(a-)thaobh** (*with gen*) concerning, regarding, touching on, in connection with, **tha duilgheadasan aige a-thaobh airgid** he has problems concerning money, **thaobh an taghaidh . . .** as for the election . . . , as far as the election is concerned . . . ; **6** *also in expr* **a thaobh (is gun)** *prep* & *conj* because of, on account of, **a thaobh sin** because of that, **a thaobh is gun chaochail e** because he died, *cf more usu* **a chionn 1** & **2**

taois, taoise, taoisean *nf* dough

taom *vti, pres part* **a' taomadh**, (*esp liquids from container etc*) pour, pour or flow out, empty; (*cookery etc*) drain, **taom na currain** drain the carrots, *cf* **dòirt** (*vti*), **ruith** (*vi*), **sil** (*vi*)

taomadh, *gen* **taomaidh** *nm* (*the act of*) pouring, emptying etc (*see* **taom** *v*)

tap, tapa, tapaichean *nmf* a (water) tap, *cf* **goc**

tapachd *nf invar, abstr noun corres to* **tapaidh** *adj*, cleverness, sturdiness etc (*see senses of* **tapaidh**)

tapadh, *gen* **tapaidh** *nm* **1** (*trad*) the state of being handy, willing, smart etc; a smart (etc) action (*see senses of* **tapaidh** *adj*); **2** *now usu in expr* **tapadh leat/leibh!** thank you!, *cf* **taing 2**

tapag, tapaig, tapagan *nf* a slip of the tongue, an exclamation

tapaidh *adj* **1** (*of persons*) willing, handy; clever, quick, smart, *cf* **deas 4**; **2** sturdy, manly, active, *cf* **calma, duineil 1, fearail**

tarbh, *gen* & *pl* **tairbh** *nm* a bull

tarbhach *adj see* **tairbheach**

tarbhaich *see* **tairbhich**

tarbh-nathrach, *gen* & *pl* **tairbh-nathrach** *nm* a dragonfly

tarcais, *gen* **tarcaise** *nf*, & **tailceas**, *gen* **tailceis** *nm*, **1** contempt, reproach, disdain, scorn, **dèan** *v* **tarcais air** despise, *cf* **tàir** *n*; **2** spite

tarcaiseach *adj* & **tailceasach** *adj* **1** contemptuous, reproachful, scornful, disdainful; **2** spiteful

targaid, targaide, targaidean *nf* **1** a target; **2** (*trad*) a targe, a shield, *cf* **sgiath 2**

tàrmachadh, *gen* **tàrmachaidh** *nm* (*the act of*) begetting, breeding etc (*see senses of* **tàrmaich** *v*)

tàrmaich *vt, pres part* **a' tàrmachadh**, **1** (*trad*) beget, *cf more usu* **gin** *v* **1**; **2** (*plants, animals*) breed, propagate; **3** produce, originate

tàrr *vi, pres part* **a' tàrradh**, *also* **tàir** *vi, pres part* **a' tàireadh**, *usu in expr* **tàrr/tàir às** escape, flee, make off, run away, *cf* **teich**

tàrradh, *gen* **tàrraidh** *nm* (*the act of*) escaping, making off etc (*see senses of* **tàrr** *v*)

tarrag *see* **tarrang**

tarraing, *gen* **tarrainge** & **tàirgne**, *pl* **tarraingean** & **tàirgnean** *nf* **1** (*the act of*) drawing, pulling, attracting etc (*see senses of* **tarraing** *v*); **2** a pull, a tug; **3** a draught (*of liquids*); **4** (*spirits*) distillation; **5** a mention, a reference, an allusion (**air** to), **cha tug e tarraing air** he made no mention of/reference to it, *cf* **guth 3, iomradh 1**

tarraing *vti, pres part* **a' tarraing**, **1** draw, drag, pull, haul, heave, tug (**air** at, on), *cf* **slaod** *v*, **spìon 1**; **2** draw (*liquids etc*), **tarraing pinnt** draw/pull a pint, **tarraing anail/fuil** draw breath/blood; **3** (*lit & fig*) approach, draw near (**gu** to), **tarraing gu crìch** draw to an end, **bha iad a' tarraing gu h-aois** they were getting on (in years), **bha an oidhche a' tarraing faisg air a' mhadainn** the night was drawing close to morning, *cf* **teann** *v* **3**; **4** (*artist etc*) draw, **tarraing dealbh** draw a picture; **5** (*person, magnet etc*) attract, *cf* **tàlaidh 1**; **6** *in expr* **tarraing à cuideigin** tease/kid someone, pull someone's leg, *cf* **farranaich 1**; **7** (*spirits*) distil

tarraingeach *adj* attractive, *cf* **tàlaidheach**

tarrang, tàirnge, tàirngean *nf, also* **tarrag, tarraig, tarragan** *nf* & **tarran, tarrain, tàirnean** *nm*, (*joinery*) a nail

tarsainn 1 *adv* (*expr position or movement*) across, over; **2** *usu as prep* **tarsainn air** (*with dat*) across, over, **bha craobh mhòr tarsainn air an rathad** a great tree was across the road, **chaidh iad tarsainn air an drochaid/na beanntan** they crossed/went over the bridge/mountains; *cf* **thairis 1** & **2, thar 1**

tart, *gen* **tairt** *nm* thirst, dryness, *cf less strong* **pathadh**

tartmhor *adj* thirsty, dry, *cf* **ìotmhor, pàiteach**

tasgadh, *gen* **tasgaidh** *nm* **1** storing, depositing etc (*see senses of* **taisg** *v*), **taigh-tasgaidh** *m* a storehouse, a museum, **ionad-tasgaidh** *m* a repository; **2** investment, **airgead-tasgaidh** *m* an investment (*ie the funds invested*), **neach-tasgaidh** *m* an investor

tasglann, tasglainn, tasglannan *nf* an archive

tasgaidh, tasgaidhe, tasgaidhean *nf* a store, a treasure, a hoard, *cf* **stòr, stòras**

tastan, tastain, tastanan *nm* (*former currency*) a shilling, *cf* **sgillinn 2**

tàth *vt, pres part* **a' tàthadh**, join or fix together (*by various means & substances*), glue (together), cement, solder, weld, bond

tathaich *vi, pres part* **a' tathaich**, (*with prep* **air**) frequent, visit (*usu frequently*); haunt, (*song*) **a fhleasgaich** (*voc*) **tha tathaich air srathan is glinn, a' mealladh nan caileag** young fellow who haunts/hangs about in straths and glens, enticing the lassies, **tathaich air càirdean** visit/call on friends, *cf* **tadhail**

tàthan, tàthain, tàthanan *nm* (*typog*) a hyphen, *cf* **strìoch**

tè *nf invar* **1** one (*denoting object or living thing having female gender, gram or phys*), **tha a' phiseag/a' chroit seo nas lugha na an tè sin** this kitten/croft is smaller than that one, *cf* **fear 3**; **2** a woman, a female, **thàinig tè gam fhaicinn an-dè** a woman came to see me yesterday, **tè-mhalairt** a business woman, *cf* **boireannach, fear 1**

teachd & **tiochd** *vi defective* **1** (*trad*) come, *virtually obs in this sense exc in set expr* **an t-àm ri teachd** the time to come, the future, *cf usu* **thig 1**; **2** fit, **an teachd e an cùl do chàir?** will it fit in the back of your car?

teachd *nm invar* an arrival, a coming, **teachd an earraich** the coming of spring, *also in exprs* **teachd-an-tìr** a living, a livelihood, **teachd-a-steach** an income (*also* an entry/entrance)

teachdail *adj* future, (*gram*) **an tràth teachdail** the future tense

teachdaire, teachdaire, teachdairean *nm* **1** a messenger, a courier; **2** a missionary, *cf less trad* **miseanaraidh**

teachdaireachd *nf invar* **1** a mission, a message, a commission, an errand, **a' dol air theachdaireachd** going on an errand/a mission (*cf* **gnothach 3**); **2** news, information etc carried (*by messenger etc*), *cf* **fios 3, naidheachd 1**

teadhair, teadhrach, teadhraichean *nf* a tether, (*calque*) **aig ceann mo theadhrach** at the end of my tether

teagaisg *vt, pres part* **a' teagasg**, **1** teach, **theagaisg mo sheanair dhomh na th' agam de ghliocas** my grandfather taught me what wisdom I have; **2** (*formally*) teach, instruct, educate, **teagaisg matamataig** teach maths, **teagaisg an ginealach ùr** teach/educate the new generation (*cf* **foghlaim**)

teagamh, teagaimh, teagamhan *nm* **1** a doubt, an uncertainty, **gun teagamh** without (a) doubt, doubtless, **an tig i a-màireach? thig gun teagamh!** will she come tomorrow? without a doubt! definitely!, *also in expr* **cuir** *v* **(an) teagamh** doubt, cast doubt on, **cha do chuir iad teagamh nach fhaca sinn e** (*note double neg*) they didn't doubt that we saw/had seen it, **cuir** *v* **teagamh ann an rudeigin** doubt (*the existence, truth etc of*) something, *cf* **amharas**; **2** *as conj* **theagamh** perhaps, maybe, **theagamh nach tig i** perhaps she won't come, *cf more usu* **dòcha 3, faod 2**

teagasg, *gen* **teagaisg** *nm* (*ed, Bibl etc*) teaching, **neach-teagaisg** *m* a teacher (*cf* **tidsear**)

teaghlach, teaghlaich, teaghlaichean *nm* a family, *cf* **caraid 2, duine 6**

teagmhach *adj* doubtful, doubting, dubious, sceptical, *cf* **amharasach**

teallach, teallaich, teallaichean *nm* a hearth, a fireside, a fireplace, **leac an teallaich** *f* a hearthstone, **teallach ceàrdaich** a forge (*in smithy*), *cf* **cagailt, teinntean**

teampall, *gen & pl* **teampaill** *nm* a temple

teanchair, teanchair, teanchairean *nm, also* **teannachair, teannachair, teannachairean** *nm*, **1** a vice, a clamp; **2** a pair of pincers; **3** a pair of tongs

teanga, teangaidh, teangan *nf* **1** a tongue, **air bàrr mo theangaidh** on the tip of my tongue; **2** (*occas*) a tongue, a language, *cf more usu* **cainnt 2, cànain**

teann *vi, pres part* **a' teannadh**, **1** (*trad*) move, go, come, proceed, (*song*) **teann a-nall 's thoir dhomh do làmh** come over here and give me your hand, *cf* **gabh 2, imich 2, rach 1, thig 1**; **2** (*lit & fig*) **teann air** approach, near, draw near to, **bha e a' teannadh air meadhan-oidhche** it was nearing midnight, *cf* **tarraing** *v* **3**; **3** begin, start, set about, set to, **theann e ri streap** he began/set to/set about climbing, *cf* **tòisich**

teann *adj* **1** tight, tense, taut, **ròpa teann** a tight rope; **2** firm, fixed, solid, **ceangail** *v* **gu teann** join firmly, *cf* **daingeann**; **3** (*person, discipline etc*) severe, strict, *cf* **cruaidh 2**; **4** close, near (*air* to), **teann air mìos air ais** close on/nearly a month ago, **bha an t-arm teann orra**

the army was hard on their heels/close by them, *cf more usu* **dlùth 1, faisg**

teannachadh, *gen* **teannachaidh** *nm* 1 (*the act of*) tightening, constricting etc (*see senses of* **teannaich** *v*); 2 constriction

teannaich *vti, pres part* **a' teannachadh**, 1 tighten, tense, tension; 2 constrict, squeeze, compress; *cf* **fàisg**

teanntachd-cuim *nf invar* constipation

teanta, teanta, teantaichean *nf* a tent, *cf more trad* **pàillean 2, puball**

Tearach *see* **Hearach**

tèarainte *adj* 1 safe, secure (*from danger etc*), **àite-falaich tèarainte** a safe/secure hide-out, *cf* **sàbhailte**; 2 secure (*ie guaranteed*), **gabhaltas tèarainte** secure tenure (*of land etc*), **inbhe thèarainte airson na Gàidhlig** secure (*legal etc*) status for Gaelic

tèarainteachd *nf invar* 1 security, safety, **an tèarainteachd** in safety; 2 security (*of tenure etc*); 3 (*IT*) **tèarainteachd dàta** data protection/security

tearc *adj* scant, scarce, few, rare, *cf* **ainneamh** & *more usu* **gann**

tèarmann, *gen* **tèarmainn** *nm* (*abstr*) protection, safeguard, refuge, sanctuary, asylum, (*con*) a refuge, a sanctuary, **fo thèarmann na cùirte** in/under the court's protection, **tèarmann poilitigeach** political asylum, **tèarmann nàdair** a nature reserve, *cf* **comraich, dìon** *n*

teàrn & **teàrnadh** *see* **teirinn**

teàrr, *gen* **tearra** *nf* tar, pitch, *cf* **bìth 1**

teas *nm invar* heat, *cf* **blàths**

teasach, teasaich, teasaichean *nf* fever, a fever, *cf* **fiabhras**

teasachadh, *gen* **teasachaidh** *nm* 1 (*the act of*) heating (*see* **teasaich** *v*); 2 (*domestic etc*) heating, **uidheam teasachaidh** *f* a heater, a heating appliance

teasaich *vti, pres part* **a' teasachadh**, heat, heat up, *cf* **blàthaich, teòthaich**

teasairg & **teasraig** *vt, pres part* **a' teasairginn** & **a' teasraiginn**, save, rescue, **is e an luchd-tadhail a theasairg an t-eilean** it was the visitors who saved the island, **bàta-teasairginn** *m* a lifeboat, a rescue boat, *cf* **sàbhail 1**

teas-mheidh, teas-mheidh, teas-mheidhean *nf* a thermometer

teatha *nf invar* & **tì** *nf invar* tea (*ie the drink*), **cupa tì** a cup of tea

teich *vi, pres part* **a' teicheadh**, flee, escape, run away, **theich na saighdearan** the soldiers fled *or* the soldiers deserted, *cf* **tàrr**

teicheadh, *gen* **teichidh** *nm* 1 (*the act of*) running away etc (*see senses of* **teich** *v*); 2 flight, escape; 3 desertion (*from army etc*)

teicneòlach *adj* technical, technological, *cf* **teicnigeach**

teicneòlaiche, teicneòlaiche, teicneòlaichean *nm* a technician, a technologist

teicneòlas, *gen* **teicneòlais** *nm* technology, (*IT*) **teicneòlas fiosrachaidh** information technology

teicnigeach *adj* technical, *cf* **teicneòlach**

tèid *pt of irreg v* **rach** (*see tables p 501*)

teine, teine, teintean *nm* fire, a fire, **taobh an teine** *m* the fireside (*cf* **cagailt, teallach, teinntean**), **teine-dealain** an electric fire, **cuir** *v* **air/cuir** *v* **às an teine** light/put out the fire, **rach** *v* **na theine** go on fire, **chaidh talla a' bhaile na theine** the village hall went on fire, **cuir** *v* **teine ri togalach** set fire to a building

teinntean, *gen* & *pl* **teinntein** *nm* a hearth, a fireplace, *cf* **cagailt, teallach**

teip, teip, teipichean *nf* 1 tape, a tape, **teip-thomhais** a measuring tape, **dùin** *v* **am parsail le teip** seal the parcel with tape, **teip-clàraidh** recording tape; 2 a tape, a cassette, a recording on tape, **an cuala tu an teip ùr aca?** have you heard their new tape?

teirce *nf invar, abstr noun corres to* **tearc**, scarceness, scarcity etc (*see senses of* **tearc**)

teirinn & **teàrn** *vti, pres part* **a' teàrnadh**, 1 come or go down, descend (*from hill etc*), **theirinn e às a' chùbaid** he came down from the pulpit, (*as vt*) **a' teàrnadh a' bhruthaich** coming down/descending the hillside; 2 alight, dismount, climb/get down (*from horse, vehicle etc*), **theirinn i bhàrr a' ghàrraidh** she climbed down from the wall; *cf* **crom** *v* **4**

teirm, teirm, teirmichean *nf* a term (*ie period, duration*), **teirm na dreuchd aige** his term of/in office, (*ed etc*) **teirm an fhoghair** the autumn term

teis-meadhan, teis-meadhain, teis-meadhanan *nm* (*also* **ceart-mheadhan**) an exact or dead centre of something, (*of earthquake etc*) an epicentre, *cf* **meadhan 1**

teisteanas, teisteanais, teisteanasan *nm* 1 testimony, a testimony, evidence, a piece of evidence (*in court etc*), *cf* **dearbhadh 2, fianais 2**; 2 (*proof of something, usu written*) attestation, an attestation, a certificate, a diploma, **teisteanas-breith** a birth certificate; 3 (*of character, qualifications etc*) a reference, a testimonial

telebhisean, telebhisein, telebhiseanan *nm*
1 television, *used with & without art,* **chunnaic
mi prògram math air (an) telebhisean**
I saw a good programme on (the) television,
cead telebhisein *m* a television licence; 2 a
television set
teòclaid & **seòclaid,** *gen* **teòclaid,** *pl*
teòclaidean *nmf* chocolate, a chocolate, *also as
adj* **teòclaid** chocolate
teòdh *see* **teòthaich**
teòiridh, teòiridh, teòiridhean *nf* theory, a
theory, **a rèir teòiridh** in theory
teodhachd & **teothachd** *nf invar* temperature,
a temperature
teòma *adj* 1 expert, skilful, adept, *cf* **ealanta
2, sgileil;** 2 ingenious, *cf* **innleachdach 1,
tionnsgalach**
teòthaich *also* **teothaich** *vti, pres part* **a'
teòthachadh,** *also* **teòdh** *vti, pres part* **a'
teòthadh,** warm, warm up, **teòthaich am
brot** warm up the soup, **teòdh ri cuideigin**
warm/take to someone, *cf* **blàthaich,
teasaich**
teth *comp* **(n)as (etc) teotha** *adj* hot, **botal-
teth** *m* a hot water bottle, *cf weaker* **blàth** *adj* 1
teud, *gen* **tèid** & **teuda,** *pl* **teudan** *nm* a string
(*of musical instrument*), **sheinneadh teudan
na fìdhle** the fiddle strings would/used to sing
tha *pt of irreg v* **bi** (*see tables p 505*)
thabhair *pt of irreg v* **thoir** (*see tables p 504*)
thàinig *pt of irreg v* **thig** (*see tables p 503*)
thairis *adv* 1 (*usu expr movement*) across,
over, beyond, **chaidh iad thairis** they went
over/across, (*trad*) they went abroad, (*now usu*)
chaidh iad a-null thairis they went abroad,
(*expr position*) **tha iad thall thairis** they
are abroad, **cuir** *v* **thairis** overflow, run over,
chuir an t-uisge thairis the water overflowed,
(*fig*) **tìr a' cur thairis le creutairean de
gach seòrsa** a land overflowing with creatures
of every kind, (*of boat*) **rach thairis** (*vi*) &
cuir thairis (*vt*), capsize, turn over, overturn,
chaidh am bàta thairis the boat capsized/
turned over, **chuir iad thairis i** they capsized
her; 2 *as prep* **thairis air** across, over, **chaidh
am plèana thairis air na beanntan** the
plane passed over the mountains, *cf* **tarsainn
2;** 3 beyond, (*fig*) **chaidh thu thairis air na
bha mi ag iarraidh** you went beyond what I
required, *cf* **thar 2**
thairis (*emph form* **thairis-san**), **thairte** (*emph
form* **thairtese**) *prep prons, see* **thar**
thall *adv* over there, (over) yonder (*usu expr
position*), (*song*) **a bhean** (*voc*) **ud thall a
rinn an gàire** woman over there who laughed,

thall 's a-bhos here and there, (*expr motion*)
hither and thither, **ann an Ameireagaidh
thall** over (yonder)/far away in America, *cf*
a-bhos, a-nall, a-null; 2 (*in exprs of time*)
expr idea furthest, latter, **mu dheireadh thall**
at long last, **aig a' cheann thall** in the end,
ultimately, at the latter end; 3 *for* **thall thairis**
see **thairis 1**
thalla *pl* **thallaibh** *imper* go, be off, get,
thalla(ibh) dhachaigh! off you go home!,
(get) away home!, *cf* **falbh 1, tiugainn,
trobhad**
thar *prep* (*with gen*), across, over: (*The prep
prons formed with* **thar,** *in the order first,
second, third person singular, first, second,
third person plural, and with the reflexive/
emphatic particles in brackets, are as follows:*
**tharam(sa), tharad(sa), thairis(san),
thairte(se), tharainn(e), tharaibh(se),
tharta(san):** across/over me, across/over
you (*fam*), etc. 1 across, over (*expr position*),
bha raidhfil aige thar a ghuailne he had
a rifle over/across his shoulder, *cf more usu*
tarsainn 2; 2 over, beyond (*expr motion*)
thoir mo shoraidh thar a' chuain carry my
greeting over/beyond the ocean, (*fig*) **tha sin
uile thar mo chomasan** all that's beyond my
capabilities, (*with numbers*) upon, **mìltean
thar mhìltean** thousands upon thousands; 3
in expr **thar a chèile** in a state of confusion,
also at loggerheads, **sgioblaich an rùm agad,
tha a h-uile càil thar a chèile** tidy your room,
everything's in a complete jumble/mess (*cf* **bun-
os-cionn**), **chuir mi thar a chèile iad** I set
them at each other's throats, **chaidh iad thar a
chèile** they fell out, *cf* **tro 2**
tharad (*emph form* **tharadsa**), **tharaibh** (*emph
form* **tharaibhse**), **tharainn** (*emph form*
tharainne), **tharam** (*emph form* **tharamsa**),
tharta (*emph form* **thartasan**) *prep prons, see*
thar
theab *v def,* 1 (*trad*) miss; 2 *now normally used
only in preterite tense, expressing the idea*
almost, nearly, **theab mi tuiteam** I almost fell,
theab iad mo sgriosadh they almost/nearly
ruined me
theagamh *see* **teagamh 2**
thèid *pt of irreg v* **rach** (*see tables p 501*)
their, theireadh, theirinn *pts of irreg v* **abair**
(*see tables p 493*)
thig *vi irreg* (*see tables p 503*), *pres part*
a' tighinn, 1 come, approach, **thig gam
fhaicinn!** come to/and see me! **cha tàinig
i còmhla rium** she didn't come with me, **a'
tighinn an taobh seo** coming this way; 2

arrive, come, get here, **cuin a thig iad?** when
will they come/get here? (*cf* **ruig**), **mus tig an
geamhradh** before winter comes, (*fig*) **thàinig
e a-steach orm nach robh iad ag èisteachd**
I realised/it occurred to me that they weren't
listening; **3** *in expr* **thig air**, *expr the onset of
an emotion, state etc*, **thàinig eagal/mulad/
acras orm** I grew afraid/sorrowful/hungry; **4**
in expr **thig do** suit, please, fit, be appropriate
for, **ciamar a tha an dreuchd ùr a' tighinn
dhut?** how's the new job suiting you?, how
do you like the new job? (*trad song*) **is tu as
fheàrr don tig deise** it is you whom a suit of
clothes best becomes/fits, *also* **thig ri** suit, **cha
tàinig an t-àite ri a shlàinte** the place didn't
suit his health, *cf* **còrd** *v*, **freagair 2**; **5** *misc
exprs* **thig beò** live, **ciamar a thig sinn beò
san àite seo?** how will we live in this place?,
thig suas/beò air live on, survive on, **cha tig
mi suas/beò air sin!** I can't live/manage/
survive on that!, **thàinig e (etc) bhuaithe** he
(etc) recovered/got over it/got better, **thàinig
orm sin a dhèanamh** I had to do that
thogras *see* **togair 2**
thoir & **tabhair**, *occas* **thabhair**, *vt irreg*
(*see tables p 504*), *pres part* **a' toirt** *occas*
a' tabhairt, **1** give (**do** to), **thug i tiodhlac
dhuinn** she gave us a present, **thoir
comhairle** give advice, **thoir dhomh do
làmh** give me your hand, **thoir an aire** pay (*lit*
give) attention, *also* take care, **thoir oidhirp**
make an attempt (**air** at), **thoir tarraing air
rudeigin** mention, touch on, allude or refer to
something (*cf* **iomradh 1**); **2 thoir seachad**
give, give away, present, deliver, hand over **bha
iad a' toirt seachad airgid air an t-sràid
an-diugh** they were giving away money in the
street today, **bheir i seachad òraid** she'll
give/deliver a speech/talk (*cf* **gabh 3**), **thoir
seachad an gunna** hand over the gun; **3** take,
bring, **thoir air falbh** take away, (*persons*)
abduct, (*song*) **thoir am fios seo thun a'
bhàird** take this news/message to the poet,
(*song*) **thoir a-nall Ailean thugam** bring Alan
over to me, **bheir mi sgrìob do Ghlaschu**
I'll take a trip to Glasgow, **a' toirt sùil air a'
phàipear-naidheachd** taking/having a look at
the paper, **thoir gu buil** bring to a conclusion,
achieve, **thoir am bith** bring into being/
existence, **thoir do chasan leat!** take yourself
off!, clear off! **thug iad na buinn asta** they
took to their heels, **thoir an t-siteag ort!** get
out! **thug i Ameireagaidh oirre** she took
herself off/off she went to America; **4** *in expr*
thoir air make, force, **thug i orm falbh** she

made me leave, **bheir e orm a dhèanamh
aig a' cheann thall** he'll force me to do it
eventually, *cf* **co-èignich**
thu, *emph* **thusa**, *pers pron* you (*sing & fam
- for note on use of* **thu** & **sibh**, *see* **sibh**);
Note: **tu** (*as opposed to* **thu**) *tends to be used
after all parts of the verb* **is** (**is tu, cha tu,
nach tu?, an tu?, bu tu** *etc*). *The form* **tu**
is also used when it is the <u>subject</u> *of a verb in
the conditional* (*eg* **bhiodh tu** you would be)
or in the relative future (*eg* **'s ann an sin a
bhitheas tu** it's there that you'll be); *contrast* **is
esan a bhuaileadh/bhuaileas thu** it's he who
would/will strike you, *where* **thu** *is the* <u>object</u> *of
the verb*
thubhairt *pt of irreg v* **abair** (*see tables p 493*)
**thuca, thugad, thugaibh, thugainn, thugam,
thuice, thuige**, *prep prons* (*see* **gu²** *prep*)
thug, thugadh, *pts of irreg v* **thoir** (*see tables
p 504*)
thuirt *pt of irreg v* **abair** (*see tables p 493*)
thun *see* **gu²** *prep*
tì *see* **teatha**
tiamhaidh *adj* melancholy, plaintive, poignant,
pulling at the heartstrings, (*song*) **'s tiamhaidh
buan dha thar nan stuaghan seinn nam
maighdeannan san àirigh** melancholy and
enduring for him, beyond the waves, is the
singing of the maidens in the sheiling
tibhre, tibhre, tibhrean *nm* a dimple
tìde, tìde, tìdean *nf* **1** time, **tha an tìde a' dol
seachad** (the) time's going by/passing, **sgrìobh
Murchadh thugainn, agus bha a thìde
aige!** Murdo wrote to us, and about time too!
bidh uisge ann fad na tìde it rains all the
time, **ri tìde** in time, in due course, eventually,
an ceann uair a (*for de*) **thìde** after an hour,
in an hour's time, *cf* **ùine 1**; **2** weather (*for more
usu* **sìde**), *cf* **aimsir**; **3** *usu with art* **an tìde**
(*also* **an tìde-mhara**) the tide, **tha an tìde
(-mhara) nar n-aghaidh** the tide's against us,
cf **seòl-mara** (*see* **muir**)
tidsear, tidseir, tidsearan *nm* a teacher, *cf*
neach-teagaisg (*see* **teagasg**)
tig, tigeadh, tiginn, *pts of irreg v* **thig** (*see
tables p 503*)
tigead, tigeid, tigeadan *nf, also* **tigeard,
tigeaird, tigeardan** *nf &* **tiogaid, tiogaid,
tiogaidean** *nf*, a ticket, *cf* **bileag 4**
tigh *see* **taigh**
tighead *see* **tiughad**
tighearna, tighearna, tighearnan *nm* **1** (*hist*)
a lord (*ie ruler*), **Tighearna nan Eilean**
Lord of the Isles; **2** a landowner, a laird, *cf*

uachdaran 2; 3 (*relig*) an Tighearna the Lord; 4 *excl* a Thighearna! (O) Lord!

tighinn *pt of irreg v* thig (*see tables p 503*)

Tìleach, *gen & pl* Tìlich *nm* an Icelander, someone from Iceland (Innis Tìle *f*), *also as adj* Tìleach Icelandic

tilg *vt, pres part* a' tilgeadh & a' tilgeil, 1 throw, fling, toss, cast (air at), na tilg clachan! don't throw stones! tilg air falbh throw away, thilg i searrach she cast/gave birth to a foal, *cf* caith 4, sad; 2 accuse of, reproach with, thilg iad orm nach robh mi dìcheallach they accused me of/reproached me with not being conscientious; 3 throw up, vomit, sick up, thilg am balach a dhìnnear the boy threw up his dinner, *cf* dìobhair, sgeith; 4 fire, shoot (*a firearm*), *cf* loisg 2

tilgeadh, tilgidh, tilgidhean *nm* 1 (*the act of*) throwing, accusing etc (*see senses of* tilg *v*); 2 a throw

till, *formerly also* pill, *vi, pres part* a' tilleadh & *formerly* a' pilleadh, return, come or go back, (*trad song*) cha till MacCruimein MacCrimmon will never return, a' tilleadh dhachaigh going back/returning home

tilleadh, *gen* tillidh *nm* returning, a return, turas-tillidh *m* a return journey

tìm, tìme, tìmean *nf* (*the abstr phenomenon*) time, (*poem*) Tha tìm, am fiadh, an coille Hallaig (Somhairle MacGill-Eain) Time, the deer, is in the wood of Hallaig, *cf more usu* (*for time as it is lived*) àm, tìde 1

timcheall 1 *adv* round, around, bha dealbh na teilidh a' dol timcheall, timcheall the picture on the telly was going round and round, cuir *v* timcheall na briosgaidean pass/send round the biscuits, *cf* cuairt 4; 2 *as prep* timcheall (*with gen*) round, around, thèid sinn timcheall an locha we'll go round the loch, tha luchd-reic a' dol timcheall a' bhaile there are salesmen going round the town, *cf* cuairt 5; 3 *as prep* timcheall air round, around, about, bha craobhan timcheall orm there were trees around me, a bheil bùithtean timcheall air an seo? are there any shops around/about here? thog iad taighean timcheall air a' ghàrradh aige they built houses around his garden, bidh timcheall air deichnear ann there'll be around/about ten people there, *cf* cuairt 5; 4 *as prep* mu thimcheall about, concerning (*with gen*), tha iad ag ràdh rudan oillteil mum thimcheall/mu timcheall they're saying dreadful/shocking things about me/her, *cf more usu* mu 3

timcheallan, *gen & pl* timcheallain *nm* (*at road junction, & in playpark etc*) a roundabout

tinn *adj* ill, sick, unwell, ailing, *cf* bochd 3, euslainteach *adj*

tinne, *gen* tinne, *pl* tinnean & tinneachan *nm* a link (*in chain*)

tinneas, tinneis, tinneasan *nm* illness, an illness, disease, a disease, sickness, tinneas-mara seasickness, tinneas cridhe heart disease, tinneas an t-siùcair diabetes, *cf* euslaint(e), galar, gearan 3

tiodhlac, tiodhlaic, tiodhlacan *nm* a gift, a present, a donation, *cf* tabhartas

tiodhlacadh, tiodhlacaidh, tiodhlacadhan *nm* 1 (*the act of*) burying, giving etc (*see senses of* tiodhlaic *v*); 2 burial, a burial, a funeral, *cf* adhlacadh 2, tòrradh

tiodhlaic *vt, pres part* a' tiodhlacadh, 1 (*of people*) bury, inter, *cf* adhlaic; 2 give as a present, donate, gift, *cf more usu* thoir 1 & 2

tiogaid *see* tigead

tiomnadh, tiomnaidh, tiomnaidhean *nm* 1 a will, a testament; 2 the act of bequeathing, a bequest, *cf* dìleab; 3 (*Bibl*) an Seann Tiomnadh the Old Testament, an Tiomnadh Nuadh the New Testament

tiomnaich *vt, pres part* a' tiomnachadh, bequeathe, leave in one's will (do to)

tiompan, *gen* tiompain, *pl* tiompain & tiompanan *nm* a cymbal

tionail *vti, pres part* a' tional, 1 (*vi*) (*esp of people*) assemble, come together, gather, congregate, collect, meet, *cf* cruinnich 1, thig còmhla (*see* còmhla *adv* 1); 2 (*vt*) (*esp of livestock*) gather, *cf* cruinnich 3, tru(i)s 3

tional, tionail, tionalan *nm* 1 (*the act of*) assembling, gathering, collecting etc (*see senses of* tionail *v*); 2 assembly, an assembly, collection, a collection, a gathering, a rally, *cf* cruinneachadh 2

tionalach *adj* cumulative

tionndadh, tionndaidh, tionndaidhean *nm* 1 (*the act of*) turning (*see senses of* tionndaidh *v*); 2 a turn (*ie a deviation or revolution*)

tionndaidh *vti, pres part* a' tionndadh, 1 (*vi*) turn (*phys & fig*), thionndaidh e chun an taoibh a thàinig e he turned towards the way/direction he had come, cò ris a thionndaidheadh e? who(m) could he turn to? tha an tìde-mhara a' tionndadh the tide's turning; 2 (*vt*) turn, cause to revolve or change orientation, cha do thionndaidh i a ceann she didn't turn her head, tionndaidh a' chuibhle(-stiùiridh) turn the steering wheel, tionndaidh an sgàthan chun a' bhalla turn the mirror to the wall; **3** (*vti*) turn (**gu** to) (*ie convert or become*), **thionndaidh an luaidhe gu òr** the lead turned to gold

tionnsgail & **tionnsgain** *vt, pres part* **a' tionnsgal** & **a' tionnsgain** & **a' tionnsgnadh**, contrive, devise, invent, *cf more usu* **innlich**

tionnsgal, tionnsgail, tionnsgalan *nm* **1** (*the act of*) contriving etc (*see senses of* **tionnsgail** *v*); **2** ingenuity, inventiveness, invention, an invention, a contraption, *cf more usu* **innleachd 1**

tionnsgalach *adj* **1** inventive, *cf* **innleachdach 1**; **2** industrial, *cf* **gnìomhachail**

tionnsgalair, tionnsgalair, tionnsgalairean *nm* an inventor

tioraidh! (*fam*) *excl on parting*, cheerio!, *cf more formal* **beannachd 4, soraidh 1**

tioram *adj* **1** dry, **seo agad tubhailte thioram** here's a dry towel, **bha an loch tioram** the loch was dry; **2** dry, thirsty, *cf* **ìotmhor, tartmhor**; **3** (*climate, landscape*) dry, arid

tiormachadh, *gen* **tiormachaidh** *nm* (*the act of*) drying, drying up

tiormachd *nf invar* **1** dryness; **2** drought, a drought, *cf less extreme* **turadh**

tiormadair, tiormadair, tiormadairean *nm* a dryer

tiormaich *vti, pres part* **a' tiormachadh**, dry, dry up, **chan eil na soithichean air an tiormachadh** the dishes haven't been dried

tiota, tiota, tiotaidhean *nm, also* **tiotan**, *gen* & *pl* **tiotain** *nm*, **1** (*clock time*) a second, *cf* **diog**; **2** an instant, a moment, a short while, a tick, a 'jiffy', *cf* **mòmaid, priobadh 2**, & *longer* **greis(eag), tacan, treis**

tiotag, tiotaig, tiotagan *nf, dimin of* **tiota**

tiotal, tiotail, tiotalan *nm* **1** a title (*of book etc*); **2** (*TV etc*) **fo-thiotalan** subtitles; **3** (*rank etc*) a title

tìr, tìre, tìrean *nf* **1** land (*as opposed to sea*), terra firma, **muir is tìr** sea and land, **tha iad a' tighinn gu tìr** they're coming ashore, (*song*) **'s truagh nach do dh'fhuirich mi tioram air tìr** it's a pity I didn't stay dry on terra firma, **tìr-mòr** a mainland, (*not usu with art*) **air tìr-mòr** on the mainland; **2** a land, a country, **tìrean cèin** distant/foreign lands, **tha mi sona san tìr seo** I'm happy/content in this country, **tìr-eòlas** geography (*cf* **cruinn-eòlas**), *cf* **dùthaich 1**; **3** an area, a region, a district, **ciamar a thig sinn beò san tìr seo?** how will we live/make a living in this area/part of the world, (*also, here*) . . . in this landscape/terrain), *cf more usu* **ceàrn, dùthaich 2, sgìre 1**; **4** land, ground, *cf more usu* **fearann, talamh 3**

Tirt, Tirteach *see* **Hiort, Hiortach**

tiugainn *imper* come along, come on ('with me' *understood*), let us go, *cf* **thalla, trobhad**

tiugh, *comp* **(n)as** (*etc*) **tighe**, *adj* **1** (*phys*) thick, dense, *cf* **dlùth 2, dòmhail 2**; **2** (*fam*) (*mentally*) thick, dense, slow-witted

tiughad, *gen* **tiughaid** *nm* & **tighead**, *gen* **tigheid** *nm* density, denseness, thickness

tlachd *nf invar* **1** pleasure, enjoyment, *cf* **toileachadh 2**; **2** affection, attachment, liking, (*trad*) **is beag mo thlachd dheth** I have little affection/liking for him, *cf* **bàidh 1, dèidh 2, spèis**

tlachdmhor *adj* **1** pleasant, pleasing, *cf* **taitneach**; **2** enjoyable, pleasurable; **3** (*of people*) attractive, likeable

tnù(th), *gen* **tnùtha** *nm* envy, jealousy; malice, *cf more usu* **eud 1, farmad**

tobar, *gen* **tobair** (*m*) & **tobrach** (*f*), *pl* **tobraichean** *nmf* **1** a spring, a (natural) well, **tobar fìor-uisge** a spring of pure water, *cf* **fuaran**; **2** a (dug) well (*unlike* **fuaran**)

tobhta, tobhta, tobhtaichean *nmf* a ruin (*of building*), (*song*) **an tobht' aig Anndra 's e làn de dh'fheanntaig** (Màiri Mhòr) the ruins of Andrew's house, overrun with nettles, *cf* **làrach 1**

tobhta, *gen* **tobhta**, *pl* **tobhtan** & **tobhtachan** *nmf* (*of boat*) a thwart

tocasaid & **togsaid**, *gen* **tocasaid**, *pl* **tocasaidean** *nf* a large barrel; (*orig*) a hogshead, *cf* **baraille**

tòchd *nm invar* a stink, a bad or foul smell

tochradh, tochraidh, tochraidhean *nm* a dowry, (*Sc*) a tocher

todha, todha, todhaichean *nm* (*tool*) a hoe, **bha obair-thodha ri dèanamh** there was hoeing to be done, *cf* **sgrìoban**

todhaig *vti, pres part* **a' todhaigeadh**, hoe

todhair *vt, pres part* **a' todhar**, **1** manure (*land*), *cf* **leasaich 3, mathaich**; **2** bleach, *cf* **gealaich 2**

todhar, *gen* **todhair** *nm* manure, dung (*to put on fields etc*), *cf* **inneir, mathachadh**

tog *vt, pres part* **a' togail**, **1** raise, lift, pick up, hoist, **tog do cheann** lift/raise your head, **togaibh na siùil** hoist the sails, **thog sin mo chridhe** that raised my spirits (*lit* heart), (*song*) **hì-ri-o-rì togaidh sinn fonn** we will sing/ strike up (*lit* raise) a song; **2** build, **thog e taigh dha fhèin** he built a house for himself, **taigh air a dheagh thogail** a well built house; **3** (*of people*) raise, bring up, rear, **thogadh mi ann an Cola** I was brought up/I grew up in Coll, (*of livestock etc*) raise, rear, breed, *cf* **àraich**; **4**

stir, rouse, *in expr* **tog ort!** rouse yourself!, stir
your stumps!, get a move on!, *also* be off with
you!; **5** pick up, acquire, **'s ann san Eilean
Sgitheanach a thog mi mo chuid Gàidhlig**
I picked up/acquired/learned my Gaelic in Skye,
cf **ionnsaich 1**

togail, *gen* **togalach** *nf* (*the act of*) raising,
building, rousing etc (*see senses of* **tog** *v*)

togair *vti*, *pres part* **a' togradh**, **1** wish for,
desire, covet, *cf more usu* **miannaich 1**; **2** *now
usu in rel fut tense*, **thèid sinn air làithean-
saora, ma thogras tu** we'll go on holiday, if
you like/want, **dìreach mar a thogras sibh**
just as you like, *cf* **iarr 1**

togalach, **togalaich**, **togalaichean** *nm* a
building

togradh, **tograidh**, **tograidhean** *nm* **1** (*the act
of*) wishing for etc (*see senses of* **togair** *v*); **2** a
wish, a desire, an inclination

togsaid *see* **tocasaid**

toibheum, **toibheim**, **toibheuman** *nm*
blasphemy, a blasphemous utterance

toigh *adj* **1** (*trad*) pleasing, agreeable, dear, *cf
more usu* **taitneach**; **2** *now in expr* **is toigh
leam** (*etc*) I (*etc*) like, find pleasing, **an toigh
leat càise? cha toil** (*for* **cha toigh leam**)! do
you like cheese? no! **nach toigh leat a bhith a'
snàmh?** is toil don't you like to swim? yes, *cf*
caomh 3, **còrd**

toil, **toile**, **toilean** *nf* **1** will, **toil Dhè** God's will,
deagh-thoil goodwill, (*prov*) **far am bi toil,
bidh gnìomh** where there's a will there's a way,
cf **miann 1**, **rùn 3**; **2** *also in expr* **mas e do
thoil/ur toil e!** please! (*lit* if it is your will)

toileach *adj* **1** willing, **tha mi toileach sin
a dhèanamh dhut** I'm willing/happy/glad
to do that for you, *cf* **deònach**; **2** (*also* **saor-
thoileach**) voluntary; **3** content, contented,
glad, *cf* **riaraichte**, **sona**, *& stronger* **toilichte**

toileachadh, *gen* **toileachaidh** *nm* **1** (*the act
of*) pleasing etc (*see senses of* **toilich** *v*); **2**
satisfaction, gratification

toileachas, *gen* **toileachais** *nm* content,
contentment, gladness

toileachas-inntinn *see* **toil-inntinn**

toilich *vt*, *pres part* **a' toileachadh**, please,
content, satisfy, *cf* **riaraich 1**

toilichte *adj* happy, well pleased or satisfied, *cf
usu weaker* **sona**

toil-inntinn, **toil-inntinne**, **toil-inntinnean**
nf **1** (*also, in this sense,* **toileachas-inntinn**,
gen **toileachas-inntinne** *nm*) (mental)
pleasure, contentment, or gladness; **2**
something that causes the foregoing, a source of
contentment etc; **3** peace of mind

toill *vt*, *pres part* **a' toilltinn**, deserve, merit

toillteanach *adj* worthy, deserving (**air** of),
(*poem*) **toillteanach air pòg** deserving (of) a
kiss, *cf more usu* **airidh**

tòimhseachan, *gen & pl* **tòimhseachain** *nm* **1**
a puzzle, a riddle, a brainteaser, a conundrum,
an enigma, **tòimhseachan-tarsainn** a
crossword puzzle

toinisg, *gen* **toinisge** *nf* sense, common sense,
'gumption', *cf* **ciall 1**, **tuigse 1**

toinisgeil *adj* **1** sensible, having common sense
and/or sound judgement or understanding, *cf*
ciallach, **tuigseach 1**; **2** mentally bright or
smart, intelligent, *cf* **geurchuiseach**

toinn *vti*, *pres part* **a' toinneadh**, twist, wind,
twine, wreathe, *cf* **snìomh 2**

tòir, *gen* **tòrach** *&* **tòire**, *pl* **tòirichean** *&*
tòirean *nf* **1** a pursuit, a chase, *cf* **ruaig 1**; **2**
now usu in expr **an tòir air** in pursuit of, in
search of, after, (*song*) **Dòmhnall dubh an
Dòmhnallaich a-nochd an tòir air Mòraig**
MacDonald's black-haired Donald tonight in
pursuit of/after Morag, **chaidh e dhan bhaile
an tòir air càr ùr** he went to the town after/
looking for a new car, *cf* **lorg** *v* **1**, **sir**

toir, **toiream**, **toireamaid**, **toiribh**, **toirt** *pts of
irreg v* **thoir** (*see tables p 504*)

toirm, **toirme**, **toirmean** *nf* noise, a noise, a
din, a hubbub, (*song*) **is toirm mum chluais**
and a din about my ear(s), *cf* **faram**, **othail**

toirmeasg, *gen* **toirmisg** *nm* **1** (*the act of*)
forbidding, prohibiting (*see senses of* **toirmisg**
v); **2** prohibition, a prohibition, a ban

toirmeasgach *adj* prohibitive, apt to prohibit or
forbid

toirmisg *vt*, *pres part* **a' toirmeasg**, forbid,
prohibit, ban

toirt *nf invar* (*the act of*) giving, taking, bringing
etc (*see senses of* **thoir** *v*)

toiseach, **toisich**, **toisichean** *nm* **1** (*in time*) a
start, a beginning, **toiseach an t-samhraidh**
the start/beginning of summer, *esp in expr* **an
toiseach** *adv* first, at first, **thàinig Flòraidh
an toiseach** Flora came first/was first to arrive,
cha bu toigh leam e an toiseach I didn't like
him at first, (*emph*) **an toiseach tòiseachaidh**
in the very beginning, originally; **2** (*in space*)
the front part of anything, a prow or bow (*of
boat*), **an comhair a thoisich** frontwards,
front end first, *also* head-on, **ann an toiseach
na làraidh** in the front (*ie cab*) of the lorry,
cas-toisich a foreleg/front leg, **toiseach an
airm** the van(guard) of the army; **3** *also in
expr* **air thoiseach air** *prep* ahead of, **bha e
a' coiseachd roimhe, fada air thoiseach**

oirnn he was walking along, far ahead/a long way in front of us, **air thoiseach air na dùthchannan eile** ahead of the other countries

tòiseachadh, *gen* **tòiseachaidh** *nm* 1 (*the act of*) beginning, starting etc (*see senses of* **tòisich** *v*), (*saying*) **is e obair latha tòiseachadh** getting started is a day's work; 2 a beginning, a start, **tòiseachadh ùr** a fresh start, *cf* **toiseach** 1

tòisich *vti, pres part* **a' tòiseachadh**, start, commence, begin, **tòisich às ùr** start afresh, make a fresh start, **tòisichidh sinn air an treabhadh a-màireach** we'll make a start at the ploughing tomorrow, **tòisich a' seinn** start singing, (*more trad*) **tòisich air/ri seinn** start to sing, *cf* **teann** *v* 3

toit, **toite**, **toitean** *nf* 1 steam, (*prov*) **cha tig às a' phoit ach an toit a bhios innte** you can't get out of the pot more steam than is in it; 2 smoke; *cf* **smùid** *n* 1 & 2

toitean, **toitein**, **toiteanan** *nm* a cigarette

toll, *gen & pl* **tuill** *nm* 1 a hole, a bore; 2 a pit, a hollow, a cavity; 3 (*vulg*) an anus, an arsehole, **'s e an t-àite seo toll an t-saoghail!** this place is the arsehole of the world!

toll *vti, pres part* **a' tolladh**, bore, hole, dig or make a hole, drill, perforate, pierce, puncture, **chaidh am bàta a tholladh** the boat was holed

tolladh, *gen* **tollaidh** *nm* (*the act of*) boring, perforating etc (*see senses of* **toll** *v*), **clàr-tollaidh** *m* a drilling platform

tolltach *adj* full of holes

toll-tòine, *gen pl* **tuill-tòine** *nm* (*vulg*) an arsehole, *cf* **toll** *nm* 3

tolman, **tolmain**, **tolmanan** *nm* (*topog*) a small knowe, knoll or mound

tom, **tuim**, **tomannan** *nm* 1 (*topog*) a small hill or hillock (*usu rounded*); 2 *now mainly in placenames*, a thicket, a bush; **Tom Beithe** Birch Thicket (*or* birch hillock)

tomadach & **tomaltach** *adj* 1 large, sizeable, bulky, ample; 2 (*of person*) big, brawny, burly, 'strapping'

tombaca, **tombaca**, **tombacan** *nm* tobacco

tomhais *vt, pres part* **a' tomhas**, 1 measure (*esp dimensions, also speed, weight*); 2 (*land etc*) survey; 3 calculate, compute (*distance, speed etc*); 4 guess, **tomhais cia mheud a th' ann** guess how many there are

tomhas, *gen* **tomhais**, *pl* **tòimhsean** & **tomhasan** *nm* 1 (*the act of*) measuring, surveying, guessing etc (*see senses of* **tomhais** *v*), **teip-thomhais** *f* a measuring tape, **neach-tomhais** *m* a surveyor; 2 measurement, a

measurement, a dimension, a size, **gabh** *v* **tomhasan** take measurements; 3 a measure (*ie measuring device*), a gauge, **tomhas-teas** a thermometer; 4 (*of land etc*) a survey; 5 calculation, a calculation, computation, a computation, **aig astar gun tomhas** at an incalculable/immeasurable speed; 6 a guess, *cf* **tuaiream**

tòn, **tòine**, **tònan** *nf* 1 an anus, a rectum, *cf* (*vulg*) **toll** *n* 3, **toll-tòine**; 2 (*fam*) an arse, a bum, a bottom, a backside, (*humorous car sticker*) **na pòg mo thòn** don't kiss my bum (*ie* keep your distance), *cf* **màs** 2; 3 the back part or section of something, **tòn an taighe/an talla** the back of the house/the hall, *cf more usu* **cùl** 2

tonn, *gen* **tuinn(e)**, *pl* **tuinn** & **tonnan** *nmf* 1 (*in sea*) a wave, **cumhachd tuinne** *m* wave power, *cf* **stuadh** 1; 2 (*physics etc*) a wave, **fuaim-thonn** a sound wave, **tonn-teasa** (*also* **teas-tonn** *m*) a heat wave

tonna & **tunna**, *gen* **tonna/tunna**, *pl* **tonnachan/tunnachan** *nm* a ton, a tonne

topag, **topaig**, **topagan** *nf* a (sky)lark, *cf more usu* **uiseag**

torach *adj* 1 (*land, plants etc*) fruitful, productive, high-yielding, fertile, (*lit & fig*) bearing fruit; 2 (*also, in this sense*, **torrach**) pregnant, with young (*cf* **trom** 4), fecund, fertilised, **ugh torrach** a fertilised egg, (*prov*) **ge b' e bhios saor, cha dèan gaoth torrach** whoever may be innocent/blameless, it's not the wind that causes pregnancy

torachadh, *gen* **torachaidh** *nm* 1 (*the act of*) fertilising etc (*see senses of* **toraich** *v*); 2 fertilisation

torachas, *gen* **torachais** *nm* fertility

toradh, **toraidh**, **toraidhean** *nm* 1 (*of land, plants etc*) produce, fruit(s), (*fin etc*) yield, **toradh na talmhainn** the produce/fruit(s) of the earth; 2 (*of action etc*) a result, a consequence, an effect, **toradh do dhol-a-mach** the consequence(s) of your behaviour, **toradh deuchainn** an exam result, **mar thoradh air sin** as a result of that, *cf* **buaidh** 4, **buil** 1, **èifeachd**; 3 (*industry etc*) output

toraich *vt, pres part* **a' torachadh**, (*gynaecology etc*) fertilise, make fertile, cause to conceive

Tòraidh, **Tòraidh**, **Tòraidhean** *nm* (*pol*) a Tory, a Conservative

Tòraidheach *adj* (*pol*) Tory (*for pol parties see* **pàrtaidh** 1)

torc, *gen & pl* **tuirc** *nm* a boar, **torc allaidh/fiadhaich** a wild boar, *cf* **cràin**, **cullach**, **muc**

torman, tormain, tormanan *nm* **1** a
continuous (*usu low*) sound, murmuring, a
murmur, droning, humming, a hum, **torman
an uillt** the murmur(ing) of the stream, *cf*
crònan 1 & *less usu* **monmhar**; **2** (*occas
louder*) rumbling, a rumble

tòrr, torra, torran *nm* **1** a heap, a mound, **tòrr
airgid** a heap of money/silver, **tòrr gainmhich**
a heap/mound of sand, *cf* **cruach** *n* **1**, **dùn 1**; **2**
(*fam*) lots, heaps, loads, many, much, (*with gen*)
tha tòrr dhaoine den bheachd sin lots of
people are of that opinion, *cf* **grunn 2**, **mòran
1**; **3** (*topog*) a hill (*esp conical or mound-
shaped*)

torrach *see* **torach 2**

tòrradh, tòrraidh, tòrraidhean *nm* a funeral,
a burial, *cf* **adhlacadh 2, tiodhlacadh 2**

tosd *nm invar* **1** silence, the state of being silent
or quiet, (*esp of persons*) **bha a' chlann nan
tosd** the children were silent, *also as command*
tosd! silence!; **2** (*music*) a rest

tosdach *adj* silent, quiet, **dh'fhalbh iad gu
tosdach** they left quietly/silently, *cf* **sàmhach 1**

tosgaid *same as* **tocasaid**

tosgaire, tosgaire, tosgairean *nm* an
ambassador, an envoy

**tosgaireachd, toisgaireachd,
tosgaireachdan** *nf* an embassy

tràchdas, *gen* & *pl* **tràchdais** *nm* a thesis, a
dissertation

tractar, tractair, tractaran *nm* a tractor

trafaig, *gen* **trafaige** *nf* (*road etc*) traffic

tràghadh, *gen* **tràghaidh** *nm* **1** (*the act of*)
draining, emptying, subsiding, ebbing etc (*see
senses of* **tràigh** *v*); **2** (*of engine*) exhaust, **pìob
thràghaidh** an exhaust pipe

tràigh, *gen* **tràgha(d)** & **tràighe**, *pl* **tràighean**
nf **1** a shore, a beach (*esp tidal*), a strand,
cf **cladach**; **2** a tide (*insofar as it covers* &
uncovers a beach), **tha tràigh mhòr ann
an-diugh** there's a very low tide today, *cf* **seòl-
mara** (*see* **muir**)

tràigh *vti, pres part* **a' tràghadh**, *also* **traogh**
vti, pres part **a' traoghadh**, *esp of liquids*, **1**
drain, empty, exhaust (*container etc*); **2** (*vi*)
subside, settle, sink, **thraogh na tuiltean** the
floods subsided, *cf* **sìolaidh 2**; **3** (*vi*) (*of sea,
tide*) ebb, subside

tràill, tràill(e), tràillean *nmf* **1** a slave; **2**
a drudge; **3** an addict, **tha e na thràill do
cheàrrachas/dhrogaichean** he's addicted to
gambling/drugs, *cf* **urra 3**

tràilleachadh, *gen* **tràilleachaidh** *nm* (*the act
of*) enslaving

tràilleachd *nf invar* & **tràillealachd** *nf invar* **1**
slavery, enslavement; **2** drudgery; **3** addiction

tràillich *vt, pres part* **a' tràilleachadh**, enslave

traisg *vi, pres part* **a' trasg(adh)**, fast

tràlair, tràlair, tràlairean *nm* a (fishing)
trawler

trang *adj* busy, (*Sc*) thrang, **trang ris an
iasgach** busy at/with the fishing, *cf* **dripeil,
sàs 2**

trannsa, trannsa, trannsaichean *nf* a
corridor, a passage (*in building*)

traogh *see* **tràigh** *v*

trasg, traisg, trasgan *nf* & **trasgadh,
trasgaidh, trasgaidhean** *nm* fasting, a fast,
latha-traisg *m* a fast day, **tha iad nan trasg**
they are fasting (*cf* **traisg** *v*)

trastanach *adj* diagonal

tràth *adj* & (*esp*) *adv* **1** early (*ie at an early
stage*), **tràth feasgar** early in the afternoon,
tràth sa mhadainn early in the morning, *cf*
moch; **2** early, in good time, soon (*ie before
time, premature*), **tràth airson na coinneimh**
early for the meeting, **ro thràth airson
ùbhlan abaich** too early/soon for ripe apples; **3**
in expr **mu thràth** (*also found as* **mar a tha** &
mar-thà) *adv* already, **leugh mi e mu thràth**
I've read it already, **mar a thubhairt mi mu
thràth** as I have said already, *cf* **a-cheana**

tràth, *gen* **tràith** & **tràtha**, *pl* **tràthan** *nm* **1**
a time, a season, a period (*incl school period*),
(*trad*) **tràth air tàileasg** a time/while spent
at backgammon, *esp an appointed, right or
habitual time*, **tràth-bìdh** a mealtime, **tràth-
ùrnaigh** prayer time, **facal na thràth** a word
in season/at the right time, *cf more usu* **àm,
greis, ràith 2**; **2** (*gram*) a tense, **an tràth
caithte** the past tense

tràthach, *gen* **tràthaich** *nm* hay, *cf more usu*
feur 2

treabh *vt, pres part* **a' treabhadh**, plough

treal(l)aich, treal(l)aich, treal(l)aichean
nf **1** jumble, lumber, assorted rubbish, trash
or junk, *cf* **truileis** & (*more worthless*)
sgudal 1; **2** (*assorted possessions etc*)
odds and ends, bits and pieces, gear, stuff,
sgioblaich do threallaich tidy your stuff; **3**
in pl **treal(l)aichean** one's luggage, baggage,
belongings

trèan *vti, pres part* **a' trèanadh**, **1** (*vt*) (*ed etc*)
train, *cf* **ionnsaich 3, oileanaich**; **2** (*vti*)
(*sport*) train

trèan(a), trèana, trèanaichean *nf* a (railway,
tube etc) train, **chaill mi an trèana** I missed
the train, **luath-thrèana** an express

treas *num adj* third, **an treas là den mhìos** the third of the month, **treas ... deug** thirteenth

trèig *vt, pres part* **a' trèigsinn**, abandon, desert, forsake, leave, quit, relinquish, **thrèig e a theaghlach** he deserted/abandoned his family, **thrèig i a dreuchd** she quit/relinquished her post, **trèigibh creideamh ur sinnsirean** forsake the faith of your forefathers, **thrèig na daoine an t-eilean** the people deserted/ abandoned the island, *cf* **dìobair, fàg**

trèigsinn *nm invar* **1** (*the act of*) abandoning, deserting etc (*see senses of* **trèig** *v*); **2** abandonment, desertion

treis, treise, treisean *nf* a while, a time, *cf* **greis**

treiseag, treiseig, treiseagan *nf* (*dimin of* **treis**), a short while *or* time, (*Sc*) a whilie, *cf* **greiseag**

treòrachadh, *gen* **treòrachaidh** *nm* **1** (*the act of*) guiding, directing, conducting, leading (*see senses of* **treòraich** *v*), **neach-treòrachaidh** *m* a (tourist *etc*) guide; **2** (*ed etc*) guidance, **tidsear-treòrachaidh** *m* a guidance teacher

treòraich *vt, pres part* **a' treòrachadh**, **1** guide, direct, conduct, **treòraich luchd-turais** *m* guide/conduct tourists, *cf* **seòl** *v* 3; **2** lead, **threòraich e a choitheanal gu Canada** he led his congregation to Canada, *cf* **stiùir** *v* 3

treubh, *gen* **trèibh** & **treubha**, *pl* **treubhan** *nf* a tribe

treud, *gen* **trèid** & **treuda**, *pl* **treudan** *nm* **1** (*animals*) a flock, a herd, *cf* **buar, greigh**; **2** (*of people*) a group, a band, *cf more usu* **buidheann 1, còmhlan**; **3** (*derog*) a gang, a crowd, (*song*) **mallachd . . . air Diùc Uilleam 's air a threud** a curse . . . on Duke William and on his gang, *cf* **gràisg, prabar**

treun, *comp* (**n**)**as** (*etc*) **treine, treise** & **treasa**, *adj* strong (*with overtones of bravery, endurance*), stout, **gaisgich threuna** stout heroes, (*poem*) **còmhdach an spioraid bu trèine** (Somhairle MacGill-Eain) garment of the bravest spirit, *cf* **calma, làidir 1**

treun *nf invar* **1** (*trad*) strength, the height of one's strength, *now usu in expr* **ann an treun a neirt** at the height of his/her powers/strength, in his/her prime

trì *num adj* three, **trì fichead** sixty, three score

triall *vti, pres part* **a' triall**, travel, make one's way, move about, journey, (*trad song*) **bha seo ort a' triall** this is what you had when on the move, (*song*) **nach fhaod mi triall do chladaichean** that I cannot travel/go along your shores, *cf* **imich 2, rach 1, siubhail 1**

trian *nm invar* a third, **chaill mi dà thrian de na shàbhail mi** I lost two-thirds of my savings

triath, triaith, triathan *nm* (*trad*) a lord, *cf now usu* **tighearna 1**

tric *adj, usu as adv* **1** often, frequent(ly), **cha tig i cho tric agus a chleachd (i)** she doesn't come as often as she used to, **is tric a rachadh sinn ann** we often used to go there, *cf* **minig**; **2** *in adv expr* **mar as trice** usually

tricead, *gen* **triceid** *nm* (*abstr*) frequency, (*elec*) a frequency

trì-cheàrnag, trì-cheàrnaig, trì-cheàrnagan *nf* a triangle

trìd 1 *prep* (*trad*) through (*cf* **tro**); **2** *now as prefix corres to Eng* trans-, *eg* **trìd-shoilleir** transparent

trì-deug *n & adj* thirteen

trioblaid, trioblaide, trioblaidean *nf* trouble (*ie misfortune, difficulties etc*), **thàinig trioblaid oirnn** trouble came upon us, **b' e call m' obrach toiseach ar trioblaidean** the loss of my job was the start of our troubles, *cf* **duilgheadas**

trìthead, trìtheid, trìtheadan *nm & num* thirty (*in alt numbering system*)

triubhas, triubhais, triubhasan *nm* a pair of trews or trousers, *cf* **briogais**

triùir *nmf invar* (*of people*) three, a threesome, (*with gen pl*) **triùir bhràithrean** three brothers, (*prov*) **bheir aon duine triùir bhàrr an rathaid** one man will lead three off the road

triuthach, *gen* **triuthaich** *nf*, *used with art*, **an triuthach** whooping cough

tro & **troimh** *prep*, through, *takes dat, & lenites following cons where possible*. (*The prep prons formed with* **tro** & **troimh**, *in the order first, second, third person singular, first, second, third person plural, and with the reflexive/ emphatic particles in brackets, are as follows*: **tromham(sa), tromhad(sa), troimhe(san), troimhpe(se), tromhainn(e), tromhaibh(se), tromhpa(san)**: through me, through you, (*fam*), *etc* **1** through, (*story collection*) **Dorcha tro Ghlainne** Through a Glass Darkly, **thàinig iad tron choille** they came through the wood, (*occas as prefix*) **tro-shlighe** *f* a thoroughfare; **2** *in expr* **troimh-a-chèile** (*of people*) at loggerheads, having fallen out (*cf* **thar 3**), *also* upset, agitated, (*of things, situations, places*) in confusion, in a mess, very untidy (*cf* **bun 2, bùrach**)

trobhad, *pl* **trobhadaibh** *imper of def verb*. **1** come, come here, come to me (*common in calling hens, pets etc*); **2** come along, come (along) with me, *cf* **tiugainn**

tròcair, tròcaire, tròcairean *nf* mercy, an act of mercy, **tròcairean Dhè** God's mercies, *cf* **iochd, truacantas, truas**

tròcaireach *adj* merciful, *cf* **iochdmhor, truacanta**

trod, *gen & pl* **troid** *nm* 1 (*the act of*) quarrelling, squabbling etc (*see senses of* **troid** *v*), **chan urrainn dhomh cadal air sgàth an troid** I can't sleep on account of their quarrelling; 2 a quarrel, a squabble, a row, **dh'èirich trod eatarra** a quarrel arose between them, *cf* **argamaid 3, tuasaid**

troich, troiche, troichean *nmf* a dwarf, *cf* **luchraban**

troid *vi, pres part* **a' trod**, quarrel, row, squabble, fight (*now usu verbally*), *cf* **sabaid** *v*

troigh, troighe, troighean *nf* 1 (*anat*) a foot, *cf* **more usu cas** *n*; 2 (*measure*) a foot, **dà throigh a dh'fhad** two feet long

troighean, troighein, troigheanan *nm* a pedal

troimh *prep, see* **tro**

troimhe (*emph form* **troimhesan**), troimhpe (*emph form* **troimhpese**) *prep prons, see* **tro**

trom *adj* 1 heavy, **parsailean troma** heavy parcels, **ceum trom** a heavy/ponderous step, (*fam*) **trom air an deoch** heavy on the booze; 2 weighty, serious, important, **cuspairean aotroma is troma** light/unimportant and serious/important matters, *cf* **cudromach 2**; 3 heavy (*in spirit*), depressed, dejected, melancholy, **le cridhe trom** with a heavy heart, *cf* **brònach; 4** pregnant, *cf* **torach 2; 5** (*typog*) bold

tromalach, *gen* tromalaich *nf* a preponderance, a majority, the greater part of something

trombaid, trombaide, trombaidean *nf* a trumpet

tromhad (*emph form* **tromhadsa**), tromhaibh (*emph form* **tromhaibhse**), tromhainn (*emph form* **tromhainne**), tromham (*emph form* **tromhamsa**), tromhpa (*emph form* **tromhpasan**) *prep prons, see* **tro**

trom-laighe, trom-laighe, trom-laighean *nmf* a nightmare, **mar neach a bhiodh fo throm-laighe** like a person in the grip of/having a nightmare

trosg, *gen & pl* truisg *nm* cod, a cod

trotan, *gen* trotain *nm* trotting, a trot, **dèan** *v* **trotan** trot

truacanta *adj* compassionate, pitying, humane, *cf* **iochdmhor, tròcaireach, daonnach**

truacantas, *gen* truacantais *nm* compassion, pity, humaneness, *cf* **iochd, truas, daonnachd**

truagh *adj* 1 poor (*ie unfortunate*), wretched, pitiable, piteous, pitiful, abject, **bochdainn**

thruagh wretched/abject poverty, (*trad*) **is truagh mo chor** wretched/piteous is my state/condition, *cf* **bochd 2; 2** sad, miserable, *cf* **brònach, muladach; 3** *with v* is, sad, a pity, a shame, **is truagh sin!** that's a pity/shame!, (*song*) **is truagh nach robh mis' ann an gleannan mo ghaoil** it is sad/a pity that I were not in my beloved little glen, *cf* **bochd 2, duilich 4**

truaghan, truaghain, truaghanan *nm* 1 a poor or wretched person, a (poor) wretch, **chaochail e aig a' cheann thall, an truaghan a bh' ann dheth** he died in the end, poor man that he was; 2 often as excl, expr pity etc, **a thruaghain!** poor man/fellow/craitur!

truaighe, truaighe, truaighean *nf* misery, woe, wretchedness, *esp in excls* **mo thruaighe!** woe is me!, (*trad*) **mo thruaighe sibh!** woe unto you!

truaill *vt, pres part* **a' truailleadh, 1** (*environment etc*) pollute, contaminate, *cf* **salaich 1 & 2; 2** (*relig, morals etc*) defile, profane; **3** (*persons*) corrupt, abuse, pervert, debauch, *cf* **claon 3, coirb**

truailleadh, *gen* truaillidh *nm* 1 (*the act of*) polluting, defiling, corrupting etc (*see senses of* **truaill** *v*); 2 pollution, corruption, defilement, contamination

truas, *gen* truais *nm* pity, compassion, **nach gabh thu truas dhìom?** won't you take pity on me?, **tha truas agam rium fhìn** I'm sorry for myself, *cf* **iochd, tròcair, truacantas**

truileis *nf invar* rubbish, junk, trash, mess, *cf stronger* **sgudal**

truimead, *gen* truimeid *nm* heaviness, the state of being heavy, (*esp emotionally*) **truimead mo chridhe** the heaviness of my heart

truinnsear, truinnseir, truinnsearan *nm* a (dinner etc) plate

tru(i)s *vt, pres part* **a' trusadh** & **a' truiseadh, 1** truss, bundle up or together; 2 (*of clothing*) tuck up, gather, roll up, **bha a còtaichean-bàna air an trusadh** her petticoats were tucked up/kilted, **thruis e a mhuilchinnean** he rolled up his sleeves; 3 gather, collect (*livestock*), **a' trusadh chaorach** gathering sheep, *cf* **cruinnich 3, tionail 2**

trusadh, *gen* trusaidh *nm* (*the act of*) bundling up, gathering etc (*see senses of* **tru(i)s** *v*)

trusgan, trusgain, trusganan *nm* 1 clothes, clothing, *cf more usu* **aodach 2; 2** a suit (*of clothes*), *cf* **culaidh 2, deise**

tu *see* **thu**

tuagh, tuaigh(e), tuaghan *nf* an axe, (*hist*) **tuagh-chatha** a battle-axe, a Lochaber axe

tuainealach *adj* dizzy, giddy

tuainealaich, *gen* **tuainealaiche** *nf* vertigo, (*lit & fig*) dizziness, giddiness, *cf* **luasgan 2**

tuaiream, tuaireim, tuaireaman *nf, &* **tuairmeas, tuairmeis, tuairmeasan** *nm,* guessing, a guess, conjecture, a conjecture, an estimate, speculation, **thoir** *v* **tuaiream air** take a guess at it, **air thuaiream** at random, *cf* **tomhas 6**

tuaireamach *adj* **1** random, arbitrary; **2** conjectural, speculative

tuairisgeul, tuairisgeil, tuairisgeulan *nm* a description (*of person or thing*), **tha tuairisgeul a' mhèirlich aig a' phoileas mu thràth** the police already have the thief's description

tuairmeas *see* **tuaiream**

tuar, tuair, tuaran *nm* (*at a given moment, not nec permanent*) complexion, hue or colour (*of features*), appearance, look, *cf* **dreach 1, fiamh 3, snuadh 2**

tuarastal & **tuarasdal**, *gen* **tuarastail**, *pl* **tuarastalan** *nm* a salary, a wage, wages, earnings; a stipend; a fee, *cf* **cosnadh 4, duais 1, pàigh** *n*

tuasaid, tuasaide, tuasaidean *nf* **1** (*verbal*) a quarrel, a squabble, a row, *cf* **argamaid 3, connsachadh 2, trod**; **2** (*more phys*) a scrap, a tussle, *cf usu more serious* **sabaid** *n*

tuath[1] *nf invar & adj* north, northern, **an àird(e) tuath** north (*ie the compass point*), **Uibhist a Tuath** North Uist, **a' fuireach/a' dol mu thuath** living in/going to the north, **oiteag on tuath** a breeze from the north, **an taobh tuath** the north, the north country, **tha Peairt tuath air Ceann Rois** Perth is north of Kinross

tuath[2], *gen* **tuatha** *nf* (*trad*) peasantry, tenantry, indigenous people of a district, (*song*) **sliochd na tuath bha gun uaill, gun ghò** (Màiri Mhòr) the native peasant stock who were without vanity, without guile

tuathal *adj* **1** anti-clockwise, *cf* **deiseil 4**; **2** contrary to the movement of the sun, (*Sc*) widdershins, *cf* **deiseil 5**; **3** awry, wrong, in a somewhat untidy or confused state, (*Sc*) agley

tuathanach, *gen & pl* **tuathanaich** *nm* a farmer

tuathanachas, *gen* **tuathanachais** *nm* (*esp the practice of*) farming, agriculture, *cf* **àiteachd**

tuathanas, tuathanais, tuathanasan *nm* a farm

tubaist, tubaiste, tubaistean *nf* an accident, a mishap, a mischance, **tubaist-rathaid** a road accident, *cf less usu* **sgiorradh 1**

tubhailte, tubhailte, tubhailtean *nf* a towel, **tubhailte-shoithichean** a tea-towel, *cf* **searbhadair**

tubhairt, tuirt *pts of irreg v* **abair** (*see tables p 493*)

tùch *vi, pres part* **a' tùchadh**, **1** make hoarse, **chaidh mo thùchadh** I have become (*lit* been made) hoarse; **2** smother, extinguish (*flame etc*), *cf* **mùch 1, smà(i)l**

tùchadh, *gen* **tùchaidh** *nm* hoarseness, the state of being hoarse; **thàinig an tùchadh oirre** she became hoarse

tùchanach *adj* hoarse

tudan & **tùdan**, *gen* **tudain**, *pl* **tudanan** *nm* **1** a stack (*of corn etc*), *cf* **cruach** *n* **1**; **2** a turd

tug *pt of irreg v* **thoir** (*see tables p 504*)

tugh *vt, pres part* **a' tughadh**, thatch

tughadh, *gen* **tughaidh** *nm* **1** (*the act of*) thatching; **2** thatch

tuig *vti, pres part* **a' tuigsinn**, understand, comprehend, 'twig'

tuigse *nf invar* **1** understanding (*ie the mental faculty or capacity*), intelligence, judgement, sense, insight, perception, *cf* **ciall 1, toinisg**; **2** (*sympathetic*) understanding

tuigseach *adj* **1** (*mentally*) understanding, sensible, intelligent, perceptive, *cf* **ciallach, toinisgeil 1**; **2** (*sympathetically*) understanding, **caraid tuigseach** an understanding friend

tuigsinn *nf invar* (*the act of*) understanding etc (*see senses of* **tuig** *v*)

tuil, tuile, tuiltean *nf* a flood, a deluge, *cf* **dìle 2**

tuilleadh *nm invar* **1** more, an additional amount or number, **(an) tuilleadh fiosrachaidh** more/additional information, **a bheil thu ag iarraidh tuilleadh?** do you want any more/some more?, **carson nach eil an tuilleadh chlàran gan dèanamh?** why aren't more records being made?, *cf* **barrachd 2**; **2** *as adv* again, any more, **na dèan sin tuilleadh** don't do that again/any more, **cha till e gu bràth tuilleadh** he won't ever come back; **3** *in expr* **a thuilleadh air** *prep* in addition to, as well as, **a thuilleadh air sin . . .** moreover . . . , **tha dà lobhta againn a thuilleadh air an taigh** we have two flats in addition to the house; **4** *in expr* **tuilleadh 's a' chòir** more than enough, too much, **pìos eile? tha tuilleadh 's a' chòir agam mu thràth**, **tapadh leat** another piece? I've more than enough already, thanks, *cf* **cus**

tuineachadh, *gen* **tuineachaidh** *nm* **1** (*the act of*) settling, dwelling (*see* **tuinich** *v*); **2** (*abstr & con*) settlement, a settlement, **tuineachadh sgaoilte/cruinn** dispersed/nucleated settlement

tuinich *vi, pres part* **a' tuineachadh**, dwell, settle, **a' chiad chinneadh a thuinich ann an Ameireagaidh** the first race that settled in America

Tuirc *nf, used with art* **an Tuirc** Turkey

tuireadh, tuiridh, tuiridhean *nm* mourning, lamentation, a lament, **dèan** *v* **tuireadh** mourn, lament, *cf* **bròn 2, caoin** *v* 1

tùirse & **tùrsa** *nf invar* sorrow, *cf more usu* **bròn 1, mulad**

tuirt *pt of irreg v* **abair** (*see tables p 493*)

tuiseal, tuiseil, tuisealan *nm* (*gram*) a case, **an tuiseal ginideach** the genitive case

tuisleadh, tuislidh, tuislidhean *nm* 1 (*the act of*) stumbling, tripping, slipping; 2 a stumble, a trip, a slip; *cf* **sgiorradh 2**

tuislich *vi, pres part* **a' tuisleachadh** & **a' tuisleadh**, stumble, trip, slip

tuit *vi, pres part* **a' tuiteam**, 1 fall, drop, tumble, **a' tuisleadh 's a' tuiteam** stumbling and falling, **thuit sèaraichean an-diugh** shares fell today; 2 happen (**do** to), befall, chance, **thuit dhomh fhaicinn air an t-sràid** I happened/chanced to see him on the street, (*more permanently*) **thuit dha a bhith na shaighdear** it was his lot/it fell to him to be a soldier, *cf* **èirich 3, tachair 1**

tuiteam, tuiteim, tuiteaman *nm* 1 (*the act of*) falling, befalling etc (*see senses of* **tuit** *v*); 2 a fall

tuiteamach *adj* accidental, fortuitous, chance, contingent, **tachartasan tuiteamach** chance occurrences

tuiteamas, tuiteamais, tuiteamasan *nm* 1 an event, a happening, an occurrence, a contingency, an incident, *cf* **tachartas**; 2 an accident (*not necessarily unpleasant, cf* **tubaist**), something happening by chance, **le tuiteamas** by chance/accident; 3 (*med*) epilepsy

tulach, *gen* **tulaich**, *pl* **tulaichean** & **tulachan** *nm* a hillock, a mound (*usu small to medium sized*), a knoll, (*Sc*) a knowe; *in placenames as* tulloch, -tilloch, -tullo etc

tulg *vti, pres part* **a' tulgadh**, 1 (*seas, ship, trees etc*) rock, roll, sway, pitch, lurch, swing, toss, *cf* **luaisg**; 2 (*also more gently*) **tulg a' chreathail** rock the cradle

tulgach *adj* 1 rocking, liable to rock, roll etc (*see senses of* **tulg** *v*); 2 (*of seat, stance etc*) unsteady, rocky, (*Sc*) shooglie, *cf* **cugallach**

tulgadh, *gen* **tulgaidh** *nm* (*the act of*) rocking, rolling etc (*see senses of* **tulg** *v*), **tulgadh a' chuain** the tossing of the ocean, **sèithear-tulgaidh** *m* a rocking-chair

tum *vt, pres part* **a' tumadh**, dip, duck, immerse, steep, plunge (*in liquid*), *cf* **bog** *v* 1

tumadh, tumaidh, tumaidhean *nm* 1 (*the act of*) dipping, immersing etc (*see senses of* **tum** *v*); 2 immersion; 3 a dip, a plunge, a ducking

tunna *see* **tonna**

tunnag, tunnaig, tunnagan *nf* a duck, *cf* **lach**

tur *adj* 1 (*trad*) whole, complete, *cf more usu* **iomlan** *adj* 2; 2 *now usu in expr* **gu tur** *adv* completely, entirely, altogether, totally, quite, **tha an dà rud gu tur eadar-dhealaichte** the two things are quite different, *cf* **iomlan** *adj* 3, **gu lèir, uile 4**

tùr[1], *gen* **tùir** *nm* sense, understanding, *cf more usu* **ciall 1, toinisg, tuigse 1**

tùr[2], *gen* & *pl* **tùir** *nm* a tower, *cf* **turaid**

turadh, *gen* **turaidh** *nm* dry, fine or fair weather, a dry spell, **is math an turadh!** it's a good dry spell!, *or* it's good to see it dry!, *cf* **tiormachd 2**

turaid, turaide, turaidean *nf* a tower, a turret, *cf* **tùr**[2]

tùrail *adj* sensible, *cf more usu* **ciallach, toinisgeil 1**

turas, turais, tursan *nm* 1 a journey, an expedition, a trip, **turas-mara** a (sea-)voyage, **turas-adhair** a flight, *cf* **cuairt 3, sgrìob** *n* 3; 2 (*now esp for holidays etc*) touring, a tour, **luchd-turais** *m coll* tourists; 3 a time, **aon turas** once, one time, **'s e seo an turas mu dheireadh** this is the last time, *cf* **uair 3**

turasachd *nf invar* tourism, **oifis turasachd** a tourist office, **Bòrd Turasachd na h-Alba** the Scottish Tourist Board

Turcach, *gen* & *pl* **Turcaich** *nm* a Turk, *also as adj* **Turcach** Turkish

tursa, tursa, tursachan *nm* a standing stone, a monolith, *in pl* **tursachan** a stone circle, **Tursachan Chalanais** the Callanish (*standing*) Stones, *cf* **carragh 2, gallan**

tùrsach *adj* sorrowful, (*song*) **dh'fhàg thu tùrsach mo chridh'** you left me with a sorrowful heart/made my heart sorrowful, *cf* **brònach, muladach**

tùs, *gen* **tùis** *nm* 1 the beginning, start or origin of something, **tùs an t-samhraidh** the start/beginning of summer, (*prov*) **'s e tùs a' ghliocais eagal Dhè** the fear of God is the beginning/origin of wisdom, *cf* **bun 3, toiseach 1**; 2 *also in expr* **o/bho thùs** from, since *or* in the beginning, originally, **tha e air a bhith ag obair an seo o thùs** he's been working here from/since the (very) beginning, **bhon a bha clann Adhaimh san àite o thùs** since the children of Adam were first/originally in the place

tùsanach, *gen* & *pl* **tùsanaich** *nm* an aborigine, a native, *cf* **dùthchasach**

tuthag, tuthaig, tuthagan *nf* a patch (*of material etc*), *cf* **brèid 2**

U

uabhann *see* uamhann

uabhar, *gen* uabhair *nm* pride (*usu excessive*), haughtiness, *cf* àrdan, pròis, uaibhreas 1 & 2

uabhas, *gen* uabhais, *pl* uabhasan *nm* 1 dread, horror, terror, *cf* oillt, uamhann; 2 a dreadful or horrible thing or action, an atrocity, a horror, uabhasan an àm cogaidh horrors/atrocities in time of war

uabhasach *adj* 1 dreadful, awful, terrible, atrocious (*cf* oillteil), (*now often with attenuated colloquial force*), chaill thu ceud not? tha sin uabhasach! you lost a hundred pounds? that's dreadful/awful/terrible!, *cf* eagalach 2, sgriosail 3; 2 *as adv* terribly, awfully, dreadfully, bha am biadh uabhasach math the food was terribly good/very very good, rinn thu uabhasach fhèin math you did amazingly well/very well indeed, *cf* cianail 3, eagalach 3

uachdar, uachdair, uachdaran *nm, opposite of* ìochdar, 1 a surface, air uachdar na talmhainn/nan tonn on the surface of the earth/the waves, thig *v* an uachdar surface, *also* manifest itself, *cf* bàrr 1; 2 the top or upper surface of anything, *cf more usu* bàrr 1, mullach 1; 3 (*of milk*) cream, top of the milk, *cf* bàrr 1; 4 (*topog*) an upland, *can occur in placenames as* auchter & ochter, *cf* bràigh *nm* 2; 5 *in expr* làmh-an-uachdair the upper hand, gheibh sinn làmh-an-uachdair orra we'll get the upper hand over them, *cf* cùis 5, gnothach 6

uachdarach *adj, opposite of* ìochdarach, 1 (*phys*) upper; 2 (*in status etc*) superior; 3 superficial; 4 creamy, *cf* barragach

uachdaran, uachdarain, uachdaranan *nm, opposite of* ìochdaran, 1 (*of status etc*) a superior; 2 a landowner, a laird, *cf* tighearna 2

uachdar-fhiaclan, uachdair-fhiaclan, uachdaran-fhiaclan *nm* toothpaste

uaibh (*emph form* uaibhse) *prep pron, see* o prep

uaibhreach *adj* 1 proud; 2 (*excessively*) proud, haughty, arrogant; *cf* àrdanach, dàna 4

uaibhreas, *gen* uaibhreis *nm* 1 pride; 2 (*excessive or insolent*) pride, haughtiness, arrogance; *cf* àrdan, pròis, uabhar

uaigh, *gen* uaighe & uaghach, *pl* uaighean *nf* a grave, (*song*) nach robh mi san uaigh! if only I were dead and buried!

uaigneach *adj* 1 (*of person*) lonely, lonesome, *cf* aonaranach; 2 (*of place etc*) solitary, lonely, deserted, secluded; 3 (*esp of place*) private, secret, *cf* dìomhair 1

uaim, *gen* uaime *nf* (*poetry etc*) alliteration

uaimh & uamh, *gen* uaimhe & uamha, *pl* uamhan & uaimhean *nf* a cave, (*trad song*) Uaimh an Òir The Cave of Gold

uaine *adj* green, *cf* glas 2, gorm 2

uainfheòil, *gen* uainfheòla *nf* lamb (*ie the meat*)

uainn (*emph form* uainne), uaipe (*emph form* uaipese) *prep prons, see* o prep

uaipear, uaipeir, uaipearan *nm* a botcher, a bungler, *cf* cearbair(e)

uair, uarach, uairean *nf* 1 (*clock time*) an hour, *esp* uair a (*for de*) thìde & uair an uaireadair an hour, cairteal na h-uarach a quarter of an hour, dè an uair a tha e? what time is it? (*lit* what hour is it?), tha e trì uairean it's three o'clock, tha e leth-uair an dèidh a ceithir it's half past four, cha dèan mi sin aig an uair seo! I won't do that at this hour/time! (*cf* àm); 2 (*as adv*) once, one time, on one occasion, bha mi ann uair I was there once/one time/on one occasion, aon uair 's gun tòisicheadh e once he got started, thig gam fhaicinn uair sam bith come and see me any time, chì mi (uair no) uaireigin thu I'll see you some time or other, air uairean (*trad* air uairibh) at times, sometimes, occasionally (*cf* uaireannan), *see also* an uair a *conj*; 3 a time (*ie a repetition*), uair is uair time and time again, again and again, over and over again, rinn sinn dà uair e we did it twice, a' chiad uair a chunna mi i the first time I saw her, *cf* turas 3

uaireadair, uaireadair, uaireadairean *nm*
1 *trad used for timepieces of various kinds, eg*
uaireadair-grèine a sundial, uaireadair-
glainne an hour-glass; 2 a clock, uair an
uaireadair an hour's (clock) time, an hour
by the clock, *cf more usu* gleoc; 3 (*now esp*) a
watch

uaireannan *adv* at times, sometimes,
occasionally, *cf* air uairean (*see* uair 2)

uaireigin *adv* (at) some time or other

uaisle *nf invar* (*abstr, of birth, character etc*)
nobility, gentility, aristocracy

uaislean *see* uasal *n* 2

uaithe (*emph form* uaithesan) *prep pron, see*
o *prep*

uallach, *gen & pl* uallaich *nm* 1 (*mostly fig*) a
burden, a load, is trom an t-uallach an aois
age is a heavy burden, (*prov*) chan fhuirich
muir air uallach the sea won't wait on a
cargo, *cf* eallach; 2 a charge, a responsibility,
an onus, chuir iad orm uallach an turais
they charged me with the responsibility for the
journey, bha uallach na dachaigh oirre
hers was the responsibility for the home,
's ann oirbhse a tha an t-uallach the
onus is on you, *cf* cùram 1, eallach, urra
2; 3 (*psych*) stress, pressure, strain, tha an
duine agam fo uallach an-dràsta air
sgàth dhuilgheadasan san fhactaraidh
my husband's under pressure/stress just now
because of difficulties in the factory; 4 worry,
bha uallach oirre air sgàth a màthar she
was worried about/on account of her mother,
gabh *v* uallach become worried, *cf* dragh 3

uam (*emph form* uamsa) *prep pron, see* o *prep*

uamh *see* uaimh

uamhann & uabhann, *gen* uamhainn *nm*
dread, horror, terror, *cf* oillt, uabhas 1

uan, *gen & pl* uain *nm* a lamb

uapa (*emph form* uapasan) *prep pron, see* o
prep

uasal *adj* 1 noble, aristocratic, (*trad*) duine-
uasal a nobleman, a gentleman, (*Sc, hist*) a
duniwassal, (*trad, formal address, in corres etc*)
a bhean-uasail Madam; 2 (*in manners etc*)
genteel; 3 precious, *esp in expr* clach uasal *f* a
precious stone

uasal, uasail, uaislean *nm* 1 (*trad*) a gentleman,
mòr-uasal a nobleman, an aristocrat; 2 *in pl*,
esp with art (*coll*) na h-uaislean the nobility,
the aristocracy

uat (*emph form* uatsa) *prep pron, see* o *prep*

ubhal, ubhail, ùbhlan *nm* an apple

ubhalghort, ubhalghoirt, ubhalghoirtean
nm an orchard

uchd, uchda, uchdan *nm* 1 a breast (*ie general
breast area*), a bosom, theannaich i am
balach ri a h-uchd she clasped the boy to her
bosom, *cf* broilleach 1, com 1; 2 a lap, bha am
balach na shuidhe na h-uchd the boy was
sitting on her lap, *cf* glùn 1; 3 *in expr* ri uchd at
the point of, on the verge of, *esp in expr* ri uchd
bàis at the point of death, at death's door; 4 *as
prefix* uchd- adoptive, pertaining to adoption,
eg uchd-leanabh *m* an adopted child, uchd-
mhacaich *vt* adopt

ud *adj* that (*usu more distant or remote than*
sin), yon, yonder, am faic thu an taigh ud,
aig ceann a' bhaile? do you see that/yon
house, at the end of the village?, (*can be slightly
pej*) cha toigh leam an duineachan ud
I don't like that/yon mannie, *cf* seo, sin, siud

ud, ud! *excl expr disapproval, reservations etc*,
tut, tut!, now, now!, no, no!, come on now! ud,
ud, a bhalaich, chan eil mi airson sin idir!
now, now/wait a minute, boy, I don't approve of
that at all!

uèir, uèir, uèirichean *nf* wire, uèir-bhiorach
barbed wire

ugan, ugain, ugannan *nm* the upper part of the
chest area

ugh, uigh, uighean *nm* an egg

ughach *adj* oval, egg-shaped

ughach, *gen & pl* ughaich *nm* an oval

ughagan, *gen & pl* ughagain *nm* custard, a
custard

ùghdar, ùghdair, ùghdaran *nm* an author

ùghdarraich, *pres part* ag ùghdarrachadh, *vt*
authorise, empower

ùghdarraichte *adj* authorised, empowered;
licensed

ùghdarras, ùghdarrais, ùghdarrasan *nm*
1 (*abstr*) authority, *cf* smachd; 2 (*con*) an
authority, ùghdarrasan ionadail local
authorities, *cf* comhairle 2; 3 authorisation,
empowerment

ughlann, ughlainn, ughlannan *nf* an ovary

Uibhisteach, *gen & pl* Uibhistich *nm* someone
from Uist (Uibhist), *also as adj* Uibhisteach
of, from or pertaining to Uist

ùidh, ùidhe, ùidhean *nf* 1 (*trad*) hope;
intention; fondness; 2 *now usu* interest, chan
eil ùidh agam ann I'm not interested in it,
gabh *v* ùidh ann take an interest/be interested
in, *cf* suim 2

uidh, *gen* uidhe *nf* 1 (*trad*) a step, a degree, a
gradation; *also* a journey; 2 *now in expr* uidh
air n-uidh step by step, bit by bit, gradually;
3 *in exprs* ceann-uidhe *m* a destination, a

terminus, a journey's end, **togalach uidhe** *m* a terminal building

uidheam, uidheim, uidheaman *nf coll* **1** (*tools, machinery etc*) equipment, gear, apparatus, tackle; **2** furnishings, accoutrements, trappings, fittings; **3** (*of horse etc*) harness; **4** (*of boat*) rigging; *cf* **acainn**

uidheamachadh, *gen* **uidheamachaidh 1** (*the act of*) equipping etc (*see senses of* **uidheamaich** *v*); **2** preparation, *cf* **ullachadh 2**

uidheamaich *vt, pres part* **ag uidheamachadh,** equip, gear up, furnish, fit out, get ready, prepare

uidheamaichte *adj* **1** equipped, geared up, fitted out, *cf* **acainneach; 2** (*of person*) qualified

uile *adj & adv* **1** all, **dh'fhalbh na saighdearan uile** the soldiers all left, **tha sin uile seachad** all that's over; **2** *often occurs as* **a h-uile** every (*precedes the noun*), **a h-uile càil/duine** everything/everybody, **a h-uile là** every day, **a h-uile fear aca** every one of them, *cf* **gach 1; 3** *as noun & pron* **na h-uile** everyone, everybody, **chaill na h-uile an cuid airgid** everyone/they all lost their money; **4** *as adv* (*trad*) **tha mi uile-thoileach** I am fully willing, *now esp in expr* **uile-gu-lèir** *adv* completely, totally, altogether, fully, absolutely, **shoirbhich leinn uile-gu-lèir** we succeeded totally, **gun fheum uile-gu-lèir** absolutely useless, *cf* **buileach, tur 2; 5** *as prefix corres to Eng* all-, omni-, *eg* **uile-chumhachdach** *adj* all-powerful, omnipotent, **uile-fhiosrach** *adj* all-knowing, omniscient

uileann & **uilinn,** *gen* **uilinn** & **uilne,** *pl* **uilnean** & **uileannan** *nf* **1** an angle, **ceart-uilinn** a right angle; **2** a corner (*usu external*), *cf* **còrnair, cùil 1, oisean; 3** an elbow

uilebheist, uilebheist, uilebheistean *nmf* a monster, **Uilebheist Loch Nis** the Loch Ness Monster

uilinn *see* **uileann**

ùilleach *adj* oily

uilleagan, *gen & pl* **uilleagain** *nm* a spoilt brat

uillnich *vti, pres part* **ag uillneachadh,** jostle, elbow, *cf* **put** *v* **2, ùpag**

uime (*emph form* **uimesan**) *prep pron, see* **mu**

uimhir *nf invar* **1** a number, an amount, a quantity, **a' cheart uimhir** the same amount/quantity, **dè uimhir 's a th' ann?** how much is there?, how many are there?, *cf* **meud 2; 2** a certain amount, a measure, a modicum of something, **bha na h-uimhir de thèarainteachd againn** we had a measure/a certain amount of security; **3** the same number,

quantity etc, **thoir dhomh uimhir eile** give me as much again/the same again, **na toir dhomh uimhir ri Seumas!** don't give me as much as James!; **4** (*also* **na h-uimhir**) a great number or quantity, so much, so many, **bha (na h-)uimhir de dhaoine ann** there were so many/such a lot of people there, **bha (na h-)uimhir de dh'airgead agam** I had so much/such a lot of money; *cf* **uiread**

uimpe (*emph form* **uimpese**) *prep pron, see* **mu**

ùine *nf invar* **1** time, **cuir** *v* **seachad ùine** spend/pass time, (*Sc*) put by time, **fad na h-ùine** all the time, **tha ùine gu leòr againn** we've plenty of time, *cf* **tìde 1; 2** a period of time, **ùine ghoirid roimhe sin** a short time before that; **3** (*fam*) *non-trad pl* **ùineachan** ages, **ùineachan is ùineachan air ais** ages and ages ago

uinneag, uinneige, uinneagan *nf* a window, **coimhead** *v* **a-mach air an uinneig** (*dat*) look out (of) the window

uinnean, uinnein, uinneanan *nm* an onion

uinnseann, *gen* **uinnsinn** *nm* (*tree & wood*) ash

ùir, *gen* **ùire** & **ùrach** *nf* **1** soil, earth, **sìol air a chur san ùir** seed sown in the earth; **2** (*trad*) *euphemism for* a grave, **chuireadh e san ùir** he was lain in the earth, he was buried, *cf* **fòid 1, uaigh**

uircean, uircein, uirceanan *nm* a piglet

uiread *nm invar* **1** a certain amount, a measure, a modicum of something, **bha na h-uiread de thèarainteachd againn** we had a certain amount/a modicum of security, *cf* **uimhir 2; 2** the same number, quantity or amount, **uiread eile** as much again, the same again, **leth uiread** half as much, **thoir dhomh uiread 's a tha aig Iain** give me as much as Ian has, *cf* **uimhir 3; 3** *in neg exprs,* **uiread is/agus** even, so much as, **gun uiread agus leth-cheud sgillinn** without even/so much as fifty pence, *cf* **eadhon, fiù** *n* **2; 4** (*also* **na h-uiread**) a great number or quantity, so much, so many, **chaill mi (na h-)uiread de thìde** I lost so much/such a lot of time, **uiread de dhaoine** so many people, *cf* **uimhir 4; 5** (*arith etc*) times, multiplied by, **a dhà uiread a dhà** two times two, twice two

uireasbhach *adj* **1** (*persons*) needy, indigent, *cf* **ainniseach; 2** needful, much needed, lacking, *cf* **dìth 2, gann 1**

uireasbhach, *gen & pl* **uireasbhaich** *nm* a needy or indigent person

uireasbhaidh, uireasbhaidhe, uireasbhaidhean *nf* **1** want, need, indigence; **2** a lack, a deficiency, a shortage, *cf* **cion 1**

uirsgeul & ùirsgeul, gen uirsgeil, pl
uirsgeulan nm 1 a fable, a legend, a myth, cf
fionnsgeul; 2 (Lit etc) fiction, a piece of fiction,
dh'fhaighnich iad am b' e uirsgeul a
bh' agam they asked if I was making it up
uirsgeulach adj 1 legendary, relating to legend;
2 (Lit etc) fictional, fictitious, made up
uiseag, uiseig, uiseagan nf a lark, a skylark, cf
topag
uisge, uisge, uisgeachan nm 1 water, deoch
uisge a drink of water, tobar fìor-uisge a well
of pure water, cf bùrn; 2 (usu with art) rain,
tha an t-uisge ann fhathast it's still raining,
sguir an t-uisge mu dheireadh thall the
rain stopped at long last, uisge-searbhaig acid
rain
uisge-beatha, gen uisge-bheatha nm whisky
uisgeachadh, gen uisgeachaidh nm 1 (the act
of) watering, irrigating; 2 irrigation
uisgich vt, pres part ag uisgeachadh, 1 water;
2 irrigate
ulaidh, ulaidhe, ulaidhean nf 1 treasure, a
treasure, a precious object; 2 (expr affection)
m' ulaidh! my darling!, precious!; cf eudail
Ulaidh n Ulster
ulbhag, ulbhaig, ulbhagan nf a large stone or
boulder
ulfhart, gen & pl ulfhairt nm (esp of dog)
howling, a howl, dèan v ulfhart howl
ullachadh, gen ullachaidh nm 1 (the act of)
preparing, providing etc (see senses of ullaich
v); 2 preparation, gun ullachadh unprepared,
impromptu, cf deasachadh 2; 3 provision,
ullachadh ionmhais provision of finance
ullaich vt, pres part ag ullachadh, 1 prepare,
get ready, cf deasaich 1 & 2; 2 (esp admin etc)
provide, ullaich ionmhas airson ospadail
ùir provide finance for a new hospital
ullamh adj 1 ready, prepared, a bheil thu
ullamh? are you ready, cf deiseil 1 & less
usu deas 3; 2 finished, bha iad ullamh de
cheasnachadh they had finished/they were
through asking questions, cf deiseil 2 & less usu
deas adj 1; 3 handy, ready to hand, airgead
ullamh m ready money, cash, cf deiseil 3,
goireasach
ultach, ultaich, ultaichean nm 1 a load (ie as
much as can be carried at one time), an armful
(cf achlasan), ultach-droma as much as can
be carried on the back; 2 a bundle
umad (emph form umadsa),umaibh (emph
form umaibhse) prep prons, see mu
ùmaidh, ùmaidh, ùmaidhean nm a blockhead,
a dolt, a dunce, a fool, cf bumailear, stalcaire

umainn (emph form umainne), umam (emph
form umamsa) prep prons see mu
umha nm invar bronze, (hist) Linn an Umha
the Bronze Age
umha(i)l adj 1 humble, meek, lowly, cf iriosal 2;
2 obedient, submissive, compliant, deferential,
umhail do a mhàthair obedient to his mother,
cf macanta; 3 obsequious
ùmhlachadh, gen ùmhlachaidh nm 1 (the act
of) becoming humble, humiliating etc (see senses
of ùmhlaich v); 2 humiliation, a humiliation,
mortification
ùmhlachd nf invar 1 humbleness, lowliness,
meekness, cf irioslachd; 2 obedience,
submissiveness, deference; 3 obsequiousness; 4
(before royalty etc) homage, obeisance, a bow
ùmhlaich vti, pres part ag ùmhlachadh, 1
become or make humble; 2 (vt) humiliate,
mortify, humble, chasten, cf irioslaich
umpa (emph form umpasan) prep pron, see mu
Ungair nf, used with art an Ungair Hungary
Ungaireach, gen & pl Ungairich nm a
Hungarian, also as adj Ungaireach Hungarian
ùnnlagh, ùnnlagha, ùnnlaghan nm a fine
unnsa, unnsa, unnsachan nm an ounce
ùpag, ùpaig, ùpagan nf (in crowd, squabble etc)
a jostle, a jab (with elbow etc), cf uillnich
ùpraid, ùpraide, ùpraidean nf 1 (noise)
uproar, an uproar, cf gleadhar, othail; 2
(in crowds, disturbance etc) confusion, a
commotion, a dispute, am measg na
h-ùpraide shiolp e air falbh amidst the
confusion/commotion he slipped away, cf
aimhreit 1
ùpraideach adj uproarious, rowdy, unruly, full of
confusion or commotion
ùr adj 1 new, fresh, recent, càr ùr m a new car,
càirdean ùra new friends, leabhar ùr m a
new/recent book, sgadan/ìm ùr fresh herring/
butter, cf nuadh; 2 modern, na h-amannan
ùra seo these modern times, cf nuadh, ùr-
nodha; 3 in expr às ùr adv afresh, anew, (for)
a second time, tòisich v às ùr start afresh/all
over again, make a fresh start; 4 occas as prefix
new, newly, fresh, freshly, eg air ùr-thighinn à
Glaschu newly arrived from Glasgow, ùr-fhàs
m new/fresh growth
ur, also less usu bhur, poss adj, pl & formal
your (corres to pron sibh), ur pàrantan your
parents, is math ur faicinn it's good to see
you, 's e ur beatha! you're welcome!, before a
vowel (bh)ur n-, eg leigibh ur n-anail take a
breather, cf sing/fam do poss adj
ùrachadh, gen ùrachaidh nm 1 (the act
of) renewing etc (see senses of ùraich v); 2

renewal; **3** modernisation; **4** a change, **bidh sin na ùrachadh dhut** that will be/make a change for you

ùraich *vti, pres part* **ag ùrachadh**, **1** become or make new or fresh, renew, refresh; **2** modernise, bring up to date

urchair, urchrach, urchraichean *nf* **1** a shot (*from firearm*), **chuala mi urchair** I heard a shot, (*distance*) **urchair gunna air falbh** a gunshot away; **2** a missile

urchasg, urchaisg, urchasgan *nm* an antidote

ùrlar, ùrlair, ùrlaran *nm* **1** a floor, **ùrlar taighe** a house floor, **ùrlar cloiche** a stone floor, **a' dannsadh air an ùrlar** dancing on the (dance) floor, **àrd-ùrlar** a stage, a platform, *cf* **làr 2**; **2** a floor (*ie storey*), *cf* **lobht(a) 1**; **3** (*music*) a theme, (*esp in pibroch*) a ground

ùrnaigh, ùrnaigh, ùrnaighean *nf* praying, a prayer, **dèan** *v* **ùrnaigh** pray (**ri** to), **Ùrnaigh an Tighearna** the Lord's Prayer, **coinneamh-ùrnaigh** *f* a prayer meeting, *cf* **guidhe** *n* **4**

ùr-nodha *adj* **1** brand new, modern, up-to-date, (*Sc*) split new

urra, urra, urraidhean *nf* **1** (*trad*) a person, an individual, *occas in expr* **an urra** *adv* each, per capita, apiece, **mìle nota an urra** a thousand pounds each/apiece, *cf* **more** *usu* **duine 2**, **neach 1**; **2** authority, responsibility (*mainly moral*), *now usu in expr* **an urra** responsible, **bha mi an urra ri Oifis a' Phuist** I was responsible for/in charge of the Post Office, *cf* **cùram 1, uallach 2**; **3** *in expr* **an urra ri** *prep* dependent on, **an urra ri drogaichean** dependent on/addicted to drugs, *cf* **tràill 3**

urrainn *nf invar* **1** (*trad*) power, ability, *cf trad* **feudar 1**; **2** *now in verbal expr* **is urrainn do** can, is able, **chan urrainn dhomh slugadh** I can't swallow, **nach urrainn dhut**

a dhèanamh? **chan urrainn** can't you do it? no, **cha b' urrainn dhomh gun a bhith brònach** I couldn't help being sad, I couldn't but be sad

urram, *gen* urraim *nm* **1** respect, deference, **àrd-urram** reverence, **thoir urram don fheadhainn a tha airidh air** respect those who are worthy of it, *cf* **meas¹ 1**; **2** honour, an honour, **cuir** *v* **urram air cuideigin** honour/confer an honour on someone (*cf* **onaraich 1 & 2**)

urramach *adj* **1** honourable, reverend, venerable, worthy of respect or honour; **2** honorary, **ball urramach** *m* an honorary member; **3** (*of minister*) Reverend, *used with art*, **an t-Urramach Uilleam Caimbeul** the Reverend William Campbell

urras, urrais, urrasan *nm* **1** (*esp in fin matters*) a guarantee, a bond, surety, **rach** *v* **an urras air** stand as surety/guarantee for, vouch for, *cf* **bar(r)antas 2**; **2** (*legal*) bail, **fuasgail** *v* **air urras** release on bail; **3** insurance, assurance, **poileasaidh-urrais** an insurance policy, *cf* **àrachas**; **4** (*legal, fin, business*) a trust, **ciste-urrais** *f* a trust fund

urrasach *adj* (*person, business etc*) trustworthy, sound, secure, dependable, *cf* **earbsach 2**

ursainn, ursainn, ursainnean *nf* **1** (*trad*) a prop, a support, (*fig, trad*) **ursainn-chatha** a champion, a staunch support in battle; **2** (*now usu*) a jamb, a doorpost

usgar, usgair, usgaran *nm* a jewel (*esp one worn as an ornament*), an item of jewellery, *cf* **seud**

uspag, uspaig, uspagan *nf* a start, (*horse etc*) a shying movement, **thoir** *v* **uspag** start, shy, *cf* **clisgeadh 2**

ùth, ùtha, ùthan(nan) *nm* an udder

ENGLISH–GAELIC

Layout of the Entries, English–Gaelic Section

Within these entries all English material for translation into Gaelic is given in bold type. Italics are used for all other text in English, ie for abbreviations, instructions such as *see* and *cf*, and all notes, comments, explanatory material and grammatical information. The Gaelic translation equivalents given for the English headwords, phrases and expressions, represent current Gaelic usage except where marked *trad* (traditional), *occas* (occasionally), etc. Gaelic spelling used corresponds to up-to-date norms. Occasionally two acceptable spellings are given for the same Gaelic word.

The examples given below show how in a typical entry the English headword is followed by its part of speech, which is abbreviated (see list of abbreviations p xiii).

> **abrupt** *adj* **1** (*sudden etc*) grad; **2** (*of persons; terse, short-tempered*) cas, aithghearr; **3** (*of slope etc*) cas

> **elder**[1] *n* **1** (*church ~*) èildear *m*, (*more trad*) foirfeach *m*; **2** (*older of two*) am fear/an tè (*etc*) as sine, **John is the** ~ is e Iain am fear as sine

These examples also show how synonyms or other indications, such as (*older of two*), are given in brackets, and often in numbered subsections, to distinguish between the senses or contexts for which a given Gaelic translation equivalent applies. In the case of **elder**[1], the superscript numeral indicates the distinction between English homonyms, that is, words with the same form but different meanings – the entry **elder**[2] refers to the elder tree.

Gaelic nouns are given in the nominative singular (radical) case, followed by the abbreviated gender of the noun, as follows:

> **safety** *n* tèarainteachd *f invar*, sàbhailteachd *f invar*, **in** ~ an tèarainteachd, ~ **equipment** uidheam sàbhailteachd *f sing coll, in expr* ~ **pin** prìne-banaltraim *m*

Some Gaelic nouns have both genders and this is shown by the abbreviation *mf*. In the example above *invar* (*invariable*) also shows that the nouns in question have only the one form, ie do not decline.

The Gaelic equivalents for many headwords are followed by common expressions involving that headword. Each repetition of the English headword is represented by the symbol ~, as in ~ **equipment** (for **safety equipment**) above. The abbreviation *in expr* (*in the expression*) is used to signal that in certain expressions, often idiomatic ones, the Gaelic equivalent for a particular English headword or phrase is different from the standard ones given earlier in the entry. This is illustrated by the example: **milk** *n* bainne *m*, *in expr* ~ **cows** crodh-eadraidh *m*

Verbs are given in the second person singular imperative form. The abbreviation *vt* (*transitive verb*) indicates that, *in the sense concerned in the entry*, a given verb is used with a direct object, while *vi* (*intransitive verb*) shows that it is used without a direct object. The following example ilustrates the difference between a transitive use of 'capsize', **they capsized her/the boat**, and an intransitive use, **the boat capsized**.

> **capsize** *v* **1** (*as vt*) cuir *vt* thairis, **they ~d her** chuir iad thairis i; **2** (*as vi*) rach *vi irreg* thairis, **the boat ~d** chaidh am bàta thairis, *also* chaidh car *m* dhen bhàta

A verb that can be used in either of these ways is labelled *vti*, as follows:

> **gather** *v* **1** (*people*) cruinnich *vti*, tionail *vi*, thig còmhla, **they ~ed/he ~ed them in the barn** chruinnich iad/chruinnich e iad san t-sabhal

Where a Gaelic verb takes a particular preposition, this is shown in brackets after the verb, as follows:

> **accentuate** *v* cuir stràc *m*, leig cudthrom *m*, (*with prep* air)

In this particular case the comma after 'cudthrom *m*' indicates that both the verbs listed take the same preposition, air, whereas in the entry below the two verbs concerned take different prepositions.

> **advise** *v* comhairlich *vt*, comhairlich *vi* (*with prep* do), thoir comhairle (*with preps* air *or* do)

A

a.m. *adv* sa mhadainn, **six** ~ sia uairean sa mhadainn

a, an *indefinite art, not expressed in Gaelic,* **I saw a man** chunnaic mi duine, **I ate an apple** dh'ith mi ubhal

abandon *v* trèig *vt*, **he ~ed his family** thrèig e a theaghlach, **the people ~ed the island** thrèig na daoine an t-eilean, ~ **the faith of your forefathers** trèig creideamh ur sinnsirean

abandonment *n* trèigsinn *m invar*

abasement *n* ìsleachadh *m*

abash *v* nàraich *vt*

abashed *adj & past part* nàraichte, air a (*etc*) nàrachadh

abate *v* lùghdaich *vi*, rach *vi* sìos, **the storm ~d** lùghdaich an stoirm *mf*, chaidh an stoirm sìos

abatement *n* lùghdachadh *m*

abattoir *n* taigh-spadaidh *m*

abbess *n* ban-aba *f*

abbey *n* abaid *f*

abbot *n* aba *m*

abbreviate *v* giorraich *vt*

abbreviation *n* giorrachadh *m*

abdicate *v* leig dheth (*etc*) an crùn, **the queen ~d** leig a' bhanrigh dhith an crùn

abdication *n* leigeil *mf* dheth (*etc*) a' chrùin, **after their ~** an dèidh dhaibh an crùn a leigeil dhiubh

abduct *v* thoir *vt* air falbh

abduction *n* toirt air falbh *f invar*

abet *v* cuidich *vti*

abettor *n* pàirtiche *m*, neach-cuideachaidh *m* (*pl* luchd-cuideachaidh *m sing coll*)

abeyance *n* stad *m*, **the scheme is in ~** tha an sgeama na stad

abhor *v*, **I ~ him/it** tha gràin *f* agam air

abhorrence *n* gràin *f*

abhorrent *adj* gràineil

abide *v* 1 (*stand, tolerate*) fuiling *vti*, **I can't ~ him/it** chan fhuiling mi e, (*also*) chan urrainn dhomh fhulang; 2 (*Lit: dwell, Sc stay*) fuirich *vi*, còmhnaich *vi*

abiding *adj* (*enduring*) maireannach

ability *n* comas *m*, ~ **to speak** comas bruidhne, **intellectual** ~ comas inntinn , **that's beyond my** ~ tha sin thar mo chomais, (*ed*) **mixed** ~ comasan measgaichte

abject *adj* truagh, (*more pej*) suarach, ~ **poverty** bochdainn thruagh

able *adj* 1 (*skilled, highly competent*) comasach, **an** ~ **man** duine comasach, **mentally** ~ comasach na (*etc*) inntinn, glic; 2 (*capable of particular activity*) is *v irreg* urrainn (*with prep* do), **I am not** ~ **to write** chan urrainn dhomh sgrìobhadh, *also* chan eil sgrìobhadh agam; 3 (*idiom: of invalid etc, fit for a particular activity*) ~ **to go out** air cothrom a dhol a-mach

-able *suffix* ion- *prefix* (*with past part of verb*), *eg* **eatable** ion-ithe, **practicable** ion-dhèanta

able-bodied *adj* corp-làidir, fallain

ablutions *n* (*ie the act*) ionnlad *m*

abnormal *adj* 1 (*unusual*) neo-chumanta, às a' chumantas; 2 (*phys* ~) meangach

abnormality *n* 1 (*state of being unusual etc*) neo-chumantas *m*; 2 (*phys* ~) meang *f*

aboard *adj* air bòrd *m* (*with gen*), ~ **the aircraft** air bòrd na plèana

aboard *adv* air bòrd *m*, **come** ~ thig *vi* air bòrd

abode *n* àite-còmhnaidh *m*, àite-fuirich *m*, **of no fixed** ~ gun àite-còmhnaidh seasmhach

abolish *v* cuir *vi* às (*with prep* do), **they ~ed the monarchy** chuir iad às don mhonarcachd

abolition *n* cur *m* às (*of* do), ~ **of the monarchy** cur às don mhonarcachd

abomination *n* 1 (*the emotion*) mòr-ghràin *f*; 2 (*a source or cause of* ~) cùis-ghràin *f*, **it's an ~!** 's e cùis-ghràin a th' ann!

aborigine *n* tùsanach *m*, dùthchasach *m*

aboriginal *adj* dùthchasach, ~ **culture** cultar dùthchasach

abortion *n* casg-breith *m invar*, casg-leatruim *m*, **she had an** ~ bha casg-breith aice

abortive *adj* (*fruitless*) gun toradh, neo-tharbhach

abound v bi vi irreg pailt, bi lìonmhor, cuir vi thairis, **a land ~ing in game** tìr a' cur thairis le sitheann

about adv 1 (around) mun cuairt, **the flu's going** ~ tha an cnatan mòr a' dol mun cuairt; **2** misc exprs **up and** ~ air a (etc) c(h)ois, **we're (just) ~ to go/leave** tha sinn gu falbh, **I'm just ~ ready** tha mi gu bhith deiseil, (up to) **what's she ~?** dè a tha i ris?

about prep **1** (around) mun cuairt & mu chuairt (with prep air), **fine views all ~ her** seallaidhean brèagha fada mun cuairt oirre; **2** (concerning) mu dheidhinn prep (takes the gen), ~ **me** mum dheidhinn, **they're saying dreadful/shocking things ~ the minister** tha iad ag ràdh rudan oillteil mu dheidhinn a' mhinisteir; **3** (concerning and around) mu (takes the dat), **a story ~ the war** sgeulachd mun chogadh (also sgeulachd mu dheidhinn a' chogaidh and sgeulachd air a' chogadh), **she put her coat ~ her** chuir i uimpe a còta (for prep prons formed with mu see p 510); **4** (approximately) timcheall air, mu (takes dat & lenites following cons where possible), **there'll be ~ ten people there** bidh timcheall air deichnear ann, bidh mu dheichnear ann

above prep **1** (position) os cionn (with gen), **clouds ~ the ocean** neòil os cionn a' chuain, ~ **me** os mo chionn; **2** (misc exprs) ~ **all** (ie especially) gu h-àraidh, ~ **board** follaiseach

abrasive adj sgrìobach

abridge v giorraich vt

abridged adj & past part giorraichte

abridgement n giorrachadh m

abroad adv **1** (expr movement) a-null thairis, **they went ~** chaidh iad a-null thairis; **2** (expr position) thall thairis, **they are ~** tha iad thall thairis; **3** (circulating, current) in expr (formal) **a rumour is ~** tha fathann a' dol mun cuairt

abrupt adj **1** (sudden etc) grad; **2** (of persons: terse, short-tempered) cas, aithghearr; **3** (of slope etc) cas

abscess n neasgaid f

abscond v teich (air falbh) vi

absence n neo-làthaireachd f invar

absent adj neo-làthaireach, (less formal) **he's ~ today** chan eil e ann an-diugh, tha e dheth an-diugh

absent v, ~ **oneself** (fail to be present or to attend) cùm vi às an làthair, cùm vi air falbh

absentee n neach m (etc) neo-làthaireach

absent-minded adj dìochuimhneach

absolute adj **1** (complete, unassailable) làn-prefix, ~ **power** làn-chumhachd; **2** (utter, complete, through & through) dearg (precedes the noun), gu chùl (follows the noun), **an ~ fool** dearg amadan, amadan gu chùl; **3** in expr **an ~ majority** mòr-chuid iomlan

absolutely adv gu h-iomlan, uile-gu-lèir

absolution n (rel) ~ **from sin** saoradh m o pheacadh

absolve v saor vt (o pheacadh)

absorb v **1** (liquids etc) sùigh vt; **2** (information) gabh vt a-steach

absorbent adj sùighteach

absorption n sùghadh m

abstain v **1** (refrain from, avoid) cùm vi (with prep o), seachain vt, ~ **from drink** cùm on deoch-làidir; **2** (at election) seachain bhòtadh, **they ~ed** sheachain iad bhòtadh

abstemious adj stuama

abstention n (pol) seachnadh bhòtaidh m

abstinence n stuamachd f invar

abstinent adj stuama

abstract adj **1** (art, noun etc) eas-chruthach; **2** in expr ~ **idea** cùis-bheachd f

abstract n (résumé of document etc) geàrr-chunntas m

abstraction n (philo etc: an absract idea or concept) cùis-bheachd f

abstruse adj deacair, iomadh-fhillte

absurd adj **1** (ridiculous) gòrach, amaideach; **2** (philo etc) mì-reusanta

absurdity n **1** (ridiculousness) gòraiche f invar, amaideas m; **2** (philo etc) mì-reusantachd f invar

abundance n pailteas m, lìonmhorachd f

abundant adj **1** (numerous) lìonmhor; **2** (plentiful) pailt

abuse n **1** (verbal) càineadh m, màbadh m; **2** (phys) droch-làimhseachadh m; **3** (sexual) truailleadh drùiseach m

abuse v **1** (persons, verbally) màb vt, dèan ana-cainnt f (with prep air); **2** (persons, phys) droch-làimhsich vt; **3** (persons, sexually) truaill vt; **4** (~ substances, position of authority etc) mì-ghnàthaich vt, ~ **drugs** mì-ghnàthaich drogaichean

abyss n àibheis f invar, dubh-aigeann m invar (used with art), **the ~** an dubh-aigeann

academic adj sgoilearach, acadaimigeach

academic n **1** sgoilear m; **2** (University teacher) neach-teagaisg oilthigh m

academy n **1** (secondary school) àrd-sgoil f, acadamaidh m; **2** (learned institution etc) acadamh mf, **The Royal Scottish Academy** Acadamh Rìoghail na h-Alba

accelerate v luathaich vti

acceleration n luathachadh m

accent n **1** (*mode of speech*) blas m, **he speaks Gaelic with an English** ~ tha blas na Beurla air a chuid Gàidhlig; **2** (*stress, accentuation*) stràc m, **the** ~ **is on the first syllable** tha an stràc air a' chiad lide m, **acute** ~ stràc geur, **grave** ~ stràc trom

accent v (*lang*) cuir stràc m (*with prep* air)

accentuate v cuir stràc m, leig cudthrom m, (*with prep* air)

accept v gabh vi (*with prep* ri), **they ~ed the situation** ghabh iad ris an t-suidheachadh

acceptable adj iomchaidh, **an** ~ **solution** fuasgladh iomchaidh, **an agreement** ~ **to all** còrdadh m ris an urrainn na h-uile gabhail

access n **1** (*way in*) inntrigeadh m, **right of** ~ còir inntrigidh, ~ **road/door** rathad/doras inntrigidh, *also* rathad/doras a-steach; **2** (*opportunity, opening*) cothrom m (**to** air), ~ **to higher education** cothrom air foghlam àrd-ìre

accessible adj **1** (*of a place*) ruigsinneach; **2** (*of a person*) fosgarra, fosgailte

accessibility n (*esp of a place*) ruigsinneachd f invar

accident n **1** (*usu unpleasant*) tubaist f, **road** ~ tubaist-rathaid f; **2** (*not nec unpleasant*) tuiteamas m, **by** ~ le tuiteamas

accidental adj tuiteamach

acclaim, acclamation n **1** (*applause, approbation*) caithream (*gen* caithreim) mf; **2** (*more abstr: renown etc*) cliù m invar

accommodation n **1** (*dwelling*) àite-fuirich m, lòistinn m, *in expr* **a night's** ~ cuid oidhche f; **2** (*arrangement, agreement*) rèite f, còrdadh m, **they came to an** ~ thàinig iad gu rèite/gu còrdadh

accompaniment n (*mus etc*) com-pàirt f, (*esp mus*) taic f

accompanist n (*mus*) neach-taice (*pl* luchd-taice m sing coll), com-pàirtiche m

accompany v **1** rach vi còmhla (*with prep* ri), **I'll** ~ **you (there)** thèid mi (ann) còmhla riut; **2** (*mus*) com-pàirtich vti, thoir taic f (*with prep* do)

accompanying adj (*associated with*) an cois prep, an lùib prep (*both with gen*), **a report and its** ~ **documents** aithisg agus na pàipearan a tha na cois/na lùib

accomplice n pàirtiche m

accomplish v thoir vt gu buil f, coilean vt, **I ~ed nothing** cha tug mi càil gu buil

accomplished adj & past part **1** (*task etc: completed, achieved*) coileanta; **2** (*of person:*

expert, skilled) ealanta, **an** ~ **linguist** cànanaiche ealanta

accord n co-aontachadh m, co-chòrdadh m

accordeon n bogsa-ciùil m, (*more fam*) bogsa m

accordance n, *in expr* **in** ~ **with** ann an co-rèir f ri

according adj a rèir (*with gen*), ~ **to your orders** a rèir nan òrduighean agaibh, **The Gospel** ~ **to Matthew** An Soisgeul a rèir Mhata

accordingly adv **1** (*as a result*) o chionn sin, air sgàth sin; **2** (*proportionately*) a rèir, **they gave five pounds to Mary, and to the others** ~ thug iad còig notaichean do Mhàiri, agus dhan fheadhainn eile a rèir

account n **1** (*fin*) cunntas m, **bank** ~ cunntas banca, **I've an** ~ **at the Royal Bank** tha cunntas agam aig a' Bhanca Rìoghail, **investment** ~ cunntas-tasgaidh, **savings** ~ cunntas-sàbhalaidh; **2** (*bill, invoice*) **an** ~ **to pay/settle** cunntas ri dhìoladh; **3** (*narrative, description etc*) cunntas m, (*in newspaper etc*) iomradh m, **an** ~ **of his life** cunntas (air) a bheatha, **an** ~ **of the strike** iomradh air an stailc

accountability n cunntachalachd f invar

accountable adj cunntachail

accountancy n cunntasachd f invar

accountant n cunntasair m

accounting n cunntasachd f invar

accoutrements npl uidheam f sing coll, acainn f sing coll

accredited adj barrantaichte

accumulate v càrn vt, cruinnich vti

accumulation n **1** (*the action*) càrnadh m; **2** (*the things accumulated*) co-chruinneachadh m

accurate adj **1** (*statements*) ceart, **what she said is** ~ tha na thubhairt i ceart; **2** (*sums, calculations*) cruinn, grinn; **3** (*of aim, weapon*) amaiseach, cuimseach

accursed adj mallaichte

accusation n casaid f, **make an** ~ dèan casaid (**against** an aghaidh, *followed by gen*)

accusative adj (*gram*) cuspaireach

accuse v **1** (*esp legal*) dèan casaid f (*with prep* an aghaidh *followed by gen*), **he ~d me** rinn e casaid nam aghaidh; **2** (*more general*) cuir vi, tilg vi, fàg vi, (*all with prep* air), cuir vi às a (*etc*) leth, **they ~d me of not being honest** chuir iad orm/chuir iad às mo leth nach robh mi onarach, **they ~d me of not being conscientious** thilg iad orm nach robh mi dìcheallach

accused adj & past part fo chasaid f (*with gen*), **he is** ~ **of murder** tha e fo chasaid-muirt

accused n neach fo chasaid m

accuser *n* neach-casaid *m*
accustom *v* cleachd *vt*, (*less usu*) gnàthaich *vt*, (**to** ri), **~ yourself to it!** cleachd thu fhèin ris!
accustomed *adj & past part* cleachdte (**to** ri)
ace *n* (*cards*), **the ~** an t-aon *m*
acerbic *adj* 1 (*of tastes etc*) geur; 2 (*of remarks, character etc*) guineach
ache *n* goirteas *m*
ache *v* bi *vi irreg* goirt, **her head ~d** bha a ceann goirt, **my back ~s** tha mo dhruim goirt
achieve *v* thoir *vt* gu buil *f*, coilean *vt*, **you never ~d anything** cha tug thu càil gu buil a-riamh
achieved *adj & past part* coileanta
achievement *n* euchd *m*, **that's a great ~** 's e euchd mòr a tha sin
acid *n* searbhag *f*
acid *adj* searbhagach, **~ rain** uisge searbhagach *m*, *also* uisge-searbhaig *m*
acidity *n* searbhachd *f invar*
acknowledge *v* aidich *vti*, **he ~d his error** dh'aidich e a mhearachd, **he ~d that he was wrong** dh'aidich e gun robh e ceàrr
acknowledged *adj* (*of expert, authority etc*) aithnichte
acne *n* cnàimhseagan *fpl*
acquaintance *n* 1 (*abstr*) eòlas *m* (**with** air); 2 (*persons*) **an ~** neach-eòlais *m*, **~s** luchd-eòlais *m sing coll*
acquainted *adj* 1 (*with persons*) eòlach (**with** air), **they're ~** tha iad eòlach air a chèile; 2 *in expr* **get ~ with someone** cuir eòlas air cuideigin; 3 (*~ with objects, ideas etc*) eòlach (**with** air), fiosrach (**with** mu), **~ with technology** eòlach air teicneolas
acquire *v* 1 faigh *vt*, (*by purchase*) ceannaich *vt*, **he ~d a house** fhuair/cheannaich e taigh; 2 (*learn, pick up*) tog *vt*, **I ~d my Gaelic in Skye** 's ann san Eilean Sgitheanach a thog mi mo chuid Gàidhlig
acquit *v* fuasgail *vt*
acre *n* acair *mf*
acrid *adj* searbh
acrimonious *adj* guineach
acrimony *n* guineachas *m*
acronym *n* acranaim (*pl* acranaimean) *m*
across *adv* (*usu expr movement*) tarsainn, thairis, **they went ~** chaidh iad tarsainn/thairis
across *prep* (*expr position or movement*) tarsainn (*with gen*), thar (*with gen*), thairis (*with prep* air), **a great tree was ~ the road** bha craobh mhòr tarsainn an rathaid, **they went ~ the bridge/the mountains** chaidh iad tarsainn na drochaid/nam beanntan, **they are/they went ~ the ocean** tha iad/chaidh

iad thar a' chuain, tha iad/chaidh iad thairis air a' chuan (*for prep prons formed with* thar, *see* p 510)
act *n* 1 (*deed, action*) gnìomh *m*; 2 (*pol*) achd *f*, **an ~ of Parliament** achd Pàrlamaid; 3 (*section of stage play*) earrann *f*
act *v* 1 gnìomhaich *vi*; 2 (*in play, film etc*) cluich *vti*
acting *adj* (*ie temporary*) an gnìomh *m*, **~ chair(person)** cathraiche *m* an gnìomh
action *n* 1 gnìomh *m*, **man of ~** fear-gnìomha *m*, **~ group** buidheann-ghnìomha *f*; 2 (*in law*) cùis-lagha *f*
active *adj* (*of persons: lively, energetic*) beothail, èasgaidh, tapaidh, deas; 2 (*industrious*) dèanadach, gnìomhach, dìcheallach; 3 (*busy, involved*) an sàs (**in** ann an), **~ in politics** an sàs ann am poilitigs; 4 (*gram*) spreigeach, **~ verb** gnìomhair spreigeach; 5 *in expr* **~ volcano** bholcàno beò
activeness *n* beothalachd *f invar*, tapachd *f invar*
activist *n* gnìomhaiche *m*
activity *n* 1 (*abstr*) gnìomhachd *f invar*; 2 (*professional ~*) dreuchd *f*; 3 (*spare time ~*) cur-seachad *m*
actor *n* actair *m*, (*more trad*) cluicheadair *m*, cleasaiche *m*
actress *n* ban-actair *f*
actual *adj* 1 (*not abstract*) nitheil, rudail; 2 (*real, true, genuine*) fìor (*precedes the n, which it lenites where possible*), **~ temperature** fìor theodhachd, **~ costs** fìor chosgaisean
acute *adj* 1 (*of faculties*) geur; 2 (*of illness*) dian; 3 *in expr* (*geometry*) **~ angle** ceàrn c(h)aol *mf*; 4 *in expr* (*lang*) **~ accent** stràc geur
adage *n* ràdh *m invar*
Adam's apple, the *n* meall *m* an sgòrnain
add *v* cuir *vt* (*with prep* ri), **~ some sugar (to it)** cuir siùcar ris
adder *n* nathair *f*
addict *n* tràill *mf*
addicted *adj & past part* na (*etc*) t(h)ràill *mf* (*with prep* do), an urra (*with prep* ri), **he's ~ to drugs** tha e na thràill do dhrogaichean *fpl*, tha e an urra ri drogaichean
addiction *n* tràilleachd *f invar* (**to** do)
addition *n* 1 (*numerical*) meudachadh *m*; 2 *in expr* **in ~ to** a thuilleadh air, **we have two flats in ~ to the house** tha dà lobhta againn a thuilleadh air an taigh; 3 *in expr* **an ~ to the family** pàiste a bharrachd san teaghlach
additional *adj* (an) tuilleadh (*with gen*), a bharrachd, **~ information** (an) tuilleadh

fiosrachaidh, **an ~ worker** obraiche a
bharrachd

address n 1 (*speech, talk*) òraid *f*, **give an ~**
thoir seachad òraid, dèan òraid; **2** (*postal ~*)
seòladh *m*

address v 1 (*speak/talk to*) bruidhinn (*with
prep* ri); **2** (*give talk*) thoir seachad òraid *f* (**to**
do), dèan òraid (*with prep* ri), **she ~ed the
local history society** thug i seachad òraid do
chomann na h-eachdraidh ionadail; **3** (*~ letter
etc*) cuir seòladh *m* (*with prep* air); **4** (*face up
to*) cuir aghaidh *f* (*with prep* ri), **he ~ed the
problem** chuir e aghaidh ris an duilgheadas

adept adj sgileil, deas, tapaidh, teòma, ealanta

adhesive adj leanailteach

adjacent adj faisg (**to** air), dlùth (**to** do *or* air)

adjective n buadhair *m*

adjourn v 1 (*as vt*) cuir vt an dàil *f*, **the chair
~ed the meeting** chuir an cathraiche a'
choinneamh an dàil; **2** (*as vi*) sgaoil vi, **the
meeting ~ed** sgaoil a' choinneamh

adjournment n cur *m* an dàil *f*, sgaoileadh *m*

adjust v 1 (*machine etc*) gleus vt, rèitich vt; **2**
(*clothing*) socraich vt

adjustment n 1 (*of machine etc*) gleusadh *m*,
rèiteachadh *m*; **2** (*of clothing*) socrachadh *m*

administer v (*~ organisation etc*) riaghail vt,
rianaich vt, seòl vt

administration n 1 (*abstr*) riaghladh *m*,
rianachd *f invar*; **2** (*con*) **the ~** luchd-riaghlaidh
m sing coll

administrative adj rianachail

administrator n rianaire *m*, neach-riaghlaidh *m*
(*pl* luchd-riaghlaidh *m sing coll*)

admissible adj (*acceptable, permissible*)
ceadaichte

adolescence n òigeachd *f invar*

adolescent n (*male*) òganach *m*, òigear *m*, (*of
either sex*) deugaire *m*

adopt v 1 (*child*) uchd-mhacaich vt; **2** (*a course
of action, plan etc*) cuir vt an gnìomh *m*

adopted adj uchd- *prefix*, **an ~ child** uchd-
leanabh *m*

adoption n 1 (*of child*) uchd-mhacachd *f invar*; **2**
(*of course of action, plan etc*) cur *m* an gnìomh
m

adorn v sgeadaich vt, sgèimhich vt

adroit adj 1 (*intellectually*) innleachdach, luath
na (*etc*) inntinn *f*; **2** (*phys*) deas, làmhach

adult adj inbhidh, **~ education** foghlam inbhidh

adult n inbheach *m*

adulterer, -ess n adhaltraiche *m*, ban-
adhaltraiche *f*

adulterous n adhaltranach

adultery n adhaltranas *m*

adulthood n inbhe *f*, **reach ~** thig vi gu inbhe

advance adj 1 (*in time*) ro-làimh, **~ payment**
dìoladh *m* ro-làimh; **2** (*of army etc*) toisich (*gen
sing of* toiseach *used adjectivally*), **~ party**
buidheann toisich

advance n 1 (*progress, improvement*) adhartas
m, piseach *m*, leasachadh *m*; **2** (*fin*) eàrlas
m, **the publisher gave him an ~** thug am
foillsichear eàrlas dha; **3** *in expr* **in ~**, ron là,
ron àm, ro-làimh, **do something in ~** dèan
rudeigin ron là/ron àm/ro-làimh

advance v 1 (*of troops etc*) rach vi air adhart; **2**
(*foster, improve*) thoir vt air adhart, adhartaich
vt, **~ the cause of freedom** thoir air adhart/
adhartaich adhbhar na saorsa

advantage n 1 (*benefit*) buannachd *f*, tairbhe *f
invar*, **it would be of great ~ to you** bhiodh
e na bhuannachd mhòr dhuibh; **2** *in expr* **take
~ of someone** (*unfairly*) gabh brath *m* air
cuideigin, (*not nec unfairly*) gabh cothrom *m* air
cuideigin

advantageous adj buannachdail, tairbheach &
tarbhach

adverb n co-ghnìomhair *m*

adverbial adj co-ghnìomhaireil

adversary n 1 (*enemy*) nàmhaid *m*; **2** (*opponent
in argument, debate etc*) co-chòmhragaiche *m*

adversity n cruadal *m*

advertise v sanasaich vti

advertisement n sanas *m*, sanas-reic *m*

advice n comhairle *f*, **give ~** thoir comhairle (**to**
air *or* do), **take/get ~** gabh comhairle

advisable adj iomchaidh, glic

advisability n iomchaidheachd *f invar*

advise v comhairlich vt, comhairlich vi (*with
prep* do), thoir comhairle (*with preps* air *or* do)

adviser n neach-comhairle *m* (*pl* luchd-comhairle
m sing coll), comhairleach *m*, **financial ~**
comhairleach ionmhais

advocate n neach-tagraidh *m* (*pl* luchd-tagraidh
m sing coll)

adze n tàl *m*

aeroplane n plèana *m*, (*more trad*) itealan *m*

aerospace n adhar-fhànas (*gen* adhar-fhànais) *m*

aesthetics n feallsanachd-maise *f invar*

affair n 1 (*matter, situation*) cùis *f*, rud *m*, nì *m*,
gnothach *m*, **how did the ~ go/turn out?**
ciamar a chaidh a' chùis?, **it was a bad ~** 's e
droch nì a bh' ann, **their divorce was a bad ~**
's e droch rud a bh' anns an sgaradh-pòsaidh aca

affect v drùidh vt (*with prep* air), **the news
didn't ~ her** cha do dhrùidh an naidheachd

oirre, (*more fam*) **it didn't ~ me in the least**
cha do chuir e suas no sìos mi

affectation *n* leòm *f*

affection *n* gràdh *m*, rùn *m*, (*less strong*) tlachd
f invar

affectionate *adj* gaolach, gràdhach, maoth

afforestation *n* coillteachadh *m*

afloat *adj*, air flod *m*, air fleòdradh *m*, air bhog *m*

afraid *adj* **1** fo eagal *m*, **a man ~** duine fo eagal;
2 (*after verb* **to be**) bi *vi irreg* an t-eagal (*with
the prep* air), **she was ~ (of me)** bha an t-eagal
oirre (romham); **3** *in expr* **become ~** gabh
eagal; **4** (*expr polite regret*) **I don't know, I'm
~** chan eil fhios (*for a fhios m*, 'knowledge of it')
agam, tha eagal orm

afresh *adv* às ùr, **start ~** tòisich *vti* às ùr

Africa *n* Afraga *f invar*

after *conj* an dèidh (*with prep* do), **~ I closed/
had closed my eyes** an dèidh dhomh mo
shùilean a dhùnadh, **~ the pub opened** an
dèidh dhan taigh-seinnse fosgladh

after *prep* **1** (*expr sequence*) an dèidh, às dèidh,
(*followed by the gen*), **~ the storm** an dèidh na
stoirme, **she came ~ him** thàinig i às a dhèidh;
2 (*expr interval of time*) an ceann (*with gen*),
~ a little while an ceann greiseig; **3** *in expr*
one ~ the other fear an dèidh fir, tè an dèidh
tè, **the policemen left, one ~ the other**
dh'fhalbh na poileasmain, fear an dèidh fir; **4** (*in
pursuit or search of*) an tòir (*with prep* air), **the
police are ~ him** tha am poileas an tòir air,
he went to town ~ a new car chaidh e dhan
bhaile *m* an tòir air càr ùr; **5** *in expr* (*of family
resemblance etc*) **take ~ someone** rach *vi* ri
taobh cuideigin

afternoon *n* feasgar *m*, **yesterday ~** feasgar an-
dè, **good ~!** feasgar math!, (*as adv expr*) **we'll
be in in the ~** bidh sinn a-staigh feasgar

afterthought *n* **1** ath-smuain *f*; **2** (*revised
opinion etc*) ath-bheachd *m*

again *adv* **1** a-rithist, fhathast, **say it ~** can
a-rithist e, can fhathast e, **I'll see you ~** chì mi
fhathast sibh, **do it ~!** dèan fhathast/a-rithist e!;
2 *in exprs* **I told him time and ~/over and
over ~** dh'innis mi dha uair *f* is uair; **3** (*after v
in the neg*) tuilleadh *adv*, **don't do that (ever)
~** na dèan sin tuilleadh; **4** (*afresh*) *in expr* **start
~** tòisich *vti* às ùr

against *prep* **1** (*contrary to, opposed to*) an
aghaidh (*with gen*), **~ the law** an aghaidh
an lagha, **dead/completely/totally ~ the
government** calg-dhìreach an aghaidh an
riaghaltais, **he turned ~ me** thionndaidh e nam
aghaidh; **2** (*expr struggle*) ri *prep* (*with dat*), **~**

the current ris an t-sruth; **3** (*expr proximity,
leaning*) ri *prep* (*with dat*), **~ the wall** ris a'
bhalla

age *n* **1** aois *f*, **(old) age is a great hindrance**
is mòr am bacadh an aois, **what age is he?** dè
an aois a tha e?; **2** (*period*) linn *mf*, (*hist*) **the
Dark ~s** na Linntean Dorcha, **the space ~** linn
an fhànais; **3** *in expr* (*fam*) **I've been here for
~s (and ~s)!** tha mi ann an seo bho chionn
ùineachan *fpl* (is ùineachan)!; **4** (*of people of
the same age*) *in expr* **they're ~s with one
another** tha iad co-aoiseach *adj*, tha iad nan
co-aoisean *mpl*

agency *n* **1** (*esp public service etc*) ionad *m*,
employment ~ ionad-cosnaidh; **2** *in expr*
travel ~ bùth-siubhail *f*

agenda *n* clàr-gnothaich *m*

agent *n* **1** (*one's representative*) neach-ionaid *m*
(*pl* luchd-ionaid *m sing coll*); **2** (*one who takes
action*) fear-gnìomha *m*

aggravate *v* **1** (*make worse*) dèan *vt* nas miosa; **2**
(*annoy*) cuir dragh *m* (*with prep* air)

aggravating *adj* draghail

aggravation (*annoyance*) dragh *m*

agile *adj* **1** (*esp phys*) clis, grad, **~ movements**
gluasadan grada; **2** (*mentally ~*) luath na (*etc*)
inntinn *f*

agility *n* cliseachd *f invar*, luas *m*, lùth *m*

agitate *v* **1** (*shake*) crath *vt*; **2** (*stir up*) gluais *vt*;
3 (*incite, provoke*) brod *vt*, spreig *vt*, stuig *vt*; **4**
(*upset*) cuir *vt* troimh-a-chèile

agitated *adj & past part* (*upset*) troimh-a-chèile

agitation *n* **1** (*stir, excitement*) gluasad *m*; **2**
(*emotional confusion*) buaireas *m*

ago *adv* **1** o chionn & bho chionn (*with gen*), **a
short time ~** o chionn ghoirid, **long ~/a long
time ~** o chionn fhada, **a while ~** o chionn
greis; **2** (*in fairy stories etc*) **long long ~** o
chionn fada nan cian, fada fada ron a seo

agree *v* **1** (*be in or come to ~ment*) co-aontaich
vi, co-chòrd *vi*; **2** *in expr* **~ to** gabh *vi* (*with prep*
ri), **we ~ to those proposals** gabhaidh sinn ris
na molaidhean sin

agreeable *adj* **1** (*esp of people*) ciatach; **2** (*of
people, also things, situations*) taitneach (**to** ri);
3 (*acceptable*) iomchaidh; **4** *in expr* **that is ~ to
me, I find that ~** tha sin a' còrdadh rium

agreeableness *n* taitneachd *f invar*, taitneas *m*

agreed *adj & past part* aontaichte

agreement *n* **1** (*abstr & con*) còrdadh *m*, aonta
m, co-aontachadh *m*, co-chòrdadh *m*, **reach/
come to an ~** thig *vi* gu còrdadh, **be in ~**
co-aontaich *vi*; **2** (*business ~, contractual ~*)
cùnnradh *m*, cùmhnant *m*

agriculture *n* **1** (*the subject*) àiteachas *m*; **2** (*the activity*) tuathanachas *m*, àiteach *m*

ahead *prep* air thoiseach (**of** air), **far ~ of us** fada air thoiseach oirnn, **~ of other countries in technology** air thoiseach air dùthchannan eile a thaobh teicneòlais

aid *n* **1** (*help*) cuideachadh *m*, cobhair *f*; **2** (*support*) taic *f*, **financial ~** taic-airgid *f*; **3** (*tool, facilitator etc*) uidheam-cuideachaidh *f*, **~s for the disabled** uidheaman-cuideachaidh do na ciorramaich

aid *v* cuidich *vti*, thoir taic *f* (*with prep* do)

aide *n* neach-cuideachaidh (*pl* luchd-cuideachaidh *m sing coll*)

aide-mémoire *n* nota *f*

ail *v* bi *vi* ceàrr (*with prep* air), **what ~s you?** dè a tha ceàrr ort?, *also* dè a tha thu a' gearan?

ailing *adj* tinn, (*more fam*) bochd, meadhanach

aim *n* **1** (*of weapon*) amas *m*; **2** (*intention, ambition*) amas *m*, rùn *m*

aim *v* **1** (*weapon etc*) cuimsich *vti*, amais *vti*, (**at** air); **2** (*intend*) bi *vi irreg* am beachd *m* (*with infin or pres part*), **I'm ~ing to go to college** tha mi am beachd a dhol don cholaiste

air[1] *n* **1** (*~ as breathed*) àile *m*; **2** (*the sky*) adhar *m*, **up in the ~** shuas san adhar, **the Air Force** Feachd *f* an Adhair

air[2] *n* (*appearance, mien, look*) coltas *m*

air[3] *n* (*tune*) fonn *m*

aircraft, **airliner** *n* plèana *mf*, (*more trad*) itealan *m*

airfield *n* raon-adhair *m*

airport *n* port-adhair *m*

airstrip *n* raon-adhair *m*

alarm *n* rabhadh *m*, **~ bell** clag-rabhaidh *m*

alas! *excl* (*trad*) och!, mo thruaighe! f, **~ and alack** och nan och!

alcohol *n* **1** (*as drink*) deoch-làidir *f*; **2** (*the chemical substance*) alcol *m invar*

alcoholic *adj* **1** alcolach; **2** *in expr* **~ drink** deoch-làidir *f*

alcoholic *n* tràill *mf* don deoch(-làidir) *f*, **he is an ~** tha e na thràill don deoch(-làidir), *also* tha e an urra ri alcol *m invar*

alcoholism *n* tinneas *m* na dighe

alder *n* feàrna *f invar*

ale *n* leann *m*

alert *adj* **1** (*mentally*) **~** grad/geur na (*etc*) inntinn *f*; **2** (*of sentry etc*) furachail; **3** (*aware*) mothachail (**to** air), **~ to the danger** mothachail air a' chunnart

alert *n* (*signal*) comharradh-rabhaidh *m*

alert *v* thoir rabhadh *m* (*with prep* do), earalaich *vt*, **they ~ed me** thug iad rabhadh dhomh

alien *n* **1** neach *m*/creutair *m* à planaid *f* eile; **2** (*foreigner*) coigreach *m*

alienate *v* cuir *vt* na (*etc*) aghaidh *nf* fhèin, **you'll ~ all your colleagues** cuiridh tu do cho-obraichean air fad nad aghaidh fhèin

alight *v* teirinn & teàrn *vi*

alike *adj* ionann (*with v* is), coltach ri chèile, **you and I are not ~** chan ionann thusa agus mise, **all the buildings were ~** bha na togalaichean air fad coltach ri chèile

alive *adj* beò

all *adj & adv* **1** (*without exception*) uile, air fad, gu lèir, (*all follow the n*) **the soldiers ~ left, ~ the soldiers left** dh'fhalbh na saighdearan uile/air fad, **~ that's over, that's ~ over** tha sin uile seachad, **~ the houses were burned** chaidh na taighean air fad/gu lèir a losgadh; **2** (*esp with periods of time*) fad (*plus gen*), **~ the time** fad na h-ùine, **I was poor ~ my life** bha mi bochd fad mo bheatha, **I'll be awake ~ night** bidh mi nam dhùisg fad na h-oidhche; **3** (*the whole*) an t-iomlan *m*, air fad, **do you want ~ of it?, do you want it ~?** a bheil thu ag iarraidh an iomlain (dheth)?, **they ravaged ~ the country** sgrios iad an dùthaich air fad; **4** (*idiom*) **that's ~ there is to it** chan eil an còrr ann ach sin

all- *prefix* uile- (*lenites following cons where possible*), (*eg*) **all-powerful** uile-chumhachdach, **all-knowing** uile-fhiosrach

alleviate *v* (*pain, suffering*) faothaich *vti*

alleviation *n* (*of pain, suffering*) faothachadh & faochadh *m*, **he experienced some ~** thàinig faothachadh air

alley *n* caol-shràid *f*

alliance *n* caidreabhas *m*

alliteration *n* uaim *f*

allocate *v* (*resources etc*) riaraich *vt*, sònraich *vt*

allocation *n* **1** (*abstr*) riarachadh *m*; **2** (*con*) cuibhreann *mf*, **we received our ~ of food** fhuair sinn ar cuibhreann de bhiadh

allot *v* (*resources etc*) riaraich *vt*, sònraich *vt*

allow *v* leig *vi* (*with prep* do *or* le), ceadaich *vti*, **he ~ed me to buy it** leig e dhomh/leam a cheannach

allowable *adj* ceadaichte

allowance *n* (*fin etc*) cuibhreann *mf*, **disability ~** cuibhreann-ciorraim

allowed *adj & past part* **1** ceadaichte; **2** (*on notices etc*) **smoking** (*etc*) **not ~** chan fhaodar smocadh (*etc*)

alloy *n* coimheatailt *f*, laghd-mheatailt *f*

allude *v* thoir tarraing *f*, thoir iomradh *m*, thoir guth *m*, (*all with prep* air), **you didn't ~ to my**

promotion cha tug sibh tarraing/iomradh/guth air an àrdachadh agam

allure *v* tàlaidh *vt*, meall *vt*

allurement *n* tàladh *m*, mealladh *m*

alluring *adj* meallach

allusion *n* iomradh *m*, tarraing *f*, guth *m*, (**to** air), **he made no ~ to it** cha tug e iomradh/ tarraing/guth air

ally *n* caidreabhach *m*

almost *adv* **1** cha mhòr, **we see her ~ every day** bidh sinn ga faicinn a h-uile là, cha mhòr; **2** cha mhòr nach *conj*, gu ìre bhig *adv*, **I ~ lost my purse** cha mhòr nach do chaill mi mo sporan, **we ~ missed the bus** chaill sinn am bus gu ìre bhig; **3** (*nearly completed action or process*) gu bhith (*plus adj*), **I'm ~ ready** tha mi gu bhith deiseil; **4** (*narrowly avoided action/event in the past*) theab *vi def*, **I ~ fell** theab mi tuiteam, **they ~ ruined me** theab iad mo sgriosadh

alms *n* dèirc *f*

alone *adj & adv* **1** nam (*etc*) aonar, leam (*etc*) fhìn/fhèin, **she was ~** bha i na h-aonar, bha i leatha fhèin, **when I'm ~** an uair a bhios mi leam fhìn; **2** (*idiom*) **let/leave them ~!** leig *vi* leotha!

along *adv* **1** air adhart, air aghaidh, **how are you getting ~** ciamar a tha thu a' faighinn air adhart?, **that's coming ~ well** tha sin a' tighinn air adhart gu math; **2** (*idiom*) **we walked ~** choisich sinn romhainn

along *prep* **1** (*expr movement*) fad (*with gen*), **~ the house/road** fad an taighe/an rathaid; **2** (*expr position*) shuas, shìos, **a short distance ~ the road** pìos beag shuas/shìos an rathad; **3** (*accompanying*) **~ with** còmhla ri, (*less usu*) maille ri, **~ with the others** còmhla ri càch

alongside *prep* ri taobh (*with gen*), **a boat ~ the quay** bàta ri taobh a' chidhe; **2** (*compared to*) an taca ri, **she's clever ~ her brother** tha i glic an taca ri a bràthair

alphabet *n* aibidil *f*

alphabetical *adj* aibidileach, **~ order** òrdugh aibidileach, *also* òrdugh na h-aibidil *m*

already *adv* mu thràth, *also found as* mar a tha & mar-thà, (*less usu*) (a-)cheana, **as I said ~** mar a thubhairt mi mu thràth/a-cheana

also *adv* cuideachd, (*less usu*) mar an ceudna, **has Ewan left? yes, and Iain ~** an do dh'fhalbh Eòghann? dh'fhalbh, agus Iain cuideachd/mar an ceudna

alter *v* atharraich *vti*, mùth *vi*

alteration *n* atharrachadh *m*, mùthadh *m*

alternate *v*, **the two of them ~d as spokesperson** bha an dithis aca nan neach-labhairt fear mu seach

alternative *adj* eile, eadar-dhealaichte, eadar-roghnach, **an ~ plan** plana eile, **~ medicine** eòlas-leigheis eadar-dhealaichte

alternative *n* roghainn *f*, **we had no ~** cha robh roghainn (eile) againn

alternatively *adv* an àite sin, air mhodh eile, **~ we could take the bus** an àite sin b' urrainn dhuinn am bus a ghabhail

although *conj* ged, **~ he wasn't ill** ged nach robh e tinn, **she didn't stop ~ she was exhausted** cha do sguir i ged a bha i claoidhte

altitude *n* àirde *f invar*

altogether *adv* uile-gu-lèir, gu tur, **she gave it up ~** sguir i dheth uile-gu-lèir, **the two things are ~ different** tha an dà rud gu tur eadar-dhealaichte

always *adv* daonnan, gun sgur, an-còmhnaidh, **she's ~ on my mind** tha i daonnan air m' aire, **she's ~ on at me!** tha i an sàs annam gun sgur/ an-còmhnaidh!

Alzheimer's disease *n* tinneas *m* Alzheimer

amalgamate *v* **1** (*companies etc*) co-aonaich *vi*; **2** (*substances: fuse*) co-leagh *vti*, (*mix*) co-mheasgaich *vti*

amalgamation *n* (*of companies etc*) co-aonachadh *m*

amaze *v* cuir mòr-iongnadh *m* (*with prep* air), **it ~d me** chuir e mòr-iongnadh orm

amazed *adj & past part*, **I** (*etc*) **was ~** ghabh mi (*etc*) mòr-iongnadh *m*

amazement *n* mòr-iongnadh *m*

amazing *adj* a chuireas/a chuireadh mòr-iongnadh *m* air duine *m*

ambassador *n* tosgaire *m*

amber *n* òmar *m*

ambiguity *n* dà-sheaghachd *f invar*

ambiguous *adj* dà-sheaghach

ambition *n* **1** (*for self-advancement*) miann-adhartais *m*, gionaiche *m invar*; **2** (*a wish, an aim*) rùn *m*, miann *f*, (*stronger*) glòir-mhiann *mf*

ambitious *adj* gionach, glòir-mhiannach

ambivalence *n* **1** (*ambiguity*) dà-sheaghachd *f invar*; **2** (*state of being in two minds*) dà-bharaileachd *f invar*

ambivalent *adj* **1** (*ambiguous*) dà-sheaghach; **2** (*in two minds*) dà-bharaileach, ann an ioma-chomhairle *f*

ambulance *n* carbad-eiridinn *m*

ambush *n* feall-fhalach *m*

amenable *adj* fosgailte (**to** ri, do)

amend v 1 (*change*) atharraich vt; 2 (*improve*) leasaich vt

amendment n 1 (*change*) atharrachadh m; 2 (*improvement*) leasachadh m

amenity n goireas m, **the club has lots of amenities** tha goireasan gu leòr aig a' chlub

America n Ameireaga f

amiss adj ceàrr, air iomrall, **something is** ~ tha rudeigin ceàrr, chaidh rudeigin air iomrall

ammunition n connadh-làmhaich m sing coll

amorous adj leannanach

amount n uimhir f invar, uiread f invar, **a certain** ~ **of something** na h-uimhir/na h-uiread de rudeigin, **give me the same** ~ **as Iain (has)** thoir dhomh uiread 's a tha aig Iain

amphibian n muir-thìreach m

amphibious adj dà-bheathach, muir-thìreach

ample adj 1 (*of quantity*) pailt, ~ **food** biadh pailt; 2 (*of person's build*) tomadach & tomaltach

amusement n 1 (*abstr*) àbhachd f invar; 2 (*fun etc*) spòrs f, dibhearsain m; 3 (*distraction, pastime, esp trivial*) caitheamh-aimsir m; 4 (*in* ~ *arcade etc*) ~**s** faoin-chleasan mpl

amusing adj èibhinn

anachronism n 1 (*abstr*) às-aimsireachd f invar; 2 (*con*) rud às-aimsireil m

anachronistic adj às-aimsireil

anaemia n cion-fala m invar

analyse v sgrùd vt, (*more rigorous*) mion-sgrùd vt

analysis n sgrùdadh m, (*more rigorous*) mion-sgrùdadh m

anatomical adj 1 (*abstr: pertainng to the subject of anatomy*) corp-eòlach; 2 (*pertaining to the actual body*) corporra

anatomist n corp-eòlaiche m

anatomy n 1 (*abstr: the science*) corp-eòlas m; 2 (*con: an actual body*) corp m, (*usu living*) bodhaig f

anchor n 1 acair(e) mf; 2 in expr **at** ~ aig acarsaid f, air an acair(e)

anchorage n acarsaid f

anchored adj & past part aig acarsaid f

and conj 1 agus, (*esp in common pairings of words*) is, **he came in** ~ **sat down** thàinig e a-steach agus shuidh e sìos, **bread** ~ **butter** aran is ìm; 2 (*other exprs*) **open the door** ~ **see if it's still raining** fosgail an doras feuch a bheil an t-uisge ann fhathast, **come** ~ **see me** thig vi gam (*for* gu mo) fhaicinn

androgynous adj fireann-boireann

anecdote n 1 sgeul m, (*esp piece of gossip*) seanchas m; 2 (~ *told at ceilidh etc*) stòiridh mf, naidheachd f

anew adv às ùr, **start** ~ tòisich vti às ùr

anger n fearg f, (*extreme*) cuthach m

angle n 1 (*geometry*) uileann & uilinn f, ceàrn mf, **a right** ~ ceart-uilinn, ceart-cheàrn, **acute** ~ ceàrn caol; 2 (*more loosely*) in expr **at an** ~ air fhiaradh m

angler n iasgair m

angling n breacach m, iasgach-slaite m

angry adj 1 feargach, (*fam*) fiadhaich, **an** ~ **man** duine feargach, **I was** ~ **after what he said to me** bha mi fiadhaich an dèidh na thuirt e rium; 2 (*other exprs*) **she grew** ~ thàinig fearg/an fhearg oirre, ghabh i an fhearg, **she made him** ~ chuir i fearg/an fhearg air

anguish n 1 (*emotional*) dòrainn f; 2 (*mental or phys*) cràdh m

anguished adj dòrainneach

animate adj beò

animate v 1 (*bring to life*) beothaich vt; 2 (*stir up*) brosnaich vt, brod vt

animated adj 1 (*lively*) beothail; 2 (*excited, in high spirits*) mear

animation n 1 (*liveliness*) beothalachd f invar; 2 (*bustle*) drip f; 3 (*high spirits*) mearachas m

ankle n caol m na coise, adhbrann m, **my/her** ~ caol mo choise/a coise

annihilate v cuir vi às (*with prep* do), (*more formal*) neonithich vt

annotate v cuir notaichean (*with prep* ri)

annoy v cuir dragh m (*with prep* air), **the noise of that music is** ~**ing me** tha fuaim mf a' chiùil sin a' cur dragh orm

annoyance n dragh m, leamhadas m

annoying adj 1 (*of person, situation*) draghail; 2 (*irritating, niggling*) leamh, **they're constantly asking me** ~ **questions** bidh iad a' cur cheistean leamha orm fad na h-ùine

annual adj bliadhnail

annual n 1 (*book*) bliadhnachan m; 2 (*flower*) flùr m aon-bhliadhnach

annul v cuir vt an neoni f invar

anonymous adj gun urra f invar, **an** ~ **letter** litir gun urra, *also* litir gun ainm m rithe

anonymously adv, **the book came out** ~ nochd an leabhar (an clò) gun ainm m ùghdair m

another adj 1 (*different*) eile, **I'd prefer** ~ **book** b' fheàrr leam leabhar eile; 2 (*additional*) eile, **I won't take** ~ **pint** cha ghabh mi pinnt eile, **I don't want** ~ **thing** chan eil mi ag iarraidh càil eile

answer *n* freagairt *f*, **I didn't get an ~ cha
d' fhuair mi freagairt, we'll give you an ~
soon** bheir sinn freagairt dhuibh a dh'aithghearr
answer *v* freagair *vti*, **won't you ~ me?** nach
freagair thu mi?, **he hasn't ~ed yet** cha do
fhreagair e fhathast
Antarctic *n, used with art*, an Antartaig *f*
anthem *n* laoidh *mf*
anthology *n* cruinneachadh *m*, co-
chruinneachadh *m*, (*esp of poetry*) duanaire *m*
anti-clockwise *adj* tuathal
antidote *n* urchasg *m*
antler *n* crò(i)c *f*, cabar *m*, **deer's ~s** cabair *mpl*
fèidh
anus *n* tòn *f*, (*vulg*) toll *m*, toll-tòine *m*
anvil *n* innean *m*
anxiety *n* **1** cùram *m*, dragh *m*, imcheist *f*,
iomagain *f*, **lack of money is causing me ~**
tha dìth airgid a' dèanamh dragh dhomh; **2** *in
expr* **prone to ~** iomagaineach, cùramach
anxious *adj* cùramach, fo chùram, fo imcheist, fo
iomagain, imcheisteach, iomagaineach
any *adj & pron* **1** gin *pron*, **have we ~
envelopes?** a bheil gin chèisean-litreach
againn?, **he was wanting nails but I hadn't
~** bha e ag iarraidh thàirngean ach cha robh gin
agam; **2** (*no matter which*) sam bith, **~ book
will do** nì leabhar sam bith an gnothach; **3** (*in
neg sentence*) sam bith, **there wasn't ~ food
(at all) in the shops** cha robh biadh sam bith
sna bùithtean; **4** *in expr* **~ more** tuilleadh, **do
you want ~ more?** a bheil thu ag iarraidh
tuilleadh?, **don't do that ~ more** na dèan sin
tuilleadh
anybody, anyone *pron* **1** duine *m*, **is there ~
there/in?** a bheil duine ann?; **2** (*no matter
who*) duine sam bith, **~ could do it** bhiodh
duine sam bith comasach air, dhèanadh duine
sam bith e; **3** (*in neg sentence*) duine, (*stronger*)
duine sam bith, **there wasn't ~ (at all) in the
church** cha robh duine (sam bith) san eaglais *f*
anything *n* **1** càil *f invar*, dad *f invar*, sìon *m*,
rudeigin *pron*, **is there ~ in the cupboard?** a
bheil càil/dad/sìon sa phreasa?, **I don't want
~ else** chan eil mi ag iarraidh càil eile, **I don't
know ~ about it** chan eil càil a (*for* de) dh'fhios
agam, **is ~ wrong?** a bheil rudeigin/càil ceàrr?;
2 (*no matter what*) rud *m* sam bith, nì *m* sam
bith, **what do you want?** **~ at all** dè a tha thu
ag iarraidh? nì/rud sam bith; **3** (*idioms*) **don't
have ~ to do with him/it!** na gabh gnothach
m ris!, **she didn't say ~ else** cha tuirt i an còrr
anyway *adv* co-dhiù, **I'm leaving ~!** tha mise a'
falbh co-dhiù!

aorta *n, used with art*, a' chuisle-chinn *f*
apart *adj* **1** (*special*) air leth, **a man ~** duine air
leth; **2** *in expr* **~ from** ach a-mhàin, **the family
left, ~ from the son** dh'fhalbh an teaghlach,
ach a-mhàin am mac
apathy *n* cion-ùidhe *m*
aperture *n* fosgladh *m*
apolitical *adj* neo-phoilitigeach
apologise *v* **1** dèan leisgeul *m*, **I want to ~** tha
mi airson leisgeul a dhèanamh, **he ~d** rinn e
leisgeul, *also* dh'iarr e a leisgeul a ghabhail; **2** *in
expr* **I ~!** gabh(aibh) mo leisgeul!
apology *n* leisgeul *m*
apostrophe *n* (*orthog*) asgair *m*
apparatus *n* uidheam *f*, acainn *f*
apparent *adj* **1** (*evident, obvious*) follaiseach, **it's
~ that he's not guilty** tha e follaiseach nach
eil e ciontach; **2** (*idiom*) **become ~** thig *vi* am
follais *f invar*
apparently *adv* a rèir c(h)oltais *m*, **he was a
scoundrel, ~** 's e slaightear a bh' ann dheth, a
rèir choltais
appeal *n* **1** (*attractiveness*) tàladh *m*; **2** (*request,
entreaty*) iarrtas (dian) *m*, guidhe *mf*; **3** (*law
etc*) tagradh *m*, **an ~ against a sentence**
tagradh an aghaidh binne *f gen*
appeal *v* **1** (*attract*) tarraing *vt*, tàlaidh *vt*; **2**
(*request*) iarr *vt* (gu dian); **3** (*law etc*) tagair *vt*,
~ against a sentence tagair an aghaidh binne
appear *v* **1** (*come into sight, arrive*) nochd
vi, **where did you ~ from?** cò às a nochd
thu(sa)?, (*book*) **~ (in print)** nochd (an clò),
also thig *vi* am follais; **2** (*seem*) bi coltach gu, **it
~s that she was married** tha e coltach gun
robh i pòsta, *also* bha i pòsta, a rèir choltais; **3**
(*look, have the appearance of*) **he ~s tired** tha
coltas *m* na sgìths air
appearance *n* **1** (*abstr: act of appearing*)
nochdadh *m*; **2** (*aspect*) cruth *m*; **3** (*of person's
features, not nec permanent*) tuar *m*; **4**
(*resemblance*) coltas *m*, **you have the ~ of a
soldier** tha coltas saighdeir *m* ort; **5** *in expr*
judging by ~s a rèir choltais, **judging by ~s,
he's guilty** a rèir choltais, tha e ciontach
appease *v* (*opposing parties etc*) rèitich *vt*
appetite *n* càil *f*, càil-bìdh (*gen of* biadh *m*)
apple *n* **1** ubhal *m*; **2** *in expr* **the ~ of the eye**
clach *f* na sùla
appliance *n* uidheam *f*, **heating ~** uidheam-
teasachaidh
applicant *n* neach-iarraidh (*pl* luchd-iarraidh *m
sing coll*), neach-tagraidh *m* (*pl* luchd-tagraidh
m sing coll)

application *n* **1** (*for job etc*) iarrtas *m*, ~ **form** foirm iarrtais; **2** (*diligence etc*) dìcheall *m*; **3** (*putting into practice or effect*) cur *m* an gnìomh *m*, **the** ~ **of new rules** cur an gnìomh riaghailtean ùra; **4** (*IT*) cleachdadh *m*, ~**s programme** prògram chleachdaidhean

apply *v* **1** (*for job etc*) cuir a-steach iarrtas *m* (**for** airson); **2** (*put into practice or effect*) cuir *vt* an gnìomh *m*; **3** (*be relevant, affect*) buin *vi* (**to** do), **this applies to you** buinidh seo dhut(sa)/dhuibh(se)

appoint *v* **1** (*select*) tagh *vt*, (*esp for job*) cuir *vt* an dreuchd *f*, **the best applicant was ~ed** chaidh an neach-iarraidh a b' fheàrr a thaghadh; **2** (*set up*) suidhich *vt*, ~ **a committee** suidhich comataidh

appointed *adj & past part* **1** (*selected*) air a (*etc*) t(h)aghadh; **2** *in expr* **before the ~ time** ron mhithich *f invar*

apportion *v* roinn *vt*, riaraich *vt*, pàirtich *vt*

apportionment *n* **1** (*abstr: the action*) roinneadh *m*; **2** (*con: a share*) cuibhreann *mf*, roinn *f*

appraisal *n* measadh *m*

appraise *v* meas *vt*, dèan measadh *m* (*with prep* air)

appreciate *v* **1** (*understand, sympathise with*) fidir *vt*, tuig *vt*, **you don't ~ the state I'm in for love of you** chan fhidir thu/cha tuig thu mar tha mise led ghaol; **2** (*be grateful*) bi *vi irreg* taingeil (**for** airson), cuir luach *m invar* (*with prep* air), **I ~ what you did for me** tha mi taingeil airson na rinn thu dhomh

appreciation *n* **1** (*gratitude*) taingealachd *f invar*; **2** (*understanding, awareness*) tuigse *f invar*, mothachadh *m*

appreciative *adj* **1** (*grateful*) taingeil (**of** airson, *with gen*), ~ **of what you did** taingeil airson na rinn sibh; **2** (*valuing, enjoying, aware*) mothachail, tuigseach

apprehend *v* glac *vt*, **the police ~ed him** ghlac am poileas e

apprentice *n* preantas *m*

approach *v* **1** (*phys*) dlùthaich *vi* (*with prep* ri), **we were ~ing the sea** bha sinn a' dlùthachadh ris a' mhuir; **2** (*fig*) teann *vi* (*with prep* ri), **it was ~ing midnight** bha e a' teannadh ris a' mheadhan-oidhche

approachable *adj* (*of person*) fosgarra, fosgailte

apron *n* aparan *m*

appropriate *adj* freagarrach, iomchaidh

appropriate *v* gabh seilbh *f* (*with prep* air)

approval *n* **1** (*agreement*) aonta *m*; **2** (*consent*) cead *m*

approve *v* **1** (*consent, agree*) bi *vi irreg* airson (*with gen*), **I ~ of that!** tha mi airson sin!; **2** (*allow*) ceadaich *vt*, ùghdarraich *vt*

approved *adj & past part* ceadaichte, ùghdarraichte

approximately *adv* timcheall air, **there'll be ~ ten people there** bidh timcheall air deichnear ann

April *n* Giblean *m*, Giblinn *f*, *used with art*, an Giblean, a' Ghiblinn

apt *adj* **1** (*appropriate*) freagarrach, iomchaidh; **2** (*liable, prone*) buailteach, dualtach, ~ **to spend money** buailteach airgead *m* a chosg, ~ **to be stingy** dualtach a bhith spìocach

aquaculture *n* tuathanachas *m* uisge

Arab *n* Arabach *m*

Arabic *adj* Arabach, ~ **numerals** figearan Arabach

arable *adj* àitich, ~ **land** talamh-àitich

arbiter *n* neach-rèiteachaidh *m* (*pl* luchd-rèiteachaidh *m sing coll*)

arbitrary *adj* **1** (*chance*) tuaireamach; **2** (*unreasonable etc*) neo-riaghailteach

arbitrate *v* (*between opposing parties etc*) rèitich *vi*

arbitration *n* rèiteachadh *m*

arch *n* stuagh *f*, bogha *m*

archbishop *n* àrd-easbaig *m*

archaeological *adj* àrsaidheil

archaeologist *n* àrsair *m*, arc-eòlaiche *m*

archaeology *n* àrsaidheachd *f invar*, arc-eòlas *m*

archaic *adj* àrsaidh

archer *n* boghadair *m*

archetypal *adj* prìomh-shamhlach

archetype *n* prìomh-shamhla *m*

architect *n* ailtire *m*

architectural *adj* ailtireach

architecture *n* ailtireachd *f invar*

archive *n* tasglann *f*

archivist *n* tasglannaiche *m*

Arctic, the *n* an Artaig *f*, **the ~ Circle** Cearcall *m* na h-Artaig, *also* An Cearcall Artach

ardent *adj* (*of persons, emotions, deeds*) dian

ardour *n* dèine *f invar*

area *n* **1** (*abstr*) farsaingeachd *f invar*; **2** (*district, locality etc*) ceàrn *mf*, **a remote ~** ceàrn iomallach; **3** (*topic, field*) raon *m*, **expert in this ~** fìor eòlach san raon seo

argue *v* **1** (*discuss, also squabble*) connsaich *vi*, (*less trad*) argamaidich *vi*; **2** (*legal etc: ~ a case etc*) tagair *vti*

argument *n* **1** (*disagreement*) connsachadh *m*, (*less trad*) argamaid *f*; **2** (*discussion*) deasbad *mf*; **3** (*sequence of ideas, points etc*) argamaid *f*

argumentative *adj* connsachail, aimhreiteach

arid *adj* **1** (*of landscape etc*) tioram, (*stronger*) loisgte, ana-thioram, ro-thioram; **2** (*uninteresting*) tioram

arise *v* èirich *vi*

aristocracy *n* **1** (*abstr quality*) uaisle *f invar*; **2** (*con*) **the** ~ na h-uaislean *mpl*

aristocrat *n* mòr-uasal *m*, duine-uasal *m*

aristocratic *adj* uasal

arithmetic *n* cunntas *m*, àireamhachd *f invar*

arm[1] *n* **1** (*part of body*) gàirdean *m*; **2** (*idiom*) **come to my ~s** thig *vi* nam chom *m*, thig nam achlais *f*

arm[2] *n* (*weapon*) ball-airm *m*

armchair *n* cathair-ghàirdeanach *f*

armful *n* achlasan *m*, ultach *m*

armour *n* **1** armachd *f invar*; **2** *in expr* **suit of** ~ deise-airm *f*

armoury *n* armlann *f*

armpit *n* achlais *f*, lag *mf* na h-achlaise

armrest *n* taic-uilne *f*

army *n* arm *m*, **when I was in the** ~ nuair a bha mi san arm

around *adv* **1** timcheall, mun cuairt & mu chuairt, **a rumour/the flu's going** ~ tha fathann/an cnatan mòr a' dol timcheall/a' dol mun cuairt

around *prep* **1** timcheall (*with gen*), timcheall air, mun cuairt air, **all** ~ **her** fada mun cuairt oirre, **we'll go** ~ **the loch** thèid sinn timcheall an locha, **they built houses** ~ **his garden** thog iad taighean timcheall air a' ghàrradh aige, **are there any shops** ~ **here?** a bheil bùithtean timcheall air an seo?; **2** (*approximately*) timcheall air, mu (*lenites following cons, takes dat*) ~ **a hundred** timcheall air ceud, mu cheud; **3** (*of garment etc*) mu, **put your coat** ~ **you** cuir umad do chota, **a bandage** ~ **his head** bann mu cheann (*for prep prons formed with* mu, *see p 510*)

Arran *n* Arainn

arrange *v* **1** (*organise, set up*) cuir *vt* air chois (*dat of* cas *f*), ~ **a meeting** cuir coinneamh air chois; **2** (*put in order*) sgioblaich *vt*, cuir *vt* an òrdugh *m*, cuir *vt* air dòigh *f*, ~ **the furniture** sgioblaich an àirneis, ~ **documents** cuir pàipearan an òrdugh

arrangement *n* **1** (*state of affairs etc*) suidheachadh *m*, **she didn't like this** ~ **at all** cha robh an suidheachadh seo a' còrdadh rithe idir; **2** (*agreement, settlement*) còrdadh *m*, rèite *f*, **they reached an** ~ thàinig iad gu còrdadh/rèite; **3** (*mus*) rian *m*

arranger *n* (*mus*) rianadair *m*

arrest *v* cuir *vt* an làimh (*dat of* làmh *f*), cuir *vt* an sàs *m*

arrival *n* teachd *m invar*, **the** ~ **of spring** teachd an earraich

arrive *v* thig *vi*, ruig *vti*, **they haven't ~d yet** cha tàinig iad fhathast, cha do ràinig iad fhathast, ~ **at Perth at 8 o'clock** ruig Peairt/thig gu Peairt aig ochd uairean

arrogance *n* dànadas *m*, uaibhreas *m*, àrdan *m*

arrogant *adj* dàna, àrdanach

arrow *n* saighead *f*

arse *n* (*fam*) màs *m*, (*fam*) tòn *f*

arsehole *n* toll *m* (*vulg in this sense*), (*vulg*) toll-tòine

art *n* ealain *f*, ~ **gallery** ealain-lann *f*, *also* taisbeanlann *f*

artery *n* cuisle *f*, **main** ~ cuisle-mhòr

artful *adj* innleachdach, carach

artfulness *n* innleachd *f*

arthritis *n* tinneas *m* nan alt

article *n* **1** (*object, thing*) rud *m*; **2** (*journalism etc*) aiste *f*, alt *m*; **3** (*gram*) alt *m*; **4** *in expr* **an** ~ **of clothing** ball *m* aodaich

articulate *adj* fileanta, pongail

articulate *v* (*express*) cuir *vt* an cèill (*dat of* ciall *f*)

artificial *adj* fuadain, brèige (*gen of* breug *f*, *used as adj*)

artisan *n* neach-ceàirde *m* (*pl* luchd-ceàirde *m sing coll*)

artist *n* neach-ealain *m* (*pl* luchd-ealain *m sing coll*)

artistic *adj* ealanta

artistry *n* ealantas *m*

as *adv* **1** (*in comparisons*) cho, **it wasn't ~ good ~ (all) that** cha robh e cho math sin, ~ **big ~ a house** cho mòr ri taigh; **2** *in expr* ~ **much ~** uiread agus/is, (*esp in neg sentences*) fiù agus/is, **give me ~ much ~ Iain (has)** thoir dhomh uiread agus a tha aig Iain, **there wasn't ~ much ~ a piece of bread left** cha robh fiù agus pìos arain air fhàgail; **3** (*distance*) ~ **far ~** gu ruige (*with nom*), ~ **far ~ the ridge** gu ruige an druim; **4** *in expr* ~ **for** (*ie concerning*) taobh, a thaobh, (*with gen*), ~ **for the election . . .** a thaobh/thaobh an taghaidh . . .

as *conj* **1** mar, ~ **they say** mar a chanas iad, **he carried on** ~ **if/as though it didn't matter** lean e air mar nach robh e gu difir, **be that** ~ **it may** biodh sin mar a bhitheas; **2** (*because*) on a & bhon a, **they put the stock on the hill** ~ **the grazing was good up there** chuir iad an sprèidh dhan mhonadh on a bha an t-ionaltradh math shuas an sin; **3** *in expr* ~ **well** (*ie also*)

cuideachd, mar an ceudna, **has Ewan left?
yes, and Iain ~ well** an do dh'fhalbh Eòghann?
dh'fhalbh, agus Iain cuideachd/mar an ceudna;
4 *in expr* ~ **well** ~ (*ie in addition to*) cho math
ri, a bharrachd air, **he had a dram ~ well ~ a
pint** ghabh e drama cho math ri pinnt
ascertain *v* faigh *vt* a-mach
ascribe *v* cuir *vt* (*with prep* às leth), ~
something to someone cuir rudeigin às leth
cuideigin
ash *n* **1** (*tree & wood*) uinnseann *m*, **mountain**
~ caorann *mf*; **2** (*fire residue*) luaithre *f invar*,
luath *f*
ashamed *adj* fo nàire *f invar*, nàraichte, air a
(*etc*) nàrachadh, **I'm** ~ tha mi fo nàire, *also*
tha nàire orm; **2** (*become* ~) gabh nàire, **I was
~ when she heard about it** ghabh mi nàire
(*also* chaidh mo nàrachadh) nuair a chuala i mu
dheidhinn
ashen *adj* bàn-ghlas
ashore *adv* **1** (*position*) air tìr *mf*; **2** (*movement*)
gu tìr, air tìr, **they're coming** ~ tha iad a'
tighinn gu tìr/air tìr
aside *adv* air leth, an dara taobh *m*, **put/set** ~
cuir *vt* air leth, cuir *vt* an dara taobh
ask *v* **1** (*enquire, question*) faighnich *vi* (*with
prep* de *or* do), ~ **Morag** faighnich de Mhòrag,
she ~ed whether there was life on Mars
dh'fhaighnich i an robh beatha air Màrt; **2**
(*request*) iarr *vti* (*with prep* air), **they ~ed for
a pay rise** dh'iarr iad àrdachadh-pàighidh, **she
~ed me to close the door** dh'iarr i orm an
doras a dhùnadh; **3** (*invite*) iarr *vt*, **they ~d me
to a party** dh'iarr iad mi gu pàrtaidh; **4** *in expr*
~ **a question** faighnich ceist, cuir ceist (*with
prep* air), **she's always ~ing questions** bidh
i a' faighneachd cheistean gun sgur, **they ~ed
me questions** chuir iad ceistean orm; **5** (*idiom*)
Iain was ~ing after you bha Iain a' gabhail do
naidheachd *f*, bha Iain gad fhaighneachd
askew *adj* claon
aslant *adj* fiar
asleep *adj* na (*etc*) c(h)adal *m*, **we were** ~ bha
sinn nar cadal
aspect *n* **1** (*appearance*) dreach *m*, cruth *m*; **2**
(*facet etc*) taobh *m*, **it's that ~ of the matter
that worries me** 's e an taobh sin den chùis
a tha a' cur dragh *m* orm; **3** (*geographical
exposure*) sealladh-aghaidh *m*
aspiration *n* (*ie desire, ambition*) miann *mf*,
mòr-mhiann *mf*, rùn *m*
aspire *v* bi *vi irreg* miannach (**to** air), ~ **to
fame/wealth** bi miannach air cliù/air beartas

assailant *n* neach-ionnsaigh *m* (*pl* luchd-
ionnsaigh *m sing coll*)
assassin *n* murtair *m*
assassinate *v* murt *vt*
assassination *n* murt *m*
assault *n* **1** ionnsaigh *mf*; **2** (*as legal term*) droch-
ionnsaigh *mf*
assault *v* thoir ionnsaigh *mf* (*with prep* air)
assemble *v* **1** (*gather, collect: of people*)
cruinnich *vti*, thig *vi* còmhla; **2** (*of people &
things*) co-chruinnich *vti*; **3** (~ *machinery, kit
etc*) cuir *vt* ri chèile
assembled *adj & past part* **1** (*of things: put
together*) co-dhèanta, air an (*etc*) c(h)ur ri
chèile; **2** (*of people: gathered*) cruinn, **the
congregation was ~ in the church** bha an
coitheanal cruinn san eaglais
assembly *n* **1** (*of people*) cruinneachadh *m*, tional
m; **2** (*of people or things*) co-chruinneachadh *m*;
3 (*abstr: putting together*) cur *m* ri chèile
assent *n* **1** aonta *m*; **2** (*permission*) cead *m invar*
assent *v* thoir aonta *m* (**to** do)
assert *v* **1** (*state, argue*) cùm a-mach *vi*, **they
were ~ing that the world wasn't round**
bha iad a' cumail a-mach nach robh an cruinne
cruinn; **2** *in expr* ~ **authority** gabh smachd *m
invar* (**over** air), **he ~ed his authority over
the country** ghabh e smachd air an dùthaich
assess *v* meas *vt*
assessment *n* **1** (*abstr: the action*) measadh *m*; **2**
(*con: an* ~) meas *m*
assessor *n* neach-measaidh *m* (*pl* luchd-
measaidh *m sing coll*)
assets *n* maoin *f*, so-mhaoin *f*
assign *n* (*resources, person to post*) sònraich *vt*
assist *v* cuidich *vti*, dèan cobhair *f* (*with prep*
air), ~ **them** cuidich *vt* iad, (*more trad*) cuidich
vi leotha
assistance *n* **1** cuideachadh *m*, cobhair *f*; **2**
(*financial* ~) taic *f* (airgid)
assistant *n* neach-cuideachaidh *m* (*pl* luchd-
cuideachaidh *m sing coll*)
associate *n* **1** companach *m*; **2** (*esp in business,
crime etc*) (com-)pàirtiche *m*
associated *adj & past part* an cois (*dat of* cas *f*),
an lùib (*dat of* lùb *f*), (*both with gen*), **poverty
and its ~ difficulties** bochdainn agus na
duilgheadasan a thig na cois, *also* bochdainn
agus a cuid dhuilgheadasan, **there is a story
~ with each building** tha sgeul an lùib gach
togalaich
association *n* **1** (*abstr*) cruinneachadh *m*, tighinn
f còmhla, **freedom of ~** còir cruinneachaidh;

2 *in expr* **in** ~ **with** an co-bhann/co-bhuinn ri;
3 (*more con: club, society etc*) comann *m*

assortment *n* measgachadh *m*, taghadh *m*, (**of** de)

assume *v* **1** (*take as fact*) gabh *vi* ris, **I** ~ **he won't do it again** tha mi a' gabhail ris nach dèan e tuilleadh e; **2** (*take on*) gabh *vt* os làimh (*gen of* làmh *f*), gabh *vt* air fhèin, **he** ~**d responsibility for the company** ghabh e os làimh/air fhèin uallach a' chompanaidh

assumption *n* **1** (*hypothesis*) tuaiream *m*; **2** (*opinion, supposition*) barail *f*

assurance *n* **1** bar(r)antas *m*, (*less formal*) gealladh *m*, **we accepted the** ~ **he gave us** ghabh sinn ris a' bharrantas a thug e dhuinn; **2** (*insurance*) àrachas *m*, urras *m*, **an** ~ **policy** poileasaidh àrachais, poileasaidh urrais

assure *v* rach an urras *m* (*with prep* do), **he** ~**d me that it was true** chaidh e an urras dhomh gun robh e fìor

asterisk *n* (*orthography*) reultag *f*

asthma *n* (*used with art*) a' chuing *f*, an sac *m*

astonish *v* cuir *vt* mòr-iongnadh *m* (*with prep* air), **it** ~**ed me** chuir e mòr-iongnadh orm

astonishment *n* mòr-iongnadh *m*

astray *adj & adv* **1** (*phys*) air fhuadan; **2** (*phys, morally*) air seachran, air iomrall; **3** *in exprs* **go** ~ (*phys, morally*) rach *vi* air seachran/air iomrall, **lead/go** ~ (*esp morally*) claon *vti*

astride *adj & adv* casa-gòbhlach (*with prep* air), ~ **the chair** casa-gòbhlach air a' chathair, **riding** ~ a' marcachd casa-gòbhlach

astrology *n* speuradaireachd *f invar*

astronaut *n* speur-sheòladair *m*

astronomer *n* reuladair *m*

astronomy *n* reul-eòlas *m*

asylum *n* (*abstr*) tèarmann *m*, **political** ~ tèarmann poilitigeach

at *prep* **1** (*position & time*) aig, ~ **home** aig an taigh, ~ **the door** aig an doras, ~ **sea** aig muir, ~ **six o'clock** aig sia uairean, ~ **dinner-time** aig àm dìnnearach, ~ **best** aig a' char as fheàrr, ~ **worst** aig a' char as miosa; **2** (*misc exprs & idioms*) ~ **Perth** ann am Peart/Peairt, ~ **that, he went home** leis a sin chaidh e dhachaigh, (*work, a task etc*) **keep/stick** ~ **it!** cùm *vi* ris!, ~ (**long**) **last** mu dheireadh (thall), ~ **all** idir (*usu with neg verb*), **are you tired? not at all!** a bheil thu sgìth? chan eil idir!, ~ **first** an toiseach, **I didn't like him** ~ **first** cha bu toigh leam an toiseach e

athletic *adj* lùthmhor

Atlantic *n*, **the**, *used with art*, An Cuan *m* Siar

atmosphere *n* (*air, earth's* ~) àile *m*

atmospheric pressure *n* cudthrom an àile *m*

atom *n* dadam *m*

atomic *adj* atamach

atone *v*, **1** (*make reparation*) dèan èirig *f* (**for** airson), **you'll** ~ **for it** nì sibh èirig air a shon; **2** (*relig: with reference to Christ's atonement*) dèan rèite *f*

atonement *n* **1** (*reparation etc*) èirig *f*, **as** ~ **for his mistakes** an èirig a mhearachdan; **2** (*relig: with reference to Christ's atonement*) rèite *f*

atrocious *adj* uabhasach, oillteil, eagalach

atrocity *n* uabhas *m*, **atrocities in time of war** uabhasan an àm cogaidh

attached *adj past part* **1** (*phys*) ceangailte (**to** ri), ~ **to the wall** ceangailte ris a' bhalla; **2** (*emotionally or in friendship*) measail, dèidheil (**to** air), ceangailte (**to** ri), **I became quite** ~ **to them** dh'fhàs mi gu math measail/dèidheil orra, dh'fhàs mi gu math ceangailte riutha

attachment *n* **1** (*phys*) ceangal *m*; **2** (*liking, friendship*) tlachd *f invar*, dèidh *f*, spèis *f*

attack *n* **1** ionnsaigh *mf*, **make/mount/launch an** ~ thoir ionnsaigh (**on** air); **2** (*verbal* ~) càineadh *m*, màbadh *m*; **3** *in expr* **heart** ~ grèim-cridhe *m*, clisgeadh-cridhe *m*

attack *v* thoir ionnsaigh (*with prep* air)

attacker *n* neach-ionnsaigh *m* (*pl* luchd-ionnsaigh *m sing coll*)

attain *v* (*an aim etc*) faigh *vt*, ruig *vt*, **he** ~**ed his wish/ambition** fhuair e a mhiann/a rùn

attempt *n* oidhirp *f*, **make an** ~ **at something** dèan oidhirp air rudeigin

attempt *v* feuch *vti* (*with prep* ri), dèan oidhirp *f* (*with prep* air), **I'll** ~ **to open the door** feuchaidh mi ris an doras fhosgladh, **they** ~**ed to lift us** dh'fheuch iad ri ar togail, **we have to** ~ **it** feumaidh sinn oidhirp a dhèanamh air

attend *v* **1** (*serve etc*) freastail *vi*, fritheil *vi*, (**on** air); **2** (*be present*) bi *vi* an làthair *f*, bi *vi* ann, fritheil *vt*, rach *vi* (*with prep* do), **they didn't** ~ cha robh iad an làthair, ~ **a meeting** rach do choinneimh; **3** (*pay attention*) thoir (an) àire *f* *invar* (**to** do); **4** *in expr* ~ **to a matter** gabh cùis *f* os làimh (*dat of* làmh *f*)

attendance *n* **1** (*service etc*) freastal *m*, ~ **at table** freastal don bhòrd; **2** (~ *on someone: at an event etc*) frithealadh *m*; **3** (*audience etc*) **there was a good** ~ bha sluagh math/mòr ann, bha luchd-èisteachd gu leòr ann

attendant *adj* na c(h)ois (*dat of* cas *f*), na lùib (*dat of* lùb *f*), **poverty and its** ~ **difficulties** bochdainn agus na duilgheadasan a thig *vi* na cois

attendant *n* neach-frithealaidh *m* (*pl* luchd-frithealaidh *m sing coll*)

attention *n* aire *f invar*, **pay** ~ thoir (an) aire (**to** do)

attentive *adj* **1** (*alert*) aireachail, furachail; **2** (*~ to task, someone's needs etc*) furachail; **3** ~ **to detail** mion-chùiseach, mionaideach

attestation *n* teisteanas *m*

attitude *n* **1** (*phys*) seasamh *m*; **2** (*mental*) gleus inntinn *mf*

attract *v* **1** (*person, magnet etc*) tarraing *vt*; **2** (*charm, entice*) tàlaidh *vt*, ~ **the customers back** tàlaidh an luchd-ceannaich air ais

attraction *n* tàladh *m*, tarraing *f*

attractive *adj* **1** tàlaidheach, tarraingeach; **2** (*esp in personality*) tlachdmhor

attribute *n* (*esp inherent*) feart *m*, **we get many ~s from our forebears/ancestors** gheibh sinn mòran fheartan bhor sinnsirean

attribute *v* (*esp with implication of guilt, blame*) cuir *vt* às leth (*with gen*), **don't ~ the rumour to me** (*emph*) na cuir am fathann às mo leth-sa

attrition *n* bleith *f*

auctioneer *n* reiceadair *m*

audacious *adj* (*more pejorative*) ladarna

audience *n* **1** (*radio, concert etc*) luchd-èisteachd *m sing coll*, **there was a good ~** bha luchd-èisteachd gu leòr ann; **2** (*meeting with important person*) coinneamh (phrìobhaideach), agallamh (prìobhaideach)

audio-visual *adj* lèir-chlaistinneach

audit *n* (*fin*) sgrùdadh *m* (chunntasan *mpl gen*)

audit *v* (*fin*) dèan sgrùdadh *m* (air cunntasan *mpl*)

auditor *n* neach-sgrùdaidh *m* (chunntasan *mpl gen*)

auger *n* drile *f*, snìomhaire *m*

augment *v* meudaich *vt*

augmentation *n* meudachadh *m*

August *n* (*used with art*) an Lùnastal *m*

aunt *n*, **my ~** (*on mother's side*) piuthar *f* mo mhàthar, (*on father's side*) piuthar *f* m' athar

au revoir! *excl* chì mi fhathast sibh/thu!

Aurora Borealis *n* (*used with art*) Na Fir Chlis *mpl*

auspices *npl*, *in expr* **under the ~** fo sgèith (*dat of* sgiath *f*) (*with gen*), **under the ~ of Creative Scotland** fo sgèith Alba Chruthachail

Australia *n* Astràilia *f*

Australian *n & adj* Astràilianach *f*

auspicious *adj* rathail, gealltanach

Austria *n* (*used with art*) an Ostair *f*

Austrian *n & adj* Ostaireach

author *n* ùghdar *m*

authorisation *n* ùghdarras *m*, cead *m*

authorise *v* ùghdarraich *vt*, ceadaich *vt*

authorised *adj & past part* ùghdarraichte, ceadaichte

authoritarian *adj* ceannsalach

authoritative *adj* ùghdarrasail

authority *n* **1** (*control, domination*) ceannsal *m*, smachd *m invar*, **under his enemy's ~** fo cheannsal a nàmhad, **she maintained ~ over the class** chùm i smachd air a' chlas; **2** (*council etc*) ùghdarras *m*, **local authorities** ùghdarrasan ionadail

autobiography *n* fèin-eachdraidh *f*

automatic *n* fèin-ghluaiseach

autonomous *adj* neo-eisimeileach, fèin-riaghlach

autumn *n* foghar *m*, **in ~** as t-fhoghar

auxiliary *adj* taiceil

auxiliary *n* cuidiche *m*, taicear *m*

avail *n* èifeachd *f invar*, buannachd *f*, tairbhe *f invar*, **of no ~** gun èifeachd

avail *v* **1** (*profit, be of use, usu in neg exprs*), **it will ~ you nothing to complain** cha leig thu a leas/cha dèan e feum (sam bith) dhut a bhith a' gearan; **2** (*make use of, take advantage of*), ~ **oneself of** cleachd *vt*, gabh cothrom *m* air, ~ **oneself of the facilities** cleachd na goireasan

available *adj* **1** (*to hand*) deiseil, ullamh; **2** (*to be had*) ri f(h)aighinn, **there is no beer ~** chan eil leann ri fhaighinn idir; **3** *in expr* **make ~** cuir *vt* an tairgse *f* (*with gen*), **make something ~ to other people** cuir rudeigin an tairgse dhaoine/muinntir eile

average *adj* **1** meadhanach, cumanta; **2** (*maths*) cuibheasach

average *n* **1** meadhan *m*; **2** (*maths*) cuibheas *m*

awake *adj* nam (*etc*) d(h)ùsgadh *m*, nam (*etc*) d(h)ùisg *m*, **she is ~** tha i na dùsgadh, tha i na dùisg

awake, awaken *v* dùisg *vti*, **I awoke at six** dhùisg mi aig a sia

awakening *n*, dùsgadh *m*, (*less usu*) mosgladh *m*

award *n* duais *f*

aware *adj* mothachail (**of** air), ~ **of the problem** mothachail air an duilgheadas

awareness *n* mothachadh *m* (**of** air)

away *adv* (*misc exprs*), ~ **from home** on taigh, **right! I'm ~** ceart! tha mi a' falbh, **she's ~** (*ie gone*) tha i air falbh, **she's ~** (*ie absent*) tha i às an làthair *f*, *also* chan eil i (ann) an seo, ~ **you go to the shop for me** thalla don bhùth dhomh, (*to dog etc*) ~ **home!** falbh/thalla dhachaigh!, **a long way ~**, **far ~** fad' air falbh,

fade ~ crìon *vi*, **keep** (*ie stay*) ~ cùm air falbh, cùm às an làthair, **keep her ~ from me!** cùm bhuam i!

awful *adj* uabhasach, eagalach, sgriosail, **that's ~!** tha sin uabhasach!

awfully *adv* 1 gu h-uabhasach, **how did you get on? ~!** ciamar a chaidh dhut? gu h-uabhasach!; 2 (*as intensifier*) uabhasach, (*stronger*)

uabhasach fhèin, **that was ~ good!** bha sin uabhasach (fhèin) math!

awkward *adj* (*person, action*) cearbach, *in expr* **an ~ person** cearbair *m*

awry *adj* 1 (*slanting etc*) claon; 2 (*wrong, not as it should be*) tuathal

axe *n* tuagh *f*, **Lochaber ~** tuagh-chatha

axle *n* aiseal *mf*

B

baa, baaing *n* mèilich *f invar*

baa *v* dèan mèilich *f invar*

babble, babbling *n* gobaireachd *f invar*

baby *n* leanabh *m*, pàiste *m*, leanaban *m*, naoidhean *m*, she had a ~ bha pàiste aice

babysitter *n* freiceadan *m* cloinne

bachelor *n* fleasgach *m*, (*usu middle-aged or elderly*) seana-ghille *m*, old ~ seann fhleasgach

back *adj* 1 (*rear*) cùil (*gen of* cùl *m*, *used adjectivally*), ~ door doras-cùil *m*, ~ room seòmar-cùil *m*, ~ stroke buille-chùil *f*; 2 (*of the anatomical ~*) droma (*gen of* druim *m used adjectivally*), a ~ support taic droma *f*, ~ pain cràdh droma *m*

back *adv* air ais, keep/hold ~ cùm air ais, (*more formal*) cuir maille *f invar* air/ann an, I won't keep/hold you ~ cha chùm mi air ais sibh, come/go ~ till (air ais), (*of time*) a month ~ mìos air ais

back *n* 1 (*the phys ~*) druim *m*, my ~'s sore tha mo dhruim goirt, the small of the ~ caol an droma *m*; 2 (*rear part of human, animal, object etc*) cùl *m*, I turned my ~ to/on him chuir mi mo chùl ris, the back of the hand/neck cùl na làimh/na h-amhaich, he shoved it in the ~ of the lorry shad e an cùl na làraidh e, chair ~ cùl cathrach; 3 (*esp of an animal*) muin *f invar*, he leapt on the donkey's ~ leum e air muin na h-asail; 4 (*~ part or section, esp of building*) tòn *f*, the ~ of the house/of the hall tòn an taighe/an talla; 5 (*of book*) còmhdach *m*, hard/soft ~ còmhdach cruaidh/bog; 6 *in expr* ~ to front cùlaibh air beulaibh

back *v* 1 (*support*) cùm taic *f* ri; 2 (*reverse vehicle etc*) rach *vi* an comhair a (*etc*) c(h)ùil; 3 (*bet*) cuir geall *m*/airgead *m* (on air)

back-biting *n* 1 (*the action*) cùl-chàineadh *m*; 2 (*the remarks etc*) cùl-chainnt *f*

backbone *n* cnà(i)mh-droma *m*, the ~ cnà(i)mh an droma

backer *n* (*fin etc*) neach-taice *m* (*pl* luchd-taice *m sing coll*)

backing *n* taic(e) *f*, financial ~ taic airgid *f*

backpack *n* màileid-droma *f*

backside *n* (*buttocks*) màs *m*, (*fam*) tòn *f*

backup *n* 1 (*support*) taic(e) *f*; 2 (*IT, to disc etc*) cùl-ghleidheadh *m*

backward *adj* deireannach

backwards *adv* an comhair a (*etc*) c(h)ùil, she fell ~ thuit *vi* i an comhair a cùil

bad *adj*, 1 droch (*cannot be used as a complement, and always precedes the noun, which it lenites, except in the case of initial c*), ~ weather droch aimsir *f*, droch shìde *f*, ~ language droch-cainnt *f*, ~ luck droch shealbh *m*, droch fhortan *m*, in a ~ state/condition ann an droch staid *f*, that's a ~ sign! is e droch comharradh *m* a tha sin!; 2 dona (*Note: can be used as a complement, unlike* droch), a ~ boy gille dona, that was ~ bha sin dona, drink is ~ for you tha deoch-làidir dona dhut; 3 (*of food etc*, off, *rotten*) lobhte, grod, go ~ lobh *vi*; 4 *in expr* in a ~ mood/temper diombach, crost(a)

badge *n* (*usu of metal*) suaicheantas *m*, bràiste *f*

badger *n* broc *m*

badly *adv* 1 gu dona, how did you get on? ~! ciamar a chaidh dhut? chaidh gu dona!; 2 *in expr* ~ behaved mì-mhodhail, mìomhail, (*usu of child*) crost(a)

bad-natured *adj* droch-nàdarrach

badness *n* donas *m*, (*stronger*) olc *m*

baffle *v* fairtlich *vi* (*with prep* air), it ~d me dh'fhairtlich e orm

bag *n* 1 poca *m*, baga *m*, sleeping-~ poca-cadail; 2 (*large ~, item of luggage etc*) màileid *f*, (*abbrev for* handbag) màileid-làimhe *f*

baggage *n* treal(l)aichean *fpl*

bagpipe *n* pìob *f*, (*Highland ~*) pìob mhòr, *frequently used with art*, a' phìob, a' phìob mhòr, ~ music ceòl *m* na pìoba, *in expr* ~ chanter feadan *m*

bail *n* urras *m*, release on ~ fuasgail *vt* air urras

bailiff *n* maor *m*

baillie *n* bàillidh *m*

bait *n* (*for fishing*) maghar *m*, biathadh *m*

bake *v* fuin *vt*

baker *n* fuineadair *m*
bakery *n* taigh-fuine *m*
baking *n* (*the action and the product*) fuineadh
m, fuine *f*, ~ **powder** pùdar-fuine *m*
balance *n* 1 (*equilibrium*) co-chothrom
m, cothrom *m*, meidh *f*, (*fig*) ~ **of power**
co-chothrom cumhachd; 2 (*set of scales
etc*) cothrom *m*, meidh *f*; 3 (*fin, abstr*)
cothromachadh *m*, ~ **sheet** cunntas
cothromachaidh *m*; 4 *in expr* **on** ~ air chothrom
m; 5 (*fin, actual sum left in hand*) còrr *m*
balance *v* 1 cuir *vt* air mheidh *f*, cothromaich
vt, **she ~ed the load/burden on her head**
chuir i an t-uallach air mheidh air a ceann; 2
(*fin*) cothromaich *vt*, ~ **a budget** cothromaich
buidseat *m*
balanced *adj & past part* 1 (*in equilibrium*) air
mheidh *f*; 2 (*fair, even-handed*) cothromach,
a ~ discussion deasbad cothromach; 3 (*fin;
budget etc*) cothromaichte
bald *adj* maol, ~ **patch** sgall *m*
baldness *n* maoile *f invar*, maoilead *m*
bale *n* (*of hay etc*) bèile *m*
bale *v* (*boat etc*) taom *vti*
baler *n* taoman *m*
ball[1] *n* (*dance*) bàl *m*
ball[2] (*for games etc*) bà(l)la *m*, ball *m*
ballad *n* bailead *m*
ballast *n* balaiste *mf invar*
ballot *n* 1 baileat *m*, taghadh *m*, **hold a ~ on
a particular question** cùm baileat air ceist
shònraichte; 2 *in expr* ~ **paper** pàipear *m*
bhòtaidh
balmy *adj* (*of evening etc*) tlàth
bamboo *n* cuilc *f* Innseanach
ban *n* toirmeasg *m*
ban *v* toirmisg *vt*
band[1] *n* 1 (*of people*) còmhlan *m*, buidheann *mf*,
(*pej*) treud *m*; 2 (*music*) còmhlan(-ciùil) *m*
band[2] *n* (*loop of material*) crios *m*, bann *m*,
rubber ~ crios-rubair *m*
bandage *n* bann *m*
bandy-legged *adj* cama-chasach, crom-chasach
bang *n* cnag *f*, brag *m*
bang *v* cnag *vti*
banish *v* fuadaich *vt*, fògair *vt*, **the people were
~ed from the glen** dh'fhògradh an sluagh às
a' ghleann
banishment *n* fuadach *m*, fuadachadh *m*,
fògradh *m*
bank[1] *n* (*fin*) banca *m*, **I've an account at the
Royal ~** tha cunntas *m* agam aig a' Bhanca
Rìoghail, ~ **loan** iasad *m* banca

bank[2] *n* 1 (*of river etc*) bruach *f*; 2 (*hillside, slope*)
bruthach *mf*
bank *v* 1 (*money*) cuir *vt* sa bhanca *m*; 2 (*idiom*)
don't ~ on it! na cuir earbsa ann!
banker *n* bancair *m*
banking *n* bancaireachd *f invar*
banknote *n* nota *f*
bankrupt *adj* briste
banned *adj & past part* toirmisgte
banner *n* bratach *f*
bannock *n* bonnach *m*
banquet *n* fèist *f*, fleadh *m*, cuirm *f*
baptise *v* baist *vt*
baptism *n* baisteadh *m*
Baptist *n & adj* Baisteach *m*
bar *n* 1 (*of wood, metal*) crann *m*; 2 (*obstacle,
impediment*) bacadh *m* (**to** air), **a ~ to
promotion** bacadh air àrdachadh, **colour ~**
dath-bhacadh *m*; 3 (*in pub etc*) bàr *m*; 4 (*music*)
car *m*; 5 (*IT etc*) ~ **chart** clàr cuilbh *m*
bar *v* 1 (*prevent, obstruct*) bac *vt*, cuir bacadh *m*
(*with prep* air); 2 *in expr* ~ **the door** cuir (an)
crann *m* air an doras *m*
barb *n* gath *m*
barbaric, barbarous *adj* borb
barbed *adj & past part* 1 gathach; 2 *in expr* ~
wire uèir-bhiorach *f*
barber *n* borbair *m*, (*more trad*) bearradair *m*
bard *n* bàrd *m*
bare *adj* 1 (*naked*) lomnochd; 2 (*uncovered*)
rùisgte, **his back was ~** bha a dhruim rùisgte,
also bha a dhruim ris; 3 (*landscape etc*) lom, **a ~
hillside** bruthach lom
bare *v* 1 (*esp body etc: strip*) rùisg *vt*, lom *vt*, **he
~d his forearm** rùisg e a ruighe *mf*; 2 (*sword*)
rùisg *vt*
bared *adj & past part* 1 (*esp of body etc: naked,
stripped*) rùisgte; 2 (*showing*) ris *prep pron*,
her forearm was ~ bha a ruighe *mf* ris
bare-faced *adj* ladarna, dàna
barefoot *adj* casruisgte
bare-headed *adj* ceannruisgte
barelegged *adj* casruisgte
barely *adv* 1 (*to a small extent, rarely, with
difficulty*) is gann (*with conj* a), **we ~ saw him**
is gann a chunnaic sinn e, **he ~ uttered two
words** is gann a leig e às dà fhacal, **we ~ made
out what she was saying** is gann a rinn sinn
a-mach dè a bha i ag ràdh; 2 (*hardly, scarcely*)
cha mhòr (*with conj* gun), **he ~ uttered two
words** cha mhòr gun do leig e às dà fhacal *m*; 3
(*esp expr difficulty*) is ann air èiginn (*with conj*
a), **we ~ made out what she was saying** is
ann air èiginn a rinn sinn a-mach dè a bha i ag

ràdh, **he ~ opened his eye** is ann air èiginn a dh'fhosgail e a shùil

bareness n luime f, lomnochd f invar

bargain n 1 (legal, official, fin etc) cùmhnant m, cunnradh m; 2 (good buy etc) bargan m

bark¹ n (of dog) comhart m

bark² n (of tree) rùsg m, cairt f

bark v dèan comhart m, tabhannaich vi, (at ri)

barking n comhartaich f, tabhannaich f

barley n eòrna m invar

barn n sabhal m, in expr ~ **owl** comhachag f

barnacle n giùran m, bàirneach f

barometer n glainne-sìde f

baron n baran m

Barra n Barraigh f

barrel n baraille m, (large ~, can be of metal) tocasaid (also togsaid & tosgaid) f, ~ **of oil** baraille ola, ~ **of a gun** baraille gunna

barren adj 1 (of land) fàs; 2 (of woman) neo-thorrach; 3 (of livestock etc) seasg

barrenness n 1 (of land) fàsachd f invar; 2 (of woman) neo-thorrachd f invar, neo-thorraichead f invar; 3 (of livestock etc) seasgachd f invar

barrier n (lit & fig) bacadh m, cnap-starra m

barrister n neach-tagraidh m (pl luchd-tagraidh m sing coll), tagarair m, tagraiche m

barter n malairt f

barter v malairtich vi, dèan malairt f

base adj suarach, tàireil

base n (bottom, foundation) bonn m, bun m

bash v (fam, in fight etc) pronn vt

bashful adj diùid, nàrach

bashfulness n diùideachd f invar, diùide f invar, nàire f invar

basic adj bunaiteach, ~ **rights** còraichean bunaiteach, ~ **Gaelic** Gàidhlig bhunaiteach

basin n mias f

basis n 1 (more usu phys) stèidh f; 2 (more usu abstr) bunait f, **the ~ of his philosophy** bunait na feallsanachd aige

basket n basgaid f

basketball n ball-basgaid m

bass n (music) beus (gen beusa) m

bastard n duine/neach m dìolain

bastard adj dìolain

bat¹ n (the animal) ialtag f

bat² (for games) slacan m, bat m

batch n dòrlach m

bath n 1 amar m, ionnaltair f; 2 in expr ~ **towel** tubhailte mhòr, searbhadair mòr

bathe v ionnlaid vti, failc vti

bathing n ionnlad m

bathroom n seòmar-ionnlaid m, rùm-ionnlaid m

battalion n cath-bhuidheann f

batter v pronn vt, dochainn vt

battery n bataraidh mf

battle n cath m, blàr m, batail m, **the ~ of Culloden** Blàr Chùil Lodair

battle-axe n tuagh-chatha f

battlefield n blàr m, àr m

battleship n long-chogaidh f

bawdy adj drabasta, draosta

bawl v glaodh vi

bay n bàgh m, camas m, òb m

bayonet n bèigleid f

be v 1 bi v irreg (cannot be used with a noun complement, cf **be 2 a**):
a) with adj complement, **it's cold, isn't it?** tha i fuar, nach eil?, ~ **quiet!** bi sàmhach!, **that's good** tha sin math
b) with adv complement, **Ian was there** bha Iain ann
c) with present participle, **is he coming?** a bheil e a' tighinn?, **they weren't singing** cha robh iad a' seinn
d) expr existence, bi with third pers prep pron ann, **there are no fairies** (ie **fairies don't exist**) chan eil sìthichean ann
e) expr state, position, occupation etc, temporary or permanent, bi with prep & poss pron nam, nad (etc), **he was alone** bha e na aonar, **they are asleep** tha iad nan cadal, **she's a nurse** tha i na banaltram/na nurs, **I'm a part-time chef just now** tha mi nam chòcaire pàirt-ùine an-dràsta (in past tenses only: visit, spend time in) **have you (ever) been to Lewis?** an robh sibh (riamh/a-riamh) ann an Leòdhas?

be v 2 is v irreg & def, past tense bu, inter an (am before b, f, m, p), past inter am bu, neg cha (chan before a vowel, or f followed by a vowel), past neg cha bu, neg inter nach, past neg inter nach bu:
a) as a copula, linking or equating two nouns/pronouns, **I am a man** is duine mi, **is she Isabel?** an ise Iseabail?, **they were the ones who did it** b' iadsan an fheadhainn a rinn e
b) expr professions, occupations, character etc, **he's a surgeon** is e lannsair a tha ann, **Fiona is a midwife** is e/i bean-ghlùine a th' ann am Fiona, **they are fools** is e amadain a tha annta (Note: this construction, with is, can express more permanence than bi with nam, nad etc, cf examples under **be 1 e**) above)
c) with adj complement (often in set exprs in Gaelic) **that's good** is math sin, **that's a shame!** is truagh sin!, **it's good that it's finished/over** 's math seachad e

d) with an emph or 'highlighted' adj or adv complement, is followed by ann *prep pron,* **she's not young, she's ancient!** chan eil i òg, is ann a tha i aosta!, **is it tomorrow we'll see her? no** an ann a-màireach a chì sinn i? chan ann

e) with an emph or 'highlighted' noun or pron complement, is followed by prep & noun/pron, **he wouldn't do that, he's a minister** (*emph*)! cha dèanadh esan sin, 's e ministear a tha ann!, **is/was it your bag** (*emph*) **that you lost?** an e do mhàileid a chaill thu? *introducing a relative clause, is followed by noun or pron,* **it's the old man who lost it** is e am bodach a chaill e, **was it you who wrote it? no!** an tusa a sgrìobh e? cha mhi!, **isn't it they who'll go (there)?** nach iadsan a thèid ann?, **isn't/wasn't it her husband who died?** nach e an duine aice a chaochail?

beach *n* tràigh *f*, (*often stony*) cladach *m*, (*shingly or pebbly*) mol *m*

bead *n* (*on necklace etc*) grìogag *f*

beak *n* gob *m*

beam *n* **1** (*ray*) gath *m*, ~ **of light** gath solais; **2** (*of timber*) sail *f*, spàrr *m*

beam *v* (*facial expr*) dèan fàite-gàire mhòr

bean, beans *n* pònair *f sing & coll*, **broad ~** pònair leathann, **French ~** pònair Fhrangach

bear *n* (*brown ~*) mathan *m*, **polar ~** mathan bàn

bear *v* **1** (*suffer, tolerate*) fuiling *vt*, **I couldn't ~ to do it** chan fhuilinginn a dhèanamh, **they had to ~ cold and hunger** b' fheudar dhaibh fuachd is acras *m* fhulang, **I can't ~ her** chan fhuiling mi i; **2** (*carry*) giùlain *vt*, iomchair *vt*; **3** (*give birth to*) beir *vt irreg*, **she bore a son** rug i mac, *also* rugadh mac dhi; **4** *in exprs* ~ **witness** thoir fianais, ~ **in mind** cùm na (*etc*) c(h)uimhne *f invar*

beard *n* feusag *f*

bearded *adj* feusagach, ròmach

bearer *n* neach-giùlain *m*, neach-iomchair *m* (*pl* luchd-giùlain/iomchair *m sing coll*), (*less trad*) portair *m*

bearing[1] *n* (*compass ~*) gabhail *mf*, (*esp nautical*) àird *f*

bearing[2] (*posture*) giùlan *m*

bearing[3] (*engineering etc*) giùlan *m*, **ball ~** giùlan-bàla *m*, *also* gràn *m*

beast *n* **1** (*animal*) ainmhidh *m*; **2** (*esp farm animal*) beathach *m*; **3** (*term of abuse*) biast *f*, brùid *mf*, bèist *f*

beat *n* (*music: rhythm*) buille *mf*

beat *v* **1** (*defeat*) fairtlich *vi*, dèan a' chùis, dèan an gnothach, (*all with prep* air), **it was the bad weather that ~ us** is e an droch aimsir a dh'fhairtlich/rinn a' chùis oirnn, **they ~ the other team** rinn iad a' chùis/an gnothach air an sgioba eile ; **2** (*strike*) buail *vt*, slac *vt*; **3** *in expr* ~ **up** (*fam, in fight etc*) pronn *vt*, dochainn(ich) *vt*

beating *n* (*thrashing, beating up*) slacadh *m*, pronnadh *m*

beautiful *adj* rìomhach, (*esp of a place, a woman, or other living beings*) bòidheach, brèagha, (*esp of a woman*) maiseach

beautify *v* maisich *vt*, sgèimhich *vt*

beauty *n* **1** maise *f invar*, bòidhchead *f*, àilleachd *f invar*; **2** *in expr* ~ **spot** (*on face*) ball-seirce *m*, (*attractive place*) àite brèagha

beaver *n* biobha(i)r *m*

becalm *v*, **the boat was ~ed** thàinig *vi* fèath *mf* air a' bhàta

because *conj* a chionn is gu, (*in neg exprs* a chionn is nach), a thaobh is gu (*in neg exprs* a thaobh is nach), ~ **he was old** a chionn 's gu robh e sean, ~ **there isn't a strike** a chionn 's nach eil stailc ann

because of *prep* a chionn, a thaobh, air sgàth, (*all with gen*), ~ **of that** a chionn sin

beckon *v* smèid *vi* (*with prep* air *or* ri), **she ~ed to me** smèid i orm/rium

become *v* **1** (*followed by adj*) fàs *vi*, **they became old/rich** dh'fhàs iad sean/beartach; **2** (*onset of emotion, sensation etc*) thig *vi* (*with n, & prep* air), **I became sorrowful/afraid/hungry** thàinig mulad/(an t-)eagal/(an t-)acras orm; **3** (*onset of emotion, sensation etc*) gabh *vt* (*followed by appropriate n*), *eg* ~ **worried** gabh dragh, gabh uallach, **4** (*adopt profession etc*) rach *vi* na (*etc*) *followed by n*, **he became a policeman** chaidh e na phoileas; **5** (*befall*) tachair *vi*, èirich *vi*, (*with prep* do), **what became of James?** dè a thachair do Sheumas?, dè a dh'èirich do Sheumas?; **6** (*suit*) thig *vi* (*with prep* do), freagair *vi* (*with prep* air), **mourning ~s Electra** thig am bròn do Electra

bed *n* **1** leabaidh *f*; **2** *in exprs* **I was in ~** bha mi san leabaidh, *also* bha mi nam laighe, **go to ~** rach a laighe, rach a chadal, **we're going to ~** tha sinn a' dol a laighe, **she took to her ~** ghabh i ris an leabaidh, thug i an leabaidh oirre; **3** (~ *of sea*) grunnd *m*

bedclothes, bedding *n* aodach *m sing coll* leapa *f*

bedfellow *n* coimhleapach *mf*

bedroom *n* seòmar-cadail *m*

bee *n* seillean *m*

beef *n* mairtfheoil *f*

beehive n sgeap f
beer n leann m
beet n biotais m invar
beetle n daolag f
befall v tachair vi, èirich vi, tuit vi, (all with prep do)
befit v 1 (suit) thig (with prep do); 2 (be incumbent on) is v irreg def cubhaidh (with prep do), as ~s a gentleman mar as cubhaidh do dhuine-uasal
befitting adj cubhaidh, iomchaidh, (to do: used with v is), an action ~ a hero gnìomh as cubhaidh (in past a bu chubhaidh) do ghaisgeach
before adv roimhe, a man we never saw ~ duine nach fhaca sinn a-riamh roimhe
before conj mus & mun, ~ the winter comes mus/mun tig an geamhradh, he didn't pay ~ he left cha do phàigh e mus do dh'fhalbh e, the night ~ she died an oidhche f mus do chaochail i
before prep 1 (space) ro (with dat), fa chomhair (with gen), standing ~ me na stad romham, na stad fa mo chomhair, ~ the door fa chomhair an dorais; 2 (time) ro (with the dat), ~ (the due) time ron àm m, ron mhithich f invar: (for prep prons formed with ro see p 510)
beforehand adv ro-làimh
beg v 1 (for money etc) dèan faoighe f invar; 2 (plead with) guidh vi (with prep air), I'm ~ging you to stay! tha mi a' guidhe ort fuireachd!, he ~ged us to let him go/set him free ghuidh e oirnn a leigeil ma sgaoil
beget v gin vt, Noah begat three sons ghin Noah triùir mhac
beggar n dìol-dèirce m, dèirceach m
begging n (for gifts of food etc) faoighe f invar
begin v tòisich vi (with prep air or ri), teann vi (with prep ri), ~ singing tòisich a' seinn, ~ to sing tòisich air/ri seinn, he began climbing theann e ri streap
beginning n 1 (in time) toiseach m, the ~ of summer toiseach an t-samhraidh, at the ~ an toiseach, at the very ~, right at the ~ aig an fhìor thoiseach, an toiseach tòiseachaidh; 2 (~ of a process etc) tòiseachadh m, a new ~ tòiseachadh às ùr, (saying) ~ is a day's work is e obair latha tòiseachadh; 3 (first or earliest stage) tùs m, (prov) the fear of God is the ~ of wisdom 's e tùs a' ghliocais eagal Dhè, he's been working here from/since the (very) ~ tha e ag obair an seo o thùs
beguile v meall vt
beguiling adj meallach
beguiling n mealladh m

behalf n, in expr on ~ of às leth (with the gen), he did it on my ~ rinn e às mo leth e
behave v 1 giùlain fhèin (etc), I wasn't behaving too well cha robh mi gam ghiùlan fhìn ro mhath; 2 (~ towards, treat) làimhsich vt, gnàthaich vt
behaviour n 1 (conduct) dol-a-mach m invar, giùlan m; 2 (treatment, ~ towards someone) làimhseachadh m, gnàthachadh m
behead v dì-cheannaich vt
beheading n dì-cheannachadh m
behind adv 1 (position) air dheireadh, air chùl, the journey was hard and the old folks were far ~ bha an turas cruaidh agus bha na seann daoine fada air dheireadh; 2 (less advanced etc) air dheireadh, ~ in technology air dheireadh a thaobh teicneolais
behind prep air cùlaibh, air cùl, (with gen), ~ the church air cùlaibh na h-eaglaise, (also fig) I left/put it ~ me dh'fhàg mi/chuir mi air mo chùlaibh e
being n 1 (abstr) bith f invar, bring into ~ thoir vt gu/am bith; 2 (living thing) creutair m; 3 in expr human ~ duine m
belch n rùchd m, brùchd m
belch v rùchd vi, brùchd vi, dèan brùchd m
Belgium n A' Bheilg nf (gen na Beilge)
belief n 1 (abstr) creideas m; 2 (esp relig) creideamh m
believe v creid vti (in ann an), thoir creideas (with prep do), I don't ~ you chan eil mi gad chreidsinn, chan eil mi a' toirt creideas dhut, I don't ~ in fairies chan eil mi a' creidsinn anns na sìthichean
belittle v cuir vt an suarachas m
bell n clag m, warning ~, alarm ~ clag-rabhaidh m
belling n (of red deer stags) langanaich f
bellow n (humans, cattle etc) geum m, beuc m, he let out a ~ leig e geum às
bellow v 1 beuc vi, geum vi, ràn vi; 2 (usu of animals) nuallaich vi; 3 (of cattle & esp of deer) langanaich vi
bellowing n 1 (of humans, cattle etc) beucadh m; 2 (of red deer stags) langanaich f
belly n 1 (abdomen) balg m; 2 (paunch) brù f, maodal f, mionach m
belly-button n imleag f
bellyful n làn broinne m, I got a ~ of it fhuair mi làn mo bhroinne dheth
belong v buin vi (to do), is v irreg & def (with prep le), does it ~ to you? am buin e dhutsa?, or an ann leatsa a tha e?, who does this ~ to?

cò dha a bhuineas seo? *or* cò leis a tha seo?, **it ~s to me** 's ann leamsa a tha e

belongings *n* treal(l)aichean *fpl*

beloved *adj* gaolach, ionmhainn

below *adv* fodha (*etc*) *prep pron*, shìos bhuaithe (*etc*), **a room with a cellar** ~ seòmar, agus seilear fodha, **we saw the river** ~ chunnaic sinn an àbhainn shìos bhuainn, **the rocks down** ~ **us** na creagan shìos fodhainn

below *prep* **1** fo (*lenites following cons where possible & takes the dat*), ~ **the surface** fon uachdar; **2** (*idiom*) **down** ~ **him** (*etc*) shìos bhuaithe (*etc*), **I saw the soldiers down** ~ **me** chunnaic mi na saighdearan shìos bhuam: (*for prep prons formed with* fo & bho *see p 509, 510*)

belt *n* crios *m*

Benbecula *n* Beinn a' Bhadhla *f*

bench *n* being(e) *f*

bend *n* **1** lùb *f*, **the stick has a big** ~ **in it** tha lùb mhòr air/anns a' bhata; **2** (~ *in a river*) camas *m*

bend *v* **1** (~ *an object*) fiar & fiaraich *vti*, lùb *vti*; **2** (~ *the body*) crom *vti*, lùb *vti*, **she bent her head** chrom i a ceann, ~ **the knee** lùb a' ghlùin

bending, bendy *adj* lùbach

beneath *prep* fo (*lenites following cons where possible & takes the dat*) ~ **the surface** fon uachdar, ~ **a tree** fo chraoibh, ~ **me** fodham(sa) (*for prep prons formed with* fo *see p 510*)

benediction *n* beannachadh *m*

benefactor *n* tabhartaiche *m*, tabhairteach *m*

beneficial *adj* tairbheach & tarbhach

benefit *n* **1** (*abstr: advantage etc*) tairbhe *f* *invar*; **2** (*usu fin*) prothaid *f*; **3** (*social security etc*) sochair *f*, **unemployment** ~ sochair cion-obrach, (*fam*) dòil *m invar*

benefit *v* buannaich *vi*, (*less usu*) tairbhich *vi*

bent *adj* crom, lùbte, **a** ~ **stick** bata crom

bent[1] *n* (*natural ability*) tàlann *m*

bent[2] (*grass*) muran *m*

bequeathe *v* tiomnaich *vt* (**to** do)

bequest *n* tiomnadh *m*, dìleab *f*

Bernera(y) *n* Beàrnaraigh *f*

berry *n* dearc *f*, dearcag *f*

beseech *v* guidh *vi* (*with prep* air), **I'm ~ing you to stay!** tha mi a' guidhe ort fuireach!

beside *prep* ri taobh (*with gen*), ~ **the quay** ri taobh a' chidhe, ~ **me** rim thaobh; **2** (*idiom*) **I was** ~ **myself (with rage)** bha mi air bhoile *f* *invar*/air bhàinidh *f invar*

besides *prep* a bharrachd air, a thuilleadh air, **he has two flats,** ~ **a house** tha dà lobht aige, a bharrachd air taigh; (*adverbial use*) **I'm tired, and** ~, **I'm broke** tha mi sgìth, agus a thuilleadh air sin, chan eil sgillinn ruadh agam

besiege *v* cuir sèist *m* (*with prep* air), **they ~d the castle** chuir iad sèist air a' chaisteal

best *sup adj* **1** feàrr *used in the exprs* as fheàrr (*for pres & fut tense*) & a b' fheàrr (*for past & conditional tense*), **the** ~ **one/man** am fear as fheàrr, **he was the** ~ **one/man** b' esan am fear a b' fheàrr, **Alan will be** ~ 's e Ailean as fheàrr a bhios (ann), **the** ~ **pen I had** am peann a b' fheàrr a bh' agam; **2** *in corres etc* **with** ~ **wishes** leis gach deagh dhùrachd; **3** *in expr* (*at wedding*) ~ **man** fleasgach *m*, fear comhailteach *m*

best *sup adv* feàrr, *with v irreg & def* is & *prep* do, **you'd** ~ **stay/you'd be** ~ **staying** b' fheàrr dhut fuireach, **you'd** ~ **be going** b' fheàrr dhuibh a bhith a' falbh, **as** ~ **I can** mar as fheàrr as urrainn dhomh, mar as fheàrr a thèid agam air

best *n* **1** (*one's best effort*) dìcheall *m*, **I did my** ~ rinn mi mo dhìcheall; **2** *in expr* **at** ~ aig a' char *m* as fheàrr (*in past tense* a b' fheàrr), **she'll be third, at** ~ bidh i san treas àite, aig a' char as fheàrr; **3** (*the* ~ *part or example of something*) brod *m*, smior *m* (*followed by gen sing of noun*), **the** ~ **of the seed** smior/brod an t-sìl, **the** ~ **of schoolmasters** smior a' mhaighstir-sgoile, **the** ~ **of crofts** brod na croite

best *v* (*fam*) dèan an gnothach, dèan a' chùis, (*with prep* air), **we ~ed them** rinn sinn an gnothach/a' chùis orra, *also* ghabh sinn orra

bet *n* geall *m*, **put/lay/place a** ~ cuir geall (**on** air)

bet *v* **1** (*put forward as probable*) cuir geall *m*, rach *vi* an geall, **I** ~ **he won't come** cuiridh mi geall nach tig e, thèid mi an geall nach tig e; **2** (*wager*) cuir geall *m* (**on** air), ~ **on a horse** cuir geall air each

betray *v* (*person, secret*) brath *vt*

betrayal *n* brathadh *m*

betrothal *n* **1** gealladh-pòsaidh *m*; **2** (*trad: involving family discussion, agreement and associated celebrations*) rèiteach *m*

better *comp adj* **1** feàrr, *used in the exprs* as fheàrr & nas fheàrr (*with pres & fut tense*) *and* a b' fheàrr & na b' fheàrr (*with past & conditional tense*), **A is** ~ **than B** tha A nas fheàrr na B, **that would be** ~ bhiodh sin na b' fheàrr, **who's** ~? cò as fheàrr?; **2** (*better in health or quality*), **make** ~ cuir *vt* am feabhas, **get** ~ rach *vi* am feabhas, **the invalid got** ~ chaidh an t-euslainteach am feabhas, **the local services are getting** ~ tha na seirbheisean ionadail a' dol am feabhas; **3** (*idioms*) **we'd be (the)** ~ **for**

a wee stroll b' fheàirrde sinn cuairt bheag, (*in a skill, activity etc*) we're getting ~ tha piseach a' tighinn oirnn

better *comp adv*, feàrr, *with v irreg & def* is & *prep* do, you'd ~ stay 's fheàrr/b' fheàrr dhut fuireach, you'd ~ be going 's fheàrr dhuibh/ b' fheàrr dhuibh a bhith a' falbh

better *n*, *in expr* get the ~ of fairtlich *vi*, faillich *vi*, (*fam*) dèan an gnothach, dèan a' chùis, (*all with prep* air), I wanted to climb the mountain but it got the ~ of me bha mi airson a' bheinn a dhìreadh ach dh'fhairtlich/ dh'fhaillich i orm

betting *n* 1 gealladh *m*; 2 *in expr* ~ shop bùth *mf* gheall *mpl gen*

between *prep* eadar (*takes the nom*), ~ us eadarainn, ~ you eadaraibh, ~ them eatarra

bevvy *n* 1 (*fam: drinking spree*) daorach *f*, on the ~ air an daoraich *dat*; 2 (*fam: booze, drink*) deoch *f*, deoch-làidir *f*, fond of the ~ dèidheil air (an) deoch(-làidir)

bevvying *n* daorach *f*, pòitearachd *f invar*

bewitch *v* cuir *vt* fo gheasaibh (*obs dat pl of* geas *f*)

bewitched *adj & past part* fo gheasaibh (*obs dat pl of* geas *f*), seunta

bewitching *adj* (*without magical association*) meallach

beyond *prep* thairis air, seachad air, (*more trad*) thar (*with gen*), ~ the ocean thairis air a' chuan, thar a' chuain, you went ~ what I required chaidh thu thairis air/seachad air na bha mi ag iarraidh, that's ~ my capabilities tha sin thar mo chomasan

bi- *prefix* dà-, *see examples below*

bias *n* claon-bhàidh *f*, taobh *m*

Bible *n* Bìoball *m*

biblical *adj* bìoballach

bibliography *n* leabhar-chlàr *m*

bicycle *n* baidhsagal *m*, (*more trad*) rothar *m*

bid *n* 1 (*at sale etc*) tairgse *f*, make a ~ thoir tairgse (for air); 2 (*an attempt at something*) oidhirp *f*, a ~ for freedom oidhirp air saorsa

bid *v* 1 (*at sale etc*) tairg *vti*, thoir tairgse *f*, (for air); 2 (*formal: request*) iarr *vt* (*with prep* air), we bade them stay dh'iarr sinn orra fuireachd; 3 (*greetings etc*) *in exprs* ~ them welcome cuir fàilte *f* orra, we bade them farewell ghabh sinn ar cead *m invar* dhiubh, *also* dh'fhàg sinn slàn aca

bidie-in (*Sc*) *n* coimhleapach *mf*

big *adj* 1 (*lit & fig*) mòr, a ~ house taigh mòr, a ~ day latha mòr, (*fam*) ~ money airgead mòr,

(*ironic*) the ~ shots na daoine mòra; 2 (*of person's build*) mòr, tomadach, calma

bigger *comp adj* 1 mò & motha, the bigger fish an t-iasg as mò, this one's bigger tha am fear seo nas mò; 2 *in exprs* grow/get ~ rach *vi* am meud *m invar*, meudaich *vi*, make ~ meudaich *vt*

bigwig *n* (*ironic*) duine mòr cudromach *m*, ~wigs na daoine mòra *mpl*, na h-urracha (*pl of* urra *f*) mòra

bilateral *adj* dà-thaobhach

bilingual *adj* dà-chànanach

bilingualism *n* dà-chànanas *m*

bill[1] *n* 1 (*fin, household*) cunntas *m*, (*fam*) bileag *f*; 2 (*parliament*) bile *m*

bill[2] *n* (*of bird*) gob *m*

binary *adj* (*IT*) dà-fhillte

bind *v* ceangail *vt*

binding *adj* (*promise etc*) ceangaltach

binoculars *n* prosbaig *f*

biodegradable *adj* so-chnàmhach

biographer *n* beath-eachdraiche *m*

biographical *adj* beath-eachdraidheil

biography *n* beath-eachdraidh *f*

biology *n* bith-eòlas *m*

biped *n* dà-chasach *m*

bird *n* eun *m*, ~s of prey eòin-àir, eòin-seilge

birth *n* 1 breith *f invar*, ~ certificate teisteanas *m* breith, premature ~ breith an-abaich; 2 (*esp the actual delivery*) asaid *f*, a difficult ~ asaid dhoirbh

birthday *n* ceann-bliadhna *m*, co-là-breith *m*, it's my ~ today tha ceann-bliadhna/co-là-breith agam an-diugh

birthright *n* (*trad*) dual *m*, that was his ~ bu dual dha sin

bishop *n* easbaig *m*

bit *adv* car, caran, rudeigin, rud beag, a ~ late car anmoch, a (little) ~ tired caran/rudeigin/rud beag sgìth

bit[1] *n* 1 mìr *m*, criomag *f*, falling/dropping to ~s a' dol na (*etc*) c(h)riomagan, a' tuiteam às a chèile, ~s and pieces criomagan *fpl*, *also* trealaich *f sing coll*; 2 (*misc exprs*) a ~ of bread pìos arain *m*, a ~ of conversation còmhradh beag, ~ by ~ uidh *f* air n-uidh, every ~ a Gael/ Highlander Gàidheal *m* gu chùl *m*, every ~ as good as X a cheart cho math ri X; 3 (*IT*) bìdeag *f*

bit[2] *n* (*ie a horse's ~*) cabstair *m*

bitch *n* 1 (*female dog*) galla *f*; 2 (*vulg: of a woman*) galla *f*, (*less trad*) bidse *f*

bite *n* **1** bìdeadh *m*; **2** (*of food*) grèim bìdh *m*, **I fancy getting/having a ~ to eat** tha mi airson grèim bìdh a ghabhail

bite *v* bìd *vti*

biting *adj* **1** geur, **~ wind** gaoth gheur, **~ tongue** teanga gheur; **2** (*of remarks, character etc*) guineach

bitter *adj* searbh, geur, goirt, **~ taste** blas searbh/geur, **~ wind** gaoth gheur, **~ distress** àmhghar ghoirt

bitterness *n* **1** (*the emotion; also ~ of taste*) gèire *f invar*; **2** (*~ directed at another person*) nimh & neimh *m*

bivouac *n* teanta bheag *f*

bivouac *v* campaich *vi* (ann an teanta bheag)

black *adj* dubh, **the night was as ~ as coal** bha an oidhche cho dubh ri gual, **a ~ woman** boireannach *m* dubh

black *n* dubh *m*, **~ and white** an dubh 's an geal

blackberry *n* **1** (*the plant*) dris ; **2** (*the fruit*) smeur *f*

blackbird *n* lon-dubh *m*

blackboard *n* bòrd-dubh *m*

blackcock *n* (*male of black grouse*) coileach-dubh *m*

blacken *v* dubh *vti*

black-haired *adj* dubh, dorcha, **a ~ woman** boireannach *m* dubh

Black Isle, the *n* An t-Eilean Dubh *m*

blackout *n* dubhadh *m*

black out *v* dubh *vt* às

blacksmith *n* gobha *m*; *in expr* **~'s shop** ceàrdach *f*

bladder *n* aotraman *m*

blade *n* lann *f*, **knife ~** lann-sgeine *f*

blame *n* coire *f*, cron *m*, **lay ~ on someone** cuir coire air cuideigin, **it's with you that the ~ for it lies** 's ann ortsa a tha a' choire

blame *v* **1**, coirich *vt*, cuir a' choire (*with prep* air), faigh cron *m* (*with prep* do); **2** (*idioms*) **it's you who are to ~ for it** 's ann ortsa a tha a' choire, *also* is tusa as coireach ris, **the parents are to be ~d** tha na pàrantan rin coireachadh

bland *adj* **1** (*food, drink*) neo-bhlasmhor, gun bhlas *m*; **2** (*character, personality*) gun smior *m*, gun bhrìgh *f invar*

blank *adj* (*paper etc*) bàn

blanket *n* plaide *f*, (*less trad*) plangaid *f*

blarney *n* cabadaich *f*, goileam *m*

blasphemy *n* (*abstr & con*) toibheum *m*, (*abstr*) dia-mhaslachadh *m*

blast *n* **1** (*of wind*) sian *m*, sgal *m*; **2** (*of noise*) toirm *f*, (*esp of noise made by people*) lasgan *m*,

iorghail *f*; **3** (*explosion*) spreadhadh *m*; **4** (*mild oath*) **~!** an donas!

blast *v* **1** (*blight*) searg *vt*, crìon *vt*; **2** (*give fierce row to*) càin/cronaich *vt* gu dian

blatant *adj* ladarna, dalma, **a ~ lie** breug *f* ladarna

blaze *n* lasair *f*

blaze *v* las *vi*

blazing *adj* lasrach, **a ~ fire** teine lasrach

bleach *v* gealaich *vti*

bleaching *n* gealachadh *m*

bleak *adj* **1** (*landscape*) lom, **a ~ moor** sliabh lom; **2** (*situation, prospects etc*) gun dòchas *m*

bleakness *n* (*of landscape*) luime *f*, dìthreabhachd *f invar*

bleary-eyed *adj* prab-shùileach

bleat, bleating *n* (*esp of sheep*) mèilich *f invar*, (*esp of goats*) miogadaich *f invar*, meigeall *m*

bleat *v* (*esp sheep*) dèan mèilich *f invar*, (*esp goats*) dèan miogadaich *f invar*

bleed *v* **1** (*general*) caill fuil *f*, **he was ~ing** bha e a' call fala; **2** (*from specific part of body*) **my finger (etc) is ~ing** tha an fhuil a' tighinn às mo chorraig (*etc*), (*of nose only*) **my nose is ~ing** tha mo shròn a' leum; **3** (*draw blood*) leig fuil (*with prep* à), **the nurse bled me** leig an nurs fuil asam

blemish *n* (*moral, of character, personality*) fàillinn *f*, (*moral or physical*) meang *f*, gaoid *f*

blend *n* coimeasgachadh & co-mheasgachadh *m*

blend *v* coimeasgaich & co-mheasgaich *vti*

bless *v* **1** beannaich *vt*; **2** *in excl* (*to someone who has sneezed*) **~ you!** Dia leat!

blessed *adj & past part* **1** beannaichte, naomh; **2** (*mild oath*) **the ~ car!** càr na croiche!

blessing *n* **1** (*in a religious context*) beannachadh *m*, beannachd *f invar*, **God's ~** beannachadh Dhè, **my ~ on you!** mo bheannachd ort!; **2** (*boon, fortunate occurrence*) beannachd *f invar*, **good health is a ~** is e/i beannachd a th' ann an deagh shlàinte

blether *n* **1** (*also ~ing*) cabadaich *f*, cabaireachd *f invar*, goileam *m*; **2** (*person who ~s*) duine cabach

blether *v* bleadraig *vi*

blight *n* **1** (*disaster etc*) sgrios *m*; **2** *in expr* **potato ~** cnàmh *m*, (*used with art*) an gaiseadh

blight *v* searg *vt*, crìon *vt*

blighted *adj & past part* **1** crìon; **2** (*fig: life, career etc*) air (a *etc*) sgrios(adh)

blind *adj* dall, **~ spot** spot dall, **a ~ person** dall *m*

blind *v* dall *vt*

blinding *adj* (*dazzling*) boillsgeach

blinding *n* dalladh *m*

blindness *n* doille *f invar*

blink *n* priobadh *m*

blink *v* priob *vi*, caog *vi*

blister *n* leus *m*, balg *m*, builgean *m*

blizzard *n* cathadh-sneachda *m*

block *n* **1** ceap *m*, cnap *m*, ~ **of wood/peat** ceap fiodha/mòna; **2** *in expr* (*usu fig*) **stumbling-~** cnap-starra *m*

block *v* **1** (*~ an aperture etc*) tachd *vt*; **2** (*stop, prevent something*) caisg *vt*

blockage *n* tachdadh *m*

blockhead *n* bumailear *m*, ùmaidh *m*, stalcaire *m*

blond(e) *adj* bàn, **blond hair** falt bàn, **a blond man** duine/fear bàn, **a blonde woman** tè bhàn, boireannach *m* bàn

blonde *n* tè bhàn, boireannach *m* bàn

blood *n* fuil *f*, ~ **relationship** càirdeas-fala *m*, ~ **is thicker than water** is tighe fuil na bùrn, ~ **pressure** bruthadh *m* fala, ~ **vessel** caochan *m* fala, **shed** ~ dòirt fuil

bloodshed *n* dòrtadh-fala *m*

bloodstream *n* ruith *f* na fala

bloody *adj* **1** (*lit*) fuil(t)each, ~ **battle** cath fuilteach; **2** (*fig, as excl, swear*) *the n concerned followed by* na croiche *or* na galla, **the ~ hammer!** òrd na croiche!, òrd na galla!

bloom *n* blàth *m*, flùr *m*

blot *n* **1** (*of ink*) smal duibh *m*, smal inc *m*; **2** (*fig: blemish etc*) smal *m*, **a ~ on his reputation** smal air a chliù

blot *v* **1** (*cause a blot*) leig *vt* inc *mf invar* (air pàipear); **2** (*soak up*) sùgh *vt*; **3** ~ **out** dubh *vt* às

blotting-paper *n* pàipear-sùghaidh *m*

blow *n* **1** (*with fist etc*) buille *f*; **2** (*disappointment, setback*) bristeadh-dùil *m*

blow *v* **1** sèid *vt*, **the wind blew** shèid a' ghaoth, **blow (up) the pipes** sèid a' phìob, ~ **up a football** sèid suas ball-coise; **2** *in expr* ~ **up** (*ie explode*) spreadh *vti*; **3** *in expr* ~ **up** (*ie enlarge photo, image etc*) meudaich *vt*

blowout *n* **1** (*tyre*) spreadhadh *m*; **2** (*food*) làn broinne *m* (de bhiadh *m*)

blubber *n* saill *f* (na) muice-mara

blubber *v* (*fam: cry, weep*) ràn *vi*

bludgeon *n* cuaille *m*

blue *adj* gorm, ~ **sky** adhar gorm, ~ **eyes** sùilean gorma

blue *n* gorm *m*

bluff *n* (*relief feature*) sròn *f*

bluff *v*, **I was only ~ing** cha robh mi ach mas fhìor

blunt *adj* **1** (*not sharp*) maol; **2** (*of person, character*) aithghearr

blush *n* rudhadh *m*, rudhadh-gruaidhe *m*

blush *v*, **she ~ed** ruadhaich *vi* a gruaidh *f*, thàinig rudhadh *m* na gruaidh

blushing *adj* ruiteach

boar *n* torc *m*, cullach *m*, **wild ~** torc allaidh/ fiadhaich

board[1] *n* **1** (*plank etc*) bòrd *m*, dèile *f*, clàr *m*; **2** (*notice ~*) bòrd *m*, **put a notice up on the ~** cuir suas sanas air a' bhòrd; **3** (*sign ~*) clàr *m*, **direction ~** clàr-seòlaidh; **4** (*for playing games etc*) bòrd *m*, **chess ~** bòrd tàileisg, ~ **game** cluich-bùird *m*; **5** (*ship, plane*) *in expr* **on ~** air bòrd

board[2] *n* (*governing etc body*) bòrd *m*

board *v* (*~ plane, boat*) rach *vi* air bòrd *m*

boast *n* bòst *m*

boast *v* dèan bòst *m*

boastful *adj* **1** (*person*) bòstail; **2** ~ **talk, tales or chatter** rabhd *m*, ràbhart *m*

boasting *n* bòstadh *m*

boat *n* **1** bàta *m*, **steam-~** bàta-smùide, **ferry ~** bàt'-aiseig; **2** (*esp a rowing boat*) eathar *or* eithear *mf*, geòla *f*

bobbin *n* iteachan *m*, piorna *mf*

bodily *adj* corporra

body *n* **1** (*of any living creature*) corp *m*, **parts of the ~** buill a' chuirp, ~ **and soul** corp is anam; **2** (*human ~*) bodhaig *f*, colann *f*; **3** (*dead ~: human*) corp *m*, (*~ usu not human*) closach *f*; **4** (*fam: a person*) creutair *m*, **a poor ~** creutair bochd; **5** (*group of people*) buidheann *mf*, **research ~** buidheann-sgrùdaidh *mf*; **6** (*collection, accumulation*) stòras *m*, cruinneachadh *m*, **a large ~ of historical material** stòras mòr de stuth eachdraidheil

bog *n* boglach *f*, fèith(e) *f*; *in expr* **peat ~** poll-mòna(ch) & poll-mònadh *m*

bog-cotton *n* canach *m* (an t-slèibh)

boil *n* neasgaid *f*

boil *v* goil *vti*

boiler *n* goileadair *m*

boiling *adj* goileach

bold *adj* **1** (*intrepid*) cruadalach, dàna; **2** (*shameless, impudent*) ladarna, dàna; **3** (*of typog*) trom

boldness *n* dànadas *m*

bolt *n* crann *m*, **nut and ~** cnò *f* is crann

bond *n* **1** (*abstr*) ceangal *m*, (*stronger*) dlùth-cheangal *m*, **there was a close/strong ~ between them** bha dlùth-cheangal eatarra; **2** (*phys: in imprisonment etc*) ceangal *m*, **he threw off his ~s** thilg e dheth a cheanglaichean; **3** (*fin etc agreement*) urras *m*

bond *v* tàth *vt*

bondage *n* **1** (*lit*) cuibhreachadh *m*, slaibhreas *m*; **2** (*more fig*) braighdeanas *m*, tràilleachd *f invar*

bonding *n* tàthadh *m*

bone *n* cnàimh & cnàmh *m*

bony *adj* cnàmhach

book *n* leabhar *m*

bookcase *n* preas-leabhraichean *m*

booklet *n* leabhran *m*, leabhrachan *m*

boot *n* **1** bròg-mhòr *f*, bròg throm; **2** (*usu Wellington ~*) bòtann *mf*; **3** (*~ of car*) ciste(-càir) *f*; **4** *in expr* **to ~** cuideachd *adv*, a bharrachd air sin, **they've a boat, and a caravan to ~** tha bàta aca, agus carabhan cuideachd

booty *n* cobhartach *mf*, (*more trad: in cattle raids etc*) creach *f*

booze *n* deoch *f*, deoch-làidir *f invar*, **he's fond of the ~** tha e measail air an deoch

boozer *n* pòitear *m*, drungair *m*

boozing *n* pòitearachd *nf invar*

border *n* **1** (*of territory etc*) crìoch *f*, **The Borders** Na Crìochan, Crìochan Shasainn; **2** (*of material etc*) oir *f*

bore[1] *v* (*~ hole etc*) toll *vti*

bore[2] *v* (*cause tedium*) is *v irreg def* liosda (*with prep* le), **you ~ me** is liosda leam thu

bored *adj* bi *vi irreg* fadachd *f invar* (*with prep* air), **I was ~ all the time he was talking** bha fadachd orm fhad 's a bha e a' bruidhinn, **a ~ little girl** caileag bheag is fadachd oirre

boredom *n* fadachd *f invar*, fadal *m*

boring *adj* fadalach, ràsanach, liosda, màirnealach

born *past part*, *usu rendered by passive forms of irreg v* beir, **he was ~** rugadh e, *also, less usu*, chaidh a bhreith, **before you were ~** mun do rugadh tusa

borrow *v* gabh/faigh *vt* air iasad *m* (**from** o/bho)

borrowed *adj & past part* air iasad *m*, **a ~ suit** deise air iasad

borrowing *n* iasad *m*

bosom *n* **1** (*general breast area*) uchd *m*, com *m*, broilleach *m*, **she clasped the boy to her ~** theannaich i am balach ri a h-uchd; **2** (*woman's ~*) cìochan (*pl of* cìoch *f*)

boss[1] *n* (*in woodwork etc*) cnap *m*

boss[2] *n* (*of firm etc*) ceannard *m*

botanical *adj* luibheach

botanist *n* luibh-eòlaiche *m*

botany *n* luibh-eòlas *m*

botcher *n* uaipear *m*, cearbair(e) *m*

both *adv & adj* **1** (*of things, actions etc*) gach cuid *f*, an dà chuid, **give me ~ sugar and salt** thoir dhomh gach cuid siùcar is salann *m*, **meat or cheese? both!** feòil no càise? an dà chuid!, **you/one can't ~ drink and drive** chan fhaod thu/chan fhaodar an dà chuid dràibheadh agus òl; **2** (*of people*) le chèile, nan dithis, **they ~ left** dh'fhalbh iad le chèile/nan dithis, *in expr* **~ of you** an dithis agaibh; **3** (*before adjs*) eadar, **they came, ~ small and great** thàinig iad, eadar bheag agus mhòr (*note that both adjs are lenited*); **4** (*as adj*) gach, **on ~ sides** air gach taobh

bother *n* dragh *m*, **I don't want to put you to any ~** chan eil mi airson dragh (sam bith) a chur oirbh

bother *v* **1** (*annoy, upset, disturb*) cuir dragh *m* (*with prep* air), (*more fam*) bodraig *vt*, (*neg exprs*) cuir *vt* suas no sìos, **the noise is ~ing me** tha am fuaim a' cur dragh orm, **it's not ~ing me** chan eil e gam bhodraigeadh, **the news didn't ~ me in the least** cha do chuir an naidheachd suas no sìos mi; **2** (*take the trouble to*) bodraig *vi*, **did you pay the bill? I didn't ~** na phàigh thu a' bhileag? cha do bhodraig mi; **3** *in expr* **you needn't ~** cha leig/ruig thu a leas *m invar*, **you needn't ~ grumbling all the time!** cha leig/ruig thu a leas a bhith a' gearan fad na h-ùine!

bottle *n* botal *m*, buideal *m*

bottom *adj* **1** as ìsle (*superlative of* ìosal *adj*), **the ~ rung** an rong *f* as ìsle; **2** *in expr* **the ~ lip** am beul-ìochdair

bottom *n* **1** (*base of something*) bonn *m*, bun *m*, **the ~ of the hill** bonn/bun a' chnuic; **2** (*lowest part*) an ceann as ìsle, **hold the ~ of it** gabh grèim air a' cheann as ìsle dheth; **3** (*of river, well etc*) grinneal *m*; **4** *in expr* **~ of the sea** grunnd *m* na mara; **5** (*backside, bum*) (*fam*) màs *m*, tòn *f*

bough *n* meang(l)an *m*, geug *f*

boulder *n* ulbhag *f*, ulpag *f*

boundary *n* crìoch *f*, **this is the ~ of my land** is e seo crìoch an fhearainn agam, **the parish ~** crìoch na sgìre, **~ wall** gàrradh-crìche *m*

bourgeois *adj & n* bùirdeasach *m*

bourgeoisie *n* bùirdeasachd *f invar*

bow[1] *n* (*before royalty etc*) ùmhlachd *f invar*

bow[2] *n* **1** (*of boat*) toiseach *m*; **2** (*weapon*) bogha(-saighde) *m*; **3** (*for stringed instrument*) bogha *m*

bow *v* **1** crom *vt*, lùb *vt*, **she ~ed her head** chrom i a ceann *m*, **~ the knee** lùb a' ghlùin; **2** (*before royalty etc*) dèan ùmhlachd *f invar*

bowed *adj* **1** lùbte; **2** (*of head*) crom

bowels *n* innidh *f invar*

bowl *n* cuach *f*, (*fam*) bobhla *m*

bow-legged *adj* camachasach, gòbbhlach

bowstring *n* taifeid *f*

box *n* bogsa *m*, bucas *m*

boxer *n* bogsair *m*

boxing *n* bogsadh & bogsaigeadh *m*

boy *n* **1** gille *m*, balach *m*, **a wee ~** gille/balach beag, **do you have a family? we have three ~s** a bheil teaghlach agaibh? tha triùir ghillean *gen* again; **2** (*fam, of a male of any age*) balach *m*, gille *m*, **you're right, ~!** tha thu ceart, a ghille (*also* 'ille)/a bhalaich!

boyfriend *n* (*fam*) car(a)bhaidh *m*, leannan *m*, (*fam*) bràmair *m* (*note that the last two of these words can be used of a sweetheart or lover of either sex*)

brace *n* (*ie pair*) càraid *f*, caigeann *f*

bracelet *n* bann-làimhe *m*

bracken *n* raineach *f*, roineach *f*

bracket *n* (*typog*) camag *f*, **square/round ~** camag cheàrnach/chruinn

braid *v* fill *vt*, dualaich *vt*

braided *adj & past part* fillte

brain, brains *n* eanchainn *f*, **she's got a good ~** tha eanchainn mhath innte

brain *v* (*fam*) cuir an eanchainn *mf* (*with prep* à), **he ~ed him** chuir e an eanchainn às

brainless *adj* faoin, baoth

brainy *adj* inntinneach

brainteaser *n* tòimhseachan *m*

brake *n* (*on wheel etc*) brèig *f*, (*more trad*) casgan *m*

bramble *n* **1** (*plant*) dris *f*; **2** (*fruit*) smeur *f*

bran *n* garbhan *m*

branch *n* **1** (*of tree, family, river, organisation etc*) meur *f*; **2** (*of tree*) geug *f*, meang(l)an *m*

branch *v* meuraich *vi*

brand *n* (*make, variety*) seòrsa *m*

brand-new *adj* ùr-nodha

brandish *v* crath *vt*, **he ~ed his fist/sword** chrath e a dhòrn/a chlaidheamh

brass *adj* **1** pràiseach; **2** *in exprs* **I don't have a ~ farthing** chan eil sgillinn ruadh agam, **~ neck** aghaidh *f*, bathais *f*

brass *n* pràis *f*

brat *n* **1** (*fam*) droch isean *m*, ablach *m*, peasan *m*; **2** *in expr* **a spoilt ~** uileagan *m*

brave *adj* **1** (*esp phys*) gaisgeil, treun, **~ heroes** gaisgich threuna; **2** (*esp rashly ~*) dàna; **3** (*esp morally ~*) misneachail

bravery *n* **1** (*esp phys*) gaisge *f invar*, gaisgeachd *f invar*; **2** (*esp rash ~*) dànadas *m*; **3** (*esp moral ~*) misneach *f*, misneachd *f invar*

brawl *n* tuasaid *f*, (*more serious*) sabaid *f*

brawl *v* sabaid *vi*, dèan sabaid *f* (**with** ri)

brawny *adj* (*of person's build*) tomadach, calma

brazen *adj* ladarna, gun nàire

breach *n* **1** (*gap*) beàrn *mf*; **2** (*infraction, contravention*) briseadh *m* (**of** air), **~ of regulations** briseadh air riaghailtean

breadth *n* farsaingeachd *f invar*, leud *m*

break *v* **1** bris(t) *vti*, **he broke the window** bhris e an uinneag, **when day broke** nuair a bhris an latha, **the marriage broke up** bhris am posadh às a chèile; **2** (*~ promise etc*) rach *vi* air ais (*with prep* air), **he broke his promise** chaidh e air ais air a ghealladh

break *n* **1** bris(t)eadh *m*; **2** (*short pause, rest*) stad (beag), *in expr* **take a ~** gabh/leig d' (*etc*) anail *f*

breast *n* **1** (*woman's ~*) cìoch *f*; **2** (*general breast area*) uchd *m*, com *m*, broilleach *m*, **she clasped the boy to her ~** theannaich i am balach ri a h-uchd, **his heart beating in his ~** a chridhe a' bualadh na chom; **3** *in exprs* **~ stroke** buille *m* uchd, **~ bone** cliathan *m*

breath *n* **1** anail *f*, **draw ~** tarraing anail, **under her ~** fo a h-anail, **get your ~ back** leig d' anail; **2** (*~ of life*) deò *f invar*, **as long as there's ~ in my body** fhad 's a bhios an deò annam; **3** *in expr* **a ~ of wind** deò gaoithe, oiteag *f*, ospag *f*

breathalyser *n* poca analach *m*

breathe *v* analaich *vi*

breather *n* (*short rest*) stad (beag) *m*, **take a ~** dèan stad, (*more colloquial*) gabh/leig d' (*etc*) anail *f*

breed *v* **1** (*plants, animals*) tàrmaich *vt*; **2** (*humans & animals*) gin *vti*

breeding *n* **1** (*of humans & animals*) gineadh *m*, (*of cattle*) dàir *f*, (*as adj*) **~ cattle** crodh-dàra *m*; **2** (*of people's manners etc: good ~*) modh *mf*

breeze *n* oiteag *f*, ospag *f*, gaoth bheag, osnadh *m*

Breton *n* (*lang*) Breatnais *f*

brewer *n* grùdair(e) *m*

brewery *n* taigh-grùide *m*

brewing *n* grùdaireachd *f invar*

bridge *n* **1** drochaid *f*, **the Skye ~** Drochaid an Eilein Sgitheanaich; **2** *in expr* **the ~ of the nose** bràigh *m* na sròine

brief *adj* goirid, **a ~ tour** cuairt ghoirid

briefcase *n* màileid *f*

brier *n* dris *f*

bright *adj* **1** (*of light etc*) soilleir; **2** (*mentally ~*) toinisgeil, eirmseach

brilliance *n* (*of light*) lainnir *f*

brilliant *adj* **1** (*of light*) lainnireach; **2** (*intellectually ~*) sàr-thoinisgeil, air leth toinisgeil

brimstone *n* pronnasg *m*

brindled *adj* riabhach

bring down *v* (*ie cause to fall*) leag *vt*

bring *v* thoir *vt* **1** (*phys & lit, also fig*) thoir *vt*, ~ **it to me** thoir thugam e, ~ **water from the well** thoir uisge on tobar, ~ **to a conclusion** thoir gu buil *f*, ~ **to an end** thoir gu crìch (*dat of* crìoch *f*), ~ **into being/existence** thoir gu/am bith *f invar*, ~ **into the open**, ~ **to light** thoir am follais *f invar*; **2** (*other phys & lit uses*) ~ **solace/comfort** furtaich *vi* (**to** air), **we will ~ you solace** furtaichidh sinn oirbh, ~ **together** cruinnich *vt*, ~ **up** (*food*) tilg *vt*, cuir *vt* a-mach **3** (*other fig uses*), ~ **a complaint** dèan casaid *f* (**against** air), ~ **out** (*book etc*) foillsich *vt*, cuir (leabhar *etc*) an clò *m*, ~ **up** (*children, livestock etc*) tog *vt*, **I was brought up in Coll** thogadh mi ann an Cola

bristle *n* (*esp on body of animals*) frioghan *m*, calg *m*

Britain *n* Breatann *mf* (*gen* Bhreatainn)

Britanny *n* A' Bhreatann Bheag (*gen* na Breatainne Bige)

broad *adj* farsaing, leathann

broadcast *n* craoladh *m*, craobh-sgaoileadh *m*

broadcast *v* craoil *vti*, craobh-sgaoil *vti*

broadcaster *m* craoladair *m*

broadcasting *n* craoladh *m*, craobh-sgaoileadh *m*

broaden *v* leudaich *vti*

broadened *adj* leudaichte

broadly *adv*, *in expr* ~ (**speaking**) san/anns an fharsaingeachd *f invar*

broadsword *n* claidheamh *m* leathann

brochure *n* leabhrachan *m*, leabhran *m*

broke *adj* gun sgillinn *f* ruadh, **I'm flat ~** chan eil sgillinn ruadh (no geal) agam

broken *adj & past part* briste

bronze *n* umha *m invar*, **the ~ Age** Linn *mf* an Umha

broth *n* brot *m*, (*trad*) eanraich *f*

brothel *n* taigh-siùrsachd *m*

brother *n* bràthair *m*

brother-in-law *n* bràthair-cèile *m*

brow *n* mala *f*, bathais *f*, clàr *m* an aodainn, maoil *f*

brown *adj* donn, **dark ~** dubh-dhonn

brown-haired *adj* donn

bubble *n* gucag *f*, builgean *m*

bucket *n* **1** bucaid *f*, peile *m*, (*more trad*) cuinneag *f*; **2** (*esp for milking*) cuman *m*

bucket *v*, *in expr* (*of weather*) **it was ~ing down** bha dìle bhàthte ann

bud *n* gucag *f*

budget *n* buidseat *m*

buffoon *n* bumalair *m*, baothair *m*

buffoonery *n* bumalaireachd *f invar*, baothaireachd *f invar*

bugger *n* **1** (*mild swear*) bugair *m*, **the ~s!** na bugairean!; **2** *in expr* (*fam*) **I don't give a ~ (for X)** cha toir mi hòro-gheallaidh *m invar* (air X)

bugle *n* dùdach *f*, dùdag *f*

build *n* (*physique*) dèanamh *m*

build *v* tog *vt*, **he built himself a house** thog e taigh dha fhèin

builder *n* togalaiche *m*, neach-togail *m* (*pl* luchd-togail *m sing coll*)

building *n* **1** (*abstr*) togail *f*; **2** (*con*) togalach *m*, **the roof of the ~** mullach an togalaich, ~ **society** comann *m* togalaich

built *adj & past part*, *in expr* **well ~ house** taigh air a dheagh thogail

bulb *n* (*plant & light ~*) bolgan *m*

bulge *n* bogha *m*, **a wall with a ~ in it** balla agus bogha air

bulky *adj* tomadach, tomaltach

bull *n* tarbh *m*

bullet *n* peilear *m*

bulling *adj* (*of cattle*) fo dhàir *f*, **a ~ cow** bò fo dhàir, **bò is an dàir oirre**

bullock *n* damh *m*

bully *n* burraidh *m*, maoidhear *m*

bullying *n* burraidheachd *f invar*, maoidheadh *m*

bulwark *n* mùr *m*, dìdean *f*

bum *n* (*ie backside: fam*) màs *m*

bundle *n* pasgadh *m*, pasgan *m*, ultach *m*

bundle *v* **1** ~ **up/together** tru(i)s *vt*; **2** (*push roughly*) brùth *vt*, sàth *vt*, **they ~d him into the car** bhrùth iad a-steach dhan chàr e

bungler *n* cearbair *m*, uaipear *m*

buoy *n* put(a) *m*

buoyancy *n* fleòdradh *m*

burden *n* (*lit & fig*) eallach *m*, uallach *m*, **love is a heavy ~** (*trad*) is trom an t-eallach an gaol

burial *n* tiodhlacadh *m*

burial ground *n* cill *f*, cladh *m*

burly *adj* (*of person's build*) tomadach, dèanta, leathann

burn[1] *n* (*injury*) losgadh *m*

burn[2] *n* (*stream*) allt *m*, sruth(an) *m*

burn *v* loisg *vti*, (*less seriously, singe*) dàth *vt*

burnt *adj* loisgte

burst[1] *n* 1 (*sudden onset of noise etc*) brag *m*, (*esp of laughter*) lasgan *m*; 2 (*of energy etc*) sgairt *f*

burst[2] *n* (*in pipe etc*) sgàineadh *m*

burst *v* 1 (*pipes etc*) sgàin *vti*, spreadh *vi*; 2 (*people out of a building, shoots from the ground etc*) brùchd *vi* (**out of/from** à)

bury *v* (*the dead*) tiodhlaic *vt*, adhlaic *vt*

bus *n* bus *m*

bush *n* dos *m*, preas *m*

business *n* 1 (*commercial ~*) gnothach *m*, gnìomhachas *m*, **set up a new ~** cuir gnìomhachas ùr air chois (*dat of* cas *f*), **~ park** raon gnìomhachais *m*, **~ card** càirt-ghnìomhachais *f*, **do/transact ~** dèan gnothach (**with** ri), **his ~ failed** dh'fhàillig an gnothach/an gnìomhachas aige, **go to France on ~** rach don Fhraing *f* air cheann ghnothaich; 2 (*commercial, but usu more abstr*) malairt *f*, **do ~** dèan malairt; 3 (*more widely, affair, matter*) nì *m*, gnothach *m*, cùis *f*, **it was a bad ~ 's** e droch nì a bh' ann, **their divorce was a bad ~ 's** e droch ghnothach a bh' anns an sgaradh-pòsaidh aca, **that's no ~ of yours!** chan e sin do ghnothach-sa!, **how did the ~ go/turn out?** ciamar a chaidh a' chùis?

businessman *n* fear-gnothaich *m*, fear-malairt *m*, fear-gnìomhachais *m*

businesswoman *n* tè-ghnothaich *f*, tè-mhalairt *f*, tè-ghnìomhachais *f*

bus-stop *n* àite-stad bus *m*

bustle *n* drip *f*, sgairt *f*

busy *adj* 1 (*of people*) trang, **I'm ~** tha mi trang, **we're ~ at the fishing** tha sinn trang ris/aig an iasgach; 2 (*of situations*) dripeil, **things are hell/heck of a ~ just now** tha cùisean garbh dripeil an-dràsta

butcher *n* bùidsear *m*, (*more trad*) feòladair *m*

butcher *v* casgair *vt*

butchering, butchery *n* spadadh *m*, casgairt *f* *invar*

Bute *n* Bòd

butt 1 (*archery etc*) targaid *f*; 2 (*fig: target, recipient etc*) cùis *f*, culaidh *f* (*followed by gen*), **they were a ~ of ridicule** bha iad nan cùis-mhagaidh/nan culaidh-mhagaidh

butter *n* ìm *m*

butter *v* 1 cuir ìm *m* (*with prep* air), **~ bread** cuir ìm air aran; 2 (*fig*) *in expr* **~ someone up** dèan miodal *m* do chuideigin/ri cuideigin

butterfly *n* dealan-dè *m*

buttock *n* màs *m*

button *n* putan *m*, **fasten/undo ~s** dùin/fuasgail putanan

buy *v* ceannaich *vti*, **~ at a good price** ceannaich air deagh phrìs

buyer *n* ceannaiche *m*

buying *n* ceannachd *nf invar*, ceannach *m*

buzzard *n* clamhan *m*

buzz *n* crònan *m*

buzz *v* dèan crònan *m*

buzzer *n* (*alarm etc*) srannan *m*

buzzing *n* crònan *m*

by *adv*, *in exprs* **put ~** cuir mu seach, **pass ~** rach seachad; **~ and ~** ri tìde *f*

by *prep* 1 (*introducing the means or the agent of an action etc*) le (*takes the dat, before the art* leis; *for prep prons formed with* le *see* p 510) **he was killed ~ a bullet** chaidh a mharbhadh le peilear, **he came by (the) train** thàinig e leis an trèan; 2 (*motion*) seachad air, **he passed ~ the house** chaidh e seachad air an taigh; 3 (*beside*) ri taobh *m* (*with gen*), **a tree ~ the road** craobh ri taobh an rathaid; 4 (*misc exprs & idioms*) **~ and large** san/anns an fharsaingeachd *f invar*, **~ the way/in the ~-going** san dol-seachad, **~ day and ~ night** a latha 's a dh'oidhche, **little ~ little** beag is beag, beag air bheag, mean air mhean, (*of time*) **~ and ~** mu dheireadh thall, ri tìde *f*, **close ~** faisg air làimh (*gen of* làmh *f*), faisg (*with prep* air), **the bank is close ~** tha am banca faisg air làimh, **close ~ the station** faisg air an stèisean

bye-law *n* frith-lagh *m*

by-election *n* fo-thaghadh *m*

by-name *n* far-ainm *m*, frith-ainm *m*

bypass *n* seach-rathad *m*

byre *n* bàthach *f*, bàthaich *m*

C

cab *n* (*ie taxi*) tagsaidh *m*
cabbage *n* càl *m*
caber *n* cabar *m*
cabin *n* 1 bothan *m*; 2 (*on ship etc*) cèabain *m*
cabinet *n* (*pol*) caibineat *m*
cabinetmaker *n* saor-àirneis *m*
cable *n* càball *m*
cache *n* stòr *m* (falaichte)
cack *n* (*fam, vulg*) cac *m*
cackle *v* gloc *vi*
cackle, cackling *n* gloc *m*, glocail *f invar*, gogail *f invar*
cadence *n* (*Lit, music*) dùnadh *m*
cadge *v* (*~ gifts of food etc*) dèan faoighe *f invar*
cadging *n* (*for gifts of food etc*) faoighe *f invar*
café *n* cafaidh *mf*, taigh-bìdh *m*
cage *n* cèidse *f*
cairn *n* càrn *m*
cake *n* cèic *f*
calamitous *adj* dosgainneach
calamity *n* dosgainn *f*
calculate *v* 1 (*distance, speed etc*) tomhais *vt*; 2 (*sums etc*) àireamhaich *vti*, obraich *vt* a-mach
calculation *n* tomhas *m*, àireamhachadh *m*
calculator *n* (*pocket etc*) àireamhair *m*
calendar *n* mìosachan *m*
calf *n* 1 (*the animal*) laogh *m*; 2 (*~ of leg*) calpa *m*
calfskin *n* laoighcionn *m*
call *n* 1 (*cry*) gairm *f*, glaodh *m*, èigh *f*; 2 (*visit*) tadhal *m*, (*esp informal ~*) cèilidh *mf*
call *v* 1 (*cry, shout: lit & fig*) gairm *vti*, glaodh *vi*, èigh *vi*, *~ing to each other* a' gairm ri chèile, they *~ed on her to do that* ghairm iad oirre sin a dhèanamh, *~ an election* gairm taghadh; 2 (*visit*) tathaich *vti*, tadhail *vi*, (*on air*), *~ on friends* tadhail air caraidean; 3 (*refer to as*) can *vi* (*with prep* ri), **Fair-haired Davie, as they ~ him** Dàibhidh Bàn, mar a chanas iad ris, **the song ~ed 'Càrlabhagh'** an t-òran ris an canar 'Càrlabhagh', (*when equivalent to* 'what's his (*etc*) name?') dè an t-ainm *with v irreg* bi & *prep* air, **what's the boy ~ed?** dè an t-ainm a th' air a' bhalach?; 4 *misc uses with*

cuir *vt*, **they ~ed off the strike** chuir iad stad *m* air an stailc *f*, chuir iad dheth an stailc, *~* **into question** cuir teagamh *m* (*with prep* an), **he ~ed my competence into question** chuir e teagamh na mo chomas, (*telephone*) **I'll ~ them tomorrow** cuiridh mi fòn *mf* thuca a-màireach, *~* **to mind** cuir na (*etc*) c(h)uimhne *f*, **it ~ed to mind the days of my youth** chuir e nam chuimhne làithean m' òige
calling *n* 1 (*shouting etc*) gairm *f*, èigheachd *f invar*; 2 (*visiting*) tadhal *m* (*with prep* air); 3 (*vocation*) gairm *f*
calm *adj* ciùin, **a ~ morning** madainn chiùin
calm *n* 1 (*esp of temperament, atmosphere*) ciùineas *m*; 2 (*esp of weather*) fèath *mf*
calm *v* ciùinich *vti*, tàlaidh *vti*, *~* **down** ciùinich *vti*, socraich *vti*
calmness *n see* calm *n* 1
calorie *n* calaraidh *m*
calumny *n* 1 (*the action*) cùl-chàineadh *m*; 2 (*the words spoken*) cùl-chainnt *f*
camel *n* càmhal *m*
camera *n* 1 camara *m*; 2 (*meetings etc*) *in expr* **(hold) in ~** (cùm *vt*) ann an dìomhaireachd *f invar*
camouflage *n* breug-riochd *m*
camp *n* campa *m*, *in expr* **~ site** ionad-campachaidh *m*
camp *v* campaich *vi*
campaign *n* (*in aid of something, to achieve something, also military*) iomairt *f*, **election ~** iomairt-taghaidh *f*
campaign *v* (*for cause, pol etc*) dèan iomairt *f*
campaigner *n* neach-iomairt (*pl* luchd-iomairt *m sing coll*)
campaigning *n* iomairt *f*
Campbell *adj* Caimbeulach, **a ~ guy/fellow/ man gave me it** thug fear Caimbeulach dhomh e
Campbell *n* 1 (*as surname*) Caimbeul, **Mr ~** Maighstir Caimbeul; 2 **a ~, someone of the name of ~** Caimbeulach *m*

camping n campachadh m, ~**ing ground** ionad-m campachaidh

can n (for drinks, food etc) cana m, canastair m

can v 1 (be permitted or allowed to) faod vi def, ~ **we go? yes** am faod sinn falbh? faodaidh; 2 (may, might) faod vi def, **it could be that there is life on Mars** dh'fhaodadh e a bhith gu bheil beatha air Màrt, **he could be ill** faodaidh gu bheil e tinn; 3 (ability, capability) urrainn f invar (with v is & prep do), bi vi irreg, followed by n & prep aig, ~ **they do it? yes** an urrainn dhaibh a dhèanamh? is urrainn, **I ~'t swallow** chan urrainn dhomh slugadh, **I couldn't help being sad** cha b' urrainn dhomh gun a bhith brònach, ~ **you read/write?** a bheil leughadh/sgrìobhadh agad?, note also exprs ~ **you swim?** an dèan thu snàmh?, ~ **you drive** (etc)? an tèid agad air dràibheadh (etc)?; 4 (expr possibility, feasibility etc) gabh vi, ~ **that be done? no!** an gabh sin a dhèanamh? (also an gabh sin dèanamh?) cha ghabh!, **as hot as ~ be** cho teth 's a ghabhas; 5 (other exprs) **she did it as well as she could** rinn i e cho math agus a rachadh aice, **she did what she could** rinn i na bha na comas

Canada nf Canada

Canadian n & adj Canèidianach m

cancel v 1 (function etc) cuir vt dheth; 2 (entry in document etc) dubh vt a-mach

cancellation n 1 (of function etc) cur m dheth; 2 (of entry in document etc) dubhadh m a-mach

cancer n aillse f invar

candid adj fosgailte, faoilidh, fosgarra

candidate n 1 (in election etc) tagraiche m, neach-tagraidh m (pl luchd-tagraidh m sing coll); 2 (at job interview etc) neach-iarraidh m (pl luchd-iarraidh m sing coll); 3 (in exam) deuchainniche m

candle n coinneal f, ~ **holder** coinnlear m

Candlemas n an Fhèill Brìde f

candlestick n coinnlear m

candour n fosgailteachd f invar, fosgarrachd f invar

cane n 1 (the material) cuilc f; 2 (~ walking-stick etc) bata(-cuilce) m

canine adj conail, ~ **teeth** fiaclan conail

canister n canastair m

Canna n Canaigh

cannabis n cainb f, (the plant) cainb-lus m

canoe n curach f Innseanach

canteen n biadhlann f

canvas n cainb f, canabhas m

canvass v, ~ **for support/votes** sìr taic/bhòtaichean

cap n (headgear) ceap m, bonaid mf

cap v 1 (limit) cuibhrich vt, ~ **a grant/expenditure** cuibhrich tabhartas/caiteachas; 2 (beat) thoir bàrr m (with prep air), **that ~s everything I ever saw** tha sin a' toirt bàrr air a h-uile càil a chunna mi (a-)riamh

capability n comas m, **all that's beyond my ~** tha sin uile thar mo chomais gen

capable adj 1 comasach (of air), **a ~ man** duine comasach, **I'm not ~ of (working) miracles** chan eil mi comasach air mìorbhailean a dhèanamh; 2 in expr **she did what she was ~ of** rinn i na bha na comas m

capacious adj 1 (of premises etc) farsaing; 2 (of vessel etc: able to take a large load/cargo) luchdmhor

capacity n 1 (abstr) tomhas-lìonaidh m; 2 in expr (more con) **a lorry with a ~ of two tons** làraidh a ghabhas (rel fut of gabh vt) dà thunna; 3 (ability, skill) comas m, ~ **of speech**, comas bruidhne f gen, **that's beyond my ~** tha sin thar mo chomais gen; 4 (role etc) dreuchd f, **in my ~ as chairman** na mo dhreuchd mar chathraiche

cape[1] n (ie headland) maol m, rubha m

cape[2] n (garment) cleòc(a) m, (esp plaid) tonnag f

caper v leum vi, ~**ing** a' leumadaich

capercaillie, capercailzie n capall-coille m

capering n leumadaich f invar

capillary n cuisle chaol f

capital n 1 (fin) calpa m, ~ **expenditure** caiteachas calpa m, ~ **gain** buannachd calpa f; 2 (~ city) ceanna-bhaile m, prìomh bhaile m; 3 (orthog) litir mhòr f

capital adj 1 (fin) calpach; 2 (first rate) anabarrach math, barraichte; 3 in exprs ~ **letter** litir mhòr f, ~ **city** ceanna-bhaile m, prìomh bhaile m

capitalism n calpachas m

capitalist n calpaiche m

capitulate v strìochd vi (to do)

capitulation n strìochdadh m (to do)

capping n (limiting) cuibhreachadh m

caprice n baogaid f

capricious adj caochlaideach, baogaideach

capsize v 1 (as vt) cuir vt thairis, **they ~d her** chuir iad thairis i; 2 (as vi) rach vi irreg thairis, **the boat ~d** chaidh am bàta thairis, also chaidh car m dhen bhàta

captain n caiptean m, (~ of boat, plane) sgiobair m

captivated adj fo gheasaibh (obs dat pl of geas f) (by le or aig), **I was ~ by it** bha mi fo gheasaibh leis/aige

captivating *adj* meallach, tàlaidheach

captive *adj* an làimh (*dat of* làmh *f*), an sàs *m*, **I am (held)** ~ tha mi an làimh/an sàs

captive *n* prìosanach *m*, ciomach *m*, (*neach etc*) an làimh (*dat of* làmh *f*), (*neach etc*) an sàs *m*, **I am a** ~ tha mi nam phrìosanach, tha mi an làimh/an sàs

captivity *n* braighdeanas *m*, ciomachas *m*

capture *n* glacadh *m*, grèim *m*

capture *v* glac *vt*, cuir *vt* an làimh (*dat of* làmh *f*), **the police** ~**d him** ghlac am poileas e

captured *adj & past part* glacte, an làimh (*dat of* làmh *f*), an sàs *m*

car *n* càr *m*, (*trad*) carbad *m*, ~ **park** pàirc chàraichean

carbon *n* gualan *m*

carbuncle *n* neasgaid *f*, guirean *m*

carcase *n* **1** corp (marbh) *m*; **2** (*usu not human: esp at butcher's etc*) closach *f*

card *n* cairt *f*, **Christmas** ~ cairt Nollaig, **playing** ~ cairt-chluiche, **a pack of** ~**s** paca chairtean, **credit** ~ cairt-iasaid, **business** ~ càirt-ghnìomhachais

cardboard *n* cairt-bhòrd *m*

cardinal *adj* prìomh, ~ **points** (*of compass*) prìomh phuingean *fpl* (combaist *f gen*)

Cardinal *n* Càirdineal *m*

care *n* **1** (*carefulness, caution*) faiceall *f*, aire *f invar*, **a lack of** ~ cion faicill *gen*, **take** ~ thoir an aire; **2** (*tending, charge, responsibility*) cùram *m*, ~ **of the elderly** cùram sheann daoine, **in Donald's** ~ air cùram Dhòmhnaill, ~ **of the sick** (*trad*) eiridinn *m invar*; **3** (*worry*) cùram *m*, iomagain *f*, **without (a)** ~ gun chùram, **full of** ~ làn iomagaine

care *v* **1** (~ *for, tend: esp the sick*) altraim *vt*, eiridnich *vt*, ~ **for the sick/ill** eiridnich na h-euslaintich; **2** (*expr affection*) bi *v irreg* measail (*with prep* air), **I** ~ **for you** tha mi measail ort; **3** (*expr disapproval, dislike*) is *v irreg def* beag orm *etc*, **she doesn't** ~ **for his house** is beag oirre an taigh aige, *note also* **I don't** ~ **much for him** chan eil mòran agam mu dheidhinn; **4** (*expr indifference*) in *exprs* **I don't** ~ tha mi coma!, **I don't** ~ **in the least** tha mi coma co-dhiù, **I don't** ~ **if he comes or not** is coma leam an tig e no nach tig

career *n* dreuchd *f*

careful *adj* cùramach, faiceallach, **be** ~ bi *v irreg* faiceallach, thoir an aire *f invar*

caress *v* cniadaich *vt*, brìodail *vt*

caressing *n* cniadachadh *m*

caretaker *n* neach-gleidhidh (*pl* luchd-gleidhidh *m sing coll*)

cargo *n* cargu & carago *m*, luchd *m*, eallach *m*

carnage *n* dòrtadh-fala *m*, bùidsearachd *f invar*, (*trad*) àr *m*

carnal *adj* feòlmhor, collaidh

carnation *n* càrnaid *f*

carnivore *n* feòil-itheadair *m*, ainmhidh feòil-itheach

carnivorous *adj* feòil-itheach

carousal, carousing *n* pòitearachd *f invar*

carouse *v* pòit *vi*

carpenter *n* saor *m*

carpentry *n* saorsainneachd *f invar*

carpet *n* brat-ùrlair *m*, brat-làir *m*

carrageen *n* cairgein & carraigean *m*

carriage *n* **1** (*vehicle*) carbad *m*; **2** (*abstr: transportation*) giùlan *m*; **3** (*the charges levied for* ~) faradh *m*

carriageway *n* rathad *m*, slighe *f*, slighe carbaid

carrier *n* **1** (*individual*) neach-giùlain (*pl* luchd-giùlain *m sing coll*); **2** (*firm; also* ~**s**) companaidh ghiùlain *mf*, companaidh iomchair

carrion *n* **1** ablach *m*; **2** *in expr* ~ **crow** feannag dhubh

carrot *n* curran *m*

carry *v* **1** giùlain *vt*, (*less usu*) iomchair *vt*; **2** *in expr* ~ **out** (*a task, process etc*) coilean *vt*, cuir *vt* an gnìomh *m*, gnìomhaich *vt*; **3** *in expr* ~ **on** (*continue, persevere*) cùm *vi*, lean *vi*, (*with prep* air), **we carried on in spite of the rain** chùm/lean sinn oirnn a dh'aindeoin an uisge; **4** *in expr* ~ **on** (*ie behave*) giùlain f(h)èin, **he was** ~**ing on as if there was no-one else in the room** bha e ga ghiùlan fhèin mar nach robh duine eile anns an rùm, *note also* **I don't like the way they** ~ **on/their way of** ~**ing on** is beag orm an dol-a-mach *m invar* (a tha) aca

carry-on, carrying-on *n* (*ie behaviour, often questionable*) dol-a-mach *m invar*, **what a carry-on!** abair dol-a-mach!

cart *n* cairt *f*

cartoon *n* dealbh-èibhinn *mf*, cartùn *m*

carve *v* **1** (*wood etc*) snaigh *vt*; **2** (*meat*) geàrr *vt*

carving *n* **1** (*of wood etc: the process*) snaigheadh *m*, (*the product*) obair-shnaighte *f*; **2** (*of meat*) gearradh *m*

cascade *n* (*waterfall*) eas *m*, leum-uisge *m*, spùt *m*

case *n* **1** (*luggage*) màileid *f*, ceas *m*; **2** (*legal*) cùis *f*, cuis-lagha *f*, **the** ~ **went against her** chaidh a' chùis na h-aghaidh; **3** (*gram*) tuiseal *m*, **the genitive** ~ an tuiseal ginideach; **4** (*fact, situation, eventuality etc*) in *exprs* **in that** ~, **if that is the** ~ mas ann mar sin a tha a' chùis, **if it is the** ~ **that he is lazy** mas e (an rud e) 's gu bheil e leisg; **5** *in expr* **in** ~ **air eagal** (*with conj* gu), mus *conj*, **he kept hold of her in** ~ **she should fall** chùm e grèim *m* oirre air eagal 's gun tuiteadh i, chùm e grèim oirre mus tuiteadh i; **6** *in expr* **in any** ~ co-dhiù, **I'm leaving in any** ~ tha mise a' falbh co-dhiù

cash *n* **1** (*as opposed to credit etc*) airgead *m*, ~ **price** prìs airgid (*gen, used adjectivally*); **2** (*ready money*, ~ *carried about one*) airgead ullamh, airgead làimhe (*gen of* làmh *f, used adjectivally*)

cask *n* baraille *m*

cassette *n* cèiseag *f*

cassock *n* casag *f*

cast[1] *n* (*in play etc*) muinntir *f*, sgioba *mf*, **the** ~ **of the play** muinntir na dealbh-cluiche

cast[2] *n* (*a throw*) tilgeadh *m*, tilgeil *f*, (*esp* ~ *of thrown weapon*) urchair *f*

cast *v* **1** tilg *vt*, caith *vt*, (**at** air), ~ **a stone** tilg clach, **she** ~ **a foal** thilg i searrach; **2** (*fig exprs*) ~ **a glance** thoir sùil (aithghearr) (**at** air), ~ **doubt on something** cuir rudeigin an teagamh, ~ **a vote** cuir bhòt

castigate *v* cronaich *vt*

castle *n* caisteal *m*, (*esp early fortified* ~) dùn *m*

castrate *v* spoth *vt*, **castrating lambs** a' spoth uan *m gen pl*

castration *n* gearradh *m*, spothadh *m*

castrato *n* caillteanach *m*

casual *adj* **1** (*pej: of person, attitude*) coma co-dhiù, mì-dhìcheallach; **2** *in expr* ~ **violence** droch-ionnsaigh(ean) gun adhbhar *m*, fòirneart gun adhbhar; **3** *in expr* **a** ~ **stroll** cuairt shocrach

casualty *n* (*in accident, war etc*) leòinteach *m*

cat *n* **1** cat *m*, **wild** ~ cat-fiadhaich; **2** (*idiom*) **it was raining** ~**s and dogs** bha dìle bhàthte ann

catastrophe *n* sgrios *m*, (*stronger*) lèirsgrios *m*, mòr-sgrios *m*

catch *v* **1** glac *vt*, **the police caught him** ghlac am poileas e, **we didn't** ~ **the plane** cha do ghlac sinn am plèana; **2** *in expr* ~ (**up with**) beir *vi irreg* (*with prep* air) **we caught (up with) him yesterday** rug sinn air an-dè; **3** (~ *illness etc*) gabh *vt*, **we caught a chill/the cold** ghabh sinn fuachd/an cnatan; **4** *in expr* ~ **sight** faigh sealladh (**of** air), (*usu at a distance*) faigh faire (**of** air)

catching *adj* (*ie infectious*) gabhaltach

catchment area *n* sgìre *f*, ~ **of a school** sgìre-sgoile, **the** ~ **of the school** sgìre na sgoile

catechise *v* (*relig*) ceasnaich *vt*

catechism *n* **1** (*relig: the book*) leabhar-cheist *m*, **the** ~ leabhar nan ceist; **2** (*the act of asking the questions*) ceasnachadh *m*

catechist *n* (*relig*) ceistear *m*

categorical *adj* (*firm, clear, definite*) deimhinne, **a** ~ **answer** freagairt dheimhinne

categorically *adv* **1** (*firmly, definitely*) gu deimhinne, gun teagamh *m* (sam bith), **I can tell you** ~ **that the moon's a balloon** faodaidh mi innse dhuibh gu deimhinne/gun teagamh sam bith gur e bailiùn a th' anns a' ghealaich; **2** (*utterly*) gu buileach, uile-gu-lèir, **I deny that** ~**ly!** tha mi ag àicheadh sin gu buileach/uile-gu-lèir!

category *n* seòrsa *m*, gnè *f*

cater *v* **1** (*in restaurant, refectory etc*) ullaich biadh *m*; **2** (*supply by way of trade etc*) solair *vti*, solaraich *vti*, (**for** do), ~ **for tourists** solar/solaraich (seirbheisean *etc*) do luchd-turais; **3** (*meet, satisfy*) coilean *vt*, leasaich *vt*, ~ **for every need** leasaich gach feum/gach easbhaidh

catering *n* ullachadh *m* bìdh (*gen sing of* biadh *m*)

cathedral *n* cathair-eaglais *f*

Catholic *n & adj* Caitligeach *m*, (*not PC*) Pàpanach *m*

cattle *n* crodh *m*, **dairy** ~ crodh-bainne, ~**-grid** cliath cruidh *f*

caught *adj & past part* an sàs, an làimh, glacte, **the robber is/has been** ~ **now** tha am mèirleach an sàs a-nise

cauldron *n* coire *m*

cauliflower *n* càl-colaig *m*

cause *n* **1** adhbhar *m*, fàth *m*, cùis *f* (*all followed by gen*), **prime** ~ màthair-adhbhar, **the** ~ **of my sadness** adhbhar/fàth mo mhulaid, ~ **for complaint** cùis-ghearain *f*; **2** (*principle, belief system etc*) adhbhar *m*, **she laboured in the** ~ **of women's rights** shaothraich i ann an adhbhar còraichean nam ban (*gen pl of* bean *f*)

cause *v* **1** is *v irreg def* adhbhar *m* (*with prep* do), is *v irreg def* coireach (*with prep* ri), **A** ~**s B** 's e A as adhbhar do B, **you** ~**d the accident** is tu a bu choireach ris an tubaist; **2** *in expr* ~ **to be** *v* cuir *vt followed by abstr n* (*with prep* air), fàg *vt followed by adj*, **you** ~**d me to be afraid** chuir sibh (an t-)eagal orm, **you** ~**d me to be sad** dh'fhàg sibh muladach mi

causeway *n* cabhsair *m*

caustic *adj* (*remarks etc*) geur, guineach, searbh

caution *n* **1** (*prudence*) faiceall *f*; **2** (*warning*) earalachadh *m*, rabhadh *m*

caution *v* **1** (*esp legal*) earalaich *vt* (**about** air); **2** (*more general*) thoir rabhadh *m* (*with prep* do), **they ~ed me** dh'earalaich iad mi, thug iad rabhadh dhomh

cautious *adj* faiceallach

cavalry *n* eachraidh *m sing coll*

cave, cavern *n* uaimh & uamh *f*

cavity *n* toll *m*

caw *n* gràg *m*, ròcail *f*

caw *v* dèan gràgail *f invar*

cawing *n* gràgail *f invar*, ròcail *f*

cease *v* 1 (*come to an end*) thig *vi* gu crìch (*dat of* crìoch *f*), sguir *vi*, **the fighting ~d** thàinig an t-sabaid gu crìch, **the noise ~ed** sguir am fuaim; **2** (*desist from, give up*) leig *vt* seachad, sguir (*with or without prep* de), **she ~d smoking** leig i seachad smocadh *m*, sguir i (de) smocadh

ceaseless *adj*, **ceaselessly** *adv*, gun sgur, ~ **noise** fuaim gun sgur, **grumbling ceaselessly** a' gearan gun sgur

ceilidh *n* cèilidh *mf*, **ceilidh-dance** cèilidh agus dannsa

ceiling *n* mullach-seòmair *m*, **the ~** mullach an t-seòmair

celebrate *v* 1 (*praise etc*) mol *vt*, luaidh *vt*; **2** (*observe festival etc*) cùm *vt*, glèidh *vt*, ~ **New Year** cùm a' Bhliadhna Ùr; **3** (*have celebratory party etc*) dèan subhachas *m*

celebrated *adj* (*renowned etc*) cliùiteach, iomraiteach

celebration *n* 1 (*observance of festival etc*) cumail-(fèille) *f*, gleidheadh *m*; **2** (*celebratory party*) pàrtaidh *m*, (*more boisterous*) hòrogheallaidh *m invar*

celebrity *n* 1 (*abstr*) ainmealachd *f invar*; **2** (*person*) neach *m* ainmeil, neach iomraiteach

celery *n* soilire *m*

celestial *adj* 1 (*incl relig senses*) nèamhaidh; **2** (*esp of phys heavens*) speurach

celibacy *n* (*esp of males*) gilleadas *m*, (*of both sexes*) seachnadh feise *m*

celibate *n* (neach *etc*) a sheachnas feise *f*

cell *n* 1 (*biol*) cealla *f*; **2** (*of saint etc*) cill *f*

Celt *n* Ceilteach *m*

Celtic *adj* Ceilteach, **the ~ languages** na cànanan Ceilteach

cement *n* saimeant *m invar*, (*more trad*) tàth *m invar*

cement *v* tàth *vt* (**together** ri chèile)

cemetery *n* cladh *m*, clachan *m*, cill *f*

censorious *adj* cronachail, coireachail

censure *n* cronachadh *m*

censure *v* cronaich *vt*

census *n* cunntas sluaigh *m*

centilitre *n* ceudailiotair *m*

centimetre *n* ceudameatair *m*, **cubic ~** ceudameatair ciùbach, **square ~** ceudameatair ceàrnagach

centipede *n* ceud-chasach *m*

central *adj* meadhanach

centralisation *n* meadhanachadh *m*

centralise *v* meadhanaich *vti*

centre *n* 1 meadhan *m*, **the town ~** meadhan a' bhaile, **right in the ~** anns a' cheart-mheadhan, **in the dead ~ of the field** ann an teis-meadhan an achaidh; **2** (*location for particular activities etc*) ionad *m*, **day ~** ionad-latha, **job ~** ionad-obrach, **health ~** ionad-slàinte, **sports ~** ionad-spòrsa, **management ~** ionad-stiùiridh, **resource ~** ionad-ghoireasan

centrifugal *adj* meadhan-sheachnach

century *n* linn *mf*

cereal *n* arbhar *m*, gràn *m*

ceremony *n* 1 (*formal event*) deas-ghnàth *m*; **2** *in expr* (*at ceilidh etc*) **the master of ceremonies** fear an taighe *m*

certain *adj* 1 (*sure, definite*) cinnteach, (*more trad*) deimhinn(e), (**of** às), **I'm ~ of it** tha mi cinnteach às, **are you ~ she'll come?** a bheil thu cinnteach gun tig i?; **2** (*Bibl, trad stories etc*) àraidh, **a ~ widow, having three sons . . .** banntrach àraidh, agus triùir mhac aice . . . ; **3** (*specified, particular*) sònraichte, **we must buy it in a ~ place on a ~ day** feumaidh sinn a cheannach ann an àite sònraichte air là sònraichte

certainly *adv* gu dearbh, **are you well? I ~ am!** a bheil thu gu math? tha gu dearbh! (*also* is mi a tha!)

certainty *n* cinnt *f*, **I can say with ~ that I am right!** faodaidh mi a ràdh le cinnt gu bheil mi ceart!

certificate *n* teisteanas *m*, **birth ~** teisteanas-breith

certify *v* thoir teisteanas *m*

cessation *n* stad *m*

chafe *v* (*skin of hand etc*) rùisg *vt*

chaff *n* càth *f*, moll *m*

chagrin *n* frionas *m*

chagrined *adj* frionasach

chain *n* cuibhreach *m*, slabhraidh *f*, *in expr* **put in ~s** cuibhrich *vt*

chain (up) *v* cuibhrich *vt*, cuir *vt* air slabhraidh *f*

chair *n* cathair *f*, (*less trad*) sèithear *m*

chairman *n* cathraiche *m*, fear-cathrach *m*

chairperson *n* cathraiche *m*, neach-cathrach *m* (*pl* luchd-cathrach *m sing coll*)

chalk *n* cailc *f*

challenge *n* dùbhlan *m*

challenge *v* **1** thoir dùbhlan (*with prep* do), **he ~d me to tell the truth** thug e dùbhlan dhomh an fhìrinn innse; **2** (*~ decision etc*) cuir *vi* an aghaidh (*with gen*)

chamber *n* seòmar *m*

champion *n* curaidh *m*

chance *adj* tuiteamach, **~ occurrences** tachartasan tuiteamach

chance *n* **1** (*luck etc*) tuiteamas *m*, **it happened by ~** thachair e le tuiteamas; **2** (*opportunity*) cothrom *m* (**of** air), **a ~ of a better life** cothrom air beatha nas fheàrr, (*idiom*) **we gave them a sporting ~** thug sinn cothrom na Fèinne dhaibh

chance *v* **1** tuit *vi* (*with prep* do), **I ~d to see her on the street** thuit dhomh a faicinn air an t-sràid; **2** *in expr* **~ upon** tachair *vi* air, amais *vi* air

chancellor *n* seansailear *m*

change *n* **1** atharrachadh *m*, caochladh *m*, (*often for the worse*) mùthadh *m*, **a ~ in the weather** atharrachadh-sìde *f*, (*idiom*) **what a ~ has come upon us!** (*trad*) nach (ann) oirnn a thàinig an dà là!; **2** (*new situation, experience etc*) ùrachadh *m*, **that will be/make a ~ for you** bidh sin na ùrachadh dhut; **3** (*money*) iomlaid *f*, **~ for/of a pound** iomlaid nota, **I didn't get any ~** cha d' fhuair mi iomlaid, *in expr* **small ~** airgead pronn

change *v* **1** atharraich *vti*, caochail *vi*, (*often for the worse*) mùth *vi*; **2** (*~ money*) **can you ~ a pound?** a bheil iomlaid *f* nota agad?

changeable *adj* caochlaideach, **~ weather/personality** sìde/pearsantachd chaochlaideach

Channel (the) *n*, *also* **the English Channel**, Caolas na Frainge *m*

Channel Islands (the) *npl* Eileanan a' Chaolais *mpl*

chanter *n* (*of bagpipe*) feadan *m*

chaos *n* **1** (*cosmology*) eu-cruth *m*; **2** (*fam: disorder, untidiness etc*) *in expr* **in ~** troimh-a-chèile, **the office was in ~** bha an oifis troimh-a-chèile

chapel *n* caibeal *m*

chapter *n* (*of book*) caibideil *mf*

character *n* **1** nàdar *m*, (*esp of humans*) mèinn *f*, (*esp hereditary*) dualchas *m*, **it's in his ~ to be proud** is e a dhualchas a bhith àrdanach, *also* tha e dualach a bhith àrdanach; **2** (*in play etc*) caractar *m*, (*less usu*) pearsa *m*

characteristic *n* (*esp inherent*) feart *m*, **we get many ~s from our forebears/ancestors** gheibh sinn mòran fheartan bhor sinnsirean

charcoal *n* gual-fiodha *m*

charge *n* **1** (*responsibility etc*) cùram *m*, **in Donald's ~** air cùram Dhòmhnaill, **in ~ of** an urra ri, **I was in ~ of the Post Office** bha mi an urra ri Oifis a' Phuist, (*idiom*) **she took ~ of the house** ghabh i an taigh os làimh (*gen of* làmh *f*); **2** (*cost, payment*) cosgais *f*, **bank(ing) ~s** cosgaisean banca(ireachd); **3** (*fee etc*) tuarastal *m*, **the lawyer didn't make a ~** cha do ghabh am fear-lagha tuarastal, *in expr* **free of ~** saor ('s an-asgaidh), **there'll be no ~ for that** bidh sin saor 's an-asgaidh, *in expr* **freight ~** faradh *m*; **4** (*legal: accusation*) casaid *f*; **5** (*military: attack*) ionnsaigh *f*

charge *v* **1** (*make responsible*) cuir uallach *m* (*with prep* air & *n in gen*), **they ~d me with the responsibility for the journey** chuir iad orm uallach an turais; **2** (*~ for goods etc*) iarr pàigheadh *m* (**for** airson); **3** (*banking etc*) **~ to an account** cuir *vt* ri cunntas; **4** (*military: attack*) thoir ionnsaigh *f* (*with prep* air), (*trad*) rach *vi* sìos; **5** (*legal*) cuir casaid *f* (*with prep* air), cuir fo chasaid

charitable *adj* **1** (*apt to give charitably*) tabhairteach; **2** (*involved in charity*) carthannach, **~ trust** urras carthannach; **3** (*of person: kindly disposed etc*) coibhneil

charity *n* **1** (*abstr*) carthannas *m*, carthannachd *f invar*; **2** (*organisation: a ~*) buidheann-carthannais, buidheann-carthannach; **3** (*con: alms, charitable gifts*) dèirc *f*; **4** (*Bibl: Christian ~*) carthannachd *f invar*, gràdh *m*

charm *n* **1** (*magical*) geas *f*, seun *m*, ortha *f*; **2** (*personal ~*) taitneas *m*, ciatachd *f invar*

charming *adj* **1** (*person*) taitneach, ciatach, tlachdmhor; **2** (*person & place*) grinn

chart *n* **1** (*map etc*) cairt *f*, **navigation ~** cairt-iùil; **2** (*table etc*) clàr *m*

charter *n* cairt *f*, cùmhnant *m* sgrìobhte

chase *n* **1** tòir *f*, ruaig *f*; **2** (*hunting*) ruaig *f*

chase *v* **1** rua(i)g *vt*, ruith *vi* às dèidh (*with gen*); **2** *in expr* **~ away** rua(i)g *vt*, fuadaich *vt*, **the dog ~d away the fox** ruaig/dh'fhuadaich an cù an sionnach, *also* chuir an cù teicheadh *m* air an t-sionnach

chaste *adj* geanmnaidh

chasten *v* ùmhlaich *vt*, nàraich *vt*

chastise *v* peanasaich *vt*

chastity *n* geanmnachd *f invar*

chat *n* **1** (*a conversation*) còmhradh (beag) *m*, **we had a wee ~** rinn sinn còmhradh beag; **2** (*words used, opinions expressed etc*) còmhradh *m*, (*fam*) craic *f*, **listening to their ~** ag èisteachd rin còmhradh

chat *v* dèan còmhradh (beag), *(idiom)* **~ting about this and that** a' còmhradh a-null 's a-nall

chattels *npl* **1** *(bits & pieces)* treal(l)aich *f sing coll*; **2** *(possessions)* **goods and ~** maoin *f*

chatter, chattering *n* cabadaich *f*, cabaireachd *f invar*, gobaireachd & gabaireachd *f invar*, goileam *m*

chatter *v* bleadraig *vi*

chatty *adj* còmhraideach, bruidhneach

cheap *adj* **1** *(in price)* saor, air bheag prìs *f*, air prìs ìseal; **2** *(derog: petty, unworthy etc)* suarach, **a ~ ploy** plòidh shuarach

cheat *n* cealgair(e) *m*, mealltair *m*, neach-foille *m*

cheat *v* **1** meall *vt*, thoir an car *(with prep* à*)*, dèan foill *f (with prep* air*)*, **they ~ed her** mheall iad i, thug iad an car aiste, rinn iad foill oirre; **2** *(as vi: in games etc)* bi *vi irreg* ri foill *f*, **they're ~ing!** tha iad ri foill!

cheated *adj* air a *(etc)* m(h)ealladh

cheating *adj* meallta(ch)

cheating *n* foill *f*, mealladh *m*

check *v* **1** *(examine for errors etc)* sgrùd *vt*, dèan ath-sgrùdadh *m (with prep* air*)*, thoir sùil *f (with prep* air*)*; **2** *(stop, restrain)* bac *vt*, cuir stad *m (with prep* air*)*, cuir bacadh *m (with prep* air*)*

check-out *n* àite-pàighidh *m*

check-up *n* àth-sgrùdadh *m*, **dental ~** àth-sgrùdadh-fhiacail, àth-sgrùdadh fhiaclan *fpl gen*

cheek *n* **1** gruaidh *f*, *(esp plump, rosy)* pluic *f*; **2** *(fam: nerve, insolence)* aghaidh *f*, bathais *f*, **what a ~!** abair aghaidh!, **what a ~ they've got!** nach ann orra a tha an aghaidh/a' bhathais!

cheep, cheeping *n* bìd *m*, bìogail *f*

cheep *v* bìog *vi*

cheer *n* **1** *(sign of approval)* iolach *f*, **raise a ~** dèan/tog iolach; **2** *(mood, spirits etc)* misneachail, **they were of good ~** bha iad misneachail, *also* bha deagh shunnd *m invar* orra

cheer *v* **1** dèan/tog iolach *f (with prep* do*)*, **the people ~ed (him)** rinn/thog an sluagh iolach (dha); **2** *in expr* **~ up** tog a *(etc)* c(h)ridhe *m*, **that ~ed me up** thog sin mo chridhe, *(as vi: idiom)* **~ up!** tog ort!

cheerful *adj* greannmhor, aighearach, cridheil, sunndach

cheerfulness *n* aighear *m*, sunnd *m invar*

cheerio! *excl* tìoraidh!

cheery *adj* *(esp person)* aighearach, *(of person, atmosphere etc)* cridheil

cheese *n* càise *mf*

chef *n* còcaire *m*, *(female ~)* ban-chòcaire *f*

chemical *adj* ceimigeach, *in expr* **~ substance** ceimig *f*

chemical *n* ceimig *f*

chemist *n* **1** ceimigear *m*; **2** *(pharmacist)* neach *m* chungaidhean, **~'s shop** bùth-chungaidh *f*

chemistry *n* ceimigeachd *f invar*

cheque *n* seic *f*

chequebook *n* seic-leabhar *m*

chess *n* tàileasg *m*, **chessboard** clàr-tàileisg *m*

chest *n* **1** *(thorax)* cliabh *m*, broilleach *m*; **2** *(furniture etc)* ciste *f*, **linen ~** ciste anairt, **treasure ~** ciste ionmhais

chew *v* **1** cnàmh *vti*, cagainn *vti*, cnuas & cnuasaich *vti*, *(fig)* **~ over** *(ideas, events etc)* cnuas & cnuasaich *(with prep* air*)*, **~ over the news** cnuasaich air an naidheachd; **3** *in exprs (of animals)* **~ing the cud**, *(also, fam, of humans)* **~ing the fat**, a' cnàmh na cìre

chick *n* isean *m*

chicken *n* *(young)* isean *m*, eireag *f*, *(mature)* cearc *f*, **roast ~** cearc ròsta

chide *v* cronaich *vt*, càin *vt*

chief *adj* prìomh, àrd, *(precede the noun, which is lenited where possible)* **~ clerk** prìomh-chlèireach, **~ justice** àrd-bhreitheamh *m*

chief *n* **1** *(leader etc)* ceannard *m*; **2** *(of clan)* ceann-cinnidh *m*, ceann-feadhna *m*, **~ of the MacDonalds** ceann-cinnidh nan Dòmhnallach

chilblain *n* cusp *f*

child *n* *(see also* **children** *below)* **1** *(abstr & general)* duine cloinne *m*, **how many ~ren do you have? one ~** cia mheud duine cloinne a th' agaibh? tha aon duine cloinne; **2** *(particular ~, generally young/infants)* leanabh *m*, pàiste *m*, leanaban *m*, naoidhean *m*, *(boy ~, esp a little older)* balach *m (beag)*, *(girl ~, esp a little older)* caileag *f (bheag)*, **she had a ~** bha pàiste aice; **3** *(misc exprs)* **unruly/badly-behaved ~** *(fam)* droch isean *m*, **~ minder** freiceadan cloinne *m*, **~ care** cùram-cloinne *m*

childhood *n* leanabas *m*

childish *adj* leanabail

childless *adj* gun chlann *f sing coll*, **~ couple** càraid *f* gun chlann

children *n* *(see also* **child** *above)* clann *f sing coll*, **little ~** clann bheaga, **two ~** dithis chloinne, **how many ~ do you have?** cia mheud duine cloinne a th' agaibh?, **the Children's Panel** Pannal *m* na Cloinne

chill *adj* *(lit & fig)* fuaraidh, fionnar

chill *n* **1** *(abstr)* fionnarachd *f invar*, *(colder)* fuachd *f invar*; **2** *(more con, a ~)* fuachd *f invar*

chill *v* fuaraich *vti*, meilich *vti*

chilly *adj* **1** (*lit & fig*) fuaraidh, fionnar; **2** (*of welcome, reception*) fuar, fionnar

chimney *n* **1** similear *m*; **2** (*marine, industrial etc*) luidhear *m*

China *n* Sìona *f*

Chinese *adj* Sìonach

chip *n* (*of wood etc, also IT*) sgealb *f*

chips *npl* sliseagan-buntàta *fpl*

chirp, chirping *n* bìd *m*, bìogail *f*

chirp *v* bìog *vi*

chisel *n* gilb *f*

chocolate *n & adj* seòclaid *f*

choice *adj* taghta

choice *n* **1** (*the thing etc chosen*) roghainn *mf*, **my own ~ of music** mo roghainn fhìn de cheòl; **2** (*alternative*) roghainn *mf*, **we've no ~** chan eil roghainn (eile) againn; **3** (*abstr: act of choosing*) taghadh *m*

choir *n* còisir *f*, còisir-chiùil *f*

choke mùch *vt*, tachd *vt*

choose *v* **1** (*select*) tagh *vt*, roghnaich *vti*, **he chose the team** thagh e an sgioba; **2** (*single out*) sònraich *vt*

chop *v* **1** (*wood etc*) sgud *vti*; **2** *in exprs* **~ off** sgath *vt* dheth, (*food etc*) **~ up** (*esp finely*) mion-gheàrr *vt*

chopper *n* làmhthuagh *f*

chosen *adj & past part* **1** (*selected*) taghta; **2** (*singled out*) sònraichte

Christendom *n, used with art,* a' Chrìosdachd *f invar*

Christian *adj* Crìosdail, **the ~ Church** an Eaglais Chrìosdail

Christian *n* Crìosdaidh *m*

Christianity *n* **1** (*the faith*) Crìosdaidheachd *f invar*; **2** (*conduct, way of life*) Crìosdalachd *f invar*

Christmas *n* Nollaig *f*, **~ Day/Eve** Là/Oidhche (na) Nollaig, **at ~ time** aig àm na Nollaig(e)

chuffed (*fam in Eng*) *adj* toilichte, (*more fam: idiom*) **he's ~** tha e air a dheagh dhòigh *m*

chunk *n* cnap *m*, geinn *m*

church *n* eaglais *f*, **the ~ of Scotland** Eaglais na h-Alba, **~ officer** maor-eaglais *m*

churchyard *n* cladh *m*, clachan *m*, cill *f*

churlish *adj* iargalt(a), droch-nàdarrach

churn *n* crannag *f*, muidhe *m*, crannachan *m*

cigarette *n* toitean *m*

cinder *n* èibhleag *f*

cinema *n* taigh-dhealbh *m*

cinnamon *n* caineal *m*

circle *n* cearcall *m*, **dancing in a ~** a' dannsadh ann an cearcall

circle *v* iadh & iath *vt, in expr* **~ around** cuartaich & cuairtich *vt*

circuit *n* **1** (*route etc*) cuairt *f*; **2** (*elec*) cuairt dealain

circular *adj* cruinn, cearclach

circular *n* (*corres*) cuairt-litir *f*

circulate *v* **1** (*as vi*) rach *vi* timcheall, rach *vi* mun cuairt, **a rumour about them was circulating** bha fathann mun deidhinn a' dol timcheall/mun cuairt; **2** (*as vt*) cuir *vt* timcheall, cuir *vt* mun cuairt, **we ~d a rumour about them** chuir sinn timcheall/mun cuairt fathann mun deidhinn

circulation *n* cuartachadh *m*, **~ of blood** cuartachadh fala (*gen of* fuil *f*)

circumspect *adj* aireach, faiceallach

circumspection *n* aire *f*, faiceall *f*

circumstance *n* **1** cùis *f*, suidheachadh *m*, **if ~s allow me** ma cheadaicheas cùisean dhomh, **in unfortunate ~s** ann an suidheachadh mì-fhortanach; **2** (*eventuality*) cor *m*, **don't sign it under any ~s** na cuir d' ainm ris air chor sam bith

citizen *n* **1** (*general*) neach-àiteachaidh (*pl* luchd-àiteachaidh *m sing coll*); **2** (*of a country*) saoranach *m*, neach-dùthcha (*pl* luchd-dùthcha *m sing coll*), **a French ~** saoranach Frangach; **3 ~s** poball *m sing*, sluagh *m sing*, **consult the ~s** cuir comhairle ris a' phoball

citizenship *n* **1** (*the status*) saoranachd *f invar*, inbhe neach-dùthcha *f*; **2** (*the associated rights etc*) còir dùthcha *m*, **seek/apply for ~** sir/iarr còir dùthcha

city *n* baile-mòr, (*esp cathedral ~*) cathair *f*

civic *adj* catharra, **~ responsibility** dleastanas catharra

civil *adj* **1** (*polite*) modhail, cùirteil; **2** (*relating to the citizens of a state*) sìobhalta, catharra, **~ servant** seirbheiseach catharra, seirbheiseach stàite, **~ war** cogadh catharra, **~ court/liberty** cùirt/saorsa chatharra; **3** *in expr* **~ engineer** innleadair-thogalach *m*

civilian *n* sìobhaltair *m*

civility n modh *mf*

civilisation *n* sìobhaltachd *f invar*

cladding *n* còmhdach *m*

claim *n* (*law, insurance etc*) tagairt *f*, tagradh *m*

claim *v* **1** (*~ rights, possessions etc: law, insurance etc*) tagair *vt*, **~ing his prize/reward** a' tagairt a dhuais; **2** (*assert*) cùm a-mach, **he ~ed that the world wasn't round** chùm e a-mach nach robh an cruinne cruinn

claimant

claimant neach-tagraidh (*pl* luchd-tagraidh *m* *sing coll*), tagraiche *m*

clamour *n* gleadhraich *f*

clamp *n* teanchair & teannachair *m*, glamradh *m*

clan *n* cinneadh *m*, clann *f*, (*more trad*) fine *f*, ~ **Donald** Clann Dòmhnaill, ~ **MacLeod** Clann MhicLeòid, ~ **chief** ceann-cinnidh *m*, *also* ceann-feadhna *m*

clang *n* gliong *m*

clang *vt* dèan gliong *m*

clanging *n* gliongadaich *f*

clannish *adj* cinneadail

clansman *n* fear-cinnidh *m*

clanswoman *n* bean-chinnidh *f*

clap *v* buail basan/(*more fam*) boisean *fpl*, **the audience ~ped** bhuail an luchd-èisteachd am basan/boisean

clapping *n* bas-bhualadh *m*, bois-bhualadh *m*

clarification *n* soilleireachadh *m*

clarify *v* soilleirich *vt*

clarity *n* soilleireachd *f invar*

clarsach *n* clàrsach *f*

clash *n* **1** (*noise*) gliongadaich *f*; **2** (*confrontation*) connsachadh *m*, connspaid *f*

clash *v* **1** (*make noise*) dèan gliongadaich *f*; **2** (*disagree etc*) connsaich *vi* (**with** le)

clasp *n* cromag *f*

class *n* **1** (*school*) clas *m*; **2** (*social ~*) seòrsa *m*; **3** (*idiom: of quality, competence etc*) **he's not in the same ~ as her** cha tig e an uisge *m* na stiùrach dhi

classical *adj* clasaigeach

classification *n* seòrsachadh *m*

classified *adj* & *past part* **1** seòrsaichte; **2** (*of document etc, confidential*) dìomhair

classify *v* seòrsaich *vt*

clattering *n* glagadaich *f*

claw *n* ìne *f*

clay *n* crèadh *f*

claymore *n* claidheamh-mòr *m*, claidheamh leathann *m*, (*less correctly*) claidheamh dà-làimh *m*

clean *adj* glan

clean *v* **1** glan *vt*; **2** ~ **out** (*byre etc*) cairt *vt*

cleanse *v* glan *vt*

cleanliness *n* glaine *f invar*

clear *adj* **1** (*of light, day etc*) soilleir; **2** (*esp of sounds, sights: audible, visible*) taisbeanach; **3** (*of area of ground etc*) rèidh; **4** (*evident etc*) follaiseach, (*more trad*) lèir (*with v irreg & def is* & *prep* do), **it's ~ that he's not guilty** tha e follaiseach nach eil e ciontach, **it was ~ to him that he was lost** bu lèir dha gun robh e air chall; **5** (*of argument, explanation etc*) soilleir

clear *v* **1** (~ *population*) fàsaich *vt*, fuadaich *vt*; **2** (~ *of obstacles etc*) rèitich *vt*, ~ **the road/way** rèitich an rathad; **3** ~ **up** (*problems, situations, relationships etc*) rèitich *vt*, (*untidiness*) rèitich *vt*, sgioblaich *vt*, ~ **up that mess!** rèitich/sgioblaich am bùrach sin!; **5** ~ **up** (*intellectual difficulties* & *misunderstandings*) soilleirich *vt*; **6** (*idiom, fam*) ~ **off/out!** thoir do chasan leat!

clearance *n* (*of population*) fàsachadh *m*, fuadach *m*, fuadachadh *m*, (*hist*) **the (Highland) ~s** Na Fuadaichean

cleared *adj* & *past part* (*area of ground etc*) rèidh

cleg *n* creithleag *f*

clemency *n* iochd *f invar*, tròcair *f*

clement *adj* **1** (*esp of weather*) ciùin, sèimh; **2** (*of judge, ruler etc*) iochdmhor, tròcaireach

clergy *n* clèir *f*, (*usu used with art*) a' chlèir

clergyman *n* ministear *m*, clèireach *m*, pears-eaglais *m*

clerical *adj* **1** (*relig*) clèireachail; **2** (*secretarial etc*) clèireachail, clèireachd (clèireachd *f invar*, *used adjectivally*), ~ **staff** luchd-obrach clèireachail, luchd-clèireachd

clerk *n* **1** (*in office etc*) clèireach *m*, (*of higher status*) clàrc *m*, ~ **of the Parliament** Clàrc na Parlamaid; **2** (*crofting*) **the township/grazings** ~ clàrc *m* a' bhaile

clever *adj* **1** (*esp mentally*) glic, eirmseach; **2** (*esp practically*) tapaidh, gleusta, deas; **3** (*resourceful*) innleachdach

cleverness *n* **1** (*esp mental*) gliocas *m*; **2** (*esp practical*) tapachd *f invar*; **3** (*resourcefulness*) innleachd *f*

cliff *n* creag *f*, bearradh *m*, stalla *m*

climate *n* clìomaid *f*

climb *v* **1** (*hill etc*) dìrich *vt*, s(t)reap *vti*; **2** *in expr* ~ **down** (*lit*) crom *vi*, teirinn & teàrn *vi*, **he ~ed down from the donkey's back** chrom e bhon asail *f*, **he ~ed down the rock** chrom e leis a' chreig *f*, **she ~ed down from the wall** theirinn i bhàrr a' ghàrraidh *m*, (*fig: give way in dispute etc*) gèill *vi*

clinking *n* gliong *m*, gliongartaich *m invar*, clagarsaich *f invar*

clip *n* (*ie for fastening*) cromag *f*, ceangal *m*

clip *v* **1** (*cut*) geàrr *vt*; **2** (~ *sheep etc*) lom *vt*, rùisg *vt*

cloak *n* cleòc(a) *m*

clock *n* gleoc *m*, cloc & cleoc *m*

clockwise *adj* & *adv* deiseil & deiseal

clod *n* (*of earth*) ploc *m*, fòid & fòd *f*

clog *v* stop *vt*

cloister *n* clabhstair *m*

close *adj* **1** (*ie near*) faisg, (*less usu*) dlùth, (**to air**), ~ **together/to each other** faisg air a chèile, ~ **to the village/township** faisg air a' bhaile; **2** *in exprs* **a** ~ **connection/link/bond** dlùth-cheangal *m* (**with** ri, **between** eadar), ~ **on a month ago** teann air mìos air ais; **3** (*of weather*) bruicheil, bruthainneach

close *n* (*Sc: in tenement etc*) clobhsa *m*

close *n* crìoch *f*, **bring to a** ~ thoir *vt* gu crìch (*dat*)

close *v* **1** (*as vt: lit*) dùin *vt*, ~ **the door** dùin an doras, (*fig*) dùin *vt*, thoir *vt* gu crìch (*dat of* crìoch *f*), crìochnaich *vt*, **the chairman will** ~ **the meeting** dùinidh am fear-cathrach a' choinneamh, bheir am fear-cathrach a' choinneamh gu crìch; **2** (*as vi*) dùin *vi*, **the shop was closing** bha a' bhùth a' dùnadh, **the window ~d with a bang** dhùin an uinneag *f* le brag *m*

closed *adj & past part* (*buildings, objects etc*) dùinte

closeness *n* faisge *f invar*, dlùths *m*

closet *n* clòsaid *f*

closure *n* dùnadh *m*

cloth *n* **1** (*material*) clò *m*, aodach *m*; **2** (*for dishes, dusting etc*) clùd *m*, clobhd *m*, brèid *m*

clothes, clothing *n* **1** (~ *in general*) aodach *m*, (*less usu*) trusgan *m*, *in expr* **a piece/an item of clothing** ball-aodaich *m*; **2** (*esp one's clothes/clothing at a given time*) cuid *f* aodaich *m gen*, **she put on her** ~ chuir i oirre a cuid aodaich; **3** (*misc exprs*) **clothes peg** cnag-aodaich *f*, **clothes-line** ròp-aodaich *m*, **suit of clothes** deise *f*, culaidh & culaidh-aodaich *f*, **bedclothes** aodach-leapa *m*, **nightclothes** aodach-oidhche *m*

cloud *n* neul *m*, sgòth *f*

cloud (over) *v* neulaich *vti*

cloudy *adj* neulach, sgòthach

clove *n* clòbha *f*

clover *n* clòbhar *m*, seamrag *f*

clown *n* **1** (*in circus etc*) cleasaiche *m*, tuaistear *m*; **2** (*ridiculous, incompetent etc person*) amadan *m*, bumailear *m*, **he's a** ~ 's e amadan/bumailear a th' ann (dheth)

club[1] *n* **1** (*weapon*) cuaille *m*; **2** (*for sport*) caman *m*, **golf** ~ (*ie driver, wedge etc, cf* **club**[2]) caman goilf *m*

club[2] *n* (*association etc*) comann *m*, club *m*, **youth** ~ comann òigridh *f*, **golf** ~ club goilf

cluck *v* dèan gogail *f invar*

clucking *n* gogail *f invar*

clump *n* bad *m*

clumsy *adj* (*person, action*) cearbach, *in expr* **a** ~ **person** cearbair *m*

cluster *n* **1** (*of nuts, fruits etc*) bagaid *f*; **2** (*of people*) grunnan *m* (dhaoine)

co- *prefix* co-, *eg* **co-education** *n* co-fhoghlam *m*, **co-operate** *v* co-obraich *vi*

coach[1] *n* (*transport*) coidse *f invar*

coach[2] *n* (*instructor etc*) neach-teagaisg *m*, (*esp sport*) neach-trèanaidh *m* (*pl* luchd-teagaisg/trèanaidh *m sing coll*)

coach *v* **1** teagaisg *vt*; **2** (*sport etc*) trèan *vt*

coal *n* gual *m*

coalition *n* co-bhanntachd *f*

coalmine *n* mèinn(e)-guail *f*

coarse *adj* **1** (*to the touch*) garbh, ~ **material** stuth garbh; **2** (*uncouth*) garbh, borb; **3** (*crude, lewd etc*) drabasta, draosta

coarseness *n* **1** (*to the touch*) gairbhe *f invar*, gairbhead *m*; **2** (*uncouthness*) gairbhe *f invar*, gairbhead *m*; **3** (*crudeness, lewdness*) drabastachd *f invar*, draostachd *f invar*

coast *n* oirthir *f*, costa *m*

coastguard *n* **1** (*the organisation*) maoras-cladaich *m*; **2** (*individual* ~) maor-cladaich *m*

coat *n* **1** (*garment, also layer, covering*) còta *m*, **a** ~ **of paint** còta peanta, còta de pheant

coat *v* còmhdaich *vt*, cuir brat *m* (**with** *prep* air)

coathanger crochadair-còta *m*

cobbler *n* greusaiche *m*

cobweb *n* lìon damhain-allaidh *m*

cock *n* **1** (*male domestic fowl or game bird*) coileach *m*; **2** (*vulg: penis*) slat *f* (*vulg/fam*)

cock *v* (*gun*) cuir *vt* air lagh *f*

cock-crow *n* gairm *f* coilich (*gen of* coileach *m*)

cocked *adj & past part* (*of gun*) air lagh *f*

cockle *n* coilleag *f*, srùban *m*

cockroach *n* càrnan *m*

cocky *adj* bragail

cocoa *n* còco *m invar*

coconut *n* cnò-bhainne *f*, cnò-còco *f*

cod *n* trosg *m*, bodach-ruadh *m*

coddle *v* (*treat too gently, spoil*) mùirnich *vt*, maothaich *vt*

code *n* **1** (*cypher etc*) còd *m*, (*IT*) **binary** ~ còd dà-fhillte, **machine** ~ còd inneil *m gen*; **2** (*rules, guidelines etc*) còd *m*, ~ **of practice** còd obrachaidh

co-education *n* co-fhoghlam *m*

coffee *n* cofaidh *mf*

coffin *n* ciste-laighe *f*

cognate *adj* dàimheil

coin *n* bonn *m* airgid

coincide *v* co-thuit *vi*

coincidence *n* co-thuiteamas *m*

coincidental *adj* **1** co-thuiteamach; **2**
(*irrelevant, unconnected*) **that's** ~ chan eil sin a'
buntainn ris a' chùis *f*

coke *n* (*fuel*) còc *m invar*

cold *adj* **1** (*phys: of weather, objects etc*) fuar, **a** ~
day là fuar, **the porridge is getting** ~ tha am
brochan a' fàs fuar; **2** (*emotionally* ~) fuar, fad'
às; **3** (*of welcome, atmosphere etc*) fionnar

cold *n* **1** (*phys*) fuachd *mf*, **I can't stand/bear
the** ~ **of winter** chan fhuiling mi fuachd a'
gheamhraidh; **2** (*the ailment: used with art*) an
cnatan *m*, (*less usu*) am fuachd *m*, **I'm getting
a/the** ~ tha an cnatan a' tighinn orm, **we
caught a/the** ~ ghabh sinn an cnatan

coldly *adv* (*of emotions, behaviour etc*) gu
fionnar, **she answered** ~ fhreagair i gu fionnar

coldness *n* (*esp phys*) fuachd *mf*, (*phys &
emotional*) fionnarachd *f invar*

Coll *n* Col(l)a *m*, **a** ~ **man/person** Col(l)ach *m*
(*also adj*)

collaborate *v* **1** (*work together*) co-obraich *vi*,
in expr ~ **with the enemy** thoir taic *f* don
nàmhaid

collaboration *n* co-obrachadh *m*

collar *n* coilear *m*

collarbone, the *n* cnà(i)mh *m* an uga, cnà(i)mh
a' choileir

colleague *n* co-obraiche *m*, companach *m*

collect *v* **1** (*esp people*) cruinnich *vi*, tionail *vi*, **a
crowd ~d in front of the house** chruinnich/
thionail sluagh (mòr) air beulaibh an taighe; **2**
(*things*) cruinnich *vt*, co-chruinnich *vt*, **he ~s
furniture** bidh e a' cruinneachadh àirneis

collection *n* **1** (*abstr & con*) cruinneachadh *m*; **2**
(*anthology*) co-chruinneachadh *m*

collective *adj* coitcheann, ~ **responsibility**
uallach coitcheann

college *n* colaiste & colaisde *f*

collide *v* co-bhuail *vi*

collision *n* co-bhualadh *m*

colon *n* **1** (*typog*) dà-phuing *f*, còilean *m*; **2** (*part
of intestine*) an caolan mòr

Colonsay *n* Colbhasa *f*

colony *n* colonaidh *m*

colour *n* **1** dath *m*, **what ~'s the coat?** dè an
dath a th' air a' chòta?; **2** (*of person's features,
complexion at a particular moment*) tuar *m*,
snuadh *m*

colour *v* dath *vt*, cuir dath *m* (*with prep* air)

colour-blind *adj* dath-dhall

coloured *adj & past part* dathte

column *n* (*architecture, newspaper etc*) colbh *m*

comb *n* **1** cìr *f*; **2** (*of game bird etc*) cìrean *m*

comb *v* cìr *vt*, ~ **your hair** cìr d' fhalt

combat *n* còmhrag *f*

combat *v* sabaid *vi*, strì *vi*, (*with prep* ri), ~
crime sabaid/strì ri eucoir *f*

combine *v* measgaich *vt*, co-mheasgaich *vti*

combination *n* measgachadh *m*

come *v* **1** *exprs with* thig *vi irreg*, ~ **in!** thig
a-steach! **she didn't** ~ **with me** cha tàinig
i còmhla rium, **coming this way** a' tighinn
an taobh seo, **before winter ~s** mus
tig an geamhradh, ~ **to an agreement/
understanding** thig gu còrdadh/gu aonta, ~ **to
a decision/conclusion** thig gu co-dhùnadh,
~ **together** thig còmhla, **the bus hasn't** ~ tha
am bus gun tighinn, ~ **out of retirement** thig
air ais bho chluaineas, ~ **to my arms!** thig nam
chom *m*/nam achlais *f*!, ~ **to be** thig gu bith,
~ **upon** thig air, tachair *vi* air, buail *vi* air, tuit
vi air, **we came upon an abandoned boat**
thachair sinn air bàta trèigte, **she came round/
came to** (*ie recovered consciousness*) thainig
i thuice fhèin; **2** (*other misc idioms & exprs*), ~
about thachair *vi*, **that's how it came about**
's ann mar sin a thachair, ~ **along/~ on** (**with
me** *understood*), *also* ~ **here**, tiugainn, trobhad
(*pl* trobhadaibh) *imper*, ~ **back** till *vi*, **coming
(back) home** a' tilleadh dhachaigh, ~ **close**
dlùthaich *vi* (**to** ri), **we were coming close to
the sea** bha sinn a' dlùthachadh ris a' mhuir,
(*expr mild protest*) ~, ~! *or* ~ **on now!** *excl*
ud, ud!, ~ **down** teirinn & teàrn *vti*, **he came
down from the pulpit** theirinn e às a' chùbaid
f, **coming down the hillside** a' teàrnadh
a' bhruthaich, **in the weeks to** ~ anns na
seachdainean (a tha) ri teachd, **the tide came
in** lìon am muir, thàinig an làn (a-steach), ~ **in
useful/handy** dèan feum *m*, **scissors would
~ in useful/handy just now** dhèanadh siosar
feum an-dràsta, (*publication*) ~ **out** nochd *vi* an
clò *m*, ~ **to light** thig *vi irreg* am follais *f invar*

comedian *n* cleasaiche *m*

comedy *n* **1** (*abstr*) àbhachd *f invar*; **2** (*amusing
film, play etc*) cleas-chluich *f*

comely *adj* ceanalta

comfort *n* **1** (*spiritual, emotional & phys*)
cofhurtachd *f invar*; **2** (~ *for pain, worry etc*)
furtachd *f invar* (**for** air), ~ **for his anguish**
furtachd air a dhòrainn

comfort *v* furtaich *vi* (*with prep* air), cofhurtaich
vt, **we will** ~ **you** furtaichidh sinn oirbh

comfortable *adj* **1** (*phys*) cofhurtail, seasgair; **2**
(*fin*) ~, **comfortably off** airgeadach, gu math
dheth

comforting *adj* (*spiritually, emotionally*)
sòlasach

comic n (*ie a comedian*) cleasaiche m

comic, comical adj èibhinn, (*less usu*) àbhachdach

coming n teachd m *invar*, **the ~ of Spring** teachd an Earraich

comma n cromag f, **inverted ~s** cromagan turrach

command n 1 (*abstr*) ceannas (**of, over** air) m; 2 (*more con, an instruction etc*) òrdugh m, reachd m *invar*

command v 1 (*order, tell*) thoir òrdugh m (*with prep* do & *infin of* v), **they ~ed me to shut the gates** thug iad òrdugh dhomh na geataichean a dhùnadh; 2 (*be in command of*) bi vi irreg an ceann (*with gen*), **the officer ~ing the regiment** an t-oifigeach (a tha/bha etc) an ceann na rèiseamaid(e)

commander n ceannard m, **~-in-chief** àrd-cheannard m

commanding adj (*personality etc*) ceannsalach

commemorate v cuimhnich vt

commemoration n 1 (*abstr*) cuimhne f invar, cuimhneachadh m, **service of ~** seirbheis f chuimhne, seirbheis cuimhneachaidh; 2 (*phys monument etc*) cuimhneachan m

commemorative adj cuimhneachaidh (*gen of* cuimhneachadh m used adjectivally), **~ medal** bonn-cuimhneachaidh

commence v tòisich vti (*with preps* air & ri), **~ work** tòisich air an obair f, **~ ploughing** tòisich a' treabhadh, tòisich ri treabhadh, tòisich air/ris an treabhadh m, **the battle ~d** thòisich am blàr

commencement n tòiseachadh m

comment v thoir (seachad) beachd m (**on** air)

commerce n ceannachd f invar, ceannach m, malairt f

commercial adj 1 malairteach, **~ sponsorship** goistidheachd f invar mhalairteach; 2 in expr **~ traveller** neach-reic siubhail m, reiceadair-siubhail m

commercial n (*on TV etc*) sanas-reic m

commission n 1 (*official task etc*) teachdaireachd f invar; 2 (*body of officials etc*) coimisean m, **the European Commission** An Coimisean Eòrpach, Coimisean na Roinn Eòrpa; 3 (*payment*) tuarastal m; 4 (*in armed services*) bar(r)antas m (oifigich m gen); 5 (*for work of art etc*) òrdugh m

commission v (*work of art, survey etc*) òrdaich vt

commit v 1 (*carry out*) dèan vt, gnìomhaich vt, **~ a crime** dèan eucoir f, **~ adultery** dèan adhaltranas m; 2 in exprs **~ suicide** cuir às dha (etc) fhèin, cuir làmh f na (etc) b(h)eatha f,

we will ~ suicide cuiridh sinn às dhuinn fhìn, cuiridh sinn làmh nar beatha, **~ to prison** cuir vt an làimh (*dat of* làmh f), cuir vt don phrìosan m, **~ to memory** meòmhraich & meamhraich vt, cùm vt air mheomhair f

commitment n dealas m (**to** airson)

committee n comataidh f, **the Housing ~** Comataidh an Taigheadais

common adj 1 coitcheann, **~ stair** staidhre choitcheann, **the ~ Market** am Margadh Coitcheann, a' Mhargaidh Choitcheann; 2 (*crofting*) **the ~ grazing** am monadh m; 3 in expr **~ sense** toinisg f, ciall f; 4 (*frequently met with*) cumanta, **a ~ occurence** tachartas cumanta; 5 (*uncouth etc*) mì-mhodhail, garbh, (*stronger*) borb

common n 1 (*common land*) coitcheann m invar, (*in crofting context: common grazing*) am monadh; 2 in expr **the House of Commons** Taigh m nan Cumantan; 3 in expr **they haven't much in ~** chan eil mòran aca an cumantas m

commonly adv gu tric, an cumantas m, am bitheantas m

commonwealth n, **the (British) Commonwealth** An Co-fhlaitheas m

commotion n ùpraid f

communal adj coitcheann, **~ facilities** goireasan mpl coitcheann

commune n co-chomann m

communicant n (*relig*) comanaiche m

communicate v 1 com-pàirtich vt, **~ information** com-pàirtich fios, cuir fios (**to** gu); 2 (*be in touch*) in expr **we still ~ with them** bidh sinn a' cur ar cuid naidheachdan fpl thuca fhathast, tha muinntireachd f invar eadarainn fhathast; 3 (*express, cause to understand*) cuir vt an cèill (*dat of* ciall f), **I cannot ~ my feelings to you** chan urrainn dhomh m' fhaireachdainnean fpl a chur an cèill dhut; 4 (*relig: receive communion*) comanaich vi

communication n 1 (*abstr*) conaltradh m, eadar-theachdaireachd f invar, **means of ~**, also **~ media** meadhanan mpl conaltraidh gen, **~ skills** sgilean mpl conaltraidh gen, **~ centre** ionad m eadar-theachdaireachd; 2 (*con, formal: an individual message*) fios m, teachdaireachd f, **we received your ~** fhuair sinn ur teachdaireachd; 3 (*the act of communicating*) com-pàirteachadh m, (*in a social context*) muinntearachd f invar,

Communion n 1 (*relig*) comanachadh m; 2 (*Presbyterianism: the ~ season, the sequence*

of services including the sacrament of ~)
òrdaighean *mpl*

communism *n* co-mhaoineas *m*

communist *n & adj* co-mhaoineach *m*

community *n* 1 (*a district & its people*)
coimhearsnachd *f*; 2 (*commune etc*) comann *m*,
co-chomann *m*

compact *adj* 1 (*dense etc*) dlùth, dòmhail &
dùmhail; 2 (*small, miniature*) mion, meanbh,
(*IT*) ~ **disc** meanbh-chlàr *m*

compact *n* (*agreement*) co-chòrdadh *m*,
cùmhnant *m*

compact *v* teannaich *vti*

companion *n* companach *m*

companionable *adj* cèilidheach, cuideachdail

companionship *n* companas *m*

company *n* 1 (*commerce etc*) companaidh *mf*,
international companies companaidhean
eadar-nàiseanta; 2 (*social*) cuideachd *f invar*,
comann *m*, **in my ~** nam chuideachd, **I
like the ~ of young people** is toigh leam
cuideachd/comann na h-òigridh, *in expr* **fond
of** ~ cuideachdail, cèilidheach; 3 (*of troops
etc*) còmhlan *m*, ~ **of soldiers** còmhlan
shaighdearan

comparable *adj* coimeasach

comparative *adj* (*gram*) coimeasach, ~
adjective buadhair coimeasach

compare *v* dèan coimeas *m* (*with prep* eadar),
coltaich *vt*, samhlaich *vt* (*both with prep* ri),
~ **X and Y** dèan coimeas eadar X is Y, ~ **X to/
with Y** coltaich/samhlaich X ri Y

compared *adj & past part*, ~ **to/with** an
coimeas ri, an taca ri, **she's clever ~ to her
brother** tha i comasach an coimeas/an taca ri
a bràthair

comparison *n* 1 coimeas *f* (**between** eadar); 2
in expr **in ~ to** an coimeas ri, an taca ri, **she's
clever in ~ to her brother** tha i comasach an
coimeas/an taca ri a bràthair; 3 *in expr* (*gram*)
adjective of ~ buadhair coimeasach

compass *n* combaist *f*

compassion *n* iochd *f invar*, truas *m*, truacantas
m, **take ~** gabh truas (**on** de), **won't you take
~ on me?** nach gabh thu truas dhìom?

compassionate *adj* 1 (*merciful*) iochdmhor,
truacanta; 2 (*sympathetic*) co-fhulangach, co-
mhothachail

compatibility *n* co-fhreagarrachd *f invar*, (*esp of
people*) co-chòrdalachd *f invar*

compatible *adj* co-fhreagarrach, freagarrach
(**with** do *or* air), **the wheel and the axle
were not ~** cha robh a' chuibhle agus an aiseal
co-fhreagarrach, **Iain and Mòrag were very ~**

bha Iain agus Mòrag glè fhreagarrach dha chèile/
air a chèile

compel *v* thoir *vi* air, co-èignich *vt*, **she ~led
me to leave** thug i orm falbh, **he'll ~ me to
do it eventually** bheir e orm a dhèanamh aig a'
cheann thall

compensate *v* (*fin*) dìol *vt*, cuidhtich *vi*

compensation *n* (*fin*) dìoladh *m*, cuidhteachadh
m

compère *n* (*at ceilidh etc*) fear an taighe *m*

competence *n* comas *m*, **beyond his ~** thar a
chomais (*gen*)

competent *adj* comasach

competition *n* 1 (*for prizes, awards etc*) co-
fharpais *f*, farpais *f*, **the Mod ~s** co-fharpaisean
a' Mhòid; 2 (*rivalry between individuals, firms,
nations etc*) còmhstri *f*

competitive *adj* 1 (*in character*) farpaiseach,
strìtheil; 2 (*in business etc*) farpaiseach, **a ~
tender** tairgse fharpaiseach, *also* tairgse air
deagh phrìs *f*

competitor *n* 1 (*for prizes, awards etc*) co-
fharpaiseach *m*, farpaiseach *m*; 2 (*rival in
business etc*) còmhstritheach *m*

compilation *n* co-chruinneachadh *m*

complain *v* 1 gearain *vi*, (*less usu*) talaich *v*,
(**about** air, **to** ri), ~ **to the manager** gearain
ris a' mhanaidsear; 2 *in expr* **apt to ~** gearanach

complaining *adj* gearanach

complaint *n* 1 (*grumble etc*) gearan *m*; 2
(*official, legal ~*) casaid *f*, **make/bring a ~**
dèan casaid (**against** air); 3 (*ailment*) gearan *m*,
galar *m*, tinneas *m*

complete *adj* 1 (*entire, intact*) iomlan, slàn, gu
lèir *adv*, **a ~ Pictish standing stone** tursa
Cruithneach iomlan/slàn, **a ~ month** mìos gu
lèir; 2 (*finished*) deiseil, ullamh, **the project
is ~** tha am pròiseact ullamh; 3 (*utter*) dearg
(*precedes the noun*), gu chùl *m*, **a ~ fool** dearg
amadan *m*, amadan gu chùl

complete *v* cuir crìoch *f* (*with prep* air), thoir
vt gu buil *f*, thoir *vt* gu crìch (*dat of* crìoch *f*),
thoir *vt* gu ceann *m*, **she ~ed her novel** chuir
i crìoch air an nobhail aice, **we ~d the project**
thug sinn am pròiseact gu buil/gu crìch/gu ceann

completed *adj & past part* crìochnaichte

completely *adv* 1 (gu) buileach, gu h-iomlan, gu
tur, **I'm ~ certain** tha mi buileach cinnteach,
also tha mi làn-chinnteach, **it was ~ destroyed**
chaidh a sgrios gu h-iomlan/gu tur, **the two
things are ~ different** tha an dà rud gu tur
eadar-dhealaichte; 2 (*more fam*) dearg, **she's
~ spoilt** tha i air a dearg mhilleadh, **~ naked**
dearg rùisgte; 3 *in expr* **~ opposed to**, ~

against calg-dhìreach an aghaidh (*with gen*), **I'm ~ against hunting** tha mi calg-dhìreach an aghaidh sealgaireachd

complex *adj* **1** (*in structure etc*) iomadh-fhillte; **2** (*hard to understand*) deacair, amalach

complex *n* (*ie group of buildings & facilities*) ionad *m*, **sports ~** ionad-spòrs

complexion *n* **1** (*of person's features*) dreach *m*, tuar *m*; **2** (*appearance, significance, interpretation*) coltas *m*, cruth *m*, **that puts a different ~ on the matter** tha sin a' cur coltais/cruth eile air a' chùis

complexity *n* **1** (*in structure etc*) iomadh-fhillteachd *f invar*; **2** (*difficulty of understanding*) deacaireachd *f invar*; **3** (*complication, problem*) duilgheadas *m*, **one of the complexities of this situation** fear de dhuilgheadasan an t-suidheachaidh seo

compliance *n* gèilleadh *m*

compliant *adj* umha(i)l, macanta, strìochdach

complicated *adj* **1** (*in structure etc*) iomadh-fhillte; **2** (*hard to understand, solve*) deacair, amalach

compliment *n* **1** moladh *m*, **I paid him a ~** rinn mi moladh air; **2** (*in corres*) **with ~s** le deagh dhùrachd *m*

compliment *v* dèan moladh *m* (*with prep* air), **she ~ed me on my Gaelic** rinn i moladh air (cho math 's a bha) mo chuid Gàidhlig

complimentary *adj* **1** luaidheach, molaidh air (*gen of* moladh *m*, *used adjectivally*), **~ words** briathran luaidheach/molaidh; **2** (*free*) an-asgaidh, **a ~ ticket** tigead an-asgaidh

comply *v* **1** (*submit etc*) gèill *vi* (**with** do); **2** (*regulations, agreements etc*) cùm *vi* (**with** ri)

comportment *n* giùlan *m*, iomchar *m*, dol-a-mach *m*

compose *v* **1** (*write etc*) dèan *vt* (suas), cuir *vt* ri chèile, **I ~d some poetry** rinn mi bàrdachd, **a song ~d by X** òran air a chur ri chèile le X; **2** (*regain composure*) socraich *vt* (mi fhìn *etc*), **she had no time to ~ herself** cha robh ùine/tìde aice i fhèin a shocrachadh

composed *adj & past part* **1** (*written etc*) dèanta; **2** (*calmed etc*) socraichte

composer *n* ùghdar *m*, sgrìobhadair *m*, (*mus*) ceòl-sgrìobhaiche *m*

compound *adj* fillte, **~ interest** riadh fillte

comprehend *v* **1** tuig *vti*, (*esp ~ people, behaviour: less usu*) fidir *vt*

comprehension *n* tuigse *f invar*

compress *v* teannaich *vt*

compressed *adj & past part* teannaichte

compression *n* teannachadh *m*

compromise *n* co-rèiteachadh *m*, còrdadh *m*

compulsion *n* co-èigneachadh *m*

compulsive *adj*, *in expr* **he was a ~ gambler** bha e na thràill *m* do cheàrrachas *m*, cha b' urrainn dha cèarrachas a sheachnadh

compulsory *adj* èigeantach, èigneachail, do-sheachainte

computation *n* tomhas *m*, àireamhachd *f invar*

compute *v* (*distance, speed etc*) tomhais *vt*

computer *n* coimpiutair *m*, *in expr* **~ terminal** ceann-obrach *m*

computerisation *n* coimpiutaireachadh *m*

computing *n* coimpiutaireachd *f invar*

comrade *n* companach *m*

con *prefix* co-, *eg* **concord** co-chòrdadh *m*

conceal *v* cuir *vt* am falach *m*, falaich *vt*, ceil *vt* (**from** air), **they ~ed the ammunition** chuir iad an connadh-làmhaich am falach, **~ it from her** ceil oirre e

concealed *adj & past part* am falach, falaichte

concealment *n* ceileadh *m*, ceiltinn *f invar*, falach *m*, cleith *f*

concede *v* **1** (*relinquish etc*) gèill *vi*; **2** (*agree, recognise*) aidich *vi*, **I ~ that I was wrong** tha mi ag aideachadh gun robh mi ceàrr

conceit *n* fèin-mholadh *m*, mòrchuis *f*, leòm *f*

conceited *adj* mòrchuiseach, mòr às (*etc*) fhèin

conceive *v* **1** (*become pregnant*) gin *vti*; **2** (*think up etc*) innlich *vt*, **~ a trick/a plan** innlich cuilbheart/plana

concentric *adj* co-mheadhanach

concept *n* bun-bheachd *m*

conception *n* **1** (*gynaecology etc*) gineamhainn *m invar*; **2** (*of plan, invention etc*) innleachadh *m*; **3** (*understanding*) fios *m*, tuigse *f*, **you have no ~ of what I mean** chan eil càil a dh'fhios agad dè a tha mi a' ciallachadh

concern *n* **1** (*interest, attention*) aire *m*, for *m invar*, (**for** air), **with ~ for nothing but his own affairs** gun aire aige/gun for aige ach air a ghnothaichean fhèin; **2** (*worry*) iomagain *f*, dragh *m*, **a cause for ~** adhbhar iomagain/dragha *gen*; **3** (*~ for others*) co-fhulangas *m*, co-mhothachadh *m*; **4** (*business, firm*) gnothach *m*, *also in expr* **that's no ~ of yours!** chan e sin do ghnothach-sa!

concern *v* **1** (*affect etc*) buin *vi* (*with preps* do & ri), **that doesn't ~ you** chan eil sin a' buntainn dhutsa/riutsa, *or* (*stronger: ie none of your business*) chan e sin do ghnothach-sa; **2** *in expr* **~ oneself** (*ie worry*) gabh uallach (**about** mu); **3** *in expr* **as far as . . . is ~ed**, a thaobh (*with* gen), **as far as the election is ~ed** a thaobh an taghaidh

concerned *adj & past part* **1** (*worried*) *in exprs* **she's ~ about the state of the world** tha uallach *m* oirre mu staid an t-saoghail, **become ~** gabh uallach (**about** mu); **2** (*relevant, involved*) *in expr* **the people ~** na daoine ris am buin a' chùis, na daoine a tha an sàs anns a' ghnothach *m*

concerning *prep* **1** (*to do with*) a thaobh (*with gen*), **he has problems ~ money** tha duilgheadasan aige a thaobh airgid; **2** (*about*) mu dheidhinn (*with gen*), **they're saying dreadful things ~ the minister** tha iad ag ràdh rudan uabhasach mu dheidhinn a' mhinisteir, **a rumour ~ing him** fathann mu dheidhinn

concert *n* cuirm-chiùil *f*

concierge *n* dorsair *m*

conciliate *v* (*opposing parties etc*) thoir *vt* gu rèite *f*

conciliation *n* rèiteachadh *m*

conciliator *n* neach-rèiteachaidh (*pl* luchd-rèiteachaidh *m sing coll*)

concise *adj* **1** (*speech etc: to the point*) pongail; **2** (*short*) goirid, **~ dictionary** faclair goirid

conclude *v* **1** (*come to a decision or conclusion*) co-dhùin *vi*; **2** (*as vt: bring to a close*) thoir *vt* gu crìch (*dat of* crìoch *f*), thoir *vt* gu ceann *m*, crìochnaich *vt*

conclusion *n* **1** (*of meeting, train of thought etc*) co-dhùnadh *m*, **come to a ~** thig *vi* gu co-dhùnadh, co-dhùin *vi*; **2** *in expr* **bring to a ~** (*project etc*) thoir *vt* gu buil *f*, (*meeting, event etc*) thoir *vt* gu co-dhùnadh *m*

conclusive *adj* deimhinnte, dearbhte, **~ evidence** fianais dheimhinnte/dhearbhte

concord *n* co-chòrdadh *m*, **~ between the nations** co-chòrdadh eadar na nàiseanan *mpl*

concrete[1] *adj* saimeant (*gen of* saimeant *m invar, used adjectivally*), **~ walls** ballaichean *mpl* saimeant

concrete[2] *adj* **1** (*actual, specific etc*) sònraichte, **a ~ example** eisimpleir shònraichte; **2** (*opposite of abstr*) nitheil

concubine *n* coimhleapach *mf*

condemn *v* **1** (*criticise severely*) cronaich *vt*, **they ~ed our conduct** chronaich iad (gu mòr) ar dol-a-mach; **2** (*sentence etc*) dìt *vt*, **~ to death** dìt *vt* gu bàs *m*

condemnation *n* dìteadh *m*

condensation *n* (*vapour*) co-dhlùthachadh *m*

condense *v* **1** (*abridge book etc*) giorraich *vt*; **2** (*of vapour*) co-dhlùthaich *vti*

condition *n* **1** (*state*) cor *m*, staid *f*, **the pitiful ~ of the refugees** cor truagh nam fògarrach; **2** (*stipulation*) cor *m*, cumha *m*, cùmhnant *m*, **on ~ that you marry me** air chor/air chumha 's gum pòs thu mi, **on this ~** air a' chùmhnant seo

conditional *adj* **1** (*gram*) cumhach, **the ~ tense** an tràth cumhach *m*; **2** (*dependent*) an crochadh (**on** air), a rèir (*with gen*), **the price is ~ on the colour** tha a' phrìs an crochadh air an dath (a th' air *etc*), tha a' phrìs a rèir an datha

condom *n* casgan *m*

conduct *n* giùlan *m*, dol-a-mach *m invar*, **I don't think much of your ~** is beag orm an dol-a-mach agad

conduct *v* **1** (*~ a legal case, an argument*) tagair *vt*; **2** (*~ tourists etc*) treòraich; **3** (*~ orchestra*) stiùir *vti*; **4** (*behave*) *in expr* **~ oneself** giùlain *vt* e/i (*etc*) fhèin, **I'm ~ing myself very well indeed!** tha mi gam ghiùlan fhìn uabhasach math!; **5** (*carry out*) cuir *vt* an gnìomh *m*, **~ an investigation** cuir sgrùdadh an gnìomh; **6** (*~ elec current*) giùlain *vt*

conductor *n* **1** (*of orchestra*) stiùireadair *m*; **2** (*of elec current etc*) stuth-giùlain *m*

cone *n* **1** (*geometry etc*) còn *m*; **2 pine/fir ~** durcan *m*

confederation *n* (*of countries*) co-fhlaitheas *m*

conference *n* co-labhairt *f invar*, còmhdhail *f*

confess *v* **1** (*to misdeed etc*) aidich *vti*; **2** (*relig*) dèan faoisid *f*, faoisidich *vti*

confession *n* **1** (*relig*) faoisid *f*, **make ~** dèan faoisid; **2** (*legal etc*) aideachadh *m*

confessor *n* (*relig*) sagart-faoisid *m*

confidant(e) *n* fear-rùin *m, pl* luchd-rùin *m sing coll*, bean-rùin *f*

confide *v* leig a (*etc*) rùn *m* (**in** ri), **don't ~ in them** na leig do rùn riutha

confidence *n* **1** (*trust etc*) earbsa *f invar* (**in** ann, às), **they have no ~ in you** chan eil earbsa aca annaibh/asaibh; **2** (*~ in oneself*) misneachd *f invar*, fèin-mhisneachd *f invar*, (*excessive*) fèin-spèis *f*, fèin-mholadh *m*; **3** (*secret etc*) rùn *m*, **let me into your ~** leig do rùn rium

confident *adj* **1** (*assured*) misneachail, **self-~** fèin-mhisneachail; **2** (*hopeful*) dòchasach, làn dòchais *m gen*, **I'm ~ about the future** tha mi dòchasach mun àm a tha ri teachd; **3** (*certain*) cinnteach, **are you ~ she'll come?** a bheil thu cinnteach gun tig i?

confidential *adj* dìomhair

confidentiality *n* dìomhaireachd *f invar*

confirm *v* **1** (*prove: truths, principles, theories etc*) dearbh *vt*; **2** (*assert, strengthen: faith etc*) daingnich *vt*, **she ~ed her faith by becoming**

a nun dhaingnich i a creideamh le a bhith a' dol na caillich-dhuibh

conflict n còmhrag f, còmhstri f, strì f

confluence n comar m, inbhir m

confront v (oppose, face up to) seas vi (with prep ri), (esp phys) seas vi mu choinneimh (with gen), **we ~ed the committee** sheas sinn ris a' chomataidh f, **she ~ed the thief** sheas i mu choinneimh a' mhèirlich

confuse v 1 (mix up) measgaich vt suas, ~ **different things** measgaich suas rudan eadar-dhealaichte; 2 (puzzle, disorientate) breislich vt, cuir vt am breisleach m, cuir vt troimh-a-chèile, **you're confusing me now** tha thu gam bhreisleachadh/gam chur troimh-a-chèile a-nis

confusion n 1 (of different things, one for the other) measgachadh m suas; 2 (in crowds: disturbance etc) ùpraid f; 3 (of things, in situations, places etc: disorder, disarray) in expr **in** ~ troimh-a-chèile, thar a chèile, **the entire house was in** ~ bha an taigh air fad troimh-a-chèile/thar a chèile; 4 (mental ~) breisleach m

congenial adj taitneach, **I find that** ~ **is** taitneach leam sin, also tha sin a' còrdadh rium

congested adj (places, buildings, gatherings etc) dòmhail & dùmhail, loma-làn

congestion n dùmhlachd f invar

congratulate v cuir meal-a-naidheachd (with prep air), **I ~d them after the wedding** chuir mi meal-a-naidheachd orra an dèidh na bainnse

congratulations excl meal do naidheachd! f (lit 'enjoy your news!')

congregate v (esp of people) tionail vi, thig vi còmhla, cruinnich vi

congregation n coitheanal m

congress n 1 (an organisation & its meetings) còmhdhail f, **Trades Union Congress** Còmhdhail nan Aonaidhean Ciùird (gen of cèard or ceàrd m); 2 (sexual ~) co-ghineadh m, cuplachadh m

conical adj cònach, air chumadh còn

coniferous adj cònach

conjectural adj tuaireamach, baralach

conjecture n tuaiream f, tuairmeas m

conjecture v thoir tuairmeas, beachdaich vi, (**about** air)

conjunction n (gram) naisgear m

conjurer n cleasaiche m, caisreabhaiche m

conjuring n cleasachd f invar, caisreabhachd f invar

connect v ceangail vt (**to** ri), (~ together) co-cheangail vt

connected adj & past part 1 (abstr & con) ceangailte, co-cheangailte, **global warming and the climate are** ~ (**to one another**) tha blàthachadh na cruinne is a' chlìomaid co-cheangailte (ri chèile); 2 (associated) ~ **with** an lùib (dat of lùb f), an cois (dat of cas), (both with gen), **theft and the loss** ~ **with it** goid agus an call a tha na lùib/na cois

connection n 1 (abstr & con) ceangal m, co-cheangal m; 2 (association, link) ceangal m, gnothach m (**with** ri), **I have no** ~ **with that firm** chan eil ceangal sam bith/gnothach sam bith agam ris a' chompanaidh sin; 3 (esp family ~) buinteanas m, **I have ~s with Skye** tha buinteanas agam ris an Eilean Sgitheanach; 4 in expr **in** ~ **with** a thaobh (with gen), **he has problems in** ~ **with money** tha duilgheadasan aige a thaobh airgid

conquer v ceannsaich vt, thoir buaidh f (with prep air)

conqueror n ceannsaiche m

conquest n ceannsachadh m

conscience n cogais f, **my** ~ **was tormenting me** bha mo chogais gam shàrachadh

conscientious adj dìcheallach, cogaiseach

conscientiousness n dìcheall m, dìcheallachd f invar

conscious adj 1 (not unconscious, in possession of one's faculties) mothachail; 2 (aware, cognisant) fiosrach, mothachail, (**of** air), ~ **of the danger** fiosrach/mothachail air a' chunnart, in expr **be** ~ **of** (ie perceive) mothaich vt (with prep do), **we were** ~ **of the movement of the boat** mhothaich sinn do ghluasad a' bhàta

consciousness n 1 (possession of one's faculties) fiosrachd f invar; 2 (awareness) mothachadh m (**of** air)

consecrate v coisrig vt (**to** do or gu)

consecrated adj & past part coisrigte (**to** do or gu), ~ (**communion**) **wafer** abhlan coisrigte

consecration n coisrigeadh m (**to** do or gu)

consecutive adj an ceann m a chèile, an sreath m f a chèile, co-leanailteach

consensus m co-aontachd f

consent n aonta(dh) m, cead m, **get your parents'** ~ faigh aonta/cead do phàrantan

consent v aontaich vti, co-aontaich vti, (**to** ri)

consequence n (of action etc) toradh m, buaidh f, buil f, **the ~(s) of your behaviour** toradh do dhol-a-mach, **as a** ~ **of that** mar thoradh air sin

conservancy n glèidhteachas m, **nature** ~ glèidhteachas nàdair

conservation n glèidhteachas m

conservationist *n* neach-glèidhteachais (*pl* luchd-glèidhteachais *m sing coll*)

conservative *adj* glèidhteach

Conservative *adj* (*pol*) Tòraidheach

Conservative *n* (*pol*) Tòraidh *m*

conserve *v* glèidh *vt*, **they're being ~d in a museum** tha iad gan gleidheadh ann an taigh-tasgaidh *m*

conserved *adj & past part* glèidhte

consider *v* **1** (*think, be of the opinion*) saoil *vi*, creid *vi*, **I ~ him to be an idiot** saoilidh mi gur e bumailear *m* a th' ann (dheth); **2** (*think over*) beachdaich *vi*, gabh beachd *m*, smaoin(t)ich *vi*, (*more fam*) cnuasaich *vi*, (*all with prep* air), **will you ~ it?** an smaoin(t)ich thu air?, am beachdaich thu air?, **~ing the events of the day** a' smaoin(t)eachadh air tachartasan an latha; **3** (*observe, contemplate*) beachdaich *vt* (*with prep* air), **~ the stars** beachdaich air na reultan

consideration *n* **1** (*~ for others*) co-fhulangas *m*; **2** (*thinking over*) beachdachadh *m* (**of** air); **3** *in expr* **take into ~** cuir *vt* san àireimh *f*, **we'll take the boy's age into ~** cuiridh sinn san àireimh aois a' ghille; **4** (*fee etc*) tuarastal *m*, duais *f*

consistent *adj* **1** (*unvarying*) seasmhach, neo-chaochlaideach; **2** (*tallying with*) co-chòrdail (**with** ri), **it's ~ with what he said** tha e co-chòrdail ris na thubhairt e

consolation *n* furtachd *f invar*, cofhurtachd *f invar*, **~ for his anguish** furtachd air a dhòrainn

console *v* (*after pain, worry etc*) furtaich *vi* (*with prep* air), cofhurtaich *vt*, **we will ~ you** furtaichidh sinn oirbh

consolidate *v* (*structure, building, situation etc*) co-dhaingnich *vt*

consonant *n* (*lang*) co-fhoghar *m*, consan *m*, connrag *f*

conspicuous *adj* faicsinneach, follaiseach, suaicheanta

conspicuousness *n* faicsinneachd *f invar*

conspiracy *n* (*plot etc*) co-fheall *f*, cuilbheart *f*

conspire *v* dèan co-fheall *f*, innlich cuilbheart *f*, (**against** an aghaidh *with gen*)

constable *n*, (*crofting, police*) constabal *m*

constancy *n* **1** (*durability etc*) maireannachd *f invar*, seasmhachd *f invar*; **2** (*loyalty*) dìlseachd *f invar*, seasmhachd *f invar*

constant *adj* **1** (*lasting*) buan, maireannach, seasmhach; **2** (*unchanging*) neo-atharrachail; **3** (*loyal*) dìleas, seasmhach, **a ~ friend** caraid

dìleas; **4** (*ceaseless*) gun sgur *adv*, **~ bickering** connsachadh *m* gun sgur

constantly *adv* gun sgur, daonnan, **they're ~ on at me** tha iad an sàs annam gun sgur

constellation *n* reul-bhad *m*

constituency *n* (*pol*) roinn taghaidh *f*, roinn-phàrlamaid *f*

constituent *n* **1** (*a part*) pàirt *mf*, earrann *f*; **2** (*pol*) neach-taghaidh (*pl* luchd-taghaidh *m sing coll*)

constitution *n* **1** (*phys, of person*) dèanamh *m*; **2** (*of country, organisation etc*) bun-reachd *m invar*, bonn-stèidh *f*

constitutional *adj* **1** (*to do with a country's etc constitution*) bun-reachdail, **~ law** lagh bun-reachdail; **2** (*in accordance with the constitution*) co-chòrdail ris a' bhun-reachd *m invar*, **the act was not ~** bha/chaidh an achd an aghaidh a' bhun-reachd

constrict *v* teannaich *vt*, fàisg *vt*, tachd *vt*

constriction *n* teannachadh *m*

construct *v* **1** cum *vt*, dealbh *vt*, dèan *vt*; **2** (*building etc*) tog *vt*

consul *n* consal *m*

consular *adj* consalach

consult *v* sir beachd *m* (*with gen*), gabh comhairle *f* (*with prep* o/bho), cuir comhairle (*with prep* ri), **he ~ed the committee** shir e beachd na comataidh

consultation *n* co-chomhairle *f*, sireadh beachd *m* (*with prep* o/bho), gabhail comhairle *f* (*with gen*)

consume *v* caith *vt*

consumer *n* (*esp of goods*) neach-caitheimh (*pl* luchd-caitheimh *m sing coll*), caitheadair *m*, (*esp of services, amenities etc*) neach-cleachdaidh *m* (*pl* luchd-cleachdaidh *m sing coll*)

consumption *n* **1** (*business, fin, spending etc*) caitheamh *f*; **2** (*the illness: used with the art*) a' chaitheamh *f*

contact *n* **1** (*phys*) beantainn *m*, suathadh *m*, (**with** ri); **2** *in expr* **in (physical) ~ with** an taice ri; **3** (*social relations, corres etc*) muinntireachd *f invar*, conaltradh *m*, **we're still in ~ with them** tha muinntireachd eadarainn fhathast

contact *v* cuir fios *m* (*with prep* gu), **~ the bank** cuir fios chun a' bhanca *m*

contact lens *n* lionsa-suathaidh *f*

contagious *adj* gabhaltach

contain *v* **1** (*have capacity for*) gabh *vt*, **it can ~ a gallon** gabhaidh e galan; **2** (*have inside*) **that cage ~s a lion** tha leòmhann sa chèidse sin

contaminate *v* (*environment etc*) truaill *vt*

contamination n (*abstr & con*) truailleadh m

contemplate v 1 (*mentally*) meòraich & meamhraich vi, (*more fam*) cnuas & cnuasaich vi, (*all with prep* air); 2 (*mentally &/or visually*) beachdaich vt (*with prep* air), ~ **the stars** beachdaich air na reultan

contemporary adj 1 (*occurring at the same period*) co-aimsireil; 2 (*modern etc*) an là m (*gen sing*) an-diugh, ~ **clothes/customs** aodach/dòighean an là an-diugh

contemporary n co-aois m, co-aoiseach m, **A and B were contemporaries** bha A agus B nan co-aoisean/nan co-aoiseachan

contempt n tàir f, tarcais f, dìmeas m, (**of, towards** air)

contemptible adj tàireil, suarach

contemptuous adj tarcaiseach, tailceasach

content adj toileach, sona, (*stronger*) riaraichte, toilichte

content[1] n (*of book, argument etc*) susbaint f, brìgh f invar (*cf* **contents** n below)

content[2], **contentment** n toileachas m, toil-inntinn f, toileachas-inntinn m

content v toilich vt, riaraich vt

contented adj toileach, sona

contention n connspaid f

contentious adj connspaideach

contentment n see **content**[2] n above

contents n, 1 na tha/bha ann, na tha/bha am broinn f (*with gen*), **the** ~ **of the chest** na tha/na bha sa chiste, na tha/bha am broinn na ciste; 2 (*list of* ~, *of book etc*) clàr-innse m; 3 (*abstr, intellectual* ~: *matter, substance of book etc*) susbaint f invar, brìgh f invar

contest n 1 strì f invar, (*esp in games etc*) farpais f

contestant n farpaiseach m

continent n 1 (*general*) roinn f, mòr-roinn f, mòr-thìr f, **the** ~ **of Europe** (An) Roinn Eòrpa; 2 (*usu from a more local point of view*) tìr-mòr m, **on the** ~ (*ie Europe from the perspective of the British Isles*) air tìr-mòr na h-Eòrpa

continental adj 1 mòr-roinneach, mòr-thìreach; 2 (*European, from the perspective of the British Isles*) Eòrpach, na Roinn Eòrpa, ~ **cheeses** càisean na Roinn Eòrpa

contingency n tuiteamas m, ~ **plan** plana tuiteamais gen

contingent adj tuiteamach

contingent n (*of troops etc*) buidheann f, còmhlan m, cuideachd f

continual see **continuous**

continue v 1 lean vi, **the bad weather** ~**d** lean an droch aimsir; 2 (*persevere, with task etc*)

lean vi (*with prep* air), cùm vi a' dol, **she** ~**d, (even) though she was tired** lean i oirre/chùm i a' dol, ged a bha i sgìth, ~! lean ort!, cùm ort!

continuity n leantalachd f invar, leanailteachd f invar

continuous, continual adj leanailteach, leantainneach, gun sgur m, ~ **rain** uisge leanailteach, ~ **stationery/assessment** pàipear/measadh leantainneach, ~ **complaining** gearain gun sgur

contraception, contraceptive n casg-gineamhainn m invar

contraceptive adj casg-gineamhainneach

contract n (*legal, official, fin etc*) cunnradh m, cùmhnant m, ~ **of employment** cunnradh-obrach m

contract v (*ie shrink etc*) teannaich vti, lùghdaich vti, fàisg vt, rach vi a-steach

contradict v cuir vi an aghaidh (*with gen*), **she** ~**ed them** chuir i nan aghaidh

contraption n inneal m, innleachd f

contrast v cuir vt an aghaidh (*with gen*), dèan eadar-dhealachadh m (*with prep* eadar), ~ **A and B** cuir A an aghaidh B, dèan eadar-dhealachadh eadar A agus B

contribute v 1 (*to charity etc*) thoir vt seachad (airgead etc); 2 (*assist in project etc*) cuidich vi (**to** le), cuir vti (**to** ri)

contribution n 1 (*to charity etc*) dèirc f; 2 (*regular payment(s) for specific purpose*) tabhartas m, **pension/National Insurance** ~**s** tabhartasan peinnsein/Àrachais Nàiseanta; 3 (*non-fin*: ~ *to project etc*) cuideachadh m (**to** le); 4 (~ *to magazine etc*) cuid-sgrìobhaidh f, làmh-sgrìobhainn mf

contrive v 1 (*invent, improvise: idea or object*) innlich vt, (*object*) dealbh vt, ~ **an emergency plan** innlich plana-èiginn m; 2 (*manage, succeed*) rach vi impersonal (*with prep* aig) (**to** air), **he** ~**d to bring them together** chaidh aige air an toirt còmhla

contrived adj & past part (*attitudes, emotions etc: insincere*) fallsa, breugach

contrivance n 1 (*abstr*) innleachdadh m; 2 (*con: the object contrived*) inneal m, innleachd f

control v 1 (*people, emotions etc: gain/regain control*) ceannsaich vt, ~ **a disturbance** ceannsaich aimhreit f; 2 (*maintain control*) cùm smachd m (*with prep* air)

controversial adj connspaideach

controversy n connspaid f

conundrum n tòimhseachan m

convene *v* gairm *vt*, ~ **a meeting** gairm coinneamh

convenience *n* (*abstr & con*) goireas *m*, **(public)** ~**s** goireasan

convenient *adj* 1 goireasach, (*more fam*) deiseil, **that will be** ~ **for you** bidh sin deiseil dhuibh; 2 *in expr* ~ **for** (*ie close to*) faisg air ~ **for the shops** faisg air na bùithtean

convent *n* clochar *m*

convention *n* 1 (*gathering*) co-chruinneachadh *m*; 2 (*document, agreement*) cùmhnant *m*, **Human Rights** ~ Cùmhnant air Còraichean a' Chinne-Daonna; 3 (*accepted practice*) gnàth *m*, cleachdadh *m*, **literary** ~ gnàth litreachail

conventional *adj* gnàthach

converge *v* co-aom *vi*

convergence *n* co-aomadh *m*

conversant *adj* eòlach (**with** air), ~ **with computers** eòlach air coimpiutairean

conversation *n* (*in more formal context*) agallamh *m*, (*more everyday*) còmhradh *m*, (*fam*) craic *f*, **we had a wee** ~ rinn sinn còmhradh beag, bha beagan còmhraidh againn

converse *v* dèan còmhradh, bruidhinn *vi* (**with** ri)

conversion *n* 1 (*esp relig*) iompachadh *m*; 2 (*of dwelling etc*) leasachadh *m*, atharrachadh *m*

convert *n* (*relig*) iompachan *m*, (*esp Presbyterianism: usu derog, implying a degree of devoutness the speaker considers excessive*) neach fo chùram *m*

convert *v* 1 (*relig*) iompaich *vt*, **she was** ~**ed** chaidh a h-iompachadh, (*esp Presbyterianism: usu derog, implying a degree of devoutness the speaker considers excessive*) ghabh i an cùram *m*; 2 (*dwelling etc*) leasaich *vt*, atharraich *vt*

converted *adj & past part* 1 (*relig*) iompaichte, (*esp Presbyterianism: usu derog, implying a degree of devoutness the speaker considers excessive*) fo chùram *m*; 2 (*dwelling etc*) leasaichte

convey *v* 1 (*transport*) giùlain *vt*, (*less usu*) iomchair *vt*; 2 (*legal*) thoir thairis còraichean *fpl* (taighe *etc*); 3 (*make understood*) cuir *vt* an cèill (*dat of* ciall *f*) (**to** do), **how will I** ~ **to you the extent of my grief?** ciamar a chuireas mi an cèill dhut meud mo bhròin?

conveyance *n* 1 (*transport*) carbad *m*, seòl-iomchair *m*; 2 (*legal: (the process)*) toirt thairis chòraichean (taighe *etc*), (*the actual documents*) còir sgrìobhte (taighe *etc*) *f*

conveyancing *n* toirt *f invar* thairis chòraichean (taighe, *etc*)

conviction *n* 1 (*legal*) dìteadh *m*; 2 (*opinion*) beachd (daingeann)

convivial *adj* 1 (*of person*) cuideachdail, cèilidheach; 2 (*of gathering etc*) làn cridhealais *m*

conviviality *n* cridhealas *m*,

coo *v* (*of doves, pigeons*) dèan dùrdail *f*

cooing *n* dùrdail *f*

cook *n* còcaire *m*, (*female* ~) ban-chòcaire *f*

cooker *n* cucair *m*, **gas/electric** ~ cucair-gas/dealain

cookery, cooking *n* còcaireachd *f invar*, *in expr* **cooking pot** prais *f*

cool *adj* (*lit & fig*) fionnar, fuaraidh, (*esp fig*) leth-fhuar, **she answered** ~**ly** fhreagair i gu fionnar, **a** ~ **welcome/reception** fàilte fhionnar/leth-fhuar, *also* fàilte gu math fuar

cool, cool down *v* fionnaraich *vti*, fuaraich *vti*

co-operate *v* co-obraich *vi*

co-operation *n* co-obrachadh *m*

co-operative *adj* co-obrachail

co-operative *n* co-chomann *m*, **crofters'** ~ co-chomann chroitearan

co-ordinate *v* co-òrdanaich *vt*

copious *adj* lìonmhor, pailt

copper *n* copar *m*

coppersmith *n* ceàrd-copair *m*

copulate *v* co-ghin *vi*, cuplaich *vi*, (*of male*) ~ **with** rach air muin *f invar* (*with gen*), **the bull** ~**d with the cow** chaidh an tarbh air muin na bà

copulation *n* co-ghineadh *m*, cuplachadh *m*

copy *n* 1 (*exact reproduction*) mac-samhail *m*, lethbhreac *m*; 2 (*one of a number of identical books, newspapers etc*) lethbhreac *m*, **he signed copies of his novel** chuir e ainm ri lethbhreacan den nobhail aige

copy *v* (*reproduce object, work of art etc*) dèan lethbhreac *m* (**of** de), (~ *written text*) ath-sgrìobh *vt*

coquette *n* guanag *f*

coquettish *adj* guanach, *in expr* ~ **girl** guanag *f*

coracle *n* curach *f*

cord *n* còrd *m*

core *n* eitean *m*, buillsgean *m*, **an apple** ~ eitean ubhail, **the earth's** ~ eitean na talmhainn

core *adj in expr* (*ed*) **a** ~ **subject** prìomh chuspair *m*, bun-chuspair *m*

cork *n* àrc *f*, (*esp for bottle*) corcais *f*, **draw/pull a cork** tarraing corcais

corn[1] *n* (*agric*) arbhar *m*

corn[2] *n* (*on foot*) còrn *m*

corner *n* 1 (*esp internal*) cùil *f*, còrnair *m*, **he was sitting in the** ~ bha e na shuidhe sa chùil/sa chòrnair; 2 (*external & internal*) oisean *m*

& oisinn *f*, **at the ~ of the house** aig oisean an taighe; **3** (*usu external*) uileann & uilinn *f*; **4** (*fig: predicament etc*) *in expr* **a tight ~** cùil-chumhang *f*

cornflakes *npl* bleideagan-coirce *fpl*

Cornish *adj* Còrnach

Cornishman *n* Còrnach *m*

corn-yard *n* iodhlann *f*

coronation *n* crùnadh *m*

corporal *adj* corporra, **~ punishment** peanas corporra

corporal *n* corpailear *m*

corporate *adj* corporra, **a ~ body** buidheann chorporra

corpse *n* corp (marbh) *m*, (*less usu*) marbhan *m*

corpulent *adj* sultmhor

correct *adj* **1** ceart, **the answers are ~** tha na freagairtean ceart; **2** (*calculations etc*) cruinn; **3** (*idiom*) **if I remember ~ly** mas math mo chuimhne *f*

correct *v* ceartaich *vt*, cuir *vt* ceart

correction *n* (*abstr & con*) ceartachadh *m*

correspond *v* **1** bi *vi irreg* co-fhreagarrach (**to** do), **X ~s to Y** tha X co-fhreagarrach do Y; **2** (*by letter etc*) co-fhreagair *vi*, sgrìobh *vi* gu chèile

correspondence *n* **1** (*abstr*) co-fhreagairt *f*; **2** (*abstr, the act of corresponding by post*) co-fhreagairt *f*, co-sgrìobhadh *m*; **3** (*con, mail*) post *m*, litrichean *fpl*

correspondent *n* **1** (*by letter etc*) co-sgrìobhadair *m*, co-sgrìobhaiche *m*; **2** (*journalism*) neach-naidheachd (*pl* luchd-naidheachd *m sing coll*), naidheachdair *m*

corresponding *adj* co-fhreagarrach (**to** ri)

corridor *n* trannsa *f*

corrie *n* coire *m*

corroborate *v* co-dhearbh *vt*

corrosion *n* **1** (*abstr*) meirgeadh *m*; **2** (*con*) meirg *f*

corrugate *v* preas

corrugated *adj* preasach

corrupt *adj* **1** (*esp financially, politically etc*) coirbte, **~ businessman/politician** fear-gnothaich/fear-poilitigs coirbte; **2** (*esp morally, sexually*) truaillte, (*esp sexually*) draosta, drabasta

corrupt *v* coirb *vt*, (*esp morally, sexually*) truaill *vt*

corrupted *adj & past part* coirbte, (*esp morally, sexually*) truaillte

corruption *n* **1** (*abstr*) coirbteachd *f invar*, (*esp moral, sexual*) truaillidheachd *f invar*; **2** (*action of corrupting*) coirbeadh *m*, (*esp morally, sexually*) truailleadh *m*

cosmonaut *n* speuradair *m*, speurair *m*

cost *n* cosgais *f*, cosg *m invar*, **the ~ of living** cosgais bith-beò *m gen*, **travel ~s** cosgaisean siubhail *m gen*

cost *v* cosg *vt*, **how much does it ~?** dè a/na chosgas e/i?, dè a/na tha e/i a' cosg?, *also* (*more fam*) dè na tha e/i?

costly *adj* cosgail, daor

costume *n* (*stage, party etc*) culaidh *f*, **fancy dress ~** culaidh-choimheach

cosy *adj* seasgair, cofhurtail

cotton *n* cotan *m*, (*more trad*) canach *mf*

couch *n* langasaid *f*

cough *n* casadaich *f invar*, casad *m*, **~ medicine** leigheas-chasad *m*

cough *v* dèan casad *m*, casadaich *vi*

coughing *n* casadaich *f invar*

council *n* comhairle *f*, **regional ~** comhairle-roinneil, **~ house** taigh-comhairle, **~ tax** cìs comhairle

councillor *n* (*local authority etc*) comhairliche *m*

counsel *n* **1** (*advice*) comhairle *f*, **take/get ~** gabh comhairle (**from** o/bho); **2** (*legal representative, advocate etc*) neach-tagraidh (*pl* luchd-tagraidh *m sing coll*)

counsellor *n* neach-comhairle (*pl* luchd-comhairle *m sing coll*)

count *v* **1** cunnt *vti*, cunntais *vti*, **~ing sheep** a' cunntadh/a' cunntas chaorach; **2** (*matter*) cunnt *vi*, **he** (*emph*) **doesn't ~** chan eil esan a' cunntadh

counter *n* (*in shop etc*) cuntair *m*

counter *v* rach *vi* an aghaidh (*with gen*)

country *n* **1** dùthaich *f*, tìr *f*, (*esp as political entity*) rìoghachd *f*, **foreign countries** dùthchannan/tìrean cèin; **2** (*territory of a given group etc*) dùthaich *f*, **the Mackay ~** Dùthaich MhicAoidh; **3** (*rural area*) dùthaich *f*, **we lived/ were living in the ~** bha sinn a' fuireach air an dùthaich

county *n* siorrachd *f*, siorramachd *f invar*

couple *n* **1** (*man & wife*) càraid *f*, **married ~** càraid phòsta; **2** (*pair, twosome*) dithis *f* (*usu used of people only*), **they came in ~s** thàinig iad nan dithisean; **3** (*fam: a few, one or two*) *the appropriate n sing followed by* no dhà, **in a ~ of days** an ceann là no dhà, **give me a ~ of apples** thoir dhomh ubhal no dhà

couple *v* **1** (*connect carriages etc*) co-cheangail *vt*; **2** (*sexually*) cuplaich *vi*

coupling *n* **1** (*carriages etc*) co-cheangal *m*; **2** (*sexually*) cuplachadh *m*, (*of cattle*) dàir *f*

coupon *n* cùpon *m*

courage *n* **1** (*phys*) gaisge *f invar*, gaisgeachd *f invar*, (*sometimes rash ~*) dànadas *m*, braisead *f*; **2** (*esp inner & moral ~*) misneach *f*, misneachd *f invar*, smior *m*

courageous *adj* **1** (*phys*) gaisgeil, (*sometimes rashly*) dàna, bras; **2** (*esp morally*) misneachail

courier *n* teachdaire *m*

course *n* **1** (*academic etc*) cùrsa *m*, **Gaelic ~s** cùrsaichean Gàidhlig; **2** (*seafaring etc*) cùrsa *m*, gabhail *mf*, (*less usu*) seòl *m*, **keeping her on ~** ga cumail air chùrsa, (*fig, fam*) **you knocked me off ~** chuir thu às mo ghabhail mi; **3** *in exprs* **in due ~, in the ~ of time,** ri tìde, **on ~** (*lit & fig*) air an t-slighe cheart; **4** (*for sports etc*) raon *m*, cùrsa *m*, **golf ~** raon goilf, **race~** cùrsa-rèis

court *n* (*royal etc*) cùirt *f*, **law ~** cùirt-lagha

court *v* **1** (*amorously*) dèan suirghe *f invar* (*with prep* air), **he ~ed a girl** rinn e suirghe air nighean; **2** (*through ambition etc*) dèan miodal *m* (*with prep* do), dèan sodal *m* (*with prep* ri), **he ~ed the important people** rinn e miodal do/rinn e sodal ris na daoine mòra

courtesan *n* siùrsach *f*, strìopach *f*

courteous *adj* cùirteil, sìobhalta, modhail, suairc(e)

courtesy *n* modhalachd *f invar*, sìobhaltachd *f invar*, modh *mf*

courting *n* suirghe *f invar*, leannanachd *f invar*

courtly *adj* cùirteil

courtship *n* suirghe *f invar*, leannanachd *f invar*

cousin *n* co-ogha *m*

cove *n* geodha *mf*, camas *m*, bàgh *m*, òb *m*

covenant *n* (*legal, official, fin etc*) cùmhnant *m*, cunnradh *m*

Covenanter *n* (*hist*) Cùmhnantach *m*

cover *n* còmhdach *m*, (*of book*) **hard/soft ~** còmhdach cruaidh/bog

cover *v* còmhdaich *vt*

covered *adj & past part* **1** còmhdaichte; **2 ~ in** (*esp natural phenomena*) fo *prep* (*lenites the following cons where possible & takes the dat*), **mountains ~ in mist/cloud/snow** beanntan fo cheò/fo sgòth/fo shneachd

covering *n* còmhdach *m*, **floor ~** còmhdach ùrlair

coverlet *n* cuibhrig *mf*

covert *adj* falaichte, dìomhair

covertly *adv* os ìosal

covet *v* sanntaich *vt*, miannaich *vt*, (*less usu*) togair *vt*

covetous *adj* sanntach

covetousness *n* sannt *m*

cow *n* bò *f*, *for pl* crodh (*m sing coll*) *can also be used*, **dairy ~s** crodh-bainne

cow *v* cuir *vt* fo eagal *m*

cowed *adj & past part* fo eagal *m*

coward *n* gealtaire *m*, cladhaire *m*

cowardice *n* gealtachd *f invar*, cladhaireachd *f invar*

cowardly *adj* gealtach, cladhaireach

coy *adj* màlda

crab *n* partan *m*, (*larger*) crùbag *f*

crabbit (*Sc*) *adj* greannach, cròst(a), diombach

crack *n* **1** (*noise*) brag *m*, pleasg *m*; **2** (*split etc*) sgoltadh *m*; **3** (*Sc/Irish fam: conversation, chat*) craic *f*

crack *v* **1** (*noise*) dèan pleasg *m*, dèan brag *m*; **2** (*split etc*) sgàin *vti*, sgoilt & sgolt *vti*

cracking *n* (*splitting etc*) sgoltadh *m*

cradle *n* creathail *f*

craft *n* ceàird *f*

craftsman *n* fear-ceàirde & fear-ciùird (*pl* luchd-ceàirde/-ciùird *m sing coll*)

crafty *adj* carach, seòlta, fiar

crag *n* creag *f*, carraig *f*

craggy *adj* creagach

cramp *n* (*used with art*) an t-orc, **I've got ~** tha an t-orc orm

crane *n* **1** (*for lifting*) crann *m*; **2** (*bird*) corra-mhonaidh *f*

crannog *n* crannag *f*

crap *n* **1** (*fam, vulg: excrement*) cac *m*; **2** (*fig: useless etc*) *in expr* **it's a load of ~** 's e tòrr *m* caca a th' ann

crash *n* **1** (*impact*) bualadh *m*; **2** (*noise*) stàirn *f*; **3** (*accident*) tubaist rathaid *f*; **4** *in expr* **~ helmet** cloga(i)d-dìona *mf*

crawl *v* snàig *vi*, crùb *vi*

creak, creaking *n* dìosgan *m*, dìosgail *f invar*

creak *v* dèan dìosgan *m*

cream *n* **1** (*of milk*) uachdar *m*, bàrr (a' bhainne) *m*; **2** (*cosmetic ~*) cè *m*, **hand ~** cè làimhe

creamy *adj* uachdarach

crease *n* preasag *f*, filleadh *m*

crease *v* preas *vti*, fill *vt*

create *v* cruthaich *vt*, innlich *vt*

creation *n* **1** (*artistic etc*) cruthachadh *m*; **2** (*of plans, devices etc*) innleachadh *m*; **3** (*relig*) cruitheachd *f*, *used with art*, **Creation** A' Chruitheachd; **4** *in expr* (*relig*) **the King/Lord of ~** Rìgh *m* nan Dùl (*gen pl of* dùil *f*)

creative *adj* **1** (*in arts etc*) cruthachail, **~ writing** sgrìobhadh cruthachail, **Creative Scotland** Alba Chruthachail *f*; **2** (*innovative, inventive*) innleachdach, tionnsgalach

creativity n (*innovation, inventiveness*) tionnsgal m, tionnsgalachd f invar, innleachd f,

creator n **1** (*esp relig*) **the Creator** An Cruthadair, An Cruthaidhear; **2** (*arts etc*) ùghdar m; **3** (~ *of more technical things*) tionnsgalair m

creature n creutair m, (*also fam, of humans*) **the poor ~!** an creutair bochd!

credibility n creideas m

credible adj so-chreidsinn

credit n **1** (*fin*) dàil f, **buy/sell on ~** ceannaich/ reic vti air dàil; **2** in expr ~ **card** cairt-iasaid f; **3** (*idiom*) **he took the ~ for what I did!** chuir e na rinn mise às a leth fhèin!

creed n (*relig etc*) creud f, creideamh m

creel n cliabh m, **lobster ~** cliabh ghiomach (*mpl gen*)

creep v èalaidh vi, snàig vi, ~ **off home** èalaidh dhachaigh

crescent n corran m

crest n **1** (*of cock; also clan etc emblem*) cìrean m, (*of other birds*) topan m; **2** (*of hill*) mala f (*cnuic etc*)

crestfallen adj gun mhisneachd f invar

crevice n còs m, sgoltadh m

crime n eucoir f, **commit a ~** dèan eucoir

criminal adj eucorach, ~ **law** lagh m na h-eucorach (*gen of* eucoir f)

criminal n eucorach m

crimson adj crò-dhearg

cringe v crùb vi, strìochd vi

cripple n crioplach m

crisis n èiginn f, cruaidh-chàs m, gàbhadh m

criterion n slat-thomhais f

critic n **1** (*one who finds fault*) cronadair m; **2** (*arts etc*) neach-sgrùdaidh (*pl* luchd-sgrùdaidh m sing coll*), sgrùdair m, breithniche m

critical adj **1** (*finding fault*) càineach; **2** (*crucial*) deatamach, riatanach

criticise v **1** (~ *adversely*) càin vti, faigh cron m (*with prep* do); **2** (*review arts etc*) sgrùd vt, breithnich vt

criticism n **1** (*adverse*) càineadh m, cronachadh m; **2** (*review of arts etc*) sgrùdadh m, breithneachadh m, in expr **piece of ~** lèirmheas m

critique n sgrùdadh m, breithneachadh m, (*esp of arts*) lèirmheas m

croak n ròcail f, gràg m

croak v dèan gràgail f

croaking n ròcail f, gràgail f invar

croft n croit & cruit f, (*in the Gaelic of some districts*) lot f

crofter n croitear & cruitear m, **a ~s' co-operative** co-chomann m chroitearan (*mpl gen*)

crofting n croitearachd f invar, **The Crofting Commission** Coimisean na Croitearachd m

cromag n cromag f

crony n seana-charaid m

crook n **1** (*person*) eucorach m; **2** (*bend in object, river etc*) lùb m, caime f; **3** (*shepherd's ~*) cromag f

crooked adj crom, fiar, **a ~ stick** bata crom

crop[1] n (*agric ~ & ~s*) bàrr m, pòr m

crop[2] n (*of bird*) sgròban m

cross adj crost(a) & crosda, (*stronger*) feargach

cross n **1** crois f, **(make) the sign of the ~** (dèan) comharradh na croise; **2** (*for crucifixion*) crann-ceusaidh m; **3** (*heraldry etc*) **St Andrew's Cross** An Crann

cross v **1** rach vi tarsainn (*with gen*), **they ~ed (over)** chaidh iad tarsainn, **they ~ed (over) the bridge/the mountains** chaidh iad tarsainn na drochaid/nam beanntan; **2** (*thwart etc*) rach vi an aghaidh (*with gen*), **don't ~ me!** na rach nam aghaidh!; **3** (*relig*) in expr ~ **oneself** dèan comharradh na croise m

crossbar n crann-tarsainn m

cross-border adj tar-chrìochail

cross-examine v cruaidh-cheasnaich vt, mion-cheasnaich vt

cross-fertilise v tar-thoraich vt

crossing n (*of water*) aiseag mf

cross-reference n tar-iomradh m

crosspiece n rong f, rongas m

crossroads n crois rathaid f

crossword n tòimhseachan-tarsainn m

crotchet n (*mus*) dubh-nota m

crouch n crùban m, crùbagan m

crouch v dèan crùban m, dèan crùbagan m, rach vi na (*etc*) c(h)rùban/c(h)rùbagan, crùb vi, **they ~ed down** rinn iad crùban, chaidh iad nan crùban/nan crùbagan, chrùb iad

crouched, crouching adj & adv na (*etc*) c(h)rùban m, na (*etc*) c(h)rùbagan m, na (*etc*) g(h)urraban m, **he was ~ed down/crouching** bha e na chrùban/na chrùbagan/na ghurraban

crow[1] n feannag f, **carrion ~** feannag dhubh, **hooded ~** feannag ghlas

crow[2] n (*of cock*) gairm f

crow v (*cock etc*) gairm vi

crowd n **1** grunn m, (*bigger*) sluagh (mòr) m, (*derog*) gràisg f, prabar m, **there was a good ~ there** bha grunn math (dhaoine) ann; **2** (*fam: 'gang' etc, can be pej*) treud m, **Ian and Alan and all that ~** Iain is Ailean agus an treud sin uile

crowd

crowd *v* 1 (*as vt*) **they ~ed the hall** lìon iad an talla; 2 (*as vi*) **they ~ed into the hall** chaidh/thàinig iad a-steach dhan talla nan ceudan *mpl*

crowded *adj* (*places, buildings, gatherings etc*) dòmhail & dùmhail, loma-làn

crowdie *n* gruth *m*, slaman *m*

crown *n* 1 (*for royalty etc*) crùn *m*; 2 (*~ of head*) mullach *m* (a' chinn)

crown *v* crùn *vt*

crowning *n* crùnadh *m*

crucial *adj* deatamach

crucifix *n* crann-ceusaidh *m*, crois *f*

crucifixion *n* ceusadh *m*

crucify *v* ceus *vt*

crude *adj* 1 (*in unprocessed state*) amh, ~ **oil** ola amh *f*; 2 (*uncouth*) gràisgeil; 3 (*obscene, coarse*) drabasta, draosta

cruel *adj* cruaidh, an-iochdmhor

cruelty *n* an-iochd *f invar*

cruisie *n* (*trad*) crùisgean *m*

crumb *n* (*of bread etc*) criomag *f*, sprùilleag *f*, ~**s** sprùilleach *m sing coll*

crumble *v* 1 (*as vt*) criomagaich, **she ~d the bread** chriomagaich i an t-aran; 2 (*as vi*) rach *vi* na (*etc*) c(h)riomagan *fpl*, **the bread ~d in the bag** chaidh an t-aran na chriomagan sa phoca

crunch, crunching *n* cnagadh *m*

crunch *v* cnag *vi*, **the shingle was ~ing beneath his feet** bha am mol a' cnagadh fo a chasan

crusade *n* cogadh-croise *m*

crush *v* preas *vt*, pronn *vt*

crust *n* plaosg *m*, rùsg *m*, **the Earth's** ~ rùsg na Talmhainn

crutch *n* 1 (*of body, trousers*) gobhal & gabhal *m*; 2 (*walking aid*) crasg *f*, croitse *f*

crux *n*, *in expr* **the ~ of the matter** cnag na cùise *f*

cry *n* 1 (*call, shout*) gairm *f*, èigh *f*, glaodh *m*; 2 (*~ of pain, anguish etc*) gaoir *f*

cry *v* 1 (*call, shout*) gairm *vi*, èigh & èibh *vi*, glaodh *vi*; 2 (*weep*) guil *vi*, gail *vi*, caoin *vi*, (*~ vigorously*)ràn *vi*

crying *n* 1 (*calling, shouting*) gairm *f*, èigheachd *f invar*; 2 (*weeping*) gul *m*, caoineadh *m*, (*usu vigorous*) rànail *m invar*, rànaich *mf invar*

crystal *n* criostal *m*

cub *n* cuilean *m*

cube *n* ciùb *m*

cubic *adj* ciùbach

cuckold *n* cèile meallta *m*

cuckold *v*, **she ~ed her husband** mheall i a cèile *m* (le fear eile)

cuckoo *n* cuthag *f*

cucumber *n* cularan *m*

cud *n* cìr *f*, **chewing the** ~ a' cnàmh na cìre

cudgel *n* cuaille *m*

Culdee *n* (*relig hist*) Cèile-Dè *m*

cull *v* tanaich *vt*

cull, culling *n* tanachadh *m*

culpability *n* coireachd *f invar*

culpable *adj* coireach, ciontach

cultivate *v* (*land*) àitich *vt*, obraich *vt*

cultivated *adj* 1 (*of land*) àitichte; 2 (*of person*) cultarail

cultural *adj* cultarach

culture *n* cultar *m*, **Gaelic** ~ cultar na Gàidhlig(e)

cultured *abj* (*of person*) cultarail

cumin *n* lus-MhicCuimein *m*

cumulative *adj* tionalach

cunning *adj* carach, seòlta, fiar, innleachdach

cunning *n* seòltachd *f invar*, innleachd *f*

cup *n* 1 cupa *m*, cùp *m*, (*dimin*) cupan *m*, copan *m*, **a ~ of tea** cupa teatha; 2 (*as trophy etc*) cuach *f*, **the World** ~ Cuach na Cruinne

cupboard *n* preas(a) *m*, **clothes** ~ preas-aodaich *m*

curb *n* bacadh *m*

curb *v* bac *vt*, cuir bacadh *m* (*with prep* air)

curd(s) *n* gruth *m*, slaman *m*

cure *n* leigheas *m*, ìocshlaint *f*, (*for* air), **a ~ for asthma** leigheas air a' chuing

cure *v* 1 (*~ the malady or the patient*) leighis *vt*, slànaich *vi*, (*~ the patient*) cuir *vt* am feabhas *m*; 2 (*bacon, fish etc*) ciùraig *vt*

curious *adj* 1 (*strange*) neònach; 2 (*desiring knowledge, information*) ceasnachail, faighneach, faighneachail

curl *n* bachlag *f*, camag *f*, dual *m*

curl *v* (*hair*) bachlaich *vt*, dualaich *vt*

curled, curly *adj* (*of hair*) bachlach, camagach, dualach

curlew *n* guilbneach *m*

curling *n* (*the sport*) crolaidh *m invar*, (*less trad*) curladh *m*

currency *n* 1 (*con*) airgead *m*, **weak/strong** ~ airgead lag/làidir; 2 (*more abstr: ~ rates*) ruith-airgid *f*, ~ **fund** ciste ruith-airgid *f*, **speculate on currencies** dèan tuairmeas air ruith-airgid

current *adj* 1 (*in effect or existence at present*) làithreach, an là (*gen*) an-diugh, ~ **legislation** reachdas làithreach, **the ~ situation** suidheachadh an là an-diugh, *also* an suidheachadh a th' ann a-nis; 2 *in expr* (*banking*) ~ **account** cunntas làithreil, cunntas ruith (*gen of* ruith *f*, *used adjectivally*)

current *n* **1** (*water*) sruth *m*, **against the** ~ ris an t-sruth, **with the** ~ leis an t-sruth; **2** (*elec*) sruth(-dealain) *m*

curriculum *n* clàr-oideachais *m*

curriculum vitae *n* cunntas-beatha *m*

curse *n* **1** (*malediction*) mallachd *f*; **2** (*swear*) mionn *mf*, mionnan *m*

curse *v* **1** (*as vt:* ~ *someone/something*) mallaich; **2** (*as vi:* swear) mionnaich, bòidich

cursed *adj* mallaichte

cursing *n* **1** (*malediction*) mallachadh *m*; **2** (*swearing*) mionnachadh *m*, speuradh *m*

cursor *n* (*IT etc*) cùrsair *m*

cursory *adj* aithghearr, cabhagach, **a** ~ **look at the accounts** sùil aithghearr air na cunntasan

curtail *v* **1** (*shorten, make shorter*) giorraich *vt*; **2** (*cut short*) cuir stad *m* (*with prep* air), **the meeting was** ~**ed** chaidh stad a chur air a' choinneimh *f* (ron àm *m*/ron mhithich *f invar*)

curtailed *adj & past part* giorraichte

curtailment *n* giorrachadh *m*

curtain *n* cùirtean *m*, cùirtear *m*

curvature *n* caime *f*, lùbadh *m*

curve *n* **1** caime *f*, lùb *f*; **2** (*in a river*) camas *m*

curve *v* crom *vti*, lùb *vti*

curved *adj* cam, lùbte, crom, **a** ~ **stick** bata crom

cushion *n* pillean *m*, cuisean *m*

custard *n* ughagan *m*

custody *n* **1** (*care, responsibility*) cùram *m*, **she had** ~ **of the child, the child was in her** ~ bha am pàiste air a cùram-se; **2** (*museum etc*) **have** ~ **of** (*an object*) glèidh *vt*; **3** (*prison etc*) in *expr* **in** ~ an grèim *m*, an làimh (*dat of* làmh *f*), **remand in** ~ cuir *vt* an grèim/an làimh

custom *n* **1** (*esp of an individual*) àbhaist *m*, cleachdadh *m*, **it was a** ~ **of mine to take a glass of brandy** b' àbhaist dhomh/bu chleachdadh dhomh glainne branndaidh a ghabhail; **2** (*more general*) cleachdadh *m*, dòigh *m*, **the** ~**s of the country** dòighean/cleachdaidhean na dùthcha; **3** (*esp trad* ~*s*) gnàth *m*, gnàths *m*, nòs *m*

customary *adj* àbhaisteach, gnàthach, (*looser*) cumanta

customer *n* **1** (*esp for goods*) neach-ceannach(d) (*pl* luchd-ceannach(d) *m sing coll*); **2** (*esp for professional services*) neach-dèilige (*pl* luchd-dèilige *m sing coll*)

customs *n* cusbainn *f invar*, ~ **officer** oifigear na cusbainn, ~ **duty** cìs-chusbainn *f invar*

cut *n* **1** (*lit & fig*) gearradh *m*, **a tax** ~ gearradh cìse, **he lost his job on account of the** ~**s** chaill e obair air sgàth nan gearraidhean

cut *v* **1** geàrr *vt*, ~ **down** geàrr sìos; **2** ~ **up** (*esp finely*) mion-gheàrr *vt*; **3** (*crops*) buain *vt*, ~ **the corn** buain an t-arbhar; **4** (*misc exprs*) **I** ~ **out smoking** leig mi seachad smocadh *m*, ~ **out the middleman** dùin a-mach am fear meadhanach, **I** ~ **him dead** chuir mi mo chùl ris, chaidh mi seachad air mar nach robh e ann

cutting *adj* **1** (*of remarks etc*) geur, guineach; **2** (*made for* ~) gearraidh (*gen of* gearradh *m*, *used adjectivally*), **a** ~ **edge** faobhar gearraidh

CV *n* cunntas-beatha *m*

cycle *n* **1** (*pedal* ~) baidhsagal *m*, (*more trad*) rothar *m*; **2** (*economics, science etc*) cuairt *f*

cyclic, cyclical *adj* cuairteach

cycling *n* baidhsagalachd *f invar*, (*more trad*) rothaireachd *f invar*

cyclist *n* baidhsagalair *m*

cymbal *n* tiompan *m*

Czech Republic (the) *n* An t-Seic *f*

D

dab *v* suath *vt*

dabble *v*, **he ~s in/with carpentry** tha làmh *f* aige ann an saorsainneachd

Daddy *n* (*fam*) Dadaidh *m*

daddy-longlegs *n* breabadair *m*

daffodil *n* lus a' chrom-chinn *m*

daft *adj* gòrach, amaideach, **don't be ~!** na bi gòrach!

dagger *n* biodag *f*

daily *adj* làitheil

daily *adv* gach là *m*, a h-uile là, **we see him ~** bidh sinn ga fhaicinn gach là/a h-uile là

dainty *adj* mìn

dairy *n* taigh-bainne *m*, *in expr* **~ cows/cattle** crodh-bainne *m*

daisy *n* neòinean *m*

dale *n* gleann *m*, (*smaller*) gleannan *m*

dam *n* dam *m*

damage *v* mill *vt*, dochainn *vt*

damage *n* milleadh *m*, cron *m*, damaiste *m invar*

damaged *adj* millte

damn *n*, (*idiom*) **I don't give a ~ for X** (*fam*) cha toir mi hòro-gheallaidh *m invar* air X, chan eil diù *m invar* a' choin agam mu X

damn *v* **1** (*lit*) dìt *vt*; **2** (*in excls*) **~ it!** mac an donais!, **~ them!** taigh na galla dhaibh!

damnation *n* dìteadh *m*

damned *adj* **1** mallaichte; **2** (*as excl, swear*) **the ~ hammer!** òrd na croiche!, **~ car!** càr na galla!

damp *adj* tais

damp *n* taiseachd *f invar*

dampen *v* taisich *vt*

dampness *n* taise *f invar*, taiseachd *f invar*, dampachd *f invar*

damp-proof *adj* taise-dhìonte, taise-dhìonach

dance *n* dannsa *m*, *in expr* **~ floor** ùrlar *m*

dance *v* danns *vti*

dancer *n* dannsair *m*

dancing *n* dannsadh *m*

dandelion *n* beàrnan-Brìde *m*

dandruff *n* càrr & càir *f*

danger *n* cunnart *m*, (*usu stronger*) gàbhadh *m*, **in ~** ann an cunnart, ann an gàbhadh

dangerous *adj* cunnartach, (*usu stronger*) gàbhaidh, *in expr* **a ~ situation** cruaidh-chàs *m*

dangle *v* **1** (*as vi*) bi *vi irreg* air bhodagan *m*, bi a' bogadan, **it ~d/was dangling at the end of a rope** bha e air bhodagan/air bhogadan aig ceann ròpa; **2** (*as vt*) cuir air bhodagan, **I ~d it above him** chuir mi air bhodagan e os a chionn

dank *adj* tais agus fuar

dare *v* **1** dùraig *vi*, **we didn't ~ (to) leave the house** cha do dhùraig sinn an taigh fhàgail; **2** (*challenge, defy to do something*) thoir dùbhlan *m* (*with prep* do & *infin of verb*), **I ~d him to steal the apple** thug mi dùbhlan dha an t-ubhal a ghoid; **3** (*idiom*) **don't (you) ~ move!** na gabh (thusa) ort gluasad!

daring *adj* dàna, (*esp rashly ~*) bras

daring *n* dànadas *m*, (*esp rash ~*) braisead *f*

dark *adj* **1** dorch(a), ciar, (*esp ~ & gloomy*) doilleir, **~ cloud** neul dorcha, **the Dark Ages** Na Linntean Dorcha *fpl*, *in expr* **the evening grew ~** chiar *vi* am feasgar; **2** (*qualifying a colour*) dubh- (*lenites the following cons where possible*), **~ blue** dubh-ghorm, **~ brown** dubh-dhonn; **3** (*of person's complexion*) ciar

darken *v* **1** ciar *vi*, doilleirich *vti*; **2** (*drawing etc: shade, make darker*) duibhrich *vt*

dark-haired *adj* dubh, dorcha, **a ~ woman** boireannach dubh

darkness *n* **1** dorchadas *m*, duibhre *f*; **2** *in expr* **shroud/cover in ~** duibhrich *vt*, sgàil *vt*

darling *adj* gaolach, **my ~ girl** mo chaileag ghaolach

darling *n* **1** luaidh *m*; **2** (*as affectionate voc expr*) **(my) ~!** a ghaoil!, a luaidh!, **my ~!** m' eudail!, m' ulaidh!

darn *v* càirich *vt*

dart *n* gath *m*, guin *m*

dash *n* **1** ruith *f*, (*usu stronger*) dian-ruith & deann-ruith *f*; **2** (*typog*) sgrìob *f*

dash *v* **1** ruith *vi*; **2** *in expr* **they ~ed off/away ~** dh'fhalbh iad nan ruith *f*

data n dàta m invar, fiosrachadh m, (IT) ~
processing obrachadh-dàta m, gnìomhachadh-
dàta m, ~ **security** tèarainteachd dàta f invar, ~
protection dìon dàta m

database n (IT) stòr-dàta m

date[1] n 1 (calendar ~) ceann-là & ceann-latha m;
2 in expr **bring up to** ~ ùraich vt

date[2] n (fruit) deit f

date v 1 (~ document etc) cuir ceann-là m (with
prep air), ~ **a letter** cuir ceann-là air litir; **2**
(become outdated) rach vi irreg às an fhasan m

dated adj sean(n)-fhasanta, às an fhasan m

dative adj (gram) tabhartach, **the ~ case** an
tuiseal tabhartach

daub v smeur & smiùr vt

daughter n nighean f

daughter-in law n bana-chliamhainn f, bean-
mhic f

daunt v cuir vt fo eagal m, cuir eagal m (with
prep air), geiltich vt

dawn n 1 camhana(i)ch an latha f, bris(t)eadh an
latha m; **2** (idiom) **from ~ to dusk** o mhoch
gu dubh

day n 1 là & latha n, **the ~s of the week**
làithean na seachdain, **what ~ is it?** dè an là
a th' ann?, **by night and by ~** a dh'oidhche 's
a là, **the other ~** an là roimhe, **one of these
~s** latha no latheigin, **a ~ off** là dheth, **~ unit**
ionad-latha m, in expr **the next/following ~**
làirne-mhàireach & làrna-mhàireach m invar; **2**
(lifetime) là & latha m, rè f invar, linn mf, **at the
end of my ~s** aig deireadh/crìoch mo là, **in my
grandfather's** ~ an rè mo sheanar, ri linn mo
sheanar

daybreak n bris(t)eadh an latha m

daylight n solas an latha m

dead adj 1 marbh, **the king is** ~ tha an rìgh
marbh, in exprs ~ **body** corp m, corp marbh m,
(less usu) marbhan m, ~ **and buried** san uaigh
f; **2** (exact) in expr **in the ~ centre of the field**
ann an teis-meadhan m/ann an ceart-mheadhan
m an achaidh; **3** (completely) in expr ~ **against**
calg-dhìreach an aghaidh (with gen)

deadline n ceann-ama m

deadly adj 1 (death-dealing etc) marbhtach,
bàsmhor; **2** in expr ~ **danger** cunnart-bàis m

deaf adj 1 bodhar; **2** (idiom) **he's as ~ as a post**
cha chluinn e bìd m

deafen v bodhair vt

deafness n buidhre f

deal n 1 (business ~) cunnradh m; **2**
(arrangement, agreement) cùmhnant m; **3**
(degree, extent) in exprs **a good ~**, **a great ~**
fada (with comp adj), **this one is a great ~**

better/bigger/stronger tha am fear seo fada
nas fheàrr/nas motha/nas trèine

deal v 1 (playing cards) riaraich vti, roinn vti;
2 ~ **with** dèilig vi (with prep ri), **I'll ~ with
it tomorrow** dèiligidh mi ris a-màireach, ~
with customers dèilig ri luchd-ceannaich; **3**
(buy & sell) dèilig vi, ~ **in shares** dèilig ann an
sèaraichan

dealer n (commerce etc) neach-dèiligidh (pl
luchd-dèiligidh m sing coll)

dear excl, ~ **oh ~** dhuine! dhuine!, obh! obh!, ~
me! O mo chreach!

dear adj 1 (expensive) daor, cosgail; **2** (of person)
ionmhainn, gaolach, caomh, **her ~ friend** a
caraid ionmhainn; **3** (affectionate address)
my ~ a ghràidh, m' eudail; **4** (in corres) ~ **Sir**
A Charaid, ~ **Sirs** A Chàirdean, ~ **Madam**
A Bhanacharaid, ~ **Mr Fraser** A Mhaighstir
Fhriseil, ~ **Morag** A Mhòrag a bhanacharaid,
~ **Donald** A Dhòmhnaill a charaid, (more
personal or affectionate) A Dhòmhnaill chòir

dearth n cion m invar, gainne f, dìth m

death n 1 bàs m, caochladh m, (trad) eug m, ~
certificate urras bàis m, ~ **throes** grèim-bàis
m; **2** in expr **I was scared to ~** bha eagal mo
bheatha orm

death-bed n leabaidh bàis f

death-dealing adj marbhtach, bàsmhor

debase v 1 (person: humiliate) ìslich vt, maslaich
vt, dèan vi irreg dìmeas m invar (with prep
air), cuir vt (ann) an suarachas m; **2** (person:
corrupt) truaill vt; **3** (~ currency) dì-luachaich
vt

debate n deasbad mf, connsachadh m, (about
air, mu, mu dheidhinn)

debate v deasbad vti, deasbair vi, connsaich vi,
(about air, mu, mu dheidhinn)

debauch v claon vt, coirb vt, truaill vt

debauchery n 1 (sexual) mì-gheanmnachd f
invar, strìopachas m; **2** (drinking) pòitearachd
f invar

debilitate v lagaich vti, fannaich vi

debility n laigse f

debris n sprùilleach m

debt n 1 fiach m, **repay a ~** dìoghail fiach; **2**
(moral etc, not fin) comain f, **I'm greatly in
your ~** tha mi fada nad chomain

debtor n fèichear m

decade n deichead m

decadence n claonadh m

decadent adj air claonadh

decapitate v dì-cheannaich vt

decapitation n dì-cheanna(cha)dh m

decay n lobhadh m, seargadh m

decay v lobh vi, caith vi, crìon vi
deceit n mealladh m, cealg f, foill f
deceitful adj mealltach, cealgach, fallsa, foilleil
deceive v meall vt, cealg vt, dèan foill f (with prep air)
deceived adj meallta
deceiver n mealltair m, cealgair(e) m
December n Dùbhlachd f invar, used with art, an Dùbhlachd, **the first of** ~ a' chiad là den Dùbhlachd
decency n beusachd f invar
decent adj 1 (of persons: moral, honest etc) còir, beusach; 2 (of persons: fair, reasonable) cothromach; 3 (of actions, arrangements etc: reasonable, appropriate) cothromach, iomchaidh, **a** ~ **salary** tuarastal cothromach/iomchaidh
deception n mealladh m, cealg f, foill f
deceptive adj mealltach
decide v 1 (make a decision) co-dhùin vi, thig vi gu co-dhùnadh m; 2 in expr ~ **on/upon** (ie choose, appoint) sònraich vt, ~ **on a day for the meeting** sònraich latha airson na coinneimh; 3 (form a plan or intention) cuir vt romham, romhad (etc) (with infin of verb), **I** ~**d to close the shop** chuir mi romham a' bhùth a dhùnadh (also rinn mi suas m' inntinn f a' bhùth a dhùnadh)
deciduous adj seargach
decimal adj deicheach, ~ **place** ionad deicheach
decimal n deicheamh m
decipher v fuasgail vt
decision n co-dhùnadh m, **come to/reach a** ~ co-dhùin vi, thig vi gu co-dhùnadh
decision-making n co-dhùnadh m
decisive adj 1 (of persons: ~ in character, actions) duineil; 2 (leading to a decision) co-dhùnaidh (gen of co-dhùnadh m), **it was he who made the** ~ **speech** is esan a rinn an òraid cho-dhùnaidh; 3 (main, crucial) prìomh, **the** ~ **element in this situation** a' phrìomh eilemaid anns an t-suidheachadh seo
decisiveness n (in character, actions) duinealas m
declare v 1 abair vti irreg, can vti def, cuir vt an cèill (dat of ciall f); 2 in expr ~ **war** gairm cogadh m
decline n lùghdachadh m, crìonadh m
decline v 1 (deteriorate etc) lùghdaich vi, crìon vi, rach vi nas miosa; 2 (turn down or refuse etc) diùlt vt; 3 (gram: ~ verbs) claoin vi
decompose v lobh vi, bris vi sìos
decomposition n lobhadh m, bris(t)eadh m sìos
decorate v maisich vt, sgeadaich vt

decoration n maiseachadh m, sgeadachadh m
decorative adj sgeadachail
decorous adj 1 (well-behaved) beusach, modhail; 2 (proper, acceptable) cubhaidh, iomchaidh
decorum n stuaim f, deagh bheus f, modh mf
decrease n lùghdachadh m
decrease v lùghdaich vti, (as vi) rach sìos
decree n òrdugh m
decree v òrdaich vi
decrepit adj (of people) breòite, anfhann
decriminalise v dì-eucoirich vt
decriminalisation n dì-eucoireachadh m
dedicate v coisrig vt (**to** gu)
dedication n coisrigeadh m (**to** gu)
deduce v dèan vt irreg a-mach, obraich vt a-mach, dèan vt irreg dheth
deduct v (subtract) thoir vt air falbh (**from** bho & o)
deduction n 1 (subtraction) toirt f invar air falbh (**from** bho & o); 2 (intellectual process) dèanamh a-mach, obrachadh a-mach m, dèanamh dheth
deed n 1 (action) gnìomh m, **bad** ~ droch ghnìomh; 2 (feat) euchd m
deep adj 1 (lit: phys) domhainn; 2 (fig: of personality, character) domhainn, dìomhair
deep freeze n reothadair m
deep n, used with art, **the** ~ an dubh-aigeann m, an doimhne f
deepen v doimhnich vti
deer n 1 (general term) fiadh m; 2 (particular ~) **red** ~ (stag) damh m, (hind) eilid f, **roe** ~ (buck) boc(-earba) m, (female) earb f; 3 in expr ~ **forest** frìth f
deface v mill vt
defamation n tuaileas m, mì-chliù m
defamatory adj tuaileasach
defame v cùl-chàin vt, mì-chliùitich vt
defeat n call m, (esp military, involving rout) ruaig f
defeat v 1 faigh buaidh f, (more fam) dèan an gnothach m/a' chùis, buadhaich vi, (all with prep air), **we** ~**ed them** fhuair sinn buaidh orra, rinn sinn an gnothach orra; 2 (esp of things one fails to achieve) fairtlich vi, faillich vi, (with prep air), **I wanted to climb the mountain but it** ~**ed me** bha mi airson a' bheinn a dhìreadh ach dh'fhairtlich/dh'fhaillich i orm
defecate v cac vi
defecation m cacadh m
defect n (moral or phys) fàillinn f, meang f
defect v trèig vi (**to** gu)

defective *adj* 1 (*having a defect*) meangail; 2 (*incomplete*) neo-iomlan, **a ~ verb** gnìomhair neo-iomlan *m*

defence *n* dìon *m*, **Centre for ~ Studies** Ionad airson Eòlas-dìona *m*

defenceless *adj* gun dìon *m*

defend *v* dìon *vt*

defendant *n* (*law*) neach-dìona *m* (*pl* luchd-dìona *m sing coll*)

defender *n* dìonadair *m*

defensible *adj* so-dhìonta

defer *v* 1 cuir *vt* air (an) ath là *m*, cuir *vt* air dàil *f*, cuir dàil (*with preps* ann an *or* air), **~ the meeting** cuir a' choinneamh air ath là, **~ construction of the bridge** cuir dàil ann an/air togail na drochaid(e); 2 (*give way*) gèill *vi* (**to** do), **he ~red to the manager** ghèill e don mhanaidsear

deference *n* urram *m*, ùmhlachd *nf invar*

deferential *adj* umha(i)l

defiance *n* dùbhlan, *m*

deficiency *n* 1 (*lack*) easbhaidh *f*, dìth *m*; 2 (*fault, failing*) fàilligeadh *m*

deficient *adj* 1 (*missing, in short supply*) easbhaidheach, a dhìth; 2 (*faulty*) easbhaidheach

deficit *n* 1 easbhaidh *f*, dìth *m*; 2 (*in balance sheet etc*) call *m*

defile *v* (*places, objects, relig, morals etc*) truaill *vt*, salaich *vt*

defilement *n* truailleadh *m*

define *v* mìnich *vt*, soilleirich *vt*, **~ your terms** mìnich na briathran a tha thu a' cleachdadh

definite *adj* cinnteach, deimhinne/deimhinnte

definitely *adv* gu dearbh, gun teagamh, **are you tired? I ~ am!** a bheil thu sgìth? tha gu dearbh!, **will she come tomorrow? ~!** an tig i a-màireach? thig gun teagamh!

definition *n* mìneachadh *m*

deflation *n* (*economics*) seargadh *m*

deforestation *n* dì-choilleachadh *m*

deform *v* cuir *vt* à cumadh *m*

deformity *n* 1 (*abstr*) mì-chumadh *m*; 2 (*specific: phys*) meang *f*

defraud *v* feallaich *vt*, dèan foill *f* (*with prep* air)

defrost *v* dì-reoth *vti*

deft *adj* deas, ealamh

defunct *adj* 1 (*of persons*) marbh, nach maireann; 2 (*of systems, ideas etc*) a chaidh à cleachdadh *m*

defy *v* thoir dùbhlan *m* (*with prep* do & *infin* of verb), **we defied them** thug sinn dùbhlan dhaibh, **he defied me to tell the truth** thug e dùbhlan dhomh an fhìrinn innse

degeneracy *n* (*moral*) coirbteachd *f invar*

degenerate *adj* (*morally*) coirbte

degenerate *v* (*phys, morally etc*) rach *vi* sìos, rach *vi irreg* am miosad *f*

degradation *n* ìsleachadh *m*

degrade *v* ìslich *vt*

degree *n* 1 (*of heat, angles*) puing *f*; 2 (*of progress, development, ability etc*) ìre *f invar*; 3 (*university ~*) ceum *m*

dehydrate *v* sgreubh *vt*, crìon *vti*, searg *vti*

dehydration *n* sgreubhadh *m*, crìonadh *m*, seargadh *m*

deity *n* 1 (*abstr*) diadhachd *f invar*; 2 (*a god*) dia *m*, **a Roman ~** dia Ròmanach, dia nan Ròmanach

dejected *adj* fo bhròn, dubhach, smalanach, fo smalan *m*, (*more fam*) sìos na (*etc*) inntinn *f*, **we were ~** bha sinn sìos nar n-inntinn

dejection *n* bròn *m*, smalan *m*, smuairean *m*

delay *n* dàil *f*, maille *f invar*, **without ~** gun dàil

delay *v* 1 (*hinder*) cuir maille *f invar* (*with prep* air *or* ann), cuir dàil *f* (*with prep* air *or* ann), cùm *vt* air ais, **that ~ed the project** chuir sin maille/dàil air a' phròiseact/anns a' phròiseact, **I don't want to ~ you** chan eil mi airson ur cumail air ais, (*idiom*) **if they're ~ed** ma thèid maille *f invar* orra; 2 (*drag one's heels*) màirnealaich *vi*, bi *vi irreg* màirnealach

delectable *adj* blasmhor

delegate *n* riochdaire *m*

delegate *v* tiomain *vt* (**to** do), **~ authority** tiomain ùghdarras *m*

delegation *n* 1 (*abstr: ~ of authority, responsibility etc*) tiomnadh *m* (**to** do); 2 (*con: a ~*) buidheann riochdachaidh *mf*

delete *v* dubh *vt* às, dubh *vt* a-mach

deliberate *adj* a dh'aon ghnothach *m*, a dh'aon rùn *m*

deliberate *v* (*reflect upon inwardly; also of committee etc, discuss*) beachdaich *vi* (**upon, about** air)

deliberately *adv* a dh'aon ghnothach *m*, a dh'aon rùn *m*

deliberation *n* beachdachadh *m* (**upon, about** air)

delicacy *n* 1 (*abstr: refinement*) fìnealtas *m*; 2 (*abstr: phys or emotional vulnerability*) maothachd *f invar*

delicate *adj* 1 (*refined etc*) fìnealta; 2 (*phys or emotionally vulnerable*) maoth

delicious *adj* ana-bhlasta

delight *n* aighear *m*, aoibhneas *m*, sòlas *m*

delight *v* toilich *vt*, riaraich *vt*

delighted *adj & past part* **1** làn-thoilichte, riaraichte, sòlasach; **2** (*idiom*) **he's** ~ tha e air a dheagh dhòigh

delightful *adj* taitneach, ciatach

delinquency *n* coire *f*, ciontachd *f invar*

delinquent *n* coireach *m*, ciontach *m*

delirious *adj* breisleachail

delirium *n* breisleach *m*

deliver *v* **1** (~ *goods etc*) lìbhrig *vt*, liubhair *vt*; **2** (*set free*) saor *vt*, fuasgail *vt*; **3** (~ *baby*) asaidich *vt*; **4** (~ *speech etc*) gabh *vt*, thoir *vt* seachad, **he ~ed a speech** ghabh e òraid *f*, thug e seachad òraid, *also* rinn e òraid

deliverance *n* saorsa *f*, fuasgladh *m*

delivery *n* **1** (*of goods etc*) lìbhrigeadh *m*, liubhairt *m*; **2** (*of baby*) asaid *f*

delude *v* meall *vt*, dall *vt*, **she was deluding herself** bha i ga mealladh fhèin

deluge *n* tuil *f*, dìle *f*, (*stronger*) dìle bhàthte

delusion *n* mealladh *m*, dalladh *m*

delusory *adj* mealltach

delve *v* rannsaich *vt*, cladhaich *vt*, **delving into his family history** a' rannsachadh eachdraidh a theaghlaich (fhèin)

demand *n* **1** iarrtas *m*; **2** (*economics, business*) fèill *f*, margadh *m*, **will there be a ~ for it?** am bi fèill/margadh air?

demand *v* iarr *vt*, **they ~ed a pay rise** dh'iarr iad àrdachadh pàighidh

demean *v* dìblich *vt*, ìslich *vt*

demented *adj* **1** air bhoile *f invar*, air chuthach *m*, (*more fam*) às a (*etc*) rian *m*, às a (*etc*) c(h)iall *f*; **2** (*idiom*) **it was nearly driving me** ~ bha e gus mo chur dhìom fhìn, *also* bha e gus mo chur às mo rian

demi- *prefix* leth-, *eg* **demigod** leth-dhia *m*

democracy *n* deamocrasaidh *m*, (*more trad*) sluagh-fhlaitheas *m*

democrat *n* deamocratach *m*

democratic *adj* deamocratach

demolish *v* leag *vt*, sgrios *vt*

demolition *n* leagail *f*, sgrios *m*

demon *n* deamhan *m*

demonstrate *v* **1** (*prove*) dearbh *vt*; **2** (~ *products, techniques etc*) taisbean *vt*; **3** (*pol etc: take part in march, rally etc*) tog *vt* fianais *f*

demonstration *n* **1** (*proof*) dearbhadh *m*; **2** (~ *of products, techniques etc*) taisbeanadh *m*; **3** (*pol etc: march, rally*) fianais-dhùbhlain *f*, (*esp march*) caismeachd *f*

demoralize *v* mì-mhisnich *vt*

demote *v* ìslich *vt*

demure *adj* stuama

den *n* **1** (*topog*) lag *mf*; **2** (*of animal etc*) garaidh *m*

denial *n* àicheadh *m*

denigrate *v* dèan dìmeas *m invar* (*with prep* air), **he ~d the First Minister** rinn e dìmeas air a' Phrìomh Mhinistear

Denmark *n* (*used with art*) An Danmhairg *f*

denounce *v* **1** (*betray*) brath *vt*; **2** (*oppose, speak out against*) cuir *vi* an aghaidh, rach *vi irreg* an aghaidh, (*with gen*), **they ~d the war** chuir iad an aghaidh a' chogaidh

dense *adj* **1** (*of trees, hair, vegetation etc*) dòmhail & dùmhail, dlùth, tiugh; **2** (*mentally ~*) maol, maol-aigneach, (*fam*) tiugh

density *n* dlùths *m invar*, tiughad *m*, tighead *m*

dent *n* beàrn *mf*, tulg *m*

dental *adj* deudach, fiaclach, *in expr* ~ **surgery** (*ie the place*) ionad fiaclaire *m*

dentist *n* fiaclair(e) *m*

dentistry *n* fiaclaireachd *f invar*

dentures *n* fiaclan-fuadain *fpl*

denunciation *n* **1** (*betrayal*) brathadh *m*; **2** (*opposition, speaking out against*) cur *m* an aghaidh (*with gen*)

deny *v* **1** (~ *accusation etc*) àicheidh *vt*, ~**ing his guilt** ag àicheadh a chionta *m*; **2** (*reject, disown*) diùlt *vti*, àicheidh *vt*, **she won't ~ her own daughter** cha diùlt i a nighean fhèin, ~**ing his faith** ag àicheadh a chreideimh; **3** (*deprive of*) cùm *vt* air ais (*with prep* o, bho), **the soldiers denied them food** chùm na sàighdearan biadh air ais bhuapa

depart *v* falbh *vi*, (*less usu*) imich *vi*, **they ~ed yesterday** dh'fhalbh iad an-dè

department *n* roinn *f*, (*ed*) **the French** ~ Roinn na Fraingis

departmental *adj* roinneil

departure *n* falbh *m*

depend *v* **1** (*accept support or help from*) cuir taic *f* (*with preps* air *or* ri), ~ **on me** cuir do thaic orm/rium; **2** (*trust*) cuir creideas *m*, cuir earbsa *f invar*, (*with prep* ann), **can we ~ on him?** an urrainn dhuinn creideas/earbsa a chur ann?; **3** (*vary according to*) bi *vi irreg* an crochadh (**on** air), **that will ~ on the price** bidh sin an crochadh air a' phrìs

dependable *adj* (*person, business etc*) urrasach

dependence *n* eisimeileachd *f invar*, eisimeil *f*

dependent *adj* **1** an eisimeil *f* (*with gen*), eisimeil (**on** air), **the company was ~ on its shareholders** bha a' chompanaidh an eisimeil an luchd-earrann aice, ~ **on her brother** an eisimeil a bràthar; **2** (*addicted*) an urra (**on** ri), na *etc* t(h)ràill *m* (**on** do), **they were ~ on**

drugs bha iad an urra ri drogaichean *fpl*, bha iad nan tràillean do dhrogaichean

dependent *n* neach-eisimeil *m* (*pl* luchd-eisimeil *m sing coll*)

depict *v* dealbh

deplorable *adj* maslach, tàmailteach

deplore *v* is *v irreg & def* beag (*with prep* air), is olc (*with prep* le), **I ~ the opinions you expressed** is beag orm na beachdan a chuir sibh an cèill

deploy *v* (*measures, strategies etc*) cuir *vt* an gnìomh *m*

depopulate *v* fàsaich *vt*

depopulation *n* fàsachadh *m*

deport *v* fuadaich *vt*, fògair *vt*

deportment *n* giùlan *m*

deposit *n* 1 (*fin: advance payment on purchases etc*) eàrlas *m*; 2 (*fin: payment into an account*) tasgadh *m*

deposit *v* taisg *vt*

depot *n* 1 (*store etc*) batharnach *m*; 2 (*base, centre, for business etc operations*) ionad *m*

deprecate *v* coirich *vt*

depress *v* 1 (*lit, phys*) brùth *vt* sìos; 2 (*sadden etc*) cuir *vt* sìos, fàg *vt* dubhach, fàg *vt* fo smalan *m*, **the news ~ed me** chuir an naidheachd *f* sìos mi, dh'fhàg an naidheachd dubhach mi

depressed *adj* fo bhròn *m*, dubhach, smalanach, fo smalan *m*, (*more fam*) sìos na (*etc*) inntinn *f*, ìosal/ìseal, **we were a bit ~** bha sinn rud beag sìos nar n-inntinn, bha sinn car ìosal

depression *n* 1 (*of mood*) bròn *m*, smalan *m*, smuairean *m*, leann-dubh *m*; 2 (*of mood or weather*) ìsleachadh *m*

deprivation *n* 1 (*the action*) cumail *f* air ais; 2 (*the state of poverty, homelessness etc*) easbhaidh *f*

deprive *v* cùm *vt* air ais (*with prep* o, bho), **the soldiers ~d them of food** chùm na saighdearan biadh air ais bhuapa

depth *n* doimhneachd *f invar*

deputation *n* buidheann-tagraidh *mf*

depute, deputy *adj* iar-, leas-, *suffixes, eg* **~ director** iar-stiùiriche *m*, leas-stiùiriche *m*

deputy *n* neach-ionaid *m* (*pl* luchd-ionaid *m sing coll*), **she appointed her ~** dh'ainmich i an neach-ionaid aice

derelict *adj* trèigte

deride *v* mag *vi*, dèan fanaid *f*, (*with prep* air)

derision *n* magadh *m*, fanaid *f*, (**of** air)

derisive *adj* 1 (*deriding, apt to deride*) magail; 2 (*~ly inadequate*) suarach

derivation *n* 1 (*abstr: the activity of etymologising etc*) freumh-fhaclachd *f invar*,

freumhachadh *m*; 2 (*con: esp ~ of words*) freumh *m*, bun *m*, tùs *m*, (*an fhacail etc*)

derivative *adj* iasadach

derive *v* 1 (*as vi*) thig *vi irreg* (**from** bho, o), **A ~s from B** thàinig A bho B; 2 (*to translate vt*) **X ~s this word from French** a rèir X, thàinig am facal seo on Fhraingis

derogatory *adj* cur-sìos, **~ statements** briathran *mpl* cur-sìos

derrick *n* crann(-togail) *m*

descend *v* 1 (*phys*) teirinn & teàrn *vti* (*with prep* à, *or direct object*), crom *vi* (*with preps* o/bho & le), thig *vi* sìos/a-nuas, **he ~ed from the pulpit** theirinn e às a' chùbaid, **~ing the hillside** a' teàrnadh a' bhruthaich, **he ~ed from the donkey's back** chrom e bhon asail, **he ~ed the rock** chrom e leis a' chreig (*dat of* creag *f*); 2 (*be a descendant of*) *see* **descendant** & **descended** *below*

descendant *n* fear *m*/tè *f* de shìol *m coll*, fear/tè de shliochd *m coll*, (*with gen of ancestor*), **she's a ~ of Diarmad** is e/i tè de shìol Diarmaid a tha innte, **~s** sìol/sliochd (*with gen of ancestor*), **(the) ~s of Diarmad** sìol/sliochd Diarmaid

descended *past part* de shliochd *m coll*, de shìol *m coll*, (*both with gen of ancestor*), **he's ~ from the Lord of the Isles** is ann de shìol Tighearna nan Eilean a tha e

descent *n* 1 (*phys*) teàrnadh *m*, cromadh *m*; 2 (*one's ancestry, genealogy*) sinnsearachd *f invar*

describe *v* thoir tuairisgeul *m* (*with prep* air)

description *n* 1 (*of person or thing*) tuairisgeul *m*, **the police already have the thief's ~** tha tuairisgeul a' mhèirlich aig a' phoileas mu thràth; 2 (*of events etc*) cunntas *m*

descriptive *adj* dealbhach, tuairisgeulach

desert *n* fàsach *mf*, (*less usu*) dìthreabh *f*, **the ~s of Africa** fàsaichean Afraga

desert *v* 1 trèig *vt*, dìobair *vt*, **he ~ed his family** thrèig/dhìobair e a theaghlach *m*, **the people ~ed the island** thrèig na daoine *mpl* an t-eilean; 2 (*soldiers etc*) teich *vi*

deserted *adj & past part* 1 (*empty, lonely*) uaigneach, fàsaichte, fàs, *in expr* **a ~ place** fàsach *mf*; 2 (*of a person, of an abandoned house etc*) trèigte

deserter *n* fear-teichidh *m* (*pl* luchd-teichidh *m sing coll*)

desertification *n* fàsachadh *m*

desertion *n* trèigsinn *m invar*, (*from army etc*) teicheadh *m*

deserve *v* 1 bi *vi irreg* airidh (*with prep* air), **they ~ praise/to be praised** tha iad airidh air moladh, (*also: idiom*) tha iad rim moladh;

2 (*idiom*) **we thoroughly ~d it** bu mhath an airidh sinn

deserving *adj* airidh, (*less usu*) toillteanach, (**of** air)

desiccate *v* tiormaich *vti*

design *n* dealbh & deilbh *mf*

design *v* (*technical & artistic objects*) dealbh & deilbh *vt*, dealbhaich *vt*, ~ **machines** dealbh/deilbh innealan *mpl*

designate *v* (*specify person or thing*) sònraich *vt*, (*esp person*) ainmich *vt*

designer *n* dealbhaiche & deilbhiche *m*, neach-deilbh *m* (*pl* luchd-deilbh *m sing coll*)

designing *n* dealbhadh & deilbheadh *m*, dealbhachadh *m*

desire *n* **1** (*abstr & con*) miann *mf*, rùn *m*, (*con*) togradh *m*, (*less usu*) dèidh *f*; **2** (*sexual ~*) miann *mf*, **a small flame of** ~ lasair bheag miann

desire *v* **1** (*wish for*) miannaich *vt*; **2** (*~ to do something*) rùnaich *vt*, togair *vti*, (*the latter is often used as vi in rel fut tense*), **just as you** ~ dìreach mar a thogras sibh

desist *v* leig *vi*, sguir *vi*, (**from** de)

desk *n* deasg *m*

desolate *adj* **1** fàsail, **a ~ land** tìr fhàsail; **2** (*of person*) trèigte, truagh

despair *n* eu-dòchas *m*

despicable *adj* suarach, tàireil

despise *v* dèan tàir *f*, dèan tarcais *f*, (*with prep* air), cuir *vt* suarach, **we ~ them** tha sinn gan cur suarach

despite *prep* a dh'aindeoin (*with gen*), ~ **the rain** a dh'aindeoin an uisge

despised *adj & past part* fo dhìmeas

despondency *n* mì-mhisneachd *f invar*

despondent *adj* gun mhisneach *f*, dubhach, smalanach

despot *n* aintighearna *m*, deachdaire *m*

despotism *n* aintighearnas *m*, deachdaireachd *f invar*

dessert *n* mìlsean *m*

dessert-spoon *n* spàin-mìlsein *f*

destabilise *v* dì-dhaingnich *vt*

destination *n* ceann-uidhe *m*

destined *adj & past part* an dàn (**for** do), **what was ~ for him** na bha an dàn dha

destiny *n* dàn *m*, crannchur *m*, **oppose/go against ~** cuir *vi* an aghaidh dàin, **if that is my ~** mas e sin mo chrannchur, *also* mas e sin a tha an dàn dhomh

destitute *adj* aireach, ainniseach

destitution *n* airc *f*, ainnis *f*

destroy *v* mill *vt*, sgrios *vt*, cuir *vi* às (*with prep* do)

destruction *n* milleadh *m*, sgrios *m*

destructive *adj* millteach, sgriosail

detach *v* dealaich *vt*

detached *adj & past part* **1** dealaichte, ~ **house** taigh dealaichte; **2** (*of personality*) fad' às, dùinte

detachment *n* **1** (*abstr*) dealachadh *m*; **2** (*~ of troops etc*) buidheann *mf*, còmhlan *m*, cuideachd *f*

detail *n* **1** mion-phuing *f*; **2** *in exprs* **attentive to ~** mion-chùiseach, **question in ~** mion-cheasnaich *vt*

detailed *adj* mionaideach, mion- (*prefix*), **a ~ enquiry/study** sgrùdadh mionaideach, ~ **knowledge/acquaintance** mion-eòlas *m* (**of/with** air)

detain *v* **1** (*delay, keep back*) cùm *vt* air ais; **2** (*~ in custody*) cùm *vt* an làimh (*dat of* làmh *f*), cùm *vt* an grèim *m*/an sàs *m*

detect *v* lorg *vt*, faigh lorg *f* (*with prep* air)

detection *n* lorg *f*

detector *n* lorgair *m*

detention *n* **1** (*abstr*) làmh *f*, grèim *m*, sàs *m*, **in ~** an làimh, an grèim, an sàs (*all dat*); **2** (*the act of detaining*) cumail *f* an làimh/an grèim/an sàs

deter *v* bac *vt*, caisg *vt*

deteriorate *v* **1** mùth *vi*, rach *vi* am miosad *m*; **2** (*of person*) rach *vi* bhuaithe (*etc*), tuit *vi* bhuaithe (*etc*), **she ~d** chaidh i bhuaipe

deterioration *n* **1** mùthadh *m*, dol *m invar* am miosad *m*, fàillinn *f*; **2** (*of person*) dol *m invar* bhuaithe (*etc*), tuiteam *m* bhuaithe (*etc*)

determination *n* daingneachd *f invar*, rùn suidhichte

determine *v* **1** (*form a plan etc*) cuir roimhe (*etc*), **they ~ed to build a house** chuir iad romhpa taigh *m* a thogail; **2** (*discover, elucidate etc*) dearbh *vt*

determined *adj & past part* **1** (*persistent, forceful*) daingeann, suidhichte, **a ~ effort** ionnsaigh dhaingeann; **2** (*firmly resolved*) mionnaichte, suidhichte, **she was ~ it wouldn't get the better of her** bha I mionnaichte nach fairtlicheadh e oirre

deterrent *n* bacadh *m*, seòl bacaidh *m*, casg *m*

detest *v* fuathaich *vt*, bi *vi irreg* gràin *f* aig (*with prep* air), **I ~ them** tha gràin agam orra

detestable *adj* gràineil, fuathach

detour *n* bealach *m*, **take/make a ~** gabh bealach

detrimental *adj* millteach (**to** air)

devalue *v* dì-luachaich *vti*

devaluation *n* dì-luachadh *m*

devastate *v* lèirsgrios *vt*

devastation *n* lèirsgrios *m*

develop *v* **1** (*as vt: improve, modernise etc*) leasaich *vt*, ~ **the town centre** leasaich meadhan a' bhaile; **2** (*as vi: make progress etc*) thig *vi* air adhart, **he/it's ~ing nicely** tha e a' tighinn air adhart gu dòigheil

developing *adj, in expr* ~ **country** tìr *mf* fo leasachadh *m*

development *n* **1** (*improvement, modernisation etc*) leasachadh *m*, **a ~ board** bòrd leasachaidh *m*, ~ **plan** plana leasachaidh *f*; **2** (*esp of persons: progress in skill, knowledge etc*) adhartas *m*, piseach *m*

deviate *v* saobh *vi* (**from** o/bho)

deviation *n* saobhadh *m* (**from** o/bho)

device *n* **1** (*mechanical*) inneal *m*, innleachd *f*; **2** (*idiom*) **leave them to their own ~s** leig *vi* leotha

devil *n* diabhal *m*, **the ~** an Diabhal, an Donas *m*

devilish *adj* diabhlaidh

devious *adj* **1** (*person, behaviour*) fiar, carach; **2** (*route etc*) cuairteach

devise *v* innlich *vt*, dealbh *vt*, (*less usu*) tionnsgail & tionnsgain *vt*, ~ **a stratagem/a machine** innlich cuilbheart/inneal

devoid (of) *adj* às aonais, às eugmhais, (*with gen*)

devolution *n* tiomnadh chumhachdan *m*, sgaoileadh-cumhachd *m*

devolve *v* tiomnaich *vt* (**to** do), ~ **power** tiomnaich cumhachd *f*

devolved *adj & past part* tiomnaichte

devote *v* coisrig *vt* (**to** gu)

devotion *n* **1** (*relig: abstr*) cràbhadh *m*, diadhachd *f invar*; **2** *in expr* ~**s** (*ie relig observances*) adhradh *m*, ùrnaigh *f*; **3** (*intense love for a person*) teas-ghràdh *m*

devour *v* glam & glamh (*also* glàm & glàmh) *vt*, sluig *vt*, ith *vt* gu glàmach

devout *adj* **1** cràbhach, diadhaidh; **2** (*idioms*) **she is very ~** tha i làn den Fhìrinn *f*, **become very ~** (*usu derog, implying a degree of devoutness the speaker considers excessive*) gabh an cùram

devoutness *n* cràbhadh *m*, diadhachd *f invar*

dew *n* dealt *mf*, dr(i)ùchd *m*

dewy *adj* dealtach

dexterity *n* deas-làmhachd *f invar*

dexterous *adj* làmhach, deas-làmhach

diabetes n tinneas an t-siùcair *m*

diabolical *adj* diabhlaidh

diagonal *adj* trastanach

diagonal *n* trastan *m*

diagram *n* diagram *m*, (*more trad*) dealbh-chumadh *mf*

dial *n* (*of clock, instruments etc*) aodann *m*, aghaidh *f*

dial *v* dèan àireamh *f* (fòn *mf gen*)

dialect *n* dualchainnt *f*

dialogue *n* co-chòmhradh *m*, còmhradh-dithis *m*

diametrically *adj, in expr* ~ **opposed to** calg-dhìreach an aghaidh (*with gen*)

diamond *n* daoimean *m*

diaphragm *n* sgairt *f*

diarrhoea *n* buinneach *f*, sgàird *f*, spùt *m*, *all used with art,* a' bhuinneach, an sgàird, an spùt

diary *n* leabhar-latha *m*

dice *n see* **die** *n*

dictate *v* **1** (~ *letter etc*) deachd *vt*; **2** (*command etc*) òrdaich *vi*

dictation *n* (*of letter etc*) deachdadh *m*

dictator *n* **1** (*pol etc*) deachdaire *m*; **2** (*of letter etc*) neach-deachdaidh *m* (*pl* luchd-deachdaidh *m sing coll*)

dictatorial *adj* deachdaireach, ceannsalach

dictatorship *n* deachdaireachd *f invar*

diction *n* labhradh *m*

dictionary *n* faclair *m*

dicy *adj* **1** (*dodgy, shaky*) cugallach; **2** (*risky*) cunnartach, *in expr* **a ~ situation** cruaidh-chàs *m*

didactic *adj* oideachail

die *v* **1** (*esp of persons*) caochail *vi*, siubhail *vi*, (*trad*) eug *vi*; **2** (*of other creatures*) bàsaich *vi* (*though this is also used by some speakers to refer to humans*), *note also* **the dog ~d** chailleadh an cù

die, *pl* **dice**, *n* (*sing*) dìsinn *m* & dìsne *mf*, (*pl*) dìsnean *m*

diesel *n* dìosail *m invar*

diet *n* riaghailt bìdh *f*

difference *n* **1** diofar *m* (*also* difir *m invar* & deifir *f*), eadar-dhealachadh *m*, **what's the ~ between A and B?** dè an diofar/an t-eadar-dhealachadh (a th') eadar A agus B?; **2** (*idiom*) **it makes no ~** chan eil e gu diofar, chan eil diofar ann

different *adj* **1** diof(a)rach, diofraichte & deifrichte, (*stronger*) eadar-dhealaichte; **2** (*idiom*) **you and I are ~** chan ionann thusa is mise

differentiate *v* eadar-dhealaich, dèan eadar-dhealachadh *m*, dèan sgaradh *m*, (**between** eadar)

differentiation *n* eadar-dhealachadh *m*

difficult *adj* **1** (~ *to do, solve etc*) doirbh, duilich, **a ~ question/problem** ceist dhoirbh/dhuilich, **that's ~ to say** tha sin doirbh a ràdh, **trigonometry isn't ~** chan eil triantanachd

doirbh; **2** (*~ to understand*) deacair, **a ~ book**
leabhar deacair; **3** (*of circumstances etc: ~ to
bear, deal with*) cruaidh, duilich; **4** *in expr* **a ~
situation** (*ie a predicament, emergency etc*)
cruaidh-chàs *m*, èiginn *f invar*
difficulty *n* **1** (*problem*) duilgheadas *m*, **we've
got difficulties where money is concerned**
tha duilgheadasan againn a thaobh airgid; **2**
(*predicament, danger*) càs *m*, (*more serious*)
cruaidh-chàs *m*, èiginn *f invar*, **an aeroplane
in ~ above the airport** itealan ann an èiginn/
na èiginn os cionn a' phuirt-adhair; **3** (*implying
effort*) *in expr* **with ~** air èiginn *f*, **it was with
~ that he opened his eye** 's ann air èiginn a
dh'fhosgail e a shùil
diffident *adj* diùid, nàrach
diffuse *adj* sgaoilte, sgapte *or* sgapta
diffuse *v* craobh-sgaoil *vti*
diffusion *n* craobh-sgaoileadh *m*
dig *v* cladhaich *vti*, ruamhair *vi*
digest *v* **1** (*lit*) cnàmh *vti*; **2** (*fig: mentally ~
information etc*) cnuasaich *vt*
digestion *n* cnàmh *m*, *used with art*, an cnàmh
digging *n* cladhach *m*
digit *n* (*arith etc*) figear *m*
digital *adj* (*IT etc*) figearail, didseatach, **~ clock**
gleoc figearail
dignified *adj* stàiteil, stòlda, stuama
dignify *v* àrdaich *vt*, urramaich *vt*
dignity *n* **1** (*abstr: rank, status*) urram.*m*,
inbhe *f*, mòralachd *f invar*; **2** (*~ of manner or
appearance*) stàitealachd *f invar*, stòldachd *f
invar*; **3** (*idiom*) **it is beneath my ~ to speak
to him** cha diù leam bruidhinn ris
digs *n* lòistinn *m*, taigh-loidsidh *m*
dilatory *adj* màirnealach, slaodach
dilemma *n* imcheist *f*, **in a ~** an/fo imcheist
diligence *n* dìcheall *m*
diligent *adj* dìcheallach
dilute *v* tanaich *vt*, lagaich *vt*
dilute *adj*, **diluted** *adj & past part*, tanaichte
dim *adj* **1** (*of light etc*) doilleir; **2** (*unintelligent*)
maol-aigneach, (*fam*) tiugh; **3** *in expr* **I take a ~
view of X** is ciar leam X, is beag orm X
dim *v* doilleirich *vti*
dimension *n* **1** (*size*) meud *m invar*, meudachd
f invar; **2** (*measurement*) tomhas *m*, **take ~s**
gabh tomhasan
diminish *v* lùghdaich *vti*, beagaich *vti*
diminution *n* lùghdachadh *m*, beagachadh *m*
diminutive *adj* meanbh, bìodach, crìon
dimple *n* tibhre *m*
din *n* ùpraid *f*, gleadhar *m*, othail *f*, iorghail *f*

dine *v* gabh dinnear *f*, **we ~ at eight** gabhaidh
sinn ar dinnear aig a h-ochd
dingy *adj* **1** (*dark*) doilleir; **2** (*grubby*) mosach,
luideach
dining-room *n* seòmar-bìdh *m*, rùm-bìdh *m*
dinner *n* dinnear *f*, (*more trad*) diathad *f*, *used
with art*, an diathad, **what have we got/what
are we getting/having for our ~?** dè a th'
againn air ar dinnear?, **she brought up her ~**
chuir i a-mach a dinnear
dinner-time *n* àm dinnearach, (*more trad*) tràth
dinnearach
diocese *n* sgìre-easbaig *f*, sgìreachd-easbaig *f*
dip *n* **1** (*the action: in liquid*) tumadh *m*, bogadh
m; **2** (*for sheep: the liquid*) dup *m*
dip *v* **1** (*~ in liquid*) tum *vt*, bog *vt*; **2** (*~ sheep*)
dup *vti*
diploma *n* teisteanas *m*
diplomacy *n* dioplòmasaidh *mf*
diplomat *n* rìochdaire dioplòmasach
diplomatic *adj* dioplòmasach
dipping *n* **1** (*in liquid*) tumadh *m*, bogadh *m*; **2** (*~
sheep*) dupadh *m*
dipsomania *n* tinneas na dighe *m*
direct *adj* dìreach
direct *v* **1** (*conduct, show way etc*) treòraich *vt*,
stiùir *vt*; **2** (*run, manage*) stiùir *vt*
direction *n* **1** taobh *m*, rathad *m*, **they're
coming in this ~** tha iad a' tighinn an taobh/
an rathad seo; **2** (*compass ~*) àird *f*; **3** *in pl* **~s**
(*instructions, guidelines etc; also for route-
finding etc*) seòladhean *mpl*, **I followed your
~s** lean mi na seòlaidhean agaibh; **4** *in expr* (*at
roadside etc*) **~ board** clàr seòlaidh *m*
directly *adv* **1** (*straight*) dìreach, **go ~ to the
office** rach dìreach don oifis; **2** (*immediately*)
gun dàil *f*, air ball, anns a' bhad *m*; **3** (*shortly*)
a dh'aithghearr, an-ceartuair, **I'll be with you
~** bidh mi agaibh an-ceartuair; **4** (*idiom*) **~
opposed to** calg-dhìreach an aghaidh (*with
gen*)
director *n* neach-stiùiridh *m* (*pl* luchd-stiùiridh
m sing coll), stiùiriche *m*, **Director General**
Àrd-stiùiriche *m*
directory *n* (*for phone etc*) leabhar-seòlaidh *m*
dirge *n* tuireadh *m*
dirk *n* biodag *f*
dirt *n* salchar *m*
dirty *adj* salach, rapach
dis- *prefix* **1** ana- *prefix, eg* **disadvantage** *n*
anacothrom *m*; **2** eas- *prefix, eg* **disobedient**
eas-umhail; **3** mì- *prefix, eg* **disadvantage** *v*
mì-leasaich *vt*, *see further examples below*

disability n ciorram m, in expr ~ **allowance** cuibhreann-ciorraim m

disabled adj ciorramach, in exprs **a ~ person** ciorramach m, neach ciorramach m (pl luchd-ciorramach m sing coll), **the ~** na ciorramaich mpl

disadvantage n anacothrom m, mì-leas m

disadvantage v mì-leasaich vt

disadvantaged adj & past part **1** (esp person) fo anacothrom m; **2** (of region etc) mì-leasaichte

disagree v rach vi an aghaidh (with gen), eas-aontaich vi, (less confrontational) **I ~** chan eil mi(se) den aon bheachd m, chan eil mi a' dol leis a sin, cha tèid mi le sin

disagreeable adj neo-thaitneach

disagreement n **1** (the act of disagreeing) dol m invar an aghaidh (with gen); **2** (abstr & con) eas-aonta f, mì-chòrdadh m, **(a) ~ arose between us** dh'èirich vi eas-aonta eadarainn; **3** (idiom) **we were in total ~** bha sinn calg-dhìreach an aghaidh a chèile

disallow v mì-cheadaich vt

disappear v rach vi à sealladh m

disappoint v meall vt, leig vt sìos

disappointment n bris(t)eadh-dùil m, mealladh-dùil m

disapproval n coireachadh m, dol m invar an aghaidh (with gen)

disapprove v **1** coirich vt, rach vi an aghaidh (with gen); **2** (idioms) **we ~ of that** chan eil sinn a' dol le sin, **I ~ of your conduct** is beag orm do dhol-a-mach

disarm v dì-armaich vti

disarmament n dì-armachadh m

disarray n mì-riaghailt f

disaster n tubaist f, mòr-thubaist f, calldachd f

disbelief n às-creideamh m

disc, disk n **1** clàr m, (IT) ~ **drive** clàr-inneal m; **2** (~ in spine) clàr m, **(a) slipped ~** (con) clàr sgiorrte, (more abstr, the medical condition) leum-droma m

discard v tilg vt air falbh

discernible adj follaiseach, so-fhaicinn

discerning adj tuigseach

discernment n tuigse f

discharge v **1** (duties, obligations etc) coilean vt; **2** (debt) ìoc vt, pàigh vt; **3** (person, from army etc) saor vt; **4** (gun) loisg vt, tilg vt; **5** (cargo etc) dì-luchdaich vti

disciple n deisciobal m

disciplinary adj smachdachaidh (gen of smachdachadh m, used adjectivally), ~ **tribunal** tribiùnal smachdachaidh

discipline n **1** smachd m invar; **2** (ed: field of study) cuspair m

discipline v **1** (assert authority over) smachdaich vt, cuir smachd f (with prep air); **2** (punish) peanasaich vt

disclose v foillsich vt, leig vt ris

disclosure n (abstr) foillseachadh m, leigeil m ris

disco n diosgo m invar

discomfort n anshocair f

disconcert v buair vt

disconnect v neo-cheangail vt, sgaoil vt

disconsolate adj brònach, dubhach

discontent n mì-thoileachadh m, diomb m invar

discontented adj mì-thoilichte, diombach

discontinue v (an activity etc) cuir stad m (with prep air), leig vt seachad, sguir vi (with prep de), **she ~d the correspondence** chuir i stad air a' cho-sgrìobhadh, **I'm discontinuing the music lessons** tha mi a' leigeil seachad nan leasanan ciùil

discord n **1** (abstr & con) eas-aonta f, mì-chòrdadh m, ~ **arose between us** dh'èirich eas-aonta/mì-chòrdadh eadarainn; **2** (music) dì-chòrda m

discount n (trade etc) lùghdachadh prìse/phrìsean m, ìsleachadh prìse/phrìsean m, **buy at a ~** ceannaich vti air prìs(ean) ìsleachaidh

discount v **1** (trade etc) leag/lùghdaich/ìslich prìs(ean) f, reic vti air prìs(ean) ìsleachaidh; **2** (ignore, not take into account) **I am ~ing everything he said** chan eil mi a' cur sùim f ann an càil sam bith a thubhairt e

discourage v **1** mì-mhisnich vt; **2** (dissuade from) thoir comhairle f (with prep air followed by gun & infin of verb), **I ~d him from joining the army** thug mi comhairle air gun a dhol dhan arm

discouragement n **1** (the action) mì-mhisneachadh m; **2** (the state of mind) mì-mhisneachd f invar

discourteous adj mì-mhodhail

discourtesy n mì-mhodh m

discover v **1** (facts etc) faigh vt a-mach; **2** (objects) lorg vt

discredit n **1** (loss of trust, credibility) mì-chreideas m; **2** (loss of reputation) mì-chliù m

discreet adj **1** (keeping confidentiality) rùnach; **2** (tactful etc) tuigseach

discrepancy n eadar-dhealachadh m, diofar m, (**between** eadar)

discretion n **1** (tact, good judgement) tuigse f, breithneachadh m; **2** in exprs **at your ~** mar

as roghnach leibh, **we left it to their own ~**
dh'fhàg sinn aca fhèin e

discriminate v 1 (*unjustly*) dèan lethbhreith
f (**against** an aghaidh, *with gen*); 2 (*neutral:
differentiate etc*) eadar-dhealaich vi, dèan eadar-
dhealachadh m, (**between** eadar)

discrimination n 1 (*unjust bias etc*) lethbhreith
f; 2 (*capacity to judge, assess*) breithneachadh
m; 3 (*abstr: making of distinctions*) eadar-
dhealachadh m (**between** eadar)

discriminatory adj (*showing unjust bias etc*)
lethbhreitheach

discuss v deasbair vi (*with prep* mu), deasbad vi,
beachdaich vi (*both with prep* air)

discussion n 1 (*abstr*) deasbaireachd f invar; 2
(*con*) **a** ~ deasbad mf

disdain n tarcais f, tailceas m, tàir f, dìmeas m

disdain v dèan tarcais f, dèan tàir f, dèan dìmeas
m (*all with prep* air)

disdainful adj tarcaiseach, tailceasach, tàireil

disease n tinneas m, galar m, (*abstr*) euslaint
f, **heart** ~ tinneas cridhe, **infectious ~s**
tinneasan gabhaltach

disembark v rach vi air tìr mf

disentangle v (*objects, situations etc*) rèitich
vt, (*objects*) fuasgail vt, ~ **this wool for me**
rèitich/fuasgail an snàth seo dhomh

disentangled adj & past part (*of wool etc*) rèidh

disgrace n 1 (*abstr*) masladh m, tàmailt f; 2
(*source of ~*) cùis-mhaslaidh f, **it's a ~!** 's e cùis-
mhaslaidh a th' ann!

disgrace v nàraich vt, maslaich vt

disgraceful adj maslach, tàmailteach, nàr, **that's
~!** is nàr sin!

disgruntled adj diombach, gruamach, mì-
riaraichte

disguise n breug-riochd m

disgust n gràin f, sgreamh m

disgust v sgreamhaich vt, cuir sgreamh m (*with
prep* air)

disgusting adj gràineil, sgreamhail

dish n soitheach m, **do/wash the ~es** nigh na
soithichean

dish-cloth n brèid-shoithichean m

dishonest adj eas-onarach, mì-onarach

dishonesty n mì-onair m

dishonour n eas-onair f, eas-urram m

dishonourable adj eas-urramach

dishwasher n nigheadair-shoithichean m

disillusion v bris(t) misneachd f, **I don't want
to ~ you** chan eil mi airson do mhisneachd a
bhris(t)eadh

disillusionment call misneachd m

disinclined adj aindeonach, leisg, **I was ~ to
follow them** bha mi aindeonach an leantainn,
(*more trad*) bu leisg leam an leantainn, *also* bha
leisg f orm an leantainn

disingenuous adj cealgach, fallsa

disinherit v thoir/cùm oighreachd f (*with prep*
bho/o), **his father ~ed him** thug/chùm athair
oighreachd bhuaithe

disinterested adj neo-thaobhach

disjointed adj 1 (*lit*) às an alt m; 2 (*of discourse
etc*) briste

disk n see **disc**

dislike n mì-thaitneamh m

dislike v, **I ~ him** is beag orm e, cha toigh leam e

dislocate v (*joint*) cuir vt às an alt m

disloyal adj mì-dhìleas, neo-dhìleas

disloyalty n mì-dhìlseachd f invar, neo-
dhìlseachd f invar

dismal adj 1 (*of weather, light*) doilleir; 2 (*of
persons: depressed etc*) dubhach, sìos na (*etc*)
inntinn f; 3 (*of condition, outlook, performance
etc*) bochd, truagh, **a ~ excuse** leisgeul bochd

dismantle v thoir vt às a chèile

dismay n mì-mhisneach f

dismay v 1 (*discourage*) mì-mhisnich vt; 2
(*alarm*) cuir eagal m (*with prep* air)

dismiss v 1 cuir vt air falbh; 2 (*employee etc*) cuir
vt à dreuchd f

dismissal n (*of employee etc*) cur m à dreuchd f

dismount v teirinn & teàrn vi (**from** bho/o)

disobedience n eas-ùmhlachd f invar

disobedient adj eas-umhail

disobey v rach vi an aghaidh (*with gen*)

disorder n 1 (*lack of orderliness*) mì-rian m, mì-
riaghailt f, in expr **in ~** troimh-a-chèile, **after
the accident everything was in ~** an dèidh
na tubaist bha a h-uile cail troimh-a-chèile; 2
(*emotional, moral ~*) buaireas m; 3 (*mental ~*)
mì-rian m; 4 (*civil ~*) aimhreit f, buaireas m

disorderly adj mì-rianail, mì-riaghailteach,
buaireasach, aimhreiteach

disown v diùlt vt, àicheidh vt, **she won't ~ her
own daughter** cha diùlt i a nighean fhèin

disparage v dèan tàir f (*with prep* air), cuir vt an
suarachas m

disparagement n 1 (*abstr*) tàir f; 2 (*the action*)
cur an suarachas m

disparaging adj tàireil

disparate adj (gu tur) eadar-dhealaichte

disparity n neo-ionannachd f invar

dispense v 1 (*supply*) solair vt, riaraich vt; 2 in
expr ~ **with** dèan vi irreg às aonais (*with gen*)

dispersal n sgaoileadh m, sgapadh m

disperse v sgaoil vti, sgap vti

display *n* (*of art, goods, techniques etc*) taisbeanadh *m*

display *v* 1 (*esp art, goods, techniques etc*) taisbean & taisbein *vt*; 2 (*IT, electronics etc*) sealladh *m*, clàr taisbeanaidh *m*, **digital ~** sealladh figearail

displease *v* mì-thoilich *vt*

displeasure *n* 1 mì-thoileachas *m*; 2 (*esp towards another person*) diomb *m invar*

disposal *n* 1 (*getting rid of*) faighinn *f invar* cuidhteas *m*; 2 (*~ by sale*) reic *m invar*; 3 (*idiom*) **I won't manage with the means at my ~** cha dèan mi a' chùis leis na tha ri mo làimh (*dat of* làmh *f*)

dispose *v* 1 (*place, arrange etc*) suidhich *vt*, socraich *vt*; 2 *in expr* **~ of something** faigh cuidhteas *m* rudeigin

disposition *n* (*temperament*) nàdar *m*, mèinn *f*, aigne *f*

dispossess *v* cuir *vt* à seilbh *f*

disprove *v* breugnaich *vt*

disputatious *adj* connsachail, connspaideach

dispute *n* connsachadh *m*, connspaid *f*

dispute *v* 1 (*as vi: argue*) connsaich *vi*; 2 (*as vt: ~ the truth etc of*) ceasnaich *vt*, cuir *vt* an ceist *f*

disqualification *n* dì-cheadachadh *m*

disqualify *v* dì-cheadaich *vt*

disquiet *n* iomagain *f*, imcheist *f*

disregard *n* 1 (*lack of concern*) neo-chùram *m* (**for** air), **~ for safety** neo-chùram air tèarainteachd *f invar*; 2 (*lack of respect*) dìmeas *m* (**for** air)

disregard *v*, *in expr* **they ~ed my instructions** (*etc*) cha robh sùim *f* aca de na h-òrduighean (*etc*) agam

disreputable *adj* 1 (*in appearance*) cearbach, luideach, grodach; 2 (*in character, behaviour*) neo-mheasail, (*fam*) fiadhaich, (*more disapproving*) tàmailteach, maslach

disrepute *n* mì-chliù *m*, **bring X into ~** tarraing mì-chliù air X

disrespect *n* dìmeas *m invar*, eas-urram *m*

disrupt *v* (*event, meeting etc*) buair *vt*, cuir *vt* troimh-a-chèile, cuir *vt* thar a chèile

disruption *n* 1 (*the action*) buaireadh; 2 (*the state of affairs*) aimhreit *f*; 3 (*relig hist*) **The Disruption** Bris(t)eadh na h-Eaglaise *m*

dissatisfaction *n* mì-thoileachadh *m*

dissatisfy *v* mì-thoilich *vt*

dissembler *n* cealgair(e) *m*

dissembling *adj* cealgach

disseminate *v* sgaoil *vt*, craobh-sgaoil *vt*

dissemination *n* sgaoileadh *m*, craobh-sgaoileadh *m*

dissent *n* (*abstr & con*) eas-aonta *f*, **~ arose between us** dh'èirich eas-aonta eadarainn

dissent *v* eas-aontaich *vi* (**from** ri)

dissenting *adj* eas-aontach

dissertation *n* tràchdas *m*

disservice *n* mì-sheirbheis *f*

dissident *adj* eas-aontach

dissident *n* eas-aontaiche *m*

dissimilar *adj* eu-coltach (**to** ri)

dissimilarity *n* eu-coltas *m*

dissimulation *n* cealgaireachd *f invar*

dissipate *v* 1 (*wealth*) struidh *vt*, caith *vt*, ana-caith *vt*; 2 (*of clouds, mist etc*) sgaoil *vi*

dissipation *n* 1 (*of wealth*) struidheadh *m*, ana-caitheamh *f*; 2 (*of clouds, mist etc*) sgaoileadh *m*

dissolve *v* 1 leagh *vti*; 2 *in expr* **~ parliament** sgaoil pàrlamaid *f*

dissuade *v* thoir comhairle *f* (*with prep* air *or* do), thoir *vt* (*with prep* air), (*both followed by* gun *and infin of verb*), **I ~d him from joining the army** thug mi comhairle air gun a dhol dhan arm, thug mi air gun a dhol dhan arm

distance *n* astar *m*

distant *adj* 1 fad' air falbh, cèin, iomallach; 2 (*of person*) fad' às

distaste *n* gràin *f* (**for** air)

distasteful *adj* gràineil, mì-chàilear

distend *v* at *vi*, sèid *vi*

distil *v* (*spirits*) tarraing *vti*

distillation *n* (*of spirits*) tarraing *f*, grùdadh *m*

distiller *n* grùdair(e) *m*

distillery *n* 1 taigh-staile *m*; 2 (*illicit ~*) taigh dubh, poit-dhubh

distinct *adj* 1 (*esp sounds, sights: clear*) taisbeanach; 2 (*different, separate*) eadar-dhealaichte, air leth, (*more trad*) fa leth, (*less strong*) diof(a)rach, **a ~ species** seòrsa eadar-dhealaichte/air leth

distinction *n* 1 (*difference*) eadar-dhealachadh *m* (**between** eadar); 2 (*pre-eminence*) àrd-urram *m*, òirdheirceas *m*

distinctive *adj* air leth, àraidh

distinctly *adv* gu taisbeanach, gu soilleir, **he saw/heard them ~** chunnaic/chuala e gu taisbeanach/gu soilleir iad

distinguish *v* eadar-dhealaich *vt*, dèan eadar-dhealachadh *m*, (**between** eadar)

distinguished *adj* (*ie pre-eminent*) barraichte, òirdheirc

distort *v* 1 (*lit: phys*) cuir *vt* à cumadh *m*; 2 (*misquote, misrepresent*) dèan mì-aithris *m*, thoir claon-iomradh *m*, (*both with prep* air),

you have ~ed what I said tha sibh air mì-aithris a dhèanamh/claon-iomradh a thoirt air na thubhairt mi

distortion *n* **1** (*lit: phys*) ath-chumadh *m*; **2** (*misquotation, misrepresentation etc*) mì-aithris *m*, claon-iomradh *m*, (**of** air)

distract *v* tarraing aire *f invar* (**from** bho/o)

distracted *adj & past part* **1** (*preoccupied*) fad' às; **2** (*in intense mental state*) às a (*etc*) rian *m*

distraction *n* **1** (*pastime*) caitheamh-aimsir *m*, cur-seachad *m*; **2** (*lack of attention or concentration*) cion aire *m*; **3** (*intense mental state*) boile *f invar*

distress *n* (*mental state, also danger*) èiginn *f invar*, **a boat in** ~ bàta *m* ann an èiginn, bàta na h-èiginn

distress *v* (*mentally, emotionally*) sàraich *vt*, cràidh *vt*, pian *vt*, tàmailtich *vt*

distressed *adj* na (*etc*) èiginn *f invar*, cràidhte, air a (*etc*) s(h)àrachadh, air a (*etc*) t(h)àmailteachadh

distribute *v* roinn *vt*, riaraich *vt*, sgaoil *vt*

distribution *n* roinn *f*, riarachadh *m*, sgaoileadh *m*

district *n* ceàrn *m*, sgìre *f*, tìr *f*, ~ **council** comhairle sgìre *f*

distrust *n* mì-earbsa *m*, amharas *m*

distrustful *adj* mì-earbsach, amharasach

disturb *v* **1** (*bother, intrude upon etc*) cuir dragh *m* (*with prep* air); **2** (*disrupt situation etc, also ~ emotionally*) buair *vt*

disturbance *n* **1** (*the action*) buaireadh *m*; **2** (*the result*) aimhreit *f*, buaireas *m*, an-fhois *f*

disunity *n* eas-aonachd *f invar*

disuse *n* mì-chleachdadh *m*, *in expr* **fall into** ~ rach *vi irreg* à cleachdadh *m*

ditch *n* clais *f*, dìg *f*

ditty *n* duanag *f*, luinneag *f*

dive *v* dàibh *vi*, dàibhig *vi*

diver *n* dàibhear *m*

diverge *v* dealaich *vi* ri chèile, **their paths ~d** dhealaich na slighean *fpl* aca ri chèile

diverse *adj* caochladh *n* (*followed by gen pl of noun*), de dh'iomadach seòrsa *m* (*follows noun*), ~ **methods** caochladh dhòighean, ~ **excuses** leisgeulan *mpl* de dh'iomadach seòrsa

diversion *n* **1** (*fun, entertainment*) dibhearsain *m*, spòrs *f*, (*more trad*) fearas-chuideachd *f*; **2** (~ *of traffic*) tionndadh slighe *m*

diversity *n* iomadachd *f invar*

divert *v* **1** (*phys, also ~ funds etc*) tionndaidh *vt* a leth-taobh *m*; **2** (*amuse etc*) thoir dibhearsain *m* (*with prep* do)

divide *v* **1** pàirtich *vt*, riaraich *vt*, roinn *vt*; **2** (*by force, through disunity etc*) sgar *vt*

divided *adj & past part* **1** (*lit*) roinnte; **2** (*of persons: ~ by force, disagreements etc*) air a (*etc*) sgaradh; **3** (*arith*) air a roinn (**by** le), **72 ~ by 3** 72 air a roinn le 3

dividend *n* **1** (*gain*) buannachd *f*, **the peace** ~ buannachd na sìthe; **2** (*from shares*) duais-shèaraichean *f*

divine *adj* **1** diadhaidh; **2** (*coming from God*) Dhè (*gen of* Dia *m*, *used adjectivally*), ~ **grace** gràs Dhè *m*

diving *n* dàibheadh *m*, dàibhigeadh *m*

divinity *n* **1** (*abstr: the attribute of a god*) diadhachd *f invar*; **2** (*the subject of study etc*) diadhaireachd *f invar*

division *n* **1** (*abstr: the process*) pàirteacheadh *m*; **2** (*through disagreement, by force etc*) sgaradh *m*; **3** (*arith etc*) roinn *f*; **4** (*con: eg in football*) roinn *f*, **the second** ~ an dàrna roinn

divorce *n* sgaradh-pòsaidh *m*

divorce *v* dealaich *vi* (*with prep* ri), **he ~d his wife** sgar e bho a mhnaoi (*dat of* bean *f*)

divot *n* fàl *m*, ploc *m*, sgrath & sgroth *f*

divulge *v* foillsich *vt*, innis *vt*

dizziness *n* tuainealaich *f*, (*less usu*) luasgan *m*

dizzy *adj* tuainealach

do *v* **1** dèan *vt irreg*, ~ **your duty** dèan do dhleastanas *m*, **don't ~ that!** na dèan sin!, **I did my best** rinn mi mo dhìcheall (**to** air *plus infin of verb*), **didn't you ~ well!**, *also* **well done!** nach math a rinn thu!, **well done!** math fhèin, math thu fhèin!, **that will ~, that will ~ the job/trick!** nì sin an gnothach, nì sin a' chùis!, ~ **business** dèan gnothach *m* (**with** ri), **it will ~ you good** nì e feum dhut, **that won't be done** cha tèid sin a dhèanamh, **that can't be done** cha ghabh sin a dhèanamh, cha ghabh sin dèanamh; **2** **don't** *neg imperative, expr by neg particle* na *followed by imperative of the relevant verb*, **don't leave it on the floor!** na fàg air an làr e!, **don't have anything to ~ with him/it!** na gabh gnothach *m* ris!; **3** (*be sufficient*) foghain *vi*, **will that ~?** am foghain sin?, (*to children etc*) **that will ~!** fòghnaidh sin!; **4** (*other idioms & exprs*) (*fam*) **how are you ~ing?** dè an dòigh (a th' ort)?, dè do chor?, **a wee stroll would ~ you good** b' fheàirrde thu cuairt bheag, **what's ~ing?** (*fam*) dè (a) tha (a') dol?, ~ **away with** cuir *vi* às do, ~ **up** (*ie renovate etc*) leasaich *vt*, nuadhaich *vt*, càirich *vt*, cuir *vt* air dòigh *f*

docile *adj* **1** sèimh, ciùin, sàmhach; **2** (*biddable*) macanta, umha(i)l

docility *n* **1** sèimhe *f invar*, ciùineas *m*; **2** (*obedience*) macantas *m*, ùmhlachd *f invar*

dock[1] *n* (*bot*) copag *f*

dock[2] *n* (*in seaport etc*) doca *m*

dock[1] *v* **1** (*cut, shorten*) giorraich *vt*, cut & cutaich *vt*; **2** (*fam: reduce*) **they ~ed my pay** lùghdaich iad am pàigheadh *m invar* agam

dock[2] (*ship etc: as vt*) cuir *vt* san doca *m*, (*as vi*) rach *vi* a-steach dhan doca

docken (*Sc*) *n* (*bot*) copag *f*

docker *n* docair *m*

doctor *n* **1** (*medical*) do(c)tair *m*, (*more trad*) lighiche *m*; **2** (*non-medical, PhD etc*) Dr *m*, ~ **Campbell** An Dr Caimbeul

doctorate *n* dotaireachd *f invar*

doctrine *n* teagasg *m*

document *n* sgrìobhainn *f*, pàipear *m*

documentary *adj* **1** sgrìobhte, ~ **evidence** fianais sgrìobhte *f*; **2** (*media etc*) aithriseach, **a ~ film** film aithriseach *m*

documentary *n* (*media etc*) film *m*/prògram *m* (*etc*) aithriseach

dodge *n* (*stratagem etc*) innleachd *f*, (*more fam*) plòidh *f*

dodgy *adj* **1** (*dubious*) cugallach; **2** (*risky*) cunnartach

doff *v* cuir *vt* (*with prep* de), **we ~ed our caps** chuir sinn dhinn ar ceapannan

dog *n* **1** cù *m*; **2** (*more trad: of any canine species*) madadh *m*

dogged *adj* **1** (*as term of praise: persistent etc*) leanailteach, dìorrasach; **2** (*as adverse criticism: stubborn, intractable*) dùr, rag, rag-mhuinealach

dogmatic *adj* (*intractable in one's opinions*) rag-bharaileach

dole *n* dòil *m invar*

dole out *v* riaraich *vt*

doleful *adj* brònach, smalanach

doll *n* liùdhag *f*, doileag *f*

dollar *n* dolair *m*

dolt *n* bumailear *m*, ùmaidh *m*, stalcaire *m*

domestic *adj* taigheil

domesticate *v* callaich *vt*

domesticated *adj* **1** (*of animals*) calla & callda; **2** (*of home-loving person*) dachaigheil

domestication *n* callachadh *m*

domicile *n* àite-fuirich *m*, àite-còmhnaidh *m*, dachaigh *f*

dominance *n* smachd *m*, làmh-an-uachdair *f*, (**over** air), **he achieved ~ over them** fhuair e smachd/làmh-an-uachdair orra

dominant *adj* **1** (*exerting power, authority*) ceannsalach, smachdail; **2** (*principal, main etc*) prìomh (*precedes the noun, which it lenites*

where possible), **the ~ group of the party** prìomh bhuidheann a' phàrtaidh

dominate *v* **1** (*achieve dominance over*) ceannsaich *vt*, smachdaich *vt*, cuir *vt* fo smachd *m*, faigh smachd (*with prep* air); **2** (*be in a position of dominance over*) cùm *vt* fo smachd, **the Romans ~d them for many years** chùm na Ròmanaich fo smachd iad fad iomadach bliadhna

domineering *adj* ceannsalach

donate *v* tiodhlaic *vt*, thoir *vt* (seachad), (**to** do)

donation *n* tabhartas *m*, tiodhlac *m*, (**to** do)

done *adj & past part* **1** dèanta & dèante; **2** (*fam: finished*) deiseil, ullamh, **are you nearly ~?** a bheil thu gu bhith deiseil?, **have you ~ with the phone?** a bheil thu deiseil den fòn?; **3** *in expr* **well ~!** math fhèin!, math thu fhèin!, nach math a rinn thu!

donor *n* tabhartaiche *m*, tabhairteach *m*

don't *neg imperative, see* **do 2**

doomsday *n* Là Luain *m*

door *n* **1** doras *m*, **the main/front ~** an doras mòr, **the ~ handle** làmh an dorais *f*, **bar the ~** cuir an crann air an doras, **living next ~** a' fuireachd an ath-dhoras, **out of ~s** a-mach air doras; **2** (*idiom*) **at death's ~** ri uchd *m* a' bhàis; *Note: traditionally* doras *was used for the door opening while the door leaf was* còmhla *mf, but* doras *is now often used for both*

doorman *n* dorsair *m*, portair *m*

doorpost *n* ursainn *f*

doorstep *n* leac (an) dorais *f*

doorway *n* doras *m* (*see Note under* **door**)

dormant *adj* na (*etc*) c(h)adal *m*, na (*etc*) t(h)àmh *m*

dormitory *n* seòmar-cadail *m*

dose *n* tomhas (ìocshlaint) *m*

double *adj* dùbailte

double *v* (*numbers, quantities etc*) dùblaich *vti*

double-barrelled *adj*, **a ~ (shot)gun** gunna dùbailte

doubt *n* **1** teagamh *m*, **without (a) ~** gun teagamh, **there's no ~ about it** chan eil teagamh ann, **cast ~ (up)on** cuir *vt* an (*prep*) teagamh, **they cast ~ on his veracity** chuir iad an teagamh an fhìreantachd aige; **2** (*perplexity, puzzlement*) imcheist *f*, iomadh-chomhairle *f*, **in ~ as to what I would do** an/fo imcheist dè a dhèanainn, ann an iomadh-chomhairle dè a dhèanainn

doubt *v* **1** (*cast ~ (up)on*) cuir *vt* an teagamh *m*, cuir *vt* an amharas *m*, cuir teagamh (*with prep* ann an), **they ~ed his innocence** chuir iad an teagamh/an amharas an neoichiontachd aige,

chuir iad teagamh san neoichiontachd aige; **2**
(*fail to believe*) **will he go back? I ~ it** an tèid e
air ais? cha chreid mi gun tèid

doubtful *adj* teagmhach

doubting *adj* teagmhach, amharasach

doubtless *adv* gun teagamh

dough *n* taois *f*

dour (*Sc*) *adj* (*stubborn, obstinate; severe, stern*)
dùr

dove *n* calman *m*

dowdy *adj* cearbach, luideach, robach

down *adv* **1** (*movement*) sìos, **my shares have
gone ~** tha mo shèaraichean air a dhol sìos; **2**
(*movement: from point of view of person(s)
making the movement*) sìos, **go ~** rach *vi* sìos,
he went ~ (towards them) chaidh e sìos
(dhan ionnsaigh); **3** (*movement: from point of
view of person(s) towards whom the movement
is made*) a-nuas, **come ~** thig a-nuas, **he came
~ (towards me)** thàinig e a-nuas (dham
ionnsaigh); **4** (*position*) shìos, **they're all ~
there** tha iad uile shìos an sin; **5** (*misc idioms &
exprs*) **sit ~** dèan suidhe *m*, (*more fam*) suidh *vi*
sìos, (*less usu*) suidh a-bhàn, **go ~** (*of sun*) laigh
vi, **knock ~, throw ~, let ~,** leag *vt*, **he let ~
the window** leag e an uinneag, **she's lying ~**
tha i na laighe, **she was a bit ~** bha i rud beag
sìos na h-inntinn, *also* bha i rud beag ìseal/
ìosal, **she walked ~ the slope** choisich i leis
a' bhruthaich, **slow ~** (*as vi*) rach *vi* am maille *f*
invar, (*as vt*) cuir maille (*with preps* air *or* ann),
slow ~ the improvements cuir maille air na
leasachaidhean

downcast *adj* smalanach, fo smalan *m*, dubhach,
(*more fam*) sìos na (*etc*) inntinn *f*, ìseal & ìosal

downhill *adv* **1** leis a' bhruthaich *mf*; **2** (*idiom:
fig*) **she went ~** chaidh *vi* i bhuaithe

downpour *n* dìle *f*, (*heavier*) dìle bhàthte,
dòrtadh *m*

downstairs *adj* **1** (*position*) shìos an staidhre
f, **they are ~** tha iad shìos an staidhre; **2**
(*movement*) sìos an staidhre, **they went ~**
chaidh iad sìos an staidhre

downstream *adv* (*movement*) leis an t-sruth

downwards *adv* **1** (*from point of view of
person(s) making the movement*) sìos; **2** (*from
point of view of person(s) towards whom the
movement is made*) a-nuas; *cf* **down 2 & 3**
above

dowry *n* tochradh *m*

doze *n* clò-chadal *m*, leth-chadal *m*, dùsal *m*,
norrag *f*

doze *v* **1** dèan dùsal *m*, dèan norrag (bheag); **2**
(*idioms*) **I ~d off** chaidh *vi* mi nam chlò-chadal
m, thàinig *vi* clò-chadal orm

dozen *n* dusan *m*

dozy *adj* **1** (*with sleep*) cadalach; **2** (*mentally
slow*) maol-aigneach

drab *adj* (*in colour*) lachdann, odhar, doilleir

draft *n* (*of document*) dreachd *f*, dreachdadh *m*

drag *v* **1** tarraing *vti*, slaod *vti*, (**at/on** air), dragh
vt; **2** (*fig*) *in expr* **~ one's heels** màirnealaich *vi*

dragonfly *n* tarbh-nathrach *m*

drain *n* **1** (*agric, plumbing etc*) clais *f*, drèana *f*;
2 (*source of fin waste or loss*) traoghadh *m* (**on**
de), **a ~ on resources** traoghadh den mhaoin *f*

drain *v* **1** (*empty a container etc*) tràigh *vt*; **2** (*~
liquids from container etc*) taom *vt*; **3** (*cookery*)
taom *vt*, **~ the carrots** taom na currain *mpl*;
4 *in expr* **~ away** sìol *vi* às, **the waters ~ed
away** shìol na h-uisgeachan *mpl* às

drainage *n* drèanadh *m*

drainpipe *n* pìob drèanaidh *f*

drake *n* ràc *m*, dràc *m*

dram *n* drama *mf*, dram *mf*, **will you take a ~?**
an gabh thu drama?

drama dràma *mf*

dramatic *adj* dràmadach & dràmatach

dramatist *n* sgrìobhaiche *m* dràma, dràmaire *m*

draught *n* (*of liquid*) tarraing *f*, (*fam*) balgam *m*,
sgailc *f*, steallag *f*

draughtboard *n* bòrd-dàmais *m*

draughts *n* (*game*) dàmais *f invar*

draw *n* (*football match etc*) geama ionannach *m*

draw *v* **1** (*pull, drag*) tarraing *vti*, slaod *vti*, (**on**
air), dragh *vt*, **~ on the rope** tarraing air an
ròpa *m*, **~ breath/blood** tarraing anail *f*/fuil *f*,
~ a pint/a cork tarraing pinnt *m*/corcais *f*; **2**
(*less lit uses*) tarraing *vt*, **~ a picture** tarraing
dealbh *m*, **~ to a close** tarraing *vi* gu crìch (*dat
of* crìoch *f*); **3** *in exprs* **~ lots** cuir croinn (*pl of*
crann *m*), tilg croinn, **~ing lots** (*ie the action*)
crannchur *m*; **4** *in expr* **~ near** dlùthaich *vi*,
teann *vi*, (**to** ri), **we were ~ing near to the
sea** bha sinn a' dlùthachadh/a' teannadh ris a'
mhuir; **5** (*~ weapon, sword*) rùisg *vt*

drawer *n* drathair *m*

drawing *n* dealbh *mf*

drawing-pin *n* tacaid *f*, tacaid-balla *f*

dread *n* uamhann *m*, oillt *f*, uabhas *m*

dreadful *adj* **1** oillteil; **2** (*often with attenuated
meaning*) eagalach, uabhasach, sgriosail,
the music was just ~! bha an ceòl dìreach
eagalach/uabhasach/sgriosail!

dreadfully *adv*, uabhasach, eagalach, garbh, **~
poor** uabhasach/eagalach bochd, **things are**

~ **busy just now** tha cùisean garbh dripeil an-dràsta

dream *n* bruadar *m*, aisling *f*

dream *v* 1 bruadair *vi* (**about/of** air), **I was ~ing about you** bha mi a' bruadar ort; 2 *in expr* **you're ~ing!** tha thu ri bruadar!, tha thu ag aisling!

dreamer *n* aislingiche *m*

dreary *adj* 1 (*mournful*) tiamhaidh; 2 (*dull, tedious*) slaodach

dregs *n* (*in liquids*) grùid *f*

drench *v* drùidh *vi* (*with prep* air), **the rain ~ed me** dhrùidh an t-uisge orm

drenched *adj & past part* drùidhte, bog fliuch

dress *n* 1 (*woman's garment*) dreasa *f*; 2 (*mode of ~*) èideadh *m*, **Highland ~** an t-èideadh Gàidhealach

dress *v* 1 (*~ oneself*) cuir *vti* (*with prep* mu), **I ~ed** chuir mi umam, chuir mi umam m' aodach *m*; 2 (*~ someone else*) cuir aodach (*with prep* air), **I ~ed him** chuir mi aodach air; 3 *in expr* ~ **up** sgeadaich *vt*

dressed *adj & past part, in exprs* **I got ~** chuir mi umam (m' aodach *m*), **well ~** spruiseil

dresser *n* (*furniture*) dreasair *m*

dressing-gown *n* còta-leapa *m*

dried *adj & past part* 1 tiormaichte; 2 *in expr* ~ **up** crìon, seac

drift *n* 1 (*of snow*) cuithe (sneachda) *f*, cathadh (sneachda) *m*; 2 (*fig: idiom*) **you made me lose my ~** chuir thu às mo ghabhail *mf* mi

drift *v* (*snow*) rach *vi irreg* na chuithe, cath *vi*

drifter *n* (*fishing*) drioftair *m*

drill[1] *n* (*tool*) drile *f*, (*more trad*) snìomhaire *m*, tolladair *m*

drill[2] *n* (*army etc*) drile *f*

drill[1] *v* toll *vt, in expr* (*oil industry*) ~ing **platform** clàr tollaidh *m*

drill[2] *v* (*army etc*) drilich *vi*, dèan drile *f*

drink *n* 1 (*of all kinds*) deoch *f*, **a ~ of milk/of water** deoch bhainne/uisge; 2 (*alcoholic ~*) deoch *f*, deoch-làidir *f invar*, **he's fond of the ~** tha e measail air an deoch

drink *v* òl *vti*, gabh *vt*, ~ **a cup of tea** òl/gabh cupan teatha; 2 (*alcoholic drinks*) òl *vti*, **I don't ~ at all** cha bhi mi ag òl idir

drinker *n* (*usu excessive*) pòitear *m*, misgear *m*

drinking *n* 1 (*general & of alcoholic drinks*) òl *m*; 2 (*of alcohol: usu excessive*) pòitearachd *f invar*; 3 *in exprs* ~ **companion** co-phòitear *m*, ~ **spree** (*now rather trad*) daorach *f*

drip, dripping *n* 1 (*abstr & con*) sileadh *m*, snighe *m*; 2 (*the sound*) gliog *m*

drive *n* 1 (*engin*) iomain *f*, ~ **shaft** crann iomain *m*; 2 (*trip in car*) cuairt bheag (sa chàr); 3 (*energy, initiative etc*) dèanadas *m*

drive *v* 1 (*~ a vehicle*) dràibh *vti*, dràibhig *vti*; 2 (*propel machinery etc*) iomain *vt*, ~ **a machine by steam** iomain inneal *m* le smùid *f*; 3 (*sport: propel*) iomain *vt*, ~ **a ball** iomain bàla *m*; 4 (*other exprs & idioms*) ~ (**on**) (*esp livestock*) iomain *vt*, ~ **on** (*people, animals*) greas *vt*, ~ **away** fuadaich *vt*, **the dog drove away the fox** dh'fhuadaich an cù an sionnach, *also* chuir an cù teicheadh *m* air an t-sionnach, ~ **out** *or* **away** *v* rua(i)g *vt*, fògair *vt*, fuadaich *vt*, **the people were ~n from/out of the glen** dh'fhògradh an sluagh às a' ghleann, (*idiom*) **it was nearly driving me mad/demented/out of my mind** bha e gus mo chur dhìom fhìn/far mo chinn/às mo rian

drivel *n* 1 seile *m invar*, ronn *m*; 2 (*fig: foolish talk, nonsense etc*) amaideas *m*, (*fam*) sgudal *m*

driver *n*, (*of a vehicle*) dràibhear *m*

driving *n* (*a vehicle*) dràibheadh *m*

drizzle *n* ciùbhran & ciùthran *m*

drizzle *v* braon *vi*

droll *adj* èibhinn, ait

drone[1] *n* (*of bagpipe*) dos *m*

drone[2] *n* 1 (*type of bee*) seillean dìomhain *m*; 2 (*sound of bee*) torman *m*

droning *n* torman *m*

droop *v* searg *vi*

drop *n* 1 boinne *f*, braon *m*, drùdhag *f*, **a ~ of milk** boinne bainne, **won't you take a ~ of tea?** nach gabh thu drùdhag tì?; 2 (*on end of nose*) boinneag *f*, **a ~ on his nose** boinneag ri shròin (*dat of* sròn *f*)

drop *v* 1 (*as vi*) tuit *vi*, **the glasses ~ped** thuit na glainneachan; 2 (*as vt: let fall accidentally*) leig *vt* às, **I ~ped the glasses** leig mi às na glainneachan; 3 (*as vt: release deliberately*) leag *vt*, ~ **bombs** leag bomaichean *mpl*; 4 (*other exprs & idioms*) ~ **to bits** rach *vi* na (*etc*) c(h)riomagan *fpl*, **the toys were ~ping to bits** bha na dèideagan *fpl* a' dol nan criomagan, **I ~ped off** (*ie dozed*) chaidh mi nam chlò-chadal *m*, thàinig clò-chadal orm

drought *n* tiormachd *f invar*, tart *f*

drove *n* 1 (*of cattle*) dròbh *m*; 2 (*fig: in pl*) ~**s** mìltean *mpl*, dròbhan *mpl*, **they came in ~s** thàinig iad nam mìltean/nan dròbhan

drover *n* (*of livestock*) dròbhair *m*

drown *v* 1 bàth *vt*, **he was ~ed** chaidh a bhàthadh *m*; 2 (*sounds*) ~ (**out**) bàth *vt*

drowsy *adj* cadalach

drudge *n* tràill *mf*, sgalag *f*

drudgery n tràilleachd *f invar*, obair sgalaig *f*

drug n 1 (*medical*) cungaidh *f*, cungaidh-leighis *f*;
2 (*medical & illicit*) droga *f*

druid n draoidh *m*

drum n (*mus*) druma *mf*

drunk *adj* 1 air mhisg *f*, air an daoraich (*dat of*
daorach *f*), leis an daoraich, **I'm** ~ tha mi air
mhisg, tha mi air an daoraich, tha an daorach
orm, tha mi leis an daoraich, (*stronger: fam*)
tha smùid *f* orm, tha mi air mo phronnadh; 2
in exprs **make** ~ cuir misg *f*, cuir an daorach
f, (*with prep* air), **they made me** ~ chuir iad
misg/an daorach orm, **half** ~ air leth-mhisg

drunkard n pòitear *m*, misgear *m*

drunkenness n daorach *f*, misg *f*, (*fam*) smùid *f*

dry *adj* 1 tioram, **here's a dry towel for you**
seo agad tubhailte thioram, **the loch was** ~
bha an loch tioram; 2 (~ *from thirst*) pàiteach,
tartmhor, ìotmhor; 3 *in exprs* ~ **spell**, ~
weather, **spell of** ~ **weather** (*esp following a*
rainy period) turadh *m*; 4 (*of dairy or suckling*
animals, giving no milk) seasg

dry v 1 tiormaich *vti*, **the dishes haven't**
been dried chan eil na soithichean air an
tiormachadh; 2 *in expr* ~ **up** (*ie wither*) crìon *vti*

dryer n tiormadair *m*

dryness n 1 tiormachd *f invar*; 2 (*from thirst*)
pathadh *m*, tart *m*, ìota *m*

dual *adj* dùbailte

dubious *adj* 1 (*having doubts*) teagmhach,
amharasach; 2 (*arousing doubts, unreliable*)
neo-earbsach, cugallach

Dublin n Baile Àtha Cliath *m*

duchess n ban-diùc *f*

duck n tunnag *f*, (*wild* ~) lach *f*

duck v (*in liquid*) tum *vt*

ducking n (*in liquid*) tumadh *m*

due *adj* 1 (*fitting*) dligheach, cubhaidh,
iomchaidh, ~ **respect** meas dligheach; 2 (*expr*
that a time limit etc has expired) bi *vi irreg*
followed by prep ri *and a verbal noun*, **this**
book is ~ **back/~ to be returned** tha an
leabhar seo ri thoirt air ais, **this bill is** ~ **(to**
be paid) tha an cunntas seo ri phàigheadh;
3 (*owed*) **you're** ~ **ten pounds from me**
tha deich notaichean agad orm; 4 *in expr* **in**
~ **course** ri tìde *f*, **we'll get it in** ~ **course**
gheibh sinn ri tìde e

due n (*what one is entitled to*) dlighe *f invar*,
dleas *m*

duel n còmhrag-dithis *f*

duet n òran-dithis *m*

duke n diùc *m*

dull *adj* 1 (*of light, colours etc*) doilleir, ciar; 2
(*tedious*) liosda, slaodach

dull v 1 (*esp light*) doilleirich *vti*; 2 (~ *pain etc*)
faothaich *vti*, lasaich *vt*

dulse n (*bot*) duileasg *m*

duly *adv* gu dligheach

dumb *adj* (*permanently or temporarily*) balbh

dumbness n balbhachd *f invar*

dump n 1 (*rubbish heap etc*) òtrach *m*; 2 (*of*
place: shabby etc) àite grodach, (*not worth*
frequenting) àite gun fheum

dun *adj* odhar, ciar, lachdann, (*less usu*) riabhach

dunce n bumailear *m*, ùmaidh *m*, stalcaire *m*

dung n (*used as manure*) innear & inneir *f*,
todhar *m*, **cow** ~ buachar *m*, ~ **heap** dùnan *m*,
òtrach *m*, siteag *f*

dunghill n dùnan *m*, siteag & sitig *f*, òtrach *m*

duodenum n beul a' chaolain *m*

dupe v thoir an car (*with prep* à), dèan foill *f*
(*with prep* air), cealg *vt*, **he ~d me** thug e an car
asam, rinn e foill orm

duplicate n 1 mac-samhail *m*, lethbhreac *m*, (**of**
de), **document** (*etc*) **in** ~ sgrìobhainn (*etc*) le
lethbhreac

duplicate v dèan mac-samhail *m*, dèan
lethbhreac *m* (*with prep* de)

duplicity n cealg *f*, foill *f*

durable *adj* buan, maireannach

duration n, *in expr* **for the** ~ **of the meeting**
fad na coinneimh, fhad 's a bha a' choinneamh
a' dol

during *prep* 1 ann an, fad, (*occas*) ri, **it was**
snowing ~ **the night** bha e a' cur an
t-sneachda san oidhche (*also* air an oidhche), **it**
was snowing ~ **the (whole) night** bha e a'
cur sneachda fad na h-oidhche, **he fell asleep**
~ **her talk** chaidh/thuit e na chadal is i a' toirt
seachad na h-òraid aice

dusk n 1 duibhre *f invar*, eadar-sholas *m*,
camhanaich *f* na h-oidhche, beul *m* na
h-oidhche; 2 (*idiom*) **from dawn to** ~ o
mhoch gu dubh

dust n duslach *m*, dust *m invar*, stùr *m*

dust v dustaig *vti*

dustbin n biona-sgudail *m*

duster n dustair *m*

dusty *adj* dustach, stùrach

Dutch *adj* Duitseach

Dutchman n Duitseach *m*

dutiful *adj* dleastanach

duty *n* **1** dleastanas *m*, (*less usu*) dleas *m*, **they did their** ~ rinn iad an dleastanas; **2** (*tax*) cìs *f*, **customs** ~ cìs-chusbainn *f invar*, ~ **free** saor o chìsean

dwang *n* rong *m*, rongas *f*

dwarf *n* luchraban *m*, troich *mf*

dwell *v* **1** (*live*) fuirich *vi*, (*less usu*) tàmh *vi*; **2** (*settle in, inhabit*) tuinich *vi*, àitich *vt*, gabh còmhnaidh *f*, **the first race that dwelt in America** a' chiad chinneadh a thuinich ann an Ameireagaidh

dweller *n* **1** (*esp in house, town etc*) neach-còmhnaidh *m* (*pl* luchd-còmhnaidh *m sing* coll); **2** (*esp in a country, continent*) neach-àiteachaidh *m* (*pl* luchd-àiteachaidh *m sing coll*), tuiniche *m*

dwelling *n* **1** (*abstr*) còmhnaidh *f*; **2** (*in adj exprs*) ~ **place** àite-còmhnaidh *m*, àite-fuirich *m*, ~ **house** taigh *m*, taigh-còmhnaidh *m*, (*more trad*) fàrdach *f*

dye *n* dath *m*

dye *v* dath *vt*, cuir dath *m* (*with prep* air)

dyed *adj* dathte

dyke *n* gàrradh *m*

dynamic *adj* innsgineach

dynasty *n* gineal *mf*, cineal *m*, sliochd *m coll*

E

each *adj* **1** gach, ~ **house** gach taigh, **I went there** ~ **day** chaidh mi ann gach là, ~ **and every** gach aon, gach uile, ~ **and every house** gach aon taigh, **she's on at me about** ~ **and every thing** bidh i an sàs annam mu gach uile nì; **2** *as pron in expr* ~ **other** a chèile, (*less usu*) cach-a-chèile, **they kissed** ~ **other** phòg iad a chèile, **talking to** ~ **other** a' bruidhinn ri chèile, **seeing** ~ **other** a' faicinn càch-a-chèile; **3** (*per capita*) an urra *f*, **they received a thousand pounds** ~ fhuair iad mìle not(a) an urra

eager *adj* **1** (*of pursuit, endeavour etc*) dian; **2** (*of person*) dealasach, (*esp of person* ~ **to work, oblige etc**) èasgaidh

eagerness *n* dealas *m*, èasgaidheachd *f invar*, dealasachd *f invar*

eagle *n* iolair(e) *f*, **golden** ~ iolair(e) bhuidhe

ear *n* **1** cluas *f*, ~ **piercing** tolladh-chluasan *m*; **2** (*idiom*) **give an** ~ dèan èisteachd *f invar* (**to do**); **3** (~ *of corn*) dias *f*

earache *n* grèim-cluaise *m*

eardrum *n* druma *mf* (na) cluaise, faillean *m*

earl *n* iarla *m*

earldom *n* iarlachd *f invar*

early *adj* moch, tràth (*advs*), (*usu Lit/poet*) òg (*adj*), **in the** ~ **morning** moch/tràth sa mhadainn *f*, san òg-mhadainn

early *adv* **1** moch, tràth, ~ **in the morning** moch/tràth sa mhadainn *f*; **2** (*before set or expected time*) tràth *adv*, ron mhithich *f invar*, ron àm *m*, ~ **for the meeting** tràth airson na coinneimh, **it's too** ~ **for ripe apples** tha e ro thràth airson ùbhlan abaich, **she retired** ~ leig i seachad/leig i dhith an obair ron mhithich/ron àm, ~ **departure** falbh ron mhithich/ron àm, **we arrived** ~ ràinig *vi* sinn ron àm

earmark *n* (*on livestock*) comharradh-cluaise *m*

earmark *v* **1** (*livestock*) cuir comharradh-cluaise *m* (*with prep* air); **2** (*fig: general*) comharraich *vt*

earn *v* coisinn *vt*, buannaich *vt*, ~**ing big money** a' cosnadh airgid mhòir

earnest *adj* **1** (*in character, personality*) dùrachdach, stòlda; **2** (*more temporary*) in *exprs* **in**~ ann an da-rìribh *adv*, **they weren't in** ~ cha robh iad ann an da-rìribh, **half in** ~ eadar fealla-dhà *f invar* is da-rìribh

earnings *n* cosnadh *m*, tuarastal *m*

ear-ring *n* cluas-fhail *f*

earth *n* **1** (*the planet*) *used with art*, **(the)** ~ an cruinne *mf*, an cruinne-cè *mf*, an talamh *m* (*f in gen sing*); **2** (*soil, ground*) talamh *m* (*f in gen sing*), (*less usu*) ùir *f*, **they put him into the** ~ chuir iad san talamh/san ùir e; **3** (*idioms*) **where on** ~ **did he go?** càit idir an deach e?, **where on** ~ **is he?** càite fon ghrèin (*dat of* grian *f*) a bheil e?, **why on** ~ **did you do it?** carson, a chiall, a rinn thu e?

earthly *adj* **1** talmhaidh *adj*, **an** ~ **creature** creutair talmhaidh; **2** (*temporal, opposite of spiritual, heavenly*) saoghalta, talmhaidh

earthquake *n* crith-thalmhainn *f*

earthworm *n* cnuimh-thalmhainn *f*, boiteag *f*

ear-wax cèir-cluaise *f*

earwig *n* gòbhlag *f*, fiolan *m*, fiolan-gòbhlach *m*

ease *n* **1** fois *f*, socair *f*, *in expr* **take your** ~ gabh fois; **2** (*in personality, character, mood*) **at (his etc)** ~ socair, socrach (*adjs*); **3** (*financial* ~) seasgaireachd *f invar*

ease *v* **1** (*suffering etc*) faothaich *vti*, lasaich *vt*; **2** (*bonds etc*) fuasgail *vt*

easel *n* sorchan-dealbha *m*

easier *comp adj* nas fhasa, (*in past & conditional tenses*) na b' fhasa, **that will be** ~ bidh sin nas fhasa

easiest *sup adj*, as fhasa (*in past & conditional tenses* a b' fhasa), **the** ~ **thing was to come back** b' e an rud a b' fhasa tilleadh

easing *n* **1** (*of pain, suffering*) faothachadh *m*, furtachd *f invar*; **2** (*of bonds etc*) fuasgladh *m*

east *adj* sear *adj*, an ear *f invar*, **the** ~ **side** an taobh sear, an taobh an ear, **an** ~ **wind** gaoth on ear

east *adv* an ear *f invar*, sear *adv*, **going** ~ a' dol an ear, ~ **of Eden** an ear air Èden, sear air Èden

east *n* ear *f invar*, **the** ~ (*ie compass direction*) an àird an ear, **in the** ~ san ear, **from the** ~ on ear, **a wind from/out of the** ~ gaoth às an ear, **the** ~ (*ie location, part of a country etc*) an taobh *m* an ear *or* an taobh sear

Easter *n* (*used with art*) a' Chàisg, ~ **Monday** Diluain na Càisge

easterly *adj* an ear *f invar*, **an** ~ **wind** gaoth an ear

eastern *adj* an ear *f invar*, sear *adj*, **the** ~ **towns** na bailtean an ear, na bailtean sear

East Indies (the) *npl* Na h-Innseachan an Ear *fpl*

eastwards *adv* an ear, chun an ear, chun na h-àirde an ear, **sailing** ~ a' seòladh (chun) an ear

easy *adj* **1** furasta, soirbh, sìmplidh, **an** ~ **job** obair fhurasta, **an** ~ **question** ceist shoirbh; **2** (*financially* ~) seasgair; **3** (*idioms*) **take things** ~ gabh *vi* air do (*etc*) s(h)ocair *f*, (*excl*) **take it** ~!, **go** ~! socair! *or* air do shocair!

easy-going *adj* **1** (*patient, apt to put up with annoyances etc*) foighidneach; **2** (*not disciplinarian*) ceadach; **3** (*nonchalant; can also be pej, implying 'couldn't care less' attitude*) coma co-dhiù

eat *v* **1** ith *vti*; **2** (*idiom*) **he came home to** ~ thàinig e dhachaigh gu bhiadh *m*

eatable *adj* ion-ithe

eating *n* ithe & itheadh *m*

eaves *n* anainn *f sing*

eavesdrop *v* dèan farchluais *f*

eavesdropping *n* farchluais *f*

ebb *n* (*of tide*) tràghadh *m*, traoghadh *m*

ebb *v* (*of tide*) tràigh *vi*, traogh *vi*

eccentric *adj* (*of person, behaviour*) neònach, às a' chumantas, rudanach

ecclesiastic, ecclesiastical *adj* eaglaiseil

ecclesiastic *n* eaglaiseach *m*, pears-eaglais *m*

echo *n* mac-talla *m*, sgailc-creige *f*

echo *v* ath-ghairm *vi*

eclectic *adj* ioma-sheòrsach, **an** ~ **collection** cruinneachadh ioma-sheòrsach

eclipse *n* dubhadh *m*, ~ **of the sun/of the moon** dubhadh na grèine/na gealaich

eclipse *v* duibhrich *vti*

economic *adj* (*related to economics, the economy*) eaconamach

economical *adj* **1** (*thrifty*) cunntach, caomhantach, cùramach (a thaobh airgid); **2** (*cheap, not excessive*) **an** ~ **price** deagh phrìs, prìs chothromach/dhòigheil

economics *n* eaconamachd *f invar*, eaconamas *m*

economise *v* caomhain *vti*, glèidh *vt*, sàbhail *vt*

economist *n* eaconamair *m*

economy *n* **1** eaconamaidh *m*, **the national** ~ eaconamaidh na dùthcha, **free market** ~ eaconamaidh saor-mhargaidh; **2** *in exprs* **domestic** ~ taigheadas *m*, banas-taighe *m invar*, **make economies** geàrr *vi* sìos, geàrr *vi* air ais, (**in air**), **make economies in our expenditure** geàrr sìos air an teachd-a-mach *m invar* againn

ecstasy *n* **1** (*the state*) mire *f*, meadhail *f invar*, meadhradh *m*, **in** ~ air mhire; **2** (*the drug*) eacstasaidh *m*

ecstatic *adj* air mhire *f*, **make someone** ~ cuir cuideigin air mhire

eddy *n* cuairteag *f*

edge *n* **1** iomall *m*, oir *f*, **the** ~ **of the wood** iomall na coille, **the** ~ **of the roof** oir a' mhullaich; **2** (*of blade, tool etc*) faobhar *m*, *in expr* **put an** ~ **on** (*blade, tool etc*) faobharaich *vt*; **3** *in expr* (*of person*) **on** ~ clisgeach

edgy *adj* clisgeach

edible *adj* ion-ithe

edict *n* riaghailt *f*, reachd *m invar*

edit *v* deasaich *vt*

editing *n* deasachadh *m*

edition *n* **1** (*abstr*) deasachadh *m*; **2** (*con*) clò-bhualadh *m*, **a new** ~ **of his novel** clò-bhualadh ùr den nobhail aige

editor *n* deasaiche *m*, neach-deasachaidh *m* (*pl* luchd-deasachaidh *m sing coll*)

educate *v* foghlaim *vt*, teagaisg *vt*, thoir sgoil *f* (*with prep* do), ~ **the new generation** teagaisg an ginealach ùr

educated *adj* foghlaimte, foghlamaichte, ionnsaichte

education *n* foghlam *m*, ionnsachadh *m*, oideachas *m*, sgoil *f*, **pre-school/nursery** ~ foghlam fo-sgoile, **adult** ~ foghlam-inbhidh, **Gaelic-medium** ~ foghlam tro mheadhan *m* na Gàidhlig, **the Education Department** Roinn *f* an Fhoghlaim, **we got our** ~ **in Lewis** fhuair sinn ar sgoil ann an Leòdhas

educational *adj* **1** (*providing education or information*) oideachail; **2** (*to do with education*) foghlaim (*gen of* foghlam *m*, *used adjectivally*) ~ **facilities** goireasan foghlaim

eel *n* easgann *f*

eerie *adj* iargalta, uaigealta

effect *n* **1** (*of action etc*) toradh *m*, buil *f*, buaidh *f*, èifeachd *f invar*, **the ~(s) of your behaviour** toradh do dhol-a-mach *m invar*, **the greenhouse** ~ buaidh an taigh-ghlainne; **2** (*impression etc made on someone*) drùidheadh *m*, *in expr* **have an** ~ **on someone** drùidh *vi* air cuideigin; **3** *in expr* **put into** ~ (*plan, ideas etc*) cuir *vt* an gnìomh *m*

effective *adj* èifeachdach

effectiveness *n* èifeachdachd *f invar*, èifeachdas *m*

effects *npl* (*one's belongings in general*) sealbh & seilbh *f sing coll*; **2** *in expr* **household** ~ àirneis (taighe) *f sing coll invar*

effeminacy *n* boireanntachd *f invar*

effeminate *adj* boireannta

effervescence *n* (*of person*) beothalas *m*

effervescent *adj* **1** (*of liquid*) builgeanach; **2** (*of person*) beothail

efficiency *n* èifeachdachd *f invar*, èifeachdas *m*

efficient *adj* èifeachdach

effigy *n* ìomhaigh *f*

effluent *n* às-shruthadh *m*

effort *n* **1** (*abstr*) saothair *f*, **it's not worth the** ~ **(to you)** chan fhiach dhut do shaothair; **2** (*con; an* ~) oidhirp *f*, (*esp a strenuous* ~) spàirn *f*, **make an** ~ thoir oidhirp (**at** air); **3** (*results of* ~) oidhirpean *fpl*, **the editor didn't like my** ~**s** cha bu toigh leis an fhear-deasachaidh na h-oidhirpean agam

effrontery *n* ladarnas *m*, (*more fam*) aghaidh *f*, bathais *f*, **what** ~**!** abair ladarnas!, abair aghaidh!

egalitarian *adj* co-ionannachail

egg *n* ugh *m*

egg-cup *n* gucag-uighe *f*

egg-shaped *adj* ughach

egg-white *n* gealagan *m*

ego *n*, *used with art*, **the** ~ am fèin *m invar*

egoist, egotist *n* fèinear *m*

egoism, egotism *n* fèineachd *f invar*

egotistical *adj* fèineil

Egypt *n* (*used with art*) An Èipheit *f invar*

Egyptian *n* & *adj* Èipheiteach

eiderdown *n* clòimhteachan *m*

Eigg *n* Eige

eight *numeral* & *adj* ochd, (*of people*) ochdnar *mf*

eighteen *numeral* & *adj* ochd-deug

eighth *adj* ochdamh

eighth *n* ochdamh *m*

eightsome *n* ochdnar *mf*, **an** ~ **reel** ruidhle-ochdnar *m*

eighty *num* & *adj* ceithir fichead, (*in alternative numbering system*) ochdad *m*

either *adv* **1** nas motha, **I won't go home! I won't** ~**!** cha tèid mi dhachaigh! cha tèid mise nas motha! (*also* cha tèid no mise!), **no-one else saw me** ~ cha mhotha (a) chunnaic duine eile mi; **2** *in expr* ~ **. . . or** an dara/dàrna cuid . . . no, (*in neg sentences*) an aon chuid . . . no,

give me ~ **meat or fish** thoir dhomh an dara cuid feòil no iasg, (*in neg sentences*) **I won't go** ~ **to Glasgow or to Edinburgh** cha tèid mi an aon chuid a Ghlaschu no a Dhùn Èideann

eject *v* tilg *vt* a-mach, cuir *vt* a-mach, (**from** à)

elaborate *adj* **1** (*involving much work*) saothrach; **2** (*detailed*) mionaideach; **3** (*multi-faceted*) iomadh-fhillte

elaborate *v* **1** (*create, develop*) innlich *vt*, tionnsgail *vt*, obraich *vt* a-mach; **2** (*give more detail*) leudaich *vi* (**on** air), **he** ~**d on his plans** leudaich e air na planaichean aige

elastic *adj* sùbailte, ~ **band** bann sùbailte

elastic *n* lastaig *f invar*

elasticity *n* sùbailteachd *f invar*

elated *adj* & *past part* aoibhneach, (*fam*) air a (*etc*) d(h)eagh dhòigh *f*, **they were** ~ bha iad air an deagh dhòigh

elbow *n* uileann & uilinn *f*

elbow *v* uillnich *vti*, thoir ùpag(an) *f* (*with prep* do)

elder[1] *n* **1** (*church* ~) èildear *m*, (*more trad*) foirfeach *m*; **2** (*older of two*) am fear/an tè (*etc*) as sine, **John is the** ~ is e Iain am fear as sine

elder[2] *n* (*the tree*) ruis *f*, droman *m*

elect *v* (*esp pol*) tagh *vt*, **they weren't** ~**ed** cha deach an taghadh *m*

elected *adj* & *past part* taghte

election *n* taghadh *m*, ~ **campaign** iomairt taghaidh *f*, ~ **expenses** cosgaisean taghaidh *fpl*

elector *n* neach-taghaidh *m* (*pl* luchd-taghaidh *m sing coll*)

electoral *adj* taghaidh (*gen of* taghadh *m*, *used adjectivally*), ~ **district** sgìre taghaidh

electorate *n* luchd-bhòtaidh *m sing coll*

electric *adj* dealain (*gen of* dealan *m*, *used adjectivally*), ~ **light/fire** solas/teine dealain, ~ **current** sruth dealain, ~ **cooker** cucair-dealain

electrical *adj* **1** dealain (*gen of* dealan *m*, *used adjectivally*); **2** *in expr* ~ **engineer** innleadair-dealain *m*

electrician *n* dealanair *m*

electricity *n* dealan *m*, **electric(al) power** cumhachd an dealain *m*

electrify *v* **1** (*lit*) dealanaich *vt*; **2** (*fig*) cuir gaoir *f* (*with prep* air), **she electrified the audience** chuir i gaoir air an luchd-èisteachd

electronic *adj* **1** eileagtronaigeach, dealanach, ~ **keyboard** meur-chlàr dealanach; **2** *in exprs* ~ **mail, e-mail** post-dealain *m*

elegance *n* grinneas *m*, snas *m*

elegant *adj* grinn, fìnealta, eireachdail

elegiac *adj* tuireach

elegy *n* cumha *m*, marbhrann *m*, tuireadh *m*

element n (*general, also science etc*) eileamaid f

elementary adj 1 bunaiteach; 2 (*not profound*) sìmplidh; 3 *in expr* ~ **knowledge** bun-eòlas m (**of, about** air)

elevate v àrdaich vt

elevator n àrdaichear m

eligibility n ion-roghnachd f *invar*, freagarrachd f *invar*

eligible adj 1 ion-roghnach, freagarrach; 2 (*qualified*) uidheamaichte

eliminate v 1 (*expel, remove, cut out etc*) thoir vt (**from** à), cuir vt a-mach (**from** à), geàrr vt às, **he was ~d from the competition** chaidh a thoirt às an fharpais, **the council is eliminating** (*financial*) **waste** tha a' chomhairle a' gearradh às ana-caitheimh; 2 (*destroy, kill*) cuir vi às (*with prep* do), **they ~d their enemies** chuir iad às do na nàimhdean mpl aca

elimination n 1 (*removal etc*) toirt f (**from** à), cur m a-mach (**from** à), gearradh m às; 2 (*destruction, killing*) cur m às (*with prep* do); 3 (*expulsion from body etc*) tilgeadh m, tilgeil f, toirt f *invar* air falbh

elision n (*gram*) bàthadh m

elm n leamhan m

elongate v sìn vti, fadaich vti

elope v teich vi (**with** còmhla ri)

elopement n teicheadh m (**with** còmhla ri)

eloquence n fileantachd f *invar*, deas-bhriathrachd f *invar*

eloquent adj fileanta, deas-bhriathrach, deas-labhrach

else adj 1 eile, **something** ~ rud m eile, **somewhere** ~ (ann an) àiteigin m *invar* eile, **who** ~ **was there?** cò eile a bh' ann?, **I don't want anything** ~ chan eil mi ag iarraidh càil m *invar* eile; 2 *in exprs* **anything** ~, **nothing** ~ an còrr m *invar*, **she didn't say anything** ~ cha tuirt i an còrr, **there was nothing** ~ **to it (than that)** cha robh an còrr ann (ach sin)

elucidate v mìnich vt, soilleirich vt

elucidation n mìneachadh m, soilleireachadh m

elude v, *see* **evade** v *below*

elusive adj doirbh a ghlacadh, doirbh a lorg

emaciated adj seang, seargte

e-mail n post-dealain m

emanate v thig (**from** a-mach à), **news emanating from Poland** naidheachdan (a tha) a' tighinn a-mach às a' Phòlainn

emancipate v saor vt, fuasgail vt, (**from** bho/o)

emancipation n 1 (*the action*) saoradh m, fuasgladh m, (**from** bho/o); 2 (*the state*) saorsa f (**from** bho/o)

emasculate v (*castrate*) spoth vt, geàrr vt

embargo n bacadh m, **trade** ~ bacadh-malairt m

embark v 1 (*as vi*) rach vi air bòrd (*with gen*), **we** ~**ed** chaidh sinn air bòrd (a' bhàta/na luinge etc); 2 (*as vt*) cuir vt air bòrd (*with gen*); 3 *in expr* ~ **on/upon** (*begin, undertake*), tòisich vi air, rach vi an sàs m ann an, gabh vt os làimh (*dat of* làmh f), **we** ~**ed on a new project** thòisich sinn air pròiseact ùr, chaidh sinn an sàs ann am pròiseact ùr

embarrass v 1 (*cause to feel shame*) nàraich vt, tàmailtich vt, maslaich vt; 2 (*make uneasy*) cuir vt troimh-a-chèile, buair vt

embarrassed adj & past part 1 (*through shame*) nàrach; 2 (*through uneasiness*) troimh-a-chèile, air (a etc) b(h)uaireadh; 3 (*through shyness*) diùid, nàrach, air a (etc) nàrachadh

embarrassment n 1 (*through shame*) nàire f *invar*, tàmailt f, masladh m; 2 (*through uneasiness*) buaireas m; 3 (*through shyness*) diùide f *invar*, nàire f *invar*

embassy n 1 (*abstr*) tosgaireachd f; 2 (*the premises & institution*) ambasaid f

embellish v maisich vt, sgeadaich vt, snuadhaich vt

embellishment n maiseachadh m, sgeadachadh m, snuadhachadh m

ember n èibhleag f

embitter v searbhaich vt

embittered adj & past part searbhta

emblem n suaicheantas m

embrace v 1 teannaich vt, **embracing each other** a' teannachadh a chèile, *also* an gàirdeanan a chèile, **she** ~**d him** theannaich i (ri a broilleach m/ri a h-uchd m) e; 2 (*include*) gabh vt a-steach, **his work** ~**s that of X and Y** tha/bidh an obair aige a gabhail a-steach obair X agus Y; 3 (*adopt enthusiastically etc*) gabh vi (*with prep* ri) **we** ~**d communism** ghabh sinn ri co-mhaoineas m

embroidery n 1 (*the activity*) grèis f; 2 (*the product*) obair-ghrèis(e) f

embryo n tùs-ghinean mf

emerald n smàrag f

emerge v 1 (*from building etc*) thig vi a-mach (**from** à); 2 (*of facts etc: become known, apparent*) thig vi am follais f *invar*, **it** ~**d this week that she was married** thàinig e am follais air an t-seachdain sa gun robh i pòsta; 3 (*come to the fore*) thig vi irreg an uachdar m, **he** ~**d as leader of the party** thàinig e an uachdar mar cheannard a' phàrtaidh

emergency *n* **1** (*situation*) cruaidh-chàs *m*; **2** (*more abstr*) èiginn *f invar*, (*often used adjectivally*) **an ~ exit** doras-èiginn *m*

emigrant *n* eilthireach *m*

emigrate *v* fàg a (*etc*) d(h)ùthaich *f* fhèin, rach *vi irreg* a null thairis, **he ~d** dh'fhàg e a dhùthaich fhèin

emigration *n* às-imrich *f*

émigré *n* eilthireach *m*

eminence *n* **1** (*rank, honour etc*) mòr-inbhe *f*; **2** (*topog*) àird(e) *f*

eminent *adj* **1** (*most important etc*) prìomh (*precedes the noun, which it lenites where possible*), **the ~ people of the town** prìomh dhaoine a' bhaile; **2** (*distinguished, famous etc*) inbheil, **an ~ surgeon** làmh-lèigh inbheil

emit *v* cuir *vt* (a-mach), leig *vt* a-mach, **~ fumes/ vapour** cuir a-mach deatach *f*

emotion *n* faireachdainn *f*, (*more extreme or troubled*) buaireas *m*

emotional *adj* **1** (*of person: affected by emotion*) gluaiste, (*more extreme or troubled*) buairte; **2** (*event etc: involving or arousing emotion*) gluasadach, drùidhteach, (*more extreme or troubling*) buaireasach; **3** *in expr* **~ arousal** gluasad *m*

emotive *adj* gluasadach, drùidhteach, (*more extreme or troubling*) buaireasach

empathy *n* co-fhaireachdainn *f*

emperor *n* ìompaire *m*

emphasis *n* cudthrom *m*, **put/lay great ~ on X** cuir/leig cudthrom mòr air X

emphasise *v* cuir/leig cudthrom *m* (*with prep* air), **~ how good her qualifications are** leig cudthrom air cho math agus a tha an t-uidheamachadh aice

emphatic *adj* deimhinn(e), deimhinnte, cinnteach, làidir, **an ~ denial** àicheadh *m* deimhinn/deimhinnte

empire *n* ìompaireachd *f*

employ *v* **1** (*use*) cleachd *vt*, (*less usu: esp* ~ *tools, weapons*) iomair *vt*; **2** (~ *workers etc*) fastaich, *also* fastaidh, *vt*, thoir obair *f* (*with prep* do)

employee *n* neach-obrach *m* (*pl* luchd-obrach *m sing coll*), obraiche *m*, cosnaiche *m*

employer *n* fastaidhear *m*, fastaiche *m*

employment *n* **1** (*abstr*) cosnadh *m*, obair *f*, **the ~ Minister** Ministear *m* a' Chosnaidh; **2** (*the act of employing people*) fastadh *m*

empower *v* thoir ùghdarras *m*, thoir cumhachd *mf*, (*with prep* do)

empowered *adj & past part* ùghdarraichte

empress *n* ban-ìompaire *f*

emptiness *n* fal(a)mhachd *f invar*

empty *adj* **1** falamh; **2** (*of place: deserted*) falamh, (*stronger*) fàs, **the glens are ~** tha na gleanntan falamh/fàs; **3** (*without substance*) dìomhain, **~ words** faclan dìomhain

empty *v* **1** falmhaich *vt*; **2** (*esp liquids from container etc*) tràigh & traogh *vt*, taom *vt*; **3** (~ *of population*) fàsaich *vt*

empty-headed *adj* faoin

enable *v* cuir *vt* na (*etc*) c(h)omas *m*, thoir comas/cothrom *m* (*with prep* do), **that ~d us to pay the bill** chuir sin nar comas/thug sin cothrom dhuinn an cunntas a phàigheadh

enamel *n* cruan *m*

enchant *v* cuir *vt* fo gheasaibh (*obs dat pl of* geas *f*)

enchanted *adj & past part* **1** (*lit*) seunta; **2** (*lit & fig*) fo gheasaibh (*obs dat pl of* geas *f*), (*by* aig), **he was ~ by the girl** bha e fo gheasaibh aig an nighean

enchantment *n* **1** (*abstr*) geasachd *f invar*; **2** (*con: a spell etc*) geas *f*

encircle *v* cuartaich *vt*

enclose *v* **1** cuartaich *vt*, iadh & iath *vt*; **2** (*esp in corres, packets etc*) cuir *vt* an cois (*dat of* cas *f*) (*with gen*), cuir *vt* an lùib (*dat of* lùb *f*) (*with gen*), **~ something in a letter** cuir rudeigin an cois litreach *f gen*

enclosed *adj & past part* **1** cuartaichte; **2** (*corres etc*) an cois (*dat of* cas *f*) (*with gen*), an lùib (*dat of* lùb *f*) (*with gen*), **~ with this letter** an cois na litreach seo

enclosure *n* **1** (*the action*) cuartachadh *m*, iathadh *m*; **2** (*con: an enclosed piece of ground etc*) lann *f*, (*esp for livestock*) crò *m*; **3** *in expr* (*corres*) **~s with this letter** (pàipearan *etc*) an cois (*dat of* cas *f*) na litreach seo

encompass *v* **1** (*encircle*) cuairtich *vt*; **2** (*embrace, contain*) gabh *vt* a-steach

encourage *v* **1** (*raise spirits etc*) misnich *vt*; **2** (*urge*) cuir impidh *m* (*with prep* air), brosnaich *vt*, coitich *vt*, **they ~d me to give away all my money** chuir iad impidh orm mo chuid airgid air fad a thoirt seachad

encouragement *n* **1** (*raising of spirits etc*) misneachadh *m*; **2** (*urging*) brosnachadh *m*, coiteachadh *m*

encouraging *adj* misneachail, brosnachail

encumber *v* uallaich *vt*

encumbrance *n* uallach *m*, eallach *m*

end *n* **1** (*the phys ~ of something*) ceann *m*, **the ~ of the bridge** ceann na drochaid(e), **the ~ of my tether** ceann mo theadhrach (*gen of* teadhair *f*); **2** (*more abstr, & esp of time*) deireadh *m*, crìoch *f*, **the ~ of the world** crìoch na cruinne,

come to an ~ thig *vi* gu crìch (*dat*), **at the ~ of my days/life** aig deireadh/crìch mo là, **the ~ of the month** deireadh a' mhìosa, **at the ~ of the day, in the ~** aig deireadh an là, aig a' cheann thall; **3** *in expr* **on ~** (*ie in succession*), an ceann a chèile, an sreath *mf* a chèile, **three days on ~** trì làithean an ceann a chèile

end *v* **1** (*complete, bring to an ~*) cuir crìoch *f* (*with prep* air), thoir *vt* gu crìch (*dat of* crìoch *f*), crìochnaich *vt*; **2** (*esp meeting*) dùin *vti*

endanger *v* cuir *vt* an cunnart *m*

endangered *adj & past part* an cunnart *m*, **an ~ species** gnè *f invar*/seòrsa *m* an cunnart

endearments *npl* faclan *mpl* gaoil, briathran *mpl* gaoil (*gen of* gaol *m*)

endeavour *n* iomairt *f*, oidhirp *f*

endeavour *v* feuch *vi* (**to** ri), dèan iomairt *f*, dèan oidhirp *f* (**to** gus *or* air)

ending *n* (*of meeting, work of art etc*) co-dhùnadh *m*, crìoch *f*, deireadh *m*

endless *adj* **1** (*continual*) gun sgur *m*, **~ criticism** càineadh gun sgur; **2** (*eternal*) sìorraidh, bith-bhuan

endorse *v* **1** (*cheque etc*) cuir ainm *m* (*with prep* ri); **2** (*support*) cuir aonta *m* (*with prep* ri)

endurance *n* cruas *m*, cruadal *m*, fulang *m*, fulangas *m*

endure *v* **1** fuiling *vti*, **they had to ~ cold and hunger** b' fheudar dhaibh fuachd is acras fhulang; **2** (*continue, last, persist*) lean *vi*

enduring *adj* **1** (*persisting*) leantainneach; **2** (*eternal*) maireannach, buan, bith-bhuan

enemy *n* nàmhaid *m*

energetic *adj* lùthmhor, brìoghmhor, sgairteil

energy *n* **1** lùth *m*, **~ conservation** caomhnadh lùtha *m*, **~ source** bun-lùtha *m*; **2** (*~ of individuals*) lùth(s) *m*, brìgh *f invar*, spionnadh *m*, sgairt *f*

enfeeble *v* lagaich *vti*, fannaich *vi*

enforce *v* cuir *vt* an gnìomh *m*, **~ the law** cuir an lagh *m* an gnìomh

engage *v* dèan *vt*, bi *vi irreg* an sàs *m* (*with prep* ann an), **~ in trade/commerce** dèan malairt *f*, *also* malairtich *vi*, **~ in politics** bi an sàs ann am poilitigs

engaged *adj & past part*, **1** (*betrothed*) **they got ~ yesterday** thug iad gealladh-pòsaidh *m* (dha chèile) an-dè; **2** (*of phone, salesperson etc*) trang, **he's ~ just now** tha e trang an-dràsta, *also* chan eil e saor an-dràsta

engagement *n* **1** (*betrothal*) gealladh-pòsaidh *m*, **~ ring** fàinne-gealladh-pòsaidh *mf*; **2** (*appointment etc*) coinneamh *f*, **I have a prior ~** tha coinneamh agam mu thràth

engine *n* einnsean *m*, **a car ~** einnsean càir

engineer *n* einnseanair *m*, innleadair *m*, **electrical ~** innleadair-dealain, **civil ~** innleadair-thogalach

engineer *v* innlich *vt*

engineering *n* einnseanaireachd *f invar*, innleadaireachd *f invar*

English *adj* Sasannach

English *n* **1** (*lang*) Beurla *f*, *often used with art*, a' Bheurla, *as adj* **an ~ word** facal Beurla *m*; **2** (*people*) **the ~** na Sasannaich *mpl*

engrave *v* gràbhail *vt*

engraver gràbhalaiche *m*

engraving *n* gràbhaladh *m*, gràbhalachd *f invar*

enhance *v* **1** (*increase, augment*) meudaich *vt*; **2** (*improve*) leasaich *vt*; **3** (*~ appearance*) sgeadaich *vt*

enhancement *n* **1** (*increase*) meudachadh *m*, *in expr* **~ of salary** àrdachadh pàighidh *m*, àrdachadh tuarastail *m*; **2** (*improvement*) leasachadh *m*; **3** (*~ of appearance*) sgeadachadh *m*

enigma *n* tòimhseachan *m*

enjoy *v* **1** gabh tlachd *f invar* (*with prep* ann an), (*less usu*) meal *vt*; **2** (*most frequently expressed using the vi* còrd, *with prep* ri) **how are you ~ing that?** ciamar a tha sin a' còrdadh ribh?, **I didn't ~ the music at all** cha do chòrd an ceòl rium idir

enjoyable *adj* **1** tlachdmhor; **2** a chòrdas (*with prep* ri), **~ music, music I find ~** ceòl a chòrdas rium

enjoyment *n* tlachd *f invar*, toil-inntinn *f*, toileachas *m*

enlarge *v* **1** (*as vt*) meudaich *vt*, leudaich *vt*; **2** (*as vi*) rach *vi irreg* am meud *m invar*, leudaich *vi*

enlarged *adj* meudaichte, leudaichte

enlargement *n* meudachadh *m*, leudachadh *m*

enlighten *v* soilleirich *vt*

enlightened *adj & past part* (*aware, broad-minded etc*) tuigseach, toinisgeil, saor-inntinneach

enlightenment *n* soilleireachadh *m*, soillseachadh *m*, (*hist*) **the Enlightenment** An Soilleireachadh, An Soillseachadh, **the Age of ~** Linn an t-Soilleireachaidh/an t-Soillseachaidh *mf*

enlist *v* (*esp in armed forces*) liostaig *vi*, gabh *vi* san arm *m* (*etc*)

enliven *v* beothaich *vt*, brosnaich *vt*, brod *vt*

enmity *n* nàimhdeas *m*

ennoble *v* uaislich *vt*

enormous *adj* ro-mhòr, (*more fam*) uabhasach mòr, eagalach mòr

enough n 1 gu leòr adv, leòr f invar, **we've ~ food** tha biadh gu leòr againn, tha gu leòr de bhiadh againn, tha gu leòr bìdh (gen of biadh m) againn, (more trad) tha ar leòr de bhiadh againn, **have you got ~?** a bheil gu leòr agad?, **I got (more than) ~ of it** fhuair mi mo leòr dheth, **right ~!** ceart gu leòr!; **2** using foghain vi, **will that be ~?** am foghain sin?, (to noisy children etc) **that's ~!** fòghnaidh (siud)!, (saying/idiom) **~ is ~, ~ is as good as a feast** fòghnaidh na dh'fhòghnas; **3** (idiom) **I've got more than ~** tha tuilleadh 's a' chòir agam

enquire v faighnich vi (**of** de or do)

enquiry n **1** ceist f; **2** (investigation) rannsachadh m, faighneachd f

enrage v cuir an fhearg (with prep air), feargaich vt, **he ~d his father** chuir e an fhearg air athair

enraged adj & past part air bhoile f invar, air bhàinidh f invar, air chuthach m

enrich v **1** beartaich & beairtich vi, saidhbhrich vt; **2** (~ soil) mathaich vt

enrol (at college etc) clàraich vti

enrolment n clàrachadh m

en route air an t-slighe f, **en ~ for the village** air slighe a' bhaile, **en ~!** togamaid oirnn!

enslave v tràillich vt

enslavement n **1** (abstr) tràilleachd f invar; **2** (act of enslaving) tràilleachadh m

ensnare v rib vt, glac vt (ann an ribe f)

entangle v amail vt, aimhreitich vt, in expr **~ oneself, get ~d** rach an sàs m (**in** ann)

enter v **1** rach/thig a-steach (with prep do), inntrig vi; **2** (on keyboard, calculator etc) put vt ann, cuir vti a-steach

enterprise n (abstr & con) iomairt f, **Highlands and Islands Enterprise** Iomairt na Gaidhealtachd is nan Eilean, **~ zone** ceàrn iomairt f

enterprising adj iomairteach, ionnsaigheach, gnìomhach

entertainment n **1** dibhearsain m; **2** (hospitality) fèisteas m

enthusiasm n **1** (in general) dealas m; **2** (about a particular thing etc) dèidhealachd f invar (**about** air)

enthusiastic adj **1** (in general) dealasach; **2** (about a particular thing etc) dèidheil (**about** air)

entice v meall vt, tàlaidh vt, breug vt

enticement n mealladh m, tàladh m

enticing adj meallach, tàlaidheach

entire adj **1** (not divided, fragmented etc) iomlan, slàn, **one was broken but the other was ~** bha an dàrna fear briste ach bha am fear eile iomlan/slàn; **2** (in its entirety) gu lèir, air fad, **the ~ army** an t-arm gu lèir, **an ~ month** mìos gu lèir, mìos air fad

entirely adv gu tur, gu buileach, gu h-iomlan, uile-gu-lèir, **the two things are ~ different** tha an dà rud gu tur/gu buileach eadar-dhealaichte, **~ useless** gun fheum uile-gu-lèir

entitled adj & past part airidh (**to** air), **she is ~ to it** tha i airidh air, also tha còir f aice air

entitlement n **1** (abstr) dlighe f invar, dleas m, còir f, airidheachd f invar; **2** (con: amount, allowance etc one is entitled to) cuibhreann mf

entrails n **1** mionach m, innidh f invar; **2** (usu of animals) greallach f

entrance n **1** (abstr) teachd-a-steach m invar, inntrigeadh m; **2** (con: way in) rathad inntrigidh (gen of inntrigeadh used adjectivally) m, slighe inntrigidh f, (by a door) doras inntrigidh m; **3** (admission to ed establishment etc) inntrigeadh m, **~ exam/test** deuchainn inntrigidh f

entrant n **1** (in competition) farpaiseach m; **2** (in exam) deuchainniche m

entreat v guidh vi, iarr vi gu dian, cuir impidh m, (all with prep air), **I'm ~ing you to stay!** tha mi a' guidhe ort fuireach!

entreaty n guidhe mf, impidh f

entrepreneur n neach-iomairt m (pl luchd-iomairt m sing coll)

entrust v earb vt (**to** ri), cuir cùram m (with gen) (**to** air), leig vt (**to** le), **don't ~ yourself to them** na h-earb thu fhèin riutha, **he ~ed his family to me** 's ann ormsa a chuir e cùram a theaghlaich, **~ the child's upbringing to her** leig leathase togail a' phàiste, leig leathase am pàiste a thogail

entry n **1** (mainly abstr) inntrigeadh m, teachd-a-steach m invar, **right of ~** còir-inntrigidh f; **2** (con) doras/rathad (etc) inntrigidh m (cf **entrance** n **2** above); **3** (Sc: ~ of tenement close) clobhsa m

entwine v suain vt

entwined adj & past part **1** air suaineadh, fillte; **2** (unintentionally, inconveniently) air amaladh

enunciate v cuir vt an cèill (dat of ciall f)

envelop v paisg vt, suain vt

envelope n cèis f, cèis litreach (gen of litir f)

envious adj **1** farmadach, **an ~ man** duine farmadach; **2** in exprs **she became/grew/felt ~ of her sister** (esp at a given moment) ghabh i farmad m ri a piuthar, **she was ~ of her sister** (ie a more permanent feeling) bha farmad aice ri a piuthar

environment n àrainneachd f invar

envoy *n* tosgaire *m*

envy *n* farmad *m*, (*less usu*) tnù(th) *m*

envy *v* gabh farmad *m* (*with prep* ri), (*more permanent feeling*) **he envied his sister** bha farmad aige ri a phiuthar

ephemeral *adj* diombuan, siùbhlach

epicentre *n* teis-meadhan *m*

epilogue *n* dùnadh *m*, faclan-dùnaidh *mpl*

episcopal *adj* easbaigeach

Episcopalian *nm* & *adj* Easbaigeach

episode *n* (*of drama series etc*) earrann *f*

epitaph *n* marbhrann *m*

equal *adj* co-ionann & co-ionnan (**to, with** ri), ~ **pay** pàigheadh co-ionann, **the scores were** ~ bha na sgòraichean *mpl* co-ionann

equal *n* 1 coimeas *m*, mac-samhail *m*, seis(e) *m*, **I never saw his** ~ chan fhaca mi a choimeas/a mhac-samhail a-riamh, **she met her** ~ fhuair i a seis; **2** *in expr* **she's not the** ~ **of** (**her mother** *etc*) chan fhiù i (a màthair *etc*)

equal *v* ionann (*with v* is), co-ionann (*with v* bi), **X** ~**s Y** is ionann X agus Y, **2 times 2** ~**s 4** tha 2 uiread 2 co-ionann ri 4, *also* tha 2 uiread 2 a' dèanamh 4

equality *n* co-ionannachd *f invar*, ~ **of opportunity** co-ionannachd cothruim *m gen*

equanimity *n* socair inntinn *f*, rèidheachd inntinn *f invar*

equation *n* (*maths*) co-aontar *m*

equator *n*, *used with art*, **the** ~ am meadhan-chearcall *m*

equidistant *adj* co-astarail (**from** bho/o)

equilibrium *n* 1 meidh *f*, cothrom *m*, **in** ~ air mheidh, **put into** ~ cuir *vt* air meidh; **2** (~ *of two objects*) co-chothrom *m*

equip *v* uidheamaich *vt*

equipment uidheam *f*, acainn *f*

equipped *adj* uidheamaichte, acainneach

equitable *adj* cothromach, dìreach, gun chlaonadh *m*

equivalence *n* co-ionannachd *f invar*

equivalent *adj* co-ionann

equivocal *adj* dà-sheaghach

era *n* linn *f*

eradicate *v* cuir às (*with prep* do), spìon *vt* (às a *etc* b(h)un *m*)

erase *v* dubh *vt* às, ~ **it** dubh às e

erect *adj* dìreach, **stand** ~ seas *vi* dìreach

erect *v* tog *vt*

erode *v* criom *vt*, cnàmh *vt*, bleith *vt*

Eriskay *n* Èirisgeigh

erosion *n* criomadh *m*, cnàmhadh *m*, bleith *f*

err *v* 1 rach *vi* air iomrall *m*, rach *vi* air seachran *m*, deàn mearachd *f*; **2** (*esp from spiritual point of view*) peacaich *vi*

errand *n* teachdaireachd *f invar*, **going on an** ~ a' dol air theachdaireachd, *also* a' dol air gnothach *m*

erratic *adj* neo-chunbhalach, caochlaideach, carach, luasganach

erring *adj* seachranach, **an** ~ **spouse** cèile seachranach

erroneous *adj* mearachdach, iomrallach, **an** ~ **rumour** fathann mearachdach

error *n* 1 (*abstr*) iomrall *m*; **2** (*con*) mearachd *f*, **make an** ~ deàn mearachd, rach *vi* air iomrall

erudite *adj* foghlaimte, foghlamaichte, **an** ~ **man** duine foghlaimte, *also* sgoilear *m*, eòlaiche *m*

erudition *n* sgoilearachd *f invar*

erupt *v* 1 brùchd *vt* (**from, out of** à, a-mach à), **the shoots** ~**ed out of the ground** bhrùchd na h-òganan a-mach às an talamh *m*; **2** (*volcano*) spreadh *vi*

eruption *n* 1 brùchdadh *m* (**from, out of** à, a-mach à); **2** (*of volcano*) spreadhadh *m*

escape *n* 1 (*abstr*, & *act of escaping*) teicheadh *m*, tàrradh & tàireadh *m* às; **2** (*means of* ~) dol-às *m invar*, **there was no** ~ **for us now** cha robh dol-às againn a-nis, ~ **route** slighe *f* dol-às, rathad *m* dol-às

escape *v* teich *vi*, tàrr & tàir *vi* às, **the soldiers** ~**d** theich na saighdearan *mpl*, thàir na saighdearan às

escort *n* (*guard etc*) coimheadach *m*, freiceadan *m sing* & *coll*, faire *f coll*

escort *v* 1 (*accompany*) rach *vi* còmhla (*with prep* ri), **he** ~**ed her back** chaidh e air ais còmhla rithe; **2** (~ *under supervision*) thoir *vt irreg* (**to** gu), **the police** ~**ed him to the frontier** thug am poileas chun na crìche e

Eskimo *adj* & *n* Easgiomach *m*

especially *adv* 1 (*as qualifying adj or adv*) air leth, ~ **good/well** air leth math; **2** (*in particular*) gu h-àraidh, gu sònraichte, **I like sport,** ~ **football** is toigh leam spòrs, gu h-àraidh ball-coise

espouse *v* (*fig*) taobh *vi* (*with prep* ri), ~ **a policy** taobh ri poileasaidh

essay *n* aiste *f*

essayist *n* aistear *m*

essence *n* (*lit* & *fig*) brìgh *f invar*, sùgh *m*, **the** ~ **of his philosophy** brìgh na feallsanachd aige

essential *adj* 1 (*indispensable*) riatanach, deatamach, do-sheachainte; **2** (*basic, fundamental*) bunaiteach

establish v 1 (*inaugurate, set up*) stèidhich vt, cuir vt air b(h)onn m, cuir vt air chois (*dat of* cas f); 2 (*of facts etc: find out, demonstrate*) dearbh vt

establishment n 1 (*abstr*) stèidheachadh m, cur m air b(h)onn m, cur air chois (*dat of* cas f); 2 (*con*) ionad m, **the proprietor of this ~** sealbhadair an ionaid seo

estate n 1 (*landed ~*) oighreachd f; 2 (*housing ~*) ionad-thaighean m, sgeama-thaighean m, *in expr* (*of council etc*) **~s office** oifig fearann-thogalach f; 3 (*misc exprs*) **~ agent** ceannaiche-seilbhe m, **industrial ~** raon gnìomhachais m

esteem n meas m, urram m, onair f

esteem v meas vt

esteemed, estimable adj measail, urramach, miadhail

estimate n meas m invar, tuaiream f, tuairmeas m, tuairmse f

estimate v 1 meas vt, thoir tuaiream f (*with prep* air); 2 (*~ value*) cuir luach m invar (*with prep* air)

estuary n beul aibhne (*gen of* abhainn m), inbhir m

eternal adj maireannach, sìorraidh, bith-bhuan, sìor-mhaireannach, **~ life** beatha mhaireannach

eternity n sìorraidheachd f invar

ethereal adj adharail, spioradail, neo-chorporra

ethical adj beusail, (*less trad*) eiticeil

ethics n beus-eòlas m, beusalachd f invar, (*less trad*) eitic f

ethnic adj (*relating to ethnicity*) cinealach

ethnicity n cinealachd f invar

ethos n 1 (*essential feature(s) of something*) brìgh f, susbaint f; 2 (*rationale behind something*) feallsanachd f invar, **the ~ of the course** feallsanachd a' chùrsa

etymology n 1 (*the discipline*) freumh-fhaclachd f invar; 2 (*~ of a particular word, name etc*) freumh m, bun m, tùs m (an fhacail, an ainm *etc*)

eulogy n 1 (*abstr*) moladh m; 2 (*con: verse ~*) dàn-molaidh m, (*prose ~*) aiste-mholaidh f, (*spoken ~*) òraid-mholaidh f

euro n euro mf (pl eurothan), **the ~ zone** ceàrn m an euro

Europe n An Roinn Eòrpa f invar, (*less usu*) Eòrpa f invar

European adj & n Eòrpach, na Roinn Eòrpa, **the European Commission** an Coimisean Eòrpach, *also* Coimisean na Roinn Eòrpa

evacuate v falmhaich vt, (*esp of people*) fàsaich vt

evacuation n falmhachadh m, (*esp of people*) fàsachadh m

evacuee n fògrach m, neach-fuadain m (pl luchd-fuadain m sing coll)

evade v, *also* **elude** v, siolp vi air falbh, èalaidh vi às, èalaidh vi air falbh, (*all with prep* air), seachain vt, **he managed to ~ me** chaidh aige air èaladh/siolpadh air falbh orm, chaidh aige air mo sheachnadh

evaluate v 1 (*monetary value*) luachaich vt, cuir luach m invar (*with prep* air); 2 (*more generally*) meas vt

evaluation n 1 (*of monetary value*) luachachadh & luachadh m; 2 (*more generally*) measadh m

evaporate v deataich vi

evaporation n deatachadh m

evasive adj (*persons, answers to questions etc*) mì-fhosgarra, fiar

eve n (*of specific days*) oidhche f, **New Year's Eve** Oidhche Challainn f

even adj 1 (*of ground, surface etc*) còmhnard, rèidh; 2 (*of numbers: not odd*) cothrom, **~ number** àireamh chothrom; 3 (*steady, regular*) cunbhalach, cothromach, **at an ~ pace** air ceum cunbhalach; 4 (*equal*) co-ionann, **the scores were ~** bha na sgòraichean mpl co-ionann

even adv 1 eadhon, fiù is/agus, uiread is/agus **I didn't ~ have two pounds** cha robh eadhon dà nota agam, cha robh fiù is/uiread is dà nota agam, **without ~ so much as a piece of bread** gun uiread agus pìos arain, **they didn't ~ look at us** cha do rinn iad fiù agus sùil a thoirt oirnn; 2 (*idiom*) **~ Calum grew afraid** thàinig an t-eagal air Calum fhèin

even-handed adj cothromach, **he is ~** tha e cothromach, *also* chan eil e taobhach

evening n feasgar m, **good ~!** feasgar math!, **Friday evening** feasgar Dihaoine, **in/during/ in the course of the ~** air an fheasgar, (*adverbial use*) **we'll be in in the ~** bidh sinn ann feasgar, **the ~ star** reul f an fheasgair

event n 1 (*occurrence*) tachartas m, tuiteamas m; 2 (*case, circumstance*) *in exprs* **in the ~ of his being guilty** mas e an rud e 's gu bheil e ciontach, **I'm not going in any ~** chan eil mise a' dol ann co-dhiù; 3 (*at sports meeting etc*) co-fharpais f

eventful adj tachartach

eventuality n (*circumstance*) cor m, **don't touch it in any ~** na buin ris air chor sam bith, *also* na buin ris ge b' e dè a thachras

eventually adv aig a' cheann m thall, mu dheireadh thall, luath no mall, **we built the house ~** thog sinn an taigh aig a' cheann thall/ mu dheireadh thall, **we'll manage it ~** thèid againn air luath no mall/aig a' cheann thall

ever *adv* **1** (*with neg v*) gu bràth tuilleadh, **he won't ~ come back** cha till e gu bràth tuilleadh; **2** *in expr* **for ~** gu bràth, gu sìorraidh, a-chaoidh, **Ben Nevis will be there for ~** bidh Beinn Nibheis ann gu bràth/gu sìorraidh, **I'll love you for ~** bidh gaol agam ort a-chaoidh, **for ~ and ~** gu sìorraidh bràth; **3** *in expr* **you'll hardly ~ see the likes of him** is gann a chì thu a leithid

evergreen *adj* sìor-uaine, (*of trees*) neo-sheargach

everlasting *adj* maireannach, **~ life** beatha mhaireannach

every *adj* a h-uile, gach, **~ day** a h-uile là *m*, **~ single day** gach aon là, **each and ~ day** gach uile là, **~ one of them** a h-uile fear aca, (*corres etc*) **with ~ good wish** leis gach deagh dhùrachd

everybody, **everyone** *pron* a h-uile duine *m*, (*esp ~ concerned*) na h-uile *pron*, **~ will die in the end** gheibh a h-uile duine bàs aig a' cheann thall, **~ lost their money** chaill a h-uile duine/ na h-uile an cuid airgid

everyday *adj* làitheil

everyone *pron, see* **everybody** *above*

everything *n* a h-uile càil *m invar*, a h-uile sìon *m*, gach (aon) rud *m*, gach (aon) nì *m*

evict *v* cuir *vt* a-mach (**from** à)

evidence *n* **1** (*testimony given*) fianais *f*, teisteanas *m*, **give ~** thoir fianais; **2** (*proof*) dearbhadh *m* (**of** air), **~ of his guilt** dearbhadh air a chionta

evident *adj* follaiseach, soilleir, **it's ~ that he's not guilty** tha e follaiseach nach eil e ciontach

evidentness *n* follais *f invar*

evil *adj* **1** olc; **2** *in exprs* **the ~ one** an Donas *m*, **the ~ eye** an droch-shùil *f*

evil *n* donas *m*, (*stronger*) olc *m*, **good and ~** am math is an t-olc

evil-natured, **evil-tempered** *adj* droch-nàdarach

evolution *n* (*of life forms etc*) meanbh-chinneas *m*, mùthadh *m*

evolve *v* **1** (*life forms etc*) mùth *vi*; **2** (*develop*) atharraich *vi* (mean air mhean), **his philosophy ~d over the years** dh'atharraich an fheallsanachd aige mean air mhean rè nam bliadhnachan

ewe *n* caora *f*, **in lamb ~** caora-uain, **~ with a lamb at foot** caora is uan *m* na cois (*dat of* cas *f*), **~ with twin lambs** caora-càraid

exact *adj* **1** (*accurate*) ceart, (*sums, figures etc*) cruinn, grinn; **2** (*of person, work etc*) pongail, mionaideach; **3** *in exprs* **in the ~ centre of**

(**the field** *etc*) ann an ceart-mheadhan *m* (an achaidh *etc*), **the ~ thing I needed** an dearbh rud *m* a bha dhìth orm

exactly *adv* dìreach, **~ as I would wish** dìreach mar a thograinn, (*expr agreement*) **~!** dìreach (sin)!

exalt *v* àrdaich *vt*, cuir *vt* an àirde *f invar*

examination *n* **1** (*in school etc*) deuchainn *f*, **entrance ~** deuchainn inntrigidh (*gen of* inntrigeadh *m*); **2** (*medical etc*) sgrùdadh *m*, **dental ~** sgrùdadh fhiaclan

examine *v* **1** (*in school etc*) ceasnaich *vt*, thoir deuchainnean *fpl* (*with prep* do); **2** (*medical etc*) sgrùd *vt*, dèan sgrùdadh *m* (*with prep* air)

examinee *n* deuchainniche *m*

examiner *n* **1** sgrùdaiche *m*; **2** (*school etc ~*) neach-ceasnachaidh *m* (*pl* luchd-ceasnachaidh *m sing coll*)

example *n* eisimpleir *m*, **for ~** mar eisimpleir (*abbrev* m.e.)

exasperate *v* leamhaich *vt*

exasperated *adj & past part* frionasach, diombach, sàraichte

exasperating *adj* frionasach, leamh

exceed *v* rach *vi irreg* thairis, rach seachad, (*with prep* air), **you ~ed my instructions** chaidh sibh thairis/seachad air na h-òrduighean a thug mi dhuibh

exceedingly *adv* anabarrach, ro- *prefix*, uabhasach (fhèin), cianail fhèin, **~ good** anabarrach math, (*more trad*) ro-mhath, (*more fam*) uabhasach (fhèin) math, **~ slow** cianail fhèin slaodach

excellence *n* feabhas *m*, (*more trad or formal*) òirdheirceas *m*

excellent *adj* air leth, air leth math, math dha-rìribh, barrail, (*more trad or formal*) òirdheirc, **an ~ bottle of wine** botal fìona air leth, **that was ~** bha sin air leth math/math dha-rìribh

exception *n*, *in expr* **with the ~ of** ach a-mhàin, **everyone returned home, with the ~ of Iain** thill a h-uile duine dhachaigh, ach a-mhàin Iain

exceptional *adj* air leth, às a' chumantas *m*, **an ~ man** duine air leth

excess *n*, cus *m*, tuilleadh 's a chòir, **an ~ of food/noise** cus bìdh/fuaim, **drink to ~** òl cus, **there was an ~ of it** bha tuilleadh 's a' chòir dheth ann

excessive *adj* **1** cus *m*, **~ noise/rain** cus fuaim/ uisge *gen*; **2** (*occas: esp with abstr nouns of feeling, psychological states etc*) ro- *prefix* (*lenites following cons where possible*), *eg* **~ anxiety** ro-chùram

excessively *adv* ro (*lenites following cons where possible*), ~ **permissive** ro cheadachail

exchange *n* 1 (*general*) malairt *f*, (*more trad*) iomlaid *f*; 2 (*currency*) iomlaid *f*, **the** ~ **rate** luach *m* na h-iomlaid, *also* co-luach *m* an airgid

Exchequer, the *n* Roinn *f* an Ionmhais

excite 1 (*esp emotions*) tog *vt*; 2 (*people*) brod *vt*, gluais *vt*, spreòd *vt*, cuir *vt* air bhioran *m*; 3 (*sexually*) brod *vt*

excited *adj & past part* air bhioran *m*, togarrach, meanmnach, (*more extreme*) am boile *f invar*, air bhoile

excitement *n* togarrachd *f invar*, meanmnachd *f invar*, (*more extreme*) boile *f invar*

exclamation *n* 1 clisgeadh *m*; 2 (*gram*) clisgear *m*, *in expr* ~ **mark** clisg-phuing *f*

exclude *v* cùm *vt* (**from** bho/o), dùin *vt* a-mach (**from** à), ~ **her** cùm a-mach i, ~ **him from the room** cùm bhon rùm e, dùin a-mach às an rùm e

exclusion *n* dùnadh *m* a-mach, às-dhùnadh *m*

excrement *n* cac *m*

excursion *n* cuairt *f*, sgrìob *f*, (**to** do), **an** ~ **to the islands** cuairt/sgrìob do na h-eileanan

excuse *n* leisgeul *m*

excuse *v* 1 gabh leisgeul *m* (*with prep* do), math *vt* (*with prep* do), **we** ~**d her** ghabh sinn a leisgeul; 2 (*excl*) ~ **me!** gabh(aibh) mo leisgeul!; 3 (*allow to leave*) thoir cead falbh *m invar* (*with prep* do), (*allow to be absent*) thoir cead *followed by* gun & *infin of the verb*, **the chairman** ~**d him from the meeting** thug an cathraiche cead dha gun a bhith aig a' choinneimh

execute *v* 1 (*a task, process etc*) thoir *vt* gu buil *f*, gnìomhaich *vt*; 2 (*kill*) cuir *vt* gu bàs *m*

executive *adj* gnìomhach

executive *n* 1 gnìomhaiche *m*; 2 (*coll*) **the** ~ an roinn-gnìomha *f*

exempt *adj* saor (**from** bho/o), neo-bhuailteach (*with prep* do), ~ **from taxes** saor o chìsean *fpl*, neo-bhuailteach do chìsean

exempt *v* saor *vt* (**from** bho/o)

exemption *n* saoradh *m* (**from** bho/o)

exercise *n* (*phys, ed etc*) eacarsaich *f*

exercise *v* 1 (*make use of*) cleachd *vt*, ~ **power** cleachd cumhachd; 2 (*put into effect*) cuir *vt* an gnìomh *m*, ~ **rights** cuir an gnìomh còraichean; 3 (*take exercise*) bi *vi irreg* ag eacarsaich

exhaust *n* (*of engine*) tràghadh & traoghadh *m*, ~ **pipe** pìob-thraoghaidh *f*

exhaust *v* 1 (*person*) claoidh *vt*; 2 (*use up resources etc*) caith *vt*

exhausted *adj & past part* 1 (*of person*) claoidhte; 2 (*of resources etc*) caithte, cosgte

exhaustion *n* 1 (*of people*) claoidheachd *f invar*; 2 (*of resources etc*) (*abstr*) caithteachd *f invar*, (*the action*) caitheamh *m*

exhibit *v* 1 seall *vt*, ~**ing signs of weariness** a' sealltainn chomharraidhean sgìths; 2 (~ *art etc*) taisbean & taisbein *vt*

exhibition *n* 1 (*of art, goods, techniques etc*) taisbeanadh *m*, ~ **hall** taisbean-lann *f*, talla-taisbeanaidh *f*; 2 (*bad behaviour*) *in expr* **what an** ~**!** abair dol-a-mach!

exhilarate *v* cuir aoibhneas *m*/sunnd *m* (*with prep* air), sunndaich *vt*

exhort *v* brosnaich *vt*, earalaich *vt*, (**to** gu)

exhortation *n* brosnachadh *m*, earail *f*, earalachadh *m*, (**to** gu)

exile *n* 1 (*abstr*) eilthireachd *f invar*; 2 (*the person exiled*) neach-fuadain *m* (*pl* luchd-fuadain *m sing coll*), fòg(ar)rach *m*, eilthireach *m*

exile *v* fuadaich *vt*, fògair *vt*, **they were** ~**d** chaidh am fuadach(adh), chaidh am fògradh

exist *v* 1 bi *vi irreg* ann, **fairies don't** ~ chan eil sìthichean ann; 2 (*live*) mair *vi* beò, bi *vi irreg* beò, **I couldn't** ~ **without music** cha mhairinn beò/cha b' urrainn dhomh a bhith beò gun cheòl

existence *n* 1 (*abstr*) bith *f*, **bring into** ~ thoir *vt* am bith, **pass out of** ~ rach *vi* à bith; 2 (*con: life*) beatha *f*, **a wretched** ~ beatha thruagh

exit *n* 1 doras dol a-mach *m*, slighe dol a-mach *f*; 2 *in expr* (*pol*) ~ **poll** cunntas sgaoilidh (*gen of* sgaoileadh *m*, *used adjectivally*)

exonerate *v* saor *vt* o choire *f*

exotic *adj* allmharach, coigreach

expand *v* 1 leudaich *vti*, meudaich *vti*; 2 (*swell*) sèid *vi*, at *vi*

expanded *adj* 1 leudaichte, meudaichte; 2 (*swollen*) sèidte, air sèid(eadh)

expansion *n* 1 leudachadh *m*, meudachadh *m*; 2 (*by swelling*) sèideadh *m*

expect *v* 1 (*anticipate*) coimhead *vi* (*with prep* ri), **we're** ~**ing storms** tha sinn a' coimhead ri stoirmean; 2 (~ *a visit*) **I** ~/**am** ~**ing her** tha dùil/sùil/fiughair (*all f*) agam rithe; 3 (*suppose*) bi *vi irreg* an dùil *f* (*with prep* aig & *conj* gu), bi *vi irreg* an dùil (*with conj* gu), **I** ~ **he'll come** tha dùil agam gun tig e, **I don't** ~ **he'll manage it** chan eil mi an dùil gun tèid aige air; 4 (*with double neg constr*) *eg*, **I'll be drunk tonight! I** ~ **you will!** bidh mi air an daoraich a-nochd! cha chreid mi nach bi!

expectation *n* dùil *f*, fiughair *f*

expedient *adj* iomchaidh, freagarrach

expedient *n* innleachd *f*, seòl *m*

expedition *n* turas *m*

expel *v* fògair *vt*, cuir *vt* a-mach, (**from** à), **the people were ~led from the glen** dh'fhògradh an sluagh às a' ghleann

expenditure *n* teachd-a-mach *m invar*, caiteachas *m*

expense *n* cosgais *f*, **travelling ~s** cosgaisean-siubhail *fpl*

expensive *adj* cosgail, daor

experience *v* 1 (*~ sensations, emotions*) mothaich *vt*; 2 (*know, live through*) fiosraich *vt*, (*esp emotions*) bi *vi irreg* fo (*prep*), **we didn't ~ poverty** cha do dh'fhiosraich sinn bochdainn *f*, **like a person experiencing fear/a nightmare** mar neach a bhiodh fo eagal/fo throm-laighe

experience *n* eòlas *m* (**of** air), **~ of the world** eòlas air an t-saoghal

experienced *adj* eòlach, fiosrach, (**in** air), cleachdte (**in** ri)

experiment *n* deuchainn *f*, dearbhadh *m*

expert *adj* 1 (*knowledgeable*) eòlach (**in, on, about** air); 2 (*~ at performing tasks etc*) teòma (**in, at** ann an)

expert *n* 1 (*knowledgeable person*) eòlaiche *m*; 2 (*~ at performing tasks etc*) ealantach *m*

expertise *n* 1 (*knowledge*) eòlas *m*; 2 (*~ in performing tasks etc*) ealantachd *f invar*, teòmachd *f invar*

expiation *n* rèite *f*

expire *v* 1 (*breath out*) analaich *vi*; 2 (*die*) bàsaich *vi*, caochail *vi*

explain *v* mìnich *vt*, soilleirich *vt*

explanation *n* 1 mìneachadh *m*, soilleireachadh *m*; 2 (*reason: idiom*) **what's the ~ for that?** dè as coireach ri sin?

explanatory *adj* mìneachail

explode *v* spreadh *vti*

exploit *n* euchd *m*, cleas *m*, (*fam*) plòidh *f*

exploit *v* 1 dèan feum *m* (*with prep* de), thoir brìgh *f invar* (*with prep* à); 2 (*~ more unfairly*) gabh brath *m*, gabh fàth *m invar*, (*with prep* air)

explore *v* rannsaich *vt*

explorer *n* rannsachair *m* (*dhùthchannan fpl gen*)

explosion *n* spreadhadh *m*

explosive *adj* 1 spreadhaidh *gen of* spreadhadh *m, used adjectivally*, **~ substance** stuth spreadhaidh *m*; 2 (*of persons; short-tempered*) cas

explosive(s) *n(pl)* stuth-spreadhaidh *m*

export *n* 1 (*abstr*) às-mhalairt *f*, **~ market** margadh às-mhalairt *mf*; 2 (*con: products etc ~ed*) às-bhathar *m sing coll*

export *v* às-mhalairtich *vti*, reic *vt* an cèin

exporter *n* às-mhalairtear *m*

expose *v* leig *vt* (*with prep pron* ris), thoir *vt* am follais *f invar*, (*esp ~ body*) rùisg *vt*

exposed *adj* ris, rùisgte, nochdte, **his back was ~** bha a dhruim ris, **~ to the sun** ris a' ghrèin (*dat of* grian *f*)

exposition *n* cunntas *m*, mìneachadh *m*

exposure *n* 1 (*bringing into view, baring*) leigeil *m* ris, toirt *f invar* am follais, (*esp ~ of body*) rùsgadh *m*; 2 (*geographical aspect*) sealladh-aghaidh *m*

express *adj* 1 (*rapid*) luath, *often as prefix in this sense, eg* **~ train** luath-thrèana *f*, **~ service** luath-sheirbheis *f*; 2 (*precise, deliberate*) **I did it with the ~ purpose/intention of annoying you** rinn mi e a dh'aon ghnothach *m*/a dh'aon rùn *m* gus dragh a chur ort

express *n* (*train*) luath-thrèana *f*

express *v* cuir *vt* an cèill (*dat sing of* ciall *f*), **~ your feelings** cuir ur faireachdainnean *fpl* an cèill

expression *n* 1 (*transient facial ~*) fiamh *m*, mèinn *f*, coltas *m*; 2 (*more permanent facial ~*) gnùis *f*; 3 (*lang: idiom, phrase etc*) abairt *f*, dòigh-labhairt *f*; 4 (*abstr: act of expressing feelings etc*) cur *m* an cèill (*dat sing of* ciall *f*)

expressly *adv* a dh'aon ghnothach *m*, a dh'aon rùn *m*, (**to** gus), **I wrote the letter ~ to bring the matter to an end** sgrìobh mi an litir a dh'aon ghnothach/a dh'aon rùn airson a' chùis a thoirt gu ceann

extend *v* 1 (*increase size*) leudaich *vti*; 2 (*hold or stretch out*) sìn (a-mach) *vti*, **~ the hand of friendship to them** sìn làmh a' chàirdeis dhaibh/thuca

extended *adj* 1 (*increased in size*) leudaichte; 2 (*held or stretched out*) sìnte (a-mach)

extension *n* 1 (*increase in size*) leudachadh *m*; 2 (*act of holding or stretching out*) sìneadh *m*

extensive *adj* 1 (*sizeable etc*) farsaing, leathann, mòr; 2 (*opposite of intensive*) sgaoilte

extent *n* 1 (*phys*) farsaingeachd *f invar*; 2 (*more abstr: degree, intensity etc*) meud *m invar*, **the ~ of her anxiety** meud a h-iomagain

exterior *n* (an) taobh a-muigh, **the ~ of the building** taobh a-muigh an togalaich

external *adj* (*phys*) an taoibh (*gen of* taobh *m*) a-muigh, (*also more fig*) **an ~ student** oileanach an taoibh a-muigh

extinct

extinct *adj* (*volcano, species etc*) marbh, à bith
f invar
extinguish smà(i)l *vt* (às), cuir *vt* às, mùch *vt*,
tùch *vt*, ~ **the fire** cuir às/smàil às an teine *m*
extinguisher *n* smàladair *m*, mùchadair *m*
extract *n* earrann *f* (**from** de *or* à)
extract *v* (*pull or take out*) thoir *vt* às, tarraing *vt*
às, **he ~ed the tooth** thug e às an fhiacail
extraordinary *adj* às a' chumantas, air leth
extravagant *adj* caith(t)each
extreme *adj* 1 anabarrach, (*occas: esp with abstr
nouns of feeling, psychological states etc*) ro-
prefix (*lenites following cons where possible*),
~ **anxiety** ro-chùram *m*; 2 (*exceptional*) **an ~
example** eisimpleir *m* air leth
extreme *n* (*eg of climate*) anabarr *m*
extremely *adv* anabarrach, air leth, (*occas: esp
with abstr nouns of feeling, psychological states
etc*) ro- *prefix* (*lenites following cons where*

possible), ~ **good** air leth math, anabarrach
math, math dha-rìribh, gu dearbh fhèin
math, ~ **willing** ro thoileach, ~ **white**
ro-gheal
extremity *n* 1 (*of extended area*) iomall *m*, crìoch
f; 2 (*of a line*) ceann *m*; 3 (*a crisis etc*) èiginn *f*
invar
exuberance *n* suilbhireachd *f invar*
exuberant *adj* suilbhir
eye *n* 1 sùil *f*, ~ **contact** glacadh sùla *m*, **the evil
~** an droch-shùil *f*; 2 *in exprs* ~ **socket** gluc *f*, ~
of a needle crò snàthaid *m*
eyeball *n* clach *f* na sùla
eyebrow *n* mala *f*
eyelash *n* fabhra *m*, rosg *m*
eyelid *n* fabhra *m*
eyesight *n* fradharc & radharc *m*, lèirsinn *f
invar*
eyewitness *n* sùil-fhianais *f*

F

fable *n* uirsgeul *m*, fionnsgeul *m*

façade *n* **1** (*of building etc*) aghaidh *f*; **2** (*outward pretence etc*) sgàil *f*

face *n* **1** (*of person*) aodann *m*, aghaidh *f*, ~ **to** ~ aghaidh ri aghaidh, **she struck me full in the** ~ bhuail i mi an clàr m' aodainn, **I told her the truth to her** ~ dh' innis mi an fhìrinn dhi an clàr a h-aodainn; **2** (*topog:* ~ *of hill etc*) aghaidh *f*, **the** ~ **of the mountain** aghaidh na beinne, **on the** ~ **of the earth** air aghaidh na talmhainn

face *v* **1** (*turn towards*) cuir a (*etc*) aghaidh *f* (*with prep* ri), **I** ~**d the wall** chuir mi m' aghaidh ris a' bhalla; **2** (*be orientated towards*) bi *vi irreg* mu choinneimh (*with gen*), (*less usu*) bi *vi irreg* fa chomhair (*with gen*), **I was facing her** bha mi mu coinneimh, **I was facing the window** bha mi mu choinneimh na h-uinneig(e); **3** *in expr* ~ **up to** seas *vi* (*with prep* ri), ~ **up to problems/enemies** seas ri duilgheadasan/ri nàimhdean

facility *n* **1** goireas *m*, **the club has lots of facilities** tha goireasan gu leòr/tha gu leòr de ghoireasan aig a' chlub; **2** (*natural bent, flair*) alt *m* (**for** air)

facing *adv* mu choinneimh, (*less usu*) fa chomhair, (*with gen*), **I sat down** ~ **the window** shuidh mi sìos mu choinneimh na h-uinneige

facsimile *n* mac-samhail *m*, lethbhreac *m*

fact *n* firinn *f*, rud *m*, **it's a** ~**!** 's e an fhìrinn a th' ann!, **the** ~ **is, I was tired** 's e an rud a th' ann gun robh mi sgìth, *or* is e gun robh mi sgìth, **if it is a** ~ **that he is lazy** mas e (an rud e) 's gu bheil e leisg

factor[1] *n* (*of estate etc*) bàillidh *m*, maor *m*

factor[2] *n* (*aspect, element*) adhbhar *m*, eileamaid *f*, **one of the** ~**s in his decision** fear de dh'adhbharan a cho-dhùnaidh, **the main** ~ **in this situation** a' phrìomh eileamaid san t-suidheachadh seo

faculty *n* comas *m*, ~ **of speech**, comas-bruidhne *m*, comas-cainnte *m*, comas-labhairt *m*

fade *v* crìon *vti*

fail *v* **1** (*as vi: person, business etc*) fàillig *vi*, (*esp business*) rach *vi* fodha, **he** ~**ed** dh'fhàillig e, **his business** ~**ed** dh'fhàillig an gnìomhachas aige, chaidh an gnìomhachas aige fodha; **2** (*as vt*) fàillig *vt*, **he** ~**ed his exams** dh'fhàillig e na deuchainnean *fpl* aige; **3** (~ *in health*) rach *vi* bhuaithe, **she is** ~**ing** tha i a' dol bhuaithe

failing *n* fàilligeadh *m*, fàillinn *f*

failure *n* fàilligeadh *m*

faint *adj* **1** fann, lag, **a** ~ **voice** guth fann, ~ **from/with hunger** lag leis an acras; **2** (*idiom*) **I haven't the** ~**est idea** chan eil càil *m invar* a dh'fhios *m* agam

faint *n* neul *m*, laigse *f*

faint *v* fannaich *vi*, fanntaig *vi*, rach *vi irreg* an laigse *f*, rach *vi irreg* an neul *m*

faint-hearted *adj* meata

fair *adj* **1** (*of hair, complexion*) bàn; **2** (*just etc*) cothromach, reusanta, **a** ~ **man** duine cothromach, **a** ~ **decision** breith chothromach; **3** (*idiom*) **we gave them** ~ **odds** thug sinn cothrom *m* na Fèinne dhaibh; **4** (*archaic: attractive*) bòidheach, maiseach

fair *n* (*market; also rides, amusements etc*) fèill *f*, faidhir *f*, **The Mull Fair** An Fhaidhir Mhuileach

fair-haired *adj* bàn

fairly *adv* **1** (*quite, pretty*) car *m*, caran *m*, (*stronger*) an ìre mhath, **we were** ~ **tired** bha sinn an ìre mhath sgìth/car sgìth; **2** (*in a fair or just manner*) gu cothromach

fairy *n* sìthiche *m*, bean-sìth(e) *f*, **the** ~ **folk, the fairies** na daoine-sìth *mpl*, na sìthichean *mpl*

faith *n* creideamh *m*, **the Islamic** ~ an creideamh Ioslamach

faithful *adj* dìleas

faithfulness *n* dìlseachd *f invar*

faithless *adj* mì-dhìleas

fake *adj* fuadain, brèige (*gen of* fuadan *m*/breug *f* used adjectivally), ~ **diamonds** daoimeanan brèige

fake *n* **1** (*person: dissembler etc*) mealltair *m*,
cealgair(e) *m*; **2** (*fake object*) rud *m* (*etc*) brèige
(*gen of* breug *used adjectivally*)

fall¹ *n* tuiteam *m*

fall² *n* (*autumn*) foghar *m*

fall *v* **1** tuit *vi*, **stumbling and ~ing** a'
tuisleadh 's a' tuiteam, **shares fell today** thuit
sèaraichean an-diugh, **it fell to him to be a
soldier** thuit dha a bhith na shaighdear, (*idiom*)
~ing **to bits** a' dol na (*etc*) c(h)riomagan *fpl*;
2 (*come to rest*) laigh *vi* (**on** air), **her shadow
fell on me** laigh a faileas orm; **3** *in exprs* ~ **into
disuse** rach *vi irreg* à cleachdadh *m*, ~ **out** (*ie
quarrel*) rach *vi irreg* thar a chèile, rach *vi irreg*
a-mach air a chèile, **I caused them to ~ out**
chuir mi thar a chèile iad, **they have ~en out**
tha iad troimh-a-chèile

fallow *adj* bàn, ~ **land/ground** talamh bàn

falls *n* (*waterfall*) eas *m*, leum-uisge *m*, linne *f*,
spùt *m*

false *adj* **1** (*deceitful etc*) meallta, mealltach,
fallsa; **2** (*artificial*) fuadain, brèige (*gen of* breug
f used adjectivally), ~ **teeth** fiaclan-fuadain *fpl*,
~ **beard** feusag bhrèige; **3** (*wrong*) ceàrr, **a ~
conclusion** co-dhùnadh ceàrr

fame *n* cliù *m invar*, (*stronger*) glòir *f invar*, **win
~** coisinn cliù

familiar *adj* **1** (*knowledgeable*) eòlach (**with** air),
~ **with computers** eòlach air coimpiutairean;
2 (*accustomed*) cleachdte (**with** ri), ~ **with her
ways** cleachdte ri a dòigh(ean); **3** (*frequently
met with*) cumanta, (*less usu*) gnàthach, **a ~
situation** suidheachadh cumanta

familiarity *n* eòlas *m* (**with** air), ~ **with
computers** eòlas air coimpiutairean

family *n* **1** (*esp immediate ~*) teaghlach *m*; **2**
(*extended ~*) càirdean (*pl of* caraid *m*), daoine
(*pl of* duine *m*), cuideachd *f*, **all my ~ are in
Stornoway** tha mo chàirdean/mo dhaoine air
fad ann an Steòrnabhagh

famine *n* gort(a) *f*

famous *adj* ainmeil, cliùiteach, iomraiteach

famously *adv*, (*idiom*) **we get on ~** tha sinn gu
math mòr aig a chèile

fan *m* (*for ventilation etc*) gaotharan *m*

fancy *v* bi *v irreg* airson, iarr *vt*, **do you ~ a cup
of tea?** a bheil thu airson/a bheil thu ag iarraidh
cupa tì?

fancy dress *n* culaidh-choimheach *f*

fank *n* (*the structure, also the activity of dipping
etc at the ~*) faing *f*, fang *m*, **there'll be a ~
tomorrow** bidh faing ann a-màireach

far *adj & adv* **1** (*phys distance*) fad(a), **how ~ is
it?** dè cho fada 's a tha e?, ~ **away/off** fad(a) air

falbh, ~ **and wide** fad' is farsaing, *in expr* **as ~
as** (*ie up to*) gu ruige *prep* (*with nom*), **we'll go
as ~ as the ridge** thèid sinn gu ruige an druim;
2 (*time*) *in expr* **so ~** (*ie up to the present*) gu
ruige seo, chun a seo, **we haven't made any
mistakes so ~** cha do rinn sinn mearachdan gu
ruige seo/chun a seo; **3** (*intensifying adv: much*)
fada, ~ **better** fada nas fheàrr, ~ **older** fada nas
sine, (*idiom*) **we had ~ too much** bha tuilleadh
's a' chòir againn

faraway *adj* fad' air falbh, cèin

fare¹ *n* (*on bus etc*) faradh *m*

fare² *n* (*provisions*) biadh *m*, lòn *m*

farewell *n* **1** cead *m*, **we bade them ~** ghabh
sinn ar cead dhiubh; **2** (*as excl*) ~! soraidh *f* leat/
leibh!, beannachd *f* leat/leibh!, slàn leat/leibh!

far-fetched *adj* (a thèid) thar na fìrinn, *in expr* ~
talk/stories/tales rabhd *m*, ràbhart *m*,

farm *n* tuathanas *m*

farmer *n* tuathanach *m*

farming *n* **1** (*the activity*) tuathanachas *m*; **2** (*the
subject, the theory of ~*) àiteachas *m*

fascinated *adj* fo gheasaibh (*obs dat pl of* geas *f*),
I was ~ by it bha mi fo gheasaibh leis, **she had
me ~** bha mi fo gheasaibh aice

fashion *n* fasan *m*, **a new ~** fasan ùr, **in ~** san
fhasan, **out of ~** às an fhasan

fashion *v* cum *vt*, dealbh *vt*

fashionable *adj* fasanta, san fhasan *m*

fast *adj* luath, **a ~ train** luath-thrèana *f*

fast *n* trasg *f*, trasgadh *m*, ~ **day** là-traisg *m*, là-
trasgaidh *m*

fast *v* bi *vi irreg* na (*etc*) t(h)rasg *f*, traisg *vi*, **they
are ~ing** tha iad nan trasg, tha iad a' trasgadh

fasten *v* ceangail *vt*

fastening *n* ceangal *m*

fast-flowing *adj* cas, bras

fastidious *adj* òrraiseach

fat *adj* reamhar, sultmhor

fat *n* **1** crèis *f*, geir *f*, saill *f*; **2** (*body ~*) sult *m*

fatal *adj* marbhtach

fate *n* dàn *m*, (*more trad*) crannchur *m*, **oppose/
go against ~** cuir *vi* an aghaidh dàin, **he
accepted his ~** ghabh e ris na bha an dàn dha,
if that is my ~ mas e sin mo chrannchur

fated *adj* an dàn (**for** do), **that was ~ for him**
bha sin an dàn dha

father *n* athair *m*

father-in-law *m* athair-cèile *m*

fatten *v* reamhraich *vti*

fatty *adj* crèiseach

faucet *n* goc *m*

fault *n* **1** (*defect in person or object*) fàillinn
f, gaoid *f*; **2** (*defect in object*) easbhaidh *f*,

cearb *f*; **3** (*moral defect in person*) meang *f*;
4 (*geological* ~, ~ *in metal etc*) sgàineadh *m*;
5 (*guilty action*) ciont(a) *m*; **6** *in exprs* **at** ~
coireach, ciontach, **it wasn't my** ~ cha mhis' a
bu choireach (ris), **find** ~ faigh coire *f* (**with** do)
favour *n* fàbhar *m*, seirbheis *f*, bàidh *f*, **he did
you a** ~ rinn e fàbhar/seirbheis/bàidh dhut
favour *v* **1** (*side with*) cùm taobh (*with prep* ri); **2**
(*prefer*) is *v irreg & def* fheàrr (*with prep* le), **I** ~
the other applicant 's e an neach-tagraidh eile
as fheàrr leam
favourable *adj* fàbharach
favourite *adj, expr by the phrase* as fheàrr (*in
past tense* a b' fheàrr) *with the pron* le, **my** ~
pastime an cur-seachad as fheàrr leam
fawn *adj* odhar
fawn *n* mang *f*
fawn *v* dèan miodal *m* (**on** do), dèan sodal *m* (**on**
ri)
fawning *n* miodal *m* (**on** do), sodal *m* (**on** ri)
fax *n* (*IT*) facs *m*, ~ **machine** inneal facsa *m*,
send a ~ cuir facs (**to** gu)
fax *v* cuir (litir *etc*) na facs *m* (*with prep* gu), **I'll**
~ **you it/I'll fax it to you** cuiridh mi thugad e
na fhacs
fear *n* **1** eagal (*occas* feagal) *m*, (*less usu*) fiamh
m; **2** *in expr* **for** ~ **that** air eagal 's/is (*with conj*
gun), mus (*also* mun & mum) *conj*, **for** ~ **that
I miss the train** air eagal 's gun caill mi an
trèana, **he held the ladder for** ~ **she should
fall** chùm e grèim air an fhàradh mus tuiteadh i
fearful *adj* eagalach
feasibility *n* ion-dhèantachd *f invar*
feasible *adj* ion-dhèanta
feast *n* **1** (*banquet*) cuirm *f*, fèisd *f*, fleadh *m*; **2**
(*idiom/saying*) **enough is as good as a** ~
fòghnaidh na dh'fhòghnas; **3** (*relig* ~) fèill *f*, **the**
~ **of St Bride/Bridget** An Fhèill Brìde
feast-day *n* latha-fèille *m*
feat *n* euchd *m*, cleas *m*
feather *n* ite *f*, (*smaller*) iteag *f*
feathered *adj* iteach, iteagach
feature *n* (*characteristic etc*) feart *m*
February *n* Gearran *m*, *used with art*, an
Gearran, *also called* a' mhìos mharbh
fecund *adj* torrach
fee *n* (*charged by lawyer etc*) tuarastal *m*
feeble *adj* fann, lag, lapach, meata, **a** ~ **voice**
guth fann
feeble-minded *adj* lag na (*etc*) inntinn *f*
feed *v* **1** (*give food to*) biath *vt*, beathaich *vt*; **2**
(*eat*) gabh *vt* biadh *m*, **they were** ~**ing** bha iad
a' gabhail am biadh

feel *v* **1** fairich *vti*, ~ **cold and heat** fairich
fuachd is teas, **how are you** ~**ing/how do
you** ~ **today?** ciamar a tha thu a' faireachdainn
an-diugh?, ~**ing disgruntled** a' faireachdainn
diombach; **2** (*be conscious of*) mothaich *vt*,
we felt the motion of the boat mhothaich
sinn gluasad a' bhàta; **3** (*touch, handle etc*)
làimhsich *vt*; **4** *in expr* ~ **the absence/lack of**
ionndrainn *vt*
feeling *adj* mothachail
feeling *n* **1** (*phys, emotional*) faireachdainn *f*; **2**
(*abstr: the sense or faculty of* ~) mothachadh *m*;
3 (*the act of* ~) faireachdainn, mothachadh *m*
fell *v* leag *vt* (gu làr *m*)
fellow *n* **1** (*man, 'guy' etc*) fear *m*, **that** ~ **over
yonder** am fear ud thall, **a** ~ **by the name of
Campbell told me** dh'innis fear Caimbeulach
dhomh (e); **2** (*misc usages*) (*compliment*)
aren't you the (**clever** *etc*) ~! nach tusa an
gille/am balach!, **the old** ~ am bodach, (*excl*)
the poor ~! an duine bochd!, an creutair
bochd!, an truaghan!, *also used in voc case* a
dhuine bochd!, a chreutair bochd!
fellow- *prefix, expressed by prefix* co-, *eg* **fellow-
worker** co-obraiche *m*, **fellow-feeling** co-
fhulangas *m*, co-bhàidh *f*
fellowship *n* **1** (*company, friendship*) comann
m, cuideachd *f*, caidreabh *m*, conaltradh *m*; **2**
(*body, association etc*) comann *m*, caidreabh *m*
female *n* (*of humans*) boireannach *m*, tè *f invar*,
a male and a ~ fireannach agus boireannach
female *adj* boireann
feminine *adj* **1** boireannta; **2** *in expr* (*gram*) **the**
~ **gender** a' ghnè bhoireann
fence *n* feansa *f*, (*more trad*) callaid *f*
fern(s) *n* raineach *f*
ferocious *adj* garg
ferocity *n* gairge *f invar*
ferret *n* feòcallan *m*
fertile *adj* **1** (*land, plants etc*) torrach; **2** *in expr*
make ~ toraich *vt*
fertilisation *n* torachadh *m*, sìolachadh *m*
fertilise *v* **1** (*ground*) leasaich *vt*, mathaich *vt*; **2**
(*egg, embryo*) toraich *vt*
fertilised *adj* torrach, ~ **egg** ugh torrach
fertiliser *n* leasachadh *m*, mathachadh *m*
fertility *n* torachas *m*
fervent *adj* (*person*) dùrachdach, (*person,
emotions, deeds*) dian
fervour *n* dèine *f invar*
festival *n* **1** fèis (*also* fèisd & fèist) *f*, **literature/
music** ~ fèis litreachais/chiùil; **2** (*esp relig* ~)
fèill *f*
festive *adj* cuirmeach

fetch *v* 1 faigh *vt*, ~ **bread from the kitchen** faigh aran às a' chidsin; 2 *in expr* go to/and ~ **something** falbh *vi*/rach *vi irreg* a dh'iarraidh rudeigin, go (*imper*) **and ~ my book** thalla a dh'iarraidh an leabhair agam

fetter *n* geimheal *m*

fetter *v* geimhlich *vt*

fettle *n*, *in expr* **he's in fine ~** tha e ann an deagh thriom *mf*/air a (dheagh) dhòigh *f*

feud *n* falachd *f invar*, connsachadh *m*

fever *n* fiabhras *m*, teasach *m*, **scarlet/yellow ~** am fiabhras dearg/buidhe

few *adj*, *in exprs* **he has very ~ friends** tha glè bheag de charaidean aige, **his friends were ~** (*trad*) bu thearc a charaidean, **as ~ as three** cho beag ri a trì

few *n* (*persons or things*) beagan *m*, (*more positive*) grunnan *m*, (*with gen*), **he has a ~ friends** tha beagan/grunnan charaidean aige, **has he any friends? only a ~** a bheil caraidean aige? chan eil ach beagan, **did you see your friends? I saw a ~ (of them)** am faca tu na caraidean agad? chunna mi beagan/ grunnan dhiubh

fickle *adj* caochlaideach, carach, luaineach

fiction *n* ficsean *m*, (*more trad*) uirsgeul *m*

fictional, fictitious *adjs* uirsgeulach

fiddle *n* fidheall *f*, **a tune on the ~** port air an fhidhill *dat*

fiddler *n* fidhlear *m*

fidelity *n* dìlseachd *nf invar*

fidgety *adj* luasganach

field *n* 1 (*mainly agric*) achadh *m*, pàirc(e) *f*; 2 (~ *for a variety of uses*) raon *m*, **playing ~** raon-cluiche, **air~** raon-adhair, **oil ~** raon-ola; 3 (*area of knowledge, expertise etc*) raon *m*, **that's not my ~** chan e sin mo raon-sa; 4 (*IT*) raon *m*

field glasses prosbaig *f sing*

fiendish *adj* diabhlaidh

fierce *adj* 1 (*of pursuit, fighting, contest etc*) dian; 2 (*of person*) garg, fiadhaich

fierceness *n* gairge *f invar*

fifteen *n & adj* còig-deug, **~ minutes** còig mionaidean deug

fifteenth *adj* còigeamh-deug, **the ~ day** an còigeamh là deug

fifth *adj* còigeamh

fifty *n* 1 leth-cheud *m*, **~ women** leth-cheud boireannach (*sing*), **the Fifties** na Leth-cheudan, **a man in his fifties** duine (is e) na leth-cheudan; 2 (*in alt numbering system*) caogad *m*

fig *n* 1 fìogais *f*, fìge *f*; 2 (*idiom*) **I don't give a ~ for X** (*fam*) cha toir mi hòro-gheallaidh air X, chan eil diu a' choin (*gen of* cù *m*) agam do X

fight *n* 1 (*esp phys*) sabaid *f*, còmhrag *f*, (**with, against** ri), (*less serious*) tuasaid *f*; 2 (*usu verbal*) trod *m*; 3 (*more abstr*) strì *f invar*, **the ~ for women's rights** an t-strì airson chòraichean nam ban

fight *v* 1 sabaid *vi*, gleac *vi*, (**with, against** ri); 2 (*usu verbally*) troid *vi* (**with** ri)

fighting *n* sabaid *f*, còmhrag *f*, (**with, against** ri)

fig-tree *n* crann-fìogais *m*, crann-fìge *m*

figurative *adj* figearach

figure *n* 1 (*shape*) cruth *m*, dealbh *mf*, **I made out the ~ of a man** rinn mi a-mach cruth duine; 2 (*person's physique*) dèanamh *m*, *in expr* **a fine ~ of a man** duine air a dheagh thogail; 3 (*arith etc*) àireamh *f*, figear *m*

file[1] *n* (*metalwork etc*) eighe *f*

file[2] *n* (*paperwork, IT etc*) faidhle *m*

fill *n* làn *m*, leòr *f invar*, **I got my ~ of it** fhuair mi mo làn/mo leòr dheth

fill *v* lìon *vti*

filled *adj* lìonta

filler *n* lìonadair *m*

filly *n* loth *f*

film *n* 1 (*thin covering*) sgàil(e) *f*; 2 (*cinema, photography*) film *m*

filter *n* sìol(t)achan *m*

filter *v* sìolaidh *vti*

filtering, filtration *n* sìoladh *m*

filth *n* salchar *m*

filthy *adj* salach

fin *n* ite *f*

final *adj* deireannach, **on the ~ day** air an là dheireannach

finally *adv* 1 (*eventually*) aig deireadh an là, aig a' cheann thall, **he managed it ~** chaidh aige air (a dhèanamh) aig a' cheann thall; 2 (*at long last*) mu dheireadh thall, **he ~ managed it** chaidh aige air mu dheireadh thall

finance *n* (*admin etc*) ionmhas *m*

financial *adj* ionmhasail, *in exprs* **~ aid/ support** taic-airgid *f*, **~ advisor** comhairleach ionmhais *m*

find *v* 1 faigh *vt irreg*, lorg *vt*, (*implying more difficulty*) faigh lorg *f* (*with prep* air), **she found a penny on the pavement** fhuair/lorg i sgillinn air a' chabhsair, **you'll ~ him in the pub** gheibh sibh san taigh-sheinns' e; 2 ~ **out** (*discover, learn*) faigh *vt* a-mach, **they found out that he was broke/bankrupt** fhuair iad a-mach gun robh e briste; 3 (*consider etc*) *in exprs* **I ~ it good** is math leam e, **I ~ that pleasing** is toigh leam sin

fine *adj* **1** (*in texture or dimensions*) mìn; **2** (*in appearance, quality*) gasta, àlainn, brèagha, grinn, **the soldiers looked ~** bha na saighdearan a' coimhead gasta, **a ~ house** taigh àlainn; **3** (*of weather*) math, brèagha, **~ weather** sìde mhath, sìde bhrèagha, **a ~ day** là brèagha; **4** (*fam: as excl*) **~!** taghta!, **your dinner's in the oven, ~!** tha do dhìnnear san àmhainn, taghta!; **5** (*fam: excellent, 'great'*) glan, gasta, **that's just ~** tha sin dìreach glan/gasta; **6** (*of person: ~ in health or spirits*) air a (*etc*) d(h)òigh *f*, gu dòigheil, **Murdo was in ~ fettle** bha Murchadh air a (dheagh) dhòigh, **how are you? I'm ~** ciamar a tha thu? tha (mi) gu dòigheil

fine *n* unnlagh *m*, càin *f*

finger *n* corrag *f*, meur *f*, **index ~** sgealbag *f*, **little ~/**(Sc)**pinkie ~** lùdag *f*, **ring ~** mac-an-aba *m*

finger *v* làimhsich *vt*

fingerprint *n* meur-lorg *f*

finish *v* cuir crìoch *f* (*with prep* air), crìochnaich *vt*, **she ~ed her novel** chuir i crìoch air an nobhail *f* aice (*cf also* **finished 2** *below*)

finished *adj & past part* **1** (*task etc*) coileanta, crìochnaichte; **2** (*of person: having completed a task etc*) deiseil, ullamh, **have/are you ~ yet?** a bheil thu deiseil/ullamh fhathast?, **have you ~ with the phone?** a bheil thu deiseil/ullamh den fòn *mf*?, **the police had ~ questioning him** bha am poileas ullamh de cheasnachadh *m*

finite *adj* crìoch(n)ach

Finland *n* An Fhionnlainn *f*

fir *n* giuthas *m*, *in expr* **~ cone** durcan *m*

fire *n* **1** teine *m*, **light/put out the ~** cuir air/cuir às an teine, **go on ~** rach *vi* na (*etc*) t(h)eine, **set ~** cuir teine (**to** ri), las *vt*, **electric ~** teine-dealain, **~ grate** cliath-theine *f*; **2** *in expr* **~ engine** einnsean-smàlaidh *m*

fire *v* **1** (*a firearm*) tilg *vt*, loisg *vti*; **2** *in expr* **~ an arrow** leig saighead; **3** (*sack, dismiss*) cuir *vt* à dreuchd *f*

fire-extinguisher *n* inneal-smàlaidh *m*

fireplace *n* teallach *m*, teinntean *m*

fireside *n* cagailt *f*, taobh *m* an teine, teallach *m*, **by the ~** ris a' chagailt

firm *adj* **1** (*constant, steady*) cunbhalach; **2** (*solid*) teann, daingeann; **3** (*in actions, character*) duineil

firm *n* companaidh *mf*

firmament *n*, *used with art*, **the ~** an iarmailt *f*

first *adj* **1** ciad, *usu with art*, **the ~ lesson** a' chiad leasan, **in the ~ place** anns a' chiad àite, **in the ~ instance** anns a' chiad dol-a-mach, **~ thing in the morning** a' chiad char *m* sa mhadainn, **~ aid** ciad-fhuasgladh *m*; **2** (*Sc pol*) **the ~ Minister** am Prìomh Mhinistear *m*; **3** *in expr* (**he fell etc**) **head ~** (thuit e *etc*) an comhair a chinn (*gen of* ceann *m*)

first *adv* **1** (*~ of a group, series etc*) an toiseach *m*, **Flora came ~** thàinig Flòraidh an toiseach; **2** (*~ in time*) **at ~** an toiseach, **I didn't like him at ~** cha bu toigh leam e an toiseach, **~ of all, at the very ~** an toiseach tòiseachaidh

firstly *adv* sa chiad àite *m*, **~, I must welcome you all** sa chiad àite, feumaidh mi fàilte a chur oirbh uile

firth *n* linne *f*

fish *n* iasg *m sing & coll*

fish *v* iasgaich *vi*

fisher, fisherman *n* iasgair *m*

fishing *n* iasgach *m*, **they're at the ~** tha iad aig/ris an iasgach, **~ net** lìon-iasgaich *m*, **fishing-boat** *n* bàta-iasgaich *m*, **~ rod** slat-iasgaich *f*, *in expr* **~ line** driamlach *mf*

fishmeal *n* min-èisg *f*

fissure *n* sgoltadh *m*, sgàineadh *m*

fist *n* dòrn *m*, (*more derog*) cròg *f*

fistful *n* làn *m* dùirn (*gen of* dòrn *m*), dòrlach *m*, **I had a ~ of coins** bha làn mo dhùirn de bhuinn airgid agam

fit *adj* **1** (*well*) slàn, fallain, (*fam*) ann an deagh thriom *mf*; **2** (*fam: ready to tackle task etc*) deiseil, ullamh, **are you ~?** a bheil sibh deiseil?; **3** (*phys able*) air chothrom (*with infin of verb*), **~ to go out** air chothrom a dhol a-mach; **4** (*suitable*) freagarrach, cubhaidh, **a land ~ for heroes** tìr a tha freagarrach do ghaisgich, **a pool ~ for swimming** linne freagarrach airson snàimh

fit *n* **1** (*outburst etc*) lasgan *m*, **a ~ of anger** lasgan feirge (*gen of* fearg *f*); **2** *in expr* **a fainting ~** neul *m*, laigse *f*

fit *v* **1** (*clothing*) thig *vi* (*with prep* do), **will it ~ me?** an tig e dhomh?; **2** (*go into available space*) teachd *vi*, **will it ~ in the back of your car?** an teachd e an cùl do chàir?; **3** (*premises, boat etc*) **~ out** uidheamaich *vt*

fitted out *adj & past part* uidheamaichte, acainneach

fitting *adj* **1** freagarrach, cubhaidh, iomchaidh, **a ~ conclusion** co-dhùnadh freagarrach/cubhaidh; **2** *in exprs* **as was ~ for you/on your part** (*trad*) mar bu chubhaidh dhut, **as was (only) ~** mar bu chòir, **he repaid it, as**

was (only) ~ dh'ath-dhìol e e, mar bu chòir (dha)

fittings *npl* (*in finished boat, building etc*) uidheam *f*, acainn *f*

five *n & num adj* (a) còig, (*of people*) còignear *mf invar* (*takes gen pl*), ~ **minutes** còig mionaidean, **how many?** ~ cia mheud? a còig, ~ **ministers** còignear mhinistearan

fivesome *n* còignear *mf invar* (*takes gen pl*)

fix *n* (*difficult situation*) èiginn *f invar*, staing *f*, cruaidh-chas *m*, **I'm in a** ~ tha mi ann an èiginn/ann an (droch) staing, tha mi nam èiginn

fix *v* **1** (*repair objects, machines etc*) càirich *vt*, cuir *vt* ceart, cuir *vt* air dòigh *f*; **2** (*sort out situations etc*) rèitich *vt*, socraich *vt*; **3** ~ **together** tàth *vt*, ceangail *vt* ri chèile

fixed *adj & past part* **1** (*firmly in place*) teann, suidhichte; **2** (*of situations etc: put right*) rèidh, socraichte; **3** (*repaired*) càirichte; **4** (*settled, consistent*) seasmhach, suidhichte, **of no** ~ **abode** gun àite-còmhnaidh seasmhach

fjord *n* loch-mara *m*

flabby *adj* (*lit: of body*) sultach, (*lit & fig*) bog

flair *n* liut *f* (**for** air)

flame *n* lasair *f*, **going up in** ~**s** a' dol na (*etc*) lasair, a' dol na (*etc*) lasraichean *fpl*

flame *v* las *vi*

flaming *adj* lasrach

flammable *adj* lasanta

flannel *n* flanainn *f*

flare *v*, ~ **up** *v* las *vi*

flash *n* **1** lasair *f*, drithleann *m*; **2** (*fam: instant of time*) plathadh *m*, **it went past in a** ~ chaidh e seachad ann am plathadh

flash *v* deàlraich *vi*

flashing *adj* lasrach, ~ **eyes** sùilean lasrach

flashy *adj* (*esp in dress*) spaideil

flask *n* searrag *f*

flat *adj* còmhnard, rèidh

flat *n* (*ie dwelling*) lobht(a) *m*

flattened *adj* leudaichte, **his nose was** ~ **against the window pane** bha a shròn leudaichte ris an lòsan

flatter *v* dèan miodal *m*, dèan brìodal *m*, (*with prep* do)

flattery *n* miodal *m*, brìodal *m*

flatulence *n*, *used with art*, a' ghaoth

flatulent *adj* gaothach

flaw *n* **1** (*moral*) meang *f*; **2** (*in object*) fàillinn *f*, easbhaidh *f*, gaoid *f*

flawless *adj* **1** (*of person*) gun mheang *f*; **2** (*of object*) gun fhàillinn *f*

flax *n* lìon *m*

flea *n* deargad *f*, deargann *f*

flee *v* tàrr *vi* às (*also* tàir *vi* às), teich *vi*

fleece *n* rùsg *m*

fleece *v* **1** (*sheep*) rùisg *vti*; **2** (*fam: rob, cheat*) spùill *vt* gu buileach

fleet *n* (*of vehicles, ships*) cabhlach *m*, (*of ships*) loingeas & luingeas *m*

fleeting *adj* **1** (*transient*) diombuan; **2** *in expr* ~ **glimpse** boillsgeadh *m*, plathadh *m*, (**of** de), **I got a** ~ **glimpse of her** fhuair mi boillsgeadh/plathadh dhith

flesh *n* feòil *f*

fleshly, fleshy *adj* feòlmhor

flex *n* (*elec*) fleisg *f*

flexibility *n* sùbailteachd *f invar*

flexible *adj* lùbach, sùbailte

flight *n* **1** (*of bird etc*) iteag *f*, **in** ~ air iteig (*dat*); **2** (*journey on plane*) turas-adhair *m*; **3** (*in battle etc*) ruaig *f*, ruith *f*, teicheadh *m*

flimsy *adj* **1** (*material etc*) tana; **2** (*easily broken*) brisg

fling *v* tilg *vt* (**at** air)

flipper *n* (*of divers*) clabar-snàimh *m*

flit (*Sc*) *v* imrich *vi*, dèan *vt irreg* imrich *f*

flitting (*Sc*) *n* imrich *f*

float *v* **1** (*as vt: set afloat*) cuir *vt* air flod *m*; **2** (*as vi*) bi *vi irreg* air fleòdradh *m*, **the ball is** ~**ing** tha am ball air fleòdradh

flock *n* **1** (*of animals*) treud *m*, greigh *f*; **2** (*of birds*) ealt(a) *f*

flock *v* **1** (*birds*) cruinnich *vi* (nan eultan *fpl*); **2** (*fig: people*) *in expr* **they** ~**ed to the fair** (*etc*) chaidh/thàinig iad dhan fhèill (*etc*) nan ceudan *mpl*/nam mìltean *mpl*

flood *n* dìle *f*, tuil *f*

floor *n* **1** ùrlar *m*, làr *m*, ~ **covering** còmhdach ùrlair; **2** (*storey in building*) lobht(a) *m*

floppy *adj* sùbailte, (*IT*) ~ **disc** clàr sùbailte

flour *n* flùr *m*, min-flùir *f*

flow *v* dòirt *vi*, sruth *vi*, ruith *vi*, sil *vi*, (*esp liquids from container etc*) taom *vi*

flow *n* **1** (*of liquids*) sruth *m*; **2** (*of conversation etc*) sruth *m*; **3** *in expr* **the minister** (*etc*) **was in full** ~ bha am ministear (*etc*) a' cur dheth

flower *n* dìthean *m*, flùr *m*, sìthean *m*

flowery *adj* (*covered in flowers*) flùranach

fluctuating *adj* caochlaideach, a' dol suas is sìos

fluency *n* (*in speech; of a second language*) fileantachd *f*

fluent *adj* (*in a lang*) fileanta, siùbhlach, ~ **in Gaelic** fileanta sa Ghàidhlig, *in expr* **a** ~ **speaker** (*of a lang*) fileantach *m*

fluently *adv* gu fileanta, *in expr* **she speaks Gaelic** ~ tha i fileanta sa Ghàidhlig, *also* tha a' Ghàidhlig aice gu fileanta

flush n (*on face*) rudhadh m, rudhadh-gruaidhe m

flushed adj (*of complexion*) ruiteach

flute n cuisle-chiùil f

flutter v (*esp wings, heart*) plap vi, (*more severe*) plosg vi

fluttering n (*esp of heart, wings*) plap m invar, (*more severe*) plosg m, plosgartaich f

fly n 1 cuileag f; 2 (*for fishing*) maghar m

fly v itealaich vi, rach vi irreg air iteig (*dat of* iteag f), sgiathaich vi, (vt, ~ as *pilot*) stiùir plèana m/ itealan m

flying adj & pres part air iteig (*dat of* iteag f)

flying n 1 (*abstr*) iteag f; 2 (*the action*) itealaich f

fly-over n (*in road system*) os-rathad m

foam cop m, cobhar m

foaming adj copach

fodder n connlach f sing coll, fodar m

foe n nàmhaid m, eascaraid m

fog n ceò mf

foggy adj ceòthach, ceòthar

fold[1] n (*for livestock: esp sheep*) crò m, (*esp for cattle*) buaile f

fold[2] n (*in material etc*) filleadh m

fold v 1 fill vt, preas vt, *in expr* ~ **up** paisg vt; 2 (*fig: fail*) rach vi fodha, **the company ~ed** chaidh a' chompanaidh fodha

folded adj & past part fillte

folder n pasgan m

foliage n duilleach m

folk n 1 (*people*) daoine mpl, **many/lots of** ~ mòran dhaoine gen, **the fairy** ~ na daoine-sìth mpl; 2 (*inhabitants of a particular area etc*) muinntir f, **Uist** ~ muinntir Uibhist gen: *see also* **folks**, *below*

folks npl (*ie relatives*) daoine mpl, cuideachd f, càirdean mpl, **my ~s** mo dhaoine, mo chuideachd, mo chàirdean

follow v lean vti

follower n 1 neach-leanmhainn m (pl luchd-leanmhainn m sing coll); 2 ~s muinntir f, cuideachd f, **his ~s left him** dh'fhàg a mhuinntir e

following n (*body of followers, adherents*) luchd-leanmhainn m sing coll

following adj 1 a leanas (*rel fut of* lean vi), **read the** ~ **words** leugh na faclan a leanas; 2 (*next*) ath (*precedes the noun, which it lenites where possible: usu used with the art*), **the** ~ **week** an ath sheachdain, *also* an t-seachdain an dèidh sin

folly n gòraiche f invar

fond adj 1 dèidheil, measail, (*of air*), **she was** ~ **of me** bha i dèidheil/measail orm; 2 (*misc exprs*) ~ **of the opposite sex** leannanach,

~ **of company** cèilidheach, ~ **of talking** còmhraideach

fondle v cnèadaich & cniadaich vt

fondness n dèidh f

food n biadh m, (*less usu*) lòn m

fool n amadan m, òinseach f (*trad of a female, but also used of males*), bumailear m, ùmaidh m, stalcaire m

foolish adj gòrach, amaideach, faoin, baoth

foolishness n gòraiche f invar, amaideas m, faoineas m

foot n 1 (*part of body*) cas f, **on** ~ de chois (dat), **on one's feet** air chois; 2 (*bottom or base of something*) bun m, bonn m, **the** ~ **of the hill** bun/bonn a' chnuic; 3 (*measurement*) troigh f, **two feet long** dà throigh a dh'fhad

football n ball-coise m

footpath n frith-rathad m

footprint n lorg(-coise) f

footstep n ceum m

footwear n caisbheart f

for prep 1 do (*takes the dat, lenites following cons where possible; for prep prons formed with do see p 509*), **I'll do that** ~ **you** nì mi sin dhut, **it's hard** ~ **me** tha e doirbh dhomh, (*trad*) is duilich leam e, **how did it go/turn out** ~ **you?** ciamar a chaidh dhut?; 2 airson (*with gen*), **she went** ~ **some eggs** dh'fhalbh i airson uighean, **don't be sorry** ~ **her** na bi duilich air a son, **she wrote an essay** ~ (*ie to oblige*) **her brother** sgrìobh i aiste airson a bràthar, **he lost his life** ~ **(the sake of) the Prince** chaill e a bheatha airson a' Phrionnsa, **are you** ~ **leaving/~ a pint?** a bheil thu airson falbh/airson pinnt?, **they voted** ~ **the government** bhòt iad airson an riaghaltais; 3 (*of time: since*) o chionn & bho chionn (*with gen*), **I've been working here** ~ **a year** tha mi ag obair an seo bho chionn bliadhna, (*idiom*) **I haven't seen you** ~ **a long time!** 's fhada o nach fhaca mi thu!; 4 (*of time: during*) fad (*with gen*), airson (*with gen*), car (*with dat*), **we were there** ~ **a fortnight** bha sinn ann fad cola-deug, **we were in Glasgow** ~ **a while** bha sinn ann an Glaschu airson greis, *also* bha sinn treis/greis an Glaschu

for conj (*rather formal: as, because*) oir, **he left,** ~ **the night was growing dark** dh'fhalbh e, oir bha an oidhche a' fàs dorch

forbid v toirmisg vt

forbidden adj toirmisgte

force n 1 (*pol etc* ~) cumhachd mf invar; 2 (*phys* ~) neart m, spionnadh m; 3 (*excessive* ~, *violence*) fòirneart m, ainneart m, èiginn f invar, **take by** ~ thoir vt air èiginn; 4 (*body of people*) feachd *f*, **the Air Force** Feachd an Adhair, **a work~** feachd obrach/oibre (*gen of* obair *f*)

force *v* thoir *vt* (*with prep* air), co-èignich *vt*, **she ~d me to leave** thug i orm falbh, **he'll ~ me to do it eventually** bheir e orm a dhèanamh aig a' cheann thall

fore- *prefix* ro- (*also* roi(mh)-) *prefix, eg* **foretaste** *n* ro-bhlasad *m*, **foretell** *v* ro-innis *vt, see further examples below*

forearm *n* ruighe *mf*

forecast *n* (*esp weather*) ro-aithris *f*

forecaster *n* tuairmsear *m*

forehead *n* bathais *f*, maoil *f*, clàr aodainn *m*

foreign *adj* cèin, coimheach, thall thairis, **~ country** dùthaich chèin, **~ language** cànan cèin

foreigner *n* coigreach *m*, eilthireach *m*, (*less usu*) coimheach *m*

foreleg *n* cas *f* toisich (*gen of* toiseach *m used adjectivally*)

foreman *n* maor *m*, maor-obrach *m*

foremost *adj* prìomh (*precedes the noun, which it lenites where possible*), **the ~ singer in Scotland** am prìomh sheinneadair ann an Alba

foresee *v* ro-aithnich *vt*

foresight *n* ro-shealladh *m*

foreskin *n* ro-chraiceann *m*

forest *n* coille (mhòr), *in exprs* **pine ~** giùthsach *mf*, **deer ~** (*trad*) frith *f*

forester *n* forsair *m*, coilltear *m*

forestry *n* forsaireachd *f invar, in expr* **~ worker** forsair *m*, coilltear *m*

forewarn *v* cuir *vt* air earalas *m*

foreword *n* ro-ràdh *m*

forge *n* ceàrdach *f*, teallach (ceàrdaich) *m*

forget *v* **1** dìochuimhnich *vt*; **2** (*idioms & exprs*) **when was that? I ~** cuine a bha sin? chan eil cuimhne *f invar* agam, **I forgot/have forgotten it** chaidh e às mo chuimhne, **the old songs were forgotten** chaidh na seann òrain air dìochuimhne *f invar*

forgetful *adj* dìochuimhneach

forgetfulness *n* dìochuimhne *f invar*

forgive *v* thoir mathanas *m* (*with prep* do), math & maith *vi*, **~ me!** thoir mathanas dhomh!

forgiveness *n* mathanas *m*

forgotten *adj & past part*, air dìochuimhne *f invar*, **be ~** rach *vi irreg* air dìochuimhne, bi *vi irreg* air a (*etc*) leigeil air dìochuimhne

fork *n* **1** gobhal & gabhal *m*, **~ in the road** gobhal san rathad, **~ of a bicycle** gobhal-baidhsagail; **2** (*table ~*) forc(a) *f*, greimire *m*; **3** (*farm or garden ~*) gòbhlag *f*, gràpa *m*

forked *adj* gòbhlach, **~ tail/lightning** earball/dealanach gòbhlach

form¹ *n* **1** (*shape*) cumadh *m*, cruth *m*, dealbh *mf*, **I made out the ~ of a man** rinn mi a-mach cumadh/cruth duine; **2** (*artistic ~*) cruth *m*, (*Lit etc*) **matter and ~** cuspair is cruth; **3** (*borrowed or copied ~*) riochd *m*, **a ghost in the ~ of a cat** taibhse an riochd cait; **4** (*mood, spirits*) dòigh *f*, gleus *mf*, **Murdo was on good ~** bha Murchadh air a (dheagh) dhòigh/air (deagh) ghleus

form² *n* (*seat*) furm *m*

form³ *n* (*to fill in*) foirm *mf*

form *v* cum *vt*, dealbh *vt*, **he ~ed an image out of the stone** chum e ìomhaigh às a' chloich

formal *adj* foirmeil, **~ language/speech** cainnt fhoirmeil

former *adj* sean(n), a bha ann (*etc*) roimhe, **a ~ policeman** seann phoileasman

forsake *v* trèig *vt*, cuir a (*etc*) c(h)ùl (*with prep* ri), **he forsook his family** thrèig e a theaghlach, **~ the faith of your forefathers** trèigibh creideamh ur sinnsirean

fort *n* **1** daingneach *f*; **2** (*hist; hill ~*) dùn *m*

fortify *v* (*structure, building etc*) daingnich *vt*

fortitude *n* misneach *f*, misneachd *f invar*, cruadal *m*

fortnight *n* cola-deug *mf invar*, **we'll be back in/after a ~** bidh sinn air ais an ceann cola-deug

fortress *n* daingneach *f*

fortuitous *adj* tuiteamach, **~ events** tachartasan tuiteamach

fortunate *adj* fortanach

fortune *n* **1** (*luck*) fortan *m*, sealbh *m*, **good ~** deagh fhortan, *in expr* **~ teller** fiosaiche *m*; **2** (*financial ~*) beartas *m*, ionmhas *m*, saidhbhreas *m*, stòras *m*, **the family ~** ionmhas an teaghlaich, *in expr* **he made a ~** rinn e airgead mòr, mòr/rinn e fortan

Fort William *n* An Gearastan *m*

forty *num* dà fhichead, (*in alt numbering system*) ceathrad *m*

forwards *adv* (*of vehicle, movement etc*) air adhart *f*, air aghaidh *f*, an comhair a (*etc*) t(h)oisich

foster brother/sister *n* co-alta *mf*

foul, foul play *n* (*sports & games*) fealladh *m*

found *v* cuir *vt* air chois (*dat of* cas *f*), cuir *vt* air bhonn *m*, **~ a business** cuir gnothach air chois/air bhonn

fountainhead *n* màthair-uisge *f*

four *n & num adj* **1** (*used of objects*) ceithir **2** (*used of people*) ceathrar *mf invar* (*with gen pl*),

there are ~ **(people) there** tha ceathrar ann, ~ **sons** ceathrar mhac; **3** *in expr* **he's** (*etc*) **on all** ~**s** tha e (*etc*) air a mhàgan/air a mhàg(a)ran *fpl*

four-legged *adj* ceithir-chasach

foursome *n* ceathrar *mf invar*

fourteen *n & num adj* ceithir-deug

fourth *n* ceathramh *m*

fourth *num adj* ceathramh

four-wheeled *adj* ceithir-chuibhleach

fox *n* sionnach *m*, madadh-ruadh *m*, balgair *m*

foyer *n* (*of public building*) for-thalla *m*

fraction *n* (*maths etc*) bloigh *f*

fragment *n* bìdeag *f*, criomag *f*, bloigh *f*

fragment *v* (*vi*) rach na (*etc*) b(h)ìdeagan *fpl*, (*vt*) cuir na (*etc*) b(h)ìdeagan

fragmented *adj* briste, na (*etc*) b(h)ìdeagan *fpl*, na (*etc*) c(h)riomagan *fpl*, pronn

fragrant *adj* cùbhraidh

frame *n* **1** cèis *f*, frèam *m*, **picture** ~ cèis-dealbha, **climbing** ~ cèis-streap, **bicycle** ~ cèis-baidhsagail; **2** *in expr* ~ **of mind** fonn *m*, gean *m*, gleus inntinn *mf*, **what** ~ **of mind is he in today?** dè am fonn/an gean a th' air an-diugh?

framework *n* frèam *m*

France *n* (*used with art*) An Fhraing *f*

frank *adj* fosgarra, fosgailte

fraud *n* foill *f*

fraudulent *adj* foilleil, fealltach

fraudulently *adv* le foill *f*, **obtain goods** ~ faigh bathar le foill

free *adj* **1** (*at liberty*) saor, mu sgaoil, mu rèir, **the prisoner is** ~ tha am prìosanach saor/mu sgaoil; **2** (*without constraints*) (*Lit*) ~ **verse** saor-rannaigheachd *f invar*, ~ **market economy** economaidh saor-mhargaidh; **3** (*at leisure*, ~ *from*) saor (**from** bho/o, is), an tàmh *m*, **are you** ~? a bheil sibh nur tàmh?, ~ **from anxiety** saor o chùram, **I'm** ~ **of debts now** tha mi saor is fiachan a-nis; **4** (~ *of charge*, *gratis*) saor, (*stronger*) saor 's an asgaidh, **I got my food (completely)** ~ fhuair mi mo bhiadh saor 's an-asgaidh

free *v* **1** (*liberate*) fuasgail *vt*, cuir *vt* mu sgaoil *m invar*, leig *vt* mu sgaoil, cuir/leig *vt* mu rèir; **2** (~ *tangled etc object*) fuasgail *vt*

freedom *n* saorsa *f invar*

free-standing *adj* neo-eisimeileach

freeze *v* reoth *vti*, (*fig*) ~ **assets** reoth so-mhaoin *f*

freezer *n* reothadair *m*

freight *n* luchd *m*, *in expr* ~ **charge** faradh *m*

French *adj* Frangach

French *n* (*lang*) Fraingis *f*, *used with art*, an Fhraingis

Frenchman *n* Frangach *m*

frequency *n* (*abstr*, *also elec*) tricead *m*

frequent *adj* cumanta, **a** ~ **occurrence** tachartas cumanta, (*or expr by adv expr*) **he was a** ~ **visitor** bhiodh e a' tadhal (oirnn *etc*) gu tric

frequent *v* tathaich *vi* (*with prep* air)

frequently *adv* (gu) tric, gu bitheanta, (*less usu*) gu minig, **he falls** ~ bidh e a' tuiteam gu tric, **she doesn't come as** ~ **as she used to** cha tig i cho tric agus a chleachd (i)/agus a b' àbhaist dhi, **he's** ~ **late** is tric a bhios e air dheireadh, *in expr* ~ **met with** cumanta

fresh¹ *adj* **i** ùr, ~ **herring/butter** sgadan/ìm ùr, **a** ~ **start** tòiseachadh ùr, **make a** ~ **start** tòisich *vi* às ùr; **2** *in expr* ~ **water** (*ie as opposed to salt water*) fìor-uisge *m*

fresh² *adj* (*of temperature*, *weather*) fionnar

fretful *adj* frionasach

friction *n* **1** suathadh *m*; **2** (*fig: between people*) mì-chòrdadh *m*

Friday *n* Dihaoine *m invar*

fridge *n* frids *m*, (*more trad*) fuaradair *m*

fried *adj & past part* ròsta, ~ **potatoes** buntàta ròsta *m sing coll*

friend *n* **1** caraid *m*, **good** ~**s of mine** deagh chàirdean/charaidean dhomh, **female/woman** ~ banacharaid; **2** (*idiom*) **we are great** ~**s** tha sinn gu math mòr aig a chèile

friendly *adj* càirdeil

friendship *n* càirdeas *m*

fright *n* **1** (*abstr*) eagal *m*, (*occas*) feagal *m*, **take** ~ gabh eagal; **2** (*con: a* ~) clisgeadh *m*, **he gave me a** ~ chuir e clisgeadh orm

frighten *v* cuir eagal *m* (*with prep* air), **he** ~**ed me** chuir e eagal orm

frightful *adj* eagalach, uabhasach, oillteil

frightfully *adv* eagalach, **that was** ~ **good** bha sin eagalach math

frill *n* fraoidhneas *m*

fringe *n* **1** (*periphery*) iomall *m*, oir *f*, **on the** ~**(s)** (*ie remote*) air an iomall; **2** (*on material*, *hair etc*) fraoidhneas *m*

frivolity *n* aotromas *m*, (*more pej*) faoineas *m*

frivolous *adj* aotrom, (*more pej*) faoin

frock *n* froca *m*

frog *n* losgann *m*

from *prep* **1** (*expr direction*, *point of origin etc*) bho & o (*takes the dat*, *lenites following cons where possible*; *for prep prons with bho/o see p 509*), **she went up** ~ **the beach** chaidh i suas bhon chladach, **get some fish** ~ **the van**

faigh iasg on bhan, a **letter from Murdo** litir
o Mhurchadh, (*much less common in this sense*)
de & dhe (*takes the dat, lenites following cons
where possible, for prep prons with* de/dhe *see
p 509*), **lift stones ~ the ground** tog clachan
den làr; **2** (*expr point of origin*) à (*before the
art* às), **food ~ Tesco's/~ the shop** biadh
à Tesco's/às a' bhùth, **a band ~ Scotland**
còmhlan-ciùil à Alba, **where are you ~?** cò às a
tha thu/sibh?, **where did he come/spring ~?**
cò às a nochd esan?; **3** (*expr a sequence of time*)
bho & o (*takes the dat, lenites following cons
where possible*), **~ morning till night** o mhoch
gu dubh, **~ that time forward/on** bhon àm sin
air adhart, **~ Monday to Friday** bho Dhiluain
gu Dihaoine

front *adj* **1** toisich (*gen of* toiseach *m used
adjectivally*), **~ leg** cas-toisich; **2** *in expr ~
door* doras mòr, doras-aghaidh *m*

front *n* **1** (*the front part of anything*) toiseach *m*,
at the ~ aig/anns an toiseach, *also* an toiseach,
in the ~ (*ie in the cab*) **of the lorry** ann an
toiseach na làraidh, **~ end first** an comhair
a thoisich; **2** (*the front surface of anything*)
beulaibh *m invar*, aghaidh *f*, **the ~ of the
building** beulaibh an togalaich, **back to ~**
cùlaibh *m invar* air beulaibh; **3** *in expr* **in ~** (*ie
ahead*) air thoiseach (**of** air), **Iain was in ~** bha
Iain air thoiseach, **a long way in ~ of us** fada
air thoiseach oirnn; **4** *in expr* **in ~** (*ie facing,
opposite a person, object etc*) mu choinneimh,
fa chomhair, (*with gen*), ro (*before art* ron), **in
~ of me** mu mo choinneimh, fa mo chomhair,
romham, **in ~ of the shop** ron bhùth; **5** (*a
weather ~*) aghaidh *f*, **a warm/cold ~** aghaidh
bhlàth/fhuar

frontier *n* crìoch *f*

frontwards *adv* an comhair a thoisich *m*, an
comhair a chinn (*gen of* ceann *m*)

frost *n* reothadh *m*

froth cop *m*, cobhar *m*

frothy *adj* copach

frown *n* mùig *m*, gruaim *f*, sgraing *f*

frown *v* cuir mùig *m*, cuir gruaim *f*, (*with prep*
air), **she ~ed** chuir i mùig/gruaim oirre

frowning *adj* gruamach, **a ~ man** duine
gruamach, duine is gruaim *f* air

frozen *adj* reòtha *and* reòthte, **my feet are ~!**
tha mo chasan reòtha!, **~ food** biadh reòtha

fruit *n* **1** meas *m*, **~ tree,** craobh mheas, measchraobh, **~ juice** sùgh-measa *m*; **2** (*crop,*

produce) toradh *m*, **the ~(s) of the earth**
toradh na talmhainn

fruitful *adj* tor(r)ach

fruitless *adj* **1** (*trees etc*) gun mheas *m*; **2** (*fig:
vain*) dìomhain, gun toradh *m*

fruity *adj* measach

fry *v* frighig *vt*, ròist & ròst *vt*

fuck *v* (*vulg/taboo*) rach *vi* air muin *f invar*, **he
~ed her** chaidh e air a muin

fuel connadh *m sing coll*

fugitive *n* fògrach & fògarrach *m*

full *adj* **1** (*filled*) làn, lìonta, **~ up, ~ to the brim**
loma-làn, **half ~** leth-làn; **2** (*complete*) làn,
iomlan, **a ~ length film** film làn-fhada, **he fell
~ length** thuit e a làn-fhad, **~-time job** obair
làn-thìde/làn-ùine, **a ~ orchestra** orcastra
iomlan; **3** *in exprs* **~ stop** (*typog*) stad-phuing
f, puing-stad *f*, **a ~ account** cunntas/iomradh
mionaideach, **~ of holes** tolltach, **he left at ~
tilt/at ~ speed** dh'fhalbh e na dhian-ruith *f*,
dh'fhalbh e aig peilear *m* a bheatha *f gen*

full *adv, in expr* **she struck him ~ in the face**
bhuail i e an clàr *m* aodainn *m gen*

full *v* (*formerly:* **~ cloth**) luaidh *vt*

full-grown *adj* **1** (*of person*) inbheach; **2** *in exprs*
~ man duine foirfe, **become ~** thig *vi* gu ìre *f
invar*

fulling *n* (*formerly:* **~ of cloth**) luadhadh *m*

full-length *adj* làn-fhada

fully *adv* **1** gu h-iomlan, uile-gu-lèir, **we
succeeded ~** shoirbhich leinn gu h-iomlan/
uile-gu-lèir; **2** (*misc exprs*) **~ grown** inbheach, **I
was ~ aware** bha làn-fhios *m* agam, **there are
~ two thousand of them there** tha dà mhìle
dhiubh ann aig a' char *m* as lugha

fulmar *n* fulmair *m*

fulness *n* lànachd *nf invar*

fumes *n* deatach *f*

fun *n* **1** spòrs *f*, dibhearsain *m*, **we had (some)
~ last night** bha spòrs againn a-raoir, **have
~ at someone's expense** faigh spòrs air
cuideigin, *in expr* **full of ~** spòrsail; **2** *in expr*
make ~ dèan fanaid *f*, mag *vi*, (**of** air), **they
were making ~ of him** bha iad a' fanaid air/a'
magadh air, *also* bha iad a' dèanamh fanaide
gen air

function *n* **1** (*purpose, use*) gnìomh *m*, feum *m*;
2 (*post, occupation*) oifis *f*, dreuchd *f*, obair *f*; **3**
(*task, action*) gnìomh *m*, **bodily ~s** gnìomhan-
bodhaig *mpl*, (*IT*) **~ key** iuchair-ghnìomha *f*; **4**
(*formal meal, event etc*) cuirm *f*

function *v* obraich, *occas* oibrich, *vti*

fund *n* 1 (*fin*) maoin *f*, *in expr* **a trust** ~ ciste-urrais *f*; 2 (*large accumulation*) stòr *m*, **a ~ of knowledge** stòr eòlais *m*

fund *v* maoinich *vt*

fundamental *adj* bunaiteach

funeral *n* tiodhlacadh *m*, adhlacadh *m*, tòrradh *m*

funnel *n* 1 (~ *of ship, industrial chimney etc*) luidhear *m*, similear *m*; 2 (*for pouring*) lìonadair *m*

funny *adj* 1 (*amusing*) èibhinn, (*less usu*) àbhachdach; 2 (*peculiar etc*) neònach, àraid

furious *adj* air chuthach *m*, air bhoile *f invar*, air bhàinidh *f invar*, (*fam*) fiadhaich, **become ~** rach *vi* air chuthach/air bhoile/air bhàinidh, **I was ~ after what he said to me** (*fam*) bha mi fiadhaich an dèidh na thuirt e rium

furlough *n* fòrladh *m*

furnace *n* fùirneis *f*

furnish *v* 1 (*fit out factory etc*) uidheamaich *vt*; 2 (~ *house etc*) cuir àirneis *f invar coll* (ann an taigh *etc*); 3 (*purvey, supply*) solair *vt*

furnishings *npl* àirneis *f*, àirneis bhog

furrow *n* 1 (*in ground*) clais *f*, sgrìob *f*; 2 (*in brow*) preas *m*, preasan *m*

furrow *v* 1 (*ground*) sgrìob *vt*, claisich *vt*; 2 (*brow*) preas *vt*

furry *adj* molach

further *adj* 1 (*additional*) a bharrachd, tuilleadh, eile, **we don't need anything ~** chan fheum sinn càil *m invar* a bharrachd, **send (us) a ~ two lorries** cuiribh dà làraidh a bharrachd thugainn, **give me ~ information** thoir dhomh tuilleadh fiosrachaidh, **she received a ~ letter** fhuair i litir eile; 2 *in expr* **~ education** foghlam *m* (aig) àrd-ìre *f invar*

furthermore *adv* a bharrachd air sin, a thuilleadh air sin

fury *n* cuthach *m*, bàinidh *f invar*

fussy *adj* 1 ro-chùramach, ro-phongail; 2 *in expr* **I'm not ~** (*ie don't mind*) is coma leam, tha mi coma co-dhiù

futile *adj* faoin, dìomhain, **the ~ endeavours of mankind** oidhirpean faoine mhic-an-duine

futility *n* faoineas *m*

future *adj* 1 ri teachd, **~ years/generations** na bliadhnachan/na ginealaich (a tha) ri teachd; 2 (*gram*) teachdail, **the ~ tense** an tràth teachdail

future *n* 1 (*with art*), **the ~** an t-àm ri teachd; 2 *in expr* **in ~** bho seo a-mach, turas *m* eile, **in ~, make sure you're wearing a safety helmet!** bho seo a-mach/turas eile, dèan cinnteach gu bheil cloga(i)d-dìona ort!

G

gable *n* stuadh *f*

Gael *n* Gàidheal *m*

Gaelic *n* **1** Gàidhlig *f*, **I speak** ~ tha Gàidhlig/a' Ghàidhlig agam, **translate English into** ~ cuir Gàidhlig air Beurla *f invar*, **where did you learn/pick up your** ~? càit an do thog thu do chuid Gàidhlig?, *also often used with art*, **speaking in** ~ bruidhinn sa Ghàidhlig; **2** (*used adjectivally*) **The Gaelic Society of Inverness** Comann Gàidhlig Inbhir Nis, **the Gaelic Association** Comunn na Gàidhlig, ~ **people/speakers** luchd *m sing coll* na Gàidhlig

gaffer *n* maor *m*, maor-obrach *m*

gain *n* (*fin*) prothaid *f*, buannachd *f*

gain *v* coisinn *vt*, buannaich *vt*, ~ **a reputation** coisinn cliù

gait *n* gluasad *m*, giùlan *m*

gale *n* gèile *m*

gallery *n* (*for exhibitions, art etc*) taisbean-lann *f*, (*less trad*) gailearaidh *m*

galling *adj* leamh, frionasach

gallon *n* galan *m*

gallows *n* croich *f*

gambler *n* ceàrraiche *m*

gambling *n* (*the act of* ~) ceàrrachadh *m*, (*abstr*) ceàrrachas *m*

game *n* **1** cluich & cluiche *m*, geam(a) *m*, **board** ~ cluich-bùird; **2** (*esp football*) geam(a) *m*, **will you be going to the** ~? am bi thu a' dol dhan gheam(a)?; **3** (*hunted creatures*) sitheann *f*, (*as food*) geam(a) *m*

gamekeeper *n* geamair *m*

gang *n* **1** (*of labourers, criminals etc*) buidheann *mf*; **2** (*fam/pej: crowd, group*) treud *m*, **the** ~ **he goes to the pub with** an treud leis am bi e a' dol dhan taigh-sheinnse *m*

gannet *n* sùlaire *m*, (*young* ~) guga *m*

gap *n* beàrn *mf*, fosgladh *m*, **a** ~ **in the wall** beàrn sa ghàrradh, **a** ~ **in the market** fosgladh sa mhargadh

garage *n* garaids *f*

garb *n* èideadh *m*, **the** ~ **of the Gael** an t-èideadh Gàidhealach

garden *n* gàrradh *m*, (*more trad*) lios *mf*, *in expr* ~ **centre** ionad-gàirnealaireachd *m*, margadh-gàrraidh *mf*

gardener *n* gàirnealair *m*

gardening *n* gàirnealaireachd *f invar*

garlic *n* creamh *m*

garrison *n* gearastan *m*

garron *m* gearran *m*

garrulous *adj* beulach, (*more fam*) cabach, gobach

garter *n* gartan *m*

gas *n* **1** deatach *f*, **emit/give out** ~ cuir (a-mach) deatach; **2** (*domestic* ~) gas *m*, ~ **cooker** cucair gas *m*

gasp, gasping *n* plosg *m*

gasp *v* (*for breath*) plosg *vi*

gate *n* geata *m*

gather *v* **1** (*people*) cruinnich *vti*, tionail *vi*, thig còmhla, **they** ~**ed/he** ~**ed them in the barn** chruinnich iad/chruinnich e iad san t-sabhal; **2** (*livestock*) cruinnich *vt*, tionail *vt*, tru(i)s *vt*; **3** ~ **together** (*people or things*) co-chruinnich *vti*; **4** (*esp of clothing: tuck up*) tru(i)s *vt*

gathered *adj & past part* (*of people*) cruinn, **the congregation was** ~ **in the church** bha an coitheanal cruinn san eaglais *f dat*

gathering *n* (*of people: abstr & con*) cruinneachadh *m*, co-chruinneachadh *m*, tional *m*

gauge *n* (*for measuring*) tomhas *m*, meidheadair *m*

gauge *v* tomhais *vt*

gear[1] *n* **1** (*assorted possessions etc: fam*) treal(l)aich *f*, **tidy up your** ~ sgioblaich do threallaich; **2** (*one's tools, equipment etc*) uidheam *f*, acainn *f*

gear[2] *n* (*engin*) gèar *f invar*, gìodhar *m*

gear up *v* uidheamaich *vt*

geared up *adj & past part* uidheamaichte, acainneach

gelding *m* gearran *m*

gender *n* **1** (*of living creatures, also grammatical* ~) gnè *f invar*, **the feminine/masculine** ~ a' ghnè bhoireann/fhireann

gene *n* gine *f*

general *adj* **1** coitcheann, ~ **knowledge/ education** eòlas/foghlam coitcheann, ~ **election** taghadh coitcheann, ~ **strike** stailc choitcheann; **2** *in expr* **in** ~ (*ie on the whole*) san fharsaingeachd *f invar*, **in** ~ **the majority are against him** san fharsaingeachd tha a' mhòrchuid na aghaidh; **3** *in expr* **in** ~ (*ie normally, usually*) an cumantas *m*, am bitheantas *m*, mar as trice

general *n* seanailear *m*

generally *adv* **1** (*on the whole,* ~ *speaking*) san fharsaingeachd *f invar*; **2** (*normally, usually*) an cumantas *m*, am bitheantas *m*, mar as trice

generation *n* **1** (*with emph on time*) linn *m*, **from** ~ **to** ~ bho linn gu linn; **2** (*with emph on people*) ginealach *m*, **two** ~**s of my family** dà ghinealach den teaghlach agam, **the Sixties** ~ ginealach nan Trì Ficheadan

generator *n* gineadair *m*

generosity *n* fialaidheachd *f invar*

generous *adj* fialaidh, fial, faoilidh, tabhartach

genitals *n* (*in general*) buill-ghineamhainn *mpl*, **female** ~ pit *f*, ròmag *f*, **male** ~ bod *m*, (*fam/ vulg*) slat *f*

genitive *adj* (*gram*) ginideach, **the** ~ **case** an tuiseal ginideach, (*as noun*) **the** ~ an ginideach

genteel *adj* (*in manners etc*) uasal

gentility *n* (*the abstr quality*) uaisle *f invar*

gentle *adj* (*of person, weather*) ciùin, sèimh

gentleman *n* duine-uasal *m*, (*trad*) uasal *m*

genuine *adj* **1** (*authentic*) fìor (*precedes the n, lenites a following cons where possible*), ~ **gold** fìor òr *m*, **a** ~ **expert** fìor eòlaiche *m*; **2** (*sincere, trustworthy etc*) neo-chealgach, dìreach

geography *n* cruinn-eòlas *m*, tìr-eòlas *m*

geology *n* geòlas *m*

germ *n* bitheag *f*

German *n & adj* **1** Gearmailteach *m*; **2** (*the language*) *used with art*, a' Ghearmailtis *f invar*

Germany *n* (*used with art*) A' Ghearmailt *f invar*

germinate *v* ginidich *vi*

germination *n* ginideachadh *m*

gesture *n* **1** gluasad *m*; **2** (*a beckoning* ~) smèideadh *m*

gesture *v* (*esp to summon or greet someone*) smèid *vi* (**to** air)

get *v* **1** (*obtain*) faigh *vt irreg*, ~ **some fish from the van** faigh iasg on bhan, **I didn't** ~ **the job** cha d' fhuair mi an obair; **2** (*become, grow*) fàs *vi* (*with adj*), rach *vi* (*often with abstr n*),

they got tired dh'fhàs iad sgìth, **she's** ~**ting old** tha i a' fàs sean, ~ **used** fàs *vi* cleachdte (**to** ri), ~ **better** (*heal & improve*) rach am feabhas *m, also* thig *vi* bhuaithe, **she got better** (*ie recovered*) chaidh i am feabhas, thàinig i bhuaithe, **the local services are** ~**ting better** tha na seirbheisean ionadail a' dol am feabhas, ~ **bigger** rach am meud *m invar*; **3** (*misc exprs & idioms*) **go to** ~ **something** falbh *vi* a dh'iarraidh rudeigin, ~ **acquainted with/**~ **to know someone** cuir aithne/eòlas air cuideigin, ~ **advice** gabh comhairle, ~ **the better of** faillich *also* fairtlich *vi* (*with prep* air), (*esp of a person: slightly fam*) dèan an gnothach *m*, dèan a' chùis *f* (*both with prep* air), **I wanted to climb the mountain but it got the better of me** bha mi airson a' bheinn a dhìreadh ach dh'fhaillich i orm, **we got the better of the other team** rinn sinn an gnothach/a' chùis air an sgioba eile, ~ **down** (*ie descend*) teirinn & teàrn *vi*, **she got down from the wall** theirinn i bhàrr a' ghàrraidh, ~ **down** (*ie into crouching position*) rach *vi* na (*etc*) c(h)rùbagan *m*, dèan crùban *m*, **they got engaged** thug iad gealladh-pòsaidh dha chèile, ~ **involved in politics** rach an sàs ann am poilitigs, ~ **a move on!** cuir car dhìot!, tog ort!, ~ **on someone's nerves** leamhaich cuideigin, ~ **on well/smoothly with someone** bi *vi irreg* rèidh ri cuideigin, **we** ~ **on well (with each other)** tha sinn gu math mòr aig a chèile, **how did you** ~ **on?** ciamar a chaidh dhut/dhuibh?, ciamar a dh'èirich dhut/dhuibh?, ~ **out!** thoir do chasan leat!, ~ **over an operation** (*etc*) faigh *vi* seachad air opairèisean (*etc*), **she got over it** thàinig i bhuaithe, ~ **rid/shot of something** faigh cuidhteas rudeigin, ~ **stuck in** teann *vi* ris an obair, crom *vi* air an obair, ~ **to** (*fam: affect, upset etc*) drùidh (*with prep* air), **the news didn't** ~ **to her** cha do dhrùidh an naidheachd oirre, (*more fam*) cha do chuir an naidheachd suas no sìos i, ~ **up** (*from bed, sitting position etc*) èirich *vi*, **I got up late yesterday** dh'èirich mi anmoch an-dè, (*more idiomatic*) bha mi fada gun èirigh an-dè, ~ **the upper hand** faigh/gabh làmh-an-uachdair (**of** air), ~ **used to it!** cleachd thu fhèin ris!, *also* faigh eòlas air!

ghost *n* taibhse *mf*, tannasg *m*

giant *n* famhair *m*, fuamhaire *m*

gibbet *n* croich *f*

giddiness *n* **1** tuainealaich *f*, luasgan *m*; **2** (*fig: of character*) guanalas *m*

giddy *adj* **1** (*lit & fig*) tuainealach, guanach; **2** *in expr* ~ **girl** guanag *f*

gift *n* **1** tiodhlac *m*, gibht *f*, tabhartas *m*; **2**
(*natural ~, talent*) tàlann *m*
gift *v* tiodhlaic *vt*, thoir *vt* seachad
Gigha *n* Giogha
gill *n* (*of fish*) giùran *m*
ginger *adj* (*of hair, animal's coat etc*) ruadh
girl *n* **1** caileag *f*, nighean *f*, **a little** ~ caileag
bheag, **~s,** ~ **children** clann-nighean *f sing coll*;
2 (*mostly found in love songs*) gruagach *f*, cailin
f, nìghneag *f*
girlfriend *n* leannan *m*, (*fam*) bràmair *m* (*note
that these words can be used of a lover or
sweetheart of either sex*)
give *v* **1** thoir (**to do**) *vt irreg*, thoir *vt* seachad,
tiodhlaic *vt*, **she gave us a present** thug i
tiodhlac dhuinn, ~ **advice** thoir comhairle *f*, ~
evidence thoir fianais *f*, ~ **me your hand** thoir
dhomh do làmh; **2** (*deliver, perform etc*) gabh
vt, ~ **a talk** gabh òraid *f*, *also* dèan òraid, thoir
seachad òraid, (**to do**), ~ **us a song!** gabh òran
m!; **3** (*misc exprs & idioms*) ~ **up** leig *vt* de &
leig *vt* seachad, **I've ~n up smoking** leig mi
seachad smocadh *m*, **he gave up his job** leig e
dheth obair *f*, **don't ~ up!** (*ie persevere*) cùm *vi*
ris!, **we didn't ~ the game away** cha do leig *vi*
sinn oirnn, ~ **a row to** càin *vt*, ~ **in,** ~ **way** gèill
vi (**to do**), (*of traffic*) ~ **way** gèill slighe *f*, ~ **out**
(*ie emit*) cuir *vt* (a-mach), ~ **out** (*ie distribute*)
roinn *vt*, riaraich *vt*
giver *n* (*to charity etc*) tabhartaiche *m*,
tabhairteach *m*
glad *adj* **1** (*happy, pleased*) toilichte, **I got the
job! I'm** ~ fhuair mi an obair! tha mi toilichte; **2**
(*willing*) toileach, **I'd be** ~ **to do that for you**
bhithinn toileach sin a dhèanamh dhut
gladness *n* gàirdeachas *m*, toileachas *m*, toil-
inntinn *f*, toileachas-inntinn *m*
glance *n* plathadh *m*, sùil (aighghearr) *f*, (**at** air)
glance *v* thoir *vt irreg* sùil *f* (aighghearr), (**at** air),
she ~d at me thug i sùil (aighghearr) orm
gland *n* fàireag *f*
glass *n* (*the material & a drinking ~*) glainne *f*
glasses *npl* (*ie spectacles*) glainneachan *fpl*,
speuclairean *mpl*
glasshouse *n* taigh-glainne *m*
glen *n* gleann *m*
glimpse *n* aiteal *m*, plathadh *m*, (**of** de)
glint *n* lainnir *f*, deàlradh *m*
glitter *n* lainnir *f*, deàlradh *m*
glitter *v* deàlraich *vi*
global *adj* **1** cruinneil; **2** *in expr* ~ **warming**
blàthachadh na cruinne
globe *n* cruinne *mf* (*f in gen sing*)

gloom, gloominess *n* **1** (*of light*) doilleireachd *f*
invar; **2** (*of mood etc*) gruaim *f*, smalan *m*
gloomy *adj* **1** (*of setting etc*) ciar; **2** (*of light*)
doilleir; **3** (*of mood etc*) doilleir, gruamach,
mùgach
glorify *v* glòraich *vt*
glorious *adj* glòrmhor, òirdheirc
glory *n* **1** (*fame*) cliù *m invar*, glòir *f*; **2** (*spiritual,
heavenly ~*) glòir *f*
gloss *n* (*lustre*) lìomh *f*
glossy *adj* lìomharra
glove *n* làmhainn *f*, miotag *f*, meatag *f*
glue *n* glaodh *m*
glue *v* glaodh *vt*
glug *v* plubraich *vi*, plub *vt*
glutton *adj* geòcaire *m*, craosaire *m*
gluttonous *adj* geòcach, craosach
gluttony *n* geòcaireachd *f invar*, craos *m*
gnash *v* gìosg *vt*, **~ing his teeth** a' gìosgail
fhiaclan *fpl gen*
gnaw *v* cagainn *vti*
go *v* **1** (*make one's way, proceed*) rach *vi irreg*,
falbh *vi*, gabh *vti*, ~ **to Glasgow** rach do
Ghlaschu, ~ **to bed** rach a chadal *m*, ~ **to
fetch/get something** rach/falbh a dh'iarraidh
rudeigin, ~ **on an errand** rach air gnothach
m, ~ **in** rach a-steach, *also* inntrig *vi*, **she went
her way** ghabh i an rathad *m*, **they went to
the hill** ghabh iad chun a' mhonaidh, *also* thug
iad am monadh orra, *note also* thalla (*for falbh*)
and theirig (*for rach*) *used as imper, eg* (**off
you**) ~ **home/to the shop!** thalla dhachaigh/
dhan bhùth!, ~ **to bed!** theirig a chadal!; **2**
(*expr changed states*) rach *vi irreg*, ~ **off/
downhill** rach bhuaithe, ~ **mad/insane** rach
air chuthach/air bhoile/air bhàinidh, ~ **astray/
wrong** (*lit or morally*) rach air iomrall *m*; **3**
(*leave*) falbh *vi*, **they went (away) yesterday**
dh'fhalbh iad an-dè, **right! I'm ~ing** ceart! tha
mi a' falbh, **she's ~ne** tha i air falbh; **4** (*misc
idioms & exprs*) **let us ~!** tiugainn! *imper of vi
def*, ~ **back** till *vi*, **~ing back home** a' tilleadh
dhachaigh, ~ **bad/rotten** lobh *vi*, ~ **to see/
visit someone** tadhail *vi* air cuideigin, **keep
~ing!** cùm *vi* ort!, **how did it ~?** ciamar a
chaidh (dhut/dhaibh *etc*)?
goal *n* **1** (*aim, ambition*) miann *mf*, rùn *m*; **2**
(*football etc*) tadhal *m*
goat *n* gobhar *mf*
gob *n* (*fam*) gob *m*, cab *m*, **shut your ~!** duin do
ghob/chab!
gobble *v* glam & glamh *vt*

God, god *m* Dia, dia *m*, **~'s grace** gràs *m* Dhè *gen*, **the ~s of the Romans** diathan nan Ròmanach

goddess *n* ban-dia *f*

godfather *n* goistidh *m*

godhead *n* diadhachd *f invar*

godliness *n* diadhachd *f invar*

gold *n* òr *m*

gold, golden *adj* òir (*gen sing of* òr *m used adjectivally*), **a gold coin/medal** bonn òir *m*

golden eagle *n* iolair(e)-bhuidhe *f*

goldsmith *n* òr-cheàrd *m*

golf *n* go(i)lf *m*, **~ club** (*ie driver etc*) caman *m* (goilf), **~ club** (*the association*) comann goilf *m*, **~ course** raon goilf *m*

good *adj* **1** math, **~ at singing** math air seinn, math air òrain, **that's ~!** 's math sin!, **very ~** glè mhath, **~ morning/night!** madainn/oidhche mhath!, **~ for you!** math thu fhèin!, **it's ~ to see you!** 's math d' fhaicinn!, **it's ~ that you're here** 's math gu bheil thu ann; **2** deagh (*precedes the noun, which it lenites where possible*), **he's a ~ singer** is e deagh sheinneadair a th' ann (dheth), **that's a ~ sign!** is e deagh chomharradh a tha sin!, **he's a ~ friend of mine/to me** tha e na dheagh charaid dhomh; **3** (*expr good measure*) pailt, **a ~ three feet in length** trì troighean pailt de dh'fhad *m*; **4** (*misc exprs*) **~ grief!** an dòlas!, O mo chreach!, mo chreach-s' a thàinig!, **~ heavens!** a chiall!, **full of ~ sense** làn cèille (*gen of* ciall *f*), (*idiom*) **a wee stroll (*etc*) would be ~ for you** b' fheàirrde thu cuairt bheag (*etc*)

good *n* feum *m*, (*occas*) math *m*, **~ and evil** am math is an t-olc, **this machine's no ~** chan eil feum anns an inneal seo, **what's the ~ of talking?** dè am feum/am math a bhith a' bruidhinn?, **do ~** dèan feum (**to do**), **the holidays will do you ~** nì na saor-làithean feum dhuibh, (*idiom*) **a drink of water (*etc*) would do you ~** b' fheàirrde thu deoch uisge (*etc*)

good- *prefix* deagh-, *eg* **~hearted** deagh-chridheach

goodbye *excl* beannachd leat/leibh!, slàn leat/leibh!, (*more fam*) mar sin leat/leibh!

goodness *n* **1** (*moral etc ~*) mathas *m*; **2** (*~ in food etc*) brìgh *f*, susbaint *f*; **3** (*as excl*) **~!** a chiall!, (**my**) **~!**, **~ me!** obh! obh!

goods *n* **1** (*merchandise*) bathar *m sing coll*, **~ vehicle** carbad-bathair *m*; **2** (*possessions*) maoin *f*, *in expr* **my worldly ~** (*trad*) mo chuid den t-saoghal *f*

goodwill *n* deagh-thoil *f*, deagh-ghean *m*

goose *n* gèadh *mf*

gooseberry *n* gròiseid *f*

gore *n* fuil *f*

gorgeous *adj* greadhnach

gorse *n* conasg *m*

gory *adj* fuil(t)each, **~ battle** cath fuilteach

gossip *n* **1** (*abstr & con*) seanchas *m*; **2** (*person who gossips*) goistidh *m*

gossip *v* bi *vi irreg* ri seanchas *m dat*

govern *v* (a country etc) riaghail *vti*, riaghlaich *vti*

government *n* **1** (*abstr*) riaghladh *m*; **2** (*con*) riaghaltas *m*, **a national/local ~** riaghaltas nàiseanta/ionadail

governor *n* riaghladair *m*

gown *n* gùn *m*

grab *v* gabh grèim *m* (*with prep* air), **he ~bed her bag** ghabh e grèim air a' mhàileid aice

grace *n* gràs *m*, **God's/divine ~** gràs Dhè (*gen of* Dia *m*)

graceful *adj* eireachdail, gràsmhor

gracefulness *n* gràsmhorachd *f invar*

graceless *adj* gun ghràs *m*

gracious *adj* gràsmhor

graciousness *n* gràsmhorachd *f invar*

grade *n* ìre *f invar*

gradient *n* **1** (*abstr*) caisead *m*; **2** (*con; hillside etc*) bruthach *mf*, leathad *m*

gradually *adv* mean (*adj as n*) air mhean, uidh *f* air n-uidh, beag (*adj as n*) air bheag

graduate *v* gabh ceum *m*, ceumnaich *vi*

graduation *n* ceumnachadh *m*

grain *n* **1** gràinnean *m*, **a ~ of salt/sugar** gràinnean salainn/siùcair; **2** (*from cereal crops*) gràn *m sing coll*, (*a single ~*) gràinne *f*

graip *n* gràpa *m*

gram(me) *n* gram *m*, **a hundred ~s of sugar** ceud gram de shiùcar

grammar *n* gràmar *m*

grammatical *adj* gràmarach

grand *adj* **1** (*important, self-important*) mòr, mòr aige (*etc*) fhèin, mòr às (*etc*) fhèin, (*ironic*) **the ~ folk** na daoine mòra; **2** (*fam: expr approval*) glan, gasta, sgoinneil, (*esp as excl*) taghta, **that was just ~** bha sin dìreach glan/gasta/sgoinneil, **We'll see you tomorrow as usual. ~!** Chì sinn a-màireach thu mar as àbhaist. Taghta!

grandchild *n* ogha *m*

granddaughter *n* ban-ogha *f*

grandeur *n* mòrachd *f invar*

grandfather *n* seanair *m*

grandmother *n* seanmhair *f*, (*fam*) granaidh *f*

grandson *n* ogha *m*

granite clach-ghràin *f*, eibhir *f*

granny n (*fam*) granaidh f
grant n (*fin*) tabhartas m
grant v builich vt (**to** air)
granular adj gràinneach
grape n fìon-dhearc f
graph n graf m
grasp n grèim m, glacadh m
grasp v **1** glac vt, gabh grèim m (*with prep* air), greimich vi (*with prep* air *or* ri); **2** (*understand*) tuig vt
grass n feur m, in expr ~ **park** faiche f, pàirc(e) f
grasshopper n fionnan-feòir m
grassy adj feurach
grate n grèata m
grate v sgrìob vti
grateful adj taingeil, buidheach
gratification n toileachadh m
grating[1] n (*scraping etc*) sgrìobadh m
grating[2] n (*grid etc*) cliath f
gratitude n taing f, taingealachd f invar, buidheachas m
grave[1] adj **1** (*of person's character*) stòlda; **2** (*of state of affairs etc*) fìor dhroch (*precedes the noun, which it lenites where possible*), ~ **news** fìor dhroch naidheachd
grave[2] adj (*lang*) trom, ~ **accent** stràc trom
grave n uaigh f
gravel n grinneal m, morghan m
gravestone n leac f, leac uaighe f, clach-chinn f
gravity n (*the force*) iom-tharraing f
graze[1] v (*skin of hand etc*) rùisg vt
graze[2] v (*livestock etc*) ionaltair vi, (*put to* ~) feuraich vt
grazing n **1** (*abstr*) feurachadh m, ionaltradh m; **2** (*con: pasture*) feurach m, ionaltradh m, clua(i)n f; **3** in exprs (*in crofting context*) **the common** ~ am monadh, **the ~s clerk** clàrc a' bhaile m
grease n crèis f
greasy adv crèiseach
great adj **1** (~ *in size, importance, prestige*) mòr, **a** ~ **crowd** sluagh mòr, **a** ~ **poet** bàrd mòr, **a** ~ **deal of money** (*fam*) airgead mòr, (*idiom*) **we are** ~ **friends** tha sinn gu math mòr aig a chèile; **2** (*expr approval etc: fam*) gasta, (*esp as excl*) taghta, **that was just** ~ bha sin dìreach gasta, **I'll do the dishes for you.** ~! Nì mi na soithichean dhut. Taghta!
great- prefix (*for family relationships: of descendants*) iar-, eg **great-grandchild** iar-ogha mf, (*of antecedents*) sinn-, eg **great-grandmother** sinn-seanmhair f
greatcoat n còta-mòr m

greater comp adj **1** mò/motha, **the** ~ **nation** an nàisean as motha/(*in past & conditional tenses*) a bu mhotha, **that nation is** ~ 's e an nàisean sin as motha; **2** in expr **the** ~ **part** a' mhòr-chuid f, **the** ~ **part of his life** a' mhòr-chuid de (a) bheatha
greatly adv gu mòr
greatness n **1** (*size, extent*) meudachd f invar, **the** ~ **of their debts** meudachd nam fiachan aca; **2** (*in prestige, reputation etc*) mòrachd f invar
Greece n (*used with art*) A' Ghrèig f
greed n (*for wealth, food*) gionaiche m invar, sannt m, (*esp for food*) geòcaireachd f invar
greedy adj (*for wealth, food*) gionach, sanntach, (*esp for food*) geòcach
Greek adj Greugach
Greek n **1** (*person*) Greugach m; **2** (*the language; used with art*), a' Ghreugais f invar
green adj uaine, gorm, (*less intense* ~) glas, ~ **grass** feur gorm/uaine, ~ **hillocks** tulaichean glasa
green n **1** (*the colour*) dath uaine m; **2** (*expanse of grass*) rèidhlean m
greenhouse n taigh-glainne m, **the** ~ **effect** buaidh an taigh-ghlainne f
greens n (*ie vegetables*) glasraich f sing coll invar
greet v fàiltich vt, cuir fàilte f (*with prep* air)
greeting n fàilte f, dùrachd f
gregarious adj greigheach, cèilidheach
grey adj **1** glas, ~ **trousers** briogais ghlas; **2** (*of landscape, hair*) liath, in expr **turn/become/go** ~ liath vi, fàs vi liath
grey v liath vi, **her hair is** ~**ing** tha a falt a' liathadh
greyhound n mial-chù m
grid n cliath f, **cattle** ~ cliath cruidh (*gen of* crodh m sing coll), (*on maps*) ~ **line** loidhne-clèithe (*gen of* cliath) f, ~ **reference** comharradh-clèithe m, ~ **square** ceàrnag clèithe f
griddle, gridiron n (*baking*) greideal f
grief n **1** mulad f, (*stronger*) dòlas m, (*excl*) **good** ~! an dòlas!, O mo chreach!, mo chreach-s' a thàinig!
grievance n cùis-ghearain f
grieve v **1** caoidh vti, (*saying*) **what the eye doesn't see the heart doesn't** ~ **over** cha chaoidh duine an rud nach fhaic e; **2** (*mourn*) bi vi irreg ri bròn m, **they are grieving** tha iad ri bròn
grievous adj crài(dh)teach
grill n (*for cooking*) grìos m

grill v 1 (*cookery*) grìosaich vt; 2 (*interrogate*) mion-cheasnaich vt

grind v 1 (*general*) pronn vt; 2 (*esp corn*) meil vt, bleith vt

grip n grèim m, glacadh m, **keep a ~ on something** cùm grèim air rudeigin

grip v gabh grèim m (*with prep* air), **~ the ladder** gabh grèim air an fhàradh, (*idiom*) **she was ~ping his hand** bha grèim aice air làimh f dat air

grizzled adj riabhach

groan n (*of pain or grief*) cnead m, **she let out a ~** leig i cnead (aiste)

groan v dèan cnead m, leig cnead, **she ~ed** rinn i cnead, leig i cnead (aiste)

grocer n grosair m

groove n clais f

grope v 1 (*in search of something*) rùraich vi; 2 (*feel one's way blindly*) smeuraich vi

gross adj 1 (*in character*) garbh, borb; 2 (*of sums of money*) iomlan, slàn, **~ interest** riadh iomlan m

grotty adj mosach, dràbhail, (*more fam*) grodach

grouchy adj crost(a) & crosda, gruamach, fo ghruaim f dat

ground adj & past part pronn

ground n 1 (*land*) talamh m (f in gen sing), fearann m, **arable/cultivated ~** talamh-àitich, **fallow ~** talamh bàn, **cultivate/till the ~** àitich am fearann, **a piece of ~** pìos fearainn m; 2 (*the surface of the ~*) làr m, **he knocked him/it to the ~** leag e gu làr e, **stretched out on the ~** sìnte air an làr; 3 (*of pibroch & other music*) ùrlar m; 4 **~s** (*ie reason(s), justification etc*) adhbhar m, **the ~s for his complaint** adhbhar a ghearain

groundless (*without justification*) gun adhbhar m

grounds[1] npl (*cause, justification*) see **ground** n 4

grounds[2] npl (*in liquids*) grùid f

group n 1 (*of people*) grunn m, (*smaller*) grunnan, **there was a ~ of people at the bus stop** bha grunn(an) dhaoine aig àite-stad nam busaichean; 2 (*esp a ~ formed for a specific purpose*) còmhlan m, buidheann mf, **a pressure ~** buidheann-strì, **a research ~** buidheann-rannsachaidh, (*music*) **a ~** còmhlan-ciùil m

grouse[1] n (*the bird*) coileach-fraoich m, in expr **red ~** cearc-ruadh f, cearc-fhraoich f

grouse[2] n (*grumble etc*) gearan m

grouse v gearain vi

grove n doire mf

grow v 1 fàs vi, **it's barley that's ~ing here** 's e eòrna a tha a' fàs ann a sheo, **the boy's ~ing pretty quickly** tha am balach a' fàs gu math luath; 2 (*become*) fàs vi (*with adj*), thig vi (*with n & prep* air), rach vi (*with prep* an/am & abstr n), **~ old** fàs sean, **they grew tired (of it)** dh'fhàs iad sgìth (dheth), **I grew afraid/sorrowful/hungry** thàinig eagal/mulad/acras orm, **~ bigger** rach am meud, **grow weary/tired** fàs vi sgìth, (*esp through tedium*) gabh fadachd f invar, **~ worse** rach am miosad; 3 **~ up** (*pass through childhood*) tog vt (*used in passive voice*), **I grew up in Coll** thogadh mi ann an Colla, (*reach maturity*) thig vi irreg gu inbhe f; 4 (*of sky etc*) **~ dark** ciar vi, fàs vi dorcha, **the evening grew dark** chiar am feasgar

growl, growling n dranndan m, dranndail f invar, grùnsgal m

growl v dèan dranndan m, in expr **apt to ~** dranndanach

grown adj & past part, **a ~ man** duine dèanta/foirfe, duine a th' air fàs suas

grown-up adj & n inbheach m

growth n (*con & abstr*) fàs m, cinneas m, **new/fresh ~** ùr-fhàs m, **economic ~** cinneas eaconamach

grub[1] n (*of insect*) cnuimh f

grub[2] n (*food*) biadh m

grumble n gearan m

grumble v 1 gearain vi (**about** air), (*less usu*) talaich vi, **you needn't bother grumbling all the time!** cha leig thu a leas a bhith a' gearan/ri gearan fad na h-ùine!; 2 in expr **apt to ~** gearanach

grumbling adj gearanach

grumbling n gearan m

grumpiness n gruaim f

grumpy adj gruamach, fo ghruaim f dat, crost(a) & crosda

grunt n 1 gnòsail f; 2 (*esp of pig*) rùchd m

grunt v 1 dèan gnòsail f; 2 (*esp of pig*) rùchd vi

guarantee n 1 (*general*) bar(r)antas m; 2 (*esp in fin matters*) urras m, **stand as ~ for someone** rach vi an urras air cuideigin

guarantee v rach vi an urras m (**that** gu)

guard n 1 (*abstr: soldier etc*) faire f, **be on ~ (duty)** dèan/cùm faire; 2 (*coll; con*) faire f, freiceadan m, **put a ~ on it** cuir faire air; 3 (*a single ~, a member of the ~*) fear-faire m; 4 in expr **put someone on his/her ~** cuir cuideigin air earalas m

guess n tuaiream f, tuairmse f, tomhas m, **take a ~ at it** thoir tuaiream air

guess *v* tomhais *vt*, thoir tuaiream *f*, ~ **how
many there are** tomhais cia mheud a th' ann
guest *n* aoigh *m*
guidance *n* **1** treòrachadh *m*, iùl *m*, (*ed*) ~
teacher tidsear-treòrachaidh *m*; **2** (*advice*)
comhairle *f*
guide *n* **1** neach-iùil *m* (*pl* luchd-iùil *m sing coll*),
(*esp tourist* ~) neach-treòrachaidh *m* (*pl* luchd-
treòrachaidh *m sing coll*); **2** *in expr* ~ **book**
leabhar-iùil *m*
guide *v* treòraich *vt*, seòl *vt*, stiùir *vt*, ~ **tourists**
treòraich luchd-turais *m sing coll*
guideline(s) *n*(*pl*) stiùireadh *m*, seòladh *m*
guilt *n* ciont(a) *m*, (*less usu*) coill *f invar*
guiltless *adj* neoichiontach
guilty *adj* ciontach, coireach, (**of** air), ~ **person**
ciontach *m*, coireach *m*
gull *n* faoileag *f*, **great black-backed** ~ farspag
& arspag *f*, **lesser black-backed** ~ (f)arspag
bheag

gullet *n* slugan *m*
gulp, **gulping** *n* glug *m*, glugan *m*
gum *n* (*plant substance & adhesive*) bìth *f*,
(*adhesive*) glaodh *m*
gum(s) *n* (*of mouth*) càireas *m*, càirean *m*
gumption *n* toinisg *f*, ciall *f*
gun *n* gunna *m*, (*artillery* ~) gunna-mòr
gunner *n* gunnair *m*
gurgle, **gurgling** *n* **1** (*of persons*) glug *m*; **2** (*of
liquids*) glugan *m*, plubraich *f*
gust *n* osag *f*, oiteag *f*
gut *n* **1** (*intestine*) caolan *m*, (*idiom: vulg*) **I
spewed my ~s up** chuir mi a-mach rùchd
m mo chaolanan; **2** (*~s of other creatures &
fam for human stomach*) mionach *m*, **fish ~s**
mionach-èisg
gut *v* (*fish etc*) cut *vti*
gutter[1] *n* (*for drainage*) guitear *m*
gutter[2] *n* (*of fish etc*) cutair *m*

H

habit *n* cleachdadh *m*, àbhaist *f*, gnàth *m*
habitat *n* àrainn *f*
habitual *adj* àbhaisteach, (*less usu*) gnàthach
hag *n* (*pej*) badhbh *f*, cailleach *f*
haggis *n* taigeis *f*
hail, hailstone *n* clach-mheallain *f*
hair *n* **1** (*coll: on human head*) falt *m sing coll*, gruag *f sing coll*, (*a single ~*) fuiltean *m*, ròineag *f*; **2** (*~ of animal*) fionnadh *m sing coll*, gaoisid *f sing coll*; **3** (*idiom*) **the ~ of the dog** leigheas na poit *m*
hairdresser *n* gruagaire *m*
hairdryer *n* tiormaichear-gruaig *m*
hairy *adj* fionnach, molach, robach, ròmach
half *adv* **1** leth, leitheach, **~ dead** leth-mharbh, **~ awake** na (*etc*) leth-dhùsgadh *m* (*also* na (*etc*) leth-dhùisg), **we were ~ awake** bha sinn nar leth-dhùsgadh/nar leth-dhùisg, **~ full** leitheach làn, **it's ~ past four** tha e leth-uair an dèidh a ceithir; **2** (*idiom*) **~ in jest/earnest** eadar fealla-dhà *f invar* is da-rìribh *adv*
half *n* **1** leth *f*, leth-chuid *f*, **the other ~** an leth eile, **a mile and a ~** mìle gu leth, **~ and ~** leth mar leth, **how much did you lose? ~ (of it)** dè na chaill thu dheth? an dàrna leth; **2** *in exprs* **~ as much** (a) leth uiread *m invar*, **~ as much again** a leth uiread eile, **~ as much as Peter has** a leth uiread agus a tha aig Peadar
half-hearted *adj* leth-fhuar, **a ~ welcome** fàilte leth-fhuar
halfway *adv* leitheach-slighe, leitheach-rathaid, (**between** eadar), **~ between X and Y** leitheach-slighe eadar X is Y
hall *n* talla *m*, **the village/town ~** talla a' bhaile
Halloween *n* Oidhche Shamhna (*gen of* Samhain *f*)
halo *n* fàinne-solais *f*
hamlet *n* clachan *m*
hammer *n* òrd *m*
hand *n* **1** làmh *f*, (*derog: of large, clumsy etc hand*) cròg *f*, **he didn't shake my ~** cha do rug e air làimh *dat* orm, **the back of the ~** cùl *m* na làimh(e), **hollow of the ~** glac *f*, **helping**

~ làmh-chuideachaidh *f*, **he's on his ~s and knees** tha e air a mhàg(ar)an, **what couldn't he turn his ~ to?** cò ris nach cuireadh e a làmh?, **take a matter in ~** gabh gnothach os làimh; **2** *in expr* **on the other ~** air mhodh *mf* eile, air an làimh eile
hand *v* **1** sìn *vt* (*with prep* gu), **she ~ed me the key** shìn i thugam an iuchair; **2** *in exprs* **~ over** thoir *vt* seachad, **~ around** thoir *vt* mun cuairt, cuir *vt* mun cuairt
handbag *n* màileid-làimhe *f*
handball *n* ball-làimhe *m*
handcuffs *n* glasan-làimhe *fpl*
handful *n* làn *m* dùirn (*gen of* dòrn *m*), dòrlach *m*, **I had a ~ of seed** bha làn mo dhùirn agam de shìol
handgun *n* daga *&* dag *m*
handicap *n* **1** (*general*) bacadh *m*, **poverty is a great ~** 's e bacadh mòr a th' anns a' bhochdainn; **2** (*phys ~*) ciorram *m*
handicapped *adj* **1** (*by a disability*) ciorramach, **mentally ~** ciorramach na (*etc*) inntinn, **a ~ person** ciorramach *n*, **the ~** na ciorramaich *mpl*; **2** (*~ socially, economically etc*) ana-cothromach
handkerchief *n* neapaigear *m*
handle *n* **1** (*of tool etc*) cas *f*, **knife ~** cas-sgeine (*gen of* sgian *f*); **2** (*of jug, mug, cup, casserole etc*) cluas *f*
handle *v* **1** (*phys*) làimhsich *vt*, (*esp tool, weapon*) iomair *vt*; **2** (*~ situations, people etc*) dèilig *vi* (*with prep* ri), làimhsich *vt*
handlebar *n* crann-làmh *m*
handshake *n* crathadh-làimhe *m*
handsome *adj* gasta, eireachdail, **a sturdy ~ man** duine calma gasta
handwriting *n* làmh-sgrìobhadh *m*
handy *adj* **1** (*convenient*) deiseil, ullamh, goireasach, **that'll be ~ for you** bidh sin deiseil/ullamh dhut; **2** *in expr* **be/come in ~** dèan feum *m*, bi *vi irreg* feumail, (**for** do), **scissors would be ~/would come in ~ (for us) just now** dhèanadh siosar feum (dhuinn)

an-dràsta, bhiodh siosar feumail (dhuinn) an-dràsta; **3** (*of person; good with one's hands*) gleusta, deas-làmhach

hang *v* (*person, picture etc*) croch *vt*

hanged *adj & past part* crochte

hanging *adj & pres part* an crochadh *m*, crochte, **a coat ~ing behind the door c**òta an crochadh air cùl an dorais

hangman *n* crochadair *m*

hangover *n* ceann daoraich *m*

happen *v* **1** (*occur, befall*) tachair *vi* (**to** do), **what's ~ing? nothing** dè a tha a' tachairt? chan eil càil, **what ~ed to James?** dè a thachair do Sheumas?, **that's how it ~ed** (*often impersonal in Gaelic*) 's ann mar sin a thachair, sin mar a thachair (e); **2** (*become of*) èirich *vi* (*with prep* do), **what ~ed to James?** dè a dh'èirich do Sheumas?; **3** (*chance: with Gaelic impersonal constrs*) tachair *vi*, tuit *vi* (*with prep* do), **I ~ed to see him on the street** thachair gum faca mi air an t-sraid e, thuit dhomh fhaicinn air an t-sràid; **4** *in expr* **~ on/upon** (*ie come across, stumble upon*) tachair *vi*, amais *vi*, (*with prep* air)

happening *n* tachartas *m*, tuiteamas *m*

happy *adj* toilichte, (*less common*) sona, **I'm ~ to do that for you** tha mi toilichte sin a dhèanamh dhut, **I hope they were ~** tha mi an dòchas gun robh iad toilichte/sona

happy-go-lucky *adj* guanach, (*can be pej*) coma co-dhiù

harass *v* claoidh *vt*, sàraich *vt*

harassment *n* sàrachadh *m*, **sexual ~** sàrachadh gnèitheasach, sàrachadh drùiseach

harbour *n* port *m*, cala *m*

hard *adj* **1** (*lit & fig*) cruaidh, **~ work** obair chruaidh, **a ~ land** tìr c(h)ruaidh, (*of book*) **~ cover/back** còmhdach cruaidh, (*IT*) **~ disc** clàr cruaidh; **2** (*difficult, painful*) duilich, **it is ~ for me to leave** is duilich leam falbh; **3** (*difficult, taxing*) doirbh, **a ~ question** cèist dhoirbh *f*, **that's ~ to say** tha sin doirbh a ràdh; **4** (*of argument, book etc: ~ to understand*) deacair; **5** (*idiom*) **the army was ~ on their heels** bha an t-arm teann orra

harden *v* cruadhaich *vti*, **don't ~ your heart!** na cruadhaich do chridhe!

hard-hearted *adj* cruaidh-chridheach

hardihood *n* cruadal *m*, cruas *m*

hardiness *n* cruas *m*, fulang *m*

hardly *adv*, *same as* **barely** *adv*

hardness *n* cruas *m*

hardship *n* cruadal *m*

hardworking *adj* gnìomhach, dèanadach, dìcheallach, èasgaidh, (*fam*) cruaidh air an obair

hardy *adj* fulangach, cruadalach, cruaidh

hare *n* maigheach *f*, geàrr *f*

harm *n* **1** lochd *m*, milleadh *m*, beud *m*; **2** (*not usu phys*) cron *m*; **3** (*idiom*) **a pint** (*etc*) **wouldn't do me any ~ just now** cha bu mhiste mi pinnt (*etc*) an-dràsta

harm *v* **1** goirtich *vt*, mill *vt*; **2** (*not usu phys*) dèan cron *m* (*with prep* air); **3** (*~ someone's feelings, situation etc*) ciùrr *vt*

harmful *adj* lochdach, cronail, millteach, cunnartach

harmonious *adj* ceòlmhor

harmony *n* **1** (*music*) co-sheirm *f*; **2** (*lack of dissension etc*) co-aontachadh *m*, co-chòrdadh *m*; **3** (*idiom*) **they lived in ~ with their neighbours** bha iad rèidh ris na nàbaidhean aca

harness *n* uidheam *f*, acainn *f*

harp *n* clàrsach *f*, (*more trad*) cruit *f*

harper *n* clàrsair *m*, (*more trad*) cruitear *m*

harpsichord *n* cruit-chòrda *f*

Harris *n*, (*used with art*), Na Hearadh *f invar*, (*as adj*) Hearach, **~ Tweed** An Clò Hearach, *also* An Clò Mòr, **a ~ man, a man from ~** Hearach *m*

harrow *n* cliath *f*

harrow *v* **1** (*agric*) cliath *vti*; **2** (*~ emotionally*) cràidh *vt*

harrowing *adj* crài(dh)teach, dòrainneach, **a ~ story** sgeulachd dhòrainneach

harsh *adj* **1** (*person, situation*) cruaidh, garbh, **a ~ land** tìr chruaidh/gharbh, **a ~ man** duine cruaidh/garbh, **a ~ voice** guth garbh; **2** (*phys sensations, words, temperament*) geur, searbh, **a ~ taste** blas geur/searbh, **~ words** briathran geura/searbha, **a ~ wind** gaoth gheur

harshness *n* cruas *m*, gèire *f invar*, searbhachd *f invar*

harvest *n* foghar *m*, buain *f*, **the barley ~** foghar an eòrna

haste *n* **1** cabhag *f*, (*stronger*) deann *f*, **in ~** ann an cabhaig *dat*, **he left in (great) ~** dh'fhalbh e na dheann, **make ~** dèan cabhag, (*as imper*) **make ~!** greas ort/greasaibh oirbh!, dèan/dèanaibh cabhag!

hasten *v* **1** (*make haste*) dèan cabhag *f*; **2** (*hurry on others*) cuir cabhag (*with prep* air)

hasty *adj* (*action etc*) cabhagach

hatch *v* **1** (*eggs*) guir *vti*; **2** (*~ a plot etc*) innlich *vt*

hatchet *n* làmhthuagh *f*, làmhadh *m*, làmhag *f*

hate *n* gràin *f*, fuath *m*

hate v fuathaich vt, more usu expr by bi vi irreg gràin f with preps aig & air, eg **I ~ him** tha gràin agam air, **they ~d her** bha gràin aca oirre

hateful adj gràineil, fuathach

hatred n gràin f, fuath m

haugh n innis f

haughtiness n àrdan m, uaibhreas m, uabhar m

haughty adj uaibhreach, àrdanach

haul v tarraing vti (**on** air), slaod vti

haulage n **1** giùlan m; **2** (the charges levied for ~) faradh m

haunt v (visit frequently, hang around in/at) tathaich vi (with prep air)

have v **1** (expr possession etc) bi vi irreg (with prep aig), **I ~ a house and a dog** tha taigh agus cù agam, **she had a headache** bha ceann goirt aice; **2** exprs with gabh vt, thoir vt, **will you ~ a cup of tea?** an gabh thu cupan tì?, **don't ~ anything to do with him/it!** na gabh gnothach m ris!, **~ pity on them** gabh truas m dhiubh, **~ a look at the newspaper** thoir sùil f air a' phàipear-naidheachd; **3 ~ to** (ie must) feum vi, 's fheudar, in past & conditional tenses b' fheudar (with prep do), **I ~ to admit that . . .** feumaidh mi aideachadh gu . . . , **do you ~ to go?** am feum sibh falbh?, **she has to/had to stop** 's fheudar/b' fheudar dhi sgur, Note also constructions such as **I ~ a lot to do** tha mòran agam ri dhèanamh, **I ~ a letter to write** tha litir agam ri sgrìobhadh; **4 ~ to** (be or feel compelled), thig vi irreg (with prep air & verbal noun), **I had to do it** thàinig orm a dhèanamh m, (also, using double neg constr) cha b' urrainn dhomh gun a dhèanamh

hay n tràthach m

hay-fork n gòbhlag f

hazardous adj cunnartach

haze n ceò m

hazel n calltainn m

hazelnut n cnò challtainn f

hazy adj ceòthach

he pers pron e, (emph form) esan, **he saw him** chunnaic e e

head adj prìomh (precedes the noun, which it lenites where possible), **the ~ clerk** am prìomh-chlèireach, **the ~ office of the company** prìomh-oifis a' chompanaidh

head n **1** ceann m, **he shook his ~** chrath e a cheann, **she bent/bowed her ~** chrom i a ceann, **~ first** an comhair f invar a chinn gen, **side of the ~** lethcheann m; **2** (~ of organisation etc) ceannard m; **3** in expr **~ of hair** gruag f; **4** in expr (of collision etc) **~ on** an comhair a thoisich; **5** in expr **a ~** (ie each) an

urra f, **we spent 50p a ~** chosg sinn leth-cheud sgillinn an urra

headache n ceann goirt m, **I have a ~** tha mo cheann goirt

headgear n ceannbheart f

heading n (in text etc) ceann m

headland n rubha m

headline n ceann-naidheachd m

headlong adj na (etc) d(h)eann-ruith f, na etc d(h)eann f, **they left in a ~ rush** dh'fhalbh iad nan deann-ruith/nan deann

headlong adv an comhair f invar a (etc) c(h)inn m gen, **she fell ~** thuit i an comhair a cinn

headstrong adj **1** (wilful) ceann-làidir; **2** (obstinate) rag-mhuinealach

head-teacher n (usu secondary school) maighistir-sgoile m

heal v slànaich vti, leighis vt, **the wound ~ed** shlànaich an leòn

healing n slànachadh m, leigheas m

health n **1** slàinte f, **~ centre** ionad-slàinte m; **2** in exprs **in good ~** slàn, fallain, **in bad ~** tinn, euslainteach, (toast) **good ~!** slàinte!

health-giving adj (of food etc) fallain

healthy adj (in good health, also health-giving) slàn, fallain

heap n tòrr m, cruach f, (small ~) cruachan m

heap v cruach vt, càrn vt

hear v cluinn vt irreg, **he can't ~ a thing** cha chluinn e bìd m/bìog f, **I ~d you were ill** chuala mi gun robh thu tinn, **it's good to be ~ing from you!** 's math a bhith a' cluinntinn bhuat!

hearing n claisneachd & claisteachd f invar, **I'm losing my ~** tha mi a' call mo chlaisneachd

heart n **1** cridhe m, **~ disease** tinneas cridhe m, **~ attack** clisgeadh-cridhe m, grèim-cridhe m; **2** in exprs **in good ~** misneachail, **the ~ of the matter** cnag na cùise f

heartbeat buille cridhe f

heartbreak n bris(t)eadh-cridhe m

heartbroken adj & past part, **she's ~** tha a cridhe m briste, **you left me ~** dh'fhàg thu mi 's mo chridhe briste

heartburn n losgadh-bràghad m

hearth n cagailt f, teallach m, teinntean m, **at the ~** ris a' chagailt dat

hearthstone n leac-theallaich f

heartiness n cridhealas m

heart-rending adj dòrainneach

hearty adj (person, atmosphere etc) cridheil, **a ~ welcome** fàilte chridheil

heat n teas m invar, **~ wave** tonn teasa mf, teas-tonn mf

heat, heat up, v teasaich vti

heater n (domestic etc) uidheam teasachaidh f

heath n 1 monadh m, sliabh m, mòinteach f; 2 (the plant) fraoch m

heathen n cinneach m

heather n fraoch m

heather-cock n coileach-fraoich m

heating n (domestic etc) teasachadh m, ~ **appliance** uidheam teasachaidh f

heave v 1 (throw) tilg vt, caith vt; 2 (haul etc) tarraing vi, slaod vi, (on air)

heaven n 1 nèamh m, flaitheas m, pàrras m; 2 in expr **the ~s** an iarmailt f; 3 (excl) **good ~s!** obh! obh!, O mo chreach!; 4 in expr **why, in ~'s name, (did you do it** etc)? carson, a chiall, (a rinn thu e etc)?

heavenly adj nèamhaidh

heaviness n truimead m, **the ~ of my heart** truimead mo chridhe

heavy adj trom, (less usu) cudromach, ~ **parcels** parsailean troma, **a ~ step** ceum trom, ~ **on the booze** (fam) trom air an deoch f, **with a ~ heart** le cridhe trom

Hebrew adj & n Eabhrach

Hebrew n (the lang) Eabhra f, (with art) an Eabhra

Hebrides n, **the ~** npl Innse Gall fpl

hectare n heactair m

hectic adj (at work etc) dripeil, **things are pretty ~ just now** tha cùisean fpl gu math dripeil an-dràsta

hedge n callaid f, fàl m

hedgehog n gràineag f

heed n aire f invar, feart & feairt f, **without paying ~ to it** gun aire/feart a thoirt air

heel n 1 sàil f, (less usu) bonn-dubh m; 2 (command to dog) **(come to my) ~!** cùl m mo chois'! (gen of cas f); 3 (idioms & exprs) **the army was hard on their ~s** bha an t-arm teann orra, **he took to his ~s** thug e na buinn mpl às, thug e a chasan fpl leis, (fig) **drag one's ~s** màirnealaich vi, bi vi irreg màirnealach, bi slaodach

height n 1 (lit) àirde f, **what ~ is it?** dè an àirde a tha ann?; 2 (fig) in expr **at the ~ of his/her powers/strength** an treun f invar a neirt (gen of neart m), also aig àird f a c(h)omais (gen of comas m)

heir n oighre m

heiress n ban-oighre f

held adj & past part 1 glèidhte; 2 (~ **in captivity**) an grèim m, an sàs m, an làimh (dat of làmh f)

helicopter n heileacopta(i)r m

hell n 1 (lit) ifrinn f, (less usu) iutharn(a) f; 2 (misc fig exprs & idioms) ~ **of a . . .** garbh adv, **things are ~ of a busy just now** tha cùisean garbh dripeil an-dràsta, **they set off ~ for leather** dh'fhalbh iad nan deann-ruith f, thog iad orra nan deann f, (with attenuated meaning) **it was sheer ~!** bha e dìreach sgriosail!, (as excl) ~! mac an donais!

hellish adj 1 (lit) ifrinneach; 2 (with attenuated fig meaning) sgriosail, **a ~ day** latha sgriosail

hello excl halò

helm n falmadair m, ailm f

helmet n cloga(i)d mf

help n 1 (relief, aid) cobhair f, (as excl) ~! (dèan) cobhair orm!, cuidich mi!; 2 (more general) cuideachadh m, **thank you for your ~** mòran taing airson ur cuideachaidh; 3 in expr **financial ~** taic f airgid (gen of airgead m); 4 (person who helps) cuidiche mf, **home ~** cuidiche-taighe

help v 1 cuidich vti, dèan cobhair f (with prep air), ~ **them** cuidich iad, (more trad) cuidich leotha, dèan cobhair orra, **a ~ing hand** làmh-chuideachaidh f; 2 (avoid, prevent oneself etc) **I can't ~/couldn't ~ . . .** chan urrainn/cha b' urrainn dhomh . . ., with conj gun, **I couldn't ~ being sad** cha b' urrainn dhomh gun a bhith brònach; 3 (idiom) **it can't be ~ed** chan eil cothrom m air

helper n cuidiche m

helpful adj cuideachail

hem n fàitheam m

hemisphere n leth-chruinne mf

hemp n cainb f

hen n cearc f, **the ~ wife** cailleach nan cearc

henceforth adv o seo a-mach

her poss adj 1 a (does not lenite a following noun), ~ **mother** a màthair; 2 aice (follows the noun and art: tends to be used with objects etc less intimately connected with the individual concerned eg ~ **pen** am peann aice (though note exceptions such as ~ **house** an taigh aice, ~ **husband** an duine aice)

her pron i, (emph form) ise

herb n luibh mf, lus m

herd n treud m, (esp of cattle) buar m

herd v (usu cattle) buachaillich vi

heritage n 1 (lit & fig) dìleab f, **the ~ of history** dìleab na h-eachdraidh; 2 (inherited property etc) oighreachd f; 3 (cultural ~) dualchas m

hermaphrodite adj fireann-boireann

hermaphrodite n fireann-boireann m

hero n curaidh m, gaisgeach m, laoch m

heroic adj gaisgeil

heroism n gaisge f invar, gaisgeachd f invar
heron n corra-ghritheach f
herself reflexive pron i fhèin, for examples of use
  cf **myself** & **-self** reflexive suffix
hesitate v 1 (through indecision) màirnealaich
  vi, bi vi irreg an imcheist f, bi eadar-dhà-lionn;
  2 (through unwillingness) is v irreg & def leisg,
  with prep le & verbal noun, **I ~ to admit it** is
  leisg leam aideachadh
hesitating adj (undecided) an imcheist f, eadar-
  dhà-lionn
heterogeneous adj ioma-sheòrsach
hibernation n cadal-geamhraidh m
hiccups n an aileag f sing, **I've got (the) ~** tha
  an aileag orm
hidden adj & past part falaichte, am falach m,
  air falach
hide¹ n (pelt) seiche f, bian m
hide² n (place of concealment) àite-falaich m
hide v 1 (as vt) cuir vt am falach m, ceil vt (**from**
  air), **~ it** cuir am falach e, **~ it from her** ceil
  oirre e; 2 (as vi) rach vi am falach m (**from**
  air), **they hid (from me)** chaidh iad am falach
  (orm)
hide-and-seek n falach-fead m
hide-out n àite-falaich m
hiding¹ n (concealment) falach m, **in ~** am falach,
  go into ~ rach vi am falach
hiding² n 1 (a beating) slacadh & slaiceadh
  m, pronnadh m, **he got a (good) ~** chaidh a
  phronnadh; 2 (a defeat in sport etc) **we gave
  them a ~!** rinn sinn a' chùis orra!
hiding place n àite-falaich m
high adj 1 (phys ~) àrd; 2 in expr **~ tide** muir-làn
  m, làn-mara m
higher adj nas àirde (in past & conditional tenses
  na b' àirde), as àirde (in past & conditional
  tenses a b' àirde), **that hill is ~** tha an cnoc sin
  nas àirde, **a ~ hill** cnoc as àirde, **that hill is the
  ~ (one)** 's e an cnoc sin as àirde
highland adj (topog) àrd-thìreach
highland n (topog) àrd-thìr f
Highland adj Gàidhealach, **~ Games**
  Geamannan Gàidhealach mpl
Highlander n Gàidheal m
Highlands n Gàidhealtachd f invar, used with
  art, **the ~** a' Ghàidhealtachd, **in the ~** air a'
  Ghàidhealtachd
highlight v 1 soillsich vt; 2 (fig: emphasise etc)
  cuir cudthrom m (with prep air)
high-ranking adj inbheil
highway n rathad-mòr m
high-yielding adj torrach
hilarity n cridhealas m,

hill n 1 (large ~, mountain) beinn f, (usu small
  to medium-sized) cnoc m, (small, usu rounded)
  tom m, (esp conical or mound shaped) tòrr m,
  (usu rounded or conical) dùn m, (usu conical)
  cruach f, (dimin) cruachan m, (stony) càrn m,
  (usu rocky) creag f, (usu lumpy) meall m; 2
  (esp agric etc: rough grazing etc) monadh m,
  (moorland) mòinteach f, sliabh m
hillock n cnoc m, cnocan m, toman m, tulach m
hillside, hillslope n leathad m, ruighe mf
hilly adj cnocach, monadail
him pron e, (emph form) esan, **he saw ~**
  chunnaic e e
himself reflexive pron e fhèin, for examples of
  use cf **myself** & **-self** reflexive suffix
hind n (female of red deer) eilid f
hinge n lùdag f, banntach f
hip n (anat) cruachann f
hippopotamus n each-aibhne m
hire v (workers) fastaich, also fastaidh, vt
hirsute adj ròmach
historian n eachdraiche m
historical adj eachdraidheil
history n eachdraidh f, **she did ~ at university**
  rinn i eachdraidh anns an oilthigh, **local ~**
  eachdraidh ionadail
hither adv 1 an seo, a-bhos, an taobh seo, an
  taobh a-bhos, a-nall; 2 in expr **~ and thither**
  thall 's a-bhos
hitherto adv gu ruige seo
hoar frost n liath-reothadh m
hoard n tasgaidh f
hoard v taisg vt
hoarse adj 1 tùchanach; 2 (idiom) **I am ~, I
  have become ~** tha an tùchadh air tighinn
  orm; 3 in expr **a ~ voice** guth garbh
hoarseness n tùchadh m
hobby n cur-seachad m
hobnail n tacaid f
hoe n todha m
hoe v todhaig vt
hoeing n obair-todha f
hog(g) n (1-2 yr old ewe lamb) othaisg f
hoist v tog vt, **~ the sails!** togaibh na siùil! mpl
hold n grèim m, **take ~ of something** gabh
  grèim air rudeigin, **keep ~ of something** cùm
  grèim air rudeigin
hold v 1 (take hold of) gabh grèim m (with prep
  air), (keep hold) cùm grèim (with prep air);
  2 (contain) cùm vt, gabh vt, **will it ~ all my
  clothes? a**n cùm e/an gabh e mo chuid aodaich
  air fad?, **the hall will ~ 300 people** gabhaidh
  an talla trì cheud duine; 3 in expr **~ back, ~ up**
  (ie delay) cùm vt air ais, cuir maille f invar (with

prep air *or* ann), **I won't ~ you back/up** cha chùm mi air ais sibh, **~ up the proceedings** cuir maille air/anns a' ghnothach, (*idiom*) **if they're held up** ma thèid maille orra; **4** *in expr* **~ on to** (*ie keep, save*) cùm *vt*, glèidh *vt*, **~ on to this for me till Friday** cùm seo dhomh gu Dihaoine; **5** (*idiom*) **she was ~ing his hand** bha grèim aice air làimh air

holding *n* (*of land*) lot *f*, croit *f*

hole *n* toll *m*, *in expr* **full of ~s** tolltach

hole *v* toll *vt*, **the boat was ~d** (*ie became holed*) chaidh am bàta a tholladh

holiday *n* **1** (*esp vacation, time off*) saor-latha *m*, **~s** làithean-saora & saor-làithean *mpl*, **on ~** air làithean-saora; **2** (*esp public ~*) latha-fèille *m*

holiness *n* naomhachd *f invar*

Holland *n* An Òlaind *f*

hollow *adj* còsach, falamh

hollow *n* **1** toll *m*; **2** (*topog*) còs *m*, glac *f*, lag *mf*

holly *n* cuileann *m*

holy *adj* **1** naomh, **the Holy Ghost/Spirit** An Spiorad Naomh *m*; **2** *in expr* **~ Communion** comanachadh *m*

homage (*before royalty etc*) ùmhlachd *f invar*

home *adv* dhachaigh, **going ~** a' dol dhachaigh, **I'm away ~!** tha mi a' falbh dhachaigh!, **the way ~** an rathad dhachaigh

home *n* **1** dachaigh *f invar*, **that's my ~** 's e sin mo dhachaigh(-sa), **old folks' ~** dachaigh nan seann daoine; **2** *in exprs* **at ~** aig an taigh *m*, **away from ~**, **not at ~** on taigh, **~ help** cuidiche-taighe *mf*, **~ farm** mànas *m*, **Home Secretary/Office** Rùnaire *m*/Oifis *f* na Dùthcha, **~ rule** fèin-riaghladh *m*

homeland *n* dùthaich *f*, **the Mackay ~** Dùthaich MhicAoidh

homesick *adj* cianalach

homesickness *n* cianalas *m*

homewards *adv* dhachaigh

homogeneous *adj* aon-sheòrsach

homonym *n* co-ainmear *m*

homosexuality *n* fearas-feise *f*

honest *adj* onarach, ionraic

honesty *n* onair *f*, ionracas *m*

honey *n* mil *f*

honeycomb *n* cìr-mheala *f*

honeymoon *n* mìos nam pòg *m*

honeysuckle *n* iadh-shlat & iath-shlat *f*, lus *m* na meala (*gen of* mil *f*)

honorary *adj* onarach, urramach, **an ~ member of the society** ball *m* onarach/ urramach den chomann

honour *n* **1** (*personal ~*) onair *f*, **on my ~!** air m' onair!; **2** (*respect, distinction*) urram *m*,

confer an ~ on someone cuir/builich urram air cuideigin; **3** (*fame, renown*) cliù *m invar*, glòir *f*

honour *v* **1** (*bestow an honour on*) onaraich *vt*, cuir/builich urram *m* (*with prep* air); **2** (*respect, revere*) onaraich *vt*; **3** (*keep, stand by, fulfil*) coilean *vt*, **he ~ed his commitment** choilean e a ghealladh *m*

honourable *adj* onarach, urramach

hood *n* (*headgear*) cochall *m*

hoodie *n* (*Sc: crow*) feannag ghlas

hoof *n* (*of horse, cattle etc*) ìne *f*, ladhar *m*

hook *n* (*for fastenings, hanging objects, fishing, etc*) cromag *f*, dubhan *m*

hoolie *n* (*fam*) hòro-gheallaidh *m invar*

hooligan *n* glagaire *m*

hooliganism *n* miastachd *f invar*, glagaireachd *f invar*

hoop *n* (*wooden*) rong *f*

hooter *n* dùdach *f*, dùdag *f*

hope *n* **1** dòchas *m*, **without ~** gun dòchas, **put one's ~ in something** cuir dòchas ann an rudeigin; **2** (*expectation*) dùil *f*, **without ~ of returning** gun dùil ri tilleadh

hope *v* bi *vi irreg* an dòchas *m*, **I ~ she won't come** tha mi an dòchas nach tig i, **it'll be a good day, I ~** bidh là math ann, tha mi an dòchas

hopeless *adj* gun dòchas

hopelessness *n* eu-dòchas *m*

horizon *n* fàire *f*, **on the ~** air fàire

horizontal *adj* còmhnard

horn *n* **1** (*of animal*) adharc *f*, (*also the material, eg*) **a ~ spoon** spàin adhairc *f*; **2** (*musical instrument, also drinking ~*) còrn *m*

hornless *adj* maol

horrible *adj* **1** uabhasach, oillteil, sgreamhail; **2** (*of behaviour*) suarach (**to** ri), **I was ~ to her last night** bha mi suarach rithe a-raoir

horrify *v* cuir oillt *f* (*with prep* air), oilltich *vt*, **that horrified me** chuir sin oillt orm

horror *n* uamhann *m*, oillt *f*, uabhas *m*, **~s of war** uabhasan cogaidh

horse *n* each *m*

horseback *n* muin eich (*gen of* each *m*), **on ~** air muin eich

horsefly *n* creithleag *f*

horsehair *n* gaoisid *f*

horseman *n* marcaiche *m*, **horsemen** marcaichean *mpl*, *also* eachraidh *m sing coll*

horsemanship *n* marcachadh *m*, marcachd *f invar*

horseshoe *n* crudha *m*

horticulture *n* tuathanachas-gàrraidh *m*

hose[1] *n* (*for water*) pìob-uisge *f*

hose[2] n (*chiefly pl*; *stockings*) osain & osanan, stocainnean (*pl of* osan *m* & stocainn *f*)

hospitable *adj* fialaidh, fial, fàilteachail, fàilteach, faoilidh

hospital n ospadal *m*, (*more trad*) taigh-eiridinn *m*, **in** ~ anns an ospadal

hospitality n aoigheachd *f invar*, furan *m*

host[1] n (*at hotel*) òstair *m*, (*at hotel, private house*) fear (an) taighe *m*

host[2] n 1 (*body of people*) mòr-shluagh *m*; 2 (*an army*) feachd *mf*

hostage n bràigh *mf*

hostel n ostail *f*

hostile *adj* nàimhdeil

hostility n nàimhdeas *m*

hot *adj* 1 teth; 2 (*idiom*) ~ **off the presses** ùr on chlò *m*

hot-blooded *adj* lasanta

hotel n taigh-òsta *m*

hotelier n òstair *m*

hot-water-bottle n botal-teth *m*

hour n uair *f*, (*as clock time, time of day*) **at this** ~ aig an uair seo, (*as lapse or passage of time*) **after (etc) an** ~ an dèidh (*etc*) uair a (*for* de) thìde, an dèidh uair an uaireadair

house n taigh *m*, (*less usu*) fàrdach *f*, **dwelling** ~ taigh-còmhnaidh *m*, **the man of the** ~ fear an taighe *m*, **the House of Commons/of Lords** Taigh nan Cumantan/nam Morairean

house v 1 (*people*) thoir taigh *m*, thoir lòistinn *m*, (*with prep* do); 2 (~ *objects in museum etc*) glèidh *vt*

housecoat n còta-leapa *m*

house-fly n cuileag *f*

housewife n bean (an) taighe *f*

housework n obair-taighe *f*

housing n 1 (*abstr*) taigheadas *m*, **the Housing Committee** Comataidh an Taigheadais *f*; 2 (*con*) taighean *mpl*, ~ **scheme** sgeama-thaighean *m*

how *inter adv* 1 ciamar, ~ **are you today?** ciamar a tha thu an-diugh?, ~ **did he do it?** ciamar a rinn e e?, ~ **did you get on** ciamar a chaidh dhuibh?; 2 (*in exprs of quantity*) ~ **many** cia mheud & co mheud, ~ **many people were there?** cia mheud duine a bha ann?, ~ **much milk have we got?** dè na tha againn de bhainne?; 3 (~ *followed by an adj*) dè cho *plus adj plus* agus/'s *plus rel pron* a *plus verb*, ~ **long will you be here?** dè cho fada 's a bhios tu ann?, ~ **useful is it?** dè cho feumail 's a tha e?; 4 (*misc idioms*) ~ **are you (doing)?** (*fam*) dè do chor *m*?, dè an dòigh *f* a th' ort?, dè

am fonn *m*?, (*cost*) ~ **much is it?** dè na tha e?, **that's** ~ **it is!** is ann mar sin a tha (e)!

howe n (*topog*) lag *mf*

however *adv* 1 ge-tà, co-dhiù, a dh'aindeoin cùise, **he didn't die,** ~ cha do chaochail e, ge-tà/co-dhiù/a dh'aindeoin cùise (*gen of* cùis *f*); 2 (*in concessive clauses*) air cho *plus adj plus* agus/is *plus conj* gu *plus verb*, ~ **tired you may be** air cho sgìth 's gu bheil thu, ~ **poor he was** air cho bochd 's gun robh e

howl n (*esp of dog*) ulfhart *m*, donnal *m*

howl v 1 (*usu of animals*) nuallaich, (*esp dogs*) dèan ulfhart *m*; 2 (*of humans: weep noisily*) ràn *vi*

howling n 1 (*usu of animals*) nuallaich *f*, (*esp of dogs*) donnalaich *f*; 2 (*of humans: noisy weeping*) rànail *m invar*, rànaich *f*

Hoy n Hòdhaigh

hubbub n ùpraid *f*, gleadhraich *f*, othail *f*, iorghail *f*, toirm *f*

hue n 1 (*colour*) dath *m*; 2 (*esp of person's complexion*) fiamh *m*, neul *m*; 3 (*of person's features: not nec permanent*) tuar *m*

hug v 1 fàisg *vt*; 2 (*idioms*) **come and let me** ~ **you!** thig nam chom!, thig nam achlais!

huge *adj* ro-mhòr, (*more fam*) uabhasach mòr, eagalach mòr

hum n crònan *m*, torman *m*

hum v dèan crònan *m*, dèan torman *m*

human *adj* 1 daonna, **the** ~ **race** an cinne-daonna, ~ **rights** còraichean daonna *fpl*; 2 *in expr* ~ **being** duine *m*

humane *adj* truacanta, iochdmhor, daonnach

humanity n 1 (*abstr: humaneness, also the quality of being human*) daonnachd *f invar*; 2 (*con, man, the human race*) an cinne-daonna *m*, mac an duine *m sing coll*

humankind n see **humanity** 2

humble *adj* 1 (*in status etc*) ìosal & ìseal, iriosal & iriseal; 2 (*self-effacing etc*) umha(i)l, iriosal & iriseal

humble v (*humiliate etc*) ùmhlaich *vt*, irioslaich & irislich *vt*, ìslich *vt*

humbleness ùmhlachd *f invar*, irioslachd & irisleachd *f invar*

humid *adj* tais

humidity n taise *f invar*, taisead *m*

humiliate v ùmhlaich *vt*, irioslaich & irislich *vt*, ìslich *vt*

humiliation n ùmhlachadh *m*, irioslachadh & irisleachadh *m*, ìsleachadh *m*

humility n irioslachd & irisleachd *f invar*

humming n crònan *m*, torman *m*

humorous *adj* èibhinn, àbhachdach

humour *n* 1 àbhachd *f invar*, àbhachdas *m*; 2 (*mood*) gleus *mf*, gean *m*, **in good** ~ air (deagh) ghleus, *also* gleusta, **good/bad** ~ deagh/droch ghean, **what sort of** ~ **is he in today?** dè an gean a th' air an-diugh?

hump *n* (*on the back*) croit & cruit *f*

hump-backed *adj* crotach

hundred *n* ceud *m*, **a/one** ~ **people** ceud duine *m sing*, ~**s of them came** thàinig iad nan ceudan, **several** ~ **years** iomadh ceud bliadhna *f sing*

hundredth *num adj* ceudamh

hung *adj* & *past part* crochte

Hungarian *n* & *adj* Ungaireach *m*

Hungary *n* (*used with art*) An Ungair *f*

hungry *adj* 1 acrach, acrasach, **a** ~ **child** leanabh acrach, leanabh is an t-acras air, *in exprs* **I am** ~ tha an t-acras orm, **I grew** ~ thàinig an t-acras orm; 2 (*fig:* ~ *for success etc*) gionach

hunt *n* sealg *f*, ruaig *f*

hunt *v* sealg *vti*

hunter, huntsman *n* sealgair *m*

hunting *n* sealg *f*

hurricane *n* doineann *f*

hurried *adj* cabhagach

hurry *n* cabhag *f*, **in a** ~ ann an cabhaig *dat*, **he ate his dinner in a** ~ ghabh e a dhìnnear ann an cabhaig, **we're in a** ~! tha cabhag oirnn!

hurry *v* 1 (*as vi*) greas *vi* (*with prep* air), dèan cabhag *f*, ~ **(up)!** greas ort! (*pl* greasaibh

oirbh!), dèan cabhag!, **they ought to** ~ bu chòir dhaibh greasad (*verbal noun of* greas *vi*) orra; 2 (*as vt*) ~ **up/on** cuir cabhag (*with prep* air), luathaich *vt*, ~ **someone (up)** cuir cabhag air cuideigin, **the teacher was** ~**ing us on** bha an tidsear gar luathachadh, *also* bha an tidsear gar putadh air adhart

hurt *adj* & *past part* (*phys or emotionally*) ciùrrte, leònta & leònte, air a (*etc*) g(h)oirteachadh

hurt *n* ciùrradh *m*, leòn *m*, goirteas *m*

hurt *v* 1 (*as vt:* ~ *phys*) goirtich *vt*, (*phys or emotionally*) ciùrr *vt*, leòn *vt*; 2 (*as vi*) bi *vi irreg* goirt, **my back** ~**s** tha mo dhruim goirt

hurtful *adj* 1 (*esp emotionally*) cronail; 2 (*of remarks etc*) guineach

husband *n* duine *m*, cèile *m*, (*trad: affectionate*) companach *m*, **my** ~ an duine agam, (*also heard, but less frequent*) mo dhuine

hush! *excl* ist!, *pl* istibh!, *also* eist!, *pl* eistibh!

hush *v* ciùinich *vt*, (*esp* ~ *a child*) tàlaidh *vt*

husk *n* cochall *m*, plaosg *m*

hydro-electricity *n* dealan-uisge *m*

hydrogen *n* hàidraidean *m*

hymn *n* laoidh *mf*, dàn spioradail *m*

hyphen *n* tàthan *m*

hypocrisy *n* cealg *f*

hypocrite *n* cealgair(e) *m*

hypocritical *adj* cealgach

hypothesis *n* beachd-bharail *f*

hypothetical *adj* baralach

I

I *pers pron* mi, *(emph)* mise, mi fhìn, ~ **did it** rinn mi e, ~ *(emph)* **did it!** is mise a rinn e!, rinn mise e!, rinn mi fhìn e!

ice *n* eigh *or* eighre *or* deigh *f*, ~ **age** linn deighe *mf*

iceberg *n* cnoc-eighre *m*, beinn-deighe *f*

ice cream *n* reòiteag *f*

Iceland *n* Innis Tìle *f*

Icelander *n* Tìleach *m*

Icelandic *adj* Tìleach

icicle *n* caisean-reòthta *m*, stob reòthta *m*

icon *n* ìomhaigh cràbhaidh *f*

Id *n* (*psych*), *used with art*, **the** ~ an t-Eadh *m*

idea *n* **1** beachd *m*, beachd-smuain *f*, smuain *f*, **abstract** ~ cùis-bheachd *m*; **2** (*idiom*) **I haven't the faintest** ~, **I've no** ~ chan eil càil a dh'fhios agam

identical *adj* co-ionann (**to** ri), ionann (**to** agus/is), ~ **to X** co-ionann ri X, (*used with v is*) **X and Y are** ~ is ionann X agus Y

idiom *n* (*lang*) gnàthas-cainnte *m*

idiomatic *adj* (*lang*) gnàthasach

idiot *n* amadan *m*, bumailear *m*, òinseach *f* (*trad a female but also used of males*)

idle *adj* **1** (*unoccupied, unemployed, not usu pej*) na (*etc*) t(h)àmh *m*, dìomhain, **the workers are** ~ **because of the strike** tha an luchd-obrach *m sing coll* nan tàmh air sgàth na stailc; **2** (*pej: lazy*) leisg, *in expr* ~ **man/person** leisgeadair *m*; **3** *in expr* ~ **talk/chatter** rabhd *m*, ràbhart *m*

idleness *n* **1** (*inactivity: not usu pej*) tàmh *m*; **2** (*pej: laziness*) leisg(e) *f*

idol *n* ìomhaigh *f*, iodhal *m*

if *conj* **1** ma, (*in neg*) mur(a), ~ **it rains** ma tha/ma bhios an t-uisge ann, **have a break** ~ **you're tired** leig d' anail ma tha thu sgìth, (*in neg exprs*) **I won't go** ~ **you're not keen on it** cha tèid mise (ann) mura bheil (*fam* mur eil) thusa air a shon; **2** (*in more hypothetical statements, with past and conditional tenses*) nan, ~ **I was/were rich I'd build you a**

castle nan robh mi beairteach thogainn caisteal dhut

ignite *v* **1** (*as vt*) cuir teine *m* (*with prep* ri), las *vt*, **they ~d the bale** chuir iad teine ris a' bhèile *f*; **2** (*as vi*) rach *vi* na t(h)eine, **the bale ~d** chaidh am bèile na theine

ignominy *n* nàire *f*, masladh *m*

ill *adj* **1** (*sick etc*) tinn, euslainteach, (*fam*) bochd; **2** *in expr* ~ **at ease** anshocrach; **3** (*bad, unfavourable etc*) **a)** *can be expressed in compounds with* droch (*adj, precedes the noun & lenites following cons where possible*), *followed by n, adj, etc, eg* ~**-natured**, ~**-tempered** *adj* droch-nàdarrach, ~**-treatment** *n* droch-làimhseachadh *m*, **b)** *can be expressed by prefixes* eu- *or* mì-, *followed by the appropriate noun, eg* ~**-health** *n* euslainte *f*, ~**-will** *n* mì-rùn *m* (*see further examples below*)

ill-bred *adj* mì-mhodhail

illegal *adj* mì-laghail

illegitimate *adj* **1** (*by birth*) dìolain; **2** (*morally, legally etc*) neo-dhligheil

illegitimacy *n* (*by birth*) dìolanas *m*

ill-health *n* tinneas *m*, euslainte *f*, anfhannachd *f*

ill-humour *n* gruaim *f*, **in an ill humour** fo ghruaim *dat*

ill-humoured *adj* gruamach

ill-mannered *adj* mì-mhodhail

illness *n* **1** (*abstr: ill-health*) tinneas *m*, euslainte *f*, **mental** ~ tinneas-inntinn *m*; **2** (*con: an* ~) tinneas *m*, galar *m*

ill-tempered *adj* **1** crost(a), diombach, gruamach, greannach; **2** (*usu more permanent characteristic*) droch-nàdarrach

ill-timed *adj* mì-thràthail

ill-treatment *n* droch-làimhseachadh *m*

illuminate *v* soilleirich *vt*

illumination *n* soilleireachadh *m*

illustrate *v* dealbhaich *vt*

illustrious *adj* ainmeil, cliùiteach, iomraiteach, òirdheirc

ill-will *n* gamhlas *m*, mì-rùn *m*

im- *neg prefix* do-, mì-, eu-, *eg* **impossible** *adj*
do-dhèanta, **impatience** *n* mì-fhoighidinn
f, **improbable** *adj* eu-coltach, *see further
examples below*

image *n* **1** (*in art, sculpture etc, in mirror etc,
also Lit, publicity*) ìomhaigh *f*; **2** (*likeness*) mac-
samhail *m*, **he was the ~ of his brother** is e
mac-samhail a bhràthar a bha ann

imagery *n* ìomhaigheachd *f invar*

imaginary *adj* mac-meanmnach

imagination *n* mac-meanmna *m*

imaginative *adj* mac-meanmnach, tionnsgalach

imagine *v* dealbh *vt*, **an event you couldn't ~**
tachartas nach b' urrainn dhut a dhealbhadh

immature *adj* an-abaich

immeasurable *adj* gun tomhas *m*, **at an ~
speed** aig astar *m* gun tomhas

immerse *v* (*in liquid*) bog *vt*, tum *vt*

immersion *n* **1** (*in liquid*) bogadh *m*, tumadh
m; **2** (*lang teaching etc*) bogadh *m*, **~ course**
cùrsa-bogaidh *m*

immigrant *n*, neach-imrich *m*, in-imriche *m*

immigration *n* imrich a-steach *f*, in-imrich *f*

imminent *adj* a tha (*etc*) a' tighinn, **they talked
of the ~ conflict** bhruidhinn iad mun chogadh
a bha a' tighinn

immoral *adj* mì-bheusach

immorality *n* mì-bheus *f*

immune *adj* saor, dìonta, (*from* o/bho)

impact *n* **1** (*lit: phys*) co-bhualadh *m*; **2** (*fig:
effect*) buaidh *f*; **3** (*fig: ~ made on someone*)
drùidheadh *m*

impartial *adj* cothromach, gun lethbhreith *f*

impatience *n* **1** mì-fhoighidinn *f*; **2** (*esp for
something to be over*) fadachd *f invar*, fadal *m*

impatient *adj* **1** mì-fhoighidneach; **2** (*esp for
something to be over: idiom*) **I was ~ all the
time he was talking** bha fadachd *f invar* orm
fhad 's a bha e a' bruidhinn

impede *v* cuir bacadh *m* (*with prep* air), cuir
maille *f invar* (*with prep* air *or* ann)

imperative *adj* **1** (*essential*) riatanach,
deatamach; **2** (*gram*) àithneach, **the ~, the ~
mood** a' mhodh àithneach

imperfect *adj* neo-choileanta

imperial *adj* ìompaireil

impermeable *adj* neo-dhrùidhteach

impersonal *adj* **1** neo-phearsanta; **2** (*of
atmosphere, person etc*) fuar, (*of person*)
fad'-às, dùinte

impersonate *v* pearsanaich *vt*, riochdaich *vt*

impertinence *n* mì-mhodh *mf*, beadaidheachd *f
invar*, dànadas *m*

impertinent *adj* mì-mhodhail, beadaidh, dàna,
bathaiseach

impetuous *adj* bras, cas

impetus *n* deann *f*, dèine *f invar*

implacable *adj* neo-thruacanta

implement *n* inneal *m*, acainn *f*

implement *v* cuir *vt* an gnìomh *m*, thoir *vt* gu
buil *f*

implicated *adj & past part*, **~ (in)** an lùib (*with
gen*), an sàs (*with prep* ann(s) an), **~ in the
plot** an lùib na cuilbheirt

impolite *adj* mì-mhodhail

import[1] *n* (*trade*) bathar a-steach *m*, in-mhalairt *f*

import[2] *n* (*meaning, significance*) seagh *m*, brìgh
f

import *v* thoir *vt* a-steach, **~ cars/food into
the country** thoir càraichean/biadh a-steach
dhan dùthaich

importance *n* **1** diofar *m*, deifir *f*, cudthrom
m, (*idiom*) **it's of no ~** chan eil e gu diofar; **2**
(*emphasis*) cudthrom *m*, **lay/put great ~ on X**
leig cudthrom mòr air X

important *adj* **1** cudthromach, trom, **~ matters**
gnothaichean *mpl* cudthromach, cuspairean *mpl*
troma, **a big ~ man** (*can be ironic*) duine mòr
cudthromach; **2** *in expr* **it's not ~** chan eil e gu
diofar

impossible, impracticable, *adjs* do-dhèanta

impractical *adj* **1** (*not in keeping with common
sense, unrealistic*) neo-phrataigeach; **2** (*cannot
be done*) do-dhèanta

impression *n* **1** (*phys mark made on something*)
comharradh *m*, lorg *f*; **2** (*~ made on someone*)
drùidheadh *m*, **make an ~** drùidh *vi* (*with
prep* air), **the news made no ~ on her** cha
do dhrùidh an naidheachd oirre (idir), (*fam:
idiom*) cha do chuir an naidheachd suas no sìos
i; **3** (*mental ~, surmise etc*) **my ~ is that he's
a liar** saoilidh mi gur e breugair a th' ann; **4**
(*printing*) clò-bhualadh *m*

impressive *adj* drùidhteach

imprint *n* **1** (*phys*) lorg *f*; **2** (*publishing*) clò *m*

imprisonment *n* braighdeanas *m*, daorsa *f
invar*, ciomachas *m*

improbable *adj* eu-coltach

impromptu *adj* gun ullachadh *m*

improper *adj* **1** (*not suitable*) mì-iomchaidh; **2**
(*indecent etc*) mì-bheusach, (*stronger*) drabasta

improve *v* **1** (*as vt*) leasaich *vt*, **~ the
company's profile/image** leasaich ìomhaigh
f na companaidh; **2** (*as vi*) rach *vi* am feabhas
m, **the local services are improving** tha na
seirbheisean ionadail a' dol am feabhas; **3** (*~ in a*

skill, activity etc: idiom) **we're improving** tha (am) piseach a' tighinn oirnn

improvement *n* **1** leasachadh *m*, **an ~ grant** tabhartas leasachaidh *m*; **2** (*in skill, activity etc*) piseach *m*

impudence *n* beadaidheachd *f invar*, dànadas *m*

impudent *adj* beadaidh, dàna, bathaiseach

impulsive *adj* bras

in *prep* **1** (*~ a position, situation*) ann an, ann am, (*with art*) anns an, anns a', sa, san (*etc*), ~ **a house** ann an taigh, ~ **the house** anns an taigh, ~ **danger** ann an cunnart, ~ **a mess** ann am bùrach, ~ **general** san fharsaingeachd *f invar*, ~ **autumn** as t-fhoghar; **2** (*into*) do, **put a bag ~ the car** cuir màileid dhan chàr, **throw a stone ~ the loch** tilg clach dhan loch; **3** (*during*) ri, air, ann an, anns an (*etc*), ~ **my grandfather's time/day** ri linn mo sheanar, ~ **the afternoon/evening** anns an fheasgar; **4** (*after*) an ceann (*with gen*), ~ **a short time** an ceann ghoirid; **5** (*with compass directions*) mu, **islands ~ the north** eileanan mu thuath; **6** (*misc exprs & idioms*) ~ **front of** ro, *before art* ron (*with the dat*), **a car was ~ front of the door** bha càr ron doras, ~ **Donald's care/ charge** air cùram *m* Dhòmhnaill, **he put a piece in his pocket ~ case he should grow hungry** chuir e pìos na phòca gun fhios nach tigeadh an t-acras air

in- *neg prefix* mì-, do-, an-, eu- (*occas* ao-), neo-, *eg* **injustice** *n* mì-cheartas *m*, **innumerable** *adj* do-àireamh, **infirmity** *n* anfhannachd *f invar*, euslainte *f*, **incapable** *adj* neo-chomasach, *see further examples below*

inaccurate *adj* mearachdach

inactivity *n* tàmh *m*

inadequacy *n* uireasbhaidh *f*

inadequate *adj* uireasbhach

inadvertent neo-aireach

inappropriate *adj* neo-iomchaidh

incalculable *adj* gun tomhas *m*, **at an ~ speed** aig astar gun tomhas

incantation *n* ortha *f*

incapable *adj* neo-chomasach

incessant *adj* leanailteach

incest *n* col *m*

incestuous *adj* colach

inch *n* òirleach *mf*, **he's every ~ a man** (*trad*) is duine gach òirleach dheth

incident *n* tachartas *m*, tuiteamas *m*

incidental *adj* tuiteamach

incisor *n* (*tooth*) clàr-fhiacail *f*

inclination *n* **1** (*desire, wish*) togradh *m*; **2** (*tendency*) aomadh *m*

incline *n* **1** claonadh *m*; **2** (*topog*) leathad *m*, bruthach *mf*

incline *v* **1** crom *vti*, claon *vti*, **she ~ed her head** chrom i a ceann; **2** (*tend*) aom *vi*

inclined *adj* dual(t)ach, buailteach, **they are ~ to be stingy/mean** tha iad dualach/buailteach a bhith spìocach

include *v* gabh *vt* a-steach, **Highland Region ~d Inverness** bha Roinn na Gàidhealtachd a' gabhail a-steach Inbhir Nis

income *n* teachd-a-steach *m invar*, *in expr* ~ **tax** cìs-chosnaidh *f*

incomer *n* coigreach *m*, srainnsear *m*

incoming *adj* a thig *vi* a-steach, *in expr* ~ **mail** post a-steach *m*

incompetence *n* neo-chomasachd *f invar*

incompetent *adj* neo-chomasach

incomplete *adj* neo-iomlan

inconsistent *adj* **1** (*liable to vary*) caochlaideach, neo-sheasmhach; **2** (*contradictory etc*) neo-chòrdail (**with** ri)

inconvenience *n* dragh *m*, **I don't want to put you to/cause you any ~** chan eil mi airson dragh a chur oirbh

inconvenience *v* cuir dragh *m* (*with prep* air), (*more fam*) bodraig *vt*, **I don't want to ~ you** chan eil mi airson dragh a chur oirbh/airson ur bodraigeadh

incorrect *adj* mearachdach, ceàrr, ~ **report** aithisg mhearachdach

increase *n* **1** meudachadh *m*; **2** (*~ in pay*) àrdachadh *m*

increase *v* meudaich *vti*, cinn *vi*, rach *vi* am meud *m invar*, ~**in length** rach *vi* am fad *m*

incumbent *adj* mar fhiachaibh (*obs dat pl of* fiach *m*) (*with prep* air), **it is ~ upon me to say a few words** (*formal*) tha e mar fhiachaibh orm facal no dhà a ràdh

indebted *adj & past part* (*financially & fig*) fo fhiachaibh (*obs dat pl of* fiach *m*) (*with prep* do), **I'm ~ to them**, tha mi fo fhiachaibh dhaibh

indecent *adj* mì-bheusach, (*stronger*) drabasta, ~ **assault** ionnsaigh dhrabasta

indecency *n* mì-bheusachd *f invar*, (*stronger*) drabastachd *f invar*

indeed *adv* **1** gu dearbh, **are you tired? I am ~!** a bheil thu sgìth? tha gu dearbh!, **he's rich! is he ~?** tha e beartach! a bheil gu dearbh? (*also* a bheil, a bheil?*); **2** (*as intensifier of an adj or adv*) gu dearbh fhèin, uabhasach fhèin, cianail (fhèin), **very good/very well ~** gu dearbh fhèin math, uabhasach fhèin math, cianail (fhèin) math, *also* math dha-rìribh

indefinite *adj* neo-chinnteach

indentation n eag f
independence n neo-eisimeileachd f invar
independent adj neo-eisimeileach
index n **1** (to contents of book etc) clàr-amais m; **2** (scale, yardstick) clàr-innse m, ~ **of industrial production** clàr-innse toradh gnìomhachais
India n (used as pl, with art) na h-Innseachan fpl
Indian n & adj Innseanach m
indicate v comharraich vt
indicative adj (gram) taisbeanach, **the ~ mood** am modh taisbeanach
indicator n taisbeanair m
Indies, the npl, **the East ~** na h-Innseachan an Ear fpl, **the West ~** na h-Innseachan an Iar fpl
indifference n **1** (the attitude of mind) neo-shuim f; **2** (idiom) **it's a matter of ~ to me** is coma leam e
indifferent adj **1** coma, (stronger) coma-co-dhiù, **it's ~ to me** is coma leam e, **in the face of her husband's anger she was (completely) ~** ro fheirg (dat of fearg f) an duine aice bha i coma-co-dhiù; **2** (of ~ quality) ach meadhanach (math), with neg v, **the meal was ~** cha robh am biadh ach meadhanach (math)
indigence n uireasbhaidh f, ainniseachd f invar
indigenous adj dùthchasach, tùsanach
indigent adj uireasbhach, in expr **an ~ person** uireasbhach m
indignant adj diombach
indignation n diomb m invar
indignity n tàmailt f
indirect adj neo-dhìreach
indispensable adj riatanach
indissoluble adj do-sgaoilte
individual adj **1** (relating to the individual) pearsanta, **~ duty** dleastanas pearsanta; **2** (separate) fa leth, **he questioned each ~ witness** cheasnaich e gach fianais fa leth
individual n neach m invar, duine m, (more trad) urra m
individually adv fa leth, **he questioned each witness ~** cheasnaich e gach fianais fa leth
Indo-European adj & n Indo-Eòrpach m
indolence n leisg(e) f
indolent adj leisg
industrial adj **1** gnìomhachail, tionnsgalach; **2** in expr **~ estate** raon gnìomhachais m
industrious adj dèanadach, gnìomhach, dìcheallach
industriousness n dèanadas m, gnìomhachas m
industry n **1** (the abstr quality) dèanadas m; **2** (manufacturing, manufacturers etc)

gnìomhachas m, **the electricity/food ~** gnìomhachas an dealain/a' bhìdh
inebriate v cuir vt air mhisg f
inebriated v misgeach, air mhisg f
inefficiency n neo-èifeachdas m
inefficient adj neo-èifeachdach
inequality n eas-aontarachd f invar, neo-ionannachd f invar
infant n leanabh m, leanaban m, pàiste m
infantile adj leanabail
infatuate v dall vt, cuir vt fo gheasaibh
infectious adj gabhaltach, **~ diseases** tinneasan gabhaltach mpl
inferior adj **1** (in rank, in phys position) ìochd(a)rach, (n)as ìsle; **2** (~ in quality) (n)as miosa (to na), **that one is ~** tha am fear ud nas miosa, also chan eil am fear ud cho math
inferior n ìochdaran m
inferiority n ìochdaranachd f invar
infernal adj ifrinneach
infertile adj neo-thorrach
infertility n neo-thorrachas m
infestation n plàigh f
infinite adj neo-chrìochnach
infinitive adj (gram) neo-chrìochnach
infinity n neo-chrìochnachd f invar
infirm adj euslainteach, anfhann
infirmary n taigh-eiridinn m
infirmity n **1** euslainte f, anfhannachd f invar; **2** (more transient) laigse f
inflame v (fig: situation etc) cuir lasair f (with prep ri)
inflammable adj lasanta
inflate v sèid vt (suas)
inflation n **1** (lit) sèideadh m; **2** (fin) atmhorachd f invar
inflexible adj rag
influence n **1** (personal, political etc) cumhachd mf invar, buaidh f; **2** in expr **under the ~ of** an lùib f, fo bhuaidh f, (with gen), **under the ~ of his friends** an lùib/fo bhuaidh a charaidean mpl gen; **3** in expr **under the ~** (ie of drink) air mhisg f
influence v thoir buaidh f (with prep air)
influential adj buadhach, cumhachdach
inform v **1** thoir fios m, cuir fios, cuir brath m, (all with prep gu), innis vti (with prep do), **he ~ed me (of it)** thug e fios thugam (mu dheidhinn)
informal adj neo-fhoirmeil
informality n neo-fhoirmealachd f invar
information n **1** fiosrachadh m, **I'd like to receive ~ about the company/firm** bu toigh leam fiosrachadh fhaighinn air a' chompanaidh,

(*IT*) ~ **technology** teicneolas fiosrachaidh *m*; **2** (*facts, news etc*) fios *m*, **is there any ~ about Mary?** a bheil fios air Màiri?

informed *adj* fiosrach, fiosraichte, (**about** air)

infra- *prefix*, fo-, bun-, *prefixes, eg* **infra-red** *adj* fo-dhearg, **infrastructure** *n* bun-structair *m*

ingenious *adj* innleachdach, teòma, tionnsgalach

ingenuity *n* innleachd *f invar*, (*less usu*) tionnsgal *m*

ingredient *n* tàthchuid *f*, **~s** *n* (*rather trad*) cungaidh *f*

inhabit *v* còmhnaich *vi*, fuirich *vi* (*with prep* ann an), àitich *vt*

inhabitant *n* neach-àiteachaidh *m*, neach-còmhnaidh *m*, **~s** luchd-àiteachaidh *m sing coll*, luchd-còmhnaidh *m sing coll*, muinntir *f*

inherent *adj* **1** (*in a person*) dual(t)ach, **it's ~ in him to be hospitable** tha e dualach dha a bhith fàilteach; **2** (*in an object, situation etc*) bunaiteach, bunasach, gnèitheach

inherit *v* sealbhaich *vt* (mar oighreachd *f*), faigh *vt* mar oighreachd

inheritance *n* **1** (*esp material ~*) oighreachd *f*, **~ tax** cìs oighreachd *f*; **2** (*esp cultural ~*) dualchas *m*

inheritor *n* oighre *m*

inimical *adj* nàimhdeil

initial *adj* ciad, *used with art*, a' chiad (*for both m & f nouns*), *precedes the noun, which it lenites where possible*, **the ~ response** a' chiad fhreagairt

initially *adv* an toiseach *m*, an toiseach tòiseachaidh *m*, sa chiad dol-a-mach *m invar*, sa chiad àite *m*

injure *v* **1** (*usu phys*) goirtich *vt*, (*phys or emotionally*) leòn *vt*, ciùrr *vt*; **2** (*not usu phys*) dèan cron *m* (*with prep* air)

injured *adj* **1** (*phys or emotionally*) leònta & leònte, ciùrrte; **2** (*as n: in accident, war etc*) **the ~** na leòintich *mpl*

injurious *adj* cronail, lochdach, millteach

injury *n* **1** (*phys or emotional*) leòn *m*; **2** (*not usu phys*) cron *m*

injustice *n* mì-cheartas *m*

ink *n* inc *m invar*, (*more trad*) dubh *m*

-in-law *adj*, *see under relationship concerned*, **brother-in-law** *etc*

inn *n* taigh-òsta *m*

innards *n* innidh *f invar*, mionach *m*, (*esp of animals*) greallach *f*

innate *adj* **1** (*in a person*) dual(t)ach; **2** (*in an object*) gnèitheach

innkeeper *n* òstair *m*, fear (an) taighe *m*

innocence *n* neoichiontachd *f invar*

innocent *adj* neoichiontach, neoichionta

innuendo *n* leth-fhacal *m*

innumerable *adj* do-àireamh

input *n* cur-a-steach *m*

input *v* **1** cuir *vt* ann; **2** (*esp at keyboard*) put *vt* ann

inquiry *n* rannsachadh *m*

inquisitive *adj* ceasnachail, faighneachail

insane *adj* air chuthach *m*, air bhàinidh *f invar*, air bhoile *f invar*, (*more fam*) às a (*etc*) c(h)iall *f*, às a (*etc*) rian *m*, **go ~** rach *vi* air chuthach/air bhàinidh/air bhoile/às a (*etc*) c(h)iall

insanity *n* cuthach *m*, bàinidh *f invar*, boile *f invar*

insect *n* frìde *f*, meanbh-fhrìde *f*

inseparable *adj* do-sgaradh

inside *adv* **1** (*expr position*) a-staigh, **they are ~** tha iad a-staigh; **2** (*expr movement*) a-steach, **come ~!** thig(ibh) a-steach!

inside *n* **1** taobh a-staigh *m*, (*esp of building*) broinn *f*; **2** (*in expr*) **~ out** caoin *f* air ascaoin *f*

inside *prep* **1** (*expr position*) a-staigh (*with prep* ann an), am broinn (*with gen*), **we were ~ the barn** bha sinn a-staigh san t-sabhal, bha sinn am broinn an t-sabhail, **there's a swimming pool ~ the house** tha amar-snàimh am broinn an taighe; **2** (*expr movement*) a-steach (*with prep* do), **come ~!** thig(ibh) a-steach! (*though note that* thig(ibh) a-staigh *is also commonly used in this sense*), **they went ~ the church** chaidh iad a-steach dhan eaglais

insight *n* **1** (*abstr: the mental faculty or capacity*) tuigse *f invar*, (*less usu*) lèirsinn *f invar*; **2** (*con: knowledge or understanding coming suddenly to someone*) geur-bheachd *m*

insignificant *adj* crìon, suarach

insipid *adj* leamhach

inspect *v* sgrùd *vt*

inspection *n* sgrùdadh *m*

inspector *n* neach-sgrùdaidh *m* (*pl* luchd-sgrùdaidh *m sing coll*)

inspire *v* misnich *vt*

instalment *n* earrann *f*

instance *n* **1** (*example*) eisimpleir *m*, **for ~** mar eisimpleir; **2** *in expr* **in the first ~** an (*prep*) toiseach *m*, anns a' chiad dol-a-mach *m invar*

instant *adj* grad (*precedes the noun, which it lenites where possible*), **~ coffee** grad-chofaidh *f*

instant *n* **1** mòmaid *f*, plathadh *m*, tiota *m*; **2** (*idiom*) **in an ~** ann am priobadh *m* (na sùla)

instruct *v* **1** (*educate etc*) teagaisg *vt*, oileanaich *vt*, **~ the new generation** teagaisg an ginealach ùr; **2** (*command etc*) òrdaich *vt* (*with* *prep* do), **they ~ed me to set fire to the house** dh'òrdaich iad dhomh teine a chur ris an taigh

instruction *n* **1** (*ed*) foghlam *m*, teagasg *m*, oileanachadh *m*; **2** (*command etc*) òrdugh *m*; **3** **~s** (*for use, assembly etc*) seòladh *m*

instrument *n* **1** (*tool, device etc*) inneal *m*, ball-acainn *m*; **2** (*musical ~*) ionnsramaid *f*, inneal-ciùil *m*

insubordinate *adj* eas-umhail

insulate *v* (*elec etc*) dealaich *vt* (**from** ri)

insulating *adj* (*ie non-conductive*) do-ghiùlan

insult *n* tàmailt *f*, tàir *f*, (**to** air)

insult *v* dèan tàir *f* (*with prep* air), tàmailtich *vt*

insulting *adj* tàmailteach, tàireil

insurance *n* àrachas *m*, urras *m*, **~ policy** poileasaidh àrachais *m*

integrity *n* ionracas *m*

intellect *n* inntinn *f*

intellectual *adj* **1** (*of book, person etc: having ~ qualities*) inntinneach; **2** (*to do with the intellect*) inntinn (*gen of* inntinn *f*), **~ ability/capacity** comas-inntinn *m*

intelligence *n* inntinn *f*, tuigse *f invar*

intelligent *adj* toinisgeil, tuigseach, eirmseach

intend *v* bi *vi irreg* airson, (*stronger resolve*) cuir *vt* roimhe (*etc*), rùnaich *vi*, **they ~ed to build a house** bha iad airson/chuir iad romhpa taigh a thogail

intense *adj* **1** (*of persons, emotions, deeds*) dian; **2** (*of heat etc*) anabarrach

intensity *n* dèine *f invar*

intensive *adj* dian, dlùth, **~ farming** tuathanachas dian, **~ care** cùram-aire *m*

intent, intention *n* rùn *m*, **that was my ~** b' e sin mo rùn, *also* b' e sin a bha mi airson a dhèanamh, **with the sole/express ~ of deceiving us** a dh'aon rùn/a dh'aon ghnothach *m* gus ar mealladh

intentionally *adv* a dh'aon rùn *m*, a dh'aon ghnothach *m*

inter- *prefix* eadar-, *eg* **interface** *n* (*IT etc*) eadar-aghaidh *f*

inter *v* tiodhlaic *vt*, adhlaic *vt*

interact *v* eadar-obraich *vi*

intercourse *n* **1** (*social ~*) conaltradh *m*, caidreabh *m*; **2** (*sexual ~*) cleamhnas *m*, feis(e) *f*, co-ghineadh *m*, cuplachadh *m*; **3** *in exprs* **have (sexual) ~** faigh muin *f invar*, co-ghin *vi*, cuplaich *vi*, **he had ~ with her** chaidh e air a muin

interest *n* **1** ùidh *f* (**in** ann), **I have no ~ in it** chan eil ùidh agam ann, **take an ~ in**

something gabh ùidh ann an rudeigin; **2** (*fin*) riadh *m*

interested *adj, in exprs* **I'm not ~ (in it)** chan eil ùidh *f* agam ann, **be ~ in something** gabh ùidh ann an rudeigin

interesting *adj* inntinneach, ùidheil

interface *n* (*IT etc*) eadar-aghaidh *f*

interfere *v* gabh gnothach *m* (**in/with** ri), buin *vi* (**in/with** do *or* ri)

interim *adj* eadar-amail

interior *n* taobh a-staigh *m*, (*esp of building*) broinn *f*

interlude *n* eadar-ùine *f*

intermarriage *n* eadar-phòsadh *m*

intermediate *adj* eadar-mheadhanach

intermingle, intermix *v* co-mheasgaich, coimeasgaich *vti*

international *adj* eadar-nàiseanta, **~ companies** companaidhean eadar-nàiseanta

internet *n* eadar-lìon *m*, **~ site** làrach eadar-lìn *f*

interpret *v* **1** (*explain etc*) mìnich *vt*; **2** (*lang*) eadar-theangaich *vti*

interpretation *n* **1** mìneachadh *m*; **2** (*lang*) eadar-theangachadh *m*

interpreter *n* (*lang*) eadar-theangaiche *m*

interrogate *v* ceasnaich *vt*

interrogation *n* ceasnachadh *m*

interrogative *adj* ceisteach

interrogator *n* neach-ceasnachaidh *m* (*pl* luchd-ceasnachaidh *m sing coll*)

interrupt *v* (*bring to a halt*) caisg *vt*, (*intrude into conversation etc*) bris(t) *vi* a-steach (*with prep* air)

interruption *n* (*bringing to a halt*) casgadh *m*, (*intrusion into conversation etc*) bristeadh a-steach *m*

interval *n* **1** (*esp in space*) beàrn *mf*; **2** (*in time*) eadar-ùine *f*

interview *n* agallamh *m*

intestine *n* **1** caolan *m*; **2** **~s** innidh *f invar*, (*esp of animals*) greallach *f*

intimate *adj* **1** dlùth, dlùth-chàirdeil; **2** *in expr* **~ knowledge/acquaintance** mion-eòlas *m* (**of/with** air); **3** (*sexually ~*) **he was ~ with her** chaidh e air a muin *f invar*

into *prep* **1** do, a-steach do, (*with dat*), **throw a stone ~ the loch** tilg clach dhan loch, **put cattle ~ the byre** cuir sprèidh a-steach don bhàthaich; **2** (*fam: interested in, keen on*) **he's ~ computing (etc)** tha ùidh mhòr aige ann an coimpiutaireachd (*etc*)

intoxicating *adj* daorachail

intoxication *n* daorach *f*, misg *f*

intrepid *adj* dàna, cruadalach

intrepidity *n* dànadas *m*, cruadal *m*

introduce *v* (*people*) cuir *vt* an aithne *f invar* (*with gen*), **I ~d them (to each other)** chuir mi an aithne a chèile *m* iad

introduction *n* **1** (*of people*) cur an aithne *m*; **2** (*in book etc*) ro-ràdh *m*

introvert *adj* dùinte

intuition *n* imfhios *m*

intuitive *adj* imfhiosach

inured *adj* dèanta (**to** ri), **~ to war/poverty** dèanta ri cogadh/bochdainn

invalid *adj* (*of documents etc*) neo-dhligheach

invalid *n* euslainteach *m*

invent *v* innlich *vt*, tionnsgail & tionnsgain *vt*

invention *n* (*abstr & con*) innleachd *f*, tionnsgal *m*

inventive *adj* innleachdach, tionnsgalach

inventiveness *n* innleachd *f*, tionnsgal *m*

inventor *n* tionnsgalair *m*, innliche *m*

invert *v* **1** (*turn over*) cuir *vt* bun-os-cionn; **2** (*maths etc: reverse position etc of*) cuir *vt* an àite a chèile, **~ X and Y** cuir X agus Y an àite a chèile

inverted *adj & past part* **1** (*turned over*) bun-os-cionn; **2** *in expr* (*typog*) **~ commas** cromagan turrach *fpl*

invest *v* (*fin*) cuir *vt* an seilbh *m*, **~ money/ capital** cuir airgead/calpa an seilbh

investigate *v* rannsaich *vt*

investigation *n* rannsachadh *m*

investment *n* **1** (*abstr, also the activity*) cur an seilbh *m*, tasgadh *m*; **2** (*con: the funds invested*) airgead an seilbh *m*, airgead-tasgaidh *m*

investor *n* neach-tasgaidh *m* (*pl* luchd-tasgaidh *m sing coll*)

invigorate *v* neartaich *vt*

invitation *n* cuireadh *m*, fiathachadh *m*, (**to** gu), **~ to a party** cuireadh gu pàrtaidh, (*idiom*) (**we got) an ~ to a wedding** (fhuair sinn) fios *m* na bainnse (*gen of* banais *f*)

invite *v* fiathaich *vt*, iarr *vt* (*sometimes with prep* air), thoir cuireadh *m* (*with prep* do), **we won't ~ you to come in** chan iarr sinn oirbh a thighinn a-steach, (**to** gu) **they ~d me to a party** dh'iarr iad mi/dh'fhiathaich iad mi/thug iad cuireadh dhomh gu pàrtaidh

invoice *n* cunntas *m*

involved *adj & past part* **1** an sàs (*with prep* ann an), **~ in politics** an sàs ann am poilitigs, **get ~ in the work** rach *vi irreg* an sàs anns an obair; **2** *in expr* **get ~** (*ie have to do with*) gabh gnothach *m* (**with** ri), **don't get ~ with those people** na gabh gnothach ris na daoine ud; **3**

(*connected with, attached to*) an lùib (*with gen*), **there's plenty of work ~ in my new job** tha obair gu leòr an lùib mo dhreuchd ùir

Iona *n* Ì, Eilean Ì, *or* Ì Chaluim Chille

ir- *neg prefix* mi-, neo-, eas-, *neg prefixes, eg* **irregular** *adj* mì-riaghailteach, *see further examples below*

Ireland *n* Èirinn (*gen* na h-Èireann) *f*

Irish *adj* Èireannach, na h-Èireann, **an ~ song** òran Èireannach, **~ Gaelic** Gàidhlig na h-Èireann, Gaeilge *f*

Irishman *n* Èireannach *m*

Irish Republic (the) *n* Poblachd na h-Èireann *f*

iron *n* (*the metal; also the household implement*) iarann *m*, **the Iron Age** Linn an Iarainn *f*

iron *v* (*clothes etc*) iarnaich & iarnaig *vti*

iron filings min-iarainn *f*

ironic(al) *adj* ìoranta

ironing *n* (*the chore and the items*) iarnachadh & iarnaigeadh *m*

irony *n* ìoran(t)as *m*

irreconcilable *adj* do-rèiteachail

irregular *adj* **1** mì-riaghailteach, mì-òrdail; **2** (*gram*) neo-riaghailteach, **~ verbs** gnìomhairean neo-riaghailteach *mpl*

irrelevant *adj* nach buin (*etc*) ris a' chùis *f*/ris a' ghnothach *m*, gun bhuntainneas *m*, nach eil (*etc*) buntainneach, **this letter is ~** chan eil an litir seo buntainneach, **that remark is ~** chan eil am facal sin a' buntainn ris a' chùis

irresponsible *adj* neo-chùramach

irreverent *adj* eas-umhail, eas-urramach

irrigate *v* uisgich *vti*

irrigation *n* uisgeachadh *m*

irritable *adj* crost(a) & crosda, dranndanach, frionasach, cas

irritate *v* cuir greann *m*, cuir an fhearg, (*with prep* air), **the music ~d me** chuir an ceòl greann orm

irritating *adj* (*situations etc*) leam, **they're constantly asking me ~ questions** bidh iad a' cur chèistean leamha orm fad na h-ùine

is *v see under* **be**

Islamic *adj* Ioslamach

island *n* eilean *m*, (*less usu*) innis *f*, **on the ~** anns an eilean, air an eilean

islander *n* eileanach *m*

Islay *n* Ìle *f invar, in exprs* **an ~ person** Ìleach *m*, **from/belonging to ~** Ìleach *adj*

isle *n* eilean *m*, **the Western Isles** Na h-Eileanan Siar, **the Western Isles Council** Comhairle nan Eilean Siar *f*, **the Isle of Man** Eilean Mhanainn *m*

isolated *adj* iomallach, ~ **areas/districts** ceàrnaidhean iomallach

Israel *n* Iosarail & Israel *f invar*

Israeli *n* Iosaraileach & Israeleach *m*

Israelite *n & adj* (*Bibl, hist*) Iosaraileach & Israelach *m*

issue *n* **1** (*matter, problem etc*) ceist *f*, cùis *f*, gnothach *m*; **2** (*outcome*) toradh *f*, buil *f* **3** (*progeny*) gineal *mf*, sìol *m sing coll*, sliochd *m sing coll*

issue *v* cuir *vt* a-mach

it *pron* (*f*) i, (*m*) e, **here's a glass, take** ~ seo glainne *f*, gabh i, **he saw** ~ (*m*) chunnaic e e, **he** (*emph*) **did** ~ rinn esan e, **that's** ~ sin e!, **can they do** ~? an urrainn dhaibh a dhèanamh?, (*impersonal* ~) ~'**s my sister who left** is i/is e mo phiuthar a dh'fhalbh

Italian *adj & n* **1** Eadailteach *m*; **2** (*lang: used with art*) an Eadailtis *f invar*

italics *npl* clò eadailteach *m*

Italy *n* (*used with art*) An Eadailt *f*

itch *n* tachas *m*

itch *v* tachais *vi*

ivy *n* eidheann *f*

J

jab *n* (*with elbow etc*) ùpag *f*
jab *v* (*esp with elbow*) uillnich *vti*, thoir ùpag *f*
  (*with prep* do)
jackdaw *n* cathag *f*
jagged *adj* eagach
jam *n* silidh *m invar*
jamb *n* ursainn *f*
janitor *n* dorsair *m*
January *n*, *used with art*, am Faoilteach *m*, *also*
  am Faoilleach *m*, **the 20th of** ~ am ficheadamh
  là den Fhaoilteach
Japan *n*, (*used with art*) an t-Seapan *f*, Iapan *f*
Japanese *n* (*lang*) Seapanais *f*, Iapanais *f*
jaundice *n* (*used with art*) a' bhuidheach *f*
jaw *n* giall *f*, peirceall *m*
jawbone *n* peirceall *m*
javelin *n* gath *m*, sleagh *f*
jealous *adj* **1** (*esp sexually*) eudach & iadach,
  eudmhor; **2** (*envious*) farmadach
jealousy *n* **1** (*esp sexual*) eud & iad *m invar*,
  eudach & iadach *m*; **2** (*envy, non-sexual* ~)
  farmad *m*
jeans *n* dinichean *fpl*
jeer *v* mag *vi* (**at** air)
jeering *adj* magail
jeering *n* magadh *m* (**at** air)
jelly *m* silidh *m invar*
jersey *n* geansaidh *m*
jest *n* fealla-dhà *f invar*, **half in** ~ eadar fealla-
  dhà 's da-rìribh *adv*
Jesus *proper name* Ìosa
Jew *n* Iùdhach *m*
jewel *n* seud *m*, àilleag *f*, leug *f*, (*esp one worn as
  an ornament*) usgar *m*
jeweller *n* seudaire *m*
Jewish *adj* Iùdhach
jiffy *n* (*instant*) priobadh (na sùla) *m*, tiota *m*,
  (*dimin*) tiotan *m*, tiotag *f*, **in a** ~ ann an tiotag,
  ann am priobadh na sùla
jingle *v* dèan gliong *m*
jingling *n* gliong *m*, gliongartaich *f invar*
job *n* **1** obair *f*, cosnadh *m*, (*usu non-manual*)
  dreuchd *f*, **out of a** ~ gun obair, gun chosnadh,

~ **centre** ionad-obrach *m*, ionad-cosnaidh *m*; **2**
in expr (*fam*) **that'll do the** ~/**that's just the**
~ nì sin an gnothach/a' chùis
Jock and Doris *n* (*ie 'one for the road'*) deoch-
an-dorais *f invar*
jog *n* (*with elbow etc*) ùpag *f*
jog *v* (*with elbow etc*) put *vt*, thoir ùpag *f* (*with
prep* do)
join *v* **1** (*fix, connect*) ceangail *vt* , tàth *vt*, (**to** ri);
2 (*enlist etc*) gabh *vi* (*with prep* ann an), **he** ~**ed
the navy** ghabh e san nèibhidh
joint *adj* co- *prefix, eg* ~ **secretary** co-rùnaire *m*,
~ **venture** co-iomairt *f*
joint *n* (*anat*) alt *m*, **the elbow** ~ alt na h-uilne,
in expr **finger-**~ rùdan *m*
jointed *adj* altach
joke *n* **1** (*usu verbal*) fealla-dhà *f invar*, (*verbal
or non-verbal*) abhcaid *f*; **2** (*humorous story*)
naidheachd *f*; **3** (*practical* ~) cleas *m*, car *m*,
they played a ~ **on me** rinn iad cleas orm,
thug iad an car asam
joke *v* bi *vi irreg* ri fealla-dhà *f invar*, **I'm not
joking!** chan ann ri fealla-dhà a tha mi!, *also* tha
mi ann an da-rìribh, tha mi ga chiallachadh
joking *n* fealla-dhà *f invar*
jollity *n* cridhealas *m*,
jostle *n* (*in crowd, in squabble etc*) ùpag *f*
jostle *v* uillnich *vti*, put *vti*
journal *n* **1** (*diary*) leabhar-latha *m*; **2**
(*periodical*) iris *f*, ràitheachan *m*
journalist *n* neach-naidheachd *m*, naidheachdair
m, ~**s** luchd-naidheachd *m sing coll*
journey *n* turas *m*, *in expr* ~**'s end** ceann-uidhe
m
journey *v* siubhail *vi*, (*less usu*) imich *vi*, triall *vi*
jovial *adj* (*person, atmosphere etc*) cridheil
joy *n* gàirdeachas *m*, àgh *m*
joyful *adj* aighearach, greannmhor, àghmhor
judge *v* **1** breithnich *vti*, thoir breith *f invar* (*with
prep* air); **2** *in expr* **judging by** a rèir, **judging
by appearances, he's a foreigner** a rèir
c(h)oltais *m gen*, 's e coigreach a th' ann (dheth)

judg(e)ment *n* **1** (*the mental faculty or capacity*) tuigse *f invar*, toinisg *f*; **2** (*legal ~*) breith *f invar*, binn *f*, breithneachadh *m*, **pass ~** thoir breith, thoir a-mach binn, (**on/upon** air)

juggler *n* cleasaiche *m*

juggling *n* cleasachd *f invar*

juice *n* sùgh *m*, **fruit ~** sùgh-measa *m*

juicy *adj* sùghmhor

July *n*, *used with art*, An t-Iuchar *m*

jumble *n* **1** (*collection of misc objects*) treal(l)aich *f*, truileis *f invar*, (*more worthless*) sgudal *m*; **2** (*state of untidiness, disorder*) bùrach *m*, **in a ~** ann am bùrach, *also* bun-os-cionn, thar a chèile, troimh-a-chèile

jump *n* leum *m*, sùrdag *f*

jump *v* **1** leum *vti*; **2** (*through fear, surprise*) clisg *vi*, **he ~ed** chlisg e, **he made me ~** chuir e clisgeadh *m* orm, chlisg e mi

jumper *n* geansaidh *m*

jumpy *adj* (*nervous etc*) clisgeach

June *n*, *used with art*, An t-Òg-mhìos, An t-Ògmhios *m*

junk *n* **1** (*misc objects, usu untidy*) treal(l)aich *f*, truileis *f invar*, **put that ~ on the floor and** sit down cuir an trealaich sin air an làr agus dèan suidhe; **2** (*rubbish*) sgudal *m*

Jura *n* Diùra(igh) *f*

jury *n* diùraidh *m*

just *adj* (*upright, fair*) dìreach, ceart, cothromach, còir, **a ~ man** duine dìreach/ceart/cothromach/còir, **a ~ decision** breith chothromach

just *adv* **1** (*simply, altogether*) dìreach, **that would be ~ great!** bhiodh sin dìreach sgoinneil!; **2** (*a moment ago*) dìreach, **he's ~ left** tha e dìreach an dèidh falbh; **3** (*expr agreement*) **~ so!** dìreach (sin)!; **4** *in expr ~* **about** (*ie practically*) cha mhòr, an ìre mhath, **we see her ~ about every day** bidh sinn ga faicinn a h-uile là, cha mhòr, **the winter's ~ about over** tha an geamhradh an ìre mhath seachad; **5** (*in comparisons*) a cheart, **A's ~ as good as B** tha A a cheart cho math ri B

justice *n* ceartas *m*, còir *f*, ionracas *m*, **the Justice Department** Roinn a' Cheartais *f*, **standing up for ~** a' seasamh na còrach (*gen of* còir)

juvenile *adj* leanabail

K

kail *n* càl *m*

keel *n* 1 (*of boat*) druim *m*; 2 (*fig*) *in expr* **put/ set on an even ~** (*situations, relationships etc*) rèitich *vt*

keen *adj* 1 èasgaidh, dùrachdach, dian, **~ to do it** èasgaidh a dhèanamh, **~ to get up in the morning** èasgaidh gu èirigh sa mhadainn; 2 *in expr* **~ on** (*ie fond of, person etc*) dèidheil air, **~ on drink/music** dèidheil air deoch-làidir *f*/air ceòl *m*; 3 (*~ for success, ambitious*) gionach

keenness *n* dèine *f invar*

keep *v* 1 cùm *vti*, **~ a grip on/~ hold of something** cùm grèim air rudeigin, **~ back!** cùm/cumaibh air ais!, **I won't ~ you back** cha chùm mi air ais sibh, **how are you ~ing?** ciamar a tha thu/sibh a' cumail?, **we didn't ~ New Year** cha do chùm sinn a' Bhliadhna Ùr, **~ going!** cùm ort!, *also* lean ort!, **~ at it!** cùm ris!, **~ time with someone** cùm caismeachd *f* ri cuideigin, **~ up/pace with someone** cùm ruith *f* ri cuideigin, **~ watch, ~ a look out** cùm faire *f*, *also* dèan faire, **~ away** (*from a specified place*) cùm às an làthair *f*, **~ away** (*from particular people, bad influences etc*) seachain(n) *vt*; 2 (*store, preserve*) glèidh *vt*, **they're being kept in a museum** tha iad gan gleidheadh ann an taigh-tasgaidh

keepsake *n* cuimhneachan *m*

kelp *n* ceilp *f*

kelpie *n* each-uisge *m*

kennel *n* taigh *m* chon (*gen pl of* cù *m*)

kept *adj & past part* glèidhte

kerb *n* (*part of pavement*) iomall cabhsair *m*

kernel *n* eitean *m*

kestrel *n* clamhan-ruadh *m*

kettle *n* coire *m*, **put the ~ on** cuir air an coire

key *n* 1 (*for locking etc; also of piano, typewriter, computer etc*) iuchair *f*, (*of pocket calculator, mobile phone etc*) putan *m*; 2 (*music: tonality*) gleus *mf*

key in *v* (*data etc*) put *vt* ann

keyboard *n* meur-chlàr *m*

khaki *adj* lachdann

kid *n* 1 (*young goat*) meann *m*; 2 (*child*) pàiste *m*

kid *v* 1 tarraing *vi* (*with prep* à), **I was ~ding you** bha mi a' tarraing asad/asaibh; 2 (*idiom*) **I was only ~ding** cha robh mi ach mas fhìor

kidney *n* dubhag *f*, àra *f*, àirne *f*

kill *v* marbh *vt*

killer *n* marbhaiche *m*, murtair *m*

killing *n* marbhadh *m*

kiln *n* àth *f*

kilo, kilogram *n* cilo *m*, cileagram *m*, **a ~ in weight** cileagram de chudthrom *m*

kilometre *n* cilemeatair *m*

kilt *n* fèile beag & fèileadh beag, èile beag & èileadh beag

kilt *v* (*ie ~ a garment*) tru(i)s *vt*, **her petticoats were ~ed** bha a còtaichean-bàna air an trusadh

kin *adj* càirdeach (**to do**), **I'm ~ to you** tha mi càirdeach dhut

kind *adj* 1 coibhneil, laghach; 2 (*in corres etc*) **with ~est regards** leis gach deagh dhùrachd *m*

kind *n* seòrsa *m*, (*less usu*) gnè *f invar*, **things of many ~s/of every ~** rudan de dh'iomadach seòrsa/de gach seòrsa, **what ~ of a day is it?** dè an seòrsa là a th' ann?, **a book of that ~** leabhar den t-seòrsa

kindle *v* 1 (*as vt*) las *vt*; 2 (*as vi*) gabh *vi*, **the fire ~d** ghabh an teine

kindliness *n* coibhneas *m*

kindly *adj* coibhneil, còir, bàidheil

kindness *n* 1 (*abstr*) coibhneas *m*; 2 (*con: an act of ~*) bàidh *f*

king *n* rìgh *m*

kingdom *n* rìoghachd *f*

kingly *adj* rìoghail

kinship *n* càirdeas *m*, (*~ by blood*) càirdeas-fala (*gen of* fuil *f*), (*~ by marriage*) càirdeas-pòsaidh *m*, *also* cleamhnas *m*

kirkton *n* clachan *m*

kirkyard *n* cladh *m*, clachan *m*, cill *f*

kiss *n* pòg *f*

kiss *v* pòg *vt*

kitchen *n* cidsin *m*

kite *n* **1** (*the flying structure*) iteileag *f*; **2** (*the bird*) clamhan-gòbhlach *m*

kitten *n* piseag *f*, isean cait *m*

knack *n* liut *f* (**of, for** air), **I haven't got the ~ for that** chan eil an liut agam air sin

knead *v* (*dough*) fuin *vt*

knee *n* glùn *f*

kneecap *n* failmean & falman *m*

knees-up *n* (*fam*) hòro-gheallaidh *m invar*

knickers *n* drathais & drathars *f invar*

knight *n* ridire *m*

knit *v* figh *vti*

knitted *adj & past part* fighte

knitter *n* figheadair *m*

knitting *n* fighe *f invar*, **~ needle** bior-fighe *m*

knob *n* cnap *m*, cnag *f*

knobby, knobbly *adj* cnapach

knock *n* **1** (*esp the sound*) cnag *f*; **2** (*deliberate ~, on door etc*) gnogadh *m*; **3** (*blow, impact*) buille *f*, bualadh *m*

knock *v* **1** (*as vi*) cnag *vi*; **2** (*as vt*) gnog *vt*, **~ at the door** gnog an doras; **3** (*strike*) buail *vt*; **4** *in expr* **~ down** *v* leag *vt*

knocking *n* (*noise, on door etc*) gnogadh *m*

knoll *n* tom *m*, cnoc *m*, tulach *m*, (*smaller*) tolman *m*

know *v* **1** (*esp people*) bi *vi irreg* eòlach (*with prep* air), is *vi irreg & def* aithne *f invar* (*with prep* do), **that's Hugh, do you ~ him?** 's e sin Ùisdean, a bheil thu eòlach air?/an aithne dhut e?, **get to ~ someone** cuir aithne/eòlas *m* air cuideigin; **2** (*of facts, information*) bi *vi irreg* fios *m* (*with prep* aig), **I ~** tha f(h)ios agam, **they didn't ~ he was ill** cha robh fios aca gun robh e tinn, **no-one ~s/it's not ~n where he is** chan eil fios càite a bheil e; **3** *in expr* **let ~** cuir fios, leig fios, (*with prep* gu), **will you let us ~?** an cuir sibh/an leig sibh fios thugainn?

knowe *n* tom *m*, cnoc *m*, tulach *m*, (*smaller ~*) tolman *m*

knowledge *n* **1** (*information*) fios *m*, **has anyone any ~ of his whereabouts?** a bheil fios aig duine càit a bheil e?; **2** (*more structured or learned ~*) eòlas *m*, **~ of computers/ history** eòlas air coimpiutairean/air eachdraidh

knowledgeable *adj* eòlach, fiosrach (**about/ on** air)

knuckle *n* rùdan *m*

kyle, kyles (*Sc*) *n* caol *m*, caolas *m*

L

label *n* bileag *f*
label *v* cuir bileag *f* (*with prep* air), bileagaich *vt*
laboratory *n* obair-lann *f*, deuchainn-lann *f*
labour *n* **1** saothair *f*, obair *f*, ~ **costs** cosgaisean
saothrach *fpl*, ~ **relations** dàimhean-obrach
mpl; **2** (*pol*) **Labour** na Làbaraich *mpl*, am
Pàrtaidh Làbarach
labour *v* saothraich *vi*, obraich *vi* (gu cruaidh)
labourer *n* obraiche *m*
lace *n* (*of shoe*) barrall *m*, iall bròige *f*
lacerate *v* reub *vt*
lack *n* dìth *m*, cion *m invar*, easbhaidh *f*, ~ **of**
practice dìth cleachdaidh, ~ **of common**
sense dìth cèille (*gen of* ciall *f*)
lack *v* **1** bi *vi irreg* às aonais (*with gen*), bi gun,
they ~ a house tha iad às aonais taighe *m gen*,
(*more usu*) chan eil taigh aca, **~ing common**
sense gun chiall *f*; **2** (*exprs where the thing*
lacked is the subject in the Gaelic sentence) bi a
(*for* de) dhìth *m*, bi a dh'easbhaidh *f*, (*with prep*
air), **they ~ a house** tha taigh *m* a dhìth orra,
what do they ~? dè a tha a dhìth orra?
lacking *adj & pres part* **1** a dhìth, a dh'easbhaidh,
food is ~ tha biadh a dhìth; **2** gun, às aonais
(*with gen*), **a family ~ a place to stay**
teaghlach gun àite-còmhnaidh, *also* teaghlach is
àite-còmhnaidh a dhìth orra
lad, laddie *n* gille *m*, balach *m*
ladle *n* ladar *m*, liagh *f*
lady *n* **1** (*polite for* **woman**) bean-uasal *f*; **2**
(*female equivalent of* **lord**) baintighearna *f*,
leadaidh *f*
ladybird *n* daolag-bhreac-dhearg *f*
lag (behind) *v* bi *vi irreg* air dheireadh
lair *n* garaidh *m*
laird *n* uachdaran *m*, tighearna *m*
lake *n* loch *m*, (*smaller*) lochan *m*
lamb *n* **1** (*the animal*) uan *m*; **2** (*the meat*)
uainfheòil *f*
lame *adj* crùbach, bacach, cuagach, **a ~ person**
crùbach *m*, bacach *m*
lament *n* tuireadh *m*, (*trad, Lit*) cumha *m*

lament *v* caoidh *vti*, caoin *vi*, dèan tuireadh *m*,
a man doesn't ~ what he doesn't see cha
chaoidh duine an rud nach fhaic e
lamentation *n* caoidh *f*, tuireadh *m*
lamp *n* lampa *mf*, (*less usu*) lòchran *m*
land *n* **1** (*territory, country*) dùthaich *f*, tìr *f*, **a**
foreign ~ dùthaich/tìr chèin, **the Mackay ~s**
Dùthaich MhicAoidh; **2** (*earth, agricultural ~*)
talamh *m* (*f in gen sing*), fearann *m*, **arable/**
cultivated ~ talamh-àitich, **cultivate/till the**
~ àitich am fearann, **fallow ~** talamh bàn, **a**
piece of ~ pìos fearainn *m*; **3** (*~ as opposed to*
sea) tìr *mf*, **on ~** air tìr
land *v* laigh *vi*, **the plane ~ed** laigh am plèana
landing-place *n* **1** (*for boats*) laimrig *f*, cidhe *m*;
2 (*for aircraft*) raon-laighe *m*
landlady *n* (*of hotel, pub, boarding house etc*)
bean-taighe *f*, **the ~** bean an taighe
landlord *n* (*of pub etc*) fear-taighe *m*, òstair *m*,
the ~ fear an taighe *m*
landmark *n* (*for navigation*) comharradh-
stiùiridh *m*, iùl *m*
landowner *n* **1** neach-fearainn *m* (*pl* luchd-
fearainn *m sing coll*); **2** (*esp member of the*
landed gentry) tighearna *m*, uachdaran *m*
landscape *n* **1** (*phys*) cruth-tìre *m*; **2** (*in art etc*)
dealbh-tìre *mf*, sealladh-tìre *m*
lane *n* caol-shràid *f*, lònaid *f*
language *n* **1** (*esp in general & abstr sense*)
cainnt *f*, **the faculty of ~** comas cainnte *m*, **bad**
~ droch chainnt, **~ laboratory** cainnt-lann *f*; **2**
(*national etc ~*) cànan *m*, cànain *f*, **the ~ of the**
Gaels cànan nan Gàidheal, **a foreign ~** cànan
cèin, **a lesser-used/minority ~** mion-chànan
or cànan beag; **3** (*IT*) cànan *m*
lanky *adj* caol, seang
lantern *n* lanntair *m*, lainntear *m*, (*less usu*)
lòchran *m*
lap² *n* (*part of body*) uchd *m*, **the boy was**
sitting on her ~ bha am balach na shuidhe na
h-uchd
lap² *n* (*in a race*) cuairt *f*
lap *v* imlich *vt*

lapwing *n* curracag *f*

large *adj* **1** mòr, (*esp bulky, burly*) tomadach &
tomaltach, **a ~ estate** oighreachd mhòr, **a ~
quantity** meud mòr, **a ~ man** duine mòr, **a
~ book** leabhar tomadach; **2** *in expr* **by and
~** san fharsaingeachd *f invar*, **by and ~, the
majority are against him** san fharsaingeachd,
tha a' mhòr-chuid na aghaidh

larger *comp adj* mò/motha

lark *n* **1** (*bird*) uiseag *f*, topag *f*; **2** (*spree, fun*)
plòidh *f*, spòrs *f*; **3** (*trick etc*) car *m*, cleas *m*

laser *n* leusair *m*, **~ beam** gath leusair *m*

lass, lassie *n* caileag *f*, nighean *f*

last *adj* mu dheireadh, deireannach, **this is the
~ opportunity you'll get** 's e seo an cothrom
mu dheireadh a gheibh thu, **on the ~ day** air an
là dheireannach, air an là mu dheireadh, **~ year**
an-uiridh *adv*

last *adv* **1** (*in final position*) air deireadh, **she
came ~** thàinig i air deireadh; **2** (*of time*) *in
expr* **at (long) ~** mu dheireadh (thall), **the
rain stopped at (long) ~** sguir an t-uisge mu
dheireadh (thall)

last *v* **1** (*survive, ~ out etc*) mair *vi*, **it won't
~ two days** cha mhair e dà là; **2** (*continue,
persist*) lean *vi*, **will the fine weather ~?** an
lean an deagh aimsir?

lasting *adj* maireannach, leantainneach, **~ peace**
sìth mhaireannach

latch *n* clàimhean *m*

late *adj & adv* **1** (*after appointed time etc*) air
deireadh, fadalach, **she came ~** thàinig i air
deireadh, **five minutes ~** còig mionaidean air
deireadh, **I was ~** bha mi fadalach; **2** (*advanced
hour*) anmoch, **~ at night** anmoch san oidhche,
it was getting ~ bha e a' fàs anmoch; **3** (*of
deceased person*) nach maireann (*verbal noun
of* mair *vi*), **the ~ Johnny Campbell** Seonaidh
Caimbeul nach maireann

Latin *adj* Laidinneach

Latin *n* (*lang*) Laideann *f*

latter *adj*, *in exprs* **at the ~ end** aig a' cheann
thall, **at the ~ day** air an là (*dat*) dheireannach

lattice cliath-uinneig *f*

laugh *n* gàire *mf invar*

laugh *v* dèan gàire *mf invar*, gàir *vi*

laughing *n* gàireachdainn *f invar*, gàireachdaich
f invar

laughing-stock *n* cùis-mhagaidh *f*, adhbhar gàire
m, **they were a ~** bha iad nan cùis-mhagaidh/
nan adhbhar gàire

laughter *n* gàire *mf invar*, gàireachdainn *f invar*

launch *v* **1** (*boat*) cuir *vt* air flod *m*, cuir *vt* air
bhog *f*; **2** (*~ company etc*) cuir *vt* air chois (*dat
of* cas *f*), cuir *vt* air bhonn *m*

laundry *n* taigh-nighe *m*

law *n* lagh *m*, **against the ~** an aghaidh an lagha

lawful *adj* **1** (*not against the law*) laghail; **2**
(*legitimate*) dligheach

lawn *n* faiche *f*, rèidhlean *m*

lawsuit *n* cùis *f*, cùis-lagha *f*

lawyer *n* neach-lagha *m* (*pl* luchd-lagha *m sing
coll*)

lay *n* (*poem, song*) laoidh *mf*

lay *v* **1** (*floortiles etc*) leag *vt*; **2** (*egg*) beir *vt*;
3 (*misc exprs*) **~ bare** lom *vt*, **~ blame** cuir
coire *f* (**on** air), **~ great emphasis on X** leig
cudthrom mòr air X

laziness *n* leisg(e) *f*

lazy *adj* leisg

lazy-bed *n* feannag *f*

lazybones *n* leisgeadair *m*

lead *adj* (*principal etc*) prìomh, **~ singer** prìomh
sheinneadair

lead *n* **1** (*example to be followed*) stiùir *f*, **give a/
the ~** thoir stiùir (**to** do); **2** (*leading position*)
in expr **he was in the ~** bha e air thoiseach; **3**
(*dog's ~*) iall *f*

lead *n* (*metal*) luaidhe *mf invar*, **a ~ soldier**
saighdear luaidhe *m*

lead *v* **1** treòraich *vt*, stiùir *vt*, **he led his
congregation to Canada** threòraich e a
choitheanal gu Canada; **2** (*as vi: be in the lead*)
bi *vi irreg* air thoiseach, **they led/were ~ing
after five minutes** bha iad air thoiseach an
dèidh chòig mionaidean; **3** *in expr* **~ astray**
(*morally*) claon *vt*, (*phys or morally*) cuir *vt* air
seachran *m*, cuir *vt* air iomrall *m*

leader *n* ceannard *m*

leadership *n* **1** (*abstr*) ceannardas *m*; **2** (*con: ie
the leaders*) na ceannardan *mpl*

leaf *n* (*of tree, plant, book*) duilleag *f*

leaflet *n* (*publicity etc*) duilleachan *m*, bileag *f*

leak *n* aoidion *m*

leaking *adj* aoidionach

leakproof *adj* (*house, boat etc*) dìonach, uisge-
dìonach

leaky *adj* aoidionach

lean *adj* **1** (*of person*) tana, seang; **2** (*of meat*)
gun saill *f*, neo-shultmhor

lean *v* **1** (*not be upright*) bi *vi irreg* air fhiaradh
m, **the post ~ed/was ~ing** bha am post air
fhiaradh; **2** (*~ for support*) cuir/leig a (*etc*) t(h)
aic *f*, cuir/leig a (*etc*) c(h)udthrom *m*, (**on** air,
against ri), **~ on me,** cuir/leig do thaic orm, **~
against a tree** cuir/leig do thaic ri craoibh

leaning adj **1** (not vertical) claon, air fhiaradh m; **2** (supported) an taic f, an tacsa m, (**against** ri), ~ **against a tree** an taic ri craoibh

leap n leum m, sùrdag f

leap v leum vti

leap year n bliadhna-lèim f

learn v ionnsaich vti, (~ less formally) tog vt, **I ~t my Gaelic in Skye** thog mi mo chuid Gàidhlig f san Eilean Sgitheanach m

learned adj foghlaimte, foghlamaichte

learner n neach-ionnsachaidh m (pl luchd-ionnsachaidh m sing coll)

learning n **1** (knowledge, scholarship) ionnsachadh m, foghlam m, oideachas m; **2** (traditional ~) beul-oideachas m

lease n gabhail mf, **the farmer took the ~ of a farm** ghabh an tuathanach tuathanas air gabhail

lease v **1** (~ out) thoir vt (seachad) air gabhail mf/air mhàl m, **the landlord ~d (out) a farm** thug an t-uachdaran seachad tuathanas air gabhail; **2** (rent, take on lease) gabh vt air mhàl m, **the farmer ~ed a farm** ghabh an tuathanach tuathanas air mhàl

leash n iall f

least 1 comp adj lugha; **2** in expr **at ~** co-dhiù, **there were 2000 there at ~** bha dà mhìle ann co-dhiù, **at ~, that's what he said** 's e sin a thubhairt e, co-dhiù; **3** in expr **at the very ~** aig a' char m as lugha, **at the very ~ we lost two thousand pounds** aig a' char as lugha chaill sinn dà mhìle nota

leather adj leathair (gen of leathar m used adjectivally), **a ~ jacket** seacaid leathair f

leather n leathar m

leave n **1** (permission) cead m invar, **by your ~** le ur cead; **2** (parting) cead m invar, in expr **take ~** gabh cead (**of** de), dealaich vi (**with prep** ri), **we took our ~ of them** ghabh sinn ar cead dhiubh, dhealaich sinn riutha; **3** (~ from army etc) fòrladh m

leave v **1** (depart) falbh vi, **they left yesterday** dh'fhalbh iad an-dè, **she's left** tha i air falbh; **2** (depart from) fàg vt, **leaving Stornoway** a' fàgail Steòrnabhaigh; **3** (put, leave behind) fàg vt, **where did you ~ the car?** càite na dh'fhàg thu an càr?; **4** (make, cause to be, with adj) fàg vt, **the journey left them tired** dh'fhàg an turas sgith iad; **5** (desert, abandon) trèig vt, **he left his family** thrèig e a theaghlach; **6** (~ in one's will) tiomnaich vt (**to** do); **7** (entrust with a task etc) leig vt (**with preps** le or do), **~ it to her to bring up the child** leig leathase am pàiste a thogail, **~ it to me** (ie I'll handle it/see to it etc) leig dhòmhsa e

leavings n fuidheall m, **he got his pick of it, I got the ~** fhuair esan a roghainn dheth, fhuair mise am fuidheall

lecher n drùisear m

lecherous adj drùiseach

lechery n drùis f

lecture n òraid f, **give a ~** thoir seachad òraid, dèan òraid

lecturer n òraidiche m

ledge n **1** (topog) leac f; **2** (of window) oir na h-uinneig(e) f

leek n creamh-gàrraidh m

lees n (in liquids) grùid f

left adj **1** clì, ceàrr, **my ~ foot** mo chas chlì; **2** in expr **on his/her ~** air a làimh (dat of làmh f) chlì

left-handed adj ciotach

leg n cas f

legacy n (lit or fig) dìleab f, **the ~ of history** dìleab na h-eachdraidh

legal adj **1** (not against the law, also, to do with the law) laghail; **2** (legitimate etc) dligheach

legend n uirsgeul m, fionnsgeul m, faoinsgeul m

legendary adj uirsgeulach

legible adj so-leughte

legislate v reachdaich vi

legislation n **1** (the action) reachdachadh m; **2** (the actual laws etc) reachdas m

legislature n reachdaireachd f

legitimate adj dligheach

leisure n **1** saor-ùine f; **2** in exprs **I am at ~** tha mi nam thàmh m, **~ pursuits/activities** cur-seachadan mpl

leisurely adj socrach, **a ~ pace** ceum socrach

lemon n liomaid f

lend v thoir vt air iasad m, thoir iasad (**with prep** de), (**to** do), **I lent James a pound** thug mi nota do Sheumas air iasad, thug mi iasad de nota do Sheumas

length n fad m, **a mile in ~** mìle a (**for** de) dh'fhad, **it flew the ~ of the house** dh'itealaich e air fad an taighe

lengthen v **1** (as vt) cuir vt am fad, **we ~ed it** chuir sinn am fad e; **2** (as vi) rach vi am fad, **it's ~ing** tha e a' dol am fad, also tha e a' fàs nas fhaide

lenite v (lang) sèimhich vt

lenition n (lang) sèimheachadh m

lens n lionsa f

leopard n liopard m

leper n lobhar m

leprosy n luibhre f invar

lesbian adj & n leasbach f

-less *suffix* mì-, eu- (*occas* ao-), *eg* **careless** mì-chùramach, **hopeless** eu-dòchasach

lessen *v* 1 lùghdaich *vti*, rach *vi* sìos, **the noise ~ed** lùghdaich am fuaim, chaidh am fuaim sìos; 2 *in expr* **his suffering/pain ~ed** thàinig faothachadh *m* air

lesser *adj* 1 as lugha, (*in past & conditional tenses*) a bu lugha, **the ~ number/quantity** an àireamh/am meud as lugha; 2 mion- *prefix*, beag, **lesser-used language** mion-chànan *m*, cànan beag; 3 (*in names of birds, animals etc*) beag, **~ black-backed gull** farspag bheag

lesson *n* leasan *m*

lest *conj* air eagal is gu, gun fhios nach, mus, **he put a piece in his pocket ~ he should grow hungry** chuir e pìos na phòca gun fhios nach tigeadh an t-acras air, **he kept hold of her ~ she should fall** chùm e grèim oirre mus tuiteadh i/air eagal 's gun tuiteadh i

let *v* 1 (*permit*) leig *vt* (*with prep* le), **he ~ me buy it** leig e leam a cheannach, **~ her be!/~ her get on with it!** leig leatha!, **will you ~ us know?** an leig sibh fios *m* dhuinn?, *also* an cuir sibh fios thugainn?; 2 *in expr* **~ go** (*ie release*) leig às *vt*, saor *vt*, fuasgail *vt*, (*esp from captivity*) leig *vt* mu sgaoil *m invar*, cuir *vt* mu sgaoil, **~ the dogs go** leig às na coin (*pl of* cù *m*), **they ~ the prisoners go** leig/chuir iad na prìosanaich mu sgaoil; 3 *in expr* **~ off/out** (*ie emit etc*) leig *vt* (*with or without adv* às), **he ~ off a fart** leig e braim *m* (às), *also* rinn e braim, **they ~ out a yell** leig iad às sgreuch *m*; 4 *in expr* **~ on** (*ie give the game away etc*) leig *vi* (*with prep* air), **we didn't ~ on** cha do leig sinn oirnn; 5 *in expr* **~ down** (*ie lower*) leag *vt*, **he ~ down the window** leag e an uinneag; 6 *in expr* **~ down** (*ie disappoint etc*) leig *vt* sìos; 7 (*idiom*) **~ me see** fuirich ort/fan ort, **that happened . . . , ~ me see now . . . , in Stornoway** thachair sin . . . , fuirich ort . . . , ann an Steòrnabhagh; 8 (**~ property etc**) thoir *vt* (seachad) air mhàl *m*, **he has ~ his house** tha e air an taigh aige a thoirt seachad air mhàl; 9 (*imper: can be archaic*) *expressed by imper forms of verb, eg* **~ us see** faiceamaid, **~ them hear** chluinneadh iad, **~ me not go** na racham

lethargic *adj* mall, slaodach, marbhanta, trom

letter *n* (*corres, orthography*) litir *f*, **~s of the alphabet** litrichean na h-aibidil(e)

lettuce *n* leiteis *f*

level *adj* 1 (*horizontal*) rèidh, còmhnard; 2 (*in election etc*) co-ionann, **the parties are ~** tha na pàrtaidhean co-ionann

level *n* 1 (*of progress, development, ability etc*) ìre *f invar*; 2 (*of rank, attainment, ability*) inbhe *f*; 3 (*of height, volume*) àirde *f*; 4 *in expr* **sea ~** còmhnard na mara *m*

lever *n* luamhan *m*

lewd *adj* drabasta, draosta, collaidh

lewdness *n* drabastachd *f invar*, draostachd *f invar*

Lewis *n* Leòdhas *or* Eilean Leòdhais *m*, (*nickname, in songs etc*) Eilean Fraoich (*gen of* fraoch *m*)

Lewisman *n* Leòdhasach *m*, **Lewis woman** ban-Leòdhasach

lexicography *n* faclaireachd *f invar*

liable *adj* buailteach, **~ to change** buailteach do chaochladh, **~ to spend money** buailteach airgead a chosg

liar *n* breugaire *m*

libel *n* tuaileas *m*

libel *v* cuir tuaileas (*with prep* air)

liberal *adj* 1 (*generous*) fialaidh, fial, tabhartach; 2 (*permissive etc*) ceadach, ceadachail; 3 (*pol*) libearalach (*m & adj*), **~ Democrat** Libearalach Deamocratach

liberate *v* saor *vt*, cuir/leig *vt* mu sgaoil, fuasgail *vt*

library *n* leabharlann *mf*

lice *see* **louse**

licence *n* cead *m invar*, **driving ~** cead-dràibhidh, **television ~** cead telebhisein

license *v* ceadaich *vt*, ùghdarraich *vt*

licensee *n* (*of public house, hotel*) òstair *m*, fear (an) taighe *m*

licensing *n* ceadachadh *m*, ùghdarrachadh *m*, *in expr* **~ board** bòrd ceadachaidh *m*, bòrd-ceadachd *m*

lichen *n* crotal *m*

licit *adj* ceadaichte, laghail

lick *n* imlich *f*

lick *v* imlich *vti*

lie *n* (*untruth*) breug *f*, *in expr* **give the ~ to** breugnaich *vt*

lie[1] *v* laigh *vi*, **~ down** laigh sìos, **I lay down** laigh mi sìos, *in expr* **lying (down)** na (*etc*) laighe *mf invar*, **she's lying down** tha i na laighe, **they were lying (down) on the ground** bha iad nan laighe air an làr

lie[2] *v* (*tell untruths*) innis/dèan breug(an) *f(pl)*

life *n* 1 (*abstr & con*) beatha *f*, (*more trad: con*) saoghal *m*, **a hard ~** beatha chruaidh, **all my ~** fad mo bheatha *gen*, **way of ~** dòigh-beatha *f*, **~ cycle** cearcall (na) beatha *m*, **~ member** ball beatha *m*, *in expr* **long ~ to you!** saoghal fada dhuibh!; 2 (*the breath of ~*) deò *f invar*, (*a spark* of ~) rong *m*, **as long as there's ~ in me** fhad 's a bhios an deò annam, **there wasn't a spark of ~ in her** cha robh rong innte; **3** (*lifespan, lifetime*) maireann *m*, beò *m*, là *m*, **he never left the island in his ~** cha do dh'fhàg e an t-eilean ri bheò/ri mhaireann, **at the end of my ~** aig crìoch mo là; **4** *in exprs* **he was running for dear ~** bha e a' ruith mar a bheatha, bha e a' ruith aig peilear *m* a bheatha, **~ expectancy** dùil aois *f*

life-belt *n* crios-sàbhalaidh *m*, crios-teasairginn *m*

lifeboat *n* bata-teasairginn *m*, bàta-coibhre *m*

life-jacket *n* seacaid-teasairginn *f*

lifelong *adj* fad-beatha

lifestyle *n* dòigh-beatha *f*

lifetime *n* maireann *m*, beò *m*, là *m*, rè *f invar*, linn *mf*, (*trad*) saoghal *m*, **in/during my ~** rim mhaireann, rim bheò, rim latha, rim shaoghal, **in my grandfather's ~** an rè mo sheanar *gen*, ri linn mo sheanar, **at the end of my ~** aig deireadh mo là *gen*

lift *n* (*ie elevator*) àrdaichear *m*

lift *v* tog *vt* (**from** de, far), **~ stones from the ground** tog clachan den làr/far na talmhainn (*gen f of* talamh *m*), **~ (up) your head** tog do cheann, **that ~ed my spirits** thog sin mo chridhe *m*

light *adj* aotrom, **~ stones/music** clachan *fpl*/ceòl *m* aotrom

light *n* (*natural or artificial*) solas *m*, **put the~ on/off** cuir air/às an solas, **electric ~** solas-dealain *m*

light *v* **1** las *vti*, **~ a cigarette** las toitean *m*, (*fig*) **his face would ~ up** bhiodh aodann a' lasadh; **2** (*~ fire, lamp etc*) cuir *vt* air, **~ the fire** cuir air an teine *m*

light upon *v* **1** (*come to rest upon*) laigh *vi* (*with prep* air), **each thing his eye would ~ upon** gach rud air an laigheadh a shùil; **2** (*come upon by chance*) amais *vi* air

light-heartedness *n* mire *f invar*, sunnd *m invar*, aighearachd *f invar*

lightning *n* dealanach *m*

like *adj* **1** (*similar*) coltach (*with prep* ri), **she's not ~ her brother** chan eil i coltach ri a bràthair, **~ each other** coltach ri chèile; **2** (*stronger: just/exactly ~*) ionann agus, *takes the v* is, **A is (exactly) ~ B** is ionann A agus B; **3** mar (*a following noun without the art is in the dat, & lenited where possible*), **singing ~ a girl** a' seinn mar chaileig, **he left, just ~ his brother** dh'fhalbh e, dìreach mar a bhràthair; *NB: Note the difference between* **he is ~** (*ie*

resembles) **his sister** tha e coltach ri phiuthar, *and* **he sings ~ his sister** (*ie sings as his sister sings*) bidh e a' seinn mar a phiuthar; **4** (*idioms*) **you look ~ a soldier** (*etc*) tha coltas *m* saighdeir (*etc*) ort, **I'm tired! you look ~ it!** tha mi sgìth! tha a choltas (sin) ort!

like *n* leithid *f*, coimeas *m*, samhail *m*, **I don't know (etc) a man the ~(s) of him** chan eil mi eòlach air (*etc*) a *poss adj* leithid de dhuine, **his/her ~ never existed** cha robh a leithid ann a-riamh, **I never saw his ~** chan fhaca mi a-riamh a leithid/a choimeas/a shamhail, **the ~(s) of that** a leithid sin

like *v* **1** *is vi irreg def* toigh (*with prep* le), (*can be stronger: be fond of*) bi *vi irreg* dèidheil (*with prep* air), **I ~ my school/the teacher** is toigh leam an sgoil agam/an tidsear, **I ~ Mary/chocolate** tha mi dèidheil air Màiri/air seòclaid; **2** (*wish, desire*) togair *vti* (*often used as vi in relative future tense*), **we'll go on holiday, if you ~** thèid sinn air laithean-saora, ma thogras tu, **just as you ~** dìreach mar a thogras sibh; **3** *in expr* (*in shop, café etc*) **what would you ~?** dè (a) tha a dhìth oirbh?

likeable *adj* tlachdmhor, taitneach, ciatach

likelihood *n* coltas *m*

likely *adj* coltach, **it's ~ that she'll come** tha e coltach gun tig i

liken *v* coimeas *vt*, dèan coimeas *m* (*with prep* eadar), **~ A and B** coimeas A agus B, dèan coimeas eadar A agus B

likeness *n* **1** (*abstr: resemblance*) coltas *m*; **2** (*con: representation in portrait, sculpture etc*) ìomhaigh *f*; **3** (*shape, disguise etc*) riochd *m*, **he appeared in the ~ of a cat** nochd e an riochd cait

likewise *adv* cuideachd, mar an ceudna, **I was good at dancing, my sister ~** bha mi math air dannsadh, (agus) mo phiuthar cuideachd/mar an ceudna

liking *n* **1** (*affection*) tlachd *f invar*, spèis *f*, bàidh *f*; **2** *in expr* **he has a ~ for (chocolate etc)** tha e dèidheil air (seòclaid *etc*)

lily *n* lili(dh) *f*

limit *n* **1** (*maximum permitted*) crìoch *f*, **speed ~** crìoch astair, astar-chrìoch *f*; **2** (*edge, boundary*) crìoch *f*, iomall *m*, **the ~(s) of the country** crìoch/iomall na dùthcha

limit *v* cuingealaich *vt* (**to** ri), cuir crìoch *f* (*with prep* ri), **~ed to five minutes** air a chuingealachadh ri còig mionaidean, **he ~ed our costs** chuir e crìoch ri ar cosgaisean

limited adj **1** (*people, attitudes*) cumhang; **2** (*business*) earranta, **a ~ company** companaidh earranta, **Birlinn ~** Birlinn Earranta

limp adj bog

limp n ceum m, **he has a ~** tha e cuagach/ bacach/crùbach

limp v bi vi irreg cuagach, bi bacach, bi crùbach, **he ~s** tha e bacach

limping adj cuagach, bacach, crùbach

line n **1** (*pencil ~, phone ~ etc*) loidhne f, (*IT*) **on ~** air loidhne; **2** (*~ of verse or prose, of people, objects*) sreath mf

line v (*curtains etc*) lìnig vt

linen n (*the material & things made from it*) anart m, **bed ~** anart-leapa m, (*adjectival use*) **a ~ shirt** lèine anairt (*gen*)

ling[1] n (*the fish*) langa f

ling[2] n (*the plant*) fraoch m

linguist n cànanaiche m

linguistic adj cànanach

linguistics n cànanachas m

lining n (*material*) lìnigeadh m

link n **1** (*con: in chain etc*) tinne f, ceangal m; **2** (*abstr: logical ~, ~ of cause & effect etc*) ceangal m (**with** ri, **between** eadar), **there is no ~ between the meat and the illness** chan eil ceangal sam bith eadar an fheòil agus an tinneas, **a close ~** dlùth-cheangal; **3** (*relationship, association*) dàimh mf invar (**with** ri), **I have no ~(s) with that firm** chan eil dàimh sam bith agam ris a' chompanaidh sin; **4** (*family etc ~*) buinteanas m, **I have ~s with Skye** tha buinteanas agam ris an Eilean Sgitheanach

link v ceangail vt, co-cheangail vt, (**to/with** ri)

linkage n ceangal m, (*esp abstr*) co-cheangal m

linked adj & past part co-cheangailte (**to** ri), **global warming and the climate are ~ (to one another)** tha blàthachadh na cruinne is a' chlìomaid co-cheangailte (ri chèile)

linn n linne f

lint n lìon m

lion n leòmhann m

lip n **1** (*of mouth*) bile f, (*less usu*) li(o)p f, in exprs **lower ~** beul-ìochdair m, **upper ~** beul-uachdair m; **2** (*~ of container, jug etc*) bile f, oir f, iomall m

lipstick n dath-lipean m

liquid adj sruthach

liquid n lionn m

liquidate v **1** (*company etc*) leagh vt; **2** (*kill, execute*) cuir vi às (*with prep* do)

liquidation n (*of company etc*) leaghadh m

Lismore n Lios Mòr m

lisp, **lisping** n liotachas m, in expr **he has a ~** tha e liotach

lisp v bi vi irreg liotach, **he ~s** tha e liotach

lisping adj liotach

list n **1** (*general*) liosta f; **2** (*in publication*) clàr m, **~ of contents** clàr-innse m, **~ of names/people** clàr-ainmean m, clàr-dhaoine m

list v dèan liosta f (*with prep* de)

listen v èist (**to** ri), **~ing to the songs** ag èisteachd ris na h-òrain mpl

listener n neach-èisteachd m, **~s** luchd-èisteachd m sing coll

literal adj litireil

literary adj litreachail

literate adj litireach

literature n litreachas m, **Gaelic ~** litreachas na Gàidhlig

litigious adj connspaideach, agartach

litre n liotair m

litter[1] n (*rubbish, untidiness*) truileis f invar, (*stronger*) sgudal m

litter[2] n (*young of animals*) cuain f, (*more trad*) àl m

little adj **1** beag, (*smaller*) meanbh, **~ by ~** beag air bheag, beag is beag, also mean air mhean, uidh f air n-uidh; **2** in expr **the Little Minch** An Cuan Sgìth

little n **1** (*a certain amount*) beagan m (*with gen*), **I have a ~ money** tha beagan airgid agam; **2** (*a very small or limited amount*) a bheag (*with prep* de), **there was only a (very) ~ room in the boat** cha robh ach a bheag de rùm sa bhàta

littoral n oirthir f, costa m

live adj beò

live v **1** (*be alive*) bi vi irreg beò, (*more trad*) is vi irreg def beò, mair vi beò, **as long as I ~** cho fad 's a bhios mi beò, cho fad 's a mhaireas mi beò, also rim mhaireann m, rim shaoghal m, (*more trad*) cho fad' 's as beò mi; **2** (*dwell etc*) fuirich vi, còmhnaich vi, fan vi, **we were living in Islay at the time** bha sinn a' fuireach/a' còmhnaidh ann an Ìle aig an àm, **~ with someone** fan/fuirich aig cuideigin; **3** (*survive, make a living*) thig vi beò, **how will we ~ in this place?** ciamar a thig sinn beò san àite seo?, **I can't ~ on that!** cha tig mi beò (*or* cha tig mi suas) air sin!

livelihood n teachd-an-tìr m invar, beòshlaint f, bith-beò f

lively adj **1** beothail; **2** (*idioms*) **look ~!** tog vi ort!, crath dhìot an cadal!

liver n adha m, (*usu of animal*) grùthan m

livestock n stoc m, (*esp cattle*) crodh m, sprèidh f

living adj 1 beò, **I didn't see a ~ soul** chan fhaca mi duine beò; **2** in expr **I'm still in the land of the ~** tha mi a' cumail beò, tha mi beò fhathast

living n 1 (abstr) bith-beò f, **the cost of ~** cosgais bith-beò f; **2** (a livelihood) teachd-an-tìr m invar, beòshlaint f; **3** (an income) teachd-a-steach m invar

lizard n laghairt mf

load n 1 (burden etc, esp as carried by humans/animals) eallach m, uallach m, (esp carried by a human) ultach m; **2** (cargo) luchd m; **3** (in pl) ~**s** (fam: a lot, lots, many) tòrr m (with gen), ~**s of people are of that opinion** tha tòrr dhaoine den bheachd sin

load v (boat, vehicle etc) luchdaich vt

loading n luchdachadh m

loads npl (ie lots, many etc) see load n 3

loaf n lof mf, (more trad: homemade bread ~, ~ of sugar etc) buileann f

loan n iasad m, **get something on ~** gabh/faigh rudeigin air iasad, **get a ~ of something** faigh iasad de rudeigin

loanword n (lang) facal iasaid m

loathe v fuathaich vt, (but usu expressed as follows) **I ~ him/them** etc tha gràin f agam air/orra

loathing n gràin f, fuath m

loathsome adj gràineil, fuathach

lobster n giomach m

lobsterpot n cliabh ghiomach m

local adj ionadail, ~ **authority/history** ùghdarras/eachdraidh ionadail

locate v (find, trace) faigh lorg f air, **the police ~ed him** fhuair am poileas lorg air

location n (site, position etc) suidheachadh m, àite m

loch n loch m, **sea ~** loch-mara m

lochan n lochan m

lock¹ n (on door etc) glas f

lock² (of hair) dual m

lock v glais & glas vt, ~ **the door** glais/glas an doras

locked adj & past part glaiste

locum n (med etc) neach-ionaid m

locust n lòcast m

lodge v 1 (as vi) fan vi, fuirich vi, ~ **with someone** fan/fuirich aig cuideigin; **2** (as vt: house, accommodate) thoir taigh m, thoir lòistinn m, (with prep do); **3** (deposit, eg in museum, bank etc) taisg vt

lodger n lòistear m

lodging(s) n 1 lòistinn m, (less usu) fàrdach f; **2** in expr **a night's ~** cuid oidhche f

loft n lobht(a) m

loggerheads n, **at ~** thar a chèile, troimh-a-chèile, **they were at ~** bha iad thar a chèile/troimh-a-chèile, **I set them at ~** chuir mi thar a chèile/troimh-a-chèile iad

London n Lunnainn

lonely, lonesome adj (person or place) aonaranach, uaigneach

long adj 1 (in time & dimension) fad(a), **how ~ is it?** dè cho fada 's a tha e? (also dè an fhad a th' ann), **don't be ~** na bi fada!, **the days were/seemed ~ for us** bha na làithean fada dhuinn; **2** (~ and weary) cian, **a ~ (weary) road** rathad cian; **3** in expr ~ **drawn out** fadalach, màirnealach; **4** (idioms) ~ **time no see!** 's fhada o nach fhaca mi (etc) thu!, (to impatient child etc) **it won't be ~ now** chan fhad' thuige a-nis

long adv 1 (of dimension) de dh'fhad (also a dh'fhad), **a mile ~** mìle mf a dh'fhad, **it's two feet ~** tha dà throigh f de dh'fhad ann; **2** (of time) fada, **as ~ as I live** cho fad(a) 's as beò mi, also (more trad) rim mhaireann m; **3** (misc exprs) **the whole night ~** fad na h-oidhche, **at ~ last** mu dheireadh thall, (in stories etc) ~ **~ ago** o chionn fada nan cian, fada fada ron a seo

long- prefix fad-, eg **long-lived** fad-shaoghalach, **long-sighted** fad-fhradharcach, **long-suffering** fad-fhulangach

long v 1 in expr ~ **for** (ie desire) miannaich vt; **2** in expr ~ **for** (ie nostalgically) ionndrainn vt

longing n 1 (desire) miann mf; **2** (with nostalgia) cianalas m; **3** (with impatience) fadachd f invar (**for** ri)

look n sùil f (**at** air), **a quick ~ at the newspaper** sùil aithghearr air a' phàipear-naidheachd m, **take/have a ~** thoir sùil (**at** air); **2** (physical appearance, aspect) dreach m, **with a ghostly ~** air dhreach taibhse; **3** (of person's features, not nec permanent) tuar m; **4** (transient, on face, in eye) fiamh m; **5** (resemblance, appearance) coltas m, **you have the ~ of a soldier** tha coltas saighdeir ort, **by the ~ of it** a rèir c(h)oltais

look v 1 coimhead vi, thoir sùil f, (**at** air), ~ **at her** coimhead oirre, ~ **out of the window** coimhead a-mach air an uinneig, **that ~s/is ~ing good!** (fam) tha sin a' coimhead math!; **2** (resemblance: idioms) ~**ing like a ghost** air dhreach taibhse, **you ~ like a soldier** tha coltas saighdeir ort; **3** in expr ~ **for** sir vt, lorg vt, bi vi irreg an tòir f (with prep air), **the company is ~ing for workers** tha a' chompanaidh a' sireadh luchd-obrach, **he went to town ~ing for his brother** chaidh e don bhaile an tòir air a bhràthair; **4**

(idiom) **I'm tired! you ~ it!** tha mi sgìth! tha a choltas (sin) ort!

loom *n (for weaving)* beart-fhighe *f*

loop *n* lùb *f*

loose *adj* **1** fuasgailte, sgaoilte, neo-cheangailte; **2** *(fig: of immoral person, behaviour)* mì-bheusach

loose *v* leig (às) *vt*, **~ an arrow** leig (às) saighead *f*

loosen *v (fastenings etc)* fuasgail *vt*, sgaoil *vt*, lasaich *vt*, **~ a knot/a shoelace** fuasgail snaidhm *m*/barrall *m*

lord *n* **1** *(ruler, landowner etc)* tighearna *m*, *(hist)* **The Lord of the Isles** Tighearna nan Eilean, *also* Triath *m* nan Eilean; **2** *(peer etc)* morair *m*, **the House of ~s** Taigh *m* nam Morairean; **3** *(relig)* **The Lord** An Tighearna; **4** *(excl)* **Good ~!** a Thighearna!

lorry *n* làraidh *f*

lose *v* caill *vti*

loss *n* call *m*

lost *adj & past part* air chall *m*, caillte, **I'm ~** tha mi air chall, **we got ~** chaidh sinn air chall

lot[1] *n* **1** *(one's fate)* crannchur *m*, **if that is my ~** mas e sin mo chrannchur; **2** *(one's ~ in life)* **it was his ~ to be a soldier (etc)** thuit dha a bhith na shaighdear *(etc)*; **3** *in exprs* **draw ~s** cuir crainn *(pl of crann m)*, tilg crainn, cuir crannchur, **drawing of ~s** crannchur *m*

lot[2] *n* **1** *(considerable quantity)* mòran *m*, *(fam)* grunn *m*, *(fam)* tòrr *m*, *(all with gen)*, gu leòr *adv (follows the noun)*, **a ~ of food** mòran bìdh *(gen of* biadh*) m*, biadh gu leòr, **I spent a ~ of years there** chuir mi seachad mòran/grunn bhliadhnachan an sin, **~s of people** mòran/tòrr dhaoine, **a ~ of money** mòran/tòrr airgid, *also (fam)* airgead mòr, **we've got a ~ of troubles** tha trioblaidean gu leòr againn; **2** *(misc exprs)* **thanks a ~!** mòran taing!, ceud *m* taing!, **a ~ better** fada/mòran nas fheàrr, **such a ~ of people there** na h-uimhir, na h-uiread, *(with prep* de*)*, **there were such a ~ of people there** bha na h-uimhir/na h-uiread de dhaoine ann

loth *adj* leisg, aindeonach, **I am ~ to sell it** is leisg leam a reic

lottery *n* crannchur *m*, **the National ~** an Crannchur Nàiseanta

loud *adj* **1** *(at high volume)* àrd; **2** *(noisy)* faramach, fuaimneach; **3** *(of style, garments etc)* spaideil

loudspeaker *n* glaodhaire *m*

louse *n* mial *f*, **lice** *npl* mialan

lout *n* duine borb

loutish *adj* gràisgeil

loutishness *n* gràisgealachd *f invar*

love *n* **1** *(esp sexual & intimate ~)* gaol *m*, *(for less intimate affection)* gràdh *m*, **she's in ~** tha i ann an gaol, **I gave my ~ to her** thug mi mo ghaol dhi, **young ~** gaol na h-òige, **my first ~** mo chiad ghaol, **the land of my ~, the land (that) I love** tìr mo ghràidh; **2** *(the person loved)* leannan *m*, **my ~** mo leannan; **3** *(in voc exprs: affectionate address)* **(my) ~!** *(esp to lovers and close family)* a ghaoil!, a luaidh!, *(usu for more general, less intimate use)* a ghràidh!, m' eudail!

love *v* **1** *(esp sexually, intimately)* bi *vi irreg* gaol *m (with preps* aig *&* air*)*, *(for less intimate affection)* bi *vi irreg* gràdh *m (with preps* aig *&* air*)*, **I ~ you** tha gaol agam ort, tha gràdh agam ort; **2** *in expr* **the land (etc) I ~** tìr *(etc)* mo ghràidh *(gen of* gràdh *m)*; **3** *(like or enjoy greatly)* is *vi irreg & def* toigh *(with prep* le*)*, **I ~ football** is toigh leam (gu mòr) ball-coise

loveliness *n (of woman, place etc)* bòidhchead *f invar*, *(esp of woman)* maise *f invar*

lovely *adj (place, weather, girl etc)* brèagha, *(woman, place etc)* bòidheach, *(esp of woman)* maiseach

lover *n* leannan *m*

loving *adj* gaolach, gràdhach, maoth

low *adj* **1** *(of phys position, status, sound)* ìosal & ìseal, **in a ~ voice** ann an guth ìosal; **2** *(~ in spirit)* smalanach, sìos na *(etc)* inntinn *f*; **3** *(~ in morale)* gun mhisneach(d) *f*

low *v (cattle)* geum *vi*, *(cattle & esp deer)* langanaich *vi*

lower *adj* **1** *(of phys position, status, quality)* ìochd(a)rach; **2** *in expr* **~ lip** beul-ìochdair *m*; **3** *(comp adj)* (n)as ìsle, *(in past & conditional tenses)* (n)a b' ìsle

lower *v (phys & fig)* ìslich *vt*, *(phys)* leag *vt*, **he ~ed the window** leag e an uinneag

lowing *n (cattle)* geumnaich *f*, *(cattle & esp deer)* langanaich *f*

Lowland *adj* Gallta, *(lang)* **~ Scots** *(usu with art)* A' Bheurla Ghallta

Lowlander *n* Gall *m*

Lowlands *n* **1** *(of Scotland)* **the ~** A' Ghalltachd *f invar*, A' Mhachair(e) Ghallta, Machair na h-Alba, **in the ~** air a' Ghalltachd, air a' Mhachair Ghallta; **2** *(as general geographical term)* còmhnardan *mpl*

lowliness *n* ùmhlachd *f invar*, irioslachd & irisleachd *f invar*

lowly *adj* umha(i)l, ìosal & ìseal, iriosal & iriseal

loyal *adj* dìleas

loyalty *n* dìlseachd *f invar*, dìlse *m invar*

lubricate *v* ùillich *vt*

lubrication *n* ùilleachadh *m*

luck *n* fortan *m*, (*usu good* ~) sealbh *m*, **good/bad** ~ deagh/droch fhortan, **good** ~! fortan leat!, sealbh ort!

lucky *adj* **1** fortanach, sealbhach; **2** (*idiom*) **he'll be** ~ (**if he isn't killed** *etc*) 's math a dh'èireas dha (mura tèid a mharbhadh *etc*)

luggage *n* treal(l)aichean *fpl*, bagaichean *mpl*

Luing *n* Luinn *m*, Eilean Luinn *m*, **a man from** ~ Luinneach *m* (*also as adj*)

lukewarm *adj* (*lit & fig*) leth-fhuar, (*welcome, attitude etc*) fionnar, ~ **tea** teatha leth-fhuar, **a** ~ **welcome** fàilte leth-fhuar *f*, fàilte fhionnar

lullaby *n* tàladh *m*, òran tàlaidh *m*

lumber *n* treal(l)aich *f*

lump *n* ceap *m*, cnap *m*, meall *m*, ~ **of peat** ceap mòna (*gen of* mòine *f*)

lumpy *adj* cnapach

lunch *n* **1** biadh meadhan-là *m*, (*trad: used with art*) an ruisean *m*; **2** (*for worker, schoolchild etc*) (**packed**) ~ pìos *m*

lung *n* sgamhan *m*

lurch *v* (*seas, ship, trees etc*) tulg *vi*, luaisg *vi*

lurching *n* tulgadh *m*

lure *v* tàlaidh *vt*, meall *vt*

lust *n* drùis *f*, ana-miann *fm*

lust *v* miannaich *vi*, ~ **after someone** miannaich *vt* cuideigin

lustful *adj* drùiseach, drùiseil

Luxemburg *n* Lucsamburg *f*

Luxemburger *n* Lucsamburgach *m* (*also as adj*)

luxurious *adj* sòghail

luxury *n* sògh *m*

lying *adj* (*ie mendacious*) breugach

M

machair, machair-land *n* (*grassy stretches of land, esp adjoining the Atlantic seaboard*) machair(e) *f in nom case, m in gen sing*

machine *n* inneal *m*, **washing ~** inneal-nigheadaireachd *m*, inneal-nighe *m* (*also* nigheadair *m*), (*IT*) **~ code** còd inneil *m*

mackerel *n* rionnach *m sing & coll*

mad *adj* **1** (*with rage, insanity*) air chuthach *m*, air bhàinidh *f invar*, air bhoile *f invar*, **go ~** rach *vi* air chuthach/bhàinidh/bhoile; **2** (*idioms*) **go quite/totally ~** (**with rage**) gabh an cuthach dearg, **it was nearly driving me ~** bha e gus mo chur dhìom fhìn/gus mo chur às mo rian *m*

Madam *n* Bean-Uasal *f*, (*voc*) A bhean-uasal

madness *n* boile *f invar*, cuthach *m*

magazine *n* **1** (*publishing*) iris *f*, (*esp a quarterly*) ràitheachan *m*; **2** (*of gun*) cèis-bhiadhaich *f*; **3** (*armoury*) armlann *mf*

maggot *n* cnuimh *f*, cnuimheag *f*

magic *adj* draoidheil, seunta

magic *n* draoidheachd *f invar*

magical *adj* draoidheil

magician *n* draoidh *m*

magistrate *n* maighstir lagha *m*

magnanimity *n* mòr-mheanmna *m*, àrd-aigne *m*

magnanimous *adj* mòr-mheanmnach

magnet *n* clach-iùil *f*, (*less trad*) magnait *f*

magnetic *adj* iùil-tharraingeach, (*less trad*) magnaiteach

magnetism *n* iùil-tharraing *f*

magnificent *adj* greadhnach, glòrmhor, (*less usu*) òirdheirc

magnify *v* meudaich *vt*, **~ing glass** glainne-meudachaidh *f*

magnitude *n* meudachd *f invar*, **the ~ of their debts** meudachd nam fiachan aca

maid *n* **1** (*servant*) searbhanta *f*; **2** (*young woman*) maighdeann *f*, **old ~** seana-mhaighdeann; **3** (*virgin*) maighdeann *f*, òigh *f*, ainnir *f*

maidenhead, maidenhood *n* maighdeannas *m*

mail *n* post *m*, **the Royal Mail** Am Post Rìoghail, **air ~** post-adhair *m*, **email** post-dealain *m*

main *adj* **1** prìomh (*precedes the noun, which it lenites where possible*), **the ~ town** am prìomh bhaile, **the ~ reason for his conduct** prìomh adhbhar a ghiùlain; **2** *in exprs* **~ door** doras mòr, **~ road** rathad mòr

mainland *n* tìr-mòr (*not usu with art*), **on the ~** air tìr-mòr

mains *n* (*agric*) mànas *m*

maintain *v* **1** (*assert*) cùm *vt* a-mach, **he ~s that Stalin was right** bidh e a' cumail a-mach gun robh Stalin ceart; **2** (*support*) cùm *vt* suas, **I've a family to ~** tha teaghlach agam ri chumail suas; **3** (*machinery etc*) gleus *vt*, càirich *vt*

maintenance *n* **1** (*abstr: financial etc support*) cumail suas *m*; **2** (*keep, feed, of livestock etc*) beathachadh *m*; **3** (*of machinery etc*) gleusadh *m*, càradh *m*

majestic *adj* **1** greadhnach, glòrmhor; **2** (*like a monarch*) rìoghail

majesty *n* **1** (*abstr: royalty*) rìoghalachd *f invar*; **2** (*splendour, grandeur*) mòrachd *f invar*, greadhnachas *m*

major *adj* **1** (*principal*) prìomh (*precedes the noun, which it lenites where possible*), **the ~ town** am prìomh bhaile, **the ~ reason for his conduct** prìomh adhbhar a ghiùlain; **2** (*of great importance, gravity etc*) mòr, glè chudthromach, **a ~ accident** tubaist mhòr, **a ~ exhibition** taisbeanadh mòr/glè chudthromach

major *n* (*military rank*) màidsear *m*

majority *n* (*of objects etc & people*) mòr-chùid *f*, **the ~ of his life** a' mhòr-chuid de a bheatha, **the ~ are in favour** tha a' mhòr-chùid air a shon

make *v* **1** dèan *vt irreg*, **I'll ~ jam tomorrow** nì mi silidh a-màireach, **they made progress** rinn iad adhartas, **~ a profit** dèan prothaid *f*, **~ war** dèan cogadh *m*, **~ fun** dèan fanaid *f*, *also* mag *vi*, (**of air**) **they were making fun of her** bha iad a' dèanamh fanaid oirre/a'

374

magadh oirre; **2** (*create, fashion*) dealbh *vt*, ~ **a statue** dealbh ìomhaigh; **3** (*cause, force to do something*) thoir *vt* (*with prep* air), **she made me leave** thug i orm falbh, **he'll ~ me do it eventually** bheir e orm a dhèanamh aig a' cheann thall; **4** (*transmit/arouse an emotion etc*) cuir *vt* (*with prep* air), **she made him angry** chuir i an fhearg air, **he made me jump** (*ie startled me*) chuir e clisgeadh *m* orm, *also* chlisg e mi; **5** (*cause to be*) fàg *vt*, **the journey made them tired** dh'fhàg an turas sgìth iad; **6** (*misc idioms & exprs*) ~ **for** (*ie head for*) dèan *vi* (*with prep* air), **he made for the boat** rinn e air a' bhàta, ~ **haste** greas *vi* (*with prep* air), ~ **haste!** greas ort!, *pl* greasaibh oirbh, **they made haste** ghreas iad orra, ~ **an impression on** drùidh *vi* (*with prep* air), **the play made an impression on me** dhrùidh an dealbh-chluich orm, ~ **a mistake** rach *vi* air iomrall *m*, *also* dèan mearachd *f*, ~ **new** *v* nuadhaich *vt*, ùraich *vt*, ath-nuadhaich *vt*, ~ **off** (*escape etc*) tàrr/tàir *vi* às, ~ **out** (*dissemble, pretend*) leig *vi* (*with prep* air), **the soldiers made out they were civilians** leig na saighdearan orra gun robh iad nan sìobhaltairean, ~ **out** (*assert*) cùm *vt* a-mach, **they are making out that the world will end tomorrow** tha iad a' cumail a-mach gun tig an saoghal gu crìch (*dat of* crìoch *f*) a-màireach, ~ **a start** tòisich *vi* (**on/at** air), ~ **a fresh start** tòisich *vi* às ùr (**on/at** air), ~ **up** (*face*) maisich *vt*, ~ **up** (*anecdote, incident etc*) **they asked (me) if I was making it up** dh'fhaighnich iad (dhomh) am b' e uirsgeul a bh' agam/an e an fhìrinn a bh' agam

maladministration *n* mì-rianachd *f invar*

malady *n* tinneas *m*, galar *m*

male *adj* fireann, fireannta, ~ **cat** cat fireann

male *n* fireannach *m*, ~**s on the right and females on the left, please!** fireannaich air an làimh (*dat of* làmh *f*) dheis is boireannaich *mpl* air an làimh chlì, mas e ur toil e!

malevolence *n* gamhlas *m*, mì-rùn *m*

malevolent *adj* gamhlasach

malice *n* gamhlas *m*, mì-rùn *m*, nimh & neimh *m*

malicious *adj* gamhlasach, nimheil

mallet *n* fairche *m*

malnutrition *n* dìth beathachaidh *m*

malpractice *n* mì-chleachdadh *m*

Mammy *n* Mamaidh *f*

man *n* **1** (*emphasising gender*) fear *m*, fireannach *m*, **a ~ and a woman** fear is bean *f*, fear/fireannach agus boireannach *m*, **the ~ of the house** fear an taighe, **men on the right and women on the left, please!** fireannaich air an

làimh (*dat of* làmh *f*) dheis is boireannaich *mpl* air an làimh chlì, mas e ur toil e!; **2** (*stressing male gender less*) duine *m*, **I met a ~ on the stair** thachair mi ri duine air an staidhre, **when I'm a ~** an uair a bhios mi nam dhuine; **3** (*mankind, humanity*) mac-an-duine *m sing coll*, an cinne-daonna *m*, ~**'s futile efforts** oidhirpean dìomhain mhic-an-duine

Man *n*, **the Isle of ~**, Eilean Mhanainn *m*

manage *v* **1** (~ *firm, organisation etc*) stiùir *vt*, riaghail *vt*; **2** (*handle situation etc*) dèilig *vi* (*with prep* ri), làimhsich *vt*, **she ~d the problem extremely well** dhèilig i ris an duilgheadas uabhasach math; **3** (*succeed in doing something, be up to a task etc*) faigh *vi* (*with prep* air), rach *vi* agam (*etc*) (*with prep* air), dèan a' chùis (*with prep* air), **I'll ~ to go back there some time or other** gheibh mi air tilleadh ann uair no uaireigin, **will you ~ to find a job?** an tèid agad air obair fhaighinn?, **the box is heavy, will you ~ it?** tha am bogsa trom, an dèan thu a' chùis air?; **4** (*live, get by*) thig *vi irreg* beò, thig suas, **I can't ~ on that!** cha tig mi beò/cha tig mi suas air sin!

management 1 (*abstr: the process*) stiùireadh *m*, riaghladh *m*, ~ **centre** ionad-stiùiridh *m*; **2** (*con: the managers etc*) luchd-stiùiridh *m sing coll*, luchd-riaghlaidh *m sing coll*

manager *n* manaidsear *m*, neach-stiùiridh *m invar*, neach-riaghlaidh *m invar* (*pl* luchd-stiùiridh & luchd-riaghlaidh *m sing coll*)

manageress *n* bana-mhanaidsear *f*

mane *n* (*of horse, lion etc*) muing *f*

mangle *v* (*lacerate etc*) reub *vt*

manhandle *v* **1** (*struggle with heavy object etc*) slaod *vi* is tarraing *vi* (*with prep* air); **2** (*handle person roughly*) droch-làimhsich *vt*

manifest *v* **1** (*show, display qualities etc*) taisbein *vt*, nochd *vt*; **2** *in expr* ~ **itself** thig *vi* an uachdar *m*, thig *vi* am follais *f invar*, nochd *vt*, **their bravery ~ed itself in wartime** thàinig an cuid gaisge an uachdar/am follais an àm cogaidh, nochd an cuid gaisge an àm cogaidh

manifold *adj* iomadh-fhillte

mankind *n* mac-an-duine *m*, an cinne-daonna *m* (*used with art*)

manliness *n* duinealas *m*, fearalachd *f invar*

manly *adj* duineil, fearail, ~ **qualities** feartan duineil/fearail *mpl*

man-made *adj* **1** (*manufactured*) saothraichte; **2** (*as substitute for the natural object etc*) fuadain, brèige

manner *n* **1** (~ *of doing something*) dòigh *m*, modh *mf*, nòs *m*, **in a particular ~** air dhòigh/

mhodh àraidh, **the traditional** ~ (*esp of singing*) an seann nòs; **2** (*manner of behaving*) dol-a-mach *m invar*, **I didn't like his** ~ bu bheag leam/orm an dol-a-mach (a bha) aige

manners *n* beus *f*, (*good* ~) modh *mf*, **good/bad** ~ deagh/droch bheus

mannish *adj* (*esp of woman*) duineil, firean(n)ta

manpower *n* **1** luchd-obrach *m sing coll*, **take on extra** ~ fastaich luchd-obrach a bharrachd; **2** (*more abstr*) sgiobachd *f invar*, ~ **planning** planaigeadh sgiobachd *m*

manslaughter *n* duine-mharbhadh *m*, murt *m*

manual *n* leabhrachan *m*, leabhran *m*, (*esp instruction* ~) leabhar-mìneachaidh *m*

manufacture *n* saothrachadh *m*

manufacture *v* saothraich *vt*, dèan *vt*

manufacturing *n* saothrachadh *m*

manure *n* **1** mathachadh *m*, leasachadh *m*, innear & inneir *f*; **2** *in expr* ~ **heap** siteag *f*, òtrach *m*, dùnan *m*

manure *v* (*land*) mathaich *vt*, leasaich *vt*, (*with seaweed*) feamainn *vt*

manuscript *n* làmh-sgrìobhainn *mf*

Manx *adj* Manainneach

Manxman *n* Manainneach *m*

many *adj* **1** mòran *m* (*with gen pl n*), iomadach *adj*, iomadh *adj*, (*both with nom sing n*), (*fam*) tòrr *m*, (*fam: usu less numerous*) grunn *m*, (*both with gen pl n*), ~ **people** mòran dhaoine, ~ **thanks!** mòran taing!, ~ **times**, ~ **a time** iomadach/iomadh uair, ~ **people are of that opinion** tha tòrr dhaoine den bheachd sin, **I spent a good** ~ **years there** chuir mi seachad grunn bhliadhnachan an sin; **2** *in expr* **so** ~ uimhir *f invar*, uiread *m invar*, na h-uimhir, na h-uiread, **there were so** ~ **people there** bha (na h-)uimhir/(na h-)uiread de dhaoine ann; **3** *in expr* **how** ~ cia mheud & co mheud (*with nom sing n*), **how** ~ **years?** cia mheud bliadhna?

many *n* mòran *m*, ~ **of them** mòran dhiubh, **there weren't** ~ **there** cha robh mòran ann, **did you buy books? not** ~ an do cheannaich sibh leabhraichean? cha do cheannaich mòran

map *n* clàr-dùthcha *m*, mapa *m*

mar *v* mill *vt*

marble *n* màrmor *m*

March *n* (*used with art*) Am Màrt *m*

march[1] *n* (*boundary, limit*) crìoch *f*, **this is the** ~ **of my land** is e seo crìoch an fhearainn agam

march[2] *n* **1** (*of soldiers etc*) màrsail *f*, mèarrsadh *m*; **2** (*music*) caismeachd *f*

marching *n* màrsail *f*, mèarrsadh *m*

mare *n* làir *f*

margarine *n* margarain *m invar*

margin *n* iomall *m*, oir *f*, **at/on the** ~**(s)** (*ie remote*) air an iomall, air an oir, *also* iomallach *adj*

marginal *adj* iomallach, air an iomall *m*

mariner *n* maraiche *m*, seòladair *m*

mark *n* **1** comharra(dh) *m*, (*school etc*) **good/ bad** ~**s** deagh/droch chomharraidhean, (*livestock*) **ear** ~ comharradh-cluaise, ~ **of respect** comharradh-urraim, **question** ~ comharradh-ceiste; **2** (~ *left by person, animal, object*) lorg *f*, comharradh *m*; **3** (*typog*) puing *f*, *eg* **exclamation** ~ clisg-phuing *f*

mark *v* **1** (*leave a mark*) fàg lorg *f*, fàg comharradh *m*, (*with prep* air); **2** (*stain*) fàg spot *m*, fàg smal *m*, (*with prep* air); **3** (*teacher etc*) ceartaich *vt*, comharraich *vt*; **4** (~ *occasions etc*) comharraich *vt*, **to** ~ **his birthday** gus an ceann-bliadhna aige a chomharrachadh

market *n* **1** margadh *mf*, marcaid *f*, (*esp for livestock*) fèill *f*, ~ **town** baile-margaidh *m*, **a common** ~ margadh coitcheann; **2** (*abstr: demand, for product etc*) margadh *mf*, fèill *f*, (**for** air), **will there be a** ~ **for it?** am bi margadh/fèill air?

marketing *n* margaideachd *f invar*

market-place *n* ionad-margaidh *m*

marking *n* (*teacher etc*) ceartachadh *m*, comharrachadh *m*, ~ **scheme** sgeama-comharrachaidh *m*

marquee *n* puball & pùball *m*

marriage *n* pòsadh *m*

married *adj* & *past part* pòsta (**to** aig *or* ri), **a** ~ **couple** càraid phòsta, ~ **to Andrew** pòsta aig/ri Anndra, **newly** ~ nuadh-phòsta, *in expr* **get** ~ pòs *vi*

marry *v* pòs *vti*

Mars *n* Màrt *m*

marsh *n* fèith(e) *f*, boglach *f*

mart[1] *n* (*Sc: beef animal*) mart *m*

mart[2] *n* (*Sc: market*) margadh *mf*, fèill *f*

marvel *n* iongnadh *m*, mìorbhail *f*

marvellous *adj* iongantach, mìorbhaileach

masculine *adj* **1** fireann, fireannta; **2** (*gram*) fireann, ~ **word/noun** facal/ainmear fireann, **the** ~ **gender** a' ghnè fhireann

mash *v* pronn

mashed *adj* & *past part* pronn, ~ **potato** buntata pronn

mask *n* **1** masg *m*; **2** (*as disguise, fancy dress etc*) aghaidh-choimheach *f*, aodannan *m*

mason *n* clachair *m*

mass adj mòr- prefix, eg ~ **production** mòr-
bhuileachadh m, ~ **media** mòr-mheadhanan
mpl

mass¹ n 1 (abstr: bulk, magnitude) tomad m; 2
(large quantity or number: of objects) meud
mòr, uimhir f invar, uiread m invar, **a ~ of**
paper meud mòr pàipeir, uimhir de phàipear; 3
(of people) sluagh mòr, meud mòr dhaoine

mass² n (relig) aifreann mf

massacre n casgairt f, murt m, (hist) **the ~ of**
Glencoe Murt Ghlinn Comhainn

massacre v casgair vt

massage n suathadh m, suathadh bodhaig

massage v suath vt

mast n (of ship etc) crann m, **radio/television**
~ crann-craolaidh m

master n 1 (one in authority, or in position of
superiority over others) maighstir m, uachdaran
m; 2 (of boat etc) caiptean m, sgiobair m; 3 in
expr (at ceilidh etc) ~ **of ceremonies** fear an
taighe m

master v 1 (people, emotions etc) ceannsaich vt,
faigh làmh-an-uachdair f (with prep air); 2 (a
topic or activity) faigh eòlas m (with prep air)

masterful adj ceannsalach, smachdail

masterly adj (at performing task, as artist etc)
ealanta, barraichte

masterwork n sàr-obair f

masticate cnàmh vt, cnuas vti, cagainn vti

masturbate v brod vt, fèin-bhrod vi

masturbation n brodadh m, fèin-bhrodadh m

match¹ n (for lighting, also football etc ~)
maids(e) m, (for lighting, trad) lasadair m

match² n (worthy or superior opponent) seis(e)
m, **she met her ~ that day!** fhuair i a seis an
là sin!

match v freagair vi, co-fhreagair vi, (with prep
do), **the coat ~es the hat** tha an còta a' co-
fhreagairt don aid (dat of ad f)

matching adj co-fhreagarrach

mate n 1 (pal) companach m, (less informal)
caraid m; 2 (on ship) meite m

mate v co-ghin vi, cuplaich vi

material adj 1 (not abstr or spiritual) corporra,
stuthail, nitheil, rudail; 2 (significant, weighty,
meaningful) cudromach, seaghach; 3 (real,
substantial) fìor, ~ **gain/advantage** fìor
bhuannachd f

material n 1 (fabric, cloth etc) stuth m; 2 (more
generally: ~ for creating or constructing
something) stuth m, adhbhar m, **building ~s**
stuthan-togalaich mpl, **collecting ~ for a book**
a' cruinneachadh stuth airson leabhair, **shoe-**
making ~(s) stuth/adhbhar bhròg

materialism n saoghaltachd f invar

materialist n duine saoghalta

materialistic adj saoghalta

materially adv 1 (ie financially) a thaobh
airgid m gen, a thaobh beartais m gen, **I'm no**
worse off ~ chan eil mi dad nas miosa dheth a
thaobh airgid; 2 (ie significantly, considerably)
gu mòr, gu ìre mhòir (f dat), **the situation**
has changed ~ tha an suidheachadh air
atharrachadh gu mòr/gu ìre mhòir

maternal adj 1 (pertaining to a mother,
motherly) màthaireil; 2 (in family relationships)
~ **uncle** bràthair-màthar m, ~ **aunt** piùthar-
màthar f, ~ **grandfather** athair-màthar m

maternity n màthaireachd f invar

mathematics, maths n matamataig m invar

mating n co-ghineadh m, cuplachadh m

matter n 1 (chem etc: material substance) stuth
m; 2 (affair etc) cùis f, gnothach m, **how did**
the ~ go/turn out? ciamar a chaidh vi a' chùis/
an gnothach?, **the nub/crux of the ~** cnag f na
cùise; 3 (subject ~) cuspair m, (Lit etc) ~ **and**
form cuspair is cruth m; 4 (something wrong)
what's the ~? dè a tha ceàrr?, **what's the ~**
with you? dè a tha a' cur ort?, (to sick person)
dè a tha thu a' gearan?; 5 (pus) brachadh m,
iongar m

matter v bi vi irreg gu diofar (freq in neg exprs),
that doesn't ~ chan eil sin gu diofar, also is
coma sin, **it doesn't ~ whether she comes or**
not is coma an tig i no nach tig

mattock n caibe m

mature adj 1 (of person) inbheach, abaich, ~
student oileanach inbheach; 2 (of fruits etc)
abaich

mature v abaich vi, (esp people) thig vi gu inbhe
f, thig vi gu ìre f invar

maturity n 1 (adulthood) inbhe f, ìre f invar,
come to/reach ~ thig vi gu inbhe/gu ìre; 2 (of
fruits etc) abaichead m

maul v 1 (with hands) garbh-làimhsich vt; 2
(fam: in fight etc) pronn vt, dochainn vt

maw n 1 (mouth, esp voracious) craos m; 2
(craw, gizzard) sgròban m; 3 (stomach, esp
greedy) maodal f, mionach m

maximum adj as motha (sup of mòr), ~ **speed**
astar m as motha

May n (used with art) An Cèitean m, (less trad) a'
Mhàigh f, **a ~ morning** madainn Chèitein (gen
used adjectivally)

may v 1 (ie be permitted, allowed to) faod vi
def, ~ **we go? yes/no** am faod sinn falbh?
faodaidh/chan fhaod; 2 (expr possibility) faod
vi def, **it ~ be that there is life on the moon**

dh'fhaodadh e a bhith gu bheil beatha *f* air a' ghealaich *f*, **he ~ be ill** faodaidh gu bheil e tinn, *in expr* **be that as it ~** biodh sin mar a bhitheas e; **3** (*trad: expr wishes etc*) gum(a) *conj*, **~ you be in good health!** fallain gum bi thu!, **long ~ you live!** guma fada beò thu! (*also* saoghal fada dhut!)

maybe *adv & conj*, is dòcha, (is) ma(th) dh'fhaodte (*also* 's mathaid), **it'll be a fine day, ~** bidh là brèagha ann, 's dòcha/ma dh'fhaodte, **~ it won't snow** 's dòcha/ma dh'fhaodte nach cuir i, **~ he's ill** 's dòcha gu bheil e tinn, *also* faodaidh gu bheil e tinn

mayor *n* mèar *m*

MC *n* (*at ceilidh etc*) fear an taighe *m*

me *pers pron* mi, (*emph*) mise, mi fhìn, **don't you know ~? It's ~** (*emph*)! nach aithnich thu mi? 's mise/'s mi fhìn a th' ann!

meadow, meadowland *n* clua(i)n *f*, dail *f*, faiche *f*, lèana *f*, (*esp beside watercourse or loch*) innis *f*

meal[1] *n* (*ground cereals etc*) min *f*

meal[2] *n* biadh *m*, (*trad*) diathad *f*, lòn *m*, **the midday ~** biadh meadhan-là *m gen, also* (*trad: with art*) an ruisean *m*

mealtime *n* tràth bìdh *m*

mean *adj* **1** (*petty, insignificant*) crìon, suarach; **2** (*stingy*) spìocach, mosach

mean *n* meadhan *m*

mean *v* **1** ciallaich *vt*, (*more fam*) minig *vt*, **what do you ~?** dè a tha thu a' ciallachadh?, (*more fam*) dè a tha thu a' minigeadh?, **what does this word ~?** dè a tha am facal seo a' ciallachadh?; **2** (*idiom: be serious*) bi *v irreg* ann an da-rìribh, **they didn't ~ it** cha robh iad ann an da-rìribh; **3** (*intend, act on purpose*) bi *vi irreg* airson, **I didn't ~ to do it** cha robh mi airson a dhèanamh, *also* cha robh mi a' ciallachadh a dhèanamh, cha do rinn mi a dh'aon rùn *m* e, cha do rinn mi a dh'aon ghnothach *m* e

meander *v* (*river etc*) lùb *vi*

meandering *adj* (*road, river, argument etc*) lùbach

meaning *n* ciall *f*, (*esp sense of words & exprs*) brìgh *f invar*, seagh *m*, **words without ~** faclan *mpl* gun chiall, **the ~ of (the) words** brìgh nam facal (*dictionary title*), **the word isn't used with that ~** cha chleachdar am facal san t-seagh sin

meaningful *adj* brìoghmhor

meaningless *adj* gun chiall

means *n* **1** dòigh *f*, meadhan *m*, **~ of transport** dòigh(ean)-siubhail, dòigh(ean)-giùlain; **2** *in expr* **by ~ of** tro mheadhan *m* (*with gen*), **by ~**

of the hammer tro mheadhan an ùird (*gen of* òrd *m*); **3** (*wealth etc*) beartas *m*, saidhbhreas *m*, *in expr* **a man of ~** duine airgeadach

meantime *n* eadar-àm *m*, **in the ~** anns an eadar-àm

meanwhile *adv* rè na h-ùine seo/sin

measles *n used with art*, a' ghriù(th)lach *f*, (*idiom*) **she has (the) ~** tha i sa ghriùlach

measure *n* **1** (*abstr, also device, tool*) tomhas *m*, **tape ~** rioban-tomhais *m*; **2** (*a certain or limited amount*) na h-uimhir *f invar*, na h-uiread *m invar*, **we had a ~ of security** bha na h-uimhir/na h-uiread de thèarainteachd againn; **3** (*expedient, solution etc*) ceum *m*, **take/implement ~s** gabh ceumannan (**to** gus), **safety ~s** ceumannan-sàbhailteachd *mpl*

measure *v* (*dimensions, speed, weight etc*) tomhais *vt*

measurement *n* tomhas *m*, **take ~s** gabh tomhasan

measuring *adj* tomhais (*gen of* tomhas *m*), **~ tape** teip tomhais *f*

meat *n* feòil *f*

mechanic *n* meacanaig *m*, (*more trad*) innleadair *m*

mechanical *adj* innealach

mechanism *n* **1** (*con, mechanical*) inneal *m*; **2** (*means, not nec mechanical*) meadhan *m*, **a ~ for collecting taxes** meadhan airson/gus cìsean a thoirt a-steach

meddle *v* gabh gnothach *m* (**in/with** ri), buin *vi* (**in/with** do, ri), **don't ~ with it** na gabh gnothach ris, na buin dha/ris

media *npl, used with art*, **the ~** na meadhanan *mpl*

medical *adj* lèigheil, (*less trad*) meidigeach

medicine *n* **1** (*abstr: the science*) eòlas-leighis *m*; **2** (*con: medication*) leigheas *m*, ìocshlaint *f*, cungaidh *f*, cungaidh-leighis *f*

medieval *adj* meadhan-aoiseil

meditate *v* meòraich & meamhraich *vi* (**on/about** air)

meditation *n* meòrachadh & meamhrachadh *m* (**on/about** air)

Mediterranean *adj* Meadhan-thìreach

Mediterranean *n*, **the ~** A' Mhuir Mheadhan-thìreach *f*

medium *adj* meadhanach

medium *n* meadhan *m*, **through the ~ of** tro mheadhan *m* (*with gen*), **education through the ~ of Gaelic, Gaelic ~ education** foghlam *m* tro mheadhan na Gàidhlig

meek *adj* umha(i)l, macanta

meekness ùmhlachd *f invar*

meet *v* **1** (*congregate*) cruinnich *vi*, coinnich *vi*, thig *vi* còmhla, tionail *vi*, **they ~ in the village hall** bidh iad a' cruinneachadh ann an talla a' bhaile; **2** (*encounter, by chance or by arrangement*) coinnich *vi*, tachair *vi*, (*with prep* ri), **I met X in the town** choinnich mi/thachair mi ri X sa bhaile, **did you ever ~ him?** an do choinnich thu a-riamh ris?; **3** *in expr* **go to ~ them** (*ie towards them*) rach *vi* nan coinneimh *f*

meeting *n* **1** (*business ~, ~ of societies etc*) coinneamh *f*, **annual ~** coinneamh bhliadhnail; **2** (*an encounter, by chance or arrangement*) coinneachadh *m*

melancholy *adj* **1** (*of person, mood etc*) gruamach, dubhach, fo ghruaim *f dat*; **2** (*of atmosphere, music etc*) tiamhaidh

melancholy *n* gruaim *f*, mulad *m*

melodious *adj* ceòlmhor, fonnmhor, binn

melody *n* port *m*, fonn *m*

melon *n* meal-bhucan *m*

melt *v* leagh *vti*

member *n* ball *m*

membership *n* ballrachd *f invar*

memorandum *n* cuimhneachan *m*, meòrachan & meamhrachan *m*

memorial *adj* cuimhneachaidh (*gen of* cuimhneachadh *m, used adjectivally*)

memorial *n* **1** cuimhneachan *m*; **2** (*in the form of a stone or monument*) clach-chuimhne *f*, clach chuimhneachain *f*, clach-chuimhneachaidh *f*

memorise *v* meòraich & meamhraich *vt*, cùm *vt* air mheomhair *f*, cùm *vt* air chuimhne *f invar*

memory *n* **1** (*the faculty and site of ~*) meomhair & meamhair *f*, cuimhne *f invar*, **commit to ~** meòmhraich & meamhraich *vt*, cùm *vt* air mheomhair, (*idiom*) **if my ~ serves me rightly/doesn't deceive me** mas math mo chuimhne, (*IT*) **random access ~ (RAM)** cuimhne thuaireach, **read only ~ (ROM)** cuimhne bhuan; **2** (*what is remembered*) cuimhne *f invar* (**of** air), **I've no ~ of him** chan eil cuimhne agam air

menace *v* maoidh *vi*, bagair *vi*, (*with prep* air), **he was menacing me** bha e a' maoidheadh orm

menace *n* maoidheadh *m*

mend *v* **1** (*repair*) càirich *vt*, càir *vt*; **2** (*remedy, improve*) leasaich *vt*

mendacious *adj* breugach

menstruation *n* fuil-mìosa *f*

mental *adj* inntinn (*gen of* inntinn *f, used adjectivally*), inntinneach, inntinneil, **~ ability/capacity** comas-inntinn *m*, **~ illness** tinneas-inntinn *m*, euslaint inntinn *m*

mention *n* iomradh *m*, guth *m*, tarraing *f*, (**of** air)

mention *v* **1** thoir iomradh *m*, thoir guth *m*, (*with prep* air), **he didn't ~ it** cha tug e iomradh/guth air; **2** *in expr* **not to ~** gun ghuth (*with prep* air), **pears are dear, not to ~ apples** tha peuran daor, gun ghuth air ùbhlan

menu *n* **1** (*in café etc*) clàr-bìdh *m*; **2** (*IT*) clàr-iùil *m*

merchant *n* ceannaiche *m*, marsanta *m*

merciful *adj* iochdmhor, tròcaireach

mercury *n* airgead-beò *m*

mercy *n* iochd *f invar*, tròcair *f*, truas *m*, **God's mercies** tròcairean Dhè (*gen of* Dia *m*), **have ~** gabh truas (**on** de)

merge *v* co-mheasgaich *vti*, co-aonaich *vti*

merit *n* **1** (*worth, value*) luach *m invar*, fiù *m invar*, (*esp of person*) airidheachd *f invar*, **without ~** gun luach, gun fhiù; **2** (*honour, reputation*) cliù *m invar*

merit *v* toill *vt*

meritorious *adj* airidh

mermaid *n* maighdeann-mhara *f*

merriment *n* cridhealas *m*, mire *f invar*

merry *adj* **1** aighearach, *in expr* **Merry Christmas/Xmas!** Nollaig Chridheil!; **2** (*tipsy*) air leth-mhisg *f*

mess *n* **1** (*litter, untidiness*) truileis *f invar*; **2** (*messy state*) bùrach *m*, **in a ~** ann am bùrach, *also* troimh-a-chèile, thar a chèile, bun-os-cionn

message *n* fios *m*, teachdaireachd *f invar*, **give him this ~** thoir am fios seo dha, **going on a ~** a' dol air theachdaireachd

messenger *n* teachdaire *m*

metal *adj* meatailt, de mheatailt *f*, **~ doors** dorsan meatailt, dorsan de mheatailt

metal *n* meatailt *f*

metallic *adj* meatailteach

metamorphosis *n* cruth-atharrachadh *m*

meteor *n* dreag *f*

meteorology *n* eòlas-sìde *m*

meter *n* meidheadair *m*

method *n* **1** (*abstr: organisation, orderliness etc*) òrdugh *m*, riaghailt *f*, rian *m*; **2** (*way of doing something*) dòigh *f*, seòl *m*, alt *m*

methodical *adj* òrdail, riaghailteach, rianail

methodicalness *n* òrdugh *m*, riaghailt *f*, rian *m*

methodology *n* dòigh-obrach *f*

meticulous *adj* (*person, work etc*) mionaideach, mion-chùiseach, pongail, **a ~ enquiry/study** sgrùdadh mionaideach

metre *n* **1** (*unit of length*) meatair *m*; **2** (*poetic rhythm*) meadrachd *f invar*, rannaigheachd *f invar*

metric *adj* meatrach

metrical *adj* meadrachail
mew *v* dèan mialaich/miamhail *f invar*
mewing, miaowing, *n* mialaich *f invar*,
miamhail *f invar*
microwave *n* meanbh-thonn *f*
midday *n* meadhan-là *m*, **the ~ meal** biadh
meadhan-là *m*, (*trad*) an ruisean *m*
midden siteag *f*, òtrach *m*, dùnan *m*
middle *n* meadhan *m*, **a belt around my ~**
crios mum mheadhan, **the very/exact ~** an '
ceart-mheadhan, an teis-meadhan, **right in the**
~ of the town ann an ceart-mheadhan/ann an
teis-meadhan a' bhaile
middle-age *n* meadhan-aois *f*
middle-aged *adj* leth-shean
middling *adj & adv* meadhanach, **I'm only ~**
well today chan eil mi ach meadhanach math
an-diugh, **you only did ~ well** cha do rinn thu
ach meadhanach math
midge *n* meanbh-chuileag *f*
midget *n* luchraban *m*
midnight *n* meadhan-oidhche *m*
midsummer *n* leth an t-samhraidh *m invar*
midwife *n* bean-ghlùine *f*
midwinter *n* leth a' gheamhraidh *m invar*
mien *n* mèinn *f*, dreach *m*, snuadh *m*
might *n* **1** (*mainly abstr: pol, military etc*)
cumhachd *mf invar*, **the ~ of the Roman**
Empire cumhachd Ìompaireachd na Ròimhe; **2**
(*abstr, but also often phys*) neart *m*, **Samson's**
~ neart Shamsoin, (*saying*) **~ before right**
thèid neart thar ceairt
might *v* **1** (*expressing possibility*) faod *vi def*, **it**
~ be that there is life on Mars dh'fhaodadh
e a bhith gu bheil beatha air Màrt, **he ~ be ill**
faodaidh gu bheil e tinn, *also* 's dòcha gu bheil
e tinn, dh'fhaodte gu bheil e tinn; **2** (*expressing*
permission) **~ I leave now? no!** am faod mi
falbh a-nis? chan fhaod!
mighty *adj* **1** (*pol, militarily etc*) cumhachdach; **2**
(*phys*) neartmhor
migrant *n* neach-imrich *m*, **~s** luchd-imrich *m*
sing coll
migration *n* imrich *f*
mild *adj* **1** (*of person, weather etc*) ciùin, sèimh, **a**
~ morning/breeze madainn/oiteag chiùin; **2**
(*of illness etc*) beag, **a ~ fever** fiabhras beag
mile *n* mìle *mf*
militant *adj* mìleanta
militant *n* mìleantach *m*
military *adj* armailteach
milk *n* bainne *m*, *in expr* **~ cows** crodh-eadraidh
m
milk *v* bleoghain *vti*

milking *n* bleoghann *f invar*
mill *n* muileann *mf*, muilinn *f*
mill *v* (*corn etc*) meil *vt*, bleith *vt*
miller *n* muillear *m*
million *n* millean *m*
millstone *n* clach-mhuilinn *f*
mimic *v* atharrais *vt*
mimicry *n* atharrais *f invar*
Minch *n, used with art,* **the ~** A' Mhaoil , **the**
Little ~ An Cuan Sgìth
mind *n* **1** inntinn *f*, **she's got a good ~** tha
inntinn mhath innte, **frame/state of ~** gleus
inntinn *mf*, *also* fonn *m*, gean *m*, dòigh *m*,
peace of ~ toil-inntinn *f*; **2** (*preoccupation etc*)
cùram *m*, aire *f invar*, **she is on my ~** tha i air
mo chùram/air m' aire, *also* tha i fa-near dhomh,
tha i nam inntinn; **3** (*decision, intention*) *in expr*
make up one's ~ cuir *vt* (*with prep* ro), **they**
made up their ~s to build a house chuir iad
romhpa taigh a thogail, *note also the idiom* **she**
had a ~ to tidy the house bha e fa-near dhi
an taigh a sgioblachadh; **4** (*memory*) cuimhne
f, **keep in ~** cùm *vt* air chuimhne, **it slipped**
my ~ chaidh e às mo chuimhne, **call to ~**
cuir *vt* na (*etc*) c(h)uimhne, **it called to ~ my**
mother's house chuir e nam chuimhne taigh
mo mhàthar; **5** (*sanity etc*) ciall *f*, rian *m*, reusan
m, **he lost his ~** chaill e a chiall, **she's out of**
her ~ tha i às a ciall/às a rian, **it was nearly**
driving me out of my ~ bha e gus mo chur às
mo rian, *also* bha e gus mo chur dhìom fhìn
mind *v* **1** (*care, be concerned*) *in exprs* **I don't**
~! tha mi coma!, **I don't ~ in the least!** tha mi
coma co-dhiù!, **never ~!** coma leat!, dad ort!; **2**
(*misc exprs*) **she was ~ed to tidy the house**
bha e fa-near dhi/bha i am beachd an taigh a
sgioblachadh, **pears are dear, never ~ apples**
tha peuran daor, gun ghuth air ùbhlan
mine *poss pron* **1** leam(sa), **it's ~** 's ann leamsa a
tha e; **2** *in exprs* **he's a good friend of ~** tha e
na dheagh charaid dhomh, **a cousin (etc) of ~**
co-ogha (*etc*) dhomh
mine *n* (*for coal etc, also explosive device*)
mèinn(e) *f*
miner *n* mèinnear *m*
mineral *adj* mèinneach & mèinneil
mineral *n* mèinnear *m*, mèinnearach *m*
mineralogy *n* mèinn-eòlas *m*, mèinnearachd *f*
invar
mingle *v* measgaich *vt*, co-mheasgaich,
coimeasgaich *vti*, **(with** ri**) ~ed together** air
am measgachadh ri chèile, *also* am measg a
chèile
Mingulay *n* Miughalaigh *f*

minimum *adj* as lugha, (*in past & conditional tenses*) a bu lugha

mining *n* mèinnearachd *f invar*

minister *n* (*religion, politics*) ministear *m*, **the First Minister** Am Prìomh Mhinistear, *in expr* **Prime ~** Prìomhaire *m*

ministry *n* (*religion, politics*) ministrealachd *f*

minor¹ *adj* **1** (*ie less important, lesser-used etc than others*) mion- *prefix*, beag, **~ language** mion-chànan *m*, cànan beag, **~ road** rathad beag; **2** (*slight, not grave*) beag, **a ~ problem** duilgheadas beag

minor² *adj* (*of person: under-age*) mion-aoiseach

minor *n* (*ie under-age person*) mion-aoiseach *m*

minority *n* **1** mion-chuid *f*, beag-chuid *f*; **2** *in expr* **~ language** mion-chànan *m*, cànan beag

minute *adj* **1** (*very small*) crìon; **2** (*detailed, meticulous*) mion- *prefix*, mionaideach, **~ questioning** mion-cheasnachadh, ceasnachadh mionaideach

minute *n* mionaid *f*, **wait a ~!** fuirich mionaid!

miracle *n* mìorbhail *f*

miraculous *adj* mìorbhaileach

mire *n* eabar *m*, poll *m*, **sinking into the ~** a' dol fodha san eabar

mirth *n* mire *f invar*

mis- *prefix* mì-, *eg* **misfortune** *n* mì-shealbh *m*, **misinterpret** *v* mì-mhìnich *vt*, *see further examples below*

miscarriage *n* breith an-abaich *f invar*

miscellaneous *adj* measgaichte, de gach seòrsa *m*

miscellany *n* measgachadh *m*

mischance *n* **1** (*abstr*) mì-shealbh *m*; **2** (*con*) tubaist *f*

mischief *n* donas *m*

misconduct *n* mì-ghiùlan *m*

miserable *adj* truagh, brònach

misery *n* truaighe *f*

misfortune *n* (*abstr*) mì-shealbh *m*, (*abstr & con*) dosgainn *f*, driod-fhortan *m*

mishap *n* tubaist *f*, driod-fhortan *m*

misinterpret *v* mì-mhìnich *vt*

misjudge *v* (*situation etc: assess wrongly*) mì-thuig *vt*

mislead *v* meall *vt*

misleading *adj* meallta

mismanagement *n* mì-rianachd *f invar*

misprint *n* clò-mhearachd *f*

Miss *n* A' Mhaighdeann(-uasal) *f*, **~ Campbell** A' Mhaighdeann(-uasal) Chaimbeul, (*voc, for corres etc*) **Dear ~ Campbell** A Mhaighdeann(-uasal) Chaimbeul, (*abbrev*) A Mh(-uas) Chaimbeul

miss *v* **1** (*fail to catch etc*) caill *vt*, **I ~ed the train** chaill mi an trèana *f*, **didn't you see the film? you didn't ~ much!** nach fhaca sibh am film? cha do chaill sibh mòran!; **2** (*pine for etc*) ionndrainn *vt*, bi *vi irreg* fadachd *f invar* orm (*etc*) (*with prep* ri), **she's ~ing you** tha i gad ionndrainn, tha fadachd oirre riut

missile *n* urchair *f*

missing *adj* a dhìth, (*less usu*) a dh'easbhaidh, **the cover of the book was ~** bha còmhdach an leabhair a dhìth

mission *n* teachdaireachd *f invar*, rùn *m*, **going on a ~** a' dol air theachdaireachd

missionary *n* teachdaire *m*, (*less trad*) miseanaraidh *m*

mist *n* ceò *m*, (*less usu*) ceathach *m*

mistake *n* mearachd *f*, iomrall *m*, **make a ~** dèan mearachd, rach *vi* air iomrall

mistaken *adj* mearachdach, iomrallach, ceàrr, **~ opinion** beachd mearachdach, **if I'm not ~** mur eil mi ceàrr

Mister *n* Maighstir *m* (*abbrev* Mgr), **~ Fraser** Maighstir Friseal, (*voc, for corres etc*) **A Mhaighstir, Dear ~ Fraser** A Mhaighstir Fhriseil, (*abbrev*) A Mhgr Fhriseil

mistress *n* **1** (*woman in authority, or in position of superiority over others*) bana-mhaighstir *f*; **2** *in expr* **school~** ban(a)-mhaighstir-sgoile *f*; **3** (*sexual partner*) coimhleapach *f*

mistrust *n* mì-earbsa *m*

misty *adj* fo cheò *m*, ceòthach, **the hills are ~** tha na beanntan (*pl of* beinn *f*) fo cheò

mitigate *v* maothaich *vt*

mitten *n* miotag *f*

mix *v* measgaich *vt*, coimeasgaich *vt*, **~ed together** air am measgachadh ri chèile, *also* am measg a chèile

mixed *adj & past part* measgaichte

mixer *n* (*for food, cement etc*) measgaichear *m*

mixing, mixture *n* measgachadh *m*, coimeasgachadh *m*

moan *v* **1** (*through grief etc*) caoin *vi*; **2** (*complain, grumble*) gearain *vi* (**about** air), **you needn't bother ~ing all the time!** cha leig thu a leas a bhith a' gearan fad na h-ùine!

mob *n* gràisg *f*, prabar *m*

mobile *adj* **1** (*moving; well able to move*) gluasadach; **2** (*eg of older person, able to get about*) **he's still ~** tha e air chothrom a dhol a-mach fhathast; **3** (*portable*) so-ghiùlain, *in expr* **~ phone** fòn-làimhe *mf*

mobility *n* (*abstr*) gluasadachd *f*, (*ability to get about*) cothrom gluasaid *m*, comas gluasaid *m*

mock *v* mag *vi*, dèan fanaid, (*with prep* air)

mockery *n* fanaid *f*, magadh *m*, (**of** air)

mocking *adj* magail

Mod *n* Mòd *m*, **local ~** Mòd ionadail, **the National Mod** Am Mòd Nàiseanta

mode *n* (*of doing something*) dòigh *f*, (*more abstr*) modh *mf*, **~s of transport** dòighean-siubhail *mpl*, **~ of governing** modh-riaghlaidh *mf*

model *n* mac-samhail *m*

moderate *adj* **1** (*not outstanding*) meadhanach; **2** (*esp of persons, behaviour, temperament: not excessive or given to excess*) measarra, stuama

modern *adj* ùr, ùr-nodha, **these ~ times** na h-amannan *mpl* ùra seo

modernisation *n* ùrachadh *m*

modernise *v* ùraich

modest *adj* **1** (*shy, self-effacing etc*) diùid, màlda; **2** (*of woman; decorous in dress, behaviour etc*) banail; **3** (*not excessive*) measarra; **4** (*not outstanding*) meadhanach; **5** (*in more positive contexts*) beag, **my mother left me a ~ legacy** thiomnaich mo mhàthair dìleab bheag dhomh, **a ~ bet on a horse** geall beag air each *m*

modicum *n* na h-uimhir *f invar*, **we had a ~ of security** bha na h-uimhir de thèarainteachd againn

modish *adj* fasanta

Mohammedan *n & adj* Mohamadanach *m*

moist *adj* tais

moisten *v* taisich *vt*

moistness, moisture *n* taise *f invar*, taiseachd *f invar*

molar *n* (*tooth*) fiacail-chùil (*gen of* cùl *m, used adjectivally*)

mole *n* **1** (*the animal*) famh *f*; **2** (*on skin*) ball-dòrain *m*

moment *n* **1** mòmaid *f*, tiota *m*, (*dimin*) tiotan *m*, tiotag *f*; **2** *in expr* **the ~** *conj* (*ie as soon as*), cho luath agus/is, **we began the ~ he came in** thòisich sinn cho luath agus a thàinig e a-steach

monastery *n* manachainn *f*

Monday *n* Diluain *m invar*

money *n* airgead *m*, **pocket ~** airgead-pòcaid, **ready ~** airgead ullamh, **that's a lot of ~!** 's e airgead mòr a tha sin!, **a waste of ~** call airgid *m*

monitor *n* (*IT*) foillsear *m*

monitor *vt* cùm sùil (*with prep* air)

monk *n* manach *m*

monkey *n* muncaidh *m*

monolith *n* tursa *m*

monster *n* uilebheist *mf*, **the Loch Ness ~** Uilebheist Loch Nis

month *n* mìos *mf*

monthly *adj* mìosach, mìosail

monument *n* clach chuimhne *f*

moo *v* geum *vi*

mood *n* **1** gean *m*, gleus *m*, fonn *m*, **what ~ is he in today?** dè an gean/ am fonn a th' air an-diugh?, **in a good ~** air deagh ghleus, **in a bad ~** diombach, dubhach, greannach; **2** (*gram*) modh *mf*, **the imperative ~** a' mhodh àithneach, **the indicative ~** a' mhodh thaisbeanach

moody *adj* **1** (*of changeable disposition*) caochlaideach; **2** (*more temporary*) dubhach, diombach, **aren't you the ~ one today!** nach tusa (a) tha dubhach/diombach/greannach an-diugh!

mooing *n* geumnaich *f*

moon *n* gealach *f*, **the harvest ~** gealach (bhuidhe) an abachaidh, **full ~** làn-ghealach, gealach (sh)làn, **the rays of the ~** gathan na gealaich *mpl*

moonshine *n* (*whisky*) poitean *m*

moor, moorland *n* mòinteach *f*, monadh *m*, sliabh *m*, aonach *m*

moral *adj* beusach, moralta

morale *n* misneach *f*, misneachd *f invar*

morality *n* moraltachd *f invar*

morals *n* beusan *fpl*, **good ~** deagh-bheusan

more *adv, pron & n* **1** tuilleadh *m invar*, barrachd *f invar*, **do you want (any/some) ~?** a bheil thu ag iarraidh tuilleadh/barrachd?, **~ information** tuilleadh/barrachd fiosrachaidh, **don't do that any ~** na dèan sin tuilleadh, **why aren't ~ records being made?** carson nach eil an tuilleadh chlàran gan dèanamh?; **2** *in expr* **~ than** barrachd air, còrr is, **~ than twenty miles** barrachd air/còrr is fichead mìle, **~ than Mary has** barrachd air na tha aig Màiri, **~ than I was expecting to see** barrachd air na bha mi an dùil fhaicinn, (*idiom*) **I've got ~ than enough** tha tuilleadh 's a' chòir agam; **3** (*corres to else*) a bharrachd, **I don't want anything ~** chan eil mi ag iarraidh càil a bharrachd; **4** (*corres to additional*) a bharrachd, **two ~ workers** dithis neach-obrach a bharrachd; **5** *in expr* **~ or less** an ìre mhath, **the winter's ~ or less over** tha an geamhradh an ìre mhath seachad

morning *n* **1** madainn *f*, **in the ~/in the course of/during the ~** anns a' mhadainn, **this ~** madainn an-diugh, **yesterday ~** madainn an-dè, **tomorrow ~** madainn a-màireach, **three in the ~** trì uairean *fpl* sa mhadainn, **the ~ star** reul *f* na maidne; **2** *in expr* **from ~ till night** o mhoch gu dubh

morose *adj* gruamach, mùgach

morrow, the *n, in expr* **on the** ~ làirne-mhàireach & làrna-mhàireach *adv*

morsel *n* (*ie to eat*) grèim *m* bìdh (*gen of* biadh *m*)

mortal *adj* **1** (*not immortal*) bàsmhor, **your** ~ **body and your immortal soul** do chorp bàsmhor is d' anam neo-bhàsmhor; **2** (*deadly, fatal*) marbhtach, bàsmhor, **a** ~ **blow** buille mharbhtach; **3** *in expr* **in** ~ **danger** an cunnart *m* bàis (*gen of* bàs *m*)

mortgage *n* morgaidse *m*

mortification *n* **1** (*humiliation*) ìsleachadh *m*, ùmhlachadh *m*; **2** (*shaming*) nàrachadh *m*

mortify *v* **1** (*humiliate*) ìslich *vt*, ùmhlaich *vt*; **2** (*shame*) nàraich *vt*

Moscow *n* Mosgo

mosque *n* mosg *m*

moss *n* (*bot*) còinneach *f*

most *n* **1** a' mhòr-chuid *f*, a' chuid-mhòr, a' chuid as mò/as motha, ~ **of his life** a' mhòr-chuid de a bheatha, ~ **people** a' mhòr-chuid, ~ **of the bread** a' chuid as motha den aran; **2** *in expr* **at** ~ aig a' char *m* as mò, **at** ~ **we will only lose twenty pounds** aig a' char as mò cha chaill sinn ach fichead nota

most *sup adj* **1** *expr by* as (*in the past & conditional tenses* a bu, *in the future* a bhitheas & a bhios*) followed by the sup form of the adj,* **she is the** ~ **beautiful woman** is ise am boireannach as bòidhche, **he will be the** ~ **famous man** is esan am fear as ainmeile a bhitheas (ann); **2** (*very, exceptionally*) anabarrach, glè, **his talk was** ~ **interesting** bha an òraid aige anabarrach inntinneach

mostly *adv* mar as trice, **we** ~ **eat porridge** mar as trice bidh sinn ag ithe lite

moth *n* leòman *m*

mother *n* màthair *f*

motherhood *n* màthaireachd *f invar*

mother-in law *n* màthair-chèile *f*

motherly *adj* màthaireil, màithreil

motion *n* (*movement; also parliamentary etc* ~) gluasad *m*

motionless *adj* gun ghluasad *m*

motive *n* adhbhar *m*, ~**less** gun adhbhar

motor *n* motair *m*

motor-bike *n* motair-baidhc *m*, (*more trad*) motair-rothar *m*

motorcar *n* càr *m*, (*trad*) carbad *m*

mould¹ *n* (*result of damp etc*) clòimh liath *f*

mould² *n* (*for forming, shaping*) molldair *m*

mound *n* **1** (*topog: rounded hill*) tom *m*, tolman *m*, tòrr *m*; **2** (*heap etc*) tòrr *m*, **a** ~ **of sand** tòrr gainmhich

mount *n* (*horse for riding*) each *m*, each dìollaid

mount *v* **1** leum *vi* air muin *f* invar (*with gen*), **he** ~**ed the horse** leum e air muin an eich; **2** (*of animals mating*) rach *vi* air muin *f* invar (*with gen*), **the bull** ~**ed the cow** chaidh an tarbh air muin na bà; **3** (*organise, set up etc*) cuir *vt* air chois (*dat of* cas *f*), **they** ~**ed an exhibition** chuir iad taisbeanadh air chois

mountain *n* beinn *f*, (*also, in some* ~ *names*) sliabh *m*

mountain ash *n* caorann *mf*

mountainous *adj* beanntach, sliabhach, monadail

mourn *v* **1** (*as vi*) bi *vi irreg* ri bròn *m*, caoidh *vi*, caoin *vi*, dèan tuireadh *m*, **they are** ~**ing** tha iad ri bròn; **2** (*as vt*) caoidh *vt*, **he is** ~**ing his parents** tha e a' caoidh a phàrantan

mourning *n* bròn *m*, **they are in** ~ tha iad ri bròn

mouse *n* luch *f*, luchag *f*

mouth *n* beul *m*, (*fam/vulg*) cab *f*, gob *m*, (*pej when used of humans*) craos *m*, **shut your** ~! dùin do bheul!, (*fam/vulg*) dùin do chab!

mouth music *n* port-à-beul *m*

mouthful *n* làn beòil *m*, **I took a** ~ **of haggis** ghabh mi làn mo bheòil de thaigeis

move *n* **1** (*flitting*) imrich *f*; **2** *in expr* **get a** ~ **on** dèan cabhag *f*!, tog ort!

move *v* **1** (*phys*) gluais *vti*, caraich *vti*, cuir car *m* (*with prep* de), **the army** ~**d towards the town** ghluais an t-arm chun a' bhaile, **don't** ~ **the table** na gluais/na caraich am bòrd, **don't** ~ **from the table** na caraich bhon bhòrd, **don't** ~ **it!** na cuir car dheth!; **2** *in expr* **unable to** ~ gun lùth/lùths *m*; **3** (~ *emotionally*) gluais *vti*, drùidh *vi* (*with prep* air), **I was** ~**d** chaidh mo ghluasad *m*, **the film** ~**d me** dhrùidh am film orm; **4** (~ *house, Sc flit*) imrich *vi*, dèan imrich *f*

movement *n* **1** gluasad *m*, **we heard a** ~ chuala sinn gluasad; **2** (*the faculty or power of* ~) lùth *m*, lùths *m*

moving *adj* **1** (*in motion*) gluasadach, siùbhlach; **2** (*emotionally* ~) gluasadach, drùidhteach

moving *n* **1** (*phys motion*) gluasad *m*; **2** (*flitting, moving house*) imrich *f*

mow *v* (*grass etc*) lom *vt*, geàrr *vt*

much *adj, adv, n,* **1** (*quantity*) mòran *m*, ~ **food** mòran bìdh (*gen of* biadh *m*), **I haven't (very)** ~ **money** chan eil mòran airgid *m gen* agam, **we didn't get (very)** ~ cha d' fhuair sinn mòran, **thank you/thanks very** ~ mòran taing *f*,

what's doing/happening? not ~ (*fam*) dè
(a) tha (a') dol? chan eil mòran; **2** *in expr* **too**
~ cus *m*, **too** ~ **talking** cus bruidhne (*gen of*
bruidhinn *f*), **I drank too** ~! dh'òl mi cus!, *note*
also idiom **far too** ~ tuilleadh 's a' chòir; **3** (*in*
various kinds of comparative exprs) mòran,
fada, fiù is/agus, uimhir *f invar*, uiread *m invar*,
~ **better** mòran/fada nas fheàrr, ~ **older**
mòran/fada nas sine, **there wasn't as** ~ **as a**
piece of bread left cha robh fiù is pìos arain
air fhàgail, **they didn't so** ~ **as look at us** cha
do rinn iad fiù agus sùil a thoirt oirnn, **give me**
as ~ **again** thoir dhomh uimhir eile (dheth),
don't give me as ~ **as James (has)!** na toir
dhomh uimhir ri Seumas!, **half as** ~ a leth
uiread, **without so** ~ **as fifty pence** gun uiread
agus leth-cheud sgillinn, **I had so** ~ **money** bha
(na h-)uimhir de dh'airgead agam; **4** (*in direct*
& indirect questions) *in expr* **how** ~ dè, **how**
~ **is there (of it)?** dè na th' ann dheth? *also*
dè an uimhir a th' ann?, **I don't know how** ~
there is chan eil fhios agam dè na th' ann dheth;
5 (*misc idioms*) **I don't think** ~ **of her hat** is
beag orm an ad aice, (*cost*) **how** ~ **is it?** dè na
tha e?

muck out *v* (*byre etc*) cairt *vt*

mucus *n* ronn *m*

mud *n* poll *m*, eabar *m*

mug *n* (*for drinking*) muga *f*

mugging *n* brath-ghoid *f*

muggy *adj* (*of weather*) bruthainneach

Mull *n* Muile, **(The) Isle of** ~ Eilean Mhuile *m*,
(*poetic, in songs*) an t-Eilean Muileach

mull over *v* cnuasaich *vi*, meòraich *vi*, (*both*
with prep air), ~**ing over what happened** a'
cnuasachadh air na thachair

multi- *prefix* ioma-, *eg* **multilingual** *adj*
ioma-chànanach, **multimedia** *adj* ioma-
mheadhan, **multinational** *adj* ioma-thìreach,
multilateral *adj* ioma-thaobhach

multiplication *n* (*maths*) iomadachadh *m*

multiply *v* **1** (*as vi: become more numerous*)
cinn *vi*, meudaich *vi*; **2** (*as vt: maths etc*)
iomadaich *vt* (**by** le), **two multiplied by four**
a dhà air iomadachadh le a ceithir, *also* a dhà
uiread a ceithir

Mummy *n* Mamaidh *f*

munitions *n* connadh-làmhaich *m sing coll*

murder *n* murt *m*

murder *v* murt *vt*

murderer *n* murtair *m*, marbhaiche *m*

murmur, murmuring *n* (*of voices, water*)
crònan *m*, monmhar *m*, (*esp of water*) torman *m*

muscle *n* fèith *f*

muscular *adj* fèitheach

muse *v* meòraich & meamhraich *vi*, (*more fam*)
cnuasaich *vi*, (**on, about** air)

museum *n* taigh-tasgaidh *m*

music *n* ceòl *m*

musical *adj* **1** ceòlmhor, fonnmhor; **2** *in expr* ~
instrument inneal-ciùil *m*, ionnsramaid *f*

musician *n* neach-ciùil *m*, ~**s** luchd-ciùil *m sing*
coll

Muslim *n & adj* Muslamach *m*, Mohamadanach
m

mussel *n* feusgan *m*

must *v* feum *vi*, (*more trad*) is/'s fheudar dhomh
(*etc*), **we** ~ **go/leave** feumaidh sinn falbh,
's fheudar dhuinn falbh, **I** ~ **admit that . .**
feumaidh mi aideachadh gu . . , ~ **you go?** am
feum sibh falbh?, (*used impersonally*) **there** ~
be a strike feumaidh gu bheil stailc ann

mutate *v* mùth *vi*

mutation *n* mùthadh *m*

mutton *n* muilt-fheoil *f*, feòil-caorach *f*

mutual *adj* **1** *can be conveyed by a prep phrase*
including (a *etc*) chèile, *eg* **their** ~ **respect/**
loathing am meas/a' ghràin a th' aca air a
chèile, **our** ~ **friend** an caraid againn, an caraid
a th' againn le chèile; **2** *can also be conveyed by*
a noun with the prefix co-, *eg* ~ **agreement** co-
chòrdadh *m*, co-aontachd *f*, co-rèiteachadh *m*,
~ **consent** co-aontachadh *m*, ~ **acquaintance**
co-eòlas *m*, ~ **assistance** co-chuideachadh *m*

my *poss adj* mo, *also very commonly expr by*
art plus noun followed by agam, ~ **mother**
mo mhàthair, ~ **home** mo dhachaigh, ~ **back**
is sore tha mo dhruim goirt, ~ **car/watch** an
càr/an t-uaireadair agam, ~ **insurance policy**
am poileasaidh-urrais agam; *as a general rule,*
the more intimate the connection, the more
likely is mo *to be used, note however examples*
such as the following, ~ **wife** a' bhean agam, ~
husband an duine agam *alongside* (*from some*
speakers) mo dhuine, ~ **house** an taigh agam
alongside mo thaigh

myself *reflexive pron* mi fhìn, **I saw** ~ **in the**
mirror chunnaic mi mi fhìn san sgàthan, **I was**
drying ~ bha mi gam thiormachadh fhìn, **by** ~
leam fhìn, **I made the cake** ~ rinn mi fhìn a'
chèic, **as for** ~ **. . .** air mo shon fhìn . . .

mysterious *adj* dìomhair

mystery *n* **1** (*abstr*) dìomhaireachd *f invar*; **2**
(*more con, a* ~, *an enigma*) tòimhseachan *m*

myth *n* uirsgeul *m*, fionnsgeul *m*, faoinsgeul *m*,
miotas *m*

N

nail¹ *n* (*of finger, toe*) ìne *f*

nail² *n* (*joinery*) tarrang *f*, tarrag *f*

naked *adj* lomnochd, rùisgte, lom

nakedness *n* luime *f invar*

name *n* **1** ainm *m*, **what's your ~?** dè an t-ainm a th' ort/oirbh?, **my ~ is Angus** 's e Aonghas an t-ainm a th' orm, **second/family ~** sloinneadh *m*, cinneadh *m*; **2** (*reputation etc*) cliù *m invar*, **he made a ~ for himself** choisinn e cliù

name *v* ainmich *vt*, thoir ainm *m* (*with prep* air)

namely *adv* is/'s e sin (*in past tense* b' e sin), **one man arrived late, ~ MacDonald** thàinig aon fhear air dheireadh, b' e sin an Dòmhnallach

nap *n* norrag *f*, norrag chadail *f*, dùsal *m*, norradaich *f*, **take a ~** gabh norrag, dèan dùsal

napkin *n* neapaigin *f*

nappy *n* badan *m*

narration *n* (*abstr & con*) aithris *f*, (*con*) cunntas *m*

narrow *adj* **1** (*phys*) caol, (*less usu*) cumhang, **a ~ bed** leabaidh chaol; **2** (*fig: in attitudes, opinions etc*) cumhang

narrow, narrows *n* caol *m*, caolas *m*

narrow *v* **1** (*as vi*) fàs *vi* caol, **the road ~ed** dh'fhàs an rathad *m* caol; **2** (*as vt; ~ down, restrict, reduce*) cuingealaich *vt* (**to** ri)

narrow-minded *adj* cumhang

nasty *adj* **1** (*esp in appearance*) mosach; **2** (*of person: in behaviour*) suarach (**to** ri), **I was ~ to her** bha mi suarach rithe

nation *n* nàisean *m*

national *adj* nàiseanta, **the ~ lottery** an crannchur nàiseanta, **~ insurance** àrachas nàiseanta *m*

nationalism *n* nàiseantachas *m*

nationalist *n* & *adj* nàiseantach *m*

nationality *n* nàiseantachd *f invar*

nationhood *n* nàiseantachas *m*

native *adj* **1** dùthchasach; **2** *in expr* **~ speaker** (*of a lang*) fileantach *m*

native *n* dùthchasach *m*

natural *adj* **1** (*in keeping with, or a product of, Nature*) nàdarra(ch), **~ selection** taghadh

nàdarra *m*, **~ gas** gas nàdarra *m*; **2** (*in keeping with a person's nature*) dual(t)ach (**for,to** do), **it's ~ for him to be proud** tha e dualtach dha a bhith àrdanach

naturally *adv* **1** (*in a natural manner*) gu nàdarra(ch); **2** (*of course*) tha f(h)ios *m*, **that will be free of charge**, ~ bidh sin saor 's an asgaidh, tha f(h)ios

nature *n* **1** (*the natural world*) nàdar *m*, **~ conservancy** glèidhteachas nàdair *m*, **~ reserve** tèarmann nàdair *m*; **2** (*a person's temperament, character*) nàdar *m*, aigne *f*, mèinn *f*; **3** (*esp hereditary ~*) dualchas *m*, **it's in his ~ to be proud** tha e na dhualchas a bhith àrdanach, *also* tha e dualtach dha a bhith àrdanach

naughty *adj* crost(a), dona, mì-mhodhail, **he's ~ today** tha e crosta an-diugh, **a ~ boy** gille dona

navel *n* imleag *f*

navy *n* **1** (*esp the force & institution*) nèibhi(dh) *mf*; **2** (*the vessels*) cabhlach *m*, loingeas *m*

Nazi *adj* & *n* Nàsach *m*

neap-tide *n* conntraigh *f*

near *adj* **1** faisg, **Christmas time is ~ now** tha àm na Nollaig(e) faisg (oirnn) a-nis

near *prep* faisg (*with prep* air), dlùth (*with prep* do *or* air), an còir (*with gen*), **~ the town** faisg air a' bhaile, dlùth don bhaile, **they didn't come ~ me** cha tàinig iad nam chòir

near *v* dlùthaich *vi* (*with prep* ri), teann *vi* (*with prep* ri *or* air), **we were ~ing the sea** bha sinn a' dlùthachadh ris a' mhuir, **it was ~ing midnight** bha e a' teannadh air meadhan-oidhche

nearly *adv* **1** faisg air, teann air, **~ a month ago** faisg/teann air mìos air ais; **2** cha mhòr *adv*, theab *v def*, **we see her ~ every day** bidh sinn ga faicinn a h-uile là, cha mhòr, **we ~ missed the bus** theab sinn am bus a chall, **I ~ fell** theab mi tuiteam, **they ~ ruined me** theab iad mo sgriosadh; **3** *note also a*) *the use of conj* gu(s) *plus adj or verbal expr*, **I'm ~ ready** tha mi gu bhith deiseil, **he was ~ dropping the parcel**

bha e gus am parsail a leigeil às, & b) *the double neg expr* cha mhòr nach (*conj*), **I ~ lost my purse** cha mhòr nach do chaill mi an sporan agam

nearness *n* faisge *f invar*

neat *adj* (*esp of person*) grinn, cuimir, (*of person, object*) sgiobalta, (*esp of objects*) snasail, snasmhor, **a ~ wee boat** eathar beag snasmhor

neatness *n* grinneas *m*, sgiobaltachd *f invar*

necessary *adj* deatamach, riatanach, (*less usu & weaker*) feumail

neck *n* **1** amha(i)ch *f*, muineal *m*

neckband, necklace *n* crios-muineil *m*

nectar *n* neactair *m*

need *n* **1** feum *m*, (*more trad*) easbhaidh *f*; **2** *in expr* **in ~** feumach, easbhaidheach, (**of** air), **in ~ of improvement** feumach air (a) leasachadh; **3** (*indigence*) airc *f*, uireasbhaidh *f*

need *v* feum *vti def*, bi *vi irreg* feum *m* agam (*etc*) (*with prep* air), bi *vi irreg* a dhìth/a dh'easbhaidh (*with prep* air), bi *vi irreg* feumach (*with prep* air), **it ~s a bit of tidying up yet** feumaidh e beagan sgioblachaidh fhathast, **I ~ money** feumaidh mi airgead, tha feum agam air airgead, tha airgead a dhìth orm, **what do they ~?** dè a tha a dhìth orra, dè a tha a dh'easbhaidh orra?, **I ~ some peace** tha mi feumach air fois; **2** (*often with implication* 'don't bother') cha leig/ruig thu (*etc*) (a) leas *m invar*, **you don't ~ to come with us** cha leig thu (a) leas tighinn còmhla rinn; **3** (*with* 'at least' *implied*) chan fhuilear *adv*, *with prep* do, **he ~s a fortnight off** chan fhuilear dha cola-deug dheth

needed *adj* (*lacking*) a dhìth, **some pepper is ~** tha piobar a dhìth

needle *n* snàthad *f*

needlework *n* **1** (*the activity*) grèis *f*; **2** (*the product*) obair-ghrèis *f*

needy *adj* feumach, easbhaidheach, uireasbhach, **a ~ person** feumach *m*

negative *adj* (*gram; also of person, attitude*) àicheil

neglect *n* dearmad *m*

neglect *v* **1** (*fail to perform an action etc*) dearmaid *vi*, cuir *vt* air dhearmad *m*, **I ~ed to inform you** dhearmaid mi fios a chur thugaibh, **~ to do something** cuir rudeigin air dhearmad; **2** (*~ something/someone*) dearmaid *vt*, leig *vt* air dhearmad *m*, **she was ~ing her studies** bha i a' leigeil a' chùrsa foghlaim aice air dhearmad

neglectful *adj* dearmadach

negligence *n* dearmad *m*, dearmadachd *f invar*

negligent *adj* dearmadach

neigh *n* sitir *f*

neigh *v* sitrich *vi*

neighing *n* sitir *f*

neighbour *n* nàbaidh *m*, coimhearsnach *m*

neighbourhood *n* coimhearsnachd *f invar*, nàbaidheachd *f invar*

neighbourly *adj* nàbaidheil

neither *adv* **1** nas motha, **I won't go home! ~ will I!** cha tèid mi dhachaigh! cha tèid mise nas motha!, *also* (*more idiomatic*) cha tèid no mise!; **2** *in constr* **~ . . . nor . . .** (*followed by nouns or proper nouns*) aon chuid *f* . . . no . . . , **he'll marry ~ Morag nor Mary** cha phòs e aon chuid Mòrag no Màiri, (*followed by adjs*) eadar, **he is ~ small nor big** tha e eadar beag agus mòr; **3** (*idiom*) **it's ~ one thing nor another** (*ie* 'six and half a dozen') tha e eadar-dhà-lionn

neither *conj* cha mhotha (a), **~ did anyone else see me** cha mhotha (a) chunnaic duine eile mi

neither *pron* (*for m nouns*) fear seach fear, (*for f nouns*) tè seach tè, **I've two sons but ~ (of them) is married** tha dà mhac agam ach chan eil fear seach fear dhiubh pòsta

neologism *n* nuadh-fhacal *m*

neophyte *n* (*relig*) iompachan *m*

nephew *n* (*brother's son*) mac bràthar *m*, (*sister's son*) mac peathar *m*, **my ~** mac mo bhràthar *or* mac mo pheathar

Neptune *n* Neiptiùn *m*

nerve *n* **1** (*anat*) lèith *f*, nèarbh *f*; **2** (*brass neck, cheek*) bathais *f*, aghaidh *f*, (*idioms*) **what a ~!** abair bathais/aghaidh, **what a ~ he's got!** nach ann air(san)/aige(san) a tha a' bhathais/an aghaidh!; **3** *in expr* **get on someone's ~s** leamhaich cuideigin

nervous, nervy *adj* clisgeach, nearbhach, frionasach

nest *n* nead *m*

net *adj* lom, **~ weight** cudthrom lom *m*

net *n* lìon *m*, (*IT*) **the ~** an lìon, (*for fishing*) lìon (-iasgaich)

nether *adj* ìochd(a)rach

netting *n* lìon *m*

nettle *n* feanntag *f*, deanntag *f*

network *n* lìonra *m*

neuk (*Sc*) *n* cùil *f*

neuter *adj* (*lang*) neodrach

neuter *v* spoth *vt*, geàrr *vt*

neutral *adj* neo-phàirteach

neutrality *n* neo-phàirteachd *f invar*

never *adv* **1** (*for past time, with a v in the neg*) a-riamh, **have you been to Egypt? ~!** an robh thu san Èipheit? cha robh a-riamh!; **2** (*for future time, with a v in the neg*) a-chaoidh, gu bràth, gu sìorraidh (tuilleadh), **they will ~ return** cha till iad a-chaoidh/gu bràth/gu sìorraidh tuilleadh; **3** (*misc exprs & idioms*) **pears are dear, ~ mind apples** tha peuran daor, gun ghuth air ùbhlan, **~ mind!** coma leat!, dad ort!, **the twelfth of ~** Là-Luain *m*

nevertheless *adv*, *also* **nonetheless** *adv*, a dh'aindeoin cùise *f gen*, a dh'aindeoin sin (*pron*), an dèidh sin, **he came last, but was pleased with himself ~** thàinig e air deireadh, ach bha e air a dhòigh a dh'aindeoin cùise/a dh'aindeoin sin

new *adj* ùr, nuadh, **~ friends** caraidean ùra, **New Year** a' Bhliadhna Ùr, **what's ~?** (*fam*) dè às ùr?, **brand/split ~** ùr-nodha, **the New Testament** An Tiomnadh Nuadh *m*

newly *adv* ùr, nuadh, **~ arrived from Glasgow** air ùr-thighinn à Glaschu, **~ published** ùr on chlò, air ùr-fhoillseachadh, **~ wed** nuadh-phòsta, **~ weds** *n* càraid nuadh-phòsta *f*

news *n* naidheachd *f*, fios *m*, guth *m*, (*TV, Radio etc*) **the ~** na naidheachdan, **is there any ~ of Mary?** a bheil fios/guth air Màiri?, **I haven't heard any ~ of him/it** cha chuala mi guth mu dheidhinn, (*idiom*) **there was (absolutely) no ~ of Murdo** sgeul *m* no fathann *m* cha robh air Murchadh

newsman *n* fear-naidheachd *m*, neach-naidheachd *m* (*pl* luchd-naidheachd *m sing coll*), naidheachdair *m*

newspaper *n* pàipear-naidheachd *m*

next *adj* **1** ath (*precedes the noun, which is lenited where possible: usu used with the art*), **~ week** an ath sheachdain *f*, **the ~ man/one** an ath fhear *m*, **living ~ door** a' fuireach an ath-dhoras; **2** *in expr* **~ to** (*phys*) ri taobh *f* (*with gen*), làmh ri (*with dat*)

next *adv* an dèidh sin, **and ~ they went to the cinema** agus an dèidh sin chaidh iad don taigh-dhealbh

nibble *v* creim *vt*, pioc *vt*

nice *adj* (*of people, objects, situations*) snog (*slightly fam*), (*esp of people*) laghach, **a ~ man** duine snog/laghach, **that was ~!** bha siud snog!, **a ~ place** àite snog

nick *n* **1** (*indentation etc*) eag *f*; **2** (*fam in Eng: form, condition*) gleus *mf*, **in good ~** air (deagh) ghleus *dat*; **3** (*Eng slang; jail*) prìosan *m*

nickname *n* far-ainm *m*, frith-ainm *m*

niece *n* (*brother's daughter*) nighean bràthar *f*, (*sister's daughter*) nighean peathar *f*, **her ~** nighean a bràthar *or* nighean a peathar

niggardly *adj* spìocach, mosach

niggling *adj* (*situations etc*) frionasach, **they're constantly asking me ~ questions** bidh iad a' cur chèistean frionasach orm fad na h-ùine

night *n* **1** oidhche *f*, **Tuesday ~** oidhche Mhàirt, **good ~!** oidhche mhath (leat/leibh)!, **a ~'s lodging/accommodation** cuid oidhche *f*, **by ~ and by day** a dh'oidhche 's a là; **2** *in expr* **from morning till ~** o mhoch gu dubh

nightgown *n* gùn-oidhche *m*

nightmare *n* trom-laighe *mf*, **like a person in the grip of/having a ~** mar neach a bhiodh fo throm-laighe

nil *n* (*in scores etc*) neoni *f invar*

nimble *adj* **1** (*in performing tasks etc*) clis, deas, ealamh; **2** (*athletic, agile*) lùthmhor

nimbleness *n* **1** (*in performing tasks etc*) cliseachd *f invar*; **2** (*phys agility*) lùth & lùths *m*

nine *num* **1** naoi *or* naodh; **2** (*of people*) naoinear *mf*, **~ sons** naoinear mhac (*mpl gen*)

nineteen *num* naoi-deug *or* naodh-deug

no *adj* **1** *expr by neg forms of the verb followed by the appropriate noun*, **we have ~ money** chan eil airgead againn, **this machine's ~ good/use** chan eil feum anns an inneal seo, **there are ~ fairies** chan eil sìthichean ann, **we eat ~ meat** cha bhi sinn ag ithe feòla (*gen of* feòil *f*), **we found ~ gold** cha do lorg sinn òr (sam bith/idir); **2** (*expr prohibition*) chan fhaodar (*present passive of* faod *vi*) *followed by the appropriate verbal noun*, **~ smoking** chan fhaodar smocadh *m*

no *adv*, *the negating word is expressed in Gaelic by putting the v of the question into the neg*, **is he there? ~** a bheil e ann? chan eil, **did you do it? ~** an do rinn thu e? cha do rinn, **is it a cat you've got? ~** an e cat a th' agad? chan e, **are you Alan? ~** an sibhse Ailean? cha mhi

nobbly *adj* cnapach

nobility *n* **1** (*abstr quality*) uaisle *f invar*; **2** (*con*) **the ~** na h-uaislean *mpl*

noble *adj* uasal, flathail

noble, nobleman *n* duine-uasal *m*, flath *m*, mòr-uasal *m*

nobody, no-one *n* duine *m* (*after neg v*), **I saw ~ (at all)** chan fhaca mi duine (sam bith), chan fhaca mi duine no duine, **there was ~ on the road** cha robh duine (beò) air an rathad *m*, **~ saw it** chan fhaca duine e

no-claims discount *n* lughdachadh neo-thagraidh *m*

nod *n* gnogadh cinn *m*

nod *v* **1** gnog a (*etc*) ceann *m*, **I ~ded** ghnog mi mo cheann; **2** *in expr* **~ off** rach *vi*/tuit *vi* na

(*etc*) c(h)lò-chadal *m*, norradaich *vi*, **they ~ded off** chaidh/thuit iad nan clò-chadal
noise *n* fuaim *mf*, (*esp louder ~*) toirm *f*, faram *m*
noisy *adj* fuaimneach, faramach
nomad *n* iniltear *m*
nominate *v* ainmich *vt*
nomination *n* ainmeachadh *m*
non- *prefix* neo-, *see examples below*
non-commital *adj* neo-cheangaltach, (*more fam*) leam-leat
none *pron* **1** (*of objects*) gin *pron, with neg v*, **he was wanting nails but I had ~** bha e ag iarraidh thàirngean ach cha robh gin agam; **2** (*of people*) aon duine *m*, aon fhear *m*, aon tè *f*, *with neg verb*, **I invited a lot of people but ~ came** thug mi cuireadh do mhòran dhaoine ach cha tàinig aon duine; **3** *in expr* **that's ~ of your business!** chan e sin do ghnothach-sa!
nonetheless *adv*, *see* **nevertheless**
non-political *adj* neo-phoilitigeach
non-renewable *adj* neo-leantainneach
non-resident *n* neo-àitiche *m*
nook *n* cùil *f*
noon *n* meadhan-là *m*
no-one *n*, *see* **nobody**
noose *n* lùb *f*, dul *m*
nor *adv*, *see* **neither** *adv*
nor *conj* cha mhotha (a), **~ did anyone else see me** cha mhotha (a) chunnaic duine eile mi
normal *adj* cumanta, àbhaisteach
normality *n* cumantas *m*
normally *adv* **1** (*generally, habitually*) am bitheantas *m*, an cumantas *m*, mar as trice, **~ it rains in the evening** am bitheantas bidh uisge ann feasgar; **2** (*as usual*) mar as àbhaist (*in past tense* mar a b' àbhaist), **he was behaving ~** bha e ga ghiùlan fhèin mar a b' àbhaist dha; **3** (*in accordance with accepted norms*) mar as còir (*in past tense* mar bu chòir), **he was behaving ~** bha e ga ghiùlan fhèin mar bu chòir (dha)
Norse *adj* Lochlannach
Norseman *n* Lochlannach *m*
north *adj* tuath, **Perth is ~ of Kinross** tha Peairt tuath air Ceann Rois, **the ~ country** an taobh tuath
north *n* **1** tuath *f invar*, **living in/going to the ~** a' fuireach/a' dol mu thuath, **the islands in the ~** na h-eileanan mu thuath, **a breeze from the ~** oiteag on tuath, **the ~** (*of an area*) an taobh tuath, **the ~ of the country** taobh tuath na dùthcha (*gen of* dùthaich *f*), ceann a tuath na dùthcha; **2** (*the compass point*) an àird(e) tuath *f*
northerly *adj* mu thuath, **the ~ islands** na h-eileanan mu thuath
northern *adj* **1** tuath, **the ~ part of the country** taobh tuath na dùthcha (*gen of* dùthaich *f*), ceann a tuath na dùthcha; **2** (*astronomy*) **the Northern Lights** Na Fir Chlis *mpl*
North Uist *n* Uibhist a Tuath
Norway *n* **1** Nirribhidh *f*, (*more trad*) Lochlann *f*; **2** *in expr* **~ spruce** giuthas Lochlannach *m*
Norwegian *n & adj* Lochlannach *m*
nose *n* sròn *f*, **my ~ is bleeding** tha mo shròn a' leum, **~ bleed** leum-sròine *m*
nostalgia *n* cianalas *m*, fadachd *f invar*, fadal *m*, (**for** ri)
nostalgic *adj* cianalach
nostril *n* cuinnean *m*
not *adv*, **1** *expressed by pre-verbal particles* cha, chan, cha do, nach, nach do, mur(a), na *etc*, **I will ~ go** cha tèid mi, **I'm ~ tired** chan eil mi sgìth, **I'm ~ doing it** chan eil mi ga dhèanamh, **I did ~ do that** cha do rinn mi sin, **he did ~ know her** cha b' aithne dha i, **I was ~ born there** cha do rugadh mi an sin, **isn't it empty?** nach eil e falamh?, **won't you go (there)?** nach tèid sibh ann?, **didn't you do it?** nach do rinn thu e?, **she said (that) she was ~ tired** thuirt i nach robh i sgìth, **if they do ~ go (there)** mur(a) tèid iad ann, **do ~ sing!** na seinn!; **2** (*rendered by* gun *followed by an infinitive in exprs such as*) **he asked me ~ to be rude** dh'iarr e orm gun a bhith mì-mhodhail
notch *n* eag *f*
note *n* **1** nota *f*, **take ~s** gabh notaichean, **send me a ~** cuir nota thugam; **2** (*music*) pong *m*
note *v* **1** (*acknowledge*) thoir fa-near (*with prep* do); **2** (*take mental note*) meòraich *vt*
nothing *n* **1** (*zero*) neoni *f invar*, (*also in fig expr*) **come to ~** rach *vi* gu neoni; **2** (*in neg exprs*) càil *m invar* (sam bith), rud *m* sam bith, **I've got ~ at all** chan eil càil/rud sam bith agam, **what did you buy? ~** dè a cheannaich thu? cha do cheannaich càil, **we've ~ to do** chan eil càil againn ri dhèanamh, **~ would make me do it** chan eil càil a bheireadh orm a dhèanamh; **3** (*idioms*) **have ~ to do with him/it!** na gabh gnothach *m* ris!, **he said ~** cha tuirt e guth *m*/ bìd *m*/smid *f* (*fam*)
notice *n* **1** (*attention*) aire *f invar*, feart *f*, for *m invar*, sùim *f*, **without taking (any) ~ of it** gun aire a thoirt dha, gun for/feart a thoirt air, **I'm not taking any ~ of what they said** chan eil sùim sam bith agam de na thubhairt iad; **2** (*information displayed*) sanas *m*, **she put up a ~ on the board** chuir i sanas an-àird/ chuir i suas sanas air a' bhòrd *m*; **3** (*advance*

notification) brath *f*, **receive** ~ faigh brath (**of** air)

notice *v* thoir an aire, thoir fa-near, (*with prep* do), mothaich *vt*, **she didn't** ~ **the car** cha tug i an aire/cha tug i fa-near don chàr, **I** ~**d it in passing** mhothaich mi dha san dol seachad

notorious *adj* (*esp of persons*) suaicheanta

nought *n* (*scores, marks etc*) neoni *f invar*, (*also in fig expr*) **come to** ~ rach *vi* gu neoni

noun *n* ainmear *m*

nourishment *n* lòn *m*, beathachadh *m*

novel *adj* **1** (*new*) ùr, nuadh; **2** (*esp unusual, odd*) annasach

novel *n* nobhail *f*

novelist *n* nobhailiche *mf*

novelty *n* **1** (*abstr*) ùrachd *f invar*; **2** (*novel object, idea etc*) annas *m*

now *adv* **1** a-nis(e), (*more immediate: just* ~, *right* ~, *at the moment*) an-dràsta, (*less usu*) an-ceartuair, **he's getting old** ~ tha e a' fàs sean a-nis, **we'll do it (right)** ~ nì sinn an-dràsta (fhèin)/an-ceartuair e; **2** (*excl: expr disapproval*) ~ ~! ud! ud!

nub *n*, *in expr* **the** ~ **of the matter** cnag *f* na cùise

nuclear *adj* niùclasach, ~ **waste** sgudal niùclasach *m*

nude *adj* lomnochd

nude *n* lom-neach *m*

nudity *n* luime *f invar*

nuisance plàigh *f*, dragh *m*

numb *adj* lapach, meilichte

numb *v* (*esp with cold*) meilich *vt*

number *n* àireamh *f*, figear *m*, ~ **four** àireamh a ceithir, **phone** ~ àireamh-fòn *f*, **a great** ~ **of people** àireamh mhòr dhaoine *mpl gen*, **cardinal/ordinal** ~ figear àrdail/òrdail

numeral *n* (*arith etc*) figear *m*

numerous *adj* lìonmhor

nun *n* cailleach-dhubh *f*

nurse *n* nurs *f*, (*more trad*) banaltram *f*, bean-eiridinn *f*

nurse *v* eiridnich *vt*, altraim *vt*

nursery *n* **1** (*in house*) seòmar-cloinne *m*; **2** (*ed:* ~ *school*) sgoil *f* àraich (*gen of* àrach *m used adjectivally*); **3** *in expr* ~ **education** foghlam fo-sgoile *m*; **4** (*gardening*) lios-àraich *m*

nursing *n* eiridinn *m invar*, banaltramachd *f invar*

nut *n* (*bot & engin*) cnò *f*, **a** ~ **and bolt** cnò is crann *m*

nutrients *npl* beathachadh *m*

nuts, nutty *adj* (*fam: mad*) às a (*etc*) c(h)iall *f*

nutty *adj* (*of taste*) cnòthach

nylon *n* nàidhlean *m*, (*as adj*) nàidhlein (*gen*), **a** ~ **shirt** lèine nàidhlein

O

oak *n* darach *m*, ~ **tree** craobh-dharaich *f*

oar *n* ràmh *m*

oath *n* (*testimony etc, also curse, (Sc) swear*) mionn *mf*, mionnan *m*, bòid *f*, **take/swear an** ~ thoir mionnan/bòid

oatmeal *n* min-choirce *f*

oats *n* coirce *m sing coll*

obedience *n* ùmhlachd *f invar*

obedient *adj* umha(i)l

obeisance *n* (*before royalty etc*) ùmhlachd *f invar*

obey *v* bi *vi irreg* umhail (*with prep* do)

object *n* **1** rud *m*, nì *m*; **2** (*butt, recipient*) cùis *f*, culaidh *f*, (*less usu*) fàth *m invar*, (*trad*) cuspair *m*, **they were an** ~ **of ridicule** bha iad nan cùis-mhagaidh *f*/nan culaidh-mhagaidh *f*, **an** ~ **of envy** culaidh-fharmaid *f*, **the** ~ **of his love** (*trad*) cuspair a ghràidh; **3** (*reason, purpose*) adhbhar *m*, **the** ~ **of his journey** adhbhar an turais aige; **4** (*gram; ~ of verb*) cuspair *m*

object *v* cuir *vi* an aghaidh (*with gen*), ~ **to the proposals** cuir an aghaidh nam molaidhean

objection *n* **1** *in expr* **I have no** ~ **to that** (*etc*), chan eil mi an aghaidh sin (*etc*); **2** (*more formal; in debate etc*) gearan *m* (**to** an aghaidh *followed by gen of noun*), **I have no** ~ **to the proposals** chan eil gearan agam an aghaidh nam molaidhean

objective *adj* cothromach, neo-phàirteach

objective *n* rùn *m*, amas *m*

objectivity *n* cothromachd *f invar*, neo-phàirteachd *f invar*

obligation *n* comain *f* (**to, towards** aig), **under an** ~ **to X** fo chomain aig X

oblige *v* **1** (*exert moral compulsion*) cuir *vi* mar fhiachaibh (*obs dat pl of* fiach *m*) (*with prep* air), **they ~d me to accept the post** chuir iad mar fhiachaibh orm an dreuchd a ghabhail; **2** (*do a favour*) dèan fàbhar *m*, dèan bàidh *f*, dèan seirbheis *f*, (*with prep* do), **they ~d me** rinn iad fàbhar/bàidh/seirbheis dhomh

obliged *adj & past part* **1** (*morally compelled*) **they made me feel** ~ **to accept the post** chuir iad mar fhiachaibh (*obs dat pl of* fiach *m*)

orm an dreuchd a ghabhail, **I was** ~ **to repay the loan** chaidh a chur mar fhiachaibh orm an t-iasad a dhìoladh; **2** (*grateful, in moral debt*) an comain (*with gen*), fo fhiachaibh (*obs dat pl of* fiach *m*) (**to** do), **I'm (very much)** ~ **to you** tha mi (fada) nad chomain, **I'm** ~ **to them**, tha mi fo fhiachaibh dhaibh

obliging *adj* (*of person*) èasgaidh, deònach

oblique *adj* claon, fiar

obliqueness *n* claonadh *m*

oblivion *n* dìochuimhne *f invar*, **pass into** ~ rach *vi* air dìochuimhne

obscene *adj* **1** drabasta, draosta; **2** (*in expr*) ~ **talk** rabhd & ràbhart *m*

obscenity *n* drabastachd *f invar*, draostachd *f invar*

obscure *adj* **1** (*poorly lit etc*) doilleir; **2** (*abstruse*) deacair; **3** (*little known*) neo-ainmeil, neo-aithnichte

obscure *v* **1** (*darken*) doilleirich *vt*, neulaich *vt*; **2** (*conceal*) ceil *vt*, falaich *vt*

obsequious *adj* umha(i)l

obsequiousness ùmhlachd *f invar*

observance *n* (*of rules, principles etc*) gleidheadh *m*

observant *adj* mothachail, furachail

observe *v* **1** (*notice*) mothaich *vt*; **2** (*follow rules etc*) glèidh *vt*; **3** (*celebrate religious festival etc*) cùm *vt*

obsession *n* beò-ghlacadh *m*

obsolete *adj* à cleachdadh *m*

obstacle *n* (*lit & fig*) bacadh *m*, cnap-starra *m*

obstinacy *n* raige *f invar*

obstinate *adj* rag, dùr, (*stronger*) rag-mhuinealach

obstruct *v* bac *vt*

obstruction *n* (*abstr & con*) bacadh *m*, (*con*) cnap-starra *m*

obtain *v* faigh *vt irreg*, ~ **employment** faigh obair/cosnadh

obvious *adj* follaiseach, soilleir, am follais *f*, **it's** ~ **he's not guilty** tha e follaiseach/soilleir nach eil e ciontach, **become** ~ thig *vi* am follais

obviously *adv* **1** tha f(h)ios, **that will be free of charge,** ~ bidh sin saor 's an-asgaidh, tha fios; **2** *also rendered by* tha e follaiseach/soilleir, **he's ~ not guilty** tha e follaiseach/soilleir nach eil e ciontach

obviousness *n* follais *f invar*

occasion *n* **1** uair *f*, turas *m*, **I was there on one ~** bha mi ann uair, bha mi ann aon turas, *in expr* **on some ~ or other** uair no uaireigin; **2** (*cause, reason*) adhbhar *m*, **we had ~ to complain** bha adhbhar-gearain *m* againn, bha adhbhar againn a bhith a' gearan; **3** (*event, function etc*) tachartas *m*, **a civic ~** tachartas catharra

occasional *adj* **1** corra (*precedes the noun, which it lenites where possible*), *also expr by adv phrase* bho àm gu àm, **I have the ~ pint with him** gabhaidh mi corra phinnt còmhla ris, *also* gabhaidh mi pinnt còmhla ris bho àm gu àm

occasionally *adv* bho àm gu àm, an-dràsta 's a-rithist, uaireannan, air uairean, (*trad*) air uairibh

occupant *n* (*of dwelling etc*) neach-còmhnaidh *m* (*pl* luchd-còmhnaidh *m sing coll*), (*esp as owner*) seilbheadair *m*

occupation *n* obair *f*, (*usu non-manual*) dreuchd *f*

occur *v* **1** (*take place*) tachair *vi*, **it ~red two years ago** thachair e o chionn dà bhliadhna/dà bhliadhna air ais; **2** (*come to mind etc*) thig *vi* a-steach (*with prep* air), **it ~red to me that they weren't listening** thàinig e a-steach orm nach robh iad ag èisteachd

occurrence *n* tachartas *m*, tuiteamas *m*

ocean *n* cuan *m*, fairge *f*

o'clock *adv* uair *f*, uairean *fpl*, **at two ~** aig dà uair, **it's three ~** tha e trì uairean, **twelve ~** dà uair dheug

octave *n* (*music*) gàmag *f*

October *n* (*used with art*) An Dàmhair *f*

odd *adj* **1** (*not even*) còrr, **~ number** àireamh chòrr; **2** (*occasional, rare*) corra (*precedes the noun, which it lenites where possible*), **the ~ person came in from time to time** thigeadh corra dhuine a-steach bho àm gu àm; **3** (*strange, unusual*) neònach, annasach

odds *npl in expr* **fair ~** cothrom *m* na Fèinne

odds and ends criomagan *fpl*, trealaich *f*

odour *n* boladh *m*

oesophagus *n* slugan *m*

of *prep* de & dhe (*takes the dat, lenites following cons where possible, for prep prons formed with de, see p 509*), **most ~ it** a' chuid as mò dheth, **at this time ~ the year** aig an àm seo den bhliadhna, **the twentieth ~ the month** am ficheadamh là den mhìos, **full ~ milk** làn de bhainne, **one ~ those who were there** fear de na bha ann, **a fool ~ a man** amadan de dhuine, **a brooch ~ silver** bràiste de dh'airgead, *Note:* de/dhe *can occur as* a, *usu in set exprs, eg* **~ one mind** (*ie unanimous*) a dh'aon rùn *m*

of course *adv* tha f(h)ios *m*, **that will be free of charge,** ~ bidh sin saor 's an-asgaidh, tha fios, **are you pleased? ~ I am!** a bheil thu toilichte? tha fios gu bheil!, *also* 's mi a tha!

off *adv* **1** dheth, **the electricity's ~** tha an dealan dheth, **turn the radio ~** cuir dheth an rèidio, **the cream's going ~** tha an t-uachdar a' dol dheth; **2** (*in phrases & idioms expr movement, departure*) be ~! tog ort!, **~ you go home!** thalla(ibh) (*imper, for* falbh) dhachaigh!, **~ you go to the shop for me!** thalla don bhùth dhomh!, **right! I'm ~** ceart! tha mi a' falbh, **she took herself ~/~ she went to America** thug i Ameireagaidh oirre; **3** (*misc exprs*) **far ~, a long way ~** fad' air falbh, **I dropped/dozed ~** chaidh mi nam chlò-chadal *m*, **make ~** tàrr *vi* às, *also* tàir *vi* às, **put something ~ (till another day)** cuir rudeigin air ath là *m*, **go ~** (*ie deteriorate*) rach *vi* bhuaithe, **she went ~** chaidh i bhuaithe, (*clothing etc*) **take ~** cuir *vt* dheth (*etc*), **take your coat ~** cuir dhìot do chòta

off *prep* bhàrr (*for* de bhàrr *m*, *lit* from the top or surface (of)), *also* far, (*takes the gen*), **he took a book ~ the table** thug e leabhar bhàrr a' bhùird, **a stone fell ~ the wall** thuit clach far a' ghàrraidh

offence *n* **1** oilbheum *m*, **give ~ to someone** thoir oilbheum do chuideigin; **2** (*illegal action*) coire *f*, eucoir *f*, **commit an ~** dèan coire, *also* ciontaich *vi*

offend *v* **1** (*give offence to*) thoir oilbheum *m* (*with prep* do), **she ~ed me** thug i oilbheum dhomh; **2** (*law: commit an illegal action*) dèan coire *f*, ciontaich *vi*

offender *n* (*law*) ciontach *m*, coireach *m*

offensive *adj* **1** (*action etc*) oilbheumach, tàmailteach; **2** (*smell etc*) sgreamhail, sgreataidh

offer *n* tairgse *f*, **make an ~** thoir tairgse (**for** air, **to** do)

offer *v* **1** tairg *vt*, tabhainn *vt*, **he ~ed his help** thairg e a chuideachadh, **he ~ed to do it** thairg e a dhèanamh; **2** (*relig: ~ up as a sacrifice*) ìobair *vt*

offering *n* **1** tabhartas *m*; **2** (*relig: sacrificial ~*) ìobairt *f*

off-hand adj **1** (*of welcome, reception etc*) fionnar; **2** (*of attitude etc: uninterested*) coma co-dhiù, (*not giving full attention*) fad' às

office n oifig *f*, oifis *f*, **the Post ~** Oifis a' Phuist, **the Scottish Office** Oifis na h-Alba

officer n **1** (*in forces etc*) oifigear *m*, oifigeach *m*; **2** *in expr* **church ~** maor-eaglais *m*

official adj oifigeil, **let them know ~ly** cuir fios thuca gu h-oifigeil

official n oifigeach *m*, **he's a Council ~** tha e na oifigeach aig a' Chomhairle

offspring n clann *f sing coll*, (*more remote generations*) gineal *mf sing coll*, sìol *m sing coll*, sliochd *m sing coll*

often adv (gu) tric, iomadach uair *f*, iomadh uair, (*more trad*) gu minig, **that ~ happens** bidh sin a' tachairt gu tric, **she doesn't come as ~ as she used to** cha tig i cho tric agus a chleachd (i)/agus a b' àbhaist, **we ~ used to go there** is tric a rachadh sinn ann, **I did it ~** rinn mi iomadach uair/iomadh uair e

oil n **1** ola *f*, ùilleadh *m*, **vegetable ~** ola-luis, **mineral ~** ola-thalmhainn; **2** *in exprs* **~ lamp** crùisgean *m*, **~ rig** crann-ola *m*, **~ tanker** tancair-ola *m*

oily adj ùilleach

ointment n ungadh *m*

OK, okay adj, adv & excl ceart gu leòr, **that's ~** tha sin ceart gu leòr, **I got on ~** chaidh dhomh ceart gu leòr, **do it tomorrow! ~!** dèan a-màireach e! ceart gu leòr!

old adj **1** (*of considerable age, also former*) sean (seann *before d, s, t, l, n or r*) *lenites following cons exc for d, s & t*, **~ people** seann daoine *mpl*, **in the ~ days** sna seann làithean *mpl*; **2** (*as prefix*) sean(n)-, *eg* **~-fashioned** seann-fhasanta; *note also the form* seana-, *eg* **~ maid** seana-mhaighdeann, **~ bachelor** seana-ghille

omen n manadh *m*

omission n dearmad *m*, **sins of ~** peacaidhean dearmaid *mpl*

omit v **1** (*fail to include*) fàg às; **2** (*through negligence, forgetfulness, fail to perform an action etc*) dearmaid *vi*, cuir *vt* air dhearmad *m*, **I ~ted to inform you** dhearmaid mi fios a chur thugaibh, **~ to do something** cuir rudeigin air dhearmad

omni- *prefix* uile-, *eg* **~potent** uile-chumhachdach

on prep **1** air, *for prep prons formed with* air, *see* p 509, **~ the table** air a' bhòrd, **a tune ~ the fiddle** port air an fhidhill (*dat of* fidheall *f*), **a book ~ history** leabhar air eachdraidh, **~ a journey** air turas, **~ my mind** air m' aire, air m' aigne, air mo chùram, **he was ~ good form** (*ie in fine fettle*) bha e air a dheagh dhòigh, **~ the spot** (*ie immediately*) anns a' bhad, an làrach nam bonn, **the television broke down ~ me** bhris an telebhisean sìos orm; **2** (*misc exprs*) **~ purpose** a dh'aon ghnothach, **~ my own** nam aonar, leam fhìn, **~ drugs** a' gabhail dhrogaichean, air na drogaichean, **dependent ~ drugs** (*etc*) an urra ri drogaichean (*etc*), na (*etc*) t(h)ràill *mf* do dhrogaichean (*etc*)

on adv **1** (*expr progression, continuity*) air adhart, **from that time ~** bhon àm sin air adhart, **how are you getting ~?** ciamar a tha thu a' faighinn air adhart, **her pupils are coming ~ well** tha na sgoilearan aice a' tighinn air adhart gu math, . . . **and so ~** . . . 's mar sin air adhart, **paper, pens, and so ~** pàipear, pinn, 's mar sin air adhart; **2** (*misc exprs*) **they get ~ well (together)** tha iad gu math mòr aig a chèile, **the light was ~** bha an solas air, **put your coat ~** cuir umad do chòta, **we walked ~** choisich sinn romhainn, **she's always ~ at me!** tha i an sàs annam an-còmhnaidh!, **he's got nothing ~** (*ie unclothed*) tha e dearg rùisgte, **I've got nothing ~ at the moment** (*ie no commitments etc*) tha mi saor an-dràsta, chan eil càil *m invar* agam ri dhèanamh an-dràsta, **what's ~ tomorrow?** dè a tha a' dol a-màireach?

once adv **1** (*at some time in the past*) uair, uaireigin, **we were there ~** bha sinn ann uair; **2** (*on a single occasion*) aon uair, aon turas *m*, **I went there ~** chaidh mi ann aon uair/aon turas, **~ or twice** uair no dhà; **3** *in exprs* **~ upon a time** fada, fada ro seo, uaireigin den t-saoghal, **at ~** anns a' bhad, air ball, gun dàil

once conj (*ie as soon as*) aon uair is/'s/agus, **~ he got started everything would be fine** aon uair 's gun tòisicheadh e bhiodh a h-uile càil air dòigh

one adj **1** (*num*) aon (*lenites following cons exc for d, t & s*), (*emph*) aonan *n*, **~ woman** aon bhoireannach, **it's ~** (*emph*) **pound he owes me, not two** 's e aon nota a th' agam air, chan e a dhà; **2** (*often in contrast to* eile **other**) an dara & an dàrna, **~ son is industrious but the other ~ is lazy** tha an dara mac èasgaidh ach tha am fear eile leisg, **put to ~ side** cuir an dara taobh; **3** (**~ of a pair**) leth-, **on ~ leg** air leth-chois (*dat of* cas *f*), **on ~ elbow** air mo (*etc*) leth-uilinn

one n **1** (*representing a m sing noun*) fear *m*, **here are some books, take ~ or two of them** seo agad leabhraichean *mpl*, gabh fear no dhà dhiubh, **which ~ do you prefer?** cò am fear as fheàrr leat?, (*idiom*) **I'm** (*etc*) **~ of them** tha mise (*etc*) air fear dhiubh, **many people are tired of it, and he's ~ of them** tha mòran dhaoine sgìth dheth, agus tha esan air fear dhiubh; **2** (*representing a f sing n*) tè *f invar*, **this ~ is smaller than that ~** tha an tè seo nas lugha na an tè sin; **3 ~s** (*pl, of people & objects*) feadhainn *f sing coll, used with art*, an fheadhainn, **these ~s are going home** tha an fheadhainn seo a' dol dhachaigh, **the ~s that are on the shelf are broken but the other ~s are OK** tha an fheadhainn a th' air an sgeilp briste ach tha an fheadhainn eile ceart gu leòr; **4** (*in succession*) **~ after another/the other** an ceann *m* a chèile *m gen*, aon an dèidh aoin *mf gen*, **three accidents ~ after the other** trì tubaistean an ceann a chèile/an dèidh a chèile; **5** (*in turn*) **~ after the other/~ by ~** fear *m*/tè *f* mu seach, fear seach fear, tè seach tè, **~ after the other/~ by ~ they went through the door** fear mu seach/fear seach fear, chaidh iad tron doras; **6** (*idioms*) **it's all ~** (*ie indifferent*) chan eil e gu diofar, **that's all ~ to me** is coma leam sin

one *pron* duine *m*, neach *m*, **it would amaze ~** chuireadh e iongnadh air duine, **a love ~ couldn't express** gaol nach cuireadh neach an cèill (*dat of* ciall *f*)

onerous *adj* trom

one-way *adj* aon-sligheach

onion *n* uinnean *m*

on-line *adj* air-loidhne

onlooker *n* neach-coimhid *m* (*pl* luchd-coimhid *m sing coll*)

onslaught *n* ionnsaigh *mf*

onus *n* uallach *m*, **the ~ is on you** (*emph*) 's ann oirbhse a tha an t-uallach

open *adj* **1** fosgailte, **an ~ window** uinneag fhosgailte, **the shop is ~** tha a' bhùth fosgailte, **an ~** (*ie public*) **meeting** coinneamh fhosgailte; **2** (*of persons: frank, approachable etc*) fosgailte, fosgarra, faoilidh; **3** *in exprs* **bring into the ~** thoir *vt* am follais *f*, **come into the ~** thig *vi* am follais

open *v* fosgail *vti*, **~ the door!** fosgail an doras!, **the door ~ed** dh'fhosgail an doras, **the shop's ~ing** tha a' bhùth *mf* a' fosgladh

opened *adj & past part* fosgailte

open-handed *adj* fialaidh, fial

opener *n* fosglair *m*

opening *n* **1** (*aperture*) fosgladh *m*, beàrn *f*; **2** (*opportunity*) fosgladh *m*, cothrom *m*, **an ~ in the market** fosgladh sa mhargadh *mf*

openness *n* (*of information, character*) fosgailteachd *f invar*, fosgarrachd *f invar*

operate *v* obraich *vt*, **~ a machine** obraich inneal *m*

operation *n* **1** (*abstr*) gnìomh *m*, **put into ~** cuir *vt* an gnìomh; **2** (*con: project etc*) gnothach *m*, **he'll be taking charge of the ~** bidh esan a' gabhail a' ghnothaich os làimh (*dat of* làmh *f*); **3** (*medical ~*) opairèisean *mf*, **she's recovering from an ~** tha i a' faighinn seachad air opairèisean

opponent *n* **1** (*sport, competition etc*) farpaiseach *m*; **2** (*politics*) neach-dùbhlain *m* (*pl* luchd-dùbhlain *m sing coll*)

opportune *adj* **1** (*timeous*) mithich, tràthail, na (*etc*) t(h)ràth *m*, **a word (spoken) at an ~ moment** facal na thràth; **2** (*appropriate, propitious*) fàbharach, freagarrach

opportunity *n* cothrom *m*, fosgladh *m*, (*less usu*) fàth *m invar*, **opportunities for higher education** cothroman air foghlam *m* àrd-ìre, **he saw an ~ in the clothing market** chunnaic e fosgladh ann am margadh an aodaich, **an ~ for some fun** fàth airson spòrsa

oppose *v* cuir *vi* an aghaidh (*with gen*), **he ~d the war** chuir e an aghaidh a' chogaidh

opposed *adj* an aghaidh (*with gen*), **I'm (completely/totally) ~ to that** tha mi (calg-dhìreach) an aghaidh sin, **they were (completely/totally) ~ to each other** bha iad (calg-dhìreach) an aghaidh a chèile

opposite *adv & prep*, mu choinneimh, fa chomhair, (*with gen*), **the man ~ (me)** an duine a bha (na sheasamh *etc*) mum choinneimh, **I was ~ her** bha mi mu coinneimh, **he stopped ~ me** stad e fa mo chomhair

opposite *n* ceart-aghaidh *f*

opposition *n* **1** (*abstr*) cur *m* an aghaidh, dùbhlan *m*; **2** (*con: esp pol*) dùbhlanaich *mpl*, **the ~** na dùbhlanaich, (*as adj*) **~ parties** pàrtaidhean dùbhlanach *mpl*; **3** (*rivals in business, sport etc*) **the ~** na còmhstrithich *mpl*, na co-fharpaisich *mpl* (*againn etc*)

oppression *n* fòirneart *m*

oppressor *n* neach-fòirneirt *m* (*pl* luchd-fòirneirt *m sing coll*)

optic, optical *adj* fradharcach

option roghainn *mf*, **we've no ~** chan eil roghainn (eile) againn

or *conj* **1** no, **war ~ peace** cogadh no sìth; **2** *in expr* **~ else** air neo, **eat your dinner, ~ else you'll be hungry** gabh do dhìnnear, air neo bidh an t-acras ort

oral

oral *adj* **1** beòil (*gen of* beul *m, used adjectivally*),
~ **evidence** fianais-bheòil *f*; **2** *in expr* ~
tradition beul-aithris *f*
orange *adj* orains, dearg-bhuidhe, **what colour
is it? (it's)** ~ dè an dath a th' air? tha orains
orange *n* **1** (*fruit*) orainsear *m*; **2** (*colour*) orains
f, dearg-bhuidhe *m*
oration *n* òraid *f*
orbit *n* cuairt *f*, reul-chuairt *f*, **the sun's** ~ cuairt
na grèine
orchard *n* ubhalghort *m*
ordain *v* **1** (*order, prescribe*) òrdaich *vt*; **2** (~ *a
minister*) suidhich *vt*
ordained *adj & past part* **1** (*ordered, prescribed*)
òrdaichte; **2** (*fated*) an dàn *m* (**for** do), **what
was** ~ **for him** na bha an dàn dha
ordeal *n* deuchainn *f*, (*stronger*) cruaidh-
dheuchainn *f*
order *n* **1** (*command, also* ~ *in café etc*) òrdugh
m, **he gave me an** ~ thug e dhomh òrdugh; **2**
(*correct sequence*) òrdugh *m*, **put in** ~ cuir *vt*
an òrdugh, òrdaich *vt*, **alphabetical** ~ òrdugh
aibidealach, **out of** ~ a-mach à òrdugh; **3**
(*orderliness, tidiness, organisation, as things
should be*) òrdugh *m*, rian *m*, **in** ~ ann an
òrdugh; **4** (*working* ~, *condition*) dòigh *f*, gleus
mf, òrdugh *m*, **in good** ~ air dòigh, air (deagh)
ghleus, *also* gleusta *adj*, **put in good** ~ cuir *vt*
air dòigh, cuir *vt* air (deagh) ghleus, **out of** ~
a-mach à òrdugh, *also* briste *adj*; **5** *in expr* **in**
~ **to** *conj* gus, **in** ~ **to clean the house** gus an
taigh a ghlanadh
order *v* **1** (*instruct*) òrdaich *vi* (*with prep* do),
they ~ed me to shut the gates dh'òrdaich iad
dhomh na geataichean a dhùnadh; **2** (*in café etc*)
òrdaich *vti*
ordered *adj* òrdail, riaghailteach, rianail
orderliness *n* òrdugh *m*, riaghailteachd *f invar*,
rian *m*
orderly *adj* òrdail, riaghailteach, rianail
ordinal *adj* òrdail, **an** ~ **number** cunntair *m*
òrdail
ordinance *n* riaghailt *f*, reachd *m invar*
ordinary *adj* **1** àbhaisteach, cumanta, gnàthach;
2 (*as n*) *in expr* **out of the** ~ às a' chumantas *m*
ore *n* mèinn(e) *f*
organ[1] *n* (*bodily* ~) ball(-bodhaig) *m*
organ[2] *n* (*mus*) òrgan *m*
organisation *n* **1** (*abstr*) òrdugh *m*, riaghailt
f, rian *m invar*; **2** (*the act of organising*)
òrdachadh *m*, cur an òrdugh *m*; **3** (*con: body
etc*) buidheann *mf*, **a charitable** ~ buidheann-
carthannachd

organise *v* **1** (*put in order*) cuir *vt* an òrdugh *m*,
òrdaich *vt*, cuir rian *m* (*with prep* air); **2** (*set up
etc*) cuir *vt* air chois (*dat of* cas *f*), cuir *vt* air
b(h)onn *m*, ~ **an investigation/a playgroup**
cuir sgrùdadh/croileagan air chois/air b(h)onn
origin *n* tùs *m*, (*prov*) **the fear of God is the** ~
of wisdom 's e tùs a' ghliocais eagal Dhè, *also* is
e eagal an Tighearna tùs an eòlais
original *adj* **1** (*innovative etc*) ùr; **2** (*first, initial*)
tùsail
originally *adv* o/bho thùs *m*, an toiseach *m*, an
toiseach tòiseachaidh *m*, sa chiad àite *m*, **they
were living here** ~ bha iad a' fuireach an seo o
thùs/an toiseach
originate *v* tàrmaich *vt*
ornament *n* ball-maise *m*
ornithology *n* eun-eòlas *m*
oscillate *v* luaisg *vi*
oscillation *n* **1** (*abstr*) luasgadh *m*; **2** (*more con:
an* ~) luasgan *m*
other *adj* **1** eile, **the** ~ **half** an leth *m invar* eile,
on the ~ **hand** air an làimh (*dat of* làmh *f*) eile,
give me the ~ **one** thoir dhomh am fear *m*/
an tè *f* eile; **2** (*often in contrast to* an dara & an
dàrna, **one**) eile, *eg* **one son is industrious
but the** ~ **(one) is lazy** tha an dara mac
èasgaidh ach tha am fear eile leisg; **3** (*in pl*) **the**
~**s** (*of persons*) càch *pron*, (*of persons & things*)
an fheadhainn *f sing coll* eile, **she did better
than the** ~**s** rinn i na b' fheàrr na càch, **I went,
along with the** ~**s** chaidh mi ann, còmhla ri
càch/còmhla ris an fheadhainn eile; **4** *in expr*
each ~ a chèile *m*, **they kissed each** ~ phòg
iad a chèile, **talking to each** ~ a' bruidhinn ri
chèile; **5** *in expr* **or** ~, *expr by the appropriate
noun followed by* air choreigin, *eg* **something
or** ~ rud air choreigin, **somebody or** ~ duine
air choreigin; **6** (*misc exprs*) **the** ~ **day** an là
roimhe *m*, **one after the** ~ (*in time or space*)
an ceann a chèile, an dèidh a chèile, **three
accidents one after the** ~ trì tubaistean *fpl* an
ceann a chèile/an dèidh a chèile
otherwise *adv* air neo, **eat your dinner,** ~
you'll be hungry gabh do dhìnnear *f*, air neo
bidh an t-acras ort
otter *n* dòbhran *m*, (*informal*) biast-dhubh &
beist-dhubh *f*
ought *auxiliary v* bu (*past/conditional of* is *v
irreg def*) chòir *f* (*with prep* do), **I** ~ **to go/
leave** bu chòir dhomh (a bhith a') falbh, **you** ~
not to smoke cha bu chòir dhut smocadh, **it's
not as good as it** ~ **to be** chan eil e cho math
agus bu chòir (dha a bhith)
ounce *n* unnsa *m*

ourselves *reflexive pron* sinn fhìn, *for examples of use cf* **myself** & **-self** *reflexive suffix*

out *adv & prep* **1** (*esp of motion: lit & fig*) a-mach (*of* à), **he went** ~ chaidh e a-mach, ~ **of here!/ get** ~**!** a-mach à seo (leat/leibh)!, **the way** ~ an t-slighe (dol) a-mach, (*by a door*) an doras (dol) a-mach, **a page** ~ **of a newspaper** duilleag a-mach à pàipear-naidheachd, ~ **of work/a job** a-mach à obair, *also* gun chosnadh, ~ **of order** a-mach à òrdugh, **my book's (come)** ~ thàinig an leabhar agam a-mach, ~ **of danger** a-mach à cunnart, **make** ~ (*ie assert*) cùm *vi* a-mach, **she was making** ~ **that Einstein was a fool** bha i a' cumail a-mach gum b' e amadan a bh' ann an Einstein; **2** *expr by* à, às (*for prep prons formed with* à, *see p 19*), **put the fire/the light** ~ cuir às an teine/an solas, **let** ~ leig *vi* (*with prep* à), **I let** ~ **a shreik** leig mi sgreuch asam, ~ **of sight** à sealladh *or* às an t-sealladh, ~ **of his mind** às a chiall, às a rian *m*, ~ **of the ordinary** às a' chumantas, **they got the hell** ~ **of it** thug iad na buinn (*pl of* bonn *m*) asta, thug iad an casan (*pl of* cas *f*) leotha, **way** ~ (*ie solution; also means of escape*) dol às *m invar*, **there was no way** ~ **for them** cha robh dol às aca; **3** (*outside*) a-muigh, **he's** ~ **in the garden** tha e a-muigh anns a' ghàrradh; **4** (*misc exprs*) ~ (*ie not at home*) on taigh, **my wife's** ~ tha a' bhean agam on taigh, ~ **in America** ann an Ameireagaidh thall, ~ **of sorts** (*ie crotchety etc*) diombach, (*usu of child*) crost(a) & crosda, ~ **of sorts** (*ie not in best of health*) ach meadhanach (*after a verb in the neg*), **he's** ~ **of sorts today** chan eil e ach meadhanach an-diugh

outburst *n* (*of noise, emotion etc*) lasgan *m*

outcome *n* toradh *m*, buil *f*

outgoing *adj* **1** (*of person: sociable etc*) faoilidh, cuideachdail, fàilteach; **2** *in expr* ~ **mail** post *a*-mach *m*

outlaw *n* neach-cùirn *m* (*pl* luchd-cùirn *m sing coll*)

outlaw *v* cuir *vt* fon choill (*dat of* coille *f*)

outlawed *adj & past part* **1** (*of person*) fon choill (*dat of* coille *f*); **2** (*of substances, practices etc*) mì-laghail, toirmisgte, fo thoirmeasg *m*, neo-cheadaichte

output *n* (*of industry etc*) toradh *m*

outrageous *adj* (*excessive, unacceptable*) uabhasach, (*scandalous*) tàmailteach, (*offensive*) oilbheumach

outside *adv* **1** (*movement*) a-mach, **go** ~ rach *vi* a-mach, (*as command*) thalla *imper* a-mach, ~ **with you!** a-mach leat!; **2** (*position*) a-muigh,

where's Iain? he's ~ càit a bheil Iain? tha (e) a-muigh

outside *n* taobh a-muigh *m* (*with gen*), **on the** ~ air an taobh a-muigh, **the** ~ **of the building** taobh a-muigh an togalaich

outside *prep* air (an) taobh a-muigh *m* (*with gen*), ~ **the building** air taobh a-muigh an togalaich

outskirts *n* iomall *m sing*, **on the** ~ **of the town** air iomall a' bhaile

outstanding *adj* **1** (*of high quality*) air leth, air leth math, **an** ~ **man** duine air leth, **that was** ~ bha sin air leth math; **2** (*bills, debts*) gun phàigheadh *m*

outwith *prep* **1** (*beyond*) thar (*with gen, for prep prons formed with* thar, *see p 20*), ~ **my competence** thar mo chomais *m gen*, thar mo chomasan *mpl gen*; **2** (*outside, furth of*) air taobh a-muigh (*with gen*), ~ **the community/the country** air taobh a-muigh na coimhearsnachd/na dùthcha (*gen of* dùthaich *f*)

oval *adj* ughach

oval *n* ughach *m*

ovary *n* ughlann *f*

over *adv* **1** (*usu expr movement*) thairis, **they went** ~ chaidh iad thairis; **2** (*misc exprs*) ~ **and** ~ **again** (*expr repetition*) uair *f* is uair, **all** ~ (*ie finished*) seachad, **that's (all)** ~ **now** tha sin seachad a-nis, **all** ~ (*ie everywhere*) anns a h-uile h-àite *m*, anns gach àite, **it will be wet all** ~ bidh i fliuch anns a h-uile h-àite

over *prep* **1** (*expr position or movement*) thar (*with gen, for prep prons formed with* thar, *see p 20*), **he had a rifle** ~ **his shoulder** bha raidhfil aige thar a ghuailne (*gen of* gualainn *f*), **they went** ~ **the ocean** chaidh iad thar a' chuain; **2** (*expr movement*) tarsainn air, thairis air, (*with dat*), **they went** ~ **the bridge/the mountains** chaidh iad tarsainn/thairis air an drochaid/air na beanntan (*pl of* beinn *f*), **the plane passed** ~ **the town** chaidh am plèana thairis air a' bhaile; **3** (*above*) os cionn (*obs dat of* ceann *m*) (*with gen*), **clouds** ~ **the ocean** neòil (*pl of* neul *m*) os cionn a' chuain, ~ **me** os mo chionn; **4** (*with exprs of time: in the course of*) rè (*with gen*), ~ **the years** rè nam bliadhnachan; **5** *in expr* **all** ~ (*in every part of*) air feadh (*with gen*), **all** ~ **the country** air feadh na dùthcha (*gen of* dùthaich *f*), **there were empty glasses all** ~ **the place** bha glainneachan falamh air feadh an àite

overcoat *n* còta-mòr *m*

overcome *v* **1** (*people, emotions etc: quell*) ceannsaich *vt*; **2** (*people, problems etc: vanquish, succeed over*) thoir buaidh *f* (*with prep* air), (*more colloquial*) dèan a' chùis *f*, dèan an gnothach *m*, (*both with prep* air), **we will ~ the enemy** bheir sinn buaidh air an nàmhaid *m*, nì sinn a' chùis/an gnothach air an nàmhaid

overexpose *v* ro-nochd *vt*

overflow *v* (*lit & fig*) cuir *vi* thairis, **the water ~ed** chuir an t-uisge thairis, **a land ~ing with creatures of every kind** tìr a' cur thairis le creutairean de gach seòrsa

overhead *adj* os-cinn, **~ cable** càball os-cinn

overhead *adv* os a (*etc*) c(h)ionn (*obs dat of* ceann *m*), **I saw a plane ~** chunnaic mi plèana os mo chionn

overload *v* an-luchdaich *vt*

overlord *n* àrd-uachdaran *m*

overseas *adv* **1** (*expr movement*) a-null thairis, **they went ~** chaidh iad a-null thairis; **2** (*expr position*) thall thairis, **they are ~** tha iad thall thairis, **~ market** margadh thall thairis

oversight *n* (*careless omission*) dearmad *m*

overt *adj* follaiseach

overtime *n* còrr-ùine *f*, seach-thìm *f*

overturn *v* **1** (*as vt*) cuir bun-os-cionn, cuir car de, (*esp of boat*) cuir thairis, **they ~ed the trailer** chuir iad an trèilear bun-os-cionn, chuir iad car den trèilear, **they ~ed the boat** chuir iad thairis am bàta; **2** (*as vi*) rach car de, (*esp of boat*) rach thairis, **the trailer ~ed** chaidh car den trèilear, **the boat ~ed** chaidh am bàta thairis

overweight *adj* ro throm

owe *v* **1** (*fin & moral debts*) bi *vi irreg* fo fhiachaibh (*obs dat pl of* fiach *m*) (*with prep* do), **we ~ them (money)** tha sinn fo fhiachaibh dhaibh; **2** (*fin debts: note that it is the person owed money who is said to 'have' the money 'on' the debtor*) **we ~ them fifty pounds** tha leth-cheud not *f sing* aca oirnn, **they ~ us fifty pounds** tha leth-cheud not againn orra

owl *n* cailleach-oidhche *f*, (*esp a barn ~*) comhachag *f*

own *adj* **1** (*using the poss formed with* aig) aige (*etc*) f(h)èin/fhìn, **their ~ house** an taigh aca fhèin, **a house of his ~** taigh aige dha fhèin; **2** (*using poss pron*) **he broke his ~ leg** bhris e a chas fhèin

owner *n* **1** sealbhadair *m*, **share ~** sealbhadair-shèaraichean (*gen pl of* sèar *m*); **2** *in expr* **who's the ~ of this lorry** (*etc*)? cò leis a tha an làraidh seo (*etc*)?

ox *n* damh *m*

ox-tail *n* earball daimh *m*

oxygen *n* ogsaidean *m*

oystercatcher *n* gille-brì(gh)de *m*, trilleachan *f*

P

Pabbay n Pabaigh f

pace n 1 (*stride, step*) ceum m, **we quickened our ~** luathaich sinn ar ceum, **take a ~ forward/back** gabh ceum air adhart/air ais; 2 (*speed*) astar m, **run at a good ~** ruith vi aig deagh astar, **they were going at/making a good ~** bha astar math aca; 3 *in expr* **keep ~** cùm ruith f (**with** ri), **keep ~ with the others** cùm ruith ri càch

pace v ceumnaich vi

Pacific, n the An Cuan Sèimh m

pacify v 1 (*calm etc*) ciùinich vt, sìthich vt, sèimhich vt, socraich vt; 2 (*subdue by force*) ceannsaich vt

pack¹ n paca m, **a ~ of cards** paca chairtean (*fpl gen*)

pack² n (*derog: mob, crowd of people*) gràisg f

pack v 1 (*parcel etc*) paisg vt; 2 *in fam exprs* **~ up/in** (*ie break down*) bris vi, **my radio's ~ed up** tha an rèidio agam briste/air briseadh/air a bhriseadh, **~ in** (*give up*) leig vt dheth (*etc*), **she's ~ing in her job** tha i a' leigeil dhith a h-obrach

package parsail m, pasgadh m, pasgan m

packed adj & past part 1 (*places, buildings, gatherings etc*) loma-làn, dòmhail & dùmhail, **the hall was ~** bha an talla loma-làn; 2 (*objects, woodland, people*) **closely ~** dlùth

packed lunch n pìos m

packet n pacaid f

packing n pasgadh m

pact n còrdadh m

paddle n pleadhag f

paddle v (*~ canoe; also ~ with feet*) pleadhagaich vti

pagan n & adj pàganach m

page n (*of a book etc*) duilleag f, **the Yellow Pages** Na Duilleagan Buidhe, (*esp for ~ numbers*) taobh-duilleig(e) m (*abbrev* d *or* td, *pl* dd *or* tdd), **~ seven** taobh-duilleige a seachd

pail n peile m, bucaid f, (*esp for milking*) cuman m, cuinneag f

pain n (*usu phys*) pian mf, (*mental/emotional or phys*) cràdh m

pain v (*usu phys*) pian vt, (*mentally or emotionally*) cràidh vt, ciùrr vt

pained adj (*emotionally or mentally*) dòrainneach

painful adj (*phys*) goirt, (*emotionally/mentally*) dòrainneach, (*mentally/emotionally or phys*) pianail, crài(dh)teach, **my back's ~** tha mo dhruim m goirt, **a ~ reminder** cuimhneachan cràiteach, **a ~ conversation/interview** agallamh dòrainneach

painstaking adj (*person, work etc*) mion-chùiseach, ro-phongail, ro-mhionaideach

paint n peant(a) m

paint v peant vti

painter n (*artist or tradesman*) peantair m

pair n 1 (*usu used of people*) dithis f, **they came in ~s** thàinig iad nan dithisean, **the ~ of you** an dithis agaibh; 2 *in expr* **~ of twins** càraid f *sing*; 3 (*of objects, creatures*) paidhir mf, **a ~ of gloves** paidhir mhiotagan *fpl gen*, **a ~ of oystercatchers** paidhir thrilleachan (*mpl gen*)

Pakistan n Pagastan f, *gen* Phagastain

pal n companach m, (*less informal*) caraid m

palace n pàileis f, (*more trad*) lùchairt f

palate n càirean m

pale-faced adj glaisneulach

palm¹ n (*of hand*) bas f, bois f, (*less usu*) glac f

palm² n (*the tree*) pailm f, craobh-phailm f

palpitate v (*esp heart*) plosg vi, (*less severe*) plap vi

palpitation n (*esp of heart*) plosg m, plosgadh m, plosgartaich f

pamphlet n leabhrachan m, leabhran m

pan n pana m

pancake n foileag f

pane n lòsan m

panel n pannal m, **a wooden ~** pannal-fiodha, **the Children's Panel** Pannal na Cloinne

pang n guin m

pannier n cliabh m

pant n plosg m

pant *v* plosg *vi*

panting *n* plosg *m*, plosgadh *m*, plosgartaich *f*

pants *n* **1** (*underwear*) drathais & drathars *f invar*; **2** (*trousers*) briogais *f*, triubhas *m*

paper *n* pàipear *m*, **wall~** pàipear-balla *m*, **news~** pàipear-naidheachd *m*

paper-mill *n* muileann-pàipeir *mf*

papist *adj* (*rather derog*) pàpanach

Papist *n* (*rather derog*) Pàpanach *m*

parable *n* cosamhlachd *f*

Paradise *n* Pàrras *m*, flaitheas *m*

paraffin *n* paireafain *m invar*

parallel *adj* co-shìnte, **~ lines** loidhnichean co-shìnte *fpl*

parcel *n* parsail *m*, pasgan *m*

parched *adj* **1** (*of person*) ìotmhor; **2** (*of ground etc*) tioram

pardon *n* mathanas *m*

pardon *v* **1** ma(i)th *vt*, thoir mathanas *m* (*with prep* do); **2** *in exprs* (*as apology*) **~ me!** gabh(aibh) mo leisgeul *m*!, (*on not catching what someone has said*) **~?** b' àill leibh?

parent *n* pàrant *m*

parenthesis *n* eadar-ràdh *m*

parish *n* sgìre *f*, sgìreachd *f*, paraiste *f*

parity *n* ionannachd *f invar*, co-ionannachd *f invar*

park *n* **1** (*recreation, agric etc*) pàirc(e) *f*, **car ~** pàirc-chàraichean *f*; **2** (*site for various activities*) raon *m*, *eg* **business ~** raon gnìomhachais

parliament *n* pàrlamaid *f*

parliamentary *adj* pàrlamaideach

parrot *n* pearraid *f*

part *n* **1** (*a proportion of a whole*) cuid *f*, pàirt *m*, **give me ~ of it** thoir dhomh cuid dheth, **the greater ~ of his life** a' mhòr-chuid de (a) bheatha, **~ of the book was good** bha pàirt den leabhar math; **2** (*section, division*) earrann *f*, **the first ~ of her novel came out** thàinig a' chiad earrann den nobhail aice a-mach; **3** (*portion, share*) cuid *f*, roinn *f*, **my ~ of the world's goods** mo chuid den t-saoghal; **4** (*in dispute etc*) taobh *m*, **she took our ~** ghabh i ar taobh, *also* chaidh i às ar leth; **5** (*misc exprs*) **spare ~s** pàirtean-càraidh *mpl*, **take ~** (*participate*) gabh pàirt, com-pàirtich *vt*, **~s of the body** buill a' chuirp *mpl*, **for my (own) ~ ...** air mo shon fhìn ...

part *v* dealaich *vti* (**from** ri), **death ~ed them** dhealaich am bàs iad, **they ~ed** dhealaich iad ri chèile, **you won't ~ him from his money!** cha dhealaich thu ri a chuid airgid e!

participant *n* com-pàirtiche *m*, (*esp in a competition*) farpaiseach *m*

participate *v* gabh pàirt *m*, gabh com-pàirt *f*, com-pàirtich *vi*

participation *n* com-pàirt *f*

particle *n* **1** mìr *m*, mìrean *m*; **2** (*gram*) mion-fhacal *m*

particular *adj* **1** àraidh, sònraichte, **it's a ~ house/one house in ~ that I want to buy** 's e taigh àraidh a tha mi airson a cheannach, **a ~ sort** seòrsa àraidh/sònraichte; **2** (*of person: precise, attentive to detail*) mion-chùiseach, pongail; **3** *in neg expr* **he's (etc) not ~** (*ie doesn't mind*) is coma leis (*etc*), tha e (*etc*) coma co-dhiù

parting *n* dealachadh *m*

partition *n* pàirteacheadh *m*

partition *v* pàirtich *vt*, roinn *vt*

partner *n* **1** pàirtiche *m*, com-pàirtiche *m*; **2** (*sexual ~*) coimhleapach *mf*, companach *mf*

party *n* **1** pàrtaidh *m*, **a political ~** pàrtaidh poilitigeach, **The Labour/Liberal Democrat/Tory Party** Am Pàrtaidh Làbarach/Libearalach Deamocratach/Tòraidheach, **The Scottish National Party** Pàrtaidh Nàiseanta na h-Alba; **2** (*social gathering*) pàrtaidh *m*, (*more boisterous; fam*) hòro-gheallaidh *m invar*

pass *n* **1** (*topog*) bealach *m*; **2** (*games*) pas *m*; **3** (*document*) cead inntrigidh *m*, pas *m*

pass *v* **1** rach *vi* seachad (*with prep* air), **the train ~ed (me)** chaidh an trèana seachad (orm), **the time ~ed quickly** chaidh an ùine seachad gu luath; **2** (*spend*) cuir *vt* seachad, caith *vt*, **~ time** cuir seachad ùine; **3** (*misc exprs*) **~ away** (*ie die*) caochail *vi*, siubhail *vi*, **~ me the salt** sìn thugam an salann, **~ the biscuits round** cuir timcheall na briosgaidean, **~ into oblivion** rach *vi* air dìochuimhne *f*, **the pain ~ed off** dh'fhalbh am pian *mf*, **~ water** dèan mùn *m*, mùin *vi*, **I noticed it in ~ing** mhothaich mi dha san dol seachad *m*

passage *n* **1** (*in building*) trannsa *f*; **2** (*in book*) earrann *f*; **3** (*through hills*) bealach *m*; **4** (*across river, strait etc*) aiseag *mf*, (*longer, maritime*) turas-mara *m*, **a rough ~** turas(-mara) garbh

passenger *n* neach-siubhail *m* (*pl* luchd-siubhail *m sing coll*)

passionate *adj* (*of person; hot-blooded*) lasanta, (*enthusiastic for a cause etc*) dìoghrasach

passive *adj* fulangach, (*gram*) **the ~ voice** an guth fulangach

passport *n* cead-siubhail *m*, cead dol thairis *m*

past *adj* & *adv* **1** seachad, **all that's ~ now** tha sin uile seachad a-nis, **~ time** an t-àm a chaidh

seachad, *also* an t-àm a dh'fhalbh; **2** *in expr* **he's
~ his best** tha e air a dhol dheth, tha e air a
dhol bhuaithe; **3** *(gram)* caithte, **the ~ tense** an
tràth caithte

past, the *n* an t-àm a chaidh seachad, an t-àm a
dh'fhalbh

paste *n (flour & water)* glaodhan *m*

pastime *n* cur-seachad *m*

pastry *n* pastra *f invar*

pasture *n* clua(i)n *f*, ionaltradh *m*, *(beside water)*
dail *f*, innis *f*

pasture *v* feuraich *vt*

patch *n* **1** *(of material etc)* tuthag *f*, brèid *m*; **2** *in
exprs* **~ of ground** pìos (beag) fearainn, **~ of
fog/mist** bad ceò *m*

Paternoster *n* paidir *f*

path *n* frith-rathad *m*, slighe *f*, {*fig, relig*} **the ~
of righteousness** slighe na fìreantachd

patience *n* foighidinn *f*

patient *adj* foighidneach

patient *n* euslainteach *m*

patron *n* neach-taice *m*, goistidh *m*

patronage *n* taic(e) *f*, goistidheachd *f invar*

patronymic *n* sloinneadh *m*

pattern *n* pàtran *m*

paunch *n* maodal *f*, mionach *m*

pavement *n* cabhsair *m*

pavilion *n* pàillean *m*

paving stone *(for cottage etc floor)* leac-ùrlair *f*,
(for pavement) leac-cabhsair *f*

paw *n* cròg *f*, spòg *f*, màg *f*

paw *v (of persons: handle improperly or
roughly)* (droch-)làimhsich *vt*

pay *n* pàigh *m invar*, pàigheadh *m*, tuarastal *m*, **a
~ rise** àrdachadh pàighidh *m*

pay *v* **1** pàigh *vti*, **~ a bill** pàigh cunntas *m*/
bileag *f*, **he left without ~ing** dh'fhalbh e gun
phàigheadh, **you'll ~ for your sins** pàighidh
tu (airson) do pheacaidhean; **2** *(misc exprs)* **~
attention** thoir an aire (**to** do), thoir fea(i)rt (**to**
air), **~ a compliment** dèan moladh (*with prep*
air), **~ X a visit** rach *vi* air chèilidh air X, dèan
cèilidh air X, tadhail *vi* air X, **~ back** *(fin or in
revenge)* dìoghail & dìol *vt*

payment *n* **1** pàigheadh *m*, dìoladh *m*; **2** *(in
reparation or in return for something: esp a
ransom)* èirig *f*

paypoint *n (in store etc)* àite-pàighidh *m*

pea *n* peasair *f*

peace *n* **1** *(opposite of war)* sìth *f*, **war or ~**
cogadh *m* no sìth, **the ~ dividend** buannachd
na sìthe; **2** *(tranquillity)* fois *f*, sìth *f*, *(esp of the
dead)* **they are at ~** tha iad aig fois, *also* tha iad
nan tàmh; **3** *in expr* **~ of mind** toil-inntinn *f*

peaceful *adj* **1** *(opposite of warlike)* sìtheil; **2**
(calm, tranquil) sàmhach, **a ~ sleep/evening**
cadal/feasgar sàmhach

peach *n* peitseag *f*

peak *n* **1** *(pointed mountaintop)* stùc *f*, binnean
m; **2** *in fig expr* **he's at his ~** tha e ann an treun
f invar a neirt *(gen of* neart *m)*, tha e aig àird a
neirt, tha e aig (a) àird

peal *n* **1** *(of bells)* seirm *f*, bualadh *m*; **2** *in expr* **a
~ of laughter** lasgan gàire *m*

peanut *n* cnò-thalmhainn *f*

pear *n* peur *f*

peasantry *n* tuath *f*

peat *n* **1** *(coll)* mòine *f sing coll*, **~ bog, ~ hag,
~ bank** poll-mòna(ch) *or* poll-mònadh *m*,
~ smoke, *(Sc)* **~ reek** ceò na mòna(ch)/na
mònadh *m*, **they're (working) at the ~(s)**
tha iad aig a' mhòine, **win/cut/gather ~** dèan/
buain mòine; **2** *(a single ~)* fòid *f*, fàd (mònach)
m; **3 ~ iron/spade** tairsgeir *f*

pebble *n* dèideag *f*, molag *f*

peck *v (of birds etc)* pioc *vti*

pedal *n* troighean *m*

pedestrian *n* coisiche *m*

pee *n* mùn *m*, **have a ~** dèan mùn, dèan dileag *f*

pee *v* dèan mùn *m*, mùin *vi*

peel *n* *(of fruit, vegetables etc)* rùsg *m*, plaosg *m*

peel *v (fruit, vegetables etc)* rùisg *vt*, plaoisg *vt*

peeled *adj & past part* rùisgte, **~ potatoes**
buntàta rùisgte *m invar coll*

peer *n* **1** *(~ of the realm)* morair *m*; **2** *(one's
equal)* seise *m*

peevish *adj* fritharra, *(usu of child)* crost(a)

peewit *n* curracag *f*

peg *n* cnag *f*, **clothes ~** cnag-aodaich *f*

pellet *n (ie as projectile)* peilear *m*

pelt *v* **1** tilg *vt*, caith *vt*, *(with prep* air*)*, **they
were ~ing me with eggs** bha iad a' tilgeil
uighean orm; **2** *in expr* **~ with stones** clach *vt*

pen[1] *n (for writing)* peann *m*

pen[2] *n (for livestock)* buaile *f*, *(esp for sheep)* crò
m

penal *adj* peanasach

penalise *v* peanasaich

penalty *n (punishment)* peanas *m*

pencil *n* peansail *m*

penetrate *v* **1** *(make one's way into)* rach *vi*
a-steach, *(more violently)* bris *vi* a-steach, *(with
prep* do*)*; **2** *(break or pierce hole(s) in)* toll *vt*;
3 *(pass or break through defences etc)* thig *vi*,
rach *vi*, *(more violently)* bris *vi*, *(all with prep*
tro, *followed by dat)*; **4** *(esp of water)* drùidh *vi*,
the rain ~ed to my skin dhrùidh an t-uisge
orm

penis n bod m, (fam/vulg) slat f

penny n 1 sgillinn f, (idiom) **I haven't a ~ to my name** chan eil sgillinn ruadh (no geal) agam; 2 (hist) **Scots ~** peighinn f

pension n peinnsean m, **retirement ~** peinnsean-cluaineis m

pensioner n neach-peinnsein m (pl luchd-peinnsein m sing coll), also peinnseanair m

Pentland Firth, the n An Caol Arcach m

people n 1 (human beings in general) daoine (pl of duine m), **many/lots of ~** mòran dhaoine mpl gen; 2 (populace) sluagh m, (esp rural: more trad) tuath f, **unrest among the ~** aimhreit am measg an t-sluaigh; 3 (the ~ of a particular place) muinntir f, poball m, **the ~ of this town(ship)** muinntir a' bhaile seo, **the ~ of Uist, Uist ~** muinntir Uibhist, **the ~ of Ireland, the Irish ~** poball na h-Èireann; 4 (one's relatives, (Sc) folks) càirdean (pl of caraid m), daoine mpl, **my ~ are in Stornoway** tha mo chàirdean/mo dhaoine ann an Steòrnabhagh; 5 (associates, followers, companions) muinntir f, cuideachd f, **he left the country but his ~ didn't go with him** dh'fhàg e an dùthaich ach cha deach a mhuinntir/a chuideachd còmhla ris; 6 (a race, tribe, etc) cinneadh m, **the Eskimo ~** cinneadh nan Easgiomach

pep up v (cooking; also fig) piobraich vt

pepper n piobar m

pepper v piobraich vt

per capita adv an urra f, (do etc) gach pearsa m, **a thousand pounds ~** mìle not(a) an urra

perceive v (visually) faic vt, (visually, mentally) mothaich vt

per cent adv sa cheud m, **four ~** ceithir sa cheud

perception n 1 (the mental faculty or capacity) tuigse f invar, lèirsinn f invar; 2 (sight) fradharc & radharc m, lèirsinn f invar; 3 (idea, view) beachd m, **his ~ of himself** am beachd a bh' aige air fhèin

perceptive adj geurchuiseach, tuigseach, mothachail

perch v (come to rest) laigh vi (**on** air)

perfect adj 1 (not usu in moral sense) coileanta, (gram) **the ~ tense** an tràth coileanta; 2 (esp morally) foirfe; 3 (fam, loosely: expr approval etc) taghta!, **that's ~!** tha sin taghta!

perfection n coileantachd f invar, (esp in moral sense) foirfeachd f invar

perforate v toll vt

perform v 1 (carry out, fulfil) coilean vt, thoir vt gu buil f, **~ a task** coilean gnìomh, coilean pìos obrach (gen of obair f); 2 (theatre, cinema) cluich vi, cleasaich vi, **~ in a play** cluich ann an

dealbh-chluich, (in orchestra, band etc) cluich vi; 3 (~ song, music etc) gabh vt, **~ a song** gabh òran; 4 (acquit oneself) **he ~ed well** 's math a rinn e

performance n (fulfilment of task etc) coileanadh m, toirt f invar gu buil

perfume n cùbhrachd f invar

perhaps adv & conj 1 is/'s dòcha, (is) ma(th) dh'fhaodte (also is mathaid), theagamh, **it'll be a fine day,** ~ bidh là brèagha ann, 's dòcha/ma dh'fhaodte; 2 (as conj) is/'s dòcha, (is) ma(th) dh'fhaodte, theagamh, faodaidh, (all followed by conjs gun/gum, nach etc), **~ he'll come tomorrow** 's dòcha gun tig e a-màireach, **~ it won't snow** math dh'fhaodte nach cuir i, **~ he's ill** faodaidh gu bheil e tinn, **~ she won't come** theagamh nach tig i

peril n gàbhadh m, (usu less strong) cunnart m, **in ~** ann an gàbhadh

perilous adj gàbhaidh, (usu less strong) cunnartach

period n 1 (of time) greis f, treis f, **he spent a ~ of time in Australia** chuir e seachad greis/treis ann an Astràilia; 2 (school lesson) tràth (-teagaisg) m; 3 (menstrual ~) fuil-mìosa f

periodical n iris f, (esp a quarterly) ràitheachan m

peripheral adj iomallach, **~ areas/districts** ceàrnaidhean iomallach

periphery n iomall m

permanent adj maireannach, buan

permeable adj so-dhrùidhteach

permissible adj ceadaichte

permission n cead m invar, **with your ~** le ur cead, **I gave them ~ to leave** thug mi cead dhaibh falbh, **planning ~** cead-dealbhaidh

permissive adj ceadachail

permit n cead m invar

permit v leig vi (with prep le or do), ceadaich vt, **he ~ted me to buy it** leig e leam a cheannach, **~ new development in the town centre** ceadaich leasachadh ùr ann am meadhan a' bhaile

permitted adj & past part ceadaichte

perplex v cuir vt an imcheist f

perplexed adj an/fo imcheist f, imcheisteach

perplexing adj imcheisteach

perplexity n imcheist f

persevere v cùm vi (with prep ri), lean vi (with prep air), **~!** cùm ris!, **she ~d** lean i oirre

persevering adj leantainneach

persistent adj 1 (of persons: tenacious etc) gramail & greimeil; 2 (of situations etc: long-lasting) leanailteach

person n (*regardless of gender*) neach m *invar*, (*less usu*) pearsa m, duine m (*see esp Gaelic-English section*, **duine 3**)

personal adj pearsanta

personality n pearsantachd f *invar*

personnel n sgiobachd f *invar*, luchd-obrach m sing coll

perspiration n fallas m

perspire v bi vi irreg fallas m (*with prep* air), cuir fallas (*with prep* de), bi vi irreg na (*etc*) f(h)allas, **I'm perspiring** tha fallas orm, tha mi a' cur fallas dhìom, tha mi nam fhallas

persuade v cuir ìmpidh f (*with prep* air), iompaich vt, **they ~d me to give up my job/ to retire** chuir iad ìmpidh orm mo dhreuchd a leigeil dhìom

persuasion n ìmpidh f

persuasive adj ìmpidheach

perverse adj **1** (*obstinate*) rag, dùr, (*stronger*) rag-mhuinealach; **2** (*morally ~*) claon

perversion n claonadh m

perversity n (*obstinacy*) raige f *invar*

pervert v **1** (*~ persons*) truaill vt, claon vt; **2** (*~ justice etc*) claon vt

pest n (*rodent etc; also fig, inconvenience etc*) plàigh f

pestiferous adj plàigheil

pestilence n plàigh f

pestilential adj plàigheil

pet n peata m

peter out v sìolaidh vi às

petition n tagradh m

petrol n peatroil & peatrail m

petticoat n còta-bàn m

petty adj **1** (*on small scale*) mion- prefix, **~ theft** mion-bhraide f; **2** (*small-minded etc*) crìon, suarach

pharmacist n neach-chungaidhean m

pharmacy n **1** (*the premises*) bùth-chungaidh(ean) f; **2** (*knowledge, profession of ~*) eòlas leigheasan m, eòlas chungaidhean m

pheasant n easag f

phenomenal adj iongantach

phenomenon n **1** (*science & philo*) sìon m; **2** (*amazing thing*) iongantas m, mìorbhail f, (*less usu*) suaicheantas m

philosopher n feallsanach m

philosophy n feallsanachd f

phlegm n ronn m

phone n fòn mf, **I was talking to him on the ~** bha mi a' bruidhinn ris air a' fòn, **what's your ~ number?** dè an àireamh-fòn a th' agad?

phone v cuir fòn mf, fòn vi, fònaig vi, (*all with prep* gu), **he ~d her** chuir e fòn thuice, dh'fhòn(aig) e thuice

photograph n dealbh mf, **take a ~** tog dealbh

physical adj corporra

physique n dèanamh m

piano n piàna & piàno m

pibroch n ceòl-mòr m, (*loosely*) pìobaireachd f *invar*

pick[1] n (*the tool*) pic m, piocaid f

pick[2] n (*choice*) roghainn f, **you'll get your ~ of it** gheibh thu do roghainn dheth

pick v **1** (*select*) tagh vt, roghnaich vt; **2** (*~ flowers etc*) cruinnich vt; **3** (*~ at food*) pioc vi, creim vi; **4** **~ up** tog vt, (*also fig*) **I ~ed up my Gaelic in Skye** (*emph*) 's ann san Eilean Sgitheanach a thog mi mo chuid Gàidhlig

pickaxe n pic m, piocaid f

pickle n picil f

picnic n cuirm-chnuic f

Pict n Cruithneach m

Pictish adj Cruithneach

picture n dealbh mf

picture v dealbh vt

piece n **1** (*bit, particle*) criomag f, bloigh f, (*smaller*) mìr m, **falling to ~s** a' dol/a' tuiteam na (*etc*) c(h)riomagan; **2** (*component part*) pìos m, earrann f; **3** (*Sc, sandwich*) pìos m; **4** (*misc exprs*) **they arrived in one ~** ràinig iad slàn is fallain, **bits and ~s** trealaich f sing coll

pierce v toll vt

piercing n tolladh m, **ear ~** tolladh-chluasan m

piety n cràbhadh m, diadhachd f *invar*

pig n muc f

pigeon n calman m

piggy-back n (*a ~ ride*) gioma-goc m

pig-headed adj rag-mhuinealach

piglet n uircean & oircean m

pigsty n fail-mhuc f

pigtail n figheachan m

pile n cruach f, tòrr m, dùn m, (*smaller*) cruachan m

pile, pile up v càrn vt, cruach vt

pilfer v dèan mion-bhraide f

pilfering n mion-bhraide f

pilgrim n taistealach m

pilgrimage n taisteal f

pill n pile f

pillar n **1** (*architecture etc*) colbh m; **2** (*~ of rock*) carragh f

pillion n pillean m

pillow n cluasag f

pilot n pìleat & paidhleat m

pimple n plucan m, guirean m

pin *n* prìne *m*, (*less usu*) dealg *f*

pincers *n* (*pair of* ~) teanchair & teannachair *m* sing

pinch *n* (*with fingers, nails*) gòmag *f*, pioc *m*

pinch *v* 1 (*with fingernails etc*) pioc *vt*; 2 (*steal*) goid *vti*, dèan braid *f*

pinching *n* 1 (*with fingernails etc*) piocadh *m*; 2 (*stealing*) goid *f*, braid *f*

pine *n* giuthas *m*, *in exprs* ~ wood/forest giùthsach *f*, ~ cone durcan *m*

pinhead *n* ploc-prìne *m*

pink *adj* pinc

pink *n* pinc *m*

pinkie (*Sc*) *n* lùdag *f*

pinnacle *n* binnean *m*

pins and needles an cadal-deilgneach *m*

pint *n* (*liquid measure, also* ~ *of beer, lager etc*) pinnt *m*

pipe *n* 1 pìob *f*, feadan *m*, water ~s pìoban-uisge, exhaust ~ pìob-thraoghaidh *f*; 2 (*for smoking*) pìob(-thombaca); 3 (*musical instrument*) cuisle *f*, cuislean *m*; 4 (*bag*~) pìob *f*, (*Highland bag*~) pìob mhòr, (*usu with art*) a' phìob mhòr, (bag)~ music ceòl na pìoba *m*

piper *n* pìobaire *m*

piping *n* (*the music & the performance*) pìobaireachd *f invar*

piss *n* mùn *m*

piss *v* dèan mùn *m*, mùin *vi*, (*involuntarily*) caill mùn, I almost ~ed myself theab mi mo mhùn a chall

pistol *n* daga & dag *m*

pit *n* 1 (*topog etc, a hollow*) lag *mf*, glac *f*, sloc *m*; 2 (*for potatoes etc*) sloc *m*; 3 (*mining*) mèinn(e) *f*

pitch[1] *n* (*tar*) bìth *f*, tèarr & teàrr *f*

pitch[2] *n* (*for football etc*) raon-cluiche *m*

pitch[3] *n* (*musical* ~) àirde (san sgàla) *f*

pitch *v* 1 (*throw*) tilg, (*esp carelessly*) sad *vt*; 2 (*movement of seas, ship, trees etc*) tulg *vi*

pitch-fork *n* gòbhlag *f*

piteous *adj* truagh, (*more pej*) suarach

pith *n* glaodhan *m*

pitiable, pitiful *adj* truagh, (*more pej*) suarach, *in expr* ~ person/creature truaghan *m*

pitiless *adj* neo-thruacanta, an-iochdmhor

pity *n* 1 iochd *f invar*, truas *m*, truacantas *m*, won't you take ~ on me? nach gabh thu truas dhìom/rium?; 2 *in expr* that's a ~! tha sin duilich!, (*more trad*) is duilich sin!, is truagh sin!, *also* (*idiom*) b' olc an airidh (e)!

pitying *adj* truasail

place *n* 1 (*general*) àite *m*, a bonny ~ àite brèagha, in its proper ~ na (h-)àite fhèin, in ~ of strife an àite strì, take ~ gabh àite, *also* tachair *vi*; 2 (*esp* ~ *where a particular activity etc is carried out*) ionad *m*, ~ of work ionad-oibre/obrach (*gen of* obair *f*), ~ of worship ionad-adhraidh

place *v* cuir *vt*, (*more carefully or elaborately*) socraich *vt*, suidhich *vt*, she ~d the book on the table chuir i an leabhar air a' bhòrd, ~ a bet cuir geall (on air), ~ a statue on a column socraich/suidhich ìomhaigh air colbh

placename *n* ainm àite *m*

plague *n* plàigh *f*, a ~ of mice plàigh de luchan

plague *v* (*exasperate*) leamhaich *vt*, sàraich *vt*

plaid *n* 1 (*esp the material & pattern*) breacan *m*; 2 (~ *blanket*) plaide *f*

plain *adj* 1 (*evident*) soilleir, follaiseach, (*more trad*) lèir, it was ~ to him that he was lost bha e soilleir/follaiseach dha gun robh e air chall, (*more trad*) bu lèir dha gun robh e air chall; 2 (*of things, situations: uncomplicated*) sìmplidh, aon-fhillte; 3 (*unpretentious*) sìmplidh, lom

plain *n* (*topog*) còmhnard *m*, machair *mf*

plaintive *adj* tiamhaidh

plait *n* dual *m*, filleadh *m*

plait *v* (*hair, rope etc*) dualaich *vt*, fill *vt*

plaited *adj & past part* fillte

plan *n* 1 (*intention; also map, diagram etc*) plana *m*; 2 (*strategy, stratagem*) innleachd *f*; 3 (*technical drawing*) dealbh-chumadh *m*

plan *v* 1 (*general*) planaig *vti*; 2 (~ *technical & artistic objects*) dealbh & deilbh *vt*; 3 (~ *a strategy, stratagem*) innlich *vt*

plane[1] *n* (*carpentry*) locair *f*, locar *m*

plane[2] *n* (*aircraft*) plèana *mf*, itealan *m*

plane[3] *n* (*geometry etc*) raon *m*

plane *v* locair *vti*

planet *n* planaid *f*

plank *n* dèile *f*, clàr *m*

planner *n* neach-dealbhaidh *m* (*pl* luchd-dealbhaidh *m sing coll*)

planning *n* dealbhadh *m*, planaigeadh *m*, ~ permission cead dealbhaidh *m*

plant[1] *n* (*botanical*) luibh *mf*, lus *m*

plant[2] *n* (*manufacturing etc*) 1 (*equipment etc*) uidheam *f*; 2 (*the premises*) factaraidh *f*

plant *v* cuir *vt*, ~ potatoes cuir buntàta

plaster *n* 1 (*for building etc*) sglàib *f invar*; 2 (*sticking* ~) plàsd & plàst *m*

plastic *n & adj* plastaig *f*

plate *n* 1 (*tableware*) truinnsear *m*; 2 (*metal etc* ~) lann *f*

platform *n* 1 (*in concert hall etc*) àrd-ùrlar *m*; 2 (*railway etc*) àrd-chabhsair *m*, còmhnard *m*; 3 (*oil industry*) clàr *m*, drilling ~ clàr-tollaidh *m*

platter n mias f

plausible adj (can imply 'smooth-talking') beulach, beulchair

play n 1 (the activity) cluich & cluiche m, (esp of children: less usu) cleas m; 2 (more con: stage ~) dealbh-chluich mf

play v 1 cluich vti, ~ **football/rugby** cluich ball-coise/rugbaidh, ~ **Rangers** cluich (an aghaidh) Rangers, ~ **Hamlet on the stage** cluich Hamlet air an àrd-ùrlar, ~ **the accordeon** cluich (air) a' bhogsa, ~ **a tune on the accordeon** gabh port air a' bhogsa; 2 in expr ~ **shinty** iomain vi, **they were ~ing shinty** bha iad ag iomain

player n (stage, games, music) cluicheadair m

playground n raon-cluiche m

playgroup n cròileagan m

playing n cluich & cluiche m, (esp of children: less usu) cleas m

plea n 1 (request) guidhe mf; 2 (law) tagradh m, tagairt f

plead v 1 guidh vi (**with** air), **he ~ed with us to let him go/set him free** ghuidh e oirnn a leigeil mu sgaoil; 2 (in court of law) tagair vti

pleasant adj (of people, also things, situations) tlachdmhor, taitneach (**to, for** ri), (esp of people) ciatach

pleasantness n taitneas m

please v 1 (content, give pleasure) còrd vi (with prep ri), toilich vt, riaraich vt, taitinn vi (with prep ri), **it ~d me** chòrd e rium; 2 (wish, prefer) togair vi, usu in expr mar a thogras (rel fut) tu/sibh, **black or white, (just) as you** ~ dubh no geal, (dìreach) mar a thogras sibh; 3 (polite request) mas e do thoil f/ur toil e, ~ **close the door** dùin an doras, mas e do thoil e

pleased adj & past part 1 (satisfied, content) toilichte, riaraichte, air a (etc) d(h)òigh f, air a d(h)eagh dhòigh, **I'm ~ to be here**, tha mi toilichte a bhith ann, **Murdo was very ~ (with himself)** bha Murchadh air a dheagh dhòigh; 2 (proud, approving) moiteil (**with** à), **we're ~ with you** tha sinn moiteil asad

pleasing adj 1 (of persons, also things, situations) tlachdmhor, taitneach, (**to** ri); 2 in expr **I find that** ~ is toigh leam sin, tha sin a' còrdadh rium

pleasurable adj tlachdmhor

pleasure n 1 tlachd f invar, taitneas m, toileachadh m; 2 (esp mental ~) toil-inntinn f, toileachas-inntinn m

pleat n filleadh m

pleat v fill vt

pleated adj & past part fillte

pledge n gealladh m, (less usu in this sense) geall m

pledge v geall vti, thoir gealladh m, rach vi an geall m

Pleiades, the n An Grioglachan m sing

plentiful adj pailt, lìonmhor

plenty n 1 (ample sufficiency, superfluity) pailteas m, **the land of** ~ tìr mf a' phailteis; 2 in expr ~ **of** gu leòr, **we've got** ~ **of time** tha ùine gu leòr againn, **there are** ~ **of people around who think that (way)** tha gu leòr ann/tha daoine gu leòr ann a tha den bheachd sin

pliable adj sùbailte, so-lùbte, so-lùbadh

pliant adj lùbach

pliers npl greimire m

plop n plub m

plop v plubraich vi, plub vi

plot¹ n 1 (conspiracy, stratagem) cuilbheart f, innleachd f; 2 (Lit) sgeul m, **the ~ of her novel** sgeul na nobhail aice

plot² n 1 (~ of ground) pìos fearainn m, pìos-talmhainn m; 2 (flower etc bed) ceapach mf

plot v innlich vt, dèan co-fheall m (**against** an aghaidh with gen), ~ **an uprising** innlich ar-a-mach, ~ **against the government** dèan co-fheall an aghaidh an riaghaltais

plough n 1 (agric) crann m; 2 (astronomy) **The Plough** An Crann-arain

plough v treabh vti

ploughing n treabhadh m

plover n feadag f, **green** ~ curracag f

ploy n 1 (activity, escapade) plòidh f; 2 (stratagem, tactic) innleachd f

pluck n (courage etc) smior m, misneach(d) f

pluck v (flower, harpstring etc) spìon vt

plug n (for sink, container etc) cnag f, (for sink, container, powerpoint etc) plucan m, (electric ~) cnag-dealain f

plumage n iteach m

plumber n plumair m

plunder n cobhartach mf, (trad: esp cattle) creach f

plunder v creach vti, spùill & spùinn vti

plunge n (into liquid) tumadh m

plunge v (into liquid) tum vt

plural adj (gram) iolra, ~ **noun** ainmear iolra m

plural n (gram) iolra m

Pluto n (planet) Pluta m invar

pm adv feasgar, **seven** ~ seachd uairean feasgar

poacher n poitsear m

pocket n pòcaid f, ~-**money** airgead-pòcaid m

pod n (of peas & beans etc) plaosg m

pod v (vegetables etc) plaoisg & plaosg vt

poem n dàn m, duan m, laoidh mf, pìos bàrdachd m

poet n bàrd m, filidh m

poetic adj bàrdail

poetry n bàrdachd f invar, rann m, (less usu) dànachd f invar

poignant adj tiamhaidh

point n **1** (of pencil, pin etc) bior m, gob m, rinn m; **2** (topog: promontory) àird f, rubha m, sròn f, rinn m; **3** (in a scale, series etc, also in an argument etc) puing f, ~ **of balance** puing-chothromachaidh f; **4** (the ~ at issue) ceist f, cùis f, rud m, **that's not the ~!** chan e sin a' cheist/a' chùis!, chan e sin an rud!, (note also the idiom) **you made me wander from the ~** chuir thu às mo ghabhail mf mi; **5** (misc exprs) **at/on the ~ of death** ri uchd m a' bhàis, **on the ~ of** gu(s), **we're on the ~ of leaving** tha sinn gu falbh, **on the ~ of losing my mind** gus mo chiall a chall, ~ **of view** (ie opinion) barail f, beachd m, ~ **of view** (ie perspective: lit & fig) sealladh m, **from the ~ of view of the old folks** bho shealladh nan seann daoine, ~**s of the compass** àirdean fpl, (usu with art) na h-àirdean

point v **1** (with finger etc) tomh vi (**at** ri); **2** in expr ~ **out** sònraich vt

pointed adj **1** (sharp) biorach; **2** (of speech etc: to the point) pongail

pointless adj dìomhain, faoin, gun fheum m, ~ **pastimes** cur-seachadan dìomhain

poison n puinnsean m, nimh & neimh m

poison v puinnseanaich vt

poisonous adj (lit) puinnseanach, (lit & fig) nimheil

poke v brodaich vt

poker n pòcair m

Poland n (used with art) A' Phòlainn f invar

polar bear n mathan-bàn m

pole n **1** (joinery etc) cabar m, pòla m; **2** (geog) pòla m, **the north/south ~** Am Pòla a Tuath/a Deas; **3** in expr **the ~ star** an reul-iùil f

Pole n Pòlach m

police n poileas m, **a ~ car** càr-poileis m

policeman n poileasman m, poileas m

policewoman n ban-phoileas f

policing n obair poileis f

policy n (government, insurance etc) poileasaidh m

Polish adj Pòlach

polish n lìomh f

polish v lìomh vt

polished adj lìomharra

polite adj modhail, cùirteil

politeness n modhalachd f invar

political adj poilitigeach, ~ **asylum** tèarmann poilitigeach m

politician n neach-poilitigs m (pl luchd-poilitigs m sing coll)

politics n poilitigs f invar

poll n **1** (election, vote) taghadh m; **2** (head) ceann m, (hist) ~ **tax** cìs-chinn f

pollutant n stuth-truaillidh m

pollute v (environment etc) truaill vt, salaich vt

polluted adj & past part truaillte

pollution n truailleadh m

poly- prefix ioma-

polygamy n ioma-phòsadh m

polyglot adj ioma-chànanach

polygon n ioma-cheàrnag f

pompous adj mòrchuiseach

pond n lochan m, lòn m, glumag f

ponder v cnuas & cnuasaich, meòraich & meamhraich vi, (more rigorously) beachd-smaoin(t)ich vi, (**about**, **upon** air)

ponderous adj **1** (heavy) trom; **2** (lumbering etc) slaodach

pony n pònaidh m

pony-tail n (on head) figheachan m

pool n lòn m, glumag f, (esp below a waterfall) linne f

poor adj **1** (indigent) bochd; **2** (unfortunate) truagh, bochd, (excl) ~ **man/fellow/creature!** a thruaghain!, a dhuine bhochd!; **3** (of ~ quality, inadequate) droch (precedes the noun, which it lenites where possible), suarach, ~ **weather** droch aimsir, droch shìde, **in a ~ state** ann an droch staid, **it was pretty ~** cha robh e ach suarach

poor n (indigent), **the ~** am bochd m sing coll, na daoine bochda mpl, na daoine uireasbhach

poorly adv **1** gu dona, **they did ~** 's ann gu dona a rinn iad, also cha do rinn iad ro mhath idir, **they fared ~** 's ann gu dona a chaidh dhaibh, also cha deach dhaibh ro mhath idir; **2** (unwell) **he's ~** tha e (gu math) bochd

Pope n Pàpa m, usu with art, Am Pàpa

popish adj (not PC) pàpanach

populace n sluagh m, muinntir f, poball m

popular adj **1** mòr-chòrdte; **2** (pertaining to the people) poibleach

population n **1** (con: the people themselves) sluagh m, muinntir f, poball m; **2** (more abstr: the people as a statistic) àireamh-sluaigh f

pork n feòil-muice f, muic-fheòil f

porpoise n pèileag f

porridge n lite f invar, brochan m

port[1] *m* **1** (*harbour etc*) port *m*; **2** (*a conurbation with a* ~) baile-puirt *m*, **Glasgow is a** ~ 's e baile-puirt a th' ann an Glaschu

port[2] *n* (*wine*) fìon-poirt *m*

portable *adj* so-ghiùlan

porter *n* **1** portair *m*; **2** (*doorkeeper*) dorsair *m*

portion *n* cuid *f*, cuibhreann *mf*, roinn *f*

portray *v* **1** (*on stage etc*) riochdaich *vt*; **2** (*in painting, drawing etc*) dealbh *vt*, tarraing *vt*

portrayal *n* **1** (*on stage, screen*) riochdachadh *m*; **2** (*in painting, drawing etc*) dealbhadh *m*, tarraing *f*

Portugal *n*, *used with art*, A' Phortagail *f*

Portuguese *n & adj* Portagaileach *m*

position *n* **1** (*job*) oifis *f*, dreuchd *f*; **2** (*phys, economic etc*) suidheachadh *m*, **the family was in a difficult** ~ bha an teaghlach ann an suidheachadh doirbh

possession(s) *n* **1** seilbh *f*, maoin *f*; **2** (*idiom*) **my worldly ~s** mo chuid den t-saoghal

possessive *adj* seilbheach

possessor *n* seilbheadair & sealbhadair *m*

possible *adj* **1** ion-dhèanta; **2** *commonly expr by* gabh *vi*, **is that ~? no!** an gabh sin a dhèanamh? cha ghabh!, **as hot as** ~ cho teth 's a ghabhas

post[1] *n* (*mail*) post *m*, **the Post Office** Oifis *f* a' Phuist

post[2] **1** (*wooden* ~) post *m*, (*fence* ~) stob *m*; **2** (*idiom*) **he's as deaf as a** ~ cha chluinn e bid *m*/bìog *f*

post- *prefix* iar-, *eg* **post-graduate** iar-cheumnaiche *m*

postal *adj* tron phost, ~ **vote** bhòt *f* tron phost

postcard *n* cairt-phuist *f*

postcode *n* còd puist *m*

postie, postman *n* post(a) *m*, **Alec the** ~ Ailig Post

postpone *v* cuir *vt* dheth, cuir *vt* air an ath là *m*, cuir *vt* air ais

postscript *n* fo-sgrìobhadh *m*

posture *n* giùlan *m*

pot *n* poit *f*, **flower~** poit-fhlùran, **tea-pot** poit-tì *f invar*

potato, potatoes *n & npl* buntàta *m invar sing & coll*, **plant potatoes** cuir buntàta, **potato blight** cnàmh *m*, gaiseadh a' bhuntàta *m*

poteen *n* poitean *m*

potent *adj* **1** (*of ruler etc*) cumhachdach; **2** (*of drink etc*) làidir; **3** (*of remedy, course of action*) èifeachdach, buadhmhor

potential *n* comas *m* (*with gen*), ~ **for growth** comas-fàis *m*

potter *n* crèadhadair *m*

pottery *n* crèadhadaireachd *f invar*

pound[1] *n* **1** (*Scots & Eng money*) not(a) *m*, (*formerly*) **Irish** ~ punnd Èireannach *m*; **2** (*weight*) punnd *m*

pound[2] *n* (*for holding animals etc*) punnd *m*

pound *v* pronn

pounded *adj* pronn

pounding *n* pronnadh *m*

pour *v* **1** dòirt *vti*, sil *vti*, ruith *vti*, **water ~ing through the roof** uisge a' dòrtadh/a' sileadh tron mhullach; **2** (~ *with rain*) sil *vi*, **it's ~ing** tha e a' sileadh

powder *n* pùdar & fùdar *m*, *in expr* **reduce to** ~ pùdaraich *vt*

powder *v* pùdaraich & fùdaraich *vt*, cuir pùdar/fùdar *m* (*with prep* air)

power *n* **1** (*might: military etc*) cumhachd *mf invar*, neart *m*, **the** ~ **of the Roman Empire** cumhachd/neart Ìompaireachd na Ròimhe; **2** (*pol & social* ~) cumhachd *mf invar*, ùghdarras *m*, smachd *m invar*, reachd *m invar*; **3** (*individual's vigour etc*) neart *m*, **he was at the height of his ~s** bha e ann an treun a neirt, *also* bha e aig àird a neirt; **4** (*electric* ~) cumhachd *mf invar*, dealan *m*, **the ~'s off** tha an cumhachd/an dealan dheth; **5** (*capacity, capability*) comas *m*, ~ **of speech** comas-bruidhne (*gen of* bruidhinn *f*), **intellectual ~s** comas-inntinn *f*, **that's beyond my ~s** tha sin thar mo chomais/mo chomasan; **6** *in expr* **the** ~ **of movement/motion** lùth *m*

powerful *adj* **1** (*phys*) làidir, neartmhor, lùthmhor; **2** (*pol, militarily*) cumhachdach

practicable *adj* ion-dhèanta, a ghabhas dèanamh

practically *adv* an ìre mhath, **the winter's ~ over** tha an geamhradh an ìre mhath seachad

practice *n* **1** (*music etc*) cleachdadh *m*, ~ **makes perfect** is e an cleachdadh a nì teòma; **2** (*habit, custom*) cleachdadh *m*, àbhaist *f*, **it was my ~ to swim every day** bha e na chleachdadh agam a bhith a' snàmh a h-uile là

praise *n* moladh *m*, luaidh *m invar*

praise *v* mol *vt*, luaidh *vt*, dèan moladh *m*, dèan luaidh *f*, (*both with prep* air)

praiseworthy *adj* ionmholta

prattle *n* goileam *m*, gobaireachd & gabaireachd *f invar*

prattling *adj* gobach

pray *v* **1** (*beseech etc*) guidh *vi* (*with prep* air); **2** (*relig*) dèan ùrnaigh *f* (**to** ri)

prayer *n* **1** (*entreaty*) guidhe *mf*; **2** (*relig*) ùrnaigh *f*, (*less usu*) guidhe *mf*, **the Lord's** ~ Ùrnaigh an Tighearna, **a** ~ **meeting** coinneamh-ùrnaigh *f*

pre- *prefix* ro-, *also* roi(mh)-, *see examples below*

preamble *n* ro-ràdh *m*

precarious *adj* **1** (*unreliable, shaky, 'dodgy'*) cugallach, **the world is (a) ~ (place)** (*trad*) is cugallach an saoghal; **2** (*risky*) cunnartach

precious *adj* **1** luachmhor, prìseil; **2** *in expr* **~ stone** clach uasal *f*; **3** *excl* **(my) ~!** m' ulaidh!, m' eudail!

precipice *n* bearradh *m*, stalla *m*

precipitate *adj* **1** (*of actions etc*) cabhagach, bras; **2** (*of stream, hillslope*) cas, (*of stream*) bras

precipitation *n* (*of liquids*) sileadh *m*

précis *n* geàrr-chunntas *m*

precise *adj* **1** (*of person, description etc*) pongail, mionaideach; **2** (*of figures etc: accurate*) grinn, pongail

precision *n* (*accuracy*) pongalachd *f invar*

precocious *adj* luathaireach

predator *n* sealgair *m*

predestination *n* ro-òrdachadh *m*

predicament *n* **1** (*difficult situation*) càs *m*, cùil-chumhang *f*, **grave/extreme ~** cruaidh-chàs *m*; **2** (*state of indecision*) ioma(dh)-chomhairle *f*, imcheist *f*, **in a ~** ann an ioma-chomhairle, an/fo imcheist

predict *v* ro-innis *vt*

predictable *adj* ro-innseach

preface *n* ro-ràdh *m*

prefer *v* is *v irreg def* (*in past & conditional tenses* b'), *followed by* fheàrr (*lenited comp adj of* math), *with* le, **I ~ meat** 's fheàrr leam feòil, **they would ~ cheese** b' fheàrr leotha càise

preference *n* roghainn *mf*, **my own ~ in music** mo roghainn fhìn de cheòl

prefix (*gram*) *n* ro-leasachan *m*

pregnancy *n* leatrom *m*

pregnant *adj* torrach, trom

prejudice *n* claon-bhàidh *f*, claon-bhreith *f*

prejudice *v* (*~ someone's situation etc*) dèan dochann, dèan cron, (*both with prep* air)

premature *adj* **1** ron àm *m*, ron mhithich *f invar*; **2** (*esp of a birth*) an-abaich

prematurely *adv* ron àm *m*, ron mhithich *f invar*

Premier *n* (*pol*) prìomhaire *m*

Premier League, the *n* (*football*) a' Phrìomh Lìog *f*

preoccupation *n* cùram *m*

preoccupied *adj* **1** (*through anxiety*) fo chùram *m*; **2** (*having one's thoughts or attention elsewhere*) fad' às

preparation *n* deasachadh *m*, uidheamachadh *m*, ullachadh *m*

prepare *v* **1** deasaich *vt*, ullaich *vt*, **~ food/a meal** deasaich biadh, **they were preparing themselves for war** bha iad gan deasachadh fhèin airson cogaidh; **2** (*by adjusting, tuning etc*) gleus *vt*; **3** (*by equipping, fitting out etc*) uidheamaich *vt*

prepared *adj & past part* **1** deiseil, ullamh, deas, **is the dinner ~?** a bheil am biadh deiseil/ullamh?; **2** (*engine, equipment etc*) air ghleus *mf*; **3** (*equipped, fitted out etc*) uidheamaichte; **4** (*willing*) deònach, **they're not ~ to do it** chan eil iad deònach (air) a dhèanamh

pre-payment *n* ro-phàigheadh *m*

preponderance *n* tromalach *f*

preposition *n* (*gram*) roimhear *m*

Presbyterian *n & adj* Clèireach *m*

Presbyterianism *n* Clèireachd *f invar*

Presbytery *n* Clèir *f*

pre-school *adj* fo-sgoile, **~ education** foghlam fo-sgoile *m*

prescribe *v* òrdaich *vt*

prescription *n* (*med*) òrdugh cungaidh *m*

pre-selection *n* ro-thaghadh *m*

presence *n* **1** làthair *f*, **(get) out of my ~!** a-mach às mo làthair!; **2** (*abstr, the fact of being present*) làthaireachd *f invar*

present *adj* **1** an làthair *f*, ann *adv*, **I knew those who were ~** bha mi eòlach air na bha an làthair/na bha ann; **2** (*current, contemporary etc*) *in exprs* **(at) the ~ time** (aig) an àm *m* seo, (*more immediate*) **I can't help you at the ~ time** chan urrainn dhomh ur cuideachadh an-dràsta, **the ~ situation** an suidheachadh sa bheil sinn a-nis/aig an àm seo, **the ~ government** riaghaltas an latha (an-diugh)

present¹ *n* tiodhlac *m*, gibht *f*

present² *n* (*ie the ~ time*) *in exprs* **the ~** an t-àm a tha an làthair, **at ~** aig an àm seo, a-nis, (*more immediate*) an-dràsta, (*more general: these days etc*) san latha an-diugh *m*

present *v* **1** (*products, techniques etc*) taisbean & taisbein *vt*; **2** (*as gift*) thoir (seachad) *vt*, tiodhlaic *vt*, (**to** do)

presentation *n* **1** (*~ of products, techniques etc*) taisbeanadh *m*; **2** (*formal ~ to official, retiree etc*) tabhartas *m*

preserve *v* glèidh *vt*, **God will ~ us** gleidhidh Dia sinn

preserved *adj & past part* glèidhte

president *n* (*of firm, company, country*) ceann-suidhe *m*

press *n* **1** (*printing ~, also publishing house*) clò *m*, **hot off the ~es** ùr on chlò, **the Ostaig ~**

Clò Ostaig; **2** *in expr* **the** ~ (*published media in general*) na pàipearan(-naidheachd) *mpl*

press *v* **1** (*phys: squeeze, compress*) fàisg *vt*, teannaich *vt*; **2** (*urge*) coitich *vt*, brosnaich *vt*; **3** (*cause to hurry*) cuir cabhag *f* (*with prep* air), greas *vt*

pressing *adj* (*ie urgent*) cabhagach, èiginneach, cudromach

pressure *n* **1** (*phys*) cudthrom, cudrom & cuideam *m*, **atmospheric** ~ cudthrom an àile; **2** (*psych: stress etc*) uallach *m*, **under** ~ fo uallach

pretend *v* **1** leig *vi* (*with prep* air), **the soldiers ~ed that they were civilians** leig na saighdearan *mpl* orra gun robh iad nan sìobhaltairean *mpl*; **2** (*esp kidding, joking*) *in expr* **I** (*etc*) **was only ~ing** cha robh mi (*etc*) ach mas fhìor

pretext *n* leisgeul *m*

pretty *adj* grinn, bòidheach, ceanalta

pretty *adv* gu math, an ìre mhath, ~ **old** gu math aosta, **we were** ~ **tired** bha sinn gu math sgìth/ an ìre mhath sgìth, **the winter's** ~ **well over** tha an geamhradh an ìre mhath seachad

prevent *v* bac *vt*, cuir bacadh *m* (*with prep* air), caisg *vt*, cuir casg *m* (*with prep* air)

prevention *n* casg *m*, casgadh *m*

preventive *adj* casgach

prey *n* cobhartach *mf*, creach *f*

price *n* prìs *f*, **high ~s** prìsean àrda, **buy at a good** ~ ceannaich *vti* air deagh phrìs

prick *v* cuir bior *m* (*with prep* an), **he ~ed me** chuir e bior annam

prickle *n* bior *m*, calg *m*, dealg *f*

pride *n* **1** (*esp legitimate* ~) pròis *f*, moit *f*; **2** (*usu more excessive* ~) àrdan, mòrchuis *f*, uabhar *m*, uaibhreas *m*

prime *adj* **1** prìomh (*precedes the noun, which it lenites where possible*), ~ **number** prìomh-àireamh *f*, ~ **minister** priomhaire *m*, **his** ~ **objective** am prìomh amas *m* a bha aige; **2** (*of high quality*) fìor mhath; **3** *in expr* (*philo*) ~ **cause** màthair-adhbhar *m*

prime *n* treun *f invar* a (*etc*) neirt (*gen of* neart *m*), **in my** ~ (ann) an treun mo neirt, *also* aig àirde *f* mo neirt

prince *n* prionnsa *m*

princely *adj* flathail

princess *n* bana-phrionnsa *f*

principal *n* (*of college, institution etc*) prionnsapal *m*, ceannard *m*

principal *adj* prìomh (*precedes the noun, which it lenites where possible*), **the** ~ **town** am prìomh bhaile

principle *n* prionnsapal *m*, **in** ~ ann am prionnsapal

print *n* **1** (*abstr & con: publications*) clò & clòdh *m*, **appear in** ~ nochd *vi* an clò; **2** (*trace, imprint of something*) lorg *f*, làrach *f*

print *v* (*books etc*) clò-bhuail *vt*, cuir *vt* an clò *m*

printed *adj & past part* clò-bhuailte, ~ **by X** clò-bhuailte le X, *also* air a c(h)lò-bhualadh le X

printer *n* clò-bhualadair *m*

printing *n* **1** clò-bhualadh *m*; **2** *in expr* ~ **error** clò-mhearachd *m*

prison *n* prìosan *m*

prisoner *n* prìosanach *m*, ciomach *m*

private *adj* **1** (*secret*) uaigneach, dìomhair; **2** (*confidential*) dìomhair, pearsanta; **3** (*of place etc; not open to all*) prìobhaideach; **4** (*not state-owned*) prìobhaideach, ~ **college** colaiste phrìobhaideach, **the** ~ **sector** an roinn phrìobhaideach

privately *adv* (*ie in secret, in confidence etc*) os ìosal & os ìseal, gu dìomhair

prize *n* duais *f*, **she won a** ~ **at the Mod** choisinn i duais aig a' Mhòd *m*

probability *n* coltachd *f invar*

probable *adj* coltach, **it's** ~ **that she'll come** tha e coltach gun tig i

probably *adv* tha (*etc*) e coltach *followed by conj* gu, **he'll** ~ **come tomorrow** tha e coltach gun tig e a-màireach

probity *n* ionracas *m*

problem *n* **1** (*point at issue*) ceist *f*, cùis *f*, **is it too costly? that's the** ~ a bheil e ro chosgail? 's e sin a' cheist/a' chùis, *also* 's e sin an rud *m*; **2** (*difficulty*) duilgheadas *m*, trioblaid *f*, **we've got ~s where money is concerned** tha duilgheadasan againn a thaobh airgid, **that won't be a** ~ **for him** cha bhi sin na dhuilgheadas dha, **social ~s** duilgheadasan sòisealta, **the loss of my job was the start of our ~s** b' e call m' obrach toiseach ar trioblaidean

proceed *v* rach *vi* air adhart (**with** le)

process *n* **1** (*industrial* ~, *also IT function or procedure*) gnìomh *m*; **2** *in expr* **the** ~ **of law** modh an lagha *mf*

process *v* **1** (*industry etc: deal with, prepare, treat materials etc, appropriately*) giullaich *vt*, gnìomhaich *vt*, saothraich *vt*; **2** (~ *information*) làimhsich *vt*, cuir *vt* an eagar *m*; **3** (*IT*) gnìomhaich *vt*, obraich *vt*, ~ **data** gnìomhaich/ obraich dàta *m invar*

processing *n* **1** (*industry etc*) giullachadh *m*, gnìomhachadh *m*, saothrachadh *m*; **2** (*IT*) *in* *exprs* **word** ~ facladaireachd *f invar*, **data** ~ gnìomhachadh-dàta *m*, obrachadh-dàta *m*

processor *n* (*IT*) gnìomh-inneal *m*, *in expr* (*IT*) **word** ~ facladair *m*

proclamation *n* gairm *f*

procrastinate *v* màirnealaich *vi*, maillich *vi*

prodigal *adj* stròdhail & struidheil, **the** ~ **Son** am Mac Stròdhail/Struidheil

produce *n* (*of land, plants, industry etc*) toradh *m*

produce *v* 1 (*industry etc*) saothraich *vt*, dèan *vt*, tàrmaich *vt*; 2 (*cinema, theatre*) riochdaich *vt*

producer *n* 1 (*of goods etc*) neach-dèanaidh *m* (*pl* luchd-dèanaidh *m sing coll*); 2 (*of film, play etc*) riochdaire *m*

product *n* 1 toradh *m*; 2 ~**s** (*ie items, goods*) bathar *m sing coll*

productive *adj* (*of land, plants etc*) torrach

profane *v* (*places, objects, relig, morals etc*) truaill *vt*

profession *n* (*ie occupation*) dreuchd *f*

professional *adj* 1 (*relating to a job or profession*) dreuchdail, ~ **terminology** briathrachas dreuchdail; 2 (*working for payment, also, having high* ~ *standards*) proifeiseanta, **a** ~ **singer** seinneadair proifeiseanta

professor *n* proifeasair *m*, ollamh *m*

proficiency *n* comas *m*

proficient *adj* comasach

profile *n* 1 (*phys*) leth-aghaidh *f*; 2 (*journalism etc: descriptive account*) cunntas *m*; 3 (*publicity etc*) ìomhaigh *f*, **improve the company's** ~ leasaich ìomhaigh na companaidh

profit *n* 1 (*esp fin*) prothaid *f*, buannachd *f*, **make a** ~ dèan prothaid; 2 (*more general*) buannachd *f*, tairbhe *f invar*

profit *v* tairbhich & tarbhaich *vi*

profitable *adj* tairbheach & tarbhach, buannachdail

profound *adj* domhainn, **a** ~ **book/thought** leabhar domhainn/smuain dhomhainn

progeny *n* 1 (*of humans*) gineal *mf*, sìol *m sing coll*, sliochd *m sing coll*; 2 (*of birds, animals*) àl *m*

program, programme *n* (*broadcasting, IT*) prògram *m*, (*IT*) **applications** ~ prògram-chleachdaidhean *m*

programming *n* prògramadh *m*, (*IT*) ~ **language** cànan prògramaidh *m*

progress *n* 1 (*the abstr concept*) adhartas *m*; 2 (*in skill, activity etc*) piseach *m*, adhartas *m*, **we're making** ~ tha (am) piseach a' tighinn

oirnn, tha sinn a' dèanamh adhartais, *also* (*more fam*) tha sinn a' tighinn air adhart

progressive *adj* adhartach

prohibit *v* toirmisg *vt*

prohibited *adj* & *past part* toirmisgte, fo thoirmeasg *m*

prohibition *n* toirmeasg *m*

prohibitive *adj* toirmeasgach

project *n* pròiseact *mf*, plana *m*

prologue *n* ro-ràdh *m*

prolong *v* sìn *vt* a-mach

promise *n* gealladh *m*, geall *m*

promise *v* geall *vti*, thoir gealladh *m* (*with prep* do), **he** ~**d me he wouldn't do it again** gheall e dhomh nach dèanadh e a-rithist e, ~ **me you'll write to me** thoir gealladh dhomh gun sgrìobh thu thugam

promised *adj* & *past part* 1 geallta; 2 *in expr* **the** ~ **land** tìr a' gheallaidh *mf*

promising *adj* gealltanach, ~ **player/student** cluicheadair/oileanach gealltanach

promontory *n* àird *f*, sròn *f*, (*esp rounded*) maol *m*, (*usu coastal*) rubha *m*

promote *v* àrdaich *vt*

prompt *adj* 1 (*on time*) an deagh àm *m*, mithich *adj*; 2 (*of person;* ~ *in performing tasks*) deas, èasgaidh, ealamh

promptly *adv*, **he did it** ~ (*quickly*) rinn e gu deas e, (*by the appointed time*) rinn e an deagh àm *m* e

prone *adj* 1 (*phys position*) air a (*etc*) b(h)eul fodha *m*, air a (*etc*) b(h)eul sìos, (*loosely*) sìnte, **they were** ~ bha iad air am beul fòdhpa/sìos; 2 (*having a tendency to*) buailteach (*with noun, & prep* do), ~ **to laughter/to change** buailteach do ghàireachdainn/do chaochladh, *also in exprs* ~ **to fear** eagalach, ~ **to anxiety/worry** *adj* cùramach, iomagaineach; 3 (*with verbal exprs*) dual(t)ach, buailteach, ~ **to spend money** dual(t)ach/buailteach airgead a chosg, ~ **to tell lies** dual(t)ach/buailteach a bhith ag innse bhreugan

pronoun *n* (*gram*) riochdair *m*

pronounce *v* (*lang*) fuaimnich *vt*

pronunciation *n* (*lang*) fuaimneachadh *m*

proof *n* dearbhadh *m* (**of** air), ~ **of his guilt** dearbhadh air a chionta

prop *n* taic(e) *f*

propagate *v* (*plants, animals*) tàrmaich *vt*

propel *v* (~ *machinery etc*) iomain *vt*, ~ **a machine by steam** iomain inneal le smùid, (*sport*) ~ **a ball** iomain bàla

propellant *n* stuth-iomain *m*

proper *adj* **1** (*suitable, fitting*) dòigheil, iomchaidh, cothromach, cubhaidh; **2** (*moral, decent*) beusach; **3** (*real, complete*) fìor, (*more pej*) dearg (*both precede the noun, which is lenited where possible*), **a ~ gentleman** fìor dhuine-uasal, **a ~ fool** fìor amadan, dearg amadan

properly *adv* gu dòigheil, **do it ~!** dèan gu dòigheil e!

property *n* **1** (*possessions*) sealbh *m*, seilbh *f*; **2** (*characteristic etc*) buadh *f*, feart *m*

prophecy *n* fàidheadaireachd *f*, fàisneachd *f*

prophesy *v* fàisnich *vti*

prophet *n* fàidh *m*, fiosaiche *m*

propitious *adj* fàbharach

proportionately *adv* a rèir

proposal *n* moladh *m*, **the government's ~s for a new bridge** molaidhean an riaghaltais airson drochaid ùire

propose *v* **1** (*intend to do something*) cuir *vi* roimhe (*etc*), rùnaich *vi*, **they ~ed to build a house** chuir iad romhpa taigh a thogail; **2** (*offer, suggest*) tairg *vi*, **he ~d to do it** thairg e a dhèanamh; **3** (*put forward idea, recommend*) mol *vti*

propped *adj & past part* an taic *f*, an tacsa *m*, (**against** ri), **~ (up) against a tree** an taic/an tacsa ri craoibh (*dat of* craobh *f*)

proprietor *n* seilbheadair & sealbhadair *m*

prose *n* rosg *m*

prospective *adj* san t-sealladh *m*, san amharc *m*

prosper *v* soirbhich *vi* (*usu used impersonally: followed by prep* le, *with dat*), **the business ~ed** shoirbhich leis a' ghnìomhachas, **we ~ed** shoirbhich leinn

prosperity *n* soirbheachas *m*, soirbheachadh *m*

protection *n* **1** (*abstr & con*) tèarmann *m*, dìon *m*, **under the court's ~** fo thèarmann/fo dhìon na cùirte; **2** (*more con*) fasgadh *m*, **seek ~ from the downpour** sir fasgadh on dìle *f*; **3** *in expr* (*IT*) **data ~** dìon-dàta *m*, tèarainteachd dàta *f invar*

protest *n* **1** (*general*) gearan *m*; **2** (*pol etc: demonstration, rally, march*) fianais-dhùbhlain *f* (**against** an aghaidh *followed by gen*)

protest *v* **1** (*general*) gearain *vi* (**about** mu dheidhinn *followed by gen*); **2** (*pol etc: demonstrate, march etc*) tog fianais *f* (**against** an aghaidh *followed by gen*)

protester *n* (*pol etc: at demonstration, march etc*) neach-togail-fianais *m* (*pl* luchd-togail-fianais *m sing coll*), (**against** an aghaidh *followed by gen*)

Protestant *n & adj* Pròstanach *m*

proud *adj* **1** (*usu legitimately*) pròiseil, moiteil, (**of** à), **we're ~ of you** tha sinn pròiseil/moiteil asad; **2** (*usu excessively ~*) uaibhreach, àrdanach, mòrchuiseach

prove *v* dearbh *vt*

proved, proven *adj & past part* dearbhte

proverb *n* seanfhacal *m*, ràdh *m invar*

provide *v* **1** (*general*) thoir *vt* seachad; **2** (*esp of traders etc*) solair *vt*, **~ accommodation for the tourists** solair lòistinn don luchd-turais; **3** (*esp admin, fin etc*) ullaich *vt*, **~ finance for a new hospital** ullaich ionmhas airson ospadail ùir

provided *conj* air chumha is (*with conj* gu), cho fad' is (*with conj* a), **~ (that) the salary is high** air chumha is gu bheil an turastal àrd, cho fad' 's a tha an turastal àrd

providence *n* sealbh *m*, freastal *m*

provision *n* ullachadh *m*, **~ of finance** ullachadh ionmhais

provisional *adj* sealach

provisions *n* lòn *m*

provost *n* pròbhaist *m*

prow *n* toiseach *m*

proximity *n* faisge *f invar*

prudence *n* faiceall *f*, earalas *m*

prudent *adj* faiceallach

PS *abbrev see* **postscript**

psychiatrist *n* lighiche-inntinn *m*

psychiatry *n* leigheas-inntinn *m*

psychologist *n* inntinn-eòlaiche *m*

psychology *n* eòlas-inntinn *m*

puberty *n* inbhidheachd *f invar*

pubes *n*, **pubic hair** *n* ròm *mf invar*, gaoisid & gaosaid *f*

public *adj* **1** (*communal*) coitcheann, poblach, **~ swimming pool** amar-snàimh coitcheann/poblach; **2** (*opposite of* private) follaiseach, poblach, **a ~ enquiry** rannsachadh follaiseach, **a ~ meeting** coinneamh fhollaiseach/phoblach, **a ~ company** companaidh p(h)oblach, **the ~ sector** an roinn phoblach, an earrann phoblach; **3** *in exprs* **~ address system** *n* glaodhaire *m*, **~ house** taigh-seinnse *m*, **~ conveniences** goireasan *mpl*

publication *n* **1** (*abstr*) foillseachadh *m*; **2** (*abstr & con*) clò-bhualadh *m*, **Birlinn ~s** clò-bhualaidhean Birlinn; **3** (*con: a periodical*) iris *f*, ràitheachan *m*

publicise *v* cuir *vt* am follais *f invar*, thoir *vt* am follais, foillsich *vt*

publicity *n* **1** (*abstr*) follaiseachd *f invar*, sanasachd *f invar*; **2** (*con: public notices etc*) sanas(an) *m(pl)*, (*commercial* ~) sanas(an)-reic *m* (*pl*)

publish *v* 1 foillsich *vt*, cuir *vt* an clò *m*; 2 *in exprs* **be/get** ~**ed** nochd *vi* an clò, **newly** ~**ed** ùr on chlò, air ùr-fhoillseachadh

publisher *n* foillsichear *m*

publishing *n* foillseachadh *m*

pudding *n* 1 mìlsean *m*; 2 (*savoury* ~) marag *f*, **black/white** ~ marag dhubh/gheal

puddle *n* glumag *f*, lòn *m*

pull *n* tarraing *f*, slaodadh *m*

pull *v* 1 tarraing *vti*, (*more heavily*) slaod *vti*, ~ **a cork** tarraing corcais; 2 (*idiom*) **they were** ~**ing my leg** bha iad a' tarraing asam

pullet *n* eireag *f*

pulley *n* ulag *f*

pullover *n* geansaidh *m*

pulp *n* glaodhan *m*, pronnadh *m*, **wood** ~ glaodhan-fiodha *m*

pulpit *n* cùbaid *f*, (*less usu*) crannag *f*

pulverise *v* pronn *vt*

pulverised *adj & past part* pronn, air a (*etc*) p(h)ronnadh

pump *n* pumpa *m*

punctilious *adj* (*of person, work etc*) mionchuiseach, pongail, mionaideach

punctual *adj* pongail

puncture *n* toll *m*

puncture *v* toll *vt*

punish *v* peanasaich *vt*, smachdaich *vt*

punishment *n* peanas *m*

punitive *adj* peanasach

pup *n* cuilean *m*

pupil *n* 1 (*ed*) sgoilear *m*; 2 (~ *of eye*) dubh (na sùla) *m*

puppet *n* fear-brèige *m*, pupaid *f*

puppy *n* cuilean *m*

purchaser *n* neach-ceannach *m* (*pl* luchd-ceannach *m sing coll*)

purchasing *n* ceannach *m*

purgatory *n* purgadair *m*

purling *n* (*of stream*) crònan *m*, torman *m*

purple *adj* corcair, purpaidh

purple *n* purpar *m*, purpaidh *f*

purpose *n* rùn *m*; 2 *in expr* **on** ~ a dh'aon rùn, a dh'aon ghnothach *m*

purring *n* crònan *m*

pursue *v* rua(i)g *vt*, lean *vt* (gu dian)

pursuit *n* 1 tòir *f*, ruaig *f*, **in** ~ an tòir (**of** air); 2 (*military*) ruith *f*; 3 (*hobby etc*) cur-seachad *m*, **my favourite** ~ an cur-seachad as fheàrr leam

pus *n* brachadh *m*, iongar *m*

push *v* put *vt*, (*more roughly*) brùth *vt*, sàth *vt*

pustule *n* guirean *m*

put *v* 1 (*exprs with* cuir *vt*) ~ **coal on the fire** cuir gual air an teine, ~ **your clothes on** cuir ort/umad do chuid aodaich , ~ **money on a horse** cuir airgead air each, ~ **the light on/ off** cuir air/às an solas, ~ **the fire out** cuir às an teine, **I had to** ~ **on weight** b' fheudar dhomh cudthrom a chur orm, ~ **one's hope in someone/something** cuir dòchas ann an cuideigin/rudeigin, ~ **into words** cuir *vt* an cèill (*dat of* ciall *f*), ~ **an end to** (*esp person*) cuir *vi* às (*with prep* do), ~ **an end to** (*a process etc*) cuir stad *m*, cuir crìoch *f*, (*with prep* air), ~ **something off (till another day)** cuir rudeigin air ath là *m*, *also* (*less trad*) cuir rudeigin dheth (gu là *m* eile), ~ **by/aside** cuir *vt* mu seach, cuir *vt* an dara taobh *m*, ~ **into action** (*plan etc*) cuir *vt* an gnìomh *m*, ~ **at risk/in danger** cuir *vt* an cunnart *m*, ~ **to flight** cuir *vt* an teicheadh *m*, cuir *vt* an ruaig *f*, (*with prep* air), **we** ~ **them to flight** chuir sinn an teicheadh/an ruaig orra, ~ **to the test** cuir *vt* gu deuchainn *f*, *also* dearbh *vt*, ~ **down** (*belittle, humiliate someone*) cuir *vt* an suarachas *m*, ~ **out** (*publish*) cuir *vt* a-mach, ~ **right** (*wrongs etc*) cuir *vt* ceart, ~ **right**, ~ **in order** (*machinery etc*) cuir *vt* air ghleus *mf*, *also* gleus *vt*, **I don't want to** ~ **you to any trouble** chan eil mi airson dragh sam bith a chur oirbh, ~ **Gaelic into French** cuir Fraingis air Gàidhlig, (*idiom*) ~ **the cat among the pigeons** cuir an ceòl air feadh na fìdhle; 2 (*other misc exprs*) ~ **down** (*rebellion etc*) ceannsaich *vt*, mùch *vt*, ~ **(great) emphasis on X** leig cudthrom (mòr) air X, ~ **right**, ~ **in order** (*situations, relationships etc*) rèitich *vt*, leasaich *vt*, ~ **to shame** maslaich *vt*, ~ **up with** fuiling *vt*, (*less trad*) cuir *vi* suas ri, **they had to** ~ **up with cold and hunger** b' fheudar dhaibh fuachd *mf* is acras *m* fhulang, b' fheudar dhaibh cur suas ris an fhuachd is ris an acras, faigh cuid-oidhche *f*/cuid *f* na h-oidhche, **we** ~ **up for the night at the hotel** fhuair sinn (ar) cuid-oidhche/fhuair sinn cuid na h-oidhche aig an taigh-òsta

putrefaction *n* grodadh *m*, lobhadh *m*, brèine *f*

putrefy *v* grod *vi*, lobh *vi*

putrid *adj* grod, lobhte

puzzle *n* tòimhseachan *m*

puzzle *v* cuir *vt* an imcheist *f*

puzzled *adj & past part* an/fo imcheist *f*

puzzling *adj* imcheisteach

Q

quadrangle *n* ceithir-cheàrnag *f*

quadrilateral *adj* ceithir-cheàrnach

quadruped *adj & n* ceithir-chasach *m*

quagmire *n* sùil-chritheach *f*, bog *m*, boglach *f*, fèith(e) *f*

quaich *n* cuach *f*

quaint *adj* neònach, annasach, seann-fhasanta

quake *n* 1 crith *f*; 2 (*earthquake*) crith-thalmhainn *f*

quake *v* bi *vi irreg* air chrith *f*, crith *vi*, **he was quaking with fear** bha e air chrith leis an eagal *m*, *in expr* **start to ~** rach *vi* air chrith

qualification *n* 1 (*for employment, study etc*) uidheamachadh *m*; 2 (*esp in written form*) ~(s) teisteanas *m*, bar(r)antas *m*; 3 (*modification of earlier statements etc*) lùghdachadh *m*, maothachadh *m*

qualified *adj & past part* 1 (*formally ~ for employment, study etc*) uidheamaichte, barrantaichte 2 (*of the standard required*) aig ìre *f invar* (na h-obrach *etc*); 3 (*of statements etc; with reservations*) le cumha *m*, le teagamh *m*, le cùl-earbsa *m*, **~ agreement** aonta le cumha

qualify *v* 1 (*be up to a particular job etc*) bi *vi* aig ìre *f invar* (na h-obrach *etc*); 2 (*esp by formal qualifications: ~ for employment, study etc*) bi *vi* uidheamaichte (airson na h-obrach/a' chùrsa *etc*); 3 (*modify earlier statements etc*) lùghdaich *vt*, maothaich *vt*

quality *n* 1 (*attribute etc*) buadh *f*, feart *m*, beus *f*, **natural qualities** buadhan nàdarra(ch), **intellectual qualities** buadhan inntinn; 2 (*degree of excellence etc*) mathas *m*

quandary *n* ioma(dh)-chomhairle *f*, imcheist *f*, **in a ~ as to what I would do** ann an ioma(dh)-chomhairle dè a dhèanainn

quantity *n* uimhir *f invar*, uiread *m invar*, meud *m invar*, **we had a (certain) ~ of food** bha na h-uimhir/na h-uiread de bhiadh againn, **give me the same ~ as Seumas (has)** thoir dhomh uimhir ri Seumas, thoir dhomh uiread 's a tha aig Seumas, *in expr* **what ~ do you require?** dè na dh'fheumas sibh dheth?

quarrel *n* 1 (*usu verbal*) trod *m*, argamaid *f*, **a ~ arose between them** dh'èirich trod eatarra; 2 (*verbal or phys*) tuasaid *f*; 3 (*phys*) sabaid *f*

quarrel *v* 1 (*squabble etc, usu verbally*) troid *vi*, connsaich *vi*; 2 (*phys*) sabaid *vi* (**with** ri); 3 (*fall out*) rach *vi* thar a chèile, **they ~led/have ~led** chaidh iad thar a chèile, tha iad troimh-a-chèile

quarrelling *n* trod *m*, **I can't sleep on account of their ~** chan urrainn dhomh cadal air sgàth an troid

quarrelsome *adj* connspaideach, connsachail, aimhreiteach

quarry[1] *n* (*for stone etc*) cuaraidh *m*

quarry[2] *n* (*of hunters etc*) creach *f*

quart *n* cairteal *m*

quarter *n* 1 ceathramh *m*; 2 (*clock time*) cairteal *m*, (*less usu*) ceathramh *m*, **a ~/three ~s of an hour** cairteal/trì chairteil na h-uarach (*gen of* uair *f*), **a ~ to four** cairteal gu ceithir; 3 (*~ of year*) ràith *f*

quarterly *n* (*periodical*) ràitheachan *m*

quarters *n* 1 (*military*) taigh-feachd *m*, gearastan *m*, cairtealan *mpl*; 2 (*non-military*) àite-fuirich *m*, lòistinn *m*,

quaver *v* crith *vi*

quay *n* cidhe *m*, laimrig *f*

queen *n* banrigh *f*, banrighinn *f*

queer *adj* neònach

quell *v* (*people, emotions etc*) ceannsaich *vt*, mùch *vt*, **~ unrest** ceannsaich aimhreit *f*

quelling *n* ceannsachadh *m*

quench *v* 1 (*thirst*) bàth *vt*; 2 (*fire, spirit etc*) mùch *vt*

querulous *adj* gearanach

query *n* ceist *f*

question *n* 1 ceist *f*, *in exprs* **~ master** ceistear *m*, fear-ceasnachaidh *m*, neach-ceasnachaidh *m*, **~ mark** comharradh-ceiste *m*; 2 (*point at issue*) ceist *f*, cùis *f*, **is it too costly, that's the ~** a bheil e ro chosgail, 's e sin a' cheist/a' chùis; 3 (*doubt*) **call into ~** cuir *vt* an teagamh *m*

question *v* 1 (*put questions*) ceasnaich *vt*, cuir ceist(ean) *f* (*with prep* air); 2 (*doubt, contest*)

411

cuir *vt* an teagamh *m*, cuir teagamh (*with prep ann an*), **they ~ed my integrity** chuir iad an teagamh an t-ionracas agam, chuir iad teagamh san ionracas agam

questionable *adj* amharasach

questioner *n* ceistear *m*

questioning *n* ceasnachadh *m*

questionnaire *n* ceisteachan *m*

queue *n* ciudha *mf*

quick *adj* **1** (*in moving from place to place*) luath, astarach; **2** (*of person, in performing tasks etc*) clis, deas, tapaidh, ealamh; **3** (*mentally ~*) luath na (*etc*) inntinn *f*, geurchuiseach, geur na (*etc*) inntinn; **4** (*brief, hurried*) aithghearr, **a ~ look/glance at the clock** sùil *f* aithghearr air a' ghleoc

quicken *v* luathaich *vti*, **our pace ~ed** luathaich ar ceum *m*, **we ~ed our pace** luathaich sinn ar ceum

quickly *adv* gu luath, **the time passed ~** chaidh an ùine seachad gu luath

quickness *n* **1** (*of person, in performing tasks etc*) luas *m*, cliseachd *f invar*; **2** (*mental or phys ~*) graide *f invar*

quick-tempered *adj* aithghearr, cas

quiet *adj* **1** (*of person, atmosphere, weather etc*) ciùin, sàmhach, sèimh; **2** (*of persons: silent, not speaking*) tosdach; **3** *in expr* **be ~!** tosd!, ist! (*pl* istibh!) & eist! (*pl* eistibh!), bi/bithibh sàmhach

quiet *n* **1** (*silence*) tosd *m invar*; **2** (*calm*) ciùineas *m*, sàmhchair *f*

quieten *v* **1** (*make silent*) tosdaich *vt*; **2** (*make calm*) ciùinich *vti*, sìthich *vti*, socraich *vti*, tàlaidh *vt*

quietly *adv* os ìosal & os ìseal

quietness *n*, *as* **quiet** *n above*

quilt *n* cuibhrig *mf*

quit *adj* saor *adj* is, cuidhteas *m* (*with or without prep de*), **we're ~ of the bad lodgers** tha sinn saor is na droch lòistearan, fhuair sinn cuidhteas (de) na droch lòistearan

quit *v* fàg *vt*, (*can be more drastic*) trèig *vt*, **she ~ her post/job** thrèig i a dreuchd, **the people ~ the island** thrèig na daoine an t-eilean

quite *adv* **1** (*completely*) (gu) buileach, gu tur, gu h-iomlan, gu leòr, **she's not ~ ready** chan eil i buileach deiseil, **~ different** gu tur eadar-dhealaichte, *in exprs* **I'm ~ certain** tha mi làn-chinnteach, **that's ~ right** tha sin ceart gu leòr, *also* (*stronger*) tha sin cho ceart ri ceart; **2** (*fairly, somewhat*) gu math, **we were ~ tired** bha sinn gu math sgìth, **~ old** gu math aosta; **3** (*expr agreement*) dìreach (sin)!, **I was wrong! ~!** bha mi ceàrr! dìreach!

quiver *v* bi *vi irreg* air chrith *f*, crith *vi*

quiz *n* ceasnachadh *m*

quota *n* cuid *f*, cuibhreann *mf*, (*less trad*) cuota *m*

R

Raasay *n* Ratharsaigh
rabbit *n* rabaid *f*, (*more trad*) coineanach *m*
rabble *n* prabar *m*, gràisg *f*
race¹ *n* **1** (*ethnicity*) cineal *m*, ~ **relations**
dàimh-chinealan *f*; **2** (*more loosely: tribe,*
people, esp supposedly of common descent) sìol
m sing coll, cinneadh *m*, gineal *mf*, **the ~ of**
Diarmaid (*the Campbells*) sìol Diarmaid; **3** *in*
expr **the human ~** an cinne-daonna *m*
race² *n* (*sports etc*) rèis *f*
racial *adj* cinneadail, cinealtais (*gen of* cinealtas
m, used adjectivally), ~ **hatred** gràin-cinnidh
f, ~ **discrimination** lethbhreith chinneadail *f*,
claonadh cinealtais *m*
racialism, racism *n* cinealtas *m*, gràin-cinnidh *f*
racialist, racist *adj* cinealtach
racist *n* neach cinealtach
racket¹ *n* (*noise*) gleadhraich *f*, (*louder*) ùpraid *f*,
othail *f*
racket² (*for sport*) racaid *f*
racket³ (*dishonest practice or transaction*) feall-
ghnìomh *m*, foill *f*, malairt fhoilleil *f*
radiance *n* deàlradh *m*, lainnir *f*
radiant *adj* deàlrach, lainnireach, boillsgeach
radiate *v* **1** (*shine*) deàlraich *vi*; **2** (*emit*) sgaoil *vt*
radio *n* rèidio *m*, **what's on the ~?** dè a th' air
an rèidio?
radioactive *adj* rèidio-bheò
raffle *n* crannchur-gill *m*
rafter *n* cabar *m*
rag *n* luideag *f*, clùd & clobhd *m*
rage *n* cuthach *m*, bàinidh *f invar*, boile *f invar*,
in a ~ air chuthach, air bhàinidh, air bhoile, **fly**
into a ~/go mad with ~ rach *vi* air chuthach,
gabh an cuthach (dearg)
ragged *adj* cearbach, luideach
raging *adj* **1** (*of persons: with madness or anger*)
air chuthach *m*, air bhàinidh *f invar*, air bhoile *f*
invar; **2** (*of seas*) doineannach
raid *n* creach *f*
rail *n* rèile *f*
railings *n* rèilichean *fpl*

rain *n* uisge *m*, (*heavy*) dìle *f*, (*torrential*) dìle
bhàthte, **the ~ stopped at long last** sguir an
t-uisge mu dheireadh thall, *in expr* **acid ~** uisge
searbhagach *m*, *also* uisge-searbhaig *m*
rain *v* **1** bi *vi irreg* an t-uisge ann, sil *vi*, (*lightly*)
fras *vi*, **it's ~ing** tha an t-uisge ann, (*usu more*
heavily) tha e a' sileadh, **it always ~ed** bha/
bhiodh an t-uisge ann an-còmhnaidh; **2** (*idiom*)
it was ~ing cats and dogs bha dìle bhàthte
ann
rainbow *n* bogha-frois(e) *m*
raincoat *n* còta-frois(e) *m*
rainfall *n* sileadh *m*
rainforest *n* coille-uisge *f*
rainproof *adj* uisge-dhìonach
raise *v* **1** tog *vt*, ~ **your head** tog do cheann,
that ~d my spirits thog sin mo chridhe, ~ **an**
issue tog cuspair, **I was ~d in Coll** thogadh mi
ann an Colla; **2** *in expr* ~ **oneself** èirich *vi*, **she**
~**d herself (up) onto one elbow** dh'èirich i
air a leth-uilinn
rake *n* (*tool*) ràcan *m*, ràc *m*
rally *n* tional *m*, cruinneachadh *m*
rally *v* (*raise spirits, encourage*) misnich *vt*, ath-
mhisnich *vt*
RAM *n* (*IT*), *see* **random access memory**
ram *n* (*tup*) rùda *m*, reithe *m*
rampart *n* mùr *m*
random *adj* **1** tuaireamach; **2** *in expr* **at ~** air
thuaiream *f*; **3** (*IT*) ~ **access memory, RAM,**
cuimhne thuaireameach
randy *adj* drùiseach, drùiseil
range *n* **1** (*scale, series*) raon *m*, sreath *mf*,
~ **of temperature** raon teothachd, ~ **of**
responsibilities sreath de dhleastanasan; **2**
(*for artillery etc practice*) raon-bualaidh *m*; **3** (~
of hills, mountains) sreath *mf*
ranger *n* maor *m*, **countryside ~** maor-dùthcha
m, **park ~** maor-pàirce *m*
rank *n* (*in hierarchy, progression, armed*
services etc) inbhe *f*
ransack *v* rannsaich *vt*
ransom *n* èirig *f*

ransom *v* fuasgail *vt* le èirig *f*, saor/saoraich *vt* le èirig

rape *n* èigneachadh *m*

rape *v* èignich *vt*

rapid *adj* **1** (*general*) luath; **2** (*of watercourse*) bras, cas; **3** (*of person's movements*) grad, aithghearr

rapier *n* claidheamh-caol *m*

rapist *n* èigneachair *m*

rare *adj* **1** (*in short supply, seldom met with*) gann, tearc, ainneamh; **2** (*unusual*) annasach; **3** (*fam: expr approval*) taghta, **that was ~!** bha sin taghta!

rarely *adv* gu tearc, *but also commonly rendered by* is *v irreg def* gann, (*less usu*) is ainneamh, (*both with conj* a), **you'll ~ see the likes of him** is gann a chì thu a leithid

rarity *n* **1** (*abstr*) gainne *f invar*, gainnead *m invar*, teirce *f invar*; **2** (*con*) **a ~** annas *m*, (*less usu*) suaicheantas *m*

rat *n* radan & rodan *m*

rate *n* **1** (*of speed*) astar *m*, luas *m*, **they were going along at a good ~** bha astar math aca; **2** (*~ of progress etc*) ruith *f*, **at this ~** air an ruith seo; **3** (*fin: level*) luach *m invar*, ìre *f*, **the ~ of exchange** luach na h-iomlaid, co-luach an airgid, **the interest ~** ìre/luach an rèidh; **4** (*local taxes*) **~s** reataichean *mpl*

rate *v* **1** (*evaluate*) meas *vt*, cuir luach *m* (*with prep* air), luachaich *vt*; **2** (*more fam*) *in expr* **how do you ~ (him/it etc)** dè do/ur b(h)eachd (air *etc*), **how do you ~ them as players?** dè do bheachd orra mar chluicheadairean?

rather *adv* **1** (*fairly, somewhat*) car, caran, beagan, rudeigin, rud beag, **~ tired** car/caran/beagan/rudeigin/rud beag sgìth; **2** (*expr preference*) b' fheàrr leam (*etc*), **they would ~ have cheese** b' fheàrr leotha càise; **3** *in expr* **~ than** seach *prep*, **give us money ~ than promises** thoir dhuinn airgead seach geallaidhean

ratify *v* daingnich *vt*

ration *n* cuibhreann *mf*

rational *adj* reusanta

rationale *n* feallsanachd *f*, **the ~ of/behind the proposals** feallsanachd nam molaidhean *mpl*

rattle¹ *n* (*ie toy etc*) clach-bhalg *f*

rattle² *n* (*ie the noise*), **rattling** *n*, (*of lighter objects*) clagarsaich *f invar*, (*louder*) glagadaich *f*, gleadhraich *f*

rattle *v* dèan glagadaich *f*, dèan gleadhraich *f*

raven *n* fitheach *m*

ravish *v* (*ie rape*) èignich *vt*

ravisher *n* èigneachair *m*

raw *adj* (*uncooked, unprocessed*) amh, **~ meat** feòil amh *f*, **~ material(s)** stuth(an) amh *m(pl)*

ray *n* gath *m*, (*less usu*) leus *m*, **~ of light** gath solais, **the ~s of the sun** gathan na grèine

raze *v*, *usu in expr* **~ to the ground**, leag *vt* gu làr *m*

razor *n* ealtainn *f*, (*less trad*) ràsair *m*

re(-) *reiterative prefix* ath- (*lenites following cons where possible*) *eg* **re-assess** *v* ath-mheas *vt also* (*more informal*) meas *vt* a-rithist, **re-count** *n* ath-chunntadh *m, see further examples below*

reach *v* **1** (*arrive at, win to*) ruig *vti*, **we ~ed Perth** ràinig sinn Peairt; **2** (*fig, abstr: arrive at, achieve*) thig *vi* (*with prep* gu), **~ an agreement/understanding** thig gu còrdadh *m*/rèite *f*, **~ a decision/conclusion** thig *vi* gu co-dhùnadh *m, also* co-dhùin *vi*; **3** (*attain with hand etc*) ruig *vi* (*with prep* air), **can you ~ the top shelf?** an ruig thu air an sgeilp *f* as àirde?, **~ for my hand** ruig air mo làimh *f*; **4** (*pass*) sìn *vt* (*with prep* gu), **~ me the sugar** sìn thugam an siùcar

read *v* leugh *vti*

reader *n* leughadair *m*

reading *n* leughadh *m*, **~ matter** stuth leughaidh *m*

ready *adj* **1** (*prepared, finished etc*) deiseil, ullamh, (*less usu*) deas, **the food's/meal's ~** tha am biadh deiseil/ullamh, **are you ~?** a bheil thu deiseil/ullamh?; **2** (*keen, willing*) èasgaidh (*to* gu), deònach, **~ to help you** èasgaidh gur cuideachadh, **~ to do it** deònach a dhèanamh, (*more trad*) deònach air a dhèanamh; **3** (*expr convenience, handiness*) ullamh, **~ to hand** ullamh, **~ money** airgead ullamh; **4** *in expr* **get ~** deasaich *vt*, ullaich *vt*, **get the food ~** deasaich am biadh, (*esp machines, equipment etc*) gleus *vt*, cuir *vt* air ghleus, uidheamaich *vt*

real *adj* **1** (*actual*) nitheil, fìor, rudail; **2** (*genuine*) fìor (*precedes the noun, which it lenites where possible*), **~ gold** fìor òr; **3** (*out & out*) fìor, dearg, (*precede the noun, which is lenited where possible*), gu c(h)ùl *m* (*follows the noun*), **they're ~ musicians** 's e fìor luchd-ciùil a th' annta, **a ~ idiot** dearg amadan, **a ~ Highlander** fìor Ghàidheal, Gàidheal gu chùl

realise *v* **1** (*comprehend, appreciate*) tuig *vti*, (*trad or formal*) fidir *vti*, **I ~ that!** tha mi a' tuigsinn sin!; **2** (*become aware*) tuig *vti*, thig *vi* a-steach (*with prep* air), **I ~d that they weren't listening** thuig mi/thàinig e a-steach orm nach robh iad ag èisteachd

realism *n* fìorachas *m*

reality n fìorachd f invar

really adv fìor (precedes the adj, which it lenites where possible), uabhasach fhèin (precedes the adj), gu dearbh, **the food was ~ good/~ excellent** bha am biadh fìor mhath/uabhasach fhèin math, **are you tired? I ~ am!** a bheil thu sgìth? tha gu dearbh!, **he's rich!, is he ~?** tha e beartach! a bheil gu dearbh?

re-animate v ath-bheothaich vt

re-appraisal n ath-bheachdachadh m (**of** air)

re-appraise v ath-bheachdaich vi (**with prep** air)

rear n 1 (of group etc) deireadh m, **she was in the ~** bha i air dheireadh, **she brought up the ~** thàinig i air deireadh; 2 (of building etc), (outside) cùl m, cùlaibh m invar, (inside) tòn f, **there were trees at the ~ of the church** bha craobhan (ann) air cùl/air cùlaibh na h-eaglaise, **the ~ (part) of the hall** tòn an talla; 3 (fam: backside, bum) tòn f, màs m

rear v 1 (children, livestock etc) tog vt, **I was ~ed in Coll** thogadh mi ann an Colla; 2 in expr **~ up** (surge upwards etc) èirich vi (suas)

reason[1] n 1 (the faculty of ~) reusan m; 2 (sanity) ciall f, rian m, reusan m, **I nearly lost my ~** cha mhòr nach deach mi às mo chiall/mo rian, theab mi a dhol às mo chiall/mo rian

reason[2] n (cause, explanation) adhbhar m, cùis f, (less usu) fàth m invar, **the ~ for my sadness** adhbhar/fàth mo bhròin; 2 in expr **what's the ~?** dè as coireach? (**for** air), **the electricity's off, what's the ~ for that?** tha an dealan dheth, dè as coireach air sin?

reason v reusanaich vi

reasoning n reusanachadh m

reasonable adj 1 (of statements, situations etc: logical, consistent with reason or common sense) reusanta, ciallach; 2 (of situations etc: fair, appropriate) cothromach, reusanta, **a ~ salary** tuarastal cothromach; 3 (of persons: amenable to, or displaying, reason or common sense) toinisgeil, ciallach

re-assess v ath-mheas vt

re-assessment n ath-mheasadh m

rebel n reubalach m

rebel v dèan ar-a-mach m invar, èirich vi (suas), (**against** an aghaidh with gen)

rebellion n ar-a-mach m invar

rebuke n achmhasan m

rebuke v cronaich vt, thoir achmhasan m (with prep do)

recall v 1 (remember) cuimhnich vi (with prep air), meòraich vti; 2 (call back, summon again) gairm vt air ais

receipt n (for money etc) cuidhteas m

recent adj ùr, **a ~ book** leabhar ùr

recently adv (bh)o chionn ghoirid

reception n 1 (welcome) fàilte f, **what sort of a ~ did you get?** dè an seòrsa fàilte a fhuair sibh?; 2 (desk in hotel etc) ionad fàilte m; 3 (function) cuirm f, **(the) wedding ~** cuirm na bainnse (gen of banais f)

receptionist n (hotel etc) fàiltiche m

recession n (fin) seacadh m, crìonadh m

recitation n aithris f

recite v aithris vt

reckon v 1 (arithmetic etc) cunnt vti; 2 (consider, think) saoil vi, meas vi, (slightly fam) **I ~ it will rain soon** saoilidh mi gum bi uisge ann a dh'aithghearr; 3 (in expr) **what do you ~?** dè do bheachd (air)?

reckoning n 1 (arithmetic etc) cunntas m, cunntadh m; 2 (sum due) cunntas m

recline v 1 (referring to the movement) laigh vi (sìos); 2 (referring to the position) bi v irreg na (etc) laighe mf invar

recognised adj & past part aithnichte

recollect v cuimhnich vi (with prep air)

recollection n cuimhne f invar (**of** air), **I've no ~ of him** chan eil cuimhne agam air idir

recommend v mol vt

recommendation n moladh m, **the government's ~s for a new tax** molaidhean an riaghaltais airson cìse ùire f gen

reconcile v (opposing parties etc) rèitich vt

reconciliation n rèite f

record n 1 (of events etc) cunntas m, clàr m; 2 (sound recording) clàr m

record v 1 (~ events etc) clàraich vt, sgrìobh cunntas (**of** air, de); 2 (~ sound) clàraich vt

recording n 1 (abstr) clàrachadh m; 2 (con) clàr m; 3 in expr **~ tape** teip chlàraidh f

recount v 1 (relate) thoir cunntas m (with prep de or air), innis vt

re-count n ath-chunntadh m

re-count v ath-chunnt vti, (more informal) cunnt vt a-rithist

recover v 1 (from illness & other ordeals etc) rach vi am feabhas m, thig vi bhuaithe, **the invalid ~ed** chaidh an t-euslainteach am feabhas, thàinig an t-euslainteach bhuaithe, (less trad) dh'fhàs an t-euslainteach na b' fheàrr; 2 (retrieve) faigh vt air ais

re-create v ath-chruthaich vt

recreation n (pastime etc) cur-seachad m

recruit v 1 (workers, staff) fastaich vt; 2 (for armed forces) tog vt

rectangle n ceart-cheàrnach m, ceart-cheàrnag f

rectangular adj ceart-cheàrnach

rectify v ceartaich vt, cuir vt ceart, leasaich vt

rectum n tòn f

recycle v ath-chuartaich vt

red adj **1** (of human hair, animal's coat) ruadh, a ~-**haired man** fear ruadh, ~ **grouse** cearc-ruadh; **2** (usu brighter ~) dearg, ~ **corpuscle** frìde dhearg, ~ **wine** fìon dearg

red n dearg m

redcoat n (hist) saighdear dearg

redcurrant n dearc-dhearg

redden v **1** (as vt: make red) deargaich vt; **2** (as vi: turn/become red) fàs vi dearg

reddish- adj prefix dearg-, eg ~**brown** dearg-dhonn

reduce v lùghdaich vti, ìslich vt

reduction n lùghdachadh m, **rent** ~ lùghdachadh màil (gen of màl m)

reed n **1** cuilc f; **2** (of musical instrument) rìbheid f

reel n **1** (for thread etc) iteachan m, piorna mf; **2** (dance) ruidhle m, ridhil m, **eightsome** ~ ruidhle-ochdnar m

redundant adj (surplus to requirements) anbharra

re-election n ath-thaghadh m

refectory n biadh-lann f

refer v **1** (admin etc) cuir vt (**to** gu), ~ **the matter to the manager** cuir a' chùis chun a' mhanaidseir, ~ **back** cuir vt air ais (**to** gu); **2** (mention, allude) thoir iomradh m, thoir tarraing f, thoir guth m, (**to** air), (**esp** ~ **to persons**) ainmich vt, ~ **to something** thoir iomradh/tarraing/guth air rudeigin

referee n (sport) rèitear m

reference n **1** (as to character, qualifications etc) teisteanas m; **2** (mention) iomradh m, tarraing f, guth m, (**to** air), **he made no** ~ **to it** cha tug e iomradh/tarraing/guth (sam bith) air

reflect v **1** (think) cnuas vi, cnuasaich vi, meòraich vi, (more rigorously) beachd-smaoin(t)ich vi, (**on/upon** air); **2** (of mirror etc) tilg vt air ais, ath-thilg vt

reflection n **1** (contemplation etc) cnuasachadh m, meòrachadh m, (more rigorous) beachd-smaoin(t)eachadh m, (**on/upon** air); **2** (reflected image) faileas m, ath-ìomhaigh f, **the** ~ **of the moon on the surface of the loch** faileas na gealaich air uachdar an locha

reformation n ath-leasachadh m, (hist, relig) **the Reformation** an t-Ath-leasachadh

reform v **1** (reshape) ath-chruthaich vt; **2** (change for better etc) leasaich vt, ath-leasaich vt

refrain n (music, poetry) sèist mf

refrain v cùm vi (**from** bho/o), seachain vt, ~ **from strong drink** cùm on deoch-làidir, seachain (an) deoch-làidir

refresh v ùraich vt

refreshment n **1** (abstr) ùrachadh m; **2** (con: meal etc) biadh m (is deoch f), lòn m, beathachadh m

refrigerate v fionnaraich vt

refrigeration n fionnarachadh m

refrigerator n frids m, (less usu) fuaradair m

refuge n (abstr & con) tèarmann m, comraich f, dìon m, fasgadh m

refugee n fògrach & fògarrach m

refusal n diùltadh m

refuse n sgudal m, (less usu) fuidhleach m

refuse v diùlt vti, **we** ~**d food** dhiùlt sinn biadh, **their father** ~**d to let them leave** dhiùlt an athair leigeil leotha falbh, **refusing to get up** a' diùltadh èirigh

refute v breugnaich vt

regal adj rìoghail

regard n **1** (respect) meas m, urram m, (**for** air), **I have a great deal of** ~ **for her** tha meas mòr agam oirre; **2** (more affectionate ~) spèis f; **3** (attention, care, concern) for m invar (**for** air), sùim f (**for** de), **he continued, with no** ~ **for me** lean e air, gun for a thoirt ormsa, lean e air, gun sùim aige dhìomsa; **4** (corres etc) **with kindest** ~**s** leis gach deagh dhùrachd m; **5** in expr **with** ~ **to** thaobh or a-thaobh (with gen), **with** ~ **to the war** (a-)thaobh a' chogaidh

regarding prep thaobh or a-thaobh (with gen), **he has problems** ~ **money** tha duilgheadasan aige (a-)thaobh airgid

regiment n rèiseamaid f

region n **1** ceàrn m, sgìre f, tìr mf; **2** (local government admin) roinn f, (formerly) **Highland Region** Roinn na Gàidhealtachd

register v clàraich vti

register n clàr m, ~ **of electors** clàr (an) luchd-taghaidh

registration n clàrachadh m

regret n aithreachas m

regret v bi vi irreg duilich, (more formal) bi vi irreg an t-aithreachas m (with prep air & conj gu), **I** ~ **having done that** tha mi duilich gun do rinn mi sin, tha an t-aithreachas orm gun do rinn mi sin

regular adj **1** (orderly, in accordance with rules etc) riaghailteach, òrdail; **2** (as regards time: consistent, evenly spaced etc) cunbhalach; **3** (gram) riaghailteach, ~ **verbs** gnìomhairean mpl riaghailteach

regularise v riaghailtich vt

regularity n riaghailteachd f invar

regulate v riaghlaich vt, riaghailtich vt, riaghail vt

regulation n **1** (abstr) riaghladh m; **2** (more con: a ~) riaghailt f

rehearsal n aithris f

rehearse v aithris vti

reign n rìoghachadh m (~ **over** air)

reign v rìoghaich vi

reject v diùlt vt, **she won't ~ her own daughter** cha dhiùlt i a nighean fhèin

rejection n diùltadh m

rejoice v dèan gàirdeachas m (**at** ri)

rejoicing n gàirdeachas m (**at** ri)

relate v **1** (recount) innis vt, aithris vt, (**to** do), **I'll ~ what I know** innsidh mi na tha a (for de) dh'fhios agam (air); **2** (be pertinent, connected) bi vi irreg co-cheangailte (**to** ri), **this ~s to what I said yesterday** tha seo co-cheangailte ris na thubhairt mi an-dè

related adj **1** (by kinship) càirdeach (**to** do), **I'm ~ to you** tha mi càirdeach dhut; **2** (linked) co-cheangailte (**to** ri), **the two things are ~** tha an dà rud co-cheangailte (ri chèile)

relation[1] n **1** (kin) caraid m, pl càirdean, (more formal) neach-dàimh m (pl luchd-dàimh m sing coll), **my ~s** mo chàirdean, mo dhaoine (pl of duine m), **a ~ of mine** caraid dhomh (note also **he's a ~ of mine** tha e càirdeach adj dhomh), **all my ~s are in Stornoway** tha mo chàirdean/mo dhaoine air fad ann an Steòrnabhagh

relation[2] **1** (relevance) buinteanas m, in expr **bear ~ to** buin vi ri, **that bears no ~ to the matter** chan eil sin a' buntainn ris a' chùis (idir); **2** in expr **in ~ to** an coimeas ri, **it's light in ~ to its bulk** tha e aotrom an coimeas ri a mheudachd

relationship n **1** (of kinship) càirdeas m, **blood ~** càirdeas-fala (gen of fuil f); **2** (not necessarily of kinship) càirdeas m, dàimh mf invar, **the ~ between the two families** an càirdeas/an dàimh eadar an dà theaghlach; **3** (~ between things, ideas etc) ceangal m, co-cheangal m, (**to** ri, **between** eadar)

relative adj **1** (dependent on circumstances) a rèir, **that's all ~!** tha sin uile a rèir!; **2** (gram) dàimheach, **~ particle** mion-fhacal dàimheach m

relative n, same as **relation**[1]

relax v **1** (rest, take one's ease) gabh fois f, bi vi irreg na (etc) t(h)àmh m; **2** (take things easily) gabh vi air a (etc) s(h)ocair f; **3** (calm down, be less stressed etc) socraich vti, as excl ~! socair!,

air do shocair!; **4** (~ grip, tension on object etc) fuasgail vt

relaxation n fois f, socair f

relaxed adj (esp people) socair, (people, atmosphere etc) socrach, **a ~ pace** ceum socrach

release v **1** (set free) fuasgail vt, cuir/leig vt mu sgaoil m invar, saor vt; **2** (fire) leig vt, ~ **an arrow** leig saighead; **3** (let out, let go/slip) leig vt às, ~ **the dogs** leig às na coin; **4** (bring out film, recording etc) cuir vt a-mach

relevance n buinteanas m (**to** ri, do)

relevant adj **1** a bhuineas (etc) (rel fut of buin vi; **to** ri, do), buntaineach, **evidence ~ to the case** fianais a bhuineas don chùis, **this letter is ~ to the question** tha an litir seo a' buntainn ris a' ghnothach

reliable adj **1** (esp morally) earbsach, urrasach; **2** (esp practically) seasmhach, cunbhalach

reliance n earbsa f invar, creideas m, **place ~ in someone** cuir earbsa ann an cuideigin, thoir creideas do chuideigin

relic n **1** (residue etc) fuidheall m, (less usu) iarmad m; **2** (keepsake etc) cuimhneachan m

relief n **1** (from pain, worry etc) furtachd f invar (**for/from** air), ~ **for/from his anguish** furtachd air a dhòrainn; **2** (from pain, suffering) faothachadh & faochadh m, **he experienced (some) ~** thàinig faothachadh air

relieve v **1** (pain, suffering) faothaich vti; **2** (pain, worry etc) furtaich vi, (with prep air), **she ~d his anguish** dh'fhurtaich i air a dhòrainn

religion n creideamh m, **the Islamic ~** an creideamh Ioslamach

religious n **1** diadhaidh, cràbhach; **2** (idiom: can imply reservations on part of speaker) **they (etc) became very ~** ghabh iad (etc) an cùram

relinquish v leig vt (with prep de), leig vt seachad, trèig vt, **she ~ed her post** leig i dhith/ leig i seachad a dreuchd f

relinquishment n leigeil seachad f, trèigsinn m invar

reluctance n leisg(e) f

reluctant adj leisg, aindeonach, in expr **be ~ is** v irreg & def leisg (with prep le), bi vi irreg leisg(e) f (with prep air), **I am ~ to sell it** is leisg leam a reic, **I was ~ to leave** bha leisg(e) orm falbh

rely v cuir earbsa f invar (**on** ann), earb thu fhèin (etc) (**on** ri), **don't ~ on them** na cuir earbsa annta, na h-earb thu fhèin riutha

remain v **1** (stay) fuirich vi, fan vi, **you ~ where you are!** fuirich/fan thusa far a bheil thu!; **2**

(*continue to be*) **it ~s a good hotel** 's e taigh-òsta math a th' ann fhathast

remainder *n* **1** (*residue*) fuidheall *m*, (*less usu*) iarmad *m*; **2** (*arithmetic*) fuidheall *m*

remark *n* facal *m*, **cutting ~s** faclan geura, *also* briathran geura *mpl*

remark *v* thoir *vt* iomradh *m* (**on, upon** air), **she didn't ~ on it** cha tug i iomradh air

remarkable *adj* air leth, sònraichte

remedial *adj* leasachaidh (*gen of* leasachadh *m used adjectivally*), **~ education** foghlam leasachaidh *m*, **~ unit** ionad leasachaidh *m*

remedy *n* **1** (*health*) leigheas *m*, ìocshlaint *f*, (**for** air), **a ~ for asthma** leigheas air a' chuing; **2** (*for problem etc*) leasachadh *m*, fuasgladh *m*, **there was no ~ for the matter** cha robh leasachadh air a' chùis, **a problem without a ~** ceist/duilgheadas gun fhuasgladh

remedy *v* (*situation etc*) leasaich *vt*, cuir *vt* am feabhas *m*, cuir *vt* ceart

remember *v* **1** cuimhnich *vti*, meòraich *vi*, (*both with prep* air); **2** (*idioms*) **I don't ~** (**him/it** *etc*) chan eil cuimhne *f* agam (air *etc*), **if I ~ rightly** mas math mo chuimhne *f*

remembrance *n* cuimhne *f*

remind *v* **1** (*recall etc*) cuir *vt* na (*etc*) c(h)uimhne *f*, **~ing me of my young days** a' cur nam chuimhne làithean m' òige; **2** (*jog memory*) cuimhnich *vi* (*with prep* do), cuir *vt* na (*etc*) c(h)uimhne, **he ~ed me to give him the key** chuimhnich e dhomh/chuir e nam chuimhne an iuchair a thoirt dha

reminisce *v* cuimhnich *vi*, meòraich *vi*, (**on, about** air)

remnant, remnants *n* fuidheall *m*, (*less usu*) iarmad *m*, **he got his pick of it, I got the ~s** fhuair esan a roghainn dheth, fhuair mise am fuidheall

remote *adj* **1** (*phys distant from centre etc*) iomallach, cèin, **~ area/district** ceàrn iomallach *m*; **2** (*~ in time or space*) cian; **3** (*of place: isolated, lonely*) uaigneach; **4** (*of person: withdrawn etc*) fad' às, dùinte

remoteness *n* (*in time or space*) cian *m*

removal *n* **1** toirt air falbh *f invar*; **2** (*from within something*) toirt às; **3** (*flitting*) imrich *f*

remove *v* **1** thoir *vt* air falbh; **2** (*from within something*) thoir *vt* às

remuneration *n* (*from employment*) pàigh *m invar*, pàigheadh *m*, tuarastal *m*, (*less usu*) cosnadh *m*

rend *v* reub *vt*, srac *vt*

renew *v* **1** (*renovate, refresh*) ùraich *vt*, ath-nuadhaich *vt*; **2** (*replace*) ath-nuadhaich *vt*; **3**

(*reaffirm etc*) ath-nuadhaich *vt*, **they ~ed their vows** dh'ath-nuadhaich iad an geallaidhean *mpl*

renewal *n* ùrachadh *m*, ath-nuadhachadh *m*

renovate *v* ùraich *vt*, nuadhaich *vt*, ath-nuadhaich *vt*, (*more colloquial*) cuir *vt* air dòigh *f*

renovation *n* ùrachadh *m*, nuadhachadh *m*, ath-nuadhachadh *m*, (*more colloquial*) cur air dòigh *m*

renown *n* cliù *m invar*, glòir *f*

renowned *adj* (*persons or things*) ainmeil, (*esp persons*) iomraiteach, cliùiteach

rent[1] *n* (*for property etc*) màl *m*

rent[2] *n* (*rip*) reubadh *m*, sracadh *m*

rent *v* **1** (*as tenant*) gabh *vt* air mhàl *m dat*; **2** (*as landlord*) thoir *vt* seachad air mhàl *m dat*

rented *adj & past part* air mhàl *m dat*, **a ~ house** taigh air mhàl

repair *n* càradh *m*

repair *v* càirich *vt*

repairer *n* neach-càraidh *m* (*pl* luchd-càraidh *m sing coll*)

repay *v* dìoghail & dìol *vt*, **~ a debt** dìo(ghai)l fiach *m*

repayment *n* dìo(gh)ladh *m*

repeat *v* **1** (*verbally*) can *vt def* a-rithist, can *vt* turas *m* eile; **2** (*actions etc*) dèan *vt* (*etc*) a-rithist/turas eile, **she ~ed the song** ghabh i an t-òran a-rithist/turas eile

replace *v* **1** (*return to its place*) cuir *vt* air ais (na (*etc*) àite *m*); **2** (*exchange, substitute*) cuir *vt* an àite *m* (*with gen*), **~ X by Y** cuir Y an àite X; **3** (*~ broken, worn out object etc*) **we ~d the fridge** (*etc*) fhuair sinn/cheannaich sinn frids (*etc*) ùr/eile

replacement *n* **1** (*stand-in etc*) neach-ionaid *m*; **2** (*for car etc*) **~ part**, pàirt-càraidh *mf*

replica *n* mac-samhail *m*, (*more trad*) lethbhreac *m*

reply *n* freagairt *f*, **I didn't get a ~** cha d' fhuair mi freagairt

reply *v* freagair *vi*, thoir freagairt *f* (**to** do), **he hasn't replied yet** cha do fhreagair e fhathast, **we'll ~ to you soon** bheir sinn freagairt dhuibh a dh'aithghearr

report[1] *n* **1** (*in newspaper etc*) iomradh *m*, aithisg *f*, cunntas *m*, **a ~ of the strike** iomradh air an stailc; **2** (*pol, business etc: formal ~*) aithisg *f*

report[2] *n* (*of gunfire*) urchair *f*

repository *n* ionad-tasgaidh *m*

represent *v* (*lawyer, spokesman, actor, artist, sportsman, politician*) riochdaich *vt*

representation *n* riochdachadh *m*

representative *n* riochdaire *m*, **(trade) union** ~ riochdaire aonaidh *m*

repress *v* (*people, emotions etc*) ceannsaich *vt*, mùch *vt*

repression *n* (*of people, emotions etc*) ceannsachadh *m*, mùchadh *m*

repressive *adj* ceannsachail

reproach *n* tarcais *f*, tailceas *m*

reproach *v* cronaich *vt*, càin *vt*, **don't** ~ **her** na cronaich i; **2** (*with following complement*) tilg *vt* (*with prep* air *followed by conj* gu *or* nach), **they** ~**ed me with not being conscientious** thilg iad orm nach robh mi dìcheallach

reproachful *adj* tarcaiseach, tailceasach

reproduce *v* **1** (*breed*) gin *vti*, tàrmaich *vti*; **2** (*copy etc*) dèan lethbhreac *m*/mac-samhail *m* (*with prep* de), ~ **this book** dèan lethbhreac den leabhar seo

reproduction *n* **1** (*breeding*) gineadh *m*, gineamhainn *m invar*; **2** (*the action of copying*) mac-samhlachadh *m*, (*con; copy of book, picture etc*) lethbhreac *m*, mac-samhail *m*, (**of** de)

reproductive *adj* gineamhainn *m invar gen, used adjectivally*, ~ **organs** buill-ghineamhainn *mpl*

reptile *n* pèist *f*

republic *n* poblachd *f*, **the Irish Republic** Poblachd na h-Èireann

republican *adj* & *n* poblachdach *m*

republicanism *n* poblachdas *m*

reputation *n* ainm *m*, cliù *m invar*

request *n* iarrtas *m*, (*less usu*) iarraidh *m*

request *v* iarr *vt*, **they** ~**ed a pay rise** dh'iarr iad àrdachadh pàighidh (*gen of* pàigheadh *m*)

rescue *n* sàbhaladh *m*, **a** ~ **boat** bàta-sàbhalaidh *m*, *also* bàta-teasairginn *m*

rescue *v* teasairg & teasraig *vt*, sàbhail *vt*

research *v* rannsaich, dèan rannsachadh *m* (*with prep* air), sgrùd *vi*, **she's** ~**ing the history of the country** tha i a' rannsachadh eachdraidh na dùthcha (*gen of* dùthaich *f*), tha i a' dèanamh rannsachadh air eachdraidh na dùthcha

research *n* rannsachadh *m*, sgrùdadh *m*

resemblance *n* samhladh *m*, coltas *m*, coimeas *m*

resemble *v* bi *vi irreg* coltach (*with prep* ri), bi *vi irreg* coltas *m* (*with gen and prep* air), **she doesn't** ~ **her brother** chan eil i coltach ri a bràthair, chan eil coltas a bràthar oirre

resembling *adj* coltach (*with prep* ri)

reservation *n* **1** (*booking*) gleidheadh *m*; **2** (*place set aside for particular group, species etc*) tèarmann *m*; **3** (*mental* ~) teagamh *m*, amharas *m*

reserve *n* **1** (*of money, goods etc*) stòr *m*, stòras *m*; **2** (*place set aside for particular group, wildlife etc*) tèarmann *m*, **nature** ~ tèarmann-nàdair *m*; **3** (*in personality: reticence etc*) diùide *f*, (*more distant*) dùinteachd *f invar*

reserve *v* (*book seat etc*) glèidh *vt*

reserved *adj* & *past part* **1** glèidhte, (*copyright*) **all rights** ~ na còraichean *fpl* uile glèidhte; **2** (*of persons: reticent etc*) diùid, sàmhach, (*more distant*) fad' às, dùinte

reservoir *n* loch-tasgaidh *m*

reside *v* còmhnaich *vi*, fuirich *vi*

residence *n* **1** (*abstr*) còmhnaidh *f*, ~ **permit** cead còmhnaidh *m*; **2** (*con*) àite-còmhnaidh *m*, àite-fuirich *m*, dachaigh *f invar*

resident *n* neach-còmhnaidh *m* (*pl* luchd-còmhnaidh *m sing coll*)

residue *n* fuidheall *m*, iarmad *m*, **he got his pick of it, I got the** ~ fhuair esan a roghainn dheth, fhuair mise am fuidheall

resolute *adj* **1** (*persevering, undaunted, determined*) gramail & greimeil, misneachail, suidhichte; **2** (*bold etc*) dàna

resolution *n* **1** (*of character*) misneach *f*, misneachd *f invar*; **2** (~ *of problem etc*) fuasgladh *m*; **3** (*aim, intention; also admin etc*) rùn *m*, **pass/adopt a** ~ gabh *vi* ri rùn

resolve *n* rùn suidhichte *m*

resolve *v* **1** (*to do something*) cuir *vt* roimhe (*etc*), rùnaich *vi*, **they** ~**ed to build a house** chuir iad romhpa taigh a thogail; **2** (~ *difficulty, situation etc*) fuasgail *vt*, rèitich *vt*

resource *n* **1** (*admin etc: esp equipment, materials etc*) goireas *m*, stòras *m*, ~ **centre** ionad-ghoireasan *m*, **natural** ~**s** stòrasan nàdarra(ch), **renewable** ~ stòras leantainneach; **2** (*admin etc: esp fin* ~**s**) ionmhas *m sing*

resourceful *adj* innleachdach, tionnsgalach

resourcefulness *n* innleachd *f*, tionnsgal *m*, tionnsgalachd *f invar*

respect *n* meas *m*, urram *m*, (**for** air), **I have a great deal of** ~ **for her** tha meas mòr agam oirre, **worthy of** ~ airidh air urram, urramach, measail, **mark of** ~ comharradh urraim *m*

respect *v* thoir urram *m*, thoir meas *m*, (*with prep* do)

respectable, respected *adj* measail

respectful *adj* modhail, cùirteil, sìobhalta

respiration *m* analachadh *m*

respite *n* (*from pain, suffering*) faothachadh & faochadh *m*, **he experienced some** ~ thàinig *vi* faothachadh air

respond *v* freagair *vt*

response *n* freagairt *f*

responsibility *n* uallach *m*, cùram *m*, dleastanas *m*, **they charged me with the ~ for the journey** chuir iad orm uallach an turais, **it's your ~** is ann oirbhse a tha an t-uallach, **under Donald's ~** air cùram Dhòmhnaill

responsible *adj* **1** (*in charge*) an urra (**for** ri, *or expr by gen*), **I was ~ for the Post Office** bha mi an urra ri Oifis a' Phuist, **they made me ~ for the journey** chuir iad orm uallach an turais; **2** (*the cause of or reason for something*) coireach (**for** ri), **there's not a soul on the street today; who's/what's ~ for that?** chan eil duine beò air an t-sràid an-diugh; cò/dè as coireach ri sin?, **James was ~ for it** is e Seumas a bu choireach ris

rest¹ *n* fois *f*, tàmh *m*, **take a ~** gabh fois, *also* (*fam*) leig d' (*etc*) anail *f*, (*esp of dead*) **they are at ~ now** tha iad aig fois/nan tàmh a-nise; **2** *in expr* **come to ~** (*on a surface*) laigh *vi*; **3** (*~ in music*) tosd *m invar*

rest² *n* **1** (*others, (the) other people*) **the ~** càch *pron*, an fheadhainn *f sing* eile, **she did better than the ~** rinn i na b' fheàrr na càch, **like the ~** coltach ri càch, coltach ris an fheadhainn eile; **2** (*the other things*) **the ~** an còrr *m invar*, **will you take the ~?** an gabh thu an còrr?; **3** (*remainder, residue*) fuidheall *m*

rest *v* gabh fois *f*, (*fam*) leig d' (*etc*) anail *f*

restaurant *n* taigh-bìdh *m*

restless *adj* (*fidgety etc*) luaisgeach

restrain *v* caisg *vt*, bac *vt*, cuir casg *m* (*with prep* air), ceannsaich *vt*

restraint *n* bacadh *m*, casg *m*, casgadh *m*

restrict *v* (*limit*) cuingealaich *vt*, cuibhrich *vt*, (**to** ri), **a speech ~ed to five minutes** òraid air a cuingealachadh/air a cuibhreachadh ri còig mionaidean

result *n* (*of action etc*) toradh *m*, buil *f*, èifeachd *f invar*, **the ~(s) of your behaviour** toradh do dhol-a-mach, **as a ~ of that** mar thoradh air sin, **exam ~** toradh deuchainn

retailing *n* meanbh-reic *m*

retain *v* glèidh *vt*, cùm *vt* (air ais)

retard *v* cuir maille (*with prep* air *or* ann), maillich *vt*

retch *v* rùchd *vi*

retching *n* rùchd *m*, rùchdail *f*

retire *v* **1** (*for night*) rach *vi* a laighe *mf invar*, rach *vi* don leapaidh *f*; **2** (*from work*) leig dheth (*etc*) obair *f*/dreuchd *f*, **I'll ~ next year** leigidh mi dhìom m' obair/mo dhreuchd an ath-bhliadhna

retirement *n* cluaineas *m*, **come out of ~** thig *vi* air ais bho chluaineas, **~ pension** peinnsean cluaineis *m*

retract *v* thoir *vt* air ais, tarraing *vti* air ais

retrospect *n* ath-bheachd *m*

return *n* tilleadh *m*, **~ journey** turas-tillidh *m*

return *v* **1** (*as vi*) till *vi*, **~ing home** a' tilleadh dhachaigh *adv*; **2** (*as vt, send or take back*) cuir *vt* air ais, thoir *vt* air ais, (**to** gu)

reveal *v* **1** (*objects*) leig *vt* ris, nochd *vt*, seall *vt*, **~ing her knees** a' leigeil a glùinean ris; **2** (*facts*) foillsich *vt*

revelation *n* (*of facts*) foillseachadh *m*

revenge *n* dìoghaltas *m*

revenue *n* teachd-a-steach *m invar*

reverence *n* urram *m*

reverend *adj* urramach, (*of minister*) **the Reverend William Campbell** an t-Urramach Uilleam Caimbeul

review *n* **1** (*critique of book*) lèirmheas *m invar* (**of** air); **2** (*study, investigation*) sgrùdadh *m*, rannsachadh *m*, (**of** air); **3** (*reappraisal etc*) ath-sgrùdadh *m*, ath-bheachdachadh *m*, (**of** air)

review *v* **1** (*book*) dèan leirmheas *m invar* (*with prep* air); **2** (*study, investigate*) sgrùd *vt*, rannsaich *vt*; **3** (*reappraise etc*) ath-bheachdaich *vi* (*with prep* air), ath-sgrùd *vt*

revile *v* màb *vt*, càin *vt*

revise *n* **1** (*for exam etc*) ath-sgrùd *vt*; **2** (*go back on*) atharraich *vt*, **I've ~d my opinion on that** tha mi air mo bheachd atharrachadh air sin

revival *n* **1** (*general*) ath-bheothachadh *m*; **2** (*relig ~*) dùsgadh *m*

revive *v* ath-bheothaich *vt*

revolt *n* ar-a-mach *m invar* (**against** an aghaidh, *with gen*)

revolt *v* èirich *vi* (suas), dèan ar-a-mach *m invar*, (**against** an aghaidh, *with gen*)

revolver *n* daga & dag *m*

reward *n* duais *f*

rheumatism *n* (*used with art*) an lòinidh *mf invar*

rhyme *n* co-fhuaim *m*

rhyme *v* dèan co-fhuaim *m* (**with** le *or* ri)

ribbon *n* rioban *m*

rice *n* rus *m*

rich *adj* **1** (*wealthy*) beartach, saidhbhir; **2** (*of soil*) torrach

riches *n* beartas *m*, saidhbhreas *m*, ionmhas *m*, stòras *m*, maoin *f*

rick *n* cruach *f*, (*small*) cruachan *m*, coc & goc *m*, ruc(a) *m*

rid *adj* & *adv* **1** saor (**of** o), **we're ~ of them at last!** tha sinn saor uapa mu dheireadh thall!;

2 *in expr* **get ~ of** faigh cuidhteas *m* (*with or without prep* de), (*less trad*) faigh clìor is/clìoras, **we got ~ of the bad lodgers** fhuair sinn cuidhteas/fhuair sinn clìor is/clìoras na droch lòisdearan

rid *v*, *in expr* **~ oneself** (*etc*) faigh cuidhteas *m* (*with or without prep* de), (*less trad*) faigh clior is, **we ~ ourselves of the bad lodgers** fhuair sinn cuidhteas/fhuair sinn clior is na droch lòistearan

riddle *n* (*puzzle etc*) tòimhseachan *m*

riddle *v* (*grain etc*) criathraich *vt*

ride *n* (*on vehicle*) cuairt *f*, **we had a ~ on a bus** ghabh sinn cuairt air bus

ride *v* **1** (*on horse*) marcaich *vi*; **2** (*on vehicle*) siubhail *vi*; (**on** air)

rider *n* marcaiche *m*

ridge *n* **1** (*topog*) druim *m*; **2** (*agric, hist: ~ of land for cultivation*) iomair(e) *f*, imire *m*, (*in the form of a 'lazybed'*) feannag *f*

ridge-pole *n* maide-droma *m*, maide-mullaich *m*

ridicule *n* fanaid *f*, bùrt *m*

ridicule *v* dèan fanaid *f* (*with prep* air)

ridiculous *adj* (*person, situation*) amaideach, gun chiall *f*

riding *n* (*of horse*) marcachadh *m*, marcachd *f invar*, **~ school** sgoil-mharcachd *f*

rifle *n* raidhfil *f*

rifle *v* rannsaich *vt*

rig[1] *n* (*agric, hist: ridge of land for cultivation*) iomair(e) *f*, imire *m*, (*in the form of a 'lazybed'*) feannag *f*

rig[2] *n* **1** (*equipment etc*) uidheam *f sing coll*, acainn *f sing coll*

rigging *n* uidheam *f sing coll*, acainn *f sing coll*

right *adj* **1** (*opposite of* left) deas, (*less usu*) ceart, **my ~ hand** mo làmh dheas, **on the ~ hand side** air an làimh dheis (*dat*); **2** (*correct*) ceart, **the answers are ~** tha na freagairtean ceart, **absolutely ~**, **as ~ as can be** cho ceart ri ceart, **~ angle** ceart-uilinn *f*, **put ~** cuir *vt* ceart, ceartaich *vt*; **3** *in exprs* **standing up for what is ~** a' seasamh na còrach (*gen of* còir *f*), **he repaid it, as was only ~** dh'ath-dhìol e e, mar bu chòir

right *adv*, *in exprs* **~ in the middle of the town** ann an teis-meadhan *m* a' bhaile, ann an ceart-mheadhan *m* a' bhaile, **the ~ Reverend William Campbell** am Fìor Urramach Uilleam Caimbeul, **~ then!** ceart, ma-thà!

right *n* **1** (*opposite of* left) an làmh dheas, **on the ~** air an làimh dheis (*dat*); **2** (*justice etc*) còir *f*, ceartas *m*, ceart *m*, **standing up for ~** a' seasamh na còrach (*gen of* còir *f*), (*prov*) **might before ~** thèid neart thar ceairt; **3** (*moral or legal entitlement*) còir *f*, dlighe *f invar*, dleas *m*, **you've no ~ to do that** chan eil còir agad sin a dhèanamh, **~ of entry/access** còir inntrigidh, **human ~s** còraichean daonna, (*copyright statement*) **all ~s reserved** na còraichean uile glèidhte

righteous *adj* ionraic, dìreach

righteousness *n* ionracas *m*

rightful *adj* dligheach

rightly *adv* **1** (*in accordance with morality etc*) mar bu chòir, **he returned the money, (quite) ~**, chuir/thug e an t-airgead air ais, mar bu chòir; **2** *in expr* **if I remember ~** mas math mo chuimhne *f invar*

rigid *adj* **1** (*lit*) rag, cruaidh; **2** (*fig: of person: in opinions, attitudes etc*) rag-bharaileach, rag-mhuinealach

rigidity *n* raige *f invar*

rig out *v* (*equip with machinery etc*) uidheamaich *vt*, beartaich *vt*

rig up *v* tog *vt*, **~ (temporary) lights** tog solais shealach

rim *n* oir *f*, bile *f*, iomall *m*

ring *n* **1** cearcall *m*, **dancing in a ~** a' dannsadh ann an cearcall; **2** (*for finger*) fàinne *mf*, **wedding ~** fàinne-pòsaidh, fainne-pòsta, **engagement ~** fàinne-gealladh-pòsaidh; **3** *in expr* **~ finger** mac-an-aba *m*

ringlet *n* dual *m*, bachlag *f*, camag *f*

ring-road *n* cuairt-rathad *m*

rinse *v* sgol *vt*

rip *n* reubadh *m*

rip *v* reub *vt*, srac *vt*

ripe *adj* abaich

ripen *v* abaich *vti*

ripeness *n* abaichead *m*

rise *n* **1** (*topog: slope*) leathad *m*, bruthach *mf*, **we climbed a slight ~** dhìrich sinn leathad/bruthach beag; **2** (*increment*) àrdachadh *m*, **a pay ~** àrdachadh pàighidh (*gen of* pàigheadh *m*); **3** *in expr* **take a ~ out of them** farranaich *vt* iad, tarraing *vi* asta

rise *v* **1** (*phys*) èirich *vi*, **he rose to his feet/to a standing position** dh'èirich e na sheasamh *m*, **she rose early in the morning** dh'èirich i tràth sa mhadainn; **2** (*become higher, lit or fig*) rach *vi* an-àird *f invar*, **prices/costs are rising** tha prìsean/cosgaisean a' dol an-àird; **3** (*rebel*) **~ (up)** èirich suas, dèan ar-a-mach *m invar*, (**against** an aghaidh *with gen*)

risk *n* cunnart *m*, **at ~** ann an cunnart, **put at ~** cuir *vt* an cunnart

risky *adj* **1** cunnartach, (*usu stronger*) gàbhaidh; **2** (*of precarious business venture etc*) cugallach

rival *n* (*in business, sport etc*) farpaiseach *m*

rivalry *n* còmhstri *f*, farpais *f*

road *n* rathad *m*, **main ~** rathad-mòr, **single/double track ~** rathad singilte/dùbailte, **~ accident** tubaist rathaid *f*, **the ~ home** an rathad dhachaigh

roar *n* beuc *m*, ràn *m*

roar *v* beuc *vi*, ràn *vi*, (*esp of animals*) nuallaich *vi*

roaring *n* beucadh *m*, rànail *m invar*, rànaich *f*

roast *adj & past part* ròsta

roast *v* ròist *vt*

roast, roasted *adj & past part* ròsta

rob *v* creach *vti*, spùill & spùinn *vti*

robber *n* mèirleach *m*, spùinneadair *m*, gadaiche *m*

robe *n* (*ceremonial*) èideadh *m*

robin *n* brù-dhearg *m*

robust *adj* (*of persons*) calma, tapaidh, rùdanach

rock *n* **1** (*the material & a ~*) creag *f*; **2** (*pillar of ~*) carragh *f*; **3** (*esp a ~ by the sea*) carraig *f*

rock *v* **1** (*as vi: seas, ship, trees etc*) tulg *vi*, luaisg *vi*; **2** (*as vt*) tulg *vt*, **~ the cradle** tulg a' chreathail; **3** *in expr* **~ to sleep** tàlaidh *vt*

rocket *n* rocaid *f*

rocking *n* luasgan *m*, tulgadh *m*

rocking-chair *n* sèithear-tulgaidh *m*

rocky *adj* creagach

roe-buck *n* boc-earba *m*

roe-deer *n* earb *f*

roll *v* **1** (*seas, ship etc*) tulg *vi*, luaisg *vi*; **2** (*as vi, of ball, wheel*) roilig *vi*; **3** *as vt*, **~ pastry, cigarette etc*) roilig *vti*; **4** (*material etc*) **~ (up)** paisg *vt*, fill *vt*; **5** (*sleeves etc*) **~ up** tru(i)s *vt*, **he ~ed up his sleeves** thruis e a mhuilchinnean; **6** *in expr* **~ over and over** rach *vi* car *m* mu char

ROM *n* (*IT*) *abbrev* **read only memory** cuimhne bhuan *f*

Roman *adj & n* **1** Ròmanach *m*; **2** *in expr* **~ Catholic** Caitligeach *m & adj*

romance *n* **1** (*romantic novel*) ròlaist *m*, nobhail romansach *f*; **2** (*love affair*) leannanachd *f invar*

Romania *n* Romàinia *f*

Romanian *n & adj* Romàinianach *m*

Rome *n* (*used with art*) An Ròimh *f*

roof *n* mullach *m*, ceann *m*

roof-tree *n* maide-droma *m*, maide-mullaich *m*

rook *n* ròcais *f*

room *n* **1** (*space*) rùm *m*, **there was no ~ in the boat** cha robh rùm sa bhàta; **2** (*apartment*) seòmar *m*, rùm *m*

root *n* (*lit & fig*) freumh *m*, **tree ~** freumh-craoibhe *m*, **he went off to the islands, in search of his ~s** thug e na h-eileanan air, an tòir air a fhreumhaichean

rope *n* ròp(a) *m*

rosary *n* (*the prayer & the beads*) conaire *f*, (*esp the beads*) paidirean *m*

rose *n* ròs *m*

rot *n* grodadh *m*, lobhadh *m*

rot *v* grod *vi*, lobh *vi*

rotate *v* **1** (*as vi*) rach *vi irreg* mun cuairt; **2** (*as vt*) cuir *vt* mun cuairt, cuir car *m* (*with prep* air); **3** (*~ crops etc*) cuartaich *vt*

rotted, rotten *adj* grod, lobhte, *in expr* **go rotten** lobh *vi*

rottenness *n* lobhadh *m*

rough *adj* **1** (*to the touch*) garbh, **~ material** stuth garbh; **2** (*fig*) garbh, **a ~ night** oidhche gharbh; **3** (*hairy, shaggy*) molach, fionnach; **4** (*uncouth, violent etc*) borb, garg

roughness *n* gairbhe *f invar*, gairbhead *m*

round *adj* cruinn

round *adv* timcheall, mun cuairt & mu chuairt, **the picture on the telly was going ~ and ~** bha dealbh an teilidh a' dol timcheall, timcheall, **pass ~ the biscuits** cuir timcheall na briosgaidean, **the cold's going ~** tha an cnatan a' dol mun cuairt

round *n* cuairt *f*, **the postman's ~** cuairt a' phosta, **a ~ of golf** cuairt-ghoilf *f*

round *prep* **1** timcheall (*with gen*), timcheall (*with prep* air), mun cuairt (*with prep* air), **we'll go ~ the loch** thèid sinn timcheall an locha, **there are salesmen going ~ the town** tha luchd-reic a' dol timcheall a' bhaile, **they built houses ~ his garden** thog iad taighean timcheall air a' ghàrradh aige, **are there any shops ~ here?** a bheil bùithtean timcheall air an seo?, **all ~ her** fada mun cuairt oirre; **2** (*esp of garment etc*) mu (*takes the dat*), **put your coat ~ you** cuir umad do chota, **a bandage ~ his head** bann mu cheann (*for prep prons formed with* mu, *see p 510*)

round up *v* (*livestock etc*) cruinnich *vt*, tionail *vt*, tru(i)s *vt*

roundabout *adj, in expr* **we went/took a ~ way** (*ie a detour*) ghabh sinn bealach *m*

roundabout *n* (*at road junction, also in playpark etc*) timcheallan *m*

roundness *n* cruinne *mf*, cruinnead *m*

rouse *v* **1** (*from sleep*) dùisg *vti*, mosgail *vti*; **2** (*arouse emotions, courage etc*) brod *vt*, brosnaich *vt*, misnich *vt*; **3** *in excl* **~ yourself!** tog ort!

rout n (*military etc*) rua(i)g f, ruith f

route n rathad m, slighe f, **they took another ~** ghabh iad rathad eile, **I didn't know the ~** cha robh mi eòlach air an t-slighe

routine adj gnàthach

routine n gnàth-chùrsa m

row¹ n 1 (*din*) gleadhraich f, othail f, faram m; 2 (*quarrel, squabble*) trod m, tuasaid f; 3 *in exprs* **they had a ~** chaidh iad thar a chèile, **give a ~ to** càin vt

row² n 1 (*line, succession etc*) sreath mf; 2 *in expr* **in a ~** (*ie in succession*) an sreath mf a chèile, an ceann m a chèile, an dèidh a chèile, **three accidents in a ~** trì tubaistean an sreath a chèile/an ceann a chèile/an dèidh a chèile

row¹ v (*~ boat*) iomair vti

row² v (*quarrel*) connsaich vi, troid vi

rowan n caorann mf

rowdy adj ùpraideach, gleadhrach

rowing n (*boat*) iomradh m

royal adj rìoghail

royalties npl (*for book etc*) dleas ùghdair m sing

royalty n 1 rìoghalachd f invar

rubber n rubair m, ~ **band** crios-rubair m

rubbish n 1 (*household etc refuse*) sgudal m, (*less usu*) fuidhleach m; 2 (*objects of little worth or value*) sgudal m, truileis f invar, trealaich f; 3 (*fam, one's odds & ends, possessions*) trealaich f, **put that ~ of mine on the floor and sit down** cuir an trealaich sin agam air an làr agus dèan suidhe; 4 (*foolish or inaccurate remarks, opinions etc*) sgudal m, **it's a load of ~!** 's e tòrr sgudail gen a th' ann!/a tha 'n sin!

rucksack n màileid-droma f, poca-droma m

ruddy adj ruiteach

rude adj mì-mhodhail, mì-shìobhalta

rugged adj garbh, **a ~ land** tìr gharbh

ruin n 1 (*~ or ~s of building*) tobhta f sing, làrach f sing; 2 (*fin ~*) bris(t)eadh m

ruin v 1 creach vt, sgrios vt, mill vt; 2 (*child etc: spoil*) mill vt, **they're ~ing that boy** tha iad a' milleadh a' bhalaich ud; 3 (*fin*) bris(t) vt

ruination n 1 creach f, sgrios m, milleadh m; 2 (*fin*) bris(t)eadh m

ruinous adj 1 (*causing ruin*) sgriosail, millteach; 2 (*of building*) a' tuiteam sìos, a' tuiteam às a chèile

rule¹ n 1 (*authority*) ceannsal m, smachd m invar, reachd m invar, **under his enemy's ~** fo cheannsal/smachd/reachd a nàmhaid; 2 (*a ~, ordinance etc*) riaghailt f, (*less usu*) reachd m invar

rule² n (*for measuring*) rùilear m

rule v 1 (*govern a country etc*) riaghail vti; 2 (*issue order, ordain etc*) reachdaich vi, òrdaich vi

ruler¹ n (*head of state etc*) riaghladair m

ruler² n (*for measuring*) rùilear m

Rum n Rùm, Eilean Rù(i)m m, Eilean Ruma

rum n ruma m

rumble, rumbling n 1 torman m; 2 (*of intestines*) rùchdail f

ruminate v 1 (*cows etc*) cnàmh a' chìr; 2 (*humans: think over etc*) cnuas & cnuasaich vi (**on, about** air)

rummage v ruamhair vi, rùraich vi, rannsaich vi, sporghail vi

rumour n fathann m, **~s are going around** tha fathannan a' dol timcheall

run n 1 ruith f, **they went away at a ~** dh'fhalbh iad nan ruith; 2 *in exprs* **he was on the ~** bha e fon choill f invar, **out of the common/ordinary ~ of things** às a' chumantas m invar

run v 1 ruith vti, **she ran two miles yesterday** ruith i dà mhìle an-dè, **the train's/the water's not ~ning** chan eil an trèana/an t-uisge a' ruith; 2 (*misc exprs*) **~ out** (*of supplies etc: come to an end*) ruith vi a-mach (**of** à), **the sugar ran out** ruith an siùcar a-mach, **we ran out of sugar** ruith sinn a-mach à siùcar, **~ out** (*of liquids: flow*) sruth vi, ruith vi, sil vi, **~ away** (*flee*) teich vi, tàrr vi, *also* tàir às, **the soldiers ran away** theich na saighdearan, thàir na saighdearan às, **~ over** (*overflow*) cuir vi thairis

rung n rong f, rongas m

running n ruith f, **I like ~** is toigh leam a bhith a' ruith

runny adj (*of liquids, foods etc*) tana

runway n (*at airport etc*) raon-laighe m

rural adj dùthchail

rush, rushes n(pl) (*ie the plant*) luachair f sing coll

rush n 1 (*haste, hurry*) cabhag f, **we're in a ~** tha cabhag oirnn, **he finished it in a ~** chuir e crìoch air ann an cabhaig (*dat*); 2 (*hurried gait*) dian-ruith & deann-ruith f, **he left in a ~** dh'fhalbh e na dhian-ruith

rush v 1 (*carry out action etc hurriedly*) expr by the appropriate verb followed by na (*etc*) d(h)ian-ruith m, or ann an cabhaig (*dat of* cabhag f), or gu cabhagach, **they ~ed home** chaidh iad dhachaigh nan dian-ruith, **they ~ed their dinner** ghabh iad an dinnear ann an cabhaig/gu cabhagach; 2 (*cause to ~*) cuir cabhag f (*with prep* air), **she ~ed the pupils at**

the end of the morning chuir i cabhag air na sgoilearan aig deireadh na maidne

Russia n Ruisia f, an Ruis f

Russian[1] n Ruiseanach m, *also as adj* Ruiseanach

Russian[2] n (*lang*) Ruiseanais f *invar*

rust n meirg f

rust v meirg *vti*, meirgich *vti*

rustproof *adj* meirg-dhìonach

rusty *adj* meirgeach

rut n (*in ground*) clais f, sgrìob f

rut, rutting n (*of deer*) dàmhair f

rutting *adj* 1 (*of deer*) dàireach; 2 *in expr* ~ time/season dàmhair f

rye n seagal m

S

sack *n* poca *m*, sac *m*

sack *v* **1** (*ransack etc*) rannsaich *vt*, creach *vt*; **2** (*dismiss from job*) cuir *vt* à dreuchd *f*

sacred *adj* naomh, coisrigte

sacrifice *n* (*relig*) ìobairt *f*

sacrifice *v* (*relig*) ìobair *vt*

sad *adj* brònach, muladach, truagh, dubhach, cianail, **that's ~!** is truagh sin!, **I'm ~** tha mi brònach/muladach, tha mulad orm, (*more trad*) tha mi fo bhròn *m*/fo mhulad *m*

saddle *n* dìollaid & diallaid *f*

sadness *n* bròn *m*, mulad *m*, cianalas *m*

safe *adj* **1** (*building, place of refuge etc*) dìonach, tèarainte; **2** (*person*) sàbhailte; **3** *in expr* **~ and sound** slàn is fallain, (*more trad*) gu slàn fallain

safeguard *n* tèarmann *m*, dìon *m*

safeguard *v* dìon *vt*

safety *n* tèarainteachd *f invar*, sàbhailteachd *f invar*, **in** ~ an tèarainteachd, ~ **equipment** uidheam sàbhailteachd *f sing coll, in expr* ~ **pin** *n* prìne-banaltraim *m*

sailor *n* seòladair *m*, maraiche *m*, **he's a** ~ tha e na sheòladair, *also* tha e aig muir *mf*/aig fairge *f*

saint *n* naomh *m*

saintliness *n* naomhachd *f invar*

saintly *adj* naomh

salary *n* tuarastal *mf*

sale *n* **1** reic *m invar*, **it's not for** ~ chan eil e ri reic; **2** (*esp of livestock*) fèill *f*, **lamb** ~ fèill-uan *f*

salesperson *n* neach-reic *m* (*pl* luchd-reic *m sing coll*)

saliva *n* seile *m invar*

sallow *adj* odhar, lachdann

salmon *n* bradan *m sing & coll*

salt *n* salann *m*

saltire *n* (*heraldry etc*) crann *m*, **the Saltire** An Crann

salutation *n* fàilte *f*

salute *n* fàilte *f*, (*bagpipe music*) **Chisholm's** ~ Fàilte an t-Siosalaich

salute *v* fàiltich *vt*

same *adj* **1** ceart, (*more emph*) ceudna, dearbh (*precede the noun, which is lenited where*

possible), fhèin, **at the** ~ **time** aig a' cheart àm, **the** ~ **amount/quantity** a' cheart uimhir, a' cheart uiread, **the (very)** ~ **man** an duine ceudna, an dearbh dhuine, *also* an aon duine, **the (very)** ~ **man I saw yesterday** an duine fhèin a chunna mi an-dè

same *n* **1** (*similar, identical*) ionann, co-ionann (*used with v is*), **you and I are not the** ~ chan ionann thusa 's mise, **it wasn't the** ~ **when we were young** cha b' ionann nuair a bha sinn òg; **2** *in expr* **the** ~ **as** ionann is/agus, co-ionann ri, **Y is the** ~ **as X** is ionann Y is/agus X, tha Y co-ionann ri X, **'bùrn' and 'uisge' are the** ~ **as each other** tha bùrn is/agus uisge co-ionnan ri chèile; **3** *in expr* (**give me etc**) **the** ~ **again** (*thoir dhomh etc*) uimhir *f invar* eile, (*thoir dhomh etc*) uiread *m invar* eile

sample *n* eisimpleir *mf*, taghadh *m*, samhla *m*

sanctity *n* naomhachd *f invar*

sanctuary *n* (*abstr & con*) tèarmann *m*, comraich *f*

sand *n* gainmheach *f*

sandal *n* cuaran *m*

sandpaper *n* pàipear-gainmhich *m*

sandwich *n* pìos *m*, (*more trad*) ceapaire *m*

sandy *adj* gainmheil

sane *adj* ciallach

sanity *n* ciall *f*, rian *m*, reusan *m*, **I nearly lost my** ~ cha mhòr nach deach mi às mo chiall/mo rian, cha mhòr nach do chaill mi mo rian

sap *n* **1** (*of tree*) snodhach *m*, sùgh *m*; **2** (*fig: essence, vigour*) brìgh *f invar*

sarcasm *n* gearradh *m*, searbhas *m*, beum *m*

sarcastic *adj* geur, searbh, beumach

sardonic *adj* searbh

satchel *n* màileid *f*

satellite *n* saideal *m*

satire *n* aoir *f*

satirical *adj* aoireil

satisfaction *n* toileachadh *m*, (*can be more physical* ~) sàsachadh *m*.

satisfied *adj & past part* riaraichte, sàsaichte, toilichte

satisfy *v* riaraich *vt*, sàsaich *vt*, toilich *vt*

Saturday *n* Disathairne *m invar*

sauce *n* **1** (*for food*) leannra *m*, (*less trad*) sabhs *m*; **2** (*fam: cheek*) aghaidh *f*, bathais *f*

saucer *n* sàsar *m*, flat *m*

saunter *v* sràidearaich *vi*

sausage *n* isbean *m*

savant *n* eòlaiche *m*, saoi *m*

save *v* **1** (*~ from danger or other difficulty*) sàbhail *vt*, teasairg & teasraig *vt*, **they were ~d by a lifeboat** chaidh an sàbhaladh le bàta-teasairginn, **it's the visitors who ~d the island** is e an luchd-tadhail a theasairg an t-eilean; **2** (*spiritually: convert etc*) tèarainn *vt*, sàbhail *vt*, **~ the heathens** tèarainn na pàganaich; **3** (*preserve, keep safe*) glèidh *vt*, **God will ~ us** gleidhidh Dia sinn; **4** (*money: put aside*) sàbhail *vt*, glèidh *vt*, cuir *vt* mu seach; **5** (*~ money, eg by spending thriftily*) caomhain *vt*

saved *adj & past part* sàbhailte

savings *n* sàbhaladh *m*, tasgadh *m*

sawdust *n* min-sàibh *f*

say *v* abair *vti irreg*, can *vti def*, **what are you ~ing?** dè a tha thu ag ràdh?, **what did you ~?** dè a thu(bha)irt thu?, **~ it again** can a-rithist e, **as they ~** mar a chanas iad, **what do you ~ in Gaelic for 'spade'?** dè a chanas sibh sa Ghàidhlig *f* ri 'spade'?, *also* dè a' Ghàidhlig a th' air 'spade'?

saying *n* seanfhacal *m*, facal *m*, (*less usu*) ràdh *m invar*, **'blood is thicker than water' is a ~** is e seanfhacal a th' ann an 'is tighe fuil na bùrn'

scab *n* sgreab *f*, càrr *f*

scale¹ *n* (*of fish, reptile etc*) lann *f*

scale² *n* **1** (*range, sequence*) raon *m*, sreath *mf*, **~ of temperature** raon teodhachd; **2** (*mus*) sgàla *f*; **3** (*in drawings etc: proportion*) sgèile *f*, tomhas *m*, **~ drawing** dealbh sgèile *mf*

scales *n* (*for weighing*) meidh *f*, cothrom *m*

scallop *n* creachan *m*, **~ shell** slige creachain *f*

Scalpay *n* Sgalpaigh

scalpel *n* sgian lèigh *f*

scandalous *adj* tàmailteach, maslach

Scandinavia *n* Lochlann *mf*

Scandinavian *n & adj* Lochlannach *m*

scant *adj* gann, tearc

scantness *n* gainne *f invar*, gainnead *m invar*, teirce *f invar*

scanty *adj* **1** gann, tearc; **2** (*esp of hair, growing crop etc*) gann, tana; **3** (*of garment*) goirid, geàrr, gann

scar *n* làrach *f*

scarce *adj* gann, tearc

scarcely *adv*, *same as* **barely** *adv*

scarceness, scarcity *n* gainne *f invar*, gainnead *m invar*, teirce *f invar*

scarecrow *n* bodach-ròcais *m*

scare *n* eagal *m*, (*weaker*) clisgeadh *m*, **I had a ~** ghabh mi an t-eagal

scare *v* cuir an t-eagal (*with prep* air), **he ~d her** chuir e an t-eagal oirre

scared *adj & past part* **1** fo eagal *m*, **a ~ man** duine fo eagal, *also* duine is an t-eagal air; **2** (*misc exprs*) **I was ~** (*became ~*) thàinig an t-eagal orm, ghabh mi an t-eagal, (*was in a ~ state*) bha an t-eagal orm, **I was ~ stiff/~ to death** bha eagal mo bheatha orm, **I never get ~** cha ghabh mi an t-eagal uair sam bith

scarlet *adj* **1** sgàrlaid; **2** *in expr* **~ fever** (*used with art*) am fiabhras dearg *m*

scarlet *n* sgàrlaid *f*

scary *adj* critheanach

scatter *v* sgap *vti*, (*less brusque*) sgaoil *vti*

scatter-brained *adj* guanach, *in expr* **~ girl** guanag *f*

scattered *adj & past part* sgapte

scenery *n* sealladh dùthcha *m*

scent *n* (*pleasant or unpleasant*) fàileadh *m*, àile *m*, boladh *m*, (*usu pleasant*) boltrach *m*

sceptical *adj* teagmhach

schedule *n* **1** clàr-tìde *m*, clàr-obrach *m*; **2** *in exprs* **ahead of ~** tràth *adv*, ron mhithich *f invar*, air thoiseach, **behind ~** fadalach, air dheireadh

scheme *n* **1** sgeama *m*, **housing ~** sgeama-thaighean *m*; **2** (*plot etc*) innleachd *f*, cuilbheart *f*

scheme *v* dèan innleachd(an) *f(pl)*

scholar *n* (*school pupil & learned person*) sgoilear *m*, (*learned person*) eòlaiche *m*

scholarly *adj* sgoilearach

scholarship *n* (*abstr: erudition; also con: bursary etc*) sgoilearachd *f*

school *n* sgoil *f*

schooling *n* sgoil *f*, foghlam *m*, **we got our ~ in Fort William** fhuair sinn ar sgoil anns a' Ghearastan

schoolmaster *n* maighstir-sgoile *m*

schoolmistress *n* ban(a)-mhaighstir-sgoile *f*

schoolteacher *n* tidsear *m*, fear-teagaisg *m*, neach-teagaisg *m* (*pl* luchd-teagaisg *m sing coll*), bean-teagaisg *f*, maighstir-sgoile *m*, ban(a)-mhaighstir-sgoile *f*, ban-sgoilear *f*

science *n* saidheans *m*, eòlas *m*

scientific *adj* saidheansail

scientist *n* neach-saidheans *m* (*pl* luchd-saidheans *m sing coll*), eòlaiche *m*

scoff¹ v (mock etc) mag vi, dèan fanaid f, (with prep air)

scoff² v (way of eating) glàm & glamh vt

scoffing adj (mocking) magail

scoffing¹ n (mockery) magadh m

scoffing² n (~ of food) glàmadh, glamhadh m

scold v càin vt, cronaich vt

scolding n càineadh m, cronachadh m

scoop n ladar m, liagh f, taoman m

scorch v dòth vt

score¹ n (in wood etc) sgrìob f

score² n (twenty) fichead m (takes the nom sing, ie radical, of the noun), **three ~ years** trì fichead bliadhna

score³ n (sports, games) sgòr m, (more trad) cunntas m

scorn n tarcais f, tailceas m, tàir f, dìmeas m invar

scorn v dèan tarcais f, dèan tàir f, dèan dìmeas m invar, (all with prep air), **they ~ed us** rinn iad tarcais/tàir/dìmeas òirnn

scorned adj & past part fo dhìmeas m invar

scornful adj tarcaiseach, tailceasach, tàireil, dìmeasach

Scot n Albannach m

Scotland n Alba f

Scots n (lang) (a') B(h)eurla Ghallta, Albais f

Scotsman n Albannach m

Scots pine n giuthas m

Scotswoman n ban-Albannach f

Scottish adj Albannach

scoundrel n slaightire m, balgair m

scourge n 1 (lit) sgiùrs(air) m; 2 (fig: destructive events etc) sgrios m, plàigh f

scourge v sgiùrs vt

scowl n drèin f, gruaim f, mùig m, sgraing f

scowl v cuir drèin f, cuir gruaim f, cuir mùig m, (all with prep air), **she ~ed** chuir i drèin/gruaim/mùig oirre, **they were sitting in the corner**, **~ing** bha iad nan suidhe anns a' chòrnair, is drèin/gruaim/mùig orra

scowling adj gruamach

scrap¹ n 1 (small piece) mìr m, bìdeag f, criomag f; 2 (left after scrapping machinery etc) fuidheall m

scrap² n (fight) tuasaid f, (usu more serious) sabaid f

scrap¹ v (fight) bi vi irreg ri tuasaid f dat

scrap² v 1 (~ worn-out machinery etc) bris(t) vt suas, cuir vi às (with prep do); 2 (~ plans etc) leig vt seachad

scrape n 1 (scratch etc) sgrìob f; 2 (tricky situation etc) (droch) staing f, cùil-chumhang f

scrape v 1 (general) sgrìob vti; 2 (involuntarily: esp skin of hand etc) rùisg vt

scratch n sgrìob f, sgròb m

scratch v 1 (damage) sgrìob vt; 2 (~ an itch) tachais vt, sgròb vt, sgrìob vt

sratchy adj sgrìobach

scream n sgreuch m, sgread m, sgiamh m

scream v leig sgread m (with prep à), sgreuch vi, sgread vi, sgiamh vi, **she ~ed** leig i sgread aiste

scree n sgàirneach f

screech n sgread m, sgreuch m

screech v sgread vi, sgreuch vi

screen n sgàilean m

screen v sgàil vt, sgàilich vt, falaich vt, ceil vt

screw n sgriubha mf, (more trad) bithis f

screwdriver n sgriubhaire m

scripture n sgriobtar m

scrotum n clach-bhalg m

scrub v sgùr vt

scruffy adj luideach, robach

scruple n imcheist f, teagamh m

scrupulous adj 1 (morally ~) ionraic, onarach, cogaiseach; 2 (punctilious etc) mion-chùiseach, mionaideach, pongail, cùramach

scrutineer n sgrùdair m

scrutinise v sgrùd vt, rannsaich vt

scrutiny n sgrùdadh m, rannsachadh m

scullery n cùlaist f

sculpture n 1 (the action) snaigheadh m; 2 (the product) ìomhaigh (shnaighte)

scurf n càrr f

scurrilous adj tuaileasach, sgainnealach, maslach

scythe n speal f

sea n 1 muir mf, cuan m, fairge f, **on land and ~** air muir 's air tìr mf, **go to ~** rach vi irreg gu muir, **he's at ~** tha e aig muir/aig fairge, **~ level** còmhnard na mara m, **~ bird** eun-mara m, **~ loch** loch-mara m; 2 in expr (fig) **all at ~** troimh-a-chèile, am breislich m

sea-bed n grunnd na mara m, grinneal m

seaboard n oirthir f

sea-chart n cairt-iùil f

seafarer n maraiche m

seagull n faoileag f

seal¹ n (sea creature) ròn m

seal² n (identifying image, ~ on document etc) seula m

seam n fuaigheal m

seam v fuaigh vt, fuaigheil vt

seaman n 1 maraiche m, seòladair m; 2 in expr **he's a ~** tha e aig muir mf

search

search *n* tòir *f*, lorg *f*, **in ~ of** an tòir air, **he went to town in ~ of his sister** chaidh e dhan bhaile (is e) an tòir air a phiuthair

search *v* **1** rannsaich *vt*, **~ the building** rannsaich an togalach; **2 ~ for** lorg *vt*, sir *vt*

seashore *n* (*esp between high- and low-water mark, esp sandy*) tràigh *f*, (*can be stony/ shingly*) cladach *m*

sea-sickness *n* cur *m invar* na mara, tinneas *m* (na) mara

season *n* **1** (*~ of the year*) ràith *f*; **2** (*less specific*) tràth *m*, **a word in ~** (*ie at the appropriate time*) facal na thràth

sea-spray *n* cathadh-mara *m*

seat *n* **1** (*phys: actual chair etc*) suidheachan *m*; **2** (*more abstr: place where one sits*) àite-suidhe *m*, **there wasn't a ~ to be had** cha robh àite-suidhe ri fhaighinn; **3** *in expr* **take a ~!** dèan suidhe *m*!; **4** (*site of an activity etc*) ionad *m*, **a ~ of learning** ionad-sgoilearachd *m*; **5** (*fam: backside*) màs *m*, tòn *f*

sea-trout *n* bànag *f*

sea-voyage *n* turas-mara *m*

seaweed *n* feamainn *f*

secluded *adj* (*of place*) falaichte, uaigneach, **a ~ glen** gleann falaichte

second *adj* **1** dara & dàrna, **the ~ day of the month** an dara là den mhìos, **he was/came ~/ he came in ~ place** bha e san dara h-àite; **2** *in expr* **~ sight** an dà shealladh *m*, taibhsearachd *f invar*

second *n* (*clock time*) diog *m*, tiota *m*, (*more loosely*) tiotag *f*, **I'll only be a ~** cha bhi mi ach diog/tiotag

second *v* (*formal meeting etc*) cuir taic *f* (*with prep* ri), **I will ~ the motion** cuiridh mi taic ris a' ghluasad *m*

secondary *adj* **1** (*subsidiary*) fo- *prefix* (*lenites following cons where possible*), *eg* **~ characteristics** fo-fheartan *fpl*; **2** (*ed: above primary*) **~ school** àrd-sgoil *f*, **~ education** foghlam àrd-sgoile *m*

second-hand *adj* cleachdte

secrecy *n* dìomhaireachd *f invar*

secret *adj* **1** (*of place*) uaigneach; **2** (*of fact, document etc*) dìomhair

secret *n* cagar *m*, rùn (dìomhair) *m*

secretarial *adj* clèireach

secretary *n* **1** (*clerical grade staff*) clèireach *m*, ban(a)-chlèireach *f*; **2** (*PA*) neach-cuideachaidh pearsanta *m*, bean-chuideachaidh phearsanta *f*; **3** (*political etc office*) rùnaire *m*, ban-rùnaire *f*, **the Secretary of State** Rùnaire na Stàite

secrete¹ *v* (*conceal*) cuir *vt* am falach *m*, falaich *vt*

secrete² *v* (*~ liquids*) sil *vti*, snigh *vti*

secretly *adv* os ìosal & os ìseal

section *n* **1** (*esp of objects*) earrann *f*, pàirt *mf*, **a ~ of his novel** earrann den nobhail aige, **a ~ of the building** earrann/pàirt den togalach; **2** (*group of people, department etc*) roinn *f*, buidheann *mf*, **the secretarial ~** an roinn chlèireach, **a ~ of soldiers** buidheann (de) shaighdearan

sector *n* roinn *f*, **the public/private ~** an roinn phoblach/phrìobhaideach

secular *adj* saoghalta, talmhaidh

secure *adj* **1** (*safe etc*) tèarainte, dìonach, **~ hide-out** àite-falaich tèarainte/dìonach; **2** (*officially/ legally recognised*) tèarainte, **~ tenure** (*of land etc*) gabhaltas tèarainte, **~ status for Gaelic** inbhe thèarainte airson na Gàidhlig; **3** (*business etc: fin ~*) urrasach

security *n* tèarainteachd *f invar*, (*IT*) **data ~** tèarainteachd dàta

sediment *n* (*in liquids*) grùid *f*

see *v* **1** faic *vti irreg*, **I can't ~ anything at all** chan fhaic mi càil sam bith, **it's good to ~ you** 's math d' fhaicinn, **I'll be ~ing you** bidh mi gad fhaicinn/gur faicinn, **I'll ~ you later/again** chì mi fhathast sibh/thu, **we'll ~!** chì sinn!; **2** (*understand, realise*) faic *vti irreg*, tuig *vti*, is *v irreg def* lèir (*with prep* do), **I ~ now!** tha mi a' faicinn/a' tuigsinn a-nis, **he could ~ that he was wrong** bu lèir dha gun robh e ceàrr; **3** (*find out, check*) feuch *vi*, faic *vi*, **I'll go and/to ~ if the potatoes are done/ready** thèid mi ann feuch a bheil am buntàta deiseil, **open the door to/and ~ if it's still raining** fosgail an doras feuch a bheil an t-uisge ann fhathast; **4** (*be sure to etc*) feuch *vi* (*with conj* gu), **~ that you're there early** feuch gum bi thu ann ron àm; **5** (*visit*) **come/go to ~** thig/rach *v irreg* air chèilidh *mf*, tadhail *vi*, (*both with prep* air), **we'll come to ~ you tomorrow** thig sinn air chèilidh oirbh a-màireach; **6 ~ to** (*tend to objects etc*) sgeadaich *vt*, cuir *vt* ceart, **~ to the fire** sgeadaich an teine; **7** (*misc exprs*) **I'll ~ to it** nì mise e, **I'll ~ you along the road** thèid mi an rathad leat/còmhla riut, **let's ~** fuirich (ort), **I saw him . . . , let's ~ . . . , yesterday** chunna mi e . . . , fuirich (ort) . . . , an-dè, **~ off** (*drive away*) rua(i)g *vt*, cuir *vt* an teicheadh *m* (*with prep* air), **the dog saw off the fox** ruaig an cù am madadh-ruadh, chuir an cù teicheadh air a' mhadadh-ruadh, (*fam*) **~ off** (*defeat etc*) dèan a' chùis/an gnothach, faigh làmh-an-uachdair *f*, (*both with prep* air), **we saw off the other**

team rinn sinn a' chùis/an gnothach air an sgioba *mf* eile, ~ **red** rach *vi* air bhoile *f invar*
seed *n* sìol *m sing coll*, fras *f sing coll*, **barley** ~ sìol-eòrna *m invar*, **sow** ~ cuir sìol
seek *v* sir *vt*, lorg *vt*
seem *v* 1 (*expr resemblance, or impression given*) bi *vi irreg* coltas *m* (*with gen & prep* air), **he ~s like a decent man** tha coltas duine chòir air; 2 *in expr* (*impersonal*) **it ~s** tha e coltach (*with conj gu*), a rèir c(h)oltais (*gen of* coltas *m*), **it ~s that he lost his job** tha e coltach gun do chaill e obair, **it ~s there'll be a storm** a rèir choltais, bidh stoirm ann; 3 (*expr experience, or impression received*) bi *vi irreg* followed by the appropriate adj (with prep do), **the days ~ed long to us** bha na làithean fada dhuinn, **it ~ed long/tedious to me** (*more trad*) b' fhada leam e
seemingly *adv* a rèir c(h)oltais (*gen of* coltas *m*)
seer *n* fiosaiche *m*, fàidh *m*
seethe *v* 1 (*liquids*) goil *vi*; 2 (*person: ~ with rage*) bi *vi irreg* air bhoile *f invar*, bi *vi irreg* air bhàinidh *f invar*
segregate *v* dealaich *vt* (**from** ri)
segregation *n* dealachadh *m* (**from** ri)
seize *v* glac *vt*, beir *vi*, gabh grèim *m*, (*all with prep* air), greimich *vt* (*with prep* air *or* ri)
seized *adj & past part* glacte
seizure *n* glacadh *m*
seldom *adv* is gann, (*more trad*) is ainneamh, (*with conj* a), **you'll ~ see the likes of him** is gann a chì thu a leithid *f*
select *v* tagh *vt*, roghnaich *vt*, **he ~ed the team** thagh e an sgioba *mf*
selected *adj & past part* air a (*etc*) t(h)aghadh, taghta
selection *n* taghadh *m*, roghainn *m*
-self *reflexive suffix* fhìn, fhèin, **myself** mi fhìn, **yourself** (*sing fam*) thu fhèin, **himself** e fhèin, **herself** i fhèin, **ourselves** sinn fhìn, **yourselves/yourself** (*pl & sing formal*) sibh fhèin, **themselves** iad fhèin; **he saw himself** chunnaic e e fhèin, **they were washing themselves** bha iad gan nighe fhèin, **take care of yourself** thoir an aire ort fhèin, **as for myself** air mo shon fhìn, **Mary herself** Màiri fhèin
self- *reflexive prefix* fèin- (*lenites following cons where possible: see examples below*)
self-abasement *n* fèin-ìsleachadh *m*
self-government *n* fèin-riaghladh *m*
self-importance *n* fèin-spèis *f*
self-indulgence *n* fèin-mhilleadh *m*
selfish *adj* fèineil, fèin-chùiseach

selfishness *n* fèinealachd *f invar*
selfless *adj* neo-fhèineil
self-love *n* fèin-spèis *f*
self-respect *n* fèin-mheas *m*
self-service *n* fèin-fhrithealadh *m*
self-sufficient *adj* fèin-fhoghainteach
sell *v* reic *vti*, **I've nothing to ~** chan eil càil agam ri reic, **~ at a good price** reic air deagh phrìs
seller *n* reiceadair *m*
semen *n* sìol *m*, sìol-ginidh *m*
semi(-) *prefix* leth- (*lenites following cons where possible: see examples below*)
semicircle *n* leth-chearcall *m*
semicircular *adj* leth-chearclach
semicolon *n* leth-chòilean *m*
semi-detached *adj* leth-dhealaichte
seminar *n* (*business, ed etc*) seiminear *m*, (*more trad*) co-labhairt *f*
semivowel *n* leth-fhoghair *m*
senate *n* seanadh *m*
senator *n* seanadair *m*
send *v* cuir *vt* (**to** gu), ~ **away/off** cuir *vt* air falbh, **I sent you a letter** chuir mi litir thugad, ~ **him word** cuir fios thuige, ~ **for someone** cuir *vi* a dh'iarraidh cuideigin, cuir fios air cuideigin, ~ **for the AA** cuir fios air an AA, ~ **on an errand** cuir *vt* air gnothach
senior *adj* 1 (*first in rank*) prìomh (*precedes the noun & lenites following cons where possible*), ~ **judge** prìomh bhritheamh; 2 (*oldest*) as sine, (*in past & conditional tense*) a bu shine; 3 *in expr* ~ **citizen** seann duine *m*, neach-peinnsein *m* (*pl* luchd-peinnsein *m sing coll*)
sensation *n* (*abstr*) mothachadh *m*, (*abstr & con*) faireachdainn *f*
sense *n* 1 (*understanding, intelligence*) tuigse *f invar*, ciall *f*; 2 (*common ~*) toinisg *f*, ciall *f*; 3 (*esp in pl: one's reason*) rian *m*, ciall *f*, **I nearly went out of my ~s** cha mhòr nach do chaill mi mo rian, theab mi a dhol às mo rian
senseless *adj* 1 (*foolish, meaningless, pointless*) gun chiall *f*, dìomhain, faoin; 2 (*stunned etc*) gun mhothachadh *m*
sensibility *n* mothachadh *m*
sensible *adj* (*having common sense*) ciallach, tuigseach, toinisgeil
sensitive *adj* 1 mothachail; 2 (*too ~*) bog, maoth; 3 (*touchy*) frionasach; 4 (*of situations: tricky, precarious*) cugallach
sensitivity *n* mothachadh *m*
sensual *adj* feòlmhor, collaidh
sensuality *n* feòlmhorachd *f invar*

sentence n 1 (*legal*) binn f, breith f *invar*, **give/ pronounce** ~ thoir a-mach binn, thoir breith, (**on** air); **2** (*gram*) seantans mf, (*more trad*) rosg-rann f

sentence v 1 thoir a-mach binn f, thoir breith f *invar*, (*with prep* air), **he** ~**d them** thug e a-mach binn orra; **2** *in expr* ~ **to death** dìt vt gu bàs m

sentiment n 1 (*feeling*) mothachadh m; **2** (*opinion: usu in pl*) beachdan mpl, smuaintean fpl, **the** ~**s you expressed** na beachdan a chuir sibh an cèill (*dat of* ciall f)

sentimental adj (*of person*) maoth-inntinneach

sentinel, sentry n neach-faire m

separate adj **1** (*apart, another*) air leth, fa leth, eile, **in a** ~ **room** ann an seòmar air leth/fa leth, ann an seòmar eile; **2** (*distinct, independent*) eadar-dhealaichte, (*less strong*) diof(a)rach, **the two questions are completely** ~ tha an dà cheist gu tur eadar-dhealaichte

separate v **1** dealaich vti (**from** ri), **he** ~**d the brothers (from each other)** dhealaich e na bràithrean mpl (bho chèile), **death** ~**d them** dhealaich am bàs iad; **2** (~ *into smaller quantities, portions etc*) roinn vt

separation n **1** dealachadh m (**from** ri); **2** (*of spouses*) dealachadh-pòsaidh m

sequence n sreath mf, ruith f

serene adj ciùin, socair, (*less usu*) suaimhneach

series n sreath mf

serious adj **1** (*important, weighty*) trom, cudromach, ~ **matters** cuspairean troma/ cudromach; **2** (*severe, extreme*) droch, **a** ~ **crime** droch eucoir; **3** (*of persons:* ~ *minded, earnest*) dùrachdach, (*sober, staid*) stòlda; **4** (*opposite of jesting*) ann an da-rìribh, **I told you I was pregnant, but I wasn't** ~! dh'innis mi dhut gun robh mi trom, ach cha robh mi ann an da-rìribh!

serpent n nathair f

serve v **1** fritheil vi (*with prep* air), ~ **someone** fritheil air cuideigin, ~ **at table** fritheil air a' bhòrd, (*more trad*) freastail vi don bhòrd; **2** (*dish out food etc*) riaraich vt, thoir vt seachad; **3** (*suffice for the task in hand etc*) **that will** ~ (**the purpose**) nì sin an gnothach; **4** (*animals mating*) rach vi *irreg* air muin f *invar* (*with gen*), **the bull** ~**ed the cow** chaidh an tarbh air muin na bà

service n **1** freastal m, frithealadh m, ~ **at table** freastal don bhòrd m, ~ **station**, ~ **area** stèisean-/ionad-frithealaidh m; **2** (*helpful action*) seirbheis f, **he rendered me a** ~ rinn e

seirbheis dhomh; **3** (*church, tennis, garage etc*) seirbheis f

service v **1** (*machinery etc*) gleus vt, cùm vt air dòigh f; **2** (*provide support, supplies etc for*) fritheil vi (*with prep* air)

servile adj tràilleil

session n (*parliament, committee etc*) seisean m, **in** ~ ann an seisean

set adj & *past part* (*fixed, established*) suidhichte, stèidhichte, ~ **procedures** dòighean-obrach suidhichte, ~ **in his ways** suidhichte na dhòighean

set n seat(a) m

set v **1** (*place, position*) suidhich vt, socraich vt, cuir vt, ~ **the statue on the column** suidhich/ socraich/cuir an ìomhaigh air a' cholbh; **2** *in various exprs with* cuir vt, ~ **up** cuir vt air chois (*dat of* cas f), cuir vt air bhonn m, **she** ~ **up a business** chuir i gnothach air chois/air bhonn, ~ **apart** cuir vt air leth, ~ **aside** cuir vt an dara taobh, cuir vt mu seach, **this** ~ **me thinking** chuir seo gu smaointeachadh mi, (*idioms*) **I** ~ **them at each other's throats** chuir mi aig ugannan a chèile iad, ~ **the cat among the pigeons** cuir an ceòl air feadh na fìdhle; **3** (*of the sun*) laigh vi, rach vi fodha; **4** (*other misc exprs*) ~ **the house on fire** leig an taigh na theine m, cuir teine ris an taigh, ~ **the table** deasaich am bòrd, ~ **free** cuir vt mu sgaoil, leig vt mu sgaoil, saor vt, fuasgail vt, **we** ~ **them free** chuir/leig sinn mu sgaoil iad, ~ **to/about** teann vi (*with prep* ri), crom vi (*with prep* air), **he** ~ **about climbing** theann e ri streap, **she** ~ **to work** chrom i air an obair, **she** ~ **off/out** ghabh i an rathad, thog i oirre, **they** ~ **about each other** ghabh iad dha chèile

setback n duilgheadas m, bacadh m

settee n sòfa f, (*more trad*) langasaid f

setting n (*context, situation*) suidheachadh m

settle v **1** (*calm, make or become comfortable etc*) socraich vti; **2** (*sort, solve*) rèitich vt, socraich vt, ~ **the matter/dispute** rèitich an gnothach/a' chonnspaid; **3** (*close, finalise*) cuir crìoch f (*with prep* air), **that** ~**s the matter!** tha sin a' cur crìoch air a' chùis!; **4** (*come to rest*) laigh vi, **the bird** ~**d on its nest** laigh an t-eun air a nead; **5** (*esp liquids*) tràigh vi; **6** (*inhabit*) tuinich vi (**in** ann an), **the first race that** ~**d in America** a' chiad chinneadh a thuinich ann an Ameireagaidh

settled adj & *past part* (*fixed, established*) suidhichte, seasmhach, ~ **in his ways** suidhichte na dhòighean fpl

settlement n 1 (*habitational: abstr & con*) tuineachadh m; 2 (*of dispute etc*) rèiteachadh m

settler n neach-tuineachaidh m (*pl* luchd-tuineachaidh m *sing coll*

sever v 1 (*cut off*) geàrr vt dheth; 2 (*fig: part, separate*) dealaich vti, sgar vti, (**from** ri)

several adj 1 (*a limited number, a few*) beagan m, (*a larger number*) grunnan m, (*both with gen pl of n*), **I met ~ people** thachair mi ri beagan/grunnan dhaoine; 2 (*a more substantial number*) iomadh, **~ hundred years** iomadh ceud bliadhna

severe adj 1 (*of person, discipline etc*) cruaidh, teann; 2 (*hard to bear*) goirt, **a ~ trial** deuchainn ghoirt; 3 (*extreme*) droch (*precedes the noun, which it lenites where possible*), **~ disadvantage** droch anacothrom m

sew v fuaigh vti, fuaigheil vti

sewage n òtrachas m, **~ works** ionad-òtrachais m

sewer n sàibhear m, giodar m

sewing n (*abstr & con*) fuaigheal m

sewn adj & past part fuaighte

sex n 1 (*gender*) gnè f invar, **the female/male ~** a' ghnè bhoireann/fhireann; 2 (*sexual activity, lovemaking*) feise f, (*less usu*) sùgradh m; 3 in expr **have ~** faigh muin f invar, co-ghin vi, cuplaich vi, **he had ~ with her** chaidh e air a muin

sexist adj gnèitheil

sexual adj 1 gnèitheach, gnèitheasach; 2 in exprs **~ equality** co-ionannachd nan gnè f, **~ activity/relations/intercourse** feise f, **~ desire** miann mf, (*more lustful*) ana-miann mf, drùis f

shabby adj 1 (*of appearance etc*) luideach, cearbach, robach; 2 (*of conduct etc*) suarach, (*stronger*) tàireil

shackle n geimheal m

shackle v geimhlich vt

shade n same as **shadow** n 1

shade v duibhrich vti

shadow n 1 (*shade*) dubhar m, sgàil(e) f, dubharachd f invar, **in the ~ of the walls** fo dhubhar(achd)/sgàil nam ballachan; 2 (*thrown ~*) faileas m, **her ~ fell on me** laigh a faileas orm

shadowy adj faileasach

shady adj dubharach

shaft n 1 (*of light*) gath m; 2 (*engin*) crann m; 3 (*of hand-tool*) cas f

shaggy adj molach, ròmach, fionnach, robach

shake n (*involuntary*) crith f

shake v 1 (*deliberately*) crath vti, **he shook his head/fist** chrath e a cheann/a dhòrn; 2

(*involuntarily*) bi vi irreg air chrith f, (*less usu*) crith vi, **he was shaking with the fever** bha e air chrith leis an fhiabhras, in expr **start to ~** rach vi air chrìth; 3 (*surfaces etc*) luaisg vi, **the building was shaking** bha an togalach a' luasgadh; 4 in expr **~ hands**, beir vi air làimh f dat (*with prep* air), **he didn't ~ hands with me** cha do rug e air làimh orm

shaking adj air chrith f, **~ with fever** air chrith leis an fhiabhras m

shaking n luasgan m

shaky adj 1 (*lit*) cugallach, critheanach, (*stronger*) tulgach, **~ on his feet** cugallach air a chasan, **~ bridge** drochaid chritheanach; 3 (*fig: dodgy, dubious*) cugallach, **don't get involved in it, it's pretty ~** na gabh gnothach ris, tha e gu math cugallach

shallow adj 1 (*lit*) eu-domhainn, (*of water*) tana; 2 (*fig: of person, activity etc*) faoin, dìomhain

shambles n bùrach m, **in a ~** ann am bùrach

shame n 1 nàire f invar, masladh m, tàmailt f, **feel ~** gabh nàire, **without ~** gun nàire, **for ~!** nàire!, **~ on you!** mo nàire ort!; 2 in exprs **put to ~** nàraich vt, maslaich vt, **that's a ~!** tha sin duilich!, (*more trad*) is truagh sin!

shame v nàraich vt, maslaich vt

shame-faced adj nàrach

shameful adj nàr, maslach, tàmailteach

shameless adj gun nàire, ladarna

shaming n nàrachadh m, maslachadh m

shamrock n seamrag f

shape n cruth m, cumadh m, dealbh & deilbh mf, **a stone in the ~ of a horse** clach air chumadh/air dhealbh/air cruth eich, **I made out his ~ in the darkness** rinn mi a-mach a chruth/a chumadh san dorchadas

shape v cum vt, dealbh vt

shapely adj cuimir

share n 1 cuid f, cuibhreann m, roinn f, **there's your ~** sin agad do chuid-sa (dheth), **a half ~** leth-chuid; 2 (*fin*) earrann f, sèar m, **~s fell today** thuit earrannan/sèaraichean an-diugh

share v 1 (**~ something with others**) co-roinn vt; 2 (**~ out**) pàirtich vt, roinn vt, riaraich vt

shared adj & past part 1 roinnte; 2 (*held or used in common*) coitcheann, **~ facilities** goireasan coitcheann mpl

sharp adj 1 geur, **~ knife** sgian gheur, **~ eye** sùil gheur, *also* sùil bhiorach, **~ taste** blas geur; 2 (*pointed*) biorach, **a ~ stick** maide biorach; 3 (*mentally ~*) geur/grad/luath na (*etc*) inntinn f, eirmseach; 4 (*remarks, tongue etc*) geur, guineach, biorach

sharpen v faobharaich vt, geuraich vt

sharpness n gèire f invar

shatter v 1 (as vi) rach vi irreg na (etc) b(h)loighdean fpl; 2 (as vt) bloighdich vt

shattered adj & past part 1 (lit) na (etc) b(h)loighdean fpl; 2 (fig & fam: exhausted) seac searbh sgìth

shave v beàrr vt, lom vt

she pers pron i, (emph form) ise, ~ **saw her** chunnaic i i

sheaf n (of corn) sguab f

shear v (sheep) rùisg vt, lom vt

shearing n (of sheep etc) rùsgadh m, lomadh m

shears n (ie a pair of ~) deamhais mf sing

shebeen n taigh-dubh m, bothan m

shed n seada mf, bothan m

shed v dòirt vt, ~ **blood** dòirt fuil f

sheep n (single ~) caora f, (pl) caoraich fpl

sheepdog n cù-chaorach m

sheepfank faing f, fang m

sheepfold n crò(-chaorach) m, faing f, fang m

sheepish adj nàrach, air a (etc) nàrachadh

sheep-shearer n lomadair m

sheep-tick n mial-chaorach f

sheet n 1 (for bed) siota m; 2 (of paper) duilleag f

shelf n 1 sgeilp f; 2 (topog: rock ~) leac f, (esp in sea) sgeir f

shell n 1 (of nuts, eggs) plaosg m, slige f; 2 (of ~fish; also artillery ~) slige f

shell[1] v 1 (nuts, eggs) rùisg vt, plaoisg; 2 (peas & beans) plaoisg vt

shell[2] v (bombard) tilg slige(ach)an fpl (with prep air)

shellfish n maorach m (sing & coll)

shelter n 1 (esp from elements) fasgadh m (**from** o & bho), ~ **belt** crios fasgaidh, **take** ~ **from the downpour** gabh fasgadh on dìle; 2 (esp protective ~) dìon m, **in the** ~ **of the castle** fo dhìon a' chaisteil

shelter v 1 (as vi: take cover etc) gabh fasgadh m (**from** bho/o), **we** ~**ed from the weather** ghabh sinn fasgadh on t-sìde; 2 (as vt, lit and fig: provide ~) thoir fasgadh m (with prep do), (esp protectively) dìon vt, **the castle** ~**ed us** dhìon an caisteal sinn

sheltered adj fasgach, (esp protectively) dìonach, ~ **spot** bad fasgach

sheltering adj fasgach, (esp protectively) dìonach, **a** ~ **wood** coille fhasgach

shepherd n cìobair m

shepherding n cìobaireachd f invar

sheriff n siorram m, **the Sheriff Court** Cùirt an t-Siorraim f

sheriffdom n (hist) siorramachd f invar

Shetland n Sealtainn m

shield n 1 sgiath f, (trad, hist) targaid f; 2 (fig) dìon m

shield v dìon vt

shieling n (hist) àirigh f, (less usu) ruighe mf, ~ **hut/bothy** bothan àirigh m

shift v caraich vt, gluais vti, cuir car m (with prep de)

shifting adj 1 (liable to move) gluasadach; 2 (inconstant, liable to change) caochlaideach, carach, luaineach

shifty adj fiar, carach

shilling n (hist) tastan m

shin n lurgann f, faobhar na lurgainn m

shine n (on shoes etc) lìomh f

shine v 1 (as vi: lights etc) deàlraich vi, deàrrs vi, **the sun's not shining** chan eil a' ghrian a' deàrrs(ach)adh; 2 (as vt: ~ shoes etc) lìomh vt

shingle n mol m, morghan m

shining adj 1 deàlrach; 2 (~ with polish etc) lìomharra

shinty n iomain f, camanachd f invar, **we were playing** ~ bha sinn ag iomain, in expr ~ **stick** caman m

shiny adj, same as **shining** adj

ship n long f, soitheach m, bàta (mòr) m

shipping n loingeas & luingeas m, luingearachd f invar

shipwreck n long-bhris(t)eadh m

shirt n lèine f

shit v (fam/vulg) cac vi

shit(e) n (fam/vulg) cac m, (fig: fam/vulg, pej) **(it's) a load of** ~! ('s e) tòrr caca m (a th' ann)!

shiver n crith f

shiver v crith vi, bi vi irreg air chrith f, **he** ~**ed** chrith e, **he was** ~**ing** bha e air chrith, **start to** ~ rach vi air chrith

shivering adj air chrith f, ~ **with cold** air chrith leis an fhuachd

shivering n crith f

shock n (through fear or surprise) clisgeadh m, **he gave me a** ~ chuir e clisgeadh orm

shocking adj oillteil, uabhasach

shoddy adj 1 luideach, cearbach, robach; 2 (of workmanship etc) dearmadach, coma co-dhiù

shoe n 1 bròg f; 2 (of horse) bròg-eich f, (more trad) crudha m

shoe v (horse) crudhaich vt, cuir crudha m (with prep air)

shoe-lace n iall bròige f, barrall m

shoemaker, shoe-repairer n greusaiche m

shoot n (of plants etc) ògan m, gas f, bachlag f

shoot v 1 (with a firearm) loisg vti, tilg vti, (**at** air); 2 (~ a person) tilg vi ann (etc), leig peilear m ann (etc), **he shot her** leig e peilear innte

shooting n losgadh m, tilgeil f

shop n bùth f, **fish** ~ bùth-èisg (gen of iasg m), **chemist's** ~ bùth-chungaidh, **craft** ~ bùth-chiùird (gen of ceàrd & cèard m), in expr **blacksmith's** ~ ceàrdach f

shopkeeper n neach-bùtha m (pl luchd-bùtha m sing coll), **the** ~ fear m na bùtha, bean f na bùtha

shore n 1 (sea~: esp between high- and low-water mark, esp sandy) tràigh f, (can be stony/shingly) cladach m; 2 (in opposition to sea) tìr f, **on** ~ air tìr

short adj 1 goirid, geàrr, ~ **story** sgeulachd ghoirid, **the days are getting** ~ tha na làithean a' fàs goirid, **a** ~ **time ago** o chionn ghoirid, **in/after a** ~ **time** an ceann ghoirid, an ùine gheàrr, **in the** ~ **term** sa gheàrr-ùine f; 2 (of person: brusque etc) aithghearr, cas; 3 in exprs **in** ~ **supply** gann, a dhìth, easbhaidheach, **food is** ~/**in** ~ **supply** tha biadh gann/a dhìth, **we won't go** ~ cha bhi dìth oirnn, ~ **cut** bealach goirid

shortage n cion nm invar, dìth m, gainne f, uireasbhaidh f

shortcoming n fàillinn f, meang m

shorten v 1 (as vt) giorraich vt; 2 (as vi: grow shorter) rach vi an giorrad m

shorter comp adj giorra, **the days are getting** ~ tha na làithean mpl a' fàs nas giorra, also tha na làithean a' dol an giorrad m

shorthand n geàrr-sgrìobhadh m

short-legged adj geàrr-chasach

shortly adv 1 a dh'aithghearr, an ceann ghoirid, (ann) an ùine gheàrr, **she'll be here** ~ bidh i ann a dh'aithghearr; 2 (brusquely) gu grad

shortness n giorrad m

shorts n 1 (trousers) briogais ghoirid; 2 (cinema) filmichean goirid mpl

short-sighted adj geàrr-sheallach

short-sightedness n geàrr-shealladh m

shot n 1 (from firearm) urchair f, **I heard a** ~ chuala mi urchair; 2 (fam: attempt) oidhirp f, ionnsaigh f, (at air), **he had another** ~ **at it** rinn e oidhirp eile air, in expr (fam) **I gave it my best** ~ rinn mi mo dhìcheall m air; 3 in expr (ironic) **a big** ~ duine mòr (cudromach), **the big** ~s na daoine mòra

shotgun n gunna-froise m

should auxiliary v bu (past/conditional of is v irreg def) chòir f (with prep do), **I** ~ **go/I** ~ **be going** bu chòir dhomh (a bhith a') falbh, **you** ~**n't smoke** cha bu chòir dhut smocadh, **it's not as good as it** ~ **be** chan eil e cho math 's a bu chòir (dha a bhith)

shoulder n 1 gualann & gualainn f, ~ **to** ~ gualainn ri gualainn; 2 in expr ~ **blade** cnàimh-slinnein m

shout n glaodh m, iolach f, èigh f

shout v glaodh vi, dèan/tog iolach f, èigh or èibh vi

shove v 1 (jostle etc) put vt; 2 (esp ~ objects) sàth vt, spàrr vt, ~ **it into the cupboard** sàth a-steach sa phreas e, ~ **your hand into the sack** spàrr do làmh sa phoca

shovel n sluasaid f

show n 1 (of art, goods, techniques etc) taisbeanadh m; 2 (ostentation etc) spaide f

show v 1 seall vt, nochd vt, (to do), ~ **me it** seall/nochd dhomh e, also leig fhaicinn dhomh e; 2 (fam: turn up etc) nochd vi, **he didn't** ~ **(up) before midnight** cha do nochd e (a-staigh) ro mheadhan-oidhche; 3 (exhibit) taisbean & taisbein vt

shower n 1 (of rain) fras f, (heavier) meall m, meall-uisge m; 2 (bathroom equipment) frasair m, (the ~ one takes) fras f; 3 in expr (fam: group of incompetents) **what a** ~! abair bumailearan mpl!

showery adj frasach

showing adv ris, **her elbow was** ~ bha a h-uileann ris

showy adj spaideil, basdalach

shrewd adj geurchuiseach, tuigseach, (less usu in this sense) seòlta

shriek n sgread m, sgreuch m

shriek v sgread vi, sgreuch vi

shrill adj sgalanta

shrimp n carran m

shrink v lùghdaich vti, teannaich vti

shrinkage n lùghdachadh m, teannachadh m

shrivel v searg vi, crìon vi

shroud n marbhphaisg f

shrub n preas m, (less usu) dos m

shrunken adj & past part crìon, seargte

shun v 1 (avoid) seachain vt, cùm vi (with prep o), ~ **her** seachain i, cùm uaipe; 2 (ostracise etc) cuir cùl m (with prep ri)

shut adj & past part 1 (buildings, objects etc) dùinte; 2 (fam: rid) cuidhteas m (with or without prep de), saor (**of** o), clìor (**of** is), **we got** ~ **of the builders** fhuair sinn cuidhteas an luchd-togalaich, **we're** ~ **of them at last!** tha sinn saor uapa/tha sinn clìor is iad mu dheireadh thall!

shut v dùin vti, ~ **the door** dùin an doras, **the shop was** ~**ting** bha a' bhùth a' dùnadh, **the window** ~ **with a bang** dhùin an uinneag le brag, (vulg) ~ **your gob!** dùin do chab/do ghob!

shy *adj* diùid

shy *v* 1 (*horse etc*) thoir uspag *f*; 2 *in expr* **apt to**
~ sgeunach

shyness *n* diùide *f invar*, diùideachd *f invar*

sick *adj* 1 (*ill etc*) tinn, euslainteach, (*less usu*)
anfhann, *in exprs* ~ **pay** pàigheadh tinneis *m*,
~ **leave** fòrladh tinneis *m*; 2 *in expr* **be** ~ (*ie
vomit*) dìobhair *vi*, sgeith *vi*; 3 (*fed up etc*) sgìth,
(*stronger*) seac searbh sgìth, (**of** de), **I'm** ~ **and
tired/heartily** ~ **of your carrying-on!** tha mi
seac searbh sgìth den dol-a-mach *m invar* agad!

sick *n* 1 (*in pl: ill people*) **the** ~ na h-euslaintich
mpl; 2 (*vomit*) dìobhairt *m invar*

sick up *v* dìobhair *vt*, tilg *vt*, cuir *vt* a-mach, **the
boy sicked up his dinner** dhìobhair/thilg am
balach a dhinnear, chuir am balach a-mach a
dhinnear

sicken *v* 1 (*become sick*) fàs *vi* tinn; 2 (*disgust*)
cuir sgreamh *m* (*with prep* air), sgreataich *vt*, **it
~s me** tha e a' cur sgreamha orm

sickle *n* corran *m*

sickly *adj* (*off colour*) bochd, (*stronger*) tinn,
euslainteach

sickness *n* tinneas *m*, gearan *m*, galar *m*, ~
benefit sochair tinneis *f*

side *n* 1 taobh *m*, (*more trad*) leth *m invar*, (*esp
of body, hill*) cliatha(i)ch *f*, **there's a pain
in my** ~ tha pian nam chliathaich, **the lorry
struck the** ~ **of the house** bhuail an làraidh
taobh/cliatha(i)ch an taighe, **the west** ~ (*of
the country etc*) an taobh siar, *also* an taobh an
iar, **at my** ~ rim thaobh, ~ **by** ~ taobh ri taobh,
put to/on one ~ cuir an dara taobh, *in expr*
~ **of the head** lethcheann *m*; 2 (*topog:* ~ *of
hill*) leathad *m*, bruthach *mf*, cliatha(i)ch *f*; 3 (*in
dispute etc*) taobh *m*, leth *m invar*, **we took her**
~ ghabh sinn a taobh-se, chaidh sinn às a leth,
chùm sinn taobh rithe; 4 (*pride*) leòm *f*

side *v in expr* **we ~d with her** ghabh sinn a
taobh-se *m*, chaidh sinn às a leth *m invar*, chùm
sinn taobh rithe

sideways *adv* an comhair a (*etc*) t(h)aoibh (*gen
of* taobh *m*), **the mare fell** ~ thuit an làir an
comhair a taoibh

siege *n* sèist *mf*, **under** ~ fo shèist, **lay** ~ cuir
sèist (**to** air)

siesta *n* dùsal feasgair *m*

sieve *n* criathar *m*

sieve, sift *v* criathraich *vt*

sigh *n* osna *f*, osnadh *m*, osann *m*, (*less usu*)
ospag *f*, **heave a** ~ leig/dèan osna, osnaich *vi*

sigh *v* leig/dèan osna *f*, osnaich *vi*

sighing *n* osnaich *f*, osnachadh *m*

sight *n* 1 (*eye~*) fradharc & radharc *m*, lèirsinn
f invar, (*less usu in this sense*) sealladh *m*; 2
(*field of vision*) sealladh *m*, (f)radharc *m*, fianais
f, **he was/he came in(to)** ~ bha/thàinig e an
sealladh/san t-sealladh, bha/thàinig e san
(fh)radharc/am fianais, **out of** ~ à sealladh, às
an t-sealladh, às an (fh)radharc, à fianais, **out of
my** ~! **a-**mach às mo shealladh/às m' fhianais!,
we lost ~ **of him** chaill sinn sealladh air, **we
were in** ~ **of the island** bha sinn am fianais an
eilein; 3 (*view, spectacle*) sealladh *m*, **beautiful
~s** seallaidhean brèagha; 4 *in expr* **second** ~ an
dà shealladh *m sing*, taibhsearachd *f invar*; 5 (~
of a gun) amharc *m*

sign *n* 1 comharra(dh) *m*, samhla(dh) *m*, **that's
a good/bad** ~! is e deagh/droch chomharradh
a tha ('n) sin!, ~ **of respect** comharradh
urraim, **'-an' is a** ~ **of the plural** is e '-an'
samhla/comharradh an iolra; 2 (*giving
information, directions etc*) soidhne *m*, **road**
~ soidhne-rathaid *m*; 3 (*hint, signal*) sanas *m*,
comharra(dh) *m*, **he gave me a** ~ **with a wink
of his eye** thug e sanas dhomh le priobadh a
shùla (*gen of* sùil *f*); 4 (*trace etc*) lorg *f*, sgeul
m, **there's no** ~ **of it/him** chan eil lorg air,
is there any ~ **of Seumas?** a bheil sgeul air
Seumas?

sign *v* (*documents etc*) cuir m' (*etc*) ainm *m* (*with
prep* ri), **she ~ed the letters** chuir i a h-ainm
ris na litrichean

signal *n* sanas *m*, comharra(dh) *m*, **he gave
me a** ~ **with a wink of his eye** thug e sanas
dhomh le priobadh a shùla (*gen of* sùil *f*)

signature *n* ainm (sgrìobhte) *m*, **append your**
~ **to the contract enclosed** cuiribh ur n-ainm
ris a' chùmhnant a tha an cois (na litreach seo)

significance *n* brìgh *f*, ciall *f*, **statements of no**
~ briathran gun bhrìgh

significant *adj* 1 (*of importance*) cudromach,
a ~ **change** atharrachadh cudromach; 2
(*meaningful*) brìgheil

signify *v* ciallaich *vt*, **what does the new
policy ~?** dè a tha am poileasaidh ùr a'
ciallachadh?

signpost *n* clàr-seòlaidh *m*, post-seòlaidh *m*,
soidhne *m*

silence *n* tosd *m invar*, sàmhchair *f*, (*as
command*) ~! tost!

silent *adj* 1 sàmhach, gun fhuaim *mf*, (*esp of
person*) tosdach, na (*etc*) t(h)osd *m invar*,
they were ~ bha iad nan tosd; 2 (*rendered
speechless*) balbh, (*stronger*) bog balbh, **he was**
~ **in the face of his wife's anger** bha e balbh
ro fheirg (*dat of* fearg *f*) na mnà aige

silk n sìoda m

silky adj sìodach

silliness n gòraiche f invar, amaideas m, faoineas m

silly adj gòrach, faoin, baoth, **don't be ~!** na bi gòrach!

silt n eabar m, poll m

silver n airgead m

silver adj airgid (gen of airgead m, used adjectivally)

silversmith n ceàrd-airgid m

similar adj coltach (**to** ri), **all the buildings were ~ (to each other)** bha na togalaichean air fad coltach ri chèile

similarity n coltas m

simile n (Lit etc) samhla(dh) m

simple adj 1 (easy) furasta, soirbh, sìmplidh, **a ~ job/question** obair/ceist fhurasta; 2 (plain, unpretentious) sìmplidh, **a ~ dwelling** àite-còmhnaidh sìmplidh; 3 (~-minded) sìmplidh, baoth

simplicity n sìmplidheachd f invar

simplify n sìmplich vt

simultaneous adj 1 co-amail; 2 in expr ~ **translation** eadar-theangachadh mar-aon m

simultaneously adv aig an aon àm m

sin n 1 peacadh m, **a mortal ~** peacadh-bàis, **original ~** peacadh-gine, (not nec in full rel sense, eg) **kissing is no ~** cha pheacadh pògadh

sin v peacaich vi

since conj 1 (causal) on & bhon (with conj a), a chionn is (with conj gu), **they put the stock on the hill ~ the grazing was good up there** chuir iad an sprèidh dhan mhonadh on a bha/a chionn 's gu robh an t-ionaltradh math shuas an sin; 2 (time) o & bho, on & bhon (with conj a), **the first letter she's sent me ~ I got to know her** a' chiad litir a tha i air a chur thugam bhon a chuir mi eòlas oirre, **it's a long time ~ I was at school** 's fhada on a bha mi san sgoil, (or, with subordinate v in neg) 's fhada o nach robh mi san sgoil, **it's a long time ~ we saw you** is fhada o nach fhaca sinn sibh

since prep (temporal) o chionn & bho chionn, **I've been working for him ~ a year ago** tha mi ag obair aige bho chionn bliadhna

sincere adj dùrachdach, fosgarra

sincerity n dùrachd mf, treibhdhireas m

sincerely adv (corres) **yours ~** le dùrachd mf, is mise le meas m invar

sinew n fèith f

sinewy adj fèitheach

sinful adj peacach

sing v 1 seinn vti, gabh vt, **will you ~ for us?** an seinn thu dhuinn?, ~ **a song!** gabh òran!, in expr ~ **to sleep** tàlaidh vt; 2 (of birds) ceileir vi

singe v dòth vt

singer n seinneadair m, ban-seinneadair f

single adj 1 singilte, ~ **track road** rathad singilte, ~ **bed** leabaidh shingilte; 2 (unmarried) singilte, gun phòsadh m, **when I was ~ and my pocket did jingle** nuair a bha mi singilte 's a bha mo phòc' a' gliongadaich; 3 in exprs **a ~ man** fleasgach m, **a ~ woman** maighdeann f; 4 (in emph exprs) aon, **we didn't see a ~ person** chan fhaca sinn fiù is aon duine, also chan fhaca sinn duine sam bith/duine beò/duine no duine, **every ~** gach aon, **it rained every ~ day** bha an t-uisge ann gach aon là

singular adj 1 (strange) àraid, neònach, (stronger) iongantach, **wasn't that ~?** nach robh sin àraid/neònach?, (trad) nach neònach sin?, **a ~ occurrence** tachartas iongantach; 2 (exceptional) sònraichte, àraid, **a ~ man** duine sònraichte/àraidh; 3 (gram) singilte, ~ **noun** ainmear singilte

sink n (kitchen etc) sinc(e) mf

sink v 1 (levels, liquids) tràigh vi, traogh vi, sìolaidh vi; 2 (send/go to the bottom) cuir vt fodha, rach vi irreg fodha, ~ **a boat** cuir fodha bàta, **the boat sank** chaidh am bàta fodha

sinner n peacach m

sip n drùdhag f, balgam m

sip v gabh drùdhag f, gabh balgam m, (**of** de)

siren n dùdach mf, dùdag f

sister n piuthar f

sister-in-law (spouse's sister) piuthar-chèile f, (brother's wife) bean-bràthar f

sisterhood, sisterliness n peathrachas m

sit v 1 (be in a sitting position) bi vi irreg na (etc) s(h)uidhe m, **you were ~ting in the corner** bha thu nad shuidhe sa chòrnair; 2 (take a seat) suidh vi, dèan suidhe m, **he sat in the corner** shuidh e sa chòrnair, ~ **down** suidh vi sìos, dèan suidhe m, ~ **(down) beside me** dèan suidhe rim thaobh; 3 (seat someone) cuir vt na (etc) s(h)uidhe, **we sat them (down) in the corner** chuir sinn nan suidhe iad anns a' chòrnair; 4 in expr ~ **an exam** feuch/suidh deuchainn f

site n 1 làrach f, ionad m, **a house ~, a ~ for a house** làrach taighe, **Site of Special Scientific Interest** Ionad de Shùim Shònraichte Shaidheansail; 2 (setting, location, position) suidheachadh m, **a good ~ for a cinema** deagh shuidheachadh airson taigh-

dhealbh; **3** (*IT*) ionad *m*, làrach *f*, **internet/web**
~ làrach-lìn *f*

sitting *n* **1** (~ *of court, parliament etc*) suidhe *m*,
seisean *m*; **2** *in expr* ~ **room** seòmar-suidhe *m*

situation *n* **1** (*circumstances*) suidheachadh *m*,
staid *f*, **our ~ was better after I found work**
bha an suidheachadh againn na b' fheàrr an
dèidh dhomh obair fhaighinn, **we were in a**
bad ~ financially bha sinn ann an droch staid
a thaobh airgid, **in a (very) difficult** ~ ann
an droch staing *f*; **2** (*setting, location, position*)
suidheachadh *m*, **a good ~ for a cinema** deagh
shuidheachadh airson taigh-dhealbh; **3** (*post,*
job) dreuchd *f*

six *n & num adj* **1** sia; **2** (*idioms*) ~ **and half a**
dozen bò mhaol odhar agus bò odhar mhaol, **at**
~**es and sevens** troimh-a-chèile

sixty *n & num adj* trì fichead *m*, (*in alt numbering*
system) seasgad *m*

size *n* **1** meud *m invar*, meudachd *f invar*,
the ~ of the house/the field meud an
taighe/an achaidh, **increase in** ~ rach *vi*
irreg am meud, **the ~ of their debts** meud/
meudachd nam fiachan aca, **about the ~ of**
a pig mu mheudachd muice (*gen of* muc *f*); **2**
(*dimensions*) tomhas *m*, **the ~ of the tractor**
tyre tomhas taidhr an tractair

sizeable *adj* tomadach & tomaltach, (*more fam*)
gu math mòr

skeleton *n* cnàimhneach *m*

skelp *n* dèiseag *f*, sgailc *f*

skelp *v* thoir *vt* sgailc (*with prep* do)

sketch *n* sgeidse *f*, ~ **book** leabhar sgeidse *m*

skewer *n* dealg *f*

ski *n* sgì *f*, ~**s** sgithean

ski *v* sgithich *vi*

skiing *n* sgitheadh *m*

skilful, skilled *adj* gleusta, sgileil, teòma, ~ **in**
the handling of weapons gleusta ann an
làimhseachadh nan arm/nam ball-airm

skill *n* sgil *m*

skin *n* **1** (*of creatures, humans*) craiceann *m*; **2**
(*hide of bovine etc*) seiche *f*, bian *m*; **3** (*of fruit,*
vegetables) plaosg *m*, rùsg *m*

skin *v* **1** (*fruit, vegetables*) rùisg *vt*, plaoisg *vt*; **2**
(*animals*) thoir an craiceann *m* (*with prep* de); **3**
(*graze etc*) rùisg, **I ~ned my hand** rùisg mi mo
làmh; **4** (~ *peat-bank*) feann *vt*

skinny *adj* **1** (*thin*) caol, tana, seang; **2** (*mean*)
spìocach, mosach

skip *n* leum *m*, sùrdag *f*

skip *v* **1** (*small jump*) leum *vi*, dèan sùrdag *f*; **2**
(*with rope*) sgiobaig *vi*; **3** (*omit*) fàg *vt* às, **we'll**

~ **the last question** fàgaidh sinn às a' cheist
mu dheireadh

skipper *n* (*of boat etc*) sgiobair *m*, caiptean *m*

skipping *n* (*with rope*) sgiobaigeadh *m*

skirt *n* sgiort *f*

skittish *adj* **1** guanach, luaineach, tuainealach, *in*
expr ~ **girl** guanag *f*; **2** (*horse etc: mettlesome*)
clisgeach, sgeunach

skivvy *n* sgalag *f*

skull *n* claigeann *m*

sky *n* speur *m*, adhar *m*, iarmailt *f*, **up in the** ~
shuas san speur/sna speuran *mpl*/san adhar

skylark *n* uiseag *f*, (*less usu*) topag *f*

slab *n* **1** (*of stone, rock*) leac *f*, *in exp* **slab-like**
leacach; **2** (~ *of cake etc*) sgonn *m*

slacken *v* (*fastenings etc*) fuasgail *vt*, lasaich *vt*

slander *n* cùl-chàineadh *m*

slander *v* cùl-chàin *vt*, càin *vt*

slanderous *adj* cùl-chainnteach

slant *n* fiaradh *m*, claonadh *m*, **at a** ~ air fhiaradh

slanting *adj* air fhiaradh, fiar

slap *n* sgailc *f*, sgealp *f*, sgleog *f*, dèiseag *f*

slap *v* sgealp *vt*

slate *n* sglèat *mf*

slaughter *n* casgairt *f invar*

slaughter *v* casgair *vt*

slaughterhouse *n* taigh-spadaidh *m*

slave *n* tràill *mf*

slaver *n* ronn *m*, seile *m invar*

slavery *n* tràilleachd *f invar*, tràillealachd *f invar*

slay *v* casgair *vt*, murt *vt*, marbh *vt*

sledge *n* slaodan *m*

sleek *adj* slìom

sleep *n* **1** cadal *m*, (*light* ~) dùsal *m*, (*usu deeper*)
suain *m*, **go to** ~! thalla a chadal!, dèan cadal!,
peaceful ~ cadal sàmhach/sèimh, **I didn't**
get a wink of ~ cha d' fhuair mi (fiù is) norrag
chadail; **2** *in expr* **sing/rock to** ~ tàlaidh *vt*

sleep *v* **1** dèan cadal *m*, caidil *vi*, ~ **now/go to**
sleep now! dèan cadal a-nis!, thalla a chadal
a-nis!, ~ **well!** caidil gu math!; **2** (*be asleep*) bi
vi irreg na (*etc*) c(h)adal, **we were ~ing** bha
sinn nar cadal

sleeping-bag *n* poca-cadail *m*

sleepless *adj* gun chadal *m*, **a ~ night** oidhche
gun chadal

sleepwalker *n* coisiche-cadail *m*

sleepy *adj* **1** cadalach, **a ~ child** pàiste cadalach;
2 *in expr* **I'm** (*etc*) ~ tha an cadal orm (*etc*), *also*
tha mi (*etc*) cadalach

sleet *n* flin & flinne *m invar*

sleeve *n* muin(i)chill & muil(i)cheann *m*, **he**
rolled up his ~s thruis e a mhuilcheannan

sleigh *n* slaodan *m*

slender *adj* caol, seang

slice *n* (*~ cut from something; also kitchen tool*) sliseag *f*, *eg* **fish-~** sliseag-èisg *f*

slide *n* (*in playpark etc, or made on ice*) sleamhnag *f*, sleamhnan *m*

slide *v* (*on slippery surface*) sleamhnaich *vi*

slight *adj* **1** beag, **a ~ cold** cnatan beag, **a ~ mist on the hill** ceò beag air a' mhonadh; **2** (*of person: ~ in build*) beag, tana; **3** (*of little value or merit*) aotrom, (*more pej*) suarach

slight *v* cuir *vt* an suarachas *m*, cuir *vt* air dìmeas *m invar*, cuir *vt* air bheag sùim *f*, dèan dìmeas (*with prep* air)

slightly *adv* beagan, **she left ~ early** dh'fhalbh i beagan ron àm, **it was raining ~** bha beagan uisge *m* ann

slim *adj* caol, tana, seang

slim *v* seangaich *vt*, (*~ deliberately, lose weight*) call cudthrom *m*, *in expr* **I had to ~** b' fheudar dhomh cudthrom a chall

slime *n* clàbar *m*

slimming *n* seangachadh *m*, call cudthruim *m*

slink *v* èalaidh *vi*, siolp *vi*, **~ off home** èalaidh/ siolp dhachaigh, **~ away** èalaidh/siolp air falbh

slip *n* **1** (*stumble etc*) tuisleadh *m*; **2** (*error*) mearachd *f*, (*less usu*) iomrall *m*; **3** *in expr* **~ of the tongue** tapag *f*

slip *v* **1** (*stumble*) tuislich *vi*, (*esp on slippery surface*) sleamhnaich *vi*; **2** (*surreptitious movement*) siolp *vi*, èalaidh *vi*, **~ inside/away** siolp a-steach/air falbh, **~ off home** èalaidh dhachaigh; **3** *in expr* **it ~ped my mind** chaidh e às mo chuimhne

slipped *adj & past part, in expr* **~ disc** clàr sgiorrte *m*

slipper *n* slapag *f*

slippery *adj* **1** (*lit*) sleamhainn; **2** (*fig: of person*) carach, fiar

slipshod *adj* (*of workmanship etc*) dearmadach, coma co-dhiù

slippy *adj* sleamhainn

slip-up *n* mearachd *f*

slit *n* sgoltadh *m*

slit *v* sgoilt & sgolt *vt*

sliver *n* sgealbag *f*

slogan *n* sluagh-ghairm *f*

slop *v* dòirt *vt*

slope *n* **1** claonadh *m*; **2** (*topog: hill~*) leathad *m*, bruthach *mf*, aodann *m*

slope *v* **1** claon *vti*; **2** (*fam; leave furtively*) **~ off** èalaidh *vi* air falbh

sloping *adj* claon

sloppy *adj* **1** (*food etc*) tana, **~ porridge** brochan tana; **2** (*of workmanship etc: careless*)

dearmadach, coma co-dhiù; **3** (*in appearance*) cearbach, luideach, robach

slosh *v* (*sound*) plubraich *vi*, plub *vi*

sloth *n* leisg(e) *f*

slothful *adj* leisg, dìomhain

slovenly *adj* luideach, rapach, robach

slow *adj* mall, slaodach, màirnealach, (*mentally ~*) mall na (*etc*) inntinn *f*

slow, slow down *v* **1** (*go/become slower*) rach *vi irreg* am maille *f invar*; **2** (*make slower*) cuir maille *f invar* (*with prep* air *or* ann)

slowness *n* maille *f invar*

slow-witted *adj* mall na (*etc*) inntinn *f*, (*fam, pej*) tiugh

sludge *n* eabar *m*, poll *m*

slug *n* **1** (*the creature*) seilcheag *f*; **2** (*fam: bullet*) peilear *m*

sluggish *adj* slaodach

slum *n* slum(a) *m*

slumber *n* suain *f*, (*usu lighter*) cadal *m*

slurry *n* giodar *m*

slut *n* **1** (*slatternly woman*) luid *f*, sgliùrach *f*, breunag *f*; **2** (*prostitute*) siùrsach *f*, strìopach *f*

sly *adj* carach, fiar

smack *n* sgailc *f*, sgealp *f*, dèiseag *f*

smack *v* sgealp *vt*

small *adj* **1** beag, mion- *prefix* (*lenites following cons where possible*), (*very ~*) meanbh, **~ girl** caileag bheag, **~ salary** tuarastal beag, **~ town** baile beag, **cut up ~** mion-gheàrr *vt*, **theft on a ~ scale** mion-bhraide *f*; **2** *in exprs* **~ change** airgead pronn, **~ intestine** caolan *m*

smart *adj* **1** (*in dress, appearance etc*) grinn, cuimir, snasail; **2** (*mentally ~*) geur/luath na (*etc*) inntinn *f*, eirmseach, geurchùiseach, toinisgeil

smash *v* smuais *vt*, smùid *vt*, spealg *vt*, bris *vt* na (*etc*) spealgan *fpl*

smashed *adj & past part* **1** smuaiste, briste, na (*etc*) spealgan *fpl*; **2** (*fam: drunk*) air a (*etc*) p(h)ronnadh, **I was ~** bha mi air mo phronnadh, *also* bha smùid (mhòr) orm

smashing *adj* (*fam: great, excellent etc*) sgoinneil, taghta, **that's ~!** tha sin sgoinneil/ taghta!, (*as excl*) **~!** taghta!, *also* math dha-rìribh!

smear *v* smiùr *vt*, smeur *vt*

smell *n* (*pleasant or unpleasant*) àile(adh) & fàile(adh) *m*, boladh *m*, (*usu pleasant*) boltrach *m*, (*bad or foul*) tòchd *m invar*, **it had a bad ~** bha droch àile (a' tighinn) dheth

smell *v* **1** (*as vt*) fairich *vt*, feuch *vt*, **can you ~ the peat reek?** am fairich thu/am feuch thu ceò na mòna?; **2** (*as vi*) **it** ~**s** tha fàileadh *m* (a' tighinn) dheth

smiddy *n* ceàrdach *f*

smile *n* faite-gàire *f*, fiamh-ghàire & fiamh a' ghàire *m*, snodha-gàire *m*, (*sly* ~) mìog *f*

smile *v* dèan faite-gàire *f*, dèan fiamh-ghàire *or* dèan fiamh a' ghàire *m*, dèan snodha-gàire *m*

smirk *n* mìog *f*

smite *v* buail *vt*

smith *n* **1** ceàrd & cèard *m*, **silver**~ ceàrd-airgid *m*, **copper**~ ceàrd-copair *m*; **2** (*black*~) gobha *m*

smithy *n* ceàrdach *f*

smoke *n* smùid *f*, ceò *m*, (*usu lighter*) toit *f*, **emit/give out** ~ cuir smùid, **peat** ~ ceò na mòna

smoke *v* **1** (*fire etc*) cuir smùid *f*, smùid *vi*, **the fire's smoking** tha an teine a' cur smùide *gen*; **2** (~ *tobacco*) smoc *vti*, **do you** ~? a bheil thu a' smocadh?

smoking *n* (*of cigarettes etc*) smocadh *m*, **no** ~, ~ **not allowed** chan fhaodar (*pres habitual passive of* faod *vi def*) smocadh

smoky *adj* ceòthach, toiteach

smooth *adj* (*surface etc*) mìn, rèidh

smoothe *v* dèan *vt* rèidh, dèan *vt* mìn

smoothly *adv*, *in exprs* **the day passed** ~ chaidh an latha seachad gu socair, **we get on/along** ~ **with them** tha sinn rèidh riutha

smother (*fire, person, dissent etc*) mùch *vt*, tùch *vt*, (*person*) tachd *vt*, (*esp fire*) smà(i)l *vt*

smoulder *v* cnàmh-loisg *vi*

smudge *n* smal *m*

smudge *v* smeur *vt*

smug *adj* toilichte leis (*etc*) fhèin, **he says we're** ~ tha e ag ràdh gu bheil sinn toilichte leinn fhìn

smuggler *n* cùl-mhùtaire *m*

smuggling *n* cùl-mhùtaireachd *f invar*

smut *n* **1** (*small dirty mark*) smal *m*, spot *m*; **2** (*suggestive talk*) drabastachd *f invar*, draostachd *f invar*, rabhd *m*

smutty *adj* (*suggestive*) drabasta, draosta

snack *n* srùbag *f*, pìos *m*

snag *n* duilgheadas *m*

snail *n* seilcheag *f*

snake *n* nathair *f*

snappy *adj* **1** (*short-tempered: of people*) aithghearr, cas, (*of dogs & people*) dranndanach; **2** (*of action etc: brisk, prompt*) deas, aithghearr

snare *n* ribe *mf*

snarl *v* dèan dranndan *m*, **the dog** ~**ed** rinn an cù dranndan, *in expr* **apt to** ~ dranndanach

snarl, snarling *n* dranndan *m*, dranndail *f invar*

snatch *v* glac *vt*, beir *vi irreg* (*with prep* air)

sneak *v* èalaidh *vi*, snàig *vi*, siolp *vi*, ~ **off home** èalaidh dhachaigh

sneer *v* dèan fanaid *f* (*at* air)

sneering *n* fanaid *f* (*at* air)

sneeze *n* sreothart *m*

sneeze *v* dèan sreothart *m*

sneezing, sneezing fit *n* sreothartaich *f*

sniff *n* boladh *m* (**at/of** de), **a** ~ **at/of the cooking pot** boladh den phrais

sniff *v* **1** (*flower etc*) gabh boladh *m* (*with prep* de); **2** *in expr* ~ **at** (*look down on*) dèan tàir *f* (*with prep* air)

snivel *v* smùch *vi*

snooze *n* dùsal *m*, norrag *f*, norrag chadail (*f gen*), **take/have a** ~ dèan dùsal/norrag

snooze *v* dèan dùsal *m*, gabh norrag *f*

snore *n* srann *f*

snore *v* srann *vi*

snoring *n* srannail *f*, **what a lot of** ~ **you were doing last night!** dè an t-srannail a bha ort a-raoir!

snout *n* soc *m*

snow *n* sneachd *m*

snow *v* cuir (sneachd *m*), **it's** ~**ing** tha e a' cur (an t-sneachda)

snowdrift *n* cathadh *m*

snowflake *n* bleideag (shneachda) *f*, pleòideag *f*

snowman *n* bodach-sneachda *m*

snowplough *n* crann-sneachda *m*

snub *v* cuir a (*etc*) c(h)ùl (*with prep* ri), **they** ~**bed us** chuir iad an cùl rinn

snug *adj* seasgair

so *adv* **1** (*before an adj*) cho, **he was** ~ **busy!** bha e cho trang!, **I'm not** ~ **good today** chan eil mi cho math an-diugh, **I'm not** ~ **young as I was** chan eil mi cho òg agus a bha mi; **2** ~ **many/much** (na h-) uimhir *f invar*, **there were** ~ **many people there** bha na h-uimhir de dhaoine ann, **I had** ~ **much money** bha uimhir de dh'airgead agam; **3** *in exprs* **and** ~ **on** 's mar sin (air adhart), **apples, pears, cherries and** ~ **on** ùbhlan, peuran, siristean 's mar sin, *also* 's a leithid sin, **she said we were lazy, rude, scruffy . . . and** ~ **on, and** ~ **on** thuirt i gu robh sinn leisg, mì-mhodhail, luideach . . . 's mar sin air adhart, ~ **far** chun a seo, gu ruige seo, **it hasn't happened** ~ **far** cha do thachair e chun a seo/gu ruige seo, **you didn't do it! I did** ~! cha do rinn thu e! rinn gu dearbh!, (*excl expr agreement*) **just** ~! dìreach!, *also* dìreach sin!

so *conj* **1** (*therefore*) mar sin, **I'm tired (and)** ~ **I'm leaving** tha mi sgìth 's mar sin tha mi a' falbh; **2** (*in order that*) gus an/am, (*neg*) gus

nach, airson, (*neg*) airson nach, ~ **(that) he**
would have some pocket money gus am
biodh airgead-pòcaid aige, ~ **(that) you can**
find the house gus an urrainn dhut an taigh
a lorg, ~ **(that) she wouldn't be hungry**
gus/airson nach biodh an t-acras oirre, (*in*
order that, also with the result that) air dhòigh
is, air chor is, (*with conjs* gu, nach), ~ **(that)**
I wouldn't be impolite air dhòigh 's nach
bithinn mì-mhodhail, **he shut the door ~**
(that) I wouldn't get in dhùin e an doras air
dhòigh is/air chor is nach fhaighinn a-steach, **he**
spoke in a low voice ~ (that) I didn't hear
him bhruidhinn e ann an guth ìosal air dhòigh 's
nach cuala mi e

so *pron* **1** (*rendered by repetition of v of*
foregoing sentence) **did he wash his hands? I**
think ~ an do nigh e a làmhan? saoilidh mi gun
do nigh, **is it gold? I don't think ~** an e òr a
th' ann? cha chreid mi gur e

soak *v* **1** drùidh *vi* (*with prep* air), fliuch *vt* (chun
na seiche), **the rain ~ed me (to the skin)**
dhrùidh an t-uisge orm, **he got ~ed to the**
skin chaidh a fhliuchadh chun na seice; **2** (*steep*
washing etc) cuir *vt* am bogadh *m*, **she put**
some clothes to ~ chuir i aodach am bogadh;
3 *in expr* ~ **up** sùigh & sùgh *vt*, **my coat ~ed**
up the rain shùigh mo chòta an t-uisge

soaked, soaking *adj* bog fliuch

soap *n* siabann *m*, **soapflakes** *npl* bleideagan
siabainn *fpl*, **soapsuds** *npl* cobhar siabainn *m*
sing

soapy *adj* siabannach

Soay *n* Sòdhaigh

sob *n* glug caoinidh *m*

sob *v* dèan glug caoinidh *m*

sober *adj* **1** measarra, stuama, stòlda; **2** (*not*
drunk) sòbar, stuama

sobriety *n* stuaim *f invar*

soccer *n* ball-coise *m*

sociability *n* conaltradh *m*

sociable *adj* cuideachdail, conaltrach, cèilidheach

social *adj* **1** (*of person*) conaltrach; **2** (*pertaining*
to society) sòisealta, ~ **security** tèarainteachd
shòisealta, ~ **work** obair shòisealta

socialism *n* sòisealachd *f invar*

socialist *adj* sòisealach

socialist *n* sòisealach *m*

society *n* **1** (*the social community*) comann-
sòisealta *m*, sòisealtas *m*, **he turned his back**
on ~ chuir e a chùl ris a' chomann-shòisealta/
ri sòisealtas; **2** (*company*) cuideachd *f*, **he likes**
the ~ of young people is toigh leis cuideachd
na h-òigridh; **3** (*club, organisation etc*) comann

m, **The Gaelic Society of Inverness** Comann
Gàidhlig Inbhir Nis

sock *n* socais *f*

socket *n* (*electric*) bun-dealain *m*

sod *n* **1** fòid & fòd *f*, fàl *m*; **2** (*coll*) fòid *f*, **when**
I'm beneath the ~ nuair a bhios mi fon fhòid
dat; **3** (*pej; unpleasant or disagreeable person*)
trustar *m*, duine gràineil *m*, duine mì-thaitneach
m

sod *v* (*swear*) ~ **the lot of them!** taigh na galla
dhaibh uile!

sofa *n* langasaid *f*

soft *adj* **1** (*to the touch*) mìn, bog, ~ **material**
stuth mìn/bog, (*of book*) ~ **cover** còmhdach
bog; **2** (*of character*) bog, maoth; **3** *in expr* ~
drink deoch lag *f*

soften *v* maothaich *vti*, bogaich *vti*

software *n* (*IT*) bathar bog, ~ **development**
leasachadh bathair bhuig

soggy *adj* bog fliuch

soil *n* talamh *m* (*f in gen sing*), ùir *f*

soil *v* salaich *vt*

solace *n* furtachd *f invar*, sòlas *m*, (*for* air), ~ **for**
his anguish furtachd air a dhòrainn, *in expr*
bring ~ furtaich *vi* (*with prep* air), **we will**
bring you ~ furtaichidh sinn oirbh

solan goose *n* sùlaire *m*

solar *adj* (na) grèine (*gen of* grian *f*), **the Solar**
System Rian na Grèine *m*, An Coras-grèine

solder *v* tàth *vt*

soldering iron *n* iarann tàthaidh *m*

soldier *n* saighdear *m*

sole *n* bonn *m*, ~ **of the foot/of the shoe** bonn
na coise/na bròige (*gen of* cas *f* & bròg *f*)

solemn *adj* sòlaimte

solicitor *n* neach-lagha *m*, (*male*) fear-lagha *m*,
(*female*) bean-lagha *f*, ~**s** luchd-lagha *m sing*
coll

solicitude *n* iomagain *f*, imnidh & iomnaidh *f*

solid *adj* **1** cruaidh, ~ **fuel** connadh cruaidh;
2 (*sound, durable*) teann, daingeann, ~
foundation bunait theann/dhaingeann, ~
structure structar daingeann; **2** (*more fig*;
well-founded, reliable) tàbhachdach, **a ~**
business gnìomhachas tàbhachdach

solidify *v* cruadhaich *vti*

solitary *adj* (*place, person*) uaigneach,
aonaranach

solitude *n* uaigneas *m*, aonaranachd *f invar*

soluble *adj* so-leaghte

solution *n* **1** (*in liquid*) leaghadh *m*, eadar-
sgaoileadh *m*; **2** (~ *to problem etc*) fuasgladh *m*

solve *v* (*problem, difficulty etc*) fuasgail *vt*, ~ **a**
crossword fuasgail tòimhseachan-tarsainn

some *adj* **1** (*not always rendered in Gaelic*) **give me ~ money** thoir dhomh airgead, **I could do with ~ peace** b' fheàirrde mi sìth; **2** (*a certain amount*) deannan (*with gen*), **he has a nice house and ~ money** tha taigh snog agus deannan airgid aige; **3** *in expr* **~ people** feadhainn *f sing coll*, cuid *f sing coll*, **~ people are in favour, others are against** tha feadhainn/cuid air a shon, tha feadhainn eile/cuid eile na aghaidh

some *pron* (*people*) feadhainn *f sing coll*, cuid *f sing coll*, **~ are in favour, ~ are against** tha feadhainn/cuid air a shon, tha feadhainn eile/cuid eile na aghaidh

some- *prefix* –eigin (*suffix*), *see* **somebody, someday, someone, something, sometime, somewhere**

somebody, someone *pron* cuideigin *mf invar*, duine *m*, **~'s come in** tha cuideigin air tighinn a-steach, **is there ~ there/in?** a bheil duine ann?

someday *adv* latheigin *m invar & adv*

someone *pron see* **somebody**

somersault *n* car a' mhuiltein *m*

something *pron* rudeigin *m invar & pron*, (*less usu*) nitheigin *m invar*, **is ~ wrong?** a bheil rudeigin ceàrr?

sometimes *adv* uaireannan *adv*, air uairean *fpl*, **~ I'm sad, ~ I'm cheerful** uaireannan bidh mi muladach, uaireannan eile bidh mi sunndach

somewhat *adv* rudeigin, rud beag, car, **she was ~ depressed** bha i rudeigin/rud beag sìos na h-inntinn, bha i rudeigin/rud beag ìseal, **~ tired** rud beag/car/rudeigin sgìth

somewhere *adv* ann an àiteigin *m invar*, **I lost it ~** chaill mi ann an àiteigin e

somnolent *adj* cadalach

son *n* mac *m*, **they have two ~s** tha dithis mhac aca

song *n* òran (*in some areas* amhran) *m*, (*less usu*) luinneag *f*, duanag *f*, **sing a ~!** gabh òran!

son-in-law *n* cliamhainn *m*

sonorous *adj* ath-fhuaimneach

soon *adv* **1** (*in a short time*) a dh'aithghearr, ann an ùine ghoirid, ann am beagan ùine, **we'll be there ~** bidh sinn ann a dh'aithghearr, **it was ~ finished/over** bha e seachad ann an ùine ghoirid/ann am beagan ùine, **they were ~ lost** ann am/an dèidh beagan ùine bha iad air chall, *also* cha b' fhada gus an robh iad air chall; **2** (*before the usual, set or expected time*) tràth, **we didn't expect you so ~** cha robh dùil againn riut cho tràth, **it's too ~ for ripe apples** tha e ro thràth airson ùbhlan abaich; **3** *in expr* **as ~**

as cho luath 's/is/agus (*with conj* a), **as ~ as he arrived the noise stopped** cho luath 's/agus a thàinig e sguir am fuaim

sooner *adv* **1** nas tràithe, (*in past & conditional tenses*) na bu tràithe; **2** *in expr* **~ or later** luath no mall, **~ or later that wall will fall down** luath no mall, tuitidh am balla sin

soot *n* sùith(e) *mf*

soothe *v* ciùinich *vt*, tàlaidh *vt*, (*esp suffering*) faothaich *vt*

soothsayer *n* fiosaiche *m*

sorcerer, sorceress *n* draoidh *m*, ban-draoidh *f*

sorcery *n* draoidheachd *f invar*

sordid *adj* **1** (*morally*) suarach, truaillidh, coirbte; **2** (*phys*) dràbhail, salach, grod, mosach

sore *adj* goirt, **a ~ head** ceann goirt, **my back's ~** tha mo dhruim goirt, **a ~ trial** deuchainn ghoirt

sorrow *adj* bròn *m*, mulad *m*, (*less usu*) tùirse & tùrsa *f invar*

sorrowful *adj* brònach, muladach, tùrsach

sorry *adj* **1** duilich, **I'm ~!** tha mi duilich!, **I'm ~ for myself** tha mi duilich air mo shon fhìn, *also* (*more trad*) tha truas agam rium fhìn; **2** (*causing sympathy, regret etc*) truagh, **it was a ~ affair** 's e rud/gnothach truagh a bh' ann; **3** (*unsatisfactory, paltry*) suarach, **a ~ excuse** leisgeul suarach

sort *n* **1** seòrsa *m*, (*less usu*) gnè *f invar*, **all ~s of things** rudan de gach seòrsa, **a book of that ~** leabhar den t-seòrsa sin; **2** *in expr* **out of ~s** (*ie grouchy etc*) diombach, (*usu of child*) crost(a)

sort *v* **1** (*classify; also ~ mail etc*) seòrsaich *vt*; **2** (*arrange, order, ~ out*) cuir *vt* an òrdugh *m*, òrdaich *vt*, cuir *vt* air dòigh *f*; **3** (*objects: put right, mend*) càirich *vt*, cuir *vt* air ghleus *mf*; **4** (*resolve/~ out situations, relationships etc*) rèitich *vt*; **5** (*tidy*) càirich *vt*, sgioblaich, rèitich *vt*, **~ your bed!** càirich do leabaidh!, **~ your room!**, sgioblaich an rùm agad!

so-so *adj* ach meadhanach (*with verb in neg*), **I'm only ~ today** chan eil mi ach meadhanach an-diugh, **the food was only ~** cha robh am biadh ach meadhanach

soul *n* **1** (*spirit*) anam *m*, **body and ~** corp is anam; **2** *in expr* **a (living) ~** duine beò, **there wasn't a (living) ~ on the road** cha robh duine beò air an rathad; **3** (*fam: usu expr sympathy*) creutair *m*, **the poor ~!** an creutair bochd!

sound *adj* **1** (*of persons: ~ in health*) fallain, **safe and ~** slàn is fallain; **2** (*of organisations etc: secure, trustworthy*) tàbhachdach, urrasach, **a ~**

business gnìomhachas tàbhachdach/urrasach; **3** (*of judgement etc: reliable*) earbsach

sound *n* **1** fuaim *mf*, **the ~ of the traffic** fuaim na trafaig, **~ wave** fuaim-thonn *mf*; **2** (*much quieter: usu in neg exprs*) bìd *f*, bìog *f*, **he can't hear a ~** cha chluinn e bìd/bìog, **he didn't utter a ~** cha tuirt e bìd/bìog

soup *n* brot *m*, (*trad*) eanraich *f*

sour *adj* goirt, searbh, geur, **~ milk** bainne goirt

source *n* bun *m*, tùs *m*, **the ~ of evil** bun an uilc (*gen of* olc *m*), (*prov*) **the fear of God is the ~ of (all) wisdom** 's e tùs a' ghliocais eagal Dhè (*gen of* Dia *m*)

south *n & adj* **1** deas *f invar & adj*, **South Uist** Uibhist a Deas, **the South Pole** Am Pòla a Deas, **the ~ of the country** an taobh deas den dùthaich, taobh a deas na dùthcha, **living in/going to the ~** a' fuireach/a' dol mu dheas, **the islands in the ~** na h-eileanan mu dheas, **a breeze from the ~** oiteag on deas, **Kinross is ~ of Perth** tha Ceann Rois deas air Peairt; **2** (*the compass direction*) **~** an àird(e) deas

southerly *adj* mu dheas, **~ islands** eileanan mu dheas, **he went in a ~ direction** chaidh e mu dheas

southern *adj* deas, mu dheas, **the ~ part of the country** taobh a deas na dùthcha, **in the ~ corner of a wood** anns a' chùil mu dheas de choille, **the ~ isles** na h-eileanan mu dheas

southerner *n* deasach *m*

South Uist *n* Uibhist a Deas

souvenir *n* cuimhneachan *m*

sovereign *n* rìgh *m*

sow *n* cràin *f*, muc *f*

sow *v* **1** (*seed*) cuir *vt*; **2** (*~ dissent, doubt etc*) sgaoil *vt*

sowing *n* **1** (*of seed etc*) cur *m*; **2** (*of dissent, doubt etc*) sgaoileadh *m*

space *n* **1** (*room*) rùm *m*, **there was no ~ in the boat** cha robh rùm sa bhàta; **2** (*opening, gap etc*) beàrn *f*, **a small ~ in the wall** beàrn bheag sa bhalla; **3** (*extra-terrestrial ~*) fànas *m*, **the ~ age** linn an fhànais *mf*, an linn-fànais *mf*

spacecraft, spaceship *n* soitheach-fànais *m*, speur-shoitheach *m*

spacious *adj* rùmail

spade *n* spaid *f*, (*more trad*) caibe *m*

Spain *n* (*used with art*) An Spàinn *f*

spanner *n* spanair *m*

spar *n* (*joinery etc*) rong *f*, rongas *m*

spare *adj* **1** (*free, available*) saor, **~ time** ùine shaor, *also* saor-ùine; **2** (*surplus*) a bharrachd, **~ money** airgead a bharrachd; **3** *in expr*

(*machinery etc*) **~ parts, ~s** pàirtean-càraidh *mfpl*

spare *v* **1** (*from punishment etc*) dèan iochd *f invar* (*with prep* ri), leig *vt* mu sgaoil, fuasgail *vt*, **the emperor ~ed her** rinn an t-ìompaire iochd rithe; **2** *in expr* (*rather trad*) **if I'm ~d** ma bhios mi air mo chaomhnadh, ma mhaireas (*rel fut of* mair *vi*) mi beò, **I'll see you tomorow, if I'm ~ed** chì mi a-màireach thu, ma bhios mi air mo chaomhnadh

spark *n* **1** sradag *f*, **give off ~s** leig sradagan; **2** (*~ of life, vital ~*) rong *m*, **there's not a ~ of life in them** chan eil rong annta

sparkle *n* drithleann *m*, lainnir *f*

sparkle *v* lainnrich *vi*

sparkling *adj* lainnireach

sparrow *n* gealbhonn *m*

sparse *adj* gann, tana, **~ crop** bàrr gann, **~ hair** falt tana

speak *v* **1** bruidhinn *vti*, (*less usu*) labhair *vi*, (**to** ri), **~ to him** bruidhinn ris, **~ing Gaelic** a' bruidhinn (na) Gàidhlig, **~ing in Gaelic** a' bruidhinn sa Ghàidhlig, *in expr* (*idiom*) **~ing with one voice** a' bruidhinn às beul a chèile; **2** *in expr* **I ~ Gaelic/English** (*etc*) tha Gàidhlig/Beurla (*etc*) agam; **3** (*address*) thoir *vt irreg* seachad òraid *f* (*with prep* do), **tomorrow I'm ~ing to the local history society** a-màireach bidh mi a' toirt seachad òraid don chomann eachdraidh ionadail; **4** *in expr* **broadly/generally ~ing** san fharsaingeachd *f invar*, **broadly/generally ~ing, the roads are good** san fharsaingeachd, tha na rathaidean math

speaker *n* **1** (*lecturer etc*) òraidiche *m*, neach-labhairt *m*; **2** *in expr* **native ~** (*of a lang*) fileantach *m*, **the native ~s' class** clas nam fileantach; **3** (*~ in parliament*) Labhraiche *m*

spear *n* gath *m*, sleagh *f*

special *adj* àraidh, sònraichte, air leth, **it's a ~ place to/for me** 's e àite àraidh/sònraichte/air leth a th' ann dhòmh(sa), **a ~ bottle of wine** botal air leth de dh'fhìon, **~ status** seasamh sònraichte

specialist *n* speisealaiche

species *n* (*biol*) gnè *f invar*, cineal *m*, seòrsa *m*

specific *adj* àraidh, sònraichte, **it's a ~ car that I'm looking for** is e càr àraidh/sònraichte a tha mi a' sireadh

specifically *adv* a dh'aon ghnothach *m*, a dh'aon rùn *m*, **I wrote the letter ~ to bring the matter to an end** sgrìobh mi an litir a dh'aon ghnothach/a dh'aon rùn gus a' chùis a thoirt gu ceann

specify

specify *v* sònraich *vt*, comharraich *vt*

specimen *n* sampall *m*

speck *n* smal *m*

speckled *adj* ballach, breac

spectacle *n* sealladh *m*

spectacles *npl* speuclairean *mpl*, glainneachan *fpl*

spectacular *adj* (*event, performance etc; impressive*) drùidhteach, (*showy, eye-catching*) basdalach, (*rich, splendid*) òirdheirc

spectator *n* neach-coimhid *m* (*pl* luchd-coimhid *m sing coll*)

spectre *n* bòcan *m*, taibhse *mf*

speculate *v* **1** (*mentally*) beachdaich *vi* (**about** air); **2** (*fin*) dèan tuairmeas *m* (**on** air)

speculation *n* **1** (*mental*) beachdachadh *m*; **2** (*fin*) tuairmeas *m*

speculative *adj* **1** (*mentally*) beachdachail, baralach; **2** (*fin*) tuairmseach

speech *n* **1** (*in general & abstr sense*) cainnt *f*, labhairt *f invar*, **~ therapist** leasaiche-cainnt *m*; **2** (*talk, oration*) òraid *f*, **give/make a ~** thoir seachad òraid, dèan òraid; **3** (*lang, gram*) còmhradh *m*, **indirect ~** còmhradh neo-dhìreach

speechless *adj* balbh, (*stronger*) bog balbh

speed *n* **1** luas *m*, luath(a)s *mf*, (*esp of vehicles*) astar *m*, **~ limit** crìoch astair *f*, **at an incalculable ~** aig astar gun tomhas, **an insane ~** astar gun chiall, **they were going (along) at a good ~** bha astar math aca; **2** (*esp of persons: haste*) deann *f*, (*stronger*) deann-ruith & dian-ruith *f*, **he left at (great) ~** dh'fhalbh e na dheann, **he left at full ~** dh'fhalbh e na dhian-ruith, *also* (*more fam*) dh'fhalbh e aig peilear a bheatha; **3** *in expr* **put on ~** luathaich *vi*

speed *v* **1** (*in car etc*) dràibhig/siubhail *vi* ro luath/aig astar *m* ro mhòr; **2** *in expr* **~ up** luathaich *vi*

speedy *adj* luath, cabhagach, (*esp of vehicles*) astarach

spell¹ *n* (*enchantment*) geas *f*, seun *m*, ortha *f*, **under a ~** fo gheasaibh (*obs dat pl of* geas)

spell² *n* **1** (*of time*) greis *f*, **a ~ of unemployment** greis gun obair, **we were in Skye for a ~** bha sinn greis san Eilean Sgitheanach, bha sinn san Eilean Sgitheanach airson/fad greis, **a ~ at/with the scythe** greis air an speal, **sunny ~** greis grèine (*gen of* grian *f*); **2** *in expr* (*esp after prolonged wet weather*) **dry ~** turadh *m*, **what a good dry ~!** is math an turadh (e)!

spell *v* litrich *vt*

spellbound *adj & past part* fo gheasaibh (*obs dat pl of* geas *f: with gen*), **~ by her beauty** fo gheasaibh a bòidhcheid (*gen of* bòidhchead *f*)

spelling *n* litreachadh *m*

spend *v* **1** (*money*) cosg *vt*, caith *vt*; **2** (*time*) cuir *vt* seachad, (*less usu*) caith *vt*, **I spent the holidays in the States** chuir mi seachad na saor-làithean sna Stàitean (Aonaichte)

spendthrift *adj* caith(t)each, struidheil & stròdhail

spendthrift *n* struidhear *m*

spent *adj & past part* **1** (*of money*) cosgte, caithte; **2** (*of energy, nuclear fuel etc*) caithte

sperm *n* sìol(-ginidh) *m*, *in expr* **~ cell** cealla-sìl *f*

spew *v* cuir *vti* a-mach, sgeith *vi*, (*fam/vulg*) **I ~ed my guts up** chuir mi a-mach rùchd mo chaolanan

sphere *n* cruinne *mf*

spherical *adj* cruinn

spice *n* spìosradh *m*

spice *v* (*lit*) spìosraich *vt*, (*lit & fig*) **~ (up)** piobraich *vt*

spicy *adj* spìosrach

spider *n* damhan-allaidh *m*

spike *n* spìc *f*, bior *m*

spill *v* dòirt *vti*, **~ blood** doirt fuil

spin *n* **1** (*revolution*) car *m*, **give the wheel a ~** cuir car den chuibhle; **2** (*drive etc*) cuairt (bheag), **we'll go for a ~ in the car** gabhaidh sinn cuairt (bheag) sa chàr

spin *v* cuir car *m* (*with prep* de), **~ the propeller** cuir car den phroipeilear

spine *n* **1** (*backbone*) (**the**) **~** cnà(i)mh (an) droma *m*; **2** (*on thistle etc*) bior *m*

spinster *n* boireannach gun phòsadh *m*, (*esp elderly ~ fam*) seana-mhaighdeann *f*

spirit *n* **1** (*relig*) spiorad *m*, **the Holy Spirit** An Spiorad Naomh; **2** (*ghostly ~*) taibhse *mf*; **3** (*courage etc*) misneach *f*, misneachd *f invar*, smior *m*; **4** (*alcoholic*) **~s** deoch-làidir *f*

spirited *adj* misneachail, smiorail/smearail

spiritual *adj* (*relig*) spioradail, **~ songs** dàin spioradail

spirituality *n* spioradalachd *f invar*

spirtle *n* maide-poite *m*

spit¹ *n* (*saliva etc*) smugaid *f*

spit² *n* (*for cooking*) bior-ròstaidh *m*

spit *v* tilg smugaid *f*

spite *n* gamhlas *m*, tarcais *f*, tailceas *m*

spite *v* dèan tarcais *f* (*with prep* air)

spiteful *adj* gamhlasach, tarcaiseach, tailceasach

spittle *n* smugaid *f*

splash *n* plubraich *f*, plub *m*, **make a ~** dèan plubraich

splash v plubraich vi, dèan plubraich f, plub vi

splendid adj gasta, greadhnach, àlainn, **the soldiers looked** ~ bha na saighdearan a' coimhead gasta, **that was ~!** bha sin gasta/àlainn!, also bha sin math dha-rìribh

splendour n greadhnachas m

split adj & past part **1** sgoilte; **2** in expr (fam) ~ **new** ùr-nodha

split n sgàineadh m, sgoltadh m

split v **1** sgoilt & sgolt vti; **2** ~ **(up)** (ie divide) roinn vt (suas), **(between** air), **the estate was** ~ **up** bha an oighreachd air a roinn suas, **we** ~ **it between them** roinn sinn orra e; **3** in expr ~ **up** (ie separate, part) dealaich vi (with prep ri), sgar vti, **the couple** ~ **up** dhealaich a' chàraid (phòsta) ri chèile

splosh v plubraich vi, plub vi

splutter v dèan plubraich f

spoil v **1** (as vi) rach vi irreg bhuaithe; **2** (as vt) mill vt; **3** (indulge child etc) mill vt

spoil, spoils n (plunder etc) cobhartach mf, spùilleadh & spùinneadh m, creach f

spoilt adj & past part **1** (lit, also fig of child, dog etc) millte; **2** in expr ~ **brat** uilleagan m

spoke n spòg f

spokesman n fear-labhairt m

spokesperson n neach-labhairt m (pl luchd-labhairt m sing coll)

sponsor n (of sporting or cultural event etc) goistidh m

sponsorship n goistidheachd f invar

spool n iteachan m

spoon n spàin f

spoonful n làn-spàine m

sport n **1** (games, also fun etc) spòrs f, **we had some** ~ **with him/at his expense** bha spòrs againn air, **football's my favourite** ~ 's e ball-coise an spòrs as fheàrr leam, ~**s complex** ionad-spòrsa m; **2** in expr **fond of/good at** ~ spòrsail

sporting adj **1** (fair) cothromach, (idiom) **a** ~ **chance** cothrom m na Fèinne; **2** (relating to sport) spòrsail

sporty adj spòrsail

spot n **1** (pimple etc) guirean m, plucan m; **2** (place) bad m, àite m, **a sunny** ~ bad grianach, **a bonny** ~ àite brèagha; **3** (stain etc) smal m, spot m; **4** in exprs **beauty** ~ (on face) ball-maise m, (place to visit) àite brèagha, **on the** ~ (ie immediately) anns a' bhad, **she did it on the** ~ rinn i anns a' bhad e, also rinn i an làrach nam bonn e

spot v (see: usu at a distance) faigh fàire f (with prep air)

spouse n cèile m invar

spout n **1** (of pot etc) feadan m; **2** (jet or flow of liquid) spùt m, steall f; **3** (large waterfall) spùt m

sprain n (of ankle etc) sgochadh m, siachadh m

sprain v (ankle etc) sgoch vt, siach vt

spray n **1** (device for watering etc) steallaire m; **2** (~ from sea) cathadh-mara m

spray v steall vti

spree n (drinking ~) daorach f

spread v sgaoil vti, **she** ~ **(out) her arms** sgaoil i a gàirdeanan, **the rumour** ~ **through the town** sgaoil am fathann air feadh a' bhaile, **fine views** ~ (past part) **out beneath us** seallaidhean brèagha air an sgaoileadh fodhainn

sprightly adj lùthmhor, clis, sgairteil, brìoghmhor

spring n **1** (leap) leum m; **2** (of water) fuaran m, tobar mf; **3** (the season) earrach m, **in (the)** ~ as t-earrach; **4** in expr ~ **tide** reothart mf

spring v **1** (leap) leum vi; **2** (appear; fam) nochd vi **(from** à), **where did you** ~ **from?** cò às a nochd thu(sa)?; **3** in exprs ~ **to mind** thig vi na (etc) inntinn f, thig vi na (etc) c(h)uimhne f invar

sprinkle v crath vt, ~ **salt on the fish** crath salann air an iasg

sprint n deann-ruith & dian-ruith f

sprout n **1** (on plant) bachlag f; **2** (veg) **Brussels** ~ buinneag Bhruisealach

sprout v (plant) cuir a-mach bachlagan fpl

spruce adj cuimir, snasail, sgiobalta

spruce n giuthas m, **Norway** ~ giuthas Lochlannach

spry adj beothail, clis, **a** ~ **old guy** bodach beothail

spur, spur on v **1** (encourage) brosnaich vt, spreig vt, stuig vt, piobraich vt; **2** (hurry on) cuir cabhag f (with prep air), greas vt, brod vt

spurt n **1** (of liquid) steall f, stealladh m, spùt m; **2** (acceleration) briosgadh m, cabhag f, **get/put a** ~ **on!** dèan cabhag!, also greas ort!

spurt v (liquids) steall vti, spùt vti

spy n **1** brathadair m, neach-brathaidh m; **2** in expr ~ **satellite** saideal brathaidh m

spying n **1** (espionage) brathadh m; **2** (eavesdropping on neighbours etc) farchluais f

spy v **1** (engage in espionage) brath vi; **2** (eavesdrop on neighbours etc) dèan farchluais f (on air)

squabble n connsachadh m, tuasaid f, trod m

squabble v connsaich vi, troid vi, **(with** ri), **they were squabbling** bha iad a' trod ri chèile

squabbling n trod m

squad *n* buidheann *mf*, sguad *m*

squalid *adj* 1 dràbhail, robach, grod, mosach; 2 (*of action, behaviour*) suarach, tàireil

squall *n* sgal *m*, meall *m*

squalor *n* mosaiche *f invar*

squander *v* caith *vt*

square *adj* 1 (*in shape*) ceàrnach; 2 (*surface area*) ceàrnagach, ~ **metre** meatair ceàrnagach

square *n* (*shape, also ~ in town etc*) ceàrnag *f*

squash *v* 1 (*lit*) brùth *vt*, preas *vt*; 2 (*fig: quash, quell*) ceannsaich *vt*, mùch *vt*

squat *n* (*position*) crùban *m*

squat *v* dèan crùban *m*, rach *vi* na (*etc*) c(h)rùban *m*, crùb *vi*, **they ~ted (down)** rinn iad crùban, chaidh iad nan crùban

squeak, squeaking *n* 1 (*of objects rubbing together etc*) dìosgan *m*, dìosgail *f invar*, gìosg *m*; 2 (*of animals etc*) sgiamh (beag)

squeak *v* 1 (*objects rubbing etc*) gìosg *vi*; 2 (*animals etc*) sgiamh *vi*

squeal *n* sgiamh *m*, sgal *m*

squeal *v* sgiamh *vi*, sgal *vi*

squeamish *adj* òrraiseach

squeeze *n* teannachadh *m*, fàsgadh *m*

squeeze *v* teannaich *vt*, fàisg *vt*, preas *vt*

squint *adj* (*aslant*) claon, fiar, air fhiaradh

squint *n* claonadh *m*, fiaradh *m*, spleuchd *m*

squint *v* seall *vi* claon, seall *vi* fiar, spleuchd *vi*

squirrel *n* feòrag *f*

squirt *n* (*of liquid*) steall *f*, stealladh *m*

squirt *v* steall *vti*

St Kilda *n* Hiort & Hirt *f invar*

St Kildan *n & adj* Hiortach, Hirteach & Tirteach *m*

stab *n* 1 sàthadh *m*; 2 (*fam: a try, a shot*) oidhirp *f*, ionnsaigh *mf*, (**at air**), **we'll have another ~ at it** bheir/nì sinn oidhirp/ionnsaigh eile air

stab *v* sàth *vti*

stabilise *v* 1 (*as vt*) bunailtich *vt*; 2 (*as vi*) fàs *vi* bunailteach

stability *n* bunailteachd *f invar*, seasmhachd *f invar*

stable *adj* seasmhach, bunailteach

stable *n* stàball *m*

stack *n* (*of corn etc*) cruach *f*, mulan *m*, coc/goc *m*, **small ~** cruachan *m*

stack *v* cruach *vt*, càrn *vt*

stackyard *n* iodhlann *f*

staff¹ *n* (*employees*) luchd-obrach *m sing coll*, **clerical ~** luchd-obrach clèireachail

staff² *n* 1 (*of bishop etc*) bachall *m*; 2 (*music*) cliath *f*

stag *n* (*red deer ~*) damh *m*

stage¹ *n* 1 (*of progress, development, ability etc*) ìre *f invar*, **at this ~ in/of my life** aig an ìre seo/aig an àm *m* seo na mo bheatha

stage² *n* (*theatre etc*) àrd-ùrlar *m*

stagger *v* 1 tuimhsich *vi*, tuislich *vi*; 2 (*fig: surprise*) cuir mòr-iongnadh *m* (*with prep* air), **I was ~ed** bha mòr-iongnadh orm

stagnant *adj* marbh, ~ **water** uisge marbh

staid *adj* stòlda

stain *n* smal *m*, spot *m*, sal *m*

stain *v* 1 dath *vt*; 2 (*accidentally*) fàg smal *m*, fàg spot *m*, (*with prep* air), **it ~ed her dress** dh'fhàg e smal air an dreasa aice

stained *adj & past part* 1 dathte, ~ **glass** glainne dhathte; 2 (*accidentally*) salaichte

stair *n* 1 (*single step*) ceum *m*; 2 (*single step & staircase, a flight of ~s*) staidhre *f*, staidhir *f*, **she went up the ~** chaidh i suas an staidhre, **she's up the ~** tha i shuas an staidhre

staircase, stairs *n* staidhir *f*, staidhre *f*

stake¹ *n* (*for fencing etc*) post *m*, stob *m*, (*more trad*) cipean *m*

stake² *n* (*in gambling*) geall *m*

stalk *n* gas *f*

stallion *n* àigeach *m*

stalwart *adj* 1 (*sturdy*) calma, tapaidh, smiorail, treun; 2 (*loyal, dependable*) seasmhach, daingeann, dìleas

stalwart *n* curaidh *m*, gaisgeach *m*

stamina *n* 1 (*strength*) neart *m*, spionnadh *m*; 2 (*staying power*) cumail-ris *f*, fulang *m*,

stamp *n* (*postage*) stamp(a) *f*

stamp *v* 1 (*letter*) cuir stamp(a) *f* (*with prep* air); 2 (*with foot*) breab *vt*, stamp *vti*, **she ~ed her foot at me** bhreab i a cas *f* rium; 3 *in expr* ~ **out** cuir *vi* às (*with prep* do), ~ **out racism** cuir às do chinealas/do ghràin-cinnidh

stance *n* (*phys, moral, philo etc*) seasamh *m*

stand *v* 1 (*rise to one's feet*) seas *vi*, èirich *vi* (na *etc* s(h)easamh *m*), **the audience stood (up)** sheas an luchd-èisteachd, **he stood up** sheas e suas, sheas e an-àird, dh'èirich e (na sheasamh); 2 (*be in a standing position*) bi *vi irreg* na (*etc*) s(h)easamh *m*, **I stood/was ~ing under a tree** bha mi nam sheasamh fo chraoibh; 3 (*tolerate, bear*) fuiling & fulaing *vti*, (*less trad*) cuir *vi* suas (*with prep* ri), **they had to ~ cold and hunger** b' fheudar dhaibh fuachd is acras fhulang, b' fheudar dhaibh cur suas ri fuachd is acras, **I can't ~ him/it!**, chan fhuiling mi e!; 4 *in expr* ~ **up for** (*ie support*) seas *vt*, **who will ~ up for you?** cò a sheasas thu?

standard *adj* **1** (*usual, normal*) suidhichte, cumanta, gnàthach; **2** (*applicable to all*) coitcheann

standard *n* **1** (*unit of comparison, a criterion*) slat-thomhais *f*; **2** (*level of achievement, ability etc*) ìre *f invar*, inbhe *f*

stand-in *n* (*theatre etc*) neach-ionaid *m*

standing *n* (*rank, prestige etc*) seasamh *m*, inbhe *f*

standing jump cruinn-leum *m*

standing stone *n* tursa *m*, carragh *f*, gallan *m*

stanza *n* rann *mf*

star *n* reul *f*, rionnag *f*

starch *n* stalc *m*

stare *n* spleuchd *m*

stare *v* spleuchd *vi* (**at** air)

starfish *n* crasgag & crosgag *f*

stark *adj* **1** (*landscape, situation etc*) garbh, cruaidh; **2** *in expr* ~ **naked** dearg rùisgte

starling *n* druid *f*, druideag *f*

start *n* **1** (*in time*) toiseach *m*, tùs *m*, **the ~ of summer** toiseach an t-samhraidh, **he's been working here from/since the (very) ~** tha e ag obair an seo o thùs; **2** (~ *of a process etc*) tòiseachadh *m*, **a fresh ~** tòiseachadh às ùr, *in expr* **make a fresh ~** tòisich *vi* às ùr; **3** (*shock, fright, nervous reaction*) clisgeadh *m*, uspag *f*, **he gave me a ~** chuir e clisgeadh orm, **he gave a ~** thug e uspag

start *v* **1** tòisich *vi* (*with preps* air *or* ri), teann *vi* (*with prep* ri), ~ **singing** tòisich a' seinn, ~ **to sing** tòisich air/ri seinn, **he ~ed climbing** theann e ri streap, ~ **afresh** tòisich às ùr, ~ **to shake/shiver** rach *vi* air chrith *f*; (*saying*) ~**ing/getting ~ed is a day's work** is e obair latha tòiseachadh *m*; **2** (*nervous reaction*) clisg *vi*, thoir uspag *f*, **he ~ed** chlisg e, thug e uspag

startle *v* cuir clisgeadh *m* (*with prep* air), clisg *vt*, **he ~d me** chuir e clisgeadh orm, chlisg e mi

starvation *n* gort & goirt *f*

starve *v* **1** (*as vi: die of starvation*) caochail *vi* leis a' ghoirt *f dat*; **2** (*as vt: deprive of food*) cuir trasg *f*, leig goirt *f*, (*both with prep* air), **they ~d me** chuir iad trasg orm, leig iad goirt orm; **3** *in expr* **he ~d them to death** chuir e gu bàs leis a' ghoirt iad

state *n* **1** (*condition*) cor *m*, staid *f*, **the pitiful ~ of the refugees** cor truagh nam fògarrach, ~ **of emergency** staid èiginneach, **in a bad ~** ann an droch staid; **2** *in expr* **he was in a good ~ of mind** bha e air a (dheagh) dhòigh *m*; **3** (*pol*) stàit *f*, **the French ~** an stàit Fhrangach, stàit na Frainge

state *v* **1** (~ *feelings, thoughts, ideas etc*) cuir *vt* an cèill (*dat of* ciall *f*), **I will ~ my opinion** cuiridh mi mo bheachd an cèill; **2** (~ *facts, details etc*) thoir *vt* (seachad), ~ **your name** thoiribh seachad ur n-ainm

stately *adj* stàiteil, ~ **gait/pace** ceum stàiteil

statement *n* **1** (*abstr*) cur *m* an cèill (*dat of* ciall *f*); **2** (*esp in pl more con; utterances, things said*) ~**s** briathran *mpl*, **foolish ~s** briathran amaideach, **I don't believe politicians' statements** cha chreid mi briathran luchd-poilitigs; **3** (*account of events, circumstances etc; verbal or written*) aithris *f*, (*esp formal & written*) aithisg *f*, (*esp for legal purposes*) teisteanas *m*

statesman *n* stàitire *m*

station *n* **1** (*transport, radio etc*) stèisean *m*

stationary *adj* na stad *m*, gun gluasad *m*

stationery *n* pàipearachd *f sing coll*, stuth-sgrìobhaidh *m*

statue *n* ìomhaigh *f*

stature *n* **1** (*height*) àirde *f*; **2** (*moral, professional etc* ~) inbhe *f*

status *n* inbhe *f*, seasamh *m*, ~ **symbol** comharradh inbhe *m*

statute *n* reachd *m invar*, riaghailt *f*

statutory *adj* **1** (*in accordance with statutes*) reachdail, dligheach; **2** (*compulsory by law/statute*) reachdail

staunch *adj* seasmhach, daingeann, dìleas, treun, làidir

staunch *v* caisg *vt*

stave *n* (*music*) cliabh *m*

stave off *v* cuir dàil *f* (*with prep* ann *or* air), cùm *vt* air falbh, ~ **the summons** cuir dàil air a' bhàirlinn, **in order to ~ hunger** gus an t-acras a chumail air falbh

stay *v* **1** (*remain*) fuirich *vi*, fan *vi*, **you ~ where you are!** fuirich/fan thusa far a bheil thu!; **2** (*dwell*) fuirich *vi*, fan *vi*, gabh còmhnaidh *f*, (**in** ann an, **with** aig), **we were ~ing in Islay at the time** bha sinn a' fuireach/a' gabhail còmhnaidh ann an Ìle aig an àm, ~**ing with Calum** a' fuireach/a' fantainn/a' fantail aig Calum

steadfast *adj* **1** (*loyal*) dìleas; **2** (*steady, enduring*) daingeann, seasmhach

steady *adj* **1** (*of structures etc: firm*) cunbhalach, bunai(l)teach, seasmhach, daingeann, teann; **2** (*of persons*) stòlda, suidhichte; **3** *as adv in exprs* ~!, ~ **on!**, socair!, **take it** ~!/**go** ~! air do shocair!, gabh *imper* air do shocair!

steady *v* daingnich *vt*

steak *n* staoig *f*

steal v **1** goid vt; **2** (corres to Eng vi) dèan mèirle f invar, bi vi irreg ri goid f; **3** in expr ~ **away** siolp vi air falbh, èalaidh vi air falbh

stealing n goid f, mèirle f invar, (usu more petty) braid f

steam n toit f, smùid f, deatach f, ~ **from the pot** toit às a' phoit, in expr ~ **boat** bàta-smùide m

steam v **1** cuir toit f, **it was ~ing** bha e a' cur toite, bha toit a' tighinn às; **2** (fam: very drunk) **I was ~ing** bha mi air mo phronnadh/air mo dhalladh

steel n stàilinn f, cruaidh f

steep adj cas, **a ~ brae** bruthach c(h)as

steep v (in liquid) tum vt, cuir vt am bogadh m

steeple n stìopall m

steer v stiùir vt

steering-wheel n cuibhle-stiùiridh f

steersman n stiùireadair m

stem n **1** (of plant) gas f; **2** (of boat) toiseach m

stench n tòchd m invar

step n **1** (pace) ceum m, **take a ~ forward/ backward** gabh ceum air adhart/air ais, ~ **by** ~ ceum air cheum, also (fig, 'bit by bit' etc) uidh air n-uidh; **2** (of stair etc: single ~) ceum m, (flight of ~s) ceumannan mpl, **go up the ~s** rach vi suas/dìrich vt na ceumannan

step v gabh ceum m, thoir ceum, ~ **forward** gabh ceum air adhart

step-brother n leas-bhràthair m

step-child n dalta mf

step-father n oide m

step-mother n muime f

stepping-stone n sìnteag f

step-sister n leas-phiuthar f

sterile adj **1** (barren) seasg, neo-thorrach; **2** (fig: fruitless) gun toradh m, gun fheum m, dìomhain, ~ **debate** deasbad gun toradh/gun fheum

stern n (of boat) deireadh m

stern adj **1** (of discipline, master etc) cruaidh, teann; **2** (unsmiling etc) dùr, gruamach, gnù, mùgach

sternum n cliathan m

stew n **1** stiubha f; **2** in expr (fam, fig) **in a ~** ann an (droch) staing f, ann an cruaidh-chàs m, ann an èiginn f invar

steward n **1** (on estate etc) maor m; **2** (on boat etc) stiùbhard m; **3** in expr **shop ~** riochdaire aonaidh m

stewardess n bana-stiùbhard f

stick n bata m, maide m, (supple ~) gad m, **walking ~** bata-coiseachd m

stick v **1** (adhere) lean vi (**to** ri); **2** (get stuck, caught) rach vi an sàs m (**in** ann an), **she stuck in the brambles** chaidh i an sàs anns na drisean; **3** (thrust, push carelessly) sàth vt, ~ **it in the cupboard** sàth a-steach dhan phreas e; **4** in expr ~ **at it!** (persevere) cùm vi ort!, cùm vi ris!, lean vi ort!

stick-in-the-mud n neach lagchuiseach m

sticky adj leanailteach

stiff adj **1** (lit) rag; **2** (fam: difficult, excessive, harsh) doirbh, cruaidh, **a ~ exam** deuchainn dhoirbh, **a ~ sentence** binn chruaidh; **3** in expr **I was scared ~** bha eagal mo bheatha m orm

stiffen v **1** (lit) ragaich vti; **2** (fig: ~ laws, conditions etc) dèan vt nas cruaidhe; **3** (~ resolve etc) daingnich vt

stiffness n raige f invar

stifle v **1** (fire etc) smà(i)l vt, mùch vt, tùch vt; **2** (person, life) mùch vt, tachd vt; **3** (uprising, spirit, opposition etc) mùch vt, ceannsaich vt

still adj **1** (weather) ciùin, sàmhach, sèimh, **a ~ morning** madainn chiùin; **2** (motionless) gun ghluasad m, na (etc) t(h)àmh, **the trees were ~ after the storm** bha na craobhan gun ghluasad/nan tàmh an dèidh na stoirme

still adv **1** fhathast, **it's ~ raining** tha an t-uisge ann fhathast; **2** (nevertheless) a dh'aindeoin sin, a dh'aindeoin cùise, air a shon sin, co-dhiù, **it's hard, but we'll manage it ~** tha e doirbh, ach nì sinn an gnothach air a dh'aindeoin cùise/air a shon sin/co-dhiù

still n (ie whisky ~) poit-dhubh f

still v ciùinich vti, sìthich vti, socraich vti

stimulate v **1** (phys, emotionally, sexually) brod vt, (emotionally) brosnaich vt; **2** (revive, revitalise) beothaich vt

sting n (of wasp etc) guin m, gath m

sting v guin vt, cuir gath m (with prep ann), **it stung me** ghuin e mi, chuir e gath annam

stinginess n spìocaireachd f invar

stinging adj **1** (sensations etc) geur, goirt; **2** (remarks etc) guineach, geur

stingy adj spìocach, mosach

stink n tòchd m invar

stint n greis f, treis f, (shorter) greiseag f, treiseag f, (at air/aig) **a ~ at the peats** greis air/aig a' mhòine

stipend n tuarastal f

stipulate v sònraich vt

stipulation n **1** (abstr) sònrachadh m; **2** (con: in contracts etc) cumha f, cùmhnant m

stir v **1** (phys) gluais vi, caraich vi, **down in the forest something ~red** shìos sa choille ghluais rudeigin; **2** (emotionally) gluais vt, drùidh vi (with prep air), **the music ~red me** ghluais an ceòl mi, dhrùidh an ceòl orm; **3** (liquids, *food*) cuir car *m* (*with prep* de), ~ **the soup** cuir car den bhrot; **4** *in exprs* ~ **up** (*enliven etc*) beothaich *vt*, **she ~red up the embers of the fire** bheothaich i èibhleagan an teine, ~ **up** (*emotionally, to action etc*) brod *vt*, brosnaich *vt*, (*fam*) ~ **your stumps!** tog ort!

stirk *n* gamhainn *m*

stirring *adj* **1** (*to action*) brosnachail; **2** (*emotionally*) gluasadach, drùidhteach

stitch *n* **1** (*needlework*) grèim *m*; **2** (*pain in side*) acaid *f*

stitch *v* fuaigh *vt*, fuaigheil *vt*

stitched *adj & past part* fuaighte

stoat *n* neas *f*, neas mhòr

stob *n* stob *m*, post *m*

stock *n* **1** (*livestock*) stoc *m*, (*esp cattle*) sprèidh *f*, crodh *m*; **2** (~ *of shop, business*) bathar *m* *sing coll*; **3** (*fin*) sèaraichean *mpl*, earrannan *fpl*, **the ~ market** margadh nan sèaraichean/nan earrannan

stocking *n* stocainn *f*, osan *m*

stolid *adj* stòlda, (*stronger*) dùr

stomach *n* stamag *f*, (*less usu*) goile *f*, (*more fam*) balg *m*, broinn *f*, brù *f*, mionach *m*, maodal *f*

stomachful *n* (*lit & fig*) làn *m* a (*etc*) broinne (*gen of* brù *f*) (**of** de), **I had a ~ of it** fhuair mi làn mo bhroinne dheth

stone *n* **1** (*individual ~, ~ in general*) clach *f*, **he threw a ~ at me** thilg e clach orm, (*used adjectivally*) ~ **walls** ballachan cloiche (*gen*), ~ **floor** ùrlar cloiche, **a memorial ~** clach-chuimhne *f*, *also* carragh-chuimhne *f*, **a plum ~** clach-phlumaise *f*, **precious ~** clach uasal, **the Stone of Destiny** Clach na Cinneamhainn, An Lia-Fàil *f*, *also* Clach Sgàin (*ie 'of Scone'*); **2** (*weight*) clach *f*, ~ **of potatoes** clach bhuntàta; **3** (*slab of ~*) leac *f*, **tomb~**, **grave~** leac-uaighe *f*, **paving-~** leac-ùrlair; **4** *in expr* (*arc*) ~ **circle** tursachan *mpl*

stone *v* clach *vt*, tilg clachan *fpl* (*with prep* air)

stonemason *n* clachair *m*

stony *adj* clachach

stool *n* stòl *m*, furm *m*, (*trad*) creapan *m*

stoop *v* crùb *vi*

stop *n* **1** (*abstr*) stad *f*, **they came to a ~** thàinig iad gu stad, **he brought the car to a ~** thug e an càr gu stad, **put a ~ to something** cuir stad air rudeigin, *in expr* **bus ~** àite-stad bus *m*; **2** (*typog*) puing *f*, **full ~** stad-phuing *f*

stop *v* **1** (*as vi*) stad *vi*, thig *vi* gu stad *m*, sguir *vi*, **the lorry ~ped** stad an làraidh, thàinig an làraidh gu stad, (*break off work etc*) **we ~ped at noon** sguir sinn aig meadhan-latha; **2** (*as vt*) stad *vt*, thoir *vt* gu stad, cuir stad (*with prep*

air), **he ~ped the lorry** stad e an làraidh, thug e an làraidh gu stad, **I'll ~ your carrying-on!** cuiridh mi stad air do dhol-air-adhart!; **3** (*prevent*) cuir bacadh *m* (*with prep* air), caisg *vt*, cuir casg *m* (*with prep* air), **her parents ~ped them getting married** chuir a pàrantan bacadh air am pòsadh; **4** (*give up, abandon an activity*) leig *vt* (*with prep* de), leig *vt* seachad, sguir *vi* (*with prep* de), **she ~ped work/working** leig i dhith a h-obair/an obair, **I'm ~ping smoking** tha mi a' sgur de smocadh/a' leigeil seachad smocadh, ~ **it!** sguir dheth!; **5** *in expr* ~ **up** (*aperture etc*) tachd *vt*, dùin *vt* suas

stopcock *n* goc *m*

stoppage *n* **1** (*cessation of activity*) stad *m*, (*through industrial action*) stailc *f*; **2** (*obstruction, blockage*) bacadh *m*, dùnadh *m*

storage *n* stòradh *m*

store *n* **1** (*repository etc*) ionad-tasgaidh *m*, tasgaidh *f*, stòr *m*; **2** (*shop*) bùth *mf*, **go to the ~ for me** thalla don bhùth dhomh; **3** (*hoard, accumulation, of objects, knowledge etc*) stòr *m*

store *v* **1** stò(i)r *vt*, (*esp in museums etc*) taisg *vt*; **2** *in expr* ~ **away** cuir *vt* air an spàrr *m*

storehouse *n* ionad-tasgaidh *m*

storey *n* lobht(a) *m*

storm *n* stoirm *f*, doineann *f*, gailleann *f*

stormy *adj* **1** (*of weather*) stoirmeil, doineannach, gailleanach, gailbheach; **2** (*of relationship, meeting etc*) aimhreiteach

story *n* **1** (*fictional*) sgeulachd *f*, **short ~** sgeulachd ghoirid; **2** (*can be factual: when fictional, often trad in content*) sgeul *m*, **a ~ about Finn** sgeul air Fionn, **the ~ of my life** sgeul mo bheatha; **3** (*usu verbal, often humorous*) stòiridh & stòraidh *m*, naidheachd *f*

story-teller *n* sgeulaiche *m*, (*of trad stories*) seanchaidh *m*

stout *adj* **1** (*brave, enduring*) treun, ~ **heroes** gaisgich threuna; **2** (*plump etc*) reamhar, sultmhor

stove *n* stòbh(a) *mf*

stow *v* **1** (*store, conserve*) taisg *vt*, glèidh *vt*; **2** (*put/tidy away*) cuir *vt* (air falbh), ~ **it in the cupboard** cuir (air falbh) dhan phreas e

straddle *v* rach *vi irreg* casa-gòbhlach, bi *vi irreg* casa-gòbhlach, rach *vi irreg* gòbhlachan, (*all with prep* air), **he ~d the chair** chaidh e casa-gòbhlach/chaidh e gòbhlachan air a' chathair *f*, **he was straddling the chair** bha e casa-gòbhlach air a' chathair

straggle *v* bi *vi irreg* air dheireadh

straggler *n* slaodaire *m*, neach *m* (a tha *etc*) air dheireadh

straight adj 1 dìreach, ~ **line** loidhne dhìreach;
2 (*honest, trustworthy*) dìreach, ceart, onarach;
3 (*idiom*) **I gave it to her** ~ thuirt mi rithe/
dh'innis mi dhi an clàr a h-aodainn *m* e

straighten v dìrich *vti*

strain n 1 (*tension: on rope etc*) teannachadh *m*;
2 (*from phys effort*) spàirn *f*; 3 (*psych* ~) uallach
m, **under a** ~ fo uallach

strain[1] v 1 (*put* ~ *on rope etc*) teannaich *vt*; 2
(*make phys effort*) dèan spàirn (mhòr), **he had
to** ~ **to lift the barrel** b' fheudar dha spàirn
mhòr a dhèanamh gus am baraille a thogail/mun
togadh e am baraille

strain[2] v (~ *liquids*) sìolaidh *vt*

strainer n 1 (*for liquids*) sìol(t)achan *m*; 2
(*tensioner*) teannaire *m*

strait n caol *m*, caolas *m*

straits npl (*ie difficulties*) droch staing *f*, cruaidh-
chàs *m*, èiginn *f invar*, **in dire** ~ ann an droch
staing, ann an cruaidh-chàs, ann an èiginn

strand[1] n (*archaic: seashore*) tràigh *f*

strand[2] n (*of material; also of argument etc*)
dual *m*

strange adj 1 (*odd, unusual, surprising etc*)
neònach, annasach, (*stronger*) iongantach; 2
(*unfamiliar*) coimheach

stranger n coigreach *m*, srainnsear *m*, coimheach
m

strangle mùch *vt*, tachd *vt*

strangulation n mùchadh *m*, tachdadh *m*

strap n iall *f*

strapping adj (*of physique*) tomadach &
tomaltach, calma

stratagem n cuilbheart *f*, innleachd *f*

strategy n ro-innleachd *f*

strath n srath *m*

straw n 1 connlach *f sing coll*; 2 (*for drinking*)
sràbh *m*

stray adj (*lost, wandering etc*) air seachran *m*,
air iomrall *m*, *in exprs* ~ **animal** ainmhidh-
seachrain *m*, ~ **dog** cù-fuadain *m* (*gen of
seachran & fuadan m, used adjectivally*)

stray v (*phys or morally*) rach *vi* air seachran *m*,
rach *vi* air iomrall *m*

straying n dol *m invar* air seachran *m*, dol air
iomrall *m*

streak n stiall *f*, srian *f*

streak v stiall *vt*

stream n 1 (*watercourse*) sruth *m*, (*often
more precipitous*) allt *m*, (*small* ~) sruthan *m*,
alltan *m*, (*large* ~) abhainn *f*; 2 (~ *of liquids in
general*) sruth *m*

stream v ruith *vi*, sruth *vi*, sil *vi*

street n sràid *f*

strength n 1 (*phys* ~) neart *m*, spionnadh *m*,
lùth & lùths *m*, brìgh *f invar*; 2 (*pol, military* ~)
cumhachd *mf invar*, neart *m*

strengthen v 1 (*esp phys*) neartaich *vt*; 2 (~
structure, buildings, beliefs, intentions etc)
daingnich *vt*

strenuous adj saothrachail

stress n 1 (*emphasis*) cudthrom & cuideam
m, **lay** ~ **on punctuality** leig cudthrom air
pongalachd; 2 (*psych* ~) uallach *m*, **under** ~ fo
uallach; 3 (*lang*) buille *f*, cudthrom & cuideam
m, **the** ~ **comes on the first syllable** thig a'
bhuille/an cudthrom air a' chiad lide

stress v (*emphasise*) leig cudthrom (mòr) (*with
prep* air), ~ **punctuality** leig cudthrom air
pongalachd

stretch n (*phys*) sìneadh *m*

stretch v sìn *vti*, **the rope is** ~**ing** tha an ròpa
a' sìneadh, **she** ~**ed (out) her left leg** shìn i
a-mach a cas chlì

stretched adj & past part sìnte, ~ **(out) on the
ground** sìnte air an làr, *also* na (*etc*) s(h)ìneadh
air an làr

strew v sgaoil *vt*, sgap *vt*, **they** ~**ed flowers on
the ground** sgaoil iad flùraichean air an làr

strict adj (*of person, discipline etc*) cruaidh,
teann

stride n 1 sìnteag *f*; 2 (*pace*) ceum *m*, **we
quickened our** ~ luathaich sinn ar ceum

strife n strì *f*, còmhstri *f*

strike n (*industrial etc*) stàilc *f*

strike v 1 (*hit*) buail *vt*; 2 (*in industry etc*) rach *vi*
irreg air stàilc *f*; 3 (*impress*) drùidh (*with prep*
air), **I was struck by her beauty** dhrùidh a
bòidhchead orm; 4 (*occur to*) thig *vi* a-steach
(*with prep* air), **it struck me that he was
a liar** thàinig e a-steach orm gun robh e na
bhreugaire; 5 *in expr* ~ **up a tune** tog fonn *m*

striking adj drùidhteach

string n 1 sreang *f*; 2 (*of musical instrument*)
teud *m*

string v 1 (*violin etc*) cuir teud *m* (*with prep* air);
2 *in expr* ~ **two words together** cuir dà fhacal
an ceann a chèile

stringency n teanntachd *f invar*

stringent adj teann

strip n (*of material etc*) stiall *f*

strip v (*body etc*) rùisg *vt*, lom *vt*

stripe n stiall *f*

stripe v stiall *vt*

striped adj stiallach

stripling n òganach *m*, òigear *m*

stripped adj & past part rùisgte

strive *v* **1** (*contend etc*) strì *vi* (**with/against** ri); **2** (*make great effort*) dèan spàirn *f* (**to** gus)

stroke *n* **1** (*blow*) buille *f*, (*less usu*) beum *m*; **2** (*sport*) buille *f*; **3** (*med*) stròc *m*

stroke *v* **1** (*dog etc*) slìob & slìog *vt*; **2** (*persons, affectionately or amorously*) cnèadaich & cniadaich *vt*

stroll *n* cuairt *f*, car *m*, **I'll take a ~ outside** gabhaidh mi cuairt a-muigh

stroll *v* coisich *vi* gu socrach, coisich air ceum socrach

strong *adj* **1** làidir, neartmhor, lùthmhor, (*can be with overtones of bravery*) treun; **2** *in expr* ~ **drink** deoch-làidir *f*

stronghold *n* daingneach *f*, (*trad*) dùn *m*

strop *n* iall *f*

structural *adj* structarail

structure *n* structair *m*

struggle *n* **1** (*abstr & con*) strì *f*, spàirn *f*, (*con*) gleac *m*, (**with**, **against** ri); **2** (*in aid of something, to achieve something*) iomairt *f*

struggle *v* strì *vi*, gleac *vi*, (**with**, **against** ri)

strut *v* spai(s)dirich *vi*

strutting *adj* spai(s)direach

stubborn *adj* **1** (*obstinate*) rag, dùr, (*stronger*) rag-mhuinealach; **2** (*tenacious*) dìorrasach

stuck *adj & past part* an sàs *m*, **he was/got ~ in the mud** bha e/chaidh e an sàs sa pholl, **get ~ into the work** rach *vi* an sàs anns an obair, *also* crom *vi* air an obair

stud *n* (*of horses*) greigh *f*

student *n* oileanach *m*, **mature ~** oileanach inbheach, **part time ~** oileanach pàirt-ùine

studies *npl* foghlam *m*, cùrsa foghlaim *m*

study *n* **1** (*learning*) ionnsachadh *m*; **2** (*investigation of a topic*) rannsachadh *m*, sgrùdadh *m*; **3** (*room*) seòmar-leughaidh *m*

study *v* **1** (*learn a particular subject etc*) ionnsaich *vt*, **~ing Gaelic** ag ionnsachadh na Gàidhlig; **2** (*investigate, research*) rannsaich *vt*, sgrùd *vt*, dèan rannsachadh/sgrùdadh *m* (*with prep* air)

stuff *n* **1** (*material etc*) stuth *m*, (*trad*) cungaidh *f*, (*fam*) **that's good ~!** 's e stuth math a tha sin!; **2** (*fam: assorted possessions etc*) trealaich *f*, **tidy up your ~** sgioblaich do threalaich

stuff *v* **1** (*~ cushion etc*) lìon *vt*; **2** (*push roughly*) sàth *vt*, dinn *vti*, (**into** a-steach do)

stumble *n* tuisleadh *m*

stumble *v* tuislich *vi*

stumbling-block *n* cnap-starra(dh) *m*

stump *n* ploc *m*, stoc *m*

stun *v* cuir *vt* na (*etc*) t(h)uaineal *m*, **the blow ~ned me** chuir a' bhuille nam thuaineal mi

stunt *n* cleas *m*

stupid *adj* **1** (*unintelligent*) gòrach, (*more fam*) tiugh; **2** (*silly*) gòrach, amaideach, baoth, faoin, **don't be ~!** na bi (cho) gòrach!

stupidity *n* **1** (*lack of intelligence*) gòraiche *f invar*; **2** (*silliness*) gòraiche *f invar*, amaideas *m*, faoineas *m*

stupor *n* tuaineal *m*

sturdiness *n* tapachd *f invar*

sturdy *adj* (*phys*) calma, (*phys & morally*) tapaidh, **a ~ handsome man** duine calma gasta

sty *n* (*agric*) fail *f*

style *n* **1** stoidhle *f*, **I like his ~!** is toigh leam an stoidhl' (a th') aige, **there's a ponderous ~ about his writing** tha stoidhle throm air a chuid sgrìobhaidh; **2** (*mode of doing things*) modh *mf*, (*more trad*) nòs *m*, **the traditional ~** (*esp of singing*) an seann nòs

sub(-) *prefix*, fo-, *see examples below*

sub-committee *n* fo-chomataidh *f*

subconscious *adj* **1** fo-mhothachail; **2** (*in Freudian sense*) fo-inntinneil

subconscious *n* fo-inntinn *f*

sub-contract *v* fo-chunnraich *vt*

subdivide *v* fo-roinn *vt*

subdue *v* **1** (*people*) ceannsaich *vt*, cuir *vt* fo smachd *f*; **2** (*spirit, uprising etc*) mùch *vt*,

subject *n* **1** (*ed*) cuspair *m*; **2** (*~ matter etc*) cuspair *m*, **the ~ of our conversation** cuspair a' chòmhraidh againn, **the ~ of his novel/talk** cuspair na nobhail(e)/na h-òraid(e) aige; **3** (*of monarchy etc*) ìochdaran *m*; **4** (*gram*) cùisear *m*, (*less trad*) suibseig *f*

subjection *n* **1** (*abstr: the state or condition*) ceannsal *m*, smachd *m invar*; **2** (*con: the action*) ceannsachadh *m*

subjugate *v* cuir *vt* fo smachd *f*, smachdaich *vt*, ceannsaich *vt*

subjugation *n* **1** (*abstr: the state or condition*) ceannsal *m*, smachd *m invar*; **2** (*con: the action*) ceannsachadh *m*

submerge *v* tum *vt*, cuir *vt* fodha

submission *n* gèilleadh *m*, strìochdadh *m*, gèill *f*

submissive *adj* macanta, umha(i)l

submissiveness *n* ùmhlachd *f invar*

submit *v* **1** (*as vi: give in etc*) gèill *vi*, strìochd *vi*, (**to** do); **2** (*as vt: present, hand in etc*) cuir *vt* a-steach, **~ a proposal** cuir a-steach moladh

subordinate *adj* ìochdarach *m*

subordinate *n* ìochdaran *m*

subscription *n* (*to magazine etc*) fo-sgrìobhadh *m*

subsection *n* fo-earrann *f*

subside *v* 1 laigh *vi*, lùghdaich *vi*, rach *vi* sìos, socraich *vi*, sìolaidh *vi*, **the wind's subsiding** tha a' ghaoth a' laighe; 2 (*esp liquids*) tràig *vi*, sìolaidh *vi*, **the floods ~d** thràigh na tuiltean

subsidence *n* fo-thuiteam *m*

subsidy *n* tabhartas *m*, (*less trad*) subsadaidh *m*

subsistence *n* teachd-an-tìr *m*, bith-beò *mf* **~ allowance** cuibhreann teachd-an-tìr, **~ agriculture** tuathanachas bith-beò

subsoil *n* fo-thalamh *m*, fo-ùir *f*

substance *n* 1 (*abstr*) brìgh *f*, susbaint *f*, **a book without ~** leabhar *m* gun bhrìgh; 2 (*material, matter*) stuth *m*

substantial *adj* 1 (*sound, solid*) tàbhachdach, **a ~ business** gnìomhachas tàbhachdach; 2 (*~ in bulk*) tomadach & tomaltach

substantiate *v* dearbh *vt*

substitute *n* (*sport etc*) neach-ionaid *m* (*pl* luchd-ionaid *m sing coll*)

substitute *v* cuir *vt* an àite *m* (*with gen*), **~ X for Y** cuir X an àite Y

subterfuge *f* cuilbheart *f*, innleachd *f*

subterranean *adj* fon talamh *mf*

subtitle(s) *n* fo-thiotal(an) *m(pl)*

subtitle *v* cuir fo-thiotalan *mpl* (*with prep* air)

subtle *adj* (*mentally*) geurchuiseach, innleachdach

subtract *v* thoir *vt* air falbh (**from** bho)

suburb *n* iomall baile *m*

subway *n* fo-rathad *m*, fo-shlighe *f*

succeed *v* 1 (*follow*) lean *vt*, thig *vi* an dèidh (*with gen*); 2 (*thrive etc*) soirbhich *vi*, *also as vi impersonal with prep* le, **the business ~ed** shoirbhich an gnìomhachas, **we ~ed totally** shoirbhich leinn uile-gu-lèir

success *n* 1 buaidh *f*; 2 (*esp material ~*) soirbheachas *m*

successful *adj* soirbheachail

succession *n* 1 (*series, sequence etc*) sreath *mf*, **a ~ of ministers preached there** shearmonaich sreath de mhinistearan an sin; 2 *in expr* **in ~** an ceann *m* a chèile, an sreath *mf* a chèile, an dèidh a chèile, fear *m* mu seach, tè *f* mu seach, **three accidents in ~** trì tubaistean an ceann a chèile/an sreath a chèile, **the Ministers resigned in ~** thug na Ministearan suas an dreuchd fear mu seach/an ceann a chèile

succinct *adj* (*report, document etc*) cuimir

such *adj* 1 de leithid *f*, den t-seòrsa *m*, (*follows the noun*), **you shouldn't read ~ trash!** cha bu chòir dhut truileis den t-seòrsa (sin)/de leithid (sin) a leughadh; 2 *in expr* **in ~ a way (that)** air dhòigh *f* is, air chor *m* is, (*with conjs* gun, nach), **in ~ a way that I couldn't get in**

air dhòigh/air chor is nach b' urrainn dhomh faighinn a-steach

such *pron* a leithid *f*, samhail *m*, **I saw ~ a thing as that once** chunnaic mi a leithid sin (a rud) aon turas, **I knew ~ a man** bha mi eòlach air a leithid de dhuine, **~ as she never existed** cha robh a leithid/a samhail ann a-riamh, a leithid cha robh a-riamh ann

such *adv* 1 *in expr* **~ a lot** na h-uimhir *f invar*, na h-uiread *m invar*, (**of** de), **there were ~ a lot of people there** bha na h-uimhir/na h-uiread de dhaoine ann; 2 *in excl* **~ a** *with adj & n*, abair, **~ a kind man!** abair duine coibhneil!

suck *v* deothail *vti*, sùgh *vti*

suction *n* deothal *m*, sùghadh *m*

sudden *adj* grad, obann, gun fhiosta, **~ noise** fuaim ghrad/obann/gun fhiosta

suddenly *adv* gu grad, gu h-obann, gun fhiosta, **he rose ~** dh'èirich e gu grad/gu h-obann/gun fhiosta

suddenness *n* graide *f*, graidead *m*

suet *n* geir *f*

suffer *v* fuiling *vti*, **he didn't ~ when he was ill** cha do dh'fhuiling e nuair a bha e tinn, **they had to ~ cold and hunger** b' fheudar dhaibh fuachd is acras fhulang

suffering *n* (*mental or phys*) cràdh *m*, fulang *m*, fulangas *m*

suffice *v* foghain *vi*, **will that ~?** am foghain sin?

sufficiency *n* leòr *f invar*, fòghnadh *m*

sufficient *adj & n* gu leòr, na dh'fhòghnas (*rel fut of* foghain *vi*), **~ time** ùine gu leòr, **have you got ~?** a bheil gu leòr agad?, **is that ~?** am foghain sin?

suffocate mùch *vt*

suffocation *n* mùchadh *m*

suffrage *n* còir-bhòtaidh *f*, guth-bhòtaidh *m*

sugar *n* siùcar *m*

suggest *v* mol *vt*

suggestion *n* moladh *m*

suicide *n* fèin-mhurt *m*

suit *n* (*of clothes*) deise *f*, (*less usu*) culaidh(-aodaich) *f*, trusgan *m*

suit *v* freagair *vi* (*with prep* air *or* do), thig *vi* (*with prep* do *or* ri), **that hat doesn't ~ you!** chan eil an ad sin a' freagairt ort!, **it doesn't ~ me to be unoccupied/idle** cha fhreagair dhomh a bhith nam thàmh, **how's the job ~ing you?** ciamar a tha an obair a' freagairt dhut?/a' tighinn riut?

suitable *adj* freagarrach, (*less usu*) iomchaidh, **the house wasn't ~ for him** cha robh an taigh freagarrach dha, **a place ~ for swimming** àite freagarrach airson snàimh

suitcase n ceas m, màileid f

sulk n gruaim f, mùig m

sulk v cuir gruaim f/mùig m (*with prep* air), **he ~ed/began to ~** chuir e gruaim/mùig air, **he was ~ing** bha gruaim/mùig air

sulkiness n gruaim f, mùig m

sulking, sulky, sullen adj gruamach, mùgach

sully v truaill vt, salaich vt, cuir smal m (*with prep* air)

sulphur n pronnasg m

sulphurous adj pronnasgail

sultry adj (*of weather*) bruthainneach, bruicheil

sum n sùim f, **a ~ of money** sùim airgid, **we did ~s at school** rinn sinn suimeannan anns an sgoil

summarise v thoir geàrr-chunntas m (*with prep* air)

summary adj (*brief, brusque*) aithghearr, bras

summary n geàrr-chunntas m (**of** air)

summer n samhradh m, **~ school** sgoil-shamhraidh f

summit n 1 mullach m, bàrr m, **~ of the mountain** mullach na beinne; 2 *in expr* **~ meeting** n coinneamh f nan ceannardan, àrd-choinneamh f

summon v gairm vt, cuir vi a' dh'iarraidh, cuir fios m (*with prep* air)

summons n 1 gairm f; 2 (*legal*) sumanadh m, (*more trad*) bàirlinn f invar

summons v (*legal*) sumain vt

sumph (*Sc*) n amadan m, òinseach f

sumptuous adj sòghail

sun n grian f, **the ~'s rays** gathan mpl na grèine

sunbathe v gabh a' ghrian

sunbeam n gath-grèine f

sunburn n losgadh-grèine m

Sunday n 1 (*trad used by Catholic communities*) Didòmhnaich m invar; 2 (*trad used by Protestant communities*) Là na Sàbaid m

sunder v 1 (*of persons: part, separate*) dealaich vt (**from** ri); 2 (*of objects: split etc*) sgàin vti

sundial n uaireadair-grèine m

sundry adj 1 (*assorted*) de gach seòrsa m, de dh'iomadach seòrsa, measgaichte adj, **~ objects** rudan de gach seòrsa/de dh'iomadach seòrsa; 2 (*various*) caochladh m (*with gen pl*), iomadach adj (*precedes the noun which is in nom sing ie radical case*), **in ~ places** ann an caochladh àiteachan, ann an iomadach àite

sunflower n neòinean-grèine m

sunlight n solas m (na) grèine

sunny adj 1 grianach, **a ~ spot** bad grianach; 2 *in expr* **~ interval/spell** greis f grèine (*gen of* grian f)

sunrise n èirigh f (na) grèine

sunset n dol-fodha m (na) grèine, laighe mf invar (na) grèine

sunshade n sgàilean-grèine m

sunstroke n beum-grèine m

sunwise adj & adv deiseal (*the opposite of this is* tuathal)

superannuation n 1 (*abstr*) peinnseanachadh m, **~ scheme** sgeama peinnseanachaidh m; 2 (*con, the income etc received*) peinnsean m

Super-Ego n, **the ~** an Sàr-Fhèin m

supercilious adj àrdanach

superficial adj uachdarach, eu-domhainn

superfluous adj thar a' chòrr, iomarcach

superior adj 1 (*in rank*) uachdarach; 2 (**~ in** *quality*) (n)as fheàrr, (*in past & conditional tenses*) (n)a b' fheàrr)

superior n (*in rank*) uachdaran m

supernatural adj os-nàdarra(ch)

supersonic adj thar-astar-fuaim

superstition n saobh-chràbhadh m

superstitious adj saobh-chràbhach

supervise v cùm sùil f (*with prep* air), stiùir vt

supper n suipear f

supple adj sùbailte, lùbach

supplier n solaraiche m

supplies n (*esp of foodstuff*) lòn m

supply n 1 (*abstr*) solar m; 2 (*more con*) *in expr* **there was a good ~ of meat** bha an fheòil pàilt, bha feòil gu leòr ann/againn (*etc*)

supply v solaraich vt

support n (*lit or fig*) taic(e) f, tacsa m

support v 1 (*assist, back*) cùm taic f (*with prep* ri), thoir taic (*with prep* do), seas vt, **who will ~ you?** cò a chumas taic riut?, cò a sheasas thu?; 2 (*side with*) cùm taobh m (*with prep* ri), gabh taobh, **we ~ed her** chùm sinn taobh rithe, ghabh sinn a taobh; 3 (*maintain*) cùm vt suas, **I've a family to ~** tha teaghlach agam ri chumail suas

supporter n fear-taice m, neach-taice m (*pl* luchd-taice m sing coll*)

supporting, supportive adj taiceil

suppose v saoil vi, **I ~ they'll be on the train** saoilidh mi gum bi iad air an trèana f, **I ~ you're right** saoilidh mi gu bheil thu ceart

suppress v (*emotions, rising etc*) mùch vt, ceannsaich vt, cùm vt fodha

suppurate v iongraich vi

supreme adj 1 (*highest in status, power*) àrd- prefix, prìomh, (*precede the noun, which is lenited where possible*), **~ power** àrd-chumhachd f; 2 (*of highest quality etc*) sàr-prefix, barraichte, **a ~ hero** sàr-ghaisgeach m sure *adj* 1 cinnteach, deimhinn(e) & deimhinnte, (of às), **are you ~ she'll come?** a bheil thu cinnteach gun tig i?, **it'll rain, I'm ~ (of it)** bidh an t-uisge ann, tha mi cinnteach/ deimhinnt' às; 2 (*in statement of agreement, or certainty*) *expressed by* creid *vi* & *double neg*, **I'll be drunk tonight! I'm ~ you will!** bidh mi air an daorach a-nochd! cha chreid mi nach bi!, **I'm ~ he'll be at the game tonight** cha chreid mi nach bi e aig a' ghèam a-nochd; 3 (*reliable etc*) earbsach, seasmhach

surety *n* (*esp in fin matters*) urras *m* (**for** air), **stand (as) ~ for someone** rach *vi* an urras air cuideigin

surface *n* uachdar *m*, bàrr *m*, **on the ~ of the earth/the waves** air uachdar na talmhainn/ nan tonn

surface *v* thig *vi* an uachdar *m*

surfeit *n* sàth *m*, leòr *f invar*, cus *m*, **we got a ~ of it** fhuair sinn ar sàth/ar leòr dheth, **a ~ of wine** cus fiona *m gen*

surge *v* brùchd *vi* (**out of** a-mach à), **they ~d out of the hall** bhrùchd iad a-mach às an talla

surgeon *n* làmh-lèigh *m*, lannsair *m*

surgery *n* 1 (*the discipline*) làmh-leigheas *m*; 2 (*surgical intervention*) obair-lèigh *f*; 3 (*the place*) lèigh-lann *m*, *in expr* **a dental ~** ionad fiaclaire *m*; 4 (*~ of politician etc*) freastal-lann *f*

surly *adj* gruamach, mùgach, gnù, iargalt(a)

surname *n* sloinneadh *m*, (*less usu*) cinneadh *m*, **what's your ~?** dè an sloinneadh a th' agaibh/a th' oirbh?, *also* dè an fhine a th' agaibh

surplus *n* còrr *m*, (*excessive*) cus *m*, **our guests have eaten, give the ~ to the neighbours** tha ar n-aoighean air ithe, thoir an còrr do na nàbaidhean, **a ~ of talking** cus bruidhne (*gen of* bruidhinn *f*)

surprise *n* 1 iongnadh *m*, (*stronger*) mòr-iongnadh *m*, iongantas *m*; 2 *in expr* **she took us by ~** thàinig i oirnn gun fhiosta

surprise *v* 1 cuir iongnadh *m* (*with prep* air), **she ~d us** chuir i iongnadh oirnn; 2 (*by arriving unexpectedly*) **she ~d us** thàinig i oirnn gun fhiosta

surprised *adj & past part*, *in expr* **I was ~** ghabh mi iongantas *m*/iongnadh *m*

surprising *adj* iongantach, **that's not ~** (*trad*) chan iongnadh *m* sin

surrender *n* gèilleadh *m*, strìochdadh *m*, (**to** do)

surrender *v* gèill *vi*, strìochd *vi*, (**to** do)

surround *v* 1 cuartaich *vt*, iadh & iath *vt*; 2 *in expr* **the house** (*etc*) **was completely ~ed by woods** (*etc*) bha an taigh (*etc*) air a chuartachadh ceithir-thimcheall le coilltean

(*etc*), *also* bha coilltean fada mun cuairt air an taigh

survey *n* 1 (*of land etc*) tomhas *m*, (*less trad*) suirbhidh *m*, **the Ordnance Survey** an Suirbhidh Òrdanais; 2 (*a study, investigation etc*) sgrùdadh *m*, rannsachadh *m*; 3 (*~ in form of questionnaire etc*) suirbhidh *m*, **postal ~** suirbhidh tron phost

survey *v* 1 (*~ land etc*) tomhais *vt*; 2 (*study, investigate etc*) sgrùd *vt*, rannsaich *vt*, dèan sgrùdadh/rannsachadh *m* (*with prep* air)

surveyor *n* fear-tomhais *m*, neach-tomhais *m* (*pl* luchd-tomhais *m sing coll*)

survive *v* thig *vi* beò, mair *vi* beò, (**on** air), cùm beò, **if I ~** ma thig mi às beò, ma mhaireas mi beò, **I can't ~ on that!** cha tig mi beò air sin!, **how are you? I'm surviving** ciamar a tha thu? tha mi beò fhathast/tha mi a' cumail beò

suspect *adj* fo amharas *m*

suspect *n* neach fo amharas *m*

suspect *v* bi *vi irreg* amharas *m* (*with prep* aig), **I ~ that these figures are wrong** tha amharas agam gu bheil na figearan seo ceàrr

suspend *v* 1 (*phys*) croch *vt*; 2 (*put in abeyance*) cuir dàil *f* (*with prep* air), **~ the work** cuir dàil air an obair; 3 (*relieve of duties*) cuir *vt* à dreuchd *f*

suspension *n* 1 crochadh *m*, *in expr* **~ bridge** drochaid-chrochaidh *f*; 2 (*~ from duties*) cur à dreuchd *m*

suspicion *n* amharas *m*

suspicious *adj* amharasach (**of** à)

sustain *v* (*feed etc*) cùm *vt* suas, beathaich *vt*

sustenance *n* lòn *m*, beathachadh *m*

swagger *v* spai(s)dirich *vi*

swallow[1] *n* (*of liquid*) balgam *m*, (*more copious*) steallag *f*

swallow[2] *n* (*bird*) gòbhlan-gaoithe *m*

swallow *v* sluig & slug *vti*

swallowing *n* slugadh *m*

swamp *n* boglach *f*, fèith(e) *f*, bog *m*

swan *n* eala *f*

swarm *n* sgaoth *m*

swarm *v* sgaothaich *vi*

swarthy *adj* (*of persons*) ciar, lachdann

sway *v* luaisg *vi*, tulg *vi*

swear *n* mionn *mf*, bòid *f*

swear *v* 1 (*legal etc*) mionnaich *vti*, *in exprs* **~ an oath** thoir mionnan *m*, *also* mionnaich bòid *f*, gabh bòid, **will you ~ to it?** an toir thu d' fhacal *m* air?; 2 (*curse etc*) mionnaich *vi*

swearing *n* 1 (*of legal oath etc*) mionnachadh *m*; 2 (*cursing, bad language*) droch-chainnt *f*, mionnachadh *m*, guidheachan *mpl*

sweat *n* fallas *m*, ~ **gland** fàireag-fhallais *f*

sweat *v* bi *v irreg* fallas (*with prep* air), cuir fallas (*with prep* de), **I'm ~ing** tha fallas orm, tha mi a' cur fallas dhìom, *also* tha mi nam fhallas

sweaty *adj* fallasach

Sweden *n* Suain (*used with art*) An t-Suain *f*

sweep *v* sguab *vti*

sweet *adj* **1** (*of tastes*) milis; **2** (*of smells*) cùbhraidh; **3** (*of sounds, music*) binn

sweet *n* **1** (*dessert*) mìlsean *m*; **2** (*sweetie*) suiteas *m*, **~s** suiteis *mpl*, siùcairean *mpl*, rudan milis *mpl*

sweeten *v* mìlsich *vt*

sweetheart *n* leannan *m*

sweetness *n* mìlseachd *f invar*

swell *v* at *vi*, sèid *vi*, (*less usu*) bòc *vi*

swelling *v* at *m*, bòcadh *m*

swift *adj* **1** (*of movement*) luath, siùbhlach; **2** (*of person: ~ in performing tasks etc*) clis, deas, ealamh; **3** (*sudden, abrupt*) grad

swim *v* snàmh *vi*, **I like to ~** is toigh leam a bhith a' snàmh

swimmer *n* snàmhaiche *m*

swimming *n* snàmh *m*

swing *n* **1** (*child's ~*) dreallag *f*; **2** (*in voting habits etc*) gluasad *m*

swing *v* (*in wind etc*) luaisg *vi*, tulg *vi*

Swiss *adj* Eilbheiseach

switch[1] *n* (*elec*) suidse *f*

switch[2] *n* (*supple stick*) gad *m*

switch *v* **1** (*lights etc*) **~ on** cuir *vt* air, **~ off** cuir *vt* às/dheth; **2** (*exchange, ~ round*) cuir *vt* an àite *m* a chèile, **she ~ed the glasses round** chuir i na glainneachan an àite a chèile

switchboard *n* suids-chlàr *m*

Switzerland *n* (*used with art*) An Eilbheis *f*

swoon *n* neul *m*, laigse *f*

swoon *v* rach *vi* an neul *m*, rach *vi* an laigse *f*, fannaich *vi*, fanntaich *vi*

sword *n* claidheamh *m*, **two-handed ~** claidheamh dà-làimh, claidheamh-mòr

swordsman *n* claidheamhair *m*

syllable *n* **1** (*lit*) lide *m*; **2** (*loosely*) bìog *f*, bìd *m*, smid *f*, *esp in expr* **they** (*etc*) **didn't utter a ~** cha tuirt iad (*etc*) bìog/smid

syllabus *n* clàr-oideachais *m*, clàr-oideachaidh *m*

symbol *n* **1** comharra(dh) *m*, **status ~** comharradh-inbhe; **2** (*Lit*) samhla *m*

symbolic, symbolical *adj* samhlachail

symbolise *v* riochdaich *vt*, samhlaich *vt*

symbolism *n* samhlachas *m*

symmetrical *adj* cothromaichte

symmetry *n* co-chothromachd *f invar*

sympathetic *adj* co-fhulangach, mothachail, co-mhothachail, tuigseach

sympathise *v* co-fhuiling *vi*, co-mhothaich *vi*

sympathy *n* co-fhulangas *m*, co-mhothachadh *m*, tuigse *f invar*

symposium *n* co-labhairt *f*

symptom *n* comharra(dh) *m*

synopsis *n* giorrachadh *m*, geàrr-chunntas *m*

synthetic *adj* fuadain

syphon *n* lìonadair *m*

syringe *n* steallair(e) *m*

system *n* **1** (*order*) riaghailt *f*, rian *m*; **2** (*mechanisms, procedures etc*) siostam *m*, modh *mf*, dòigh *f*, **~ of government** siostam riaghlaidh, modh-riaghlaidh

systematic(al) *adj* riaghailteach, òrdail

T

table *n* **1** bòrd *m*; **2** (*in book etc*) clàr *m*, ~ **of contents** clàr-innse *m*

tacit *adj* tosdach, ~ **approval** aonta tosdach

taciturn *adj* tosdach, dùinte, (*through shyness*) diùid

tack[1] *n* (*sailing*) gabhail *mf*, taca *f*

tack[2] *n* (*small nail*) tacaid *f*

tacket *n* tacaid *f*

tackle *n* (*gear, equipment*) uidheam *f sing coll*, acainn *f sing coll*

tackle *v* thoir ionnsaigh *f*, thoir oidhirp *f*, (*with prep* air), rach *vi* an sàs *m* (*with prep* ann an), **tomorrow we'll ~ Sgùrr Alasdair** a-maireach bheir sinn ionnsaigh/oidhirp air Sgùrr Alasdair, **she ~d her new job full of optimism** chaidh i an sàs san obair ùr aice 's i làn dòchais

tactic *n* innleachd *f*

tactical *adj* innleachdach

tadpole *n* ceann-pholan *m*, ceann-simid *m*

tail *n* earball *m*, **a dog wagging its** ~ cù (is e) a' crathadh earbaill

tailor *n* tàillear *m*

taint *v* **1** (*sully*) truaill *vt*, salaich *vt*; **2** (*flavour*) thoir droch bhlas *m* (**to** do)

take *v* **1** *exprs with* gabh *vti*, ~ **place** (*ie happen*) gabh àite *m, also* tachair *vi*, ~ **leave** gabh cead *m invar* (**of** de), ~ **in** (*ie comprise, include, also* ~ *in mentally*) gabh *vt* a-steach, ~ **in hand**, ~ **on** (*work etc*) gabh *vt* os làimh (*dat of* làmh *f*), ~ **pity** gabh truas *m* (**on** de & ri), (*food etc*) **will you ~ a cup of tea?** an gabh thu cupan tì?, ~ **counsel/advice** gabh comhairle *f*, ~ **a rest/ break** gabh fois *f*, ~ **things easily** gabh air a (*etc*) s(h)ocair *f, in expr* (*excl*) ~ **it easy!** socair! *or* air do shocair!, ~ **a stroll/walk** gabh cuairt *f*, **she took to her bed** ghabh i ris an leabaidh *f*, ~ **advantage of X** (*not nec unfairly*) gabh cothrom *m* air X, ~ **(unfair) advantage of X** gabh brath *m* air X, **the hall will ~ 300 (people)** gabhaidh an talla trì ceud (duine); **2** *exprs with* thoir *vt*, ~ **it to him** thoir thuige e, ~ **it away** thoir air falbh e, **I'll ~ a trip to Glasgow** bheir mi sgrìob *f* do Ghlaschu, ~ **a look** thoir sùil *f* (**at** air), ~ **care (of yourself)** thoir an aire (ort fhèin), ~ **yourself off!** thoir do chasan *fpl* leat!, *also* tog ort!, **they took to their heels** thug iad na buinn (*pl of* bonn *m*) asta, **she took herself off to America** thug i Ameireagaidh oirre, *also* thog i oirre gu Ameireagaidh; **3** *misc exprs* ~ **a breather** leig d' anail *f*, ~ **a photograph** tog dealbh *mf*, (*in family etc*) ~ **after someone** rach *vi* ri taobh cuideigin *mf*, ~ **an exam** feuch deuchainn *f*, ~ **my hand** beir *vi* air mo làimh (*dat of* làmh *f*), ~ **to someone** teòth *vi* ri cuideigin *m*, ~ **your coat off** cuir *vt* dhìot do chòta *m*, ~ **part** gabh pàirt *mf* (**in** ann), com-pàirtich *vi*, ~ **(Holy) Communion** comanaich *vi*, ~ **on** (*workers*) fastaidh *vt*, ~ **in** (*understand*) tuig *vt*, (*deceive*) meall *vt*

taken in *adj & past part* (*deceived*) meallta

tale *n* sgeulachd *f*, (*esp trad* ~) sgeul *m*

talent *n* tàlann *m*

talented *adj* tàlantach, ealanta

talk *n* **1** (*abstr*) bruidhinn *f*; **2** (*conversation*) còmhradh *m*, **we had a** ~ rinn sinn còmhradh (beag), *also* (*more fam*) chuir sinn ar cinn còmhla, **a bit of a** ~ còmhradh beag, bonn còmhraidh; **3** (*address, speech*) òraid *f*, **give a** ~ thoir *vt* seachad òraid, dèan *vt* òraid, (**to** do)

talk *v* **1** bruidhinn *vi*, (*less usu*) labhair *vi*, (**to** ri); **2** (*converse*) dèan còmhradh *m*; **3** *in exprs* ~**ing of this and that** a' còmhradh a-null 's a-nall, *also* a' cnàmh na cìre, **the chairman was ~ing away** bha am fear-cathrach a' cur dheth

talkative *adj* còmhraideach, bruidhneach, (*more pej*) beulach, cabach, gabach

talking *n* bruidhinn *f*, (*less usu*) labhairt *f*

tall *adj* (*of people, buildings etc*) àrd, (*of people, less usu*) fad(a), **a ~ woman/building** boireannach/togalach àrd, **a ~ lanky woman** boireannach fada caol

talon *n* spu(i)r *m*, ìne *f*

tame *adj* **1** (*of animal etc*) calla & callda, solta; **2** (*insipid, unexciting*) gun bhrìgh *f*, gun smior *m*

tame *v* callaich *vt*, ceannsaich *vt*

tamper *v* **1** bean *vi*, buin *vi*, (**with** do *or* ri), **don't ~ with the radio** na bean ris an rèidio; **2** (*more maliciously*) **~ with** mill *vt*

tan *v* **1** (*~ leather*) cairt *vt*; **2** (*sunbathe*) gabh a' ghrian

tangible *adj* beanailteach

tank¹ *n* (*for water etc*) amar *m*

tank² *n* (*warfare*) tanca *f*

tanker *n* tancair *m*

tanning *n* (*of leather*) cartadh *m*

tannoy *n* glaodhaire *m*

tap¹ *n* (*plumbing*) tap *mf*, goc *m*

tap² *n* (*light blow*) cnag *f*

tape *n* teip *f*

tar *n* teàrr *f*, bìth *f*

tardy *adj* **1** (*late*) fadalach; **2** (*slow*) mall, màirnealach, (*less usu*) athaiseach

targe, target *n* targaid *f*

target *n* **1** (*archery etc*) targaid *f*, cuspair *m*; **2** *in expr* (*publicity etc*) **~ audience** luchd-amais *m sing coll*

tariff *n* clàr-phrìsean *m*

tarnish *v* smalaich *vt*, dubhaich *vt*, (*esp fig*) cuir smal *m*, cuir sgleò *m*, (*both with prep* air)

tart *adj* **1** (*of tastes*) geur, searbh; **2** (*of remarks etc*) geur, searbh, guineach

tart *n* (*pastry*) pithean *m*

tartan *n* breacan *m*

tartan *adj* breacanach, tartanach, **~ cloth/clothing** aodach breacanach/tartanach

task *n* **1** obair *f*, pìos obrach *m*, gnìomh *m*, gnothach *m*, **the ~ before us** an obair/an gnìomh/an gnothach a tha romhainn, **~ force** buidheann-gnìomha *m*; **2** *in expr* **take to ~** thoir achmhasan *m* (*with prep* do), **I must take them to ~** feumaidh mi achmhasan a thoirt dhaibh

taste *m* **1** (*flavour*) blas *m*, **the ~ of honey** blas na meala (*gen of* mil *f*); **2** (*small quantity*) blasad *m*, **a ~ of honey** blasad meala; **3** (*artistic etc discernment*) tuigse *f invar* (a thaobh ealaine *etc*)

taste *v* **1** (*as vt*) blais *vt*, feuch *vt*, **~ this beer** blais/feuch an leann a tha seo; **2** (*as vi*) *in exprs* **it doesn't ~ of anything** chan eil blas *m* (sam bith/idir) air, **it ~s of paint** tha blas a' pheanta air, **cake tasting of honey** cèic air blas na meala (*gen of* mil *f*)

tasteless *adj* mì-bhlasta, gun bhlas *m*

tasty *adj* blasta, (*stronger*) blasmhor

tatter *n* luideag *f*, cearb *f*, **the curtains are in ~s** tha na cùirtearan nan luideagan

tattered *adj & past part* luideach, cearbach, nan (*etc*) luideagan *fpl*, reubte

tatty *adj* luideach, cearbach

taunt *n* beum *m*, magadh *m*

taunt *v* mag *vi* (*with prep* air), **they were ~ing her** bha iad a' magadh oirre

taut *adj* teann

tavern *n* taigh-òsta *m*

tawdry *adj* suarach, grodach, dràbhail

tawny *adj* lachdann, odhar, ciar

tax *n* cìs *f*, càin *f*, **~ avoidance** seachnadh cìse *m*, **~ cut** gearradh cìse *m*, **~ rate** ìre cìse *f*

tax *v* **1** (*cause to pay tax*) cuir/leag càin *f* (*with prep* air), **~ the population** cuir càin air an t-sluagh; **2** (*levy tax on goods etc*) cuir cìs *f* (*with prep* air), **~ tobacco** cuir cìs air tombaca

taxable *adj* cìs-bhuailteach

taxation *n* cìs *f*, càin *f*

taxi *n* tagsaidh *m*

tea *n* **1** (*the drink*) tì *f invar*, teatha *f invar*, **a cup of ~** cupa tì *m*; **2** (*the meal*) biadh feasgair *m*

teach *v* teagaisg *vti*, ionnsaich *vti*, (**to** do), **my grandfather taught me what wisdom I have** theagaisg mo sheanair dhomh na tha agam de ghliocas, **~ maths** teagaisg matamataig, **~ boys** teagaisg gillean, **~ boys maths/~ maths to boys** teagaisg matamataig do ghillean

teacher *n* fear-teagaisg *m*, neach-teagaisg *m*, bean-teagaisg *f*, tidsear *m*, maighstir-sgoile *m*, ban(a)-mhaighstir-sgoile *f*, **~s** luchd-teagaisg *m sing coll*

teaching *n* teagasg *m*, (*less usu*) oileanachadh *m*, **the ~ staff** an luchd-teagaisg *m sing coll*

team *n* buidheann *mf*, (*esp sport*) sgioba *mf*, **research ~** buidheann-rannsachaidh, **football ~** sgioba ball-coise

tear¹ *n* (*a rip*) reubadh *m*, sracadh *m*

tear², **teardrop** *n* deur *m*

tear *v* **1** (*rip*) reub *vt*, srac *vt*; **2** (*snatch*) spìon *vt* (**from** à), **~ it (away) from him** spìon às e; **3** (*rush etc*) falbh (*etc*) na (*etc*) d(h)ian-ruith *f*, **she tore out of the house** dh'fhàg i an taigh na dian-ruith, *also* dh'fhàg i an taigh aig peilear a beatha

tearful *adj* deurach

tease *v* tarraing *vi* (*with prep* à), farranaich *vt*, **he's teasing the other boy** tha e a' tarraing às a' bhalach eile

teat *n* sine *f*

tea-towel *n* tubhailte-shoithichean *f*

technical *adj* teicnigeach

technician *n* teicneòlaiche *m*

technique *n* dòigh(-obrach) *f*, alt *m*

technological *adj* teicneòlach

technologist *n* teicneòlaiche *m*

technology *n* teicneòlas *m*

tedious *adj* fadalach, liosda, màirnealach

tedium *n* fadachd *f invar*, fadal *m*, fadalachd *f invar*, liosdachd *f invar*

teem *v* cuir *vi* thairis (**with** le), **the woods ~ed/ were ~ing with creatures of every kind** bha na coilltean a' cur thairis le creutairean de gach seòrsa

teenager *n* (*of either sex*) deugaire *m*

teens *npl* deugan *mpl*

telephone *n* fòn *mf*, **I was talking to him on the ~** bha mi a' bruidhinn ris air a' fòn, **what's your ~ number?** dè an àireamh-fòn *f* a th' agad?

telephone *v* cuir fòn *mf*, fòn *vi*, fònaig *vi*, (*all with prep* gu), **he ~d her** chuir e fòn thuice, dh'fhòn e thuice

telescope *n* prosbaig *mf*

television *n* telebhisean *m*, *used with & without art*, **I saw a good programme on (the) ~** chunnaic mi prògram math air an telebhisean, **~ licence** cead telebhisein *m*

tell *v* **1** (*command*) òrdaich *vi* (*with prep* do), **they told me to shut the gates** dh'òrdaich iad dhomh/(*less formal*) thuirt iad rium na geataichean a dhùnadh; **2** (*recount, relate*) innis *vti*, **~ me about it!** innis dhomh mu dheidhinn!, **~ a story** innis sgeulachd, **I'll ~ what I know (about it)** innsidh mi na tha a (*for* de) dh'fhios agam (air), **to ~ (you) the truth, I don't know** leis an fhìrinn innse, chan eil fhios a'm

temper *n* **1** nàdar *m*, **bad ~** droch nàdar; **2** *in expr* **in a bad ~** diombach, crost(a)

temperament *n* mèinn *f*, nàdar *m*

temperance *n* stuamachd *f invar*

temperate *adj* **1** (*of weather*) sèimh; **2** (*of people*) measarra, stuama

temperature *n* teòthachd *f invar*

tempest *n* doineann *f*, gailleann *f*

tempestuous *adj* gailbheach, doineannach

temple[1] *n* (*relig*) teampall *m*

temple[2] *n* (*anat*) lethcheann *m*

temporal *adj* aimsireil, talmhaidh, saoghalta

temporary *adj* sealach, **~ accommodation** àite-còmhnaidh sealach *m*

tempt *v* buair *vt*, meall *vt*, (*with milder overtones*) tàlaidh *vt*, **the devil/evil one ~ed me** bhuair/mheall an diabhal mi, **~ the customers back** tàlaidh an luchd-ceannach air ais

temptation *n* buaireadh *m*, mealladh *m*

ten *n & adj* **1** deich; **2** (*of people*) deichnear *mf invar* (*with gen pl*), **~ sons** deichnear mhac

tenacious *adj* dìorrasach

tenacity *n* dìorrasachd *f invar*

tenancy *n* gabhaltas *m*

tenant *n* màladair *m*

tend[1] *v* (*care for*) eiridnich *vt*, **~ the sick/ill** eiridnich na h-euslaintich

tend[2] *v* **1** (*be liable to*) bi *vi irreg* buailteach, bi dual(t)ach, (*with infin of verb or with prep* air), **he ~s to be mean** tha e dualach/buailteach a bhith spìocach, **we ~ to spend money** tha sinn dualach/buailteach airgead a chosg, **they ~ to get tired** tha iad buailteach air fàs sgìth; **2** (*habit, routine*) *in expr* **~ to** mar as trice bi *vi irreg, with participial construction*, **we ~ to get up very late on Sunday** mar as trice, bidh sinn ag èirigh glè anmoch (air) Là na Sàbaid

tendency *n* **1** (*trend*) aomadh *m*, **economic ~** aomadh eaconamach; **2** (*propensity*) buailteachd *nf invar, in expr* **he** (*etc*) **has a ~ to complain** (*etc*) tha e (*etc*) buailteach/dual(t)ach a bhith a' gearan (*etc*)

tender *adj* (*phys or emotionally*) maoth, (*emotionally*) bog, **a ~ heart** cridhe bog

tender *n* (*commerce etc: offer*) tairgse *f*

tender *v* (*commerce etc: offer*) tairg *vti*

tendril *n* ògan *m*

tense *n* (*gram*) tràth *m*, **the present ~** an tràth làthaireach, **the past (preterite) ~** an tràth caithte, **the imperfect ~** an tràth neo-choileanta, **the perfect ~** an tràth coileanta, **the future ~** an tràth teachdail, **the conditional ~** an tràth cumhach

tense *adj* **1** (*phys*) teann, rag; **2** (*emotionally, nervously*) nèarbhach, clisgeach, frionasach

tense *v* teannaich *vti*

tension *n* **1** (*esp phys*) teannachadh *m*; **2** (*emotional, nervous*) frionas *m*

tent *n* teanta *f*, (*large*) pàillean *m*, (*larger still*) puball & pùball *m*

tenterhooks *npl, in expr* **on ~** air bhioran *mpl*

tenth *adj* deicheamh

tenure *n* gabhaltas *m*

tepid *adj* (*lit & fig*) leth-fhuar, flodach, **~ soup** brot leth-fhuar, **the relationship between us had become ~** bha an dàimh a bha eadarainn air fàs leth-fhuar

term[1] *n* **1** (*condition*) cumha *f*, **the ~s of the contract** cumhachan a' chùmhnaint; **2** (*terminology*) briathar *m*, **what/which ~ do you use for 'ministerial'?** cò am briathar a th' agaibh air 'ministerial'?, **technical ~s** briathran teignigeach; **3** (*in relationships*) *in exprs* **be on good ~s with someone** bi *vi irreg* rèidh ri cuideigin, **they are on bad ~s** tha iad troimh-a-chèile/thar a chèile, *also* chan eil iad a' tarraing ro mhath

term² n (*period of time*) teirm f, **the autumn ~** teirm an fhoghair, **his ~ of office** teirm na dreuchd aige

terminal n (*IT*) ceann-obrach m

terminate v cuir crìoch f (*with prep* air), thoir vt gu crìch (*dat*), **~ a lease** cuir crìoch air gabhail

terminology n **1** (*abstr*) briathrachas m; **2** (*con: in form of lexicon etc*) briathrachan m

terminus n ceann-uidhe m

terra firma n tìr mf, talamh tioram m

terrible adj (*with full or attenuated meaning*) eagalach, uabhasach, sgrìosail, **it was just ~!** bha e dìreach eagalach/uabhasach/sgrìosail!

terribly adv **1** uabhasach, anabarrach, eagalach, **~ good** uabhasach/ anabarrach math, *also* uabhasach fhèin math; **2** in exprs **how did it go? it went absolutely ~!** ciamar a chaidh dhut/dhuibh? cha deach(aidh) ach gu dubh dona!, **things are ~ busy just now** tha cùisean garbh dripeil an-dràsta

terrier n abhag f

terrify v cuir oillt f, cuir eagal mòr, (*with prep* air), oilltich vt

territory n dùthaich f, tìr mf, **the Mackay ~** Dùthaich MhicAoidh

terror n uamhann m, oillt f, uabhas m

terse adj aithghearr, **a ~ reply** freagairt aithghearr f

tertiary education n foghlam (aig) àrd-ìre m

test n **1** dearbhadh m, deuchainn f, **~s on a new car** dearbhaidhean air càr ùr, **put to the ~** cuir vt gu deuchainn, dearbh vt; **2** (*ed*) deuchainn f, **entrance ~** deuchainn-inntrigidh

test v cuir vt gu deuchainn f, dearbh vt, **they ~ed the new machines** chuir iad na h-innealan ùra gu deuchainn

testament n (*legal etc, Bibl*) tiomnadh m, **the Old Testament** An Seann Tiomnadh, **the New Testament** An Tiomnadh Nuadh

testicle n magairle mf, clach f

testify v thoir fianais f

testimonial n teisteanas m

testimony n fianais f, teisteanas m, dearbhadh m

testy, tetchy adj frionasach, cas

tether n feist(e) f, teadhair f, in exprs **~ post** cipean m, (*calque*) **at the end of my ~** aig ceann mo theadhrach

text n **1** teacsa f; **2** (*of sermon etc*) ceann-teagaisg m

textual adj teacsail

than conj na, **they are older ~ I** tha iad nas sine na mise

thank v **1** thoir taing f (*with prep* do), **I want to ~ you** tha mi airson taing a thoirt dhut/dhuibh;

2 in exprs **~ you!** tapadh leat/leibh!, (*less usu*) taing dhut/dhuibh!, **~ you very much!** mòran taing!, ceud taing!

thankful adj taingeil, buidheach

thanks n taing f, **many ~!**, **~ a lot!** mòran taing!, **give ~** thoir taing (**to** do)

that adj sin, a tha 'n sin, (*usu more distant or remote*) ud, **~ book** an leabhar sin/ud, an leabhar a tha 'n sin, (*adv use*) **it wasn't ~ good** cha robh e cho math sin

that rel pron a, (*in neg*) nach, **the drink ~ I drank** an deoch a dh'òl mi, **the film ~ I didn't see** am film nach fhaca mi

that pron sin, (*usu more distant or remote*) siud, **what's ~?** dè a tha sin/siud?, **~'s my house** sin an taigh agam, **~'s the point** is e sin an rud/a' chùis, **~ is my hope**, **~'s what I hope** 's e sin mo dhòchas, **~'s a lot of money** 's e airgead mòr a tha sin, **it wasn't as good as ~!** cha robh e cho math sin!, **are you tired? I am ~!** a bheil thu sgìth? tha mi sin! (*also* 's mi a tha!), **~'s it!** sin e!

that conj **1** gu, gun, (*before b, f, m, p*) gum, (*neg*) nach, (*with v is*) gur, **it's certain/definite ~ she's lost** 's cinnteach gu bheil i air chall, **I'm glad ~ you came** tha mi toilichte gun tàinig sibh, **they said ~ they weren't ready** thuirt iad nach robh iad deiseil, **is it gold? I don't think ~ it is** an e òr a th' ann? cha chreid mi gur e; **2** in expr **so ~** (*ie with the intention ~*), gus am, gus an, (*neg*) gus nach, **so ~ he would have some pocket money** gus am biodh airgead-pòcaid aige, **so that you can find the house** gus an urrainn dhut an taigh a lorg, **so ~ she wouldn't be hungry** gus nach biodh an t-acras oirre; **3** in expr **so ~** (*ie with the result ~, also, with the intention ~*) air dhòigh f is, air chor m is, (*with conjs* gu, gun, gum, (*neg*) nach), **she didn't lock the door so ~ I could get in** cha do ghlas i an doras air dhòigh/air chor 's gum faighinn a-steach, **he spoke in a low voice, so ~ I didn't hear him** bhruidhinn e ann an guth ìosal, air dhòigh/air chor is nach cuala mi e

thatch n tughadh m

thatch v tugh vt

thaw n aiteamh m

thaw v leagh vti

the *definite art* an etc, *for full list of forms see table p 491*

theatre n taigh-cluiche m

theft n goid f, mèirle f invar

them pron mpl & fpl iad, (*emph form*) iadsan

theme *n* **1** cuspair *m*, **the ~ of her talk** cuspair na h-òraid aice; **2** (*mus*) ùrlar *m*

themselves *reflexive pron* iad fhèin, *for examples of use cf* **myself**, & **-self** *reflexive suffix*

then *adv* **1** (*at that time*) aig an àm sin, **I was young ~**, bha mi òg aig an àm sin; **2** (*next*) an uair sin, **he read the paper and ~ he went to bed** leugh e am pàipear(-naidheachd) 's an uair sin chaidh e a chadal/don leabaidh; **3** (*in that case*) ma-thà & ma-tà, **the door's open! close it ~!** tha an doras fosgailte! dùin e, ma-tà!, **right ~!** ceart, ma-thà!

theologian *n* diadhaire *m*

theology *n* diadhachd *f invar*

theory *n* **1** (*a surmise etc*) beachd *m*, beachd-smuain *m*; **2** (*hypothetical conclusions*) teòiridh *f*, **in ~** a rèir teòiridh

therapist *n* leasaiche *m*, teiripiche *m*

there *adv* **1** an sin, sin, (*usu more distant or remote*) an siud, (*more emph*) ann an sin, ann an siud, **I was born ~** rugadh mi an sin, **where's my book? it's ~/~ it is** càit a bheil an leabhar agam? sin e, **what are you doing ~?** dè a tha thu a' dèanamh ann an sin?; **2** (*over*) **~** (*usu expr position*) thall (an sin), **here and ~** thall 's a-bhos, an siud 's an seo, **over ~ in America** (*etc*) ann an Ameireagaidh (*etc*) thall, **what are they doing over ~?** dè a tha iad a' dèanamh thall an sin?; **3** (*present*) ann, an làthair *f*, **I knew those who were ~** bha mi eòlach air na bha ann/na bha an làthair

there *pron* **1** (*expressed by the v irreg* bi, & *a prep phrase*) **~'s a man at the door** tha duine aig an doras, **~'s not a lot of peace in the world** chan eil mòran sìthe san t-saoghal; **2** (*expressed by the v irreg* bi & *a prep pron*) **~'s a strike** tha stailc ann, **~ was no petrol** cha robh peatrail ann; **3** (*expressed by the v irreg* bi & *a verbal expr*) **~'s something happening** tha rudeigin a' tachairt, **~'s nothing to be done** chan eil dad ri dhèanamh (*can also expressed by* chan eil cothrom air)

therefore *adv* a chionn sin, air sgàth sin, mar sin, do bhrìgh sin, uime sin, **we've no money, ~ we've no food** chan eil airgead againn, (agus) mar sin/air sgàth sin chan eil biadh againn

thereupon *adv* le sin, leis a sin, **the bar closed, ~ he went home** dhùin am bàr, (is) leis a sin chaidh e dhachaigh

thermometer *n* teas-mheidh *f*, tomhas-teas *m*

these *pron*, *see* **this**

thesis *n* tràchdas *m*

they *pron mpl & fpl* iad, (*emph forms*) iadsan, iad fhèin

thick *adj* **1** (*phys*) tiugh; **2** (*of trees, hair, vegetation etc: dense*) dlùth, dùmhail; **3** (*mentally ~: fam*) tiugh, maol

thicket *n* doire *mf*, bad *m*

thickness *n* tighead *m*

thickset *adj* tomadach & tomaltach

thief *n* gadaiche *m*, mèirleach *m*

thieve *v* goid *vti*, dèan mèirle *f invar*, (*usu more petty*) dèan braid *f*

thieving *n* goid *f*, mèirle *f invar*, (*usu more petty*) braid *f*, **are you still at your ~?** a bheil thu ri goid fhathast?

thigh *n* sliasaid *f*, (*less usu*) leis *f*

thimble *n* meuran *m*

thin *adj* **1** (*of persons*) caol, tana, seang; **2** (*of substances: ~ in consistency*) lom, tana, **~ porridge** brochan lom/tana; **3** (*of trees etc: sparse*) tana, gann, lom

thin *v* (*crops etc*) tanaich *vt*

thing *n* **1** (*object*) rud *m*, nì *m*, **a stone is a ~** 's e rud a tha ann an clach; **2** (*more fam & general*) càil *m invar*, sìon *m*, dad *m invar*, **what's in the cupboard? not a ~** dè a th' anns a' phreas? chan eil càil/sìon/dad; **3** (*matter, affair etc*) cùis *f*, rud *m*, **~s are pretty busy just now** tha cùisean gu math dripeil an-dràsta, **their divorce was a bad ~** 's e droch rud a bh' anns an sgaradh-pòsaidh aca; **4** (*point at issue*) cùis *f*, gnothach *m*, **did he steal it or didn't he? that's the ~** an do ghoid e e no nach do ghoid? 's e sin a' chùis/an gnothach; **5** *in exprs* **first ~ in the morning** a' chiad char *m* sa mhadainn, **I haven't heard a ~ about him** cha chuala mi guth *m* mu dheidhinn

think *v* **1** (*consider, contemplate: philosopher etc*) beachd-smaoin(t)ich *vi*, beachdaich *vi*, (*less rigorously*) smaoin(t)ich *vi*, cnuas & cnuasaich *vi*, meòraich & meamhraich *vi*, (**about** air); **2** (*be of the opinion*) creid *vi*, saoil *vi*, bi *vi irreg* den bheachd *m*, **I ~ that you are right** tha mi a' creidsinn/saoilidh mi/tha mi den bheachd gu bheil sibh ceart; **3** *in exprs* **I ~ it good** (*etc*) (*trad*) is math (*etc*) leam e, **~ over** cnuas & cnuasaich *vi* (*with prep* air), **~ over what happened** cnuasaich air na thachair

thinking *n* **1** (*the process, faculty, activity*) smaoin(t)eachadh *m*, beachdachadh *m*; **2** (*rationale*) feallsanachd *f*, **the ~ behind the proposals** feallsanachd nam molaidhean

think-tank *n* buidheann-beachdachaidh *mf*

thinning *adj* tana, **~ hair** falt tana

third *n* trian *m invar*, **I lost two ~s of my savings** chaill mi dà thrian de na shàbhail mi

third *num adj* **1** treas, **the ~ (day) of the month** an treas là den mhìos; **2** *in expr* (*insurance etc*) **~ party** an treas neach *m*

thirst *n* pathadh *m*, (*stronger*) tart *m*, ìota(dh) *m*

thirsty *adj* **1** pàiteach, (*stronger*) tartmhor, ìotmhor; **2** *in exprs* **I was/I grew ~** bha/thàinig am pathadh *m* orm

thirteenth *num adj* treas deug, **the ~ (day) of the month** an treas là deug den mhìos

thirty *num & ad* deich ar (*for* thar) fhichead, fichead 's a deich, (*in alternative numbering system*) trithead *m*

this, these *pron* **1** seo, **who's this?** cò (a) tha seo?, **this is my wife, and these are the boys** seo a' bhean agam, agus seo na gillean; **2** (*as demonstrative adj*) seo, *also* a tha seo, **this boy** am balach (a tha) seo, **this one** (*m*) am fear (a tha) seo, (*f*) an tè (a tha) seo, **these ones** an fheadhainn *f sing coll* (a tha) seo, iad seo, **these (ones) are going home** tha an fheadhainn seo/iad seo a' dol dhachaigh

thistle *n* cluaran *m*, fòghnan *m*, giogan *m*

thither *adv* **1** ann, a-null, **I'm going ~** tha mi a' dol ann/a-null; **2** *in expr* **hither and ~** thall 's a-bhos, a-null 's a nall

thong *n* iall *f*

thorax *n* cliabh *m*

thorn *n* **1** (*the plant*) droigheann *m*; **2** (*the prickle*) dealg *f*, bior *m*

thorny *adj* **1** (*lit*) droighneach; **2** (*fig: tricky, sensitive etc*) duilich. doirbh, **a ~ problem** duilgheadas doirbh/duilich

thorough *adj* **1** (*of person*) pongail, dìcheallach, dealasach; **2** (*of job of work etc*) mionaideach, **a ~ enquiry/study** sgrùdadh mionaideach, *also* mion- *prefix, with appropriate n, eg* **~ knowledge/acquaintance** mion-eòlas *m* (**of/with** air); **3** (*out and out, utter*) dearg (*precedes n*), gu c(h)ùl *m* (*follows the n*), **a ~ scoundrel** dearg shlaightear, slaightear gu chùl

thoroughfare *n* tro-shlighe *f*

though *adv* ge-tà & ged-thà, **I was at the fank all day, I'm not tired ~** bha mi aig an fhaing fad an là, chan eil mi sgìth, ge-tà

though *conj* ged, **~ he wasn't ill** ged nach robh e tinn, **she didn't stop ~ she was exhausted** cha do sguir i ged a bha i claoidhte

thought *n* **1** (*the process, faculty, activity*) smaointeachadh *m*, beachdachadh *m*; **2** (*a ~*) smuain & smaoin *f*, (*can be more rigorous ~*) beachd *m*, beachd-smuain *m*, **melancholy ~s** smuaintean dubhach, **~s on the coming war**

smuaintean/beachdan/beachd-smuaintean air a' chogadh a tha romhainn; **3** (*interest, concern*) for *m invar* (**for** air), **he had no ~ for anything but his own affairs** cha robh for aige ach air a ghnothaichean fhèin

thoughtful *adj* **1** (*pensive etc*) smuainteachail; **2** (*considerate*) tuigseach, suimeil

thousand *n* mìle *m* (*followed by nom sing ie radical of n*), **a ~ men** mìle duine

thrash *v* slaic *vt*

thrashing *n* slaiceadh *m*

thrawn (*Sc*) *adj* rag, dùr, (*stronger*) rag-mhuinealach

thread *n* **1** (*single ~*) snàthainn *m*; **2** (*coll*) snàth *m sing coll*

threadbare *adj* lom

threat *n* maoidheadh *m*, bagairt *f*, bagradh *m*, **a ~ of war** bagairt cogaidh

threaten *v* maoidh *vi*, bagair *vi*, (*with prep* air), **he was ~ing me** bha e a' maoidheadh/a' bagairt orm

three *num adj* **1** trì; **2** (*of people*) triùir *mf invar* (*with gen pl*), **~ brothers** triùir bhràithrean

threefold, three-ply *adj* trì-fillte

threesome *n* triùir *mf invar* (*with gen pl*)

thresh *v* buail *vti*, **~ing the corn** a' bualadh an arbhair

threshold *n* stairs(n)each *f*

thrifty *adj* **1** cùramach (a thaobh airgid *m*), glèidhteach; **2** *in expr* **be ~ (with)** caomhain *vti*

thrill *n* gaoir *f* (*can be pleasant or unpleasant*), **give a ~** cuir gaoir (**to** air)

thrill *v* cuir gaoir *f* (*with prep* air)

thrilling *adj* gaoireil

thrive *v* **1** soirbhich *vi*, **the business ~d** shoirbhich an gnìomhachas; **2** soirbhich *vi* (*as impersonal v, with prep* le), **he ~d** shoirbhich leis

throat *n* **1** amha(i)ch *f*, sgòrnan *m*

throb *n* (*esp of heart*) plosg *m*

throb *v* (*esp heart*) plosg *vi*, dèan plosgartaich *f*, (*less severe*) plap *vi*

throbbing *n* (*esp of heart*) plosgadh *m*, plosgartaich *f*

throne *n* rìgh-chathair *f*

throng *n* sluagh mòr, mòr-shluagh *m*

throng *v* rach (*etc*) *vi* nan (*etc*) ceudan *mpl*/nan (*etc*) mìltean *mpl*/nan (*etc*) dròbh(an) *m*(*pl*), **we ~ed to the meeting** chaidh/thàinig sinn dhan choinneimh nar ceudan/nar mìltean/nar dròbh

throttle *v* mùch *vt*, tachd *vt*

through *adv* **1** (*fam: finished etc*) deiseil, (*less usu*) ullamh, deas, (**with** de), **are you ~?** a bheil thu deiseil?, **they aren't ~ with the phone**

yet chan eil iad deiseil den fòn fhathast, **they were ~ asking questions** bha iad ullamh de cheasnachadh; **2** *in expr* ~ **and** ~ gu c(h)ùl *m*, **a Gael/Highlander** ~ **and** ~ Gàidheal gu chùl

through *prep* tro, *with art* tron (*takes dat, & lenites following cons where possible*; *for prep prons formed with* tro, *see p 510*), ~ **a glass darkly** dorcha tro ghlainne, **they came ~ the wood** thàinig iad tron choille

throw *n* tilgeadh *m*

throw *v* **1** tilg *vt*, caith *vt*, (**at** air), **he threw it at me** thilg e orm e, **don't ~ stones!** na tilg clachan!; **2** *in exprs* ~ **away** tilg *vt* air falbh, ~ **down** (*ie demolish, fell*) leag *vt* (gu làr *m*), ~ **up** tilg (suas) *vti*, dìobhair *vti*, sgeith *vti*, **he threw up his dinner** chuir e a-mach a dhinnear

thrush *n* (*the bird*) smeòrach *f*

thrust *n* **1** sàthadh *m*, **a ~ of the knife** sàthadh den sgithinn; **2** (*fig: essence, 'drift'*) brìgh *f invar*, comhair *m*, **the ~ of his argument** brìgh na h-argamaid(e) aige

thrust *v* **1** sàth *vti*, spàrr *vt*, (**into** a-steach do, an), ~ **your hand into the sack** sàth/spàrr do làmh a-steach don phoca, **he ~ the knife into him/it** shàth e an sgian ann; **2** *in expr* (*fig*) ~ **upon** spàrr *vt* (*with prep* air), **the new law was ~ upon us** chaidh an lagh ùr a sparradh oirnn

thumb *n* òrdag *f*

thump *n* buille *f*, buille-dùirn *f*

thump *v* dòrn *vt*, slaic *vt*

thunder *v* tàirneanaich & tàirnich *vi*

thunder *n* tàirneanach *m*

Thursday *n* Diardaoin *m invar*

thus *adv* air an dòigh *f* seo, air an dòigh a leanas, (*less formal*) mar seo, **open the packet ~** fosgail a' phacaid air an dòigh seo/air an dòigh a leanas/mar seo

thwart *v* cuir bacadh *m*, cuir stad *m*, (*with prep* air), **we ~ed his schemes** chuir sinn bacadh/stad air a chuid innleachdan

tick¹ *n* (*marking etc*) strìochag *f*

tick² *n* **1** (*sound of clock*) diog *m*; **2** (*fam*; *instant*) diog *m*, tiota *m*, (*dimin*) tiotan *m*, tiotag *f*, **I'll be with you in a ~** bidh mi agaibh/leibh ann an diog/ann an tiotag

tick³ *n* (*the parasite*) mial *f*, **sheep-~** mial-chaorach *f*

ticket *n* tiogaid *f*, tigeard *f*

tickle *v* diogail *vti*

ticklish *adj* diogalach, ciogailteach

tide *n* **1** seòl-mara *m*, làn-(mara) *m*, **there's a big ~ today** tha làn mòr ann an-diugh; **2** (*usu with art*) **the ~,** an tìde-mhara *mf*, **the ~'s**

against us tha an tìde-mhara nar n-aghaidh; **3** *in exprs* **high** ~ muir-làn *m*, làn-mara *m*, **spring-~** reothart *mf*, **neap-** ~ conntraigh *f*, **the ~ came in** lìon *vi* am muir

tidings *n* naidheachdan *fpl*, (*more fam*) sgeul *m*, guth *m*, ~ **from the battlefield** naidheachdan on bhlàr, **are there any ~ of Iain?** a bheil sgeul/guth air Iain?

tidy *adj* **1** (*of person, figure: well turned-out; also of objects: trim, well-made etc*) cuimir, grinn, sgiobalta, snasail, snasmhor; **2** (*of room, space, objects etc; neat, not untidy*) sgiobalta, (*less usu*) cunbhalach

tidy *v* sgioblaich *vt*, òrdaich *vt*, cuir *vt* an òrdugh *m*, cuir *vt* air dòigh *f*, rèitich *vt*

tie *n* **1** (*necktie*) taidh *f*; **2** (*for fastening, securing*) ceangal *m*, bann *m*; **3** (*link(s) of relationship, friendship*) dàimh *mf invar*, càirdeas *m*, **the ~s between the two families** an dàimh/an càirdeas eadar an dà theaghlach

tie *v* ceangail *vt* (**to** ri), ~ **together** ceangail ri chèile

tier *n* sreath *mf*, **two ~s of government** dà shreath de riaghaltas

ties *n* (*of kinship, friendship*) dàimh *mf invar*, càirdeas *m* (*see also* **tie** *n* **3**)

tight *adj* **1** (*lit*) teann, **a ~ rope** ròpa teann; **2** (*leaving little leeway*) teann, **a ~ budget/timescale** buidseat *m*/raon-ama *m* teann; **3** (*in short supply etc*) gann, **money's ~ this month** tha (an t-) airgead gann air a' mhìos seo; **4** *in expr* (*fig*) **a ~ corner** cruaidh-chàs *m*, cùil-chumhang *f*, cruadal *m*, staing *f*

tighten *v* teannaich *vti*

tightening *n* teannachadh *m*

tile *n* leac *f*, (*smaller*) leacag *f*

till *conj, see* **until** *conj*

till *prep, see* **until** *prep*

till *n* (*in shop etc*) cobhan(-airgid) *m*, (*checkout, paypoint*) àite-pàighidh *m*

till *v* àitich *vt*, obraich *vt*, ~ **the soil/land/ground** àitich/obraich am fearann

tiller *n* **1** (*of boat*) failm *f*, ailm *f*; **2** (~ *of land*) fear-àitich *m*

tilt¹ *n* (*slant*) claonadh *m*, fiaradh *m*

tilt² *n*, *in expr* **at full ~** na (*etc*) d(h)ian-ruith *f*, (*more fam*) aig peilear *m* a (*etc*) b(h)eatha, **they left at full ~** dh'fhalbh iad nan dian-ruith/aig peilear am beatha

tilt *v* claon *vi*, aom *vi*, rach *vi* air fhiaradh *m*

tilted, tilting *adjs* air fhiaradh *m*

timber *n* fiodh *m*, **a ~ house** taigh-fiodha *m*

time *n* **1** (*the abstr phenomenon*) tìm *f*; **2** (*clock* ~) uair *f*, **what ~ is it?** dè an uair a tha e?,

at this ~ aig an uair seo; **3** (~ *as it is lived/ experienced*) tìde *f*, ùine *f*, (**the**) ~'s **passing** tha an tìde a' dol seachad, **spend** ~ cuir seachad tìde/ùine, **all the** ~ fad na tìde, fad na h-ùine, **plenty of** ~ tìde/ùine gu leòr, **a waste of** ~ call ùine *m*, **an hour's** ~ uair a (*for* de) thìde, **about** ~ **too!** bha a thìde aige!, **he took his** ~ thug e fada gu leòr!, **in** ~ (*ie eventually*) ri tìde, ri ùine; **4** (*specific moments or periods of* ~) àm *m*, linn *mf*, rè *f invar*, **at this** ~ aig an àm seo, **at the** ~ **of the Great War** aig àm a' Chogaidh Mhòir, **she was poorly at the** ~ bha i bochd aig an àm, **from** ~ **to** ~ bho àm gu àm, **at** ~**s he's naughty and at other** ~**s he's good** aig amannan bidh e crosta agus aig amannan eile bidh e glè mhath, **olden** ~**s** na làithean/an t-àm a dh'fhalbh, **these modern** ~**s** na h-amannan ùra seo, **in our ancestors'** ~ ri linn ar sinnsirean, **in my grandfather's** ~ ri linn/an rè mo sheanar; **5** (*an appointed or appropriate* ~) àm *m*, (*less usu*) tràth *m*, **she arrived before** ~ thàinig i ron àm, **it's** ~ **for us to leave** tha an t-àm againn falbh, **it's high** ~/**not before** ~ tha an t-àm ann, **meal** ~ tràth-bìdh *m*, **prayer** ~ tràth-ùrnaigh *m*, **a word at the right** ~ facal na thràth; **6** (*a period or stretch of* ~) ùine *f*, greis *f*, treis *f*, (*less usu*) tamall *m*, (*shorter*) ùine ghoirid, greiseag *f*, treiseag *f*, (*less usu*) tacan *m*, **for a** ~ airson greis, car uair, **after a** ~ an ceann greise/ tamaill, **a short** ~ **before that** ùine ghoirid roimhe sin; **7** (*occasion, repetition*) uair *f*, turas *m*, **I was there one** ~ bha mi ann aon uair/aon turas, **any** ~ uair sam bith, **many** ~**s, many a** ~ iomadach uair, iomadh uair, ~ **and** ~ **again** uair is uair, **the first** ~ **I saw her** a' chiad uair a chunna mi i, **at** ~**s** uaireannan, air uairean, **the last** ~ an turas mu dheireadh; **8** *in exprs* **some** ~ uaireigin *m & adv*, **I'll see you some** ~ chì mi uaireigin thu, **some** ~ **or other** uair no uaireigin

timely, timeous *adj* mithich, an deagh àm *m*, tràthail

timepiece *n* uaireadair *m*

times *adv* (*arith etc*) uiread *m invar*, air iomadachadh (*with prep* le), **two** ~ **two** a dhà uiread a dhà, a dhà air iomadachadh le a dhà

timescale *n* raon-ama *m*

timetable *n* clàr-tìde *m*, clàr-ama *m*

timid *adj* **1** (*shy, bashful*) diùid, nàrach, màlda; **2** (*jumpy, nervous*) clisgeach; **3** (*fearful*) meata, (*usu stronger*) gealtach

timidity *n* **1** (*shyness*) diùide *f invar*, nàire *f invar*; **2** (*fearfulness*) meatachd *f invar*, (*stronger*) gealtachd *f invar*

tin *n* **1** (*the metal*) staoin *f*; **2** (*can for drinks, food etc*) cana *m*, canastair *m*

tinge *n* **1** fiamh *m*, dath *m*; **2** (*esp of complexion*) fiamh *m*, tuar *m*

tinker *n* ceàrd *m*

tinkle *v* dèan gliong *m*, dèan gliongartaich *f invar*

tinkling *n* gliong *m*, gliongartaich *f invar*

tint *n* **1** fiamh *m*, dath *m*; **2** (*esp of complexion*) fiamh *m*, tuar *m*

tiny *adj* crìon, (*less usu, & used mainly as prefixes*) meanbh, mion

tip *n* (*slender end of anything*) bàrr *m*, **on the** ~ **of my tongue** air bàrr mo theangaidh

tippler *n* pòitear *m*, misgear *m*

tippling *n* pòitearachd *f invar*

tipsy *adj* air leth-mhisg *f*, **I was** ~ bha mi air leth-mhisg

tiptoe *n* corra-biod *m invar*, **on** ~ air a (*etc*) c(h)orra-biod

tire *v* **1** sgìthich *vti*; **2** (*as vi*) fàs *vi* sgìth; **3** *in expr* ~ **out** claoidh *vt*

tired *adj & past part* **1** sgìth, ~ **of x** sgìth de x; **2** *in exprs* ~ **out** claoidhte, **sick and** ~/**heartily** ~ **of x** seac searbh sgìth de x

Tiree *n* Tiriodh *and* Tiridhe

tiresome *adj* draghail, sàrachail

tissue *n* stuth *m*

title *n* (*of book etc* ~, *rank etc*) tiotal *m*

tittle-tattle *n* goileam *m*, cabaireachd *f invar*

tizzy *n*, *in expr* **in a** ~ troimh-a-chèile, am breisleach *m*

to *conj* **1** (*in order* ~) gus, airson, **she bought a broom** ~ **clean the house** cheannaich i sguab gus/airson an taigh a ghlanadh, **he found a job** ~ **get some money** fhuair e obair gus/airson airgead fhaighinn, **come** ~ **see me** thig gam fhaicinn; **2** *in expr* (*idiom*) **he came home** ~ **eat** thàinig e dhachaigh gu (a) bhiadh

to *prep* **1** gu & gus, *with gen, when followed by art becomes* thun & chun (*for prep prons formed with* gu, *see p 509*), **he went** ~ (*esp to the outskirts of, as far as*) **Glasgow** chaidh e gu Glaschu, **I'll send a book** ~ **her** cuiridh mi leabhar thuice, **we went** ~ **the gate** chaidh sinn chun a' gheata; **2** do, *takes the dat, lenites following cons where possible* (*for prep prons formed with* do, *see tables p 509*), **give it** ~ **Iain** thoir do dh'Iain e, **tell it** ~ **Mary** innis do Mhàiri e, **he's a good friend** ~ **me** tha e na dheagh charaid dhomh, **what happened** ~ **you?** dè a thachair dhut?, **he went** ~ (*ie into*)

Glasgow chaidh e do/a Ghlaschu, **I'll go ~ (the) church** thèid mi don (*or* dhan) eaglais, **a trip ~ the islands** sgriob/cuairt do (*or* dha) na h-eileanan; **3** (*with compass directions*) mu, **he went ~ the south** chaidh e mu dheas; **4** (*expr that something is or needs to be done*) ri, **I've lots ~ do** tha mòran agam ri dhèanamh, **that house is ~ be sold** tha an taigh sin ri reic, **they are ~ be/deserve ~ be praised** tha iad rim moladh; **5** (*when equivalent to part of the English infinitive*) a (*followed by the verbal noun, which is lenited where possible*), **I'm going ~ swim** tha mi a' dol a shnàmh, **you ought not ~ hit your brother** cha bu chòir dhut do bhràthair a bhualadh

toad *n* muile-mhàg *f*

toast[1] *n* (*drink*) deoch-slàinte *f*

toast[2] *n* (*~ed bread etc*) tost *m*

tobacco *n* tombaca *m*

today *adv* an-diugh

toe *n* òrdag *f*, òrdag-choise *f*, **the big ~** an òrdag mhòr

together *adv* **1** còmhla, le chèile, **living ~** a' fuireach còmhla (ri chèile), a' fuireach le chèile, **they left ~** dh'fhalbh iad còmhla (ri chèile); **2** *in exprs* **~ with** còmhla ri, **she left ~ with the others** dh'fhalbh i còmhla ri càch, **join ~** ceangail *vt* (ri chèile), **come ~** (*congregate, unite*) thig *vi* còmhla, coinnich *vi*, cruinnich *vi*, **bring ~** cruinnich *vt*, **pulling/working ~** (*idiom*) a' tarraing air an aon ràmh *m*, **string/ put two words ~** cuir dà fhacal an ceann a chèile/an altaibh a chèile

toil *n* saothair *f*, obair chruaidh

toil *v* saothraich *vi*, bi *vi irreg* ag obair gu cruaidh

toilet *n*, (*public or private*) taigh-beag *m*, (*public*) goireasan *mpl*

tolerable *adj* meadhanach math

tolerably *adv* meadhanach math, **you only did ~ well** cha do rinn thu ach meadhanach math

tolerance *n* ceadachas *m*

tolerant *adj* ceadach

tolerate *v* fuiling *vt*, (*more fam*) cuir *vi* suas (*with prep* le *or* ri)

tomb *n* uaigh *f*, tuam *m*

tombstone *n* leac uaighe *f*

tomcat *n* cat fireann *m*

ton *n* tunna *m*

tongs *n* (*pair of ~*) clobha *m sing*

tongue *n* **1** teanga *f*; **2** (*a language*) cànain *f*, cànan *m*, **the ~ of the Gael(s)** cànan nan Gàidheal

tonne *n* tunna *m*

too[1] *adv* (*ie also*) cuideachd, mar an ceudna, **has Ewan left? yes, and Iain ~** an do dh'fhalbh Eòghann? dh'fhalbh, agus Iain cuideachd

too[2] *adv* **1** (*to an excessive extent*) ro (*lenites following adj where possible*), **it's ~ late to go for a walk** tha e ro anmoch airson cuairt a ghabhail, **~ keen on gambling** ro dhèidheil air ceàrrachadh; **2** *in expr* **~ much** cus (*with gen*), (*stronger*) tuilleadh 's a' chòir, **~ much talking** cus bruidhne (*gen of* bruidhinn *f*), **I ate ~ much** dh'ith mi cus, **here's some ironing for you; I've ~ much already!** seo iarnaigeadh dhut; tha tuilleadh 's a' chòir dheth agam mar a tha!

tool *n* inneal *m*, ball-acfhainn *m*

tooth *n* fiacail *f*, **~ of a saw** fiacail sàibh

toothache *n* dèideadh *m* (*used with art*), **I've got (the) ~** tha an dèideadh orm

toothbrush *n* bruis-fhiaclan *f*

toothed *adj* fiaclach

toothpaste *n* uachdar-fhiaclan *m*

toothy *adj* fiaclach

top *adj* **1** (*phys*) as àirde, **the ~ floor** an lobht' as àirde; **2** (*best, foremost etc*) prìomh (*precedes the noun, which is lenited where possible*), barraichte, **the ~ player** am prìomh chluicheadair, **a ~ restaurant** taigh-bìdh barraichte

top *n* **1** bàrr *m*, mullach *m*, ceann *m* as àirde, **~ of the milk** bàrr a' bhainne, **the ~ of a tree** bàrr craoibhe, **the ~ of a mountain** mullach beinne, **~ of the ladder** mullach an àraidh, *also* ceann shuas an àraidh, **a great stone with a bird on ~ of it** clach mhòr is eun air a mullach; **2** (*in exprs*) **on ~ of** air muin *f invar* (*with gen*), **she put on a blouse and on ~ of that a jacket** chuir i blobhs oirre agus air muin sin seacaid, **he was singing at the ~ of his voice** bha e a' seinn (aig) àird a chlaiginn (*gen of* claigeann *m*)

top *v* (*beat, cap*) thoir bàrr *m* (*with prep* air), **that ~s everything I ever saw!** tha sin a' toirt bàrr air a h-uile càil a chunna mi a-riamh!

topic *n* cuspair *m*

topography *n* cumadh-tìre *m*

topsy-turvy *adj* bun-os-cionn, troimh-a-chèile

torch *n* leus *m*, lòchran *m*

torment *n* (*mental/emotional*) dòrainn *f*, (*mental/emotional or phys*) cràdh *m*

torment *v* (*mentally/emotionally or phys*) cràidh *vt*, sàraich *vt*, (*weaker*) pian *vt*, **my conscience was ~ing me** bha mo chogais gam chràdh/gam shàrachadh

torrent *n* **1** (*watercourse etc*) bras-shruth *m*, dòrtadh *m*; **2** (*downpour*) dìle *f*, (*heavier*) dìle bhàthte

torso *n* com *m*

tortuous *adj* (*road, river, argument etc*) lùbach

torture *n* (*mental or phys*) cràdh *m*, (*weaker*) pianadh *m*, **put to** ~ cuir *vt* an cràdh

torture *v* (*esp phys*) cuir *vt* an cràdh *m*, ciùrr *vt*, (*mentally or phys*) cràidh *vt*, (*weaker*) pian *vt*

Tory *adj* Tòraidheach, **the** ~ **Party** am Pàrtaidh Tòraidheach

Tory *n* Tòraidh *m*

toss *n* **1** (*a throw*) tilgeadh *m*; **2** *in expr* (*fam*) **I don't give a** ~ **for X** cha toir mi hò-ro-gheallaidh *m invar* air X

toss *v* **1** (*as vi: seas, ship, trees etc*) tulg *vi*, luaisg *vi*; **2** (*as vt: throw*) tilg *vt*, ~ **the caber** tilg an cabar; **3** *in expr* ~ **a coin** cuir crainn (*pl of* crann *m*), **they** ~**ed a coin to see who would pay** chuir iad crainn feuch cò a phàigheadh

total *adj* **1** iomlan, uile-gu-lèir, ~ **cost** cosgais iomlan/uile-gu-lèir; **2** (*utter, complete*) dearg (*precedes the noun, which it lenites where possible*), gu c(h)ùl *m* (*follows the noun*), **a** ~ **fool** dearg amadan, amadan gu chùl

total *n* (*result of addition*) sùim *f*, iomlan *m*

totally *adv* gu tur, (gu) buileach, gu h-iomlan, uile-gu-lèir, **the two things are** ~ **different** tha an dà rud gu tur eadar-dhealaichte/(gu) buileach eadar-dhealaichte, **I'll defeat him** ~ nì mi an gnothach air gu buileach/gu h-iomlan, **we succeeded** ~ shoirbhich leinn uile-gu-lèir/gu h-iomlan/gu buileach

touch *v* **1** (*phys*) bean *vi* (*with prep* ri *or* do), làimhsich *vt*, **don't** ~ **the pictures** na bean ris na dealbhan, *also* na teirig faisg air na dealbhan; **2** (*fig, have to do with etc*) bean *vi* (*with prep* ri), buin *vi* (*with prep* do *or* ri), gabh gnothach *m* (*with prep* ri), **it's a dodgy business, don't** ~ **it** 's e gnothach cugallach a th' ann, na bean ris/na buin dha/na buin ris/na gabh gnothach ris idir; **3** (~ *emotionally*) gluais *vti*, drùidh *vt* (*with prep* air), **the song** ~**ed them** ghluais an t-òran iad, dhrùidh an t-òran orra, *also* bha buaidh mhòr aig an òran orra; **4** *in expr* ~ **on/ upon** (*ie mention, refer to*) thoir iomradh *m*, thoir tarraing *f*, (*with prep* air), **in his talk he** ~**ed upon the state of the economy** anns an òraid aige thug e iomradh/tarraing air staid an eaconomaidh

touching *adj* (*emotionally affecting*) gluasadach, drùidhteach

touchy *adj* frionasach

tough *adj* **1** (*of persons*) cruaidh, fulangach, buan; **2** (*of materials, food etc*) righinn

toughen *v* rìghnich *vti*

toughness *n* **1** (*of persons*) cruas *m*, fulang *m*, fulangas *m*; **2** (*of materials, food etc*) rìghnead *m*

tour *n* cuairt *f*, turas *m*, **a** ~ **to the islands** cuairt/turas do na h-eileanan

tourism *n* turasachd *f invar*

tourist *n* **1** (*holidaymaker etc*) neach-turais *m*, ~**s** luchd-turais *m sing coll*; **2** (*adj uses*) ~ **office** oifis turasachd *f*, **the Scottish Tourist Board** Bòrd Turasachd *f* na h-Alba

towards *prep* **1** (*when followed by a noun*) a dh'ionnsaigh (*with gen*), chun & thun (*with gen*), ~ **the town(ship)** a dh'ionnsaigh a' bhaile, chun/thun a' bhaile; **2** (*when followed by a pers pron*) a dh'ionnsaigh; *the prep prons formed with* a dh'ionnsaigh *are:* ~ **me** dham ionnsaigh, ~ **you** (*fam sing*) dhad ionnsaigh, ~ **him/it** (*m*) dha ionnsaigh, ~ **her/it** (*f*) dha h-ionnsaigh, ~ **us** dhar n-ionnsaigh, ~ **you** (*pl or formal sing*) dhur n-ionnsaigh, ~ **them** dhan ionnsaigh, **the boy was running** ~ **her** bha am balach a' ruith dha h-ionnsaigh

towel *n* tubhailte *f*, searbhadair *m*

tower *n* tùr *m*, turaid *f*

town *n* baile *m*, (*bigger*) baile mòr, ~ **hall** talla-baile *m*, **the** ~ **hall** talla a' bhaile

township *n* baile (croitearachd) *m*, **the** ~ **clerk** clàrc a' bhaile *m*

toy *n* dèideag *f*

trace *n* **1** lorg *f*, làrach *f*, sgeul *m*, **it didn't leave a** ~ cha do dh'fhàg e lorg/làrach, **there's no** ~ **of it** chan eil lorg/sgeul air; **2** (*idiom*) **there was (absolutely) no** ~ **of Murdo** sgeul no fathann *m* cha robh air Murchadh

trace *v* faigh lorg *f* (*with prep* air), lorg *vt*, **the police** ~**ed them** fhuair am poileas lorg orra

track *n* **1** (*path etc*) ceum *m*, frith-rathad *m*, ùtraid *f*; **2** (*with more abstr connotations*) slighe *f*, **a** ~**less wilderness** fàsach gun slighe; **3** (~ *left by person, animal, object*) lorg *f*, **on the** ~ **of the deer** air lorg an fhèidh (*gen of* fiadh *m*)

track, track down *v* faigh lorg *f* (*with prep* air), **the police** ~**ed him down** fhuair am poileas lorg air

tract *n* (*pamphlet etc*) tràchd *mf*

tractable *adj* soitheamh, (*excessively so*) socharach

tractor *n* tractar *m*

trade *n* **1** (*a craft*) ceàird *f*, ~**(s) union** aonadh-ciùird *m*; **2** (*commercial exchange*) malairt *f*, ceannachd *f invar*, **engage in** ~ dèan malairt, malairtich *vi*

trade *v* dèan malairt *f*, malairtich *vi*

trader *n* neach-malairt *m* (*pl* luchd-malairt *m sing coll*), marsanta *m*, ceannaiche *m*

tradesman *n* **1** (*practitioner of a trade*) fear-ceàirde *m*; **2** (*retailer, merchant etc*) marsanta *m*, ceannaiche *m*

trading *n* ceannachd *f invar*, ceannach *m*, malairt *f*

tradition *n* **1** (*cultural heritage: in terms of one's descent/ancestry*) dualchas *m*, (*or the place one belongs to*) dùthchas *m*; **2** (*oral ~; esp song & story*) beul-aithris *f invar*, (*oral ~; esp trad lore & learning*) beul-oideachas *m*, beul-oideas *m*; **3** *esp in pl* (*customs, practices etc*) cleachdaidhean *mpl*

traditional *adj* traidiseanta, dualchasach, ~ **music** ceòl traidiseanta, ceòl dualchasach

tradition-bearer *n* seanchaidh *m*

traffic *n* **1** (*transport*) trafaig *f*; **2** (*trade*) malairt (mhì-laghail) *f*

traffic *v* dèan malairt (mhì-laghail) *f*

tragic *adj* dòrainneach, mìcheanta, **a ~ story** sgeulachd dhòrainneach

trail *n* (*abstr & con*; *~ left by person, animal*) lorg *f*, **on the ~ of the deer** air lorg an fhèidh (*gen of* fiadh *m*)

trailer *n* (*transport*) slaodair *m*

train *n* (*railway, tube*) trèan(a) *f*

train *v* **1** (*sport, mil*) trèan *vti*; **2** (*teach a trade, skill etc*) teagaisg *vt*, oileanaich *vt*

trained *adj* ionnsaichte, uidheamaichte

training *n* **1** (*sport, mil*) trèanadh *m*; **2** (*ed, & for trade, skill etc*) teagasg *m*, oileanachadh *m*, uidheamachadh *m*

trait *n* (*of character*) fea(i)rt *m*

traitor *n* brathadair *m*

trample *v* saltair *vt*

trance *n* neul *m*, **go into a ~** rach *vi* an neul

tranquil *adj* ciùin, sàmhach, sìtheil, sèimh

tranquillity *n* ciùineas *m*, sàmhchair *f*, sìth *f*, fois *f*

tranquillizer *n* tàmhadair *m*

transact *v* dèan *vt*, ~ **business** dèan gnothach *m*, dèan malairt *f*, (**with** ri)

transaction *n* (*business*) gnothach *m*

transgress *v* **1** ciontaich *vi*; **2** (*usu in relig sense*) peacaich *vi*

transgression *n* **1** ciont(a) *m*; **2** (*in relig sense: abstr & con*) peacachadh *m*, peacadh *m*

transient, transitory *adj* diombuan, siùbhlach

translate *v* eadar-theangaich *vti* (**into** gu), cuir *vt* (*with prep* air), ~ **into English** eadar-theangaich gu Beurla, ~ **English into Gaelic** cuir Gàidhlig air Beurla

translation *n* (*abstr & con*) eadar-theangachadh *m*

translator *n* eadar-theangair *m*

transmission *n* **1** (*broadcasting*) craobh-sgaoileadh *m*, craoladh *m*; **2** (*engin, abstr; drive*) iomain *f*

translucent *adj* trìd-shoillseach

transmit *v* craobh-sgaoil *vti*

transmitter *n* crann-sgaoilidh *m*

transparent *adj* trìd-shoilleir

transport *n* **1** (*general & abstr*) còmhdhail *f*; **2** (*more con, for people: travel from place to place*) siubhal *m*, (*con*) **means/modes of ~** dòighean siubhail *fpl*; **3** (*for goods etc: carriage from place to place*) giùlan *m*, (*less usu*) iomchar *m*, (*con*) **means/modes of ~** dòighean giùlain *fpl*

transport *v* giùlain *vt*, (*less usu*) iomchair *vt*

trap *n* ribe *mf*

trap *v* rib *vt*, glac *vt*

trapped *adj & past part* glacte, an sàs *m*

trappings *n* uidheam *f coll*, acainn *f coll*

trash *n* trealaich *f*, truileis *f invar*, (*more worthless*) sgudal *m*

travel *n* siubhal *m*, *in exprs* ~ **agency** bùth-turais *f*, ~ **centre** ionad-siubhail *m*

travel *v* siubhail *vi*, (*also as vt, rather trad, eg*) ~**ling (over) the moor** a' siubhal na mòintich, (*less usu*) triall *vi*

traveller *n* neach-siubhail *m*, ~**s** luchd-siubhail *m sing coll*

travelling *adj* siubhail (*gen of* siubhal *m, used adjectivally*), ~ **bank** banca siubhail *m*

trawler *n* tràlair *m*

tray *n* sgàl *m*

treacherous *adj* **1** (*esp of persons*) foilleil, cealgach; **2** (*of ground, situations etc*) cunnartach, (*less strong*) cugallach

treachery *n* brathadh *m*, cealgaireachd *f invar*, foill *f*

tread *v* (*eg grapes etc*) saltair *vt*

treason *n* brathadh *m*

treasure *n* ionmhas *m*, ulaidh *f*, tasgaidh *m*

treasurer *n* ionmhasair *m*

treasury *n* (*department of government*) roinn an ionmhais *f*

treat *n* cuirm *f*

treat *v* **1** (*behave towards*) làimhsich *vt*, gnàthaich *vt*, dèilig *vi* (*with prep* ri), **he ~ed his wife badly** is dona a làimhsich e/a ghnàthaich e a' bhean aige, **how does he ~ the customers?** ciamar a bhios e a' dèiligeadh ris an luchd-ceannaich?; **2** (*med*) leighis *vt*

treatise *n* tràchd *mf*, tràchdas *m*

treatment n 1 (*way of behaving towards someone*) làimhseachadh m, gnàthachadh m; 2 (*med*) leigheas m

treaty n co-chòrdadh m, cunnradh m

treble adj trìbilte

tree n 1 craobh f; 2 (*now usu in names of trees only*) crann m, eg **fig** ~ crann-fiogais, **olive** ~ crann-ola

tremble n crith f

tremble v bi vi irreg air chrith f, crith vi, **he was trembling** bha e air chrith, **(start to)** ~ rach vi irreg air chrith

trembling adj air chrith f, ~ **with fear** air chrith leis an eagal

tremendous adj 1 (*in size*) uabhasach mòr; 2 (*in quality*) uabhasach (fhèin) math, (*fam*) **that was** ~! bha sin taghta!

tremor n crith f

trench n clais f, (*esp battlefield* ~es) trainnse f

trend n aomadh m, **economic** ~ aomadh eaconomach

trendy adj fasanta

trespass n (*on land*) bris(t)eadh chrìochan (*fpl gen*)

trespass v 1 (~ *on land*) bris(t) crìochan *fpl*; 2 (*in relig sense*) peacaich vi, ciontaich vi

trespassing n (*on land*) bris(t)eadh crìochan (*fpl gen*)

trews n triubhas m

tri(-) prefix trì(-), see examples below

trial n 1 dearbhadh m, ~**s on a new car** dearbhaidhean air càr ùr m; 2 (*ordeal*) deuchainn f, **my mother's illness was a** ~ **for me** bha tinneas mo mhàthar na dheuchainn dhomh

triangle n trì-cheàrnag f, triantan m

triangular adj trì-cheàrnach, triantanach

tribe n treubh f, cinneadh m, fine f

tribulation n trioblaid f, deuchainn m

tribute n moladh m, in expr **pay** ~ **to** mol vt

trick n 1 (*usu playful*) cleas m, (*can be less playful*) car m, **play a** ~ dèan cleas (**on** air), thoir an car (**on** à), **they played a** ~ **on me** rinn iad cleas orm, thug iad an car asam; 2 in expr (*fam*) **that'll do the** ~! nì sin an gnothach!, nì sin a' chùis!

trick v meall vt, (*can be less serious*) thoir an car m (*with prep* à), **they** ~**ed her** thug iad an car aiste

trickle n sileadh (beag)

trickle v sil vi

trifling adj crìon, suarach

trilingual adj trì-chànanach

trim adj cuimir, sgiobalta, snasail, snasmhor

trim n gleus mf, **in good** ~ air ghleus

trip[1] n (*journey*) turas m, cuairt f, sgrìob f, **a** ~ **to the islands** turas/cuairt/sgrìob do na h-eileanan

trip[2] n (*a stumble*) tuisleadh m

trip v 1 (*stumble*) tuislich vi; 2 (*cause to stumble*, ~ *up*) cuir camacag f (*with prep* air) **he tripped me (up)** chuir e camacag orm

tripartite adj trì-phàirteach

triple adj trì-fillte, trìbilte

triumph n buaidh f

triumphant adj buadhmhor

trivial adj 1 (*pointless, empty*) faoin, dìomhain; 2 (*without significance*) crìon, suarach

troop n 1 (*of soldiers etc*) buidheann mf, cuideachd f; 2 (*of actors*) còmhlan m

Tropic of Cancer n Tropaig Chansar f

Tropic of Capricorn n Tropaig Chapricorn f

tropical adj tropaigeach

trot n trotan m

trot v dèan trotan m

trotting n trotan m

trouble n 1 (*inconvenience, bother, worry*) dragh m, **I don't want to put you to any** ~ chan eil mi airson dragh a chur oirbh; 2 (*misfortune, difficulties etc*) trioblaid f, duilgheadasan mpl, (*droch*) staing f, (*can be more serious*) èiginn f invar, ~ **came upon us** thàinig trioblaid oirnn, **the loss of my job was the start of our** ~**s** b' e call m' obrach toiseach ar trioblaidean, **I'm in** ~ tha mi ann an droch staing, tha mi nam èiginn, tha mi ann an èiginn, **an aeroplane in** ~ **above the airport** itealan ann an èiginn os cionn a' phuirt-adhair; 3 (*effort, putting oneself out*) saothair f, **it's not worth the/your** ~ chan fhiach dhut do shaothair; 4 (*disturbance, disorder, unrest*) aimhreit f, buaireas m

trouble v 1 (*inconvenience*) cuir dragh m (*with prep* air), (*more fam*) bodraig vt, **I don't want to** ~ **you** chan eil mi airson dragh a chur oirbh/airson ur bodraigeadh; 2 (*harass, vex*) sàraich vt, **they were** ~**d with/by debts/ bad neighbours** bha iad air an sàrachadh le fiachan/le droch nàbaidhean; 3 (*disturb, upset*) buair vt, **the bad news** ~**d me greatly** bhuair an drochd naidheachd mi gu mòr; 4 in expr **what's troubling you?** dè (a) tha a' gabhail riut?, dè (a) tha a' cur ort?

troubled adj 1 (*anxious*) fo iomagain f, fo chùram m; 2 (*vexed, harassed*) air a (*etc*) s(h)àrachadh; 3 (*upset*) air a (*etc*) b(h)uaireadh, air a (*etc*) t(h)àmailteachadh

troublesome *adj* (*person, situation*) draghail, buaireasach

trounce *v* **1** (*thrash*) slaic *vt*; **2** (*sport: defeat*) dèan an gnothach/a' chùis (*with prep* air), **we ~d them this time!** rinn sinn an gnothach/a' chùis orra an turas seo!

troupe *n* còmhlan *m*, **~ of actors** còmhlan de dh'actairean

trousers *n* (~ *in general, also a pair of* ~) briogais *f*, triubhas *m*

trout *n* breac *m*

truce *n* fosadh *m*, **call/declare a ~** gairm fosadh

truck[1] *n* (*transport*) làraidh *f*

truck[2] *n* (*ie dealings etc*), **have ~** bean *vi* (**with** ri), buin *vi* (**with** do *or* ri), gabh gnothach *m* (**with** ri), **have no ~ with them** na bean riutha, na buin dhaibh/riutha, na gabh gnothach riutha, *also* cùm *vi* bhuapa

true *adj* **1** (*factual, accurate, truthful*) fìor, fìrinneach, **the rumour/story is ~** tha am fathann/an sgeul fìor, **a true account of what happened** cunntas fìrinneach air na thachair; **2** (*genuine, authentic, real*) fìor (*precedes the noun, which it lenites where possible*), (*of person*) gu c(h)ùl *m*, **~ gold** fìor òr, **a ~ Scot** fìor Albannach, Albannach gu chùl; **3** (*loyal*) dìleas

truly *adv* fìor (*lenites a following adj where possible*), **the food was ~ good** bha am biadh fìor mhath

trumpet *n* trombaid *f*

trunk *n* **1** (*of human body*) com *m*; **2** (*of elephant etc*) sròn *f*; **3** (*luggage etc*) ciste *f*; **4** (*of tree*) stoc *m*, bun craoibhe *m*

trust *n* **1** earbsa *f invar*, creideas *m*, **put one's ~ in something/someone** cuir earbsa ann an rudeigin/cuideigin; **2** (*legal, fin, business: a* ~) urras *m*, **set up a ~** stèidhich urras, **a ~ fund** ciste-urrais *f*

trust *v* **1** thoir creideas *m* (*with prep* do), earb *vti* (*with prep* à), **do you ~ me? no!** an toir thu creideas dhomh? cha toir!, *also* a bheil earbsa agad annam/asam? chan eil!, **they didn't ~ their neighbours** cha robh iad ag earbsadh às na nàbaidhean aca, cha robh earbsa aca às na nàbaidhean aca; **2** *in expr* **~ in** cuir earbsa *f invar* (*with prep* ann), **~ in providence** cuir earbsa anns an fhreastal

trusting *adj* earbsach

trustworthy *adj* (*person, business etc*) earbsach

trusty *adj* dìleas

truth *n* **1** fìrinn *f*, **to tell (you) the ~/~ to tell, I don't know** leis an fhìrinn innse, chan eil fhios a'm

truthful *adj* fìrinneach

try *n* **1** (*attempt*) oidhirp *f* (**at** air), **he had another ~ at it** thug e/rinn e oidhirp eile air; **2** *in expr* **give it a ~** (*ie sample it*) feuch *vt* e, feuch *vi* ris

try *v* **1** feuch *vti* (**to** ri), **I'll ~ to open the door** feuchaidh mi ris an doras fhosgladh, **they tried to lift us** dh'fheuch iad ri ar togail *f*, **~ this beer** feuch an leann a tha seo, **~ it (out)** (*ie sample it*) feuch ris, **~ to be there early** feuch gum bi sibh ann ron àm *m*, **be good! I'll ~** bi math! feuchaidh mi; **2** (~ *out, test etc*) cuir *vt* gu deuchainn *f*, dearbh *vt*, **they tried out the new machines** chuir iad na h-innealan *mpl* ùra gu deuchainn; **3** (*pain, vex etc*) cuir *vt* gu deuchainn *f*

trying *adj* (*vexing, worrying etc*) deuchainneach

tub *n* ballan *m*, (*less trad*) tuba *mf*

tube *n* (*small*) feadan *m*, (*of various sizes*) pìob *f*

tuberculosis *n* (*used with the art*) a' chaitheamh *f*

tuck up *v* (*garment*) tru(i)s *vt*, **her petticoats were tucked up** bha na còtaichean-bàna aice air an trusadh

Tuesday *n* Dimàirt *m invar*

tug *n* tarraing *f*

tug *v* tarraing *vti* (**at** air)

tuition *n* teagasg *m*, (*less usu*) oideachas *m*

tumble *n* tuiteam *m*

tumble *v* **1** (*as vi*) tuit *vi*, **he ~d to the ground** thuit e gu làr *m*; **2** (*as vt*) leag *vt*, **he ~d him to the ground** leag e gu làr *m* e

tumour *n* at *m*

tumult *n* ùpraid *f*, iorghail *f*, othail *f*

tumultuous *adj* ùpraideach, iorghaileach

tune *n* **1** (*air, melody*) port *m*, fonn *m*, **strike up a ~ on the fiddle** cuir port air an fhidhill (*dat of* fidheall *f*), **a song to the tune 'The Thistle of Scotland'** òran air fonn 'Fòghnan na h-Alba', **raise/strike up a ~** tog fonn; **2** (*correct tuning*) gleus *mf*, **in ~** air gleus

tune *v* (*musical instrument, machine etc*) gleus *vt*, cuir *vt* air gleus *mf*

tuned *adj & past part* air ghleus *mf*

tuneful *adj* ceòlmhor, fonnmhor, binn

tuning *n* (*the pitch*) gleus *mf*, (*the action*) cur *m* air ghleus

tuning-fork *n* gobhal-gleusaidh *m*

tup *n* reithe *m*, rùda *m*

turbulence *n* **1** (*unruliness etc*) gairge *f invar*, aimhreit *f*, buaireas *m*; **2** (*of sea etc*) luaisgeachd *f invar*, tulgadh *m*

turbulent *adj* **1** (*of people, situations etc: unruly, troublesome*) garg, aimhreiteach, buaireasach; **2** (*of seas, flight etc*) luaisgeach, tulgach

turd *n* tudan & tùdan *m*

turf *n* **1** (*a single ~*) fàl *m*, sgrath *f*, ceap *m*, ploc *m*; **2** (*coll & individual*) fòid & fòd *f*, **when I'm beneath the ~** nuair a bhios mi fon fhòid *dat*

Turk *n* Turcach *m*

Turkey *n* (*used with art*) An Tuirc *f*

turkey *n* eun-Frangach *m*, cearc-Fhrangach *f*

Turkish *adj* Turcach

turn *n* **1** (*circular movement*) car *m*, tionndadh *m*, **give the wheel a ~** cuir *vt* car den chuibhle, **a turn of the wheel** car/tionndadh den chuibhle; **2** (*stroll*) car *m*, cuairt *f*, **I'll take a ~ outside** bheir/gabhaidh mi car/cuairt a-muigh; **3** (*in games, queue etc*) cuairt *f*; **4** (*deviation*) tionndadh *m*, **a ~ to the left** tionndadh chun na làimh chlì; **5** *in expr* **in ~** mu seach, fear *m* mu seach, tè *f* mu seach, **they each spent a while in ~ in the kitchen** thug iad greis mu seach anns a' chidsin, **they went in ~ through the door** fear mu seach/tè mu seach, chaidh iad tron doras, **she picked up the cards in ~** thog i na càirtean tè mu seach

turn *v* **1** tionndaidh *vti*, (*as vi*) (*phys & fig*) **the tide's ~ing** tha an tìde-mara a' tionndadh, **whom could he ~ to?** cò ris a thionndadh e?, **he ~ed against me** thionndaidh e nam aghaidh, **the lead ~ed to gold** thionndaidh an luaidhe na h-òr/gu òr, (*as vt*) **she didn't ~ her head** cha do thionndaidh i a ceann, **~ the steering wheel** tionndaidh a' chuibhle (-stiùiridh), *also* cuir car *m* den chuibhle (-stiùiridh), **~ the mirror to the wall** tionndaidh an sgàthan ris a' bhalla; **2** (*expr with*) cuir *vti*, **I ~ed my back to/on him** chuir mi mo chùl ris, **~ over** cuir *vti* thairis, *also* cuir *vt* a (*etc*) c(h)eann fodha, cuir *vt* bun-os-cionn, **~ them away** cuir air falbh iad, **he ~ed against me** chuir *vi* e nam aghaidh; **3** *misc exprs* **~ out** (*ie happen, 'go'*), tachair *vi*, rach *vi irreg*, (*both can be used impersonally*) **as it ~ed out** mar a thachair (e), **how did it ~ out (for you)?** ciamar a chaidh dhut?, **~ up** (*appear, arrive etc*) nochd *vi*, tionndaidh *vi* suas, tionndaidh *vi* an-àird', **he didn't ~ up last night** cha do nochd e/cha do thionndaidh e suas a-raoir, **she ~ed up** (*ie at the house*) **unexpectedly** thàinig i a-steach gun dùil againn rithe

turret *n* turaid *f*

tussle *n* tuasaid *f*

tut tut! *excl* ud, ud!

tweed *n* clò *m*, **Harris ~** An Clò Mòr, An Clò Hearach

tweezers *n* greimiche *m*

twelfth *adj* dara-deug, **the ~ day** an dara là deug *m*

twelve *n & adj* **1** d(h)à-dheug, **~ men** dà fhear dheug, **~ o'clock** dà uair dheug; **2** (*fam*) dusan *m* (*takes sing n*), **~ years old** dusan bliadhna a (*for* de) dh'aois

twentieth *adj* ficheadamh

twenty *num* fichead *m*, *takes the nom sing* (*radical*) *of the noun*, **~ pence/years** fichead sgillinn/bliadhna

twice *adv* **1** (*repetitions*) dà uair *f*, dà thuras *m*, **we did it ~** rinn sinn dà uair/dà thuras e, **once or ~** uair no dhà; **2** (*quantity*) **~ as much** a dhà uiread *m invar* (*as* agus/is), **give me ~ as much as Màiri has** thoir dhomh a dhà uiread agus a tha aig Màiri

twig *v* (*understand*) tuig *vti*

twilight *n* (*morning or evening*) eadar-sholas *m*, camhana(i)ch *f*, **morning ~** camhana(i)ch an latha, bris(t)eadh *m* an latha, **evening ~** ciaradh *m*, camhana(i)ch na h-oidhche, *also* duibhre *f invar*

twin *n* leth-aon *m*, leth-chàraid *f*, **a pair of ~s** càraid *f sing coll*

twine *v* toinn *vti*

twinkle *v* priob *vi*

twinkling *n* (*lit & fig*) priobadh *m*, *in expr* (*fig*) **in the ~ of an eye** ann am priobadh na sùla

twist *n* car *m*, snìomh *m*, toinneamh *m*

twist *v* snìomh *vt*, dualaich *vt*, toinn *vti*

twisted *adj & past part* snìomhte, toinnte

twitter *v* ceilearaich *vi*

two *n & adj* **1** d(h)à (*takes the dat, lenites a following noun where possible*), **~ dogs** dà chù, **~ stones** dà chloich, **a time or ~** uair no dhà; **2** (*usu used of people only: with gen pl of following noun*) dithis *f*, **there were ~ people at the table** bha dithis aig a' bhòrd, **~ soldiers** dithis shàighdearan, **they came in ~s** thàinig iad nan dithisean, **the ~ of you** an dithis agaibh; **3** (*as prefix*) **two-** dà(-), *see examples below*

two-eyed *adj* dà-shùileach

two-legged *adj* dà-chasach

twosome *n* dithis *f* (*cf* **two** *n & adj, rubric* 2)

two-tier *adj* dà-shreathach

type[1] *n* (*kind etc*) seòrsa *m*, gnè *f invar*

type[2] *n* (*in printing etc*) clò *m*

type *v* clò-sgrìobh *vti*

typed *adj & past part* clò-sgrìobhte

typescript *n* clò-sgrìobhainn *f*

typewriter *n* clò-sgrìobhadair *m*

typical *adj* **1** (*representative*) samhlachail, àbhaisteach; **2** (*of person: characteristic, in character*) dual(t)ach (**of** do), **it's ~ of you to tell lies** tha e dualtach dhut a bhith ag innse bhreugan

typist *n* clò-sgrìobhaiche *m*

tyrannical *adj* aintighearnail

tyranny *n* aintighearnas *m*

tyrant *n* aintighearna *m*

tyre *n* taidhr *f*

U

udder *n* ùth *m*
ugliness *n* gràndachd *f invar*
ugly *adj* grànda
uileann pipes *n* pìob-uilne *f*
Uist *n* Uibhist *f*
ulcer *n* neasgaid *f*
Ulster *n* Ulaidh
ultimate *adj* 1 (*final*) deireannach, mu
dheireadh; **2** (*best, unsurpassed etc*), brod
m (*with gen art plus n*), gun samhail, gun
choimeas, barraichte *adj*, **the ~ car** brod a'
chàir, càr air nach toireadh duine bàrr
ultimately *adv* aig a' cheann thall
umbilical *adj* imleagach
umbilicus *n* imleag *f*
umbrage *n*, (*idiom*) **take ~ at something** gabh
rudeigin anns an t-sròin (*dat of* sròn *f*) (*the
Gaelic expr is fam*)
umbrella *n* sgàilean-uisge *m*
un(-) *prefix* (*see numerous examples below*), **1**
eu- *prefix*; **2** mì- *prefix*; **3** neo- *prefix*; **4** ain-
prefix; **5** ana- *prefix*; **6** *the neg idea of* **un-** *is
also rendered by* gun *followed by a noun or
verbal noun, eg* **unemployed** *adj* gun obair
f, **unsolved** *adj* gun fhuasgladh *m*; **7** *the
prefix* do- *indicates that something cannot
be done, eg* **uncountable** *adj* do-àireamh,
ungovernable *adj* do-riaghlaidh; **8** *however,
though dictionaries give very many words
beginning with the prefixes listed above, and
a good number are given below, it is often
more natural in Gaelic to use instead a verbal
construction in the negative, or a noun constr
with* gun: *rubric* **2** *of the next entry below
exemplifies this*
unable *adj* **1** eu-comasach; **2 I was ~ to lift
it** cha robh e comasach dhomh a thogail, cha
b' urrainn dhomh a thogail, **~ to move** gun
lùth *m*, **~ to speak** gun chainnt *f*
unaccustomed *adj* neo-chleachdte (**to** ri)
unadventurous *adj* lagchuiseach
unanimity *n* aon-inntinn *f*

unanimous *adj* aon-inntinneach, aon-ghuthach,
aon-toileach
unasked *adj* gun iarraidh *m*, **come ~** thig *vi
irreg* gun iarraidh
unassuming *adj* iriosal
unattainable *adj* do-ruigsinn
unavoidable *adj* do-sheachanta
unceasing *adj*, **unceasingly** *adv* gun sgur *m*
uncertain *adj* mì-chinnteach
uncertainty *n* teagamh *m*, mì-chinnt *f*
uncivil *adj* mì-shìobhalta
uncle *n* (*on mother's side*) bràthair-màthar *m*,
(*on father's side*) bràthair-athar *m*
unclothed *adj* lomnochd, rùisgte, (*less usu*) lom
uncommon *adj* neo-chumanta, tearc
unconcerned *adj* (*ie indifferent etc*) coma
unconditional *adj* gun chumhachan *fpl*, **~
surrender** gèilleadh gun chumhachan
unconscious *adj* gun mhothachadh *m*
uncountable *adj* do-àireamh
uncouth *adj* borb, garbh, gràisgeil
uncouthness *n* gràisgealachd *f invar*
uncultivated *adj* fàs, bàn, **~ ground** talamh
fàs/bàn
undecided *adj & past part* ann an iomadh-
chomhairle *f*, eadar-dhà-lionn *m sing*, **~ as to
what I would do** ann an iomadh-chomhairle
dè a dhèanainn
under(-) *prefix* **1** (*referring to lower phys level
etc*) fo-; **2** (*expr subordination*) fo-, iar-; *see
examples below*
under *prep* **1** fo (*lenites following noun where
possible & takes the dat; for prep prons formed
with* fo *see p 510*), **~ the surface** fon uachdar, **~
a tree** fo chraoibh, **~ an obligation** fo chomain
(**to/towards** aig), **~ control** fo smachd, **~ a
spell** fo gheasaibh (*obs dat pl of* geas *f*); **2** (*adv
usage*) **the boat went ~** chaidh am bàta fodha
under-clerk iar-chlèireach *m*
underclothes *npl* fo-aodach *m sing coll*
underdeveloped *adj* dì-leasaichte
under-gamekeeper iar-gheamair *m*

undergo v 1 (*endure etc*) fuiling vt, ~ **hardship** fuiling cruadal m; 2 *in expr* ~ **surgery** rach vi fo obair-lèigh f

undergraduate n fo-cheumnaiche m

underground adj fo-thalamh

undergrowth n fo-fhàs m

underhand adj cealgach, os ìosal & os ìseal

underline v 1 (*lit*) cuir loidhne f (*with prep* fo); 2 (*fig: confirm, emphasise*) comharraich vt, leig cudthrom m (*with prep* air), daingnich vt

underling n ìochdaran m

underpants n drathais & drathars f invar

underpass n fo-rathad m, fo-shlighe f

under-secretary n 1 (*clerical grade*) iar-chlèireach m; 2 (*government office*) fo-rùnaire m, **Under-Secretary of State** Fo-rùnaire na Stàite

understand v tuig vti, lean vti, **do you ~/are you ~ing me?** a bheil sibh gam thuigsinn/gam leantainn?

understanding adj tuigseach, mothachail, **an ~ friend** caraid tuigseach

understanding n 1 (*the mental faculty or capacity; also sympathetic ~*) tuigse f invar; 2 (*good sense, judgement, intelligence*) ciall f, toinisg f, tùr m; 3 (*agreement between parties*) còrdadh m, **we had an ~ about that** bha còrdadh againn/eadarainn mu dheidhinn sin, **reach/come to an ~** thig vi gu còrdadh

undertake v 1 (*take on*) gabh vt os làimh (*dat of* làmh f); 2 (*guarantee, promise to do something*) geall vi

undertaker n neach-adhlacaidh m (*pl* luchd-adhlacaidh m sing coll)

undertaking n 1 (*project etc*) gnothach m; 2 (*commitment, assurance etc*) gealladh m

underwear n fo-aodach m sing coll

undo v 1 neo-dhèan vt; 2 (*untie etc*) fuasgail vt, lasaich vt, ~ **a knot/a shoelace** fuasgail snaidhm/barrall

undoubtedly adv gun teagamh m (sam bith)

undress v 1 (*as vt*) rùisg vt; 2 (*as vi*) cuir dheth (*etc*) a (*etc*) c(h)uid aodaich f, **we ~ed** chuir sinn dhinn ar cuid aodaich

undressed adj lomnochd, rùisgte

unease n an-shocair f, imcheist f

uneasy adj anshocrach, an-fhoiseil, fo imcheist f

unemployed adj gun obair f, gun chosnadh m

unemployment n cion cosnaidh m, ~ **benefit** sochair cion cosnaidh f, (*fam*) dòil m invar

unenterprising adj lagchuiseach

unequal adj neo-ionann

unexpected adj, **unexpectedly** adv, gun dùil f ris (*etc*), gun sùil f ris (*etc*), gun fhiosta, **an ~**

visit cèilidh ris nach robh dùil/sùil, **he arrived** ~**ly** thàinig e gun dùil/sùil againn (*etc*) ris, thàinig e gun fhiosta (dhuinn *etc*)

unfair adj mì-chothromach

unfairness n ana-cothrom m, mì-chothrom m

unfaithful adj neo-dhìleas

unfamiliar adj coimheach

unfashionable adj neo-fhasanta

unfavourable adj neo-fhàbharach

unfeeling adj fuar, neo-mhothachail

unfeigned adj fìor, neo-chealgach

unfit adj 1 (*in health*) euslainteach, (*less usu*) anfhann; 2 *in expr* **he's ~ for the job** (*through lack of ability etc*) chan eil e aig ìre f invar na h-obrach, (*more fam: calque*) chan eil e suas ris an obair

unfold v sgaoil vti, fosgail vti

unforeseen adj gun dùil f, gun sùil f, **an ~ occurrence** tachartas m ris nach robh dùil/sùil (againn *etc*)

unfortunate adj mì-fhortanach, mì-shealbhach

unfounded adj (*of claim etc*) gun bhunait mf

unfriendly adj neo-chàirdeil

unfruitful adj neo-tharbhach, neo-thorrach

unfurl v sgaoil vti, fosgail vti

ungainly adj cearbach

ungodly adj neo-dhiadhaidh

ungovernable adj do-riaghlaidh

ungrateful adj mì-thaingeil, mì-bhuidheach

unhappiness n mì-shonas m

unhappy adj mì-shona, mì-thoilichte

unhealthy adj 1 (*in poor health*) tinn, euslainteach, (*less usu; infirm*) anfhann; 2 (*bad for health*) mì-fhallain, (*more fam*) dona (dhut *etc*)

unholy adj 1 (*not holy*) mì-naomh; 2 (*satanic etc*) diabhlaidh

unhurt adj slàn, slàn is fallain

unification n co-aonachadh m

unified adj & past part (co-)aonaichte

uniform adj cunbhalach, aon-fhillte

uniform n èideadh m, deise f

unify v co-aonaich vt

unilateral adj aon-taobhach

unimportant adj gun chudthrom m, gun bhrìgh f, neo-chudromach

uninjured adj slàn, slàn is fallain

unintelligent adj neo-thoinisgeil

unintelligible adj do-thuigsinn

uninteresting adj liosta, tioram, neo-inntinneach

uninterrupted adj (*ie continual*) gun stad m, gun sgur m, leanailteach, leantainneach

uninvited *adj & adv* gun iarraidh *m*, **come ~ thig** *vi* gun iarraidh

union *n* aonadh *m*

unique *adj* gun samhail *m*, gun seis(e) *m*, air leth

unit *n* (*team, organisation etc*) aonad *f*, **development ~** aonad-leasachaidh

unitary *adj* aonadach

unite *v* **1** (*join*) ceangail *vt*, co-cheangail *vt*, (**to/with** ri), aonaich *vti*; **2** (*join together, cooperate*) thig *vi* còmhla

united *adj & past part* aonaichte, **the United Nations** Na Dùthchannan Aonaichte, **the United States** Na Stàitean Aonaichte

unity *n* aonachd *f invar*

universal *adj* (*common to all*) coitcheann, uile-choitcheann, **~ suffrage** còir-bhòtaidh choitcheann

universe *n* **1** (*used with art*) an domhan *m*, an cruinne-cè *mf*, A' Chruitheachd *f*; **2** *in expr* **the King/Lord of the Universe** (*ie the Deity*) Rìgh *m* nan Dùl (*gen pl of* dùil *f*)

university *n* oilthigh *m*, **Glasgow University** Oilthigh Ghlaschu, **the Open University** An t-Oilthigh Fosgailte, **she's at ~** tha i aig an oilthigh

unjust *adj* mì-cheart, ana-ceart

unkempt *adj* luideach, cearbach, robach

unkind *adj* neo-choibhneil

unkindness *n* neo-choibhneas *m*

unknowable *adj* do-aithnichte

unknown *adj* **1** neo-aithnichte; **2** *in exprs* **~ to** (*ie without someone's knowledge*) gun fhios *m* (*with prep* do *or* aig), **~ to Mary, he sold the house** gun fhios do Mhàiri/gun fhios aig Màiri, reic e an taigh; **3** *in expr* **a book/man** (*etc*) **~ to me** (*ie that I have no knowledge of*) leabhar/duine (*etc*) nach eil mi eòlach air/air nach eil mi eòlach

unlawful *adj* mì-laghail

unless *conj* **1** *can be expressed by the conjs* ach & mur(a), **I won't go ~ you're agreeable/ in favour** cha tèid mi ann ach ma tha thusa air a shon, cha tèid mi ann mura bheil thusa air a shon; **2** *note also the cumbersome construction* **he wouldn't be satisfied ~ I went with him** chan fhòghnadh leis gun mise a dhol còmhla ris

unlicensed *adj* gun cheadachd *f invar*

unlike, unlikely *adj* eu-coltach

unlimited *adj* neo-chrìochnach

unload *v* falmhaich *vt*, aotromaich *vt*

unlucky *adj* mì-shealbhach, mì-fhortanach

unmanageable *adj* do-stiùiridh, do-cheannsachaidh

unmanly *adj* neo-fhearail

unnecessary *adj* neo-riatanach

unobtrusive *adj* neo-fhollaiseach

unoccupied *adj* **1** (*of land etc*) fàs, falamh; **2** (*of person*) na (*etc*) t(h)àmh, dìomhain

unofficial *adj* neo-oifigeil

unpaid *adj* **1** (*of bill etc*) neo-dhìolta; **2** (*of worker etc*) gun phàigheadh *m*, gun tuarastal *m*

unparalleled *adj* gun choimeas *f*

unpleasant *adj* mì-thaitneach, mì-chàilear

unpolluted *adj* neo-thruaillidh

unprepared *adj* neo-ullamh, gun ullachadh *m*

unproductive *adj* neo-tharbhach

unprofitable *adj* (*esp fin*) neo-bhuannachdail, (*more generally*) neo-tharbhach

unprotected *adj* neo-thèarainte

unrecognised *adj* neo-aithnichte

unreasonable *adj* mì-reusanta

unreliable *adj* neo-earbsach, cugallach, **the world is (an) ~ (place)** (*trad*) is cugallach an saoghal

unresolved *adj* gun fhuasgladh *m*, **an ~ problem/question** ceist *f* gun fhuasgladh

unripe *adj* an-abaich

unrivalled *adj* gun seis(e) *m*, gun choimeas *m*

unruliness *n* gairge *f invar*, aimhreit *f*, buaireas *m*

unruly *adj* (*of people*) garg, aimhreiteach, buaireasach, ùpraideach

unsafe *adj* mì-shàbhailte

unsaleable *adj* do-reicte

unsavoury *adj* **1** (*lit*) mì-bhlasta; **2** (*fig; in bad taste etc*) mì-chiatach

unselfish *adj* neo-fhèineil

unsettled *adj* neo-shuidhichte, *in expr* **~ weather** sìde chaochlaideach

unsheathe *v* (*sword etc*) rùisg *vt*

unskilled *adj* neo-ealanta, neo-uidheamaichte

unsociable *adj* neo-chuideachdail

unsolved *adj* gun fhuasgladh *m*, **an ~ problem/ question** ceist *f* gun fhuasgladh

unsound *adj* **1** (*in health, condition*) neo-fhallain; **2** (*not reliable*) neo-earbsach

unsparingly *adv* gun chaomhnadh *m*

unspeakable *adj* do-labhairt

unstable *adj* neo-sheasmhach, critheanach, cugallach

unsteady *adj* critheanach, cugallach, tulgach, **~ on his feet** cugallach air a chasan

unsuitable *adj* mì-fhreagarrach, neo-iomchaidh

untidy *adj* **1** (*of places, objects*) mì-sgiobalta, troimh-a-chèile; **2** (*esp of person's appearance*) cearbach, luideach, robach

untie *v* fuasgail *vt*, **~ a knot/a shoelace** fuasgail snaidhm *m*/barrall *m*

until *conj* gus an, gus am, (*neg*) gus nach, **I won't get the meal ready** ~ **you come home** cha deasaich mi am biadh gus an tig thu dhachaigh, **I'll earn money** ~ **we've got enough of it** coisnidh mi airgead gus am bi gu leòr againn dheth, **keep it** ~ **you don't need it any more** cùm e gus nach bi an còrr feum agad air

until *prep* **1** gu & gus (*with dat*), **we'll wait/stay** ~ **six o'clock** fanaidh sinn gu sia uairean, **I can't keep/save it** ~ **tomorrow** chan urrainn dhomh a ghleidheadh gu(s) a-màireach; **2** (*up* ~) gu ruige (*with nom*), **we'll be busy** ~ **New Year** bidh sinn trang gu ruige a' Bhliadhna Ùr

untimely *adj* neo-thràthail

untruth *n* breug *f*

untruthful *adj* breugach

unusual *adj* **1** neo-àbhaisteach, neo-chumanta; **2** (*novel*) annasach

unwell *adj* tinn, (*more fam*) bochd

unwilling *adj* **1** leisg, aindeonach; **2** *in expr* **I am** ~ **to sell it** (*etc*) chan eil mi deònach (air) a reic (*etc*), is leisg leam a reic (*etc*)

unwillingly *adv* an aghaidh a (*etc*) t(h)oil *f gen*, **I stood up** ~ sheas mi (suas) an aghaidh mo thoil

up *adv & prep* **1** (*expr position*) shuas, **there's a plane** ~ **there** tha plèana shuas an sin, **she's** ~ **the stair** tha i shuas an staidhre; **2** (*expr movement: from point of view of person(s) away from whom the movement is made*) suas, **she went** ~ chaidh i suas, **she went** ~ **the stair/the street** chaidh i suas an staidhre/an t-sràid; **3** (*expr movement: from point of view of person(s) towards whom the movement is made*) a-nìos (*lit 'from below'*), **come** ~ **to us!** thig *vi* a-nìos thugainn!; **4** (*misc idioma & exprs*) **is he** ~ **to the job?** a bheil e aig ìre na h-obrach?, (*also*) a bheil e suas ris an obair?, **what are you** ~ **to?** dè a tha sibh ris?, (*fam*) **what's** ~? dè a tha ceàrr (ort *etc*)?, ~ **and about** air chois (*dat of* cas *f*), ~ **the hill/slope** ris a' bhruthaich, **dry** ~ (*ie wither*) crìon *vti*, **get** ~ (*from bed, sitting position etc*) èirich *vi* (suas), **I got** ~ **late yesterday** dh'èirich mi anmoch an-dè, (*more colloquially*) bha mi fada gun èirigh an-dè, **don't give** ~! cùm *vi* ris!, **grow** ~ (*ie mature*) thig *vi* gu inbhe, **grow** ~! na bi cho leanabail!, **hurry** ~! (*ie be quick*) greas ort/ (*pl*) greasaibh oirbh!, dèan/dèanaibh cabhag, **keep it** ~! cùm *vi* ort!, **put** ~ **a notice** cuir suas sanas, cuir sanas an-àirde, **rise** ~ (*rebel etc*) èirich *vi* suas, **shut** ~! dùin do bheul!, **stand** ~ seas *vi*, seas *vi* suas, seas *vi* an-àird, èirich *vi* (na *etc* s(h)easamh), **we stood** ~ sheas sinn (suas/

an-àird), dh'èirich sinn nar seasamh, **wake** ~ dùisg *vti*

up to *prep* (*of movement up as far as*; *of time up until*) chun & thun (*with gen*), gu ruige (*with nom*), **we went** ~ **the gate** chaidh sinn chun a' gheata, **the floods came (right)** ~ **the house** thàinig na tuiltean gu ruige an taigh, **it hasn't happened** ~ **now** cha do thachair e chun a seo/ gu ruige seo, **we'll be busy (right)** ~ **New Year** bidh sinn trang gu ruige a' Bhliadhna Ùr

upkeep *n* **1** cumail suas *f*; **2** (*of livestock etc*) beathachadh *m*

uphill *adv* ris a' bhruthaich *mf dat*

uphold *v* cùm *vt* suas

upland *n* aonach *m*, monadh *m*, (*esp in place-names*) bràigh *m*, uachdar *m*

uplifting *adj* brosnachail, a thogas an cridhe *m*

upon *prep* **1** (*lit & fig*) air, ~ **the table** air a' bhòrd, **we came** ~ **him on the hill** thachair *vi* e oirnn/thachair sinn air anns a' mhonadh, **it is incumbent** ~ **you** tha e mar fhiachaibh (*obs dat pl of* fiach *m*) oirbh; **2** (*in addition to*) thar (*with gen*), **thousands** ~ **thousands** mìltean thar mhìltean

upper *adj* **1** (*lit & fig*) uachdrach, (*politics, law court etc*) **the** ~ **chamber** an seòmar uachdrach, (*of river*) ~ **reaches** cùrsa uachdrach; **2** *in exprs* ~ **lip** beul-uachdair *m*, **get the** ~ **hand** faigh làmh-an-uachdair *f*, dèan an gnothach *m*, dèan a' chùis *f*, (**of/over** air), **we got the** ~ **hand over them** fhuair sinn làmh-an-uachdair orra, rinn sinn an gnothach/a' chùis orra

upright *adj* **1** (*phys & morally*) dìreach, **stand** ~ seas *vi* dìreach; **2** (*of person, morally* ~) onarach, ceart, ionraic

uproar *n* ùpraid *f*, gleadhar *m*, othail *f*, iorghail *f*

uproarious *adj* ùpraideach

upset *v* **1** (*knock over, overturn*) leag *vt*, cuir *vt* bun-os-cionn; **2** (*put objects, situations etc into disarray*) cuir *vt* troimh-a-chèile; **3** (~ *someone emotionally*) buair *vt*, cuir *vt* troimh-a-chèile, **the news** ~ **us** chuir an naidheachd troimh-a-chèile sinn, bhuair an naidheachd sinn

upsetting *adj* (*of situations etc*) buaireasach, frionasach

upside down *adj* bun-os-cionn

upstairs *adv* **1** (*expr motion*) suas an staidhre *f dat*, **they went** ~ chaidh iad suas an staidhre; **2** (*expr position*) shuas an staidhre, **they're** ~ tha iad shuas an staidhre

upstream *adv* (*expr motion*) ris an t-sruth *f dat*, **she went** ~ chaidh i ris an t-sruth

up-to-date *adj* ùr-nodha

upturn *n* (*in fortunes, economy etc*) car math
urban *adj* bailteil, ~ **development** leasachadh
bailteil, ~ **sprawl** sgaoileadh bailteil
urbane *adj* suairc(e)
urbanity *n* suairceas *m*
urge *v* 1 (~ *to do something*) cuir ìmpidh *f* (*with
prep* air), spreig *vt*, stuig *vt*, coitich *vt*, **they
~d me to give up my job/to retire** chuir
iad ìmpidh orm mo dhreuchd a leigeil dhìom;
2 ~ **on** (*encourage*) brosnaich *vt*, piobraich *vt*,
(*hurry on, drive on*) greas *vt*, (*esp livestock*)
iomain *vt*
urgency *n* deifir *f*, cabhag *f*
urgent *adj* deifireach, cabhagach
urging *n* impidh *m* & ìmpidh *f*, spreigeadh *m*
urinate *v* dèan mùn *m*, mùin *vi*
urination *n* mùn *m*, dèanamh mùin *m*
urine *n* mùn *m*, fual *m*
usage *n* (*custom, habit etc*) cleachdadh *m*, àbhaist
f, nòs *m*, gnàth(s) *m*
use *n* 1 (*utilisation*) feum *m*, **make ~ of** cuir *vt*
gu feum, dèan feum (*with prep* de), **we made ~
of it** chuir sinn gu feum e, rinn sinn feum dheth;
2 (*value, usefulness*) feum *m*, (*occas*) math *m*,
this machine's no ~ chan eil feum (sam bith)
anns an inneal seo, **what's the ~ of talking?**
dè am feum a bhith a' bruidhinn?, dè am math a
bhith a' bruidhinn?
use *v* 1 cleachd *vt*, dèan feum *m* (*with prep* de),
~ **a hammer** cleachd òrd; 2 (*expr habitual
situation in the past*) cleachd *vi*, **I ~d to be
bad-tempered** chleachd mi a bhith droch-
nàdarrach, **it's not as cold as it ~d to be** chan
eil e cho fuar agus a chleachd e a bhith, *also* chan
eil e cho fuar 's a b' àbhaist
used *adj* & *past part* 1 cleachdte, ~ **car** càr
cleachdte; 2 (*accustomed*) cleachdte (**to** ri), **I'm**

not ~ to it chan eil mi cleachdte ris; 3 *in expr*
get ~ to it! cleachd *vt* thu fhèin ris!
useful *adj* 1 feumail, **a ~ book** leabhar
feumail; 2 *in expr* **be ~** dèan feum *m* (**to** do),
scissors would be ~ just now dhèanadh
siosar feum an-dràsta, bhiodh siosar feumail
an-dràsta
useless *adj* gun fheum *m*, **a ~ man/job** duine/
obair gun fheum
user *n* neach-cleachdaidh *m*, ~**s** luchd-
cleachdaidh *m sing coll*
usual *adj* àbhaisteach, cumanta, gnàthach
usually *adv* mar as trice, an cumantas *m*, am
bitheantas *m*
uterus *n* machlag *f*
utilise *v* cleachd *vt*, cuir *vt* gu feum *m*, dèan feum
(*with prep* de)
utility *n* 1 (*abstr*) feum *m*, feumalachd *f invar*;
2 (*con: water, electricity etc companies*) *in
expr* **the ~ industries/the utilities** na
gnìomhachasan-seirbheis *mpl*
utter *adj* dearg (*precedes the noun, which it
lenites where possible*), gu c(h)ùl *m*, **an ~ fool**
dearg amadan, amadan gu chùl
utter *v* abair *vt irreg*, can *vt def*, cuir *vt* an cèill
(*gen of* ciall *f*)
utterly *adv* 1 gu tùr, gu h-iomlan, gu buileach,
uile-gu-lèir, air fad, ~ **different** gu tùr eadar-
dhealaichte, **they were ~ destroyed** chaidh an
sgrios gu h-iomlan/gu buileach/uile-gu-lèir/air
fad; 2 (*idiomatic uses with* dearg & dubh) **she's
~ spoilt** tha i air a dearg mhilleadh, ~ **naked**
dearg rùisgte, **he's ~ lazy** tha e leisg agus dubh-
leisg
u-turn *n* car iomlan *m*
uvula *n* cìoch an t-slugain *f*

V

vacancy n dreuchd f/àite m (etc) ri lìonadh

vacant adj 1 (of site etc) falamh, bàn; 2 (of post, job vacancy) ri lìonadh

vacuous adj faoin

vacuum n falmhachd f invar

vagina n faighean m, pit f

vague adj (not precise) neo-phongail, (not clear) neo-shoilleir

vain adj 1 (futile) faoin, dìomhain, **the ~ endeavours of mankind** oidhirpean faoine/ dìomhain mhic-an-duine; 2 (conceited) mòr às (etc) fhèin, mòrchuiseach, **I'm not ~** chan eil mi mòr asam fhìn

valid adj èifeachdach, tàbhachdach, **a ~ driving licence** cead-dràibhidh èifeachdach

validate v dearbh vt

valley n gleann m, (small, narrow ~) glac f

valour n gaisge f invar, gaisgeachd f invar

valuable adj luachmhor, prìseil

valuation n luachachadh m, meas m

value n 1 luach m invar, (esp in neg exprs) fiù m invar, **what's its ~?** dè an luach a th' ann?, **it's of no ~** tha e gun fhiù, also chan fhiach e; 2 in expr **is this of ~ to/for you?** an fhiach vi seo dhut? **no** chan fhiach

value v 1 (estimate value of) luachaich vt, meas vt; 2 (prize) cuir luach m invar (with prep air)

valued adj measail

valueless adj gun fhiù m invar, gun luach m invar

valve n cìochag f

vandal n milltear m

vanguard n toiseach m, **the ~ of the army** toiseach an airm

vanity n 1 (futility) faoineas m, dìomhanas m, (Bibl) ~ **of vanities** dìomhanas nan dìomhanas; 2 (conceit etc) mòrchuis f

vapour n deatach f, smùid f

variable adj caochlaideach

variation n atharrachadh m

variety n 1 (abstr) caochladh m, **a ~ of** caochladh (with gen pl), **a ~ of occupations** caochladh dhreuchdan; 2 (sort, kind, genus) seòrsa m, gnè f

various adj expr by caochladh m (with gen pl), **in ~ places** ann an caochladh àiteachan

varnish n falaid m

varnish v falaidich vt

vary v atharraich vti

vat n dabhach f

vault n (architecture; burial ~) crùisle m, (underground space) seilear-làir m, (arched structure) druim-bogha m

veal n laoigh-fheòil f

veer v claon vi

vegetable, vegetables n glasraich f invar, sing & coll

vehemence n dèineas m

vehement adj dian

vehicle n carbad m

vein n cuisle f, (less usu) fèith f

velocity n luaths m, astar m

velvet n meileabhaid f

vendor n reiceadair m

venerable adj urramach

vengeance n dìoghaltas m

vennel n caol-shràid f

venom n (fig & lit) nimh & neimh m, (lit) puinnsean m

venomous adj (fig & lit) nimheil, (lit) puinnseanach, puinnseanta

venture n (business etc) iomairt f

verb n gnìomhair m, **regular ~s** gnìomhairean riaghailteach, **irregular ~s** gnìomhairean neo-riaghailteach

verbal adj 1 beòil (gen of beul m, used adjectivally), **a ~ agreement** còrdadh beòil; 2 in expr (gram) ~ **noun** ainmear gnìomhaireach m

verbatim adj & adv facal m air an fhacal

verbose adj faclach, briathrach

verdict n breith f invar

verge n 1 oir f, iomall m, crìoch f, **the ~ of the wood** oir/iomall na coille; 2 (at roadside) fàl f

verify v dearbh vt

vernacular *n* cainnt (na) dùthcha *f*, cainnt dhùthchasach *f*

vernacular *adj* (*of lang etc*) dùthchasach

versatile *adj* iol-chomasach

versatility *n* iol-chomas *m*

verse *n* 1 (*ie poetry*) bàrdachd *f invar*, rann *m*, dànachd *f invar*; 2 (*esp contrasted with prose*) rann *m*, **prose and** ~ rosg *m* is rann; 3 (*a single* ~) rann *m*

versification *n* rannaigheachd *f invar*

vertical *adj* dìreach

very *adv* 1 glè, fìor, (*stronger*) ro, (*all lenite a following cons where possible*), ~ **old** glè shean, ~ **quickly** glè luath, **the food was** ~ **good** bha am biadh fìor mhath, **the** ~ **Reverend William Campbell** An Ro-urramach/Am Fìor Urramach Uilleam Caimbeul; 2 *in expr* ~ (*plus adj or adv*) **indeed** cianail fhèin, uabhasach fhèin, ~ **good indeed/~ well indeed** cianail fhèin math; 3 (*exact, identical*) dearbh, ceart, ceudna, fhèin, **the** ~ **man!** an dearbh dhuine!, an ceart dhuine!, an duine ceudna!, an duine fhèin!, **the** ~ **thing I needed** an dearbh rud a bha dhìth orm; 4 (*even*) fhèin, **I lost the** ~ **lace out of my shoe** chaill mi am barrall fhèin às mo bhròig (*dat of* bròg *f*)

vessel *n* 1 (*sailing* ~) soitheach *m*, long *f*, bàta *m*; 2 (*dish*) soitheach *m*

vest *n* fo-lèine *f*, peitean *m*

vestige *n* lorg *f*, **there's no** ~ **of it** chan eil lorg air

vet *n* bheat *m*, (*more trad*) lighiche-bheathaichean *m*, lighiche-sprèidh *m*

vet *v* sgrùd *vt*

veto *n* bhìoto *m*

veto *v* dèan bhìoto *m* (*with prep* air)

vex *v* sàraich *vt*, claoidh *vt*, farranaich *vt*

vexing *adj* (*of situations etc*) frionasach, leamh, **they're constantly asking me** ~ **questions** bidh iad a' cur cheistean frionasach orm fad na h-ùine

vice¹ *n* 1 (*immorality, wickedness*) aingidheachd *f invar*; 2 (*undesirable trait or habit*) droch-ghnàths *m*, droch-bheus *f*, droch-bheart *f*

vice² *n* (*clamp*) teanchair & teannachair *m*

vice- *prefix* iar- (*lenites following cons where possible*), *eg* **vice-president** iar-cheann-suidhe *m*, **vice-chairman** iar-chathraiche *m*, iar-fhear-cathrach *m*

vice versa *adv*, **(and)** ~ agus a chaochladh *m*, **he gave her a present**, **and** ~ thug e tiodhlac *m* dhi, agus a chaochladh

vicious *adj* 1 aingidh; 2 (*hurtful etc*) guineach, nimheil, ~ **criticism** càineadh guineach/

nimheil; 3 (*phys violent*) brùideil, **a** ~ **beating** slacadh brùideil

victim *n* 1 (*of accident*) leòinteach *m*; 2 (*of misfortune, injustice etc*) fulangaiche *m*

victor *n* buadhaiche *m*, buadhair *m*

victory *n* buaidh *f*

video *n* bhidio *mf*

view *n* 1 (*attractive scenery etc*) sealladh *m*, sealladh dùthcha (*gen of* dùthaich *f*), **beautiful** ~**s** seallaidhean brèagha; 2 (*a field of vision*) fradharc, sealladh *m*, fianais *f*, **come into** ~ thig *vi* san fhradharc, thig an sealladh *or* san t-sealladh, thig am fianais; 3 (*opinion*) beachd *m*, **I take the** ~ **that . . .** tha mi den bheachd gu **. . .** , **that is not my** ~**!** chan e sin mo bheachd-sa!; 4 *in expr* **in** ~ **of** (*ie considering*) a' cur san àireamh *f* (*followed by gen*), leis mar a tha/bha (*followed by noun*), **in** ~ **of the rent, we took the house** a' cur a' mhàil san àireamh/leis mar a bha am màl, ghabh sinn an taigh

viewer *n* (*TV etc*) neach-coimhid *m*, ~**s** luchd-coimhid *m sing coll*

vigilance *n* furachas *m*

vigilant *adj* furachail

vigorous *adj* 1 (*phys*) lùthmhor, brìoghmhor, sgairteil; 2 (*in argument, discussion etc*) sgairteil, **a** ~ **exposition of his views** mìneachadh sgairteil air na beachdan aige

vigour *n* 1 (*phys*) lùth & lùths *m*, neart *m*, sgairt *f*; 2 (*intellectual*) sgairt *f*

vile *adj* 1 (*disgusting etc*) gràineil, grànda; 2 (*abject*) dìblidh

vilify *v* màb *vt*, dubh-chàin *vt*

vine *n* crann-fìona *m*, fìonan *m*

vinegar *n* fìon-geur *m*

violence *n* fòirneart *m*, ainneart *m*

violent *adj* brùideil, fòirneartach

violin *n* fidheall *f*

violinist *n* fidhlear *m*

viper *n* nathair-nimhe *f*

virgin *n* òigh *f*, ainnir *f*, maighdeann *f*

virginal *adj* òigheil

virginity *n* (*phys & abstr*) maighdeannas *m*

virility *n* fearachas *m*

virtue *n* 1 (*moral conduct*) subhailc *f*, deagh-bheus *f*; 2 (*Lit: inherent quality, value*) brìgh *f invar*, **a food without** ~ biadh gun bhrìgh; 3 *in expr* **by** ~ **of** do bhrìgh, air sgàth, a chionn, (*all with gen*), **she got the job by** ~ **of her qualifications** fhuair i an obair air sgàth nan teisteanasan (a bh') aice

virtuous *adj* (*of moral conduct*) subhailceach, deagh-bheusach

virulent *adj* nimheil

visible *adj* ri f(h)aicinn, ris, faicsinneach, lèirsinneach, **there was nothing** ~ cha robh càil ri fhaicinn, **her elbow was** ~ bha a h-uileann ris

vision *n* 1 (*eyesight*) fradharc *m*, lèirsinn *f invar*; 2 (*foresight etc*) lèirsinn *f invar*; 3 (*supernatural dream etc*) aisling *f*

visit *n* 1 (*esp to a person*) tadhal *m*, cèilidh *mf*, **pay X a** ~ dèan cèilidh air X, *also* tadhail *vi* air X; 2 (*to a place*) turas *m*, sgrìob *f*, (**to** do), **a** ~ **to Uist** turas/sgrìob do dh'Uibhist, **on a** ~ air turas

visit *v* 1 (~ *people*) tadhail *vi*, rach *vi* a chèilidh, rach air chèilidh *mf*, (*all with prep* air), ~**ing my parents** a' tadhal air mo phàrantan, ~ **friends** tadhail air caraidean, rach a/air chèilidh air caraidean; 2 (~ *places*) rach *vi* air turas *m* (*with prep* gu), **we** ~**ed the Isle of Man** chaidh sinn air turas gu Eilean Mhanainn, *also* bha turas againn gu Eilean Mhanainn

visitor *n* 1 neach-tadhail *m* (*pl* luchd-tadhail *m sing coll*); 2 (*holidaymaker etc*) fear-turais *m*, neach-turais *m* (*pl* luchd-turais *m sing coll*)

vital *adj* 1 (*lively etc*) beothail, brìoghmhor, lùthmhor; 2 *in expr* ~ **spark** rong *f*; 3 (*indispensable*) riatanach, deatamach, ro chudromach

vitality *n* beothalachd *f invar*

vivacious *adj* beothail, meanmnach

vivacity *n* beothalachd *f invar*, meanmna *m*

vocabulary *n* 1 (*abstr*) faclan *mpl*, briathran *mpl*; 2 (*con: in book form etc*) faclair *m*, briathrachan *m*

vocation *n* 1 (*esp a calling, eg the church*) gairm *f*; 2 (*occupation*) dreuchd *f*

vocational *adj* dreuchdail, ~ **training** oideachas dreuchdail

vocative *adj* (*gram*) gairmeach, **the** ~ **case** an tuiseal gairmeach

voice *n* 1 guth *m*, **in a low** ~ ann an guth ìosal/ìseal; 2 *in expr* **singing at the top of my** ~ a' seinn *vi* (aig) àird mo chlaiginn (*gen of* claigeann *m*); 3 (*gram*) guth *m*, **the passive** ~ an guth fulangach

voice *v* cuir *vt* an cèill (*gen of* ciall *f*), **she** ~**d her own anxiety** chuir i an cèill a h-iomagain fhèin

void *n* fal(a)mhachd *f invar*, fànas *m*, fàsalachd *f invar*

volatile *adj* caochlaideach

volcanic *adj*, bholcànach

volcano *n* bholcàno *m*, beinn-theine *f*

volume¹ *n* 1 (*capacity*) tomhas-lìonaidh *m*; 2 (*loudness*) àirde-fuaime *f*

volume² (*book*) leabhar *m*, ~ **one** leabhar a h-aon

voluntary *adj* saor-thoileach

volunteer *n* saor-thoileach *m*

vomit *n* dìobhairt *mf invar*

vomit *v* dìobhair *vti*, sgeith *vti*, cuir *vti* a-mach

vomiting *n* dìobhairt *mf invar*, sgeith *m*

voracious *adj* craosach, geòcach, gionach

vote *n* bhòt(a) *f* (**for** airson)

vote *v* 1 bhòt *vi* (**for** airson); 2 *in expr* ~ **into office** tagh *vt*

voter *n* neach-bhòtaidh *m* (*pl* luchd-bhòtaidh *m sing coll*)

voting *n* bhòtadh *m*, ~ **rights** còraichean bhòtaidh *fpl*

vouch *v* rach *vi* an urras *m* (**for** air), ~ **for someone** rach an urras air cuideigin

voucher *n* cùpon *m*

vow *n* gealladh *m*, bòid *f*

vow *v* geall *vti*, thoir gealladh *m*, gabh bòid *f*, bòidich *vi*, **he** ~**ed he wouldn't do it again** bhòidich e nach dèanadh e a-rithist e

vowel *n* fuaimreag *f*

voyage *n* turas-mara *m*, bhòids(e) *f*

vulgar *adj* 1 (*uncouth etc*) gràisgeil, garbh, borb; 2 (*indecent*) draosta, drabasta; 3 (*belonging to the people*) coitcheann, cumanta, ~ **tongue** cainnt choitcheann/chumanta

vulgarity *n* 1 (*uncouthness*) gràisgealachd *f invar*; 2 (*indecency*) draostachd *f invar*, drabastachd *f invar*

vulnerable *adj* so-leònte

vulva pit *f*

W

wafer *n* (*as food*) sliseag *f*; **2** (*relig*) **a communion** *or* **consecrated** ~ abhlan coisrigte *m*

wag *v* **1** (*as vi*) bog *vi*, **the dog's tail was ~ging** bha earball a' choin a' bogadh; **2** (*as vt*) crath *vt*, **a dog ~ging his tail** cù (is e) a' crathadh earbaill

wage, **wages** *n* tuarastal *m*, pàigheadh *m*, (*less usu*) duais *f*, cosnadh *m*

wage *v* dèan *vt*, ~ **war** dèan cogadh *m*

wager *n* geall *m*, **put/lay/place a** ~ cuir geall (**on** air)

wager *v* **1** (*lit*) cuir geall *m* (**on** air); **2** (*fig*) cuir *vi* geall *m*, rach *vi irreg* an urras *m* (*with conj* gu/ nach), **I'll** ~ **he won't come** cuiridh mi geall nach tig e, thèid mi an urras nach tig e

wail *v* caoin *vi*, guil *vi*

waist *n* meadhan *m*

waistcoat *n* peitean *m*

wait *v* **1** fuirich *vi*, feith *vi*, (**for** ri), **you** ~ **here!** fuirich thusa an seo!, **I was ~ing for you** bha mi a' fuireach riut/a' feitheamh riut, ~ **a minute!** fuirich mionaid!, **~ing for the bus** a' feitheamh ris a' bhus; **2** *in expr* **the bus was ~ing** bha am bus na stad *m*; **3** (*serve*) fritheil *vi* (**on** air), ~ **on the guests** fritheil air na h-aoighean

waiter *n* gille-frithealaidh *m*

waiting list *n* liosta-feitheimh *f*

waitress *n* caileag-fhrithealaidh *f*

wake, **waken** *v* **1** dùisg *vti*, **I wakened/woke (up) at six** dhùisg mi aig (a) sia, **wake me up/ waken me in two hours** dùisg mi an ceann dà uair *f gen* a (*for* de) thìde *f*; **2** *in excl* ~ **up!** dùisg!/dùisgibh!, (*to slow or sleepy person*) crath dhìot an cadal!

wakened *adj & past part* na (*etc*) d(h)ùisg, na (*etc*) d(h)ùsgadh

Wales *n* Cuimrigh *f*, *used with article*, A' Chuimrigh

walk *n* cuairt *f*, **go for/take a** ~ gabh cuairt, rach *vi irreg* air chuairt

walk *v* **1** coisich *vi*, **I ~ed along/on/onwards** choisich mi romham; **2** (*as opposed to driving/ riding*) rach *vi irreg* de chois (*dat of* cas *f*), **I'll** ~ **there** thèid mi ann dhem chois, *also* 's e coiseachd *f invar* a nì mi (ann)

walker *n* coisiche *m*

walking *n* coiseachd *f invar*, ~ **stick** bata-coiseachd *m*

wall *n* **1** (*esp defensive or fortified*) mùr *m*; **2** (*usu inner or outer ~ of building, but occas freestanding*) balla *m*; **3** (*freestanding ~, eg of garden*) gàrradh *m*

wallpaper *n* pàipear-balla *m*

walnut *n* **1** cnò Fhrangach *f*, gall-chnò *f*; **2** (~ *tree*) crann ghall-chnò *m*

walrus *n* each-mara *m*

wan *adj* glaisneulach

wand *n* slat *f*, slatag *f*

wander *v* **1** (*travel far & wide, at random, or like an exile*) rach *vi irreg* air fhuadan *m*, bi *vi irreg* air fhuadan, (*more trad*) rach/bi air allaban *m*; **2** (*get lost, stray*) rach *vi irreg* air seachran *m*, rach *vi* air iomrall *m*; **3** *in expr* **you made me ~ from the point** chuir thu às mo ghabhail *mf* mi

wandering *adj* **1** (*lost, astray*) air iomrall *m*, air seachran *m*; **2** (*like an exile, a traveller*) air fhuadan *m*, air allaban *m*

wandering *n* **1** (*when lost, astray*) seachran *m*, iomrall *m*; **2** (*like an exile, a traveller*) fuadan *m*, allaban *m*

want *n* **1** (*lack*) dìth *m*, cion *m invar*, uireasbhaidh *f*, easbhaidh *f*; **2** (*poverty*) bochdainn *f*, (*less usu*) aìnnis *f*

want *v* **1** (*require, wish for*) iarr *vt*, (*more fam*) bi *vi* airson (*with gen of n*), **do you** ~ **a/some coffee?** a bheil thu ag iarraidh cofaidh?, **the children ~ed me to buy a kitten** bha a' chlann ag iarraidh orm piseag a cheannach, **I don't** ~ **you to be on your own** chan eil mi airson gum bi thu nad aonar; **2** (*require, look for*) sir *vt*, **the company ~s workers** tha a' chompanaidh a' sireadh luchd-obrach; **3** (*in shop etc*) **what do you** ~**?** dè tha a dhìth *m* oirbh?, **I ~ a coat** tha còta a dhìth orm; **4** (*lack, need*) bi *vi irreg* a dhìth, bi a dh'easbhaidh *f*, (*with prep* air), **what do they ~ (for)?** dè a tha a dhìth/a dh'easbhaidh orra?; **5** (*like, wish*) togair *vi* (*often used in rel fut tense*), **we'll go on holiday, if you ~** thèid sinn air laithean-saora, ma thogras tu

wanting *adj* a dhìth *m*, a dh'easbhaidh *f*, easbhaidheach, **food is ~** tha biadh a dhìth

war *n* cogadh *m*, **the First (World) War** a' Chiad Chogadh, An Cogadh Mòr, **make/wage ~** dèan cogadh, **on a ~ footing** air ghleus cogaidh *mf*

warble *v* ceileir *vi*

warcry *n* gairm-cogaidh *f*, sluagh-ghairm *f*

wardrobe *n* preas-aodaich *m*

warehouse *n* batharnach *m*

wares *n* bathar *m sing coll*, **selling their ~** a' reic an cuid bathair *f*

warfare *n* cogadh *m*

warlike *adj* **1** (*as term of praise*) cathach; **2** (*more pej: belligerent etc*) cogach

warm *adj* **1** (*of weather, objects*) blàth, **it's ~ today** tha i blàth an-diugh, **~ milk** bainne blàth; **2** (*of people, emotions, atmosphere*) blàth, cridheil, càirdeil, **a ~ welcome** fàilte chridheil

warm *v* **1** teasaich *vt*, teòth *vt*, blàthaich *vt*, **~ (up) the soup** teasaich am brot; **2** (*fig: emotionally*) teòth *vi* (**to** ri), **~ to someone** teòth ri cuideigin

war-memorial *n* cuimhneachan-cogaidh *m*

warm-hearted *adj* blàth-chridheach

warming *n* teasachadh *m*, blàthachadh *m*, teòthadh *m*

warmth *n* **1** (*lit*) blàths *m*; **2** (*of people, emotions, atmosphere*) blàths *m*, cridhealas *m*

warn *v* thoir rabhadh *m* (*with prep* do), earalaich *vt*, (**about/against** air), **they ~ed me about/against her** thug iad rabhadh dhomh oirre

warning *n* rabhadh *m*, earalachadh *m*, **a ~ bell** clag-rabhaidh *m*

warrant *n* (*ie authorisation*) barantas *m*, **building ~** barantas-togail *m*, **arrest ~** barantas-glacaidh *m*

warranty *n* (*ie guarantee*) bar(r)antas *m*, urras *m*;

warrior *n* **1** fear-cogaidh *m* (*pl* luchd-cogaidh *m sing coll*); **2** (*as trad term of praise*) gaisgeach *m*, laoch *m*, curaidh *m*, seud *m*

warship *n* long-chogaidh *f*

wart *n* foinne *m*

wary *adj* **1** (*alert*) faiceallach, cùramach; **2** (*mistrustful*) amharasach, teagmhach

wash *v* nigh *vt*, ionnlaid *vt*, **~ the baby** nigh an leanabh *m*, **I was ~ing** bha mi gam nighe fhìn

washbasin *n* mias-ionnlaid *f*

washer[1] *n* (*for screw or bolt*) cearclan *m*

washer[2] *n* (*for clothes*) nigheadair *m*

wash house *n* taigh-nighe *m*

washing *n* (*abstr*) nighe *m invar*, ionnlad *m*, (*con: a batch of washing*) nigheadaireachd *f invar*

washing-machine *n* nigheadair *m*, inneal-nigheadaireachd *m*

wasp *n* speach *f*, **~'s sting** gath speacha *m*

waste *adj* fàs, **~ ground** talamh fàs

waste *n* **1** call *m*, cosg *m invar*, **a ~ of money** call/cosg airgid; **2** (*refuse*) sgudal *m*, **~ collection** togail sgudail *f*

waste *v* (*esp money*) caith *vt*, cosg *vt*, struidh *vt*

wasteful *adj* caith(t)each, struidheil

waster *n* struidhear *m*

watch[1] *n* **1** (*abstr: guard*) faire *f*, caithris *f invar*, **keep ~** dèan/cùm faire, **the night ~** faire na h-oidhche, caithris (na h-oidhche); **2** (*con: ie the people on ~*) luchd-faire *m sing coll*, freiceadan *m sing coll*, **a (single) ~/a member of the ~** fear-faire *m*; **3** *in expr* **The Black Watch** Am Freiceadan Dubh

watch[2] *n* (*timepiece*) uaireadair *m*

watch *v* coimhead *vt*, **~ a film/TV** coimhead film/an TBh

watcher *n* neach-coimhid *m* (*pl* luchd-coimhid *m sing coll*)

watchful *adj* furachail

watchfulness *n* furachas *m*

watchman *n* fear-faire *m*, fear-coimhid *m*

water *n* uisge *m*, (*esp in Lewis Gaelic*) bùrn *m*, **~ mill** muileann-uisge *mf*

water *v* uisgich *vt*

waterfall *n* eas *m*, leum-uisge *m*, linne *f*, spùt *m*

waterfowl *n & npl* eun-uisge *m*, *pl* eòin-uisge

watering can *n* peile-frasaidh *m*

waterproof *adj* dìonach, uisge-dhìonach

watershed *n* **1** (*topog*) druim-uisge *m*; **2** (*fig; crucial, defining stage, moment etc*) sgarachdainn *f*

watertight *adj* (*house, boat etc*) uisge-dhìonach

waterway *n* slighe-uisge *f*

watery *adj* uisgeach

waulk *v* (*full cloth with the hands or feet*) luaidh *vti*

waulking *n* (*fulling of cloth with the hands or feet*) luadhadh *m*, **~ songs** òrain luadhaidh & òrain luaidh *mpl*

wave *n* (*in sea, physics etc*) tonn *mf*, ~-**power** cumhachd *mf invar* tuinne (*gen of* tonn), **sound** ~ fuaim-thonn *mf*, **heat** ~ teas-tonn *mf*

wave *v* **1** (*oscillate etc*) luaisg *vi*, tulg *vi*; **2** (*signal with the hand*) smèid *vi*, crath a (*etc*) làmh(an) *f(pl)*, (**to/at** ri), **they were waving to her** bha iad a' smèideadh rithe/a' crathadh an làmhan rithe

wax *n* cèir *f*

waxen, waxy *adj* cèireach

way *n* **1** (*route, road*) rathad *m*, (*sometimes with more abstr sense*) slighe *f*, **the** ~ **home** an rathad dhachaigh, **we met them on the** ~ thachair sinn riutha air an rathad/air an t-slighe, **give** ~ gèill slighe, **right of** ~ còir-slighe *f*, ~ **out** (*ie exit*) slighe dol a-mach, (~ *out via a door*) doras dol a-mach; **2** (*direction*) taobh *m*, rathad *m*, **they're coming this** ~ tha iad a' tighinn an taobh/an rathad seo, **they went that** ~ chaidh iad an rathad sin, ghabh iad an t-slighe sin; **3** (*distance*) astar *m*, **a long** ~ fada *adj*, **that's a fair/a long** ~**!** 's e astar mòr/math a tha sin!, 's fhada sin!, **a long** ~ **away** fad' air falbh; **4** (~ *of doing something*) dòigh *f*, modh *mf*, seòl *m*, **do it (in) this** ~ dèan air an dòigh seo e, **in a particular** ~ air mhodh àraidh, ~ **of life** dòigh-beatha; **5** *in expr* (*fam*) **there's no** ~ **that will work!** chan obraich sin idir idir!, chan eil dòigh air gun obraich sin; **6** (*custom(s) etc*) dòigh *f*, **they aren't used to our** ~**s** chan eil iad cleachdte ri ar dòighean; **7** *in exprs* ~ **out** (*ie from predicament etc*) dol-às *m invar*, **there was no** ~ **out for us now except . . .** cha robh dol-às againn a-nis ach . . . , **that's the** ~ **it is!** is ann mar sin a tha (e)!

weak *adj* **1** (*phys* ~) lag, (*faint*) fann, (*less usu*) lapach, ~ **from hunger** lag/fann leis an acras, **a** ~ **voice** guth fann; **2** (*emotionally* ~, ~ *in character*) bog, meata, maoth, gun smior

weaken *v* lagaich *vti*, (*less usu*) fannaich *vti*

weakening *n* lagachadh *m*, fàillinn *f*

weak-minded *adj* lag na (*etc*) inntinn *f*

weakness *n* laigse *f*

wealth *n* beartas *&* beairteas *m*, saidhbhreas *m*, ionmhas *m*, stòras *m*, (*less usu*) maoin *f*

wealthy *adj* beartach *&* beairteach, saidhbhir

weapon *n* ball-airm *m*

wear *n* **1** (*abstr*) caitheamh *f*; **2** (*con: apparel*) aodach *m*, *eg* **evening** ~ aodach-feasgair

wear *v* **1** (*clothes*) cuir *vt* (*with prep* air *or, more trad*, mu), ~ **your coat today** cuir (ort/umad) do chòta an-diugh; **2** *in expr* **a man** ~**ing a suit** (*etc*) fear is deise (*etc*) air

wear out *v* **1** (*clothing etc*) caith *vt*; **2** (*of people: exhaust, weary*) claoidh *vt*, sgìthich *vt*

weariness *n* **1** (*through fatigue*) sgìths *f invar*, claoidheadh *m*, claoidh *f invar*; **2** (*through tedium etc*) fadachd *f invar*, fadal *m*

weary *adj* **1** (*through fatigue*) sgìth, claoidhte, (*esp through stress, worry etc*) sàraichte, **grow** ~ fàs *vi* sgìth; **2** (*causing weariness*) cian, **a** ~ **road** rathad cian; **3** **grow** ~ (*esp through tedium*) gabh fadachd *f invar*

weary *v* claoidh *vt*, sgìthich *vt*, (*esp by harassment, pressure etc*) sàraich *vt*

wearying *adj* sgìtheil

weasel *n* neas (bheag) *f*

weather *n* **1** aimsir *f*, sìde (*also less usu* tìde) *f*, ~ **forecast** tuairmse (na) sìde *f*; **2** *in expr* **appalling/terrible/atrocious** ~ sìde nan seachd sian *fpl*

weather-beaten *adj* (*of complexion*) air dath nan sian, (*of exposed landscape etc*) sian-bhuailte

weathercock *n* coileach-gaoithe *m*

weave *v* figh *vti*

weaver *n* breabadair *m*, figheadair *m*

weaving *n* fighe *mf invar*, breabadaireachd *f invar*, ~ **loom** beart-fhighe *f*

web *n* **1** (*of spider etc*) lìon *m*; **2** (*IT*) *usu with art*, **the (worldwide)** ~, lìon na cruinne, ~ **site** làrach-lìn *f*

wed *adj & past part* pòsta, **get** ~ pòs *vi*

wedder *n* mult *&* molt *m*

wedding *n* banais *f*, ~ **reception** cuirm bainnse, *in expr* ~ **ring** fàinne-pòsaidh *mf*, fàinne-pòst(a) *mf*

wedge *n* geinn *m*

wedlock *n* pòsadh *m*

Wednesday *n* Diciadain *m invar*

wee *adj* **1** beag, **a** ~ **boy** balach beag; **2** *in expr* **a** ~ **bit** (*adv*) caran *m*, rud beag, **a** ~ **bit tired** caran sgìth, rud beag sgìth

weed *n* luibh *mf*, lus *m*

week *n* seachdain *f*, **a** ~ **today** seachdain on diugh

weekend *n* deireadh-seachdain *m*, **at the** ~ aig deireadh na seachdaine

weekly *adj* seachdaineach, seachdaineil, (*adv*) a h-uile seachdain *f*

weep *v* caoin *vi*, guil *vi*, gail *vi*, (*esp* ~ *vigorously*) ràn *vi*

weeping *n* caoineadh *m*, gul *m*, gal *m*, (*usu vigorous*) rànail *m invar*, rànaich *f invar*

weigh *v* **1** (*as vt*) cothromaich *vt*, cuideamaich *vt*; **2** (*as vi*) **what's it** ~**?** dè an cudthrom *m* a tha ann?, **it** ~**s a kilogram** tha cileagram de

chudthrom ann; **3** (*mentally*) ~ (**up**) beachdaich
vi, gabh beachd *m*, (*with prep* air), **~ing up the**
situation a' beachdachadh/a' gabhail beachd
air an t-suidheachadh

weight *n* cudthrom *m*, **a kilogram in ~**
cileagram de chudthrom, **I had to put on ~**
b' fheudar dhomh cudthrom a chur orm

weighty *adj* cudromach, trom, **~ matters**
cuspairean cudromach/troma

weir *n* cairidh & caraidh *f*

weird *adj* neònach

welcome *adj* **1** (*as excl*) ~! fàilte *f* oirbh/ort!, ~
to my house! fàilte oirbh/ort don taigh agam!,
they bid us ~ chuir iad fàilte oirnn; **2** (*after*
expr of thanks, appreciation etc) **you're ~** is/'s
e do bheatha *f*, is/'s e ur beatha, **thank you**
very much! you're ~ mòran taing! 's e do
bheatha/ur beatha

welcome *n* fàilte *f*, gabhail *mf*, **we got a hearty/**
lukewarm ~ fhuair sinn fàilte chridheil/leth-
fhuar, **what sort of a ~ did you get?** dè an
seòrsa fàilte a fhuair sibh?

welcome *v* cuir fàilte *f* (*with prep* air), fàiltich *vt*,
they ~ed us chuir iad fàilte oirnn

welcoming *adj* fàilteachail, fàilteach

weld *v* tàth *vt*

welfare *n* **1** (*material & psychological*
circumstances) cor *m*, **he became anxious**
about the ~ of the refugees ghabh e cùram
mu chor nam fògarrach; **2** (*social security,*
benefits etc) sochair (shòisealta), **~ state** stàit-
shochairean *f*

well *adj* gu math, fallain, slàn, **I'm ~, thank**
you tha (mi) gu math, tapadh leat, **he's not a ~**
man chan e duine fallain a th' ann (dheth)

well *adv* **1** gu math, **she did the work ~** 's math
a rinn i an obair; **2** (*in passive constructions*)
expressed by air *plus* deagh *adv, and the verbal*
noun, eg **it's ~ made/done** tha e air a dheagh
dhèanamh, (*also* tha e air a dhèanamh gu math);
3 (*other idioms & exprs*) **~ done!** math thu
fhèin!, nach math a rinn thu!, **he's ~ off** tha
e glè mhath dheth, **as ~ as** (*ie in addition to*)
cho math ri, a thuilleadh air, a bharrachd air,
we have two flats as ~ as the house tha dà
lobhta againn cho math ris/a thuilleadh air/a
bharrachd air an taigh, **we get on (very) ~**
(with each other) tha sinn gu math mòr aig
a chèile, tha sinn rèidh ri chèile, tha sinn a'
tarraing glè mhath

well *n* tobar *mf*, fuaran *m*

well-behaved *adj* beusach, modhail, sìobhalta

wellbeing *n* (*material & psychological*
circumstances} cor *m*, math *m*, **he became**

anxious about the ~ of the refugees ghabh e
cùram *m* mu chor nam fògarrach *mpl gen*

well(-)built *adj* **1** (*of person: sturdy etc*)
tomadach, tapaidh, calma; **2** (*of building*) air a
dheagh thogail

well-informed *adj* fiosrach (**about** air)

wellington (boot) *n* bòtann *mf*

well-known *adj* ainmeil, (*esp of persons*)
iomraiteach

well-liked *adj* mòr-thaitneach, mòr-chòrdte

well-mannered *adj* modhail

well-ordered *adj* dòigheil, òrdail, riaghailteach

well-timed *adj* an deagh àm *m*

Welsh *adj* Cuimreach

Welshman *n* Cuimreach *m*

west *adj* siar *adj*, an iar *f invar*, **the ~ wind**
a' ghaoth an iar, **the ~ coast/~side (of the**
country) an taobh an iar, an taobh siar

west *adv* an iar *f invar*, **we're going ~** tha sinn
a' dol an iar, **~ of the island** an iar air an eilean,
siar air an eilean

west *n* iar *f invar*, **breezes (etc) from the ~**
oiteagan (*etc*) on iar, **the ~** (*ie point of compass*)
an àird an iar *f*, **the ~** (*ie location*) an taobh an
iar, *also* an taobh siar

westerly *adj* **1** (*from the west*) on iar *f invar*, **a ~**
wind gaoth on iar; **2** (*towards the west*) (chun)
an iar, **going in a ~ direction** a' dol (chun)
an iar

western *adj* siar *adj*, an iar *adv*, **the Western**
Isles Na h-Eileanan an Iar *or* Na h-Eileanan
Siar

West Indies (the) *npl* Na h-Innseachan an Iar
fpl

westward(s) *adv* an iar, chun an iar, chun na
h-àirde an iar, **going ~** a' dol (chun) an iar

wet *adj* fliuch, **a ~ day** là fliuch, **I'm ~ through/**
soaking ~ tha mi bog fliuch

wet *v* **1** fliuch *vt*, **the water overflowed, ~ting**
everything chuir an t-uisge thairis, a' fliuchadh
a h-uile càil, (*fam*) **~ your whistle!** fliuch do
ribheid!; **2** *in expr* **he ~ himself** chaill e a mhùn
m

wether *n* mult & molt *m*

whale *n* muc-mhara *f*

what *inter pron* dè, **~'s your name?** dè an
t-ainm a th' oirbh?, **~'s happening?** dè a tha a'
tachairt?, **~'s the good/use of talking!** dè am
math a bhith a' bruidhinn!, **~ do you think?**
dè do bheachd *m* (air)?, **I don't know ~ I'll do**
chan eil fhios agam (gu) dè a nì mi; **2** *in expr* **~**
(did you say)? b' àill leat/leibh?, (*less polite*)
dè an rud?; **3** (*esp when 'what' could be replaced*
in Eng by 'which') cò, **~ books do you like**

best? cò na leabhraichean *mpl* as fheàrr leat?;
4 *in exprs* ~ **for?** carson?, ~ **did you do that
for?** carson a rinn thu sin?, ~ **a** (*followed by
a noun*) abair (*imperative of* abair *vti irreg*),
followed by a noun, eg ~ **a fool!** abair amadan!,
~ **a mess!** abair bùrach!

what *rel pron* na, **I gave him** ~ **I had** thug mi
dha na bha agam, **they lost** ~ **food they had**
chaill iad na bha aca de bhiadh

whatever *pron* **1** (*envisaging multiple
possibilities*) ge b' e *with the appropriate pron,
usu* dè, ~ **I did there I don't remember it** ge
b' e dè a rinn mi (ann) an sin, chan eil cuimhne
agam air, ~ **the weather may be like** ge b' e
dè an aimsir/an t-sìde a bhios ann; **2** (*as object
of main verb*) càil sam bith *f invar*, rud sam bith
m, nì sam bith *m*, *also* càil (*etc*) air bith, **you
will get** ~ **you want** gheibh thu càil/rud/nì
sam bith a thogras tu; **3** (*emph for* **what**) dè fon
ghrèin (*dat sing of* grian *f*), dè air an t-saoghal,
~ **do you mean?** dè fon ghrèin/dè air an
t-saoghal a tha thu a' ciallachadh?, (*trad*) gu dè
as ciall dhut?

wheat *n* cruithneachd *m invar*

wheel *n* cuibhle *f*, (*more trad, less usu*) roth *mf*,
the ~ **of fortune** cuibhle an fhortain

wheelchair *n* cathair-cuibhle *f*, sèithear-cuibhle
m

wheeled *adj* rothach

wheesht! *excl* ist! (*pl* istibh!) & eist! (*pl* eistibh!),
tosd!

whelk *n* faochag *f*

whelp *n* cuilean *m*

when *adv* (*inter*) cuine (*before a vowel* cuin), ~
was that? cuin a bha sin?, **I don't know** ~ **it
was ...** chan eil fhios am cuin a bha e . . .

when *conj* (*non-inter*) an uair a & nuair a, **give
me it** ~ **you've finished with it** thoir dhomh e
an uair a bhios tu deiseil dheth

whenever *pron* **1** (*where there is doubt about
the time of occurrence etc*) ge b' e cuin(e), ~ **it
happened, I don't remember it** ge b' e cuin
a thachair e, chan eil cuimhne *f* agam air,; **2**
(*where the time of occurrence is unimportant or
undefined*) uair sam bith, **come and see us** ~
you like thig gar faicinn uair sam bith a thogras
tu; **3** (*emph for* **when**) cuin air bith, ~ **did you
say that?** cuin air bith a thuirt thu sin?

where *adv* **1** (*inter*) càite (*before a vowel* càit),
~**'s Iain?** càit a bheil Iain?; **2** *in expr* ~ **...
from?** cò às . . . ?, ~ **are you from?** cò às a tha
thu?, ~ **did he** (*emph*) **spring from?** cò às a
nochd esan?

where *conj* (*non-inter*) far a, **you'll find it** ~
you left it gheibh thu e far na (*for* far an do)
dh'fhàg thu e

wherever *pron* **1** (*where there is doubt about
the place of occurrence etc*) ge b' e càit(e), ~ **it
happened, I don't remember it** ge b' e càit
an do thachair e, chan eil cuimhne agam air; **2**
(*where the place of occurrence is unimportant
or undefined*) àite sam bith *m*, **we'll go** ~ **the
sun's shining** thèid sin do dh'àite sam bith
far a bheil a' ghrian a' deàrrsadh; **3** (*emph for*
where) càit air bith, ~ **did you see that?** càit
air bith am faca tu sin?

whereupon *adv* (is) leis (a) sin, **the bar closed,
~ he went home** dhùin am bàr, is leis a sin
chaidh e dhachaigh

whether *conj* co-aca, co-dhiù, **I don't care ~
you come or not** tha mi coma co-aca/coma
co-dhiù a thig thu no nach tig

which *pron* cò, ~ **books do you like best?** cò
na leabhraichean as fheàrr leat?, **I'm not sure
~ of them I'll marry** chan eil mi cinnteach cò
aca a phòsas mi

while *conj* fhad 's a ~ **she was in France she
learnt French** fhad 's a bha i anns an Fhraing
dh'ionnsaich i an Fhraingis

while *n* greis *f*, treis *f*, tamall *m*, tràth *m*, (*short* ~)
greiseag *f*, treiseag *f*, tacan *m*, **for a** ~ fad greis/
tamaill, airson greis/tamaill, *also* car uair *f*, **a** ~
ago o chionn greis/tamaill

while *v in expr* ~ **away time** cuir seachad ùine
(gu dìomhain)

whim *n* saobh-smuain *f*

whimper *n* sgiùgan *m*

whimper *v* dèan sgiùgan *m*

whinny *n* sitir *f*

whinny *v* dèan sitir *f*

whin(s) *n* conasg *m sing & coll*

whip *n* cuip *f*

whip *v* cuip *vt*, (*less usu*) sgiùrs *vt*

whipping *n* cuipeadh *m*

whisky *n* uisge-beatha *m*, (*nickname for* ~) mac-
na-bracha *m*

whisper *n* cagar *m*

whisper *v* cagair *vti*

whispering *n* cagar *m*, cagarsaich *f*

whistle *n* **1** (*the noise*) fead *f*; **2** (*the instrument:
penny* ~, *Irish* ~ *etc*) feadag *f*, fideag *f*, **he
played a tune on the** ~ ghabh e port air an
fheadaig *dat*; **3** *in expr* (*fam*) **wet your** ~ fliuch
do ribheid *f*

whistle *v* **1** (*a single whistle*) dèan fead *f*, leig
fead (*with prep* à), **I ~d** rinn mi fead, leig mi
fead asam; **2** (*more continuous whistling*)

feadaireachd *vi*, **the wee boy was whistling** bha am balach beag a' feadail

whistling *n* **1** fead *f*, **the ~ of the wind** fead na gaoithe; **2** (*continuous, with the mouth*) feadaireachd *f invar*, feadalaich *f invar*, feadarsaich *f invar*

white *adj* **1** (*general*) geal, **black and ~** dubh is geal, **~ wine** fìon geal; **2** (*esp of hair, & of colouring of humans & animals*) bàn, (*trad*) fionn, **the ~ dog/horse** an cù/an t-each bàn

white *n* **1** geal *m*, **the ~ of the eye** geal na sùla; **2** *in expr* **the ~ of an egg** gealagan *m*

whiten *v* gealaich *vti*

whiteness *n* gile *f invar*, gilead *m*

whiting *n* cuidhteag *f*

who *inter pron* cò, **~'s he?** cò esan?, **~ did it?** cò a rinn e?, **I don't know ~ it is** chan eil fhios agam cò a th' ann

who *rel pron* a, (*in neg sentence*) nach, **the man ~ sang and the woman ~ wasn't listening to him** am fear a sheinn agus an tè nach robh ag èisteachd ris

whoever *pron* **1** (*where there is doubt about the identity of the person*) ge b' e cò, **~ did it, I don't remember it** ge b' e cò a rinn e, chan eil cuimhne agam air; **2** (*where the identity of the person is unimportant or undefined*) duine *m* sam bith, **we'll welcome ~ comes to the house** cuiridh sinn fàilte air duine sam bith a thig dhan taigh; **3** (*emph for* who) cò air bith, cò fon ghrèin (*dat sing of* grian *f*), **~ told you that?** cò air bith/cò fon ghrèin a dh'innis sin dhut?

whole *adj* **1** (*an object, period etc in its entirety*) gu lèir, air fad, uile, **the ~ army was captured** chaidh an t-arm gu lèir/air fad/uile an sàs, **a ~ month** mìos gu lèir/air fad, **they ravaged the ~ country** sgrios iad an dùthaich air fad/gu lèir; **2** (*intact, undivided*) slàn, iomlan, **the (standing) stone isn't ~** chan eil an tursa slàn/iomlan, **a ~ word** facal slàn, **a ~ number** àireamh shlàn; **3** (*of periods of time*) fad (*with the gen*), **the ~ time** fad na h-ùine, **I was poor my ~ life** bha mi bochd fad mo bheatha, **I'll be up the ~ night** bidh mi air mo chois (*gen of* cas *f*) fad na h-oidhche

whole *n* **1** *used with art*, an t-iomlan *m*, **do you want the ~ of it?** a bheil thu ag iarraidh an iomlain (dheth)?; **2** *in expr* **on the ~** san fharsaingeachd *f invar*, **on the ~ the majority are against him** san fharsaingeachd tha a' mhòr-chuid na aghaidh

wholeness *n* slàine *f invar*

wholesome *adj* slàn, fallain, **~ food** biadh fallain

whooping-cough *n* (*used with art*) an triuthach *f*

why *inter adv* carson, **~ did he leave?** carson a dh'fhalbh e?, **~ isn't Màiri at work? don't ask** ~ carson nach eil Màiri ag obair? na faighnich carson

wicked *adj* olc, (*less usu*) aingidh

wickedness *n* olc *m*, donas *m*, (*less usu*) aingidheachd *f invar*

widdershins (*Sc*) *adj* tuathal

wide *adj* farsaing, leathann, **far and ~** fad' is farsaing

widen *v* leudaich *vti*

widened *adj* leudaichte

widow *n* banntrach *f*

widower *n* banntrach *f*

widowhood *n* banntrachas *m*

width *n* farsaingeachd *f invar*, leud *m*

wield *v* (*tool, weapon etc*) làimhsich *vt*, iomair *vt*

wife *n* **1** bean *f*, bean-phòsta *f*, **my ~** mo bhean; **2** *in expr* (*fam*) **the ~** a' chailleach

wife, wifie *n* (*Sc*) (*fam for* **woman**) cailleach *f*

wig *n* gruag-bhrèige *f*

wild *adj* **1** (*not domesticated*) fiadhaich, **~ goat** gobhar fhiadhaich; **2** (*weather, landscape etc*) garbh, **a ~ night** oidhche gharbh, **~ country** tìr gharbh; **3** (*unruly, turbulent*) garbh, garg, borb, **a ~ people** sluagh garbh/garg/borb; **4** (*fam: angry*) fiadhaich, **I was ~ after what he said to me** (*fam*) bha mi fiadhaich an dèidh na thuirt e rium; **5** (*fam: hard-living, hard-drinking etc*) fiadhaich, garbh, **he's a ~ man, right enough!** 's e duine fiadhaich/garbh a th' ann dheth, ceart gu leòr!; **6** *in expr* **~ and woolly** molach

wildcat *n* cat-fiadhaich *m*

wilderness *n* fàsach *mf*, (*less usu*) dìthreabh *f*

wildness *n* gairbhe *f invar*, gairbhead *m*, gairge *f invar*, buirbe *f invar*

wile *n* cuilbheart *f*, innleachd *f*, car *m*

wilful *adj* ceann-làidir, rag, rag-mhuinealach, dùr

will *n* **1** toil *f*, **God's ~** toil Dhè (*gen of* Dia *m*), (*prov*) **where there's a ~ there's a way** far am bi toil, bidh gnìomh; **2** (*for making legacy*) tiomnadh *m*, **he didn't make a ~** cha do rinn e tiomnadh

willing *adj* deònach, èasgaidh, toileach, **they're not ~ to do it** chan eil iad deònach (air) a dhèanamh, chan eil iad èasgaidh/toileach a dhèanamh

willingly *adv* a dheòin, **~ or not/or otherwise, ~ or un~** a dheòin no a dh'aindeoin

willingness *n* deòin *f*

willow *n* seileach *m*

willy-nilly *adv* a dheòin no a dh'aindeoin

wily *adj* carach, fiar, seòlta, (*less usu*) caon
win *v* **1** (*as vt*) coisinn *vt*, faigh *vt irreg*,
buannaich *vt*, ~ **fame** coisinn/buannaich cliù,
~ **a prize** coisinn/faigh/buannaich duais; **2** (*as
vi: in battle, race, competition etc*) buannaich *vi*,
buinnig *vi*, **we won** bhuannaich sinn, (*fam: eg
to someone working at a task*) **are you ~ning?**
a bheil thu a' buinnig?; **3** *in expr* ~ **to** (*ie reach,
make it to*) buannaich *vt*, **we won to the
village at dusk** bhuannaich sinn am baile am
beul na h-oidhche
wind *n* **1** gaoth *f*; **2** (*intestinal ~*) *used with art*, a'
ghaoth; **2** *in expr* ~ **and watertight** dìonach
wind *v* toinn *vt*
windfall *n* turchairt *f*
winding *adj* (*of road, river etc*) lùbach
winding-sheet *n* marbhphaisg *f*
windmill *n* muileann-gaoithe *mf*
window *n* **1** uinneag *f*, ~ **bars** cliath-uinneige *f*; **2**
in expr ~ **pane** lòsan *m*
windowsill *n* oir (na h-)uinneige *f*
windsock *n* muincheann-gaoithe *m*
windy *adj* **1** gaothach, **a ~ day** latha gaothach; **2**
in expr **it's ~ today** tha gaoth *f* ann an-diugh
wine *n* fìon *m*, **red/white** ~ fìon dearg/geal
wing *n* **1** sgiath *f*; **2** *in expr* **on the ~** air iteig (*dat
of* iteag *f*)
wink *n* **1** priobadh (na sùla) *m*; **2** *in expr* ~ **of
sleep** norrag chadail *f*, **I didn't get a ~ of
sleep** cha d' fhuair mi norrag chadail
wink *v* priob *vi*, (*less usu*) caog *vi*
winkle *n* faochag *f*
winner *n* buannaiche *m*
winter *n* geamhradh *m*
wintry *adj* geamhrachail
wipe *v* suath *vt*, siab *vt*
wiper *n* siabair *m*
wire *n* uèir *f*
wisdom *n* **1** gliocas *m*; **2** *in expr* ~ **tooth** fiacail-
forais *f*
wise *adj* glic
wish *n* **1** (*a ~ to achieve, acquire etc something,
an ambition*) miann *mf*, rùn *m*, togradh *m*, (*less
usu*) dèidh *f*; **2** (*~ directed towards others*)
guidhe *mf*, **a good/ill ~** deagh/droch ghuidhe,
(*a good ~, a greeting*) dùrachd *m*, (*corres etc*)
with best ~es leis gach deagh dhùrachd
wish *v* **1** (*desire something, ~ for something*)
miannaich *vt*, rùnaich *vt*; **2** (*~ that something
were the case*) is miann leis (*etc*), bu mhiann
leis (*etc*), **I ~ I could win a prize in the
lottery** bu mhiann leam gum faighinn duais sa
chrannchur; **3** (*often used as vi in rel fut tense*)
togair *vi*, **we'll go on holiday, if you ~** thèid

sinn air làithean-saora, ma thogras tu, **just as
you** ~ dìreach mar a thogras sibh; **4** (*directing a
good or bad ~ at someone*) guidh *vt* (*with preps
air & do*), **I ~ a curse on him** guidhidh mi
mallachd air, **~ing him a Happy Christmas**
a' guidhe Nollaig Chridheil dha, **I ~ you health
and happiness** (*trad*) guidheam (*pres imper*)
slàint' is sonas dhut
wishing well *n* tobar m(h)iann *mf*
wisp *n* (*esp of straw, hay*) sop *m*
wit *n* **1** (*witty humour*) eirmse *f*; **2** (*common
sense*) toinisg *f*, ciall *f*; **3** (*in pl: mind, sanity*) ~**s**
ciall *f*, rian *m*, reusan *m*, **he lost his ~s** chaill e
a chiall, **she was at her ~s' end** bha i gu bhith
às a ciall
witch *n* **1** bana-bhuidseach *f*; **2** *in expr* **old ~**
(*pej*) cailleach *f*
witchcraft *n* buidseachd *f*
with *prep* **1** (*accompanying, in the company of*)
còmhla ri, le (*takes the dat; before the art*, leis),
(*less usu, more trad*) cuide ri, mar ri, maille ri,
I went ~ the others chaidh mi ann còmhla ri
càch *pron*, **where's Eilidh? ~ the old folks**
càit a bheil Eilidh? còmhla ris na seann daoine,
~ **compliments** le deagh dhùrachd, *Note:
the use of* le/leis *for this sense of* with, *when
refering to people, is not always considered to
be good style*; **2** (*by means of*) le (*takes the dat:
before the art*, leis), **he hit it ~ a hammer/~
the hammer** bhuail e e le òrd/leis an òrd; **3**
(*expr direction, esp in the exprs*) (**going** *etc*)
~ **the slope/~ the current** (a' dol *etc*) leis a'
bhruthaich/leis an t-sruth; **4** (*as a consequence
of*) leis, **I can't see you ~ it being so dark**
chan fhaic mi thu leis cho dorch 's a tha e
withdraw *v* tarraing *vti* air ais, thoir *vt* air ais
withdrawn *adj* (*of persons*) fad' às, dùinte
wither *v* crìon *vti*, searg *vti*
withered *adj* & *past part* crìon, seargte
withhold *v* cùm *vt* air ais
without *prep* gun (*takes dat, lenites following
cons except for d, n & t*), ~ **peace/rest** gun
fhois, ~ **delay** gun dàil, **she bought it ~ my
knowledge/~ me knowing** cheannaich i e
gun fhios dhòmhsa
withstand *v* **1** (*resist*) seas *vi* (*with prep* ri); **2**
(*bear, put up with*) fuiling *vt*
witness *n* **1** (*abstr*) fianais *f*; **2** (*con: a ~ at scene
of crime, at trial etc*) neach-fianais *m* (*pl* luchd-
fianais *m sing coll*)
witness *v* **1** faic *vt*, bi *vi irreg* na (*etc*) f(h)ear-
fianais *m*; **2** (*legal: ~ a document etc*) dèan
fianais *f* (*with prep* do)
witty *adj* eirmseach

wizard n buidseach m, draoidh m

wizardry n draoidheachd f invar

wizened adj crìon

wobbly adj cugallach, **a ~ table** bòrd cugallach

woe n 1 (grief) bròn m, mulad f; 2 (grief & misfortune) dòlas m, truaighe f; 3 in excls ~ **is me!** an dòlas!, mo thruaighe!, mo sgrios!, ~ **to/~ betide** (trad) is mairg adj (with rel pron a), ~ **to/~ betide anyone who would come near him** (trad) is mairg a thigeadh faisg air

woeful adj brònach, muladach, truagh

wolf n madadh-allaidh m, (less usu) faol m

woman n boireannach m, tè f, (less usu) bean f, **women on the left, please!** boireannaich air an làimh chlì mas e ur toil e!, **the ~ who sang** am boireannach/an tè a sheinn, **the ~ of the house** bean an taighe, **an old ~** seann bhoireannach, (fam) cailleach f, (fam, of one's wife) **the/my old ~** (fam) a' chailleach

womanly adj banail

womb n machlag f, brù f, broinn f

wonder n iongnadh m, (stronger) iongantas m, mìorbhail f, **no ~ he's pleased!** chan iongnadh gu bheil e toilichte!

wonderful adj iongantach, mìorbhaileach

wood n 1 (the material: ~ in general, ~ not worked) fiodh m, **put ~ on the fire** cuir fiodh air an teine m; 2 (usu for shaped or worked ~) maide m; 3 (a group of trees) coille f, (small ~) doire mf

woodcock n coileach-coille m

woodcutter n coillear m, gearradair-fiodha m

wooden adj fiodha (gen sing of fiodh m), **a ~ house** taigh fiodha

wood-louse n reudan m

wool n clòimh f, olann f

woollen adj de chlòimh f

woolly adj 1 (lit) clòimheach, ollach; 2 (of unkempt human hair) (wild and) ~ molach, ròmach; 3 (fig, of thinking etc) ceòthach

word n 1 (written or spoken) facal m, **'eaglais' is a feminine ~** is e facal boireann a tha ann an 'eaglais', **she said a ~ or two/a few ~s in Gaelic** thubhairt i facal no dhà anns a' Ghàidhlig, **we didn't speak a ~ of Gaelic on the ferry** cha do bhruidhinn sinn facal Gàidhlig air a' bhàt'-aiseig, ~ **for ~** facal air an fhacal; 2 (esp in pl, statements, pronouncements etc) briathran (pl of briathar m), **foolish/sensible ~s** briathran amaideach/ciallach, **don't believe politicians' ~s** na creid briathran luchd-poilitigs; 3 (promise, ~ of honour) facal m, **will you give me your ~ (on it)?** an toir thu dhomh d' fhacal (air)?; 4 (information, news) fios m, guth m, sgeul m, **we sent him ~** chuir sinn fios thuige, **is there any ~ of Mary?** a bheil fios/sgeul air Màiri?, **I didn't hear a ~ about her** cha chuala mi guth mu deidhinn; 5 (esp in neg sentences: a sound, a syllable etc) bìd f, bìog f, smid f, **he didn't say a ~** cha tuirt e bìd/bìog/smid, **he didn't hear a ~** cha chuala e bìd/bìog; 6 in exprs (IT) ~ **processor** facladair m, ~ **processing** facladaireachd f invar

wordy adj faclach, briathrach

work n 1 (abstr & con) obair f, (usu more abstr) cosnadh m, **I've got ~ to do** tha obair agam ri dhèanamh

work v 1 (as vi) obraich vi, **the washer isn't ~ing** chan eil an t-inneal-nighe ag obrachadh, **we tried to play a trick on her but it didn't ~** dh'fheuch sinn car a chur aiste ach cha do dh'obraich e; 2 (as vt) obraich vt, ~ **a machine** obraich inneal, ~ **land/a croft** obraich fearann/croit, also àitich fearann/croit; 3 (to be at ~) bi vi irreg ag obair, **he's ~ing today** tha e ag obair an-diugh; 4 (to have ~) bi vi irreg obair f (with prep aig), **are you ~ing just now?** a bheil obair agad an-dràsta?

worker n 1 neach-obrach m, obraiche m, ~s luchd-obrach m sing coll

workforce n luchd-obrach m sing coll

workhorse n each-obrach m

working party n buidheann-obrach mf

workman n obraiche m, fear-obrach m

workshop n bùth-obrach mf

work station n (IT etc) ionad-obrach m

world n 1 (esp the ~ as man's abode, and as opposed to heaven) saoghal m; 2 (esp the ~ as the physical globe, the planet) cruinne mf (used with art: m in nom sing, f in gen sing), **the ~** an cruinne, **the end(s) of the ~** crìoch na cruinne, (sport) **the World Cup** Cuach na Cruinne; 3 (a particular sphere of activity) saoghal m, **the business ~/the ~ of business** saoghal a' ghnìomhachais; 4 in expr (emph) **where in the ~** càit air an t-saoghal, **where in the ~ are they going?** càit air an t-saoghal a bheil iad a' dol?

worldly adj 1 (as opposed to heavenly, spiritual etc) saoghalta, talmhaidh; 2 in exprs ~ **goods/wealth** maoin f, **my ~ possessions/goods** (trad) mo chuid den t-saoghal f

worm n boiteag f, cnuimh f

worn adj & past part 1 caithte; 2 (of clothing, fabrics: threadbare etc) lom, **a ~ coat** còta lom; 3 in expr ~ **out** (of objects) caithte, (of living creatures: exhausted etc) claoidhte

worried *adj* **1** fo chùram *m*, draghail, fo iomagain *f*, iomagaineach, (**about** mu), **she was** ~ bha i fo chùram/fo iomagain, *also* bha uallach *m* oirre; **2** (~ *in a nervy, niggly way*) frionasach

worry *n* dragh *m*, uallach *m*, **lack of money is causing me** ~ tha dìth airgid a' dèanamh dragh dhomh

worry *v* **1** (*as vi: be worried, begin to worry*) gabh dragh *m*, gabh uallach *m*, **don't** ~! na gabh dragh!, *also* (*more fam*) dad ort!, coma leat!, na gabh ort!; **2** (*as vt: cause worry*) cuir dragh *m* (*with prep* air), dèan dragh (*with prep* do), ~ **someone** cuir dragh air cuideigin, dèan dragh do chuideigin, **lack of money is ~ing me** tha dìth airgid a' dèanamh dragh dhomh; **3** *in expr* **it didn't ~ me in the least** cha do chuir e suas no sìos mi (*fam*)

worrying *adj* (*of person, situation*) draghail, iomagaineach, imcheisteach

worse *comp adj* **1** nas miosa, (*in past tense*) na bu mhiosa, **the father is wicked but the son is** ~ tha an t-athair olc ach tha am mac nas miosa, **get/become** ~ fàs *vi* nas miosa, *also* rach *vi irreg* am miosad *f*; **2** *in expr* **the ~ for** miste (*with v irreg & def* is), **I am the ~ for it** is miste mi e, **you'd be none the ~ for a dram** cha bu mhiste sibh drama

worship *n* adhradh *m*

worship *v* dèan/thoir adhradh *m* (*with prep* do)

worst *superlative adj* **1** as miosa, (*in past tense*) a bu mhiosa, **you were the** ~ is tusa a bu mhiosa, **the ~ man/one** am fear as miosa; **2** *in exprs* **the ~ of** diù *m invar* (*with gen*), **the ~ of jobs/professions** diù nan dreuchdan, **at** ~ aig a' char *m* as miosa, **we'll only spend four pounds at** ~ cha chosg sinn ach ceithir notaichean aig a' char as miosa

worth fiach *nm* (*with v* is), luach *m invar*, **one more time? it's not** ~ **it!** aon uair eile? chan fhiach e!, **a thing** ~ **seeing** rud as fhiach fhaicinn, **is this** ~ **anything to/for you? no!** an fhiach seo dhut? chan fhiach!, **for what it's** ~ airson na 's fhiach e, **it's not** ~ **our while/~ our effort** chan fhiach dhuinn ar saothair, **what's it** ~ dè a luach?, **it's not** ~ **10p** chan fhiach e deich sgillinn

worth *n* fiach *m*, **give me two pounds'** ~ **of it** thoir dhomh fiach dà nota dheth

worthless *adj* **1** (*without value*) gun fhiù *m invar*, gun luach *m invar*; **2** (*of no use*) gun fheum *m*

worthwhile *adj* fiach *adj*, with *v irreg & def* is (**to/for** do), **is it** ~ **for us?** an fhiach e dhuinn?, *also* an fhiach dhuinn ar saothair *f*?

worthy *adj* **1** airidh, toillteanach, (**of** air), ~ **of a kiss** airidh/toillteanach air pòg; **2** (*decent*) còir, **a ~ man** duine còir

wound *n* (*phys or emotional*) leòn *m*, (*less usu*) lot *m*, creuchd *f*

wound *v* (*phys or emotionally*) leòn *vt*, (*less usu*) lot *vt*, creuchd *vt*

wounded *adj* **1** leònta & leònte; **2** *in expr* **the** ~ na leòintich *mpl*

wounding *adj* (*remarks etc*) guineach, beumnach

woven *adj & past part* fighte

wrangle *n* conas *m*

wrangle *v* connsaich *vi*, connspaid *vi*

wrangling *n* connspaid *f*

wrangling *adj* connspaideach

wrap *v* **1** (*envelop etc*) suain *vt*; **2** ~ (**up**) (*parcel etc*) paisg *vt*, fill *vt*

wrapping *n* pasgadh *m*

wrath *n* fearg *f*

wrathful *adj* feargach

wreathe *v* toinn *vt*

wreck *n* (*of ship*) long-bhriseadh *m*

wreck *v* **1** sgrios *vt*, mill *vt*; **2** (*fig:* ~ *someone's plan etc*) mill *vt*

wren *n* dreathan-donn *m*

wrestle *v* gleac *vi* (**with, against** ri)

wretch *n* **1** (*poverty-stricken, unfortunate etc person*) truaghan *m*; **2** (*despicable etc person*) duine suarach, duine tàireil

wretched *adj* **1** (*pitiable*) truagh, ~ **poverty** bochdainn thruagh, *in expr* ~ **person/creature** truaghan *m*; **2** (*despicable etc*) suarach, tàireil

wring *v* fàisg *vt*

wrinkle *n* preas *m*, preasag *f*, (*less usu*) roc *f*

wrinkle *v* preas *vt*

wrinkled, wrinkly *adj* preasach

wrist *n* caol an dùirn *m*, **my** ~ caol mo dhùirn

writ *n* sgrìobhainn-cùirte *f*

write *v* **1** sgrìobh *vti* (**to** gu), **she wrote me a letter** sgrìobh i litir thugam, **he ~s poetry** bidh e a' sgrìobhadh bàrdachd; **2** *in expr* ~ **off debts** cuir fiachan às a' chunntas

writer *n* **1** sgrìobhadair *m*, sgrìobhaiche *m*; **2** *in expr* **writer-in-residence** filidh *m*

writing *n* sgrìobhadh *m*, (*hand~*) làmh-sgrìobhadh *m*

wrong *adj* **1** (*of statements, opinions etc: incorrect, inappropriate*) ceàrr, mearachdach, iomrallach, **a ~ answer** freagairt cheàrr, **you are ~!** tha thu ceàrr!, **the ~ train** an trèana cheàrr, **far ~** fada ceàrr; **2** (*morally ~*) eucorach, (*stronger*) olc, ~ **actions** gnìomhan eucorach

wrong *adv* **1** (*not as it should be, awry*) ceàrr, tuathal, (**with** air), **there's something** ~ **with my back/my radio** tha rudeigin ceàrr air mo dhruim/air an rèidio agam; **2** *in expr* **what's** ~ **with you**? dè a tha a' gabhail riut?, dè a tha thu a' gearan?; **3** *in expr* **go** ~ (*ie make a mistake*) rach *vi* air iomrall *m*; **4** *in expr* **go** ~ (*morally*) rach *vi* air iomrall *m*, rach *vi* air seachran *m*

wrong *n* eucoir *f*, coire *f*

wrong *v* dèan eucoir *f* (*with prep* air), **they** ~**ed me** rinn iad eucoir orm

wrongful *adj* eucorach

wynd *n* caol-shràid *f*

X

xenophobia *n* gall-ghamhlas *m*

Xmas *n* (*usu used with definite art*) An Nollaig *f*, ~ **time** àm na Nollaig(e)

x-ray *n* x-ghath *m*, gath-x *m*, ~ **therapy** leigheas x-ghath

xylophone *n* saidhleafòn *m*

Y

yacht *n* sgoth-long *f*, (*less trad*) gheat *f*

yard¹ *n* 1 (*enclosed space*) cùirt *f*; 2 (*school play area etc*) raon-cluiche *m*; 3 (*agric: for corn, straw etc*) iodhlann *f*

yard² *n* (*unit of measurement*) slat *f*

yardstick *n* (*lit & fig: ie criterion etc*) slat-thomhais *f*

yawl *n* geòla *f*

yawn *n* mèaran & mèanan *m*

yawn *v* dèan mèaranaich/mèananaich *f*, you're ~ing a lot today! 's ann ort a tha a' mhèaranaich an-diugh!

yawning *n* mèaranaich & mèananaich *f*

year *n* bliadhna *f*, four ~s old ceithir bliadhna a dh'aois, (*advs*) this ~ am-bliadhna, next ~ an ath-bhliadhna, last ~ an-uiridh, the ~ before last a' bhòn-uiridh

yearling *adj* bliadhnach

yearling *n* bliadhnach *m*

yearly *adj* bliadhnail

yearning *n* fadachd *f invar*, fadal *m*, (for ri)

yeast *n* beirm *f*

yell *n* sgairt *f*, glaodh *m*, ràn *m*, (*esp shrill & sudden*) sgal *m*, sgiamh *m*

yell *v* dèan sgairt *f*, glaodh *vi*, ràn *vi*, (*esp shrilly & suddenly*) sgal *vi*, sgiamh *vi*

yelling *n* sgreuchail *f invar*, rànail *m invar*, rànaich *f invar*, sgaladh *m*

yellow *adj* buidhe, the Yellow Pages Na Duilleagan Buidhe *fpl*

yes *adv* 1 (*as affirmative response*) *rendered by repetition of the main verb used in the question*, are you tired? ~ a bheil thu sgìth? tha, did you believe it? ~ an do chreid thu e? chreid, will you go? ~ an tèid thu ann? thèid, did you see him? ~ am faca tu e? chunnaic; 2 (*as a non-affirmative response to a statement, or on being addressed etc*) seadh *adv* (*v irreg & def* is, *plus obs neuter pron* eadh), Iain! ~? Iain! Seadh?, I saw Màiri yesterday. ~? Chunna mi Màiri an-dè. Seadh?

yesterday *adv* an-dè

yet *adv* 1 fhathast, the rain hasn't stopped ~ cha do sguir an t-uisge fhathast, is breakfast ready? not ~ a bheil a' bhracaist deiseil? chan eil fhathast, we'll get the better of it/crack it ~ nì sinn a' chùis air fhathast; 2 *in expr* the bus (*etc*) hasn't come (*etc*) ~ tha am bus (*etc*) gun tighinn (*etc*) fhathast

yet *conj* ge-tà, air a shon sin, ach, they got engaged, ~ they didn't get married thug iad gealladh-pòsaidh dha chèile; cha do phòs iad, ge-tà/cha do phòs iad air a shon sin/ach cha do phòs iad

yew *n* (*wood & tree*) iubhar *m*, (*tree*) craobh-iubhair *f*

yield *n* (*of crops, investment etc*) toradh *m*

yield *v* 1 (*submit*) gèill *vi*, strìochd *vi*, (to do); 2 (*as vt*) thoir *vt* suas (to do), he ~ed his power thug e suas a chumhachd *mf invar*; 3 (*give, provide*) thoir *vt* seachad, this investment ~s five per cent bidh an tasgadh seo a' toirt seachad còig sa cheud, *also* 's e toradh *m* an tasgaidh seo còig sa cheud

yielding *adj* (*of ground etc, soft*) bog, tais; (*of person, character*) sochar, meata

yielding *n* gèilleadh *m*, strìochdadh *m*

yobbish *adj* gràisgeil

yobbishness *n* gràisgealachd *f invar*

yoke *n* cuing *f*, (*also fig*) beneath the tyrant's ~ fo chuing an aintighearna

yolk *n* buidheagan *m*

yon, yonder (*Sc*) *adj* ud, ann an siud, ~ house an taigh ud, an taigh ann an siud

yonder *adv* 1 an siud, ann an siud; 2 *in expr* over ~ thall, thall an siud, over ~ in America ann an Ameireagaidh thall, thall an Ameireagaidh, it's raining over ~ tha e a' sileadh thall an siud

you *pers pron* (*sing fam*) thu, (*pl & formal sing*) sibh, (*emph*) thusa, sibhse & thu fhèin, sibh fhèin, I'm well, how are ~? tha mi gu math, ciamar a tha thu fhèin/sibh fhèin?, good for ~! 's math thu fhèin!, (*Note Gaelic constr with poss adj & verbal noun eg*) **it's good to see** ~ is math d' fhaicinn/ur faicinn

young *adj* 1 òg, **a** ~ **girl** caileag òg, **a** ~ **man** duine òg (*also* gille *m*, òganach *m*), ~ **people/ folk** daoine òga, *also* òigridh *f sing coll invar*; 2 *in exprs* **my** ~ **days** làithean m' òige, ~ **love** gaol na h-òige

young *n* 1 (~ *of animals, birds*) àl *m*; 2 *in expr* **the** ~ (*ie young people*) na daoine òga

youngster *n* (*male*) òganach *m*, (*of either sex*) òigear *m*, ~**s** òigridh *f sing coll invar*

your *poss adj* 1 (*sing, fam*) do (*lenites following cons where possible*), (*pl & formal sing*) ur, bhur, ~ **parents** do phàrantan *or* ur pàrantan, **get** ~ **breath back!** leig d' anail! *or* leigibh ur n-anail; 2 *also expressed by prep prons* agad (*sing, fam*) & agaibh (*pl & formal sing*), *appended to the noun*, ~ **house** an taigh agad/ agaibh; *Note that as a general rule the poss*

adjs mo, do, *etc tend to be used in preference to* agam, agad *etc where the connection with the object concerned is more intimate*

yours *poss pron* 1 (*sing, fam*) leat(sa), (*pl & formal sing*) leibh(se), **is it** ~**?** an ann leatsa/ leibhse a tha e?; 2 (*in corres*) ~**s sincerely** le dùrachd, is mise le meas

yourself, yourselves *reflexive pron* (*sing, fam*) thu fhèin, (*pl & formal sing*) sibh fhèin, **take care of** ~ thoir an aire ort fhèin, thoiribh an aire oirbh fhèin; *for further examples cf* **myself**, & **-self** *reflexive suffix*

youth *n* (*abstr*) 1 òige *f invar*, **the days of my** ~ làithean m' òige; 2 (*young male person*) **a** ~ òigear *m*, òganach *m*, gille *m*; 3 (*coll: young people*) òigridh *f sing coll invar*, **the** ~ **of today/today's** ~ òigridh an là an-diugh, **a** ~ **club/group** buidheann òigridh

Z

zeal *n* dìoghras *m*, dealas *m*, eud *m invar*
zealous *adj* dealasach, dùrachdach, dìcheallach
zero *n* neoni *f invar*
zestful *adj* brìoghmhor

zinc *n* sinc *m*
zone *n* sòn *m*, **war** ~ sòn cogaidh, **tropical** ~ sòn tropaigeach
zoo *n* sutha *mf*

The Forms of the Gaelic Article

		Singular		Plural
		Masculine	**Feminine**	**Both Genders**
Nom & Acc		**an** (*before consonants, exc b,f, m, p*) **am** (*before b, f, m, p*) **an t-** (*before a vowel*)	**a'** (*before b, c, g, m, pl, which are lenited*) **an t-** (*before s followed by l, n, or r, or by a vowel*) **an** (*before all other letters; f is lenited*)	**na** **na h-** (*before a vowel*)
e.g.		**an** taigh, **an** sìol, **an** sruth **am** bodach, **am** fraoch, **am** mol **an t-**eilean	**a'** chraobh, **a'** ghaoth, **a'** phìob **an t-**side, **an t-**sròn **an** ite, **an** fhras	**na** caileagan, **na** rudan **na h-**òrain, **na h-**uairean
Gen		**a'** (*before b, c, g, m, p, which are lenited*) **an t-** (*before s followed by l, n, r or by a vowel*) **an** (*before all other letters; f is lenited*)	**na** (**na h-** *before a vowel*)	**nan** (**nam** *before b, f, m, p*)
e.g.		**a'** bhodaich, **a'** ghliocais, **a'** mhadaidh **an t-**sìl, **an t-**sruith **an** eilein, **an** taighe, **an** fhraoich	**na** gaoithe, **na** craoibhe, **na** sròine **na h-**ite	**nan** taighean, **nan** òran **nam** bodach, **nam** figean
Dat		**a'** (*before b, c, g, m, p, which are all lenited*) **an t-** (*before s followed by l, n, r or by a vowel*) **an** (*before all other letters; f is lenited*)	**a'** (*before b, c, g, m, p, which are lenited*) **an t-** (*before s followed by l, n, r, or by a vowel*) **an** (*before all other letters; f is lenited*)	**na** (**na h-** *before a vowel*)
e.g.		**a'** bhodach, **a'** chù, **a'** gheall **an t-**sìol, **an t-**sruth, **an t-**salann **an** eilean, **an** taigh, **an** fhraoch	**a'** ghaoith, **a'** chraoibh **an t-**sùil, **an t-**slait, **an t-**sròin **an** tràigh, **an** fhàire	**na** caileagan, **na h-**òrain

Note: In the Dative Singular, for both genders, after a preposition ending in a vowel the article is shortened to 'n or 'n t-, and combined with the preposition. E.g. don bhùth, on taigh, bhon t-sìol, tron choille, fon t-sruth, mun bhòrd.

The More Common Forms of the Gaelic Irregular and Defective Verbs

ABAIR

abair say (*pres part* **ag ràdh** saying, *infin* **a ràdh** to say)

Important Note: It is very common for the forms of this verb, except for the Past (Preterite), to be supplied by the defective verb **can** (see p495, 496 below).

IMPERATIVE

abram let me say

na h-abram let me not say

abair (*sing*) say

na h-abair (*sing*) don't say

abradh e/i let him/her say

na h-abradh e/i let him/her not say

abramaid let us say

na h-abramaid let us not say

abraibh (*pl*) say

na h-abraibh (*pl*) don't say

abradh iad let them say

na h-abradh iad let them not say

FUTURE (AND HABITUAL PRESENT)

their mi I will say, I say

chan abair mi I won't say, I don't say

an abair mi? will I say? do I say?

nach abair mi? won't I say? don't I say?

RELATIVE FUTURE

dè a their mi? what will I say?

PAST (PRETERITE)

thuirt mi I said

cha tuirt mi I didn't say

an tuirt mi did I say?

nach tuirt mi? didn't I say?

Note: **thuirt** also occurs as **thubhairt** (for emphasis); **tuirt** occurs as **tubhairt**

PERFECT AND PLUPERFECT

tha mi air ràdh I have said

bha mi air ràdh I had said

tha mi air a ràdh I have said it
 (*m or f*)

bha mi air a ràdh I had said it
 (*m or f*)

Note: In the Future, Relative Future, Past, Perfect and Pluperfect tenses, the same forms of the verb are used for all persons.

CONDITIONAL

theirinn I would say	**chan abrainn** I wouldn't say
theireadh* tu you would say	**chan abradh* tu** you wouldn't say
theireamaid we would say	**chan abramaid** we wouldn't say
an abrainn? would I say?	**nach abrainn?** wouldn't I say?
an abradh* tu? would you say?	**nach abradh* tu?** wouldn't you say?
an abramaid? would we say?	**nach abramaid?** wouldn't we say?

The forms marked * are used for all persons except the first singular, I. The forms in -**maid** are alternative forms for the first person plural, we.

BEIR

beir bear, catch (*pres part* **a' breith** bearing/catching, *infin* **a bhreith** to bear/catch)

IMPERATIVE

beiream let me bear	**na beiream** let me not bear
beir (*sing*) bear	**na beir** (*sing*) don't bear
beireadh e/i let him/her bear	**na beireadh e/i** let him/her not bear
beireamaid let us bear	**na beireamaid** let us not bear
beiribh (*pl*) bear	**na beiribh** (*pl*) don't bear
beireadh iad let them bear	**na beireadh iad** let them not bear

FUTURE (AND HABITUAL PRESENT)

beiridh mi I will bear, I bear	**cha bheir mi** I won't bear, I don't bear
am beir mi? will I bear? do I bear?	**nach beir mi?** won't I bear? don't I bear?

RELATIVE FUTURE

dè a bheir/bheireas mi? what will I bear?

PAST (PRETERITE)

rug mi I bore	**cha do rug mi** I didn't bear
an do rug mi did I bear?	**nach do rug mi?** didn't I bear?

PERFECT AND PLUPERFECT

tha mi air breith I have borne	**bha mi air breith** I had borne
tha mi air a bhreith I have borne it (*m*)	**bha mi air a bhreith** I had borne it (*m*)

CONDITIONAL

bheirinn I would bear

cha bheirinn I wouldn't bear

bheireadh* tu you would bear

cha bheireadh* tu you wouldn't bear

bheireamaid we would bear

cha bheireamaid we wouldn't bear

am beirinn? would I bear?

nach beirinn? wouldn't I bear?

am beireadh* tu? would you bear?

nach beireadh* tu? wouldn't you bear?

am beireamaid? would we bear?

nach beireamaid? wouldn't we bear?

The forms marked * are used for all persons except the first singular, I. The forms in -**maid** are alternative forms for the first person plural, we.

PAST PASSIVE

rugadh e he was born

cha do rugadh e he wasn't born

an do rugadh e? was he born?

nach do rugadh e? wasn't he born?

Note: In the Future, Relative Future, Past, Perfect, Pluperfect and Past Passive, the same forms of the verb are used for all persons.

CAN

can say (*pres part* **a' cantainn** saying, *infin* **a chantainn** to say)
Note: The following forms of this defective verb are very commonly used instead of the corresponding forms of **abair** (see p493, 494).

IMPERATIVE

canam let me say

na canam let me not say

can (*sing*) say

na can (*sing*) don't say

canadh e/i let him/her say

na canadh e/i let him/her not say

canamaid let us say

na canamaid let us not say

canaibh (*pl*) say

na canaibh (*pl*) don't say

canadh iad let them say

na canadh iad let them not say

FUTURE AND HABITUAL PRESENT

canaidh mi I will say, I say

cha chan mi I won't say, I don't say

an can mi? will I say? do I say?

nach can mi? won't I say? don't I say?

RELATIVE FUTURE

dè a chanas mi? what will I say?

PERFECT AND PLUPERFECT

tha mi air cantainn I have said

tha mi air a chantainn I have said it (*m*)

bha mi air cantainn I had said

bha mi air a chantainn I had said it (*m*)

Note: In the Future, Relative Future, Perfect and Pluperfect, the same forms of the verb are used for all persons.

CONDITIONAL

chanainn I would say

chanadh* tu you would say

chanamaid we would say

an canainn? would I say?

an canadh* tu? would you say?

an canamaid? would we say?

cha chanainn I wouldn't say

cha chanadh* tu you wouldn't say

cha chanamaid we wouldn't say

nach canainn? wouldn't I say?

nach canadh* tu? wouldn't you say?

nach canamaid? wouldn't we say?

The forms marked * are used for all persons except the first singular, I. The forms in -**maid** are alternative forms for the first person plural, we.

CLUINN

cluinn hear (*pres part* **a' cluinntinn** hearing, *infin* **a chluinntinn** to hear)

IMPERATIVE

cluinneam let me hear

cluinn (*sing*) hear

cluinneadh e/i let him/her hear

cluinneamaid let us hear

cluinnibh (*pl*) hear

cluinneadh iad let them hear

na cluinneam let me not hear

na cluinn (*sing*) don't hear

na cluinneadh e/i let him/her not hear

na cluinneamaid let us not hear

na cluinnibh (*pl*) don't hear

na cluinneadh iad let them not hear

FUTURE AND HABITUAL PRESENT

cluinnidh mi I will hear, I hear

an cluinn mi? will I hear? do I hear?

cha chluinn mi I won't hear, I don't hear

nach cluinn mi? won't I hear? don't I hear?

RELATIVE FUTURE

dè a chluinneas mi? what will I hear?

PAST (PRETERITE)

chuala mi I heard

an cuala mi? did I hear?

cha chuala mi I didn't hear

nach cuala mi? didn't I hear?

PERFECT AND PLUPERFECT

tha mi air cluinntinn
I have heard

tha mi air a chluinntinn (*m*)
I have heard it (*m*)

bha mi air cluinntinn
I had heard

bha mi air a chluinntinn
I had heard it (*m*)

Note: In the Future, Relative Future, Past, Perfect and Pluperfect, the same forms of the verb are used for all persons.

CONDITIONAL

chluinninn I would hear

chluinneadh* tu you would hear

chluinneamaid we would hear

an cluinninn? would I hear?

an cluinneadh* tu? would you hear?

an cluinneamaid? would we hear?

cha chluinninn I wouldn't hear

cha chluinneadh* tu you wouldn't hear

cha chluinneamaid we wouldn't hear

nach cluinninn? wouldn't I hear?

nach cluinneadh* tu? wouldn't you hear?

nach cluinneamaid? wouldn't we hear?

The forms marked * are used for all persons except the first singular, I. The forms in -**maid** are alternative forms for the first person plural, we.

DEAN

dèan do/make (*pres part* **a' dèanamh** doing/making, *infin* **a dhèanamh** to do/make)

IMPERATIVE

dèanam let me do

dèan (*sing*) do

dèanadh e/i let him/her do

dèanamaid let us do

dèanaibh (*pl*) do

dèanadh iad let them do

na dèanam let me not do

na dèan (*sing*) don't do

na dèanadh e/i let him/her not do

na dèanamaid let us not do

na dèanaibh (*pl*) don't do

na dèanadh iad let them not do

FUTURE AND HABITUAL PRESENT

nì mi I will do, I do

an dèan mi? will I do? do I do?

cha dèan mi I won't do, I don't do

nach dèan mi? won't I do? don't I do?

RELATIVE FUTURE
dè a nì mi? what will I do?

PAST (PRETERITE)

rinn mi I did

an do rinn mi? did I do?

cha do rinn mi I didn't do

nach do rinn mi? didn't I do?

PERFECT AND PLUPERFECT

tha mi air dèanamh I have done

tha mi air a dhèanamh

I have done it (*m*)

bha mi air dèanamh I had done

bha mi air a dhèanamh

I had done it (*m*)

Note: In the Future, Relative Future, Past, Perfect and Pluperfect, the same forms of the verb are used for all persons.

CONDITIONAL

dhèanainn I would do

dhèanadh* tu you would do

dhèanamaid we would do

an dèanainn? would I do?

an dèanadh* tu? would you do?

an dèanamaid? would we do?

cha dèanainn I wouldn't do

cha dèanadh* tu you wouldn't do

cha dèanamaid we wouldn't do

nach dèanainn? wouldn't I do?

nach dèanadh* tu? wouldn't you do?

nach dèanamaid? wouldn't we do?

The forms marked * are used for all persons except the first singular, I. The forms in -**maid** are alternative forms for the first person plural, we.

FAIC

faic see (*pres part* **a' faicinn** seeing, *infin* **a dh'fhaicinn** to see)

IMPERATIVE

faiceam let me see

faic (*sing*) see

faiceadh e/i let him/her see

faiceamaid let us see

faicibh (*pl*) see

faiceadh iad let them see

na faiceam let me not see

na faic (*sing*) don't see

na faiceadh e/i let him/her not see

na faiceamaid let us not see

na faicibh (*pl*) don't see

na faiceadh iad let them not see

FUTURE AND HABITUAL PRESENT

chì mi I will see, I see

am faic mi? will I see? do I see?

chan fhaic mi I won't see, I don't see

nach f(h)aic mi? won't I see? don't I see?

RELATIVE FUTURE

dè a chì mi? what will I see?

PAST (PRETERITE)

chunnaic/chunna mi I saw

am faca mi? did I see?

chan fhaca mi I didn't see

nach f(h)aca mi? didn't I see?

PERFECT AND PLUPERFECT

tha mi air faicinn I have seen

tha mi air fhaicinn I have seen it (*m*)

bha mi air faicinn I had seen

bha mi air fhaicinn I had seen it (*m*)

Note: In the Future, Relative Future, Past, Perfect and Pluperfect, the same forms of the verb are used for all persons.

CONDITIONAL

chithinn I would see

chitheadh* tu you would see

chitheamaid we would see

am faicinn? would I see?

am faiceadh* tu? would you see?

am faiceamaid? would we see?

chan fhaicinn I wouldn't see

chan fhaiceadh* tu you wouldn't see

chan fhaiceamaid we wouldn't see

nach f(h)aicinn? wouldn't I see?

nach f(h)aiceadh* tu? wouldn't you see?

nach f(h)aiceamaid? wouldn't we see?

The forms marked * are used for all persons except the first singular, I. The forms in -**maid** are alternative forms for the first person plural, we.

FAIGH

faigh get (*pres part* **a' faighinn** getting, *infin* **a dh'fhaighinn** to get)

IMPERATIVE

faigheam let me get   **na faigheam** let me not get

faigh (*sing*) get   **na faigh** (*sing*) don't get

faigheadh e/i let him/her get   **na faigheadh e/i** let him/her not get

faigheamaid let us get   **na faigheamaid** let us not get

faighibh (*pl*) get   **na faighibh** (*pl*) don't get

faigheadh iad let them get   **na faigheadh iad** let them not get

FUTURE AND HABITUAL PRESENT

gheibh mi I will get, I get   **chan fhaigh mi** I won't get, I don't get

am faigh mi? will I get? do I get?   **nach f(h)aigh mi?** won't I get? don't I get?

RELATIVE FUTURE

dè a gheibh mi? what will I get?

PAST (PRETERITE)

fhuair mi I got   **cha d' fhuair mi** I didn't get

an d' fhuair mi? did I get?   **nach d' fhuair mi?** didn't I get?

PERFECT AND PLUPERFECT

tha mi air faighinn I have got   **bha mi air faighinn** I had got

tha mi air fhaighinn I have got it (*m*)   **bha mi air fhaighinn** I had got it (*m*)

Note: In the Future, Relative Future, Past, Perfect and Pluperfect, the same forms of the verb are used for all persons.

CONDITIONAL

gheibhinn I would get   **chan fhaighinn** I wouldn't get

gheibheadh* tu you would get   **chan fhaigheadh* tu** you wouldn't get

gheibheamaid we would get   **chan fhaigheamaid** we wouldn't get

am faighinn? would I get?   **nach f(h)aighinn?** wouldn't I get?

am faigheadh* tu? would you get?   **nach f(h)aigheadh* tu?** wouldn't you get?

am faigheamaid? would we get?   **nach f(h)aigheamaid?** wouldn't we get?

The forms marked * are used for all persons except the first singular, I. The forms in -**maid** are alternative forms for the first person plural, we.

RACH

rach go (*pres part* **a' dol** going, *infin* **a dhol** to go)

IMPERATIVE

racham let me go	**na racham** let me not go
rach (*sing*) go	**na rach** (*sing*) don't go
rachadh e/i let him/her go	**na rachadh e/i** let him/her not go
rachamaid let us go	**na rachamaid** let us not go
rachaibh (*pl*) go	**na rachaibh** (*pl*) don't go
rachadh iad let them go	**na rachadh iad** let them not go

FUTURE AND HABITUAL PRESENT

thèid mi I will go, I go	**cha tèid mi** I won't go, I don't go
an tèid mi? will I go? do I go?	**nach tèid mi?** won't I go? don't I go?

RELATIVE FUTURE

cuin a thèid mi? when will I go?

PAST (PRETERITE)

chaidh mi I went	**cha deach(aidh) mi** I didn't go
an deach(aidh) mi? did I go?	**nach deach(aidh) mi?** didn't I go?

PERFECT AND PLUPERFECT

tha mi air dol/air a dhol, bha mi air dol/air a dhol I have gone, I had gone

Note: In the Future, Relative Future, Past, Perfect and Pluperfect, the same forms of the verb are used for all persons.

CONDITIONAL

rachainn I would go	**cha rachainn** I wouldn't go
rachadh* tu you would go	**cha rachadh* tu** you wouldn't go
rachamaid we would go	**cha rachamaid** we wouldn't go
an rachainn? would I go?	**nach rachainn?** wouldn't I go?
an rachadh* tu? would you go?	**nach rachadh* tu?** wouldn't you go?
an rachamaid? would we go?	**nach rachamaid?** wouldn't we go?

The forms marked * are used for all persons except the first singular, I. The forms in -**maid** are alternative forms for the first person plural, we.

RUIG

ruig *as vi* arrive, *as vt* reach (*pres part* **a' ruigsinn** arriving *etc*, *infin*
a ruigsinn to arrive *etc*)

IMPERATIVE

ruigeam let me arrive	**na ruigeam** let me not arrive
ruig (*sing*) arrive	**na ruig** (*sing*) don't arrive
ruigeadh e/i let him/her arrive	**na ruigeadh e/i** let him/her not arrive
ruigeamaid let us arrive	**na ruigeamaid** let us not arrive
ruigibh (*pl*) arrive	**na ruigibh** (*pl*) don't arrive
ruigeadh iad let them arrive	**na ruigeadh iad** let them not arrive

FUTURE AND HABITUAL PRESENT

ruigidh mi I will arrive, I arrive	**cha ruig mi** I won't arrive, I don't arrive
an ruig mi? will I arrive? do I arrive?	**nach ruig mi?** won't I arrive? don't I arrive?

RELATIVE FUTURE

cuin a ruigeas mi? when will I arrive?

PAST (PRETERITE)

ràinig mi I arrived	**cha do ràinig mi** I didn't arrive
an do ràinig mi? did I arrive?	**nach do ràinig mi?** didn't I arrive?

PERFECT AND PLUPERFECT

tha mi air ruigsinn I have arrived	**bha mi air ruigsinn** I had arrived
tha mi air a ruigsinn I have reached it (*m or f*)	**bha mi air a ruigsinn** I had reached it (*m or f*)

Note: In the Future, Relative Future, Past, Perfect and Pluperfect, the same
forms of the verb are used for all persons.

CONDITIONAL

ruiginn I would arrive	**cha ruiginn** I wouldn't arrive
ruigeadh* tu you would arrive	**cha ruigeadh* tu** you wouldn't arrive
ruigeamaid we would arrive	**cha ruigeamaid** we wouldn't arrive
an ruiginn? would I arrive?	**nach ruiginn?** wouldn't I arrive?
an ruigeadh* tu? would you arrive?	**nach ruigeadh* tu?** wouldn't you arrive?
an ruigeamaid? would we arrive?	**nach ruigeamaid?** wouldn't we arrive?

The forms marked * are used for all persons except the first singular, I. The
forms in -**maid** are alternative forms for the first person plural, we.

THIG

thig come (*pres part* **a' tighinn** coming, *infin* **a thighinn** to come)

IMPERATIVE

thigeam let me come	**na tigeam** let me not come
thig (*sing*) come	**na tig** (*sing*) don't come
thigeadh e/i let him/her come	**na tigeadh e/i** let him/her not come
thigeamaid let us come	**na tigeamaid** let us not come
thigibh (*pl*) come	**na tigibh** (*pl*) don't come
thigeadh iad let them come	**na tigeadh iad** let them not come

FUTURE AND HABITUAL PRESENT

thig mi I will come, I come	**cha tig mi** I won't come, I don't come
an tig mi? will I come? do I come?	**nach tig mi?** won't I come? don't I come?

RELATIVE FUTURE

cuin a thig mi? when will I come?

PAST (PRETERITE)

thàinig mi I came	**cha tàinig mi** I didn't come
an tàinig mi? did I come?	**nach tàinig mi?** didn't I come?

PERFECT AND PLUPERFECT

tha mi air tighinn/a thighinn, bha mi air tighinn/a thighinn I have come, I had come

Note: In the Future, Relative Future, Past, Perfect and Pluperfect, the same forms of the verb are used for all persons.

CONDITIONAL

thiginn I would come	**cha tiginn** I wouldn't come
thigeadh* tu you would come	**cha tigeadh* tu** you wouldn't come
thigeamaid we would come	**cha tigeamaid** we wouldn't come
an tiginn? would I come?	**nach tiginn?** wouldn't I come?
an tigeadh* tu? would you come?	**nach tigeadh* tu?** wouldn't you come?
an tigeamaid? would we come?	**nach tigeamaid?** wouldn't we come?

The forms marked * are used for all persons except the first singular, I. The forms in -**maid** are alternative forms for the first person plural, we.

THOIR

thoir give/take/bring (*pres part* **a' toirt** giving *etc*, *infin* **a thoirt** to give *etc*)

IMPERATIVE

thoiream let me give	**na toiream** let me not give
thoir (*sing*) give	**na toir** (*sing*) don't give
thoireadh e/i let him/her give	**na toireadh e/i** let him/her not give
thoireamaid let us give	**na toireamaid** let us not give
thoiribh (*pl*) give	**na toiribh** (*pl*) don't give
thoireadh iad let them give	**na toireadh iad** let them not give

Note: In the first person sing and pl imperative **t(h)ugam** and **t(h)ugamaid** are also found, and in the third person sing and pl **t(h)ugadh**.

FUTURE AND HABITUAL PRESENT

bheir mi I will give, I give	**cha toir mi** I won't give, I don't give
an toir mi? will I give? do I give?	**nach toir mi?** won't I give? don't I give?

RELATIVE FUTURE

dè a bheir mi? what will I give?

PAST (PRETERITE)

thug mi I gave	**cha tug mi** I didn't give
an tug mi? did I give?	**nach tug mi?** didn't I give?

PERFECT AND PLUPERFECT

tha mi air toirt I have given	**bha mi air toirt** I had given
tha mi air a thoirt I have given it (*m*)	**bha mi air a thoirt** I had given it (*m*)

Note: In the Future, Relative Future, Past, Perfect and Pluperfect, the same forms of the verb are used for all persons.

CONDITIONAL

bheirinn I would give	**cha toirinn** I wouldn't give
bheireadh* tu you would give	**cha toireadh* tu** you wouldn't give
bheireamaid we would give	**cha toireamaid** we wouldn't give
an toirinn? would I give?	**nach toirinn?** wouldn't I give?
an toireadh* tu? would you give?	**nach toireadh* tu?** wouldn't you give?
an toireamaid? would we give?	**nach toireamaid?** wouldn't we give?

The forms marked * are used for all persons except the first singular, I. The forms in -**maid** are alternative forms for the first person plural, we.

Note: **toir**, **thoir** and **toirt** are occasionally found as **tabhair**, **thabhair** and **tabhairt**

BI

bi be (*infin* **a bhith** to be)

IMPERATIVE

bitheam let me be	**na bitheam** let me not be
bi (*sing*) be	**na bi** (*sing*) don't be
biodh/bitheadh e/i let him/her be	**na biodh/bitheadh e/i** let him/her not be
biomaid/bitheamaid let us be	**na biomaid/bitheamaid** let us not be
bithibh (*pl*) be	**na bithibh** (*pl*) don't be
biodh, bitheadh iad let them be	**na biodh, bitheadh iad** let them not be

PRESENT

tha mi I am	**chan eil mi** I am not
a bheil mi? am I?	**nach eil mi** am I not?

FUTURE AND HABITUAL PRESENT

bidh/bithidh mi I will be, I am	**cha bhi mi** I won't be, I'm not
am bi mi? will I be? am I?	**nach bi mi?** won't I be? am I not?

RELATIVE FUTURE

ma bhios, ma bhitheas mi if I will be, if I am

PAST (PRETERITE)

bha mi I was	**cha robh mi** I wasn't
an robh mi? was I?	**nach robh mi?** wasn't I?

PERFECT AND PLUPERFECT

tha mi air a bhith I have been	**bha mi air a bhith** I had been

Note: In the Future, Relative Future, Past, Perfect, and Pluperfect, the same forms of the verb are used for all persons.

CONDITIONAL

bhithinn I would be

bhiodh*/bhitheadh tu you would be

bhiomaid/bhitheamaid we would be

am bithinn? would I be?

am biodh*/bitheadh tu? would you be?

am biomaid/bitheamaid? would we be?

cha bhithinn I wouldn't be

cha bhiodh*/bhitheadh tu you wouldn't be

cha bhiomaid/bhitheamaid we wouldn't be

nach bithinn? wouldn't I be?

nach biodh*/bitheadh tu? wouldn't you be?

nach biomaid/bitheamaid? wouldn't we be?

The forms marked * are used for all persons except the first singular, I. The forms in -**maid** are alternative forms for the first person plural, we. *See also following page.*

Constructions Using Bi As an Auxiliary Verb

PRESENT AND PAST CONTINUOUS (ACTIVE, REFLEXIVE AND PASSIVE)

tha/bha e a' bualadh he is/was striking

tha/bha e gam bualadh he is/was striking them

tha/bha e ga bhualadh fhèin he is/was striking himself

tha/bha e ga bhualadh he is/was being struck (*also* he is/was striking him *or* it *m*)

PERFECT TENSES (PRESENT, PLUPERFECT, FUTURE AND CONDITIONAL), ACTIVE AND PASSIVE

tha/bha e air bualadh he has/had struck

tha/bha e air am bualadh he has/had struck them

tha/bha e air a bhualadh he has/had been struck (*also* he has/had struck him *or* it *m*)

bidh e air bualadh he will have struck

bidh e air am bualadh he will have struck them

bidh e air a bhualadh he will have been struck (*also* he will have struck him *or* it *m*)

bhiodh e air bualadh he would have struck

bhiodh e air am bualadh he would have struck them

bhiodh e air a bhualadh he would have been struck (*also* he would have struck him *or* it *m*)

IMPERSONAL PASSIVE

thathar ag ràdh it is said *and* it is being said

bhathar ag ràdh it was said *and* it was being said

bithear ag ràdh it is said *and* it will be said

bhite/bhithist ag ràdh it would be said *and* it used to be said

The Gaelic Prepositional Pronouns

Below are given the principal Gaelic pronouns, followed by the forms of the prepositional pronouns to which they give rise. These are formed by combining a given preposition with each of the personal pronouns (*eg* **aig** combined with **mi** gives **agam**, **ri** combined with **sinn** gives **rinn**). The emphatic/reflexive particles -**sa**, -**se** *etc* (*as in* **agadsa** 'at yourself' *or* **dhìse** 'to *or* for herself') are shown in brackets. Cross-references from the English-Gaelic section of the dictionary refer the reader to the table below, and the prepositional pronouns are also listed in the Gaelic-English section of the dictionary, under the preposition concerned, where some examples of their use are also given.

à, às, from, out of: **asam(sa), asad(sa), às(-san), aiste(se), asainn(e), asaibh(se), asta(san),** from me, you *etc*

aig, at: **agam(sa), agad(sa), aige(san), aice(se), againn(e), agaibh(se), aca(san),** at me, you *etc*; *also* my *etc*, *as in* **an cù agam** my dog

air, on: **orm(sa), ort(sa), air(san), oirre(se), oirnn(e), oirbh(se), orra(san),** on me, you *etc*

an, ann an/am, in: **annam(sa), annad(sa), ann(san), innte(se), annainn(e), annaibh(se), annta(san),** in me, you *etc*

bho, from: **bhuam(sa), bhuat(sa), bhuaithe(san), bhuaipe(se), bhuainn(e), bhuaibh(se), bhuapa(san),** from me, you *etc*

chun, to: **chugam(sa), chugad(sa), chuige(san), chuice(se), chugainn(e), chugaibh(se), chuca(san),** to me, you *etc*

de & **dhe,** of, from: **dhìom(sa), dhìot(sa), dheth(san), dhith(se), dhinn(e), dhibh(se), dhiubh(san),** of/from me, you *etc*

do, to, for: **dhòmh(sa), dhut(sa), dhà(san), dhì(se), dhuinn(e), dhuibh(se), dhaibh(san),** to/for me, you *etc*

eadar, between: *combines with the pl pers prons* **sinn, sibh, iad** *to give the prep prons* **eadarainn, eadaraibh, eatarra,** between us, you, them

fo, under, beneath: **fodham(sa), fodhad(sa), fodha(san), fòidhpe(se), fodhainn(e), fodhaibh(se), fòdhpa(san),** under/beneath me, you *etc*

gu, to: **thugam(sa), thugad(sa), thuige(san), thuice(se), thugainn(e), thugaibh(se), thuca(san),** to me, you *etc*

le, with: **leam(sa), leat(sa), leis(-san), leatha(se), leinn(e), leibh(se), leotha(san),** with me, you *etc, also* 'mine', 'yours' *etc, as in* **is ann leamsa a tha e** it's mine, it belongs to me

mu, about, around; concerning: **umam(sa), umad(sa), uime(san), uimpe(se), umainn(e), umaibh(se), umpa(san),** around/concerning me, you *etc*

o, from: **uam(sa), uat(sa), uaithe(san), uaipe(se), uainn(e), uaibh(se), uapa(san),** from me, you *etc*

ri, to; against: **rium(sa), riut(sa), ris(-san), rithe(se), rinn(e), ribh(se), riutha(san),** to/against me, you *etc*

ro, before: **romham(sa), romhad(sa), roimhe(san), roimhpe(se), romhainn(e), romhaibh(se), romhpa(san),** before me, you *etc*

thar, across, over: **tharam(sa), tharad(sa), thairis(san), thairte(se), tharainn(e), tharaibh(se), tharta(san),** across/over me, you *etc*

tro, through: **tromham(sa), tromhad(sa), troimhe(san), troimhpe(se), tromhainn(e), tromhaibh(se), tromhpa(san),** through me, you *etc*